CONSUMER SALES LAW

Cavendish
Publishing
Limited

London • Sydney

CONSUMER SALES LAW

The Law Relating to Consumer Sales and Financing of Goods

John Macleod, PhD, LLB
Barrister, Professor of Law, University of Liverpool

Cavendish
Publishing
Limited

London • Sydney

First published in Great Britain 2002 by Cavendish Publishing Limited, The Glass House, Wharton Street, London WC1X 9PX, United Kingdom

Telephone: +44 (0)20 7278 8000   Facsimile: +44 (0)20 7278 8080

Email: info@cavendishpublishing.com

Website: www.cavendishpublishing.com

British Library Cataloguing in Publication Data

Macleod, JK (John Keith)

Consumer sales law

1 Consumer protection – law and legislation – Great Britain

I Title

343.4'1'071

ISBN 1 85941 700 0

Printed and bound in Great Britain

PREFACE

Since the publication of the first edition (1989) by Butterworths, perhaps the single most important change in this area of the law has been a practical one: the methods of financing consumer supplies of goods has largely been reduced to two forms:

(a) Direct financing, where the individual transaction is set up by direct contact between the financier and consumer, the financier contracting to supply the goods to the consumer. This is the traditional formula, normally used for items of high unit value, such as motor vehicles.

(b) Loan financing, where the financier sets up a loan contract with the consumer, which the consumer then uses to obtain goods from a retailer. This is commonly done by way of a personal loan or credit card and is typically used for items of smaller unit value.

Thus, loan financing has almost supplanted indirect financing (block discounting), which has been largely confined to specialist factoring businesses and excised from this work. To this extent, the financed supply of goods has been simplified.

Whether the supply of goods be financed or not, perhaps the most significant post-1989 changes have been these. First, the divergence in legal treatment of domestic and international sales continues apace. Second, Parliament has begun the process of amending the basic code, the Sale of Goods Act 1979 by discrete pieces of legislation: eventually, we can expect to see a new code, incorporating the changes. Third, the degree of interference in this field brought about by our membership of the European Union continues remorselessly (now some 80% of DTI-sponsored statutory instruments); but this is not always obvious because of the manner in which these European Union initiatives are assimilated into English law, usually by difficult-to-find statutory instruments, which nevertheless have the power to overturn English statutes, eg, the Weights and Measures Acts, Part III of the Fair Trading Act, Part II of the Consumer Protection Act. Fourth, whilst the draftsmen of English-inspired statutes and statutory instruments seems to offer no respite from the modern practice of legislating in detail, rather than trusting the courts to implement policies stated in generalised terms, the increasingly pervasive EU Directives and English statutory instruments made under them are drafted in the continental more generalised style. Fifth, with the continued development of different areas of law applicable to domestic supplies of goods, more frequently the crucial legal issue in a consumer supply dispute concerns which area of law to apply, rather than the murky details of any one area: to that extent, the issue is sometimes which statute/text to go to, rather than what it means when you get there; and to this extent monographs on single legal subjects are less useful. Indeed, with the passage of time, those different areas of the law have become increasingly inter-twined, a situation with which I have endeavoured to cope by increasingly generous cross-referencing. Sixth, it is increasingly difficult to keep up with the accelerating plethora of EU and Whitehall reform proposals, many overlapping, some contradictory. My only claim is I tried, aided by my many patient friends in the credit industry and credit trade organisations, such as the Finance and Leasing Association, Consumer Credit Trade Association and Consumer Credit Association. Seventh, I have tried to make this work more relevant to practitioners in the field, whether or not they be qualified lawyers and have increased the number of references to non-legal works.

My thanks are due to the relays of typists in the Faculty Office, especially Mrs Cathy Owens. Over the years since the earlier edition published by Butterworths in 1989, they have patiently made the myriad of amendments as I endeavoured to keep up with changes in this area of the law. When this or my insufficient computer literacy has caused computer or internet difficulties, Steve Cooper has patiently sorted things out. Last, but not least, my editors, Jon Lloyd and Lucia Rae, have patiently saved me from all manner of minor mistakes; and Cavendish Publishing has had the faith to publish the work. However, I remain responsible for such errors as remain.

In this edition, I have endeavoured to state the law as at 1 February 2002 with the resources then available to me. However, the indulgence of my publisher has allowed a few later references.

John Macleod
11 March 2002

CONTENTS

PART 1
THE NATURE OF CONTRACTS FOR THE SUPPLY OF GOODS

CHAPTER 1   INTRODUCTION

CHAPTER 2   SUBJECT MATTER OF THE SUPPLY CONTRACT:
                         GOODS AND PRICE

PART 2
CONSUMER PROTECTION

CHAPTER 3   REGULATION OF BUSINESS

CHAPTER 4   CONSUMER PROTECTION AND THE CRIMINAL LAW

CHAPTER 5   CONSUMER PROTECTION AND INSTALMENT CREDIT

CHAPTER 6   LICENSING

PART 4
THE CONTENTS OF A CONTRACT FOR THE SUPPLY OF GOODS

CHAPTER 11   CONTRACTUAL TERMS

CHAPTER 12   UNDERTAKINGS AS TO TITLE

CHAPTER 13   UNDERTAKINGS AS TO QUANTITY AND QUALITY

CHAPTER 14   UNDERTAKINGS AS TO FITNESS AND
SATISFACTORY QUALITY

CHAPTER 15   OTHER IMPLIED TERMS, TRANSACTIONS AND
OBLIGATIONS

Contents

PART 5
THE CONVEYANCE IN SUPPLY CONTRACTS:
THE EFFECTS OF THE CONTRACT

CHAPTER 22   RISK AND IMPOSSIBILITY

PART 6
PAYMENT IN SUPPLY CONTRACTS

CHAPTER 23   DELIVERY AND PAYMENT

CHAPTER 24   POSSESSION AND REPOSSESSION BY THE SUPPLIER

PART 7
DISCHARGE, ENFORCEMENT AND REMEDIES

CHAPTER 26   DISCHARGE OF CONTRACTUAL OBLIGATIONS

CHAPTER 27   REMEDIES OF THE SUPPLIER – 'CREDITOR OR OWNER'

TABLE OF CASES

Note: Bold references indicate that a direct quote from the judgment has been used.

B

I

M

N

Y

Z

NB Those sections set out in the text are denoted in bold print. Abbreviations found in the text for statutes are to be found here in square brackets.

TABLE OF STATUTORY INSTRUMENTS

NB Statutory instruments made under the Consumer Credit Act 1974 have their titles abbreviated (CC = Consumer Credit) and the text of them will be found in the following; Goode, *Consumer Credit Law and Practice*; Guest, *Encyclopedia of Consumer Credit*. Most of the other statutory instruments lists below will be found in Thomas, *Encyclopedia of Consumer Law*.

TREATY OF ROME

TABLE OF EEC DIRECTIVES

PART 1

THE NATURE OF CONTRACTS FOR THE SUPPLY OF GOODS

CHAPTER 1

INTRODUCTION

Suppose a newspaper street-seller (S). A consumer wishing to obtain a newspaper will approach S and hold out the cover price: nothing is said, but price and paper exchange hands. For his price, the consumer will obtain immediate delivery (possession) and ownership (property) of the newspaper. That is a simple cash sale of goods.

SCOPE OF THE ENQUIRY

[1.01] This book is concerned with what laymen might term 'sales of goods' within England and Wales; that is, with domestic – rather than international (cross-border) – supplies of goods.[1] Its object is to trace the legal life-history of goods within this country, starting from manufacture, growth or import, through the chain of distribution (see post, para 17.01), to their eventual consumption (whether by a business or a private person). Such transactions will normally be governed by English law (see post, para 18.13).

The fundamental transaction in such activity must be that which is technically characterised as a sale of goods (see post, para 1.02). This is a specialised area of the common law which largely developed in the 18th and 19th centuries and was first codified in the Sale of Goods Act 1893 and was subsequently re-enacted with amendments in the UK[2] in the Sale of Goods Act 1979 (SGA). Unless otherwise stated, subsequent references to the SGA refer to the SGA 1979:[3] the 1979 Act in fact only consolidated all the statutory amendments previously made to the 1893 Act, for example, by the Supply of Goods (Implied Terms) Act 1973, and the Unfair Contract Terms Act 1977.

Since then, Parliament has pursued a policy of piecemeal amendment,[4] including some special SGA amendments for 'consumer sales' (see post, para 14.01).

Yet, in the modern world, this is by no means the whole story. Perhaps the single most important complicating factor is the need for 'buyers' to finance the acquisition of goods (see post, para 1.03) and, as there have evolved completely different techniques for the financing of domestic and international sales respectively, this provides one justification for concentrating here on the former. Another is that modern domestic sales may bring into play a whole range of specialised statute-based rules of criminal law, largely introduced as ancillary supports for the civil law (see para 1.03), and so the totality of the transaction must inevitably involve consideration of the interplay of civil and criminal 'remedies' (see post, para 1.04).

[1.01]

1 For international sales generally, see Schmitthoff, *The Export Trade* (10th edn); Bridge, *International Sale of Goods*.

2 The modern American sales code is to be found in Art 2 of the Uniform Commercial Code (UCC); as to which, see generally Hawkland, *Sales and Bulk Sales* (3rd edn, 1976); *Williston on Sales* (4th edn); Mitchell (2001) 117 LQR 645 at 656–61. As to the UCC, see generally post, para 25.33.

3 For the contracts to which the 1979 Act applies, see s 1 and Sched 1.

4 By the Sale of Goods (Amendment) Act 1994; the Sale and Supply of Goods Act 1994; the Sale of Goods (Amendment) Act 1995.

The categories of contract

[1.02] Basic sales. In terms of legal analysis, no doubt the greater number of sales are achieved within the scope of the SGA by way of a simple sale of goods with payment on delivery (s 28: set out post, para 23.16). The SGA purports to do no more than 'codify the law relating to the sale of goods' and expressly leaves the general principles of the common law untouched save insofar as they are inconsistent with the terms of the Act (s 62(2): set out post, para 10.18). The overall effect is to emphasise that the sale of goods is merely a chapter of the general law of contract. The SGA has never applied to contracts for the sale of other types of property, such as realty, negotiable instruments or choses in action; nor does it refer to all dispositions of goods, expressly excluding from its ambit 'any transaction in the form of a contract of sale, which is intended to operate by way of mortgage, pledge, charge or other security' (s 62(4): set out post, para 1.07). Moreover, subsequent statutes have steadily reduced the role of the common law in the regulation of sales.

Within the context of sales of goods, the draftsman of the SGA 1893 (Sir MacKenzie Chalmers)[1] endeavoured to capture the spirit of the common law rules, leaving alterations in the common law of England to be made by Parliament.[2] The underlying philosophy behind the 19th century rules was that their function was to hold the ring between two equal parties whilst they achieved a true bargain,[3] the rules themselves being displaceable by contrary agreement: this attitude is often described as *laissez-faire*.[4] Whilst Chalmers for the most part succeeded in embodying this philosophy in his draft, for example, *caveat emptor* (see post, para 15.22), it may be questioned, however, whether (a) the optimum moment was chosen for codification in terms of common law development, and (b) Chalmers was as successful in achieving his objective as is sometimes traditionally held.[5] *A fortiori*, the continued universal use of the philosophy as regards sales of goods, may itself be criticised. The assumption of equality of bargaining power must clearly be erroneous in some cases, and it would seem an almost impossible task to formulate a set of even *prima facie* rules which would do justice to all parties in all the circumstances obtaining at the time of codification, let alone subsequently.[6]

Consumer sales. Indeed, statute has already introduced notions of consumer contracts in several different contexts, which, perhaps unfortunately, utilise different criteria. First, in the context of exclusion clauses, there has been established the concept of 'dealing as consumer' (s 12 of the UCTA: see post, para 18.18); and this has subsequently been

---

[1.02]

1 He produced a commentary on the SGA. Chalmers also drafted the Bills of Exchange Act 1882 and Marine Insurance Act 1906.

2 See Chalmers' Preface to his 1894 edition. Some changes were made by Parliament, particularly during the course of extending the Bill to Scotland, eg, the requirement as to notice in SGA s 18, rr 2 and 3. See further Lord Diplock in *Ashington Piggeries Ltd v Christopher Hill Ltd* [1972] AC 441 at 501. See also Greig, *Sale of Goods*, 1–2 and Kerr (1978) 41 MLR at 17–18; Rodger (1992) 108 LQR 570.

3 *Per* Jessel MR in *Printing and Numerical Registering Co v Sampson* (1875) LR 19 Eq 462 at 465. But see standard form contracts: post, para 11.08.

4 Is it true to say that in modern consumer sales the SGA is still interpreted neutrally by the courts? See further post, para 1.04; and generally *Chitty on Contracts* (28th edn), vol 1, para 1-010.

5 Cf Williston's US Sales Act 1906 and Goode, *Commercial Law* (2nd edn), 9.

6 See Bridge [1991] LM and CLQ 52 at 53. For further discussion as to whether there are any general principles of commercial law and whether the subject should be codified as a whole, see Goode, *ibid*, Chapter 40.

utilised in amendments to the SGA (see post, para 11.05A). Second, for credit transactions there has been introduced the regulated agreement (see post, para 1.03). Third, Euro-legislation has imported its own version of the 'consumer', within which context there has been seen the death of freedom of contract (see post, para 11.12), especially as regards inequality of information as between seller and buyer.[7] The basic issues for parliamentary draftsman in the next few years are as follows:

(1) Whether there should be a separate consumer sales code,[8] or a single code for all sales.[9] In any event, the well-known standard forms of trade associations (see post, para 11.08) have been characterised as almost a separate Act for each trade.[10]

(2) For the purposes of those provisions which distinguish consumers from non-consumers, which of the above definitions should be preferred?

(3) Bearing in mind the pressures on the parliamentary timetable, how should the new statutory provisions be kept up to date, for example, E-commerce?[11] This appears to involve at least two major policy decisions: (a) whether any code should be drafted in general or detailed form; and (b) to what extent (if any) the details should be fleshed out by statutory instrument.

It would seem that the spirit of the times favours piecemeal reform, as does the UK approach to EEC Directives (see post, para 1.03).

[1.03] Consumer supplies. Whilst the basic transaction considered above rightly envisages the parties making a simultaneous exchange of the price for the goods, it is a fact of life that many persons wishing to obtain goods in England and Wales do not have within their own resources the cash to pay for them on delivery. Broadly speaking, such persons have available to them the following alternative methods of immediate acquisition:

(a) a cash sale (see post, para 1.07) financed by a loan (see post, para 7.01 *et seq*); or

(b) an instalment contract, which may take any of these forms—

    (i)   a credit or conditional **sale** (see post, para 1.10), or

    (ii) a simple **hiring**, rental or leasing (see post, para 1.18), or

    (iii) **a hire-purchase agreement** (see post, para 1.20).

It is submitted that it is unrealistic to look at the law relating to domestic sales without examining all these alternative forms of supply contract used to attain the same objective. It will be noted at once that the above forms of contract utilise two different types of contract to transfer the use-value of goods to consumers: (1) sales (see post, para 1.06 *et seq*); and (2) hiring (see post, para 1.17 *et seq*).

---

7   Hedley [2001] JBL 114, at 124–25.

8   Sale and Supply of Goods (1987, Law Com No 160) paras 1.09; 1.11; 1.14–15; and see generally Borrie and Diamond, *Consumer Society and the Law* (4th edn).

9   For a possible model, see the US Uniform Commercial Code, Art 2: see ante, para 1.01, note 2.

10 For a possible model, see the Australian Trade Practices Act 1974 (as amended). For a commentary, see Taperell, Vermeesch and Harland, *Trade Practices and Consumer Protection* (2nd edn, 1978); Bridge, *op cit*, note 6, at 58.

11 See Brownsword and Howells (1999) 19 LS 287; and post, para 8.17A.

For a long time it was a fundamental weakness of our law that these different solutions to the same problem were governed by disparate pieces of legislation, or in some cases were subject to no legislative control at all. However, this weakness was tackled by the enactment of the Consumer Credit Act 1974 (CCA).[1] Whilst the SGA codified the pre-existing common law of sale and hence replaced it (see ante, para 1.02), the CCA assumes the existence of the common law relating to supplies of goods and then makes detailed changes to it: so, to understand the CCA, the underlying common law must first be appreciated. The CCA, because it has to deal with a number of different legal transactions which may be used to achieve the same objective, is necessarily complicated. Indeed, it is a monument to the drafting skills of the author, Mr Francis Bennion,[2] who had planned to draft in layman's language[3] a comprehensive scheme built of brand-new concepts (see post, para 5.26). Whereas the SGA 1893 was in a sense typical of the 19th century in its reflection of the notion of freedom of contract,[4] the CCA is a leading example of 20th century legislation with an axe to grind,[5] and increasingly reliant on criminal sanctions.[6]

With our accession to the EEC in 1973 (see post, para 1.03A), there has been introduced an entirely new factor. In the 1970s, the EEC began the process of evolving its own community-wide policy on consumer affairs (see post, para 3.10); and of mixed EEC and domestic origins has been the enactment of the Consumer Protection Act 1987 (CPA), containing both civil and criminal provisions relating to three distinct aspects of consumer supplies.[7] By 1990, the centre of thinking and activity on reform of consumer protection law had passed to Brussels. Apart from the potentially significant domestic Deregulation Act 1994, the major development has been the Sale of Goods Directive (see post, para 14.01).

[1.03A] The European Union (EU). In 1973, the United Kingdom became a member of the EEC, thereby undertaking all the rights and obligations arising, *inter alia*, from the Treaty of Rome, the Articles of which have unfortunately been renumbered (old numbers in brackets where appropriate). Under this Treaty, the Community must strive towards the approximation of laws (Art 3(h)) and harmonise legislation (Art 94 [ex 100]), including the progressive approximation throughout the EEC of the different national policies and laws. Whilst the original Treaty of Rome did not lay down a clear basis for an EEC consumer protection policy, the EEC promoted a number of uniform consumer laws (see post, para 3.10) indirectly justified on the basis of various provisions of the Treaty.[1] The Maastricht Treaty 1991 introduced two relevant changes. First, it added to the Treaty of

---

[1.03]

1 See the Preamble to the CCA. For the objectives of this Act, see further the *Crowther Report* upon whose recommendations it was substantially based: post, para 5.03.

2 He has produced a monumental looseleaf commentary on the Act: Consumer Credit Control – set out according to an entirely novel pattern.

3 Criticised by Hahlo (1975) 38 MLR at 23. See further post, para 5.06.

4 It has been pointed out that the apparent simplicity of the drafting of the SGA is misleading: Goode, *Commercial Law* (2nd edn), pp 198–99.

5 See Nicol (1981) 44 MLR 21.

6 For the interpretation problems to which this gives rise, see post, para 1.05.

7 (a) Consumer safety (see post, para 4.31 *et seq*); (b) misleading pricing (see post, para 8.09 *et seq*): (c) product liability (see post, para 17.21 *et seq*).

[1.03A]

1 Mostly justified under old Arts 36, 100, 100A, 235. See generally Goode, *Consumer Credit Law and Practice*, Part II.

Rome a new objective of strengthening consumer protection to safeguard the 'economic interests of consumers' and provide 'adequate information to consumers' (Art 153 [ex 129A]). They do not preclude more stringent such national protective measures as are compatible with the Treaty. Second, it asserted the new principle of subsidiarity, which was supposed to restrict the organisation (now designated EU) from more enthusiastic intervention in fields so far occupied by national laws (Art 3B).

Under the Treaties, Member States must give effect to Community law, which takes precedence over English law, for example, s 1(1) of the CPA (see post, para 17.23). Those Community laws extant at the time of our accession were given the force of law within the UK by the European Communities Act 1972 (ECA), subsequent changes in the Treaties being similarly incorporated. For our purposes, EU attempts to harmonise consumer law of Member States may be roughly divided into two types.

1   *Positive harmonisation.* Positive Community law is of two sorts:

(a) 'Self-executing' laws which take direct internal effect in precedence to the domestic law of Member States.[2] These include provisions of the Treaties and Regulations, which have general applications, whereas decisions deal only with an individual case.[3] These may be enforced in the UK by way of actions for breach of statutory duty (see post, para 3.21).

(b) Directives, which are only valid provided *intra vires* the Article of the Treaty under which they are made.[4] The Directive will specify only the result to be achieved in domestic law, but leave to the national authorities the choice of form.[5] The UK has adopted the practice of fulfilling its Community obligations by the enactment of statutes or statutory instruments,[6] which should simplify public enforcement (see post, para 28.02).

There are also EU Codes of conduct (see post, para 3.14).

2   *Negative harmonisation.* This comes into play where national measures ostensibly adopted to protect, say, consumers, are incompatible with the Treaty. Theoretically, consumers adversely affected may complain to the EU Commission direct so that the latter may take up the matter before the European Court of Justice (Art 226 [ex 169]), in which case the decision of that Court is binding on the UK and overrides national

---

2   ECA s 2(1). Eg, *Conegate Ltd v Customs and Excise* [1987] QB 254, CJEC, old Arts 30, 36; Sunday trading (see post, para 8.13). Directly applicable provisions of Community law should prevail over future Acts of Parliament: ECA s 2(4); and see below.

3   Art 249 [ex 189], eg, exempted from old Art 85 under Community Regulation 17. See generally Morris [1989] JBL 233; and post, para 2.13.

4   *Germany v European Parliament; R v Secretary of State for Health ex p Imperial Tobacco Ltd* [2000] All ER (EC) 769, ECJ (tobacco advertising).

5   See Art 249 [ex 189] of the Treaty of Rome. For a current list of EEC Directives relating to consumer protection, see Thomas and Clarke, *Encyclopedia of Consumer Law*, part 5. For the process of making directives, see post, para 3.10. For 'Minimum Directives', see Stapleton (1994) 110 LQR 213.

6   As to statutes, eg, Weights and Measures Act 1979 (subsequently re-enacted in the 1985 Act: see post, para 4.24). As to statutory instruments, see ECA, ss 2(2), (4) and Sched 2, eg, Doorstep-Selling Regulations (see post, para 10.21); package holidays (see post, para 15.20 and post, para 3.10). For an (allegedly invalid under Community law) attempt to vary by statute the rules of a Directive, see CPA 1987 s 4(1)(e): see post, para 17.30. As to the repeal of UK statutes by statutory instrument, see post, para 5.10.

legislation.[7] In practice, such UK consumers are more likely to seek remedies within the UK courts, as the Community treaties and law are directly enforceable in Member States, for example, competition law (see post, para 2.12), taking precedence over domestic law: according to s 2(4), post-1972 UK legislation 'shall be construed and have effect subject to' UK statutes and statutory instruments incorporating EU law into UK law (see above).[8] The breach of Community law may be used as a cause of action, for example, for breach of statutory duty (see post, para 3.21); or as a defence, where a party is sued in the UK courts, for example, for breach of contract where relevant English statute contravenes Art 12 [ex 6] of the Treaty.[9] Sometimes, it will be appropriate for the aggrieved consumer to apply for judicial review or damages against the State,[10] as where the State has neglected to implement a Directive,[11] so narrowing the distinction between Directives and Regulations (see above). However, it would seem that an aggrieved consumer cannot rely on Community law rights as against a private defendant in respect of an unimplemented directive.[12] In all cases, reference or appeal lies from the courts of the United Kingdom to the European Court of Justice (CJEC; Art 234 (ex 177)).

Interpretation of the Acts[1]

[1.04] Civil statutes. In the preface to his commentary on the SGA 1893, Chalmers says[2] that the pre-Act cases are only law insofar as they illustrate the words of the statute,[2a] though the effect of this statement has since been complicated by the 1979 almost verbatim re-enactment of the SGA. In the 19th century, the typical judicial attitude to codifying Acts, such as the SGA, was that they should be interpreted according to the literal rule of statutory construction;[3] but in the 20th century the courts have not, in respect of all issues arising under the SGA, maintained such a lofty impartiality,[4] as witness their treatment of the issue of *caveat emptor* (see post, Chapters 13–14) and the

---

7   The EU Commission is empowered to bring such actions as guardian of the Treaties and sometimes does so upon individual complaints. But see Thomas (1989) 139 NLJ 1485. For the EU Ombudsman, see post, para 3.25. For an example when such a claim failed to topple a national law, see the Sunday trading disputes (post para 2.13).

8   Section 2(4) of the 1972 Act. This is an example of a 'Henry VIII clause' (see post, para 5.10) and has been used to overrule, for example, Part II of the CPA (see post, para 4.32).

9   See Burbidge (2000) 150 NLJ 1544, citing s 26 of UCTA (see post, para 18.13).

10 *R v Secretary of State for Transport ex p Factortame* [1999] 4 All ER 906, HL (damages); *Three Rivers DC v Bank of England* [2000] 3 All ER 1, HL (misfeasance in public office).

11 Eg, the UK and the Sale of Goods Directive (see post, para 14.01). On such 'vertical direct effect' of directives, see Goode, *op cit*, note 1, Part X, para 4; Gordon and Miskin (1996) 146 NLJ 1055; Craig (1997) 113 LQR 67.

12 'Horizontal direct effect', eg, *El Corte Inglès SA v Cristina Blezquez Rivero* [1996] CLY 1175, ECJ (Consumer Credit Directive); *R v Secretary of State for Employment ex p Seymour-Smith* [1997] 2 All ER 273, HL. But there may be some help from the rules of interpretation where there is a relevant national provision (see post, para 1.04).

[1.04]

1   See generally, Interpretation Act 1978.

2   See Chalmers, *Sale of Goods* (18th edn), vii. Cf Atiyah, *Sale of Goods* (9th edn), p 1; Goode, *Commercial Law* (2nd edn), pp 192–93, 195. See also *per* Lord Herschell in *Bank of England v Vagliano Brothers* [1891] AC 107, at 144–45, HL. For an application of this philosophy, see *Re Wait* (set out post, para 20.22).

2a So rendering otiose discussion of prior common law rules not embodied in the 1893 Act: see ante, para 1.02.

3   See generally, Allen, *Law in the Making* (7th edn), pp 482–593; Willis (1938) 16 Can BR 1.

4   See Goode, *op cit*, note 2, pp 23–25, 198.

exceptions to the *nemo dat* rule (see post, Chapter 21). *A fortiori,* it may be doubted whether the old impartiality will be visited upon the consumer protection legislation of later centuries. For instance, we shall see later that the implication of terms as to the quality and fitness of goods supplied were substantially amended in favour of the consumer by the Supply of Goods (Implied Terms) Act 1973 (SOGIT) and the Supply of Goods and Services Act 1982 (SGSA), which were enacted specifically as measures of consumer protection.[5] In such cases, it is at least arguable that the evident bias of the legislation should lead to the adoption of the mischief rule of statutory interpretation.[6] Thus, in a tax case, *Pepper v Hart,*[7] the House of Lords allowed such reference where: (a) the legislation is ambiguous or obscure or the literal meaning leads to absurdity; (b) the material relied on consists of statements by a minister or other promoter of the Bill; and (c) the statements relied on are clear.[8] A similar approach has been adopted where the CCA clashed with Convention rights.[9]

The interpretation of uniform statutes enacted or authorised by Parliament and derived from treaties or similar arrangements, for example, EU Directives, is another matter entirely: in part, this is because these are more likely to be drafted according to the Continental, rather than the English model;[10] in part, it seems to follow from the ECA;[11] in part, it is attributable to the tendency of the UK Government, especially in statutory instruments, to copy out the English language version of Directives more or less verbatim, for example, the Unfair Terms in Consumer Contracts (UTCC) Regulations (see post, para 11.12 *et seq*); and in part from a rule of interpretation for UK courts to try to interpret national legislation,[12] where possible, consistently with EU rules.[13]

[1.05] Criminal statutes. However, the matter of interpretation is further complicated because, particularly in recent years, Parliament has sought to put more effective teeth into its consumer protection statutes by imposing criminal sanctions for breach of their provisions in such profusion as almost to overshadow the civil law.[1] Some of these

---

5   See respectively the following final Law Commission Reports: *First Report on Exemption Clauses* (Law Com No 24, 1969); *Implied Terms in Contracts for the Supply of Goods* (Law Com No 95 1979).

6   Compare *Stevenson v Rogers* (set out post, para 14.04); *R & B Customs Brokers Ltd v United Dominions Trust Ltd* (set out post, para 18.18). See generally the authorities referred to in note 3, above. For a fascinating discussion of the relationship of statute and case law, see Atiyah (1985) 48 MLR 1, particularly citing examples as follows: breach of statutory duty (see post, para 3.21); SGA s 11 and innominate terms (see post, para 11.05); SGA, s 14 and implied terms in analogous transactions (see post, para 15.26); UCTA and both fundamental breach and interpretation (see post, paras 18.07–08); Bills of Sale Acts and sale and re-hirings (see post, para 25.39).

7   [1993] AC 593, HL. It has been said that parliamentary statements by ministers may also be used: Borrie [1999] JBL 205 at 206.

8   For an example in our context, see *Warwickshire CC v Johnson* (set out post, para 8.09) at 305a–306a (discussed Scott [1993] JBL at 494–98).

9   *Wilson v First County Trust Ltd* (set out post, para 9.20), at 147–49.

10   Insofar as EU Directives are implemented within the UK by our own legislation (see ante, para 1.03A), English courts could adopt their ordinary approach to interpretation, though perhaps at the risk of defeating the harmonisation intent lying behind the enactment, unless such an approach is expressly excluded (eg, CPA s 1(1): see post, para 17.24). See generally, Mann (1983) 99 LQR 376.

11   Section 2(4) and see *Three Rivers D C v Bank of England (No 2)* [1996] 2 All ER 363; *U v V* [1977] Eu LR 342 (not a sale case; *Hansard* admitted).

12   Eg, UTCC Regulation 7; Stop Now Orders (see post, para 6.06). See also, Maltby (1993) 109 LQR 301.

13   It seems that the mischief rule of interpretation should be used: see *per* Lord Steyn in the *First National Bank* case (set out post, para 7.03A); and post, para 11.12.

[1.05]

1   See Borrie, *The Development of Consumer Law and Policy*, p 45.

statutes, such as the Trade Descriptions Act 1968 (TDA), impose only criminal sanctions for breach of their provisions (s 35: set out post, para 10.19); and it is a well-known maxim that penal provisions are to be interpreted restrictively in favour of freedom of the subject.[2] Yet this will not necessarily preclude the courts from looking at the mischief in need of a remedy,[3] though such an approach has been explicitly rejected with regard to the CCA.[4]

Indeed, the CCA not only forbids the parties from contracting out of its provisions (s 173: see post, para 18.11), but contains a mixture of civil and criminal sanctions, sometimes even in respect of the same prohibited conduct,[5] and expressly limits the sanctions to those specifically provided in the Act (s 170: see post, para 10.19). Yet another approach is to be found in the CPA, where some whole topics are regulated by civil obligations and others by criminal sanctions.

Finally, there must be borne in mind the possible effect on consumer protection statutes of the Human Rights Act 1998 and the 'convention rights' it introduces (see post, para 3.09). Suppose the courts are faced with a UK statute or statutory instrument inconsistent with convention rights, whether passed before or after the 1998 Act. First, the 1998 Act requires the court to give effect to the consumer protection statute in a way that is compatible with convention rights 'so far as it is possible to do so'.[6] Second, it will try to do so even if this is inconsistent with a previous Court of Appeal interpretation.[7]

The basic categories of contract employed to effect a consumer supply (see ante, para 1.03) are sale, hire and hire-purchase (hp), all discussed below. Into which of these categories a particular transaction falls is a matter of substance, not form: see *Forthright Finance Ltd v Carlyle Finance Ltd* (set out post, para 1.22).

DEFINITION OF A CONTRACT OF SALE

Sales in general[1]

[1.06] Introduction. The contract of sale is defined by s 2 of the SGA,[2] and Chalmers suggests that this definition is merely declaratory of the common law (see s 62(2)). Traditionally, the contract of sale was rigidly distinguished from several other contracts

---

2   Eg, *Davies v Sumner* (set out post, para 4.03A). See, generally, Glanville Williams, *Criminal Law, The General Part* (2nd edn), para 76; *per* McNeil J in *Miller v FA Sadd & Son Ltd* (set out post, para 4.05) at 270c; *per* Ormrod LJ in *Westminster CC v Ray Allen (Alanshops) Ltd* [1982] 1 All ER at 774B.

3   *Attorney General's Reference (No 1 of 1988)* [1989] 2 All ER 1, HL (insider trading); *R v Deegan* [1998] 2 Crim App R 121, CA (flick-knives).

4   See *National Westminster Bank v Devon CC* (1996) 13 Tr LR 70, DC, esp *per* Kennedy LJ at 75D; *Coventry City Council v Lazarus* [1996] CLY 1165. But compare *Scarborough BS v East Riding of Yorkshire CC* [1997] CCLR 47, DC (see post, para 8.25).

5   Eg, entering into consumer credit agreements whilst an unlicensed trader: CCA, ss 39, 40. These provisions are discussed post, para 6.28.

6   Eg, *Wilson v First County Trust Ltd* (set out post, para 9.20).

7   Emmerson (1999) 149 NLJ 1899 at 1900.

[1.06]

1   See generally, Atiyah, *Sale of Goods* (10th edn, 1995); *Benjamin's Sale of Goods* (5th edn, 1997); *Blackburn on Sale* (3rd edn, 1910); Chalmers, *Sale of Goods* (18th edn, 1981); *Chitty on Contracts* (28th edn), vol 2, Chapter 41.

2   For the sale contracts to which the 1979 Act applies, see ante, para 1.01; and for the definition of sales, see post, para 1.07.

which it resembled, but which had their own common law rules (see post, para 15.21 *et seq*). Yet the distinction should not today be over-emphasised for the following reasons:[3]

(a) As the SGA 1893 was supposed to be a codification of the common law, the latter's rule for the analogous transaction may well be the same as the comparable SGA rule.[4]

(b) There is a modern tendency to enact statutory provisions for all transactions for the supply of goods which are virtually identical with those applicable to sales of goods: this has already happened in relation to the statutory implied terms in hire-purchase agreements in the SOGIT 1973 (see post, Chapters 12–16), the statutory restrictions on exclusion clauses in the Unfair Contract Terms Act 1977, ss 6–7 (see further Chapter 18) and the statutory implied terms in quasi-sales and simple hirings in the SGSA (see further Chapters 12–16).

(c) There are a number of hybrid transactions which involve elements of both sale and an analogous transaction, for example, sale and fitting of a carpet, installation of central heating, sale of patented goods under licence. *Prima facie*, the following analyses would appear possible: (i) there is a single contract, which may be categorised according to the predominant aspect;[5] (ii) there are two separate contracts, one of sale, and the other of, for example, labour; (iii) there is a single hybrid contract, partly of sale or quasi-sale and partly of, for example, labour[6] or hiring.[7] See further post, para 15.26.

[1.07] Definition. Like most commercial law statutes, the SGA contains a definition section which describes the ambit of the Act (s 2), what may be termed its 'gateway'. A contract of sale is defined by s 2(1) of the SGA as follows:

> A contract of sale of goods is a contract whereby the seller transfers or agrees to transfer the property in goods to the buyer for a money consideration, called the price.

This definition requires that *all* the following components should be present before a transaction passes through the gateway and falls within the SGA:[1]

1   *A contract.* The Act makes no attempt to interfere with the ordinary rules concerning the formation of contracts governed by English law. It just requires that there should be a contract (see post, Chapter 10). But, even this apparently simple requirement may give rise to problems. First, what is the position of drugs supplied under the NHS (see post, 4.29)? As between dispensing chemist and the patient there would appear to be

---

3   Certain contracts for the supply of goods must still be evidenced in writing: see post, para 9.02.
4   Eg, *Young and Marten Ltd v McManus Childs Ltd* [1969] 1 AC 454, HL (implied term as to fitness in the unamended SGA); and see further post, paras 15.24–25.
5   Eg, *Vigers v Cook* [1919] 2 KB 475, CA (funeral); *Dawson (Clapham) Ltd v Dutfield* (set out post, para 2.09 – sale); *Young & Marten Ltd v McManus Childs Ltd* (supra – analogous transaction); *Common Services Agency v Purdie and Kirkpatrick* 1995 SLT (Sh Ct) 34 (photocopier rented at cost per copy).
6   Eg, *Watson v Buckley* [1940] 1 All ER 174, at 179–80. See further Atiyah, *op cit*, note 1, p 9. But see post, para 1.07, note 3. As to quasi-sale, see post, para 2.10.
7   Eg, *The Saint Anna* [1983] 2 All ER 691 (charterparty held to include sale of oil on board at commencement of charter).
[1.07]
1   Can a contract fall within the SGA definition where it contains all these elements, plus some additional ones, eg, installation? See ante, para 1.06.

no contract at all;[2] but would the court imply analogous terms as to the quality of the drugs supplied?[3] Second, account must be taken of the modern practice of franchising, which may make it difficult for the consumer to determine the identity of his retail supplier.[4] Even if the consumer is aware that he is dealing with a 'franchise', the expression covers a wide variety of business arrangements, including business-format franchising[5] and licences to supply[6] or to occupy premises. The fact situation may vary between (a) an entirely independent business-concession, for example, shop-within-a-shop or a market hall, (b) a joint operation between the owner of the premises and the franchise-holder, and (c) the latter as a mere promoter of stock owned by the tenant of the premises. Is it significant who remunerates the salesman? Third, there is the problem of 'free gifts' (see below). Fourth, the parties may *prima facie* assign their contractual rights (see post, para 7.16).

2 *Made in respect of 'goods'.* The meaning of the term 'goods' will be dealt with later (post, para 2.01 *et seq*). However, the insistence on a supply of 'goods' distinguishes a sale of goods from a supply of services (see post, para 2.05). Nor is a contract for the supply of services turned into a sale of goods just because under that contract the general property in some goods is incidentally transferred from one to another.[7] There should also be distinguished pyramid sales (see post, para 1.09).

3 *To transfer the 'property' in those goods.* The object of the contract must be to transfer the property in those goods (see post, para 1.08) from seller to buyer (see post, para 1.09), delivery not being an essential element. Thus, the Act provides that '"Sale" includes a bargain and sale as well as a sale and delivery' (s 61(1))[8] and sharply distinguishes between the contract and the transfer of property in the goods (see post, para 1.10).

4 *In exchange for the price.* Section 2(1) requires that the transfer of property be for 'a money consideration, called the price'. The concept of price is considered later (see post, para 2.06). Property and price must be exchanged, though not necessarily simultaneously (s 28: see post, para 23.22). Further, one who merely finances a sale by provision of the price does not thereby become a buyer of the subject matter.[9] Normally, the insistence on consideration will clearly distinguish a sale from a gift (see post, para 2.08), though there may be difficulties in drawing the borderline in respect of so called 'free gifts', and under the inertia selling rules, the recipient of unsolicited goods may treat those goods as a gift rather than the offer to sell that their supplier intended (see post, para 8.18). Moreover, the requirement that the

---

2 *Pfizer Corp v Ministry of Health* [1965] AC 512, HL (see further post, para 4.29). *Contra* drugs supplied under private prescription, where a price is paid. The presence or absence of a retail supply contract may have implications for product liability: see post, para 17.04. As to the supply of electricity, see post, para 3.07.

3 See post, para 15.25; and further Atiyah, *Sale of Goods* (10th edn), p 9; Treitel, *Law of Contract* (10th edn), p 91, note 76; Woodroffe, *Goods and Services – The New Law*, para 2.06; and post, para 4.29.

4 As to franchising, see generally Adams and Jones, *Franchising* (3rd edn); [1986] JBL 206. For the control of franchising by competition law, see post, para 2.13.

5 This type of franchising involves the sale of business knowledge and experience, coupled with a licence to use or sell a particular product, brand name, logo, etc. See also post, para 1.09.

6 The supply may be of goods, eg, motor trade distributorships, or of services, eg, credit card franchises (see post, para 7.09).

7 Eg, *Appleby v Sleep* [1968] 2 All ER 265, DC (supply of drugs under NHS: see further post, para 4.30).

8 And see *Watts v Seymour* [1967] 2 QB 647, DC.

9 *Ebeling v Theo & Jos Van Der Aa, SA* [1955] 2 LIR 641. For financing of price, see further post, paras 2.20–24.

consideration for a sale be money, termed the 'price' (see post, para 2.06), distinguishes a sale from a barter or exchange (see post, para 2.10).

[1.08] The object of the contract. The substance of the contract[1] must be 'to transfer the property in goods' from the seller to the buyer, though the SGA does not insist on an immediate transfer of property (see post, para 1.10). The Act provides that 'property' means 'the general property in the goods, and not merely a special property'.[2] However, the general property in the goods is not always the most important consideration. Thus, the Act distinguishes between property and title (see Chapter 19), and sometimes allows a person to pass a good title even though he does not possess the property in the goods (see Chapter 21). Moreover, the Act contemplates that the parties may contract out of the implied obligation on the part of the seller that he will transfer a good title.[3] Particularly after the SOGIT Act in 1973 imposed obligatory implied terms as to title, there was a very real problem with regard to whether or not a contract which purported to oust completely the implied undertakings as to title was a contract for sale of goods at all.[4] However, the importance of this issue was lessened by the SGSA: if such a transaction is not a sale of goods, it may be an analogous transaction (quasi-sale) within the later Act.[5]

The insistence of the SGA on at least an agreement to transfer the general property in goods (see post, para 1.10), combined with its evident indifference as to whether there is any transfer of possession (see ante, para 1.07), is underlined by s 62(4), which lays down that:

> The provisions of this Act about contracts of sale do not apply to a transaction in the form of a contract of sale which is intended to operate by way of mortgage, pledge, charge, or other security.

Thus, there must be distinguished from sale all the following:

(a) *Bailments*, for example, hirings, where the essence of the transaction is the transfer of possession whilst the bailor retains the general property in the goods (see post, para 1.17).

(b) *Security transactions*, where the secured party will have something less than the unfettered general property in the goods.[6] But this exception does not include a sale with a reservation of title,[7] nor a genuine sale rather than a charge.[8]

[1.08]

1   *Contra* where the 'goods sold' are a mere token: see *Lipkin Gorman v Karpnale Ltd* [1992] 4 All ER 512, HL (gambling chips). Are the chips a form of money (see post, para 2.02)?

2   Section 61(1). As to 'special property', see below. This emphasis of English sales law on the passing of property has been described as 'obsessional': Goode, *Commercial Law* (2nd edn), p 200.

3   It will be argued later that the Act only insists that the seller promises to transfer the general property in the goods to the buyer insofar as he is able to do so: see post, para 12.17.

4   See the dispute between Preston and Carr: (1974) 37 MLR at 599–600. If the transaction could not be classed as a sale of goods, then it appeared to escape the statutory prohibition against contracting out of the implied terms as to title: see post, para 12.17.

5   See post, para 2.10. *Quaere* whether s 1 of the SGSA is subject to this same limitation as s 2 of the SGA?

6   With a lien he will have only possession, with a pledge he will have possession plus a special property; and with a mortgage or charge his general property will he subject to an equity of redemption: see post, para 25.02.

7   *Armour v Thyssen* (set out post, para 20.28).

8   *Welsh Development Agency v Export Finance Co Ltd* [1992] CLY 2541, CA; and see generally post, para 25.33.

[1.09] The parties. The essence of a sale is the transfer of the property in goods from one person (the 'seller') to another (the 'buyer').[1] Indeed, the common law rule was that a man could not purchase his own goods;[2] but this would seem to be amended to the extent that the Act allows one part-owner to sell to another.[3] Moreover, it is clear that the SGA will cover the situation where an owner of goods buys them back from one who has a legal right to dispose of them, such as a sheriff (see post, para 19.16). The requirement seems to be that the buyer must stand to gain some part of the general property in the goods from the seller; and for this reason it is essential to distinguish carefully a contract of sale from a contract of agency – one who sells from one who acts as an agent in effecting a sale.[4] Thus a franchise to sell goods may create just an agency, to which the SGA is inapplicable,[5] with separate contracts for the sale of goods made within that regime.[6] Alternatively, a franchise agreement may itself provide for the supply of goods to the franchise-holder (distributor).[7] One particular variant of franchising is pyramid-selling.[8] Such direct selling of goods, also known as 'Network Marketing', can be a legitimate form of self-employment, whereby participants earn both by recruiting other participants and selling goods to end-users. Unfortunately, such form of business can also be used to fleece participants, as where a participant's earnings depend almost entirely on his recruitment of others. Attempts to control such abuses were first introduced in Part XI of the Fair Trading Act (FTA) 1973; but, this proving inadequate, its provisions have been bolstered by the Trading Schemes Act 1996. These controls are based on the widely defined 'trading schemes' (s 118 of the FTA (as substituted); on the power to make detailed regulations controlling 'trading schemes';[9] and on the imposition of a number of criminal sanctions on scheme promotions.[10]

[1.10] Contract and conveyance. It has already been pointed out that the two elements of **contract** and **conveyance** are both present in the one transaction of a contract of sale (see

---

[1.09]

1   According to s 61(1), '"seller" means a person who sells or agrees to sell goods' and '"buyer" means a person who buys or agrees to buy goods'.

2   Atiyah, *Sale of Goods* (10th edn), p 30, citing cases on the old liquor licensing Acts (see generally post, para 6.05).

3   Section 2(2). As to whether a sale by a part-owner of his interest is a sale of goods, see post, para 20.22A.

4   *AMB Imballaggi Plastici SRL v Pacflex Ltd* [1999] 2 All ER (Comm) 249, CA. There may be practical difficulties, as where the alleged agent is a commission agent, or a *del credere* agent (one who guarantees performances by his principal), or acts in both capacities (eg, mail order catalogue agent). Cf *Potter v Customs and Excise Comrs* [1985] STC 45, CA (Tupperware parties); comp-u-card (1985 Which? 3).

5   Eg, *B Davis Ltd v Tooth & Co Ltd* [1937] 4 All ER 118, PC. See also Murdoch (1975) 91 LQR at 365. See generally ante, para 1.07.

6   *Rose and Frank Co v Crompton Bros* [1925] AC 445, HL (franchise agreement prevented from being a contract by the 'honourable pledge clause': see generally post, para 10.01).

7   *Decro-Wall International SA v Practitioners in Marketing Ltd* [1971] 2 All ER 217, CA, esp *per* Salmon LJ at 222.

8   The principal legitimate trade body is the Direct Selling Association, which has its own Code of Practice (see post, para 3.13). Distinguish direct selling from franchising (see ante, para 1.07).

9   See the Pyramid Selling Scheme Regulations 1989, SI 2195 (as amended), set out in Thomas, *Encyclopedia of Consumer Law*, Part 2, para 1139.

10 FTA, ss 120(1) (as amended), 120(2), 122. These are the same enforcement arrangements as for Part II of the FTA (s 123: see post, Chapter 28), with special defences for an innocent advertiser or supplier (see post, para 28.16).

ante, para 1.07). Indeed, the Act uses different terminology according to whether or not the property has passed under the contract. Section 2 says:

(4) Where under a contract of sale the property in the goods is transferred from the seller to the buyer the contract is called a sale.

(5) Where the transfer of the property in the goods is to take place at a future time or subject to some condition thereafter to be fulfilled the contract is called an agreement to sell.

(6) An agreement to sell becomes a sale when the time elapses or the conditions are fulfilled subject to which the property in the goods is to be transferred.

Thus, a sharp distinction is drawn between a sale and an agreement to sell: the one is an executed contract, the other executory.[1] The distinction is important, because the executory contract creates only personal rights between the parties whereas an executed contract gives the buyer an interest in the goods themselves.[2] Where it is convenient to avoid making such a judgment it is normal to use some neutral expression such as 'contract of sale'.

[1.11] Absolute and conditional sales. Finally s 2(3) of the SGA recognises that 'A contract of sale may be absolute or conditional'. 'Conditional' in this subsection does not refer to conditions in the sense of essential promises in the contract (see post, para 11.04), nor usually to conditions precedent to the existence of the contract (see post, para 15.21), but to conditions precedent or subsequent to **performance** of the contract itself:[1]

(a) *Conditions precedent.* These may suspend the passing of the property in the goods which are the subject matter of the contract[2] until some act is performed either:

(i) *by one of the parties.* This act may be a conditional performance,[3] but need not necessarily be so;[4] and the contract may make that act precedent to performance by the other party either expressly[5] or impliedly;[6]

(ii) *by some third party.* Thus, in *Marten v Whale*,[7] M agreed to buy a plot of land from T, subject to M's solicitor's approval of title; and, in consideration of this agreement, T agreed to buy M's car. T took possession of the car 'on loan' and sold it to a *bona fide* purchaser. Subsequently, M's solicitor disapproved T's title to the land.

[1.10]

1 For examples of the utilisation of the dichotomy between 'sale' and 'agreement to sell', see SGA, ss 5(3), 6, 7.

2 For further consideration of the conveyancing effect of the contract, see post, Chapter 19.

[1.11]

1 Eg, *Bentworth Finance Ltd v Lubert* (set out post, para 15.23); *Financings Ltd v Stimson* (set out post, para 10.08).

2 The condition is normally precedent only to performance, but it could go further and be precedent to formation of the contract itself: see generally post, para 15.21.

3 Eg, *Trans Trust SPRL v Danubian Trading Ltd* (set out post, para 27.35); or the type of 'conditional sales' considered below, para 1.14.

4 Eg, certificates of quality and inspection; some prize competitions (see post, para 8.16).

5 Eg, the type of 'conditional sale' considered below in para 1.14.

6 Eg, a sale of goods not then in a deliverable state: see the SGA, s 18, r 2 (post, para 20.11).

7 [1917] 2 KB 480, CA: see further post, paras 15.21 and 21.46.

The Court of Appeal held that the two sales were interdependent, so that there was a conditional sale of the car within s 2(3); and that, even though the condition had never materialised, T was able to pass a good title as a buyer in possession (see post, para 21.46).

(b) *Conditions subsequent.* In *Total Gas Marketing Ltd v Arco British Ltd*,[8] A operated a North Sea oilfield and T refined petrol from several such oilfields. A and T entered into an agreement for T to buy A's oil as from a given date. This agreement was made conditional on A before that date becoming party to an allocation agreement with other oil producers for the commingling of their oils at T's delivery terminal. By the given date, A had not entered into such an allocation agreement. T argued that this entitled him to terminate his agreement with A; but A claimed that their obligations under the contract were merely suspended until A entered the allocation agreement.

The House of Lords held that, particularly because A's entry into the allocation agreement was to happen before first delivery (see post, para 23.25), it was clearly intended to be a contingent condition; and A's failure to do so meant that T was no longer bound by the contract. Examples of such conditions subsequent in the retail trade may include some situations where the supplier grants an unfettered right to return goods without cause;[9] or direct financing where there is an initial contract of sale between dealer and consumer (see post, para 10.09).

One particular form of contract of sale whose performance is conditional is that where the seller's duty to transfer the *property* in the goods is made conditional upon the buyer's prior observance of all the terms of the agreement; and, in particular, his payment by instalments of part or all of the price. So common has this situation become that there has developed a tendency to describe only such situations as a 'conditional sale': they are dealt with below (see post, para 1.14).

Instalment sales

[1.12] Introduction. The parties may enter into a contract (commonly by retail) which, whilst satisfying the definition of a contract of sale above considered, differs from an ordinary sale in some fundamental characteristics. First, it provides for payment of the price by (normally approximately equal) instalments and usually after an initial deposit. Second, it may oust the ordinary presumption that delivery and payment are concurrent terms (s 28 of the SGA: see post, para 23.16), providing for early delivery and subsequent payment of the price by instalments.[1] Third, the transactions are normally conducted by way of standard-form contracts (see post, para 11.08). Since 1938, the legislature has recognised that such sale contracts have much in common with hire-purchase (hp) agreements,[2] and accordingly the Hire Purchase Act 1938 (HPA 1938) sought to extend

---

8   [1998] 2 Lloyd's Rep 209, HL, where the obligation to enter the allocation agreement was termed a 'contingent condition or a condition precedent'. See also Smith and Thomas, *Casebook on Contract* (10th edn), p 410.

9   For further discussion of sale or return transactions, see post, para 20.23 *et seq.*

[1.12]

1   Distinguish instalment deliveries and matching payments where the rule in s 28 of the SGA is observed. For instalment contracts, see post, para 23.23 *et seq.*

2   For argument that, until the conditions are fulfilled, a conditional sale is a type of bailment, see post, para 1.14.

some hp controls to such sales. The Hire Purchase Act 1964 (HPA 1964) introduced a further refinement:[3]

(1) *Conditional sales.* Where the contract suspended the passing of property until such conditions as to the payment of instalments or otherwise as may be specified in the agreement are fulfilled, the transaction was to attract almost all the restrictions applicable to hp (see post, para 1.14).

(2) *Credit sales.* Where the property passed at latest on delivery, it attracted only a few of the restrictions (see post, para 1.13).

The result of this momentous innovation was as follows: henceforth, the crucial distinction in consumer instalment transactions was frequently no longer whether the customer had agreed to buy at the outset, but whether the property passed on, or before, delivery. Unfortunately, the position was not quite so simple as this. First, statutory conditional sales were not assimilated in to statutory hp agreements for all purposes, so that a new hybrid was created.[4] Second, the Acts did not cover all transactions.[5] Third, the distinction between conditional sale and hp has begun to break down: see *Forthright Finance Ltd v Carlyle Finance Ltd* (set out post, para 1.22).

[1.13] Credit sales. Where the property in goods passes on or before delivery, the buyer clearly has a good title which he can pass to another under the *nemo dat* rule (see post, para 19.11), or which might fall into his insolvency (see post, para 19.23). For the purpose of the statutory control of instalment contracts, the Hire Purchase Act 1938 (since replaced) introduced a category now termed a 'credit sale agreement' and defined in the CCA as:[1]

> An agreement for the sale of goods, under which the purchase price or part of it is payable by instalments, but which is not a conditional sale agreement.

However, the purpose of this definition is not clear as the term 'credit sale' nowhere features in the body of the CCA, though it figures in Sched 2.[2] On the other hand, many 'credit sales' will amount to regulated consumer credit agreements (see post, para 5.19), in which case they will be subject to restrictions as to the following matters: seeking business[3] and antecedent negotiations;[4] entry into the agreement;[5] cancellation;[6] during

---

3   The HPA 1964 was itself consolidated in the HPA 1965: see post, para 1.24.

4   See Zeigel (1964) 108 Sol Jo 788, at 790.

5   Accordingly, the distinctions in existence before the HPA 1938 were still important so that there existed at least six categories, three at common law and three under the HPA. Matters were the more complicated when property passed part-way through payment of the instalments.

[1.13]

1   See s 189(1). These agreements may be constituted by two or more documents: s 189(4). See also the Health and Safety at Work Act 1974 s 53; and CPA s 45(1).

2   Example 5. As to the effect of these statutory examples, see post, para 5.06.

3   CCA, ss 43–47: see further post, para 8.21 *et seq*.

4   CCA, s 56: see further post, para 16.08.

5   CCA, ss 55, 60–63: see further post, para 9.06 *et seq*.

6   CCA, ss 67–73: see further post, para 10.29 *et seq*.

the currency of the agreement;[7] guarantees and indemnities;[8] preliminary notices before enforcement;[9] death of the buyer;[10] negotiable instruments;[11] and extortionate credit bargains (CCA, ss 137–40: see post, para 29.40). But, to save imposing burdens on suppliers out of all proportion to the monetary amounts involved, the provisions as to entry and cancellation do not apply to small agreements.[12]

Conditional sales[1]

[1.14] Introduction. This paragraph is concerned with the situation where there is an instalment sale (see ante, para 1.12) which satisfies the definition contained in the SGA (see ante, para 1.07) but also contains a reservation of the property in the goods – usually until payment of the full price. In such circumstances, unless and until that condition is satisfied, the buyer obtains no general property in the goods to transfer to another,[2] whether for value (see post, para 1.15), or upon execution, bankruptcy or distress (see post, para 19.15 et seq). Not only will the property remain in the unpaid supplier,[3] but the deposit[4] and payment terms will normally be arranged to confer throughout the contract a 'residual value' on the buyer.[5] The contract may also include two further provisions. First, in the event of the buyer's default, the seller would be granted an express right to recover possession of the goods (see post, para 1.14A), which might be exercised either just to encourage the buyer to make good his default, or to enable the seller to resell the goods to recoup his loss;[6] and any such resale should be free of any interest of the buyer in the goods.[7] Second, to preserve the market value of this right of repossession and resale, the agreement would contain provisions for the maintenance of the goods (see post, para 11.09).

[1.14A] The licence to seize. For some time, there were anxieties that this licence for the seller to repossess the goods (see ante, para 1.14) might bring the transaction within the purview of the Bills of Sale Act 1882. This Act, which is dealt with later (see post,

---

7   CCA, ss 77, 81, 82, 94–97: see further respectively post, paras 15.17, 15.16, 26.22, 26.19.
8   CCA, ss 105–13: see further post, paras 25.11–13.
9   CCA, ss 76, 89, 98: see further post, paras 24.28–32, 26.10.
10 CCA, ss 86(2): see further post, para 24.47.
11 CCA, ss 123–25: see further post, paras 25.08–09.
12 CCA, s 74(2). For 'small agreements' within the CCA, see post, para 5.17.

[1.14]

1   See generally, Melville (1974) 124 NLJ 615; Jones, *Chattel Mortgages* (6th edn, 1933), Chapter 19; Goode, *Commercial Law* (2nd edn), pp 763–67.
2   Whilst the buyer is in possession before the passing of property, it has been pointed out that the transaction is a form of bailment: Jones, *ibid*, para 932; and the *Romalpa* case (see post, para 25.29). *Contra* Bridge LJ in *Borden (UK) Ltd v Scottish Timber Products Ltd* [1981] Chapter 25 at 35D.
3   The commercial principle is the same for hp: see post, para 1.20. The supplier's security in an unregulated agreement is ultimately recaption and resale: see post, para 27.02. For restrictions in respect of regulated agreements, see post, para 24.27 et seq.
4   The size of the deposit will normally be calculated to cover at least the drop in value on supply of the goods, eg, the market price drop from new to second-hand.
5   See post, para 27.12. As to the supplier's interest in the goods, see post, para 24.22.
6   Eg, *Hewison v Ricketts* (set out post, para 27.19).
7   Because the buyer (unlike a mortgagor: see ante, para 1.08) has no equity of redemption: see post, para 24.22.

Chapters 9 and 25), rendered void almost every chattel mortgage by an individual which was not in the statutory form; and, as the statutory terms did not provide adequate security, creditors would normally seek to avoid the Act altogether. The 1882 Act was expressed to apply to any transaction evidenced by a written bill of sale granted by way of security for a loan (s 3); and the term 'bill of sale' is defined to include 'licences to take possession of personal chattels as security for any debt' (see post, para 9.04). The issue was settled in *McEntire v Crossley Brothers*:[1]

> Crossley agreed to let one of their gas-engines to a trader under an agreement which provided as follows: when the trader had paid £240 the engine was to become his, but until then it was to remain the sole and absolute property of Crossley. The agreement also empowered Crossley to repossess and resell the engine, retaining any deficiency but paying over any surplus, upon the happening of certain stated events, which included the trader's bankruptcy.[2] The engine was claimed by the trader's assignee in bankruptcy.

Whilst a trustee will normally have no greater rights to property than the bankrupt trader (see post, para 19.23), the trustee here claimed that the property in the engine had passed to the trader and that Crossley's right to repossess was avoided as being a licence to seize within the 1882 Act. However, the House of Lords held that such a conditional sale did not fall within the 1882 Act because Crossley as owner was not **granting**, but **reserving**, a licence to seize (see post, para 25.27). Lord Herschell explained (at 462):

> If the property never passed to the bankrupt [trader], he can never have ... given the right to seize ... within the meaning of the Bills of Sale Act. The ... Act relates to ... rights to seize given or conferred by the person who owns the property.

Thus, the House of Lords confirmed that an ordinary *bona fide* two-party[3] conditional sale agreement would avoid the Bills of Sale Act 1882, simply because the agreement did not pass to the conditional buyer during the period when the licence to seize was operative any proprietary rights either at law[4] or in equity.[5] The position would, of course, be otherwise if the property passed before the licence to seize expired,[6] or if the agreement was not genuine, as with some of the sale and rehiring transactions (see post, para 25.27).

As we shall see later, this distinction is important for English law (see post, para 25.01); but it should be noted that US law has long foresworn such sophistry, treating conditional sales as a type of chattel mortgage.[7]

[1.15] Dispositions by the buyer. Whilst the reservation of property by a conditional seller was a sensible first step to protect him against non-payment by the buyer (see ante,

---

[1.14A]

1 [1895] AC 457, [1895–96] All ER Rep 829, HL.
2 This looks remarkably like a summary of the rights of a mortgagor and mortgagee: see post, para 25.20.
3 Distinguish the three-party transactions involved in lender credit (see post, para 2.20), where the issue may be more difficult (see post, para 25.33 *et seq*).
4 Notwithstanding that the trader had a contractual right to call for the property in the goods on due completion of the payments: see further post, paras 16.17; 24.22.
5 The Lord Chancellor expressly pointed out that, whilst the result might be similar to that achieved by a mortgage (see note 2 above), that in itself did not bring the Bills of Sale Acts into operation (at 465–66).
6 *Re Hawkins ex p Emerson* (1871) 41 LJ Bky 20.
7 See Jones, *Chattel Mortgages* (6th edn, 1933), Chapter 19; and post, para 1.26.

para 1.14), an ever-present danger was that the conditional buyer might contract to dispose to a third party either of (i) the title to the goods or (ii) his interest in them.

1   *Dispositions of title.* Suppose the conditional buyer sold or pledged the goods to a *bona fide* third party. It is true that, because the conditional buyer did not himself have a good title to the goods, as a general rule he could not pass one to that third party: this is because of the *nemo dat* rule (see post, para 19.11). However, he may be able to pass a good title to a *bona fide* purchaser or pledgee by way of one of the following exceptions to the *nemo dat* rule:

(a) Buyers in possession (see post, para 21.43). The matter was litigated in *Lee v Butler*:[1]

> Under an agreement made with a furniture dealer (A), B was to take immediate possession of some furniture in return for a promise to pay 'as and by way of rent' £1 on May 6th and £96 on the following August 1st. *Inter alia*, the agreement provided that, if B removed the goods, A might repossess them,[2] and all sums previously paid should be appropriated to rent only; but, if B performed all the terms of agreement, the rent should cease, and the goods should then, but not before, become the property of B. Before all the instalments were paid, B sold the furniture to a *bona fide* purchaser (bfp). The Court of Appeal found that B had 'agreed to buy' the furniture, and therefore passed a good title to the bfp under s 9 of the Factors Act 1889.

It was, of course, to meet this threat that the hp form of agreement was invented (see post, para 1.20), though subsequent case law has cast doubts on the ambit of the threat.[3] Nevertheless, it was thought that conditional sales had so much in common with hp agreements that this case law distinction between the two types of contract was therefore partially destroyed by statute (see ante, para 1.12): where a conditional sale falls within the CCA definition (see post, para 1.16) but not otherwise, the buyer is deemed not to be a person who has 'agreed to buy' within the meaning of s 9 (see post, para 21.46).

(b) A further limited exception to the *nemo dat* rule was created for dispositions of motor vehicles to 'private purchasers' (see post, para 21.55) made by one who was a conditional buyer or a hirer under an hp agreement (see post, para 1.22). In neither case does it matter whether or not the agreement is regulated by the CCA 1974 (see post, para 5.13).

Recognising that there will be some circumstances where a reservation of property may be insufficient to defeat the claim of a *bona fide* purchaser or pledgee to whom the conditional buyer has transferred the goods, the unpaid conditional seller may at this point attempt to transfer his claim to (or 'trace') the proceeds of that disposition (see post, para 27.14).

2   *Dispositions of his interest.* Suppose the conditional buyer (Z), instead of trying to dispose of a good title to the goods (see above), instead merely attempts to assign his

---

[1.15]

1   [1893] 2 QB 318, [1891–94] All ER Rep 1200, CA.

2   This licence to seize probably would not infringe the Bills of Sale Acts: see ante, para 1.14A.

3   See *Newtons of Wembley Ltd v Williams* (set out post, para 21.51). It has even been suggested that a transfer by one who has only agreed to buy cannot be a sale within s 2 of the SGA: *Re Interview* [1975] IR 382 at 395. *Sed quaere?* See further post, para 21.49.

interest in them to X.[4] He has contractual rights under the conditional sale; namely, to present possession of the goods and later acquisition of the property in them.[5] The result of such an assignment would be that X (the 'assignee') would *prima facie* 'stand in the shoes of' Z (the 'assignor'), taking over his position as conditional buyer (see post, para 2.22).

Vehicle transfer agencies. First appearing about 1990, these purport to arrange such assignments for impecunious hirers,[6] though this service causes difficulty by reason of the standard prohibition against assignment normally found in conditional sale and hp agreements (see post, para 1.23) and of the failure by the agency to keep up the promised payments.[7] To pursue a transaction in the face of such a prohibition may render the Agency unfit to hold a CCA licence:[8] sometimes, the Agency may succeed in passing a good Part III title if the assignee is in fact a 'private purchaser' (see above); but, in most cases the original owner is likely to be entitled to repossess the vehicle.[9]

[1.16] Statutory definition. For the purposes of the statutory control of instalment contracts, there was introduced in 1964 a category termed a 'conditional sale' and now defined by the CCA as:[1]

> ... an agreement for the sale of goods or land under which the purchase price or part of it is payable by instalments, and the property in the goods or land is to remain in the seller (notwithstanding that the buyer is to be in possession of the goods or land) until such conditions as to the payment of instalments or otherwise as may be specified in the agreement are fulfilled.

Typically, the contract will provide that the property is not to pass until the whole of the purchase price has been paid.[2] Further, it should be noted that the definition has been extended to include conditional sales of land.[3]

---

4   The rights of the conditional buyer may not be assignable: see the discussion of the similar issues which may arise with regard to a hirer under an hp agreement (post, para 1.23).

5   These contractual rights amount to a chose in action (see post, para 7.16), which may *prima facie* be assigned either in equity or under statute (see post, para 7.17 *et seq*).

6   Such Agencies tend to advertise (wrongly) that for a commission the hirer/lessee is relieved of any further obligation to keep up the payments, whereas in law the hirer/lessee can only be so released with the consent (normally withheld) of the owner/lessor. The advertisements also attract would-be hirers who would be unlikely to obtain finance facilities.

7   Over 90% of such agencies have been found to fail to make the payments.

8   The OFT considers the Agencies are licensable as debt-adjusters (see post, para 5.43): see (1991) Beeline, No 91/3, p 7. As transfer will normally interfere with the original hp or lease agreement, there will usually be reasons for doubting the fitness of the Agency to hold a licence (see generally post, para 6.18): see (1992) 46 CC 6/11.

9   Even if the vehicle were 'protected goods' under a regulated agreement, the hirer will have lost protection under the CCA by voluntarily parting with possession: see post, para 24.37.

[1.16]

1   See s 189(1): these agreements may be constituted by two or more documents (s 189(4)). With the addition of a reference to land, this definition is taken verbatim from the HPA 1964, s 29(1). For an example, see Sched 2, Example 4. See also SOGIT, s 15(1); CPA, s 45(1).

2   Suppose the agreement provides that the property is to pass when part of the price has been paid. When that point is reached, does it become a 'credit sale agreement'? (see ante, para 1.13); does it cease to be a 'conditional sale agreement'?

3   Conditional sales of land are uncommon: Goode, *Consumer Credit Law and Practice*, para 38.5. Distinguish mortgages of land, in respect of which the CCA restrictions are considered post, para 25.23.

However, the CCA is not applicable to all conditional sales within the foregoing definition: for the most part, the provisions of the Act extend only to regulated agreements (see post, para 5.13). Where there is a regulated conditional sale, it is subject to all the same statutory restrictions as a credit sale agreement (see ante, para 1.13) plus the following: first, it has already been seen that a buyer under such a conditional sale is not one who has 'agreed to buy' (see ante, para 1.15); and second, such conditional sales have been largely assimilated to hp agreements (see post, para 1.24), being subject to the statutory restrictions in respect of the buyer's death (ss 86, 128 of the CCA: see post, para 24.44/46), his default,[4] his right to terminate[5] and the seller's right to repossess (ss 87–93 of the CCA: see post, para 24.27 *et seq*).

BAILMENT AND HIRING

[1.17] Bailment generally.[1] In English law, bailment is the transfer (delivery) of **possession** of goods by one person (the bailor) to another (the bailee) on condition, express or implied, that the goods shall be returned to the bailor (or dealt with according to his instructions) as soon as the purpose for which they were bailed is ended.[2] It is distinguished from sale by reason of the fact that the normal objective of a bailment is to effect a transfer of the **possession** of goods, whereas the objective of a sale is to effect a transfer of the general **property** in goods.[3] Exceptionally, under a bailment the bailee may acquire the property in the goods from his erstwhile bailor, as where there is a hire-purchase agreement (see post, para 1.20) or perhaps a sale or return transaction (see post, para 20.23); or the bailee may have the right to mix and substitute other identical goods, for example, in a grain store.[4] Moreover, where under a contract for the sale of goods the property and possession of goods are for some time separated, as English law allows (see post, para 19.01), for that space of time there may also be a bailment: if possession passes before property, the buyer will be in possession as bailee of the seller;[5] whilst if the property passes before possession, the seller will be in possession as bailee of the buyer. The separation of property and possession under a contract of sale may have implications for risk (see post, para 22.01).

There are many everyday transactions of bailment, such as the deposit of goods for safe custody or storage, the leaving of goods for the purpose of cleaning or repair, the hiring out of goods (post, para 1.18), a pledge (post, para 25.15), the carriage of goods, a

---

4   CCA, ss 87–89, 90–93, 129–36: see post, respectively paras 24.30; 24.34; 24.39.
5   CCA, ss 99–100, 102–03: see post, respectively paras 26.05; 26.04. But not in the case of land after title has passed to the debtor: CCA, s 99(3).

[1.17]

1   See generally, *Chitty on Contracts* (28th edn), vol 2, Chapter 32; Palmer, *Bailments* (2nd edn); Bell, *Personal Property*, Chapter 5.
2   *Wincanton Ltd v P&O Trans European Ltd* [2001] 9 CL 123, CA; and *Winfield and Jolowicz on Tort* (15th edn) 16. Distinguish a mere contractual licence to park a caravan on a site: *Hinks v Fleet* [1986] CLY 151, CA.
3   For the duty of delivery in relation to goods sold, see post, para 23.03.
4   *Mercer v Craven Grain Storage Co* (1994) *The Times*, 17 March, HL (see 111 LQR 10); and Bridge, *Sale of Goods*, pp 54–57.
5   As under a conditional sale: see ante, para 1.14. Nevertheless, that bailment will cease when some later event causes the property in the goods to pass to the buyer: see post, para 25.20.

supply of software on licence.[6] Whilst the relationship between bailor and bailee is frequently based on contract (see post, para 1.18); this is not necessarily the case,[7] as where a carrier or repairer acts gratuitously (without consideration), or goods are delivered before contract (see post, para 10.09). Indeed, there may also be a bailment where the bailee sub-bails the goods in such a way that there is no contract of bailment between bailor and sub-bailee.[8] The rights of the bailor and bailee to sue a third party in respect of the wrongful retention, destruction of, or damage to, goods will be dealt with later (post, paras 19.06; 19.10); but, whichever of the two recovers, he may have a duty to account to the other to the extent of that other's interest in the goods.[9]

[1.18] Simple hiring agreements. The English contract to hire chattels may be defined as one whereby the hirer obtains a right to use the chattel hired, in return for the payment to the owner of the price of the hiring, this price usually being termed 'rent' or 'hire-rent'. Leaving aside charterparties of ships, the common law rules are the same for all forms of simple hiring: basically, these will mostly be the same as for bailments generally (see ante, para 1.17), of which simple hiring is but a species; but they may be varied or ousted by the terms of the contract of bailment and there will frequently be found a standard-form contract spelling out the obligations of bailor and bailee in considerable detail (see post, para 11.08) – and hence leaving little scope for the common law rules. Moreover, whilst the contract of hiring gives the hirer an interest which is *prima facie* assignable (see post, para 1.23), the absence of an option to purchase means that the hirer has no such interest in the goods which could be seized by way of execution or upon which distress can be levied;[1] and treatment of simple hiring agreements is likely to be materially different for the purposes of taxation (especially capital allowances and VAT) and grants (especially the system of regional development grants). The terms statutorily implied in a 'contract for the hire of goods' in favour of the hirer will be dealt with later (see post, Chapters 12–15). Because the essence of a bailment is a transfer of possession (see ante, para 1.17), the hiring, with its obligation to pay rent, does not commence until delivery and the bailee is *prima facie* under a duty to return the goods when the agreement is determined (see post, para 27.21).

Distinguish simple hiring from hp. Hire-purchase does, but simple hiring does not, include an option to purchase,[2] though this apparently simple distinction has given rise to difficulty with perpetual hiring agreements (see post, para 1.24) and has a number of consequences. First, the exception to the *nemo dat* rule is applicable in respect of motor vehicles let on hp, though not under simple hiring agreements.[3] Second, the Bills of Sale Act 1882 will not usually apply to either hp or simple hirings: despite the normally-present licence for the bailor to seize the goods in default (see post, para 9.04), the chattel

---

6   *Watford Electronics Ltd v Sanderson CFL Ltd* (set out post, para 18.24A; unappealed point).
7   The obligations of the bailee to take care of goods is grounded in the tort of negligence: *Graham v Voigt* [1990] CLY 4310, Aust. See generally post, Chapter 17. Cf involuntary bailees: post, para 8.18.
8   *The Pioneer Container* [1994] 2 All ER 250, PC (see [1996] JBL 329).
9   *O'Sullivan v Williams* [1992] 3 All ER 385, CA. As to where the hirer is in administration, see post, para 19.19.

[1.18]
1   See Goode, *Hire Purchase Law and Practice* (2nd edn), pp 633, 893.
2   The distinction may be vital: *Galbraith v Mitchenall Estates Ltd* (set out post, para 27.21). For the option to purchase in hp agreements, see post, para 1.22.
3   As to the *nemo dat* rule, see post, para 19.11; and as to this exception thereto, see post, para 21.55.

mortgage legislation will not catch either a genuine bailment (with or without option to purchase) for the same reasons as in the case of conditional sale (see ante, para 1.14A); nor a genuine sale and rehiring (see post, para 25.26). Third, there are some differences in treatment as between simple hirings and hp as regards both minimum payment clauses (see post, paras 27.37; 27.50) and the measure of damages in claims against the other party by a bailor (see post, para 27.31) or bailee (see post, para 29.25).

[1.18A] Commercial categories of lease.[1] The commercial world has developed the practice of describing simple hiring agreements in respect of goods (see ante, para 1.18) by different appellations according to context, of which the following are examples:

(a) *'Charter'* is the expression that has long been used in relation to the hiring of ships, and over the years a separate body of law has developed relating to charterparties which is beyond the scope of this work.[2]

(b) An *'equipment lease'* is a contract between two commercial parties, lessor and lessee, giving the lessee possession and use of a specific asset on payment of rentals over a primary period: the lessor retains ownership of the asset, which will never pass to the lessee, unlike in hp.[3] Such leases are commonly divided according to whether or not the asset value is amortised (recovered) by the lessor over the primary period.

  (i) *'Finance (or full payout) leases'* are the most common type. Here, the primary period may be (say) 75% of the expected useful life of the asset,[4] for example, of plant and machinery to be used as part of the fixed assets of a business and extending to 'big-ticket' items such as jumbo jets and oil platforms. It will transfer substantially all the risks and rewards of ownership to the lessee and has much in common with conditional sales (see ante, para 1.14), hire-purchase (see post, para 1.20) and chattel mortgage.[5] The asset will usually be chosen by the lessee from the stock of a third party supplier and then sold to the lessor, making this a form of direct financing (see post, para 2.21). Sometimes, a manufacturer and lessor will get together to offer a leasing package form of finance.[6] The commercial attractions of finance leases tend to be influenced significantly by taxation and accounting standards.

  (ii) In *'operating leases'*, the primary period will be for substantially less than the expected life of the asset. Such schemes are commonly used, together with a

---

[1.18A]

1 See Goode, *Hire Purchase Law and Practice*, pp 880–83; Soper and Munro, *The Leasing Handbook*, esp Chapter 19 for the terms of the leasing contract; Davies, *Equipment and Motor Vehicle Leasing and Hiring*.

2 'Large ticket' ship leases are properly 'demise charters'. As to the leasing of ships and oil rigs, see generally Soper and Munro, *ibid*, pp 317–18.

3 See post, para 1.24. This ownership technicality is crucial for the tax-treatment of the two types of contract – particularly who is to claim the capital allowance of 'big-ticket' items (see below) – and as to the incidence of VAT between VAT-registered businesses.

4 See generally Davies [1984] JBL 468; Goode, *Commercial Law*, Chapter 31; Soper and Munro, *op cit*, note 1, p 58 *et seq*, 319–21 (vehicle fleet management).

5 Where there is an option to purchase, such transactions are sometimes termed 'industrial hp' or 'equipment leasing', or 'lease purchase', or 'personal leasing', regardless of legal niceties. For sub-leasing, see ante, para 1.17. Distinguish the (normally longer term) lease of land, governed by the law of real property: for fixtures, see post, para 25.23.

6 Eg, of computers or office equipment: see post, para 16.06A. See generally Soper and Munro, *op cit*, note 1, pp 325–28. For the sales and leasing code of practice, see post, para 3.13.

supply of services, for those types of goods which enjoy an active second-hand market, for example, crane and driver; aircraft and crew,[7] or for specialist equipment suffering high obsolescence rates, for example, computers and software.

(c) *'Contract hire'* (or car leasing) is a specialised form of operating lease, used for self-drive fleets of motor vehicles, where the lessor undertakes some of the responsibility for the management and maintenance of the vehicles. At the end of the (typically) two or three year hire period, the trade supplier may agree to repurchase the vehicle.[8]

(d) *'Rental agreement'* is the expression normally reserved for retail business and used in relation to the short-term hiring to private consumers of motor vehicles and the indefinite hiring of televisions, videos and furniture. The rental agreement may be block discounted (see post, para 2.22).

[1.19] Statutory definition. For the purposes of the statutory control of instalment contracts, there was introduced by the CCA a category termed 'consumer hire agreement' and defined as:[1]

an agreement made by a person[2] with an individual (the hirer)[3] for the bailment or (in Scotland) the hiring of goods to the hirer, being an agreement which

(a) is not a hire-purchase agreement (see post, para 1.24), and

(b) is capable of subsisting for more than three months,[4] and

(c) does not require the hirer to make payments exceeding £x.[5]

This careful definition is aimed primarily at situations where a consideration is payable before the expiry of the bailment: typically, it will extend to periodic domestic rental/hire and the leasing of business equipment and vehicles (see ante, para 1.18A). Whether the lessor ('owner') is leasing office equipment to solicitors, medical instruments to doctors, plant and machinery to builders, cars to businessmen or television sets to consumers, the Act and regulations will apply if the agreement is within the financial limits, is not exempt and the lessee or hirer is not a company (see Chapter 5). Some further points may be noticed about this definition. First, it relates only to goods let as such and does not

---

7   'Plant hire' is for relatively short periods. In all such cases, the lessor commonly looks to the resale for much of his profit.

8   For Vehicle Transfer Agencies, see ante, para 1.15.

[1.19]

1   Sections 15(1), 189(1): these agreements may be constituted by two or more documents – s 189(4). Eg, see CCA, Sched 2, Examples 20, 24. See generally Palmer and Yates [1979] 38 CLJ 180.

2   Presumably, the draftsman used the expression 'person' to cover both leasing and sub-leasing. But he then appears to deal with the same point again in his s 189(1) definition of 'owner'. Cf the description of the transferor under s 8 as 'creditor' (see post, para 5.19); and as to 'creditor', see further post, para 5.25. For contracts governed by foreign law, see post, para 18.13.

3   For the meaning of 'individual', see below and post, para 5.24. 'Hirer' is defined by s 189(1). For discussion of the similar definition of 'debtor', see post, para 5.24.

4   See *Dimond v Lovell* (below).

5   In computing liability, the hirer's statutory right of termination (see below) must be ignored: Lindgren (1977) 40 MLR at 167. This upper rental figure is the same as the amount of credit under a regulated consumer credit agreement (as to which, see post, para 5.22), but unlike the latter, it includes deposits or rentals payable before delivery and VAT.

extend to leases of land.[6] Second, whilst it clearly comprehends all the types of simple hiring agreements considered above, in England it would also appear to cover gratuitous bailments.[7] Third, it seems that the crucial thing for s 15(1)(c) is the value of the rentals at the time the agreement is made, ignoring any subsequent variation.[8] Fourth, in *Dimond v Lovell*:[9]

> D was an innocent driver in a road traffic accident. Whilst D's car was being repaired, she hired a replacement, for a period which turned out to be eight days, from accident hire company (A) upon the following terms: the rental period must not exceed 28 days; D would not have to pay the hire charges immediately; instead, A was given authority to sue the negligent driver (L) and recover its charges from him.

In the House of Lords, the case primarily concerns consumer credit (see post, para 5.13), but in relation to whether the accident hire agreement amounted to a consumer hiring within the above definition the Court of Appeal held as follows: s 15 was also capable of applying to a single period of hiring and where the charges were paid upon completion of the litigation against D many months later; but the accident hire agreement fell outside s 15 because the bailment was not capable of subsisting for more than three months (s 15(1)(c)). Fifth, there are proposals to exclude from the definition agreements based on a flat fee for a hire period of up to one week with no penalty for a change in the agreed period of hire.[10]

CCA provisions. Where a 'consumer hire agreement' does fall within the ambit of the CCA, in which case it is termed 'regulated' (see post, para 5.13), the legislature has sought to reduce the advantages to be derived from utilisation of this form instead of an instalment sale or hp agreement. Accordingly, the CCA has made applicable almost all the same restrictions as obtain in the case of credit sales (see ante, para 1.13), except that the extortionate credit bargain provisions do not apply to consumer hirings (see post, para 29.40). However, despite the similar retention of ownership of goods let on hire, it was not possible to utilise all the further rules in respect of conditional sales (see ante, para 1.16). Instead, the CCA introduced separate provisions as follows: the hirer is granted a special, more limited right of termination (s 101: see post, para 26.07); and there are limited restrictions upon the owner's right of recaption,[11] together with some financial relief to the hirer in that event (s 132: see post, para 27.50). There has been debate as to whether more, or less, of these commercial leases should be regulated (see post, para 5.11).

---

6   *Contra* conditional sales: see ante, para 1.15. As to 'goods', see ante, para 2.01. Does 'goods' include credit cards (see post, para 5.30)?
7   As to which, see ante, para 1.17. Could this lead to the application of the CCA rules as between bailor and sub-bailee?
8   Spicer and Munro, *The Leasing Handbook*, 272.
9   [1999] 3 All ER 1, CA (see [1999] JBL 452, at 454–58).
10 This should prevent short-term hirers, eg, of power tools, from holding over beyond three months and then claiming that the agreement is regulated and unenforceable: DTI, *Clarification and Simplification of UK Consumer Credit Law* (Feb 1988) Chapter 5; and see further post, para 5.11.
11 Recaption is subject to the notice procedure (see post, para 24.28) and time orders (see post, para 24.40) but not the protected goods rules (see post, para 24.35). Court actions for recovery of the goods are brought under the Torts Act 1977, s 3 (see post, para 24.26).

DEFINITION OF A CONTRACT OF HIRE-PURCHASE[1]

Development of the Common Law Form

[1.20] Background. As will be seen below, the English contract of hire-purchase (hp) started life as a form of sale, switched to a form of bailment towards the end of the 19th century, and has evolved into such a specialised form of bailment as now to be regarded as something *sui iuris*.[2]

Hire-purchase is in economic terms (see ante, para 1.14), but perhaps not in legal theory, a fiction:[3] historically, evolution consists of increasingly sophisticated attempts by legal draftsmen to devise on behalf of suppliers under instalment contracts a form of contract which would preserve for the supplier such rights in the goods supplied as would provide adequate security for the subsequent payment of the 'price'. There are three major dangers which the supplier must face. First, he must secure his rights to the goods against the consumer and the latter's creditors (see post, para 1.21). Second, he must try to prevent the consumer overriding his possessory or proprietary interest in the goods in favour of a *bona fide* purchaser (bfp) or other transferee (see post, paras 1.22–23). Third, when the supplier has secured his legal interest in the goods, he must take steps to ensure that these rights continue to be of adequate value (see post, para 11.09). Throughout the 19th century, the legal form of the contract was evolving to meet these requirements;[4] and it was not until 1895 that the major characteristics of the form were settled.[5] By reason of its complicated nature, the transaction was almost always in writing[6] and commonly in standard form (see post, para 11.08).

[1.21] Other creditors. Any appropriate form of words will create a debt in the consumer, so that in the event of default the supplier may levy execution on any of the consumer's goods.[1] However, as the supplier also wishes to obtain a preferential claim to the goods supplied as against the consumer's other creditors, one of the following forms was normally used:

(a) A conditional sale; that is, an agreement to sell with a reservation of property until the price was paid (see ante, para 1.14); or

---

[1.20]

1 See generally, Diamond, *Commercial and Consumer Credit*; Dunstan, *Law Relating to HP* (4th edn, 1939); Earengay, *Law Relating to HP* (2nd edn, 1938); Goode, *HP Law and Practice* (2nd edn); Guest, *Law of HP* (1966); Wild, *The Law of HP* (2nd edn, 1965); Goode, *Commercial Law* (2nd edn), pp 767–73; Cranston, *Consumers and the Law* (3rd edn), pp 232–34; and further post, para 1.25.

2 See further post, para 1.25. But see the persistent use of the terminology for 'industrial hp' (ante, para 1.18) and consumer contracts termed 'option to own'.

3 Hire purchase has been described as a legal fiction: the *Crowther Report on Consumer Credit* (Cmnd 4596) para 5.2.3. But is it?

4 Perhaps an early example was the Scots case of *Cowan v Spencer* (1828), as explained in the judgment of Lord Keith in *Armour v Thyssen* (set out post, para 20.28).

5 The major characteristics of hp could be said to have been settled by the HL in 1895 with the following cases: *McEntire v Crossley Bros* (set out ante, para 1.14A); *Helby v Matthews* (set out post, para 1.22).

6 The courts were reluctant to accept oral hp contracts: *Scammell & Nephew v Ouston* (set out post, para 10.03). But see *Hitchens v General Guarantee Corp* [2001] 4 CL 291, CA.

[1.21]

1 Eg, *Chubb Cash Ltd v John Crilley & Sons* [1983] 2 All ER 294, CA. For levying execution, see generally post, para 19.15. To levy execution on the goods of a third party is an act of conversion: see post, para 19.06.

(b) A hp agreement; that is, a letting of the goods with an option to purchase.[2]

Because they both reserve the property in the goods to the supplier, either type of contract would usually keep the goods supplied out of the consumer's insolvency[3] or any execution levied on the consumer;[1] and it might also give a right to trace.[4] However, the supplier's security might still be vulnerable because of the legislation mentioned below.

1   *The Bills of Sale Act 1882* (see generally post, Chapters 9 and 25). It has already been seen that in *McEntire v Crossley Bros* the House of Lords decided that this legislation did not catch the ordinary two-party conditional sale (see ante, para 1.14A). *A fortiori*, this would save the ordinary *bona fide* two-party hp or simple hiring agreement.

2   *The Law of Distress Amendment Act 1908*. To meet the threat posed to their security by s 4 of the 1908 Act (see post, para 19.17), draftsmen invented the verbose *Smart v Holt* clause (see post, para 26.09).

[1.22] The *bona fide* purchaser or pledgee. In the mid-19th century, the conditional sale with a reservation of property was sufficient to defeat the claims of a *bona fide* purchaser or pledgee because of the rule *nemo dat quod non habet* (see post, para 19.11). However, an important exception to that rule was enacted in s 9 of the Factors Act 1889 (FA): this provided that, generally speaking, one who had 'agreed to buy' goods should be able to pass a good title to a *bona fide* purchaser or pledgee (see post, para 21.43). Almost immediately, the Court of Appeal decided that this new exception applied in the case of a conditional buyer (*Lee v Butler*: see ante, para 1.15). This decision immediately threw the instalment credit trade into turmoil; and the new form of contract drafted with a view to avoiding this consequence was litigated in *Helby v Matthews*:[1]

> The terms of the agreement between the dealer (A) and customer (B) were somewhat similar to those in *Lee v Butler*. B agreed to pay 10/6 per month as rent for hire of a piano, and the property was not to pass until 36 of these instalments had been paid. However, the agreement further provided that B might at any time determine the hiring by delivering the piano to A upon which he should remain liable for all arrears of rent. During the continuance of the agreement, B pledged the piano to C who took bf and for value, and pleaded title under s 9.

The House of Lords unanimously held, reversing the Court of Appeal, that C had not obtained a good title. Lord Macnaughten explained:[2]

> The contract ... on the part of the dealer was a contract of hiring coupled with a conditional contract or undertaking to sell. On the part of the customer it was a contract of hiring only until the time came for making the last payment. It may be that at the inception of the transaction both parties expected that the agreement would run its full course, and that the piano would change hands in the end. But an expectation, however confident and however

---

2   Eg, *Pearce v Brooks* (1866) LR 1 Ex 213; *City Motors (1933) Pty Ltd v Southern Aerial Super Service* (1961) 106 CLR 477, Aust HC, esp *per* Kitto J at 486–87.

3   The rule extending the ambit of a bankruptcy beyond goods owned by a bankrupt to include also those of which he was the reputed owner has now been abolished: see post, para 26.09.

4   See Goode (1976) 92 LQR 360, at 376. Tracing is considered further post, paras 27.13–14.

[1.22]

1   [1895] AC 471, [1895–99] All ER Rep 821, HL. The result is the same even if the customer gives a promissory note as collateral security: *Modern Light Cars Ltd v Seals* [1934] 1 KB 32.

2   At 482. The reasoning is criticised by Atiyah, *Sale of Goods* (10th edn), p 16.

well-founded, does not amount to an agreement, and even an agreement between two parties operative only during the pleasure of one of them is no agreement on his part at law.

Their Lordships distinguished *Lee v Butler* on the grounds that in that case, as soon as the agreement was made, there was a binding agreement to buy on the part of B and he had no option to return the goods,[3] though their Lordships might not have been so adamant if the *Helby v Matthews* agreement had contained a modern minimum payments clause.[4] Indeed, *Helby v Matthews* was itself distinguished in *Forthright Finance Ltd v Carlyle Finance Ltd*:[5]

> Forthright supplied a Ford Cosworth car to Senator Motors, a limited company dealer, under a contract described as a 'Hire Purchase Agreement': it required Senator to pay all the instalments of hire-rent and conferred the usual option to purchase on it when all the instalments had been paid; but it added that the option was deemed to have been exercised when all instalments had been paid, whereupon the property in the car passed to Senator, unless it has told Forthright before completion of the payments that such is not the case. Before it had paid all the instalments, Senator sold the car to CF Ltd, who successfully claimed a good title under the above exception (see post, para 21.52).

Delivering the unanimous judgement of the Court of Appeal, Phillips LJ pointed out that Senator was bound to complete all the payments of hire-rent and held that it was a conditional sale agreement:[6] he distinguished *Helby v Matthews*, where the hirer was not bound to continue with the hiring for any particular number of months (at 97) and pointed out that (at 98):

> The option not to take title, which one would expect only to be exercised in the most unusual circumstances, does not affect the true nature of the agreement.

His Lordship expressly refrained from deciding whether the agreement would have been a conditional sale if it had contained a positive nominal option, rather than a negative option.[7] The result is that, if the supplier wishes to enter an hp agreement, rather than a conditional sale, it would seem that he cannot legally bind his customer to complete the allotted span of the 'hiring' and hence pay an amount of rent which is equivalent to the deferred price:[8] all he can do is to so arrange the payment terms that it is in the customer's interest to complete the hiring (see post, para 1.25).

[1.23] Other *bona fide* transferees. Besides an outright disposition of the general or special property in the goods by way of sale or pledge respectively (see ante, para 1.22), the hirer under a hp agreement may seek to utilise such interest as he has by way of assignment or lien.

---

3   See also *Hull Ropes Co Ltd v Adams* (1895), 65 LJQ 114.

4   The object of such a clause (see post, para 11.09) has been said to be to place the owner in at least as favourable position as a conditional seller: *Crowther Report on Consumer Credit* (Cmnd 4596) para 5.1.3.

5   [1997] 4 All ER 90, CA. The agreement was not regulated because Senator was a limited company (see post, para 5.24); and the transaction was therefore capable of falling within the modern equivalent of s 9 of the FA, s 25(1) of the SGA (see post, para 21.45).

6   He cited the argument that it should be a conditional sale if the customer bound himself to complete all the payments in Goode, *Consumer Credit Legislation*, para 218.

7   This has significance for the drafting of the agreement: see post, para 1.25.

8   *Close Asset Finance v Care Graphics Machinery Ltd* [2000] 4 CLY 849. What would be the effect of an acceleration clause (see post, para 26.19)?

1   *Assignment.*[1] The form of an hp agreement being a hybrid between bailment and sale, the hirer *prima facie* has two contractual interests each capable of independent assignment:[2]

(a) His right to hire the goods, which is similar to the right of a hirer under a simple bailment (see ante, para 1.17).

(b) His option to purchase, which may be compared with the right of a conditional buyer (see ante, para 1.13), though it is worth less because there is no guarantee that the hirer will exercise his option (see post, para 1.25).

Despite the fact that the supplier will normally make careful enquiries into the character of the would-be transferee before entering the agreement (see post, paras 8.35–39), the courts have taken the attitude that this does not evince an intention to restrict the *prima facie* right of assignment.[1] For this reason, most modern conditional sale and hp agreements expressly forbid assignment by the transferee of his rights under the agreement.[3] Such a clause may limit or exclude the rights which the assignee can acquire against the supplier (see post, para 7.26), which should render otiose the activities of Vehicle Transfer Agencies (see ante, para 1.15); but the purported assignee may have a remedy against the assignor.[4] In practice, the supplier will frequently relinquish his interest in the goods to the assignee on payment of the outstanding balance due under the agreement.[5]

2   *Liens.*[6] Essentially, a lien is just a right granted by common law to retain possession of goods as security for the performance of particular obligations,[7] though lienees have been granted a special power of sale by the Torts Act 1977 (ss 12–13). In respect of goods supplied on conditional sale, simple hiring or hp, perhaps the most commonly claimed lien is that of a repairer.[8] Whilst at common law, no man can create a lien on goods of another without the other's consent, it has been held that a supply on conditional sale, simple hiring or hp normally gives the transferee an implied authority to create a lien for repairs,[9] but only whilst the instalment agreement remains in force (as to which, see post, paras 26.08–10). To counteract this, the agreement will normally expressly prohibit the transferee from creating any lien over the goods,[10] though the transferee may still be left with an ostensible authority to do

---

[1.23]

1   For assignments of choses in action generally, see post, para 7.16 *et seq.*

2   *Whiteley Ltd v Hilt* [1918] 2 KB 808, CA. See generally Goode, *HP Law and Practice* (2nd edn), pp 525–26, 586–88.

3   Because the two rights of the hirer are independent, the clause must be carefully examined to see whether it has forbidden assignment of either or both the rights of hiring and option: see further Goode, *ibid*, pp 526–29.

4   Eg, *Butterworth v Kingsway Motors Ltd* (set out post, para 12.06). What if, at the time the agreement is made, the transferee makes it clear that he is obtaining the goods as a gift for a third party?

5   What is termed a 'settlement figure'; as to which, see further post, paras 26.19; 26.22.

6   See generally Crossley Vaines, *Personal Property* (5th edn), Chapter 7.

7   Eg, the lien of the unpaid repairer (below), auctioneer (see post, para 10.11) seller (see post, para 24.08) or cancelling debtor (see post, para 10.33).

8   *Tappenden v Artus* [1964] 2 QB 185, CA. *Semble*, the lien probably does not extend to towing and garaging charges: see *Re Southern Livestock Products Ltd* [1963] 3 All ER 801; *Hatton v Car Maintenance Co Ltd* [1915] 1 Chapter 621. As to storage charges, see post, para 24.09.

9   *Green v All Motors Ltd* [1917] 1 KB 625, CA (hp).

10   Such a provision may be ineffective where contradicted by an express duty in the bailee or conditional buyer to keep in good repair. It may also amount to an unfair term under the UTCC Regulations: see post, para 11.15.

so provided that the repairer knows that the goods are supplied on conditional sale, simple hiring or hp.[11]

[1.24] Statutory definitions. Upon this common law form of hp, a number of statutory definitions have been imposed. The leading modern definition is to be found in identical form in both SOGIT (s 15) and the CCA:[1]

'hire-purchase agreement' means an agreement,[2] other than a conditional sale agreement, under which –

(a) goods are bailed or (in Scotland) hired in return for periodical payments by the person to whom they are bailed ..., and

(b) the property in the goods will pass to that person if the terms of the agreement are complied with and one or more the following occurs –

    (i) the exercise of an option to purchase by that person,

    (ii) the doing of any specified act by any party to the agreement,

    (iii) the happening of any other specified event.

This definition is more satisfactory than its predecessors in several ways: it makes it clear that the statutory category of hp cannot include credit sale (see ante, para 1.13), pledges (see post, para 25.02) or deliveries on sale or return (see post, para 20.23). Moreover, it expressly excludes conditional sales (see ante, para 1.14), which exclusion is considered later (see post, para 1.25).

Perpetual hiring agreements. In modern times, there has been a tendency to use simple hiring as an alternative to instalment sales (see ante, para 1.12) or hp agreements (see post, para 1.20). If the agreement is truly a simple hiring agreement, it will be treated as such by the courts.[3] In 1954, it was held that a hiring under which the option was not exercisable until the happening of a future uncertain event was not within an earlier statutory hp definition;[4] but it seems likely that such facts would fall within the above CCA definition.[5] However, the question is a matter of substance, not words, as witness the so called 'perpetual hiring agreements', which provide that all the incidents of property[6] will pass to the bailee except the outward shell of ownership,[7] in which case the agreement might be regarded as hp or conditional sale.[8] If so, they are subject to much the

---

11   *Albermarle Supply Co Ltd v Hind* [1928] 1 KB 307, CA (hp). What if the repairer does not know for certain that the goods are on hp, but merely that they are likely to be so?

[1.24]

1   Section 189(1). The agreement may be constituted by two or more documents: s 189(4). See, eg, Sched 2, Example 10. Cf *Kay's Leasing Corp Pty Ltd v Fletcher* (1964) 116 CLR 124, Aust HC. See also s 53 of the Health and Safety at Work Act 1974; SOGIT s 15(1); CPA s 45(1).

2   See generally post, para 5.15.

3   See *Galbraith v Mitchenall Estates Ltd* (set out post, para 27.21); cf *Baker v Monk* (1864) 4 De GJ & SM 388.

4   *R v RW Profitt Ltd* [1954] 2 QB 35 (option exercisable 'subject to the enactment of the necessary legislation'; not within the definition in the HPA 1938, s 21): see the discussion by Turner in (1974) 48 ALJ 63. The contract might be regarded as a type of conditional sale: see *Jones on Chattel Mortgages* (4th edn), para 960.

5   Within para (b)(iii), not present in the 1938 definition: see Goode, *Consumer Credit Law and Practice*, para 23.144.

6   For the incidents of property which normally pass on sale, see post, para 19.10.

7   See *Domestic Electric Rentals Ltd v Dawson* [1943] LJNCCR 31; *Carroll v Credit Services Investments Ltd* [1972] NZLR 460.

8   See *Jones on Chattel Mortgages* (4th edn), paras 952–55 and the *Crowther Report*, para 5.2.7.

same statutory restrictions (see ante, para 1.16); but, if not, they are subject only to the lesser restrictions on consumer hire agreements (see ante, para 1.19). There is presently debate as to whether more, or less, of these transactions should be regulated (see post, para 5.11).

[1.25] Difficulties. It is now possible to consider a number of the difficulties arising from the dual nature of hp.

1   *As to the hiring.* There were two ways in which this might be arranged:

(a) The hirer might agree to take the goods on hire from, for example, month to month, what is termed a **'periodic hiring'**. From the viewpoint of the supplier, this form suffers from the disadvantage that the hirer might elect to return the goods.

(b) The hirer might agree to take the goods on hire for a given number of months (a **'fixed-term'** hiring). From the viewpoint of the supplier, this has the attraction that he is sure to achieve the whole of his hp price, apart from the (usually nominal) option fee. However, this form was thought to be a conditional sale in *Forthright Finance Ltd v Carlyle Finance Ltd*.[1]

2   *Turning to the option,* there were again two possible forms of contract:[2]

(a) The hirer was granted an **option** to purchase which he might exercise once he had paid a stipulated amount of hire rent, exercisable on payment of a further sum (usually nominal),[3] which in practice was usually added to the last instalment.[4]

(b) The price of the **option** was paid at the outset, or included in the hire rent, so that the property in the goods would necessarily pass automatically but for the hirer's express power to terminate. However, the negative option in this form might now turn it into a conditional sale, following *Forthright Finance Ltd v Carlyle Finance Ltd* (above).

It seems to follow that the only safe form of hp remaining is the **periodic hiring** with a **positive option** (see further post, para 1.26).

Because of the above dual nature of the hp agreement, the courts have frequently been faced with the problem of whether to apply to it the rules of sale or bailment. It purports to be a species of bailment; and the courts have so treated it when deciding such issues as the owner's measure of damages in contract (see post, para 27.37), who may maintain an action for wrongful interference with goods (see post, para 19.06), or whether to imply extra terms in favour of the hirer (see post, para 15.23). Yet the economic object of

---

[1.25]

1   Set out ante, para 1.22, *per* Phillips LJ at 98, without expressly deciding the point. *Contra Close Asset Finance Ltd v Care Graphics Machinery Ltd* [2001] GCCR 2617 (held hp).

2   Where the agreement falls within the CCA, form (a) may cause difficulty with the truth-in lending provisions (see post, para 8.22). As to calculating the APR when levying documentation and option fees, see (1993) 48 CC3/2.

3   The amount should be kept within the 'exempt supply' limit (£10) so as not to attract VAT (see generally post, para 2.06): (1989) 44 CC2/21. As to methods of payment, see post, para 23.13.

4   Suppose a hirer announced during the currency of the agreement that he would not exercise his option when the time came, would he be bound by that announcement, perhaps as a waiver (see post, para 26.17) or election (see post, para 26.23)? Cf *Marseille Fret SA v D Oltmann Schiffahrts GmBH & Co KG* [1981] Com LR 277, DC.

the traditional simple transaction is normally to effect a sale;[5] and the courts have looked exclusively at this element when determining such issues as the tort damages to which the owner is entitled as against the hirer or his assignee (see post, paras 27.22; 27.31), or the hirer is entitled in respect of breach by the supplier (see post, para 29.34), or when the hirer may plead a total failure of consideration (see post, para 29.12). Similar inconsistencies of approach may be found in the decisions in relation to hp agreements in respect of such matters as risk (see post, para 22.01) and illegality (see post, para 10.20). As it is apparently impossible to decide whether hp has more in common with sale or bailment,[6] it has sometimes simply been labelled as a form of contract *sui generis*.[7] That this is a sensible way to view the transaction is, perhaps, confirmed by modern developments in, for example, motor finance by way of so called 'Personal Contract Purchase'.[8]

The hirer's interest in the goods. The above problems are neatly illustrated by the difficulty of deciding the extent of the hirer's proprietary interest in the goods before he exercises his option to purchase. As we shall see later, the courts have decided that the hirer does not have an equity of redemption in the goods (see post, para 24.22). However, whilst he does not have an interest recognised by law, during the continuance of the hiring he has an interest whose economic value may be measured by the proportion of the hp price which has been paid: every instalment *pro tanto* reduces the value of the supplier's interest and increases that of the hirer. Yet this hirer's interest is of a peculiarly uncertain nature, inasmuch as the supplier, by lawfully terminating the agreement in accordance with its terms, will automatically bring the hirer's interest to an end (see post, paras 26.08–10).

[1.26] The future. It has been seen that hp evolved as a hybrid form of contract, incorporating elements of both bailment and sale, in order to secure for the supplier the greatest possible amount of security that the 'price' will be paid as promised. In a sense, it typifies the 19th century attitude of freedom of contract (*laissez-faire*: ante, para 1.02). Yet this hybrid has unsurprisingly given rise to a number of conceptual problems (see ante, para 1.25). Moreover, subsequent case law has demonstrated that the creation of hp was largely unnecessary for the purposes for which it was created;[1] in the important area of implied terms, there has already been imposed an almost uniform statutory system (see post, Chapters 11–16); and the CCA treats bailment, hp and sale on credit in a very similar manner.[2] It has been suggested that these developments raise the following issues:[3]

---

5   Recently, there have been developed variations under which the hirer in effect pays the rental appropriate to a simple lease for the duration of the agreement and is then given the choice of making a larger ('balloon') option payment: see [2000] Which? Car 11.

6   See the *dicta* of the CA in *Felston Tile Co Ltd v Winget Ltd* [1936] 3 All ER 473, CA, criticised *obiter* in *William Cory and Son v IRC* [1964] 3 All ER 66, at 71, 75. But see Goldberg (1972) 88 LQR 21.

7   Eg, *per* Goddard J in *Karflex Ltd v Poole* [1933] 2 KB 251, at 264, 265. See also post, para 27.31.

8   [2000] Which? Car 11. These are (say) two year leases under which during that two years the lessee pays rent calculated to be the depreciation of the vehicle. At the end of the period, the lessee may exercise an option to buy (the option fee being the capital value) or return the vehicle (cf personal leases: see ante, para 1.18). See further (1995) 49 CC 5/20; and post, para 3.26.

[1.26]

1   Eg, *Newtons of Wembley Ltd v Williams* (set out post, para 21.51); *Aluminium Industrie Vaassen BV v Romalpa Aluminium* (set out post, para 25.29).

2   For the CCA treatment of conditional sales, see ante, para 1.16. Such uniformity was recommended by the *Crowther Report on Consumer Credit* (Cmnd 4596), paras 5.2; 5.6.

3   Macleod and Cronin in Chapter 22 of *Consumer Credit* (ed Goode, 1978).

(a) Should hire-purchase be abolished, by enacting that all hp agreements shall be deemed conditional sales? This would appear to have certain advantages and to be the way matters have gone in the United States of America[4] and Australia.[5] Within the CCA, it would make little substantive difference, whilst enabling a modest simplification of that Act; it would make possible the abolition of the separate rules for implied terms in hp agreements found in the SOGIT; and outside the CCA it would cut the Gordian Knot in the shape of the common law rules of damages. Or could we go even further and replace both hire-purchase and conditional sale by a workable chattel mortgage system?[6]

(b) Should there be approved statutory forms of contract, possibly in consumer-understandable language? We may be moving in that direction with the application by the Office of Fair Trading of the UTCC Regulations (see post, para 11.12 *et seq*).

[1.27] Postscript. There are a number of general lessons to be learnt about this subject from the above concerning the applicability of statutes and common law:

(1) There are a number of different statutes to contend with, for example, the SGA, CCA and the SGSA.

(2) Sometimes, it is simply a matter of asking what is the essence of the transaction so as to decide which of those statutes to apply, for example, cash sales are dealt with by the SGA.

(3) Each of them assumes a common law background, so the answer may be found in the relevant statute or the common law, for example, different issues in hire-purchase are governed by the common law, the SOGIT and the CCA.

(4) Sometimes more than one statute is applicable to different aspects of a transaction, for example, a credit sale is governed by the SGA as to its sale aspect and the CCA as regards its credit aspect.

(5) The statutes apply to our transactions a mixture of civil and criminal law, for example, the CCA.

---

4   See ante, paras 1.18; 1.24. Except for Pennsylvanian 'bailment-leases': see Jones, *Chattel Mortgages* (6th edn, 1933), para 960; but see para 955, note 72.

5   Australian Consumer Credit Code 1996, s 10.

6   Such a move was resisted on grounds of freedom of contract: the *Crowther Report* (above) para 5.2.15, though it did recommend that all the various forms of contract should be subject to the proposed chattel mortgage legislation (as to which see post, para 25.34).

SUBJECT MATTER OF THE SUPPLY CONTRACT: GOODS AND PRICE

THE GOODS

[2.01] Introduction. As a species of bailment (see ante, para 1.17), the contracts of both hp and simple hiring (leasing) are only applicable to goods; and, of course, the term 'goods' is used in the SGA definition of a sale (s 2(1): set out ante, para 1.07) and in the CCA definitions of 'credit sale', 'conditional sale', 'hire purchase' and 'consumer hiring'.[1] Moreover, the expression 'goods' is also to be found in the Trade Descriptions Act 1968 and in Parts I–III of the Fair Trading Act 1973 (see post, Chapter 4). Whilst the last-mentioned Acts contain their own (non-exclusive) definition of 'goods',[2] the CCA expressly defines goods by reference to the SGA (s 189(1)), as does the Unfair Contract Terms Act 1977 (s 14), and the SGSA sets out an almost identical definition.[3] Thus, the major definition for our purposes is the SGA one (see post, para 2.02), which is further sub-divided (see post, para 2.03) and distinguishes sales of services (see post, para 2.05).

[2.02] SGA definition. Section 61(1) of the SGA (as amended) provides that, unless the context otherwise requires (italicised words introduced by s 2(c) of the Sale of Goods (Amendment) Act 1995):

> 'goods' includes all chattels personal other than thing in action and money ...; and in particular 'goods' includes emblements, industrial growing crops, and things attached to or forming part of the land which are agreed to be severed before sale or under the contract of sale *and includes an undivided share in goods*.

This definition may be analysed as follows:

1 *Chattels personal other than things in action and money*. The term 'chattels personal' covers all tangible,[1] moveable,[2] property,[3] and even water, oil, gas and air, eg, compressed air, though electricity is more doubtful (see post, para 3.07). In relation to computer supplies, the English courts have taken the following *prima facie* view:[4] sales of tangibles, *viz*, the hardware, instruction manual and floppy discs carrying the software, are supplies of 'goods', whereas sales of the (intangible) software itself are

---

[2.01]

1 These definitions are respectively set out ante, paras 1.13; 1.16; 1.24, 1.19.

2 These two definitions also vary as between themselves: see Trade Descriptions Act 1968, s 39(1); Fair Trading Act 1968, s 137(1); and see the criticism in Cmnd 6628, para 68; and Bragg, *Trade Descriptions*, Chapter 2. See also the (again different) definitions in the Factors Act 1889, s 1(3) (see post, para 21.29); the Torts (Interference with Goods) Act 1977, s 14; the Trading Stamps Act 1964, s 10(1); Counter-Inflation Act 1973, s 21(1); Companies Act 1985 (see post, para 25.28A); Consumer Protection Act 1987, s 45 (see post, para 4.32). Are all these differences in definition justifiable?

3 Section 18(1)). Contrast the definition of 'personal chattels' in the Bills of Sale Acts: see post, para 9.04.

[2.02]

1 As to the controversy whether in the case of a motor vehicle, 'goods' includes the registration document, see post, para 21.29. As to supplies of services, see post, para 15.15.

2 *Contra* real (immoveable) property. For the distinction between the sale of goods and land, see post, para 9.03. For houseboats, see *Chelsea Yacht and Boat Co Ltd v Pope* [2001] 2 All ER 409, CA.

3 Including animals. As to human remains, see *Benjamin's Sale of Goods* (5th edn), para 1-088.

4 *Watford Electronics Ltd v Sanderson CFL Ltd* (set out post, para 18.24A; unappealed point).

not;[5] but this dichotomy has been criticised for paying too much attention to the medium of supply, viz whether the software is supplied on floppy disc or on-line.[6] The following types of personal property are excluded by the definition:

(a) *Things (or choses) in action.* The English law of property other than realty divides that property into two types: choses in possession, which can be enjoyed by taking possession of them, eg, goods; and choses in action, which can be enjoyed only by court action, eg, a debt (see post, para 7.16). The effect of this exclusion of choses in action from the definition is that an assignment (transfer) of a chose in action, for example, a debt for the price of goods sold (see post, para 2.06), can never amount to a sale of goods.[7]

(b) *Money.* This probably refers only to that which is transferred in the UK by way of legal tender for its face value at the time of contracting (see post, para 23.14). Thus, 'money' does not seem to include coins valued only by their substance,[8] or by way of their curio or rarity value,[9] or coins which have ceased to be legal tender,[10] or imitation or stage money, or trading stamps (see post, para 15.17). Payment cards are often inaccurately described as 'plastic money' when referring to their use by a card-holder (see post, para 2.27); but presumably the sale of blank plastic cards is a sale of goods.

2 *Emblements and industrial growing crops.* These are incorporated in the old term *fructus industriales*, and include growing crops of the soil which are produced by the labours of the cultivator, eg, wheat, barley, potatoes.[11]

3 *Things attached to or forming part of the land.* This phrase covers both fixtures (see post, para 25.23) and what was known as *fructus naturales*, the latter expression comprehending natural products of the soil, such as grass and trees, provided the contract of sale intends their severance, eg, hay, timber. As to the extent to which these may amount to sales of interests in land, see post, para 9.03.

4 *An undivided share.* Whilst a sale of a **divided** share of goods, eg, half a lamb carcass by a food business, has long been regarded as a sale of goods, under the amendments introduced into the SGA in 1995 the sale of an **undivided** share in goods (see post, para 20.20A) is also to be regarded as a sale of goods, eg, a half share of a racehorse to a punter.[12]

---

5   The *St Albans* case (set out post, para 18.24), *per* Glidewell LJ at 493f–j; and see 16 Tr L 387, but see Thornton J in the *Watford Electronics* case (above) where, on an unappealed point, his Lordship doubted the distinction drawn by Glidewell LJ between computer programs and software.

6   See *Beta Computers (Europe) Ltd v Adobe Systems (Europe) Ltd* 1996 SLT 604; and Atiyah, *Sale of Goods* (10th edn), pp 66–71.

7   For the borderline between sales of goods and of contractual rights, see *Couturier v Hastie* (set out post, para 22.10).

8   *Allgemeine Gold-und Silberscheideanstadt v Customs and Excise Comrs* [1980] QB 390, CA (Krugerrands), discussed [1985] JBL 97. But see the case cited in note 10 below. Neither of these cases actually involved the SGA definition.

9   *Moss v Hancock* [1899] 2 QB 111, DC (1897 Jubilee £5 gold pieces).

10 *R v Thompson* [1980] QB 229, CA (half-crowns, sixpences). The case also dealt with Krugerrands as to which see above, note 8.

11 Nowadays, the expression 'emblements' appears to add nothing to the definition: Benjamin, *op cit*, note 3, para 92. *Contra* Chalmers, *Sale of Goods* (18th edn), p 268.

12 See *Sale of Goods Forming Part of a Bulk* (1993, Law Com 215), paras 2.3–2.6; 4.2; 5.3.

Different categories of goods

[2.03] The expressed scheme. One of the oddities in the drafting of the SGA lies in the manner in which it deals with the different categories of goods. Section 5 of the SGA appears to envisage the following three different 'types' of goods:

1   *'Existing goods'*. This term is explained by s 5(1) as goods 'owned or possessed by the seller ...'. Thus, the seller does not have to be the owner of the goods so long as they are in his possession at the time the contract is made;[1] and vice versa, eg, an owner of goods currently in transit by an independent carrier.

2   *'Future goods'*. This term is defined by ss 5(1) and 61(1) in exactly the same terms[2] as 'goods to be manufactured or acquired by the seller after the making of the contract of sale'. Whereas the property may pass immediately in the case of 'existing goods', the Act explicitly recognises that in the case of 'future goods' there must initially be only an agreement to sell (s 5(3)). The property in future goods cannot pass unless and until the seller does some act irrevocably appropriating them to the contract.[3] The difficult question whether, prior to this stage, the buyer has an equitable interest in the goods will be examined later (see post, para 20.22). As to frustration, see post, para 22.15.

3   *'A chance'*. The distinction between the sale of 'a chance' and of 'future goods' is not at first sight very clear, for both may depend on a contingency (s 5(2)). However, the distinction probably lies in whether or not the seller promises that he will manufacture or obtain the goods:[4] if he does so promise, there is a sale of future goods; but, if he does not, there is only the sale of a chance,[5] which does not even raise a presumption that the transaction amounts to wagering within the Gaming Act 1845.[6] Perhaps a modern example is futures trading.[7]

Whereas s 5 sets out a clear scheme, very little will be found to turn upon it, whilst the all-important distinction between specific and unascertained goods receives scant mention in the Act (see post, para 2.04).

[2.04] Specific goods. In practical terms, far more important that s 5 of the SGA (see ante, para 2.03), is the dichotomy between 'specific' and 'unascertained' goods.

[2.03]

1   The question of whether there can be a sale of goods in which the seller does not promise to transfer the title is considered post, para 12.17.

2   For a more elaborate classification, see Benjamin's *Sale of Goods* (5th edn), para 1-101.

3   It has been said that the effect of s 5 is that, in specific future goods, the passing of property is governed by s 18: see Goode, *Commercial Law* (2nd edn), p 232; Chalmers, *Sale of Goods* (18th edn), p 271. But see post, para 20.02.

4   Does the seller have to promise to supply the goods to an identifiable buyer? Is a draw or raffle for a bottle of whisky a sale of goods?

5   Eg, *Langton v Higgins* (set out post, para 20.18); *Howell v Coupland* (set out post, para 22.15); *Sainsbury Ltd v Street* (set out post, para 22.15). For further discussion, see Atiyah, *Sale of Goods* (10th edn), pp 73–74; Benjamin, *op cit*, note 2, paras 1-108–1.111.

6   See *Ellesmere v Wallace* [1929] 2 Ch 1, CA. As to statutory intervention, see post, para 8.16.

7   On sales of futures, see further Benjamin, *op cit*, para 1-103; and Schmitthoff [1984] JBL 303. What is the effect of a supply of goods which includes an entry form for a competition, the 'prize', being further goods? As to where those further goods are winnable by the exercise of skill, see post, para 8.16. For the relationship between futures and string sales, see Bridge [1991] LM & CLQ 52 at 60–62.

1 '*Specific goods*'. These are defined by s 61(1) (as amended), which lays down that, subject to a contrary intention:[1]

> 'specific goods' means goods identified and agreed upon at the time a contract of sale is made *and includes an undivided share, specified as a fraction or percentage, of goods identified and agreed upon as aforesaid.*

The key requirements are that the goods must be **identified and agreed upon** at the time of contracting. Further, the italicised phrase will bring within the definition of specific goods a sale of an undivided share (see ante, para 2.02) of identified goods, eg, a quarter share of an identified horse or boat.[2] As to identifiable goods, see post, para 20.03.

2 '*Unascertained goods*'. These are nowhere defined by the SGA, but the Act does use the expression by way of contrast to 'specific' goods, so that 'unascertained' goods must, *prima facie*, be goods which are not identified and agreed upon at the time when the contract is made, but will become identified and agreed upon (ascertained) at some later stage. 'Unascertained' goods may be of any of the following types: (a) to be manufactured or grown by the seller; (b) generic goods, that is, of a designated type; (c) an unascertained part of a specific bulk.[3]

The distinction between specific and unascertained goods is to be drawn at the moment of contracting, when it should be asked whether or not the contract goods are identified and agreed upon.[4] If yes, the goods are specific. If no, the goods are unascertained, regardless how soon **after** contracting they become ascertained. Except by making a fresh contract of sale in place of an earlier one (a novation),[5] unascertained goods will **never** become specific, though they should become ascertained. On the other hand, the distinction between 'specific' and 'unascertained' goods will frequently only be one of degree: contracts for the sale of any hundred tons of wheat, for the sale of 99 tons out of a particular stock of 100 tons, or for the sale of **that** 100 tons may look similar, but the first two are for the sale of 'unascertained' goods and the last for the sale of specific goods. The distinction is important in the contexts of the passing of property and impossibility of performance.[6]

[2.05] Sale of skill and labour (services).[1] The insistence that the transaction of sale, hp and hiring require that in exchange for money there shall be transferred 'goods' theoretically enables these transactions to be distinguished from the supply of skill and labour. However, the importance of the requirement was substantially lessened by Parliament with the repeal of the rule requiring certain sales to be evidenced in writing

---

[2.04]

1 Italicised words introduced by the Sale of Goods (Amendment) Act 1995, s 2(d).

2 Sale of Goods Forming Part of a Bulk (1993, Law Com 215), paras 2.26; 5.4. This should remove such sales from the ambit of those SGA provisions based on possession or physical delivery (ie ss 18, 27–37): *ibid*, paras 5.5–5.7.

3 For a suggestion that this category might need special treatment, see Nicol (1979) 42 MLR 129, at 142. See further post, paras 20.20 and 21.49.

4 The fact that a written contract or invoice contains a 'specification' is ambiguous for this purpose.

5 Discharge of the earlier contract by such subsequent mutual agreement is considered post, para 26.18.

6 See post, paras 20.01; 22.14. *Contra* specific performance: see post, para 29.38.

[2.05]

1 See generally *Benjamin's Sale of Goods* (5th edn), paras 1-041–47; Cranston, *Consumers and the Law* (3rd edn), Chapter 6.

(see post, para 9.02) and the enactment in 1982 of Part II of the SGSA.[1a] Furthermore, the common law has also contributed to this process by its tendency to apply the rules of sale of goods by analogy to supplies of services, eg, in relation to delivery[2] and the implied term as to fitness (see post para 15.26). Yet there would still appear to be differences, eg, with regard to the passing of property[3] and the effects of frustration.[4]

Assuming the parties have not settled by their contract the issue of whether or not a transaction is to be, or involve, a sale of goods (see ante, para 1.06), the following points should be borne in mind:

(1) Where the work involves the 'seller' in affixing materials to the land or goods of the 'buyer', the position is as follows: if the seller (workman) supplies the materials, the issue is whether the contract is substantially to improve the buyer's existing real property,[5] or one of sale of goods with an incidental obligation to affix;[6] or one of quasi-sale (see post, para 2.10). But where the 'buyer' supplies the materials, it will normally be a contract only of skill and labour.[7]

(2) Where the work is substantially independent of the creation or supply of the goods, the position is this: ancillary services will not prevent a contract from amounting to a sale of goods,[8] and vice versa;[9] and where there is a supply of goods plus subsequent maintenance, there may be two separate contracts. In this context, it may be significant whether the parties stipulate for one global consideration, eg, a new car, or two separate ones, eg, TV tube plus insurance.

(3) Where the work is wholly a component of the goods created and supplied, the courts appear to have changed their minds. The earlier relatively simple view was that there was a sale of goods so long as 'a chattel is ultimately to be delivered';[10] whereas the more recent view is that everything depends on the substance of the contract, the commissioning of a portrait from an artist being held a supply of skill and labour, notwithstanding the incidental supply of a canvas.[11] A similar problem arises with the supply of computer software, where there may be a single package supply, eg, of goods plus training.[12]

1a   See post, para 15.15. For false statements as to qualifications, see post, para 4.16.

2   *Charles Rickards Ltd v Oppenheim* (set out post, para 26.25).

3   For the passing of property on the sale of goods, see post, Chapter 20; for the passing of property on affixing one chattel to another (usually termed 'accessio'), see post, para 19.05, and for the passing of property in goods becoming affixed to realty, see post, para 25.23.

4   Because the Law Reform (Frustrated Contracts) Act 1943 does not apply to certain contracts for the sale of goods (s 2(5)(c)): see post, para 22.18.

5   Eg, *Stewart v Reavell's Garage* [1952] 2 QB 545 (fitting new brake-linings to a car).

6   Eg, *Philip Head & Sons Ltd v Showfronts Ltd* [1970] 1 Lloyd's Rep 140 (sale and fitting of carpet); *Parsons (Livestock) Ltd v Uttley, Ingham & Co Ltd* (set out post, para 27.42 – sale and installation of a hopper); *Truk (UK) Ltd v Tokmakidis GmbH* (set out post, para 29.07; fitting lifting gear to chassis).

7   What if some of the materials are provided by each party? See Benjamin, *op cit*, note 1, paras 1-044–45.

8   Eg, *Lockett v A & M Charles Ltd* [1938] 4 All ER 170 (sale of meal in restaurant). What of a meal supplied to a lodger?

9   Eg, *Dodd v Wilson & McWilliam* [1946] 2 All ER 691 (vet making diagnosis and supplying drug). See Atiyah, *Sale of Goods* (10th edn), p 26.

10   *Lee v Griffin* (1861) 30 LJKB 252, at 253 (supply of false teeth by a dentist).

11   *Robinson v Graves* [1935] I KB 579, CA (criticised by Samek [1962] 36 ALJ 66); Benjamin, *op cit*, note 1, para 1-041. Cf *Cammell Laird & Co Ltd v Manganese Bronze & Brass Co Ltd* (set out post, para 14.14). What of an undertaker?

12   *Watford Electronics Ltd v Sanderson CFL Ltd* (set out post, para 18.24A; unappealed point, at para 50).

A contract to supply services may also attract criminal liability under s 14 of the TDA or Part II of the CPA (see post, paras 4.16; 8.09).

THE PRICE AND CREDIT

Statutory definitions

[2.06] The price of goods sold. In order that the SGA can apply to a transfer of goods, the SGA requires that the property in those goods be transferred for 'a money consideration, called the price';[1] and it is clear that *prima facie* that price must be paid in legal tender[2] by, or on behalf of, the buyer.[3] Section 8 provides for the manner in which that price is to be determined, laying down the following rules:

(1) The price in a contract of sale may be fixed by the contract,[4] or may be left to be fixed in a manner thereby agreed,[5] or may be determined by the course of dealings between the parties.[6]

(2) Where the price is not determined in accordance with the foregoing provisions the buyer must pay a reasonable price.[7]

Thus, s 8 assumes that a contract has been made.[8] However, it must be borne in mind that the determination of the price is often an important factor in deciding whether a contract has been concluded, particularly if reliance is being placed on s 8(2) (see post, para 10.03). To the extent that s 8 is a codification of the ordinary common law rules, it will represent the *prima facie* rules applicable to other supply contracts.[9] Agreements to sell at a

---

[2.06]

1　Section 2(1): set out ante, para 1.07. See also the definition in the Fair Trading Act 1973, s 137(2). For the distinction between money and goods for the purposes of the SGA, see ante, para 2.02. For price as a means of distinguishing sales of goods from certain other transactions, see post, para 2.08 *et seq.* These rules say nothing of the effect of inflation: as to which, see Downes (1985) 101 LQR 98.

2　As to which, see post, para 23.14; and as to decimalisation, see post, para 4.24. Distinguish the promise to pay money (legal tender) from the discharge of that promise, which may be accomplished by set-off, part-exchange, cheque or credit card (see post, para 23.13A), or perhaps even by trading stamp or voucher (see post, para 2.10, note 7).

3　*Bennett v Griffin Finance* [1967] 2 QB 46, CA (see 92 LQR at 193). This is an aspect of the rule of privity of contract.

4　*Anangel Atlas Compania Naviera SA v Ishikawajima-Harima Heavy Industries Co (No 2)* [1990] 2 Lloyd's Rep 526 ('most favoured customer' status). For express provisions as to price, see post, para 11.07.

5　The clause of the Sale of Goods Bill 1888 originally provided that the price might be 'left to be fixed by subsequent arrangement'; but these words were struck out in Committee. For the difficulties which price adjustment clauses may cause, see post, para 10.05.

6　Eg, *Finland Steamship Co v Felixstowe Dock Co* [1980] 2 Lloyd's Rep 287; *Agip SpA v Navigazione Alta Italia SpA* [1984] 1 Lloyd's Rep 353, CA.

7　What is a reasonable price is a question of fact (s 8(3)): see eg, *British Coal Corp v South of Scotland Electricity Board* 1991 SLT 302. For similar provisions in relation to the supply of services, see s 15 of the SGSA 1982 (see post, para 15.15).

8　If so, s 8(2) does **not** enable an aggrieved party to re-open the amount simply because he thinks the agreed price unreasonable; but he may be able to do so if it is extortionate: CCA, s 137: see post, para 29.40A). For variation of contract, see post, para 26.21.

9　Eg, hp and simple hiring contracts, where, however, the rules may have less scope because of the greater tendency to employ standard form contracts. Moreover, where an hp agreement is regulated, the issue is largely academic because of the requirement to state in writing the price or rent: see post, para 9.13.

valuation are dealt with later (s 9: see post, para 10.05), as are lowest price guarantees (see post, para 11.07).

On top of the price as above defined there will *prima facie* have to be added value added tax (VAT) on most goods.[10] Payment of the price is dealt with later (see post, para 23.13 *et seq*), as are restrictions on the pricing of goods and price variations (see post, para 26.21). In a consumer supply contract, the price *per se* is a core term and thus cannot be an unfair term (see post, para 11.12A–14); but a price increase clause may be unfair (Grey List (l): see post, para 11.17). There are also rules dealing with price displays (see post, para 8.08).

Bar coding. The code is a simple system of machine readable product identification.[11] It is normally used by retailers in conjunction with a computer database, eg, to enable check-out machines in supermarkets to register the sale automatically for the purposes of identifying and recording the price of the goods sold (as to mis-pricing, see post, para 8.09A).

Electronic point of sale (EPOS). This is an electronic till, that is, one connected to a telephone line, which can read bar coding (see above). In its simple state, EPOS generates sales bills, records sales data and can be used to automatically order up replacement goods to the shelves for those sold. It can also be used to effect payment by plastic card (EFTPOS: see post, para 2.17).

[2.07] Credit within the CCA. Like the HPA, the CCA intended to protect private consumers rather than transactions between businessmen. Sometimes when Parliament wishes to draw such a distinction it adopts the 'purpose of use' test, eg, s 12 of the UCTA (see post, para 18.18). However, the HPA had preferred the dual test of a financial ambit and exclusion of corporate consumers. The HPA therefore had to be far more explicit on 'price' than the SGA, because its ambit depended in part on the 'price' of the goods supplied on hp, conditional or credit sale falling within certain specified ranges. A similar approach is to be found in the CCA,[1] which applies almost exclusively to regulated agreements (see post, para 5.13): these fall into two categories, consumer credit agreements (see post, para 5.19) and consumer hire agreements (see ante, para 1.19). However, the major category is that of consumer credit agreement, in relation to which the CCA treatment differs in two important respects from the HPA. First, the key to its application turns on the provision of credit (see post, para 5.21), a notion comprehending far more types of contract than fell within the HPA (see post, para 5.19). Second, the ambit of the CCA is largely regulated not by the 'price', but by the credit element in the transaction (see post, para 5.22): the difference between the 'price' (plus VAT) and 'credit' may for the moment be thought of as likely to be the deposit and credit charge: both these items were included in the 'price' under the HPA but excluded from the 'credit' within the CCA.[2]

---

10 See Value Added Tax 1994. For the effect on the price where the rate of VAT is changed between contract and delivery, see s 89.

11 Bar coding may be replaced by radio tags: (1994) *The Times*, 12 January. Some supermarkets are experimenting with allowing their customers to self-scan their shopping (1996) *The Times*, 27 April).

[2.07]

1   See also the Doorstep-selling Regulations: see post, para 10.21. *Contra* the EEC Directive on Consumer Credit, which has a purpose of use test with no financial ceiling: see post, para 5.12.

2   *Contra* consumer hirings, where the deposit is included: see ante, para 1.19.

It should be borne in mind that there are statutory difficulties in supplying goods on credit to minors (see post, para 10.18). A popular marketing tool is the offer of credit at 0% finance,[3] though such deals are commonly hedged about with restrictions, either positive[4] or negative (see post, para 5.09).

Price distinguishes other transactions

[2.08] Gifts. A gift involves an unconditional transfer of the property in goods without any consideration. It does not extend to unintended extras supplied with goods (*Wilson v Rickett Cockerell Ltd*: set out post, para 14.03); nor to the packaging in which the goods may be supplied, even though both parties may expect that it will be thrown away (*Geddling v Marsh*: set out post, para 14.03). However, the contract may provide for some sorts of packaging, eg, a bottle, to be returnable, in which case it would appear to have been bailed.

Unlike sales, hp and simple hiring agreements, a gift of goods is incomplete until delivery, unless accomplished by deed (see post, para 9.01) or declaration of trust.[1] Thus, where a retail buyer obtains goods for the purpose of giving them to another, that gift cannot normally be effective until delivery, upon which the retail buyer's right to reject the contract goods used to be lost before any effective inspection (s 35 of the SGA: see post, para 29.06).

'*Free gifts*'. The question arises whether the so called 'free-gifts' commonly made in the course of retail business are genuinely gifts or are supplied for a consideration.[2] If the 'free gift' or 'sample' is supplied without there being any obligation on the transferee to do anything, there will be no contractual relationship between transferor and transferee.[3] However, in commerce, items described as 'free gifts' are frequently advertised as being available only where other goods or services are bought under a contract. In some retail trades, such 'free gifts' can be of substantial value: they may take the form of either an immediate delivery of goods, eg, a free portable TV with each car or bedroom suite supplied; or a voucher for a price reduction off a later purchase of goods or services.[4] The question of the status under which such 'free gifts' are delivered was considered in *Esso Petroleum Ltd v Comrs of Customs and Excise*:[5]

> Esso devised a 'World Cup coin' sales promotion for use by garages selling their petrol. Garages would advertise that, for every 4 gallons of petrol sold, it would supply a motorist

---

3   There are two common forms: (a) the price without interest is simply payable by instalments; or (b) the price plus interest is initially payable by instalments, but the interest subsequently refunded.

4   Frequently difficult for the consumer to fathom or execute, a high interest rate payable on default: see [2000] 12 Which? 10. Such limitations may be unfair terms (see post, para 11.12 *et seq*).

[2.08]

1   See *Milroy v Lord* (1862) 4 De GF & J 264; *Cochrane v Moore* (1890) 25 QBD 57, CA.

2   Such gift, made to one who is employed to buy, may amount to a bribe or secret profit, eg, *R v Braithwaite* [1983] 2 All ER 87, CA.

3   For such promotional activities, see generally post, para 8.14. If 'free gifts' are offered at an auction, there may be an offence: see post, para 10.11.

4   Does this amount to the provision of a credit note? Is it *prima facie* assignable? Can any valid restrictions be placed upon its use? A 'free gift' coupon will not attract VAT (*Boots v Customs and Excise Comrs* [1991] CLY 3668, CJEC; and as to such vouchers generally, see post, para 15.18.

5   [1976] 1 All ER 117, HL. See generally Atiyah (1976) 39 MLR 335; Lawson, *Advertising Law*, pp 155–57.

with a coin bearing the likeness of a member of the English soccer team playing in the 1970 World Cup.

Two Law Lords, Lords Dilhorne and Russell, agreed with the Court of Appeal that the coins were of so little value that there was no intention to create legal relations, Lord Russell suggesting an analogy with a garage's offer of 'Free Air'; but this may be distinguishable where the 'gift' has a significant value.[6] However, the majority held that there was a contractual promise by the garage to transfer the coins in consideration for the motorist agreeing to buy the petrol (see post, para 8.05): according to Lords Wilberforce and Simon, as the consideration was not the price, but entry into the petrol sale contract, the coins were the subject of a collateral contract (see generally post, para 11.06); but Lord Dilhorne held that the coins were the subject of a sale.[7]

None of these views affect the legal position with regard to the major goods or services purchased; that is, the petrol in the *Esso* case. However, suppose the 'free gift' supplied by the petrol-seller[8] is not of satisfactory quality: if it is really supplied by way of gift, the supplier incurs no contractual liability; if it is supplied by way of sale, there may be liability under the SGA;[8a] but, if it is supplied by way of collateral contract, any liability would be under the SGSA (see post, para 2.10). In some circumstances, there may be criminal liability, eg, failure to supply the 'free gift',[9] or cause an advertisement so promising to amount to misleading advertising (see post, para 8.12A). Furthermore, if the 'free gift' supplied to a consumer is dangerous, that may engender both civil and criminal liability.[10] Commonly, the 'free gift' will in fact be supplied by a third party:[8] unless the latter acts so as to create privity of contract in respect of that 'free gift' between the main supplier, eg, petrol-seller, and consumer, there will in reality be two independent transactions, so that the consumer may be able to rescind one without rescinding the other.

[2.09] Barter or exchange. Section 2(1) of the SGA envisages that the consideration for the promise to transfer goods shall be money, for it calls that consideration 'the price'; and, in defining 'goods', s 61(1) explicitly excludes money.[1] Therefore, where each party merely promises to transfer goods to the other, then the contract is one of barter and hence outside the SGA; but it will instead amount to a quasi-sale (see post, para 2.10). The more

---

6   See *AG v LD Nathan & Co Ltd* [1990] 1 NZLR 129, CA (criminal case; a 'free' bottle of wine offered with sales of 'family packs' of beef).

7   Within the Purchase Tax Act 1963, a view supported by Atiyah (1976) 39 MLR at 336. The Advertising Standards authority now forbids the description of any offer as 'free' if there is any cost to the consumer beyond that of delivery: Code of Advertising Practice, para 4.4 (generally post, para 3.14).

8   The 'free gift' may actually be supplied by a third party direct to the consumer, eg, *AG v LD Nathan & Co Ltd* (above; wine owned by Nobilos and supplied on N's behalf to consumers as a promotion of a new brand).

8a   See post, para 15.25. The 'free gift' would be supplied under the contract of sale: see post, para 14.03.

9   If the 'free gift' is a supply service, eg, free insurance, there may be an offence under s 14 of the TDA: *Kinchin v Ashton Park Scooters Ltd* (1984) 148 JP 540; and see post, para 4.16. If the free offer is to supply goods, there is no offence under s 20 of the CPA: Griffiths and McIntyre (1993) 14 Jo MLP 109 at 111; and see generally post, para 8.09.

10   As to civil liability, see CPA Part I (see post, para 17.24 *et seq*); and as to criminal liability, see CPA Part II and the GPS Regulations (see post, para 4.32 *et seq*). In the CPA, 'supply' is defined to catch not only sales, but also collateral contracts and gifts (CPA, s 46(1)); and the GPS Regulations define 'product' to include a gift (reg 2).

[2.09]

1   See ante, para 2.02. For other possible approaches, see *Benjamin's Sale of Goods* (5th edn), para 1-34, note 30. What is the position with regard to hp and hiring agreements?

difficult situation is where a money value is put by the parties upon the goods to be exchanged (valued barter).[2] In *Dawson (Clapham) Ltd v Dutfield*:[3]

> D agreed to buy from P two lorries for £475, of which £250 was to be paid in cash and the rest made up by two other lorries taken in part-exchange, provided they were delivered within one month. The money was paid, but D failed to deliver the two lorries within the stipulated time. If this had been a contract of barter P would have had to frame his action in detinue for the two lorries promised; but Hilberry J held that this was an entire contract of sale, on which P was entitled to sue for the balance of the price.

It is submitted that the case did not turn upon whether the greater proportion of the price was payable in cash or kind; but upon whether the parties intended the transaction to be a sale or barter. Indeed, it has been suggested that 'there is nothing to prevent the parties from expressly agreeing that what might have been a barter shall take the form of reciprocal sales, with a mutual set-off of prices and, if necessary, a cash adjustment'.[4]

Part-exchange. Particularly in respect of motor vehicles and other consumer durables, it is common for other goods (usually of a similar type) to be 'traded-in' in part-exchange, in which case a value will normally be assigned by the parties to the trade-in goods.[5] Further complicating factors often found are: (i) that the goods traded-in were owned by a third party finance company under an instalment credit contract (see ante, para 1.03), it being envisaged that the third party's interest in the goods will (as part of the overall package) be bought out by payment to him of his 'settlement figure' (see post, para 26.19A); and (ii) that the acquisition of the new goods may itself be on instalment terms[6] financed by a fourth party (see post, para 2.20). But it is clear that neither of these possibilities will necessarily interfere with the basic analysis of the transaction.[7] Returning to the central transaction, there would appear to be two plausible analyses:

(a) There may be one contract to supply the new goods, coupled with a subsidiary arrangement that the price may be partially satisfied (at an agreed amount) by delivery of the old goods.[8] If this is correct, it may be that the transaction should be regarded as a single quasi-sale (see post, para 2.10); but the difficulty with this view arises where the consumer has no title to the old goods or misdescribes them (see post, Chapters 12 and 13).

(b) There may be reciprocal contracts of sale with a set-off of prices: the consumer sells the 'trade-in goods' to the retailer; and the retailer sells the 'new goods' to the

---

2   In international trade, this is termed 'countertrade': see Schmitthoff [1985] JBL 115.

3   [1936] 2 All ER 232 (as to detinue, see post, para 19.04). See also *Aldridge v Johnson* (set out post, para 20.16).

4   Benjamin, *op cit*, note 1, para 1-037. But see *per* Lord Reid in *Chappell & Co Ltd v Nestle & Co Ltd* [1960] AC 87 at 109, HL.

5   Eg, *Oscar Chess Ltd v Williams* [1957] 1 All ER 325, CA. For what the CCA terms a 'part-exchange allowance': see s 73, discussed post, para 10.34. For a case where no such values were assigned, see *Flynn v Mackin* [1974] IR 101, noted 39 MLR 589.

6   The part-exchange allowance will normally be utilised as the whole or part of the deposit. If the transaction in respect of the 'new' goods is also financed, that deposit may be credited to the financier: see post, para 16.05.

7   Eg, *Bennett v Griffin Finance* [1967] 2 QB 46, CA. See also Palmer (1983) 46 MLR 621.

8   This analysis is preferred by Goode, *HP Law and Practice* (2nd edn), p 305. It is said to explain most of the cases: Benjamin, *op cit*, para 1-039. It seems to have been adopted in the criminal law (see *Metsoja v Pitt & Co* (1989) 8 Tr LR 155, DC.

consumer.[9] This view has the attraction that it is apparently easy to work out the respective rights of the parties by treating matters as two separate but interdependent sales of goods, each within the SGA, cf *Marten v Whale* (set out ante, para 1.11).

[2.10/11] Quasi-sales. Section 1(1) of the Supply of Goods and Services Act 1982 (SGSA) refers to a 'contract for the transfer of goods', which this gateway section defines as:[1]

> A contract under which one person transfers or agrees to transfer to another the property in goods, other than an excepted contract.

The two major elements of this definition are (1) a contract (2) to transfer the property in goods. This insistence on a transfer of goods is clearly apt to cover a barter transaction[2] and perhaps LETS.[3] However, s 1(3) makes it clear that the consideration for the supply of goods does not, as in the case of a sale (see ante, para 1.07), require a monetary price, but instead may be constituted by (or include) a supply of goods and services (see post, para 15.26). So the category might cover 'free gifts',[4] part-exchanges (see ante, para 2.09) and the replacement of defective goods (see post, para 29.03A). The section draws the same distinction between contract and conveyance as the SGA (see ante, para 1.10), though it contains no rules as to the passing of property equivalent to those found in the SGA.[5] On the other hand, the section is restricted to contracts involving the transfer of property in goods: whilst it may be applicable even where that transfer is conditional,[6] it is difficult to see how it can be applied to materials consumed in the course of their application by the supplier.[7] Further, s 1 expressly excludes all the following types of property-transferring ('excepted') contract (s 1(2)):

(a) a contract of sale of goods;[8]

(b) a hire purchase agreement;[9]

---

9   This analysis is preferred by Greig, *Sale of Goods*, pp 11–12; Woodroffe, *Goods and Services – The New Law*, paras 4.11–13.

[2.10/11]

1   As amended. Section 18 defines 'goods' and 'property' in terms identical to those employed in the SGA: as to which see respectively ante, paras 2.01 and 1.08. As to the SGSA generally, see post, para 15.02.

2   Eg, *Widenmeyer v Burn Stewart & Co Ltd* 1966 SLT 215. For the rules applicable to barter, see *Benjamin's Sale of Goods* (5th edn), paras 1-035–36. For vouchers and trading stamps, see post, paras 15.17–18; Woodroffe, *Goods and Services – The New Law*, paras 4.02–04.

3   L(ocal) E(xchange) T(rading) S(ystem). Under these systems, a locally-invented 'money' is used by groups whose members swap goods and services without cash necessarily changing hands. Each member holds an account which is credited or debited whenever an exchange takes place. See (1994) *The Times*, 17 October; (1997) *The Times*, 10 November.

4   'Free gifts' are usually supplied under contract: see ante, para 2.08 and post, para 15.18. Do they fall within the SGSA or the SGA (see Woodroffe, *op cit*, note 2, para 4.05)?

5   It may be that the passing of property depends on the intention of the parties (Benjamin, *op cit*, para 5-031) or cannot pass until the job is completed (Woodroffe, *op cit*, note 2, para 3.17). For the passing of property, see generally Chapter 20.

6   As where the contract contains a *Romalpa* clause (as to which, see post, para 25.29). *Dubitante* Palmer (1983) 46 MLR at 622.

7   Eg, dyes, lotions, solvents, shampoos. It would appear that such transactions are still governed by the common law: see post, para 15.26.

8   For definition, see ante, para 1.07.

9   For definition, see ante, para 1.20 *et seq*.

(c) a contract under which the property in goods is (or may be) transferred in exchange for trading stamps on their redemption;[10]

(d) a transfer or agreement to transfer which is made by deed and for which there is no consideration other than the presumed consideration imported by deed;[11]

(e) a contract intended to operate by way of mortgage, pledge, charge or other security, an exemption identical to that employed in the SGA (s 62(4): see ante, para 1.08).

In respect of quasi-sales, Part I of the SGSA imports implied terms as to title, fitness, quality and sample which are closely modelled on those in ss 12–15 of the SGA (see post, Chapters 12–15). It also deals with hybrid contracts (see ante, para 1.06), expressly stating that the transaction remains a quasi-sale, notwithstanding that services are also provided (s 1(3)), eg, a plumber fitting a new tap (see post, para 15.15).

STATUTORY CONTROL

[2.12] **Statutory control of prices**. At the outset, a distinction must be drawn between the following types of control in relation to prices.

1 *Price levels*. In 1973, there was introduced a general statutory power to control **directly** the level of prices which might be charged. This was replaced by the Competition Act 1980, which established the following scheme: as regards the private sector, prices were to be controlled **indirectly** by the competition rules; but there were reserve powers to investigate pricing by public utilities.[1] This public/private divide was maintained by the Competition Act 1998 (see below).

2 *Price displays*. The power to control price displays is dealt with elsewhere (see post, para 8.08).

3 *Price discrimination*. Where a single supplier exercises price discrimination between his customers, this may amount to an anti-competitive practice (see below) or discrimination, eg, on grounds of race or sex (see post, para 4.23).

4 *Restraints on trade*. As from 1956, the UK legislature started to make more comprehensive attacks on agreements between businesses as to prices and terms of trade.[2] When the UK joined the EU (see ante, para 1.03A), there was introduced the EU system for regulating competition as between different Member States (ECA, ss 2,10). Accordingly, there commenced the following dual system, detailed consideration of which is beyond the scope of this work.

(a) *EU controls*. At the Community level, apart from State aid which may distort competition by conferring competitive advantage (Art 89 [ex 94]), economic

---

10 For definition, see post, para 15.17. *Aliter*, if the coupon does not amount to a trading stamp, when the transaction will fall within s 1 of the SGSA.

11 For gifts, see generally ante, para 2.08. Note that there is no comparable exception in respect of the provisions of hire (see post, para 15.13) and services (see post, para 15.15).

[2.12]

1 Sections 11–13 (now repealed). Price increases by public utilities may also be challengeable in their own committee structure (see post, para 3.07) and subject to codes of practice (see post, para 3.14). As to the price of credit, see post, para 29.40.

2 Under the Restrictive Trade Practices Acts 1956–77 (now repealed). There were earlier piecemeal provisions, eg, Auctions (Bidding Agreements) Act 1927 (see post, para 10.13).

activity between businesses which distorts competition or restricts the free movement of goods between Member States may contravene the EU Treaty itself (see post, para 2.13), or regulations made under it, eg, the Merger Regulations.[3] The European Commission has broad powers to police these rules and impose fines of up to 10% of turnover,[4] but tends only to investigate matters which raise issues significant at Community level; and in respect of these, local investigation within the UK would usually be conducted on behalf of the European Commission by the Director General of Fair Trading (DG).[5] Alternatively, civil action may be brought by third parties in the UK courts[6] for breach of statutory duty (see post, para 3.21).

(b) *UK controls.* The UK system pre-dated the 1972 accession of the UK to the EU and the two systems were conceptually inconsistent. This being thought undesirable, the UK competition system has now been replaced by the Competition Act 1998 (CA). The new UK system for regulating competition within the UK is modelled on the EU system: it is outlined later (see post, para 2.14) and is to be interpreted so far as possible consistently with the EU competition system,[7] which will include its case law. Monopolies, mergers and anti-competitive practices are to be supervised by the Competition Commission (s 45 of the CA), whilst the powers of the DG have been enhanced to give him (and the utility regulators) a domestic position in competition law similar to that of the European Commission at the Community level (though subject to appeals to the Competition Commission) and dovetailed with the specific powers of the regulators of the utilities (s 54 of the CA: see post, para 3.07). The DG is granted wide powers of investigation (ss 25–31 of the CA) and enforcement (ss 32–44 of the CA): failure to comply is an offence (s 42), enabling the Director to impose fines up to 10% of UK turnover (s 36);[8] but it also seems likely that aggrieved third parties may take proceedings for breach of statutory duty.[9]

[2.13] EU controls on businesses. Of particular relevance for our purposes are the following Community rules:

1 *The free movement of goods.* Government activity which restricts the free movement of goods between Member States, eg, quotas, may contravene Art 28 [ex 30] of the Treaty of Rome, unless it is saved by Art 30 [ex 36] on 'grounds of public morality, public

---

3 See further *Chitty on Contract* (27th edn), para 40-344.

4 See Chitty, *ibid*, para 40-344.

5 Competition Act 1998, ss 61–65. For the DG, see post, para 3.03; and enforcement, see further, Chapter 28.

6 *Garden Cottage Foods v Milk Marketing Board* [1984] AC 130, HL; and Chitty, *op cit*, note 3, para 40-344.

7 CA, s 60. This was intended to ensure so far as possible that the UK and EU prohibitions 'are interpreted and developed consistently with the Community competition system': Lord Simon, *Hansard*, HL, vol 583, col 960. For the overall Government intention, see *Modern Markets: Confident Consumers* (1999, Cm 4410), paras 2.1–2.6.

8 The DG claims to be able to use these powers to control indirectly the abuse of price levels, the so called 'rip-off Britain' campaign: OFT, 2000 AR, 11–12. For the price level controls of the utility regulators, see post, para 3.07.

9 In Parliament, the Government stated that there would be such a right similar to that under the Treaty of Rome; but it refused to expressly so provide in the CA. As to statutory interpretation generally, see ante, para 1.04. As to actions for breach of statutory duty, see post, para 3.21.

policy or public security'.[1] As EU rules *pro tanto* prevail in the event of conflict with UK legislation (see ante, para 1.03A), the former have sometimes been pleaded with little justification simply to avoid (or delay the imposition of) UK legislation. For instance, it was sought to avoid UK Sunday trading laws (see post, para 8.13) as contravening the EU free movement provisions: but the European Court decided that this was a matter for national law; and the UK courts have confirmed that our Sunday trading laws are consistent with the Treaty.[2] Further, any rules regarding 'selling arrangements' could go unchallenged, provided they apply to all traders within the territory of the Member State.[3]

2   *Competition controls.* Restrictive practices by businesses ('undertakings') which may affect inter-State trade may infringe the competition rules contained in Arts 81–82 [ex 85–86] of the Treaty of Rome, which are to be read in the light of the other policy objectives of the Treaty.[4]

Article 81 [ex 85] prohibits agreements or concerted practices (eg, gentlemen's agreements) between undertakings which 'prevent, restrict or distort competition' insofar as they may affect trade between Member States and contains an indicative list of types of agreement which may be covered, eg, price-fixing, control of production, market-sharing. Subject to a *de minimis* principle, these provisions have been widely interpreted by the Commission and the courts to cover both horizontal and vertical agreements:[5] for instance, they have been invoked to strike down restrictions on the import of goods,[6] franchise agreements dividing markets,[7] advertisements (see post, para 8.06), dealers' rings (see post, para 10.13) and origin marking (see post, para 4.10). As this rule is cast so widely, there is provision in the Treaty for the Commission to exempt agreements which meet certain criteria and are, on balance, beneficial (Art 81(3)): such agreements can be registered with the Commission with a view to obtaining individual exemption; and, even in advance of such application, the Commission has granted some block exemptions.[8]

[2.13]

1   Eg, *R v Henn* [1980] 2 All ER 166, CJEC & HL (import of pornography); *Quietlynn Ltd v Southend-on-Sea BC* [1991] 1 QB 454, CJEC (sex shops: see post, para 6.02); *Konsumentombudsmannen (KO) v Gourmet International Products AB* [2001] All ER (EC) 308, CJEC (advertisement for alcohol).

2   *Stoke-on-Trent City Council v B & Q plc* [1993] AC 900, HL. Cf *Chisholm v Kirklees MBC* [1993] ICR 826 (no sex bias in Sunday trading law: see generally post, para 4.23).

3   As to alcohol advertising, see Tayleur (2001) 151 NLJ 859.

4   See generally Benjamin, *Sale of Goods* (5th edn) para 3-041; *Chitty on Contract* (28th edn) para 42-003 et seq. They may be enforced by injunction: see post, para 29.39.

5   *Consten and Grundig v Commission* [1966] ECR 299. 'Horizontal' agreements are those between competitors at the same level in the distribution chain (see post, para 17.01); and 'vertical' agreements are between those at different levels in the chain.

6   *Ford Werke AG etc v EC Commission* [1985] 3 CMLR 528, CJEC (action to prevent Ford restricting the import of new Ford cars into the UK. Ford have subsequently given an undertaking to the OFT: see 1986 AR 77; and note 8, below). See also *British Leyland v EC Commission* [1987] 1 CMLR 185, CJEC.

7   *Pronuptia de Paries GmbH etc v Schillgalis* [1986] I CMLR 414, CJEC. See generally, Adams [1986] JBL 205, esp 214–17.

8   Eg, EU Regulation 123/85 exempts new motor vehicle distribution agreements, which allow motor manufacturers to impose restrictions on competition between their dealers; but see *Modern Markets: Confident Consumers* (1999, Cm 4410) para 2.15; and [2001] 9 Which? 5. Block exempt agreements may still fall foul of Art 82. See further Benjamin, *op cit*, note 4, para 3-041; Chitty, *op cit*, note 4, para 42-042.

Article 82 [ex 86] prohibits those who hold a dominant market position within the Community from abusing that position: the Treaty gives a number of examples of such abusive conduct, eg, unfair buying or selling prices, predatory pricing, import/export bans. However, Art 82 does not extend to refusing to supply an insolvent buyer.[9]

The above directly applicable rules (see ante, para 1.03A) render automatically null and void not the whole agreement, but only those parts of agreements which restrict competition between Member States;[10] but they do not extend to agreements which effect trade exclusively (a) within one Member State,[11] or (b) outside the EU,[12] though these may be subject to the UK domestic rules (see post, para 2.14). To reinforce the above rules, the Commission has the ultimate power to fine an enterprise up to 10% of their annual, global turnover in the sector concerned (EU Regulation 17/62).

[2.14] UK competition controls on business. At common law, as between the immediate parties to a contract for the supply of goods, the position is this. As regards vertical restrictions,[1] they may be binding insofar as they relate to the goods supplied but unenforceable as being in restraint of trade where they relate to goods other than those supplied under that agreement;[2] and as between the more remote parties in the chain of distribution, there is no privity of contract and the English Courts rejected the notion that contractual restrictions on the use of goods could run with those goods.[3] As regards horizontal restrictions,[1] such agreements were subject to the restraint of trade doctrine,[4] though auction rings were upheld.[5]

The Competition Act 1998 (CA). The CA provides a new set of competition rules modelled on the EU provisions (see ante, para 2.13) and should be read consistently with them (s 60 of the CA).

Chapter I prohibitions (cf Art 81 [ex 85]). Replacing the Restrictive Trade Practices Acts (s 1 of the CA), the CA prohibits agreements which are implemented in the UK and whose purpose or effect is 'the prevention, restriction or distortion of competition within the UK' (s 2(1) of the CA). Such agreements are to be notified to the Director General of Fair Trading (DG: see post, para 3.03). Certain classes of agreement are excluded from the

---

9   *Leyland Daf v Automotive Products* [1993] BCC 389, CA. Cf SGA, s 41(1): see post, para 24.10.
10   UK courts will apply the familiar 'blue pencil' test to it: *Chemidus Wavin v TERI* [1978] 3 CMLR 514; and Chitty, *op cit*, note 4, para 42-065.
11   *Tepea BV v EU Commission* [1978] 2 CMLR 392.
12   Unless the agreement made outside Member States is to fix charges within Member States: *Re Wood Pulp Cartel* [1988] 4 CMLR 392.

[2.14]

1   See ante, para 2.13, note 5.
2   See *Palmolive Co (of England) v Freedman* [1928] Ch 264, CA; *Esso Petroleum Co Ltd v Harper's Garage (Stourport) Ltd* [1968] AC 269, HL.
3   Eg, purported restrictions in wholesale contracts as to the retail get-up of goods: *Taddy v Sterious* [1904] 1 Ch 354; *McGruther v Pitcher* [1904] 2 Ch 306, CA. But consider the tort of wrongful interference with contract and industrial property rights, eg, patents or trade marks (see post, para 12.03).
4   *AG of Commonwealth of Australia v Adelaide Steamship Co* [1913] AC 781, PC; trade codes of practice (see post, para 3.12).
5   *Rawlings v General Trading Co* [1921] I KB 635. However, such rings are now a criminal offence (see post, para 10.13), and therefore unenforceable.

Act (s 3 of the CA and Scheds 1–4, eg, mergers), the Director has power to grant individual exemptions[6] and there are also arrangements for block exemptions.[7]

Chapter II prohibitions (cf Art 82 [ex 86]). Replacing parts of the Competition Act 1980 (s 17 of the CA), the CA will prohibit the abuse by an undertaking of a dominant market position in the UK (s 18). Again, notification of abuses may be made to the DG (ss 20–24 of the CA) and certain cases are excluded (s 19 of the CA and Scheds 1 and 3, eg, mergers).

Having determined that the above rules have been broken, the DG may apply to the court for an order to secure observance of his determination (s 34 of the CA); and he also has the power to fine an enterprise up to 10% of turnover (s 36). The new Competition Commission has two functions: (1) to replace the old MMC (see ante, para 2.12), eg, to report breaches to Parliament, which may then make a statutory instrument;[8] and (2) to act as an appeals tribunal for the enforcement of the above Chapter I and Chapter II provisions (s 45 and Sched 7) under the mechanism laid down.[9] Findings of fact by the Director may be relied on in civil proceedings (s 58). The Secretary of State has largely been removed from any active role in UK competition law, except that he still retains a crucial control in relation to monopolies and mergers (see ante, para 2.12); and, as regards competition controls, he may modify by regulation the application of Chapters I and II as regards vertical agreements.[10]

FINANCING THE PRICE

[2.15] The consumer's obligation. The consumer's need to pay the price in order to acquire legitimately the object of his desire gives rise to two different issues.

1 *Transmission of the price.* Assuming that the consumer has at his disposal sufficient money, he can safely enter into a cash sale under which he agrees to pay the price demanded (see post, para 23.01) by way of a lump sum at the moment the goods are delivered to him (see post, para 23.16). If the price is relatively small, it is likely to be so paid by handing over money.[1] In consumer transactions, larger sums were commonly paid by cheque (see post, para 7.28), but nowadays are more likely to be effected by payment card (see post, para 2.23): both of these are devices for transmitting money from the consumer's bank account to the supplier's bank account. The providers of such money transmission services are the mainstream financial intermediaries described below (see post, para 2.17), whose activities are co-

---

6 CA, s 4, provided they meet the criteria laid down in s 9, eg, the Link scheme (see post, para 2.24). He may vary or cancel these exemptions.
7 CA, ss 6–9. These will automatically include all the EU block exemptions, and are known as 'parallel exemptions'.
8 Eg, the New Cars Order 2000, SI 2088, which may not be entirely effective (see [2001] 4 Which? 5).
9 CA, ss 46 and 48 and Sched 8. Third parties may intervene (s 47); and further appeal on questions of law lie to the Court of Appeal (s 49).
10 CA, s 50. The intention is to keep in step with the EU, which is conducting an ongoing review of vertical restraints policy at EC level.
[2.15]
1 As to legal tender, see post, para 23.14. Alternatively, supermarket check-outs may offer cashback facilities: the consumer deliberately overpays for goods purchased, eg, by plastic card, and is given the difference in cash from the till.

ordinated by APACS;[2] and the ubiquitous nature of such services put at a considerable disadvantage that relatively small proportion of the population which does not have a money transmission account (the unbanked).[3] In an increasingly cashless society, life can be difficult without a bank account,[4] though some banks are beginning to experiment with simple money transmission accounts, operated through ATMs (see post, para 2.24) and without overdraft facility or credit checks.[5] Alternatively, the unbanked may obtain access to money transmission by way of a credit union (see below) or cheque casher (see post, para 7.28). Credit unions are financial co-operatives which provide low interest loans (see post, para 15.19). The Post Office has now been restructured[6] and there are also plans for a universal bank based in sub-post offices.[7]

2   *Financing the price.* Particularly in relation to larger value items, consumers may not be able or willing to pay the price by way of a single lump sum at delivery of the goods (see above); and saving the price can be difficult for the unbanked.[8] For those consumers with a bank account,[3] it is possible to pay by regular instalments transmitted from that account by way of either standing orders or direct debits (see post, para 23.14). We have already examined the types of transaction which may then be used to facilitate immediate acquisition of the goods (see ante, para 1.03). But somebody has to finance such arrangements: most consumers are likely to apply to one of the mainline financiers (see post, para 2.16); but alternative sources of credit currently sometimes available to the unbanked include: credit unions (above); local Christmas clubs (see post, para 15.18); home shopping catalogues (see post, para 8.19); moneylenders (see post, paras 6.09; 7.02–04A); and cheque cashers (see post, para 7.28). The Government hope[9] that the financially disadvantaged without access to mainstream financiers[3] will in future be serviced as follows: the employed will be served at below market rates of interest by credit unions (above), part-financed by the banks;[10] and the unemployed on social security will look to the Social Fund.[11]

---

2   The Association for Payment Clearing Services (APACS) *inter alia* oversees the clearing of paper cheques and plastic cards.

3   The unbanked is usually estimated at about 15% of the population. Only about 10% of employees are now paid in cash. See OFT, *Vulnerable Consumers and Financial Services* (1999), 24–25; 51 QA 4; Collard, Kempson and Whyley, *Tackling Financial Exclusion* (June 2001).

4   OFT, Vulnerable Consumers and Financial Services (1999), 6; 54 QA 1; OFT, 2000 AR 21; (2001) CCA News, Winter, 20.

5   (2000) *The Times,* 28 July; [2001] 5 Which? 29. Because of the legal constraints on minors repaying credit (see post, para 10.18), these facilities would also be more suitable for minors.

6   See the Postal Services Act 2000.

7   There are plans for local post offices to act as subsidised universal banks, providing cash machines and simple accounts without overdraft facility: Ryder [2001] JBL 510, at 519–21; Field (2001) 86 Adviser 44.

8   Kempson and Whyley, *Understanding and Combatting Financial Exclusion* (1999).

9   Announcement by the Treasury (reported in (1999) *The Times,* 17 November) aimed at boosting the 1% of UK adult membership of credit unions to nearer the Irish 45%.

10   It is hoped that the Banks will provide or pay for a basic centralised infrastructure of the (voluntary) credit unions. This might replicate the infrastructure of the successful credit unions. The scheme would be regulated by the FSMA (see post, para 3.02).

11   Under the Social Security Act 1986, ss 32–35.

The financiers

[2.16] Introduction. This section is concerned with the situation where the would-be consumer desirous of obtaining early enjoyment of goods, whether that consumption be for business or private purposes, does not wish to pay the full price on or before delivery of the goods.[1] From the viewpoint of that consumer, the necessary credit facilities may be extended to him by one of two persons.

1   *His goods-supplier*. If the goods-supplier seeks to provide such credit facilities to consumers in respect of a significant part of his turnover, he could raise the necessary capital from a third party[2] and provide what is here termed 'vendor credit' to the consumer (see post, para 2.19). Alternatively, he could simply act as agent for a third-party financier,[3] in which case, although the situation may look the same to the consumer, the transaction does in fact fall within the second category (below).

2   *A financier*. A third-party financier may be invited to extend credit facilities to the consumer rather than to the goods-supplier in what is here termed 'lender credit' (see post, paras 2.20–24) by financiers whose normal economic function is to act as financial intermediaries (see post, para 2.17).

Surveying this field in 1971, the *Crowther Report on Consumer Credit* (see generally post, para 5.03) made the following fundamental observations (para 1.2.2):

(1)   In respect of both vendor and lender credit,[4] there are two possible methods of financing: an instalment credit contract, or a cash sale plus loan (see ante, para 1.03).

(2)   Whilst some loans are entirely independent of the acquisition of goods (loan credit), eg, bank overdraft, moneylender's or pawnbroker's loan, others are closely related thereto (sale credit),[5] this distinction being taken up later (see post, paras 5.29; 7.05; 25.01).

(3)   It may also be relevant to consider in relation to lender credit whether or not the goods and finance are being supplied as part of one single package, that is, whether the vendor and financier are connected in what is really a joint enterprise, the financier then being described as a 'connected lender'.[6]

[2.16]

1   For the historical development of consumer credit see the *Crowther Report* on *Consumer Credit* (Cmnd 4596), Chapter 2.1. For the factors influencing the selection and popularity of the forms of credit, see *Consumer Credit* (ed Goode), pp 273–75.

2   The legal ramifications of raising finance mostly fall outside the scope of this work. But see indirect financing: post, para 2.22; and for the discounting of post-dated cheques, post, paras 23.24A; 25.08.

3   Either utilising one of the traditional forms of lender credit (see post, paras 2.20–24) or 'private label schemes' (see post, para 2.24).

4   The expressions 'vendor credit' and 'lender credit' are here used in the sense seemingly utilised in para 5.2.1 *et seq* of the *Crowther Report*, and not that adopted when describing the pre-CCA law (paras 1.2.2; 4.1.2).

5   Eg, bank personal loan, instalment credit contracts, all trade credit. Instead of sale or loan credit, the *Crowther Report* (para 5.2.12) uses the terminology 'purchase-money credit' and 'non-purchase-money credit', which is derived from the American UCC, Art 9-107.

6   See post, para 5.32. It has been pointed out that, whilst most loans by connected lenders will be purchase-money loans and most loans by independent lenders will not, this will not necessarily be the case: *Crowther Report*, para 6.2.23.

[2.17/18] Financial intermediaries. In the lender credit situation (see ante, para 2.16), the financier is unlikely to finance such loans from his own resources, but may himself raise that money on the market.[1] All such deposit-taking will be supervised by the Financial Services Authority (see post, para 3.02). This paragraph is concerned with the most important types of such financial intermediary operating in our field.[2]

1   *The clearing banks*. Traditionally, these banks operated money transmission[3] through chequeing accounts and lent by way of overdraft on current account, sometimes with a provision for collateral security (see post, Chapter 25). In modern times, they have sought to mechanise personal banking by the large-scale use of computers and telephones.[4] Thus, cash withdrawals are increasingly accomplished by automatic teller (see post, para 2.24); the old paper-based transmission systems, eg, cheques (see post, para 7.24) are being replaced by the electronic transfer of funds (EFT), eg, debit cards, charge cards (see respectively post, paras 2.25; 2.27); and telephone and internet banking (see post, para 8.17) may displace branch transactions.[5] The banks have also sought to compete in the business of financing the acquisition of goods for consumption by three means:

(a) They instituted the Personal Loan, by which they meant an unsecured loan for a stipulated period made for the express purpose of, and tied to, the acquisition of goods. At the same time, the banks accepted the utilisation of overdrafts for similar purposes.

(b) They began to compete in the provision of payment cards (see post, para 2.24) and of finance for the acquisition of dwelling houses (see below).

(c) They made arrangements with supermarkets to set up banking operations, especially making deposits and granting loans, within the supermarket halls.

For bankers' duties, see post, para 7.03.

2   *Finance companies*. Such companies first developed in the 19th century to meet the needs of businesses to acquire on instalments plant and machinery, eg, the wagon companies; and later similar companies were founded to satisfy the wants of consumers, eg, for motor vehicles. The absence of a high-street branch network in modern times has contributed to their emphasis on doing business by way of direct financing (see post, para 2.21). More recently, they have developed business lending (asset financing) on both fixed and current assets, eg, factoring (see post, para 2.22) and equipment leasing (see ante, para 1.18). The 1980s witnessed expansion into payment cards (see above), mortgages (usually second) of dwelling houses and unsecured personal loans, eg, for white goods. In the 1990s, finance companies begun

---

[2.17/18]

1   As to alternative methods of raising money by 'unitisation', see Ferran, *Mortgage Securitisation*. As to centralised lenders, see (1993) 14 CCA News 2/8.

2   In relation to the quotation of interest rates by the financial intermediary, there is this difference: the quotation of rates to consumer-borrowers is carefully controlled by the CCA (see post, para 8.25); but the quotation of rates to consumer-depositors falls under s 32 of the Banking Act 1987.

3   The use of money transmission services by criminals to conceal the criminal source of funds may now constitute the offence of money laundering, a topic beyond the scope of this work.

4   See generally, the *Jack Report on Banking Services* (1989, Cm 622) Chapters 9 and 10; and Arora, *Electronic Banking and the Law* (2nd edn), Chapter 5; Guest and Lloyd, *Consumer Credit Law*, para 2-188.

5   Telephone and internet banking particularly raise issues within the Data Protection Act 1998, such as the security of data: see further post, para 8.17.

to operate current accounts for consumers[6] and to issue cheque-books on them. They have their own industry base interest rate, Finance House Base Rate (FHBR).

3   *Building societies.*[7] As recently as 1965, building societies were a specialist form of financial intermediary (with a mutual status) and high-street branch network, which concentrated on loans to finance the acquisition of dwellings: they were required by law to take security in the form of (in practice usually first) mortgages on land (see generally Chapter 25). However, under the Building Societies Act 1986 (as amended), building societies are now able to make unsecured loans and offer almost a full range of consumer banking services, eg, current accounts, overdrafts, money transmission; and many large building societies have turned themselves into banks.

4   *Credit unions* (see post, 15.19).

5   *Collected (or home) credit* (see post, para 5.02).

Vendor credit

[2.19] Where one person supplies both the goods and the 'loan' of their price (see ante, para 2.16) that may be done in either of the following ways:[1]

(1) The supplier and consumer enter into one of the forms of instalment credit contract in relation to goods (see ante, para 2.16). This form was commonly used by high-street retailers (see below) and is still popular with mail-order houses (see post, para 8.19) and doorstep sellers (see post, para 5.02).

(2) The supplier and consumer enter into both a cash sale of goods (see ante, para 1.06) **and** a contract of loan.[2] In the case of retail stores, it is becoming common for the retailer to supply the private consumer with a 'store card',[3] though, particularly with corner shops, there is still to be found instead the system of saving in advance through a club (see post, para 15.18). Where the retailer is making a loan to a private consumer, one of the following accounting systems is commonly used:[4]

(i) *An open account*, eg, monthly, whereby the consumer pays the entire price for all the goods purchased during the preceding month on a designated day.[5]

---

6   Insofar as finance companies allow consumers to accumulate credit balances on these accounts, they will also need banking licences: (1999) 53 CC5/37.

7   Although financial intermediaries, building societies are exempt from the Banking Act 1987 (s 4 and Sched 2 (as amended)), provided they fall within the Building Societies Act 1986 (as amended). The 1986 Act controls both the borrowing and lending of these institutions, though the latter is overridden by the CCA in respect of regulated loans (see post, para 5.13 *et seq*).

[2.19]

1   See generally the *Crowther Report on Consumer Credit* (Cmnd 4596), Chapter 2.5.

2   As to contracts of loan, see generally post, Chapter 7. In the trade, it was customary to treat the sale and loan together, as giving rise to a credit sale, but it seems likely that English law would regard the transaction as a separate sale and loan: the trade view was prompted by urgent need to avoid the now repealed Moneylenders Acts (see post, para 6.09). Some traders, eg, supermarkets, have even begun to allow cash withdrawals.

3   Store or Budget Cards tend to charge comparatively high rates of interest; and some stores will accept only their own cards for payments otherwise than in cash.

4   Under a private-label scheme, the loan is in fact provided by a third party: see post, para 2.24.

5   See the *Crowther Report* (above), para 2.5.1–2.

(ii) *A revolving or budget account*, whereby the consumer agrees to make regular payments to the retailer of an agreed amount (eg, £10 by monthly direct debit) and is then allowed to purchase goods from that retailer up to the value of a designated multiple (say 24 times) of that sum (eg, £240), it being agreed that the credit shall never exceed that sum (the credit line), but that new purchases on credit may be made insofar as the outstanding credit falls below that amount.[6] Modern forms tend to utilise a 'budget card':[3] it may involve loans of money to the consumer,[2] or in some cases to the retailer.[7]

This form of business will be discussed later (post, para 7.08).

(iii) *An option account*, which is an open account with a retailer whereunder the customer has the option, when presented with the (say) monthly statement, to defer payment under the above revolving credit system.[8] Frequently, interest is not charged if the entire balance is discharged each month;[9] and, where most of the retailer's business is done on credit, any rate of interest charged may be nominally reduced by assimilating it into the cash price of the goods (but see post, para 8.27).

Lender credit[1]

[2.20] Introduction. Where the goods and 'loan' are to be supplied by two separate people (see ante, para 2.16), the obvious pattern would be for the goods supplier (dealer) to enter into a contract of sale of the goods for the price to be paid immediately by the consumer and for the financier to lend that price to the consumer.[2] However, this pattern had the disadvantage that it usually fell within the now-repealed Moneylenders Act 1900–27: whilst this did not affect the clearing banks, which were exempt from those Acts,[3] it did deter other financiers who consequently adopted the following traditional forms of business:

1 *Direct financing*. For items of large unit value such as would justify the cost of setting up for each transaction a separate agreement directly with a customer, eg, a motor vehicle, direct financing was used (see post, para 2.21).

2 *Indirect financing*. For items of smaller unit value, where it would be uneconomic to set up separate transactions but where the size of turnover would compensate for less

---

6   See *ibid*, para 2.5.3; Goode, *HP Law and Practice*, pp 896–98. This form of business is regarded as a useful way of keeping the customer psychologically tied to a particular outlet; but it is rigid in that the amount of the regular payment is fixed: compare credit cards (see post, para 7.09).

7   Some variants allow the consumer to continue making periodic payments even though his entire debt has been repaid ('save and borrow' accounts): at this stage, the consumer may become the creditor.

8   Goode, *op cit*, note 6, 898. Cf three-party credit cards: post, para 2.24. These are sometimes mistaken for fixed sum credit: (1993) 48 CC 2/12.

9   This may produce up to five weeks' 'free credit' in respect of goods or services, but is unlikely to be offered in respect of cash advances.

[2.20]

1   In North America this is termed 'sales financing': see Geva: *Product Defences*, 3–4.

2   For the general rules as to the payment of the price and other debts, see post, para 23.13. The financier may himself finance this business by factoring the consumer debts: see generally post, para 2.22.

3   The Moneylenders Act 1900, s 6(d) obviously exempted banks, but was shown to have no general application to even the largest finance company: *United Dominions Trust Ltd v Kirkwood* [1966] 2 QB 431, CA.

individual control, it was common to bundle transactions together in what became know as block discounting or indirect financing (see post, para 2.22).

However, with the removal in 1974 of the artificial restriction represented by the Moneylenders Acts, financiers became free to conduct their business by way of their making loans to consumers (see post, para 2.23). This immediately threw into prominence the issue of security: was the financier prepared to make an unsecured loan to the consumer; or did he require the comfort of rights in some assets before parting with his money? In direct financing, the financier would automatically attain such security because he became the owner of the goods financed (asset financing); and thus direct financing has continued unabated for higher priced items, eg, cars. However, the (albeit impaired) security of indirect financing has been largely relinquished for the (even cheaper to administer) simple loan,[4] commonly effected by credit card (see post, para 2.28).

[2.21] Direct financing[1]

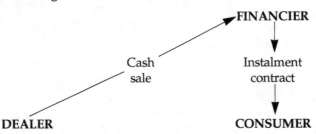

Under this system, the goods-supplier (dealer) makes a cash sale of the goods to the financier, who then enters into an instalment contract (see ante, para 1.03) with the consumer.[2] The normal course of events is that the consumer selects his goods, typically a motor vehicle, from the dealer's stock and then completes an instalment contract and sometimes other[3] forms in respect of the goods.[4] In addition, the consumer may have to find a surety (see post, para 25.04 et seq) and will normally have to pay a substantial deposit to the dealer.[5] The next step is for the dealer to forward the completed forms (plus any surety required) to the finance company, together with an invoice, which will contain details of the goods and their cash price, and will constitute an offer by the dealer to sell

---

4   See post, para 16.03. For the mortgaging of land and goods, see generally post, Chapter 25. But see the comment post, para 2.23.

[2.21]

1   See Goode, *HP Law and Practice* (2nd edn), pp 124–51, 129–132b; *Commercial Law* (2nd edn), pp 758–59, 783–85.

2   In the case of simple hiring, this will take the form of an equipment lease (see ante, para 1.18): see Goode [1981] JBL 239; Soper and Munro, *The Leasing Handbook*, pp 50–52.

3   The financier will usually require information about the consumer for their credit-vetting procedures (see post, para 8.35). Sometimes this information is included in the instalment contract form; but in others, a separate 'proposal form' is used.

4   For express terms, see generally post, para 11.07. In law the consumer's signature thereon will usually amount to an offer to take the goods on those terms: see post, para 10.08.

5   For the liability of the finance company for the return of that deposit if the proposal is not accepted, see post, para 16.05.

the goods to the finance company, commonly with full recourse.[6] If the finance company decides to accept the business, the agreement-form will usually be signed by one of its officers; and a copy dispatched to the consumer, which will normally amount to the company's acceptance (see post, para 10.08). At the same time, the finance company will notify the dealer that the proposal has been accepted, and that it is in order for him to deliver the goods.[7] The result of this complicated transaction will thus be that (a) the finance company will normally acquire title to the goods financed from the dealer (see post, para 16.03) and (b) there will be no primary contractual relationship between the dealer and the consumer, although there may be a collateral contract between them (see post, para 16.18). Sometimes, the dealer collects the instalments on behalf of the financier (agency collection).[8]

[2.22] Indirect financing.[1] Here, the goods-supplier (dealer) enters into an instalment contract (see ante, para 1.03) with the consumer,[2] typically in respect of a domestic appliance, so initially extending the credit to the consumer, just as in vendor credit (see ante, para 2.19).

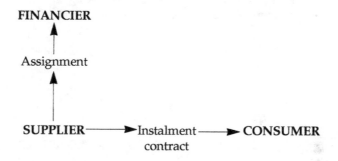

The dealer would then have two rights:

1 *His contractual right to the instalments.* Thus, the cash price due under a credit or conditional sale is a present legal chose in action (see ante, para 2.02) in the hands of the dealer, as is the hire rent due under a fixed-term hiring; but the rent which may become due under a periodic hiring (see ante, para 1.25), whether under a simple hiring or hp, is only a future chose (see post, para 7.18).

2 *His residuary proprietary rights to the goods.* A conditional seller, or one who supplies goods on hp or simple hiring *prima facie* retains the general property in the goods, which he may reclaim by suing in tort (see post, para 19.04).

The dealer would collect all his instalment agreements over a given period, eg, a month, and then assign his interest in them to a financier in a block (hence the term 'block discounting'). That (say monthly) assignment might be absolute, that is, a transfer of the

---

6   The invoice may contain the conditions of the proposed sale, or be subject to a Master Agreement (as to which see Macleod, *Consumer Sales Law*, 1989, Butterworths, para 16-28, though this is more usual in indirect financing. For recourse provisions, see post, para 16.16.

7   Normal finance company practice is to pay out the dealer only against the consumer's signed receipt.

8   Goode, *op cit*, note 1, 125.

[2.22]

1   See Goode, *HP Law and Practice* (2nd edn), pp 125–26; *Commercial Law* (2nd edn), pp 759–63.

2   See Macleod, *Consumer Sales Law*, 1989, para 16.22 *et seq.*

dealer's entire interest; or it might be by way of security, that is, by way of mortgage, charge or trust.[2] Normally, this monthly assignment would be closely regulated by a complicated Master Agreement (see ante, para 2.21). Instalments are normally collected on behalf of the financier by the dealer unless and until the dealer defaults, so enabling the dealer to continue regular contact with the consumer.

Factoring. Analytically similar to indirect financing, factoring is a form of business under which the dealer raises money on the debts owed to him by his customers ('accounts receivable') by selling them to a 'factor'.[3] Unfortunately, 'factoring' is one of those confusing expressions which has acquired several different meanings: a 19th century factor would be a businessman who either sold goods (usually by retail) on his own behalf or as agent of another;[4] whereas the modern factor referred to here tends instead to specialise primarily in the sale and purchase of commercial debt (see post, para 2.27).

Indirect financing and the similar factoring have become so specialised that they are now beyond the scope of this work.

[2.23] Loan financing and payment cards. This paragraph is concerned with the financing of consumer transactions by way of a loan to the consumer.

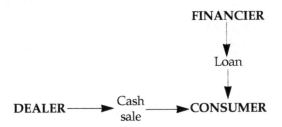

Of all the various types of consumer loan financing (see post, para 15.17), by far the most important is payment cards,[1] which in the UK really started with the launch of Barclaycard in 1966. The late 20th century mushroom growth in the use of embossed plastic payment cards is part of the worldwide developments of retail banking. There is a global technical specification for payment cards laid down by the International Standards Organisation (ISO), the ISO rules being embodied in British Standards (see post, para 3.08). To try and combat counterfeiting, cards normally embody elaborate holograms. Nevertheless, the unscrupulous still seem to acquire supplies of blank cards and then persuade, eg, a waiter to run a customer's card through a swipe machine twice, so generating personal card details ('skimming') from which a card may be counterfeited.[2]

---

3   Eg, *Re Charge Card Services Ltd* (set out post, para 2.27). See generally Goode, *Commercial Law* (2nd edn), p 802 *et seq*; Adams, *Factoring*; Biscoe, *Law and Practice of Credit Factoring*; Salinger, *Factoring* (3rd edn).

4   If entrusted with possession of his principal's goods. Compare a 'broker' who tended not to be entrusted with possession: see Fridman, *Agency* (7th edn), pp 40–44. The 'factor' in this 19th century sense gave his name to a series of Acts of Parliament: see post, para 21.24.

[2.23]

1   See Arora, *Electronic Banking* (2nd edn), pp 108–09. There are EU Codes of Conduct relating to electronic payments (87/598/EEC) and systems (88/590/EEC): set out in Goode, *Consumer Credit Law and Practice*, Part X, para 2.21 *et seq*.

2   See [2001] 5 Which? 14.

An important problem for bankers is to identify the person applying for payment by card, so reducing fraud.[3] Several forms of identification have been developed. Originally, reliance was placed on the human comparison of the signature which the card-holder was supposed to place on the card. Not only is signature comparison unreliable, eg, the signature stripe may be replaced and depends on human recognition, but it can be entirely circumvented by the theft of blank cards and cannot be used for telephone and internet sales. So, there was introduced the personal identification number (PIN) system, where a machine compared the information on the magnetic stripe on a card with a matching PIN typed in by the card-holder: a unique four-digit number will be secretly issued to the card-holder, so that supposedly only the holder could type that number when inserting his card in a machine,[4] eg, an ATM (see post, para 2.24). More recently, there have developed other identification devices: since 1991 card-issuers have been experimenting with the photograph of the card-holder printed on the card; and in the late 1990s they have begun to utilise 'smart-card' technology[5] to replace (insecure) magnetic stripes with information contained in a chip, so as to allow machine comparison of eye, voice finger-print or digital signature. There are also systems helping retailers detect stolen ('hot') cards.[6] Modern payment cards tend to be marketed with a range of perquisites.[7]

In a fast-developing market,[8] UK payment cards now include various functions, sometimes combined on multi-purpose cards.[9] These cards fall into two groups:

(1) A two-party card issued by the supplier of the goods or services (see post, para 2.24);

(2) A three-party card issued by a third party financier (see post, para 2.25).

The EU is beginning to think in terms of introducing their own legislative control over such electronic payment mechanisms.[10]

[2.24] Two-party cards. The following types of two-party card may be noticed.

Cash cards with which the card-holder can, by use with appropriate security (see ante, para 2.23), withdraw cash from an Automated Teller Mechanism (ATM).[1] The debt will be

---

3 For card-notification organisations, see the *Jack Report on Banking Services* (1989, Cm 622), paras 11.13–17; and for counterfeit cards, see paras 11.18–22.

4 See further Arora (1992) 9 Tr L 91. The card user has the practical difficulty of remembering his PINs without writing them down: unlike a signature system, this tends to put the risk on the card-holder: see post, para 7.01.

5 Visa issued its first 'smart card' in 1998. 'Smart cards' contain a micro-processor and memory chip, so dispensing with human intervention: see the *Jack Report, op cit*, note 3, paras 11.24–28; *Banking Ombudsman, Annual Report* 1995/6, para 12.4; (1998) 52 CC5/29; (1998) CCA News Spring 24; (2001) *The Times*, 19 May. For Electronic Fund Transfer, see ante, para 2.17.

6 Originally based on circulated lists, modern systems depend on lower floor levels and almost instantaneous telephone access by the retailer to the computerised records of credit bureaux: see post, para 8.36.

7 See [2000] 7 Which? 20.

8 Eg affinity cards, where the issuer pays a percentage of each transaction to a charity, eg, the RSPCA, RSPB; shareholders' discount cards; points systems (see post, para 15.18).

9 See the *Jack Report, op cit*, note 3, paras 11.10–12. From the viewpoint of consumer security, is a single all-purpose card desirable? The problem is compounded with high-value ('gold') cards.

10 Electronic money: Commission proposes clear regulatory framework (1998): press release IP/98/727; (2002) 56 CC5/11.

[2.24]

1 See Arora, *Electronic Banking* (2nd edn), Chapter 5; the *Jack Report on Banking Services* (1989, Cm 622), para 9.08; Guest and Lloyd, *Consumer Credit Law*, para 2-015.

electronically debited to the card-holder's current account by EFT (see ante, para 2.17), usually immediately. Since the various ATM systems have been linked together so that customers of any bank may use any machine, ATMs have become an increasingly popular method of withdrawing cash.[2] In effect, the cash card is a two-party debit card (see post, para 2.25), even if it can be used in ATMs owned by third parties.[3]

Pre-payment cards, where the card-holder pays for the value to be held on a disposable card: although it is not legal tender (see post, para 23.14), the card-holder is in effect paying in advance for services, so that the card may be considered as akin to cash, eg, a phone card,[4] or payment card for minors.[5] There are also being introduced a new generation of rechargeable ('stored value') smart cards (see ante, para 2.23): not only could these be used to obtain goods and services, but they would also enable the creation of so called 'electronic' or 'digital' money, which operates as a sort of 'cashless purse' to be used by insertion into a card-reader;[6] and, if that reader is linked to a telephone, it could work like an ATM in reverse.[7]

Budget or store cards, enabling the card-holder to charge purchases in the issuing store to his account there, the card functioning as a verification of the customer's signature.[8] Such cards are sometimes a form of vendor credit (see ante, para 2.19). Alternatively, they may function as a three-party card (see post, para 2.25), as where the retailer operates the card through a separate company, eg, jointly with a bank; or that separate company is in fact run by a financier (private-label schemes), this being a disguised form of lender credit.[9]

[2.25] Three-party cards. These involve the introduction of a third-party financier (see ante, para 2.17), who normally sets up a revolving credit account (see ante, para 2.19) for the consumer, which the latter operates by way of a plastic payment card.[1] Such accounts may be divided according to whether or not the extension of credit is an integral part of the system. If so,[2] they are properly termed 'credit cards'.[3] However, in the following types of three-party card, any element of credit granted to the consumer is incidental:

Cheque guarantee card, for use where the card-holder pays for goods or services by cheque, which is a form of bill of exchange, as to which see generally post, para 7.24. In

---

2   The pricing of this service has given rise to competition issues; but the OFT has accepted the Link scheme as being in the public interest: [2001] 11 CL 60; 31 Fair Trading 7; and generally ante, para 2.14.

3   The third party usually merely acts as agent: Goode, *Consumer Credit Legislation,* para 549.5.

4   See (2000) QA 4.

5   [2001] 3 Which? 43; (2001) *The Times,* 21 April. For the legal difficulty with extending credit to minors, see post, para 10.18.

6   Eg, the Mondex card (see (1994) *The Times,* 5 September; (1997) *The Times,* 24 February). The system is being developed for use on the internet (see (1996) *The Times,* 9 January).

7   By extracting value from the card and passing it by phone to the supplier's bank account: see [1998] 6 Which? 41.

8   Eg, M & S, Dixons, Miss Selfridge. An attraction to retail issuers is that these cards have been shown to be a good way of enhancing customer loyalty: see (1994) 49 CC 1/27.

9   See ante, para 2.20. Cf eponymous subsidiaries (see post, para 16.06A). Distinguish loyalty cards: see post, para 8.13A.

[2.25]

1   See ante, para 2.24. Additionally, card-issuers sometimes also issue the consumer with a cheque book, so that the account may be operated like a traditional bank account: as to which, see ante, para 2.17.

2   Use of that credit may be encouraged by the awarding of 'points' (see post, para 15.19).

3   See post, para 2.28. In 2001, there were in issue 48 m credit cards and 49 m debit cards.

exhibiting to the supplier of goods or services a cheque card with matching signature, the consumer is proffering the bank's promise that a cheque with that signature will be met up to the amount and on the conditions specified (see post, para 2.26).

Debit card,[3] which the card-holder presents at the point of sale (with either verifying signature or PIN), enabling the supplier of goods or services to debit electronically the sale to the card-holder's bank account within a pre-set limit.[4] These will be examined later (see post, para 23.15), but for now may be thought of as a sort of electronic cheque.[5] A subsequent innovation has been the corporate purchase card designed to enable big business to buy low value supplies.[6] It is Bank of England policy to modernise money transmission by replacing (paper-based) cheques with (electronic-based) debit cards.

Charge card, by production of which (with signature verification) the card-holder can obtain the immediate supply of the goods or services (see post, para 2.27); and the card-holder is normally expected to settle his bill to the card-issuer in full at the end of each month,[7] though if he is entitled to roll over his debt it becomes a credit card.[3]

[2.26] Cheque guarantee cards.[1] The commercial purpose of these cards is to persuade retailers to release goods against customer's cheques.[2] There are two dangers to the retailer in so releasing the goods: (a) the customer may have insufficient funds in his bank account to meet the cheque;[3] and (b) the customer may have forged the signature of the signatory to the bank account.[4] The question of whether a cheque guarantee card protected the retailer in event (b) was considered in *First Sport Ltd v Barclays Bank plc*:[5]

> A cheque book and cheque card issued by the Bank to a Mr Kahn were stolen from the latter. The trial judge found it likely that the genuine signature was removed from the card and replaced by the signature of the person who presented the cheque and card to the retailer. It followed that the alteration was probably undetectable. The Bank refused to meet the cheque when presented by the retailer on the valid grounds that the cheque had not been signed by Mr Kahn. Accordingly, the retailer sued the Bank on the cheque guarantee card.

---

4   Eg Switch, Visa Delta. These cards may be used in conjunction with EFTPoS facilities at the cash-out, which machine-read the card and then debit the card-holder's bank account like an ATM. See further post, para 23.15.

5   Campbell (1994) 13 Tr L 18 at 19.

6   A smart card (see ante, para 2.23) whose chip will deal with the VAT implications of each transaction, this form of debit card will significantly cheapen and accelerate the process of placing small orders: see (1994) *The Times*, 14 November; (1995) 16 CCA News 4/19.

7   Eg American Express (Amex). Alternatively, these card are sometimes described as 'Travel and Entertainment' (T & E) cards, eg, Diners. Another variation is a bank budget account, under which the card-holder contracts to make regular payments (cf ante, para 2.19).

[2.26]

1   See generally *Chitty on Contract* (28th edn), vol 2, para 38-441. Partly because of the amount of fraud, some card-issuers have resisted increasing the upper limit of their obligation above the original £50: *Jack Report on Banking Services* (1989, Cm 622) para 7.65.

2   Ie, to give up their right of lien on the goods until the cheque is met (see post, para 24.03).

3   In which case, the bank is usually entitled to refuse to meet the cheque: Bills of Exchange Act 1882, s 53(1).

4   In which case, that forged signature is a nullity: Bills of Exchange Act 1882, s 24.

5   [1993] 3 All ER 789, [1993] 1 WLR 1229, CA.

The Court of Appeal held that the effect of the card was to convey a unilateral offer by the Bank to enter a collateral contract with the retailer. The terms of that contract were that, if the retailer complied with certain conditions, the Bank would meet the cheque.[6] Accordingly, the court carefully construed the terms written on the card. The Bank argued that the cheque-form signed was not a cheque in the technical sense because the signature on it was a forgery; but the majority construed the conditions of the card as requiring only an apparently genuine signature.[7] The question is: how liberal will the courts be with the use of these cards?[8] The Banks are refusing to pay such cheques where the forgery is blatant.[9] If the banks try to change the terms of the guarantee, these changes will have to pass the statutory tests of fairness and reasonableness.[10] Beyond that, the Banks may have to rely on the tort of negligent mis-statement (see post, para 17.20).

[2.27] Three-party charge cards.[1] The operation of these cards was judicially considered in *Re Charge Card Services Ltd*:[2]

> An unsuccessful charge card operation, CCS Ltd, was set up to operate a 'Fuel Card' Scheme as follows: account-holders could present a Fuel Card to a franchised garage exhibiting the logo and thereby pay for fuel by signing a sales voucher; one copy of the voucher was sent by the franchisee garage to CCS Ltd, who paid the franchisee the face value of the voucher less a commission; and CCS Ltd billed the account holder monthly. Because CCS Ltd would normally pay the franchisee before receiving payment from the account holder, the business was financed by factoring (see ante, para 2.22).

The dispute was between the factor and franchisees over money collected by the liquidator of CCS Ltd from account-holders, technically the account-holders not being parties to the proceedings.[3] Nevertheless, Millett J carefully considered the whole legal structure of charge and credit cards, making the following points (in which he was broadly supported by the unanimous Court of Appeal):

(1) The charge card operation involved three separate bilateral contracts between the account-holder (consumer),[4] CCS Ltd (card-issuer) and franchisee (retailer), each being a party to only two of the contracts (see post, para 7.09).

---

6   Evans LJ said that this was not strictly a 'guarantee' but 'a separate and independent obligation which is not dependent in any way on default by the customer' (at 795c–d). As to guarantees, see post, para 25.05.

7   This crucial wording on Barclays cheque guarantee cards has since been changed so as to give the retailer only protection (a): see (1993) 143 NLJ 430; 48 CC 2/20.

8   Eg if the card is used to 'back' a cheque in excess (say £275) of the limit (say £50), will the guarantee be good for £50 if the card limit is circumvented by drawing several cheques for the card limit?

9   (1994) *The Times*, 29 December.

10 As to fairness, see UTCC reg 4 (see post, para 11.15); and as to reasonableness, see UCTA, s 3 (see post, para 18.24).

[2.27]

1   See generally, Jones, *Credit Cards*, esp Chapter 10; Goode, *Consumer Credit Law and Practice*, Chapter 39; Goode, *Instalment Credit* (ed Diamond), pp 86–90; *Chitty on Contract* (27th edn), vol 2, para 36-388.

2   [1987] Ch 150, [1986] 3 All ER 289 (discussed (1987) 2 BFLR 119); affd [1989] Ch 497, [1988] 3 All ER 702, CA.

3   The propriety of the omission was confirmed by Millett J, who held that consumers were neither party nor privy to the relevant contracts.

4   The cards could be operated by the account-holder (commonly a registered company) or his authorised agents (usually employees). Millett J thought that for present purposes account-holders were liable as principals, disclosed or undisclosed, of card-holders, eg, employees.

(2) Goods were supplied by the retailer to the consumer under a supply contract concluded at the pump or till (see post, para 10.02). Rather than constituting a quasi-sale within the SGSA,[5] this supply contract probably amounted to a sale within the SGA (see ante, para 1.07), the display of the logo simply adding a term allowing for payment by charge card.[6] Refusal by the retailer to accept a properly produced card is presumably a breach of contract and may amount to an offence under the TDA (s 14: see post, para 4.16).

(3) *Prima facie*, use of the card constitutes absolute payment (see post, para 23.14), not conditional payment as would a cheque (s 38(1) of the SGA: see post, para 24.03). This reflects the popular perception of credit and charge cards as substitutes for cash, being frequently referred to as 'plastic money'.[7]

(4) Thereafter, the retailer must look exclusively to the card-issuer for payment[8] and the latter was entitled to debit the consumer's account[9] in respect of all transactions of which he was notified of card use.[10]

(5) It follows that the consumer carried no risk of the card-issuer's insolvency, a matter of dispute wholly between the retailer and factor.[11]

[2.28] Credit cards.[1] Under this essentially three-party system of payment card (see ante, para 2.25), a credit card is issued by the 'card-issuer' to a consumer (the 'card-holder') who uses that card to obtain goods or services from a merchant (retail-supplier) recruited by the merchant-acquirer (see below). Many card contracts allow for the issue of an extra card on the same account to an 'additional user', eg, relative, employee. It is presumed that the legal analysis of the scheme is similar to that for charge cards (see ante, para 2.27).

The retail-supplier will advertise his willingness to supply his goods or services on this system by displaying a logo; and the card-holder will initiate the system by signing a sales voucher, the basic security being provided by a signature test.[2] The card and sales

---

5   See Tiplady [1989] LM and CLQ 22. For quasi-sales, see ante, para 2.10.

6   See Dobson [1989] JBL at 341–42. This displaces the general rule requiring cash on delivery (s 28): see post, paras 23.16; 23.22. What if the holder closes his account before the retailer demands payment?

7   *Per* Browne-Wilkinson, VC, delivering judgment of the CA: at 705h–711d. Is this because the card company guarantee payment to the retailer? What if the card holder resigns his card before the retailer presents his account to the erstwhile card-issuer?

8   It has been argued that if the card-holding contract were a regulated cancellable agreement (which it was not: see below) and cancelled, this could leave the franchisee without means of redress: Sayer (1986) 136 NLJ 1030.

9   Both charge and credit cards would appear to constitute a provision of credit (see post, para 5.22); but the fuel card scheme could not give rise to regulated agreements insofar as the debtors were registered companies (see post, para 5.24). The additional (ie, employee) card-holders are irrelevant for this purpose in that they are not co-debtors (see post, para 7.08).

10   By the retailer presenting to the card-issuer a copy of the sales voucher signed by the consumer. Cf *Customs and Excise Comrs v Diners Club Ltd* [1989] 2 All ER 385, CA (VAT case).

11   This concerned the right of the factor to the retention fund without infringing the insolvency legislation (see post, para 19.22), or amounting to an unregistered charge over its own indebtedness (see post, para 25.25), or infringing the set-off rules (see post, para 7.23). It was not appealed.

[2.28]

1   See generally Jones, *Law Relating to Credit Cards* (1989), Chapter 1; *Chitty on Contract* (28th edn), vol 2, paras 38-433/36. The first credit card introduced into the UK was by American Express in 1963.

2   As to signature comparison, see ante, para 2.23. The retailer should also check his 'stop list' and will have a 'floor-limit', ie, if the transaction exceeds a nominated amount, he must phone the card-issuer for prior authorisation. As to telephone sales see post, para 8.17.

voucher will then be 'wiped' through a machine to transfer the details from the card onto the sales voucher. In service industries, eg, hotels, it is becoming common to wipe a card in blank before the service is provided. Does this provide the supplier with any security?

At the end of each accounting period (usually a month), the card-issuer presents an account to the card-holder who is automatically given a choice: he may make full payment within a set period, in which case probably no interest is charged, except perhaps for cash withdrawals;[2a] or he may elect to defer payment and pay interest, in which case he may pay any amount he chooses in excess of a stipulated minimum. Meanwhile, the merchant-acquirer/card-issuer will reimburse the retail supplier (often at a discount) against presentation of sales vouchers; and, insofar as this is done before they are put in funds for that purpose by the card-holder, the card-issuer is probably lending money to the card-holder.[3]

In practice, the credit card system is a bit more complicated than above, involving up to four principal trade parties.[4] Besides the retail-supplier, these are:

1   *Payment card organisations*, eg, Mastercard, Visa. Their role is to set and administer internationally the scheme rules, hold the trade mark in the credit card and issue licences to merchant-acquirers and/or card issuers. Key rules imposed by card organisations have included to honour all cards, not to discriminate between retail purchasers by cash or credit card and minimum volumes.[5] They also have 'charge back' arrangements by which a payer on a queried transaction may obtain reimbursement, eg, the card-issuer may credit the card-holder and then seek reimbursement from the merchant-acquirer, who may in turn seek reimbursement from the supplier. This mechanism may be used to operate the statutory indemnity, where applicable.[6]

2   *Merchant-acquirers*. These are intermediaries (see ante, para 2.17) who obtain licences from the above organisation and then recruit (acquire) merchants (retail-suppliers) to the organisation under merchant agreements.[7] The clearing banks have all become merchant-acquirers for both the major payment card organisations (see above).

3   *Card-issuers*. Some card-issuers offer (either on a single or separate cards), the facilities of more than one card organisation, eg, a card which is both an Access and a Visa card. Nowadays, most cards are issued in the UK in return for an annual charge: for the legal effect of this, see post, para 7.11. Besides making the card-holding (loan)

2a About 25% of credit card debts are paid off during the interest-free period and are not generally regarded as borrowing: (2001) 29 Credit Finance 13.

3   Goode, *HP Law and Practice* (2nd edn), p 902; Geva, *Financing Consumer Sales and Product Defences*, 11-6. Chitty, *op cit*, note 1, para 3757. For the consumer's statutory protection, see post, para 17.09 *et seq*.

4   See Goode, *Consumer Credit Law and Practice*, paras 2.61–64; OFT, *Connected Lender Liability* (1994) Chapter 3. For the chain of indemnities between them, see (1994) 7 Fair Trading 14.

5   These terms were referred to the Monopolies and Merger Commission (see ante, para 2.12), who reported that the latter two were restrictive trade practices: *Credit Card Services* (1989, Cmnd 718). Visa having unsuccessfully applied for judicial review (*R v MMC* [1991] Tr LR 97, CA) and refused to give voluntary undertakings (OFT, 1990 AR, 81-2), the Commission's recommendations were implemented by two Orders: Credit Cards (Merchant Acquisition) Order 1990/2158; Credit Cards (Price Discrimination) Order 1990/2159.

6   Under the Consumer Credit Act 1974, s 75(2): see OFT, *Connected Lender Liability* (1994), paras 3.16–19; and post, para 16.17.

7   See the OFT account in (1993) 2 Fair Trading 8; 10 Tr LR 105–06. For the retailer, there must be compared the cost of clearing cheques with the merchant charge on credit, charge, and debit cards.

contract with the consumer and collecting payments from him, card-issuers will also act as merchant-acquirers, sometimes for the very merchant to whom the credit card is presented.[8] Conduct of these arrangements are subject to the Banking Code of Practice (see post, para 3.13). Further developments are that some card-issuers enable their card-holders to operate their accounts like bank accounts (see post, para 7.03) by supplying them with cheques which they can use to draw on the account.[9]

---

8   Some UK card-issuers, eg, Lloyds, Midland and NatWest, have collaborated to set up the Joint Credit Card Company to act as their merchant-acquirer (see above). Provisions in the merchant contract restricting card issuers from acting as merchant-acquirers have now been declared unlawful monopolies: 1990 SI 2158; and see generally ante, para 2.12.

9   These will be subject to all the rules for cheques: see post, para 7.28. Credit-issuers sometimes use them, together with 'teaser rates', to attract new consumer business by way of transferred balances: see [1999] 12 Which? 44.

PART 2

CONSUMER PROTECTION

REGULATION OF BUSINESS

[3.01] Introduction. In 1995, the United Nations passed a resolution setting our eight basic consumer rights,[1] against which the English system described in this book may be tested.

In Part 1 of the book, the nature of the contracts used for the domestic supply of goods was examined. Part 2 is concerned with the different types of consumer protection that are available even before the parties start to negotiate a particular transaction for the domestic supply of goods. Chapter 3 deals with four topics: first, it outlines the various types of consumer watchdog (see post, paras 3.02–08); secondly, it looks at the statutory and voluntary control of supplies of goods to consumers (see post, paras 3.09–14); thirdly, it outlines the means of achieving consumer redress (see post, paras 3.15–25); and fourthly, it summarises the controls on the power of traders to accumulate personal information about consumers (see post, paras 3.26–28).

However, from the outset, it must be borne in mind that any system of controls is really only as good as the understanding of the people using it. Thus, on the trader's side much of the effect of legislation is diluted if traders simply do not know of, understand or implement, the legal norms with which they are supposed to comply: acceptance of this by the first Director General of the OFT (see post, para 3.03) lay behind the impetus which he gave to the voluntary codes (see post, para 3.11 *et seq*). Indeed, historically, one of the reasons for legislating has not been just to change the law, but to publicise it with the object of securing adherence.[2] In modern times, this process has been taken a step further: to take criminal or civil proceedings against a trader for acting in ignorance of the law has sometimes been thought counter-productive; and one of the justifications for the modern extensive use of voluntary codes of practice (see post, para 3.11 *et seq*) has been claimed to be its educative function as regards traders. It is also a much cheaper and more flexible way of securing trader compliance. However, a disadvantage to consumers is that a trader may simply decide to ignore consumer rights as a matter of policy.[3]

Turning to consumers, on the one hand there is considerable pressure for them to be provided with more information, whether as to their legal rights, product information at point of sale, or redress mechanisms; and the next step is to make consumers more demanding.[4] On the other hand, for even the ablest there is clearly a maximum limit of information that may be absorbed: it may be asked whether the English system of consumer protection is approaching that limit; and each extra protection should be weighed against the further complication it may introduce.[5] Furthermore, it is not the

---

[3.01]

1 The right to: safety; be informed; satisfaction of basic needs; choose; redress; consumer education; be heard; and a healthy environment (see OFT, AR-96, p 11).

2 For a modern example, see the work of the OFT in relation to traders and the UTCC Regulations: see OFT, UCT Bulletin No 5, p 7; and generally post, para 11.12A *et seq*.

3 See *Modern Markets: Confident Consumers* (1999, Cm 4410) paras 3.1; 3.4. Much government information is now published on the Internet.

4 Eg, passing consumer-complainants back to the manufacturer ([2001] 6 Which? 7); denying liability under s 75 of the CCA ([2001] 5 Which? 42).

5 Current government policy sees the present body of consumer law as broadly adequate: *Modern Markets, op cit*, note 3, para 6.2.

case that all consumers start from a basis of equal knowledge of their rights; and there are distinct limitations on the extent to which legislation can equalise differences between classes of consumers.[6] Indeed, it may be that consumer protection legislation should therefore be limited in aim to remedying the imbalance in bargaining power between consumers and suppliers as a whole;[7] optimising simplicity and transparency in transactions;[8] and educating against overindebtedness (see post, para 27.01).

Complementary to this is the dual policy of putting the burden of enforcement of consumer rights on officialdom[9] and steps taken to improve consumer awareness of their rights: the desirability of educating children in knowledge of their rights as consumers is at last being taken seriously;[10] and the Office of Fair Trading has an important official function in this regard,[11] as do the directly sponsored bodies and local authorities (see post, para 3.03 *et seq*); but there are also voluntary bodies concerned with consumer protection (see post, para 3.08) and education.[12] Finally, the traditional English obsession with redress by way of damages is at last being supplemented by the introduction of a continental-inspired system for injunctions to be obtained on behalf of consumers against traders (see post, para 28.03); and, as against public bodies and private bodies carrying out public functions, consumers may sometimes be able to invoke the Human Rights Act 1998 (see post, para 3.09).

CONSUMER WATCHDOGS

The government

[3.02] **Whitehall**. 'The role of central government in consumer protection is to promote legislative policy, oversee the implementation of legislation and oversee the work of the various government agencies.'[1] Actual enforcement is frequently left to local authorities (see post, para 3.05) or government agencies, eg, Office of Fair Trading (see below), Information Commissioner (see post, para 3.27). However, within Whitehall, central government responsibility for consumer protection is spread between a number of different Departments of State, in a pattern which tends to change with the complexion of each government.[2] Hence, the usual draftsman's formula in a statute that something shall

---

6 Cayne and Trebilcock (1973) 23 UTLJ 396, at 407–11; OFT, *Vulnerable Consumers and Financial Services* (1999) paras 200, 700; Modern *Markets, op cit*, note 3, paras 1.6; 3.31; OFT, AR-99, 9.

7 Cayne and Trebilcock, *ibid*, at 427.

8 It should be remembered that virtually all measures of consumer protection have costs, which will have to be met – generally by way of higher charges for the relevant goods or taxation.

9 For the officials concerned with consumer credit, see Goode, *Consumer Credit Law and Practice*, Directory.

10 *Modern Markets, op cit*, note 3, paras 3.32–34; OFT, AR-98 21; AR-99, 23; [2000] 5 Credit Today 21. For initiatives aimed at credit education for 14 to 16-year-olds, see 46 CC 5/22; OFT, AR-90, 20, 27; Consumers' Association, 1994/95 AR 21. There seems to be some support for NVQ recognition for money advice.

11 See OFT, AR-95, 17; [2001] 4 Credit Today 32; and see further post, para 3.16. For FSA educational initiatives, see post, para 3.02.

12 Eg, the National Consumer Education Partnership (see (1997) 16 Tr LR 520). Citizenship is due to become part of the national curriculum, Key Stage 4: [2000] CCA News, Winter 16.

[3.02]

1 Harvey, *Consumer Protection and Fair Trading* (6th edn), p 49.

2 Harvey, *ibid*, pp 49–52.

be done by 'the Secretary of State' tends to refer even as regards consumer protection statutes to different Secretaries of State in respect of different functions and at different dates. Under this formal umbrella, there is likely to be a politician at Minister of State level responsible for day-to-day issues.

As from summer 2002, residential house loans secured by way of a first charge, including non-status lending (see post, para 7.04A), will be controlled by the Treasury, overseeing the operation of the Financial Services and Markets Act 2000 (FSMA) and the activities of the Financial Services Authority (FSA): whilst largely beyond the scope of this work, *inter alia*,[3] the FSA will control deposit-taking by financial intermediaries (see ante, para 2.17); promote consumer financial education;[4] and ensure consumer protection, as by advertising controls (cf post, para 8.29), cooling-off periods (cf post, para 10.28), restrictions on repossession (cf post, para 25.24) and an ombudsman system (see post, para 3.25), what the FSMA terms 'regulated activities'.[4a] So, ordinary residential mortgages will usually be outside the Consumer Credit Act 1974 (CCA),[5] being subject to different educational initiatives[6] and a different set of consumer protection rules, though the latter are likely in some respects to parallel those of the CCA.[7] Establishing the borderline between the operation of the FSMA and the CCA is therefore likely to be vital.[8]

The Department of Trade and Industry (DTI) deals with the supply of goods on credit and oversees the CCA, including regulated loans, whether unsecured or secured on houses ('second mortgages'), eg, home improvement loans. Within the DTI, day-to-day responsibility being divided between several of his Ministers of State,[9] the Department also being responsible for the Office of Fair Trading (see post, para 3.03). Additionally, the various Departments of State also sponsor a number of other functions[10] and bodies (see post, para 3.04). In 1994, the Government empowered themselves to contract out certain ministerial functions under the deregulation initiative (see post, para 5.10); and, in the absence of new primary legislation, this procedure may be used to effect a number of statutory alterations beneficial to consumers.[11] Indeed, it has been estimated that over

---

3   Currently, the FSA is not to control mortgage advice, nor the brokers who normally give it, these matters being left to codes of conduct: see post, para 3.13.

4   Section 4. It seems likely to concentrate these activities on the mainstream market and largely ignore lower income groups: see (1999) 52 *Quarterly Accounts* 6.

4a Section 22. This should not be confused with 'regulated agreements' under the CCA: see post, para 5.13.

5   Either because it exceeds the financial limit (see post, para 5.22) or is exempt from the CCA (see post, para 5.15).

6   Under FSMA, ss 4, 5. Eg, the booklets *Money Counts* (2000), *You and Your Money* (2001).

7   FSMA, s 428. The EU Commission has adopted a recommendation that as from 2002 there should be a voluntary code of conduct on pre-contractual information, including a 'European standardised information sheet'.

8   See the FSMA (Regulated Activities) Order 2001, SI 544. The FSMA will apply to most first mortgages and some second mortgages, but probably not to any mortgages regulated by the CCA: see Rosenthal (2001) 30 Credit Finance 22. The Treasury intend that, where there is any overlap, FSMA regulation will take precedence.

9   For the exercise of his functions under the CCA, see Goode, *Consumer Credit Law and Practice*, Directory.

10 There should also be borne in mind the specialist functions in respect of such as discrimination, food, medicines and weights and measures. Co-ordination across government is promised: *Modern Markets: Confident Consumers* (1999, Cm 4410), para 9.2.

11 Including making some of the changes recommended in *Modern Markets* (above). Other alterations in commercial behaviour may be forced by use of the CCA licensing system: see post, para 6.18.

80% of DTI legislative initiatives are nowadays exercised by statutory order made under either the ECA (see ante, para 1.03A) or Deregulation Acts (see post, para 5.10).

[3.03] Office of Fair Trading. Section 1 of the Fair Trading Act 1973 (FTA) created a new government agency, the Office of Fair Trading (OFT), headed by the Director General of Fair Trading (the Director). The Director is subject to the control of the Secretary of State (s 12: see ante, para 3.02); and there are Government plans to interpose an OFT management board.[1] Despite the name of his Office, the Director was not given a free hand to interfere whenever he considered there to be unfair trading, but was instead strictly confined within the specific powers granted to him by the FTA and other statutes. The FTA itself envisaged two major strands of consumer protection: prices and products. First, he was to protect the economic interests of consumers by the promotion of economic efficiency and competition policy (see ante, paras 2.12–14); but this large area of specialist law is mostly beyond the scope of this work. Second, he was to protect the economic and social interests of consumers other than in the price of goods and services supplied. Currently, the major elements of the latter consumer protection function are as follows:[2]

1   *Information collection.* To keep under review, and to collect, receive and collate information concerning commercial activities in the United Kingdom affecting the interests of consumers;[3] and make recommendations for action to the Secretary of State.[4]

2   *Estate agency.* To superintend the working and enforcement of the Estate Agents Act 1979, a matter beyond the scope of this work.

3   *Rogue traders.* To seek assurances from traders and obtain court undertakings from rogue traders that they will mend their ways under what are now called Stop Now Orders (Part III, FTA: see post, paras 6.06–08).

4   *Unfair contract terms.* Since 1994, to consider complaints that certain classes of standard contract terms are unfair. If so, as lead-enforcer to seek suitable undertakings from the *proferens* (see post, para 11.12 *et seq*); or, failing that, take court action (see below).

5   *Consumer education.* To publish information[5] and advice to consumers,[6] and to encourage trade associations to prepare codes of practice for guidance in safeguarding and promoting the interests of UK consumers.[7]

[3.03]

1   OFT, 2000-AR, 12. See the draft Enterprise Bill 2002: see post, para 5.11.

2   A formalised strategic re-statement of the Director's consumer functions is discussed in OFT, 1990 AR, 18–21; 1994-AR, 19; 2000-AR, 14–15. The government proposes to strengthen the position of the OFT: *Modern Markets: Confident Consumers* (1999, Cm 4410) paras 8.12–13. For the OFT's thoughts, see 1998-AR 9-11; 1999-AR 17.

3   FTA, ss 2(1), (2), 131; CCA, s 1(2). As to the classification of complaints, see OFT, Annual Report, Appendix K.

4   FTA, s 2. For the powers of the Secretary of State to make statutory orders, see post, paras 4.20–24.

5   Eg, Fair Trading (a quarterly published digest for consumer protectors and advisers); and an OFT website ((1999) 23 Fair Trading 8). As to restrictions on the disclosure of information, see ss 124, 133 (as amended); and post, para 28.06.

6   FTA, s 124; CCA, s 4. The OFT publishes a substantial number of leaflets and booklets: a current list is to be found in the latest Annual Report, eg, *A Buyer's Guide.* For a new OFT consumer information strategy, see OFT, 1991 Annual Report, 22.

7   FTA, s 124(3). The OFT sponsors a substantial number of codes of practice: see further post, para 3.11.

6   *Reports to Government.* To make annual and other reports to the Secretary of State in respect of the scope of his duties under the CCA[8] and any other enactment so requiring,[9] such reports to be published and laid before Parliament.

7   *Licensing.* To administer the licensing system under the Consumer Credit Act 1974 (see post, para 6.11 *et seq*) and in respect of estate agency (see above). The former powers have been extended in relation to European businesses (ss 203–04 of the FSMA: see post, para 6.12).

8   *Central co-ordinator.* To act as the central co-ordinator (see post, para 28.03) for enforcement of the Trade Descriptions Act 1968 (see post, para 4.02 *et seq*) and the Consumer Credit Act 1974 (s 2 of the CCA; and see Chapter 5).

9   *Enforcement.* By applying to court for Stop Now Orders, to act as primary enforcer of the Unfair Terms Regulations (see post, para 11.19), long-stop enforcer of the Misleading Advertisement Regulations (see post, para 8.12A) and lead-enforcer for other consumer protection legislation (see below; and post, paras 28.03).

10 *Registers of convictions.* To keep central registers of convictions which is available to local authorities, but not the public.[10]

11 *Distance Selling.* To enforce the Distance Selling Regulations (see post, para 8.17) and publish information and advice about them (reg 29; and above).

Further, the Government have announced that the forthcoming Enterprise Bill will broaden the OFT's duties to promote self-regulation through codes of practice.

[3.04] Directly sponsored bodies.[1] Whitehall has sponsored a number of bodies whose remit is to aid the protection of consumers.

1   *The National Consumer Council (NCC).* The first Consumer Council was recommended by the Molony Committee.[2] After its demise in 1971, the present body was set up in 1975 with a government grant 'to give a vigorous and independent voice to consumers in the United Kingdom',[3] though not to give advice to the individual consumers.[4] Whilst the Secretary of State has a general responsibility for its work, it is non-statutory and independent of the Government. It does not deal directly with consumer complaints, but seeks to influence policy affecting consumers by

---

8   FTA, s 125; CCA, s 5. Substantial Annual Reports (AR) have been published every year since 1974. The OFT has also published such as the *Review of the Trade Descriptions Act* (see post, para 4.02).

9   Eg, under the Courts and Legal Services Act 1990, ss 29, 31–33, 45–46, 105, 107. The Act refers to him or 'the Director' (s 119(1)). Primarily, the Director must report to the Lord Chancellor on the effect on competition of the provision of the Act as to legal services. He has defamation protection under s 69(2).

10 See OFT (1995/96) 12 Fair Trading, 4.

[3.04]

1   See generally Harvey, *Consumer Protection and Fair Trading* (6th edn), pp 56–58.

2   *Committee on Consumer Protection* (1962, Cmnd 1781), Chapter 20.

3   For the functions of the Council, see the statement 'About the NCC' in its Annual Reports. Reliance on a grant is, of course, relevant to its independence. See also Cranston, *Consumers and the Law* (3rd edn), pp 17–18.

4   Though NCC gives much help to other consumer bodies which do advise individual consumers – see NCC, Annual Reports.

conducting research, making representations,[5] producing reports[6] and publishing general consumer advice.[7] Unfortunately, Government thinking seems no closer to clarifying the relationship of this body to the OFT.[8]

2 *The Consumer Protection Advisory Committee (CPAC)*. Established by s 3 of the FTA (see ante, para 3.03) the function for which this committee was set up was to examine consumer trade practices referred to it. After an initial burst of activity (see post, para 4.21), it was dissolved in the early 1980s.[9]

[3.05/06] Local Authorities (LA). Over the centuries, legislators have found that it was necessary to call upon the criminal law to provide effective measures of consumer protection (see post, para 28.01). However, in developing that trading standards legislation (see Chapter 4) it has been said that the UK was probably unique amongst EU Member States in relying upon enforcement by LA.[1] In modern times, the departments of local authorities administering these functions tend to be called 'Consumer Protection' or 'Trading Standards' Departments (see post, para 28.03) and have developed two distinct types of activity:

1 *Enforcement of the criminal law*. As it evolved, the above system developed two features: first, statutes increasingly imposed a **duty**, rather than a power, of enforcement on local authorities; and second, that duty tended to be exercisable by the local authority in its own right rather than simply as agent of the central government. To encourage more uniformity of enforcement, central oversight has in recent times been entrusted to the OFT (see ante, para 3.03). The LAs and OFT also co-operate in the enforcement of the Unfair Terms Regulations (see post, para 11.19).

2 *Advice in relation to the civil law*. Acting under statutory permission to provide **advisory** services for the general public,[2] and encouraged by the Consumers' Association (see post, para 3.08), since 1969 LAs have been setting up Consumer Advice Centres[3] and have provided support for neighbourhood law centres (see post, para 3.16). In some instances, they also help consumers to obtain redress by guiding them through the County Court Small Claims Scheme (as to which, see post, para 3.24) and have offered advice where the complaint concerns 'misleading advertisements', which may be referred to the OFT (see post, para 8.12A). As ever, the availability of such discretionary services tends to be subject to the availability of local authority finance, a consideration which tends to reduce the stability of such service-provision. Under the deregulation initiative, Ministers are empowered to contract out designated non-judicial local authority functions (see post, para 5.10).

---

5 Sometimes supporting new legislation, eg, the Credit Unions Act 1979 (see ante, para 2.21); Supply of Goods and Services Act 1982 (see post, paras 15.12–14). It is also active in BEUC (see post, para 3.10).

6 Eg, *Report on Origin Marking* (1979); *Ordinary Justice* (1989).

7 It publishes a considerable range of very cheap or free publications advising consumers: see the list in the NCC Annual Report.

8 *Modern Markets: Confident Consumers* (1999, Cm 4410), paras 8.6–8.8.

9 OFT, 1998-AR 24.

[3.05/06]

1 Harvey, *Consumer Protection and Fair Trading* (6th edn), p 54.

2 Local Government Act 1972, ss 137, 142, 201(8).

3 See further Harvey, *op cit*, note 1, pp 55–56. As to money advice, see post, para 3.08.

Other watchdogs

[3.07] Privatised utilities. This paragraph is concerned with the special rules relating to the privatised utilities concerned in the supply of goods to consumers, eg, gas, electricity or water. It omits utilities wholly or largely concerned with the supply of services, eg, telephony (see post, para 8.17), the post office (see post, para 2.15). Although gas, electricity and water may be 'goods' (see ante, para 2.01), it has been held that their supply does not amount to the sale of goods (see ante, para 1.07) because the terms of the supply do not depend on contract.[1] Instead, the methods by which citizens might seek to control the excesses of utilities were administrative, the terms of supply being laid down compulsorily by statute.[2] After 1945, the major public utilities were nationalised, with provisions to restrain their ability to employ their monopoly power over the supply of goods and services in a manner oppressive to consumers, eg, pricing (see below), the special statutory powers to enter premises, and of gas and electricity utilities to disconnect unilaterally services for non-payment (see post, para 27.02). Parliamentary control of nationalised industries was later replaced by regulation of the privatised public utilities,[3] each industry being subject to oversight by a separate public official, now called a Regulator, and a licensing system.[4] Among the common responsibilities of the Regulators in relation to the protection of consumer interests are the following: the level of prices charged to consumers generally are regulated[5] and subject to the OFT and the Competition Commission;[6] the social obligation to poor consumers;[7] to make regulations prescribing standards of performance;[8] to direct suppliers as to the provision of information; and a complaints-handling machinery.[9] Additionally, the utilities have been made subject to such as in respect of their advertisements the ASA rules (see post, para 3.14); or, under the deregulation initiative, the Minister may instead accept an undertaking from the utility (see post, para 5.10). Because of the foregoing public accountability system, it was thought inappropriate to make these utilities subject to the CCA licensing system (s 21(3): see post, para 6.12), but their equipment contracts with consumers remain regulated under the CCA transaction rules (see post, para 5.13). The privatised utilities include the following:

[3.07]

1   *Norweb plc v Dixon* [1995] 3 All ER 952, DC; and hence a demand for payment cannot amount to unlawful harassment (see post, para 24.24) nor an unfair term (see post, para 11.12A). In certain cases, there may be a deemed contract: Gas Act 1995, Sched 2, para 8.

2   The utilities may therefore be subject to public law remedies: see Cranston, *Consumers and the Law* (3rd edn), p 198.

3   As to the efficacy of relying on large numbers of small shareholders to control public utilities, see Harvey and Parry, *Consumer Protection and Fair Trading* (6th edn), p 82.

4   See Cranston, *op cit*, note 2, pp 463–64.

5   Gas Act 1986, s 4(2)(a) (as substituted); Electricity Act 1989, s 3(2)(a) (as amended); Water Industry Act 1991, ss 2(3)(a), (5). For the pricing mechanism, see Harvey and Parry, *op cit*, note 3, p 83.

6   Competition Act 1998, s 54, which grants concurrent powers to the Director General of the OFT (see ante, para 3.03). For the Competition Act 1998, see generally ante, para 2.12.

7   For discussion of the social obligation, see (2000) 55 QA 6. For disconnection, see post, para 27.02. Also bear in mind the Fuel Direct scheme administered by the DSS and the Benefits Agency.

8   There are also standard-form offences of providing false information in the utilities statutes (Gas Act 1986, s 43, Electricity Act 1989, s 59; Water Industry Act 1991, s 207) and the consequent liability of corporate officers (1986 Act, s 45; 1989 Act, s 108; 1991 Act, s 210: and see generally post, para 28.11).

9   Under the Utilities Act 2000, s 2. The body will be known as GECC or 'Energywatch'. For its powers to make investigations and deal with consumer complaints, see ss 22, 23. Unsatisfied complaints may be reported to GEMA: see note 10, below.

1   *Gas*. The Gas Act 1986 (as amended) made provision for the removal of the monopoly of supplying gas through pipes (ss 3, 5–8) and established a dual system of control. First, it appointed a public official to deal with matters affecting the public generally[10] and allowed him to make references to the Competition Commission (see ante, para 2.12). Second, it created a Consumers' Council to deal with individual complaints.[9]

2   *Electricity*. Under the Electricity Act 1989, electricity is to be treated as goods for the purposes of UK competition law (s 100 of the 1989 Act: see ante, para 2.12). By the Utilities Act 2000, there was established a dual system of control modelled on that for gas (above); that is, a public Regulator, whose office is known as GEMA,[10] and a Consumers' Council (GECC) to look into individual complaints.[9]

3   *Water*. The water industry was privatised by the Water Act 1989, which introduced the notion of a public Regulator. With powers subsequently re-enacted in the Water Industry Act 1991,[11] the Regulator may make references to the Competition Commission (s 14). The consumer interest is protected by service committees, who look into individual complaints (ss 28, 29, 194). Unlike the above utilities, there is a public health consideration in the provision of water, which results in some different statutory controls, some of which are relevant for our purposes: for instance, the utility is under a duty to supply water to domestic premises (s 52) and it is an offence for a utility to supply water unfit for human consumption (s 70) or to unilaterally disconnect water supplies (s 63), without following the statutory procedure.[12]

With the increase of competition between utilities providing gas and electricity, the Government is intending to protect consumers by relying more on the ordinary competition rules (see ante, para 2.12) and less on the above special rules. Thus, there are circumstances where the utilities supply by contract domestic equipment, eg, gas fires, electric cookers; and in respect of these transactions the supplier-utility will attract rules applicable to all suppliers, eg, under the CPA, SGA, TDA, CCA (see above). Moreover, the agreements the utilities make with consumers are being policed under the Regulations in respect of Distance Selling and Unfair Terms (see post, paras 8.17; 11.12), including by Stop Now Orders (see post, para 6.07).

[3.08] Voluntary organisations.[1] There are a number of organisations which offer information and guidance to consumers, either nationally or locally.

1   *Citizens' Advice Bureaux (CABx)*. These bureaux, the first of which was set up in 1939, have a much wider remit than consumer protection in relation to the supply of goods with which we are concerned.[2] Their National Association receives central government financial support, whilst autonomous local CABx are often grant-aided

---

10   Under the Utilities Act 2000, s 1, this is the Gas and Electricity Markets Authority (GEMA).

11   Section 1 provides for a Director General of Water Services, whose office is known as OFWAT. For the duties of the Director, see ss 7, 8, 27, 30, 31, 193, 195. For the supply code, see post, para 3.14.

12   Under s 62, must first follow a statutory code of conduct and then apply to the county court.

[3.08]

1   See generally Harvey, *Consumer Protection and Fair Trading* (6th edn), p 58 *et seq*. As to other Marks of Approval, see [2001] 4 Which? 30.

2   See Cranston, *Consumers and the Law* (3rd edn), p 107. For the scope of their services, see the *Report of the Royal Commission on Legal Services* (1979) Cmnd 7648, Chapter 7. Only about one-fifth of their work is concerned with consumer problems: see the Annual Reports of the National Association of CABx.

by local authorities, even though their functions overlap with Consumer Advice Centres (see ante, para 3.05). Besides referring consumers to solicitors or barrister as appropriate, the CAB also has an office in the Royal Court of Justice in London to help litigants in person (see post, para 3.17).

2   *Consumers' Association (CA)*. The CA was set up in 1957 as a company limited by guarantee, and it became a charity in 1987. The primary aim of the CA is to provide information to the consumer about products and services by reporting the results of its tests[3] in its magazine, Which?, and online (see post, para 8.17). Besides numerous other publications[4] and an individual advice service,[5] it also lobbies on behalf of the consumer interest in Westminster, Whitehall[6] and Brussels;[7] and has spawned a network of local consumer groups.[8] It is a qualifying body under the UTCC Regulations (see post, para 11.19) and will probably be able to apply to court for Stop Now Orders on behalf of consumers (see post, para 28.03).

3   *British Standards Institution (BSI)*. Under its present name, the BSI was incorporated by Royal Charter in 1929. Its objects include: the setting of standards for goods and services; setting dimensions and date-marking for manufactured goods; and the maintaining and promoting a register of such 'British Standard' specifications, which now exceed 7,000 in number.[9] Whilst a manufacturer may simply claim that his goods comply with a certain British Standard,[10] the BSI also run a certification scheme, whose application to goods may be signified by application to them of a 'Kitemark'. Compliance with these standards by manufacturers is usually voluntary: but a false claim of compliance may be an offence under the TDA (s 2(1)(g): see post, para 4.02); and in some cases standards are compulsory, eg, under some safety regulations (see post, para 4.35). Since 1972, the traditional work of the BSI in laying down standards has been to some extent side-lined by our entry into the EU, which has its own system of certified standards (CE marks);[11] but in recent years the BSI has acquired a new lease of life testing compliance with standards through the expansion of its Kitemarking, eg, operating a register of approved traders, and complaint-handling.[12]

---

3   Established in 1971, the CA Survey Unit provides a centralised system for conducting survey work and user trials about matters such as product safety and reliability. For a history of the CA, see [1987] Which? 106.

4   Eg, *Directory of Consumer Information Organisations; Handbook of Consumer Law*; Which? Guides, eg, to car buying, the way to complain; legal advice leaflets on behalf of the Legal Services Commission (see post, para 3.17).

5   The 'Personal Service' offers both subscription advice to individual members and an advisory service for local authority advice centres (see ante, para 3.05). For criticism, see (2000) 150 NLJ 952.

6   Eg, it played a substantial part in promoting the Litigants in Person (Costs and Expenses) Act 1975; Unfair Contract Terms Act 1977 (see post, para 18.12 *et seq*); Unsolicited Goods and Services Act 1971 (see post, para 8.18). A record of their campaigns is to be found in the Annual Reports.

7   It is a member of the European Office of Consumers' Unions (see post, para 3.10). See also ante, para 2.13.

8   Harvey and Parry, *op cit*, p 61; Cranston, *op cit*, note 2, pp 18–19.

9   Eg, the BSI for PINS and the ISO rules (see ante, para 2.24); payment practice (see post, para 7.03A). For the BSI and Administration, see (1994) 6 Fair Trading 14.

10 See [1991] Which? 201. Compliance may bring a tax advantage, eg, zero VAT rating for safety boots (for VAT, see generally ante, para 2.06).

11 See post, para 8.06. For complaint that the CE marks are too voluntary, see [1998] 10 Which? 14.

12 As to the register, see (1998) 17 Tr L 52. As to complaint-handling, see OFT, 1998-AR 23; *Modern Markets: Confident Consumers* (1999, Cm 4410), para 5.2.

4   *Other organisations.* There are a large number of other organisations concerned with consumer guidance, including the following: the Design Council, a body established in 1944 in an attempt to improve the aesthetic, functional and engineering design of consumer products, eg, safety (see post, paras 4.33; 14.20; 17.28); the Advertising Standards Authority (see post, para 3.14); numerous trade and professional associations whose functions include an element of consumer protection (see post, para 3.11) and consumer advice bodies (see post, para 3.16).

TYPES OF CONTROL

Compulsory controls

[3.09] Statutory.[1] There are several major ways in which Parliament has sought to protect the consumer interest in the supply of goods. First, Parliament and government have played a substantial part in the creation and support of many of the consumer watchdogs (see above). Second, in legislating Parliament has made extensive use of the techniques of strict liability criminal offences (see Chapter 4) and the licensing of suppliers (see Chapter 6), with special provisions for licensing moneylenders (see Chapter 7). Third, there have been frequent statutory alterations made to the civil law relating to the supply of goods, all of them leaning one way: they are designed to derogate from the even-handed, *laissez-faire* 19th century position (see ante, para 1.02), instead giving the consumer some advantage to try to redress a real or imagined imbalance of bargaining-power.[2] Fourth, there are some statutory codes of practice, eg, the pricing code (see post, para 8.10A), from which must be distinguished the ordinary voluntary codes (see post, para 3.11). Fifth, there is a growing amount of EU intervention (see post, para 3.10). Sixth, the Council of Europe has a membership which extends beyond that of the EU to include also most other countries in Western Europe. Unlike EU legislation which is binding, proposals by the Council of Europe can only have national effect insofar as a state voluntarily ratifies its draft conventions, and implements these and other recommendations by national legislation.[3] From 1993, those European countries not members of the EU are pledged to adopt its conventions. Seventh, there is the possible effect on consumer law of the Human Rights Act 1998. This Act introduces into UK law the over-arching principles of the European Convention on Human Rights (Sched 1), sponsored by the Council of Europe (above). Whilst largely beyond the scope of this work, the Act provides that the courts will be under a duty so far as possible to interpret UK legislation 'in a way which is compatible with Convention rights' (s 3(1): see ante, para 1.05): if it cannot do this, under s 4 it is to make a declaration of incompatibility,[4] in

---

[3.09]

1   The many statutes and statutory instruments are to be found in convenient up-dated form in Thomas, *Encyclopedia of Consumer Law*, Parts I and 2.

2   It is for consideration whether the present statutory provisions are both too elaborate and lacking in system. The further possibility of a Consumer Sales Act has already been mentioned (see ante, para 1.02).

3   Eg, the Conventions on Product Liability (see post, para 17.23); Retention of Title (see post, para 24.21); and the Resolution on Access to Justice (14 May 1981).

4   See *Wilson v First County Trust Ltd* (set out post, para 9.20). See also Bamforth (2001) 117 LQR 34; Loveland (2000) 150 NLJ 1595.

which case a Minister may make a statutory order amending the offending legislation.[5] Whilst this is primarily intended to give the private citizen rights against public authorities,[6] it has also been interpreted to give private citizens justiciable rights against one another. Amongst the convention rights possibly relevant to consumers are the following: a fair trial (Art 6: see post, paras 3.19; 3.22; 3.24; 3.25); privacy (Art 8: see post, paras 3.26; 24.23); free speech (Art 10: see post, para 3.14).

[3.10] The European Union.[1] It has already been noted that the EU has begun to promote consumer interests generally; that at first it used indirect justifications for very specific interventions;[2] but that the Maastricht Treaty 1991 has given it a direct basis for such interventions (see ante, para 1.03A). To administer this programme the EU has a Consumer Protection Directorate, advised by a Consumers' Committee and lobbied, *inter alia* by the European Office of Consumers' Organisations (BEUC).[3] This Directorate has engendered a number of Directives, in each of which there has been a two-stage process: the first stage is to produce (usually over a period of years) a Draft Directive; and, if acceptable, this progresses to a full Directive.[4] Early directives tended to involve detailed provisions as to harmonisation in the fields of safety, quality standards and weights and measures.[5] However the Single European Act of 1986 led to completion of the internal market and has allowed a more generalised approach. Under the 1986 Act, purely national laws can only apply to purely national goods, and not to those imported from elsewhere in the EU.[6] The Commission has since undertaken an ambitious programme of reform,[7] including a scheme requiring each member state to choose national bodies which would be entitled to seek injunctions on behalf of consumers in respect of infringement of relevant Directives (see post, para 28.03). The UK Government have indicated a desire to see a reduction in the pace of change, with more emphasis on enforcement[8] and regular reviews of existing rules.[9] However, the stream of Draft Directives shows no signs of

---

5   Section 10 and Sched 2.
6   Defining 'public authority' to include courts (s 6(3)), the Act provides that no 'public authority' may act in a manner incompatible with Convention rights (s 6(1)).

[3.10]
1   For introductions, see Goode, *Consumer Credit Law and Practice*, Part 1J; Harvey and Parry, *Consumer Protection and Fair Trading* (6th edn), pp 39–45.
2   Eg, consumer information about such as the labelling of food (see ante, para 1.27), pharmaceutical products (see post, para 4.29); or cosmetics (see post, para 4.31).
3   Commission Decision (95/260/EEC). The early history is to be found in the Commission's *First Report on Consumer Protection and Information Policy*, set out in paras 5-751 of Thomas, *Encyclopedia of Consumer Law*. BEUC produces its own magazine, BEUC Legal News.
4   These include the following: consumer credit (see post, para 5.08); misleading advertisements (see post, para 8.06); product liability (see post, para 17.23); price displays (see post, para 8.08); unfair terms (see post, para 11.12); the supply of services (see post, para 5.15); data protection (see post, para 3.27); distance selling (see post, para 8.19); consumer sales and guarantees (see post, paras 14.01; 17.09A). The texts of relevant Directives will be found set out in Goode, *Consumer Credit Law and Practice*, Part X.
5   See note 2, above. These were designed from the industry standpoint to permit the free circulation of goods. For criticism of EU safety standard, see [1993] 12 Which? 46.
6   See (1992) Tr L 12. See the directives referred to in note 4, above.
7   See the Consumer Policy Action Plan (COM/98/696).
8   *Modern Markets: Confident Consumers* (1999, Cm 4410) para 1.8. Except in relation to e-commerce: see post, para 8.17.
9   *Modern Markets: Confident Consumers* (1999, Cm 4410) para 6.19.

abating and currently includes the following: consumer credit (see post, para 5.12); consumer financial services; and payment card fraud.[10]

Voluntary codes

[3.11] Business self-regulation.[1] A growth area in recent decades has been that of collective business self-regulation. Some business have even gone so far, usually under the aegis of a trade association, as to launch codes of ethical and social practice: this has commonly been done to create a good self-image for a trade, to distance its members from the more disreputable elements[2] and sometimes to stave off legislation, eg, water disconnection code (see ante, para 3.07); advertising codes (see post, para 3.14); tobacco advertising.

Statutory recognition of the value of this process came with the FTA, which imposed a duty on the Director 'to encourage relevant associations to prepare, and to disseminate to their members, codes of practice for guidance in safeguarding and promoting the interests of consumers in the United Kingdom'.[3] Urgency was given to the implementation of this duty when the Director recognised the very limited capacity of traders to absorb new legislation (see ante, para 3.01), and that further effective changes in trading habits were more likely to be achieved through the medium of voluntary codes.[4] Accordingly, since 1974 a substantial number of codes of practice (about 50) have been encouraged and approved by the OFT,[5] which has even gone to the length of publishing guides for trade associations in drawing up their codes, eg, for credit scoring (see post, para 8.39).

The OFT is in a good position to monitor the adoption and implementation of such codes because they have always been registrable with it.[6] In persuading trade organisations to adopt them, the OFT has some powers: the carrot is that the Director may recommend that approved codes be exempt from the competition rules (see ante, para 2.12); and the stick lies in his powers to recommend legislation. Of course, some codes have statutory force;[7] and the local operation of codes can be monitored via the annual returns made by local authorities to the OFT (see ante, para 3.05). Additionally, failure to

---

10   Documents 598PC0468; 599PC0438.

[3.11]

1   See generally, Harvey and Parry, *Consumer Protection and Fair Trading* (6th edn), p 360 *et seq*; Cranston, *Consumers and the Law* (3rd edn), Chapter 2.

2   Eg, the Finance and Leasing Association's Credit Scoring (see post, para 8.39) and Code of Practice the Visa Credit Code.

3   Section 124(3): see generally ante, para 3.03.

4   See the Second (1975) Annual Report of the OFT. On the other hand, the publicity surrounding new legislation does have an educative effect.

5   See post, para 3.13. In granting their approval, the OFT will only do so 'if satisfied that the code safeguards and promotes the interests of the consumer and that the trade association intends to make it a success': 1976-AR, 11.

6   Previously, as restrictive trade practices, now under the competition rules: see ante, para 2.12.

7   Eg, the pricing code (CPA, s 25: see post, para 8.10A); or general safety requirement (CPA, s 10(2)(b): see post, para 4.33); or advertising (see post, para 8.12A); or any enforcement codes (see post, para 5.10). Reports on the monitoring of codes are made in the Annual Reports of the OFT.

observe other codes might lead the OFT to take one of the following types of action against the perpetrator: to seek Part III assurances (see post, para 6.08); to make issue of a credit licence depend on observance of a code (see post, para 6.19); to seek changes in standard-form terms (see post, para 11.08) by threatening use of the UTCC Regulations (see post, para 11.12). Nor is official sponsorship of codes of practice confined to the OFT (see post, para 3.14).

[3.12] Assessment of codes of practice. From an early stage the OFT realised that codes of practice could not directly raise the quality of products and so concentrated in relation to codes on the provision of information, the abandonment of unfair trading practices and the way complaints were handled (see post, paras 3.16; 3.23). To some extent, the codes referred to above supplement gaps in the law.[1] For instance, these codes may supplement the law relating to the supply of goods and provide the flexibility so difficult to build into modern legislation: if a supplier fails to honour his previously announced adherence to a code, his supply contracts may have been induced by misrepresentation or amount to a breach of an express promise to abide by the code;[2] whereas the fact that a supplier has adhered to a code may help his defence to one of the strict liability offences considered in Chapter 4, by supporting a general statutory defence,[3] or could be embodied in a Part III Assurance (see post, para 6.08). Moreover, codes may be useful for matters less appropriate to legislation, eg, dealing expeditiously with complaints; conciliation by way of arbitration or ombudsman (see post, paras 3.24–25).

However, it cannot be said that the voluntary codes adequately supplement the law in all respects. Such codes lack bite in the drafting and are sometimes adopted for less than altruistic motives, such as insulation from competitive forces; indeed some codes have sometimes been dealt with by the courts as unreasonable restraints of trade.[4] Even where the rules of the relevant code do tend to favour the consumer, its operation may be less than satisfactory in practice. Whilst some codes recognise the possibility of the relevant trade association imposing sanctions for breach,[5] few associations seem prepared to invoke them; and in any event they cannot apply to non-members, a category which will usually include the more disreputable operators from whom the consumer is in greatest need of protection.

In practice, much of the responsibility for policing the codes seems to have fallen on the OFT (see ante, para 3.11). Particularly in the period 1974–83, the codes referred to above were promoted and adopted by the OFT as an alternative to legislation in what it perceived to be problem sectors, such as travel, electrical goods and the motor trade.[6] By the mid-1980s, the OFT emphasis had switched from negotiating new codes to

---

[3.12]

1   By causing the courts to take into account any relevant code in establishing: (a) customary terms and trade usage (see post, para 15.11); (b) unfair terms (see UTCC Regulations, reg 4: post, para 11.15); (c) unreasonable terms (see UCTA, s 3: see post, para 18.24).

2   See *Bowerman v ABTA* [1995] Tr LR 246. It may make any exclusion clause unreasonable: Circus, *Towards a General Duty to Trade Fairly?*, pp 63–65.

3   It may support the general statutory defence (see post, para 28.13): see Bragg, *Trade Descriptions*, pp 188–89.

4   *Pharmaceutical Society of Great Britain v Dickson* [1970] AC 403, HL. See now the Competition Act 1998, s 2; and generally ante, para 2.14.

5   A 'fine' was upheld in *Thorne v Motor Trade Association* [1937] AC 797, HL.

6   OFT, *Voluntary Codes of Practice* (1996), paras 2.3; 2.5. For the 1996 Guidelines, see Appendix A.

monitoring existing ones and by then its revised 'minimum requirement' for codes had been developed.[6] After some disillusionment with codes of practice in the late 1980s, from 1993 the OFT began to insist, as one condition of its support, that codes contain an element of independence in both redress and disciplinary procedures; and from the next year it started to require that codes expressly refer to the Unfair Terms Regulations (see above). In 1996, the OFT reached the conclusion that, 'with a few notable exceptions, [codes] do not appear to have been effective in reducing either malpractice or consumer dissatisfaction. Yet the speed and flexibility of the best self-regulation are highly attractive, and we have therefore continued to seek ways of bringing them to bear on a wider range of consumer problems'.[7] However, by 1999 the Government had decided that codes of practice were a good thing and were once again encouraging their development.[8] Since then, the mortgage industry has found official pressure on it in relation to the operation of the mortgage code such that it has begun to lobby for replacement of that code by statutory regulation under the FSA.[9] The OFT has begun to lobby for its approval of codes to be put on a stronger statutory basis[10] and there is some indication that the EU might accept codes of practice.[11]

[3.13] OFT sponsored codes of practice.[1] Leaving aside the codes for the privatised utilities (see post, para 3.14) and telephone-selling (see post, para 8.17), the OFT has at one time or another sponsored versions of the following codes of practice, which substantially reflect the highest level of consumer complaints it has received.[2]

1   *Domestic electrical appliances.*[3] In 1974, the manufacturers of domestic electrical appliances introduced a code in respect of servicing and complaints; and an AMDEA Consumer Relations Department provides expert help and advice to CABx, Consumer Advice Centres and Trading Standard Departments. More recently, there has been introduced a code on extended warranties (see post, 17.09).

---

7   OFT, *ibid*, para 3.1. The key factors for the success of a code of practice are: the availability of a strong sanction; a plausible threat of statutory regulation; a clear wish by the good players in the industry to distinguish themselves from others; and obvious benefits to consumers, sufficient to affect their choice of trader: para 3.5.

8   *Modern Markets: Confident Consumers* (1999, Cm 4410) paras 4.3–12; OFT 1999-AR 22.

9   See [1999] 11 Credit Today 24; and see ante, para 3.02. Similarly with debt management (see post, para 5.42; [2001] 3 Credit Today 6.

10   OFT, 2000-AR 8; (2001) 30 Fair Trading 15; [2001] 7 Credit Today 13.

11   The EU has accepted 'guidelines' for mortgage sales: [2001] 3 Credit Today 8.

[3.13]

1   See generally, Lowe and Woodroffe, *Consumer Law and Practice* (5th edn), para 10.04 *et seq*; Harvey and Parry, *Consumer Protection and Fair Trading* (6th edn), pp 364–76. For a current list of such codes, see Thomas, *Encyclopedia of Consumer Law*, paras 4-751. For the addresses of the trade associations sponsoring these codes, see Lowe and Woodroffe, App 1.

2   Complaint levels are listed in the Annual Reports of the OFT, which also contain records of the OFT monitoring exercises, and forecasts of areas of industry where new codes may be developed. See also Borrie [1988] JBL 116.

3   OFT, First Annual Report, 23; 1975-AR, 25; 1995-AR 15; 1997-AR, 19. Disconnection of supply will not be used where the debt relates to the supply of goods. For an OFT warning about extended warranties, see (1996) 15 Tr LR 258; and generally post, para 17.09.

2   *Motor industry*.[4] In 1975, the motor industry adopted a code, subsequently revised:

(a) In relation to new cars, it dealt with pre-delivery inspections; fair terms in order forms, especially as to cancellation and total price; manufacturers' guarantees; and recalls of models found to be defective.

(b) In relation to used cars, it covers defects on an approved pre-sales check list, minimum warranties, verification of mileage (see post, para 4.09) and repairs. Additionally, there are separate codes dealing with vehicle body repairs, motor cycle retailers and reconditioned engines. Subsequent dissatisfaction with used car sales has led to calls for replacement of these codes by a positive licensing system (see post, para 6.03).

3   *Footwear*. In 1976, the Footwear Distributors Association took steps to remedy their unfortunate image, a major feature of their code being the setting up of a footwear testing centre.

4   *Direct marketing*.[5] In 1992, there was formed the Direct Marketing Association (DMA) from a merger of the former mail order publishers and direct sellers. In 1997, the DMA published a revised code, notably including a 14-day cooling-off period, since overtaken by legislation (see post, para 8.19). Because of the way the industry solicits business, it may also be subject to codes for: media (see post, para 3.14); junk mail;[5a] and cold-calling (see post, para 8.17).

5   *Furniture and carpets*. In 1978, the manufacturers and retailers of furniture introduced a code covering advertising, prices, deposits, labelling and disputes. This was replaced in 1992 by the 'Qualitas' scheme for the furniture and carpet industries; and this scheme has since been extended to home improvements.[6]

6   *Antiques*. In 1992, the antique dealers association (LAPADA) drew up a code dealing with pricing information, valuations and conciliation.

7   *Double glazing*. In 1981, there was launched a revised version of a code dealing with the installation of double-glazing, covering such matters as a cooling-off period, price increases, product and installation standards and dates, guarantees, deposit indemnity and complaints.

8   *Instalment credit*.[7] Since 1987, the instalment credit industry has sponsored a code which emphasised pre-contract enquiries to avoid over-indebtedness (see post, para 8.38), the use of plain English (see post, para 11.08), ethical debt collection procedures (see post, para 27.02), CPI insurance (see post, para 24.48) and an arbitration scheme (see post, para 3.24). There have also been separate codes on equipment (sales-aid) leasing (see post, para 16.06A) and holiday caravans.

---

4   As to new cars, see OFT, 1975-AR 26–28; 1990-AR 25. As to a code for vehicle renting, see OFT, 1995-AR 17. As to used cars, see OFT, 1997-AR 21–22. As to the ABI Code on vehicle write-offs, see (1996) 17 CCA News 2/20. As to the text of the motor industry code of practice, see Lowe and Woodroffe, *op cit*, pp 409–18.

5   OFT, 1977-AR 11; 1987-AR 19; OFT, 1997-AR, p 20. For direct marketing, see post, para 8.19. There is also a code in respect of automatic vending machines: (1994) 13 Tr L 236.

5a   As such operations depend on computerised lists of names and addresses, consumers registering not to receive junk mail can enforce matters under the DPA, s 11, 55–57; see post, para 3.27.

6   OFT, 2000-AR 45; and see post, para 23.22.

7   For the text of the Codes, see Goode, *Consumer Credit Law and Practice*, Part VIII. For over-indebtedness, see post, para 3.15; for pre-contract enquiries, see post, para 8.35, for the Plain English Campaign, see post, para. 11.08; for debt collection, see post, paras 5.42 and 27.01; and for arbitration schemes, see post, para 3.23. For holiday caravans, see OFT, 1997-AR 19.

9   *Banking.*[8] Following the Report of the Jack Committee (see ante, para 2.17), in 1991 the clearing banks and building societies adopted a code of banking practice, subsequently updated. This dealt, *inter alia,* with confidentiality and references (see post, para 7.03), restraints on marketing, limitations of customers' liability for losses at ATMs and on payment cards (see post, paras 7.01; 7.13), charges, health warnings for guarantors, the use of plain English and references to the Banking Ombudsman (see post, para 3.25). There is also a special mortgage code subscribed to by most mortgage lenders, be they banks, building societies, or direct lenders (see ante, para 3.12).

10 *Debt collecting.*[9] In 1991, the debt collecting code supplemented the CCA (see post, paras 5.42–43) by setting out guidelines of good business conduct in the collection of debts. The Money Advice Trust (see post, para 3.16) has since published a code for money advisers and there are two competing codes for debt managers.

11 *Non-status lending.*[10] To try to protect that vulnerable group who seek credit whilst having an impaired credit-rating, in 1997 the OFT issued revised guidelines to lenders and brokers who operate in this market, principally requiring greater transparency and the cessation of dual interest rates (see post, para 7.04A).

12 *Energy suppliers.*[11] The privatised utilities (see ante, para 3.07) got together to launch a code of practice concerning the selling of gas and electricity.

13 *E-shopping.* In 2001 there was launched 'TrustUK', a scheme under which retail websites can exhibit a logo indicating adherence to a code of conduct.[12]

[3.14] Other codes. These include codes relating to the following:

1   *Broadcasting.* For our purposes, the rules relating to broadcasting by television or radio are only relevant insofar as they concern advertisements for the supply of goods. The BBC is forbidden by the terms of its licence to broadcast any commercial advertising or sponsored programme without the permission of the Home Secretary.[1] Independent television and local commercial radio are governed by the Broadcasting Act 1990 (as amended), which allows the broadcasting of advertisements under certain conditions: the Act itself sets out the general rules for programmes[2] and advertisements (s 8). It also casts upon the Independent Broadcasting Authority (IBA) the duty to 'draw up and from time to time review, a code governing standards and practice in advertising' (s 7(1)). A statutory duty to secure observance of the IBA Code

---

8   OFT, 1997-AR 3. For the text of the current Code, see Goode, *ibid,* VIII. Compare the DTI views as to what the code should do: (1990) Cm 1026, Annexe C. For areas where the Code has been criticised as inadequate, see [1998] 9 Which? 42.

9   OFT, 1991-AR 25–26. For the money advisers code, see (1994) 48 CC 6/27.

10   See (1998) 52 CC 6/3. There are problems of definition as to what amounts to 'non-status lending': (1998) 53 CC 6/2; and post, para 7.04A.

11   OFT, 1997-AR 20.

12   (2000) 27 Fair Trading 4.

[3.14]

1   For an unsuccessful attempt to obtain an injunction against broadcasting, see *Cambridge Nutrition Ltd v BBC* [1990] 3 All ER 523, CA.

2   Eg, no subliminal advertising (s 6(1)(e)), as recommended by the *Molony Report* (1962), Cmnd 1781, para 782). Breach is not a criminal offence: *R v Horseferry Road Magistrates' Court ex p IBA* [1986] 2 All ER 666, DC.

is placed on the Authority.[3] Additionally, the transmissions of both the BBC and ITV are subject to the oversight of the Broadcasting Standards Commission and the code of conduct it is required to produce.[4] Misleading advertisement are within the broadcasting codes and also subject to Stop Now Orders (see post, paras 6.06; 8.12A; 28.04).

2   *Privatised utilities.* Whether directly by statute, or as a condition of their authorisation, the public utilities are required to observe codes of practice in dealing with consumer debt, including water disconnections.[5] They have also entered into a voluntary code (see ante, para 3.13).

3   *Advertising.* Under the threat of statutory intervention recommended by the *Molony Report on Consumer Protection* (1962, Cmnd 1781), the non-broadcasting advertising industry set up the Advertising Standards Authority (ASA) to supervise and enforce a code of practice.[5a] The essence is that 'All advertisements should be legal, decent, honest and truthful'.[6] The main sanctions relied upon by the ASA are publicity, the agreement of the media to refuse publication to non-conforming advertisements,[7] and the back-up powers of the OFT with regard to misleading advertisements (see post, para 8.12A). The ASA administers two codes:[8] the British Code of Advertising Practice; and the British Code of Sales Promotion Practice. The ASA's decisions are subject to judicial review; but the court can interfere only on grounds of irrationality, illegality or procedural impropriety.[9] Nor can such judicial proceedings be used to temporarily gag the ASA, as the ASA will not usually be restrained from publishing its reports in the interim;[10] nor do its normal activities breach the European Convention on Human Rights.[11]

---

3   Section 9(1)(b). For the IBA Code, see Cranston, *Consumers and the Law* (3rd edn), p 60. For the IBA complaints procedure, see [1998] 4 Which? 25.

4   Broadcasting Act 1996, Part V. This procedure is subject to the European Convention on Human Rights (see ante, para 3.09): *R v Broadcasting Standards Commission ex p BBC* [2000] 3 All ER 989, CA. See further the Office of Communications Bill 2001.

5   Gas Act 1995 Sched 2; Electricity Act 1989, s 24 and Sched 6; conditions of appointment under the Water Industry Act 1991. See generally Howells, *Consumer Debt*, Chapter 8; and ante, para 3.07.

5a   Does it extend to Internet advertisements?

6   Paragraph 1.1, eg, misleading bank advertising (see [1999] 10 Credit Today 6). See generally Cranston, *op cit*, note 3, p 48. For mail order trading, see further post, para 8.19. For reviews of the effectiveness of the ASA, see Thompson in *Consumer Law in the EEC* (ed Woodroffe), Chapter 4 ; Clucas, *Systems of Control of Advertising Standards* (1987, Advertising Assoc); [1999] 2 Which? 4.

7   The courts have indirectly supported this code by banning third parties from placing inserts (which may not be amenable to ASA control) in newspapers as amounting to passing-off: see post, para 17.17. As to the ASA, see Cranston, *op cit*, note 3, pp 55–60.

8   For the text, see Goode, *Consumer Credit Law and Practice*, Part VIII. See Circus, *Sales Promotion Law* (2nd edn), p 198. There is also a media code in the newspaper industry: see (1994) 13 Tr L 246.

9   *R v ASA ex p The Insurance Service* [1990] TLR 169, DC (see 139 NLJ 1161); *R v ASA, ex p DSG Retail Ltd* [1997] CLY 3558; *R v ASA, ex p Charles Robertson Ltd* [2000] CLY 4146; *R (on the Application of SKB plc) v ASA* [2001] 6 CL 70.

10   *R v ASA ex p Vernons Organisation Ltd* [1993] 2 All ER 202.

11   *R v ASA ex p City Trading Ltd* [1997] CLY 3559 (claim that the Code contravened the free speech provisions of the European Convention on Human Rights failed). See also *R v ASA ex p Matthais Rath* [2001] 2 CL 450; and Lawson (2001) 151 NLJ 526.

4   *Other codes*. The EU promulgates codes of conduct, eg, relating to electronic payments (see ante, para 2.24); the DTI is to promote a code on environmental claims;[12] and the Consumers' Association co-sponsors the e-commerce code (see ante, para 3.13).

CONSUMER REDRESS[1]

Information and advice

[3.15] Introduction. It is an old adage that before entering a transaction a consumer tends to suffer from 'buying fever',[1a] whereas after the event this is replaced by 'buyer's remorse'.[2] At both stages, the consumer may need information and advice as to the product and any associated credit.[3]

1   *The pre-contract stage*. Broadly speaking, the role of consumer product information both generally and at the point of sale will be largely regulated by the law relating to such matters as trade descriptions, labelling, packaging and pricing dealt with in Chapter 4, and that relating to advertising which is surveyed in Chapter 8.[4] A leading example of such protection concerns the pre-contract disclosure of specified information required in respect of regulated agreements under the Consumer Credit Act 1974 (see post, para 9.06). Independent providers of free advice to consumers generally include the NCC (see ante, para 3.04), the OFT (see ante, para 3.03), the Consumers' Association[5] and the media.[6]

2   *The post-contract stage*. Much of the remainder of this work is concerned with the rights available to the consumer in the event that the goods supplied do not meet his expectations. However, the mere existence of such rights is not enough in itself. First, a consumer unaware that one of his rights has been infringed is unlikely even to seek redress; and this has led to a sustained programme of consumer education (see ante, para 3.01). Second, the consumer, aware that his rights have been infringed should be encouraged in the first instance to approach his supplier with a complaint: this requires the supplier to have an adequate complaints procedure and the consumer be

---

12   Green Claims (1998); and see *Modern Markets: Confident Consumers* (1999, Cm 4410) paras 3.17–18. For a voluntary green scheme for cars, see [2000] 1 Which? 7; and for dodgy green claims, see [2001] 1 Which? 17.

[3.15]

1   See generally, Cranston, *Consumers and the Law* (3rd edn), p 102 *et seq*; OFT, Developments in Consumer Redress (1996); Lowe and Woodroffe, *Consumer Law and Practice* (5th edn), Chapter 10.

1a   A difficulty is that in this state the consumer may deliberately avoid thinking about the disadvantages of the transaction – which blunts consumer education.

2   For a survey by the OFT, see *Developments in Consumer Redress* (1995).

3   The case for information and advice in relation to consumer credit is put in Chapters 9.2–3 of the *Report on Consumer Credit* (1971, Cmnd 4596). Codes of conduct (see ante, para 3.11 *et seq*) can also be seen as having a consumer redress function: OFT, 1984-AR, 11.

4   Many of the developments in the area were given significant impetus by the Molony Committee *Report on Consumer Protection* (1962, Cmnd 1781), especially Chapters 6–10, 15–18.

5   See [1984] Which? 22; getting action on complaints. For the CA, see generally ante, para 3.08.

6   One commentator even puts the media as the consumers' major source of advice and assistance: Cranston, *op cit*, note 1, p 107.

taught how to use it.[7] Only if this fails does the dissatisfied consumer need specific legal advice relating to his particular problem (see post, paras 3.16–17). Third, armed with this information, the consumer needs convenient,[8] cheap[9] and efficient machinery[10] for the enforcement of those rights (see post, para 3.18 *et seq*). Fourth, there is the very real problem of consumer over-indebtedness,[11] especially with regard to the prevalence of multiple indebtedness.[12] Effective total records of individual consumer credit industry indebtedness may be necessary (see post, para 8.36) and the need for money advice centres becomes greater (see post, para 3.16). To some extent, creditors can help by not over-lending (see the instalment credit code: ante, para 3.13) and pre-contract credit assessment (see post, para 8.35 *et seq*). Fifth, credit insurance is sometimes possible (see post, para 24.44–45), as is litigation insurance (see post, para 3.18).

[3.16] Consumer legal advice.[1] Consumer sales law is a challenging, complicated subject; and it has proved difficult to ensure across-the-board, consistent, high level legal advice. Whilst some consumers are likely to receive adequate advice from organisations to which they belong, eg, a trade union, or by paying an adviser,[2] there is undoubtedly a continuing consumer demand for local, readily accessible, free advice. In the first instance this tends to be met for the most part by the traditional local authority-funded organisations: Trading Standards Offices (see ante, para 3.05), sometimes termed Consumer Advice Centres; and CABx (see ante, para 3.08). To these should be added the utilities regulators (see ante, para 3.07); and ombudsmen (see post, para 3.25). Frequently, one of these services may be able to settle a problem between a trader and a consumer.[3] But, if that proves impossible, then they may act as a filter for the forwarding of complaints to a solicitor, a step which immediately raises the question of cost. Of course, not all complaints follow this pattern: for instance, an advice centre will sometimes follow a dispute right through to litigation, eg, the CAB office in the Royal Courts of Justice (see ante, para 3.08); some CABx operate with a panel of solicitors on a rota scheme,

---

7   See (1991) 8 Tr L 242–45; (1999) 54 CC 1/8; and the regular consumer dissatisfaction surveys which appear in the Annual Reports of the OFT. For an EU template complaints form for consumers, see OFT, 1998-AR 23. For a code on telephone call queuing, see [1998] 10 Which? 7.

8   This might include more consumer-friendly court/tribunal sittings, eg, evenings: see Harvey and Parry, *Consumer Protection and Fair Trading* (6th edn), p 234.

9   This might include more *pro bono* legal advice (see post, para 3.16) and legal assistance by McKenzie friends (see post, para 3.17).

10   This might include more trial by paper and easier enforcement of judgments (see post, para 27.04).

11   The remorseless increase in instalment credit (see post, para 5.01) is just one symptom of the increasing indebtedness *per capita*: see also Borrie [1986] JBL 181; Social Security Advisory Committee; Credit, Debt and Poverty (1989); Whitton (1998) 50 Quarterly Account 4; OFT, Vulnerable Consumers and Financial Services (1999) 5, 16. In 2000, the NCAB (see ante, para 3.08) detected a significant increase in consumer indebtedness (+ 9%) and begun to press the Government for action: for DTI action, see further post, para 27.01.

12   It should be remembered that consumer indebtedness is likely to extend beyond the credit industry to include, eg, Council Tax, debts to the Social Fund and utilities (see antes, para 2.15; 3.07) and loans under the Education (Student Loans) Act 1990.

[3.16]

1   *Modern Markets: Confident Consumers* (1999, Cm 4410), para 5.1 *et seq*.

2   Eg, the Which? Personal Service (see 1991–92 Annual Report 28; and [1994] 1 Which? 26); the Citizens Debt Counselling Service (see (1997) CCA News, Summer 18).

3   See Borrie, *The Development of Consumer Law and Policy*, 36. The Plain English Campaign may help: see post, para 11.08.

commonly on a *pro bono* (no fees) basis;[4] or perhaps the more educated consumer may initially consult a solicitor privately, whilst the disadvantaged can do so on legal aid (see post, para 3.17) or may go to a neighbourhood law centre.

The concept of the law centre was imported from the United States in the 1970s. Such centres 'existing mainly in deprived communities to give free legal advice and representation to people in that community, to assist and represent groups such as tenants' associations, and to help to educate individuals and groups in the community about the law and its impact on them'.[5] Most law centres tend to be constituted as charities and run by a local management committee which includes a strong user representation; and many of them are financially supported by their local authority[6] or the Government scheme (see post, para 3.17). Each tends to employ a number of full-time workers, including qualified lawyers, so they will therefore require a waiver of Practice Rules from the Law Society or Bar Council, which may in turn involve the goodwill of the local profession. Consumer problems are likely to form a fairly small part of their workload.

Nevertheless, it is clear that there is never likely to be enough free advice to meet demands; and this is especially true in relation to debt advice. Accordingly, in recent years attention has been focused on other ways of financing further advice free to the consumer at the point of use[7] and subject to OFT licensing as ancillary credit businesses (see post, para 5.43). In the absence of sufficient public money being available, the income of advice agencies is likely to have to come from creditors. Broadly, there are three competing funding philosophies: first, industry support gathered centrally, as with the Money Advice Trust,[8] which in turn set up the National Debtline;[9] second, a US-style deduction from debts collected by the centre;[10] and third, there have developed businesses which charge debtors for advice.[11] To bring together these varied debt advice schemes, there has been set up the Money Advice Liaison Group;[12] and, with the recent increase in funding of Money Advice charities, there are signs of the development of more permanent paid advisers, with the skills retention which that implies.

---

4   See Sweet (1999) 149 NLJ 1588; (2000) 150 NLJ 253; Boon and Whyte (2000) 150 NLJ 1564. The College of Law may participate to give students a 'clinical' training: (1999) *The Times*, 25 October.

5   *Law Centres A Practical Guide* (1980) by the Law Centres Federation. See Morton (1988) 138 NLJ 141. (1991) 141 NLJ 1249.

6   The relationship tends to be uneasy because many of the complaints are against their own local authority; and in recent years there have been question marks over the financing: (1999) 149 NLJ 278. For an attempt to restrict Brent Law Centre to giving advice rather than supporting litigation, see Pearson (1992) 142 NLJ 1165. For recent expansion in the number of Law Centres, see (2001) 151 NLJ 1632.

7   An early model was the Birmingham Settlement (see [2000] 8 Credit Today, Extra). As to how money advice works, see Chambers (1991) 46 CC 2/24; (1996) 17 CCA News 2/12.

8   Eg, the Money Advice Trust. This body was set up in response to an appeal by the Director of the OFT (see OFT, 1990-AR 28 and continues to be supported by the OFT (OFT, 1997-AR, 24). For the terms of membership, see (2001) 60 QA 1. For the Paylink Trust, see post, para 5.42.

9   Eg, with grant-aid ((1998) 53 CC 1/38); (2001) 59 QA 15. For a plea that counsellors widen their range of expertise, see (2000) 55 QA 15.

10 Eg, the Consumer Credit Counselling Service (CCCS): see D'Ingeo (1995) 145 NLJ 190. For debt management plans, see post, para 5.42.

11 See [2001] 2 Credit Today 5.

12 As to the Money Advice Liaison Group, see (1993) 48 CCI/26; (1994) 15 CCA News 1/21; (1996) 50 CC 6/20; 53 CC2/32.

[3.17] Financing legal advice and proceedings. Like the Ritz hotel, the legal system is open to everybody; but obtaining legal advice and taking legal proceedings can be expensive. For many years, the State offered modest financial support under the Legal Aid Acts, though that system has been entirely replaced by the Access to Justice Act 1999. This (perhaps misnamed) Act aims to restrict State financial support only to 'individuals' (s 7(1)), so that registered companies are not eligible for support. The State support is to be overseen by the Legal Services Commission (ss 1–3), which has two arms: the Criminal Defence Service (CDS) and Community Legal Service (CLS). The CDS (ss 12–18, as amended) deals predominantly with the cost of defence in criminal proceedings, so that it is of little use to an aggrieved consumer (see post, para 3.19), but may be relevant to the small unincorporated trader charged with a strict liability offence (see Chapter 4). The CLS (ss 4–11) is intended to ensure that the poor and disadvantaged can access the civil law services and benefits to which they are entitled on a means-tested basis (s 7): the individual may have to make a contribution (ss 10–11) and will be funded according to statutory criteria set out in a code (s 8). Initially, no more Government money will be available than under the previous legal aid scheme, which will clearly circumscribe the services provided; and the effect would appear to be that it is unlikely to be available to owner-occupiers. To achieve all this, the Commission may set the priorities (s 6(1)) and the CLS must work in co-operation with 'other authorities, bodies and persons' (s 4(6)), eg, Local Authorities (see post, para 28.02), CABx and the Consumers' Association (see ante, para 3.08) and law centres.[a] The CLS support is restricted to those costs of litigation which are proportionate to the issue;[1] and it limits the matters litigated to those which are within the public interest (s 8(2)(g)) and fall within the Funding Code criteria.[2] The Act envisages that primarily it will not support the types of litigation listed in Sched 2, eg, negligence, apart from clinical negligence, and defamation.[3] Of the many matters which do primarily fall within the scope of the Act, those of importance to this text include contract, consumer and debt. However, the Act also empowers the Lord Chancellor to bring even scheduled matters back within the Act in particular circumstances (s 6(8)); and it may be that this will enable the CLS to fund test cases, eg, in product liability claims (see Chapter 17). Apart from the foregoing, consumers wishing recourse to the civil law are left to rely on the following: (1) the services of lawyers paid for by a combination of conditional fees and 'after-the-event insurance' (ss 27, 28: see post, para 3.18); or (2) litigants in person (see below), relying on advice agencies (see ante, para 3.16) to help them through a new simplified court system (see post, para 3.22).

Under the above access to civil justice scheme, instead of solicitors applying for State funds when a client problem arises, the CLS will contract with particular 'persons' (franchisees) to provide the CLS-funded services within an agreed area of law:[4] to ensure their expertise within the contracted area of law, the Act provides for quality control standards (s 4(8)), which will be apparent to the public by way of the logo for a CLS Quality Mark; and the provision is deliberately drafted widely enough so that the CLS

[3.17]

a   See also Ardill (2001) 151 NLJ 1842.

1   Section 8(2)(a). The 'concept of proportionality': see LCD, *Access to Justice* (1996) 79.

2   Section 8(1). The Funding Code is issued by the CLS; and the LC may order its amendment from time to time: s 8(2)(h). For criticism, see Stein (2001) 151 NLJ 998. For litigation, see post, para 3.22.

3   See Sched 2, which *inter alia*, generally excludes matters arising from the carrying on of a business.

4   Section 6(3). The contracted 'persons' will be publicised in CLS Directories. For initial progress, see Lock (2001) 151 NLJ 613.

may contract not only with professional lawyers, but also with the not-for-profit sector. In our context, this last has enabled the CLS to employ the services of consumer advisers, eg, CCCS (see ante, para 3.16).

1   *Legal help.* Replacing the old 'green-form scheme', this provides 'first aid' work involving the writing of letters or negotiations for a settlement, as well as legal advice. The scheme is stringently means-tested (as above); and, where a particular client is ineligible, many solicitors operating this scheme may offer a similar amount of advice on a *pro bono* basis, perhaps regarding that advice as a sort of loss leader to legal assistance (see below).

2   *Legal assistance.* Under the 1999 Act, legal assistance in the form of representation by a solicitor and barrister paid for by State funds is available on a means-tested basis (see above) to bring or defend civil litigation within the scope of the Act (see above) in the County and High Court (Sched 2); but it is not available for arbitrations (see post, para 3.23), nor for most tribunals, which will exclude ombudsmen (see post, para 3.25). The applicant must persuade the administering body that his claim falls within the Funding Code (see above): this prescribes the type (see above) and levels of service which may be provided by a franchisee, including (a) Help at Court and (b) Legal Representation.[5]

Litigants in person. Parallel to the development of the small claims procedure in the county court (see post, para 3.23), there has been a movement to encourage consumers to litigate in person. The Lord Chancellor's Office has produced an explanatory booklet for litigants in person;[6] and in practice considerable support and advice in individual actions has been provided in recent years by organisations such as Consumer Advice Centres (see ante, para 3.05). Furthermore, in those cases where costs are at issue, eg, ordinary High Court or county court actions, the position of the consumer has been considerably improved in relation to costs by the Litigants in Person (Costs and Expenses) Act 1975. Prior to that Act, the litigant in person was not entitled to remuneration in respect of his time and labour,[7] whereas under the Act he may be.[8] Moreover, whilst solicitors and barristers have a right of audience in court, even if acting *pro bono* (see ante, para 3.16), any litigant may instead represent himself.[9] Alternatively, it has long been clear that he may be represented by a friend without right of audience, usually known as a McKenzie friend.[10] A litigant in person has a *prima facie* right to the 'quiet and unobtrusive' assistance in open court of a McKenzie friend;[11] but a judge has a discretion to exclude such a friend from

---

5   For criticism of the new service, see: Hudson (2000) 150 NLJ 529; and the riposte 150 NLJ 636.

6   See the leaflets produced by the Lord Chancellor's Office and widely available at CABx and Advice Centres. See also *How to Sue in the County Court* by the Consumers' Association. As to whether the legal aid of litigant-in-person statutes infringe the Human Rights Convention, see Birch (2001) 151 NLJ 162 and 277.

7   *Buckland v Watts* [1970] 1 QB 27, CA.

8   *Hart v Aga Khan Foundation (UK)* [1984] 2 All ER 439, CA. Costs are not usually allowed in small claims in the County Court: see post, para 3.22.

9   See the Courts and Legal Services Act 1990, ss 27, 28, 29, 31, 31A, 31B, 31C (as amended, substituted and added by the Access to Justice Act 1999).

10 *McKenzie v McKenzie* [1971] P 33, CA (matrimonial case). See now the Courts and Legal Services Act 1990, s 27(2)(c); and *Izzo v Philip Ross & Co* [2001] 9 CL 82 (Stephenson 151 NLJ 1726).

11 *R v Leicester City Justices ex p Barrow* [1991] 2 QB 260, CA (community charge case).

private proceedings in chambers.[12] Moreover, it has been established that the privilege is that of the litigant in person, not the friend.[12]

Enforcement of consumer rights

[3.18] Introduction. Even when armed with advice as to his legal rights (see ante, paras 3.15–17), the consumer faces a number of difficulties. If the trader against whom he is complaining refuses redress, he will need a considerable effort of sustained will-power to achieve his rights. Even more significant is likely to be the issue of financial resources. The basic assumption of the English Legal System appears to be that anybody seeking legal advice or participating in court proceedings is likely to utilise the services of lawyers; that costs will normally follow the event, that is, the loser pays the costs of both sides;[1] and, as such services are normally provided on the basis of an expensive piece-rate, it is usually very important to consumers to consider ways of cheapening the process.

Perhaps the most obvious solution to these problems might appear to be to look for a parallel criminal offence (see Chapter 4), persuade another to undertake the prosecution,[2] and then seek compensation from the convicting court (see post, paras 3.19–20). Alternatively, or subsequently, the consumer may pursue civil proceedings through the courts (see post, para 3.22), perhaps using a prior conviction to cheapen the civil proceedings (see post, para 3.21). A policy of using civil test cases brought by public authorities might be helpful to consumers,[3] as may the wider availability of class actions, which allow a whole class of persons severally injured by a defendant to sue that defendant together in a single action.[4] The Lord Chancellor has announced his intention to allow class actions by persons injured and representative actions by bodies such as consumer groups.[5] Further, a litigant in person may reduce his costs by use of advice centre support.[6] Alternatively, an aggrieved consumer may choose to pursue his complaint in an alternative forum which is likely to involve him in no or reduced costs, such as arbitration or an ombudsman (see post, paras 3.23–25).

However, having looked at all the above, an aggrieved consumer may find that the only effective avenue for redress is to employ lawyers to bring or defend civil proceedings on his behalf. In this context, there becomes relevant the game-plan of the Access to Justice Act 1999. This Act assumes the State financial assistance is unlikely to be available to the ordinary consumer (see ante, para 3.17), who **instead** will finance the

---

12 *Clarkson v Gilbert* [2000] CLY 537, CA (chambers); *Noueiri v Paragon Finance plc (No 2)* [2001] 11 CL 47, CA (open court).

[3.18]

1   The availability of criminal test-cases depends on the good of offices of the OFT or Local Authority (see post, para 3.19) and has budgetary implications.

2   In our context, that would commonly be the Local Authority: see post, para 28.03.

3   Such schemes are widely available on the Continent. They were introduced here with the UTCC Regulations (see post, para 11.19); and have since been generalised by the introduction of consumer injunctions (see post, para 28.03).

4   Eg, an action against a manufacturer in respect of a design fault: see post, paras 14.18; 17.02. See Harvey, *Consumer Protection and Fair Trading* (6th edn), p 237 *et seq*; Cranston, *Consumers and the Law* (3rd edn) pp 121–33. Costs should be shared: *BCCI v Ali (Assessment of Costs)* [2001] 4 CL 82.

5   *Modern Markets: Confident Consumers* (1999, Cm 4410) paras 5.25; 7.10. The LC has issued a Consultation Paper (2001). But they cannot use Stop Now Orders (see post, para 28.03).

6   Eg, by Local Authority Consumer Advice Centres (see ante, para 3.05), or by Law Centres (see ante, para 3.16). See the *Money Advice Handbook on Court Procedures* (2nd edn).

considerable financial costs of litigation by one or both of conditional fees (see below) and legal expenses insurance.[7] The consumer may have taken out such insurance before the event (BTE insurance), eg, as part of his household or motor insurance; or, more likely, he may have to enter such a policy after the dispute has arisen (ATE insurance).[8]

Conditional fees. Traditionally, any arrangement by which a solicitor's entitlement to his fee was contingent on his client winning the case was considered reprehensible. So English common law treated any such solicitor-client contract as illegal on grounds of maintenance and champerty (see post, para 7.26), whether the agreement was that the solicitor recovered (a) some of his client's winnings, (b) his normal fee plus a success uplift, or (c) only his normal fee. However, in the 1980s, perceptions of this public policy began to change when it was appreciated that some form of conditional fee might facilitate access to justice by those earning too much to qualify for State financial assistance for litigation (see ante, para 3.17). Accordingly, the outright statutory prohibition on solicitors entering any kind of conditional fee arrangement in the Solicitors Act 1974 (s 59(2)(b)) was first replaced by a provision in the Courts and Legal Services Act 1990, which enabled the Lord Chancellor by regulation to allow solicitors sometimes to charge what it called 'conditional fees' (s 58); and this provision has since been enhanced to become a central plank of the Access to Justice Act 1999, ss 27–28. The enhanced provisions (1990 Act, ss 58, 58A) broadly allows arrangements of above types (b) or (c), but not (a);[9] and it extends to virtually any civil claim.[10] However, the Act expressly says that any other contingent fee arrangement shall remain 'unenforceable'.[11] It has been claimed that these statutory conditional fees 'are a halfway-house or hybrid grafted on to the existing litigation system by a Government determined to increase access to justice but too squeamish to go the whole hog and introduce US-style contingency fees'.[12]

[3.19] Criminal proceedings. Particularly in Chapter 4, there will be considered a large number of statutory provisions imposing criminal sanctions in attempts at consumer protection.[1] Many of these are offences of strict liability (see post, para 28.08) and must nowadays be consistent with the Defendant's Convention rights (see ante, para 3.09). Most of these offences are triable either on indictment (usually by jury) before the Crown Court or summarily (without a jury) by a magistrates' court,[2] frequently involving a heavier maximum penalty if trial is on indictment (see post, para 28.07). An analysis of the types of complaint and numbers of convictions are to be found in the Annual Reports of the Office of Fair Trading (see ante, para 3.03). As State financial assistance is not available to prosecute such complaints (see ante, para 3.17), a consumer is likely to wish

---

7   The 1999 Act confirms that these insurance premiums are recoverable from the other side: ss 30–32.

8   See *Callery v Gray (No 2)* [2001] 4 All ER 1, CA (BTI; 151 NLJ 1373); *Sarwar v Alam* [2001] 4 All ER 541, CA (BTE). These are recoverable as costs under s 29.

9   There is provision for the CLS (see ante, para 3.17) to fund such conditional fee arrangements in what are called 'legal funding agreements': new s 58B.

10   See the Conditional Fee Agreements Regulations 2000, SI No 692. For the steps to be followed in making a conditional fee agreement, see Harrison (2000) 150 NLJ 895. For defects, see Moorhead and Sherr (2001) 151 NLJ 274.

11   New s 58(1). See *Awwad v Geraghty & Co* [2000] 1 All ER 608, CA (discussed 116 LQR 371).

12   See Bawdon (1999) 149 NLJ 1890.

[3.19]

1   For a comparative survey within the EEC, see the Commission's *Consumer Redress* (12.12.84), Annex 2.

2   The procedure to be adopted is laid down in the Magistrates Court Act 1980, ss 17–28: see further Harvey, *Consumer Protection and Fair Trading* (6th edn), pp 246–48.

to persuade somebody else to prosecute, typically the local Trading Standards Department.[3] However, conviction is not normally the sole aim of the consumer: he may seek a compensation order from the convicting court (see post, para 3.20); or he may subsequently take civil proceedings (see post, para 3.21 *et seq*). It is for consideration how far public authorities should go in bringing prosecutions where the primary objective is to make possible a compensation order or facilitate a civil claim (see ante, para 3.18).

[3.20] Compensation orders. Assuming a supplier is prosecuted to conviction, it may be possible for any consumer injured by commission of the offence to obtain a compensation order from the convicting court. Such a procedure has long been available in respect of convictions under the Theft Act (s 28, as amended); and later a general procedure was introduced in the Powers of Criminal Courts Act 1973.[1] However, these statutory powers do not provide for any compensation where civil proceedings are concluded before conviction;[2] nor do they contain any interim power to freeze the defendant's assets pending conviction,[3] though there is power under the Supreme Court Act 1981 to apply for an injunction to this effect.[4]

Section 35(1) of the 1973 Act (as amended) provides that:

> ... a court by or before which a person is convicted of an offence, instead of or in addition to dealing with him in any other way, may on application or otherwise make an order (in this Act referred to as 'a compensation order') requiring him to pay compensation for any personal injury, loss or damage resulting from that offence or any other offence which is taken into consideration by the court in determining sentence.

Under this section, it is not strictly necessary that the person injured makes an application; nor is the court bound to make an order.[5] However, it is necessary that there be a conviction and loss;[6] and there is a restriction on the maximum amount of compensation which a magistrates' court may order.[7] Whilst the 1973 Act followed the traditional practice that compensation to the injured individual could only be additional to another form of punishment,[8] it may be that the courts will find some encouragement

---

3   See ante, para 3.05. For prosecution by LAs, see post, Chapter 28.

[3.20]

1   The order must be made by the convicting court: *R v Blackpool Justices ex p Charlson* [1972] 3 All ER 854, DC. What, if any, is the effect on such powers of provisions in consumer protection statutes creating offences but forbidding any civil redress (see post, para 3.21)?

2   *Hammerton Cars Ltd v London Borough of Redbridge* [1974] 2 All ER 216, DC.

3   *Malone v Metropolitan Police Comr* [1980] QB 49, CA.

4   Section 37(1): *Chief Constable of Kent v V* [1983] QB 34, CA. But see *Chief Constable of Hampshire v A* [1984] 2 All ER 385, CA.

5   The appellate courts have insisted that such orders are not to be made where the issues are complex or disputed: *R v Swan and Webster* (1984) 6 Cr App R(S) 22. As to presentation of claims by trading standards officers (see post, para 28.03), see (1993) 10 Tr L 187. As to Government encouragement for greater use of such orders, see *Modern Markets: Confident Consumers* (1999, Cm 4410) para 5.22.

6   *R v Boardman* [1987] CLY 892, CA (conditional sale; goods recovered undamaged). But distress may be sufficient: *Bond v Chief Constable of Kent* [1983] 1 All ER 456, DC.

7   This has serious implications where other offences are taken into account: see Weatherill (1986) 136 NLJ 459.

8   Indeed, the Act does not even require the presence of an independent civil remedy: *R v Chappell* (1984) 80 Cr App R 31, CA (criticised 48 MLR 706; Atiyah, *Sale of Goods* (10th edn), p 295).

in the subsequent amendments: that made in 1982 which allows such compensation **instead** of punishment with preference to be given the compensation;[9] and one enacted in 1988 requires a court to give reasons if refusing compensation (1988 Act, s 104(1)). In making the order, the court is directed to have regard both to the means of the convicted person and the amount considered appropriate (s 35(1)(A)); and the courts continue to insist on proof of the precise amount of any loss or damage.[10] The court has power to allow the convict time for payment[10] or order payment by instalments (s 34). The instalment orders may be a real disadvantage to recipients needing to replace capital equipment, but this is only likely to be a problem where the poverty of his convicted supplier induces the court to make an instalment order. Finally, if there is subsequently any civil litigation in respect of the same damage, the damages awarded must be reduced by the amount of compensation paid.[11]

Civil proceedings

[3.21] Prior convictions. Notwithstanding that the consumer does not obtain any, or sufficient, compensation thereby, it may still be of advantage to a consumer to obtain a conviction of his supplier for a criminal offence (see ante, paras 3.18–20) before commencing civil proceedings.

1   *Evidential value.*[1] According to s 11(1) of the Civil Evidence Act 1968:

In any civil proceedings the fact that a person has been convicted of an offence by or before any court in the United Kingdom ... shall ... be admissible in evidence for the purpose of proving, where to do so is relevant to any issue in those proceedings, that he committed that offence ...

Leaving aside defamation actions (s 11(3)), it is not conclusive evidence,[2] though the Act provides no guidance as to the standard of proof required to disprove the conviction, and little in identifying the conduct which is the subject matter of the conviction (see s 11(2)(b)). However, it is clear that, following conviction, s 11 will tend to reduce the cost and increase the certainty of subsequent civil litigation.[3]

2   *Statutory duties.* There are likely to be a significant number of cases where a person in the chain of distribution (see post, para 17.01) has committed a criminal offence by breaching one of the statutory provisions designed for the protection of consumers, see eg, Chapter 4, but it does not prove possible to obtain a compensation order (see ante, para 3.20) and there is no privity of contract (see post, para 10.01). In the

---

9   Section 35(4A) of the 1973 Act, as introduced by the Criminal Justice Act 1982 Act. It is still not possible for the court to make both a compensation order and a criminal bankruptcy order (s 39(1)); but it is possible to combine the latter with a restitution order (as to which see post, para 24.25): *R v James* (1984) 6 Cr App R(S) 370, CA. For insolvency, see generally post, para 19.18 *et seq.*

10 *R v Horsham Justices ex p Richards* [1985] 2 All ER 1114, DC.

11 Section 38 (as substituted by s 105 of the Criminal Justices Act 1988). *Quaere* whether the compensation order is evidence that the injury was caused by the offence, and what affect it may have on costs in the civil proceedings?

[3.21]

1   See generally *Cross on Evidence* (9th edn), pp 96–99.

2   Section 11(2)(a). See *J v Oyston* [1999] 1 WLR 694; *McCauley v Hope* [1999] 1 WLR 1977, CA.

3   Eg, under the Road Traffic Acts (see post, para 4.37), where conviction for supplying a vehicle contravening the regulations might then support of civil claim for unsatisfactory quality (see post, para 14.22).

foregoing circumstances, the consumer may wish to bring an action in tort for breach of statutory duty.[4] Thus, it has been said that:[5]

> *Prima facie* a person who has been injured by the breach of a statute has a right to recover damages from the person committing it unless it can be established by considering the whole of the Act that no such right was intended to be given.

A few statutes expressly grant such a right of action[6] whilst a number of others expressly rule out such an action.[7] Where statute is silent on the point, as regards domestic legislation the courts have usually preferred to refuse such a tort action on the grounds that a right of action was already available under the statute or some other rule of contract or tort: for instance that food is not of the nature and quality demanded or is unfit for human consumption;[8] or that a vehicle was supplied in breach of the construction and use regulations or in an unroadworthy condition (see post, para 4.37). Nor does it seem likely that such an action will lie for breach of the Trade Descriptions Act (see generally post, paras 4.02–17): contrary to the recommendation of the Molony Committee,[9] s 35 of the Act is deliberately unclear on the point and it has subsequently been argued that an action should be denied because no personal injury is likely to be occasioned by breaches.[10] However, such tort actions have been allowed to give an individual damages for breach of EU law.[11]

[3.22] Civil litigation. Assuming that a consumer does wish to proceed with a civil claim in the courts, the action is likely to be in contract or tort, or in respect of an extortionate credit bargain under the CCA (see below); and the proceedings must nowadays be consistent with Convention rights (see ante, para 3.09). If the dispute is between two businessmen and worth over £100,000, it is likely to be taken to the High Court, perhaps that sitting known as the Commercial Court.[1] However, if the claim involves a consumer and is worth only £10,000, it is likely to start in the County Court. These courts were first created in 1846 to try, on a local basis, claims involving a small sum of money, the jurisdiction of each court being normally limited to disputes in some way connected with its defined geographic area. However, it was recognised that this approach was unduly restrictive, particularly to large commercial or public bodies (some two-thirds of business of county courts) who were required to issue proceedings in all or most county courts and also where proceedings were undefended (see below): so the rules were altered to allow

---

4   See generally *Street on Torts* (10th edn), Chapter 16; Winfield and Jolowicz, *Torts* (12th edn), Chapter 8; Buckley (1984) 100 LQR 204; Stanton, *Breach of Statutory Duty* (1986).

5   *Mark v Warbey* [1935] 1 KB 75 at 81, Greer LJ (Road Traffic Act 1930, s 35). The courts have been criticised as unnecessarily unhelpful to consumers in this regard: Harvey, *Consumer Protection and Fair Trading* (6th edn), p 263, note 12.

6   Eg, Mock Auctions Act 1961, s 3(6); Weights and Measures Act 1985, s 33(6); CCA, ss 92(3), 72(11); CPA, s 41(1).

7   Eg, Medicines Act 1968, s 133(2)(a); FTA, s 26(a); CCA, s 170(1); CPA, s 41(2).

8   See *Square v Model Farm Dairies (Bournemouth) Ltd* [1939] 2 KB 365, CA; *Buckley v La Reserve* [1959] Crim LR 451, Cty Ct.

9   *Report of the Committee on Consumer Protection* (1962, Cmnd 1781), para 459.

10   *Review of the Trade Descriptions Act 1968* (1976, Cmnd 6628), para 251. Cf *Mid Kent Holdings plc v General Utilities plc* [1996] 3 All ER 132.

11   *Garden Cottage Foods v Milk Marketing Board* [1984] AC 130, HL.

[3.22]

1   See Goode, *Commercial Law* (2nd edn), Chapter 38.

the claimant to choose a venue,[2] but with an automatic transfer to the defendant's local court on his filing a defence. The jurisdiction of the latter is laid down in the County Courts Act 1984 (as amended): this includes 'any action founded on contract or tort where the debt, demand or damage does not exceed' the 'county court limit' or any greater sum by agreement of the parties (s 18). The Courts and Legal Services Act 1990 gave the Lord Chancellor power (s 1) to adjust by order the jurisdiction limits of the High Court and County Court.[3]

As from April 1999, the Woolf reforms have made important changes to the court handling of **defended** claims: the High and County Court structure has been unified under a single system of Civil Procedure Rules (CPR);[4] the new system has been designed to encourage early settlement of disputes,[4a] eg, by offers to settle and payments into court, case conferences between parties; to minimise disputes by early openness, eg, by disclosure of documents, pre-action protocols[5] and jointly-instructed experts; to make the proceedings proportional to the dispute, eg, choice of court, timetable, costs; and to encourage the parties to behave reasonably, eg, when deciding costs. The objective is to achieve faster, cheaper justice by pushing defended claims as high up the following three litigation routes below High Court level as possible under the following unified structure:

(1) *Small claims (CPR Part 27).* The Small Claims Court will hear most straightforward claims, eg, for debt, under £5,000, frequently by litigants in person (see ante, para 3.17). The procedure is relatively informal, with hearings in public, but with the possibility of written submissions. Disputes are heard by a District Judge, allow only lay (non-lawyer) representation,[6] further simplify procedure and with a 'no-costs' rule.[7] For practical purposes, his decision is final on the facts,[8] though there is a limited right of appeal on matters of law.

(2) *Fast track (CPR Part 28).* The Circuit Judge will hear the middle-value band of claims, which includes debt claims for £5 to £15,000. The procedure used includes a provision for entering judgment in default of appearance (default judgment: see below), the hearing of minor matters before the District Judge[9] and fixed scales of costs.[10] The big

---

2 This enables the claimant to take an undefended case through to judgment and enforcement (see post, para 27.03) in the venue of his choice. There has also been introduced the Northampton Bulk Centre to enable major plaintiffs to centralise their proceedings there.

3 The system for non-CCA cases is as follows: the High Court has exclusive jurisdiction over a certain figure (currently £50,000); the county court has exclusive jurisdiction below a certain figure (currently £25,000); and both courts have concurrent jurisdiction in between.

4 For a summary of the rules, see Goode, *Consumer Credit Law and Practice*, Part XIIA. There have also been significant increases in many court fees, which may act as a barrier to consumers: [1999] 11 Which? 6.

4a For speedy resolution of disputes, see Michaelson (2002) 152 NLJ 24.

5 A formal system for identifying the issues in a particular type of dispute. Four protocols are currently in force, more are in the pipeline; and a draft debt protocol is under consultation, but may be abandoned in favour of a general pro-action protocol.

6 For the manner in which a solicitor may assist his client in small claims, see Frenkel (1998) 148 NLJ 623.

7 The rule is not absolute: see Foster (1998) 148 NLJ 1266.

8 Harvey and Parry, *Consumer Protection and Fair Trading* (6th edn), pp 231–34; Appleby, *A Practical Guide to the Small Claims Court*. For research into the operation of the system, see OFT, 1994-AR 24.

9 Below the small claims limit (see above), or where the defendant is not expected to appear. He also deals with the pre-trial review of cases expected to go before the Circuit Judge.

10 To combat the costs problems in, eg, *Kasler and Cohen v Slavouski* [1928] 1 KB 78 (multiple parties).

feature of this track is that the court will at an early stage set a trial date and allocate only one day: if the trial requires more than one day, it is transferred to the multi-track (see below).

(3) *Multi-track (CPR Part 29).* The greatest value claims will be distributed as appropriate between the County and High Court, except that all CCA disputes must go the County Court (CCA, s 141: see post, para 24.39). There are procedures for transferring cases between multi-track trial before a Circuit Judge and trial in the High Court, including at the stage of execution of judgment. A feature of multi-track trials is the case management conference: personal attendance by the parties may be required; they will be encouraged to co-operate to minimise the issues; and the opportunity may be taken to try to settle the case. In some circumstances, only fixed costs will be awarded, eg, claims for debt or under the CCA; but in any event multi-track costs are likely to be substantially less than those in the High Court.

Undefended claims. If no legally significant defence is put in, application may be made for default or summary judgment (CPR Parts 12 and 24). For undefended claims, see post, para 27.03. Which court deals with a claim, eg, for debt (after judgment termed a 'judgment debt'), may have implications as to the venue of proceedings (see above) and as to the methods of enforcing judgment (see post, para 27.04).

[3.23] Arbitration.[1] Whereas the courts (see ante, para 3.22) may be a more suitable venue for the resolution of a test case, or to establish a precedent, the various forms of arbitration (see below) usually offer the advantages of relative speed, flexibility, cheapness and privacy. There should be distinguished from both the foregoing the various methods of resolving disputes which usually ultimately depend on the agreement of the parties for the efficacy of their solutions, such as Alternative Disputes Resolution (ADR),[2] mediation[3] and Ombudsman (see post, para 3.25).

1   *Commercial arbitration.*[4] In the realms of formal commercial contracts, it has long been common for the agreement to provide that any disputes between the parties should be settled by arbitration.[5] Such a clause will usually expressly refer to disputed matters of fact; in which case, any attempt by a party to dispute in court related matters of fact will usually be stayed by the court,[6] provided the conditions of the arbitration clause are observed.[7] At common law, the jurisdiction of the courts in matters of law could not be ousted;[7] but under Part I of the Arbitration Act 1996, the

---

[3.23]

1   See Rutherford (1990) 140 NLJ 1600. Arbitration clauses are not within UCTA: (see s 13(2): (post, para 18.16); but in relation to consumer supplies, they fall within the Unfair Contract Terms Regulations: see Grey List (q), post, para 11.18.

2   (1993) 10 Tr LR 250. See Practice Statement [1994] 1 All ER 34; Banking Ombudsman, 1995/96 AR para 1.14; NCC, *Settling Consumer Disputes*; Naughton (1995) 145 NLJ 383; the LCD Discussion Paper (2000). The Government prefers to settle disputes in which it is involved by adrs: [2001] 4 CL 4. Our courts sometimes try to bring adrs within our arbitration system: *Channel Tunnel Group v Balfour Beatty Construction* [1993] AC 334, HL.

3   LCD, *Resolving Disputes* (1995); Trent (1999) 149 NLJ 410; Genn, *Mediation in Action* (1999). Unlike arbitration clauses, mediation clauses are unlikely to inhibit litigation: *Halifax Financial Services Ltd v Intuitive Systems Ltd* [1999] 1 All ER (Comm) 303. See further post, para 3.24.

4   See Goode, *Commercial Law* (2nd edn), Chapter 39.

5   It is also competent for the parties to make an arbitration agreement to similar effect after a dispute has arisen.

6   *Scott v Avery* (1856) 5 HLC 811; *Jones v Sherwood Computers* [1992] 2 All ER 170, CA.

7   *Veba Oil Supply and Trading GmbH v Petrotrade* [2002] 1 All ER 703, CA.

parties may enter into an agreement excluding the jurisdiction of the High Court.[8] However, in the case of a 'domestic arbitration agreement',[9] the courts can usually do so only where the applicant is dragging his feet over the arbitration (s 86(3)), or the arbitration agreement was made after commencement of the arbitral proceedings (s 87). Further discussion is beyond the scope of this work.

2   *Court arbitration.* In a High Court action, the Rules allow in particular circumstances the whole or any part of a case to be referred for trial to the referee or other official of the court, it being envisaged that this power should be used in particular when prolonged examination of documents or local examination is required or where matters of account are involved. Further, a judge in the Commercial Court now has power to postpone his hearings until the parties have attempted to settle their dispute through ADR or mediation (see above).

3   *Consumer arbitration* (see post, para 3.24).

[3.24] Consumer arbitration. Perhaps because of the deficiencies in the then county court small claims procedure (see ante, para 3.23), there arose various voluntary arbitration schemes, either by geographical area or trade, and normally on a documents only basis and instead of court action.[1] These must all be consistent with Convention rights (see ante, para 3.09).

1   *Local schemes.* The two schemes which attracted the most notice failed when local authority funding was withdrawn.[2]

2   *Trade codes of practice.* A noticeable feature of many of the codes of practice (see ante, paras 3.12–14) has been a provision for conciliation and arbitration in the event of dispute between trader and consumer. The envisaged first stage is usually an attempted conciliation by the trade association;[3] and, if that fails, traders supporting the code promise in advance to accept arbitration if requested.[4] Such arbitrations usually proceed on documentary evidence only to keep the cost to a minimum.[5] Whilst some of the above schemes offer consumers definite advantages, it was found that others contained an agreement to submit to arbitration (a *Scott v Avery* clause: see ante, para 3.23), which bound consumers wishing to prosecute a claim to a high cost arbitration.[6]

Accordingly, since 1988 a consumer arbitration agreement has generally been unenforceable even with the consumer's consent. The present rules are to be found in the

---

8   Treitel, *Law of Contract* (10th edn), p 409.

9   1996 Act, s 85. These provision may be unlawful under the Treaty of Rome (see generally ante, para 1.03A) unless the concept is extended beyond UK nationals to include EU nationals: see *Phillip Alexander Securities and Futures Ltd v Bamberger* [1996] Eu LR 63, CA.

[3.24]

1   See Borrie, *The Development of Consumer Law and Policy* (1984), pp 38–39. For the relative merits of a court or voluntary arbitration, see [1993] 2 Which? 52.

2   See Lowe and Woodroffe, *Consumer Law and Practice* (5th edn), paras 10.08; 10.60; Harvey and Parry, *Consumer Protection and Fair Trading* (6th edn), pp 231–32.

3   Such conciliation tends to be free, but is not legally binding. See further Lowe and Woodroffe, *ibid*, para 10.08; and ante, para 3.23.

4   Eg, by codes of practice of FLA, CCTA (see ante, para 3.13). The OFT agreed a model arbitration scheme with the Chartered Institute of Arbitrators: OFT, 1983-AR, 15.

5   Harvey and Parry, *op cit*, note 2, pp 360–64; Goriely (1991) 141 NLJ 535.

6   This might amount to an unfair term (see below): OFT, Unfair Terms Bulletin No 8, 25.

Arbitration Act 1996: whilst this Act is primarily concerned with commercial arbitrations (see ante, para 3.23), ss 89–91 lay down special rules for consumer[7] 'arbitration agreements'.[8] Section 89(1) provides that such consumer arbitration agreements are to be governed by the terms of the Unfair Terms Regulations,[9] whatever the law applicable to the arbitration agreement (s 89(3)). Moreover, the Act expressly deems unfair any arbitration agreement relating to small claims for amounts less than a specified figure (s 91), currently £5,000.[10] With regard to claims in excess of that figure, it may be expected that the provisions will catch, *inter alia*, unreasonable time limits on claims.[11]

[3.25] Ombudsman.[1] The term 'ombudsman' comes from a Swedish word, loosely meaning 'grievance man'. The notion was originally imported into the UK to deal with complaints by private citizens against Government Departments;[2] and separate ombudsman schemes were subsequently set up for other public authorities, eg, local and health authorities. More recently, this successful notion has been first transmuted into the Directors of the overseeing authorities for the privatised utilities (see ante, para 3.06) and also transplanted into the private commercial sector, eg, insurance industry and banking industry.[3] Subsequently, statutory ombudsman schemes have been set up for building societies[4] and legal services.[5] Unlike public service arbitration schemes (see ante, para 3.24), commercial sector ombudsmen have a dual role: they both investigate individual grievances and report their findings, eg, in Annual Reports, so as to improve the services they monitor.[6] Under the Financial Services and Markets Act 2000, all those Ombudsmen involved with financial services have been unified under a single statutory scheme.[7] EU Ombudsman have been set up to deal with EU institutional maladministration[8] and are being considered to investigate cross-border consumer complaints.

Most of the Ombudsman schemes work in a similar manner. They have carefully defined terms of reference, outside which the ombudsman will not step.[9] Within those terms of reference and subject to the complainant exhausting the businesses' internal complaints system, the scheme will provide a cheap (to the consumer) and informal method of providing redress for valid consumer complaints: this will normally try to put

---

7   The definition of this concept in s 3 is virtually identical with that of 'dealing as consumer' in s 12 of UCTA, including the burden of proof (see post, para 18.18), but is extended to include not just natural persons, but also legal persons: s 90.

8   'Arbitration agreement' means an agreement to submit to arbitration present or future disputes or differences (whether or not contractual)': s 89(2).

9   Eg, a clause granting the supplier a unilateral right to refer disputes to arbitration has been found unfair: OFT, Bulletin 14, case 4. See generally post, para 11.12 *et seq*.

10   Unfair Arbitration Agreements (Specified Amount) Order 1999, SI 2167.

11   As a Grey Term within the 1999 Regulations, Sched 2, para 1(q): see post, para 11.18.

[3.25]

1   See generally Lowe and Woodroffe, *Consumer Law and Practice* (5th edn), paras 10.53–59.

2   Under the Parliamentary Commissioner Act 1967 (as amended).

3   See the *Jack Report on Banking Services*, 1989, Cm 622, Chapter 15.

4   Under Part IX of the Building Societies Act 1986.

5   Under the Courts and Legal Services Act 1990, ss 21–26.

6   They may pay attention to relevant Codes of Practice (see generally ante, para 3.13).

7   Part XVI. Under a Chief Financial Services Ombudsman these replaced eight previous organisations, including those for banks and building societies. The new scheme does not yet extend to home repayment mortgages, not to all unsecured personal loans, eg, store cards.

8   The remedy is intended to be political rather than judicial: see (1994) 144 NLJ 609.

9   For current Terms of Reference, see Goode, *Consumer Credit Law and Practice*, Part VIII.

the consumer back into the position he was before the complained conduct.[10] This whole service is paid for by the trade party to the dispute, so in effect by the extra overheads passed on to non-complaining customers of the trade party. In any event, any ombudsman scheme must now comply with the individual's right to a fair trial.[11]

In the UK, many of the functions that in other Member States are performed by ombudsmen here fall within the remit of the OFT (see ante, para 3.03).

INFORMATION ABOUT CONSUMERS

[3.26] Amongst that segment of commerce and industry providing goods and services to individual consumers, the last quarter of the 20th century saw an explosion of interest in the collection of information about those individuals. Such information is primarily required by them for three purposes: (1) to contact potential customers deemed likely to be interested and suitable for receipt of those goods and services; (2) to facilitate checks on those persons before supplying goods or services, eg, credit; and (3) to trace defaulters. Many suppliers of goods and services themselves accumulate such information; but much of the information is accumulated by third party specialist credit bureaux for onward transmission to suppliers.

Originally, credit bureaux were very much a locally-based activity usually conducted by a manual card-index system. Their nature was transformed by the introduction of powerful computers: these are able not only to store vast amounts of information, but also to dispense it on-line (by telephone line to the trade customer's terminal). Since 1965, there have gradually been established nationwide computerised credit bureaux.[1] They hold personal records, such as the electoral roll (see below), county court judgments for debt (see ante, para 3.22), disqualified directors (see post, para 19.24), other adverse and creditable information (see post, para 8.36) and the land registry records of titles to land.[2] Almost all the relevant finance companies, mortgage-providers, brokers and dealers subscribe to these services, supplying them with details of their own transactions,[3] and, before entering into any such transaction, they can for a small fee search (usually on-line) the register.[4] As they have become more confident in their systems, the credit reference agencies have expanded into related sectors, the assimilation by one of them of HPI being an early example (see above). The HPI service is also available to non-members, including the general public; and it is a matter for consideration as to whether its functions should

---

10 This is nearer to the measures of damages in tort than contract: see post, para 27.28.

11 Human Rights Act 1998, incorporating into English law the European Convention on Human Rights, Art 6 (see Sched 1 of the Act): see generally ante, para 3.09.

[3.26]

1 For the leading agencies specialising in consumer credit, see McNeil Greig, *The Growth of Credit Information*; (1998) CCA News, Summer 8–13. There is now a routine exchange of information between the credit reference agencies, so improving the comprehensiveness of the data: FLA, 1998 Annual Report, p 10.

2 The Land Registry has not made public mortgages on land, which information is only available in respect of company borrowers via the companies register (see post, para 25.28). For adverse and creditable information, see post, para 8.36.

3 What can happen when this practice is not adhered to was demonstrated in *Moorgate Mercantile Co Ltd v Twitchings* (set out post, para 21.57).

4 Supplying information to bureaux for this purpose is not a breach of a bank's duty of confidentiality (see post, para 7.03): *Turner v Royal Bank of Scotland* [2001] 1 All ER (Comm) 1057, CA.

be taken over by the government as the basis for a statutory title-registration system for goods (see post, para 21.61).

Because of their modern effectiveness, these credit reference agencies and HPI have been made subject to special statutory control, with limited waivers in the interest of combating fraud.[5] The first place where Parliament intervened in connection with the activities of credit bureaux was in the Consumer Credit Act 1974,[6] which termed these bureaux 'credit reference agencies'.[7] Subsequently, concern with the recording of information led to the wider statutory control of computerised records ('data') in the Data Protection Act 1984,[8] which was intended to strike a balance between the free flow of information and individual privacy. In the Human Rights Act 1998, Parliament for the first time enshrined in English law the **right** of an individual to privacy.[9] That same year, the 1984 Act was replaced by the Data Protection Act 1998 (see post, para 3.27). Under the Representation of the People Act 2000, electors may be given the option of indicating whether or not they wish registered information about them to be available for commercial purposes:[10] the 'full' register will continue to be available to credit reference agencies for credit applications;[11] but, when an elector chooses to be placed on the 'edited' register, his particulars would not be available to commercial organisations for other purposes, including purposes (1) and (3) above.

[3.27] The Data Protection Act 1998 (DPA).[1] The DPA is based on the Data Protection Directive, which requires Member States to protect the fundamental rights and freedoms of natural persons.[2] As amended,[3] the DPA applies to any 'personal data',[4] whether computerised or manual,[5] concerning living persons ('data subjects').[6] It will give special

---

5   Launched in 1988 under the aegis of the CCTA (above), in 1991 the Credit Industry Fraud Avoidance System (CIFAS) became a separate company limited by guarantee and housed at the Registry Trust Ltd (see ante, para 3.22). It provides a special reporting system by way of the ordinary credit reference agencies which creditors promise to trigger when fraud is suspected: see further post, para 8.39.

6   See generally post, para 5.05 *et seq.*

7   Section 145(8): see post, para 8.36.

8   Section 1(2) defined 'data' in a manner which covers computerised records but excludes manual (paper) ones.

9   Human Rights Act 1998, incorporating into English law the European Convention on Human Rights, Art 8 (see Sched 1 of the Act); and generally ante, para 3.09.

10   Section 9. The draft regulations were intended to be laid at the end of 2001; but the Government is having second thoughts (see below).

11   Whilst this provision is designed to curb fraud, *R (On the Application of Robertson) v Wakefield MCC* [2001] All ER (D) 243 suggests that it may infringe the right to privacy under Art 8 (see above).

[3.27]

1   See the DPC, *Guidelines*; and see further Mas and Church (2002) 152 NLJ 147; and Charlton and Gaskill, *Encyclopedia of Data Protection*.

2   Directive (95/46/EC), Art 1, which may be linked up with the Human Rights Act 1998 (see ante, para 3.26). For the text of the Directive see Goode, *Consumer Credit Law and Practice*. It follows that the 1998 Act must be read in the light of the Directive: see ante, para 1.04. For the junk mail directive, see post, para 8.17.

3   The DPA was significantly amended by the Freedom of Information Act 2000 as regards information held by a 'public authority'; but most of those amendments are beyond the scope of this work. For a relevant provision of the latter Act, see post, para 17.05.

4   This means 'data which relate to a living individual who can be identified ...' (s 1(1)), eg, customer lists. Such data is protected by copyright: see generally ante, para 8.02.

5   'Data' is defined by s 1(1) (as amended) in a manner which includes computerised records and also (unlike the 1984 Act: see ante, para 3.26) **some** manual (paper) records which fall within a 'relevant filing system', eg, default files. What about application forms?

6   Section 1(1). The requirement of living persons excludes from the DPA information about registered companies but includes that on sole traders and partnerships. Cf CCA: see post, para 5.24.

protection to 'sensitive personal data' (s 2), some of which is likely to be of relevance to commerce for the purposes outlined above (see ante, para 3.26), eg, racial origins, commission of any offence. That data may be 'processed'[7] by any UK 'data controller',[8] that is, somebody who determines the processing, eg, creditor or supplier; or somebody who executes that policy on his behalf and is termed a 'data processor', eg, computer bureau.[9] In processing this personal data (usually under licence: see below), these parties must in relation to the data subject observe the Data Protection Principles (see post, para 3.28). Further, the Act grants the following rights to data subjects: access to the information held on them (ss 7–9: see post, para 3.28); to prevent processing likely to cause damage or distress (s 10), or for the purposes of direct marketing (s 11; see post, para 8.19); in relation to automated decision taking (s 12; see post, para 8.39); to compensate for damage caused by contravention of the Act by the data controller (s 13); to rectify, block, erase or destroy inaccurate data (s 14); and to request the Commissioner's help (see below). The foregoing principles are subject to various exemptions of different widths: the more important of these are contained in the Act;[10] and lesser exemptions in Sched 7.

The Act establishes (s 6) a public authority to promote and enforce the Act, the Data Protection Commissioner, who has since been renamed the Information Commissioner (IC):[11] *inter alia*, data controllers must register ('notification') with the IC specified particulars about themselves, the personal data that they hold and the uses to which that data may be put (ss 16, 18–20), this regularly renewable information to be held by the IC on a public register; enquire into compliance with the Act at the behest of data subjects (s 42); serve on data controllers notices requiring information (ss 43–46); and to help enforce all this, the IC has powers of entry and inspection (s 50 and Sched 9: see post, para 28.05). The major sanction available to the IC is to serve enforcement notices on data controllers contravening the data protection principles (ss 40–41), in which case an appeal lies to the Information Tribunal.[12] To give this process teeth, the Act creates a number of offences by a data controller: *inter alia*, these include the processing of data without notifying the IC (ss 17, 21); failure to notify the IC of changes in notifiable matters (ss 20, 21); failure to comply with an enforcement notice (s 47); obstruction of entry and inspection (Sched 9); unlawfully obtaining, procuring, disclosing or selling personal data (s 55); forcing a data subject to agree to access to his personal data (ss 56, 57); and

---

7   'Processing' is widely defined to mean 'obtaining, recording or holding the information or data or the carrying out any operation ... on the data ...': s 1(1). But it does not appear to fit with the common industry practice of delegating the collection of information locally: see [2001] 6 Credit Today 24.

8   'Data controller' is one who alone or with others 'determines the purposes for which and the manner in which any personal data are, or are to be, processed': s 1(1). For data controllers outside the UK, see s 5.

9   'Data processor', in relation to personal data, means any person (other than an employee of the data controller) who processes the data on behalf of the data controller: s 1(1).

10 The more far-reaching exemptions are contained in Part IV of the Act and include data processed for the purposes of prevention of crime (s 29), eg, CIFAS (see ante, para 2.18); public watchdogs (s 31), eg, the OFT and local authorities (see ante, para 3.03–06), OFGAS (see ante, para 3.07), charities (see ante, para 3.08), ombudsmen (see ante, para 3.25); information available under public enactment (s 34, as amended), eg, registries of company charges, court judgments, insolvencies; in connection with legal proceedings (s 35); domestic purposes (s 36).

11 Freedom of Information Act 2000, s 18. The Commissioner must promote good practice under the DPA (s 51), ie, support the spirit of the Act, including taking account of the Human Rights Act 1998 (see ante, para 3,26).

12 Sections 6, 48–49, Sched 6 (as amended). There is a right of further appeal on law to the appropriate court (s 49(6). Cf post, para 6.24.

unlawful disclosure of information by the IC or his staff (ss 58, 59). The IC is empowered to bring prosecutions against businesses contravening the Act (s 60), or their corporate officers (s 61: see post, para 28.11). Can information obtained in breach of the above rules be used in a court action?

[3.28] The Data Protection Principles. Like the 1984 Act (though in slightly different form), the DPA 1998 lays down eight 'data protection principles', applicable where data is 'processed'. Unless he falls within one of the exemptions and whether or not registered or exempt (see ante, para 3.27), 'it shall be the duty of a data controller to comply with the data protection principles in relation to all personal data with respect to which he is the data controller' (s 4(4)). The Data Protection Principles are a curious mixture of generalisation and specific instance. They are as follows (s 4(1), Sched 1):

First Principle.[1] 'Personal data shall be processed fairly[2] and lawfully and, in particular, shall not be processed unless:

(i) In the case of ordinary personal data, it complies with one of the conditions set out in Sched 2, eg, the data subject has given his consent,[3] the processing is **necessary** for the administration of justice;[4] **and**

(ii) In the case of sensitive personal data (an expression which does not include financial data), it **also** complies with one of the conditions set out in Sched 3, eg, the data subject has given his **explicit** consent,[5] the processing is **necessary** for the purposes of legal proceedings or equal opportunities.[6]

Second Principle. Personal data shall be obtained only for one or more specified and lawful purposes, and shall not be further processed in any manner incompatible with that purpose or those purposes.[7]

Third Principle. Personal data shall be adequate, relevant and not excessive in relation to the purpose or purposes for which they are processed. This will exclude third party data, eg, adult children of the data subject.[8] For host mailing, see post, para 8.06.

Fourth Principle. Personal data shall be accurate and, where necessary, kept up to date (see Sched 1, Part II, para 7).

[3.28]

1   The first Principle is particularly relevant to direct marketers and the finance industry, eg, *British Gas Trading Ltd v DPR* [1999] CLY 823. As to proposal forms, see post, para 8.35.

2   The Act also contains a 'fair processing code': Sched 1, Part II, paras 1–4, eg, whether the data subject in giving the information was 'deceived or misled', or is himself notified of the identity of the data controller. As to third party data, see note 8, below.

3   It would appear to follow that information given in good faith and marked 'confidential' cannot be used.

4   This would justify the holding of public records as to, eg, insolvency, court judgment.

5   The data subject must give explicit consent in relation to sensitive data; but presumably he can give implied consent in other cases. The Act does not define his 'consent'; but the Directive refers to 'any freely given specific and informed indication of his wishes by which the data subject signifies his agreement to personal data relating to him being processed'. As to third party data, see note 8, below.

6   As to legal proceedings, see post, Chapters 27, 29. As to equal opportunities, see post, para 4.23.

7   See Sched 1, Part II, paras 5–6. As to using data, see *R v Brown* [1996] 1 All ER 545, HL. For the disclosure/sharing of data in relation to credit reference agencies, see post, para 8.38. As to 'host mailing', see ante, para 8.06.

8   On the difficult issue of recording third party data with that of the data subject, the IC has reached a compromise with the industry: see [2000] 12 Credit Today 18; (2001) 28 Credit Finance 2.

Fifth Principle. Personal data processed for any purpose or purposes shall not be kept for longer than is necessary for that purpose or those purposes.

Sixth Principle. Personal data shall be processed in accordance with the rights of data subjects under this Act,[9] so that he may access that information (ss 7–9: see post, para 8.38).

Seventh Principle. Appropriate technical and organisational measures shall be taken against unauthorised or unlawful processing of personal data and against accidental loss or destruction of, or damage to, personal data (Sched 1, Part II, paras 9–12). This requirement of security is particularly relevant as regards the reliability of the data controller's staff (para 10); or where one party is processing information on behalf of another, eg, any computer bureau he uses (para 9), or in direct financing,[10] or sending only encrypted e-mails.

Eighth Principle. Personal data shall not be transferred to a country or territory outside the European Economic Area, unless that country or territory ensures an adequate level of protection for the rights and freedoms of data subjects in relation to the processing of personal data (see Sched 1, Part 2, paras 13–15. For exceptions, see Sched 4).

The DPC publishes a series of Guidance Notes on the application of the DPA to particular commercial activities.[11]

---

9 A person will contravene this principle if, but only if, they fail to comply with ss 7, 10, 11, 12: Sched 1, Part II, para 8.

10 There must be a suitable written contract between the controller and processor (paras 11–12). As to direct financing, see ante, para 2.21. As to debt collection agencies, see post, para 5.42.

11 Eg, DPA 1998 – *Legal Guidance*; the *Guidance Note for Direct Marketers* (see generally post, para 8.19); *Guidance Note for Users of Document Image Processing Systems* (digitised storing of commercial records); *Guidance On Credit References* (see post, para 8.38). Some of these notes are set out in Goode, *op cit*, Part VIII.

CHAPTER 4

CONSUMER PROTECTION AND THE CRIMINAL LAW

[4.01] Introduction. This chapter is concerned with those parts of the criminal law which regulate the supply of goods to consumers.[1] When considering redress for such consumers, there are significant practical advantages in first examining such criminal provisions, which frequently arise on the same facts as a civil right of action. First, it may be possible to persuade the appropriate public authority, eg, the local authority (see ante, para 3.05), to bring the criminal proceedings, so obviating costs and stress for the consumer (see ante, para 3.18). Second, on conviction, it may be possible to persuade the criminal court to award compensation to the consumer under the Powers of Criminal Courts Act 1973 (see ante, para 3.20); but if not, the conviction may assist subsequent civil proceedings, either as (i) having an evidential value in a civil cause of action, or (ii) as giving rise to a civil action for breach of statutory duty (see ante, para 3.21).

Whilst the law of theft requires proof of *mens rea*,[2] it has long been recognised in this context that widespread effectiveness requires the imposition of strict criminal liability (see post, para 28.08). Consequently, since the Middle Ages there have been a series of such measures;[3] and their scope was considerably enhanced as a result of the recommendations of the *Molony Report* in 1962,[4] especially the Trade Descriptions Act 1968 (TDA: see post, para 4.02), the Fair Trading Act 1973 (see post, para 4.18) and the consumer safety legislation (see post, para 4.31). It will be noticed that the statutory arrangements for the enforcement by public authorities of these strict liability offences have a substantial degree of similarity (see Chapter 28) and that the authorities can obtain injunctions to prevent continued infringement by minor offences (see post, para 28.03). Further, the consumer terrorist who announces, eg, that baby food has been spiked, may commit blackmail[5] or an offence under the Public Order Act 1986.[6] On the civil side, Molony led to a number of consumer protection statutes;[7] and there are also a number of mixed civil and criminal statutes.[8]

Nowadays, there is also an EU dimension to UK criminal law, designed to protect consumers. First, such UK laws must be compatible with the (general) provisions of the

---

[4.01]

1   See generally Cartwright (1996) 59 MLR 225; Thomas and Clarke, *Encyclopedia of Consumer Law*. For statistics on supplier convictions and consumer complaints, see the Annual Reports of the OFT.

2   Eg, *R v Morris* [1984] AC 320, HL (consumer switching price labels in self-service store): *R v Lambie* [1982] AC 449, HL (abuse of credit card). See also Phillips [1982] JBL 377; Leigh (1985) 48 MLR 167; Goode, *Consumer Credit Law and Practice*, Div IE, para 70.1 *et seq*; Law Commission, Consultation Paper on *Fraud and Deception* (1999, No 155),which would reverse the burden of proof.

3   Designed to regulate, eg, weights and measures (see post, para 4.24) and food and drugs (see post, para 4.26).

4   Report of the Committee on *Consumer Protection* 1962, Cmnd 1781. For a summary of its recommendations, see Harvey, *Consumer Protection and Fair Trading* (6th edn), pp 22–23.

5   Under s 21 of the Theft Act 1968. See *R v Telford* (1992) 13 Cr App R (S) 676, CA; and further, Smith and Hogan, *Criminal Law* (9th edn) 605–11.

6   Under ss 5(1) or 38. As to s 5(1), see the annotation in Current Law Statutes; and generally Smith and Hogan, *op cit*, p 750. As to s 38, see post, para 4.23.

7   On the civil law side, see SOGIT, SGSA, UCTA (see post, paras 12.01; 18.12).

8   See, eg, the CCA (post Chapter 5), CPA (post, para 17.23).

Treaty of Rome (see ante, para 1.03A), which may leave scope for challenge.[9] Second, as from 1992 the approximation drive (see ante, para 3.10) impinged increasingly on areas hitherto regulated only by UK statute, though this should be less noticeable here to the extent that it is imported by amendment of the relevant UK legislation (see ante, para 1.03A).

TRADE DESCRIPTIONS[1]

[4.02] Introduction. The Trade Descriptions Act 1968 grew out of, but is much wider than, the old Merchandise Marks Acts 1887–1953, which it repealed. Whereas the primary purpose of the Merchandise Marks Acts was to protect businessmen against the passing-off as theirs of goods made by others, the chief objective of the Trade Descriptions Act was the protection of consumers as against manufacturers and traders.[2] The legislation is intended to deter misleading statements in the business supply of goods and services to consumers by making such statements criminal offences[3] without affecting the civil rights of the parties.[4] However, it contains this major difference in treatment:[5] whereas there is strict criminal liability in relation to mis-statements made in the business supply of goods (see post, para 4.03), the criminal liability in respect of the business supply of services was not intended to be so strict (see post, para 4.17). Notwithstanding some unforeseen judicial interpretation making the latter liability stricter,[6] there is still pressure for statutory amendment to impose 'the full measure of strict liability' on supplies of services,[7] though this would already seem to have been achieved where a service is performed on the bailor's goods.[8] Meanwhile control of false and misleading pricing has been removed to other legislation (see post, para 8.09 *et seq*). Recently, it has become possible to have this legislation enforced by Stop Now Orders (see post, para 6.08).

---

9   Eg, Sunday trading (post, para 8.13); sex shops (post, para 6.02); and generally, Bentil (1992) 9 Tr L 23.

[4.02]

1   See generally Harvey and Parry, *Consumer Protection and Fair Trading* (6th edn), Chapter 12; Lowe and Woodroffe, *Consumer Law and Practice* (5th edn), Chapter 13; Bragg, *Trade Descriptions*.

2   For suggestions for reform, see the Methven Committee *Review of the 1968 Act* (1976, Cmnd 6628).

3   About half the convictions under this Act tend to be against the motor trade: see the OFT Annual Reports. For enforcement of this Act, see post, Chapter 28.

4   Section 35: see post, para 10.19. However, the power to make compensation orders (see ante, para 3.20) is fairly widely used in TDA cases.

5   It has been recommended that this distinction be removed by making them all offences of strict liability: the Methven Review (see above), paras 49, 105.

6   Principally in *Wings Ltd v Ellis* (set out post, para 4.17).

7   Bragg, *op cit*, p 171. Government action is promised: *Modern Markets: Confident Consumers* (1999, Cm 4410) para 3.19.

8   *Formula One Autocentres Ltd v Birmingham CC* [1999] RTR 195, DC (car service; some promised items not checked. *Held*: s 1 offence by garage).

False statements as to goods

Prohibition of false trade descriptions

[4.03] The key offences. The gateway provisions and principal offences to be found in the Trade Descriptions Act 1968 (TDA) are contained in s 1(1), which provides that:

Any person who, in the course of a trade or business –

(a) applies a false trade description to any goods; or

(b) supplies or offers to supply any goods to which a false trade description is applied;

shall, subject to the provisions of this Act, be guilty of an offence.

This section is designed to protect from the blandishments of errant traders both innocent private persons and innocent traders.[1] But it only applies to blandishments uttered in relation to '**goods**',[2] which expression probably does not include the price of goods;[3] nor does it include land. However, a false statement made in relation to the building of a house may amount to a supply of services within another TDA provision;[4] and such a statement made in respect of the contents of a built house may be within the above section as relating to goods.[5] There are entirely separate provisions designed to control the sale of houses by estate agents (see ante, para 3.03) and misdescription of houses by them.[6]

It will be observed that s 1(1) actually creates two distinct classes of offence of strict liability:[7]

(a) Applying a false trade description to goods (see post, para 4.04), eg, the offence of the actively unscrupulous;[8]

(b) Supplying goods to which a false trade description has been applied (see post, para 4.05), eg, the offence of culpable failure to check what another said.[9]

Of these two offences, the former is the more heinous and therefore non-excludable (see post, para 4.09) and subject to less statutory defences (see post, para 28.17). Notwithstanding that the former offence can be committed innocently,[10] its prosecution

---

[4.03]

1 See *R v Ford Motor Co Ltd* (set out post, para 4.08). *Contra* misleading pricing: see below.

2 See the definition in the TDA, s 39(1). Cf the SGA definition of goods: ante, para 2.02.

3 For offences in relation to false or misleading pricing, see post, para 8.09 *et seq*.

4 Under TDA, s 14 (see post, para 4.15): see *Beckett v Cohen* [1973] 1 All ER 120, DC; and further the TDA Review (1976, Cmnd 6628), para 90. What of a meal in a restaurant?

5 Eg, fitted carpets sold with a house. What if the carpets are described as 'prizes' or 'gifts' (see ante, para 2.08)? For fixtures and fittings, see post, para 25.23.

6 An offence is provided by the Property Misdescriptions Act 1991, s 1, which also grants power to make regulations.

7 See post, para 4.04. This may lead to some harsh results. What about the mechanic who innocently replaces a faulty odometer?

8 *Per* Lawton LJ in *R v Hammerton Cars Ltd* [1976] 3 All ER 758 at 765, CA.

9 *Per* Woolf LJ in *Lewin v Fuell* (1991) 10 Tr LR 126, at 128, DC. For s 6, see post, para 4.05.

10 Eg, *Clode v Barnes* [1974] 1 All ER 1166, DC (conviction of innocent partner with no knowledge or means of knowledge); and see post, para 4.09.

tends to be reserved for cases of dishonesty.[11] There are provisions allowing for substitute prosecution of the person really at fault (see post, para 28.11–12).

Both classes of offence are limited by a number of common requirements (see post, para 4.03A).

[4.03A] The common ingredients. Both principal offences (see ante, paras 4.03) are limited by all the following requirements:

(a) There must be a **false trade description** (see post, paras 4.06–08).

(b) That false trade description must be **applied** to goods (see post, para 4.04).

(c) The primary offence must be committed by a defendant '**in the course of a trade or business**', which apparently includes the professions.[1] So, private transactions are excluded *per se*,[2] though they may be caught indirectly, as where a private seller applies a false trade description and his buyer (a dealer) commits an offence by sub-selling under the same description: the private seller may be prosecuted under s 23 (see post, para 28.12). There are some doubts over unincorporated associations.[3] However, where the defendant has a business, the offence does not need to be part of the primary activity of that business.[4] Thus in *London Borough of Havering v Stevenson*:[5]

> The operator of a car-hire business usually sold vehicles for which he no longer had a use in his business. The odometer having under-represented the mileage in one such sale, he was held to have committed an offence under s 1(1)(b) because such sales were an integral (though secondary) part of the business.

On the other hand, in *Davies v Sumner*:[6]

> A self-employed courier purchased a car and used it almost exclusively in his business. When sold by the courier in part-exchange, the car had a false odometer reading. It was held that the courier had not committed an offence under s 1(1)(a).

Their Lordships had little difficulty in distinguishing the *Stevenson* case: whilst denying that the regularity of sales of stock-in-trade are necessarily required by the provision, they pointed out that this was the first such sale by the courier of his business equipment and would not necessarily be repeated.[7]

---

11 Bragg, *Trade Descriptions*, pp 6–7.

[4.03A]

1 *Roberts v Leonard* [1995] Tr LR 536, DC. As to the NHS, see Bragg, *Trade Descriptions*, p 52.

2 *Blackmore v Bellamy* [1983] RTR 303, DC; and see Bragg, *ibid*, pp 59–60. Cf post, paras 4.19; 14.04; and generally Holgate [1984] JBL 263; Stephenson, *Criminal Law and Consumer Protection*, pp 3–6.

3 As to a member buying from an association, see *John v Matthews* [1970] 2 All ER 643, DC (doubted by Bragg, *op cit*, note 1, pp 62–63). As to indirect offences, see Dixon (1994) 13 Tr LR 297.

4 As to supply by a business agent (even without commission), see *Kirwin v Anderson* (1992) 11 Tr LR 33, 156 JP 301, DC (discussed 9 Tr L 151, at 152–53). For discussion of the situation where the defendant is not otherwise trading, see Bragg, *op cit*, note 1, pp 57–62.

5 [1970] 3 All ER 609, [1970] 1 WLR 1375, DC.

6 [1984] 3 All ER 831, [1984] 1 WLR 1301, HL. *Devlin v Hall* [1990] RTR 320, DC (D prosecuted in respect of first of several sales: acquittal criticised by comparison with the test in civil cases (see post, paras 14.04; 18.18) by Dobson in [1991] JBL 68).

7 Lord Keith (p 834) envisaged that a 'one-off adventure in the nature of trade' might fall within s 1(1); but he added that 'the occasional sale of some worn out piece of shop equipment would not fall within the enactment'. As to reform, see Bragg, *op cit*, note 1, p 64.

(d) That offence must be committed by a **'person'**, that is, personally, even if he is an employee (see post, para 28.08); and in the last case an offence may also be committed by his employer (see post, para 28.10).

(e) That offence can only be committed in relation to an **actual supply** of goods. Thus, the mere issue of an inaccurate test certificate in relation to goods will not amount to the offence; but, it may do so if the certificate is issued in connection with the supply of goods.[8] Further, mere preparatory acts showing only an intention to apply a trade description to goods is insufficient, though the description does not need to be uttered contemporaneously with the supply.[9] Once it has been shown that the trade description has been made in relation to a supply of goods, it is unnecessary to prove either dishonesty by the defendant or that anybody has actually been deceived. As to what amounts to a supply, see post, para 4.05. As to attempts to disclaim, see post, para 4.09.

(f) The prohibited acts must involve statements made to induce the customer to **enter** into the transaction relating to the supply contract for the goods:[10] it is insufficient that the customer returns the goods and the statement is then made to pacify him.[11] On the other hand, the offence can be committed by either transferor or transferee. In *Fletcher v Budgen*:[12]

> In negotiating the purchase of a car from a private seller, a car dealer stated that the car was only fit for scrap. He was then able to buy it for £2, repair it, and sell it at a large profit. Held: the car dealer committed an offence under s 1(1)(a).

[4.04] Applying a false trade description to goods. For a s 1(1) offence to be committed, a false trade description must be applied to goods at the moment of supply, whether or not by their supplier. This notion of applying is widely defined by s 4(1) as follows:

(1) A person applies[1] a trade description to goods if he –

    (a) affixes or annexes it to or in any manner[2] marks it on or incorporates it with –

        (i) the goods themselves or

        (ii) anything in, on or with which the goods are supplied,[3] or

---

8   *Wycombe Marsh Garage Ltd v Fowler* [1972] 2 All ER 248, DC (inaccurate diagnosis of tyre defect led to refusal of an MOT certificate); *Roberts v Leonard* (above; veterinary certificate wrongly issued in respect of calves not inspected to allow their export).

9   *R v Haesler* [1973] RTR 486, CA. As to advertisements, see post, para 8.07.

10 *Norman v Bennett* [1974] 3 All ER 351, DC. It would appear that the test is wider than under s 13 of the SGA (see post, para 13.11): Dobson [1990] JBL at 436–37.

11 *Wickens Motors (Gloucester) Ltd v Hall* [1972] 3 All ER 759, DC. But compare the offence under s 14, which may be committed by statements made after the supply of services: see post, para 4.15; and Stephenson, *op cit*, pp 9–10.

12 [1974] 2 All ER 1243, [1974] 1 WLR 1056, DC (criticised in 141 NLJ at 890 and 897).

[4.04]

1   For application by advertisement (s 5), see post, para 8.07.

2   This would appear to include attempts to disguise defects by repair (being a positive statement), but not sale of goods which another has so repaired because that would impose criminal liability for silence: see post, para 4.07.

3   *Swithland Motors v Peck* [1991] RTR 322, DC (goods themselves: odometer). Paragraph (a) will include statements made on any label, packaging container or instructions: *Haringey LBC v Piro Shoes* [1976] Crim LR 462 (label on shoes); *R v Ford Motor Co Ltd* (set out post, para 4.08 – order form).

(b) places the goods in, on or with anything which the trade description has been affixed or annexed to, marked on or incorporated with, or places any such thing with the goods;[4] or

(c) uses the trade description in any manner likely to be taken as referring to the goods.[5]

Of particular significance is s 4(2): whilst the old Merchandise Marks Acts probably applied only to written misdescriptions, the TDA clearly extends to oral misdescriptions by either seller or buyer.[6] Nor need the speaker be a party to the contract for the supply of goods. Thus, in *Fletcher v Sledmore*:[7]

D was a repairer of, and dealer in, cars. D sold a car to another dealer, X, on the basis that the car would remain on D's premises for repair. P, whom D knew to be a possible purchaser, was brought to D's premises to inspect the car; and D told P that the engine was all right. P, having purchased the car, found the engine to be defective. Held: D was guilty of the offence of applying by means of an oral statement a false trade description to the car.

One particularly common case is where the trade description is actually put forward by the transferee. To meet this case, s 4(3) provides:

(3) Where goods are supplied in pursuance of a request in which a trade description is used and the circumstances are such as to make it reasonable to infer that the goods are supplied as goods corresponding to that trade description, the person supplying the goods shall be deemed to have applied that trade description to the goods.

The effect of this was considered in *Shropshire County Council v Simon Dudley Ltd*:[8]

The Council put out a specification for tender of a fire engine. On this basis, SD made the successful tender; but subsequently the parties agreed to amend the tender. The fire engine supplied complied neither with the original specifications, nor with the agreed modifications. The Divisional Court held that both the original and amended specification were trade descriptions and SD was convicted of offences under s 1(1)(b) in relation to both of them.

In relation to s 4(3), Phillips LJ pointed out that it was 'designed to cover the situation where the supplier made no express application of a trade description to goods, but made an *implicit trade description* by supplying them pursuant to a request for goods of their description' (p 81). As to the original specification, his Lordship had no difficulty in applying s 4(3), saying that the test was a simple test of fact and did not depend on whether or when the trade description became a term of the contract (p 79). In also bringing the modification within s 4(3), Phillips LJ admitted to a slight extension of its literal meaning; but he held that, where 'the trade description used in the original request was varied by a subsequent request, and the goods were supplied in circumstances such

---

4   Eg, *Roberts v Seven Petroleum and Trading Co* [1981] RTR 312, DC. Cf *Donnelly v Rowlands* [1971] 1 All ER 9, DC.

5   'Uses' is very wide: it presumably extends to a retailer just displaying in his window a poster which may be taken as a trade description of stock on the premises: see Lawson, *Advertising Law*, p 206.

6   'An oral statement may amount to the use of a trade description': s 4(2). Eg, *Fletcher v Budgen* (set out ante, para 4.03A). There is a shorter time-limit for prosecutions in respect of an oral trade description (s 19(4)): see post, para 28.07.

7   [1973] RTR 371, (1973) 71 LGR 179, DC.

8   (1997) Tr LR 69, DC (no s 24(2) notice was served: see post, para 28.14).

as to make it reasonable to infer that they correspond to the description as varied, the person supplying the goods had to be deemed to have applied to the goods the trade description as varied' (p 80). In this case, the Council had originally commenced a civil action and only later initiated a prosecution: Phillips LJ regretted the prosecution, on the grounds that the facts were not within the mischief at which the Act was aimed (p 82); but Hooper J was in no doubt that s 1(1) offences extended to express promises,[9] even as to the future.[10]

[4.05] Supplying or offering to supply goods. It is now settled that s 1(1)(b) creates two separate offences in respect of goods to which a false trade description is applied.

1   *Supplying goods*,[1] eg, selling a vehicle on which another has replaced the odometer. In *Miller v FA Sadd and Sons Ltd*:[2]

> D had made a successful tender to supply to the schools of a local authority such fruit and vegetables as might be ordered at the prices then quoted in the fruit trade journal. In response to an order, D supplied the fruit and vegetables to a particular school together with invoices quoting a higher price than those obtaining in the trade journal.

The court held that no offence had been committed under s 1(1)(b): D's tender was a standing offer; and each order by the authority an acceptance, and hence, the court said, an actual supply.[3] Each invoice was merely a post-contract record of price which could not amount to a trade description (see post, para 4.06).

2   *Offering to supply*. This expression was deliberately given a wide meaning by s 6, which laid down that:

> A person exposing goods for supply or having goods in his possession for supply shall be deemed to offer to supply them.

Thus to facilitate enforcement, the Act has made it unnecessary to prove an actual offer to supply,[4] or even exposure for supply at business premises.[5] It is sufficient if the goods are in the defendant's possession in a stockroom. The result is that the *prima facie* offence may be committed very early in the negotiations,[5] so reducing the scope for disclosure (see post, para 4.09).

Note that the supplier of the goods does not himself need to apply the trade description to commit an offence under s 1(1)(b), though the offence overlaps with s 1(1)(a) insofar as the supplier himself does so.[6] Thus, in a typical case a retailer

---

9   At 74–75. This clearly comprehends express and logically implied terms (see post, paras 11.07; 11.10); but does it extend to the statutorily implied terms (see post, para 11.11)?

10   At 72. Compare the s 14 offences, where the courts have confined the offence to promises of existing fact: see Milne (1997) 113 LQR 383; and post, para 4.15.

[4.05]

1   This will comprehend sale, hire and hire-purchase: *Cahalne v Croydon LB* (1985) 4 Tr L 199, DC. It has also been held to cover part-exchange: *Davies v Sumner* (set out ante, para 4.03A). Does it cover 'free gifts' (see post, para 8.18) or prizes (see post, para 8.15) or supply under NHS prescription (see ante, para 1.07)? See Bragg, *Trade Descriptions*, p 18. Cf 'supplying' in the CPA: see post, para 4.34.

2   [1981] 3 All ER 265, DC. See also *Formula One Autocentres Ltd v Birmingham CC* [1999] RTR 195, DC (car service; some promised items not checked. *Held*: s 1 offence by garage).

3   But in the uncited case of *Rees v Munday* [1974] 3 All ER 506, DC, it was held that 'supplied' in s 1(1)(b) refers rather to delivery.

4   A window display is sufficient. Cf *Fisher v Bell* [1961] 1 QB 394, DC.

5   *Stainthorpe v Bailey* [1980] RTR 7, DC (upon mere inspection of car at dealer's home). As to 'expose for sale', see post, para 4.27.

6   *Telford and Wrekin Council v Jordan* [2001] 3 CL 110, DC; see ante, para 4.04.

commits a s 1(1)(b) offence in supplying goods to which a manufacturer has applied a trade description, perhaps in an advertisement (see further post, para 8.07). In recognition that the retailer has here committed a less heinous offence than if he himself had applied the trade description, the Act allows him a wider range of defences (see post, para 28.17); and it has been decided that the offence has only been committed where the supplier knows of the trade description,[7] though he does not need to be aware of its falsity.[8] Can the offence be committed by a retailer who has simply run out of the advertised goods?[9]

False trade description

[4.06] A trade description. The TDA continues the policy of the previous Acts in that it provides an exhaustive list of those matters which are to be regarded as part of the trade description.[1] Section 2(1) provides:

> A trade description is an indication, direct or indirect, and by whatever means given, of any of the following matters with regard to any goods or part of goods, that is to say:[2]

(a) 'Quantity, size or gauge' (see further TDA, s 2(3)). Compare the undertakings as to quantity: see post, para 13.03 *et seq*. An average weight (see post, para 4.25) is not a trade description.[3]

(b) 'Method of manufacture, production, processing or reconditioning', eg, 'immaculate'; 'in excellent condition throughout'; 'home-grown'; 'rust-proof'; 'free range'; 'organic'.

(c) 'Composition'.[4]

(d) 'Fitness for purpose, strength, performance, behaviour or accuracy'.[5]

(e) 'Any physical characteristics not included in the preceding paragraphs', eg, misdescriptions as to components, such as a car being 'fitted with disc brakes' or having a 'tool-set'. Does it apply to garment washing instructions?

---

7   *Cottee v Douglas Seaton (Used Cars) Ltd* (set out post, para 28.17).

8   *Tarleton Engineering Co v Nattrass* [1973] 3 All ER 699, DC.

9   See Bragg, *op cit*, note 1, p 20; and post, para 4.16. What about switch selling?

[4.06]

1   *Cadbury v Halliday* (set out post, para 4.08). But see TDA, s 3(3): post, para 4.08. However, trade descriptions do extend to approval marks made under the Road Traffic Act 1988, s 80: see post, para 4.37.

2   In relation to livestock, see also TDA, s 2(2). It has been claimed that most of the difficulties have concerned statements involving an element of subjectivity: Stephenson, *Commercial Law and Consumer Protection*, pp 11–12. See generally Bragg, *Trade Descriptions*, pp 22–23.

3   Weights and Measures Act 1985, s 48(4). For overlap with the 1985 Act, see TDA, s 22(2): see post, para 28.16.

4   *British Gas Corp v Lubbock* [1974] 1 All ER 188, DC (discussed by Lawson, *Advertising Law*, 217–18); *Queensway Discount Warehouses v Burke* [1985] CLY 3112, DC (knock-down goods pictured assembled). Cf the undertakings as to quality: see post, para 13.09 *et seq*. As to the composition of textiles, see regulations made under ECA 1972, s 2(2); and see also TDA, ss 8 and 9 (see post, para 4.10).

5   Eg, *Sherratt v Geralds, the American Jewellers Ltd* (1970) 68 LGR 256, DC ('Divers watch', 'waterproof'). For civil liability for breach of the undertaking as to fitness, see post, para 14.07 *et seq*. Could s 2(1)(d) extend to misleading instructions for assembly or use (see post, para 18.29)? For a pessimistic view generally, see Stephenson, *op cit*, note 2, pp 12–14. As to unroadworthy vehicles, see OFT, 1987-AR, 20; and post, paras 4.07 and 4.37.

(f) 'Testing by any person and results thereof', eg, 'MOT Certificate'; and see post, para 8.03. As to the information on an MOT certificate, see ante, para 4.03A.

(g) 'Approval by any person or conformity with a type approved by any person', eg, compliance with a British Standard (as to which, see ante, para 3.08). It also overlaps with TDA, ss 12, 13 (see post, para 4.10). Non-existent standards are caught by s 3(4).[6]

(h) 'Place or date of manufacture, production, process or reconditioning'.[7] This overlaps with the special provisions in relation to imported goods, see post, para 4.10.[8]

(i) 'Person by whom manufactured, produced, processed or reconditioned'.[9] What about own-brand goods; or goods described generally by a manufacturer's name, eg, biro, hoover? In respect of counterfeit goods (see also post, paras 8.05; 13.11), there are suggestions that this may not be an entirely appropriate form of control.[10]

(j) 'Other history, including previous ownership or use'. In respect of motor vehicles, common complaints include the clocking of odometers or vehicles described as 'new'.[11]

Section 2(1) is discussed below (post, para 4.07), except for the special rules for advertisements (see post, para 8.07). As to misleading pricing, see post, para 8.09 *et seq*.

[4.07] To some extent the concept of a trade description is wider than 'direct or indirect' indications as to listed matters (see ante, para 4.06), extending to include anything likely to be taken as an indication of them (s 3(3): set out post, para 4.08). Thus, it is well-established that an odometer reading is an indirect trade description;[1] and the widespread practice in the motor trade of winding back odometers ('clocking') has led to attempts to disclaim odometer readings (see post, para 4.09). Nevertheless, despite the generous wording of the Act, the courts have insisted that there will be no offence without a positive statement: this will avoid criminal liability for silence[2] and usually also for breach of express promises as to the future and implied promises.[3] With regard to express statements, mere puffs are probably outside the statute (see post, para 4.08), but not promises as to present facts. In *Denard v Smith*:[4]

---

6 See post, para 4.08. See also the Hallmarking Act 1973, s 1; Video Recordings Act 1984, s 14.

7 *Routledge v Ansa Motors* (1979) 123 Sol Jo 735, DC (date of manufacture).

8 What about 'Cheddar cheese'? See also Anglo-Portuguese Commercial Treaty Acts 1914 and 1916 (port wine); Scotch Whisky Act 1988.

9 *Roberts v Severn Petroleum and Trading Co* [1981] RTR 312, DC (other petrol sold from an Esso station).

10 For civil claims in respect of passing off, see post, para 17.17. As to representations that goods have been made by disabled persons, see post, para 8.13. See generally Bragg, *op cit*, note 2, pp 33–35.

11 Car owned by a leasing company described as having had 'one owner': see post, paras 4.07–08.

[4.07]

1 Within s 2(1)(j): *Tarleton Engineering Co v Nattrass* [1973] 3 All ER 699, DC; *R v Hammerton Cars Ltd* (set out post, para 4.09).

2 *Per* Widgery LCJ in *Cottee v Douglas Seaton (Used Cars) Ltd* [1972] 3 All ER 750 at 757a, DC. This supports the civil law rule *caveat emptor*: as to which, see post, para 15.22. Cf misrepresentations: see post, para 11.01. For negotiations to require mileage statements, see OFT, 1987-AR, 20.

3 *R v Lloyd* [1976] CLY 2472 (express warranty as to future performance). Except insofar as they amount to promises as to present facts (see s 2(1)(d)), it follows that the concept of trade descriptions does not extend to implied terms (see post, Chapters 12–15): *per* Bridge J in *R v Ford Motor Co Ltd* (set out post, para 4.08), at 491j–492a. It has been recommended that it remain so: Review of the TDA (1976, Cmnd 6628) paras 140–45. As to false implications of endorsement, see post, para 8.03.

4 (1991) 10 Tr LR 86, DC.

Dixons, an electrical retailer, advertised at the point of sale a computer package with certain specified computer games software. When the specified software was out of stock, Dixons continued to sell the package with different games without taking any steps to alert customers to that fact. Dixons and their manager were charged with an offence under s 1(1)(b).

The defence argued that the computer was accurately described and there was an intention to deliver the advertised software package at a later date, unless customers could be persuaded to accept substitute games, so that at most there was only a breach of promise to supply the software with the computer. However, the Divisional Court held that the advertisement (see generally post, para 8.07) was to supply the computer and software as a package; that this amounted to a broken trade description; and that Dixons must have known that the software package was out of stock and therefore could not rely on the due diligence defence (see post, para 28.15). On the other hand, it seems that, if all the advertised goods (computer and software) had been sold out, Dixons would not have committed an offence.[5]

Whilst the court is looking for a direct or indirect indication of one of the listed matters of fact, the test is objective: the Act does not extend to subjective statements, eg, of worth or value; but it does not matter if a particular consumer is not misled when an ordinary consumer would be. Thus, in *Holloway v Cross*:[6]

> In 1978 a dealer bought a 1973 Triumph car whose odometer read 716 miles. A prospective customer asked the car's true mileage. The dealer truthfully replied that he did not know but gave a written estimate of 45,000 miles. The car had actually done 73,000 miles.

The dealer's conviction for supplying a car to which a false trade description had been applied (see ante, para 4.05) was upheld on the basis that his estimate was an indirect indication of mileage by way of opinion.[7]

In concentrating on a list of matters which may amount to trade descriptions, it may be regretted that s 2 did not expressly mention goods described as 'new', an expression capable of a number of meanings.[8] There is also power to exempt goods sold for export (s 32); and the Act itself deems not to be trade descriptions certain descriptions properly made[9] under statutes relating to food and drugs[10] and some other cases.[11] Finally, it is for

---

5   *Robins and Day Ltd v Kent CC* [1996] CLY 1168, DC.

6   [1981] 1 All ER 1012, [1981] RTR 146, DC. See also *Cadbury v Halliday* (set out post, para 4.08); *Furniss v Scott* [1973] RTR 314, DC (actual private purchaser aware car not 'mechanically superb' as described); *R v Veys* (1993) 137 SJ 785 (football club coat of arms).

7   It may be that the same view would not be taken of the same words spoken to a trade purchaser: see *Norman v Bennett* [1974] 3 All ER 351, DC. What of a DIY enthusiast? Cf the civil law dichotomy between misrepresentations and terms: see post, para 11.02.

8   Eg, meaning first retail sale, or current model, or new as opposed to old, used, damaged or second-hand. See Bragg, *Trade Descriptions*, pp 37–41; Andrew [1996] Tr LR 284; and post, para 4.08. As to the civil law, see post, para 13.11.

9   But if the description is not properly used within the statutes, there may be an offence under the TDA: *R v Inner London Justices ex p Wandsworth LBC* [1983] RTR 425; *Benfall Farm Produce v Surrey CC* [1983] 1 WLR 1213, DC.

10 Section 2(5), as amended by the following: (a) as to food, see post, para 4.27 *et seq*; (b) as to drugs, see post, para 4.29; and (c) as to safety (see below).

11 Section 2(4), as amended by the following: (a) as to agriculture, see the Agriculture Act 1970, and the European Communities Act 1972, Scheds 3 and 4; and (b) as to safety, see the CPA (see post, para 4.32 *et seq*).

consideration whether it might not be more satisfactory to replace the specific list approach with a general misdescription clause.[12]

[4.08] Falsity. The *Molony Report* did not intend that every inaccurate statement relating to a supply of goods should amount to a trade description (Cmnd 1791, para 634): mere statements of opinion of the character of a 'trade puff' were to remain outside the Act;[1] and there should only be an offence where the error was 'of such substance that it could fairly be regarded as capable of inducing a purchase'.[2] Parliament attempted to capture this distinction in s 3(1), which provides that:

> A false trade description is a trade-description which is false to a material degree.

Frequently, the issue of falsity will turn on the exact words used and the context in which they are used,[3] in which connection any disclaimer may be relevant (see post, para 4.09); and the court is not interested in whether the bargain is a fair one overall.[2] The words 'material degree' were considered by the Court of Appeal in *R v Ford Motor Co Ltd*:[4]

> A car manufactured by F was damaged whilst in the care of forwarding agents. It was repaired and supplied to the dealer as a 'new car'. Held: the damage was sufficiently limited and repairs sufficiently perfect for the car still to be a 'new car'.

Thus, it seems that 'material' relates to the degree of deception and that the test will usually be whether an ordinary man will be deceived, eg, whether a trade term has acquired general usage.[5] Section 3 then seeks to plug three possible loopholes as follows:

1　*The literally true, but misleading, statement*. Section 3(2) provides that:[6]

> A trade description which, though not false, is misleading, that is to say, likely to be taken for such an indication of any of the matters specified in section 2 of this Act as would be false to a material degree, shall be deemed to be a false trade description.

The effect of this subsection is illustrated by the attitude of the courts to disclaimers (see post, para 4.09) and has been held to include the situation where a car which had

---

12　This suggestion was rejected by the Review of the TDA (above), which instead suggested a new order-making power (paras 119–39). As to the difficulty with vague and meaningless claims, see *Modern Markets: Confident Consumers* (1999, Cm 4410) para 3.16.

[4.08]

1　Eg, *Cadbury Ltd v Halliday* (see below); 'best on the market'; and see Bragg, *Trade Descriptions*, p 43. But for some cases which seem to bring puffs within the Act, see Bragg, p 27; and see s 3(3) (below).

2　*Furniss v Scholes* [1974] RTR 133, DC (car described as being in 'exceptional condition throughout').

3　Eg, *Donnelly v Rowlands* [1971] 1 All ER 9, DC (milkman using another's embossed bottles). Cf the *de minimis* rule: see post, para 13.12.

4　[1974] 3 All ER 489, [1974] 1 WLR 1200, CA: discussed by Harvey, *Consumer Protection and Fair Trading* (6th edn), pp 399–400; Lawson, *Advertising Law*, 214–17; and Bragg, *op cit*, note 1, pp 39–40, 44. See also *Simmons v Ravenshill* [1983] Crim LR 749, DC. *Distinguish Cottee v Douglas Seaton (Used Cars) Ltd* (set out post, para 28.17).

5　See *Chidwick v Beer* [1974] RTR 415, DC; Lawson, *Advertising Law*, 208, 212–13; and see Bragg, *op cit*, note 1, pp 44–45.

6　Eg, *Robertson v Dicicco* [1972] RTR 431, DC ('beautiful car'); *Chidwick v Beer* (above; car 'in exceptional condition'). But cf *Kensington and Chelsea (Royal) LBC v Riley* [1973] RTR 122, DC.

belonged to a leasing company was described as having had 'one previous owner',[7] though not that goods were 'new'.[8]

2   *The indirect indication.* At common law, 'a nod or a wink, or a shake of the head, or a smile' may amount to a misrepresentation.[9] However, according to s 3(3):

> Anything which though not a trade description, is likely to be taken for an indication of any of those matters and, as such an indication, would be false to a material degree, shall be deemed to be a false trade description.

In *Holloway v Cross*,[10] this was held to bring within the Act an 'estimate' given by a car dealer of the actual mileage and recorded as such on the invoice. Thus, s 3(3) may extend trade descriptions beyond the common law notion of misrepresentation, compare s 14(2)(a) (see post, para 4.15); injurious falsehood (see post, para 17.17). However, the courts have generally been cautious in applying the provision to indirect indications of trade descriptions. For instance, in *Cadbury v Halliday*:[11]

> Chocolate manufacturers (M) sought to take advantage of the fact that, following the replacement of purchase tax by VAT, they were able to supply more chocolate at the same price. Accordingly, M stamped the wrappers of their chocolate bars with the legend 'extra value', and were charged with an offence contrary to s 1(1)(b) of the TDA.

The Court held that M had not committed that offence, because 'extra value' was neither a trade description (see ante, para 4.06), nor likely to be taken as an indication of one under s 3(3); and that in any event the manufacturers had a good defence under s 23 (see post, para 28.12). In a later case, it was said that the distinction between s 3(2) and s 3(3) is between 'an indication which tells a lie about itself' (s 3(2)) and 'one which, whilst accurate on its face, misleads by its associations in the mind of the customer' (s 3(3)).[12]

3   *Non-existent standards.* Section 3(4) enacts that:

> A false indication, or anything likely to be taken as an indication which would be false, that any goods comply with a standard specified or recognised by any person or implied by the approval of any person shall be deemed to be a false trade description, if there is no such standard so specified, recognised or implied.

[4.09] Disclaimers.[1] It has been decided that, where a party is charged with applying a false trade description to goods (s 1(1)(a): see ante, para 4.04), he cannot escape conviction

---

7   *R v Inner London Justices ex p Wandsworth LBC* [1983] RTR 425, DC. See also *Surrey CC v Clark* (1992) 11 Tr LR 147, DC.

8   *R v Ford Motor Co Ltd* (above); but compare *R v Anderson* (1987) *The Times*, 31 December, CA. Newness is not a specific requirement of s 2, though recommended by the *Molony Report* (1962, Cmnd 1781) para 636. Cf the civil law: see post, para 13.12.

9   *Per* Lord Campbell in *Walters v Morgan* (1861) 3 De GF and J718 at 723–24. For misrepresentation, see post, para 11.01.

10   [1981] 1 All ER 1012; [1981] RTR 146, DC.

11   [1974] 2 All ER 226; [1974] 1 WLR 649, DC. See also Lawson, *op cit*, note 4, pp 209–11; Stephenson, *Criminal Law and Consumer Protection*, 17; Bragg, *op cit*, note 1, p 42.

12   *Per* Taylor LJ in *Surrey CC v Clark* (above)

[4.09]

1   See generally Bragg, *Trade Descriptions*, Chapter 3; Roberts (1990) 7 Tr L 66.

by a disclaimer on the grounds that he cannot disclaim his own fraud;[2] but it would seem that this ban on disclaimers applies even where the description was made innocently.[3]

On the other hand, a party may disclaim liability where he is charged with supplying goods to which another has applied a false trade description (s 1(1)(b): see ante, para 4.05). The issue here is not quite the same as with the exclusion of civil liability (see post, para 18.04): for TDA purposes, constructive knowledge is insufficient and the issue has been said to be whether or not the disclaimer made before the goods are supplied is 'as bold, precise and compelling as the trade description itself'.[4] The point has most commonly arisen in connection with false odometer readings on motor vehicles. In *R v Hammertons Cars Ltd*:[5]

> The dealer (D) argued that, during the negotiations prior to the sale, the purchaser had been orally informed that the odometer readings were not guaranteed; and he further relied upon a printed 'guarantee' supplied at the time of delivery which included an express disclaimer. Held: if D wished to avoid conviction for 'clocking', he should have taken positive steps to negate the effect which such a reading might have upon the mind of a purchaser; and that neither a casual remark made in the course of oral negotiations nor the 'small print' in a contractual document were sufficient to save him from conviction under s 1(1)(b).

The TDA does not expressly permit disclaimers but there would seem to be two possible ways in which this judge-made rule may offer protection: first, it may be that it modifies the description that would otherwise relate to the goods;[6] or second, it may provide a defence once a trade description has been given.[7] There are important differences between the two views. Not only does the former view provide the supplier with a much wider protection because it is not limited to the terms of the defences;[8] but it also postulates that no offence has been committed so that nobody else, eg, the person who 'clocked' the car, can be charged under the by-pass provision in respect of that supply (see post, para 28.12).

---

2   *R v Southwood* [1987] 3 All ER 556, CA (odometer returned to zero). But see *Newham LBC v Singh* [1988] RTR 359, DC.

3   *May v Vincent* (1991) 10 TLR 1, DC (painting-auction catalogue); *Southend BC v White* (1992) 11 Tr LR 65, DC (damaged dashboard replaced: see 157 JP 294). For an unusual case, see *R v Shrewsbury Crown Court ex p Venables* [1994] CLY 524, DC.

4   *Per* Widgery LCJ in *Norman v Bennett* [1974] 3 All ER 351 at 354a, DC. See also *Zawadski Sleigh* (below); *Holloway v Cross* (set out ante, para 4.07: 'estimate' overrode disclaimer); *Lewin v Fuell* (1991) 10 Tr LR 126, DC (being prepared to tell potential customers that the goods were fakes 'if they asked' was wholly inadequate). As to offences under s 6 (where there is no supply), see *Lewin v Fuell* (above; car boot sale: oral disclaimer too late).

5   [1976] 3 All ER 758, [1976] 1 WLR 1243, CA. See also *Waltham Forest LBC v TG Wheatley (Central Garage)* [1978] RTR 333, DC.

6   *Crook v Howells Garages Ltd* [1980] RTR 434 at 439, *per* Donaldson LJ; *Kent CC v Price* [1993] CLY 484, DC ('Brand copy'; decision affd by CA and described as 'counterfeiter's charter': see Whisson (1994) 13 Tr L 44); *Bury MBC v Real* [1994] CLY 523, DC; *R v Bull* [1996] CLY 1199, CA.

7   *Lewin v Fuell* (above). 'The disclaimer is not one that negatives the description, but one that says enough to put a potential purchaser on guard': Bragg, *op cit*, note 1, p 75. The disclaimer must then be proved by the defendant to comply with all the requirements of a defence: see post, paras 28.13; 28.17.

8   'A disclaimer' is not a defence at all in the strict sense of s 24(1), because a disclaimer is saying 'I am not making any representation at all': *per* Lane LCJ in *Wandsworth BC v Bentley* [1980] RTR 429 at 433H; and see Holgate (1990) 154 LGR at 571; Harvey and Parry, *Consumer Protection and Fair Trading* (6th edn), p 395.

Presumably because of the easy profit to be made from mis-stating a vehicle's mileage (the price being normally based on that mileage) and the difficulty of detection, 'clocking' continues to be widespread. This has led to a revised Motor Code of Practice (see ante, para 3.13) and the suggestion that a misleading disclaimer might itself amount to a false trade description,[9] or an unfair term.[10] The Director of the OFT has tried to stem the flood by the exercise, or the threat of exercise, of his powers to demand Part III assurances or revoke credit licences (see post, paras 6.05; 6.09). The effect of generalised disclaimers prominently displayed in retail establishments remains problematic.[11] The Government have proposed to reduce the scope for clocking by mandatory recording of mileage on vehicle documents.[12]

[4.10/14] Other offences in connection with the supply of goods.

(a) *Definition and marking orders*.[1] The Government has power by statutory order[2] to assign definite meanings to expressions used in relation to goods. Where such meaning is assigned to an expression it shall be deemed to have that meaning when used in a trade description or in such other circumstances as may be specified in the order.[3] There is also power to require by order that goods be marked with or accompanied by any information[4] or instructions[5] and to regulate or prohibit the supply of non-complying goods.[6] Similarly, an order may be made that an advertisement contain or refer to any information relating to the goods (s 9).

(b) *Imported goods*. The United Kingdom has a long history of trying to distinguish imported goods in the UK market-place. The TDA contains both negative and positive provisions to this effect, though some of these provisions are overshadowed by EU rules (see ante, para 2.13). On the negative side, s 2(1)(h) makes it an offence to state falsely the origin of goods (see ante, para 4.06); the Act contains separate prohibitions against the importation into the UK of any goods bearing a false indication of origin (s 16) or an infringing trademark (s 17); and s 36 attempts to deal with the difficult problem of defining the origin of assembled goods.[7] On the positive side, attempts were made to specify that imported goods must be marked with their

---

9 See *Corfield v Starr* [1981] RTR 380, DC.

10 OFT, Unfair Contract Terms Bulletin No 4, p 32; and see generally post, para 11.12 *et seq*.

11 See *Zawadski v Sleigh* [1975] RTR 113, DC (auction-room notice insufficient); and generally Bragg, *op cit*, note 1, p 72. Insofar as it purports to disclaim civil liability a disclaimer might amount to an offence under another provision: see post, para 4.22.

12 OFT, 1999-AR 21.

[4.10/14]

1 Section 36(2). The OFT *Review of the TDA* (1976, Cmnd 6628) reported that these order-making powers were too tightly drawn for widespread use, and that they should be amended to introduce greater flexibility (paras 289–94).

2 For the manner in which Orders should be made, see s 38. This has been criticised for causing potential difficulties with EU Directives by the *OFT Review* (above), paras 295–98.

3 Section 7. There are similar powers to make definition orders in relation to the supply of services in s 15: see further post, para 4.15.

4 Eg, Trade Descriptions (Sealskin Goods) (Information) Order 1980, SI No 1150.

5 For the legal effect of instructions generally, see post, para 18.28.

6 Sections 8, 10. This power has been used to, eg, require origin-marking of specified classes of goods. The EEC has successfully sued the UK before the European Court on the grounds that such orders interfere with free trade: see ante, para 1.03A; and 138 NLJR 240.

7 Perhaps EU considerations have inhibited the use of powers under s 36(2) to make regulations: Bragg, *Trade Descriptions*, pp 31–32.

origin in both the TDA 1972 and orders made under s 8 of the 1968 Act; but the European Court forced revocation of the orders[8] and the 1972 Act was repealed after warnings by the Commission.[9]

(c) *False pricing* (see post, para 8.09).

(d) *False claims as to approval, etc.* In relation to the supply of both goods and services, it is an offence to give a false indication of royal approval or award (s 12) or to make a false representation that goods or services are of a kind supplied to any person.[10] It is argued that these anomalous offences should instead be subsumed under ss 2 and 14.[11]

False statements as to service

[4.15] Introduction. Contrary to the recommendations of the *Molony Report* that the offences should be restricted to representations made in connection with the supply of goods, the gateway s 14 of the Act set out to regulate the supply of services.[1] However, in recognition that this was a new development, liability was made rather less strict. Leaving aside for the moment both the state of mind in which the representor makes his statement and also the subject matter of the statement (see post, paras 4.16–17), it will be observed that the offences under s 14 are like those under s 1 in all the following matters: the statements must be made in the course of trade or business (see ante, para 4.03A); they must be false to a material degree (s 14(4): see ante, para 4.08); and liability may be avoided by an adequate disclaimer;[2] or by invoking the statutory defences even though, unlike the other provisions creating offences, s 14 is not expressed to be 'subject to the provisions of the Act'.[3] The nub of s 14 offences concerns 'statements made' as to the 'provision' of certain matters.

(a) *Statements*. Section 14 is primarily directed at 'statements', which expression is amplified by the following provision:[4]

> ... anything (whether or not a statement as to any of the matters specified in [s 14(1)]) likely to be taken for such a statement as to any of those matters as would be false shall be deemed to be a false statement as to that matter.

---

8   Section 13. Eg, see post, para 8.15. As contravening Art 28 [ex 30] of the Treaty of Rome (see post, para 8.06): *EEC v UK* [1985] 2 CMLR 259, CJEC.

9   CPA, s 48(2)(a). As to whether indirect attempts to preserve origin-marking under a new s 8 order effectively escapes the EU, see Bragg, *op cit*, note 7, pp 225–27.

10   Section 13. See, eg, post, para 8.15.

11   See Bragg, *op cit*, note 7, p 175.

[4.15]

1   Cmnd 1781 (1962) para 5. For TDA, ss 12 and 13, which apply to both goods and services, see ante, para 4.10. For implied terms as to services, see post, para 15.15; and as to codes of conduct, see ante, paras 3.11–14.

2   *Edward A Savory and Associates Ltd v Noel Dawson* (1976) 26.2, DC referred to in Cmnd 6628, App 3. Cf ante, para 4.09. See Bragg, *Trade Descriptions*, p 158.

3   *Sunair Holidays Ltd v Dodd* [1970] 2 All ER 410, DC; cited by Lord Hailsham in *Wings Ltd v Ellis* (set out post, para 4.17). For the defences, see post, Chapter 28.

4   TDA, s 14(2)(a); *R v Bevelectric* (1993) 12 Tr LR 19, CA (servicer's policy to say replacement motor required). Cf TDA, s 3(3): see post, para 5.08.

Unfortunately, the draftsman has not there made clear whether the test is subjective (likely to be taken by the addressee) or objective (likely to be taken by the reasonable man).[5] Further, the emphasis throughout s 14 is on false or misleading statements of existing fact, eg, that a service has been provided: promises as to opinion or future performance *prima facie* fall outside the section;[6] but they may constitute offences where the speaker does not currently have that opinion or intention.[7] This dichotomy between present and future has caused particular difficulty in relation to the advertising of holidays at hotels and timeshares not then completed: forecasts as to what the facilities at the hotel will be like when completed are not false trade descriptions, but an offence is committed in so far as the brochure suggests an existing fact, eg, that the hotel is already complete and conforming to those standards.[8] Nor is it any defence that the service is offered subject to contract, so that alteration is no breach of contract.[8]

(b) *Made.* In *Wings Ltd v Ellis* (set out post, para 4.17), the House of Lords explained that the expression 'statement made' does not necessarily import that a statement is communicated to anyone; but their Lordships affirmed that there will be an offence every time it is communicated to a different consumer.[9] Each communication is therefore a separate offence, allowing multiple prosecutions in respect of each statement 'made'. It has also been decided that the offence may be committed even though the statement is not made until after the parties have entered the contract.[10]

(c) *Provision.* The word 'provision' in s 14 is concerned only with the fact of providing services, etc.[11] The price at which they are provided is irrelevant for TDA purposes,[12] though it may amount to a pricing offence under the CPA (see post, para 8.09).

Subsequently, there have been introduced separate regulations to provide additional protection in respect of package holidays, a subject beyond the scope of this work.

[4.16] The subject matter. Section 14(1) refers to statements made about any of the following matters:

(i) the provision in the course of any trade or business of any services, accommodation or facilities;

(ii) the nature of any services, accommodation or facilities provided in the course of any trade or business;

---

5 See Bragg, *op cit*, note 2, pp 157–58.

6 *Beckett v Cohen* [1973] 1 All ER 120, DC (promise by builders as to completion date). *Contra* where it implies an assertion of existing fact: *R v Avro* (1993) 12 Tr LR 83, CA.

7 *British Airways Board v Taylor* [1976] 1 All ER 65, HL (double-booking, plane seats; see Cmnd 6628, para 106); *James Ashley v Sutton LBC* (set out post, para 4.16; and see the following note).

8 *R v Clarksons Holidays* (1972) 57 Cr App R 38, CA. Or a statement that a flight has been scheduled for a certain time: *R v Avro plc* (1993) 12 Tr LR 83, CA (subject to contract). See Lawson, *Advertising Law*, pp 222–25.

9 *R v Thompson Holidays Ltd* [1974] QB 592, CA. *Semble*, the statement may also be 'made' when the brochure is read by traders in the chain of distribution: *per* Lord Hailsham in *Wings Ltd v Ellis* [1985] AC at 285E, HL. See also *per* Lords Keith, Scarman and Brandon.

10 *Breed v Cluett* [1970] 2 QB 459, DC (NHRBC guarantee). *Contra* goods; see ante, para 4.03.

11 This extends to false statements about services already provided: *R v Bevelectric Ltd* (above: see [1993] JBL at 46–47; 156 JPN 759; 13 Tr LR 55).

12 *Newell and Taylor v Hicks* [1984] RTR 135, DC ('free' offer).

(iii) the time at which, manner in which or persons by whom any services accommodation or facilities are so provided;

(iv) the examination, approval or evaluation by any person of any services accommodation or facilities so provided; or

(v) the location or amenities of any accommodation so provided.

Whilst none of the expressions 'services', 'accommodation' or 'facilities' is fully defined in the Act, there is power to make definition orders (s 15):

(a) *Services*. The Act expressly extends the notion of 'services' to include the effect of any 'treatment, process or repair' (s 14(3)). However, it carefully distinguishes the provision of services, eg, waterproofing, from anything done under a contract of employment (s 14(4)). The expression 'services' has been interpreted fairly widely to include not only a false statement that a guarantee existed,[1] but also a misdescription of the terms of the supplier's guarantee;[2] a mail order house's ambiguous offer to supply goods on approval 'carriage free',[3] though not to promises of refunds;[4] and a s 14 offence is committed when the provider of a service falsely claims a relevant qualification.[5] On the other hand, it has been decided that a false claim as to the provision of a 'free gift' of goods with other goods cannot amount to the provision of a service within s 14(1) since the 'free gift' of goods is not a service.[6] However, a 'free gift' of services may be within the section. In *James Ashley v Sutton LBC*:[7]

> There was advertised at prices between £55 and £179 sales of a book containing a football pools formula with a money-back guarantee which the seller refused to honour.

It was held that there was both a sale of goods (the book) within s 1 (see ante, para 4.03) and a service (the formula) within s 14; and that the blanket refusal to honour the money-back guarantee constituted a s 14 offence (see ante, para 4.15).

(b) *Accommodation*. As with the other two expressions, s 14(1) allows accommodation claims to be made in a number of respects, eg, as to its nature or amenities.[8]

(c) *Facilities*. Whereas 'services' connotes doing something for somebody, a 'facility' enables him to do it for himself. The expression 'facilities' was considered by the Divisional Court in *Westminster City Council v Ray Allen (Manshops) Ltd*:[9]

> A retailer placed a newspaper advertisement indicating that goods were on sale in his London shop at a lower price than previously charged, when the higher price had been

---

[4.16]

1 *Breed v Cluett* [1970] 2 QB 459, DC (NHRBC guarantee).

2 *Bambury v Hounslow LBC* [1971] RTR 1, DC (second-hand car); doubted by Bragg, *Trade Descriptions*, p 169.

3 *MFI Warehouses Ltd v Nattrass* (set out post, para 4.17). Does it extend to statements of adherence to Codes of Practice (ante, para 3.11)? See also *R v Avro plc* (1993) 12 Tr LR 83, CA.

4 *Dixons Ltd v Roberts* (1984) 82 LGR 689, DC (retailer made a false claim that the difference would be refunded if goods could be bought more cheaply elsewhere). But see the CPA: post, para 8.09.

5 *R v Breeze* [1973] 2 All ER 1141, CA (architect); *R v Piper* [1995] CLY 1054, (master craftsman).

6 *Newell and Taylor v Hicks* [1984] RTR 135, DC. For the contractual effects of 'free gifts', see ante, para 2.08.

7 (1995) 14 Tr LR 350, DC (see Clayson (1995) 14 Tr LR 387; Cartwright [1996] JBL 58.

8 *Wings Ltd v Ellis* (set out post, para 4.17); *R v Thompson Holidays Ltd* [1974] QB 592, CA.

9 [1982] 1 All ER 771; [1982] 1 WLR 383, DC (criticised 45 MLR 711–12).

charged at his Leeds branch. He also displayed a sign outside his London shop saying 'Closing Down Sale' when in fact the sale was not a closing down sale and the retailer continued to trade at the shop.

The court held that the retailer had committed no offence in relation to his closure notice, as 'facilities' did not extend to shopping facilities. Ormrod LJ suggested that 'facilities' must be read *eiusdem generis* 'services' and 'accommodation', and Woolf J explained that the facts fell outside the mischief aimed at by the offence.[10] It seems unlikely that 'facilities' extends to the availability of goods, but that it would extend to free insurance[11] or willingness to accept credit cards by exhibiting the logo (see ante, para 2.27).

The problem of price claims in relation to services, accommodation and facilities are now dealt with by the CPA (see post, para 8.09).

[4.17] The representor's state of mind. According to s 14(1) it is an offence in the course of trade or business (see ante, para 4.03A) in relation to any of the matters there listed (see ante, para 4.16) for a person:[1]

(a) to make a statement which he knows to be false; or

(b) recklessly to make a statement which is false.

At one time, it was thought that this required *mens rea* for a s 14 offence; but that view has been shown to be too narrow.

(a) The expression 'make a statement which he knows to be false' was considered by the House of Lords in *Wings Ltd v Ellis*:[2]

> W Ltd, a holiday tour operator, mistakenly published a brochure describing certain accommodation in Sri Lanka as air-conditioned. In May 1981, W Ltd discovered the mistake and instructed all staff and agents to inform customers of the error. In 1982, a customer booked that holiday without being so informed. W Ltd did not plead any of the defences apparently available under the Act, but instead sought to show that they had not committed an offence under s 14.

The Divisional Court quashed the conviction under both paragraphs (a) and (b).[3] However, on appeal in respect of the s 14(1)(a) acquittal only, the House of Lords unanimously held that there might be a conviction where W Ltd had no knowledge of the falsity of the statement at the time of its publication,[4] but knew of its falsity at the

---

10 All ER at 775, WLR at 388B, criticised by Cartwright (1992) 9 Tr L at 3–5. As to whether such conduct would now be caught by the CPA, see post, para 8.09.

11 *Kinchin v Ashton* (1984) 148 JP 540, DC. See generally Cartwright, *ibid*; Bragg, *op cit*, note 2, pp 166–67.

[4.17]

1 It has been said that this creates two separate offences, which are not interchangeable: *per* Lords Wilberforce, Dilhorne, Simon, Edmund-Davies and Fraser in *British Airways Board v Taylor* [1976] 1 All ER 65, HL at 68, 71, 72, 74–75, 78. As to whose state of mind is relevant where the defendant is a corporation, see Cartwright [1997] JBL at 469–71; and generally post, para 28.10.

2 [1985] AC 272, [1984] 3 All ER 577, HL 2. As to the defences, see post, Chapter 28.

3 [1984] 1 All ER 1046, DC. As to s 14(1)(a), it was held that there had been created a 'result crime', which only occurs where a defendant fails to take any available opportunity to counteract the effect of publication.

4 As to constructive knowledge of falsity through a servant, see Bragg, *Trade Descriptions*, pp 62–63. Note that he does not need to know the statement has been 'made': see below.

time when the statement was read by the complainant.[5] On this reasoning, it would appear that there will still be an acquittal where a defendant has not become aware of the falsity of the statement by the time it is made.[6] However, the effect is to introduce semi-strict liability: D did not need to know that the statement was made, nor need he be dishonest, before conviction; but he was required to know that the statement was untrue.[7]

(b) 'Recklessly made a statement which is false'. By itself, this phrase might be thought to refer to a *Derry v Peek* test of dishonesty (see post, para 17.18). However, it is amplified by s 14(2)(b), which provides that:

> a statement made regardless of whether it is true or false shall be deemed to be made recklessly, whether or not the person making it had reasons for believing that it might be false.

Thus, a statement may be made 'recklessly' within s 14 whether or not there is any dishonest intent, so that the standard is much nearer to negligence.[8] In *MFI Warehouses Ltd v Nattrass*:[9]

> D advertised the sale by mail order of louvre doors on fourteen days' free approval, after which the price and carriage charges were payable. The advertisement also offered folding door gear on approval 'carriage free': D intended that the gear should be supplied only with the doors, and did not appreciate that the advertisement could be read so that the gear might be taken to be offered separately. Held: in refusing to supply the door gear alone carriage free, D recklessly committed an offence under s 14.

In this case, Lord Widgery said that it sufficed for conviction that the advertiser 'did not have regard to the truth or falsity of the advertisement, even though it cannot be shown that he was deliberately closing his eyes to the truth' (p 313. Cf *Derry v Peek* (see post, para 17.18); s 20 of the CPA (see post, para 8.09)). On the other hand, in *Wings Ltd v Ellis* the Divisional Court held that there was no offence committed under s 14(1)(b) because there was no evidence that any one or more of the natural persons who constituted the directing mind and will of W Ltd were reckless.[10]

Whereas it had originally been envisaged that s 14 would only impose *mens rea* liability (see ante, para 4.03) so that the general statutory defence (see post, para 28.13) would normally be ineffective,[11] that does not now appear to be the case.[12] Accordingly, once a semi-strict liability offence under s 14(1)(a) has been made out, the accused may plead the general statutory defence; but, where a *prima facie* s 14(1)(b) offence is shown, that will

---

5 'The subsection says not that it is an offence knowingly to make a false statement but that it is an offence to make the statement': *per* Lord Scarman at 295F. See also *per* Lord Hailsham LC at 289 who regretted his decision because of the absence of fault by W Ltd, and further (1985) 101 LQR 3. But see the criticism in (1985) 48 MLR 340; and (1991) 141 NLJ at 889.

6 *Coupe v Guyett* [1973] 2 All ER 1058, DC (sleeping partner).

7 Bragg, *op cit*, note 4, p 161.

8 Bragg, *op cit*, note 4, p 159. As to recklessness, see Smith and Hogan, *Criminal Law* (9th edn), p 60 *et seq*.

9 [1973] 1 All ER 762, DC; discussed in Lawson, *Advertising Law*, pp 219–20. See also *Dixons v Roberts* (1984) 82 LGR 689, DC.

10 Compare *Cowburn v Focus Television Rentals* [1983] Crim LR 563, DC; *Yugotours v Wadsley* (1989) 8 Tr LR 74, DC.

11 Eg, *Coupe v Guyett* (above). However, if s 14 is a pure *mens rea* offence, how can one say that he has exercised due diligence, etc (s 24)?

12 *Wings Ltd v Ellis* (above), which does not suggest how to overcome the *Coupe v Guyett* problem (above).

normally be inconsistent with the defence (see post, para 28.15). There is a proposal to make s 14 a straightforward strict liability offence (see ante, para 4.02).

FAIR TRADING

[4.18/21] Introduction. The Fair Trading Act 1973 (FTA) marks an entirely new departure in the field of consumer protection: the appointment of an officer of national status – the Director – backed by an adequate centralised Office of Fair Trading (OFT) with extensive new powers of intervention in the field of trade.[1] Whilst the Act had several principal objects (see ante, para 3.03), the present chapter is interested only in the consumer protection provisions, which are encompassed by Parts II and III of the Act. If the Director discovers a business activity which he considers to be detrimental to consumers, he is given the following powers:

1 *Undesirable practices*. Where he considers that the type of conduct is not, but should be, regulated the Director may initiate the process under Part II of the Act for the promulgation of a statutory order to deal with that conduct, which orders are enforced by the local authorities (see post, para 28.03). This power is circumscribed in the following respects: (1) the conduct must amount to a 'consumer trade practice' (s 13); (2) it must 'adversely affect the economic interests of consumers in the United Kingdom' (s 14(1)); and (3) be unfair within the meaning of s 17(2). In these circumstances, the Director was to refer the practice to the CPAC (see below), which may initiate a statutory instrument (ss 19–22), breach of which will be a criminal offence.[2] After an initial burst of enthusiasm in the use of this machinery[3] led to the promulgation of a number of statutory instruments (see post, para 4.22), the machinery fell into disuse and the CPAC was dissolved (see ante, para 3.04). Could it ever have done more than cope with yesterday's problems?

2 *Undesirable traders*. Where the type of conduct is already regulated by law, but a particular business is finding it worthwhile to break that law persistently, the Director may under Part III of the Act obtain a court order requiring the cessation of that activity (see post, para 6.06).

It has been pointed out that most of the existing consumer protection crimes are drafted very precisely in order to deal with specific mischiefs; and that this necessarily entails burdensome complexity, a risk of under-inclusion of unregulated abuses, anomalous distinctions and variations in enforcement.[4] Accordingly, it was suggested that it may be desirable to introduce an additional general statutory duty to trade fairly supported by codes of practice.[5] Subsequently, the Government have suggested amendment to give the

---

[4.18/21]

1   Part 1: see ante, para 3.03. The OFT is not specifically created or mentioned in the Act.

2   FTA, s 23. See further Chapter 28.

3   For the procedure by which it was intended to operate, see Macleod, *Consumer Sales Law*, Butterworths edn, 1989; and Harvey and Parry, *Consumer Protection and Fair Trading* (6th edn), pp 349–55.

4   It is claimed by the OFT that Part II of the FTA is of limited assistance in this regard because of the restrictive definition of consumer trade practices: *A General Duty to Trade Fairly* (1986), para 2.17.

5   OFT, *ibid*, para 5.11 *et seq*. See generally Dobson [1986] JBL 487; Circus (1986) 136 NLJ 948, 1043; Puttick (1986) 7 BLR 299; Borrie [1988] JBL at 123–26. Alternative suggestions to introduce into English contracts a general duty of good faith have now borne fruit in the UTCC Regulations (see post, para 11.12 *et seq*).

Secretary of State a new power by statutory order to specify that certain unfair practices should become criminal offences, eg, one-day sales,[6] as well as making improvements to Part III (see post, para 6.06).

[4.22] Statutory orders made under Part II.[1]

(a) *Restrictions on statements*. Whilst clauses purporting to limit or exclude the terms implied in favour of a consumer in a contract for the supply of goods are already avoided by statute (see post, Chapter 18), nevertheless they have continued to appear and to mislead consumers as to their rights.[2] Whilst this practice has subsequently been deemed unfair in 'consumer supply contracts',[3] the Restrictions on Statements Orders make it an offence to include any of the following types of clause in a 'consumer transaction'[4] for the supply of goods:[5]

(i) A term rendered void by s 6 of the Unfair Contract Terms Act 1977 or s 4 of the Trading Stamps Act 1964 (see post, paras 18.19; 15.17), whether that term operates by way of display at his business premises, advertisement, statement on the goods or their packaging, or in any invoice or receipt.[6] On the other hand, it is not an offence to exclude undertakings in those sections in favour of a business transferee; nor to exclude undertakings not referred to in those sections, eg, of a buyer to exchange goods on whim, or of a hirer to any of the implied terms granted by the SGSA, or any of the other exclusions rendered void by UCTA.[7]

(ii) A written statement of his rights furnished to the consumer which does not also refer to his inalienable statutory rights (Art 4), eg, an express guarantee of parts only, which would leave the consumer relying on his statutory rights as to the labour cost of any repair (see post, para 17.09). In a 'consumer supply', a failure to state adequately the consumer's statutory rights may also be an unfair term (UTCC reg 7: see post, para 11.13).

(iii) A statement on the goods or packaging of a business supply contract where that statement might be 'reasonably supposed' to be passed on to a consumer and does not refer to the consumer's inalienable statutory rights (Art 5). This was

---

6   *Modern Markets: Confident Consumers* (1999, Cm 4410) para 7.6.

[4.22]

1   For the text of the orders currently in force, see Thomas, *Encyclopedia of Consumer Law*, Part 2.

2   Eg, 'no cash refunds', 'credit notes only', 'sale goods may not be returned'. See generally, Borrie, *The Development of Consumer Law and Policy*, pp 49–50; OFT, 1983-AR, 14.

3   Under reg 7 (see post, para 11.13): OFT, Unfair Contract Terms Bulletin No 12, case 16.

4   Consumer Transactions (Restrictions on Statements) Order 1976 SI 1813 (as amended), Art 2(1). This definition is closely modelled on that of the concept of 'dealing as consumer' in s 12 of UCTA: see post, para 18.18.

5   These provisions comprehend transactions by way of sale, hp or a trading stamp, do not cover quasi-sales or simple hirings.

6   Article 3. Eg, *Hughes v Hall* [1981] RTR 430, DC ('as seen and inspected' held capable of interfering with legal rights). Compare *Cavendish-Woodhouse v Manley* (1984) 82 LGR 376, DC ('bought as seen'), discussed by Dobson [1984] JBL 500. See further Lowe and Woodroffe, *Consumer Law and Practice* (5th edn), paras 17.12–16.

7   For the implied terms granted by the SGSA, see post, para 15.12 *et seq*. For the other exclusions rendered void by the UCTA, see post, para 18.22 *et seq*.

intended to apply to manufacturer's guarantees which might otherwise foster the common presumption amongst consumers that the guarantee was somehow instead of his rights against the retailer.[8]

(b) *Mail order transactions*. This Order has been replaced by the Distance Selling Regulations (see post, para 8.17).

(c) *Business advertisements*.[9] In contracts for the supply of goods certain terms are implied only where the supply is made in the course of business (see post, para 14.04); and the practice had developed in some trades of advertising goods for sale in such a manner that there appeared to be a private sale, and hence misleading the consumer into believing that his contract did not contain these implied terms, eg, antique or car dealers. Additionally, it will be less obvious that the transaction is regulated by the Trade Descriptions Act (see ante, paras 4.03; 4.15). Accordingly, the Business Advertisements (Disclosure) Order provides that a person 'seeking to sell goods ... in the course of a business' shall not for that purpose publish an advertisement unless it is there made reasonably clear that the 'goods are to be sold in the course of a business'.[10] This offence may be committed without any resort to roguery[11] and should ensure that newspaper classified advertisements are properly categorised.

OTHER STATUTORY PROVISIONS

[4.23] Introduction. Apart from the TDA (see ante, para 4.02 *et seq*) and the FTA (see ante, para 4.18 *et seq*), there are many other statutory provisions which seek to protect consumers of goods by the imposition of strict criminal liability. Leaving aside consumer credit (see post, Chapter 5) and provisions relating to the seeking of business generally,[1] those dealt with in this chapter include the following: weights and measures (see post, para 4.24 *et seq*), food and drugs (see post, para 4.26 *et seq*) and other dangerous goods including motor vehicles (see post, para 4.31 *et seq*). Apart from these, there are a host of miscellaneous provisions including those relating to the following:[2] selling to children, eg, tobacco to persons under 16;[3] hallmarking;[4] energy consumption of motor

---

8 For manufacturer's guarantees, see post, para 17.09. For curbs on attempts by a manufacturer in such a guarantee to exclude his own liability, see post, para 18.26.

9 See generally Lowe and Woodroffe, *op cit*, note 6, paras 17.18–19; and further paras 8.19, 14.04.

10 1977 SI 1918, Art 2(1). It does not apply to advertisements of sale by auction or competitive tender, nor to some farm-gate sales: Art 2(3).

11 But it is normal only to charge this offence in conjunction with one under another of the major statutes considered in this chapter: Bragg, *Trade Descriptions*, p 58, note 31.

[4.23]

1 Eg, advertisement (see post, para 8.07), price displays (see post, para 8.08), false or misleading pricing (see post, paras 8.09–10), unsolicited goods (see post, para 8.18); circulars to minors (see post, para 8.33); age (see post, para 8.35).

2 See also the statutes mentioned later as rendering contracts illegal (see post, para 10.20) and those mentioned in the checklist in the *Encyclopedia of Forms and Precedents* (5th edn), vol 34, title Sale of Goods, paras 521–25.

3 Children and Young Persons Act 1933, s 7 (as amended). See *St Helens MBC v Hill* (1991) 11 Tr LR 94, DC. As to the general rule in contract law, see post, para 10.18.

4 Under the Hallmarking Act 1973; see *Chilvers v Rayner* [1984] 1 All ER 843, DC. This is the system for informing the public of the proportion of precious metal contained in alloys of gold, silver and platinum; see further Harvey, *Consumer Protection and Fair Trading* (6th edn), pp 284–85. The CA (see ante, para 3.08) has campaigning for the EU to adopt a Community-wide hallmarking system ([1992] 12 Which? 4); but the EU has so far rejected the idea: (1995) *The Times*, 31 March.

vehicles;[5] mock auctions (see post, para 10.11); trading stamps (see post, para 15.19); unlawful harassment of debtors (see post, para 24.24); discrimination in the supply of goods, facilities or services on grounds of sex,[6] race[7] or disability,[8] matters also relevant to credit licensing (see post, para 6.19); the sale of some kinds of wildlife;[9] tampering with retail goods;[10] sale of human organs;[11] and health and safety.[12]

Weights and measures

[4.24] General. From earliest times, Parliament has sought to protect both honest traders and consumers against the advantages conferred on unscrupulous traders by their giving short measure; and this included a system for ensuring that minimum weights were supplied, enforced locally.[1] However, from 1972 when we joined the EU (see ante, para 1.03A), there has also been a stream of Directives on the matter. As has been seen (see ante, para 3.10), early Directives in the consumer protection field tended to be very detailed and one of the areas covered was weights and measures.[2] Their main purpose was to require certain products to be sold by average quantity;[3] some pre-packed foods to be marked with an indication of quantity (see post, para 8.11); and to ensure that stated quantities can be relied upon as being accurate and not misleading. Moreover, as part of a Directive on price displays (see post, para 8.08), there were promulgated rules on unit pricing, that is, prices per kilogram, litre, etc (see post, para 8.08). Of course, these Directives overrule inconsistent UK provisions (see ante, para 1.03).

The two streams of rules on the subject have been brought together in the Weights and Measures Act 1985, which makes provision for their consolidation over a period of time by regulations, so enabling the UK government to introduce the EU aspects here slowly, and some would say, surreptitiously. The 1985 Act divides its operation between central and local government. The central government function is to set the primary and

---

5   Energy Act 1976; Passenger (Car Fuel Consumption Order 1996, SI 1486 (as amended), esp to meet EU Directive 93/116). For motor vehicles, see generally post, para 4.37.

6   Sex Discrimination Act 1975, s 29. See *Quinn v Williams Furniture* [1981] 1 CR 328, CA (credit facilities); *Gill v El Vino* [1983] QB 425, CA (service in bar); and as to credit scoring, see post, para 8.39. The Equal Opportunities Commission is campaigning for positive discrimination in favour of women.

7   Race Relations Act 1976, s 20. See OFT, *Vulnerable Consumers and Financial Services* (1999) para 600.

8   Disability Act 1995, ss 19–21. This extends to the provision of goods, facilities or services (s 19(2)), including banking, loans, credit or finance (s 19(3)(e)), eg, a blind loan applicant. See also OFT, *ibid*, para 500. A Code of Practice is planned.

9   Eg, Wildlife and Countryside Act 1981, s 6 (as amended); Endangered Species (Import and Export) Act 1976, s 4 and see the Control of Trade in Endangered Species (Enforcement) Regulations 1985, SI 1155 (eg, rhino horn): see (1989) *The Times*, 18 February.

10 Public Order Act 1986, s 38. This is intended to cover actual or claimed contamination of goods at the point of retail sale.

11 Human Organ Transplants Act 1989, s 1. As to offences by corporate officers, see s 4; and post, para 28.11.

12 Health and Safety Regulations are made under s 15 of the Health and Safety at Work Act 1974 (as amended). For Health and Safety Regulations relevant to this text, see Thomas, *Encyclopedia of Consumer Law*.

[4.24]

1   See generally, Harvey and Parry, *Consumer Protection and Fair Trading* (6th edn), pp 2–7, 455.

2   Eg, Average Quality Packaged Goods Directives 75/106, 76/211 (implemented by 1986 SI 2049: see below); Food Labelling Directive 79/112.

3   For an account of the complicated method by which the Directive determined average weights, see Harvey and Parry, *op cit*, note 1, pp 454–55.

other standards of goods (ss 8–10) and coinage,[4] and deal with matters such as the decimalisation of the currency[5] and metrication[6] and standardising of quantities of goods. For instance, central government will approve types of weighing and measuring machines and test prepacked goods at the point of packing or import (Parts II, III and V). However, the essence of the Act is to be found in the functions placed upon local authorities, which have to ensure that retailers 'use for trade'[7] only approved types of machine and also to test non-prepacked goods (see post, para 4.25).

As the law presently stands, much of the detail of the above law is found in Regulations and codes of practice (some with statutory force).[8] Presently, opponents of metrication ('the Metric Martyrs') are taking advantage of this legislative confusion to defy what on paper should be compulsory metrication of weights and measures on retail sales.[9] The UK Government hopes to improve the clarity of this branch of the law in due course;[10] and this could be achieved by statutory instrument under the Deregulation Act (see post, para 5.10).

[4.25] The local authority function: consumer protection offences. Under the Weights and Measures Act 1985 (see ante, para 4.24), the duty of local enforcement is placed upon the local authorities (see post, para 28.02). In particular, this relates to policing the use by retailers of weights and measures machines[1] for the supply of goods (Part IV). This last function is of considerable importance to consumers. It involves the creation of a number of strict liability offences (see below), whilst allowing a defaulting retailer to plead several defences.[2] For weights, measures, food and drugs, special defences are created with regard to reliance on false warranties.[3] To some extent, consumer vigilance as to how a retailer uses equipment regulated by the Weights and Measures Act (see ante, para 4.24) combined with the law of theft will serve to protect consumers from dishonest traders. However, Parts IV and V of the 1985 Act goes much further, providing *prima facie*[4] strict criminal liability as follows:

(a) *Selling goods by quantity*. The Act empowers the Secretary of State to impose by regulation requirements as to how particular goods (see Scheds 4–7) may be sold

---

4   See Part I of the 1985 Act; the Coinage Act 1971 (as amended); and Harvey and Parry, *op cit*, note 1, pp 443–44. For further discussion of the price of goods supplied, see ante, para 2.06.

5   See the Decimal Currency Acts 1967 (repealed) and 1969.

6   See the Units of Measurement Regulations of 1986, 1994 and 1995, implementing EU Directives: these regulations *pro tanto* overrule the provisions of the 1985 Act referring to imperial measurements. See further, Harvey and Parry, *op cit*, note 1, pp 458–59.

7   As to 'use for trade', see s 7, which effectively extends to all retail contracts for the supply of goods by quantity.

8   See the Weights and Measures (Packaged Goods) Regulations 1986. This incorporates the Code of Practical Guidance for Packers and Importers and the Manual of Practical Guidance for Inspectors.

9   The use of unapproved weighing or measuring machinery is an offence (s 17). Eg, *Steve Thorburn* (see (2001) *The Times*, 19 February; 10.4 (use of imperial measure). Convicted by High Court).

10   *Modern Markets: Confident Consumers* (1999, Cm 4410) para 3.11.

[4.25]

1   Or have in his possession for use: see *Bellerby v Carle* [1983] 2 AC 101, HL. Some of the requirements have been loosened under the deregulation initiative: 1999 SI 503; and see generally post, para 5.10.

2   For the enforcement provisions and defences, see post, Chapter 28.

3   See post, para 28.18. As to civil claims for breach of warranty, see post, para 11.06.

4   These offences are all subject to the statutory defences, which are considered in Chapter 28.

(s 22(1)) and to prescribe the manner in which such information is displayed.[5] In relation to goods sold loose, it contains alternative methods of satisfying the quantity provisions.[6] However, a more modern practice in many trades is to sell goods pre-packed: particularly with an eye to large-scale machine-packing, the Act therefore includes a system for average weights and measures.[7] 'Offering or exposing for sale' goods in breach of the above quantity rules will amount to a criminal offence.[8] Their pricing is dealt with later (see post, para 8.08).

(b) *Short weight.* According to s 28(1):

... any person who, in selling or purporting to sell any goods by weight or other measurement or by number, delivers or causes to be delivered to the buyer –

(a) a lesser quantity than that purported to be sold, or

(b) a lesser quantity than corresponds with the price charged, shall be guilty of an offence.

This offence is not confined to scheduled goods (see above), nor to retailers. Whilst not expressly so limited, this provision puts the primary liability in respect of goods that will be consumed by the public on the retailer;[9] and facts falling within it may also amount to the offence of applying a false trade description to goods[10] or give rise to civil liability under s 30 of the SGA (see post, para 13.04). A contentious issue has been the quantity of beer supplied by publicans and, in particular, whether to include the head (s 43: repealed by the Deregulation Act: see post, para 5.10). The Act also contains a number of other offences of misrepresenting the quantity of goods in connection with their sale or purchase,[11] such misrepresentations incurring strict criminal liability.[12]

Food and drugs

[4.26] Introduction. Perhaps the two types of goods most obviously dangerous to the ordinary consumer are food and drugs. There has been criminal legislation[1] against the supply of impure food for human consumption since 1266.[2] The increasing number of enactments on this subject were consolidated in the Food and Drugs Act 1955. Yet these two aspects sat uneasily together in one statute: medicine is supposed to do the consumer good; whereas food is expected not to do him harm.

---

5   Sections 23–24. For the detailed provisions, see O'Keefe, *Law of Weights and Measures* (2nd edn).

6   Sections 44–46. Where the goods are not delivered at the time of sale, the quantity may have to be stated in writing (ss 26–27).

7   Sections 47–49; and see ante, para 4.24. For unit pricing, see post, para 8.08.

8   Sections 22(1), 25, 26(3). For defences and enforcement, see ss 32–40, 69–84; and generally, Chapter 28.

9   Eg, *Bennett v Markham* [1982] 3 All ER 641, DC (head on glass of beer: see Clayson (1993) 137 SJ 1192).

10   Eg, *Kinchin v Haines* [1979] Crim LR 329, DC: for s 1(1) of the TDA, see ante, para 4.03.

11   Sections 28(2), 29(1), 30(1), 31(1). As to misrepresentations by third parties, see *Collett v Co-operative Wholesale Society Ltd* [1970] 1 All ER 274, DC.

12   *Winter v Hinkley Co-Operative Society Ltd* [1959] 1 All ER 403, DC.

[4.26]

1   See generally Harvey and Parry, *Consumer Protection and Fair Trading* (6th edn), p 431 *et seq*; Butterworth, *Law of Food and Drugs*; Baylis, *Food Safety – Law and Practice* (1994); Lauterburg, *Food Law: Policy and Ethics* (2001).

2   For civil action in respect of defective food, there may be an action under the SGA, eg, *Frost v Aylesbury Dairy Co* (set out post, para 14.08), for negligence, eg, *Donaghue v Stevenson* (see post, para 17.13) or under Part I of the CPA (see post, para 17.24 *et seq*).

Subsequently, the control of drugs was removed to the Medicines Act 1968 (see post, para 4.29) and the law relating to food re-enacted in the Food Act 1984.[3] From our perspective, the more important parts of the 1984 Act were replaced in 1990 (see below), but those parts of the 1984 Act still in force include those dealing with the following: the regulation of markets (Part III: and see below) and some minor enforcement provisions (ss 93–95; 121 (as amended); and see below). In the late 1980s, there was a spate of food scares[4] and concern about the use in relation to food of certain additives, ingredients, pesticides and irradiation. To deal with these concerns, Parliament enacted the Food Safety Act 1990. Whereas earlier statutory definitions proved inadequate, the 1990 Act contains no general definition of 'food', but merely provides that it 'includes' (s 1(1)):

(a) drink;[5]

(b) articles and substances of no nutritional value which are used for human consumption;[6]

(c) chewing gum and other products of a like nature and use; and

(d) articles and substances used as ingredients in the preparation of food or anything falling within this subsection.

According to s 1(2), it does **not** include: (a) live animals, birds or fish, unless consumed alive, eg, oysters; (b) animal fodder and foodstuffs – which are governed by the Agriculture Act 1970, etc; (c) licensed medicines and controlled drugs (see post, para 4.29). From our viewpoint, the most important exception is (c): its effect is that natural preparations which consumers ingest with the expectation that they will do them good, but have no discernable therapeutic effect, are not medicines, but 'food', eg, vitamins, dietary supplements and herbal tea, slimming preparations and perhaps chewing tobacco.

Apart from the major offences created by the 1990 Act (see post, paras 4.27–28), it is largely an enabling measure, containing wide powers for the Minister (s 4) to make regulations as to food safety and consumer protection,[7] whether inspired by UK or EU sources;[8] and the powers also including the registration and licensing of food premises[9]

---

3   There is a separate power to make statutory orders where there is an emergency threat of contamination to the food chain, eg, by radioactivity or pesticides: Food and Environment Protection Act 1985 (as amended).

4   Eg, salmonella, listeria, botulism and BSE. See Thomas (1989) 139 NLJ 1762; and *Food Safety – Protecting the Consumer* (1989, Cmnd 732). As to antibiotics in food, see [1997] 3 Which? 18.

5   This will include water from the point of supply to premises (s 55: before this, it was governed by the Water Act 1989 (see ante, para 3.07)).

6   Eg, slimming aids. As to 'human consumption', see s 53(1). For claims that preparations are food rather than drugs, see post, para 4.29.

7   Section 13. These powers are extended (s 18(1)) to 'novel foods' (s 18(3)) or 'food sources' (s 1(3)), eg, new slimming products, and to 'genetically modified food sources' (s 18(4)), eg, yeast.

8   Sections 16 (and Sched 1) and 17 respectively. UK-inspired regulations will usually first be referred to the Food Advisory Committee; and for irradiation, see [1991] JBL at 329. Hitherto, EU-inspired regulations have been made under the ECA, s 2 (see ante, para 1.03A). For EU Directives on GM foods, see O'Rourke (1997) 147 NLJ 1578; and for a failed challenge to a Directive, see *Ministry of Agriculture, etc v Webbs Country Foods Ltd* [1998] Eu LR 359.

9   Section 19. The intention is to register all (including Crown) premises used for a 'food business' (s 1(3)), but largely confine the licensing to those food businesses which give rise to a risk to health. As to licensing of food markets, see above; and generally post, para 6.02. As to enforcement powers, see post, para 28.05.

and the issue of codes of practice.[10] The enormous volume of regulations made under earlier food legislation is to continue in force for the time being (s 59(3) and Sched 4). Whilst Parliament took the opportunity of the 1990 Act to create a more systematic structure of enforcement powers and penalties (see post, Chapter 28), further food scares in the 1990s, eg, BSE (mad cow disease), led to the introduction of a Food Standards Agency to protect public health in relation to both human and animal food.[11] There are also EU proposals for a European Food Authority.[12]

[4.27] Food: composition and sale. Part II of the Food Safety Act 1990 contains general provisions relating to the composition and sale of 'food' (see ante, para 4.26). Repeated breaches may lead to proceedings under Part III of the FTA (see post, para 6.06). Any breach may also give rise to prosecution under the General Product Safety Regulations (see post, para 4.32) or a civil claim for breach of an implied term under the SGA (see post, Chapters 13–14). Besides widely defining 'sale',[1] the Act creates certain presumptions, such as that:[2]

> Any food commonly used for human consumption shall, if sold or offered, exposed or kept for sale, be presumed, until the contrary is proved, to have been sold or, as the case may be, to have been or to be intended for sale for human consumption.

The principal provisions of the 1990 Act are as follows:

(i) *Rendering food injurious to health.* Section 7 introduces a new offence for any person to 'render any food injurious to health' by the addition or use of any 'article or substance' (s 53(1)), the abstraction of any constituent (which will presumably cover abstraction from milk, but not its mere dilution), or subjecting the food to any other process or treatment.[3] To commit an offence under s 7, a person must **render** the food injurious: it is not sufficient that he merely sells injurious food, eg, poisonous mushroom, though this may be an offence under s 8 (see below); and he must do something positive to the food.[4] In determining whether food is **injurious to health**, regard shall be had not only to the probable effect of that food on the person consuming it,[5] but also the cumulative effect of his consuming similar food in ordinary quantities.[6]

---

10 Section 40. Food authorities must observe these codes (s 40(2)). For commentary on some food codes, see Roberts (1992) 9 Tr L 66. Cf the pricing code: see post, para 8.10A.

11 Food Standards Act 1999. In the light of BSE, is the Agency sufficiently able to disclose information?

12 See O'Rourke (2000) 150 NLJ 230.

[4.27]

1 According to s 2, 'sale' includes any supply of food in the course of a business, including food given, eg, free meals or condiments, or offered as a prize or reward.

2 Section 3(2). There are similar presumptions in respect of food or ingredients found on premises used for the manufacture, preparation, storage or sale of food (s 3(3), (4)).

3 The section provides a useful benchmark for food control and may give rise to strict civil liability (see post, para 17.24): Harvey and Parry, *Consumer Protection and Fair Trading* (6th edn), pp 433–34.

4 Most additives and treatments are likely to be covered by the detailed regulations (see ante, para 4.26); but s 7 should fill any gaps.

5 For definition of 'injury' and 'injurious to health', see s 7(3). This may also amount to an offence under the GPS Regulations (see post, para 4.32A): Cartwright (1995) 58 MLR 222 at 229–30.

6 Section 7(2). This is not as wide as, but is excluded from, the general safety requirement (see post, para 4.33) and there may be proof problems: see [1989] Which? 557; [1990] JBL at 322–23.

(ii) Selling food not complying with safety requirements. Section 8 makes it an offence for any person to sell, offer, expose or advertise,[7] food which 'fails to comply with the food safety requirements'. According to s 8(2), food fails this test if either:

(a) it has been rendered injurious to health by reason of any of the operations mentioned in s 7 (above); or

(b) it is unfit for human consumption;[8] or

(c) it is so contaminated (whether by extraneous matter or otherwise) that it would not be reasonable to expect it to be used for human consumption in that state.[9]

The test also *prima facie* taints any other food in the same 'batch, lot or consignment' (s 8(3)).

(iii) *Selling food not of the nature, etc, demanded* (s 14: see post, para 4.28).

(iv) *Falsely describing or presenting food* (s 15: see post, para 8.11).

As will be seen later, powers are given to the authorised officers of a food authority to inspect, seize and condemn food which does not comply with the food safety requirements (see post, para 28.06). However, to try to intercept such food before it does too much harm, the 1990 Act introduces a new scheme of notices and orders (with criminal sanctions) in respect of any food business (s 1(3)):

(a) an *improvement notice* by an authorised officer, when it is suspected that an offence under certain regulations has been committed (s 10. For the regulations within this scheme, see s 10(3). For appeals, see ss 37 and 39).

(b) a *prohibition order* by the court following such conviction where there is a risk of injury to health, the order being mandatory as regards defective premises,[10] but discretionary as to any human culprit.[11]

(c) a temporary *emergency order* without conviction where there is an imminent risk of such injury (s 12), which enables an *emergency prohibition notice* to be issued by an authorised officer, usually to be followed quickly by an *emergency prohibition order* by the court. For more generalised food scares, s 13 allows the Minister to issue an *emergency control order* on any 'food source' (s 1(3)), eg, substandard poultry farm, or 'contact materials' (s 1(3)), eg, packaging or equipment.[12]

[4.28] Nature, substance and quality.[1] Substantially repeating earlier legislation dating back to 1875, s 14(1) of the Food Safety Act 1990 provides that:

---

7   As to 'advertise' and 'human consumption', see s 53(1).

8   See note 7, above, and animals slaughtered in a knacker's yard (s 8(4)).

9   Eg, food which is mouldy, rancid or stale. Otherwise, it may be necessary to wait until an offence is committed under s 14.

10 Section 11; or upon a court issuing (s 11(a)) an emergency prohibition order (see below). For the health risk condition, see s 11(2). For the appropriate prohibition, see s 11(3). For the lifting of the order after the health risk has abated, see s 11(6)–(8).

11 Section 11(4) talks of prohibiting the 'proprietor' (s 53(1)) from participating in the management of a 'food business' (s 1(3)); but the Act allows proceedings against any culpable manager (s 11(10) and (11)): see [1991] JBL at 325.

12 As to ministerial use of s 13 powers, see *R v Secretary of State for Health ex p Eastside Cheese Co* [1999] CLY 2590, CA.

[4.28]

1   See generally Harvey and Parry, *Consumer Protection and Fair Trading* (6th edn), pp 434–38. As to 'food' and 'sale', see ante, paras 4.26–27.

Any person who sells to the purchaser's prejudice any food which is not of the nature or substance or quality demanded by the purchaser shall be guilty of an offence.

An offence under this section will be committed by the person who in law is the seller, although on many occasions the sale will actually be conducted by an employee.[2] Its essence is to sell as food for human consumption (s 14(2)) to the **purchaser's prejudice**:[3] the Act expressly provides that 'it shall not be a defence that the purchaser was not prejudiced because he bought for analysis or examination' (s 14(2)); and earlier case law establishes that the offence includes sale of an inferior article, whilst having difficulty with disclaimers.[4] In fact, it would seem that s 14 creates three distinct but overlapping offences;[5] namely, as to compliance of the food with the demand[6] as regards:

1 The nature of the food. This appears to refer to the type of food requested. So it is no answer to supply another sort of food or even something that is not food at all.[7]

2 The substance of the food. Whilst primarily a reference to the constituents or ingredients of food,[8] this is also apt to cover the situation where food is adulterated or contains some foreign body.[9]

3 The quality of food. It would seem that this is not just a matter of description,[9] but relates to the essential characteristics of the food,[10] including its composition and water content.[11]

[4.29] Medicines and drugs. The law relating to medicinal products was consolidated in the Medicines Act 1968 (as amended). In the wake of the thalidomide tragedy, medical products are broadly defined by s 130 with regard to potent substances. By ss 104–05, other articles not falling within s 130 may by statutory order be treated as medicinal products; and it is for consideration whether this power should be invoked to control (frequently highly priced, but imported) natural (herbal) medicines (see below). Parts II and IV of the 1968 Act relate to a licensing system for the manufacture of medicines and for retail pharmacies (see post, para 6.05). Parts V and VI are concerned with the packaging and labelling of medicinal products (see post, para 8.12). Part III of the Act regulates dealings with licensed medicinal products, making provision for the

---

2 *Goodfellow v Johnson* [1966] 1 QB 83, DC.

3 The prejudice is that of the ordinary hypothetical buyer not the actual purchaser: *Pearks, Gunston and Tee Ltd v Ward* [1902] 2 KB 1, DC. See Gibbons (1993) 143 NLJ 515.

4 See Lawson (1991) 141 NLJ at 1103–04. Cf disclaimers under the TDA: see ante, para 4.09.

5 So separate charges should be laid where it is thought that the case falls under more than one head: *Bastin v Davies* [1950] 2 KB 579, DC; *Shearer v Rowe and Rowe* (1985) 4 Tr L 206, DC. For food fraud generally, see [1996] 4 Which? 26.

6 *McDonald's Hamburgers Ltd v Windle* (1987) 151 JP 333, DC (diet cola demanded; ordinary cola supplied).

7 *Meah v Roberts* [1978] 1 All ER 97, DC (lemonade ordered; caustic soda supplied). Cf a false trade description: see ante, para 4.06.

8 The standard to be applied is a reasonable one: *Goldup v John Manson Ltd* [1982] QB 161, DC.

9 *Smedleys Ltd v Breed* [1974] AC 839, HL (caterpillar in tinned peas).

10 As where the food includes extraneous matter: *Newton v West Vale Creamery Co Ltd* (1956) 120 JP 318, DC (dead fly in milk); *Lindley v GW Horner and Co Ltd* [1950] 1 All ER 234, DC (nail in sweet).

11 *Rodbourn v Hudson* [1925] KB 225 (general bar notice insufficient reference on sale of watered spirits). On water weight added to food, see [1996] 4 Which? 29.

appropriate Minister to designate medicines as being available in one of the following categories:[1]

(a) By doctor's prescription only. Medicines on this list may be sold or supplied by retail[2] only by a registered pharmacy acting on prescription by an appropriate practitioner, contravention of this rule being a strict liability offence.[3] For controlled drugs, see below.

(b) At a registered pharmacy. If the item appears on the pharmacy only list, then generally speaking[4] it may be sold or supplied by retail[2] without prescription, but only by or 'under the supervision of' a registered pharmacist.[5]

(c) As general sales list medicines. Medicines on this list may be sold or supplied by retail[2] without prescription or the supervision of a registered pharmacist[6] from any premises meeting the prescribed conditions,[4] eg, supermarkets or garages.

Part III also contains provisions relating to the composition of medicinal products (see post, para 4.30) and there are separate provisions in relation to false warranties (see ante, para 4.24). Under the central control of the Minister, the 1968 Act is to be enforced at a local level by the Pharmaceutical Society or local authority (s 108) and their powers of enforcement will be considered later (Chapter 28). Where goods may be classified as food (see ante, para 4.26) or medicine, there may be attempts to bring goods within the former category so as to escape the more rigorous controls of the Medicines Act.[7]

Drugs. From those items classed as medicinal because of their therapeutic purpose (see above) are to be distinguished the law relating to the misuse of poisons[8] or drugs. The 'traditional' drugs are governed by the Misuse of Drugs Act 1971 (as amended): terming these prescription-only (see above) items 'controlled drugs',[9] the 1971 Act places

---

[4.29]

1 Section 51. Sale of unlicensed medicines is generally prohibited (ss 7, 43; and for offences, see s 45). Unfortunately, it is currently not an offence simply to possess licensed medicines, eg, steroids, so that it is difficult to secure a conviction, except where the defendant is caught in the act of supplying. Cf TDA, s 6 (see ante, para 4.05).

2 The expression is 'sell by retail ... or supply in circumstances corresponding to retail sale': ss 53(1), 58(2)(a). This presumably covers both sales and dispensing under the NHS (see *Pfizer Corp v Ministry of Health* [1965] AC 512, HL) and sales by internet (see [2001] 10 Which? 7). For warnings, see post, para 8.12. For wholesaleing, see ss 61, 62.

3 Sections 58, 59. For offences, see s 67; and *Pharmaceutical Society v Storkwain* [1986] 2 All ER 635, HL. There are exceptions for medical, dental and veterinary practitioners (s 55) and in respect of herbal remedies (56). For the gradual move of medicines from category (a) to categories (b) or (c), see below.

4 There are special provisions dealing with automatic vending machines (s 54) and herbal remedies (s 56); exemptions for doctors, dentists and vets (s 55); and a power to extend or modify exemptions (s 57).

5 Section 52; and for offences, see s 67. Eg, *Pharmaceutical Society of GB v Boots* [1953] 1 QB 401, CA.

6 Section 53. The proportion of licensed medicines included in this list has been expanded rapidly: see [1999] 4 Which? 22.

7 Eg, *Optident Ltd v Secretary of Trade and Industry* (2001) *The Times*, 2 July, HL (tooth-bleaching agent held a cosmetic); herbal medicines (see [2001] 5 Which? 13).

8 Under the Pharmacy and Poisons Act 1933; Poisons Act 1972 (as amended). See also the Farm and Garden Chemicals Act 1967 (as amended).

9 The Secretary of State has wide powers to make regulations (s 10). See Jason-Lloyd (2000) 150 NLJ 1401. For an attempt to control 'glue-sniffing' by prohibiting the supply by retailers of intoxicants, eg, typewriter correction fluid, aerosols, or varnish to minors, see the Intoxicating Substances (Supply) Act 1985.

them in different classes according to their relative harmfulness.[10] It imposes severe, but graded,[9] restrictions on their production, importation,[11] prescription by medical practitioner (ss 11–17), supply and possession.[12] There are extensive criminal sanctions backed up by wide powers of search, seizure, forfeiture and arrest (ss 18–27). As to offences by corporations, see post, para 28.11; and as to the right of an innocent owner of goods, eg, let on hp, to contest forfeiture because, eg, the hirer, has secreted drugs in them, see s 27(2). For confiscation, see the Drug Trafficking Offences Act 1986.

[4.30] Composition of medicines. Under the Medicines Act 1968 (see ante, para 4.29), there are a number of offences connected with the supply of medicines (s 67).

1   *Compliance with standards.* Section 65 prohibits the sale or supply in the course of a business of a medicinal product which does not comply with the standard laid down for a product of that name.[1]

2   *Safety prohibitions.* In the interests of safety,[2] Ministers are empowered by s 62 to make orders prohibiting the sale or supply[1] or importation of medicinal products of any kind, or animal feeding stuffs containing such products.[3]

3   *Adulteration.* Along the general lines of s 7 of the Food Safety Act 1990 (see ante, para 4.27), s 63 creates several general prohibitions on the adulteration of medicines intended for sale or supply[1] in that state. However, unlike the 1990 Act, s 63 requires that the adulteration must injuriously affect, not the consumer, but the 'composition of the product'.

4   *Nature, substance and quality.* By way of close parallel to s 14 of the Food Safety Act 1990 (see ante, para 4.28), s 64(1) provides that:

> No person shall to the prejudice of the purchaser, sell[4] any medicinal product which is not of the nature or quality demanded by the purchaser.

'Prejudice' is likewise extended to goods purchased for analysis or examination (s 64(2)). However, to the above offence (see s 67) there are two special defences:[5] first, insofar as the product contains some extraneous matter, it is a defence to show that this 'was an

---

10   They are classified by s 2 and Sched 2 into classes A, B and C, the most serious being Class A, eg, heroin. In 2001, the Government announced it was considering reclassifying cannabis from Class B to Class C: (2001) *The Times*, 24 October .

11   Section 3. But this limitation may contravene Art 3 of the Treaty of Rome (see generally ante, para 2.13): *R v Secretary of State for the Home Dept ex p Evans Medical* [1995] All ER (EC) 481, ECJ.

12   Sections 3–9. Do the provisions extend to the 'mimic' drugs, eg, heroin substitutes? The Secretary of State is also given power to make regulations and issue directions (ss 10–17). As to the meaning of 'supply', see *R v Maginnis* [1987] 1 All ER 907, HL (return to bailor).

[4.30]

1   For 'medicinal products', and for 'sale or supply', see ante, para 4.29.

2   As to 'interest of safety', see s 132. See also the General Product Safety Regulations (post, para 4.33).

3   Section 67(3) extends the offence to persons in possession of such goods and 'knowing or having reasonable cause to suspect that it was sold, supplied or imported in contravention of the order'. Exception to the prohibitions is generally made in favour of, eg, sales by doctors, or to a public analyst.

4   There is an express extension to 'supply' (s 64(5)), which increases the scope of the section to NHS prescriptions: see *Appleby v Sleep* [1968] 2 All ER 265, DC.

5   For the more general defences, see post, para 28.13 *et seq*. For discussion of the Food Act 1984, s 3 (now repealed), defences similar to s 64(3) and (4), see Stephenson, *Criminal Law and Consumer Protection*, pp 119–22.

inevitable consequence of the process of manufacture';[6] or secondly, that there was an additional or subtracted ingredient which did not injuriously affect the composition of the product, that the operation was not done fraudulently and that the product carried an adequate notice.[7]

Other dangerous goods

[4.31] Introduction. It will be seen later that the civil law regulating supplies of goods does enforce some general minimum standards, eg, the tort of negligence (see post, para 17.14 *et seq*), Part III orders (see post, para 6.06); and, where there is a contractual *nexus* between the parties, there is compulsory strict liability in respect of both shoddy and unsafe goods (Chapters 14–15). However, the criminal law contains no counterpart for shoddy goods; and only in relation to unsafe goods has there been significant statutory intervention. Leaving aside licensing (see post, para 6.05), even here governments have been reluctant to fix too many compulsory detailed standards, preferring to leave the detail to voluntary standards.[1] Indeed, the Food Safety and Medicines Acts are perhaps unusual in prescribing in general terms minimum standards as to product or performance only to safeguard human health or safety.[2] Otherwise, governments have only shown themselves willing to legislate in relation to unusually hazardous activities[3] or products, examples of the latter being motor vehicles (see post, para 4.37), explosives,[4] petroleum,[5] weapons[6] and, especially as supplied to young people, such as alcoholic liquor (see post, para 6.05) and tobacco (see ante, para 4.23).

The major drawback to much of the foregoing legislation was that, each time a new standard was fixed or an old one revised, a fresh Act of Parliament was generally required. The Molony Committee therefore recommended that statutory power to deal with dangerous goods 'should exist in advance of demonstrable need'.[7] This resulted in the Consumer Protection Acts 1961 and 1971, which gave the Secretary of State an extensively used general power to make regulations as to **any** class of **dangerous** goods, and allowed enforcement by local authorities (see post Chapter 28). In due course, these Acts were replaced by the Consumer Safety Act 1978, which introduced a power to intercept and ban such goods before they reached retail outlets (see post, para 4.36). All

---

6 Section 64(3). Cf *Smedleys Ltd v Breed* [1974] AC 839, HL (s 3(2) of 1984 Act; 'unavoidable consequences').

7 Section 64(4). For what amounts to adequate notice, see s 64(4)(b); and cf Stephenson, *op cit*, note 5, pp 71–73; and ante, para 4.09.

[4.31]

1 Eg, BSI standards (see ante, para 3.08). See Cranston, *Consumers and the Law* (3rd edn), pp 377–80; and *Modern Markets: Confident Consumers* (1999, Cm 4410) paras 4.18–19.

2 See also Rag Flock and Other Filling Materials Act 1951 (as amended). The legislation frequently takes into account any relevant research by the British Standards Institute (see above).

3 Eg, Road Traffic Act 1988, s 145 (as amended) (discussed in Harvey and Meisel, *Auctions* (2nd edn), pp 233–38; Burton (1995) 145 NLJ 882); Health and Safety at Work Act 1974, s 6 (as amended, controlling the safety of articles for use at work). Cf UCTA 1977, s 2(1) (see post, para 18.23).

4 See the Explosives Act 1875, as amended, eg, by the Explosives (Age of Purchase) Act 1976 (raising to 16 minimum age for purchase of fireworks); and *Sarwan Singh Deu v Dudley MBC* [1987] CLY 836.

5 Petroleum (Consolidation) Act 1928 (as amended).

6 Firearms Acts 1968–1997; Crossbows Act 1987. Flick-knives were dealt with by the Restriction of Offensive Weapons Act 1959; but see *Fisher v Bell* [1961] 1 QB 394, DC (invitation to treat). See also Criminal Justice Act 1988, s 141A (sale of offensive weapons).

7 Interim Report on *Consumer Protection* (1961, Cmnd 1010).

these powers were supplemented and consolidated in Part II of the Consumer Protection Act 1987 (CPA), which makes it clear that those powers in respect of 'unsafe' goods[8] can be exercised in relation to 'safety provisions',[9] whether or not any prohibited act has yet occurred (see now post, para 4.36). Additionally Part II introduced a general safety requirement (see post, para 4.33).

However, the foregoing pattern has been substantially changed by the EU, both in relation to general safety principles (see post, para 4.32) and the labelling of dangerous goods (see post, para 18.29). Recently, it has become possible to have this legislation enforced by Stop Now Orders (see post, para 6.08).

[4.32] EU intervention. In parallel to the above developments, in the 1980s the EU developed its own rules to protect consumers from unsafe goods as follows:

1 *Civil law.* In 1985, the EU promulgated a Directive designed to ensure that the consumer injured by unsafe goods obtained adequate **civil** compensation. This was enacted into English law by Part I of the CPA.[1]

2 *Criminal law.* In 1992, there appeared an EU General Product Safety Directive (GPSD) which attempted by way of **criminal** provisions to prevent injury to the consumer being caused by unsafe goods (92/59/EC). This was incorporated into English law in 1994 by Regulations,[2] which were made under s 2 of the ECA and hence take precedence over English law (see ante, para 1.03A). They introduced the 'general safety requirement' (see post, para 4.33) and contain certain key definitions (see post, para 4.32A). This GPS scheme overlaps considerably with Part II of the CPA (see ante, para 4.31). Unfortunately, the Government chose not to assimilate unambiguously the two streams of law into one coherent scheme: much of Part II of the CPA was left standing (ss 12–18 of the CPA: see post, paras 4.35–36) and to these sections the CPA definitions continue to apply; but, as they were entitled to do (see above), the GPS Regulations repealed part of s 10(3)(b)(ii) of the CPA (see post, para 4.33) and regulations made under the CPA (GPS, reg 6). Even worse, as regards the centrepiece of Part II of the CPA, the 'general safety requirement' found in s 10,[3] the GPS Regulations introduced its own 'general safety requirement' (see post, para 4.33) and dealt with any conflict by providing for the paramountcy of the Regulations over the 'general safety requirement' by 'disapplying' the latter.[3] Presumably, this means that the GPS Regulations *pro tanto* overrule Part II of the CPA as regards the general safety requirement, but that, insofar as not repealed, the general safety requirement in s 10 still stands.[4]

[4.32A] Definitions. As was seen in the previous paragraph, there are presently two sets of (overlapping) **criminal** provisions applicable where a consumer is injured because

---

8   'Safe', 'unsafe' and 'safer' are defined in s 19(1): see the discussion in my Butterworths edn, 1989, para 4.32.

9   'Safety provision' means 'the general safety requirement in s 10 ... or any provision of safety regulations, a prohibition notice or a suspension notice': s 46(1).

[4.32]

1   See post, para 17.24. Where the civil and criminal law overlap there should be borne in mind the advantages of first seeking criminal proceedings: see ante, para 4.01.

2   General Product Safety Regulations 1994, SI 2382. See generally Hodges, Tyler and Abbott, *Product Safety* (1995); Mildred, *Product Liability*, para 6.12 *et seq*.

3   For an account of the CPA general safety requirement, see Butterworths edn, 1989, paras 4.33–34.

4   See further *Parry* [1995] JBL 268 at 278; Mildred, *op cit*, note 2, para 6.30; and see post, para 4.33.

chattels are unsafe. Whilst they are both confined to the area of personal safety (see ante, para 4.32), unfortunately they even differ as to some key definitions.

1   *Consumer products.* The 1994 Regulations apply to consumer products. Thus, reg 2(1) lays down that 'consumer' means one 'acting otherwise than in the course of a commercial activity';[1] and 'product' is defined as:[2]

> ... any product intended for consumers or likely to be used by consumers, supplied whether for consideration or not in the course of a commercial activity and whether new, used or reconditioned.

Thus, both the CPA and the Regulations are confined to consumers, albeit with different definitions of consumer; but, unlike the CPA, the Regulations contain no specific restrictions regarding the types of product.[3] On the other hand, the Regulations contain an exclusion from the category of consumer product, saying that any:[4]

> ... product which is used exclusively in the context of a commercial activity even if it is used for or by a consumer shall not be regarded as a product for the purposes of these Regulations provided always and for the avoidance of doubt this exception shall not extend to the supply of such a product to a consumer.

Thus, products used only by businesses are outside the Regulations, eg, a crane, printing press or articulated lorry; but, as regards products used also by consumers, a distinction is drawn: if such dual use goods are **supplied** to, and **used** by, a consumer they are within the regulations, eg, DIY goods, such as a wall-paper stripper, rotavator, box van or washing machine supplied to a launderette; whereas, if they are only **used** by a business, they are outside the regulations, eg, an industrial washing machine supplied to a laundry. Finally, even if supplied to consumers, the following types of product are excluded by reg 3: second-hand products which are antiques (undefined); products supplied for repair or reconditioning before use;[5] any product where there are specific EU provisions governing all its safety aspects (see post, para 4.33).

2   *Consumer safety.* As compared with the CPA's 'safe' goods[5a], Regulation 2 likewise produces a general definition of 'safe', followed by some specific instances. Thus, the opening words provide that:

> ... 'safe product' means any produce which, under normal or reasonably foreseeable conditions of use, including duration, does not present any risk or only the minimum risk compatible with the product's use, considered as acceptable and consistent with a high level of protection for the safety and health of persons ...

[4.32A]

1   This excludes, eg, soft toys made for a child by a relative: Parry [1995] JBL 268 at 270.

2   Regulation 2. This definition is taken verbatim from Art 2 of the Directive. It will cover any form of supply, eg, sale, quasi-sale, and explicitly extends to free gifts and samples.

3   There is no list of excluded types of goods, such as is found in the CPA s 10(7): see Butterworths edn, 1989, para 4.33; so the Regulations extend to, eg, tobacco, food (see ante, para 4.27).

4   Regulation 2(1). This exclusion is derived from the recitals to the Directive. But it is argued that this interpretation is too narrow and would exclude, eg, a hairdresser's shampoo: see Cartwright (1995) 58 MLR 222 at 223.

5   Provided that the supplier clearly informs the consumer of this. Must the information be supplied before the supply of goods? Cf the specified defects exception to the implied terms (see post, para 14.25).

5a   The CPA definition of 'safe' (s 19) is discussed in the Butterworths edn, 1989, para 4.32.

As in the case of the CPA, for the Regulations the chattel is safe where the risks to humans arising from use are **reduced to a minimum**, so that inherently unsafe goods, eg, a kitchen knife, may be 'safe', balancing risk with utility (see post, para 17.02). However the injury might arise directly or indirectly from that risk, eg, goods which self-destruct; and the regulation explicitly extends use beyond normal use to reasonably foreseeable misuse, eg, superglue for children's play; sniffing correction fluid or aerosols. Whilst the CPA speaks simply of the chattel causing death or personal injury to any person whatsoever,[6] the Regulation limits this to risks which are (1) unacceptable and (2) consistent with a high level of protection for the safety and health of persons.[7] Regulation 2 then sets out the following list of non-exclusive factors to be considered in determining whether or not products are unsafe:

(a) the characteristics of the product, including its composition, packaging, instructions for assembly and maintenance;

(b) the effect on other products, where it is reasonably foreseeable that it will be used with other products;

(c) the presentation of the product, the labelling, any instructions for its use and disposal and any other indication or information provided by the producer; and

(d) the categories of consumers at serious risk when using the product, in particular children and the fact that higher levels of safety may be obtained or other products presenting a lesser degree of risk may be available shall not itself cause the product to be considered other than a safe product ...

It will be noted that this list is similar to, but more elaborate than, that contained in s 19 of the CPA[5a]; but neither contain any explicit reference to **cost**.[8] Finally, the definition allows that a product may be 'safe', even though there are safer products on the market[9] or other ways of making this product safer, cf s 10(2)(c) of the CPA.

[4.33] The GPS Regulation general safety requirement. The relationship of the GPS general safety requirement to compliance of the goods with other requirements is this: (a) so far as 'Community' law is concerned, the GPS Regulations do not apply where there is a specific EU provision governing the safety of a product (see ante, para 4.32), but do apply insofar as that EU law does not make provision for an aspect of the safety of the product;[1] (b) where the product conforms with other UK rules which lay down specific mandatory health and safety requirements for the product, there is a presumption that it is a safe product;[2] whereas, (c) in the absence of such mandatory UK rules, in assessing

---

6   So extending beyond the user to injury to any third party. Is there to be criminal liability for any caused human injury; or should there be a test equivalent to the civil test of remoteness (as to which, see post, para 27.41)?

7   Cf the Health and Safety at Work Act 1974, s 6.

8   Eg, that cost of safety features of a car. It is claimed that the regulations may be wide enough to include this factor: Cartwright, *op cit*, note 4, p 224.

9   'The fact that higher levels of safety may be obtained or other products presenting a lesser degree of risk may be available shall not of itself cause the product to be considered other than a safe product' (reg 2(1), 'safe product', closing words).

[4.33]

1   Regulations 3 and 4 (see ante, para 4.32A). As to EU safety regulations, see post, para 4.35.

2   This transfers to the prosecution the burden of proving that, say, a pushchair complying with UK safety regulations, is unsafe: Parry [1995] JBL 268 at 273.

the safety of a product, a court may take into account compliance of the product with other standards[3] and 'the safety which consumers might reasonably expect'.[4]

Whereas the similar CPA provision is aimed primarily at the retail supplier, the GPS Regulations concentrate on the 'producer' of the product (see ante, para 4.32A), whilst imposing only secondary responsibility on 'distributors'.[5]

1 *Producer liability.* Regulation 7 lays down that:

> No producer shall place a product on the market unless the product is a safe product.

The basic scheme is to distinguish according to whether or not the producer is 'established in the Community', a notion which extends beyond the EU to the European Economic Area (reg 2(2)).

(i) *EU producer.* If so established, reg 2 lays down that 'producer' means the manufacturer of the product. However, it proceeds to extend that category to include own-branders of goods,[6] wherever manufactured.[7] Further, the Regulations also extend to other 'professionals' in the chain of EU distribution whose activities so interfere with the goods as to 'affect the safety properties of a product', eg, a retailer misassembling a product.[8] It is for consideration whether activities includes inaction, eg, a shopkeeper who fails to refrigerate perishables.

(ii) *Non-EU producer.* If not so established, the Regulations distinguish according to whether or not that non-EU producer has a representative within the Community: if so, that representative is the 'producer'; if not, the 'producer' is the importer of the goods into the EU (reg 2).

2 *Distributor liability.* Whereas a producer is responsible that a product is safe (above), a 'distributor', such as a retailer, is only required by reg 9 to 'act with due care to ensure compliance with ... regulation 7'.[9] However, reg 9(a) contains two extensions of this duty, laying down that:

> a distributor shall not supply products which he knows, or should have presumed, on the basis of information in his possession and as a professional, are dangerous products.

---

3 These are listed in reg 10(2) in order of priority: (1) EU standards, whether or not embodied in UK voluntary standards; (2) other UK standards, codes of conduct (cf *P and M Supplies Ltd v Walsall MBC* [1995] CLY 748, DC; and see ante, paras 3.08; 3.11), or the state of the art and technology. Under the repealed CPA, s 10(3)(b)(ii), compliance with UK standards would have been a complete defence.

4 Bear in mind that the mere fact that there are safer products does not make a product unsafe: see the closing words of the definition of 'unsafe product' (see ante, para 4.32A). Is the test relative, so that consumers of more expensive models with additional safety features are entitled to a higher standard? See Parry, *op cit*, note 2, p 273.

5 'Distributor' means any professional in the supply chain whose activity does not affect the safety properties of a product (reg 2). Does this include a finance company?

6 Paragraph (a) of the definition refers to 'any person presenting himself as the manufacturer by affixing to the product his name, trade mark or other distinctive mark, or the person who reconditions the product'. For a discussion of own-branders, see post, para 17.27.

7 There is no mechanism for making a retailer disclose the identity of his supplier (cf CPA, s 2(3): see post, para 17.27).

8 Regulation 2(1), definition of 'producer', para (c), eg, a car dealer's pre-delivery check. *Contra* where he properly assembles the product, but may be liable as its distributor (see below). Presumably, this is not intended to catch employees? For chains of distribution, see generally post, para 17.01.

9 Cf the objective standard of driving without due care under s 3 of the RTA 1988, as substituted by s 2 of the RTA 1991: discussed in Smith and Hogan, *Criminal Law* (9th edn) 485–91.

First, reg 9(a) imposes strict liability on those with knowledge that the product is dangerous.[10] Second, it establishes liability on the basis of what the distributor should have known 'as a professional', presumably an objective test. Further, reg 9(b) requires the distributor 'within the limits of his activities'[11] to:

> participate in monitoring the safety of products placed on the market, in particular by passing on information on the product risks and co-operating in the action taken to avoid those risks.

So, the reluctant distributor can no longer take refuge in inertia and ignorance. Presumably, it will be enough for the Trading Standards Officer (TSO: see post, para 28.02) to write to the distributor outlining the dangers of a product.

[4.34] Breach of the GPS general safety requirement. Where the 'producer' or 'distributor' contravenes the GPS general safety requirement (see ante, para 4.33) he commits an offence under reg 12. Similarly, reg 13 also makes it criminal to do certain preparatory acts to a reg 12 offence, such as offering or agreeing to place on the market or supply any dangerous product.[1] For both provisions, the penalty tariff is laid down by reg 17;[2] the Regulations deal with the liability of persons other than the principal offender;[3] and there is the usual due diligence defence (reg 14: see post, para 28.13). Enforcement is in the hands of the relevant local authority;[4] and many of the enforcement provisions of the CPA also apply to these Regulations.[5]

Apart from the above general safety requirement, the Regulations also impose further duties on both the 'producer' and 'distributor', as already defined (see ante, para 4.33).

1   *Information and measures by a producer.* 'Within the limits of his activity',[6] reg 8 imposes two such duties on the producer. First, reg 8(1)(a) deals with consumer **information**, requiring that a producer shall:

> ... provide consumers with the relevant information to enable them to assess the risks inherent in a product throughout the normal or reasonably foreseeable period of its use, where such risks are not immediately obvious without adequate warnings, and to take precautions against those risks ...

---

10   Cf s 10(4)(b) of the CPA, which establishes strict liability, subject to a specific limited defence for retailers.

11   As to the differential standard which this may impose on large and small distributors, see Cartwright (1995) 58 MLR 222 at 226–27. It may impose lesser standards on charity shops, jumble sales and car boot sales.

[4.34]

1   Or exposes or possess a product for any such purpose: see *Caerphilly CBC v Stripp* [2001] 2 CMLR 5. This is likely to be particularly relevant to retailers and mean that they may be *prima facie* liable, irrespective of their knowledge, for stocking dangerous goods. As to changes in the wording of the final version of reg 13, see Parry [1995] JBL 268 at 276. For a suggestion that reg 13 is stricter than reg 12, see Caldwell (1995) 58 MLR 222 at 227.

2   The maximum custodial penalty differs from that under the CPA: see Parry [1995] JBL 268 at 269. As to the time-limit for prosecutions (reg 16): see post, para 28.07. The penalties have been criticised as inadequate: Cartwright, *op cit*, p 230.

3   There is a standard bypass provision (reg 15(1): see post, para 28.12) and sanction for the prosecution of corporate officers (regs 15(2),(3): see post, para 28.11).

4   Regulation 11(c): see post, para 28.03. Notice must be given to the Minister (reg 18).

5   By reg 11, the following CPA provisions (see post, para 4.36) apply to products under the Regulations, sometimes with a reduced penalty (reg 11(d)): prohibition notices and notices to warn (s 13); suspension notices (ss 14 and 15); forfeiture orders (s 16); power to obtain information (s 18).

6   See Mildred, *Product Liability*, para 6.35. Does this protect the small manufacturer without any research facilities? Is this too wide an escape clause?

So, the producer has no need to mention obvious risks, eg, that sharp knives cut, but has a continuing obligation to issue adequate warnings in respect of less obvious risks.[7] Second, reg 8(1)(b) insists that a producer shall take **measures**,[8] saying that he must:

> adopt measures commensurate with the characteristics of the product which he supplies to enable him to be informed of the risks which these products might present and to take appropriate action, including, if necessary, withdrawing the product in question from the market to avoid those risks.

This provision is concerned with the producer detecting safety problems before goods leave his factory, which is relevant to the general defence (see post, para 28.15); and, if any product escape that safety net, instituting a safety recall.[9]

2   *Information and measures by a distributor.* 'Within the limits of his activities',[10] reg 9(b) requires that a distributor shall:

> participate in monitoring the safety of products placed on the market, in particular by passing on information on the product risks and cooperating in the action taken to avoid those risks.

Presumably, these duties placed upon a distributor are intended to dovetail with the (above) duties placed upon a producer.

In the case of neither regs 8 or 9 (above) is there any express sanction for breach.[11] There are two possible explanations. First, the draftsman may have intended that any breach of regs 8 or 9 shall be treated as a breach of regs 12 or 13. Second, he may have planned that regs 8 and 9 should be indirectly enforced by deprivation of the due diligence defence.[12]

[4.35] Safety regulations. There are two streams of safety regulation, which in theory should gradually coalesce.

1   *UK-inspired safety regulations.* Under earlier safety legislation (see ante, para 4.31), there had been built up a considerable volume of safety regulations laying down compulsory minimum detailed standards of safety which retailed goods must meet.[1] However, unlike the previous situation, it will now be in the interests of trades to expedite the promulgation of such regulations to provide them with shelters from the general safety requirement.[2] Building on the previous legislation, but not confined to

---

7   See Mildred, *ibid*, para 6.36. As to risks to third parties, see Caldwell, *op cit*, note 1, at 225–26. Cf *Vacwell Engineering Ltd v BDH Chemicals Ltd* (set out post, para 18.29).

8   Regulation 8(2) gives some examples of such measures, eg, batch marking, sample testing, complaints investigation.

9   As to product recalls generally, see Stone (1991) 8 Tr L 2 at 22–24. The consumer lobby is disappointed that there is no compulsory process for product recall: Parry, *op cit*, note 1, pp 274–75. Product recalls may also be relevant for civil liability: see post, para 17.02.

10   For a suggestion that there may be a lesser duty on a corner shop, see Mildred, *op cit*, note 6, para 6.41.

11   This may amount to a failure of the UK to implement the Directive: see Mildred, *op cit*, note 6, para 6.37.

12   This explanation would dovetail with reg 14(5), which explicitly removes the defence in respect of a reg 9(b) offence: see Parry, *op cit*, note 1, 276. As to the defences, see Cartwright, *op cit*, at 227–29; and generally post, para 28.13 *et seq*. There may also be an action for breach of statutory duty: as to which, see ante, para 3.21.

[4.35]

1   See Thomas and Clarke, *Encyclopedia of Consumer Law*, Part 2. For kitemarks, see ante, para 3.08.

2   'Safety regulations' are defined by s 45(1) of the CPA as those made under s 11. For regulations relating to motor vehicles see post, para 4.37.

'consumer goods',[3] s 11(1) of the CPA provides that regulations may be made for the purposes of securing:

   (a) that the goods to which this section applies are safe;[4]

   (b) that goods to which this section applies which are unsafe, or would be unsafe in the hands of persons of a particular description, are not made available to persons generally or, as the case may be, to persons of that description;[5] and

   (c) that appropriate information is, and inappropriate information is not, provided in relation to goods to which this section applies.[6]

In general, the minister has a duty to consult before laying any regulations,[7] though in some cases of urgency he can introduce temporary regulations with a shelf-life of up to 12 months without consultation (s 11(5)). Some idea of the scope of his power to devise regulations may be gathered from the detailed statutory list of types of control.[8] For the time being, regulations made under earlier Acts continue in force (s 50(5)), contravention of both those and regulations made under the CPA amounting to criminal offences.[9] Offences are also committed by failure to test goods for compliance with safety regulations, or to mark goods as required, or to give relevant information as required.[10] Finally, the CPA is particularly favourable to civil action by consumers injured through breach of safety regulations: breach is expressed to give rise to an action for breach of statutory duty;[11] and any supply contract remains fully enforceable.[12]

2   *EU-inspired safety regulations.* From an early stage, the EU begun to produce Directives in the field of consumer safety (see ante, para 3.10) and had its own scheme for marking goods (the CE mark: see ante, para 3.08). The normal way in which these were enacted in the UK was by way of statutory instrument (see ante, para 1.03A). For most purposes, there is nowadays no need to distinguish these EU-inspired safety regulations from the UK-inspired ones (see above). Unfortunately, such a distinction

---

3   CPA, s 10(7): see Macleod, *Consumer Sales Law*, Butterworths edn, 1989, para 4.33.

4   As to 'safe' and 'unsafe' so CPA, s 19(1): see Butterworths edn, 1989, para 4.32.

5   This new power to prohibit goods to particular sections of the community, eg, fireworks to the under-aged, removes a doubt that such regulations might be *ultra vires*: Bragg, *Consumer Safety*, 1987, unpublished paper.

6   As to instructions for use, see generally post, para 18.28 *et seq.*

7   Section 11(5): see *R v Secretary of State for Health ex p US Tobacco International Inc* [1992] QB 353, DC (oral snuff).

8   Section 11(2), (4). Section 11 is not confined to consumer goods; but s 11(7) contains an exemption list shorter then its counterpart in s 10(7).

9   'Where safety regulations prohibit a person from supplying or offering or agreeing to supply any goods or from exposing or possessing any goods for supply ...' (s 12(1)). The CPA empowers the minister to impose restrictions as to who may prosecute (s 11(3)). For penalties, see s 12(5). For the general defence, see s 39(5): see post, para 28.13.

10 Sections 12(2), (3), 18. Some of the offences (s 12(1)–(3)) are of strict liability like s 1 of the TDA (see ante, para 4.03), whereas others (ss 12(4), 18) introduce a formula very like that found in s 14 of the TDA (see ante, para 4.17). For penalties, see ss 12(5), 18(4).

11 Section 41(1), (3), (5), (6). Is the civil action based on breach of s 11 limited to personal injury damage? This may provide an alternative to a civil action under Part I of the CPA: see post, para 17.03. As to actions for breach of statutory duty, see ante, para 3.21.

12 Section 41(3): for illegality, see post, para 10.19. Apart from when a safety regulation so allows, it is forbidden to contract out of civil liability for breach of that regulation (s 41(4)); and see generally post, para 18.10.

is drawn for the purposes of deciding whether compliance with a UK safety regulation is a good defence to criminal proceedings for breach of the GPS general safety requirement (see ante, para 4.34): if behind those regulations is an EU Directive covering all aspects of product safety, the product is exempt from the GPS Regulations (reg 3: see ante, para 4.33); whereas, if the regulations are UK-inspired, the matter is treated differently (reg 4: see ante, para 4.34).

[4.36] Other provisions. Besides the general safety requirement and safety regulations (see ante, paras 4.33–35), the safety legislation also contains several other types of control in respect of unsafe goods (see ante, para 4.32). Before 1986, when something dangerous appeared on the market, the enforcing authority was a largely ineffectual reactor after personal injury to the public: there was no early-warning system that dangerous goods were about to come onto the UK market; and there were no effective sanctions against traders who continued to dispose of such stock. However, the CPA system introduced a real chance that the enforcing authority will receive such advance notice of import[1] and can adequately trace both imported and home-produced unsafe goods: the Minister has power to obtain information (s 18), whilst the enforcing authorities can make test purchases, enter and search premises, and seize goods and documents (see post, para 28.05). Armed with this information, the authority can put a temporary freeze on distribution by itself issuing a suspension notice; ask the court for a forfeiture order to remove goods permanently from circulation; and also request from the minister prohibition and warning notices (see below). This system has been extended beyond what the CPA termed 'safety provisions'[2] to include the GPS general safety requirement (reg 11: see ante, para 4.34).

1   *Suspension notices.*[3] Under the 1978 Act, the enforcing authorities were constantly frustrated by finding that, by the time their laboratory tests had proved seized samples were unsafe, the unscrupulous trader had disposed of his remaining stock. Accordingly, s 14(1) of the CPA provides that:

> Where an enforcement authority has reasonable grounds for suspecting that any safety provision has been contravened in relation to any goods, the authority may serve a notice ('a suspension notice')[3] prohibiting [for a maximum period of six months] the person on whom it is served,[4] from doing any of the following things without the consent of the authority, that is to say, supplying the goods, offering to supply them, agreeing to supply them or exposing them for supply.

Eg, in *R v Birmingham City Council ex p Ferrero Ltd:*[5]

> F Ltd manufactured chocolate eggs, each of which contained a plastic capsule which itself contained a kit which could be assembled to make a small toy representing a well-

---

[4.36]

1   For the power of HM Customs to inform enforcing authorities of the import of unsafe goods, see s 37. The likely effect of this important section is discussed by Caldwell (1987) 50 MLR at 628–29.

2   According to CPA, s 45(1), these include safety regulations and suspension or prohibition notices.

3   'Notice' means notice in writing: s 45(1). As to the information which must be contained in a suspension notice, see s 14(2); and for extensions of time, see s 14(4). The notice may also require that the LA is kept informed of the whereabouts of the goods (s 14(3)). Contravention is an offence (s 14(6)); and for defences, see s 39(5) and post, para 28.13.

4   As to the dilemma this may cause other traders not served with a notice, see Stone (1991) 8 Tr LR 2, at 20–21.

5   [1993] 1 All ER 530; (1991) 10 Tr LR 129, CA.

known cartoon character, eg, the Pink Panther. In 1989, a little girl accidentally swallowed part of such a Pink Panther toy and died of asphyxiation as a result. The LA immediately issued a s 14 suspension notice and F Ltd applied for judicial review.

The Court of Appeal refused judicial review on the grounds that F Ltd should have followed the statutory appeal system under s 15, saying that the LA is under no implied duty to consult a trader either before or after the service of a suspension order. Alternatively, the LA could have obtained from the Minister a temporary order pending promulgation of a safety regulation (s 11(5): see ante, para 4.35); or, if there were several suppliers of the same unsafe goods, mount a test prosecution against another supplier.[4] However, if the LA does make a s 14 order, it may grant conditional consent to the disposal of unsafe goods (s 14(5)) and consent to their disposal for scrap or repair.[6] If the authority wrongly serves a notice, it is liable to pay compensation to 'any person having an interest in the goods' (s 14(7), (8)).

2 *Forfeiture orders.* According to s 16(1):

> An enforcement authority ... may apply (to a magistrates' court) ... for an order for the forfeiture of any goods on the grounds that there has been a contravention in relation to the goods of a safety provision..

Note that such an order can be sought on evidence that a representative sample of the goods is unsafe,[7] and that the authority does not need to also secure a conviction.[8] Potentially, use of this procedure could both effectively remove unsafe goods from the market permanently and financially penalise their stockist.[9]

3 *Minister's prohibition notices.* Section 13 deals with future and past stock considered unsafe,[10] described here as 'relevant goods' (s 13(6)), as follows:[11]

(a) If there is a danger that a manufacturer or stockist is likely to obtain further supplies of the unsafe goods, the Minister may:

> ... serve on any person a notice ('a prohibition notice') prohibiting that person ... from supplying, or from offering to supply, agreeing to supply, exposing for supply or possessing for supply, any relevant goods.

(b) If goods already supplied by that manufacturer or stockist may endanger consumers, the Minister may:

> ... serve on any person a notice ('a notice to warn') requiring that person at his own expense to publish ... a warning about any relevant goods.

---

6   As to 'supply', etc, see ante, para 4.34. Thus the notice cannot prevent the simple relocation of goods, though the authority can insist on notice of that fact (s 14(3)).

7   Section 16(4). This renders viable mass detention of suspect goods on the basis of sample testing: Caldwell, *op cit*, p 633. What if the test results are inconsistent?

8   If satisfied of contravention (s 16(3)), the court may order destruction of the goods (s 16(6)) or their release on terms (s 16(7)).

9   The likely outcome is thus that, provided the retail stockist stops distribution when warned of the unsafe nature of his goods, he is likely to avoid prosecution but suffer forfeiture of stock, a loss he may seek to recoup by civil action against his supplier: see Chapter 14.

10 By the Secretary of State. For 'unsafe', see Butterworths edn, 1989, para 4.33. What if goods satisfy the general safety requirement and yet are 'unsafe'?

11 Section 13(2), (5) imports the detailed provisions of Sched 2 as to these notices and also allows for the introduction of regulations. As to offences, see s 13(4); and as to defences, see s 39(5) (above).

There are still no compulsory procedures for safety recalls (see ante, para 4.34); nor may the LA use publicity to achieve a similar effect.[12]

[4.37] Road traffic. Among the many statutory requirements imposed on the manufacturer or importer of motor vehicles[1] are the construction and use requirements: under powers now embodied in the amended s 41 of the Road Traffic Act 1988 (RTA), the Secretary of State has made extensive regulations as to both the construction and use of motor cars[2] and equipment.[3] More significant for our purposes, are the provisions which make it an offence to supply a motor vehicle or vehicle parts which contravene the s 41 regulations.[4] In relation to an offending motor vehicle, the strict liability offence[5] may be committed by either a trade or private supplier (s 75(5)). In relation to offending spare parts, it is also made an offence to supply such parts either by way of fitting to a vehicle or where the supplier has reasonable cause to believe that it will be so fitted (s 76) and this is additional to any contractual liability (s 76(10)). Special provision is made for motor cycle helmets[6] and silencers (see the Motor Cycle Noise Act 1987). In some circumstances, the foregoing may overlap with TDA offences[7] or offences under safety requirement or regulations (see ante, paras 4.33–35); or there may be infringements of Codes of Practice (see ante, para 3.13). But still there are calls for yet more statutory protection for the consumer motorist.[8]

Civil law rights. Sometimes the injured consumer can obtain compensation by awaiting prosecution for one of the above offences and then asking the convicting court for a compensation order (see ante, para 3.20). The consumer should be aware of the special rules concerning instalment contracts (see ante, Chapter 1) and purchase by auction (see post, paras 10.10–13). As regards a buyer at auction, there are special rules for supply by dealer (see post, para 14.04) and exclusion clauses (s 12(3) of the UCTA: see post, para 18.18). All motor vehicles and spares must be as described (see post, Chapter 13); in most cases the supplier will undertake to give a good title (see post, Chapter 12) or a Part III title may be obtained (see post, para 21.55); and where the car is paid for by credit card, the private consumer may also have a right of action against the credit card issuer (s 75 of the CCA: see post, para 16.11). As regards offences, the RTA also expressly

---

12   *R v Liverpool CC, ex p Baby Products Assoc* [2000] CLY 853, DC.

[4.37]

1   Under RTA 1988, s 63, there have been made regulations relating to the manufacturing specification of vehicles and making breach an offence under the TDA (see below). So the sale of a second-hand vehicle altered from that specification is an offence.

2   According to RTA, s 185(1), 'motor car' means 'a mechanically propelled vehicle intended or adapted for use on roads'. See *Percy v Smith* [1986] RTR 262, DC.

3   Under RTA, ss 40A–42 (as inserted by RTA 1991, s 8), it is an offence both to construct vehicles contravening the regulations and to use such vehicles on the road. *Inter alia* these regulations require vehicles to comply with some British Standards (see generally ante, para 3.08).

4   RTA, ss 75, 76 (as amended), which contains savings for vehicles sold as scrap. As to 'expose for sale', eg, ante, para 4.27.

5   RTA, s 75(5) (as amended), *Sandford Motor Sales v Hapgood* [1962] CLY 2730 (under RTA 1960). It is a defence to prove that the vehicle was supplied for export, or under a reasonable belief that it would not be used on the road: s 75(6).

6   RTA, s 17, eg, *Loseix v Clarke* [1984] RTR 174, DC. There is no express saving for contractual rights.

7   Eg, TDA, s 1(a) offence (see ante, para 4.03), as by applying a forged MOT certificate (see ante, para 4.06), or clocking a vehicle (see ante, para 4.09). See further OFT (1999) 23 Fair Trading 10.

8   Especially in relation to purchase of used vehicles: see (1991) 8 Tr LR 171; OFT, (1998) 18 Fair Trading 8.

saves the transferee's contractual remedies[9] and it would therefore seem that every breach of the construction and use regulations by a trade supplier is likely also to give rise to a civil claim for breach of the undertakings as to fitness and quality because the ordinary purpose for which a car is required is driving on the highway.[10] Manufacturers and trade warranties may also provide significant protection (see post, paras 17.09–09A). For certificates of title, see post, para 21.60; and for Stop Now Orders, see post, para 6.08.

---

9   RTA, s 75(7). This reverses the decision that such contracts were tainted with illegality (*Vinall v Howard* [1953] 2 All ER 515), so that a supplier might now recover on a stopped cheque; but it would not allow an action for breach of statutory duty (see ante, para 3.21).

10 Would it not be more satisfactory if the motorist could ascertain before his accident that he was driving a rebuilt car or on rebuilt tyres?

CHAPTER 5

CONSUMER PROTECTION AND INSTALMENT CREDIT

INTRODUCTION

[5.01] The background. In the 20th century, there was an explosive growth in the use made of instalment credit both by business (asset finance) and by private consumption.[1] On the consumer side, this to a considerable degree appears to be linked to the development of the affluent society and mass production of consumer durables.[2] Especially since the 1950s the amount outstanding on instalment credit generally has grown remorselessly, though it is difficult to put precise figures on the volume, or make accurate comparisons over time, because of the ever-changing institutional providers and forms of credit.[3] In 1971, the then shape of the credit market was surveyed by the *Crowther Report* (see post, para 5.03): in terms of loans outstanding, over 40% was vendor credit (see ante, para 2.19) provided by retailers; whereas some 50% was lender credit (see ante, para 2.20) supplied by banks and finance houses.[4] A decade later, the position had changed substantially: banks, finance houses and building societies (see ante, para 2.17) directly provided over 65% of all consumer credit and indirectly extended another 12% by way of three-party cards (see ante, para 2.25). In the 1980s, lender credit increased to over 80% of the market: this was largely achieved by the expansion in the use of three-party cards in retail outlets at the expense of traditional forms of vendor credit, the latter falling below 5% of amounts outstanding.[5]

Whilst the banks, finance companies and building societies dealt mainly in large advances to prosperous customers (see above), other lenders, such as check-traders, moneylenders and pawnbrokers (see post, para 15.17), more often lent modest amounts to poor families.[6] Vendor credit to poor families would typically be supplied by mail order (see post, para 8.19); or door-to-door traders. Developing out of the credit drapers and tallymen or 'Scotch drapers' of the 18th century,[7] these businesses provided goods on credit on a door-to-door basis in low-income areas. Providing small amounts of finance and flexible home collection, their services are relatively expensive and disadvantaged by the APR rules (see post, para 8.23), the doorstep selling regulations (see post, paras 10.21–22) and the cancellable agreements regime for regulated agreements (see post, para 10.28 *et seq*).

[5.01]

1   This would scarcely have been possible without the use of computers: see ante, paras 3.26–28.
2   Reviews of the credit scene were carried out by NOP surveys as follows: (1) In 1969 for the *Crowther Report* (Cmnd 4596) Chapter 3.5 and Appendix II; (2) In 1979 for the OFT: see its 1979-AR, 33.
3   Rapid increases in consumer per capita indebtedness has led to a substantial increase in consumers who find themselves in financial difficulties: see below.
4   OFT, *Consultation Document on the Working and Enforcement of the Consumer Credit Act 1974* (1993), Annex 1. See also OFT, *Connected Lender Liability* (1994), para 3.1 *et seq*.
5   For a breakdown of ways in which members of that Association provide credit, see the Annual Reports of the FLA (see generally ante, para 2.18).
6   See Rowlingson, *Money Lenders* (1994) 17; OFT *Vulnerable Consumers* (1999) esp 16, 29.
7   Rowlingson, *ibid*, 23. For a fascinating enquiry as to why poor people use moneylenders, see Rowlingson, pp 81–99. For controls on peddling, see post, para 6.02.

The converse method of business at that level is for the consumer to pay instalments in advance of delivery under a club scheme, eg, Christmas Club Stamps (see post, para 15.18) or utility advanced payment scheme (see ante, para 3.07). This involves the consumer giving credit (see post, para 5.21) to the trader. Such credit is normally discharged at a stroke by the subsequent delivery of goods, so that it is exempt from the CCA,[8] but would in any event be a non-commercial agreement (see post, para 5.18).

[5.02] Legislative history. The economic purpose of instalment credit is to advance the price of goods to the consumer for consumption before payment.[1] However, historically society's hostility to moneylending led to its being subject to legal restrictions (see post, para 6.09) and to the development of other legal forms of transaction which would achieve the same end whilst attracting less opprobrium, such as disguising the loan as a deferred sale (see ante, para 1.03).

1 *Tradesmen's credit.* Shopkeepers in the towns (credit or scotch drapers)[2] and itinerant pedlars in the countryside (tallymen) began to supply goods on credit in a growing and systematic way. In the 19th century, this led to the evolution of sophisticated forms of instalment sales (see ante, para 1.12) and the invention of hp (see ante, para 1.20), with its many opportunities for technical default.[3] Eventually statutory controls were developed in the form of the Hire Purchase Act 1938 and its successors, until by 1970 there were extant the following: Hire Purchase Act 1964, Part III (see post, para 21.55 *et seq*); Hire Purchase Act 1965; Advertisements (Hire Purchase) Act 1967.[4]

2 *Moneylending.* Having experienced difficulty in collecting their debts,[5] shopkeepers supplying goods on credit began to take pledges (see post, para 25.15) and a series of Pawnbroking Acts were introduced from 1603 onwards in an attempt to provide regulation, culminating in the Pawnbrokers Acts 1872 and 1960. Meanwhile, in 1854 statutory control over the rate of interest charged by moneylenders was removed, though as regards restrictions on the form of security moneylenders might take over goods, widespread abuses eventually led to the Bills of Sale Acts 1878 and 1882 (see post, para 9.04). Moneylending itself remained uncontrolled until the end of that century, when the Moneylenders Acts 1900–27 introduced a system whose most notable facet was the total exclusion of banks from control (see post, para 6.09). Since the repeal of the Moneylenders Acts, credit card business (see ante, para 2.24) undertaken by the banks and others has boomed, whilst a shift towards non-purchase money lending secured by house mortgage[6] led to late amendments in what became

---

8 It would usually come within a CCA exempt category: see post, para 5.15.

[5.02]

1 The converse method is for the consumer to save in advance of delivery, eg, by paying by instalments under a club scheme (see post, para 15.18).

2 See Goode, *HP Law and Practice* (2nd edn), pp 900–01; *Crowther Report* (above), paras 2.5.9–15; (1995) 16 CCA News 5/12; (1996) 17 CCA News 1/10; (1997) CCA News Summer 16. For attempts to disguise pawnbroking as selling: see Macleod [1995] JBL 155; and post, para 25.17.

3 As to the sort of practice against which the 1938 Act was aimed, see the account of 'snatch backs', post, para 26.08.

4 See further the *Crowther Report*, Appendix V.

5 What started as a 'secondary trade' frequently developed into a separate business: the *Crowther Report*, para 2.1.15.

6 In the case of building society and bank lenders, these loans have tended to be secured by tacking an additional loan onto a first mortgage, whereas finance companies particularly have expanded second mortgage lending. For purchase money loans, see generally ante, para 2.16.

the Building Society Act 1986. At the same time, there was a steady development of weekly home credit (see ante, para 2.17), where it is relatively common both for the loan to be in default[7] and for loans to be rolled-over (see post, para 7.04A).

The net effect of the foregoing was a clear dichotomy of legislative control. If the supplier of goods chose to do business on credit, he should look to the Hire Purchase Acts for his controls; whereas, if the loan transaction was separate from the supply of goods, it might be governed by the Pawnbrokers Acts or the Moneylenders and Bills of Sale Acts. Eventually, the anomalous pattern of these statutory controls led to the creation in 1968 of the Crowther Committee (see post, para 5.03).

[5.03/04] The *Crowther Report*. The radical two volume Report of the Crowther Committee was published in March 1971.[1] Besides commenting on the economic and social aspects of consumer credit,[2] the Report pointed to serious deficiencies in the then existing law.[3] In the light of these findings, it opted for sweeping changes, resting on recognition of two points: first, that the extension of credit in sale or hp was in reality a loan, the reservation of title in conditional sale, hp and finance leases in reality being a chattel mortgage securing that loan; and second, that there should be introduced a uniform set of rules for all security devices. To implement this thesis, the Report proposed two new statutes **as a package:**[4]

1   *The proposed Lending and Security Act.* Other than loans secured on land, this was to apply to all credit transactions generally.[5] It would deal not just with the rights of the parties under the 'loan' contract, but also with registration of the security interest and conflicts between the secured party and any third party.[6]

2   *The proposed Consumer Sale and Loan Act.* This would fuse together all the various forms of existing legislation relating to consumer credit into one rationally coherent enactment: whereas the proposed Lending and Security Act would apply to all transactions of the types mentioned, the proposed Consumer Sale and Loan Act was designed to catch only those types of transaction when applied to consumers.[7]

After taking two years to digest these sweeping proposals, the government produced the following conclusions:[8] a Consumer Sale and Loan Bill should be introduced immediately (see CCA: post, para 5.05), but the proposed Lending and Security Bill

---

7   It is argued that this is not really default, in that technical default is normal, but not treated by either debtor or creditor as such: CCA, *Mirage or Reality* (1992), p 20.

[5.03/04]

1   *Report of the Crowther Committee on Consumer Credit* (1971, Cmnd 4596). It contains a mine of information on the then state of the industry, all carefully indexed and conveniently summarised in Chapter 1.3. See the account in Goode, *Consumer Credit Law and Practice*, Div 1A, paras 1.41–43.

2   Paragraphs 1.3.2–5. The matter is set out in more detail in Part 3 of the Report.

3   Paragraph 1.3.6. The then-existing state of credit law is set out in Part 4 of the Report.

4   Paragraph 5.2.20. The Report also dealt with administrative and fiscal measures, including the appointment of a credit commissioner, licensing, the statutory control of credit terms and the future: Chapter 1.3 and Parts 7, 8 and 9.

5   Including unsecured loans; the loan aspect of all instalment sales, revolving credits, check-trading and credit cards; hp and conditional sales; finance leases; mortgages and charges of goods, documents and intangibles; and pledges of goods and documents.

6   Paragraphs 1.3.12–21. The details of these proposals are set out in Part 5 of the Report.

7   Paragraphs 1.3.23–47. The proposals are set out in some detail in Part 6 of the Report.

8   *Reform of the Law on Consumer Credit* (1973, Cmnd 5427).

shelved indefinitely (see post, para 25.34). Central co-ordination of this new consumer protection system was to be placed in the hands of the Director General of the Office of Fair Trading (see ante, para 3.03), together with a new licensing system (see post, para 6.10).

THE CONSUMER CREDIT ACT

[5.05] Introduction.[1] Though amended substantially during its passage through Parliament, the Consumer Credit Act 1974 (CCA) was essentially a bi-partisan measure. Indeed, MPs almost killed the measure with kindness, as they competed with each other to give ever-more protection to their consumer-voters. The eventual Act was of very substantial proportions: 193 sections and five schedules, occupying some 174 pages in the Queen's Printer's copy; and a significant number of those provisions were simply enabling ones.[2] Indeed, it was the policy of the Act to confine itself to general principles, leaving the details to be filled out by statutory instruments;[3] and so great was the task that some of these instruments were not promulgated for 10 years.[4] In *Dimond v Lovell* (set out ante, para 1.19), Scott VC confirmed the application of the orthodox cannons of interpretation to this legislative scheme as follows (at 88g): '... the Act is to be construed as a whole; but it should not be construed in the light of the regulations' (the 'Henry VIII' principle: see post, para 5.10).

The resulting body of legislation is compulsory,[5] being at once both radical (see post, para 5.06) and traditional (see post, para 5.07). To some extent, the formidable bulk[6] is misleading, being derived from an attempt to cover every conceivable transaction and variation: if the individual provision is approached with particular examples in mind and the surplus words jettisoned, its general effect is frequently fairly easily apparent, even though the total weight of the legislation is undoubtedly formidable. In the 1990s, the Government seriously considered removing the protection of the Act from unincorporated business debtors, that is, sole traders and partnerships (see post, para 5.11). Subsequently, it contemplated a more general simplification of the Act by way of the deregulation initiative (see post, para 5.10). Account must also be taken of the changes wrought by the EU, in particular through the consumer Credit Directives (see post, para 5.12).

[5.05]

1 See generally Lindgren (1977) 40 MLR 159.

2 An unsuccessful attempt has been made to challenge some CCA regulations as being *ultra vires*: *First National Bank v Secretary of State* (1990) 10 TR LR 184, CA (advertising regulations made under s 44(1): see post, para 8.30).

3 The text of most relevant current statutory instruments will conveniently be found set out in the encyclopedias referred to below.

4 Unless otherwise stated, in the Regulations words have the same meaning as in the CCA: Interpretation Act 1978, s 11.

5 CCA, s 173; see further, post, para 18.11.

6 'An Act of extraordinary length and complexity': see Goff LJ in *Jenkins v Lombard North Central plc* (set out post, para 8.29) at 829e.

Moreover, because of its size, complexity and changing nature, the CCA can really only be satisfactorily consulted via one of the looseleaf encyclopedias,[7] or at very least a looseleaf annotated version of the statute,[8] though there are some monographs that attempt to put the Act in context.[9]

[5.06] The radical aspect. The CCA is self-consciously radical. Some idea of its scope may be gained from the list of enactments wholly or partially repealed (s 192 and Sched 5). The Act is certainly radical in the sense that it seeks to make a new start with newly-invented terminology. The purpose was to make it difficult for practitioners to ignore the new law by simply assuming that it only re-enacts previous law:[1] much of the new terminology will be found listed and explained by way of helpful examples in Sched 2;[2] and all the old Acts remaining in force are set out in the new terminology in Sched 4.[3] The CCA is also radical in that it extends its protection into fields hitherto uncovered, eg, licensing of all credit-granters (see post, Chapter 6), restricting of canvassing of all credit (see post, para 7.05), and on second mortgages (see post, para 25.23).

[5.07] The traditional aspect. In another sense, the CCA is traditional. First, whereas the SGA 1893 was intended to embody the common law concepts by codifying them, the CCA merely assumes the basic common law concepts: so, whilst a coherent pattern of law can often be divined simply by reading the SGA and the previous common law largely discarded, with the CCA the reader must constantly bear in mind the underlying common law, to which the Act makes, often detailed, changes.

Second, at the statutory level many of the provisions in the CCA simply build on ideas found in previous legislation. Thus, many of the ideas of the old Hire Purchase Acts and Moneylenders Acts have simply been re-cast in the new terminology and adapted to cover a greater range of transactions, eg, the provisions in relation to advertising (see post, para 8.27), cancellation (see post, para 10.29) and repossession (see post, para 24.27). Furthermore, the CCA does **not** do any of the following:

(a) make chattel mortgaging easier (see post, para 25.25); nor

(b) deal with the implied terms in contracts for the supply of goods (see post, Chapters 12–15); nor

(c) affect third party rights (see post, Chapter 21); nor

(d) interfere with the general fair trading rules (see ante, Chapter 4).

---

7   See Bennion, *Consumer Credit Control* (see ante, para 1.03); Goode, *Consumer Credit Law and Practice*, (unless otherwise stated, all subsequent references are to Div 1); Guest and Lloyd, *Encyclopedia of Consumer Credit*. The last is the smallest of these works, and the one perhaps best suited to undergraduate needs.

8   A good working annotation is by Guest and Lloyd, *ibid*, Part 2. See also Goode, *ibid*, Div II.

9   See Diamond, *Commercial and Consumer Credit*; Dobson's *Concise College Text, Sale of Goods and Consumer Credit* (6th edn).

[5.06]

1   See the *Crowther Report*, para 5.2.20.

2   But see s 188: in the event of conflict, the CCA prevails over Sched 2; and see Lindgren (1977) 40 MLR at 163. If difficulty is experienced in locating any of the new concepts of the CCA, a good place to start is often the Act's definition section (s 189(1)).

3   What is the effect, if any, on the statutes set out in the Schedule insofar as they deal with unregulated agreements, eg, Part III of the HPA 1964 (see post, para 21.55); s 14(3) of the SGA (see post, para 14.12)?

[5.08] The major areas of CCA control. Leaving aside licensing (see, post Chapter 6), the major areas in which the CCA imposes changes on the ordinary laws are as follows:[1]

(a) *The machinery of enforcement.* Breach of many of the provisions of the CCA (or regulations made thereunder) is a criminal offence of strict liability, imposed on an extended range of persons but subject to a number of defences.[2] Enforcement is placed in the hands of local weights and measures authorities (see ante, para 3.05) working under a uniform system (see post, Chapter 28) and subject to the centralised control of the OFT,[3] which also operates the above all-embracing licensing system.

(b) *Truth-in-lending.* In attempting to force the disclosure of the true cost of credit, the CCA enables the Secretary of State to make regulations governing the components to be taken into account in calculating the 'total charge for credit' (see post, para 8.23). This concept is important for a number of reasons: to fix the low cost credit category of exempt agreement (see post, para 5.15); to establish the amount of credit, and hence, whether an agreement is regulated (see post, para 5.22); to decide whether or not a credit bargain is extortionate (see post, para 29.40); and to publicise the total charge for credit.[4]

(c) *Transactional control prior to default.* Besides the truth-in-lending provisions (above), the CCA seeks to regulate all the following aspects of the transaction: advertising for such business (see post, para 8.20 *et seq*); the formalities required in the making of agreements within its ambit (see post, Chapter 9); the formation of the agreement, including cancellation[5] and contracting out;[6] the right to terminate the agreement;[7] and the persons liable for breach of undertaking or misrepresentation (see post, Chapter 16).

(d) *Transactional 'default' control.* In favour of a defaulting debtor or hirer,[8] the CCA imposes the following restrictions on the freedom of action on his creditor or owner: obligatory preliminary notices;[9] and enforcement[10] or Time Orders[11] or Stop Now Orders (see post, para 28.03) by a court.[12]

[5.08]

1 There are also important provisions dealing with pawnbroking (see post, para 25.15), contracts of surety (see post, para 25.03) and consumer credit intermediaries (see post, para 5.36).

2 For strict liability crimes, see generally ante, para 4.01. However, the CCA criminal liability does not of itself lead to any further sanctions (s 170); and see post, para 10.19. For the defences, see post, para 28.13 *et seq.*

3 See ante, para 3.03. For the OFT's current *General Notices and Determinations, Circulars and Official Forms*, see Goode, *Consumer Credit Law and Practice*, Div IV, XIII; Guest and Lloyd, *Encyclopedia of Consumer Credit*, Part 4.

4 Expressed both as a sum of money and as a percentage by way of the advertisement and documentation regulations (see post, Chapters 8–10).

5 Under ss 67–73: see post, para 10.29 *et seq.*

6 Under s 173: see post, para 18.11.

7 Under ss 99–102: see further post, paras 26.04–07. As to accelerated settlement, see post, para 26.19.

8 Whilst the expression 'default' is used here, it will be seen later that the CCA provisions go far beyond the situation where the debtor or hirer is technically in default to include such as his death.

9 Before a creditor or owner takes any of the specified major steps, eg, to terminate the agreement, he is required to give the debtor or hirer a seven day notice: ss 76, 87, 98 (see post, paras 24.28–32; 26.10).

10 In certain cases, before he can enforce an agreement, the creditor or owner must obtain from the court an enforcement order: ss 90–92, 96, 126, 127 (see post, paras 24.34–38; 24.44; 25.23; 24.33).

11 These orders will frequently be granted by the court in proceedings after 'default', see post, para 24.40.

12 Under s 189(1), in England and Wales 'court' in the Act *prima facie* means county court; as to which see generally post, para 24.39.

[5.09] Post-1974 credit practice. In 1974 the greater amount of consumer credit was probably of finite sums, whether linked to a supply of goods in an instalment credit contract (see ante, para 1.03), or by way of loan. However, since the enactment of the CCA there have been some major changes in the consumer market.[1]

1 *Revolving credit*. The notion of revolving credit has long been familiar to consumers in this country in both the following contexts: the bank overdraft (see ante, para 2.17) and store budget accounts (see ante, para 2.19). However, the 1980s saw a significant switch in the forms of credit used, from contracts in respect of a definite sum to revolving credit, particularly by the use of credit cards (see ante, para 2.28). Whilst finite amounts of credit for higher value items is still likely to be granted by a way of Personal Loan (see ante, para 2.17) or instalment credit contract (see above), smaller items tend to be obtained through revolving credit based on a credit card. By 2001, the number of credit cards in use had risen to 48 million, covering some 14 million individuals (see ante, para 2.25).

2 *Bank accounts*. This move towards revolving credit has been linked with the spread of bank accounts and use of overdrafts. In 1969, only one-third of adults had a bank account with a cheque book, whilst the unbanked two-thirds tended to rely on instalment credit from retailers and loans from pawnbrokers, moneylenders and check traders.[2] By the 1990s, over 80% of the population had bank accounts:[3] such accounts have traditionally been operated by the use of cheque books (see post, para 7.28); but the authorities seem anxious to replace such a paper-based system by an electronic one, the debit card (see ante, para 2.25). The remaining unbanked part of the population are normally insufficiently creditworthy to qualify for a debit card or credit card, frequently being forced back on the more expensive home credit (see ante, para 5.01): they also tend to use check traders (see post, para 15.17), mail order catalogues (see post, para 8.19) and estate-based credit unions if available (see post, para 15.19); they may have to discount any cheques received;[4] and are particularly likely to suffer over-indebtedness.[5]

3 *Leasing*. As an alternative to bank overdraft to raise funds for purchase, there has been an increased willingness to lease goods (see ante, para 1.18), a market significantly influenced by issues of taxation.

4 *E-Commerce*. The wide-spread availability of shopping by internet in the 21st century and payment for such items by credit card has posed new problems (see post, para 8.17), because the CCA assumes a paper-based system.

The formidable size of the CCA was partly based on the premise that there was so little parliamentary time likely to be granted for reform in this area that the opportunity should

---

[5.09]

1 See OFT, *Consultation Document on the Working and Enforcement of the Consumer Credit Act 1974* (1993), Annex 1, para 13.
2 *Ibid*, para 9; and see ante, para 2.23.
3 *Ibid*, para 10. Sometimes, such a cheque will be supported with a cheque guarantee card (see ante, para 2.25).
4 In particular, discounting the new instruments under the Cheques Act 1992 may be expensive.
5 See OFT, (1992) Beeline 1/8; and post, para 29.01.

be taken to make sufficient changes to last a generation – what may be termed the 'big bang' theory. Certainly, it is a tribute to the structure of the CCA, and to the *Crowther Report* on which it was based, that the CCA has coped so well with the above changes in the structure of the credit industry. However, it may be questioned whether the 'big-bang' strategy has proved as successful as the more piecemeal approach adopted in relation to reform of the SGA (see ante, para 1.02). Certainly, the Government now has a shopping-list of changes to the CCA which it would like to see implemented;[6] not all of these are likely to find their way into a new EU Directive (see post, para 5.12), nor are amendments to existing legislation, but perhaps they can be dealt with under the deregulation powers (see post, para 5.10), eg, the practice of advertising '0% credit' where interest is charged from the outset, but reclaimable under a deliberately complicated procedure that the consumer is unlikely to be able to invoke[7] and may be unfair (see post, para 11.12 *et seq*).

[5.10] Deregulation. Government initiative in the 1990s to reduce red-tape across Whitehall led to the discovery that many of the desired changes could not be made because they required primary legislation. To remove this parliamentary bottle-neck, there was enacted the Deregulation and Contracting Out Act 1994.[1] The success of this Act led to the enhancement of the deregulatory powers in the Regulatory Reform Act 2001.[1] As its name implies, the 1994 Act has two major strands:

1　*Deregulation*. Within Part I of the Act, Chapter 2 contains a list of miscellaneous statutory provisions whose requirements are simplified or removed, including those relating to the following: weights and measures;[2] licensed premises;[3] and shop opening hours.[4] Of far wider significance are the two sorts of general power to be found in Part I. First, whilst one statutory instrument can always be repealed or altered by another statutory instrument, it has been an accepted part of our constitutional law that primary legislation cannot generally be amended by a subsequent statutory instrument, a 'Henry VIII clause' (see ante, para 5.05), although there is already an exception as regards statutory instrument implementing EU laws.[5] However, under s 1 of the 2001 Act ministers are empowered by statutory order to amend or repeal **existing** primary legislation (of any date) that imposes an unnecessary burden on business.[6] So, the powers cannot be used to create an entirely **new** provision. Only some of the orders already made are relevant here;[7] and for us the most significant proposals are those in the field of in consumer credit (see post,

---

6　The DTI have consulted since 2000 on: early settlements; advertising; financial ceilings; extortionate credit; e-commerce. See further post, para 5.11.

7　On '0% credit', see ante, para 2.07 and post, paras 8.27; 8.30.

[5.10]

1　For valuable introductory notes on the 1994 and 2001 Acts, see Current Law Statutes. The first two years after enactment in 1994 saw a wealth of detailed change: [1996] 15 Tr L 343.

2　Section 14 of the 1994 Act: see ante, para 4.25.

3　Section 19 of the 1994 Act: see post, para 6.05.

4　Sections 23–24 of the 1994 Act: see post, para 8.13.

5　Under s 2(2) of the ECA: see ante, paras 1.03A; 4.24; 4.32.

6　Sections 1–3 of the 2001 Act. The manner in which order-making power may be exercised is dealt with in ss 4–8 of the 2001 Act which includes preliminary public consultation (ss 5, 7).

7　Eg, credit unions (see post, para 15.19); truncation of cheques (see post, para 23.14A).

para 5.11) and UCTA.[8] Unlike the powers under the 1994 Act, those under the 2001 Act can be used to impose burdens in limited circumstances (s 1(1) of 2001 Act). Second, the Act contains powers to 'improve' the 'fairness, transparency and consistency' of enforcement procedures,[9] which for our purposes is likely to be particularly significant in relation to the enforcement of consumer protection statutes by local authorities (see post, para 28.03). The 2001 Act enables the promulgation of statutory codes of practice:[10] these are mandatory on local authorities in the sense that, where there is a local authority prosecution, any relevant code may be taken into account by the tribunal 'in deciding how to deal with the failure to comply with' the provision (s 9(3) of 2001 Act; and see post, para 28.06). Whilst the court or tribunal can take the LA's failure to comply with any relevant code into account at the sentencing and costs stage (see post, para 28.07), the provision seems unclear as to whether that failure is relevant before conviction.[11]

2   *Contracting out.* Part II of the 1994 Act confers powers on Ministers to provide for the contracting out to private contractors of certain functions which other statutes have placed upon Ministers (ss 69, 71: see ante, para 3.02), office holders,[12] and local authorities (ss 70, 71: see ante, para 3.05/06), subject to restrictions on the disclosure of information (Sched 15: see post, para 28.06).

[5.11] Amendment of Consumer Credit Act. The OFT has long kept a wish-list of reforms to the CCA.[1] If the DTI, as the sponsoring Government Department (see ante, para 3.02), chooses to amend the CCA it broadly has two choices. First, it may effect amendments by way of statute, though this will require heavy use of scarce parliamentary time: it may effected by including amendments in a statute which is primarily designed to achieve some other purpose;[2] or it may promote a new statute for the purpose (see below), though a Department will seldom obtain such an opportunity. Second, it may lay before Parliament a statutory instrument (SI), which will generally take up much less parliamentary time:[2a]

1   *Statutory instruments.* It has already been noted that, under the terms of the CCA, many of its principles may be fleshed out by SI (see ante, para 5.05); and, of course, those SIs may be further varied by subsequent SIs, eg, the raising of the financial

---

8   The Government has remitted to the Law Commission the possibility of replacing the UTCC Regulations (see post, para 11.12) and UCTA (see post, para 18.12) with a single coherent code: DTI, *Sale of Consumer Goods: First Consultation* (4.1.01), Question 2.

9   Section 9(1)(b) of the 2001 Act. There is still in force an amended s 6 of the 1994 Act, empowering the Government to make model enforcement provisions.

10   Section 10 of the 2001 Act. For codes of practice, see generally ante, para 3.11.

11   Eg, to exclude evidence unfairly obtained; or a general defence (see post, para 28.14).

12   Sections 69, 71, 74. According to s 79 'office holder' includes an office created by statute, eg, OFT (see ante, para 3.03).

[5.11]

1   OFT, *Consumer Credit Deregulation* (June 1994). Some of the ideas in this document not taken up in the DTI response (see below) include the following: (a) increase in Part V exemption powers (see post, para 9.07); (b) rules relating to advertisements simplified (see post, para 8.31); (c) copies of documentation for land mortgages (see post, para 9.17A) reduced; (d) category of cancellable agreements (see post, para 10.29) shrunk; (e) simplified procedure for modifying regulated agreements (see post, para 26.22); and (f) licensing categories system should be simplified (see post, para 6.15).

2   Eg, CCA, s 3 (see post, para 6.25); s 74 (see post, para 9.07); s 187 (see post, para 5.33).

2a   As of February 2002, this looks to be quite a likely route for early reform: (2002) 56 CC 5/4.

limits (see post, para 5.22). However, on general principles, those SIs made under the CCA cannot vary the CCA itself (a 'Henry VIII clause': see ante, para 5.10). By way of exception, the following types of SI may vary the text of the CCA:

(a) *Euro-SIs*. These are SIs implementing EU Directives generally (see ante, para 1.03A); and in particular the amendments to the Consumer Credit Directive (see post, para 5.12). These SIs made to implement Directives may have both a negative and positive effect on the CCA: the SIs may delete provisions of the CCA; and they may add new principles to the CCA. However, from the viewpoint of the DTI, these SIs suffer from the disadvantage that the DTI cannot directly control what goes into the Directive and hence, what must appear in the SI.

(b) *Deregulation SIs* (see ante, para 5.10). Since 1994, the DTI has proposed a number of deletions from the CCA via this route in two Consultation Papers in 1995 and 1998:[3]

(i) *Lending and hiring to unincorporated businesses*. Because of the difficulty of distinguishing between the business and personal affairs of such persons, the CCA presently extends to unincorporated businesses by reason of its definition of 'individual' (see post, para 5.24). A draft statutory order foundered in a House of Commons Committee.[4]

(ii) *Quotations*. The CCA regulated the documents in which creditors and owners give prospective debtors and hirers full information about the nature and prices of their services; but these have been replaced (see post, para 8.32).

(iii) *Early settlement rebates*. If a debtor under a regulated agreement elects to repay his debt early, CCA regulations ensure that he receives a rebate on that early settlement (see post, para 26.19A). The OFT recommended that the method of calculating rebates should be made more equitable; but this has been rejected.[5]

(iv) *Short-term hire agreements*. It will be recalled that the definition of a consumer hire agreement excludes agreements of less than three months (see ante, para 1.19). Tool hire businesses argue that some customers hire goods from day-to-day, retain them for more than three months and then argue that the hiring is an unenforceable regulated hiring. The DTI recommends the exclusion of such indefinite hirings from the CCA.

(v) *Unsigned mail order agreements*. The agency mail order business has been run for many years with the agent, usually a housewife, making repeated oral credit agreements with family and friends (see post, para 8.19). Some customers have begun to argue that these are unenforceable regulated agreements; and the DTI questions whether they deserve exemption (Chapter 6 of the 1998 Paper). A similar problem has since arisen with E-commerce (see post, para 8.17).

It will be observed that all the above deregulation initiatives are negative, in the sense that they seek to derogate from an existing CCA provision; for as previously pointed out, the deregulation powers cannot be used to create an entirely new provision (see ante, para 5.10). To do that, a statute is needed.

---

3   *Deregulation of United Kingdom Consumer Credit Legislation* (DTI, 1995); *Clarification and Simplification of UK Consumer Credit Law* (DTI, February 1998).
4   See (1997) 52 CC 1/2.
5   See (1997) 51 CC 5/23.

2   *Statutes*. The CCA has served well for an entire generation, but is now beginning to show its age, eg, some case law has raised difficulties of interpretation.[6] After the General Election, the new Consumer Affairs Minister made a fresh announcement in July 2001 that the DTI would review the CCA: it was envisaged that this review would be in addition to following up the Overindebtedness Task Force recommendations (see post, para 27.01), but largely leaving aside those matters likely to be dealt with in the (perhaps more long-term EU review of the Consumer Credit Directive (see post, para 5.12). The DTI has secured a slot for a draft Enterprise Bill 2002.[7] It has identified the following priority areas to be included in the Enterprise Bill:[8] enhancing the powers of the OFT and adding a new statutory Board (see ante, para 3.03); enabling consumers to conclude credit agreements on-line and bring competition claims; increase the CCA financial limits and change the exemption categories; amend the early settlement regulations; simplify the advertising regulations; make more effective the extortionate credit provisions, perhaps by adding a new element of unconscionability; change the licensing regime, perhaps in the hope of restraining heavy-handed debt collection; lightening the insolvency laws (see post, para 19.19); repealing Parts II and III of the FTA; and dovetailing all these developments with the new regime for house mortgages, etc, being constructed under the FSMA (see ante, para 3.02). Further, one might ask whether enforcement of the amended CCA rules might be tightened to combat routine non-compliance by some creditors?[9]

[5.12] EU developments. Since the late 1970s the EEC has been moving towards the harmonising of consumer credit laws (see generally ante, para 3.10). The first Directive on this subject was dated 1987; and in 1990 that Directive was amended to add provisions on the computation of the annual percentage rate of charge.[1] The Directive was modelled on the CCA, but was short and general in character. It allowed Member States to 'introduce or retain more stringent provisions to protect consumers' (Art 15), so that it did not prove necessary to make any alterations to the CCA.[2]

However, the 1987 Directive did contain the (common) provision for the Commission to review its operation by the mid-1990s (Art 17). Accordingly, the EU promulgated further amendments to the Consumer Credit Directive,[3] which will require amendment to English law in the following areas:

1   The extension of its scope to consumer credit where the purpose is to launch a business.[4]

---

6   Especially on s 18 (see post, para 5.27) and on s 75 (see post, para 16.11).

7   Due before Parliament in March 2002: (2002) *The Times*, 14 January.

8   DTI, *Consultation Document on Modernising the CCA* (July 2001). See further (2001) 31 Fair Trading 17; DTI, *Empowering Consumers in the Enterprise Economy* (2002).

9   This could partly be a matter of consumer education (see ante, para 3.01) and partly a matter of putting the onus on litigating creditors to provide evidence of their CCA compliance: see (2001) 61 QA 13.

[5.12]

1   Directive 87/102/EEC, as amended by Directive 90/88/EEC.

2   Goode, *Consumer Credit Law and Practice*, Part IJ, para 125.2.

3   Directive 98/7/EC. The text of Directive 87/102, as amended by Directives 90/88 and 98/7 is set out in Goode, *ibid*, Part X, para 1.91; Guest, *Encyclopedia of Consumer Credit Law*, para 9-126.

4   *Modern Markets: Confident Consumers* (1999, Cm 4410), para 6.12.

2   A Directive relating to mortgage credits (see post, para 7.04A).

3   Specifying the rules governing the use of credit cards (see post, paras 7.09; 16.11).

4   Revision of the maximum limit upwards or to be removed entirely (see post, para 5.22).

5   Considering retention of the exemption of four instalment agreements (see post, para 5.15).

6   A Code of Conduct on advertisements aimed at 'young' consumers (see post, para 8.33).

7   Maximum interest rates (see post, para 29.40).

8   The annual percentage rate of charge (see post, paras 8.23–26).[5]

9   A Directive relating to compulsory credit insurance (see post, para 24.44).

In 2001, there was another round of consultations concerned with the production of a further Directive on consumer credit, *inter alia*, perhaps with a view to excluding business lending and tightening the licensing of consumer credit.[6] The Commission have announced plans to publish a new draft Directive in February 2002, which they say would 'involve contemplating moving on from minimum harmonisation to maximum and optimal harmonisation which would guarantee a high level of consumer protection across the whole of the European Union', eg, interest rate capping.

The ambit of the Act

Regulated agreements

[5.13/14] Regulated agreements. The CCA for the most part applies only to '**regulated agreements**'. Thus, to ascertain whether any transaction is regulated by the CCA, the first task is normally to identify any 'regulated agreement', this expression being defined by s 189(1) as follows:

> ... 'regulated agreement' means a consumer credit agreement, or consumer hire agreement, other than an exempt agreement, and 'regulated' and 'unregulated' shall be construed accordingly.

This small section describes a vital two-stage intellectual process as regards **agreements**, whether actual or prospective (see below).

Stage 1. The draftsman has first identified for most purposes the permanent outer limits of the CCA by reference to the two key concepts of a **consumer credit** agreement (s 8) and a **consumer hire** agreement (s 15), both of which he deliberately defined too widely.

Stage 2. Then he has reduced their scope by introducing the, variable by statutory instrument, notion of **exempt** agreements (see below).

The result is that regulated agreements may be one of two sorts:[1]

---

5   *Modern Markets*, para 3.25.
6   See respectively post, paras 5.25; 6.11.
[5.13/14]
1   The agreement may be gathered from more than one document: s 189(4).

(a) non-exempt (s 8(3)) consumer credit agreements (see post, para 5.19 *et seq*), which is usually thought of as the main category within the Act;

(b) non-exempt (s 15(2)) consumer hire agreements (see ante, para 1.19), which is aimed at finance leases (see ante, para 1.18A), so that suppliers could not use that route to avoid the Act.[2]

Since the inception of the Act, most commentators have assumed that the above two categories are mutually exclusive; but this assumption was rebutted in *Dimond v Lovell*:[3]

> This case involved an accident hire agreement entered into by the innocent motorist (D) in a traffic accident, on terms previously described (see ante, para 1.19). It had already been decided in a previous case that this form of agreement was not void as amounting to maintenance.[4] The present proceedings raised many issues; and the Court of Appeal decision in favour of the negligent driver (L) was affirmed on a narrower range of issues by the House of Lords. On an unappealed point, the Court of Appeal unanimously decided that in principle the agreement could amount to **both** consumer credit[5] **and** consumer hire, but was saved from the latter category by the 28-day restriction.[6]

Referring to the distinct danger that the two sets of CCA provisions may be incompatible, Scott VC said:

> If any genuine case of incompatibility were to arise, the Act provides a remedy via an application under section 60(3) for a waiver or variation of the requirements.

Dimond v Lovell is a leading case concerned with the following two branches of the law:

(i) The effect on the accident hire agreement of the CCA. Both courts held that the accident hire agreement was a regulated consumer credit agreement (see post, para 5.21), but not exempt (see post, para 5.15). On unappealed issues, the Court of Appeal held that the agreement amounted to running account-credit;[7] and that, because the agreement did not comply with the documentation rules,[8] it was unenforceable.[9]

(ii) The measures of damages recoverable by D because of L's admitted negligent damage to D's car, which led to the hiring of a replacement (see post, para 27.28). The issue was strictly *obiter*, because the agreement was unenforceable under the CCA (see above). However, the majority of the Court of Appeal would have allowed D to recover the sum claimed on the grounds that she had properly mitigated her loss by entering into the accident hire agreement (see post, para 27.44); but the House of Lords would have reduced the damages under the rules of causation (see post, para 27.29) and also refused a restitutionary remedy for unjust enrichment by reason of s 170 (see post, para 10.18).

Prospective agreements. The Act sometimes bites before there comes into existence what the common law would recognise as a binding contract, referring to a 'prospective agreement' (see post, para 5.20).

---

2   Goode, *Consumer Credit Law and Practice*, Part 11B, para 5.25.
3   [1999] 3 All ER 1, CA (see [1999] JBL 452); affd [2000] 2 All ER 897, HL (see [2001] JBL 14).
4   *Giles v Thompson* [1994] 1 AC 142, HL; see post, para 7.26.
5   Under s 9(1): see post, para 5.21.
6   Under s 15(1)(c): see ante, para 1.19.
7   Under s 10(1)(a): see post, para 5.28.
8   Under ss 60–61: see post, para 9.10.
9   Under s 65: see post, para 9.19.

Exempt agreements. Broadly, the draftsman has saved from the CCA agreements which he terms 'unregulated' because they are 'exempt' (see above). According to the Act (s 189(1)), an 'exempt agreement' means one specified in or under s 16, which in turn sets out different classes of exemption for the two main categories:

(a) Exempt consumer credit agreements, a category in respect of which s 16 has been significantly amended over the years (see post, para 5.15).

(b) Exempt consumer hire agreements as specified by statutory instrument.[10]

Whilst the Act has little application to exempt agreements (see below), except in relation to the extortionate credit provisions (see post, para 29.40 *et seq*) and advertisements (s 43(1)(b): see post, para 8.29), in relation to regulated agreements it also creates some special categories (see post, para 5.16).

[5.15] Exempt consumer credit agreements. Even though a transaction amounts to a consumer credit agreement (see post, para 5.19), it may be an exempt agreement (see ante, para 5.14) if it falls within one of the following categories under s 16 and its Regulations:[1]

1 *Short-term consumer credit*.[2] This exempt category covers consumer credit agreements for the supply of goods or services (dcs agreements: see post, para 5.34) within either of the following types:

(a) For fixed-sum credit (see post, para 5.28) of up to 12 months duration[3] in respect of goods supplied and where the number of instalments does not exceed **four**,[4] eg, a 28-day trade credit for goods supplied, where the price is payable 28 days after delivery of the goods; a purchase from a department store of a bedroom suite by a deposit and not more than three post-delivery instalments.

(b) For running-account credit (see post, para 5.28) where the credit provided in each period, eg, weekly or monthly, *must* be repayable in **one** amount,[4] eg, the weekly milk bill; a purchase from a department store of a radio by a customer with a monthly account, or using a charge card.[5]

2 *Low-cost credit*. This category is restricted to pure loans (dc agreements: see post, para 5.35) extended on a non-commercial basis (see post, para 5.18) and does not apply to loans connected with the supply of goods or services, which will usually only be exempt under the above short-term category. It exempts only the following categories (s 16(5)(b); and Art 4):

---

10 Section 16(6). See Consumer Credit (Exempt Agreements) Order 1989, SI 869, Art 6.

[5.15]

1 The Consumer Credit (Exempt Agreements) Order 1989, SI 869 (as amended). This account ignores some of the less common exempt classes.

2 Section 16(5)(a) and Art 3(1)(a). This category does not include finance for the purchase of land, or conditional sales or hp or pledges of goods: Art 3(2). It does not apply to unsecured cash loans, which can only achieve exemption under category 2, below.

3 *Zone v Rouamba* [2000] 2 All ER 620, CA; *Ketley v Gilbert* (2001) 151 NLJ 20, CA. This category did not extend to *Dimond v Lovell* (set out ante, para 5.13) because the credit hire agreement for fixed-sum credit (see post, para 5.28) could last more than 12 months in that the payment of rental could be delayed beyond that time.

4 Article 3(1)(a). Only counted are repayments of capital (*contra* category 4, below) without option to extend the number of payments or without later variation to that effect.

5 As to open accounts, see ante, para 2.19. As to charge cards, see ante, para 2.24.

(a) loans by credit unions (see post, para 15.19) where the rate of interest in effect does not exceed 12.7% APR;[6]

(b) fixed loans which are not 'offered to the public generally', but only 'offered to a particular class, or particular classes, of individuals',[7] and the APR[6] does not exceed 1% more than the highest bank base rate as that rate varies. Confined to loans at below a commercial rate of interest, this category will cover such as low-cost mortgages to employees.[8]

3 *Finance for foreign trade.* The effect of this exemption is that credit agreements made in connection with the export or import of goods or services are exempt,[9] and therefore largely beyond the control of the Act, whilst remaining subject to the extortionate credit bargain provisions.[10]

4 *Responsible mortgage lenders.* As they are assumed to be responsible lenders, there are automatically exempt by s 16(2) most consumer credit agreements secured on land where the lender is a local authority (ss 16(1), (2)), or housing association (s 16(6A)) or other responsible mortgage lender. See further below.

5 *Residential first mortgages.* By summer 2002, residential house purchase loans are likely to be governed by the FSMA (see ante, para 3.02) and be exempt from the CCA.[11] In effect, that will leave residential second mortgages within its financial limit to be regulated by the CCA: but, where the lender is a body specified in or under s 16(1) (as amended) and the loan is by way of mortgage within s 16(2) (see above), the loan is exempt if it *also* satisfies the conditions laid down in the Regulations.[12]

[5.16] Special categories. Whilst exempt agreements are, as their name suggests, almost wholly exempt from the provisions of the CCA (see ante, para 5.15), the Act also contains a number of special categories which are either exempted from particular (different) provisions, or additionally subject to some further ones.

1 *Small agreements* (see post, para 5.17).

2 *Non-commercial agreements* (see post, para 5.18).

3 *Bank overdrafts.* These may be exempted by the Director (see ante, para 3.03) from all the documentation provisions of the CCA (see post, para 9.07).

4 *Second mortgages of land.* Instead of the agreement being subject to the cancellation provisions, the debtor entering such mortgages is given a special opportunity to withdraw before the agreement is concluded (s 58: see post, para 10.27).

---

6 For APRs, see post, para 8.26. The proposition in the text is an over-simplification, because, even ignoring the special rules applicable during 1998/99, Art 4 gives a special meaning to the tcc (as to which, see post, para 8.24): see further Guest and Lloyd, *Encyclopedia of Consumer Credit*, para 3-338.

7 This requirement derives from Art 2(2) of the EU Consumer Credit Directive 87/102 and may be difficult to interpret: see Guest and Lloyd, *ibid.* Loans of variable amounts of capital are excluded by Art 4(2).

8 Eg *BCCI v Ali (No 2)* [2000] CLY 2594.

9 Section 16(5)(c) and Art 5: see Goode, *Consumer Credit Law and Practice*, para 49.92. But see Lindgren (1977) 40 MLR at 168–69. Compare s 27(2) of UCTA 1977: see post, para 18.14.

10 Sections 137–40: see post, para 29.40 *et seq.*

11 Sections 16(6C)–(6E), as inserted by the FSMA: 2001 SI 544, Art 90(2).

12 Section 16(2) and Art 2. See further, Guest and Lloyd, *Encyclopedia of Consumer Credit*, para 3-336.

5   *Pledges of documents of title.* The CCA restrictions as to the taking of pledges[1] are designed to protect consumers rather than businessmen, and therefore do not apply to pledges of documents of title.[2]

6   *Conditional sale and hp agreements.* As important types of consumer credit agreement (see post, para 5.19 *et seq*), they are subject to many of the CCA controls. Additionally, there are some provisions which apply exclusively to regulated conditional sales and hp: they cannot be small agreements (see post, para 5.17); they may involve protected goods,[3] and also be subject to the prohibition on entering premises;[4] the buyer or hirer has a statutory right to terminate the agreement;[5] there is a special rule for showing adverse possession of goods let on hp;[6] and the court has special powers to make transfer or return orders (s 133: see post, para 24.43).

[5.17] Small agreements. According to s 17(1), this expression means:

(a)   a regulated consumer credit agreement for credit not exceeding [£x], other than a hire-purchase or conditional sale agreement; or

(b)   a regulated consumer hire agreement which does not require the hirer to make payments exceeding [£x],

being an agreement which is either unsecured or secured by a guarantee or indemnity only (whether or not the guarantee or indemnity is itself secured).

This section extends to running-account credit with the same small credit limit;[1] and it includes an anti-avoidance device.[2] Overall, s 17 is drafted with three qualifications:

(1)   Its ambit is limited by a figure. Section 17 originally referred to £30, though like many of the Act's financial limits, it may be amended by statutory order;[3] and the figure has now been raised to £50.[4] However, in relation to the two types of regulated agreement the figure refers to different things: with regard to consumer credit agreements (see post, para 5.19 *et seq*), it is speaking of the amount of credit, eg, sum borrowed; whereas in respect of consumer hire agreements (see ante, para 1.19), the important thing is the total amount the hirer is **required** to pay under the agreement, eg, deposit, plus rentals and VAT. Nor is it possible to evade the financial limits by utilising running-account credit;[1] nor by splitting up the transaction into two or more agreements.[2]

[5.16]
1   Sections 114, 122: see post, para 25.15 *et seq*.
2   Section 114(3), as amended by the Banking Act 1979, s 38 (see above); and for trust receipts, see post, para 25.16.
3   Within s 90: see post, para 24.35.
4   Section 92: see post, para 24.34.
5   Sections 99–100: see post, para 26.05–07.
6   Section 134: see post, para 24.42.

[5.17]
1   Section 17(2), referring to s 10(3)(a), but not s 10(3)(b): see post, para 5.28.
2   Sections 17(3) and (4): this is to prevent a transaction from being artificially split into two or more small agreements.
3   Section 181. The intention behind the provision is to allow Parliament to inflation-proof the figure. This device is copied from s 3 of the HPA 1965.
4   Consumer Credit (Increase of Monetary Limits) Order 1983, SI No 1878.

(2) It cannot include conditional sales (see ante, para 1.16) nor hp agreements (see ante, para 1.24). Such agreements may amount to consumer credit agreements (see post, para 5.23); but, however small the amount of credit, they cannot fall within s 17(1).

(3) The agreement must be unsecured, or secured only by a guarantee or indemnity (see post, para 25.10). Thus, however small the amount of money involved, s 17(1) does not comprehend transactions supported by real security, eg, a pledge for £5.

Examples of small agreements will include all the following: a credit sale (see ante, para 1.13) where the credit does not exceed the designated figure; a bank overdraft or credit-card facility for less than that figure;[5] a consumer hire agreement for an indefinite period, but giving the hirer the option to terminate before his total payments reach the stipulated figure. The major exemption enjoyed by small agreements is from most of Part V of the CCA (s 74(2)), dealing with entry into credit or hire agreements (see post, para 9.07). Additionally, small agreements are exempt from provisions as to the following: the unsolicited mailing of credit cards,[6] copies of card agreements[6] and the duty to supply periodic statements of accounts.[7] The rationale of all these exemptions would appear to be that the relieved duties would amount to too great a burden on the creditor as against the advantage to the debtor.

[5.18] **Non-commercial agreements**. According to s 189(1), this expression:

... means a consumer credit agreement or consumer hire agreement not made by the creditor or owner in the course of a business carried on by him.

Clearly, if the creditor carries on a business[1] of entering into regulated agreements, none of the regulated agreements which go through the books of the firm could be regarded as non-commercial. Equally clearly, a creditor not engaged in any business would have his regulated agreements classed as non-commercial.[2] But what of a creditor who is primarily engaged in some business not necessarily connected with entry into regulated agreements, eg, a solicitor, but who does occasionally enter into regulated agreements?[3]

Non-commercial agreements not only obtain the same exemptions from the CCA as small agreements (see ante, para 5.17), but are also totally exempt from the connected lender liability of s 75 (s 75(3)(a): see post, para 16.11). Additionally, non-commercial agreements are exempt from the following: the creditor or owner is exempted from the licensing requirements (see post, para 6.09 et seq) so that by the absence of a licence he neither commits an offence (s 39) nor has his agreements rendered unenforceable (s 40); both parties are released from the duty to supply information during the continuance of the agreement as to respectively the state of accounts to debtor/hirer or surety,[4] or

---

5   See Sched 2, Examples 16 and 17. See also Example 22.
6   Sections 51(2), 85(3). As to these duties, see post, para 7.12.
7   Section 78(7). As to these duties, see post, para 7.08. Note that the creditor remains liable in respect of the other duties to supply information contained in ss 77 and 78.

[5.18]
1   'Business' includes a profession or trade: s 189(1). Cf SGA, s 61(1) (see post, para 14.04); UCTA, s 14 (see post, para 18.18).
2   Cf Part III of the HPA 1964: see post, para 21.56.
3   See s 189(2), set out post, para 5.36; and Goode, *Consumer Credit Law and Practice*, para 23.141. Does it matter whether or not the regulated agreements are put through the books of the practice? Cf *Newton v Pyke* (1908) 25 TLR 127.
4   Sections 77–79, 107–10: see post, paras 7.08, 15.17.

whereabouts of the goods,[5] or variation of the regulated agreement,[6] or termination statements;[7] and the transaction is saved from the restrictions in respect of the realisation of security,[8] and as regards pawn-tickets (s 114: see post, para 25.18).

Consumer credit agreements

[5.19] Consumer credit agreements. This is one of the key concepts of the CCA, embracing all forms of contractual credit and including hp,[1] conditional sale,[2] credit sale,[3] check trading,[4] credit cards,[5] budget accounts,[6] overdrafts, personal loans,[7] mortgages[8] and pledges (see post, para 25.15). The concept is defined in s 8: as with most of the CCA, s 8 applies only to regulated agreements,[9] which excludes exempt agreements (s 8(3): see ante, para 5.15).

In respect of non-exempt agreements, the concept of a **consumer credit agreement** is defined in a complicated manner involving a number of constituent parts. Moreover, in order to differentiate fixed-sum credit for running-account credit (see post, para 5.28), the draftsman has separated out the amount of credit into a second stage.

Stage 1. A personal credit agreement. Whilst some other statutes in the consumer field define their applicability by reference to the purpose of the transaction,[10] the CCA instead concentrates on the status of the parties. Accordingly, s 8(1) provides that:

> A personal credit agreement is an agreement between an individual ('the debtor') and any other person ('the creditor') by which the creditor provides the debtor with credit of any amount.

This contains the following four requirements:

(a) there must be **an agreement** (see post, para 5.20);

(b) for the **provision of credit** (see post, para 5.21);

---

5 Section 80: see post, para 15.17.
6 Section 82: see post, para 26.22.
7 Section 103: see post, para 26.04.
8 Section 112: see post, para 25.13.

[5.19]
1 See ante, para 1.24.
2 See ante, para 1.16.
3 See ante, para 1.13.
4 See post, para 15.17.
5 See ante, para 2.28.
6 See ante, para 2.19.
7 See ante, para 2.17.
8 See post, para 25.19.
9 But not the extortionate credit bargain provisions (see post, para 29.40). Why is s 8(3) needed in view of the definition of 'regulated agreement' in s 189(1)? In view of this, it is difficult to resist the inference that s 8 is unnecessarily complicated.
10 Eg 'dealing as consumer' within s 12 of UCTA, which employs both a status of the parties and a status of the goods test (see post, para 18.18). The status of the supplier is relied upon in implied undertakings (see post, para 14.04). The 'purpose of the loan' test is used in the EEC Directive on Consumer Credit (Art 2(a)).

(c) between **the debtor** (see post, para 5.24); and

(d) **the creditor** (see post, para 5.25).

Stage 2. The amount of credit. Following the old HPA, the CCA wished to define its ambit by reference to the amount of money involved in the transaction: within the designated amount the agreement might be regulated; but above that amount it would be unregulated. However, this caused the draftsman problems in the modern market-place, where many credit agreements are for revolving credit under which it is of the essence of the transaction that the agreement should not specify the amount of credit (see ante, para 2.19). To meet this problem, he therefore divided regulated credit agreements into the following two sorts:

(i) *Fixed-sum credit*. This is the simpler situation where the amount of credit is known at the outset and the draftsman can therefore stipulate the amount of credit which will determine whether a transaction is regulated. For this situation, s 8(2) provides as follows:

> A consumer credit agreement is a personal credit agreement by which the creditor provides the debtor with credit not exceeding £x.

In order to determine whether fixed-sum credit is regulated, one therefore has to satisfy the above four tests for a personal credit agreement and then add a fifth test; namely whether the transaction is within the statutory credit ceiling (see post, para 5.22).

(ii) *Running-account credit*. Where there is a revolving credit agreement, which does not specify an amount of credit granted, but rather lays down the maximum amount of credit which can be obtained, the Act adopts the following scheme: in s 10 it christens that agreement a 'running-account' and the maximum sum the 'credit limit'; and then determines whether or not that agreement is regulated according to whether that credit limit exceeds the £x specified in s 8(2) (see above).

[5.20] An agreement. A consumer credit agreement (see ante, para 5.19) requires an **agreement**, meaning a binding contract between at least two parties made in accordance with the general law,[1] or prospective agreement (see below); and it does not include non-contractual arrangements, eg, supply of gas or electricity (see ante, para 3.07).

Furthermore, it must be an agreement to grant credit (see post, para 5.21): it is not sufficient that the agreement grants a **facility** under which another is in breach of contract able to obtain credit, eg, an unauthorised overdraft on a bank account;[2] he must have the **right** under the agreement to obtain credit,[3] though it would seem sufficient if the bank simply honours a cheque which allows the account to go overdrawn.[4] Nor need the bank customer exercise immediately any right to an overdraft facility. The effect of this may be

---

[5.20]

1 Goode, *Consumer Credit Law and Practice*, para 23.43. As to unregulated agreements treated by the parties as regulated, see Goode, paras 23.4b–d.

2 Such as a building society account which expressly prohibits the holder from overdrawing. Cf *Nejad v City Index Ltd* [2000] CLY 2597, CA.

3 The right to credit may be granted expressly, eg, a Personal Loan Account (see generally, ante, para 2.17); or it may be granted impliedly (see CCA, Sched 2, Examples 17, 18).

4 Goode, *op cit*, note 1, para 11.72.

to bring any payment cards issued on an account with an overdraft facility within the CCA,[5] whether they be a debit,[6] cash,[6] cheque guarantee card,[7] or multi-function card.[8]

For the moment, we may ignore any formalities required of such a contract (see post, Chapter 9) and any special rules required for its formation (see post, Chapter 10), though we should note two special situations provided for by the Act. First, there are some circumstances where it is intended that the Act shall apply not just to actual agreements, but also to inchoate ones:[9] in these situations only, the Act refers to 'prospective agreements' and the persons who will become parties to them.[10] This rule has special significance in relation to revolving credit agreements, eg, an overdraft facility, where the alleged agreement may in fact only amount to a standing offer (see post, para 7.11). Second, the Act reinforces the common law (see post, para 10.03) and continues the general prohibition[11] previously found in the HPA against the consumer binding himself to enter into a regulated agreement.[12] It provides that (s 59(1)):

> An agreement is void if, and to the extent that, it purports to bind a person to enter as debtor or hirer into a prospective regulated agreement.

This prohibition does not extend to the creditor or supplier binding himself, so that s 59(1) does not avoid options to enter into a regulated agreement granted to the debtor or hirer; nor does it extend to modified agreements (see post, para 26.12). For credit proposal forms, see post, para 8.35.

[5.21] The provision of credit. Credit is the amount of money of which the debtor has the use. According to s 8 (see ante, para 5.19), what is required by that section is an agreement by which a prospective creditor binds himself to provide non-exempt credit,[1] which may be either of a fixed amount, eg, a Personal Loan (see ante, para 2.17), or a revolving credit, eg, an overdraft (see post, para 5.28).

The meaning of 'credit' under the CCA is to be found in s 9(1), which lays down that:

---

5   For debit and cash cards, see generally ante, para 2.24. Where overdraft facilities are absent see post, para 5.21.

6   See Dobson [1984] JBL 350; the Banking Ombudsman, Annual Report 1990/91, para 10.6; but *contra* Goode, *op cit*, note 1, para 24.83.

7   Logically, it would seem that wherever the number of cheque forms issued to the customer times the card limit exceeds the credit balance in the account, the customer has a credit facility. See Sched 2, Example 21; Jones, *Credit Cards*, 10.

8   In the case of use of a multi-function card, each function may be treated as a separate agreement: s 18(2); and see post, para 5.27. See also the Banking Ombudsman, Annual Report 1990/91, para 10.7, case 10.

9   Eg ss 57, 58: see post, Chapter 10. As to the ambit of 'prospective regulated agreements', see post, para 10.26.

10 See the warning against applying the concept of a prospective agreement too widely: Goode, *op cit*, note 1, para 23.23; and post, para 5.24. At common law, such agreements may be difficult to achieve: see post, para 10.03.

11 Section 59(2) contains a power to exempt by regulation to meet anticipated difficulties with business consumers: see further Guest and Lloyd, *Encyclopedia of Consumer Credit*, para 2-060.

12 Eg, the New Vehicle Order Form under which the consumer promises to enter an hp agreement.

[5.21]

1   For criticism of the use of the word 'provides' in s 8, see Goode, *Consumer Credit Law and Practice*, para 23.50; Lindgren (1977) 40 MLR at 164. For the granting of credit to an undischarged bankrupt, see post, para 19.21.

In this Act, 'credit' includes[2] a cash[3] loan and any other form of financial accommodation.

The 'cash loan' does not need to be paid direct to the debtor, for it may suffice that the money is paid at the debtor's request to a third party (see post, para 7.02). According to Goode, the ingredients of **credit** granted by a supplier [A] to a consumer [B] are as follows:[4]

(a) *The receipt by B of a benefit*, eg, goods. The CCA concentrates on the provision of credit under an agreement, as where **purchased** goods are delivered in advance of payment; but picking up goods in a self-service store does not involve credit because the contract is not made until the cash desk. Thus, in the ordinary cash sale, payment of the price and delivery of the goods are concurrent terms (s 28 of the SGA: see post, para 23.16), so that there is no element of credit; and this remains true where payment and delivery are by matching instalments, eg, a book club (see post, paras 23.23; 26.16).

(b) *Attracting to B a contractual duty of payment*, eg, an overdraft. There is no credit if the recipient of the benefit is left under no contractual duty to pay for it, eg, a gift (see ante, para 2.08), or a sale of book-debts (see post, para 7.18) or bills of exchange,[5] or payment by cheque,[6] or a quasi-contractual claim (see post, para 29.12).

(c) *In money to A*. The contractual duty must be to pay money, not some other obligation. Thus, actual payment before delivery of goods sold does not constitute credit to B, eg, a Christmas club (see post, para 15.18); nor does an agreement to barter, though a part-exchange deal may involve credit (see ante, para 2.09).

(d) *Significantly contractually deferred*. As to the **deferring** of payment, Goode explained that:[7]

> Debt is deferred and credit is extended, whenever the contract provides for the debtor to pay, or gives him the option to pay, later than the time at which payment would otherwise have been earned under the express or implied terms of the contract ... It is necessary ... to ask when, but for [the express] stipulation, payment would have had to be made. It is the difference between the two dates that constitutes the credit.

In *Dimond v Lovell* (set out ante, para 5.13), the Court of Appeal expressly approved the above passage. All the judges in both the Court of Appeal and House of Lords held that the accident hire agreement involved credit for the following reason: the nub of the contract was for the provision of services in the form of the hire of a car; leaving aside the terms of the agreement, the common law required that payment for those services be made at latest by the end of the hiring (see post, para 27.21); whereas clause 5 of the

---

2   However, s 9(1) is probably comprehensive: see Goode, *ibid*, para 24.4.

3   According to s 189(1), 'cash includes money in any form'. It need not be money which is legal tender in England (see ante, paras 2.03, 2.06): s 9(2).

4   Goode, *op cit*, note 1, para 24.8 *et seq*. See also Guest and Lloyd, *Encyclopedia of Consumer Credit*, para 2-010. When does mere non-enforcement of a creditor's rights amount to a granting of financial accommodation by him?

5   As to discounting bills, see Goode, *op cit*, note 1, paras 11.76; 24.47. Distinguish bills created as part of a credit transaction (CCA, ss 123–25: see post, para 25.09).

6   Payment by cheque is conditional payment (see post, para 24.03), so that notionally there is no credit, even though the cheque takes time to clear (as to whether a cheque is nevertheless a credit token, see post, para 5.30). Cf credit and charge cards, which have been held to amount to absolute payment to the retail supplier (see ante, para 2.25). As to cheque cashing businesses, see post, para 7.28.

7   Cited in *Dimond v Lovell* (above) by the CA, at para 57; and cited by Lord Hoffman in the HL at 903e.

agreement allowed that payment to be deferred until damages had been recovered from L (see ante, para 1.19).

Further, the above definition requires that the payment be **significantly** deferred. Presumably, the momentary deferment of payment for goods supplied does not amount to credit, as where a shopkeeper [A] hands goods to his customer [B] before B hands the price to A. Similarly, where B pays A by cash card or debit card,[8] there may be a momentary deferment before the sum is electronically debited to B's account, but this is not usually thought to amount to credit (s 187(3A): see post, para 5.33). Further, even a significant deferment of payment is disregarded if non-contractual, as where A delays sending out his bills or B is tardy in paying them. On the other hand, there is credit where A binds himself to **grant** credit, even where B does not bind himself to take it: it is sufficient that B has the option to take credit, eg, a budget or option account (see ante, para 2.19) or a three-party credit card or charge card (see ante, para 2.24). Credit cards are expressly caught by the Act;[9] and so may debit, cash, charge and cheque guarantee cards where there is the necessary right to an overdraft facility (see ante, para 5.20). Whilst charge cards allow up to a month's credit, they are exempt (see ante, para 5.15). There have been government proposals that cash, charge and debit cards be given their own consumer protection provisions.[10]

Wider still is the concept of '**financial accommodation**' in s 9(1), which s 9(3) of the Act expressly extends to include the hire-rent in hp (see post, para 5.23). Although the expression 'financial accommodation' has been seen as an anti-avoidance device,[11] its essence would seem to be that the consumer is **given time to pay**. On this analysis, s 9(3) was necessary because in hp the rental for each period is usually payable at latest by the first day of each period of hire so that, without s 9(3), there would be no 'financial accommodation' in hp.

[5.22] The credit ceiling. An agreement for the provision of credit (see ante, paras 5.20–21) will only be a consumer credit agreement (see ante, para 5.19) where the amount of credit to which the debtor has a contractual right at the moment of contracting falls within a specified maximum[1] financial limit for that moment (see ante, para 2.07). Originally, that upper figure was fixed at £5,000, perhaps aiming at a new family car. However, copying a device found in the HPA to inflation-proof such limits, the CCA contains power to increase the limit by statutory order (s 181): in the 1983 that power was utilised to increase the limit to £15,000; and in 1998 the limit was further raised to £25,000.[2] Leaving aside the complication of revolving credit (see post, para 5.28), this paragraph concentrates on the amount of 'credit'. This is a two-stage enquiry, because 'credit' denotes, not the total

---

8 Goode, *op cit*, note 1, para 24.25.
9 Section 14(3): see post, para 5.30. This is so even if the debtor only uses his credit card as a charge card by paying it off in full each month: Jones, *Credit Cards*, p 79.
10 These recommendations of the Jack Committee were taken up by the White Paper (see generally ante, para 2.17), paras 4.6.
11 Goode, *op cit*, note 1, II para 5.9. *Contra* Guest and Lloyd, *op cit*, note 4, para 2-010. Would it extend to activities within the (now repealed) Pawnbrokers Act 1872, s 6 (see Macleod [1995] JBL 155, esp at 170)?

[5.22]
1 If the amount of credit falls below a minimum figure, there may only be a small consumer credit agreement: see ante, para 5.17.
2 Consumer Credit (Increase in Monetary Limits)(Amendment) Order 1998, SI 996.

amount the debtor has to pay, but rather the element of 'financial accommodation' (see ante, para 5.21).

Stage 1. There must first be ascertained the total amount which the debtor has contracted to pay under the personal credit agreement in sterling.[3] In the case of an hp or conditional sale agreement, this will be the 'total price' (see post, para 5.23). In *National Westminster Bank plc v Story:*[4]

> Mr S and Miss P were joint owner-occupiers of a house from which Mr S carried on a carpentry business. In November 1986, the Bank agreed to lend a total of £35,000 on three separate credit facilities: an overdraft of £15,000 to Mr S to cover his business expenditure and secured by mortgage; a joint mortgage of £5,000 to Mr S and Miss P intended to refinance existing borrowing (separated to qualify for tax relief); and a joint loan of £15,000. On appeal, the issue was confined to the two joint loans: if they were provided under separate agreements, they were irrecoverable for non-compliance with the CCA, the then limit being £15,000.

The unanimous judgment of the Court of Appeal was delivered by Auld LJ. His Lordship first considered whether the banking facilities constituted one or more contracts. He held that this matter was one of ordinary contract law: the court accepted that each of the three facilities could be drawn upon independently; but nevertheless it agreed with the County Court Judge that the three facilities were negotiated and documented as a single package which was subject to 'common conditions' set out in a single covering letter. Second, Auld LJ considered whether that single agreement was regulated by reason of ss 18 and 11 of the CCA (see post, paras 5.27; 5.29).

Stage 2. From the foregoing total, there must be deducted **both** the following sums (if any):

(a) The 'deposit', which is commonly a part-exchange allowance (see ante, para 2.09), is defined as (s 189(1)):

> ... any sum payable by the debtor or hirer by way of deposit[5] or down-payment, or credited or to be credited to him on account of any deposit or down-payment, whether the sum is to be or has been paid to the creditor or owner or any other person,[6] or is to be or has been discharged by a payment of money or a transfer or delivery of goods or by any other means.

(b) The total charge for credit (TCC), eg, the interest charge, is excluded by s 9(4) in the following terms:

> For the purposes of this Act, an item[7] entering into the total charge for credit shall not be treated as credit even though time is allowed for its payment.

---

3   If the financial accommodation is granted otherwise than in sterling, eg, a foreign currency loan, then the sterling equivalent must be taken: s 9(2). What of VAT?

4   [2000] GCCR 2381, CA.

5   For deposits, see generally post, para 23.27. *Contra* consumer hirings where the deposit is included: see ante, para 1.19.

6   The reference to 'any other person' takes account of both vendor and lender credit: as to which see ante, para 2.16.

7   This does not necessarily have to benefit the creditor, eg, insurance premiums, survey fees.

This complicated concept of TCC will be considered later (see post, para 8.23). In the case of a conditional sale, the amount of credit granted is basically as follows: Credit = Total price minus (deposit + TCC), as is demonstrated by *Humberclyde Finance Ltd v Thompson*:[8]

> At a time when the CCA limit was £15,000, T agreed to buy from HF on conditional sale a Ford Sierra car. The deposit was provided by a trade-in, which left a balance of £14,497 of the cash price to be financed. The agreement also contained a 'payment waiver option', priced £796: under this option, if T died before completing the payments, the balance of the price was waived. T elected to pay this extra sum, so that the total financed was some £15,293. After more than one third of the total price had been paid, T defaulted and the car was repossessed.

Leaving aside the protected goods issue (see post, para 24.35), the Court of Appeal had to decide whether the agreement was regulated. Obviously, the trade-in was to be ignored, because it was a sum credited on account of the deposit; and the issue was whether the payment waiver option was: (i) part of the credit, in which case the credit totalled £15,293 and the agreement was unregulated; or (ii) part of the TCC and thus to be ignored for this purpose (see post, para 8.24), in which case the credit totalled £14,497 and the agreement was regulated. The court took the latter view.

[5.23] Credit: the special hp rule. To meet the technical objection that the hire-rent in hp is not credit[1] within s 9(1) (see ante, para 5.22), s 9(3) provides that:

> Without prejudice to the generality of subsection 1, the person by whom goods are bailed ... to an individual under a hire purchase agreement shall be taken to provide him with fixed-sum credit to finance the transaction of an amount equal to the total price of the goods less the aggregate of the deposit (if any) and the total charge for credit.

'Total price' is defined for the purposes of hp or conditional sale by s 189(1);[2] but what of a credit sale (as to which, see ante, para 1.13)? The effect of the foregoing rules on the computation of credit is illustrated elsewhere,[3] but may have unexpected results where there are multiple agreements (see post, para 5.27) and does not apply to credit limits under running account credit (as to which, see post, para 5.28).

[5.24] The debtor. A consumer credit agreement is an agreement to extend credit within the requisite financial limit (see ante, paras 5.22–23) to an individual (the debtor) (see s 8(1): ante, para 5.19): this may be termed a 'status of customer' test.

Individual is defined as including (s 189(1)):

> ... a partnership or other unincorporated body of persons not consisting entirely of bodies corporate.

Thus, like the HPA, the CCA has no application where the debtor is an artificial person, but may apply whenever the debtor is not a body corporate, this last expression meaning a company registered under the Companies Acts,[1] or created by Royal Charter or Act of

---

8   (1997) Tr LR 242, CA. See also *Wilson v First County Trust Ltd* (set out post, para 9.20).

[5.23]

1   Cf *R v Miller* [1977] 3 All ER 986, CA.

2   See post, para 24.35. What if a dealer, as part of a promotion, agrees to pay the first instalment to the financier on behalf of the debtor?

3   CCA, Sched 2, Example 10; and Goode, *Consumer Credit Law and Practice*, para 24.150.

[5.24]

1   Eg, *Re Charge Card Services Ltd* (set out ante, para 2.27).

Parliament.[2] On the other hand, the expression 'individual' is apt to include an unincorporated club, or charity, trade union or small business (whether partnership or sole trader). After determined attempts to exclude small businesses from the definition, in 1997 Parliament rejected the proposed change (see ante, para 5.11).

Debtor is defined as meaning (s 189(1)):

> ... the individual receiving credit under a consumer credit agreement or the person to whom his rights and duties under the agreement have passed by assignment or operation of law,[3] and in relation to a prospective consumer credit agreement includes the prospective debtor.

Note that this definition of 'debtor' includes his assignees[4] and also extends to prospective agreements (see ante, para 5.20).

Finally, s 185 contains special provisions to deal with the situation where there are joint debtors or hirers.[5] Notwithstanding that the CCA ordinarily applies only where the debtor or hirer is an 'individual', s 185(5) provides that:

> An agreement for the provision of credit, or the bailment or (in Scotland) the hiring of goods, to two or more persons jointly where:
>
> (a) one or more of those persons is an individual, and
>
> (b) one or more of them is body corporate,
>
> is a consumer credit agreement or consumer hire agreement if it would have been one had they all been individuals; and the body corporate or bodies corporate shall accordingly be included among the debtors or hirers under the agreement.

Such cases are thus brought within the general CCA rule for co-parties (see post, para 25.08) that any right conferred on the debtor must be observed in relation to each of them,[6] whilst any duty cast on the debtor may be discharged by any of them.[7]

[5.25] The creditor. A consumer credit agreement is an agreement to extend credit within the requisite financial limitation by any other person (the creditor) (s 8(1)).

Person. Unlike the definition of debtor (see ante, para 5.24), the creditor does not need to be an 'individual', and may therefore be either an artificial or natural person.[1] Except

---

2   Eg, Limited Liability Partnership Act 2000.

3   Eg, personal representative; trustee in bankruptcy. For comment on 'and duties', see post, para 5.25. Cf the definition of 'hirer': ante, para 1.19.

4   For attempts by a debtor to assign his interest under an instalment credit agreement, see ante, para 1.23. For assignment generally, see post, para 7.16 *et seq*.

5   The provision does not extend to joint and several debtors/hirers: see Goode, *Consumer Credit Law and Practice*, para 44.21.

6   Eg, pre-contract disclosure under s 55 (see post, para 9.08); personal signature of regulated agreements under s 61 (see post, para 9.13); the copies rules under ss 62–64 (see post, para 9.18); withdrawal and cancellation rights under ss 57, 60, 63 (see post, paras 10.26; 9.10; 9.17); rights to information and documents under ss 77–79 (see post, paras 7.08; 15.17); notices under ss 76, 87 and 98 (see post, para 24.28); statutory rebates under s 95 (see post, para 26.19A).

7   Eg, services of notices of cancellation under s 69 or termination under ss 99 or 101 (see post, paras 10.31; 26.05; 26.07); early settlement under s 94 (see post, para 26.19); information as to the whereabouts of the goods under s 80 (see post, para 15.16); application to the court by the debtor or hirer under s 129 or 132 (see post, paras 24.40; 27.23). Can one act against the wishes of the other?

[5.25]

1   Interpretation Act 1978, s 5 and Sched 1.

for the purpose of exempt agreements (see ante, para 5.15), the Act is not concerned with the status of that person.

Creditor. According to the Act (s 189(1)):

> ... 'creditor' means the person providing credit under a consumer credit agreement or the person to whom his rights and duties[2] under the agreement have passed by assignment or operation of law,[3] and in relation to a prospective consumer credit agreement, includes the prospective creditor.

First, it should be noticed that, as with 'debtor', the definition extends to prospective creditors (see ante, para 5.20). Second, by reason of the explicit extension to assignees,[4] the concept of creditor includes a financier to whom an assignment has been made by way of indirect financing.[5] Third, s 186 provides for the situation where goods are supplied by more than one person jointly in the following terms:

> Where an actual or prospective regulated agreement has two or more creditors or owners, anything required by or under this Act to be done to, or in relation to, or by, the creditor or owner shall be effective, if done to, or in relation to, or by, any one of them.

Thus, any right conferred on the creditors may be exercised by any one of them,[6] whilst any duty cast on the creditors may also be discharged by any of them.[7]

NEW CONCEPTS

[5.26] Introduction. As already noted (see ante, para 5.06), the CCA consciously introduced much new terminology. Its primary differentiation is between regulated and unregulated agreements (see ante, para 5.13), though s 189(1) also defines a number of different sorts of agreement, eg, conditional sale, credit sale, hire-purchase agreements.[1] Part II of the Act (ss 8–20) creates a number of new concepts, some of which have already been mentioned in this chapter. These include the following two key components of regulated agreements (see ante, para 5.13). The first is personal credit/consumer credit[2] and consumer hire[3] agreements. The second is the system for exempting categories of agreement from the Act by introducing (i) a classification of almost wholly exempt agreements[4] and (ii) the partially exempt small agreements.[5] Additionally, Part II also

---

2   It has been pointed out that 'and duties' departs from the HPA formulation 'or liabilities', and that the common law (see post, para 7.27) does not allow the assignment of duties: Goode, *Consumer Credit Law and Practice*, para 23.21.

3   For involuntary assignment by operation of law, see post, para 7.27.

4   The CCA draftsman has acknowledged his misuse of the word 'assignees' because duties may not be assignable (see post, para 7.27): Bennion, *Consumer Credit Control* I: 920.

5   For voluntary assignments, see post, para 7.27 *et seq*.

6   See the other examples cited in para 5.24, note 6, except in relation to ss 61, 95.

7   See the examples cited in para 5.24, note 7, except in relation to ss 80, 129, 132.

[5.26]

1   For the definitions, see respectively ante, paras 1.16; 1.13; 1.24.

2   Section 8: see ante, paras 5.19–25.

3   Section 15: see ante, para 1.19.

4   Section 16: see ante, para 5.15.

5   Section 17: see ante, para 5.17.

introduces a number of other important concepts: fixed-sum and running-account credit;[6] restricted-use and unrestricted-use credit;[7] debtor-creditor-supplier and debtor-creditor agreements;[8] credit token agreements;[9] and linked transactions.[10] There is also the multi-concept of ancillary credit business.[11] Many of these new concepts are modelled on the proposals contained in the *Crowther Report* (see ante, para 5.03), and an explanation of them will be found there (see para 1.2.12).

With all these different classifications, it is not surprising that there is some overlap, where a single agreement falls simultaneously within more than one of the above categories, in which case the CCA christens it a 'multiple agreement' and deals with it in the very complicated, over-compressed and much criticised s 18 (see post, para 5.27). This notion of 'multiple agreement' does **not necessarily** refer to whether more than one item is supplied, eg, a credit sale of a stereo system plus speakers. Instead, the draftsman intended this section to achieve the following two purposes:

(i) to prevent avoidance of the CCA by combining in one agreement transactions the Act intends to regulate with others it does not, eg, contract-hire of a car with periodical maintenance included. However, in *National Westminster Bank plc v Story* (set out ante, para 5.22), the Court of Appeal unanimously held that s 18 did not affect the common law position that the three facilities there formed part of one single agreement whose combined value fell outside the CCA.

(ii) to deal with the obvious fact that many regulated agreements will fall within more than one of the 'categories' mentioned in the Act, eg, a consumer credit agreement may be for fixed-sum restricted-use credit.

Part II concepts

[5.27] Multiple agreements. According to s 18(1), a multiple agreement is one whose terms are such as:

(a) to place a part of it within one category of agreement mentioned in this Act, and another part of it within a different category of agreement so mentioned, or within a category of agreement not so mentioned, or

(b) to place it, or a part of it, within two or more categories of agreement so mentioned.

This highly compressed definition does not define what it means by a 'part' of an agreement or a 'category of agreement mentioned in the Act'. In *National Westminster Bank plc v Story* (set out ante, para 5.22), Auld LJ said *obiter*:[1]

My inclination, without formally deciding the matter, is that the word 'part' in this context includes, but it is not restricted to, a facility that is different as to some of its terms from

---

6   Section 10: see post, para 5.28.
7   Section 11: see post, para 5.29.
8   Sections 12–13: see post, para 5.32 *et seq.*
9   Section 14: see post, para 5.30.
10   Section 19: see post, para 5.31.
11   See post, para 5.36 *et seq.*
[5.27]
1   For difficulties with payment protection insurance (see post, para 24.44), see Guest and Lloyd, *Encyclopedia of Consumer Credit Law*, para 2–019(i).

another facility granted under the same agreement or one that can stand on its own as a separate contract or bargain ...

Having held that under this test the two separate loan facilities (for £5,000 and £15,000) were separate 'parts' of the single agreement (see above), his Lordship continued, *obiter*:[2]

... there is then the question of whether they are placed within separate 'categories' of agreement in the [s 18] sense. My inclination here, influenced in part by the positioning of that provision in Part II of the Act, and again without needing to decide the matter, is that the word 'category' should be construed in the more narrow sense. That is, it applies to different 'categories' within Part II of the Act rather than as between every type of agreement for which the Act, in its various Parts, provides its own legal regime.

It will be noted that s 18(1) contains two paragraphs which may be applied cumulatively so that an agreement creates the following four, perhaps overlapping, situations:

Case 1: s 18(1)(a), first portion. Part A of the agreement is within one CCA category, whilst Part B is within a different CCA category, eg, two loan facilities under a regulated loan, one part of which (Part A) is to pay off existing indebtedness (restricted-use credit) and another part (Part B) which the borrower may spend as he likes (unrestricted-use credit).

Case 2: s 18(1)(a), second portion. Part C of the agreement is within a CCA category, whilst Part D is within a non-CCA category, eg, a furnished letting;[3] bank savings account with overdraft facility (see Sched 2, Example 18); a credit card with points;[4] goods sold on credit sale with an extended warranty (see post, para 17.09); a multi-function card (see ante, para 2.23).

Case 3: s 18(1)(b), first portion. The whole of the agreement is within two or more disparate[5] CCA categories, eg, a single regulated loan may be restricted-use and debtor-creditor credit.

Case 4: s 18(1)(b), second portion. Part of the agreement is within two or more disparate[5] CCA categories, eg, one of two loan facilities under a regulated loan is restricted-use and debtor-creditor credit.

Not every multiple agreement within s 18(1) is affected by that section, eg, Case 2: so, in *Dimond v Lovell*, where an accident hire agreement amounted to a regulated consumer credit agreement (Part C: see ante, para 5.21), the House of Lords held that, even though the agreement also amounted to a consumer hiring (Part D: see ante, para 1.19), because it was exempt consumer hiring s 18 had 'no relevance' (*per* Lord Hoffman at 905b).

On the other hand, Cases 1, 3 and 4 will be affected by s 18. For these situations, s 18(2) provides as follows:

Where a part of an agreement falls within subsection (1), that part shall be treated for the purposes of this Act as a separate agreement.

Thus, in Case 1 Part A of the agreement must obey the CCA rules for restricted-use credit, whereas Part B must follow those for unrestricted-use credit;[6] but there is some doubt as

---

2   In referring to s 19, the Report is clearly mistaken.
3   The lease of premises is outside the Act, whilst the lease of furniture is within it: see s 18(6).
4   As to a credit card, see ante, para 2.28; and as to points, see post, para 15.18.
5   *Aliter*, if all the Parts fall within the same category, eg, *Story* (see below).
6   For difficulties, see Guest and Lloyd, *op cit*, note 1, para 2-019(ii).

to how far this notion of treating each Part 'as a separate agreement' should be taken.[7] For Cases 3 and 4, s 18(3) explains:

> Where an agreement falls within subsection (1)(b), it shall be treated as an agreement in each of the categories in question, and this Act shall apply to it accordingly.

It has already been seen that a regulated consumer credit agreement will commonly fall within more than one category, eg, Case 3: if so, s 18(3) is saying that it must comply with all the CCA requirements for each of them, eg, all the requirements for restricted-use credit and all the requirements for debtor-creditor agreements. An important instance of this for our purposes is a three-party credit card.[8] Special provision is made by s 18 for both the following cases: by s 18(4) for apportionment, eg, in calculating the 'total price' to determine if there are 'protected goods';[9] and by s 18(5) for running-account credit where the credit limit is temporarily exceeded. However, in *Story* (above) s 18(2) had no effect because both the loan facilities were for fixed-sum, unrestricted-use credit.[10]

The OFT have canvassed reform.[11]

[5.28] Running-account credit. It may be a positive advantage to a creditor (see ante, para 5.25) to persuade a debtor to undertake revolving credit (see ante, para 2.19) rather than a fixed amount of credit: he may thereby hope for repeat business without further separate credit checks,[1] but is unlikely to have any real security.[2] Section 10 seeks to ensure that both types of credit fall within the Act.

(a) *Revolving credit*. According to s 10(1)(a):

> ... running-account credit[3] is a facility under a personal credit agreement[4] whereby the debtor is enabled to receive from time to time (whether in his own person, or by another person) from the creditor or a third party cash, goods and services (or any of them) to an amount or value such that, taking into account payments made by or to the credit of the debtor, the credit limit (if any) is not at any time exceeded.

---

7   Eg, does it apply to documentation matters arising during the course of the agreement (see post, para 15.16); or exempt agreements (see ante, para 5.15)?

8   See Sched 2, Example 16; and post, para 7.10. For difficulties, see Guest and Lloyd, *op cit*, note 1, para 2-019(iii).

9   Section 18(4) reverses the decision in *Mutual Finance Ltd v Davidson* [1963] 1 All ER 133, CA. For protected goods, see post, para 24.36.

10 Decision of fact by the judge and accepted by the CA. Criticised by MacDonald (1999) 149 NLJ 962 at 964.

11 Discussion paper on *Multiple Agreement and section 18* (1995) Chapter 7. Amendment of the Regulations, rather than the Act, has been supported: (1996) 50 CC5/29. As to difficulties with flexible mortgages, see Vaughan (2000) 55 CC3/12.

[5.28]

1   There will, of course, be no need to credit score a new proposal, the creditor normally having the advantage of behavioural scoring: see generally post, para 8.35. It also creates opportunities for enclosing mail advertising with (monthly) statements.

2   For real security, see post, para 25.01. It would seem possible to combine running-account credit with a retention of title by way of conditional sale: *Armour v Thyssen* (set out post, para 20.28); but not in respect of regulated agreements ((1985) 40 CC 2/21).

3   For criticism of the expression 'running-account credit', see Goode, *Consumer Credit Law and Practice*, para 25.24.

4   For personal credit agreements, see s 8(1): set out ante, para 5.19.

Whilst the notion looks complicated, the basic idea is simple, comprehending lines of credit, such as an ordinary bank overdraft,[5] some credit card arrangements, eg, Master or Visa cards, and store and mail order budget accounts (see ante, para 2.19). It does not require that at any particular time the debtor by indebted: indeed, he may even be in credit; but the credit facility continues until terminated by the parties. However, it is crucial that the debtor is 'enabled to receive from time to time' credit, etc; that is, that the debtor 'has a facility on which he can draw at pleasure'.[6] For the special rules applicable to running-account credit, see post, para 7.08.

(b) *Fixed amount credit.* According to s 10(1)(b):

> ... fixed-sum credit is any other facility under a personal credit agreement whereby the debtor is enabled to receive credit (whether in one amount or by instalments).

Into this category fall hp, conditional sales, credit sales, check and voucher trading and personal loans.[7] Even an overdraft may occasionally be fixed amount credit – as when the right to draw is exhausted. Unlike running-account credit, when the fixed-sum debt is paid off, the agreement normally terminates automatically, eg, unauthorised overdraft (Sched 2, Example 17). Moreover, as fixed-sum credit is the residuary category, any consumer credit agreement which is not running-account must be fixed sum. This may have some unexpected results: so in *Dimond v Lovell* (set out ante, para 5.13), where an uncertain amount of credit was to be repaid all at once, the Court of Appeal held that it was fixed-sum credit.[8]

The credit limit. In the case of fixed-sum credit, it has been seen that there may be a regulated consumer credit agreement where that credit is within a specified figure (see ante, para 5.22). However, it is necessary for the Act to deal separately with running-account credit because, unlike fixed-sum credit, the amount of credit which will be utilised by the debtor is not known at the outset of an arrangement so that the Act can only refer to a credit ceiling. Section 10(2) provides that:

> ... in relation to running-account credit, 'credit limit' means, as respects any period, the maximum debit balance which, under the credit agreement, is allowed to stand on the account during that period, disregarding any term of the agreement allowing that maximum to be exceeded merely temporarily.

By s 10(3)(a), running-account credit may amount to a consumer credit agreement where the credit limit does not exceed the amount specified in s 8(2) (see ante, para 5.19); or only does so temporarily.[9] By way of an anti-avoidance device, s 10(3)(b) provides that the same result will follow if:

---

5 See Sched 2, Example 18 (authorised overdraft). As to overdrafts, see generally ante, paras 2.17 and 2.23, item 1.
6 Goode, *op cit*, note 3, para 25.25. Does it include a milk account, or a newspaper account?
7 For hp, see ante, para 1.24; for conditional sale, see ante, para 1.16; for credit sales, see ante, para 1.13; for check and voucher trading, see ante, para 2.23, item 2; and for personal loans, see ante, para 2.17.
8 See [1999] JBL 452 at 459–60. Point conceded before HL.
9 Sections 10(2), 18(5), 82(4); Sched 2, Examples 22, 23. *Contra*, if the debtor is allowed to exceed that credit limit as a matter of course (see Lindgren (1977) 40 MLR at 165) and that credit limit includes credit charges (see Jones, *Credit Cards*, p 83. Cf fixed sum credit: ante, para 5.23).

... whether or not there is a credit limit, and if there is, notwithstanding that it exceeds the specified amount –

(i) the debtor is not enabled to draw at any one time an amount which, so far as (having regard to section 9(4)) it represents credit, exceeds the specified amount,[10] or

(ii) the agreement provides that, if the debit balance rises above a given amount (not exceeding the specified amount), the rate of the total charge for credit increases or any other condition favouring the creditor of his associate comes into operation,[11] or

(iii) at the time the agreement is made it is probable, having regard to the terms of the agreement and any other relevant considerations, that the debit balance will not at any time rise above the specified amount.[12]

[5.29] Restricted-use/unrestricted-use credit. A person who borrows cash may well be doing so to meet existing commitments, which will put him in a particularly vulnerable position. Section 11 sets about identifying him by creating another dichotomy within the category of regulated consumer credit agreements (see ante, para 5.19), this one being directed to the mechanism of payment.

1   *Restricted-use (RU) credit*. According to s 11(1):

A restricted-use credit agreement is a regulated consumer credit agreement –

(a) to finance a transaction between the debtor and the creditor, whether forming part of that agreement or not, or

(b) to finance a transaction between the debtor and a person (the 'supplier') other than the creditor, or

(c) to refinance any existing indebtedness of the debtor's, whether to the creditor or another person,

and 'restricted-use credit' shall be construed accordingly.

The above three categories of RU credit are as follows:

(a) Both types of vendor credit (see Sched 2, Example 10; and ante, para 2.19).

(b) This category is meant to deal with lender credit (see ante, paras 2.20–28) and therefore introduces a third character, whom it terms the 'supplier'.[1] All three forms of lender credit can amount to RU credit within this category, provided only that the creditor controls the application of the credit, eg, by paying the supplier direct,[2] or by furnishing the debtor with a redeemable token.[3]

---

10   See Sched 2, Example 19.
11   See Sched 2, Example 6.
12   See Sched 2, Example 7. For the burden of proof, see s 171(1); and further Lindgren (1977) 40 MLR at 166–67; Guest and Lloyd, *Encyclopedia of Consumer Credit Law*, para 2–011; Jones, *op cit*, note 9, pp 85–86.

[5.29]
1   See the definition of 'supplier' in s 189(1): set out post, para 5.34. Particularly significant for indirect financing, the Act confirms that it is irrelevant that, when the regulated agreement is first made, the identity of the eventual creditor may be unknown to the debtor (s 11(4)).
2   As in direct financing: see ante, para 2.21. Or perhaps to finance the provision of cash: see Guest and Lloyd, *Encyclopedia of Consumer Credit*, para 2–012.
3   The token may be redeemable only at designated outlets, as in check or voucher trading: see ante, para 2.23, item 2.

(c) Refinancing (see post, para 7.04A), whether by way of rescheduling an existing debt between the parties[4] or not, eg, Sched 2, Example 13. This category does not include credit hire because the charges were payable and the indebtedness created under the same transaction as provided for postponement of the time of payment.[5]

2   *Unrestricted-use (UU) credit*. According to s 11(2), this is:

> a regulated consumer credit agreement not falling within subsection (1).

The obvious example of this category is where money is passed to the debtor, whether by cash or cheque, eg, Sched 2, Example 8, and whether or not the agreement under which it is passed is for fixed-sum credit.[6] However, a credit card can be RU or UU, depending on how it is used: if it is used to purchase goods, there is RU credit; but if it is used to obtain money, there is UU credit (see Sched 2, Example 16; and post, para 7.10).

However, to some extent the foregoing three categories of RU credit are overridden by the provision that (s 11(3)):

> ... an agreement does not fall within subsection (1) if the credit is in fact provided in such a way as to leave the debtor free to use it as he chooses, even though certain uses would contravene that or any other agreement.

In *National Westminster Bank plc v Story* (set out ante, para 5.22) the debtor expected that the £5,000 would be used to discharge his existing indebtedness; but the first instance judge held that there was no term of the contract to that effect. Auld LJ held that what mattered was the ordinary common law test of contractual intention (see post, para 11.07): whatever the debtor expected, because there was no contractual term restricting his use of the £5,000, it was unrestricted-use credit. Thus, the crucial thing is whether the debtor (see ante, para 5.24) is **entitled** to get his hands on the money:[7] if he is, the transaction does not amount to RU credit even though it appears to fall within one of the three categories.

The effect of the RU/UU dichotomy. This is particularly relevant in deciding whether a credit facility can be canvassed: an RU facility can be canvassed with a special licence (s 23(1): see post, para 6.14) whereas a UU facility may not be canvassed in any circumstances (s 49: see post, para 7.07). There are also a number of situations where special treatment is given to RU credits: these include linked transactions (s 19(1)(c): see post, para 5.31), land mortgages (s 58(2): see post, para 25.23), cancellation[8] and exclusions from Part V of the CCA (s 74(2): see post, para 9.07). The dichotomy also figures substantially in the debtor-creditor-supplier/debtor-creditor concepts (see post, para 5.32 *et seq*).

[5.30] Credit tokens.[1] The extension of credit by way of credit cards or check trading (see respectively ante, para 2.28 and post, para 15.17) led to the creation of yet another

---

4   Eg *National Westminster Bank plc v Story* (see below).
5   *Dimond v Lovell* (set out ante, para 5.13), where the transaction was held to fall within s 11(1)(a).
6   What of a cashback (as to which, see post, para 8.13A)?
7   Eg overdrafts, whether of a fixed-sum (Sched 2, Example 17) or running-account (Sched 2, Example 18).
8   Sections 69(2), 71: see respectively post, paras 10.32; 10.33.
[5.30]
1   See the recommendation of the *Crowther Report*, paras 6.12.1–12; 6.13.10–11.

category of consumer credit agreement (see ante, para 5.19). Section 14(1) of the CCA christens them 'credit tokens' and explains that:

> A credit-token is a card, check, voucher, coupon, stamp, form, booklet or other document or thing given to an individual by a person carrying on a consumer credit business, who undertakes—
>
> (a) that on the production of it (whether or not some other action is also required)[2] he will supply cash, goods and services (or any of them) on credit, or
>
> (b) that where, on the production of it to a third party (whether or not any other action is also required),[2] the third party supplies cash, goods[3] and services (or any of them), he will pay the third party for them (whether or not deducting any discount or commission), in return for payment[4] to him by the individual.

'In essence a credit token is a piece of paper or plastic which unlocks the door to credit'[5] and is 'given to an individual by a consumer credit business'.[6] Whilst widely defining what items might amount to credit tokens, to fall within s 14(1) the giver of that item must on its 'production' 'undertake' either (a) or (b) above; but, as the agreement may be prospective (see ante, para 5.20), there does not need to be a binding contract (see post, para 10.01). In *Elliott v DG*:[7]

> Retailers by way of an advertising scheme sent out unsolicited plastic cards, each expressed to be a credit card available for immediate use upon the recipient signing it. They did not disclose that, before honouring the card, a customer would have to enter into a credit sale with them and sign a direct debit mandate.

The retailers were convicted of supplying an unsolicited credit token,[8] notwithstanding that the 'undertaking' was intended to be conditional and to amount only to an invitation to treat which had no contractual force. A successful defence would have meant that the card amounted to a false statement as to the provision of services within s 14 of the TDA (as to which, see ante, para 4.15).

Section 14 is designed to deal with both two- and three-party credit transactions (see ante, para 2.19 *et seq*); and it is expressed to be applicable whether the user presents the card to a person, or a machine (s 14(4)), eg, an ATM (see ante, para 2.24).

(a) *Two-party transactions* (s 14(1)(a)), where the issuer is the supplier. These will include store budget accounts (see ante, para 2.19) and cards enabling the holder to draw cash

---

2   Eg, signing a receipt; entering a PIN (see ante, para 2.24).

3   For 'goods', see s 189(1): see ante, paras 2.01–02. Does 'goods' include a credit token, so arguably bringing credit-tokens within consumer hirings (see ante, para 1.19)?

4   'Payment' includes tender: s 189 (1). See generally post, para 23.12 *et seq*.

5   Goode, *Consumer Credit Law and Practice*, para 25.68. It has been argued that the following are not credit tokens: (a) an application form (see post, para 8.35; Goode); (b) a cheque form, even where there is an overdraft agreement (Guest and Lloyd, *Consumer Credit Law*, para 2.015). *Sed quaere*?

6   For 'individual' and 'consumer credit business', see ante, para 5.24 and post, para 6.12. But a 'credit token' need not be regulated, though a 'credit token agreement' (see below) must be: Guest and Lloyd, *ibid*.

7   [1980] 1 WLR 977, DC. Both the director and the company were prosecuted: see further post, para 28.11.

8   Section 51: see post, para 7.12. There was no offence under s 46 (see post, para 8.27) because the section was not in force at the time: Jones, *Credit Cards*, pp 40, 98.

from a bank dispenser (see Sched 2, Example 16). However, it may not include a cheque guarantee card, because of the express reference in the section to credit.[9]

(b) *Three-party transactions* (s 14(1)(b)), where the holder uses a card issued by a financier to obtain cash, goods or services from a third party. Section 14(1)(b) does not mention credit but s 14(3) deems him to obtain credit within s 9(1) when the item is supplied.[10] This had led to differing academic views as to whether or not a requirement of credit is to be read into s 14(1)(b):[11] this in turn has caused disagreement as to whether cash cards, debit cards and gift tokens (see ante, paras 2.24–25 and post, para 15.18) can fall within s 14(1)(b) when there is no previously agreed credit arrangement.[12]

Credit token agreements (see post, para 7.10) will, of course, be subject to all the ordinary rules applicable to regulated agreements, plus some additional rules applicable even if there is no agreement at all (see post, para 7.09 *et seq*).

[5.31] Linked transactions. The CCA, in interfering with freedom contract in relation to regulated agreements (see ante, para 5.13), is drafted so that it also affects any satellite agreement. To do so, it creates in s 19 a new concept, for which it borrows[1] the expression 'linked transaction'. According to s 19(1):

> A transaction entered into by the debtor or hirer,[2] or a relative of his,[3] with any other person ('the other party'), except one for the provision of security,[4] is a linked transaction in relation to an actual or prospective regulated agreement (the 'principal agreement') of which it does not form part if …

any *one* of the three following criteria are satisfied:

(a) 'A contract entered into in compliance with a term of the principal agreement' (s 19(1)(a)), such as a contract for the maintenance of goods supplied under a credit or hire agreement. This can only be satisfied where the principal agreement is entered into first and makes the satellite agreements compulsory: it cannot extend to such contracts offered as an optional extra.

(b) Vendor or lender credit connected with the supply of goods or services, as in the case of budget accounts, loan financing or check trading: the contract for the retail supply of goods is a linked transaction if it 'is financed, or to be financed, by' that credit agreement.[5] However, this category cannot extend to direct financing, because the

---

9   Goode, *op cit*, note 5. *Contra* Guest and Lloyd, *op cit*, note 5, both citing Sched 2, Example 21. For credit generally, see ante. para 5.12.

10 Eg Master and Visa cards used to obtain goods (see Sched 2, Examples 3 and 16); trading checks and vouchers (see Sched 2, Example 14). As to charge cards, see Guest and Lloyd, *op cit*, note 5.

11 See Goode, *op cit*, note 5, para 25.70 (yes); Guest and Lloyd, *op cit*, note 5 (no).

12 See Goode, *op cit*, note 5, paras 25.82–85 (no); Guest and Lloyd, *op cit*, note 5 (yes).

[5.31]

1   The expression 'linked-on' agreement had previously been used in an entirely different context, which would now fall within s 82: see post, para 26.22.

2   'Debtor' and 'hirer' are both defined by s 189(1): see respectively ante, paras 5.24 and 1.19.

3   See ss 184(1), 189(1): see post, para 5.33.

4   Eg, contracts of surety, as to which see Chapter 25.

5   Section 19(1)(b). It seems to follow that, if the parties agree a cash supply and only subsequently talk about credit, the cash supply is still within s 19.

credit there 'forms a part' of the supply contract, and hence does not include the sale from dealer to financier.[6]

(c) This category involves three separate cases and looks rather complicated (ss 19(1)(c), (2)) but may be illustrated by the following examples:[7] where entry into a satellite agreement is **insisted** upon before the creditor or owner will enter the principal agreement; or is **suggested** by the creditor or owner; or is for a purpose **related** to the principal agreement.

The major restriction on linked transactions is to be found in s 19(3), which provides that:[8]

> A linked transaction entered into before the making of the principal agreement has no effect until such time (if any) as that agreement is made.

Additionally, the category of a linked transaction is relevant for the following reasons: computing the total charge for credit;[9] withdrawal and cancellation;[10] rebates for early settlement (ss 95(1), 96: see post, para 26.19A); to prevent the evasion of the Act by the use of security[11] or contracting out (s 113(8): see post, para 25.12); and extortionate credit bargains (ss 137–40: see post, para 29.40). Although not expressly mentioned by the Act, linked transactions may be affected by connected-lender liability (s 75: see post, para 16.09), or the fact that a regulated agreement is improperly executed (s 65: see post, para 9.19), or terminated (s 99: see post, para 26.05) or otherwise discharged,[12] or where the court exercises one of its powers under Part IX of the Act (see post, para 24.27).

Debtor-creditor-supplier/debtor-creditor agreements

[5.32] The *Crowther Report* (see ante, para 5.03) defines a connected lender as 'one who, pursuant to a regular business relationship with one or more sellers, makes a loan which is used to buy goods or services from one such seller' (para 6.2.22). It will be observed that this definition contains two distinct elements. First, the 'connected' loan must be utilised to obtain goods or services. Secondly, assuming the financial accommodation (see ante, para 5.21) is so utilised, the crucial matter is whether there is a business connection between the supplier of the goods to the consumer (the goods-supplier) and the financier. In a vendor credit situation (see ante, para 2.19), the connection is obvious because the goods and finance are supplied by the same person; whereas in the case of lender credit (see ante, paras 2.20 *et seq*) it is necessary to define that business relationship, a task undertaken by s 187 (see post, para 5.33). Building upon that s 187 connection, the Act seeks in ss 12 and 13 to distinguish whether a regulated agreement (see ante, para 5.13)

---

6   Is this a drafting mistake? Does the reasoning necessarily prevent part-exchange goods from being supplied under a linked transaction? See the analysis of part-exchange goods ante, para 2.09.

7   Goode, *Consumer Credit Law and Practice*, paras 43.21–23. Particularly for the latter two, the fact that s 171(2) puts the burden of proof on the party mentioned in s 19(2), eg, creditor, may be significant.

8   Subject to any transaction excluded by regulation: s 19(4) and the regulations made thereunder, eg, insurance (see post, para 25.07A) or guarantee of goods (see post, para 17.09). See further post, paras 10.32; 24.44; 26.19A.

9   Section 20(2): see post, para 8.24. As to the effect of the regulations made thereunder in narrowing the ambit of the concept of linked transactions, see Bennion [1986] JBL 294.

10   Sections 57(1), 69(1): see post, respectively paras 10.26; 10.32.

11   Section 173: see post, para 18.11. Thus, the linked transaction cannot impose any greater liability than the regulated agreement.

12   Eg, for misrepresentation. For discharge, see generally Chapter 26.

amounts to a connected or unconnected loan,[1] though it should be noted that the distinction is drawn between two or three functions rather than two or three people.[2]

(a) *Debtor-creditor-supplier agreements* are elaborately defined by s 12 (see post, para 5.34). Here, the Act regards the s 187 connection as sufficient justification for interfering with the contract for the supply of goods or services by classifying that supply as a linked transaction within s 19(1)(b) (see ante, para 5.31). This is particularly important to the goods-supplier upon withdrawal or cancellation of the regulated agreement[3] and to the financier with regard to connected-lender liability (s 75: see post, para 16.11).

(b) *Debtor-creditor agreements* are likewise elaborately defined by s 13 (see post, para 5.35). The *Crowther Report* observed that 'where goods are bought for cash provided by an independent lender there is no reason to regard the sale as any different from a normal cash sale or to treat the loan as other than a normal loan' (para 6.2.24). In such a case, the pre-occupation of the Act is with the raising of the loan, and hence the prohibition on canvassing, approaching minors or supplying unsolicited credit tokens.[4]

[5.33] The s 187 connection (business link). The easiest way to understand this rather complicated concept is to bear in mind its object. It is concerned with the situation where goods or services are supplied to a debtor by two separate people as follows: the effective retailer of goods to the debtor is termed the 'supplier'; and the person who finances that supply on credit is termed the 'creditor' (see ante, para 5.25). Section 187 defines whether the supplier and creditor are engaged in a joint venture. The two may be thought of as two oarsmen, and contravention of the Act as pulling the bung on a boat: if the two are engaged in a joint venture and sharing one single boat, they will both get wet; whereas, if they are rowing separate boats, one may sink without affecting the other.

The scope of the three parties for the purposes of s 187 is extended to their 'associates'.[1] The debtor's associates include certain specified relatives[2] and also partners (s 184(2)). In the usual case, the supplier and creditor will be corporations, in which case the Act defines as an associate any interlocking company[3] and the controller of either company (s 184(4)). Concentrating on the supplier and creditor (plus their associates) and

---

[5.32]

1 Additionally, the distinction between debtor-creditor-supplier and debtor-creditor agreements is significant for the following purposes: the criteria for exemption under s 16 (see ante, para 5.15); and the disclosure requirements with regard to the formalities and formation of the agreement (see post, Chapters 9 and 10).

2 These definitions are a good example of the over-elaboration which detracts from the many merits of the CCA. For a diagrammatic explanation, see Bennion, *Consumer Credit Act Manual* (3rd edn), p 13.

3 Sections 57(1), 69(1): see respectively post, paras 10.26; 10.31.

4 See respectively ss 49, 50, 51, discussed post, paras 7.07; 8.33; 7.12.

[5.33]

1 Section 187(4). The concept of an 'associate' is principally important for the purposes of licensing (s 25: see post, para 6.19).

2 Sections 184(1),(5), 189(1), eg, second husband of a businessman's divorced wife. The concept of a 'relative' is also important for the following purposes: linked transactions (s 19(1): see ante, para 5.31); total charge for credit (s 20(2): see post, para 8.23); the return of goods on cancellation (s 72: see post, para 10.34); credit brokerage (see post, para 5.38); extortionate credit bargains (s 138(1): see post, para 29.41).

3 Section 184(3). See the examples in Guest and Lloyd, *Encyclopedia of Consumer Credit Law*, para 2-185.

leaving aside debit and cheque guarantee cards,[4] s 187 distinguishes two ways in which there may be a joint venture between them for the supply of goods or services to consumers:

1   *A pre-existing arrangement.* According to s 187(1):

> A consumer credit agreement shall be treated as entered into under pre-existing arrangements between a creditor and a supplier if it is entered into in accordance with, or in furtherance of, arrangements[5] previously made between ... [them].

Typically, this will cover the situation where a creditor has, before the appearance of the debtor, provided the supplier with a stock of his documentation or logo to exhibit.[6]

2   *A contemplated future arrangement.* According to s 187(2):

> A consumer credit agreement shall be treated as entered into in contemplation of future arrangements between a creditor and a supplier if it is entered into in the expectation that arrangements will subsequently be made between ... [them] ... for the supply of cash, goods and services (or any of them) to be financed by the consumer credit agreement.

This will extend s 187 to the following credit card situation (see ante, para 2.28): the card-holder uses his card at a retailer/merchant[7] who is not, at the time the card is issued, within the scheme, but joins it later.[8] Whilst s 187(2) refers only to 'future arrangements',[9] it seems that 'arrangements' here refers to **credit** arrangements dealt with in s 12 (see post, para 5.34–35), not **payment** arrangements between creditor and supplier referred to in s 11.[10]

With the introduction of Electronic Fund Transfer (see ante, para 2.17), the banks were afraid that the arrangements set up to allow the operation of that system would be held to amount to a s 187 connection with the operator of the other terminal. Accordingly, they procured the passage of s 187(3A), which provides that:[11]

> Arrangements shall be disregarded for the purposes of subsections (1) and (2) if they are arrangements for the electronic transfer of funds from a current account at a bank ...

---

4   Section 187 has no application to cheque guarantee cards (s 187(3)) nor to debit cards (see below). See further ante, para 5.30; and Dobson [1988] JBL at 167.

5   Does this extend to one-off transactions? And see Sched 2, Examples 8 and 16.

6   'Where the creditor is an associate of the supplier's, the consumer credit agreement shall be treated, unless the contrary is proved, as entered into under pre-existing arrangements between creditor and the supplier' (s 187(5)).

7   Section 187(2) actually refers to a supply of cash by one other than the creditor. Is this a mistake? Section 187(2) does not apply to s 12(c) (see post, para 5.34) and the draftsman obviously intended it to be DC credit where a credit card is used to obtain cash from an agent (see Sched 2, Example 16).

8   For an explanation of why s 187(2) is narrower than might at first sight appear, see Goode, *Consumer Credit Law and Practice*, para 25.63. *Contra* Howells, *Consumer Debt*, pp 8–9.

9   For the reasons referred to post, para 5.34, note 10.

10 So that it does not include one-off RU agreements within s 11(1)(b) (see ante, para 5.29), eg, creditor promises to pay the supplier direct against his invoice, with no element of joint-venture between creditor and supplier: Goode, *op cit*, note 8, IIB para 5.368.

11 Section 187(3A), inserted by the Banking Act 1987, s 89, eg, a debit or cash card; see Guest and Lloyd, *op cit*, note 3, para 2-015.

This will save banks[12] from a s 187 connection with the operator of an ATM or a retailer accepting a debit card (ante, para 2.24): the result is that any credit arising because of an overdraft agreement will remain DC credit (see post, para 5.35) so that bank will escape any s 75 liability (see past, para 16.11) and the bank is exempted from documentation requirements by s 74(3A) (see post, para 9.07).

[5.34] Debtor-creditor-supplier (DCS) agreements. The DCS category is crucial to many important provisions of the Act, being its equivalent of Crowther's connected lender (see ante, para 5.32). In looking for a joint venture as to the supply of goods (or services) and credit, s 12 identifies three separate types of regulated consumer credit agreement (see ante, para 5.19 *et seq*).

Paragraph (a). Section 12(a) covers:

An RU[1] credit agreement to finance a transaction between the debtor[2] and the creditor, whether forming a part of that agreement or not.

This obviously comprehends all forms of vendor credit (see ante, para 2.19), where the creditor and supplier are, of course, the same person; and it specifically deals with both variants of vendor credit, *viz* whether the goods and credit are supplied under a single instalment credit contract[3] or a cash sale and separate loan. Turning to lender credit, at first sight greater difficulty is caused by direct financing (see ante, para 2.21), because of doubt as to the meaning of the word 'supplier'. The physical supplier of the goods or services to the debtor is the retailer, which might appear to take direct financing into paragraphs (b) or (c) below;[4] but the Act elsewhere makes it clear that 'creditor' for this purpose means the legal supplier,[5] from which it follows that direct financing falls within this category.[6]

Paragraph (b). Section 12(b) covers:

An RU[1] credit agreement to finance a transaction between the debtor and supplier and made by the creditor under a s 187 arrangement between himself and the supplier.

This paragraph appears to require the existence of three separate parties[7] and is essentially dealing with loan financing: it insists on a contract of loan[8] and a s 187 connection (see ante, para 5.33), but also requires the creditor to make payment direct to the supplier (RU credit). Examples include credit cards used to purchase goods or

---

12 Not every creditor who operates current accounts will amount to a bank: see *United Dominions Trust Ltd v Kirkwood* [1966] 2 QB 431, CA.

[5.34]

1 For RU and UU credit, see ante, para 5.29.

2 For 'debtor', see generally ante, para 5.24.

3 Thus ordinary hp, conditional or credit sales within the Act will be properly described as: DCS agreements for RU fixed-sum credit within ss 10(1)(b), 11(1)(a) and 12(a). Is this degree of complication really necessary?

4 For the significance of this in relation to s 75, see post, para 16.12.

5 The definition of 'supplier' in s 189(1) for the purposes of s 11(1)(a) also includes his assignee (see below).

6 See Goode, *Consumer Credit Law and Practice*, para 25.48.

7 See the definition of 'supplier' in s 189(1), which for this purpose cross refers to s 11(1)(b): see ante, para 5.29.

8 For loan financing, in general, see ante, paras 2.23–28; and for contracts of loan, see post, para 7.01 *et seq*.

services, eg, Master and Barclaycards (see Sched 2, Example 16), check or voucher trading and personal loans where the creditor makes out a cheque to the supplier.

Paragraph (c). Section 12(c) covers:

A UU[1] credit agreement which is made by the creditor under a pre-existing arrangement between himself and the supplier[9] in the knowledge that the credit is to be used to finance a transaction between the debtor and the supplier.

This is an anti-avoidance device, aimed at the situation where there is in reality a joint venture for the supply of goods (or services) within s 187 (see ante, para 5.33), but the debtor is technically free to use the credit as he wishes (UU credit),[10] eg, a double glazing company introduces the debtor to a creditor who makes an advance to the debtor for the purchase of windows (see Sched 2, Example 8).

[5.35] Debtor-creditor (DC) agreements. The DC category is required for a number of important provisions of the Act, being its equivalent of Crowther's 'unconnected lender' (see ante, para 5.32). All that is really required is the absence of any joint venture between the creditor and any supplier, and thus something which is not a DCS agreement.[1] Unfortunately eschewing this simple course, s 13 identifies three[2] other types of regulated consumer credit agreement (see ante, para 5.19 *et seq*).

Paragraph (a). Section 13(a) covers:

An RU[3] credit agreement to finance a transaction between the debtor and the supplier[4] but not made by the creditor under a s 187 arrangement between himself and the supplier.

This comprehends the situation where the debtor searches out his own personal source of funds with which he intends to obtain goods (or services), but the creditor insists on paying the supplier direct, eg, a personal loan. Even if there is co-incidentally an apparent s 187 connection between the creditor and supplier, the transaction is saved from that section because the creditor would be prepared to make a similar payment to any supplier (ss 187(3), (3A): see ante, para 5.33).

Paragraph (b). Section 13(b) covers:

An RU[3] credit agreement to refinance any existing indebtedness of the debtor's, whether to the creditor or another person.

This category deals with two situations, in neither of which does the debtor see any cash. First, it comprehends book transactions between debtor and creditor, as where a fixed-sum credit is converted into a running-account facility.[5] Second, it deals with refinancing

---

9   In defining 'supplier', s 189(1) here has yet another variant, this time referring back to s 12(c).

10   Section 12(c) does not extend to credit agreements made in contemplation of future arrangements between creditor and supplier: for the reasons, see Goode, *op cit*, note 6, para 25.50.

[5.35]

1   Goode, *Consumer Credit Law and Practice*, para 25.65. See also Guest and Lloyd, *Encyclopedia of Consumer Credit Law*, para 2-013. What should be done with a transaction which does not fit within any of the six categories of ss 12 and 13? Suppose a retailer wrongly exhibited a Visa logo?

2   What is the point of differentiating between these three categories?

3   For RU and UU credit, see ante, para 5.29.

4   For the purposes of s 13(c), 'supplier' is defined by reference back to that provision: s 189(1). But what is to be done about the meaning of 'supplier' in s 13(a)?

5   See post, para 7.04A. For fixed-sum and running-account credit, see ante, para 5.28. *Contra* a rescheduling of existing indebtedness? See Goode, *op cit*, note 1.

(see post, para 7.04A), where a creditor agrees to take over one or more debts which a debtor already owes to third parties,[6] eg, where the debtor transfers his credit card debts to another card issuer.

Paragraph (c). Section 13(c) covers:

A UU[3] credit which is not made by the creditor under a pre-existing arrangement between himself and the supplier in the knowledge that the credit is to be used to finance a transaction between the debtor and the supplier.

This category covers all personal loans where the debtor is entitled to get his hands on the cash, so he may do with it as he pleases,[7] eg, a bank overdraft or pledge (see Sched 2, Examples 8, 16, 17, 18). Does s 13(c) apply whether or not the supplier knows the credit is to be used, eg, to buy goods?

ANCILLARY CREDIT BUSINESSES

Introduction

[5.36/37] Whilst the major thrust of the CCA is to regulate the operations of creditors and owners under consumer credit and consumer hire agreements, it does not stop there. Instead, following the recommendations of the *Crowther Report* (see generally ante, para 5.03), the CCA seeks to regulate a wide range of other types of business which participate in the credit and hire industry. The Act christens these others 'ancillary credit businesses', and s 145(1) lists them:

An ancillary credit business is any business[1] so far as it comprises or relates to –

(a) credit brokerage[2]

(b) debt-adjusting[3]

(c) debt-counselling[3]

(d) debt-collecting[3] or

(e) the operation of a credit reference agency.[4]

Note that s 145(1) places an emphasis on there being a business and s 189(2) explains that:

A person is not to be treated as carrying on a particular type of business merely because occasionally he enters into transactions belonging to a business of that type.

In *R v Marshall*,[5] the issue of at what point 'occasionally' becomes a 'type of business' was said to be a matter of fact and degree and not simply denote more than one transaction. A

---

6   This will amount to debt-adjusting within s 145(5): see further post, para 5.43.

7   Section 11(3): set out ante, para 5.29.

[5.36/37]

1   'Business' includes a profession or trade: s 189(1), which also refers to s 189(2).

2   See post, para 5.38.

3   See post, para 5.43.

4   See post, para 8.37 *et seq*.

5   (1989) 90 Cr App R 73, CA, *per* Taylor LJ at 77 (this case involved an unsuccessful prosecution for unlicensed credit broking under ss 39, 147(1): see post, para 6.28); *Hare v Schurek* [1993] CLY 456, CA. Cf *Litchfield v Dreyfus* [1906] 1 KB 584; *Conroy v Kenny* [1999] 1 WLR 1340, CA (Moneylenders Acts).

similar limitation is to be found in respect of non-commercial agreements (see ante, para 5.18) and licensing (see post, para 6.12).

The types of business listed in s 145(1) are later defined in that section and must also be read in conjunction with the exceptions set out in s 146 (see post, paras 5.39; 5.43). All these ancillary credit businesses are subject not only to the licensing provisions (s 147(1): see post, Chapter 6) but also to the CCA provisions relating to seeking business,[6] canvassing[7] and formalities of the agreement (s 156. See generally post, para 9.09 *et seq*). Additionally, there are some special rules relating to credit reference agencies and one in respect of credit-brokers. Should a new category be created for money advisers (see post, para 5.42)?

Credit brokerage

[5.38] Introduction. Of all the various types of ancillary credit business (see ante, para 5.36), credit brokerage is probably the most important group. Pressure for the regulation of this type of business first arose in the 1960s from abuses by mortgage brokers operating in the second mortgage field.[1] However, the *Crowther Report* casts its net wider: it suggested a system of control for all persons carrying on business as brokers or other agents in connection with the making of consumer loans, whether or not connected with mortgages (para 6.4.25). The CCA went one better, and also included hire transactions as well. The result is most retailers and other dealers in consumer durables who do not carry their own credit rank as credit-brokers.[2] Thus, the prime mover in the retail supply of goods on credit or hire[3] will usually be a credit-broker (see post, para 5.39). He will require a category C standard licence[4] and be subject to several controls (see post, para 16.19). Unlicensed credit-broking attracts severe penalties.[5]

[5.39] The definition. According to s 145(2):

Subject to section 146(5),[1] credit brokerage is the effecting of introductions –

(a) of individuals desiring to obtain credit[2]–

    (i) to persons carrying on business to which this sub-paragraph applies,[3] or

    (ii) in the case of an individual desiring to obtain credit to finance the acquisition or provision of a dwelling occupied or to be occupied by himself or his relative,[4] to

---

6   Sections 151–52. See generally post, paras 8.29; 8.34.
7   Sections 153–54. See generally post, para 7.05 *et seq*.
[5.38]
1   See the *Crowther Report*, paras 2.4.47–53; 6.4.22–24; and ante, para 5.37.
2   Bennion, *Consumer Credit Manual* (3rd edn), 150.
3   See Sched 2, Example 2.
4   See post, para 6.15. Is it of any legal effect for the creditor to require the broker to warrant that he is licensed?
5   (a) it is an offence under s 39 – see post, para 6.28; (b) the agreement for the broker's services may be unenforceable under s 148 – see post, para 6.27; (c) the credit agreement he introduces may be unenforceable under s 149 – see post para 6.28.
[5.39]
1   Section 146(5): set out post, para 5.41.
2   For 'individuals' and 'credit', see respectively ante, paras 5.24; 5.21.
3   This category is explained in s 145(3): see post, para 5.40.
4   For 'relative', see ante, para 5.33.

any person carrying on a business in the course of which he provides credit secured on land, or

(b) of individuals desiring to obtain goods on hire to persons carrying on businesses to which this paragraph applies,[5] or

(c) of individuals desiring to obtain credit, or to obtain goods on hire, to other credit-brokers.

This definition is complicated because it attempts to ensure that it catches all the desired categories of broker, but none of the ones it wishes to exempt. In essence, this form of ancillary credit business (see ante, para 5.36) consists in making a business (see ante, para 5.37) of effecting introductions (see post, para 5.41), an activity which may be broken down as follows:

1   *The individual consumer introduced.* First, it is necessary to have an 'individual' (see ante, para 5.24) who desires to obtain credit of any kind (see ante, para 5.21), or to obtain goods on hire (see ante, para 1.19). It should be noted that the normal credit limit (see ante, para 5.22) does not apply here; nor is it relevant whether the individual requires the goods for business or private purposes; nor whether the individual is consciously looking for credit – he may simply be looking for goods or services and not have considered the means of payment.

2   *The credit or hire trader* to whom he is introduced (see post, para 5.40).

3   *The intermediary* (credit-broker) effecting the introduction (see post, para 5.41).

[5.40] The credit or hire trader. Introductions of an individual will only fall within the definition of credit brokerage (see ante, para 5.39) if they are to a person carrying on at least one of the following categories of business (ss 145(2), (3) (as amended)):

1   *A consumer credit business.*[1] The most common example, where a shopkeeper asks a finance company to finance a purchase by his customer within the credit limit.[2]

2   *An exempt DCS agreement business* (s 145(2)(a)(i)). This is defined as (s 145(3)(b)):

> a business which comprises or relates to consumer credit agreements being, otherwise than by virtue of section 16(5)(a), exempt agreements.

The effect is that, whilst the credit trader who only enters exempt agreements largely escapes the Act (see ante, para 5.15), a credit-broker who makes a business of introducing individuals to such traders is caught by the CCA unless the individual is only granted normal trade credit (*ibid*).

---

5   This category is explained in s 145(4): see post, para 5.40.

[5.40]

1   Sections 145(2)(a)(i), 145(3)(a). For consumer credit businesses, see post, para 6.12. It has been suggested that, because of the reference to 'persons' in s 145(2)(a)(i), introductions channelled through a single creditor are not credit-broking: Guest and Lloyd, *Encyclopedia of Consumer Credit*, para 2-146. *Sed quaere?*

2   For a debate as to whether this category extends to unregulated agreements, see Guest and Lloyd, *ibid*. *Contra* where a private supplier makes such a request direct to a financier, though not a 'private transaction' (explained post, para 25.35).

3 *A mortgage to purchase a dwelling-house* granted by a mortgagee who does not have a s 16 exemption. This will typically cover the second mortgage lender making a loan of any amount for home improvements.[3]

4 *An agreement with a foreign element.*[4] Caught under this anti-avoidance device are introductions to foreign creditors, eg, in Dublin, in circumstances under which, had the creditor been resident in England, he would have been carrying on a consumer credit business.

5 *A consumer hire business.*[5] Eg, where an electrical dealer arranges the hire of a TV set from a rental company within the credit limit.

6 *Another credit broking business.*[6] This is an anti-avoidance provision: a person who would be a credit-broker if he introduced the individual directly to the creditor or owner cannot avoid that label simply by doing such business indirectly through another credit-broker.[7]

[5.41] The intermediary (credit-broker). A middleman (intermediary) will not be a credit-broker within the meaning of the Act (see ante, para 5.39) unless he carries on a business of credit brokerage, so that introductions by friends or relatives will not do. The Act does not require a s 187 relationship (see ante, para 5.33), but simply refers to 'the effecting of introductions' between an individual consumer (see ante, para 5.39) and a credit or hire trader (see ante, para 5.40). The sense of the provision is that the intermediary must not be the employee of either of the other two, but an independent conduit pipe acting on his own account.[1] However, the introduction could be to another company in the same group.[2] Further, it should be noted that the individual must be introduced to the source of credit or hire: it follows that it is not credit-broking for a retailer simply to advertise credit or hire facilities, or even to stock the forms of the creditor or owner; but his forwarding a completed proposal form to the creditor or owner will amount to credit-broking.[3]

The Act specially exempts two particular categories of intermediary.

1 *Lawyers involved in contentious business.* The difficulty here is for a lawyer wishing to rely on this category rather than a group licence (see post, para 6.16) to be certain at the outset that the matter he takes on will be contentious (s 146(1)–(4)).

2 *Housewife canvassers.* The foregoing definition would catch the army of housewives who, armed with a mail order catalogue, solicit business from neighbours and friends (see post, para 8.19). The *Crowther Report* recommended that they should be exempt even if carrying on a part-time business (para 6.4.20). Accordingly, s 146(5) provides that:

---

3 Section 145(2)(a)(ii). See Goode, *Consumer Credit Law and Practice*, para 48.19. Compare the negative licensing power of the Director with regard to estate agents to be found in the Estate Agents Act 1979: see post, para 6.04.
4 Sections 145(2)(a)(i); 145(3)(c), as amended.
5 Section 145(2)(b),(4). For consumer hire businesses, see post, para 6.12.
6 Section 145(2)(c).
7 *Hicks v Walker* [1984] CLY 555, DC.
[5.41]
1 Does s 146(5)(a) support or detract from this?
2 Guest and Lloyd, *Encyclopedia of Consumer Credit*, para 2-146. Or perhaps an in-house franchise (see ante, para 1.07) offering business to his franchisor?
3 *Brookes v Retail Credit Cards Ltd* [1986] CLY 370, DC (discussed [1986] JBL 234; 40 CC3/12).

For the purposes of section 145(2), introductions effected by an individual by canvassing off trade premises either debtor-creditor-supplier agreements falling within section 12(a) or regulated consumer hire agreements shall be disregarded if –

(a) the introductions are not effected by him in the capacity of an employee,[4] and

(b) he does not by any other method effect introductions falling within section 145(2).

Leaving aside consumer hire agreements, it should be noticed that the exemption is restricted to canvassing off trade premises[5] the supply of goods under DCS agreements within s 12(a): it does not exempt canvassing goods on trade premises, nor DC loans anywhere (see ante, para 5.35); and with regard to goods, it does not save DCS agreements within s 12(b) or (c).[6]

Debt collection agencies

[5.42] There are a number of firms who make a business of collecting the debts of third parties.[1] Sometimes, the debt collector will act as agent for the creditor,[2] perhaps collecting on a 'no collection, no fee' basis, perhaps managing sales ledgers for creditors, tracing absconding debtors ('gone-aways')[3] and conducting legal action on behalf of creditors. In other cases, once a debt has reached a certain stage of default, it may be sold by the creditor at a substantial discount to a specialist debt collecting company,[4] which in practice runs a very different sort of business from the factor who buy good debts (see ante, para 2.22). Parliament has attempted to curb the worst excesses used by debt-collectors in attempting to recover debts from consumers by making them an offence under s 40 of the Administration of Justice Act 1970 (see post, para 24.24); and, insofar as any collection document/letter may be mistaken for an official one emanating from the county court ('look-alikes'), amount to specific offences.[5] Such debt collectors also require a CCA licence, with significant further penalties for illegal loan sharks (see post, para 6.20) and should comply with the relevant voluntary codes of practice (see ante, para 3.13). In the light of the foregoing, the *Crowther Report* recommended (para 6.12.15) and the CCA accepted that such activities should be regulated (see post, para 5.43). An

---

4   This exemption may also be available to some self-employed direct salesmen who would otherwise required their own credit-broking licence.

5   Sections 48, 153, 189(1): see post, para 7.06. The words 'off trade premises', would appear to be tautologous; and the limitation to 'canvassing', leaves the housewife unprotected either when she is (a) invited to visit her customers in their own homes, or (b) taking orders in her own home: see Dobson (1980) 130 NLJ 528.

6   As to DCS agreements, see ante, para 5.34. Hence, it cannot save agents for check traders. *Contra* Goode, *Consumer Credit Law and Practice*, para 48.33.

[5.42]

1   Sometimes as an adjunct to other business, eg, a credit reference agency (see post, para 8.37) or a firm specialising in repossessions (see post, para 24.23).

2   Eg, trade protection societies. They will often make regular door-to-door collections from debtors.

3   This activity will be controlled by the Representation of the People Act 2000 (electoral roll: see ante, para 3.26) and the DPA (see ante, para 3.28).

4   What have been termed 'dealers in the bad debts of others': the *Crowther Report*, para 2.6.12; see generally ante, para 5.03. Why is the debt worth more in the hands of the agency than in the hands of the creditor?

5   Under the County Courts Act 1984, ss 135, 136: do these rules preclude the creditor from sending to the debtor a photocopy of a completed (but not yet lodged in court) summons? See also unlawful harassment under the AJA (see post, para 24.24); the Protection from Harassment Act 1997; and for telephone harassment, see post, para 8.17.

alternative route sometimes recommended by debt-collectors is an Individual Voluntary Arrangement (see post, para 19.20).

Money advice. From those third parties who collect debts (above) may be distinguished those who merely advise consumers on the payment of debts (see ante, para 3.16), an activity particularly relevant to over-indebtedness (see post, para 27.01). Charitable organisations operating in this field tend to supply only advice and possibly offer to make arrangements with his creditors on the debtor's behalf,[6] under what are known as debt-management-plans (DMEs),[6a] eg, CABx (see ante, para 3.08), the Paylink Trust.[7] On the other hand, businesses in this field sometimes go further and offer to take over from the multiple debtor responsibility for all his debts,[8] or otherwise re-finance his debts;[9] and their terms are subject to the UTCC Regulations (see post, para 11.12). Some of these activities fall within debt-collecting (see above) or one or more of the other existing categories of 'ancillary credit business' (see post, para 5.43): the significance of this is that only where the money adviser is an ancillary credit business is it subject to the discipline of the OFT's powers over licensing[10] and advertising (see post, para 8.20 *et seq*). However, it maybe that what is required is new legislation[11] and perhaps a compulsory (statutory) code of practice.[8]

Whether or not a money adviser is used, any default on re-scheduling of his debts by a consumer will normally be treated by the creditor as a default: this is likely to be registered with a credit bureau;[3] and will probably result in the debtor being unable to obtain further credit under that name, except perhaps on impaired terms.[12]

[5.43] Ancillary credit businesses.[1] The activities described below have also been brought by the CCA within the rubric of 'ancillary credit businesses'.[2]

(a) *Debt-adjusting*. This is defined by s 145(5) as follows:

> Subject to s 146(6),[3] debt-adjusting is, in relation to debts due under consumer credit agreements or consumer hire agreements –
>
> (a) negotiating with the creditor or owner, on behalf of the debtor or hirer, terms for the discharge of a debt,[4] or

---

6 Cranston, *Consumers and the Law* (3rd edn), pp 267–68.

6a See [2001] 12 Credit Today, Extra. Possibly without the debtor realising, these may damage his credit record: see post, para 8.36.

7 Set up by the Money Advice Trust (see ante, para 3.16): (2001) 30 Credit Finance 21.

8 See Whyley and Collard, *Fee or Free?* (1999); [1999] 10 Credit Today 13; [2001] 5 Credit Today 31. Sometimes absconding with the debtor's payments: see the *Crowther Report*, para 6.12.14.

9 For an example of such activities, see the part played by Auto Finance in *Snook v London and West Riding Investments Ltd* [1967] 2 QB 786, CA: for criticism of this decision, see Cranston, *op cit*, note 6, p 268.

10 See post, para 6.11 *et seq*. Partly to remedy government refusal to statutorily regulate debt management plans, the OFT has issued 'Guidelines' on debt management.

11 See the Regulation of the (pm) Debt Management and Credit Repair Services Bill 2001.

12 'Non-status' lending: see post, para 7.04A.

[5.43]

1 See generally Goode, *Consumer Credit Law and Practice*, Part 1, Chapter 48.

2 See ante, para 5.36. As to the types of standard licence ordinarily required, see post, para 6.15.

3 Note that a housewife within s 146(5) (set out ante, para 5.41) is expressly saved from all these categories of ancillary credit business as well: s 146(6)(e).

4 Eg, the dealer taking goods in part-exchange (see ante, para 2.09) who obtains a settlement figure from a finance house (see post, para 26.19A).

(b) taking over, in return for payments by the debtor or hirer, his obligation to discharge a debt,[5] or

(c) any similar activity concerned with the liquidation of a debt.

This would cover both debt advice and management (see ante, para 5.42) and also debt consolidation (see post, para 7.04A). However, s 145(5) is wider than might appear at first sight.[6] First, it applies in relation to any consumer credit and consumer hire agreements, whether regulated or not.[7] Second, the activity need only be aimed at some rearrangement of a debt[8] arising from such agreements, whether or not the rearrangement is legally binding or the debts have yet accrued due, eg, a dealer arranging a part-exchange (see ante, para 2.09); money advisers (see ante, para 5.42).

(b) *Debt-counselling*. This is defined by s 145(6) as follows:

Subject to s 146(6)[3] debt-counselling is the giving of advice to debtors or hirers about the liquidation of debts due under consumer credit agreements or consumer hire agreements.

Once more this extends to both unregulated agreements[7] and debts[8] not yet accrued due under existing agreements.[9] Not only does s 145(6) cover persons who advise for reward,[10] but also those who do so as a 'profession', so that it would appear to extend to those organisations which offer free advice.[11]

(c) *Debt-collecting*. This is defined by s 145(7) as follows:

Subject to s 146(6),[3] debt-collecting is the taking of steps to procure payment of debts due under consumer credit agreements or consumer hire agreements.

Again embracing unregulated agreements[7] and debts[8] not yet due, this category will comprehend not just commercial debt-collecting agencies (see ante, para 5.42), but also professional collectors of debts owed to others,[12] eg, repossession agents with authority to accept payments (see post, para 24.23); but it does not include those who buy debts, eg, factors (see ante, para 2.22). Normally, debt-collectors are not employed by the public, so that on principle the CCA should not be concerned with how they obtain their business from creditors. However, where a contract for his services is made by an unlicensed debt-collector, it will be unenforceable without an OFT order (s 148): this is admittedly illogical, but is said to help re-enforce the licensing system.

---

5   Eg, an overdraft granted to pay off existing obligations. Because the debtor does not pay the financier to take the assignment, s 145(5)(b) does not catch either indirect financing or the factoring of good or bad debts.

6   Goode, *op cit*, note 1, para 48.36.

7   For exempt agreements, see ante, para 5.15.

8   For debts, see post, para 7.04A. See also vehicle transfer agencies (see ante, para 1.23).

9   It does not extend to advice to those about to enter into such agreements: Goode, *op cit*, note 1, para 48.39. For the formation of supply agreements, see generally post, Chapter 10.

10 Eg solicitors, accountants, bankers, fee-charging debt counsellors. There are exemptions for the legal profession whilst engaged in contentious business: s 146(1)–(4).

11 By reason of the definition of 'business' in s 189(1): Goode, *op cit*, note 1, eg, CABx (see ante, para 3.08); neighbourhood law centres (see ante, para 3.16); money advisers (see ante, para 5.42). Group licences have been issued to CABx and Age Concern.

12 Eg, solicitors, receivers. Group licences for debt-collecting have been issued to solicitors. For the separate litigation exemption, see above, note 11. A debt-collecting licence is not needed by one who was the credit-broker for a debt: (1992) 13 CCA News 5/11. See generally [2000] 7 Credit Extra.

CHAPTER 6

LICENSING

INTRODUCTION[1]

[6.01] This chapter is concerned with the use of administrative regulation to attain consumer protection. Even assuming all the ordinary consumer protection rules are enforced,[2] there are always likely to be situations where a trader may make a net profit by ignoring the rules and paying any fine or damages. Of course, there is a general power for the Attorney General to seek an injunction to restrain persistent breaches of commercial law;[3] Part III of the Fair Trading Act grants the Director a similar power in respect of some persistent breaches of both criminal and civil law (see post, paras 6.06–08); and the subsequent proliferation of ombudsmen to oversee various parts of commerce is intended to meet similar needs.[4] However, at best such proceedings are likely to remain a stable-bolting exercise, making no attempt to weed out the unscrupulous trader before he harms consumers. By contrast,[5] the technique of licensing has the advantage that it can be set up so that such traders may be precluded from lawfully trading before consumers can be harmed (see post, para 6.02). As always, there is the dilemma that too Draconian controls may simply divert consumer demand into the arms of illegal traders (see post, para 6.20).

[6.02] Licensing. For centuries, governments have used licensing as a technique for controlling the activities of their citizens, though its efficacy is in part dependent on the availability of resources to operate it.[1] Frequently, the objectives of a licensing system are economic, or a mixture of economic and political: export and import licensing;[2] photocard licences for motor vehicles, issued by the Driving Licence Authority (DVLA) and a useful identity check frequently used when granting retail credit. The holding of markets and fairs is controlled in part by custom and the common law and in part by statute.[3] Sometimes, licences are a form of planning control, as with the licensing of public

---

[6.01]

1 See generally Borrie, *The Development of Consumer Law and Policy*, Chapter 4.

2 See the general protections offered by statutes in Chapter 4; the special statutory protections in respect of consumer credit in Chapter 5; and the rules of civil law enumerated throughout.

3 *AG v Harris* [1961] 1 QB 74, CA; and see generally post, para 29.39.

4 See ante, para 3.25; and generally Morris [1987] JBL 131 and 199.

5 For a discussion of the advantages of licensing, see Borrie, *op cit*, note 1, pp 90–97.

[6.02]

1 Eg, the (now repealed) Moneylenders Acts 1900 and 1927: see post, para 6.09. See generally Goode, *Consumer Credit Law and Practice*, para 27.1; Cranston, *Consumers and the Law* (3rd edn), p 449.

2 See generally, Atiyah, *Sale of Goods* (10th edn), Chapter 22; *Benjamin's Sale of Goods* (5th edn), para 18-247 *et seq.*

3 See Hill (1985) 5 Legal Studies 320. Many of the private rights to hold markets have passed to local authorities; and the others are subject to planning permission. As to what is a market, see *Kingston upon Hull CC v Greenwood* (1984) 82 LGR 586; *Manchester Cty Council v Walsh* (1985) 50 P & CR 409, CA.

markets, eg, car boot sales,[4] street traders[5] or sex shops.[6] Other control systems are introduced as a protection for public health[7] or safety (see post, para 6.05) or other interests of consumers, as with the regulation of the supply of gaming machines,[8] or door-to-door traders peddling goods,[9] eg, home credit, or money (see post, para 6.09), or collecting donations for charity.[10] Plainly, many of these forms of licensing could in their operation tend towards restraint of trade;[11] and the administration of all such licensing systems is *prima facie* subject to control of the courts.[12] The various types of licensing are analysed below (post, para 6.04).

[6.03/04] Licensing persons. From the viewpoint of consumer supplies, perhaps the most significant form of licensing is that of persons, rather that of places or goods. Broadly speaking, a personal licensing system may belong to one of two types:

1 *Positive licensing*. These are systems which require that a licence is obtained before undertaking the relevant activity. In fact, it is possible to distinguish between different types of positive licensing systems according to an ascending order of severity with which they interfere with activities within their ambit:[1]

(a) registration,[2] frequently proved by way of a receipt;[3]

(b) certification, which requires an applicant to demonstrate an appropriate standard before registration;[4] and

---

4   Eg, *Newcastle-upon-Tyne City Council v Noble* (1991) 89 LGR 618.

5   See the Local Government (Miscellaneous Provisions) Act 1982, s 3 and Sched 4; *Wandsworth LBC v Rosenthal* [1996] CLY 4142, DC; *Kempin v Brighton and Hove C* [2001] 4 CL 504. A pedlar's certificate (see note 9, below) is no substitute: *Watson v Malloy* [1988] 3 All E R 459, DC (see 132 SJ 1654); *Chichester DC v Wood* [1997] CLY 3534; *South Tyneside MBC v Jackson* [1998] EHLR 249, DC.

6   See the Local Government (Miscellaneous Provisions) Act 1982, s 2 (see 45 MLR 676). These rules do not infringe the Treaty of Rome: see ante, para 2.13.

7   Eg, the Public Health Act 1936, s 107 (offensive trades); Pet Animals Act 1951, s 1 (as amended). As to food premises, see ante, para 4.26. As to damages, see 152 LGR 883.

8   The Gaming Act 1968, s 27, requires a licence to be held not only by suppliers of amusement machines but also by those directly financing the transaction on lease, though not other forms of instalment credit.

9   See the Pedlars Act 1871 (as amended). For the scope of this provision, see *Murphy v Duke* [1985] 2 All ER 274; *Stevenage BC v Wright* [1996] CLY 4144, DC. Furthermore, special registration is required before one can purport to supply on behalf of blind or otherwise disabled persons: Trading Representations (Disabled Persons) Acts 1958 and 1972. See generally Bragg [1985] Jo of Social Welfare Law 103; and Bragg [1986] Jo of Social Welfare Law p 302; Papworth (1998) 17 Tr L 201. For canvassing, see further post, para 8.17.

10 See the House to House Collections Act 1939 (as amended); and post, para 8.13A.

11 *R v Basildon DC ex p Brown* (1981) 79 LGR 655, CA (discussed 79 LGR 588). For the monopoly effects of licensing, see Cranston, *op cit*, note 1, pp 454–57; and generally ante, para 2.13.

12 *R v Wear Valley DC ex p Binks* [1985] 2 All ER 699. See 102 LQR 24; and generally De Smith, *Judicial Review of Administrative Law* (5th edn), Chapter 8. For injunctions, see generally post, para 29.39.

[6.03/04]

1   Cranston, *Consumers and the Law* (3rd edn), pp 460–62.

2   Registration is where individuals need only list their names in an official register, eg, Explosives Act 1875; Wildlife and Countryside Act 1981, s 6 (as amended); Scrap Metal Dealers Act 1964 (as amended); Data Protection Act 1998 (see ante, paras 3.27–28).

3   Eg, the licences required by retailers of game (Game Act 1831, s 18; Game Licences Act 1860, ss 13–15).

4   Eg, Poisons Act 1972, s 3 (non-medicinal poison); Road Traffic Act 1988, Part III (as amended: driver's licences; used in credit checks (see post, para 8.35)).

(c) licensing proper. The last predicates that only those who meet the appropriate standard and are licensed may practice (see post, para 6.05); but its effectiveness depends on regular review,[5] whose cost-implications sometimes make government reluctant to employ the technique.

2 *Negative licensing.*[6] In the United States, the technique of the 'cease and desist' power was developed, whereby orders can be obtained against businesses to prevent them engaging in conduct detrimental to consumers. The effect of these powers is therefore negative in this sense: any businessman within the ambit of the system may act as he wishes unless and until an order is made against him that he 'cease and desist' from that activity. UK examples include estate agents,[7] food safety[8] and Part III of the Fair Trading Act 1973 (see post, para 6.06). Whilst negative licensing has cost advantages both to businesses and government, it still requires for its effective implementation that a monitoring system be established to collect information[9] and may amount only to a stable-bolting exercise.

[6.05] Types of personal licensing. Confining discussion to proper positive licensing systems relating to persons (see ante, para 6.03), there are a number of different licensing systems of significance to consumers of goods.

1 *The Consumer Credit Act* (see post, para 6.09 *et seq*).

2 *Intoxicating liquor.*[1] Since medieval times, the troublesome subject of intoxicating liquor has been the province of local magistrates, whose control has been partly exercised by means of a licensing system.[2] The current basis of the system is the Licensing Act 1964 (as amended), which makes it an offence to 'sell or expose for sale by retail any intoxicating liquor' except under a licence at the place stipulated in that licence.[3] The licensing procedure is under the control of the licensing justices (s 1) and distinguishes according to whether it is 'a licence authorising sale for consumption off those premises only' (an off-licence) or also allows consumption on those premises (an on-licence). Special provision is made for the sale and supply of intoxicating liquor in such as club premises (Part II), restaurants and guest houses (Part IV). The licensing system concentrates not only on the fitness of the licence-holder,[4] but also on the premises from which the liquor is supplied by retail: there is power to require structural alterations in respect of on-licences (s 19) and an elaborate system to control the hours during which sales are permitted;[5] and applications for a new licence must

---

5   If positive licensing does not include regular review, the distinction from negative licensing is substantially lessened: see post, para 6.11.

6   Cranston, *op cit*, note 1, pp 448, 439–40.

7   Estate Agents Act 1979, s 3 (supervised by the OFT: see ante, para 3.03).

8   Food Safety Act 1990, s 19(i)(b) (see ante, para 4.26).

9   Cranston, *op cit*, note 1.

[6.05]

1   Current laws have their origin in emergency powers introduced during the First World War to ensure that munitions workers were not drunk at work.

2   See the definition of 'intoxicating liquor' (1964 Act, s 201(i) (as amended)).

3   Section 160. Eg, *French v Hoggett* [1967] 3 All ER 1042, DC. For 'sale by retail', see Licensing (Retail Sales) Act 1988. For vicarious criminal liability, see post, para 28.09.

4   Section 3. Further, the applicant must not have been disqualified (s 9(6)).

5   Part III. Compare ordinary retail shop hours: see post, para 8.13.

prove need.[6] There is a general prohibition of door-to-door sales (s 163), of on-licence sales on credit unless supplied with a meal or to residents[7] and of supplies to young persons.[8] The Government has proposed reform.

3   *Dangerous goods*. The supply of many types of dangerous goods are subject to licensing systems, eg, petroleum,[9] firearms (Firearms Acts: see further ante, para 4.31), explosives,[10] medicines,[11] food safety (see ante, para 4.26). Previously considered and rejected was the licensing of garages to control vehicle servicing and repair.

4   *Privatised utilities* (see ante, para 3.07).

THE FAIR TRADING ACT 1973, PART III

[6.06] Rogue traders. To combat the situation where a trader finds it advantageous to break the law persistently and pay any fines or damages, there was introduced by Part III of the FTA a system by which the Director-General of the Office of Fair Trading (see ante, para 3.03) might seek a cessation of such activities (see post, para 6.08). As originally drafted, this power was available only in respect of conduct detrimental to consumers (see post, para 6.07). According to s 34(1), the OFT Director may exercise his powers under Part III of the FTA:

> where it appears to [him] that a person carrying on a business has in the course of that business persisted in a [designated] course of conduct ...

This introduction was tightly worded. First, it required that an activity was carried on by a 'person', which may, of course, be a natural or artificial person.[1] Where it appears to the Director that the conduct within s 34 has been carried on by a body corporate 'with the consent or connivance' of what the Act terms an 'accessory', the Director might also proceed against the accessory.[2] Second, s 34 insisted that that 'person' must be 'carrying on a course of business', which requires that what he is doing amounts to a business.[3] Third, proceedings must be brought by the Director of the OFT (see ante, para 3.03). Fourth, the defendant must have 'persisted' in a designated course of conduct: that persistence must be established at each stage (see post, para 6.08); but, in establishing

---

6   See Light (2000) 150 NLJ 926.

7   Section 166. Does this make it an offence for an ordinary public house to accept payment by credit card?

8   Generally, persons under 14 years are not allowed within on-licensed premises (s 168, as amended), 168A: see ante, para 5.10 and those under 18 may not be served with intoxicating liquor (s 169, as amended).

9   Petroleum (Consolidation) Act 1928 (as amended).

10   Explosives Acts 1875 and 1923 (as amended).

11   Medicines Act 1968, Parts I–IV (as amended). See Cranston, *Consumers and the Law* (3rd edn), p 469 *et seq*; Teff (1984) 47 MLR 303; and generally ante, para 4.29.

[6.06]

1   This has caused difficulty with phoenix businesses (see post, para 19.25).

2   Sections 38, 39; and see post, para 6.08. This is a point of some significance where a business may be transferred to a new company: Borrie, *The Development of Consumer Law and Policy*, 73. Compare how modern statutes make corporate officers liable: see post, para 28.11.

3   'Business' is defined by s 137(2) to include 'a professional practice and ... any other undertaking which is carried on for gain or reward or which is an undertaking in the course of which goods or services are supplied otherwise than free of charge'. There has been difficulty in showing that, eg, car boot sellers, were carrying on business.

persistence, s 34(2) helps the Director by instructing him to have regard to both 'complaints' and 'other information'.[4] In practice, the OFT has found it a difficult hurdle to marshall sufficient such evidence of persistence about a particular complaint within a reasonable time-span.[5] These requirements have now been significantly eased by new Regulations (see below), but in a manner which looks most odd to an English lawyer: what are in effect amendments to Part III of the FTA are to be found in Sched 2 of the Stop Now Orders Regulations 2001 (SI No 1422) implementing an EU Injunctions Directive (98/27/EC). Significantly copying out the terms of the Directive (see ante, para 1.04) and without expressly repealing any of the sections of Part III, Sched 2 of the Regulations introduces what is in effect an entirely new code, leaving the courts to piece together the two streams of legislation.

In seeking to ascertain the presence of such conduct, the Director relies heavily, although not exclusively,[6] on the submission of information by local authority consumer protection departments.[7] A central registry of convictions is kept to enable the OFT to identify businesses for possible action. The OFT usually publicises any action it takes under Part III, a weapon whose efficacy should not be underestimated.

[6.07] Stop Now Orders. Under the original Part III of the FTA, conduct will only fall within s 34(1) where a person persisted in a course of conduct which satisfies both the following criteria:

1 *Detrimental.* It must be shown that the conduct 'is **detrimental** to the interests of consumers in the United Kingdom, whether those interests are economic interests or interests in respect of health, safety or other matters'.[1] So, inter-business practices are excluded, eg, photocopier malpractices (see post, para 16.06). As to consumers, it is for consideration whether this requires an overall view to be taken as to the extent to which the conduct must affect consumers.[2] Can a national organisation pursue in one of its areas a course of conduct which would bring a local trader within s 34?

2 *Unfair.* It is unfair to consumers in that it consists of breaches of either–

   (a) The criminal law. Section 34(2) provides that a course of conduct shall be regarded as unfair to consumers if it consists of:

   ... contraventions of one or more enactments which impose duties, prohibitions or restrictions enforceable by criminal proceedings, whether any such duty, prohibition or restriction is imposed in relation to consumers as such or not and whether the person carrying on the business has or has not been convicted of any offence in respect of any such contravention.

---

4   Section 34(4) makes it clear that the complaints do not have to be from consumers and that the OFT can use information collected for whatever purpose; and see post, para 6.08.

5   See Cranston, *Consumers and the Law* (3rd edn), p 440.

6   Other sources of information include consumer organisations (see ante, para 3.07 *et seq*), the mass media and the courts.

7   See s 34(4). For details of complaints made by consumers to local authorities, see the OFT, Annual Reports; and further Harvey and Parry, *Law of Consumer Protection and Fair Trading* (6th edn), pp 355–59.

[6.07]

1   Section 34(1)(a). As to the FTA concept of 'consumers', see ante, para 4.19.

2   OFT, *Trading Practices* (1990), paras 4.30–31.

It probably does not extend to unrelated serious crime; but examples would include[3] breaches of the Trade Descriptions Act 1968 (see ante, paras 4.03–17), of safety legislation (see ante, paras 4.31–37), of misleading pricing or advertisements (see post, paras 8.10; 8.12A), or of licensing provisions (see ante, paras 6.02–05). But see below.

(b) The civil law. Section 34(3) provides that a course of conduct on the part of the person carrying on a business shall be regarded as unfair to consumers if it consists of:

> things done, or omitted to be done, in the course of that business in breach of contract or in breach of a duty (other than a contractual duty) owed to any person by virtue of any enactment or rule of law and enforceable by civil proceedings, whether (in any such case) civil proceedings in respect of the breach of contract or breach of duty have been brought or not.

Examples would include failure to return money to which the consumer was entitled; failure to deliver goods, to carry out services, or perform a money-back guarantee in breach of contract; breach of a statutory implied term; failure to pay damages; deceit or misrepresentation; carrying out unauthorised repairs.[4]

However, the above requirements in general, and the requirement of persistence in particular, have been substantially eased by reg 3 of the Stop Now Orders (EC Directive) Regulations 2001 (see post, para 28.03). Not only does Sched 2 to these Regulations enable any qualified entity to bring Part III proceedings (para 1), but reg 3 in effect assumes that the Part III requirements of persistence in detrimental and unfair conduct are satisfied by 'Community infringements', an expression which covers virtually all the statutory consumer protections. The Regulations have also enhanced the procedure (see post, para 6.08).

But still the OFT seeks new statutory powers: these would seem to go beyond what might be achievable by statutory instrument under the deregulation initiative (see ante, para 5.10) and require new primary legislation.[5] The Government proposes new legislation to amend Part III of the FTA in the following respects:[6] new powers to ban traders for a period; and to ban unfair practices (see ante, para 4.20).

[6.08] The amended procedure. Where the Director or other qualified entity is satisfied that a trader is **persistently** (see ante, para 6.07) indulging in conduct within the enhanced Part III of the FTA,[1] it enjoins on him an accelerated, three-stage procedure.

---

3   Other examples might include offences under the Mock Auctions Act 1961; CCA; CPA 1987, Part III (misleading prices); AJA 1980, s 40 (unlawful harassment of debtors).
4   For some of the difficulties encountered in prosecuting, see OFT, AR-1996, 29.
5   The DTI has promoted a draft Enterprise Bill 2002: see ante, para 5.11.
6   *Modern Markets: Confident Consumers* (1999, Cm 4410), paras 7.6–9.
[6.08]
1   Enhanced by the Stop Now Order Regulations: see post, para 28.03.

Stage 1: A voluntary assurance. Section 34(1) instructed the Director that he should first:

> use his best endeavours, by communication with that person or otherwise, to obtain from him a satisfactory written assurance that he will refrain from continuing that course of conduct and from carrying on any similar course of conduct in the course of that business.

In practice, the OFT found this a difficult hurdle:[2] traders procrastinate; they avoid assurances by temporarily altering their conduct; and assurances are only negative in effect, not committing the trader to do anything positive. Nevertheless, a gradually increasing number of undertakings given annually is to be found in the OFT Annual Reports.[3] The Regulations make the following changes: unless the matter is urgent, they invite the Director or other qualified body in the first instance to consult the person against whom proceedings are contemplated (paras 2, 3), with a view to the latter giving such an assurance (para 14). However, 'if the cessation of the infringement is not achieved within two weeks after the request for consultation is received, the qualified entity may bring proceedings without further delay' (para 4).

Stage 2: Court action. Where, but only where, he is unable to obtain satisfactory written assurances as above, or such assurances are broken, the Director may bring proceedings before the court.[4] In these proceedings, the Director will have to prove that the respondent's conduct is within s 34 or amounts to a 'Community infringement', the decision of any court being *prima facie* evidence for this purpose.[5] The court then has a choice:

(a) it may accept any suitable **undertaking** from the respondent to refrain from 'continuing' that or any similar course of conduct.[6] As the undertaking is as to 'continuing' conduct (s 34(1)), it looks solely to the future; so, the longer the respondent can prevaricate before giving an undertaking, the longer he can continue with the complained conduct. However, under the Regulations the defendant shall be liable to civil proceedings in respect of any failure to fulfill the undertaking (para 15).

(b) or it may **order** that he do so (s 37(2)), this Order being known as a 'Stop Now Order'.[7] This Order 'shall be made with all due expediency, and in circumstances where it would grant an interim injunction ... to a public authority seeking to enforce the law where it has power to do so, the court may make an interim order' (para 8). With both the full and interim order, the court may order publication of its decision and a suitable corrective statement by the defendant (para 9).

Where the Director has additionally, or instead, brought an accessory before the court, it has similar powers;[8] and there are wide powers to prevent avoidance of the process by

---

2   Cranston, *Consumers and the Law* (3rd edn), pp 441.
3   A consolidated set of texts is to be found in Part 4 of the *Encyclopedia of Consumer Law* by Thomas. For illustrative cases, see Harvey, *Consumer Protection and Fair Trading* (6th edn), pp 356–57.
4   Section 35 (as amended); Regulations, Sched 2, para 16. See generally ante, paras 2.12–14.
5   Section 36; Regulations, Sched 2, para 5. Cf s 11 of the Civil Evidence Act 1968: see ante, para 3.21.
6   Section 37(3); Regulations, Sched 2, para 6.
7   Regulations, Sched 2, para 7. If the case is brought by a 'Community qualified entity', the court may examine whether that entities' purposes justifies taking action in the particular case: para 10.
8   Sections 38, 39; Regulations, Sched 2, paras 11, 12, 13. Cf post, para 28.11. It may be possible to seek a disqualification order against a director under other legislation: see post, para 19.25.

transferring business between continuing companies in a group of companies (s 40). Legal assistance is available in these proceedings (s 43) and appeal on fact or law lies to the Court of Appeal.[9] Unfortunately, assurances given under Part III bind only the person giving the assurance, so that there is often scope to side-step the procedure by incorporation.[10]

Stage 3: Contempt. Under the original version of Part III, breach of such an undertaking or court order will amount to a contempt of court, a procedure likely to be effective in respect of the person against whom it is made.[11] However, it would seem that contempt proceedings no longer apply to breaches of undertakings (see above), but are to be confined to breaches of a court order; but, if granted, it might put the defendant trader out of business.

A list of the assurances, undertakings, court orders and contempt orders given or made each year is to be found in the OFT Annual Report.[12] It seems that an injured consumer could not obtain a compensation order in any of the above proceedings, because there is no 'conviction' (see ante, para 3.20).

STATUTORY CONTROL OF MONEYLENDERS

[6.09/10] The background: usury.[1] Even before the time of Christ, usury was condemned as an evil practice, especially where the loan was not for some business purpose but to relieve poverty. However, in Tudor times, the medieval prohibition of usury was replaced by statutory regulation of maximum interest rates (what are today termed 'rate-ceilings'), even that control being removed by the Usury Laws Act 1854. Nevertheless, the authorities did feel the need to control the security taken by lenders. As the earlier transactions commonly took the form of a pawn or pledge, there were a series of statutes regulating pawnbroking.[2] In the 19th century, chattel mortgaging became popular and the Bills of Sale Acts sought to control the individual transactions (see post, para 9.04). However, it was not until the 20th century that a separate, statutory system was introduced for moneylenders in the (now repealed) Moneylenders Acts 1900–27.[3] Finding their desires balked (as they were intended to be by these three sets of Acts), in the 20th century parties increasingly turned to the alternatives offered by the new forms of instalment credit contract (see ante, para 1.03) and finance (see ante, para 2.19 *et seq*) which fell outside the ambit of those Acts.

The Crowther Report. Contemplating the foregoing pattern, the Report (see generally ante, para 5.03) rejected rate-ceilings (see further post, para 29.40), but did recommend a

9   Section 42. But see *DG of FT v Stuart* [1991] 1 All ER 129, CA.
10   OFT, *Trading Malpractices* (1990), paras 4.34–37. As to phoenix companies, see post, para 19.25.
11   For example of imprisonment of a mechanic continuing to do shoddy work, see (1999) 24 Fair Trading 3.
12   See *R v DG ex p FH Taylor and Co Ltd* [1981] 1 CR 292, DC (publicity).
[6.09/10]
1   See generally the *Crowther Report* (Cmnd 4596) para 2.1.1 *et seq*; Livingston (1993) 14 CCA News 2/11.
2   These were consolidated in the (now repealed) Pawnbrokers Act 1872 (as amended). For the present control of pawnbroking, see post, para 25.17.
3   To prevent repetition of the activities of Isaac Gordon: see *Gordon v Street* [1899] 2 QB 641. For details, see Butterworths edn, 1989, para 6.09A.

new unified positive licensing system that would be both wider and simpler in its control of lending:[4]

1   The licensing system should catch a much wider selection of those who make a business of lending money to consumers, whether by way of secured or unsecured loan, whilst excluding lenders to business.

2   The new licensing system should be centrally administered,[5] positive in nature[6] and co-exist with the possibility of enforcement by prosecution in respect of individual transgressions (see post, para 28.04).

Such a licensing system has a number of advantages over enforcement only by prosecution in respect of individual transgressions:[7] it provides an extremely powerful sanction against deliberate law-breaking, for its exercise may prohibit the law-breaker from pursuing his business; the centralised OFT administration engenders uniformity; and there can be administrative flexibility in granting and removing licences.[8] Yet, these very advantages carry within them the seeds of their own disadvantage: such novel breadth (for the UK) of administrative discretion (see post, para 6.18) ought to be counter-balanced by an adequate system of judicial control.[9]

Perhaps inevitably, these controls do not go far enough for some:[10] there have been calls for improved alternative lending sources to the poor, eg, credit unions, social fund (see ante, para 2.15); and for strengthened extortionate credit bargain rules (see post, para 29.42).

The principles of the CCA system

[6.11] **Introduction.** The justification for selecting consumer credit for special treatment over other areas of consumer protection is said to be that it is particularly prone to abuses from which consumers can do little to protect themselves.[1] Following the White Paper,[2] an elaborate licensing system was established for creditors and owners in Part III of the CCA, together with special licensing provisions for ancillary credit businesses.[3] The object

---

4   Paragraphs 7.2.3–7. This system should be carefully distinguished from the regulation of the acceptance of deposit by financial intermediaries, eg, borrowing by banks, now governed by the Banking Acts: see ante, para 2.17.

5   It actually recommended the creation of a new Credit Commissioner; but the government decided instead to graft the functions onto the OFT: see ante, paras 3.03 and 5.03.

6   For a justification, see Borrie, *The Development of Consumer Law and Policy*, pp 85–88. For positive licensing systems generally, see ante, para 6.04. But see the *Crowther* suggestion for simplifying the initial administration by granting the application virtually as a matter of course on the first occasion: para 7.2.9.

7   See Goode, *Consumer Credit Law and Practice*, para 27.2.

8   This dovetails well with the continental approach to consumer protection: see Goode, *ibid*, para 27.3.

9   It has been claimed that UK administrative law is as yet insufficiently developed for this purpose: Goode, *ibid*, para 27.5.

10   [2000] 5 Credit Today 6.

[6.11]

1   Cranston, *Consumers and the Law* (3rd edn), p 465.

2   *Reform of the Law on Consumer Credit* (1973) Cmnd 5427, paras 93–101.

3   See post, para 6.27. There are proposals to replace the present positive licensing system for credit brokers with a negative one (see ante, para 6.03).

was to ensure that, so far as practicable, only fit persons became and remained licensed to continue to operate in the consumer credit industry. When the system was first set up, it was predicted that 50,000 licences would be requested but in the event the figure increased to over 300,000.[4] In the 1980s, these unexpected numbers threatened to overwhelm the system: it led to extensions in the licensing period (see post, para 6.14), computerisation of the OFT licensing administration and OFT reliance on other parts of the CCA;[5] and the unexpected cost made the Government wary of positive licensing (see ante, para 6.04). However, by the early 1990s, the OFT began to feel comfortable with the computerised licensing system, in part because of the steady decline of licence applications.[6] This led to a shortening of the licensing period; and the OFT began to favour the use of licensing rather than detailed new legislation.[7]

Within its wide ambit (see post, para 6.12), the CCA establishes a system of different classes of licence (see post, para 6.13 *et seq*) and lays down the businessman's rights and duties with regard to that system (see post, para 6.17 *et seq*). Control of the system is centralised in the hands of the Director-General of Fair Trading (the Director):[8] licensing is administered by his Office and is a matter of public record (see post, para 6.26); and in conducting this operation the Director will have the benefit of the reports by local authorities and others (see ante, paras 3.05; 3.08) on transgressions in relation to a whole range of statutes designed to protect consumers by means of the civil and criminal law.[9] In 1999, there was a government review of licensing, which led to pressure on the OFT to tighten up administration of the system.[10] The EU have begun to ponder improvements to the system (see ante, para 5.12).

[6.12] Ambit. The key provision is s 21, which lays down as follows:

(1) Subject to this section, a licence[1] is required to carry on a consumer credit business or consumer hire business.

(2) A local authority does not need a licence to carry on a business.

(3) A body corporate empowered by a public general Act naming it to carry on a business does not need a licence to do so.

Thus, the major thrust of the licensing provisions is aimed at those who carry on consumer credit or consumer hire businesses.[2] These are defined by s 189(1) as any business so far as it comprises or relates to the provision of credit or bailment of goods under regulated agreements (see ante, para 5.36).

---

4   OFT, *Consultation Document on the Working and Enforcement of the CCA* (Aug 1993), para 2.10.

5   This seems to have suited the style of the second Director (Borrie), an academic lawyer.

6   Since 1996, the number of applications has begun to rise again: see OFT, AR-1997, 26.

7   The third Director (Carsberg), an accountant, was of this view: (1993) 14 CCA News 2/9. Eg, inertia selling of credit (see post, para 24.22).

8   See the definition of 'Director' in s 189(1). For the functions of the Director, see generally ante, para 3.03. For administration, see the OFT Annual Reports.

9   For the setting up of this central register, see the First Annual Report of the OFT, 25–26.

10 By the National Audit Office: OFT, 1999-AR 25; [2000] 9 Credit Today 5, 13; OFT, 2000-AR 16.

[6.12]

1   Section 189(1) makes it clear that 'licence' extends to that required by an ancillary credit business.

2   For consumer credit agreements, see ante, para 5.19; for consumer hire agreements see ante, para 1.19; for examples of consumer credit business and consumer hire business, see post, para 6.15. The *Crowther Report* (ante, para 5.03) recommended against licensing consumer hire businesses (para 7.2.7).

Whilst this primary definition encompasses all those who enter into regulated agreements as creditor or owner, s 21 goes on to exclude creditors or owners falling into any of the following categories:

1   *Those activities outwith the industry*, so that the licensing provisions usually do not extend to those activities beyond the scope of the Act.[3] Moreover, the Act excludes those who do not make a business of entering into such agreements, eg, private lenders, or businesses who only occasionally enter such transactions.[4]

2   *The usual exemptions.* As usual, this part of the Act excludes those who only supply credit or goods above the financial limits laid down by the Act (see ante, para 5.22), or only to companies,[5] or only under exempt agreements, eg, friendly societies (see generally ante, para 5.14); but small agreements are now caught.[6] There were proposals (now failed) that credit agreements made with business debtors shall remain subject to licensing but free of the other CCA provisions (see ante, para 5.11).

3   *Public bodies.* Local authorities (defined in s 189(1)) and public corporations,[7] eg, the privatised utilities (see ante, para 3.07). The reason for excluding both categories from licensing provisions has been said to be that Parliament has conferred powers on such bodies under separate Public General Acts.[8] Whilst local authorities also have the protection that their individual agreements with consumers are exempt (see generally ante, para 5.13), the actual credit agreements made by privatised utilities are regulated (see generally ante, para 5.13).

4   *EU law.* The CCA system has subsequently been amended by EU law as follows:[9] to enable banks and other financial institutions authorised in other EU Countries to carry on certain activities covered by the CCA[10] without the need to obtain a CCA licence;[11] and in relation to UK registered banks and building societies to require the OFT, before granting a CCA licence, to notify the banking/building society regulator.

---

3   Other than regulated agreements made by (a) creditor-individuals (b) for amounts below the floor limit: see Sched 3, para 5 (as amended). *Contra* credit-brokers, who must be licensed even though only introducing exempt agreements: see ante, para 5.40.

4   Section 189(2): set out ante, para 5.36 and cf the Moneylenders Acts (see ante, para 6.09). How infrequent is 'occasionally': see *Wills v Wood* (1984) 128 Sol Jo 222, CA (discussed by Palmer 26 Credit 47); *R v Marshall* (see ante, para 5.36/37)? See further Goode, *Consumer Credit Law and Practice*, para 27.42; Guest and Lloyd, *Encyclopedia of Consumer Credit Law*, para 2-022.

5   Who are not 'individuals', as is required for debtors or hirers under regulated agreements. For 'individuals', see s 189(1): set out ante, para 5.24.

6   Small loans were originally exempt from licensing (Sched 3, para 5, as substituted). After several reports of such small loans (sometimes regularly topped up) by unlicensed lenders at upwards of 14 million % pa (say 40p in the £ per week), this exemption was removed for consumer credit business (1989 SI 1128). But the small loans licensing exemption remains for credit brokers: see post, para 6.28.

7   Section 21(3). Because they are not named therein, this formula does not extend to companies incorporated under the Companies Acts, or formed under such as the Friendly Societies Acts Industrial and Provident Societies Acts, Building Society Acts or Trade Union Acts. Nor would the exemption appear to extend to chartered companies or those established by private Act.

8   Goode, *op cit*, note 4, para 27.46. Is this a sufficient answer?

9   By Directive 89/646, incorporated into UK law by regulation. See generally Goode, *op cit*, note 4, Part III, para 22.

10 Certain other provisions apply to such banks as if they were licensed.

11 Eg, lending (post, para 7.04), issuing credit cards (post, para 7.10), credit reference services (post, para 8.37).

The types of licence

[6.13] Where a business conducts activities which fall within the ambit of the licensing system (see ante, para 6.12), s 22(1) makes available the following types of licence:[1]

(a) a standard licence, that is a licence, issued by the Director to a person named in the licence on an application made by him, which during the prescribed period, covers such activities as are described in the licence, or

(b) a group licence, that is a licence, issued by the Director (whether on the application of any person or of his own motion), which, during such period as the Director thinks fit or, if he thinks fit, indefinitely, covers such persons and activities as are described in the licence.

Thus, the Act formally envisages two major types of licence: (a) standard licences (see post, para 6.14); and (b) group licences (see post, para 6.16). On the other hand, it might be more helpful to think of group licences rather as an exemption device: bearing in mind the huge number of businesses that require a standard licence, and the even greater number who operate at the periphery of the credit industry, the group licence scheme was devised to obviate the need for separate licensing of those peripheral categories. However, if a particular member of that peripheral class were engaged in a substantial amount of business within the Act, the Director is empowered to exclude that named person from a particular group licence (s 22(6): set out post, para 6.16), so encouraging him to apply for a standard licence.[2] A previous Government looked into whether it may be possible to reduce significantly the volume of standard licences by increasing the number of group licences to include trade associations on behalf of their members.[3]

[6.14] Standard licences. The characteristics of a standard licence, which requires individual application,[1] are as follows:

1 *It is issued to a named person only.* The licence does not authorise the licensee to carry on a business under any other than the specified name (s 24), to do so being an offence.[2] In the case of a sole trader or registered company, the licence shall not be issued to more than one person[3] and, in the case of a partnership or other unincorporated body

---

[6.13]

1 'Director', 'licence' and 'prescribed' are all defined by s 189.

2 See s 22(5): set out post, para 6.16. This power may also be used to weed out undesirables who only operate occasionally within the purview of the Act.

3 OFT, 1995-AR 22.

[6.14]

1 Section 22(1)(a): set out ante, para 6.13. *Contra* group licences, which do not require (though they allow for) individual application.

2 Section 39(2): see post, para 6.20. However, that would not appear to invalidate agreements made by the licensee other than under his licensed name (s 170(1): see post, para 10.19): Goode, *Consumer Credit Law and Practice,* para 27.187.

3 Section 22(3). Thus, even if operating under a franchise name (see ante, para 1.07), each sole trader or company in the group requires a separate licence.

of persons, the licence shall be issued in the name of the partnership or body.[4] It follows from these rules that, if a sole trader or partnership incorporates, a new licence is required; and, if the business is operated through a group of companies, each such company carrying on licensable activity requires a licence.[5] However, once a licence is issued to the principal in a business, it covers the activities of all persons, eg, employees, acting on behalf of the licensee, including even part-time independent commission salesmen.

2   *It covers only the activities described.* As the licence is to carry on a particular type of business, it covers all lawful activities done in the course of that business, whether by the licensee or other persons on his behalf (s 23(1)); but, where the debtor is introduced to the creditor by an unlicensed credit-broker, the agreement is enforceable against the debtor only where the Director so orders (s 149(1); and see post, para 6.28). The Act allows that the licence may limit the activities it covers, whether by authorising the licensee to enter into certain types of agreement only, or in any other way (s 23(2)); and the Director has in fact specified seven different categories of business (see post, para 6.15). Additionally, there are the following limitations, which may be particularly relevant to the home credit trade:[6] first, whilst DC[7] agreements may not be canvassed at all off-trade premises (s 49: set out post, para 7.07), DCS[7] agreements and consumer hirings may be so canvassed – but only if, and to the extent that, the licence specifically so provides;[8] and second, there is power by regulation to specify other activities which may only be practised if covered by the express term of the licence (s 23(4)).

3   *It is operative only for the prescribed period.* Originally, it was envisaged that a normal standard licence would be granted for three years; and the Director instituted the practice of carefully vetting applicants before licences were granted.[9] However, the administrative burden proved so great (see ante, para 6.11) that the Director extended the licence period to 15 years,[10] a matter which increased the significance of the provisions for suspending or revoking licences (see post, para 6.23) where wrong-

---

4   But where a change in the partnership results in a change in the partnership name, the licence shall cease to have effect: s 36(5). This rule appears to be a trap for a sole trader taking a relative into his business as a partner.

5   This is because each registered company is a separate legal person: see *Salomon v Salomon Ltd* (set out post, para 19.25).

6   For weekly collected credit, see ante, para 2.18. This successor to the tallyman (see ante, para 5.02) inevitably has higher overheads, which reflects unfavourably in his APR (see post, para 8.24–25). The market seems to depend largely on wages being paid weekly in cash. See Cayne and Trebilcock (1973) 23 UTLJ 396, esp at 404, 406, 423.

7   For DC and DCS agreements, see respectively ante, paras 5.35; 5.34.

8   Section 23(3); and see the *Crowther Report*, para 6.4.20. The result is that a creditor must have such a separate endorsement on his licence before he can utilise door-to-door sales techniques, but may also require a pedlar's licence (see ante, para 6.02). For other restrictions on door-to-door sales, see further post, para 10.21. As to whether door-to-door agents require a separate licence on their own account, see Guest and Lloyd, *Encyclopedia of Consumer Credit Law*, para 2-024.

9   Compare the recommendation of the *Crowther Report*: see ante, para 6.10.

10 The three-year period put in the 1975 Regulations on the recommendation of the *Crowther Report* (para 7.2.10) was extended to 10 years by regulations made in 1979, and to 15 years by regulations made in 1986.

doing is detected.[11] After computerisation of the system, the OFT were able to reduce the licensing period to five years.

[6.15] Categories of standard licence. It has been decided to administer standard licensing (see ante, para 6.14) by what may be termed the driving-licence principle; that is, standard licences are divided into six categories:

Category A – Consumer credit businesses.[1]

Category B – Consumer hire businesses.[2]

Category C – Credit brokerage.[3]

Category D – Debt-adjusting and debt-counselling.[4]

Category E – Debt-collecting.[5]

Category F – Credit reference agencies.[6]

Applications may be made for one or more categories of licence according to whether the applicant considers he may conduct business within that category and the relatively small fee and high penalty for unlicensed trading (see post, para 6.20) will normally indicate that the applicant should err on the side of applying for more, rather than less, categories.[7] For instance, a retailer may need a licence covering the following categories: insofar as he provides his own credit and hire facilities, categories A and B, with or without a canvassing endorsement (see ante, para 6.14); insofar as he introduces his customers to finance companies to provide credit, category C; insofar as he collects instalments and follows up arrears on behalf of a finance company, category E; and insofar as he takes goods in part-exchange, category D. Statistics and a report on licence applications will be found in the most recent Annual Report of the OFT.

[6.16] Group licences. As it is an exemption device (see ante, para 6.13), the Act lays down that (s 22(6)):

> The persons covered by a group licence may be described by general words, whether or not coupled with the exclusion of named persons, or in any other way the Director thinks fit.

---

11   Cranston, *Consumers and the Law* (3rd edn), pp 467–68.

[6.15]

1   Eg, retailers, finance houses, pawnbrokers, moneylenders, check traders, mail order firms, credit card companies, banks, building societies. For consumer credit businesses, see generally ante, para 6.12.

2   Eg, business leasing or hiring out TVs, cars, caravans, vending machines, office or factory equipment. For consumer hire businesses, see generally ante, para 6.12.

3   Eg, mortgage and insurance brokers, retailers who introduce customers to category A licensees. For credit brokerage, see generally ante, para 5.38.

4   Eg, accountants, solicitors, mortgage and insurance brokers, consumer agencies who advise about debt problems. For debt-adjusting and debt-counselling, see generally ante, para 5.43.

5   Eg, trade protection societies, finance houses which discount the debts of others. For debt-collecting, see generally ante, para 5.43.

6   Eg, trade protection societies, one of a group of companies which supplies information to other members of the group. For credit reference agencies, see generally post, para 8.37.

7   This policy now receives official encouragement: OFT, 1996-AR 26. As to applications for licences, see post, para 6.22.

Furthermore, a group licence differs from a standard licence (see ante, para 6.14) in all the following ways: it does not **require** an individual application;[1] it cannot include a special licence to canvass DCS agreements off trade premises;[2] and it may be issued for an indefinite period of time. On issuing a group licence, the Director must give a 'general notice'.[3] It has become the practice for the period of these licences *prima facie* to be brought into line with that for standard licences.[4] The Act envisages that a person may be covered by both a standard and a group licence, even in respect of the same activities (s 22(7)). Nevertheless the two types of licence are obviously designed for different sorts of situation; and it is clear that in the ordinary case a standard licence will be appropriate, for the Act provides that:[5]

> The Director may issue a group licence only if it appears to him that the public interest is better served by doing so than by obliging the persons concerned to apply separately for standard licences.

The scope of this power would appear limited by the Director's subjective view of the 'public interest'.[6] Group licences have already been issued to such as the Law Society, the Accountancy Institutes, Age Concern and the National Association of Citizen's Advice Bureaux.[7] However, in 2000 the Law Society was threatened with loss of its group licence because of concerns over its inability to deal with complaints,[8] a move which would force solicitors involved in regulated business to apply for individual standard licences (see ante, para 6.14).

The position of creditors and owners

[6.17] The basic rule of Part III of the CCA is that 'a licence is required to carry on a consumer credit business or a consumer hire business' (s 21(1): see ante, para 6.12)). This rule will apply to both vendor and lender credit (see ante, para 2.19 *et seq*); and, as regards the latter, will apply to the financier (creditor), whether engaged in direct or loan financing. The basic step which the creditor will have to take is to apply under s 22 for a standard licence of the requisite categories, together with any desired specific authorisation to canvas (see ante, paras 6.14–15). Unless the licence is expressly limited (s 23(2)), it will cover 'all lawful activities done in the course of that business, whether by the licensee or other persons on his behalf' (s 23(1)). In applying for a standard licence to conduct such businesses, a creditor or owner has to show that he is a 'fit person' (see post,

---

[6.16]

1 But if there is an individual applicant for a group licence, the group licence shall be issued to that person: s 22(8).

2 Section 23(3): for licensing to canvass, see ante, para 6.14.

3 That means 'a notice published by the Director at a time and in a manner appearing to him suitable for securing that the notice is seen within a reasonable time by persons likely to be affected by it': s 189(1).

4 OFT, 1979-AR 26. For the period of standard licences, see ante, para 6.14.

5 Section 22(5). For the criteria utilised by the OFT in the issue of group licences, see 1976 Annual Report, 22–23. Compare standard licences, in respect of which s 25(1) requires the Director to issue a licence if satisfied of certain matters: see post, para 6.18.

6 Does 'public interest', include the minimising of a would-be licensee's overheads? On 'satisfied', cf post, para 6.18.

7 For the terms of these licences, see Goode, *Consumer Credit Law and Practice*, Div IV.

8 See OFT (2000) 28 Fair Trading 4.

paras 6.18–19). If he fails to do so and yet continues to operate within the ambit of the CCA, it lays down some Draconian penalties for unlicensed trading (see post, paras 6.20–21). However, there always remains the temptation to operate outside the law; and a typical example which is occasionally highlighted by the media is that of the back-street moneylender, perhaps illegally taking child benefit books by way of security.[1]

With regard to the conduct of a licensed, but not an unlicensed, business, s 26 allows the making of regulations as to the conduct of business,[2] a power which is extended by s 54 (see post, para 8.20). Insofar as regulations may be made under s 26 with regard to the seeking of business,[3] breach may constitute an offence.[4] Consideration has been given to use these powers in relation to the following: banning negative option insurance (see generally post, para 8.20); strengthening the rules against sending credit circulars to minors (see post, paras 8.20; 8.33); unsolicited credit circulars (see post, para 8.18); and unilaterally increasing the credit limit in relation to running-account credit (see ante, para 5.28).

[6.18] Fit persons. Whilst the early versions of the Consumer Credit Bill contained no right to a licence,[1] s 25(1) provides that:

> A standard licence shall be granted on the application of any person if he satisfies the Director that –
>
> (a) he is a fit person to engage in activities covered by the licence, and
>
> (b) the name or names under which he applies to be licensed is or are not misleading or otherwise undesirable.[2]

Accordingly, it would appear that an applicant has a right to the issue of a standard licence[3] provided only that the two conditions as to fitness and name are satisfied,[4] rather than that issue being in the discretion of the Director. However, this position is blurred by the fact that the Director has to be **satisfied** as to those two conditions, a matter necessarily involving a value judgment on his part.[5] In reaching such a decision, it is not clear whether the Director is acting in a manner which is executive, administrative, judicial or a mixture of these;[6] nor whether his duty is delegable.[7] In practice, the Director

---

[6.17]

1 See Borrie, *The Development of Consumer Law and Policy*, 86–87; OFT, 1983-AR, 19.

2 Regulations have been made with regard to the conduct of credit reference agencies (see post, para 8.38) and pawnbrokers (see post, para 25.18).

3 A list of regulations made will be found in the looseleaf encyclopedias (see ante, para 5.05).

4 In the case of registered companies, such regulations might supplement those made under the Companies Acts. See generally, Gower, *Company Law* (6th edn), Chapter 19.

[6.18]

1 Goode, *Consumer Credit Law and Practice*, para 27.81.

2 See also the Companies Act 1985, ss 26, 28; Banking Act 1987, s 67.

3 There is no equivalent provision for a group licence. But compare ss 22(5), (6): see ante, para 6.13.

4 The Director cannot refuse a licence on any other ground, eg, that there is already a sufficiency of such services, or that the creditor is underfunded. See Cranston, *Consumers and the Law* (3rd edn), p 467. Can he grant one if he is not satisfied as to the listed matters?

5 See Guest and Lloyd, *Encyclopedia of Consumer Credit Law*, paras 2-004, 2-026; Goode, *op cit*, note 1, para 22.22.

6 Presumably, s 170 (see post, para 10.19) precludes any action against the Director by any customer of a miscreant licensee, claiming that the licence was negligently issued?

7 See *Vine v National Dock Labour Board* [1957] AC 488, HL.

has taken advantage of the position to issue to credit traders what he terms 'guidelines',[8] with the implication that he will exercise his licensing powers if that advice is not heeded (see post, para 6.22 *et seq*): the guidelines may be general or sector specific.[9]

The Act does lay down a number of criteria for the determination of fitness (see post, para 6.19); but it is to be noted that these do not require the OFT to investigate whether a potential licensee is solvent or competent to run a credit business.[10] In the 1990s there was criticism of the lax application of these criteria by the OFT.[11] The laxer the issue of licences, eg, for an indefinite period, and the more Draconian their removal (see post, para 6.23), the more the system resembles negative licensing (see ante, para 6.04).

[6.19] Criteria of fitness. Whilst providing no exclusive criteria for fitness to hold a standard licence (see ante, para 6.18), s 25(2) directs that:

> In determining whether an application for a standard licence is a fit person to engage in any activities, the Director shall have regard to any circumstances appearing to him to be relevant,[1] and in particular any evidence tending to show[2] that the applicant, or any of the applicant's employees, agents or associates[3] (whether past or present) or, where the applicant is a body corporate, any person appearing to the Director to be a controller of the body corporate or an associate of any such person ...

has done any number of acts. The criteria referred to in s 25(2) are that any of the persons there referred to have:

(a) committed any offence[4] involving fraud or other dishonesty,[5] or violence;[6]

(b) contravened any provision made by or under this Act, or by or under any other enactment regulating the provision of credit to individuals or other transactions with individuals;[7]

---

8   Eg, the 'guidance' to debt collectors: see [2000] CCA News, Summer 14; 55 QA 2; and see generally ante, para 5.42.

9   OFT, 2000-AR 7, 16. General guidelines were issued Feb 2001; and the Director said sector guidelines are planned, eg, for debt-collection, credit-broking, used cars [2001] CCA News, Spring, 5.

10   But if such evidence became available to the OFT, it may be relevant: see (1995) 9 Fair Trading 14.

11   In the absence of serious convictions or insolvency, the OFT is likely to grant a licence: (2001) 61 QA 5.

[6.19]

1   See also s 170(2). These two provisions would appear to leave the Director unfettered discretion as to the sources of his evidence. See Borrie, *The Development of Consumer Law and Policy*, p 88.

2   Including relevant evidence inadmissible in court: Borrie [1982] JBL at 95–96. What weight of evidence and standard of proof are required? What of an offence which has expired under the Rehabilitation of Offenders Act 1974?

3   For 'associates', see s 184: see ante, para 5.33. For the purpose of this section, 'associate' includes a business associate (s 25(3)), eg, an undesirable credit-broker or controller.

4   See Guest and Lloyd, *Encyclopedia of Consumer Credit Law*, para 2-026.

5   Thus, s 25(2)(a) does not include strict liability offences, as to which see below. For suggested tests of fraud and dishonesty, see Guest and Lloyd, *ibid*, para 2-026. See also Borrie [1982] JBL at 95.

6   Eg, some of the acts which amount to unlawful harassment of debtors (see post, para 24.24); and see OFT, 1981-AR 21. Does the violence have to amount to an offence?

7   As to the CCA, see esp s 170(2); but note the limitation suggested by Guest and Lloyd, *op cit*, note 4, para 2-026. The OFT take the view that this provision covers the strict liability offences protecting consumers, eg, TDA: see 1979-AR 29–30; 1980-AR 33.

(c) practised[8] discrimination on grounds of sex, colour, race or ethnic or national origins in, or in connection with the carrying on of any business;[9] or

(d) engaged in business practices appearing to the Director to be deceitful, or oppressive,[10] or otherwise unfair or improper (whether unlawful or not).[11]

If the Director decides that the applicant is fit to carry out some types of activity but not others, there is nothing to stop the Director limiting the licence accordingly (s 23(2): see ante, para 6.14). The powers thus given to the Director are astonishingly wide, arbitrary and uncertain, raising issues far beyond the scope of this work.[12] It seems a matter for his discretion how much the Director invokes these wide licensing powers rather than proceeding under some other (probably more limited) statutory power.

[6.20] Loan-sharking. Where a person engages in activities for which a CCA licence is required, either standard or group (see ante, para 6.13), without at that time being covered by such a licence, the Act imposes a number of cumulative criminal and civil sanctions. Leaving aside the situation where an unlicensed ancillary credit business has participated in a transaction (see post, para 6.27), this paragraph will concentrate on the situation where a creditor or owner has engaged in such unlicensed trading. Here, it will usually be the case that a category A or B standard licence (see ante, para 6.15) is absent, or does not cover the requisite activity, eg, canvassing without a specific endorsement, as required by s 23(3) (see ante, para 6.14).

1 *Criminal sanctions.* According to s 39:[1]

(1) A person who engages in any activities for which a licence is required when he is not a licensee under a licence covering those activities commits an offence.

(2) A licensee under a standard licence who carries on business under a name not specified in the licence commits an offence.[2]

(3) A person who fails to give the Director or a licensee notice under section 36 within the period required commits an offence.[3]

---

8   This appears to require a degree of repetition and continuity. Cf s 189(2): see ante, para 5.37.

9   See further ante, para 4.23. It need not necessarily be a business connected with the credit industry.

10 Do the tests of 'deceitful' and 'oppressive' refer to the intention behind, or result of, the business practice?

11 Eg, persistently clocking cars (see ante, para 4.09); selling credit to those who cannot afford it; driving extortionate credit bargains (see post, para 29.40); using high pressure sales techniques (see post, para 10.28); purporting to exercise contractual or common law powers they have not got; obtaining poor resale values on repossessed goods; taking customers' pension or allowance books; incompetence in the conduct of business; charging debtors for collecting their debts; failure to make refunds due (see post, para 29.04); inertia selling of credit insurance (see post, para 24.24); misleading advertisements (see post, para 8.12A); unfair terms (see post, para 11.12); eponymous subsidiaries (see post, para 16.06A).

12 Cooper (1988) 138 NLJ 589.

[6.20]

1   For penalties, see s 167 and Sched 1. See *R v Carr* (1980) 2 Cr App R 153; *R v Priestly* (1983) 5 Cr App R 344, CA. For s 36, see post, para 6.26.

2   For trading name requirements, see s 24: see ante, para 6.14.

3   Section 36 deals with the licensee's duty to notify the Director of changes in his circumstances: see post, para 6.26.

Unlike under the old Moneylenders Acts,[4] unlicensed trading does not render the regulated agreements illegal and void: instead, it only has the additional civil effects referred to below,[5] and then probably only where there is a degree of repetition of the unlicensed activity. So, not only must the trader be carry on a licensable activity (see ante, para 6.12), but the drafting of s 39 would seem to require his entry into sufficient regulated agreements outside his licence to amount to an 'activity'.

2   *Civil sanctions*. Section 40(1) provides that:

> A regulated agreement, other than a non-commercial agreement,[6] if made when the creditor or owner was unlicensed, is enforceable against the debtor or hirer only where the Director has made an order under this section which applies to the agreement.

Prima facie, there is rendered unenforceable both the regulated agreement[7] and any security (s 113(2): see post, para 9.19). An elaborate machinery is provided for the making by the Director[8] of such validation orders (see post, para 6.21), which it is his practice to make for specific agreements only.[9] Of course, faced with this situation a loan shark is more likely to employ illegal methods of debt collection[10] that will negative any defence of consent (see s 173(3): post, para 18.11).

[6.21] Validation orders. Suppose an unlicensed activity is enforceable only by order of the Director (see ante, para 6.20). Section 40(2) provides that:[1]

> Where during any period an unlicensed person (the 'trader') was carrying on a consumer credit business or consumer hire business, he or his successor in title may apply[2] to the Director for an order that regulated agreements made by the trader during that period are to be treated as if he had been licensed.

In such a case, s 40(5) says that:

> If the Director thinks fit, he may in an order under subsection (2) –
>
> (a) limit the order to specified agreements, or agreements of a specified description or made at a specified time;
>
> (b) make the order conditional on the doing of specified acts by the applicant.

Particulars of any such order are one of the matters recorded in the Public Register (see post, para 6.26) and do not prevent prosecution, eg, of the broker (s 149: see post, para 6.28). According to s 40(4):

---

4   Eg, *Cornelius v Phillips* [1918] AC 199, HL. For the Moneylenders Acts, see generally ante, para 6.09.
5   *Booth and Phipps Garages Ltd v Milton* [2000] CLY 2601, Cty Ct. See s 170(1); post, para 10.19. Does this prevent the contract being frustrated?
6   For non-commercial agreements, see ante, para 5.18.
7   See *Hertfordshire Investments Ltd v Bubb* [2000] 1 WLR 2318, CA.
8   Distinguish enforcement orders made by the court: see post, para 24.33.
9   OFT, 1990-AR, 32.
10 Commonly systematic assault and intimidation. See also post, para 24.49. For difficulties of prosecution, see (1996) 51 CC 1/3.

[6.21]
1   The fees for validation orders are on a sliding scale, which relates to the agreements covered and may cost significant sums: (1991) 46 CC 1/25.
2   He may only apply on the designated form, and must then answer the questions indicated in Guest and Lloyd, *Encyclopedia of Consumer Credit Law*, para 2-041. Is this not to admit an offence?

In determining whether or not to make an order under subsection (2) in respect of any period the Director shall consider, in addition to any other relevant factors –

(a) how far, if at all, debtors or hirers under regulated agreements made by the trader during that period were prejudiced by the trader's conduct,

(b) whether or not the Director would have been likely to grant a licence covering that period on an application by the trader, and

(c) the degree of culpability for the failure to obtain a licence.

Section 40(3) lays down a procedure to be followed where the Director is minded to refuse such an application: there are rules governing representations that may be made to the Director (see post, para 6.22); and there are also provisions relating to appeals (see post, paras 6.24–25). This has led to the characterisation of the whole process as judicial, rather than administrative.[3] The OFT receive a trickle of such applications.[4]

The operation of the licensing system[1]

[6.22] Applications for a licence. Like any other application to the Director under the CCA, an application for a licence:[2]

> must be in writing, and in such form, and accompanied by such particulars, as the Director may specify by general notice, and must be accompanied by the specified fee.

Not only is the provision of false information in such an application an offence,[3] but the Act provides that (s 6(1)):

> An application to the Director under this Act is of no effect unless the requirements of this section are satisfied.

As the Act stipulates that a standard licence may only be granted on application,[4] an invalid application, eg, by payment of the wrong fee, or giving incorrect information, would appear to invalidate the licence thereby obtained,[5] so that the applicant will be operating as an unlicensed trader (see ante, para 6.20).

Once the Director has received a valid application, he has three choices:

(i) To grant the application as requested, on the grounds that he is satisfied as to the matters referred to in s 25(2) (see ante, para 6.19).

(ii) To grant the application in terms different from those applied for.[6]

---

3   Guest and Lloyd, *ibid*. Support may be found for this in s 170(3).

4   OFT, 1995-AR 25.

[6.22]

1   See generally the OFT Booklet, *Do You Need a Licence?* Used car dealers attract the most adverse decisions: OFT, 1986-AR 21; 1989-AR 31.

2   Section 6(2). The Director has power to call for further and better particulars and require the information supplied to be verified (s 6(3)) and also to require the applicant to publicise details of his application (s 6(4)). See further Goode, *Consumer Credit Law and Practice*, paras 27.106–07.

3   Section 7. For penalties, see s 167 and Sched 1. See further OFT, 1983-AR 19.

4   Sections 22(1), 25(1): set out respectively ante, paras 6.13; 6.18.

5   Borrie [1982] JBL at 92.

6   Section 27(2). Eg, without the sought permission to canvass.

(iii) To refuse the application altogether.[7]

Unless the Director takes the first choice, s 27(1) requires him to serve on the applicant a 'minded to refuse' notice, giving his reasons and inviting representations.[8] If still dissatisfied, the applicant may have recourse to the appeals procedure (see post, para 6.24).

[6.23] Existing licences. Where a licence has already been issued to an applicant (see ante, para 6.22), there are a number of situations in which the licensing machinery may again be invoked.

(a) *Renewal.* Applications may be made to the Director[1] for renewal of any licence (s 29(1)). Generally speaking, all the previously discussed rules relating to first issue of a licence apply to renewals thereof, including the sweeping fitness powers granted to the Director (see ante, para 6.19). In the event of an application for renewal not being granted:[2]

> ... the Director may give directions authorising a licensee to carry into effect agreements made by him before the expiry of the licence.

(b) *Variation.* This may be made by request, or compulsorily. Where there is an application to vary a standard licence,[3] the Director may, if he thinks fit, grant the request;[4] but on refusal, the disappointed applicant has similar rights to reasons and representations as on original application (s 30(4)). Alternatively, the Director is empowered to make a compulsory variation on the basis that:[5]

> ... if the licence had expired at that time, he would, on an application for its renewal or further renewal on the same terms (except as to expiry), have been minded to grant the application but on different terms.

But such a compulsory variation shall not take effect before the end of the appeal period (s 31(7)) and gives the Director no power to validate agreements already made.

(c) *Suspension and revocation.* The Director has power to suspend or revoke any licence on the basis that he (s 32(1)):

> ... is of the opinion that if the licence had expired at that time he would have been minded not to renew it.

Again, there are safeguards similar to those on variation as to the period before the order takes effect, but this time including a power to validate agreements (s 32(5)).

---

7   See the *Crowther Report*, para 7.2.11; and Borrie [1982] JBL at 94–100.
8   See the procedure set out in Goode, *op cit*, note 2, paras 27.144–47. As to the raising of standards and quantity of information by the OFT, see ante, para 6.11.

[6.23]
1   Section 6: see ante, para 6.22. But the Director may also renew any group licence of his own motion by giving general notice: ss 29(2), (6). See the reports by the OFT in its Annual Reports.
2   Section 29(5). On a refusal to renew, then until expiry of the 'appeal period' (see post, para 6.24) the licence continues in force: s 29(4). See the comment below.
3   He has similar powers to vary a group licence on application: ss 30(2), (3), (5).
4   Section 30(1). Eg, to add a new category of licensable activity or record a change of business name. Where a business changes its name and does not apply in time for variation or renewal of its licence, it would appear to be engaged in unlicensed trading (see ante, para 6.20). Subject to any validation order (see ante, para 6.21), for the effect of this see (1986) 41 CC 1/26.
5   Section 31(1). Eg, the licensee is breaking his licence, employing undesirables, or has been convicted of relevant offences. This power exists in relation to both standard and group licences: ss 31(2)–(6).

The Act then makes some further provisions in respect of suspensions.[6] The suspension or revocation does not in any event take effect until expiry of the 'appeal period',[7] leaving a period for negotiation.[8]

(d) *Termination*. The standard licence obtained by the successful applicant is clearly a very personal thing: it cannot be assigned, nor is it generally transmissible on death or in any other way.[9] There is also power by regulation both to specify other events causing automatic termination of a standard licence, and to defer such termination by up to 12 months.[10]

It has been pointed out that it is a serious weakness of the Act that the only ultimate sanction available to the Director is the slow but drastic procedure of revocation of licence; that there is an intermediate power of compulsory variation, or suspension of licence, which may be supplemented by informal warnings; but that it might be desirable if the Director also had power to compel licensees to take specified action.[11] However, subsequent events seem to show that the OFT have some room for manoeuvre: the OFT have managed to extract promises as to the management of a licensee as the price for their not contesting an appeal;[8] and it now has available the Stop Now Orders (see ante, para 6.08). The OFT hopes that its actions can be accelerated where there is a failure to comply with a relevant guideline[12] or the issue of private warning letters.[13] However, the OFT seem to feel overly constrained by their view that such actions must be proportionate under the CPR.[14]

[6.24] Licence appeals. The *Crowther Report* argued that, since it is protection of the individual debtor that is at stake, enforcement should not be made too difficult.[1] The Report therefore recommended that the licensing authority should be entitled to refuse to renew, revoke or suspend a licence (see ante, para 6.23) if satisfied that 'the applicant has been conducting his business in repeated or flagrant breach of the law, or in such a way as to mislead the public, or that he has persistently made excessive charges, or that he has acted oppressively towards his debtors'.[1] However, the other side of the coin is that in so acting the Director can affect a businessman's livelihood. The CCA therefore lays down a

---

6 For the effect of suspension, see s 32(8); and for applications to end a suspension, see s 33.

7 Section 32(7); and for the 'appeal period', see s 189(1), and post, para 6.24. It has been pointed out that this period may be unmeritoriously used solely to prolong the legality of nefarious activities: Borrie, *The Development of Consumer Law and Policy*, 87.

8 Eg, such a determination to revoke has been used to negotiate swingeing changes to an electrical retailer, Colorvision: see (1996) 16 Tr L 339; CC6/12; 17 CCA News 2/19.

9 Section 22(2). The licence generally terminates automatically if the licensee dies, is adjudicated bankrupt or becomes a mental patient: s 37(1). This section does not apply to group licences: s 37(4). On s 37, see generally Goode, *Consumer Credit Law and Practice*, paras 27.206–08; and the *Crowther Report*, para 7.2.11.

10 Section 37(3). Thus, there may be a 'holding period', during which the licensee's representative could himself apply for a standard licence should he wish to continue the business. See further Goode, *ibid*, paras 27.215–16.

11 Borrie, *op cit*, note 7, pp 89–90. As to informal warnings, see Borrie [1982] JBL at 100–01; OFT, 1978-AR 26.

12 (2001) 30 Fair Trading 7. For OFT guidelines, see ante, para 6.18.

13 (2001) 61 QA at 6. The information may not be published (CCA, s 174: see post, para 28.06).

14 Deputy DGFT [2001] 12 Credit Today 9. As to litigating proportionately, see ante, para 3.22.

[6.24]

1 Paragraph 7.2.11. Note the recommendation that the licensing procedure should allow for informal consultation to facilitate, eg, changing business practices (para 7.2.13), something the Director appears to be doing.

careful system of appeals, being especially lenient to persons already engaged in an existing business. Thus, in every case where the Director determines not to renew, to make a compulsory variation of, or to suspend or revoke, a licence, the Act provides that the licence shall continue in force until the end of the 'appeal period';[2] but this is not the case where the application is to start a business.

Where the Director indicates by a minded to refuse notice (see ante, para 6.22) to the applicant/licensee that he is contemplating making a decision in regard to any of the foregoing matters that person will not like,[3] s 34(1) anticipates that the applicant/licensee may wish to make written and oral representations to him.[4] Taking into account those representations, the Director[5] shall reach a determination (s 34(2)); and then he shall both give notice thereof to the applicant/licensee (s 34(3)) and enter his determination in the public register (see post, para 6.26). That determination is judicial in nature[6] and may then be challenged by the applicant/licensee (see post, para 6.25).

[6.25] Challenging a determination of the Director. Where a person is aggrieved by the final determination[1] of the Director (see ante, para 6.24), he may take one of two courses:

(a) Follow the appeal procedure laid down in the CCA and considered in this paragraph; or

(b) Apply to the court to exercise its inherent jurisdiction over administrative tribunals, a course of action which more properly belongs within the realms of administrative law, or perhaps complain to the ombudsman (see ante, para 3.25).

The CCA envisages a formal appeal to the Secretary of State by an aggrieved licensee/applicant only:[2] it says nothing as to appeals by the Director or any third party, eg, by competitors or objectors, though an informal approach could be made by the latter to the Secretary of State, requesting that he give 'specific directions' to the Director as to the carrying out of his functions (s 2(2): see ante, para 3.02). The appeal from a decision of the Director to the Secretary of State will not be heard by the latter personally, but by assessors on his behalf. Regulations govern the formal and elaborate appeal procedure before the assessors.[3] The Secretary of State is not bound by the recommendations of his assessors; and he can reach a decision either more or less adverse to the licensee/applicant than the determination of the Director from which he is appealing.[4] On a point of law only, appeal from the decision of the Secretary of State may be made to the High Court.[5]

---

2   Sections 29(4), 31(7), 32(7). For 'appeal period', see s 189(1). See the comment thereon in ante, para 6.23.

3   To refuse a standard licence in the terms of the application (s 27(1)(b)); to exclude any named person from a group licence (s 28(b)); to refuse an application to end a suspension (s 33(2)(b)) or by an unlicensed trader to enforce his agreements (ss 29(5), 32(5)), or validate unenforceable agreements (ss 40, 148, 149).

4   Such representations may include undertakings as to future conduct: OFT, 1994-AR, 28.

5   The work is done for him by adjudicating officers: see OFT, 1994-AR, 14.

6   See ante, para 6.21. It is accordingly subject to review by the Council of Tribunals: s 3 of the CCA was repealed and replaced by the Tribunals and Enquiries Act 1992, s 1 and Sched 1, Part 1.

[6.25]

1   For inactivity by the Director, see Goode, *Consumer Credit Law and Practice*, para 27.219.

2   Section 41 requires that the appellant must be (a) listed in the table to that section and (b) aggrieved.

3   See the Consumer Credit Licensing (Representations) and (Appeals) Regulations, 1976 SI 191 and 1998 SI 1203. See further Goode, *op cit*, note 1, para 27.231 *et seq*.

4   Goode, *op cit*, note 1, paras 27.279; 27.291.

5   Tribunals and Inquiries Act 1992, s 11, replacing CCA, s 41. See Goode, *op cit*, note 1, paras 27.301–324.

[6.26] Publicity. To ensure adequate publicity for the administration of the licensing system, the *Crowther Report* recommended a publicly available register of licences (para 7.2.10). Accordingly, express right of public access to the register[1] is laid down (ss 35(3)–(5)); and that register now includes minded to revoke or refuse notices, reasons for revocations and undertakings by traders.[2] Further it has been decided that publication in a newspaper that the Director of the OFT is minded to revoke a licence does not infringe s 174.[3]

As the Act also requires the holders of standard licences to notify the Director of various material changes (s 36), the result is to provide a sort of publicly available compendium of current 'credit-drivers' licences'.[4] If acting for the debtor or hirer in a contentious regulated matter, it is usually advisable to make such a register check as a matter of routine: it may truncate the proceedings if the other side is unlicensed.

Licensing ancillary credit businesses

[6.27] Introduction. Following the recommendations of the *Crowther Report* (para 6.4.25), s 147(1) makes applicable to ancillary credit businesses[1] all the licensing provisions governing creditors or owners (see ante, paras 6.11–26) with one necessary adaption with regard to the civil sanction for unlicensed trading (see post, para 6.28). Such businesses will mostly[2] require either a group licence (see ante, para 6.16) or a standard licence of categories C–F (see ante, para 6.15). There are some rules created specially with regard to the activities of unlicensed ancillary credit businesses:

1 *Agreement for services.* Section 148 prevents the unlicensed ancillary credit business (trader) from claiming under an agreement for his services[3] commission or other fees from a 'customer', eg, a member of the public,[4] without an order of the Director.[5] This rule will be particularly relevant to second mortgage brokers and commercial debt-adjusters.[6]

2 *Credit-brokers* (see post, para 6.28).

3 *Debt collectors* (see ante, para 5.43).

[6.26]

1 The Director shall give general notice of matters required to be included in the register: s 35(2).

2 Goode, *Consumer Credit Law and Practice*, paras 22.62; 27.22; 27.146.

3 *Murtagh v Newspaper Publishing plc* [1990] CCLR 64 (see 44 CC 2/9). For s 174, see post, para 28.06.

4 It may only be inspected by personal callers, but postal and telex requests may be made for copies of clearly identified documents.

[6.27]

1 For ancillary credit businesses, see generally ante, para 5.36 *et seq*.

2 For exceptions see generally ante, para 6.12.

3 Should this be restricted to agreements for the traders' ancillary credit services (Goode, *Consumer Credit Law and Practice*, IIB, para 5.288), so allowing him to recover commission on that part of his business which does not require a CCA licence? See Howells, *Consumer Debt*, para 3.04.

4 'Customer' will be wide enough to include a creditor: Guest and Lloyd, *Encyclopedia of Consumer Credit Law*, para 2-149.

5 See post, para 8.38. The validation procedure is very similar to that obtaining in respect of unlicensed consumer credit businesses (s 148(2)): see ante, para 6.21.

6 For the limitation on fees in respect of licensed credit-broking, see post, para 16.19.

4   *Credit reference agencies.* Section 147(2) contains a special power to make regulations with regard to the collection and dissemination of information by credit reference agencies[5] along similar general lines to that found in s 26 (see ante, para 6.17).

As the first two rules both vest a discretionary power of validation in the Director, they are both subject to the same rules relating to appeals as those which obtain with regard to his licensing powers generally (see ante, paras 6.24–25), there being provided an express right of appeal by the disappointed applicant from the Director to the Secretary of State (s 150).

[6.28] Unlicensed credit-brokers. If a trader carries on an unlicensed credit-broking business,[1] not only does he commit an offence,[2] but the business he introduces is tainted.[3] According to s 149(1):

> A regulated agreement made by a debtor or hirer who, for the purpose of making that agreement, was introduced to the creditor or owner by an unlicensed credit-broker is enforceable against the debtor or hirer only where –
>
> (a) on the application of the credit-broker, the Director has made an order under section 148(2)[4] in respect of a period including the time when the introduction was made, and the order does not (whether in general terms or specifically) exclude the application of this paragraph to the regulated agreement, or
>
> (b) the Director has made an order under subsection (2) which applies to the agreement.

The effect of this important provision is to import a measure of trade policing:[5] no creditor or owner is likely to accept business introduced by a credit-broker[6] without first satisfying himself that the latter is licensed.[7] If the creditor or owner does accept business from an unlicensed credit-broker,[8] any agreement[9] that the broker introduces is *prima facie* unenforceable,[10] regardless of how careful the creditor has been in accepting that business.[11] The regulated agreement may, however become enforceable upon order of the Director in either of two ways: either the credit-broker may successfully apply to the Director,[4] or the creditor or owner may do so.[12]

[6.28]

1   Even where exempt agreements are introduced: see ante, para 5.40. There are exceptions for introducing small dcs agreements: see 1977 SI 2163.
2   Sections 39, 147(1): see *Brookes v Retail Credit Cards* [1986] CLY 370, DC.
3   Eg, if the broker is bankrupt (s 37(1)): see ante, para 6.23.
4   See ante, para 6.27.
5   For a justification, see Borrie, *The Development of Consumer Law and Policy*, 86; Borrie [1982] JBL at 101. For credit-brokers, see generally ante, paras 5.39–41.
6   *Aliter*, where the debtor makes the introduction: (1993) 48 CC2/28.
7   The creditor or owner aids and abets the credit-broker's offence, see *Brookes* (above).
8   But what if the creditor or owner accepts business from a licensed credit-broker who has in turn obtained it from an unlicensed credit-broker? See Guest and Lloyd, *Encyclopedia of Consumer Credit Law*, para 2-150.
9   Is this limited to regulated and linked agreements? See Howells, *Consumer Debt*, para 3.05.
10   And any security will be unenforceable (s 113(2)): see post paras 9.19; 25.13.
11   This liability without fault has parallels with the creditor's liability under s 75: see post, para 16.11 *et seq*.
12   Under s 149(2). For suggestions as to what factors the Director may take into account, see s 149(4). For the validation procedure, see ante, para 6.21.

CHAPTER 7

MONEYLENDING

[7.01] Introduction. Whilst this book is primarily about the retail supply of goods, adult consumers frequently press for early delivery with subsequent payment, typically by instalments.[1] We have already seen (ante, para 2.16) that payment may be financed by either the retail supplier of the goods (vendor credit) or by a third party (lender credit), using a number of different methods. Some of these methods are, or involve, what in law amounts to a loan of money; others do not (see post, para 7.02). If a loan contract is utilised, the two functions of a retail supply of goods and loan to the consumer[2] may be separated. Thus, a vendor credit transaction may be achieved by a cash sale and a separate loan contract between the same two parties (see ante, para 2.19), whereas lender credit may involve a cash supply of goods financed by a loan from a third party financier (see ante, para 2.20). In either case, the funds under the loan contract (see post, para 7.02) may be transmitted in one of several ways:

(a) By a delivery of cash to the consumer. For security reasons, this method is likely to be used only in relation to relatively small sums of money. The consumer-borrower may go to the lender, as where the consumer goes to a bank, building society or pawnbroker;[3] or he may go to the lender's ATM (see ante, para 2.24). Or the lender may go to the borrower, as in home credit (see ante, para 5.02).

(b) By delivery to the supplier of a cheque or other instrument (see post, para 7.24), whether by hand or post. For instance, in loan financing the financier may post a cheque to the retail supplier.

(c) By funding the consumer's existing current account (see ante, para 2.17). At simplest, this might involve a clearing bank providing its existing customer with a personal loan (fixed-sum credit) or an overdraft facility (running-account credit): the customer may then access that credit by –

   (i) drawing cash, usually by inserting a cash card in an ATM (see below);

   (ii) writing cheques, or utilising its modern equivalent, the debit card (see post, para 23.15).

(d) By opening a new loan account for the consumer. Funds in the loan account may be accessible by furnishing the customer with a cheque-book (as in (c) above); but a more popular modern alternative is for the account to be operable by way of a payment card (see ante, para 2.24), eg, a cash card for use in an ATM, credit card, debit card or store card. Such new accounts are particularly common for regulated loans (see post, para 7.04 *et seq*).

[7.01]

1   There are further difficulties in supplying goods and/or money on credit to minors (see post, para 10.18), unless supported by an adult indemnifier: see post, para 25.06.

2   See the *Crowther Report*, paras 4.1.3–4. For this Report, see generally ante, para 5.03.

3   As to bank and building society Personal Loans, see ante, para 2.19. As to pawnbroking, see post, para 15.17.

Suppose a customer has set up one of the above forms of account to be operated by a payment card. A matter which has caused difficulty is where a third party has used the card to obtain funds. On ordinary principles, the card-issuer may debit the card-holder's account where the third party is acting, or can be treated as acting, as the card-holder's agent (see post, para 10.06). The transaction may also be governed by either or both of the CCA and the Distance Selling Regulations.[3a]

Case 1. If the account out of which the unauthorised payment was made was already, or thereby became, overdrawn, it may be regulated by the CCA. If the third party uses an ATM card, the matter will fall within CCA, s 83 (reg 21(4): see post, para 7.07A); and if he uses a credit card it will be dealt with by s 84 (see post, para 7.13), unless within case 2 (reg 21(5)).

Case 2. If the unauthorised payment[4] arose under a fraudulent distance-selling transaction (see post, para 8.17), the Regulations entitle the card-holder to cancel the payment and be re-credited with the funds (regs 21(1), (2)). This rule would appear to cover the use of an ATM card to withdraw funds from an account in credit, though not an overdrawn one (reg 21(4); s 83 of the CCA: see above); and it would also extend to goods ordered with a stolen debit, charge or store card (reg 21(6)) over the telephone, internet or by mail order (see post, para 8.17; 8.17A; 8.19).

Case 3. Other cases may arise which are not within the previous two cases; that is, where an unregulated transaction does not amount to distance selling, a company credit card is used, or a business uses mail order. Here matters would still appear to be governed by the reasonable terms of the contract[5] and the Banking Code of Practice.[6] The issue will frequently turn on whether the card-holder has been negligent.[7] Statutory control has been proposed by the Treasury.[8]

LOANS GENERALLY

[7.02] Definition. 'A contract of loan of money is a contract whereby one person lends or agrees to lend money to another, in consideration of a promise express or implied to repay that sum on demand, or at a fixed or determinable future time, or conditionally upon an event which is bound to happen, with or without interest.'[1] An executory contract to make a loan is not specifically enforceable,[2] but breach may give rise to an

---

3a   See respectively post, paras 7.07A; 8.17. Could a case be made for consolidating these two sets of provisions into one?

4   The burden of proving authorised use is on the card-issuer: reg 21(3).

5   The terms will be subject to the reasonableness test under ss 2 and 3 of UCTA: see post, paras 18.17; 18.24.

6   For the Codes, see generally ante, para 3.13. *Inter alia*, Part C of the Banking Code limits the card-holder's liability on unregulated cards in a manner similar to that which the CCA applies to regulated cards (see post, para 7.13) and also provides for disputes to be referred to an Ombudsman (see generally ante, para 6.01).

7   See the Banking Ombudsman, 1993–94 AR, Case 10A; and post, para 7.07A. The precise legal position was litigated: see (1994) *The Times*, 30 July; 44 CC 2/21.

8   (2001) 30 Fair Trading 3.

[7.02]

1   See *Chitty on Contracts* (28th edn), vol 2, para 38-221. For interest, see post, para 7.03A.

2   *South African Territories v Wallington* [1898] AC 309, HL. But see the Companies Act 1985, s 195.

action for damages,[3] except perhaps where the borrower is a minor.[4] The obvious example of a loan is where B pays money to C, not intending to effect a gift or trust.[5] However, the notion of a loan from B to C also extends to where B pays money to A at the request of C.[6] Whether two or three parties are involved, the issue remains the same: whatever the legal form of the transaction, do the parties intend that its real legal nature shall be one of loan?[7] Or more shortly, is the transaction a mere cloak for a loan?[8]

Prima facie, it may be thought that some vendor and lender transactions were really loans. Much depends on which of the methods of financing the transaction is utilised:

1   *Instalment credit contract utilised.* Taking first vendor credit, it is clear that the various forms of instalment credit contract (see ante, para 1.03) will not by themselves normally amount to loans.[9] With regard to lender credit, it is well established that a genuine directly financed transaction will not amount to a loan by the financier to the consumer (see post, para 25.28).

2   *Payment card utilised.* As regards vendor credit, most budget or store cards will enable the consumer to obtain goods in advance of paying for them (see ante, para 2.19); and, insofar as he does so, it has been argued that the consumer will not be taking a loan from the vendor but entering a series of sales on running-account.[10] On the other hand, a payment card may be used by the consumer to obtain finance from a third party (see ante, para 2.25): so the use of a cash, charge, credit, debit or cheque guarantee card will amount to loans where there is the necessary element of an overdraft facility (see ante, para 5.21).

3   *Other cases.* Whilst some transactions are clearly presented as loans to the consumer, whether the loan be paid to the consumer on his behalf to the supplier, others do not purport to be loans. Nevertheless, it seems fairly clear that check or voucher trading does amount to lending money (see post, para 15.17).

[7.03] Terms of loan. Where a transaction amounts to a loan within the above definition (see ante, para 7.02), the law will attach a number of terms to it:

1   *The general common law.* Where money is lent without any stipulations as to time of repayment, a present debt is created which is repayable immediately and without previous demand.[1] However, the parties may expressly or impliedly agree that the

---

3   See Chitty, *op cit*, note 1, paras 38–228/29.

4   Minors' Contracts Act 1987, s 3: see generally, post, para 10.18.

5   *Prima facie* an obligation to repay arises from the fact of payment, and the onus is on C to prove B intended a gift: *Seldon v Davidson* [1968] 2 All ER 755, CA; and ante, para 2.08. For trusts, see post, para 19.03.

6   *Law v Coburn* [1972] 3 All ER 1115. See further post, para 7.15.

7   Chitty, *op cit*, note 1, para 38–224. It is irrelevant that the economic purpose of the transaction is to effect a loan, eg, direct financing (see ante, para 2.21).

8   *Re Securitibank (No 2)* [1978] 2 NZLR 136. See also the cases cited post, para 7.03A, and also those on the ambit of the Bills of Sale Acts (see post, para 25.25 *et seq*).

9   *Chow Yoong Hong v Choong Fah Rubber Manufactory* [1962] AC 209 at 216, PC.

10   See Goode, *Consumer Credit Law and Practice*, para 11.78.

[7.03]

1   *Re George* (1890) 44 Ch D 627. The action to recover the sum lent should be in debt, not quasi-contract: *Spargos Mining NL v Atlantic Capital Corp* [1996] CLY 772.

loan will only be repayable on demand, eg, an overdraft on a bank current account,[2] or on some stipulated date, eg, under a bank personal loan (see ante, para 2.17). As to interest, see post, para 7.03A.

2   *Banks as lenders.* If the lender is a bank, there are statutory requirements to maintain confidentiality with regard to information relating to the business or other affairs of any person, enforced by criminal sanctions (see s 82 of the Banking Act 1987; DPA: see ante, para 3.27). Additionally, in the absence of any formal written agreement with its customer, the bank owes its customer certain well-established implied contractual duties: (i) to conform to the customer's mandate, eg, to honour/stop his cheques; only to debit a customer's account where appropriate[2a], as on a cheque he personally signed, proper operation of a standing order or direct debit;[3] or insertion in an ATM of a card plus PIN;[4] (ii) to render accounts;[5] (iii) to act with proper care and skill (s 13 of the SGSA: see post, para 15.15); and (iv) a qualified duty of secrecy as laid down in *Tournier v National Provincial and Union Bank,*[6] the most important qualifications for our purposes being compulsion by law[7] and express or implied consent by the customer.[8]

3   *Secured loans.* The fact that a loan is secured, as by mortgage (see below), pledge or surety (see post, para 25.02), does not mean that the lender is bound to look only to the security for repayment of the debt: the lender may nevertheless sue on the debt (see post, para 19.22). Now, the security offered by a (first) mortgage (see post, para 25.20) may justify a lower rate of interest (see post, para 7.03A); but first mortgages will usually be beyond the scope of this work (see ante, para 3.02). Because of the priority rules (see post, para 25.22), a further advance from the same lender, eg, for home improvements, may attract a similar rate because it may grant the same priority. On the other hand, a third party mortgagee may require a higher rate to compensate for the lower priority, eg, where he is granting a second mortgage for home improvements.

In many cases the lender will not be content to leave his rights to the above common law presumptions, but will spell them out – often in a standard-form contract (see generally post, para 11.08) – dealing with such matters as: the application process (see post, para 8.35); the amount loaned, which may bring it within the ambit of the CCA (see ante, para

---

2   *Joachimson v Swiss Bank Corp* [1921] 3 KB 110, CA; *Williams and Glyn's Bank Ltd v Barnes* [1980] Com LR 205. For overdrafts, see Goode, *Payment Obligations in Commercial and Financial Transactions,* p 69.

2a *Patel v Standard Chartered Bank* [2001] 10 CL 22 (ambiguous mandate).

3   The difference is that by a standing order a customer operates his account, whereas by a direct debit he authorises his creditor to do so. For payment by these systems, see further post, para 23.14.

4   *Aliter,* if the underlying transaction is illegal: *Spector v Ageda* [1971] 3 All ER 417; and generally post, para 10.20.

5   A banker may be estopped if he renders an inflated account upon which his customer acts. As to estoppel, see post, para 21.10 *et seq.*

6   [1923] 1 KB 461, CA; and see *Jackson v Royal Bank of Scotland* [2001] 1 CL 154, CA. Do the duties laid down in this case also apply to finance and leasing companies, whose dealings with customers are transaction-based rather than relationship-based (see (1994) 49 CC 3/21)? For further discussion, see generally Howells [1995] JBL 343 at 348–50; and *Paget's Law of Banking* (11th edn), Chapter 10.

7   Eg, court orders for attachment of debt or earnings (see post, paras 27.04–05) and tracing (see post, para 27.13).

8   Including to a credit reference agency (see ante, para 3.26). Is this consistent with the data protection principle (see ante, para 3.28)? See the *Jack's Report on Banking Services* (1989, Cm 622), Chapter 5; (1989) 44 CC2/31.

5.22); the rate of interest (see post, para 7.03A); the precise date(s) of repayment,[9] commonly making time of payment of the essence (see post, para 23.20), that is, making it a condition of the contract (see post, para 11.07); and the position of any security.[10] Furthermore, where the loan is repayable by instalments, the agreement will commonly provide that, if the debtor makes default in respect of any instalment, all the instalments shall be repayable immediately, thus enabling the creditor to sue at once for the entire sum outstanding (an acceleration clause).[11] Normally, as an optional extra, insurance cover may be offered to the debtor (see post, para 24.44).

Such standard-form terms will be subject to two sets of rules in respect of burdensome contract terms: (i) the Unfair Terms Regulations (see post, para 11.12 *et seq*); (ii) s 3 of UCTA (see post, para 18.24). Moreover, there may also be relevant the rules relating to undue influence (see post, para 29.40) and possibly also the Banking Code of Practice.[12] But the contract will contain none of the implied terms in favour of the customer found in contracts for the supply of goods (see post, Chapters 11–15). Only by using s 75 of the CCA can such implied terms be used against the lender (see post, para 16.11).

[7.03A] Interest. This is the charge which the borrower pays for the use of the money borrowed. At common law,[1] the *prima facie* rule is that interest *per se* is not payable on a debt or loan by way of general damages,[2] though interest incurred as a result of default may be recoverable as non-remote special damage.[3] Whilst the SGA does not impede any such claim (s 54), as a general rule interest is not payable on the price of goods sold,[4] unless the buyer has given a cheque for the price (s 57 of the Bills of Exchange Act 1882: see generally, post, para 7.28).

Of course, it is otherwise where the agreement expressly provides for the payment of interest (see below), or where such an obligation may be inferred from the course of dealings or trade usage (see post paras, 18.04; 15.11). Further, compound interest is usually only payable at common law by agreement,[5] though this may be implied, as in the case of bank overdrafts;[6] and there is a special rule where a statutory rebate is available on early settlement (see post, para 26.19A).

---

9   Including to/from a credit reference agency (see ante, para 3.26): *Turner v Royal Bank of Scotland plc* [2001] 1 All ER (Comm) 1057, CA. For the risk in transmission of payments, see post, para 23.14. For the CCA right to complete payments ahead of time, see post, para 26.19.

10 Loans secured on realty may or may not be purchase-money (see ante, para 2.16). For regulated loans, see post, para 7.04; for refinancing, see post, para 7.04A; and for security, see post, paras 25.19A; 25.24.

11 Eg, cl 8 in *White and Carter (Councils) Ltd v McGregor* [1962] AC 413, HL (S). See further post, para 26.19.

12 Part B of the Code is addressed to banks, building societies and other card issuers. See generally ante, para 3.13.

[7.03A]

1   Interest is sometimes payable in equity even in the absence of a promise to pay it, eg, on a mortgage debt, or a surety's indemnity: see *Al-Wazir v Islamic Press Agency* [2001] 11 CL 222; and *Chitty on Contracts* (28th edn), vol 2, para 38-248; and generally Goode, *Payment Obligations in Commercial and Financial Transactions*, 79–89.

2   Ie the damages claimable without proof of the real loss incurred. See *President of India v La Pintada Compania Navigacion SA* [1985] AC 104, HL. See further Mann (1985) 101 LQR 30; Bowles and Whelan (1985) 48 MLR 229.

3   Ie on producing evidence of the real loss incurred, eg, interest charges suffered. See *Wadsworth v Lydall* [1981] 2 All ER 401, CA. As to remoteness of damage, see post, para 27.41.

4   *Benjamin's Sale of Goods* (5th edn), para 16-006 *et seq*.

5   Eg, *Kitchen v HSBC Bank plc* [2000] 1 All ER (Comm) 787, CA.

6   Chitty, *op cit*, note 1, para 38-250. As to the interest on bank overdrafts, see Paget, *Law of Banking* (11th edn), 181 *et seq*.

With regard to the rate of interest chargeable under the loan agreement, the position is as follows: apart from the old equitable jurisdiction to re-open harsh and unconscionable bargains (see post, para 29.40), the general control is now to be found in the following: increased rates of interest payable on default may amount to a penalty at common law (see post, para 27.25); or it may be avoided by the CCA (s 93: see post, para 26.19); or in a consumer supply it may amount to an unfair term (see below). However, variable rates of interest according to a formula are legitimate, eg, x% over bank rate or FHBR for the time being, unless unreasonable.[7]

Statutory powers. These powers to award interest on late payment of debts depend on the stage reached:

(1) **Contractually late.** The Late Payment of Commercial Debts (Interest) Act 1998 provides that, as regards most domestic (but not international: s 12) contracts between two **businesses** for the supply of goods or services (s 2), but not consumer credit agreements (s 2(5)(a)), there is *prima facie* an implied term that simple interest shall be payable on any qualifying debts.[8] The Act sometimes allows this implied term to be ousted by express contractual provision (see ss 7–10); but s 14 makes even such permitted ousters subject to the UCTA statutory reasonableness test (s 3(2)(b); and see post, para 18.24).

(2) **Judgment debts.** At common law, once judgment is obtained on a loan, *prima facie* the contract merges in the judgment, including any provision for interest (see post, para 26.17). There are statutory powers for a court to award simple interest on any **unregulated** debt in excess of £5,000 from the moment the sum is due under the judgment; or anytime on the debtor's insolvency.[9]

However, in relation to **regulated** loans, the case must be heard before the county court (see post, para 24.39) and there is no right to statutory interest.[9a] It has therefore become common for lenders to include in their loan agreement a provision under which contractual interest on the capital lent (**not** on the interest) remains due until payment **after as well as before any judgment**. In a regulated agreement, such a clause might be void under s 173 of the CCA (see post, para 18.11), as contravening ss 93–95 (see post, paras 26.19–19A); and the debtor could apply for a variation of the clause under s 136 (see post, para 9.20). However, another avenue of attack was explored in *Director General of Fair Trading v First National Bank plc*:[10]

> Clause 8 of FNB's unsecured regulated loan for home improvements contained such a provision for simple contractual interest on the capital lent to be paid in respect of the period before and after judgment; and by this FNB intended to prevent defaulters obtaining a discount. This would have left the debtor liable to pay contractual interest even though he

---

7 *Lloyds Bank plc v Voller* [2000] 2 All ER (Comm) 978, CA. For FHBR, see ante, para 2.18; for the CCA treatment of consensual variations, see post, para 26.21; and for possible dangers, see post, para 10.05. As to unreasonable terms, see Unfair Contract Terms Act 1977, s 3 (see post, para 18.24).

8 Section 1. As to qualifying debts, see s 3; as to the interest period, see ss 4, 5, 11; and as to the rate of interest, see s 6. As to the ineffectiveness of the Act, see (1999) 11 Credit Today 13; (2000) 6 CT 8; [2001] 10 CT 17; 56 CC 3/36. For a BSI on payment practice, see ante, para 3.08.

9 See Chitty, *op cit*, note 1, paras 27-151; 38-256.

9a For recommendations in the *First National* case that it would simplify matters if statutory interest was so available, see Lord Hope (at paras 47, 52); or if the Agreement Regulations required the agreement to draw attention to s 136, see Lord Rodger (at para 66). For a suggestion that the former is currently English law anyway, see Lord Millett (at para 61).

10 [2001] 2 All ER (Comm) 1000; [2001] 3 WLR 1297; [2002] 1 All ER 97, HL.

had satisfied any judgment, perhaps to pay by instalments with interest. If the debtor failed to pay, FNB would apply for a charging order on his house (see post, para 27.04); but, inexplicably, few debtors would invoke the above CCA defences, or ask for a Time Order (see post, para 24.40).

The DG applied for an injunction on the grounds that cl 8 was unfair under the 1994 version of the UTCC Regulations (see post, para 11.19), which were *pro tanto* the same as the present Regulations. It was not in dispute that (i) the Regulations apply to regulated agreements and (ii) cl 8 was not individually negotiated (see post, para 11.14). Reversing the Court of Appeal, the House of Lords accepted that the effect of cl 8 was to prevent the interest provision merging in the judgment (Lord Bingham at 1005, paras 3–4: see post, para 26.17); and, whilst agreeing that cl 8 fell within the UTCC Regulations, held that it satisfied the fairness test there laid down (see post, paras 11.14–15). However, bearing in mind the prevalence of versions of cl 8 in the industry (para 24) and of the availability to the courts of existing CCA provisions to control them (see above), their Lordships recommended various steps which might be taken to publicise these provisions to litigating debtors.[11] If these steps are taken, the direct effect of the *First National* case should be small.[12]

REGULATED LOANS

[7.04] Introduction. The circumstances in which a loan contract (see ante, paras 7.02–03) amounts to a regulated loan within the CCA have already been examined (see ante, para 5.13 *et seq*). In relation to moneylenders, this has meant a change of policy: instead of commencing with a list of persons totally exempt from the legislation (see ante, para 6.09), the CCA starts by comprehending all persons who make a business of lending money, and then granting exemption from particular provisions.[1] This it does as follows: all loans to non-corporate borrowers within the upper financial limit are consumer credit agreements (see ante, para 5.19); but they are not regulated agreements if they are exempt (see ante, para 5.15), and are saved from some of the provisions of the Act if they are non-commercial or small agreements (see ante, paras 5.17; 5.18). Additionally, some lenders, eg, large banks, are expressly saved from much of Part V of the Act[2] or the Director empowered to exclude them.[3] Loans within the ambit of the CCA are further subject to the following (overlapping) classifications:

(1) Restricted-use (RU) or unrestricted-use (UU) agreements;[4]

(2) Debtor-creditor-supplier (DCS) or debtor-creditor (DC) agreements;[5] and

---

11   Eg, in County Court Forms (para 23); by notice in the agreement form (para 66). The suggestions may form part of the DTI Review of the CCA: see ante, para 5.11.

12   But it may cause more debt recovery actions to be defended and hence transferred to the debtor's local county court: see ante, para 3.22.

[7.04]

1   As under the previous legislation, occasional transactions are ignored and there must still be the requisite degree of repetition: see CCA, s 189(2); and ante, para 6.12.

2   Eg, s 74(1)(b): see post, para 9.07.

3   Eg, ss 60(3); 74(3): see post, paras 9.09; 9.07.

4   This largely depends on whether or not the debtor *de facto* acquires freedom to use the credit as he wishes: see ante, para 5.29.

5   This depends on whether or not there is a business connection between the suppliers of goods and finance: see ante, para 5.32.

(3) Credit-token agreements (see post, para, 7.09).

Thus, the typical cash-loan which used to fall within the Moneylenders Acts will under the CCA be a regulated DC agreement for UU credit; and, if that loan is obtained through the medium of a credit-card, it will amount to a UU loan obtained under a DC credit-token agreement (see ante, para 5.30). However, a loan to re-finance existing indebtedness is likely to amount to a regulated DC agreement for RU credit (see post, para 7.04A).

Whilst the rules applicable to regulated agreements generally are examined elsewhere,[6] there must here be considered certain special rules applicable only to regulated loans: these include canvassing (see post, para 7.05); revolving credit (see post, para 7.08); and credit-tokens (see post, para 7.09). Section 179 contains power to make regulations as to the form and content of secondary documents,[7] laying down that the effect of contravention shall from that moment be as if the regulated agreement had been improperly executed under s 60(1).[8] Additionally, s 83 saves the debtor from liability for misuse of a credit facility (see post, para 7.07A). Considered elsewhere are the very important connected lender provisions (see post, para 16.11 *et seq*).

[7.04A] Refinancing and debt consolidation. Amounting to RU credit (see ante, para 5.28), the consolidation of a number of earlier debts, perhaps with statutory rebate (see post, para 26.19A), into one large debt is termed by the CCA 'refinancing', though without formal definition.[1] It may be achieved in two ways:

(a) the refinancing of credit agreements between the same two parties, as by a variation of one agreement,[2] or a consolidation of several agreements;[3]

(b) the refinancing of one or more debts owed to third parties,[3] as where the creditor pays off the earlier creditors from one new loan to the debtor, eg, where a credit card company attracts a new customer by paying off his existing card debts.

A particular problem has been the refinancing of existing debts in default, especially where (as is frequently the case) the debtor is no longer creditworthy, eg, he lacks a steady income or has county court judgments (CCJs) against him. This is termed 'non-status' or 'sub-prime' lending and is made to borrowers who fail to meet the normal commercial test of creditworthiness and hence are legitimately charged much higher rates of interest.[3a] This tends to be a specialist class of business, much of it concentrated in the hands of certain small banks, building societies, finance companies and moneylenders, often operating through a network of brokers. In this class of business, it is common for

---

6 See especially the rules as to licensing (ante, para 6.11 *et seq*), advertising (see post, para 8.27 *et seq*) and extortionate credit bargains (see post, paras 29.40–42). Should automatic periodic statements be required for fixed sum credit (cf s 78: see post, para 7.08)?

7 According to s 179(1), these secondary documents are 'credit cards, trading-checks, receipts, vouchers and other documents or things issued by creditors, owners or suppliers under or in connection with regulated agreements or ... linked transactions'. No regulations have yet been made.

8 Section 179(2). As to s 60(1), see post, para 9.10; and as to improperly executed agreements, see post, para 9.19.

[7.04A]

1 Goode, *Consumer Credit Law and Practice*, para 25.65.

2 Eg, granting more time to pay (roll-over loans; see below); granting top-up loans. For criticisms, see OFT, *Unjust Credit Transactions*, para 4.12; Rowlingson, *Money Lenders* (1994) 162. For variations, see generally post, para 26.22.

3 This will usually amount to a novation (see post, para 7.27).

3a For description of the 'non-status' category, see (2001) 62 QA 3. For definitional problems, see ante, para 3.13.

the creditor to insist on a secured loan: this gives the creditor more effective remedies (see post, para 27.04).

Where the refinancing includes a mortgage on the debtor's home, it will normally be for an amount which exceeds the CCA limit (see ante, paras 5.22; 3.02), though it is likely to be within the extortionate credit provisions[4] and the Advertising Regulations (see post, para 8.30). Perhaps because of the financial pressure such debtors already face,[5] in seeking refinance they have shown themselves insufficiently conscious of the APR quoted (see post, para 8.22), the level of fees charged by brokers and lenders,[6] and that entry into secured financing puts their homes at risk.[7] The OFT has issued a code of practice for non-status lending,[8] backed up by the threat of credit licence revocation.[9] Moreover, whether or not regulated the terms of such loans may be attacked as unfair terms.[10] Some of these controls may be transferred to the FSMA (see ante, para 3.02).

Canvassing credit

[7.05] Introduction. The *Crowther Report* sought to draw a distinction between the doorstep peddling on the one hand of goods on credit and on the other of money.[1] The Report recommended that the doorstep peddling[2] of money, already illegal under the Moneylenders Acts (see ante, para 6.09), should continue to be banned, whilst the doorstep peddling of loans to purchase goods embraced many perfectly legitimate forms of business, eg, check trading and mail order. However, foreseeing that the peddling of goods[3] might be used as a cloak for the peddling of money, the Report recommended that the former should only be allowable under a supplementary licence (see ante, para 6.14). These ideas were adopted by the CCA: it defined doorstep peddling as 'canvassing' (see post, para 7.06) and sought to prohibit most canvassing of DC agreements (see post, para 7.07).

[7.06] Definition. Seeking to enact the *Crowther* recommendation (see ante, para 7.05), s 48(1) provides:

---

4   Where the loan is secured, rates quoted are unlikely to be extortionate. Even the higher rates usually charged for unsecured refinancing are unlikely to be extortionate, except at the lower end of the market. See further post, para 29.41.

5   See further my Butterworths edn, 1989, para 7.04A.

6   These are sometimes called 'arrangement fees'. For attempts to bring such fees within the APR, see post, para 8.24.

7   This is particularly the case with non-status borrowers (see post, paras 8.22; 8.35): OFT, *Unjust Credit Transactions* paras 1.6; 4.11. Such consumers are sometimes encouraged to capitalise on the tremendously increased equity in their homes by taking out a second mortgage. As to foreclosure, see post, para 25.20; and as to second mortgages, see post, para 25.24. Further protection of such debtors is under consideration.

8   *Guidelines for lenders and brokers in the non-status lending market* (1997): see Goode, *op cit*, note 1, VIII, para 16.1. For Codes of Practice, see generally ante, para 3.13.

9   See (1997) 16 Tr L 143. As to renewal and termination of licences for creditors and credit-brokers, see respectively ante, paras 6.23; 5.40.

10 *Falco Finance Ltd v Michael Gough* (set out post, para 8.22; see Rosenberg 52 QA 9). As to unfair terms, see post, para 11.12.

[7.05]

1   Paragraphs 6.4.17–20. For this Report, see generally ante, para 5.03.

2   But not postal advertising: *ibid*, para 6.4.21.

3   Peddling goods may require a pedlar's licence and/or a street trader's licence: see ante, para 6.02.

An individual[1] (the 'canvasser') canvasses a regulated agreement[2] off trade premises if he solicits the entry (as debtor or hirer)[3] of another individual (the 'consumer') into the agreement by making oral representations[4] to the consumer or any other individual,[5] during a visit by the canvasser to any place (not excluded by subsection (2)) where the consumer, or that other individual, as the case may be, is, being a visit–

(a) carried out for the purpose of making such oral representations to individuals who are at the place, but

(b) not carried out in response to a request made on a previous occasion.

Thus, the essence of canvassing is the oral soliciting of entry by the consumer into a regulated agreement by the individual canvasser during a visit to non-business premises. This is very carefully drafted and **none** of the following will amount to canvassing:

1 Section 48(2) expressly excludes soliciting, etc, at any permanent or temporary **business premises** of the financier (creditor or owner), goods supplier, canvasser or consumer, eg, stall at a trade fair, mobile display at roadside, retail premises. The exclusion here of the consumer's business premises may be compared with their inclusion within the cancellation provisions (see post, para 10.29).

2 The soliciting, etc, involves **no oral communication**, thus excluding wholly written communications, whether delivered by post or otherwise. Mail drops offering credit facilities have become an increasingly common feature of modern life, the sale of lists of potential customers being a substantial business. However, a circular sent to a minor may amount to another offence (see post, para 8.33). What about sign language to the deaf?

3 The soliciting, etc is not made during the course of a **visit** to non-business premises, as where a financier from his office telephones a consumer.[6]

4 The visit must be **unsolicited**, so that it is not canvassing if the visit is made in response either to a reply-paid signed postcard sent in by the consumer[7] or even a prior[8] oral request. But a visit made in response to an oral request, whilst it will not amount to canvassing, may constitute an offence under s 49(2).[9]

5 The visit is unrequested, but not carried out for the **purposes** of soliciting (s 48(1)(a)); for instance, where a discussion spontaneously develops about a loan either during a home visit to service a previous loan or at an independent party or round of golf.[10]

[7.06]

1 For 'individual' see the definition in s 189(1): set out ante, para 5.24.

2 For regulated agreements, see ante, para 5.13 *et seq*.

3 For 'debtor' and 'hirer', see the definition in s 189(1): set out ante, respectively paras 5.24 and 1.19.

4 'Representation' is defined in s 189(1), discussed post, para 16.08.

5 Eg, spouse or other member of household.

6 For special cases, see Goode, *Consumer Credit Law and Practice*, para 28.87, item (c). For telephone selling generally, see post, para 8.17.

7 Section 48(1)(b). This does not stipulate by whom the request must be made: see Guest and Lloyd, *Consumer Credit Law*, para 2-049.

8 The request must be genuinely previous: it would be insufficient if on the doorstep the consumer signed a back-dated request.

9 See post, para 7.07. As to the delivery of unsolicited goods, see further post, para 8.18.

10 *Aliter*, if the home visit or social event was set up or attended for the purpose of soliciting, a matter which may be difficult to prove. *Quaere*, if the visit was to solicit a DCS agreement?

[7.07] The prohibitions. In accordance with the *Crowther* recommendations (see ante, para 7.05), two acts are prohibited in relation to canvassing (see ante, para 7.06).

1 *To canvass loans of money*. Section 49(1) provides that:

> ... it is an offence to canvass debtor-creditor agreements off trade premises.

The effect of the restriction to DC agreements (see ante, para 5.35) is to prohibit the unrequested doorstep peddling of cash, but not of trading checks or vouchers, nor any form of vendor credit.[1] It creates an offence in the canvasser,[2] but does not give rise to any further sanctions:[3] so any regulated agreement resulting from the canvassing is not affected. Moreover, the section expressly exempts the soliciting of overdraft facilities on existing current accounts;[4] nor does it apply to the doorstep 'peddling' of goods on credit (DCS agreements) or hire (consumer hirings), though a canvassing endorsement is required on licences.[5]

2 *Orally solicited visits*. Whilst not amounting to canvassing, s 49(2) enacts that:

> It is also an offence to solicit the entry of an individual (as debtor) into a debtor-creditor agreement during a visit carried out in response to a request made on a previous occasion, where–
>
> (a) the request was not in writing signed by or on behalf of the person making it, and
>
> (b) if no request for the visit had been made, the soliciting would have constituted the canvassing of a debtor-creditor agreement off trade premises.

The draftsman could have simply amended the definition of canvassing to include under s 48(1)(b) only signed written requests; but, because he wished to use the definition of canvassing for other purposes as well, he chose to create this extra offence with the same limited sanctions[3] and banking exemption.[4] The effect of s 49(2) is that new home credit business can only be lawfully obtained by either (a) the consumer visiting the trader's business premises, or (b) indirectly at the consumer's house, eg, by newspaper coupons or telephone calls.

Finally, it should be noted that just as the foregoing relate to the door-step soliciting of regulated agreements, the Act also seeks to control the doorstep soliciting of certain ancillary credit services. Section 154 makes it an offence[2] to canvass off trade premises[6] the services of a person carrying on a business of credit-brokerage (see ante, paras 5.38–41), debt-adjusting[7] or debt-counselling;[8] but there is no prohibition in respect of orally solicited visits.

[7.07]

1 Because they are DCS agreements under s 12: see ante, para 5.34.
2 For penalties, see s 167 and Sched 1. See further Chapter 28.
3 Section 170(1): see post, para 10.19.
4 Sections 49(3)–(5), 183. For details, see Guest and Lloyd, *Consumer Credit Law*, para 4-4800; and for an explanation, see Bennion, *Consumer Credit Control*, para 4.10.
5 For the doorstep peddling of goods on credit, see ante, para 6.14.
6 As defined by s 153, which contains a definition of canvassing slightly different from that in s 48 in relation to the type of premises involved.
7 See ante, para 5.43. It is not made an offence to solicit the service of debt-collectors or credit reference agencies because these services are only likely to be employed by creditors and suppliers.
8 See ante, para 5.43. It is not made an offence to solicit the services of debt collectors or credit reference agencies because these services are only likely to be employed by creditors and suppliers.

[7.07A] Liability for misuse of credit facilities. Whether the customer has a fixed or running-account (see ante, para 5.28) with a financier, there may be circumstances where a third party wrongfully withdraws money from that account. According to the general law, the financier can only charge that wrongfully withdrawn amount to the customer's account where he has a contractual right to do so.[1] However, s 83(1) of the CCA grants the consumer a special statutory immunity from such a contractual provision in the following terms:

> The debtor under a regulated consumer credit agreement shall not be liable to the creditor for any loss arising from the use of the credit facility by another person not acting, or to be treated as acting, as the debtor's agent.

This general CCA rule is carefully limited as follows:

(1) The account between the consumer and financier must involve a **consumer credit agreement**,[2] so that it has no application as regards a simple customer's account containing a credit balance, eg, a bank or building society account without overdraft facility which contains a £70 balance (see ante, para 7.01). Section 83 is intended to give a customer/debtor an **immunity** from liability, not to protect a customer/debtor from **loss**:[3] so, if a thief pretends to be the account-holder to abstract that £70 balance, the section offers the account-holder no protection.

(2) This immunity applies only in respect of a **credit** facility, eg, £100: it may be a fixed or running-account, eg, a bank Personal Loan (fixed-sum) or overdraft (running-account). It can have no application to consumer **hirings**, as where a third party impersonates another to hire goods.

(3) The indemnity is limited to loss arising from **use** of the credit facility, eg, abstraction of £50 from the £100 facility. If the thief merely uses an ATM card (see ante, para 7.01) to draw down a customer's balance, eg, abstraction of £50 from customer's £70 balance, the matter is outside s 83,[4] but governed by the general law (see above). However, insofar as the thief utilises the customer's credit facility, eg, sending him into unauthorised overdraft by abstracting £80 from an account £70 in credit, the matter may fall within s 83 as to the £10,[5] unless a credit-token was used (s 84: see post, para 7.14).

(4) Section 83 has no application where the withdrawal is made by a third party who is acting as the customer's **agent**, or to be treated as such. Thus, if the customer 'loaned' his ATM card and PIN to a spouse to make a withdrawal, the customer cannot claim the s 83 protection, even if the spouse drew more than was authorised.[6]

(5) By s 83(2), the above indemnity does not apply to non-commercial agreements (see ante, para 5.18); nor does it affect the bankers' statutory protection in collecting cheques.[7]

[7.07A]

1 Ie under the account mandate (see ante, para 7.03). Or where the customer is estopped from denying this (see generally post, para 21.10).

2 So it cannot apply where the third party misrepresents that there is a consumer credit agreement.

3 Goode, *Consumer Credit Law and Practice*, para 39.9.

4 It has been promised that all payment cards will be brought within ss 83 and 84: *Banking Services* (1990, Cm 1026) paras 4.6; 8.3.

5 Goode, *op cit*, note 3, para 39.10.

6 Goode, *op cit*, note 3, para 39.8.

7 Section 83(2). Under s 4 of the Cheques Act 1957: see post, para 7.28.

Banking code. Issuers of payment cards who subscribe to the Banking Code of Practice (see generally ante, para 3.13) undertake, irrespective of ss 83 and 84 of the CCA, to pay the full loss incurred through use of a card: (a) when it has not been received by a customer;[8] (b) for all unauthorised transactions after the card issuer has been told that the card has been lost or stolen or that someone else may know the PIN (see generally post, para 7.13), including money transferred to his electronic purse (see ante, para 2.24); (c) if faults have occurred in the machine or other system used, causing customers to suffer direct loss, unless the fault was obvious or advised by a message or notice on display.[9] Customers will remain liable for all loss so caused where they are shown to have acted fraudulently or with gross negligence.[10]

[7.08] Revolving credit generally. It has already been seen that a loan may be either a finite sum or a revolving credit; and that these two types of loan are respectively christened by the Act 'fixed-sum credit' and 'running-account credit' (see ante, para 5.28). In respect of all running-account credits, the CCA has to make some adjustments to bring them into line with fixed-sum credit: this is so in relation to the 'credit limit' necessary for determining the ambit of the Act (see ante, para 5.28); and with regard to the information to be supplied to the debtor during the currency of the agreement. The Act makes it clear that the running-account debtor is entitled not just (on payment) to comparable information **on request;**[1] but also **gratis** to **automatic** periodic statements of account,[2] typically a monthly statement showing the opening and closing balances, any movements (debits/credits) and the minimum payment due. There are special rules for credit-tokens (see post, para 7.09 *et seq*); and, where more than one consumer is a party to the transaction, it may be a question whether they are co-principals[3] or one is just an additional permitted user of the other's facility.[4] Unfortunately, the Act does not appear to deal clearly with 'application form agreements',[5] a form of business common in some types of running-account credit:[6] this may give rise to difficulties both as regards execution[7] and cancellation.[8]

---

8   See generally post, para 7.11. Would it be fairer if the burden of proof were transferred to the creditor (cf s 171)?

9   Paragraph 20.4. The burden of proof is on the issuer (para 20.5). For the concept of 'gross negligence', see the Banking Ombudsman, Annual Report 1994/95 paras 10.4–6.

10 Eg, by writing a PIN on the card. See further the Banking Ombudsman, 1995–96 Annual Report, paras 12.6; 12.7.

[7.08]

1   Sections 78(1)–(3): see generally post, para 15.16.

2   Sections 78(4)–(5); and see [1999] 12 Which? 44. The rule does not extend to small agreements (see ante, para 5.17): s 78(5). The complicated regulations as to periodic statements are considered by Goode, *Consumer Credit Law and Practice*, paras 34.18–31. No sanction is prescribed for breach of ss 78(4): s 170(1); and see post, para 10.19.

3   In the case of joint accounts (see generally ante, para 5.24), the Act allows the debtors to forego their right to one statement each by signing a 'dispensing notice': s 185(2), as amended. Presumably it is not possible for all joint debtors to submit dispensing notices, the last in time being ineffective.

4   For the effect of use by an 'additional card-holder', see post, para 7.09.

5   The practice of promoting schemes by way of a leaflet, part of which consists of an application form, the leaflet being available from a dispenser: (1984) 39 CC 1/19.

6   Eg, store budget cards (see ante, para 2.19), credit cards (see post, para 7.09 *et seq*). 'Application form' agreements for fixed-sum credit are effectively ruled out: Guest and Lloyd, *Encyclopedia of Consumer Credit*, para 2-062.

7   For the purposes of s 61(1)(c) (see post, para 9.12), is the leaflet extracted by the consumer from the dispenser 'presented' to him?

8   For the purposes of s 67 (see post, para 10.29), is the shop-assistant's direction of the consumer to the dispenser an 'oral representation'?

Finally, and quite apart from the CCA, it should be borne in mind that, where goods are obtained through a running-account facility, there is no inherent right of recaption of goods (see post, para 24.23) as there would be if an hp agreement was utilised;[9] and credit balances on running-accounts may give rise to yet further problems.[10]

Credit cards (tokens)

[7.09] **Introduction**. The three separate bilateral contracts in a credit or charge card operation (see ante, para 2.27) may be analysed as follows:[1]

1   *Supply contract*. Between the retail supplier of goods or services and the consumer there will be a contract for the supply of those goods or services, the consideration being satisfied by means of a credit or charge card (plastic money). In the case of goods, this may amount to a sale with a special arrangement to pay by card; and with either goods or services the supplier may insist at the outset on either of the following:

(a) taking an imprint of the card, which raises the question of whether there is then a preliminary contract; or have the parties not yet finished agreeing (see post, para 10.03)? If there is a preliminary agreement, does it contravene s 59 (see ante, para 5.20)?

(b) the card-holder signing in blank. It might be argued that there is (a) an open contract to pay whatever the supplier deems fit, or (b) a contract to pay only a reasonable price (see ante, para 2.06). The supply contract follows all the ordinary rules as to express and implied terms and exclusions (see Part 4). On the analogy of a cheque, is the card-holder under any tortious duty of care to ensure that the slip is so drawn that it is not possible afterwards for another to insert extra charges?

2   *Card-holding contract*. The credit or charge cards will have been issued to the account-holder (principal debtor) and any other card-holder, eg, spouse, by one of the following: with a two-party card, whether simpliciter or private label, the card-issuer will be the retail-supplier; whereas with a three-party card, the issuer (merchant-acquirer) will be a financier (see ante, paras 2.24–25). In most cases, it would appear that the card contract will in essence be one of loan for revolving credit.[1] Leaving aside the formation of that contract (see post, para 7.11), its terms are likely to include the following:[2] the time-limited card must be signed by the card-holder, is usually subject to an annual fee (see post, para 7.11) and may only be used subject to the conditions for the time being in force (see post, para 11.07) and within the credit

---

9   For alternative means of obtaining security, see post, Chapter 25.

10   Where the consumer has a credit balance on his running-account, the question arises whether he has made a 'deposit' with the system-operator within s 5 of the Banking Act 1987. Whilst fixed-sum credits would seem exempted (s 5(2)), running-account credits would appear not to be so: see (1987) 41 CC 4/30.

[7.09]

1   See *Re Charge Card Services Ltd* (set out ante, para 2.27). Distinguish where there is a cheque card; or a debit card without overdraft facility (see ante, para 5.21).

2   See Kiely [2001] 1 Credit Today 33; 2 CT 39. For some model forms, see Guest and Lloyd, *Encyclopedia of Consumer Credit*, para 8-228 *et seq*. As standard-form contracts, any exclusion or disclaimer must be reasonable: see post, para 18.24.

limit;[3] the issuer will debit the holder's account[4] with the amount of all card transactions effected by him or his authorised agent (see post, para 7.13); interest is payable on the balance outstanding after due date;[5] the card-holder must make a minimum specified payment each month, as compared with the fixed regular payment under a budget account (see ante, para 2.19), but in default of such minimum payment, there is likely to be an acceleration clause (see generally ante, para 7.03); or he may pay more at his option (cf post, para 26.19); the card remains the property of the issuer[6] and the holder may terminate the agreement by surrendering the card to the issuer (cf post, para 26.03); and in the case of unregulated three-party cards no claims by the holder may be offset against the issuer by reason of the so called cut-off clause (see post, para 7.25); the card-issuer does not guarantee that the card will be honoured by any supplier[7] and may disclose to its agents information about the card account, eg, the retailer (as to consent to such disclosure under the DPA, see ante, para 3.27). This contract will usually be regulated by the CCA (see post, para 7.10); and its express terms are subject to the statutory tests of reasonableness under s 3(1) of the UCTA 1977 (see post, para 18.24) and fairness under the UTCC Regulations (see post, para 11.15).

3   *Merchant contract.* Provisions commonly found in such franchise contracts between the supplier/merchant and the financier include the following: a derogation from the signed voucher provision for distance sales;[8] arrangements for refunds to account-holders (cf post, para 29.04); and a commission payable to the card issuer. There also used to be a promise to supply card-holders at the same price as cash customers; but such provisions have now been rendered unlawful.[9] The contract will usually provide for termination on breach[10] and a 'charge-back clause', designed to put the risk of fraud on the merchant by relieving the merchant-acquirer/financier of the obligation to pay out the merchant in respect of particular sorts of transaction, eg, where a fraudulent third party acquires goods or services by way of a card-not-present transaction, which is one where goods or services are ordered by telephone or mail order (as to which, see post, paras 8.17; 8.19). The express terms will usually be subject to the statutory test of reasonableness (s 3 of UCTA: see above) which may cause

---

3   If the card is used above the limit, strictly the issuer is entitled to refuse to honour the retailer that use, rather than honour it *pro tanto*. Use above the limit may amount to the offence of obtaining pecuniary advantage by deception: *R v Lambie* [1982] AC 449, HL (Barclaycard).

4   Additional card-holders, eg, employees or spouses, are sometimes made to underwrite their own card expenditure. This may make them personally liable as indemnifiers (see post, para 25.06) if the card-holder becomes insolvent (see post, para 19.18).

5   For interest, see generally ante, para 7.03A. If the debt is not completely cleared by due date, interest is normally payable from billing. Cash advances may attract interest from the date of advance. A lower rate of interest may be obtained if the indebtedness is secured, eg, by a mortgage.

6   Eg, *Tony Mekwin MTV and Co v National Westminster Bank plc* [1998] CLY 2512, CA. This may be advantageous where the issuer wishes to stop someone using the card, whether a holder or third party. For the action of conversion, see post, para 19.04.

7   Is this an exclusion clause (cf post, para 18.16)? What would be the measure of damages?

8   This is to cover supply contracts made by telephone or mail order (see post, para 8.19), where it would be impractical to obtain the card-holder's signature on a sales voucher. Whilst highly convenient, this variation facilitates fraud.

9   As a monopoly: 1990 SI 2159; and see generally ante, para 2.12.

10 See, eg, *Naheem v National Westminster Bank plc* [1998] CCLR 10, CA.

difficulty, *inter alia*, as regards the application of 'charge-back clauses' to 'card-not-present' transactions.[11]

[7.10] Application of the CCA. Whilst both credit- and charge card-holding contracts are in essence loans (see ante, para 7.01), charge cards are exempt from the CCA (s 16: see ante, para 5.21). On the other hand, a credit card contract is likely to amount to a regulated agreement within the CCA, being a loan to an 'individual'[1] within the 'credit limit'.[2] It will then amount to a regulated consumer credit agreement (see ante, para 5.19) for the provision of running-account credit (see ante, para 5.28) under which the account-holder is the debtor (see ante, para 5.24), the card-issuer is the creditor (see ante, para 5.25), the card-contract is a credit-token agreement[3] and the card issued under it a credit-token (see ante, para 5.30). If such a card is used to obtain cash, there will be a DC agreement for UU credit under ss 11(2) and 13(c) (see ante, paras 5.29; 5.35; and Sched 2, Example 16). However, if the card is used to obtain goods or services, then there is RU credit (see ante, para 5.29) and the position is as follows: in the case of a two-party card,[4] there is a DCS agreement[6] within s 12(a); whereas in the case of a three-party card,[5] there is a DCS agreement[6] within s 12(b) (see s 187(3), considered ante, para 5.33), the retailer being the supplier (see Sched 2, Examples 3, 16), and the supply contract a linked transaction.[7] The whole transaction is subject to all the normal rules applicable to regulated agreements considered later,[8] and is additionally subject to certain special rules (see post, para 7.12). Normally, the card-issuer will require a category A licence (see ante, para 6.15), whereas the retail supplier will not need any CCA licence.[9]

Authorised users. If the debtor accepts the frequently proffered invitation to add another member of his family as an 'authorised user' or 'additional card-holder' (usually with a separate card issued to that user), the legal position would be as follows: unless a co-debtor,[10] the authorised user has none of the CCA protections,[11] but the debtor remains liable for the latter's use of the card (see post, para 7.13).

[7.11] Formation of card contract. Whilst the terms of the card contract between the consumer and card-issuer have already been outlined (see ante, para 7.09), there remains

---

11   See Brownsword (1999) 19 LS at 311. Also (1997) 147 NLJ 1806; (1998) 148 NLJ 7 and 133.

[7.10]

1   But see *Re Charge Card Services Ltd* (set out ante, para 2.27).

2   See ante, para 5.28. For the complications that may be caused by the small agreement rules, see Jones, *Credit Cards*, 64–65.

3   Section 14(2). Depending on whether or not a binding contract is made at the outset (see post, para 7.11), it will amount to either a prospective or actual credit-token agreement (see ante, para 5.20). What if creditors dispense with plastic cards and merely require a number verbally repeated, eg, telephone sales?

4   Because it falls within two categories, it is a multiple agreement: see ante, para 5.27 and Sched 2, Example 16.

5   Two- and three-party cards are explained ante, para 2.24.

6   See ante, para 5.34.

7   See ante, para 5.31. As regards the exemption of insurance policies under s 19(4), see post, para 24.44.

8   Eg, formalities (see Chapter 9), s 56 liability (see post, para 16.08). See generally Jones, *op cit*, note 2, Chapter 5.

9   Because he does not effect introductions, he is not a credit-broker (see ante, para 5.41): Jones, *op cit*, note 2, p 15.

10   He may be required to indemnify the card-issuer: see ante, para 7.09.

11   See Jones [1988] JBL 457. For co-debtors, see ante, para 5.24. See generally Jones, *op cit*, note 2, pp 106, 109.

the issue of how that credit-token contract (see ante, para 5.30) is made. Where the card-issuer charges a fee[1] there will be a bilateral contract, under which the credit-card is then issued; and each replacement card, sent with a fresh set of terms (see post, para 7.12), will usually discharge the old contract by subsequent agreement (see post, para 26.18) and replace it with a new agreement on those fresh terms.[2] However, where no such fee is charged, the position would appear to be this:[3] in so far as the antecedent card 'agreement' in fact amounts merely to an offer by the issuer to enter into a unilateral contract,[4] there is only a separate acceptance of the issuer's continuing offer each time the card is used by the holder,[5] a view which has been characterised as 'absurdly complicated'.[6]

Insofar as the credit card contract may be regulated (see ante, para 7.10), s 66(1) lays down the earliest moment at which the card-holder may become civilly liable under it:

> The debtor shall not be liable under a credit-token agreement for use made of the credit-token by any person unless the debtor had previously accepted the credit-token, or the use constituted an acceptance of it by him.

Under this important provision, the burden of proof is on the creditor;[7] and s 66(2) goes on to explain that:

> The debtor accepts a credit-token when –
>
> (a) it is signed,[8] or
>
> (b) a receipt for it is signed,[9] or
>
> (c) it is first used,
>
> either by the debtor himself or by a person who, pursuant to the agreement is authorised by him to use it.

The effect is to protect the debtor in the event of the card being stolen in course of post to him and *pro tanto* overrides s 84 (see post, para 7.13); but it is not clear what happens if an additional card is stolen.[10] Aside from the statutory protection, similar rules may be applied to unregulated payment cards under the Banking Code (see post, para 7.13).

[7.11]

1   To convert a card issued free into one for which a fee is charged may not be lawful: Borrie (1990) 44 CC 5/20.

2   OFT, *Equal Liability*, 7. See Campbell (1994) 13 Tr L 18 at 23–24. For the historical importance of this issue, see Butterworths edn, 1989, para 7.14.

3   For the burden of proof in respect of the lawful supply of credit-tokens, see s 171(4)(a). 'Lawful supply' seems to refer to s 51: see post, para 7.12.

4   It may be doubted whether this represents the reality of the transaction, because the offeree (consumer) is under an obligation to make payments as stipulated (see ante, para 7.09).

5   Is the reality a hybrid contract, under which the unilateral offer matures into a bilateral contract?

6   It may make some uses of a card small agreements (see ante, para 5.17): Jones, *Credit Cards*, p 64. It may convert each use of the card into fixed-sum credit (see ante, para 5.28): Jones, p 74.

7   See s 171(4)(a); and Jones, *ibid*, pp 146–47.

8   Distinguish signature of the agreement: see post, para 9.13.

9   It is suggested that the receipt must be for the credit-token as such, and not merely for any package containing it, eg, recorded-delivery letter: Goode, *Consumer Credit Law and Practice*, para 39.6.

10   As to theft of an authorised user's card, see Goode, *ibid*, IIB para 5.126. What of theft of one joint debtor's card?

[7.12] Special CCA provisions. Where the use of a credit card amounts to a regulated transaction (see ante, para 7.10), it is subject to special CCA rules as follows:

1   *Unsolicited mailing.* The early 1970's saw the launch of the two major three-party credit card systems in the UK by way of unsolicited mass mailing.[1] In s 51, an outraged Parliament sought to prevent repetition of this exercise by making it a criminal offence,[2] but made the rule subject to several exceptions: (a) small DCS agreements;[3] or (b) tokens given to companies or for amounts above the CCA limit; or (c) the credit-token is given in response to a signed request by its recipient;[4] or (d) it is given for use under a credit-token agreement already made;[5] or (e) it is given in renewal or replacement.[6] In practice, new card-issuers have found these exemptions sufficiently generous to enable the effective marketing of new brands of card. Nor does the prohibition touch the over-relaxed issue of cards, nor the overgenerous increase of credit limits on cards already issued.

2   *Copy of card-holding contract.* Unlike the general rule as to copies on execution of the regulated agreement, a copy of the credit-token agreement (see ante, para 7.10) can be given to the debtor with the credit-token (see post, para 9.15). Except for small agreements (see ante, para 5.17), on each subsequent issue of a credit-token to the debtor (but not to an additional card-holder),[7] the creditor must give the debtor a further copy of any executed agreement and of any other document referred to in it (s 85). Further, during the life of the card, the creditor must also supply the debtor with information (see ante, para 7.08).

3   *Cancellation rights.* There are two variations from the ordinary cancellation rules (see generally post, para 10.28 *et seq*). First, notice of his right of cancellation may be given to the debtor with the first credit-token (s 64(2)). Second, the debtor is not entitled to repayment of any sum payable for the issue of a credit-token until that token has been returned to the creditor or supplier.[8]

4   *Use and misuse.* The Act establishes both the earliest moment at which a holder can become liable under a credit-token agreement (see ante, para 7.11), and the extent to which he can be liable for misuse by another of the token (see post, para 7.13).

[7.12]

1   Access and Barclaycards. Today, each are members of worldwide schemes: respectively the MasterCard and Visa networks.

2   *Elliott v DG* (set out ante, para 5.30). For the tariff see s 167 and Sched II; and see generally post, para 28.07. 'Give' means deliver or send by post': s 189(1). Section 51 does not preclude the giving of advertising literature.

3   Section 51(2). For small agreements, see ante, para 5.17. This exception is likely to save most trading-check operations: as to which, see generally ante, para 2.23.

4   Section 51(2). Provided it does not amount to canvassing (see ante, para 7.06), it is therefore possible to solicit the consumer in writing to apply for a credit card either by personal letter or general advertisement.

5   Section 51(3)(a). This enables an unsolicited card to be sent to an authorised user, eg, spouse, as an additional card-holder: see ante, para 7.10.

6   Section 51(3)(b). Is this consistent with s 82(2)(a)?

7   For joint debtors, see s 185(2) as amended by s 38(3) of the Banking Act 1979. See generally ante, para 5.24; and post, para 25.08.

8   Section 70(5). Note that this refers not to credit acquired by use of a credit-token, but only to sums payable for issue of the token.

5   *Reimbursement*. A consumer can achieve reimbursement by the charge-back mechanism (see ante, para 7.09) or through connected lender liability (see post, para 16.11 *et seq*).

6   *Multiple agreements* (see ante, para 5.27).

[7.13/14] Misuse of credit-tokens. The general rule under s 83 is that a debtor cannot be made liable for another's **unauthorised** use[1] of his regulated credit facility: whilst this rule does not usually apply to other payment cards, ss 83 and 84 have been informally extended to all payment cards by the Banking Code (see ante, para 7.07A). However, within the context of credit-tokens, s 84 provides that a debtor may within limits be liable for another's use of his card, though it should be remembered that this liability can only arise after acceptance of the credit-token (see ante, para 7.11) and does not apply where the token is used in distance selling.[2]

At common law, such liability for unauthorised user could arise either by virtue of the credit-token agreement (see ante, para 7.09) or in the tort of negligence.[3] However, the Act provides that s 84 liability (see below) shall only last until 'the creditor has been given oral or written notice that [the card] is lost or stolen, or is for any other reason liable to misuse'.[4] Furthermore, that liability cannot arise unless the credit-token agreement prescribes details of the persons who must be notified of that loss, theft or misuse.[5]

Within these limitations, s 84 distinguishes two cases for liability on a genuine credit-token:[6]

1   *Unauthorised user*. Whilst the general rule in s 83 is that the card-holder is not liable for unauthorised user of his card facility by another (see ante, para 7.07A), s 84(1) provides as follows:

> Section 83 does not prevent the debtor under a credit-token agreement from being made liable to the extent of £x (or the credit limit if lower) for loss to the creditor arising from use of the credit-token by other persons during a period beginning when the credit-token ceases to be in the possession of any authorised person and ending when the credit-token is once more in the possession of an authorised person.

[7.13/14]

1   This may amount to the offence of evading liability by deception on the part of the unauthorised user (*R v Jackson* [1983] Crim LR 617, CA); or of procuring the execution of a valuable security by deception (*R v Beck* [1985] 1 All ER 571, CA). As to where the card-holder signs a blank slip and an unauthorised amount is subsequently entered, see post, para 10.16.

2   Section 84(3A), as inserted by the Distance Selling Regulations: see ante, para 7.01.

3   But see Goode, *Consumer Credit Law and Practice*, para 39.62; and generally post, para 17.14.

4   Section 84(3). The burden of proof is on the creditor: s 171(4)(b)(ii). 'Liable to misuse' might extend to a negligently disclosed PIN. Where oral notice is given, it must be confirmed in writing within 7 days (s 84(5)), which should protect the creditor against false assertions of oral notification: and see further Goode, *ibid*, para 39.45. For card protection plans, see post, para 25.14.

5   Section 84(4). For standards of legibility, see the Consumer Credit (Credit-Token Agreement) Regulations 1983, SI 1555.

6   If two or more tokens are given under one credit-token agreement, each token is treated separately for the purposes of this section: s 84(8). See also s 84(6). There may be real difficulties in proving whether or not the use is authorised: [1985] Which? 539, in which case the burden of proof is on the creditor: s 171(4)(b)(i).

Suppose his card is lost or stolen from a card-holder.[7] By s 84(1), his maximum liability for unauthorised user[8] of his genuine card is the lesser of his credit limit (see ante, para 7.10), or the prescribed sum – which is currently £50[9] – per period of use.[10] However, this liability is only in respect of card transactions made whilst the card is not in the hands of any 'authorised person', which expression will usually comprehend the card-issuer, his servants and agents and the card-holder or any authorised user.

2   *Authorised user.* Where possession or use of the card by another[11] is authorised by the debtor, his liability on ordinary agency rules is reinforced by s 84(2), which removes the above monetary limit protection, enacting that:

> Section 83 does not prevent the debtor under a credit-token agreement from being made liable to any extent for loss to the creditor from use of the credit-token by a person who acquired possession of it with the debtor's consent.

The most obvious categories of authorised user within s 84(2) are (a) the person to whom the debtor hands a credit card and (b) the additional card-holder (see ante, para 7.10). In neither situation does the card-holding debtor have any protection whatever against any transactions that the third party initiates with the genuine card (see post, para 16.12); and he may have difficulty in cancelling the authority of the additional card-holder before the renewal date.[12]

TRIPARTITE TRANSACTIONS

[7.15/17] Assignment of debts.[1] It has already been seen that a chose in action is a type of personal property which can be enjoyed by the obligee [A] only by court action, eg, a claim by a buyer [A] of defective goods under s 14 of the SGA (see post, para 14.01). However, by far the most common form of chose in action is a claim by a creditor [A] in debt (see ante, para 2.02), eg, by a seller of goods [A] for the price. In practice, in our field transfer of debt is used in two very different situations: transfer of a good debt (where the debtor is willing and able to pay) is a method of financing (see ante, para 2.22), whereas transfer of a bad debt is a method of collection (see post, para 27.02).

---

7   Distinguish where a genuine card is stolen in course of post to him: see ante, para 7.11; or where a duplicate card is used: Banking Ombudsman, AR 1994/95, para 10.3.

8   The debtor, the creditor, and any person authorised by the debtor to use the credit-token, shall be authorised persons for the purposes of subsection (1): (s 84(7)). Does this apply to s 84(2)?

9   Section 84(1) originally stipulated £30; but there is a power to alter the limit by regulation (s 181). The current figure of £50 was introduced in 1983: see now the Consumer Credit (Further Increase in Monetary Limits) (Amendments) Order 1998, SI 997. In some cases, the consumer is offered insurance to cover this risk.

10   For illuminating examples of how this works, see the Banking Ombudsman, Annual Report 1990/91, para 10.3.

11   Eg, by 'additional card-holders', typically the account-holder's spouse; or a person to whom the account-holder has 'loaned' his card. See also above and ante, para 7.10.

12   [1989] Which? 612. Can the card-holding contract be cancelled without returning to the card-issuer all cards issued under it? See the Banking Ombudsman, AR 1990/91, p 24.

[7.15/17]

1   For assignments of choses in action, see generally Treitel, *Law of Contract* (10th edn), Chapter 16; *Chitty on Contracts* (28th edn), vol I, Chapter 20. For attornment of debts, see Oditah, *Accounts Receivable*, pp 88–90.

Transfer of a chose in action is usually by way of 'assignment' (see below), except in the case of negotiable instruments (see post, para 7.24). Whereas the common law refused to recognise attempts to transfer debts or other choses in action, equity would normally enforce such an assignment[2] from the creditor (the assignor) to a third party (the assignee), whether the chose be present or future (see post, para 7.18) and without the consent of the debtor.[3] To constitute a voluntary[4] equitable assignment, generally no particular form is required, since equity looks to the intent rather than the form; and in the commercial context that would generally[5] be accomplished simply by a contract to assign.[6] That contract would be made between assignor [A] and assignee [B]: in equity, notice to the debtor [C] was unnecessary to perfect an equitable assignment; but such notice was necessary to constitute a statutory assignment[7] and may be needed for other purposes.[8] Both an equitable and statutory assignee will always take subject to the equities.[9]

Where the chose in action arises out of a regulated agreement, the CCA provides that the expressions 'debtor', 'creditor', 'hirer' and 'owner' shall include their assignees.[10]

[7.18] Present and future chose. Taking by way of example a debt, a chose in action may be classified as follows:

1 *Present chose.* This category will comprehend not just debts presently owing,[1] but also sums of money payable at a later date (perhaps conditionally) under a present contract.[2] Thus, the price due under a cash, credit or conditional sale is a present chose in the hands of the seller (A), as is hire rent due or growing due to the bailor (A) under a **fixed-term** hiring, a category which seems no longer to include hp agreements (see ante, para 1.25).

2 *Future chose.* There will be a future chose in either of the following two circumstances:

    (a) the assignor (A) does not own the chose at the time of assignment, eg, where A purports to assign a debt presently owed by C to X.

---

2 For the exceptional case of non-assignable rights, see post, para 7.26.

3 It is thereby distinguishable from novation, a transaction to which the debtor must be a party: see generally post, para 26.18. For other explanations of the effect of assignment, see Geva, *Financing Consumer Sales and Product Defences*, 61–64.

4 For compulsory assignment on death, see post, para 24.44.

5 Statute sometimes requires registration of assignment for the benefit of the assignor's other creditors: see Insolvency Act 1986, s 344 (for individual assignors: see post, para 19.24); Companies Act 1985, s 395 (for company assignors: see post, para 25.28).

6 *Brandt's Son and Co v Dunlop Rubber Co* [1905] AC 454, HL; *Karsales (Harrow) Ltd v Wallis* (set out post, para 18.07). Except that a disposition of an equitable interest must be in writing: see post para 25.21. For perfection, see generally post, para 25.19.

7 Law of Property Act 1925, s 136; and see further Treitel, *op cit*, note 1, 622 *et seq*.

8 Eg, the data protection rules (see ante, para 3.28); to avoid harassment (see post, para 24.24).

9 See post, para 7.23. *Contra* negotiation: see post, para 7.24.

10 Section 189(1). For debtor and creditor, see ante, paras 5.24–25. For assignment of the burden of the contract, see post, para 7.27.

[7.18]

1 Eg, *Brandt's Son and Co v Dunlop Rubber Co* [1905] AC 454, HL (A purchased rubber with money provided by B and resold it to C; to repay B, A assigned to B the price due from C); and see post, para 16.19.

2 *Hughes v Pump House Hotel* [1902] 2 KB 190, CA (as security for an overdraft, A made an absolute assignment of all moneys due and becoming due under his existing building contracts); and see post, para 16.18.

    (b) there is no presently existing chose, eg, where A purports to assign future rentals which may become due to him under a **periodic** hiring[3] whether under a simple hiring or hp agreement.[4]

Whereas there can be an immediate equitable assignment of a present chose,[5] a purported assignment of a future chose can only operate as a contract to assign. In *Tailby v Official Receiver*:[6]

> Packing-case manufacturer (A) was short of money and sought to raise a loan from B. As security for the loan, A *inter alia* mortgaged all his book-debts[7] both due and falling due.[8] Later, a book-debt of £11 became due to A from C for goods supplied; and B gave C notice of the assignment. A having become bankrupt, the issue arose whether the Official Receiver (standing in the shoes of A) or B was entitled to the £11.

The House of Lords held that the assignment of future book-debts passed the equitable interest to B in debts arising after assignment: whilst it could not pass any interest immediately as the debt did not then exist, it operated as a contract to assign which equity would regard as an assignment binding on the subsequent debt **from its creation** by way of a floating charge (see post, para 25.02).

[7.19/22] Notice.[1] Starting from the basic principle that equity is looking for an intention to assign (see ante, para 7.17), it follows that the parties must have done everything which the law deems necessary to implement that intention. Normally, notice to the assignee (B) is necessary to perfect the assignment:[2] such notice could be by the assignor (A) or by someone with his authority, eg, the debtor (C).[3] Once perfected, the assignment will bind not just A, but also all those who stand in his shoes, eg, A's trustee in bankruptcy or judgment creditor.[4]

---

3   The distinction is probably whether the hirer (C) is contractually bound to pay the hire-rent: see *Chitty on Contracts* (28th edn), vol I, para 20-028; Treitel, *Law of Contract* (10th edn), p 629; and ante, para 1.25.

4   *Blakey v Trustees of Pendlebury* [1931] 2 Ch 255, CA (hp; case on s 38(c) of the Bankruptcy Act 1914, now repealed).

5   On the vexed question of the effect of a voluntary equitable assignment, see Treitel, *op cit*, note 3, p 629 *et seq*.

6   (1888) 13 App Cas 523, [1886–90] All ER Rep 486, HL. See also *Holroyd v Marshall* (set out post, para 9.05, involving after-acquired goods).

7   Book-debts are debts arising out of the ordinary course of a company's business, whether actually entered in the books or not: *per* Erle J in *Shipley v Marshall* (1863) 14 CB (NS) 566 at 571. It might include modern equivalents, eg, computer records: Goode, *Legal Problems of Credit and Security*, 92.

8   Ie, a bill of sale assigning by way of mortgage all present and future book-debts. For bills of sale, see post, para 9.05.

[7.19/22]

1   According to the rules of equity, notice may be given in any form, so that even oral notice of assignment, eg, of a debt, is sufficient. But a written notice is necessary to secure priority over successive assignees of equitable interest (Law of Property Act 1925, s 137(3)); and registration of charges is notice (see post, para 25.28).

2   *Morrell v Wootten* (1852) 16 Beav 197. Where A is a registered company, registration under s 395 of the Companies Act 1985 may constitute notice to a subsequent encumbrancer: see post, para 25.25. For perfection, see generally post, para 25.19.

3   Treitel, *Law of Contract* (10th edn), p 627.

4   *Gorringe v Irwell Works* (1886) 34 Ch D 128.

Whilst notice does not need to be given to C to perfect an equitable assignment,[4] it does need to be given for several other reasons.[5] First, notice to C is necessary to bind him: before receipt of notice, C may obtain a good discharge by paying his debt to A;[6] whereas, upon notice of the assignment, C ceases to be liable to A and may thereafter secure his release only by paying B.[7] Secondly, notice to C completes a statutory assignment (s 136 of the LPA) and establishes priority as between assignees (see below).

Priorities. Where there are successive transfers of the same property to innocent purchasers for value, it will be necessary to establish their order of priority to the property. For goods, priority is established by the historical order in which the transfers were made, the *nemo dat* rule (see post, para 19.11). However, in the case of equitable assignments of choses in action, priority is established by the order of notice to the debtor [C]: under the rule in *Dearle v Hall*,[8] generally speaking,[9] the first assignee [B1] to give notice[1] to C is the one entitled to enforce the debt against C,[10] though in the case of assignment of a future chose, eg, future hire rent under a periodic hiring agreement (see ante, para 7.18), notice can only be given as from the time the chose comes into existence.[11]

[7.23] Subject to the equities. Whether the assignment be equitable or statutory (see ante, para 7.17), it is a general principle that the assignee (B) takes 'subject to the equities';[1] that is, the debtor (C) may plead against B claims that C had against the creditor/assignor (A).[2] The object of the rule is that C shall not be prejudiced by the assignment;[3] and it has a number of effects. First, B takes subject to any defect in A's title to the chose which may have existed at the time of the assignment, which may be seen as an aspect of the doctrine *nemo dat* (see post, para 19.11): if no money ever became due from C to A, B takes nothing;[4] and the same will follow if a contract of debt between C and A is void for

---

5 See Goode, *Legal Problems of Credit and Security*, p 90. *Contra* negotiable instruments: see post, para 7.24.

6 *Bence v Shearman* [1898] 2 Ch 582; *Warner Bros Records Inc v Rollgreen Ltd* [1976] QB 430 (assignment of option).

7 *Brice v Bannister* (1878) 3 QBD 569 (Oditah, *Accounts Receivable*, p 241); *the Attica Hope* [1988] 1 Lloyd's Rep 439. *Contra* UCC, Art 9-318(2).

8 (1828) 3 Russ 1. See generally, *Snell on Equity* (27th edn), pp 62–68; Crossley Vaines, *Personal Property* (5th edn), pp 274–76; Oditah, *ibid*, 130–33, pp 140–42, 265; and in the context of real property post, para 25.22. *Contra* negotiable instruments (as to which, see post, para 7.24) and other personal property (as to which, see post, para 25.25).

9 This will not be so if: (a) the assignee is a volunteer; or (b) he takes with notice of a prior assignment, eg, a registered company charge (above); or (c) the chose is held under a declaration of trust or shares in a registered company; or (d) purchase-money security, eg, *Romalpa* clauses (see post, para 25.30); or (e) appropriation of debt or sub-rent (see post, para 23.12) or (f) priority agreements (see post, para 19.14). See generally Oditah, *op cit*, note 7, pp 135–40; 163–85.

10 *Marchant v Morton* [1901] 2 KB 829.

11 *Johnstone v Cox* (1880) 16 Ch D 571. This makes life difficult for factors (see ante, para 2.22).

[7.23]

1 *Security Trust Co v Royal Bank of Canada* [1976] AC 503, PC. See generally, Geva, *Financing Consumer Sales and Product Defences*, 50–54; Oditah, *Legal Aspects of Receivables Financing*, pp 224–25.

2 *Contra* negotiable instruments: see post, para 7.24. Distinguish the 'mere equities' considered here, from equitable interests in property (eg, ante, para 7.16): see Goode, *Commercial Law* (2nd edn), pp 30–31.

3 The rule seems to apply to both present and future choses: Oditah, *op cit*, note 1, pp 239–40.

4 *Tooth v Hallett* (1869) LR 4 Ch App 242.

mistake[5] or illegality, or voidable for misrepresentation.[6] Second, there are the notice rules (see ante, para 7.19). Third, C may *prima facie* plead by way of set-off as against B all claims arising out of the chose in action,[7] whether arising before or after assignment,[8] and whether liquidated or unliquidated,[9] and whether arising before or after C has notice of the assignment.[10] Fourth, C may also plead as against B even claims arising dehors the chose in action, provided that such claims arose before C had notice of the assignment;[11] but, because C is essentially setting up against the innocent B a claim he has against A, C's set-off can never exceed his debt to A.[12]

[7.24] Negotiability. Mercantile custom (see post, para 11.10) has recognised certain categories of choses in action by written contract as amounting to negotiable instruments, including the following important categories, none of which amount to 'goods' within the SGA (see ante, para 2.02):

1   *A bill of exchange.* The rules relating to these instruments were codified in the Bills of Exchange Act 1882.[1] It defines a bill of exchange as an unconditional[2] order in writing, addressed by one person (A: the drawer) to another (C: the drawee),[3] signed by A, requiring C to pay on demand or at a determinable future time[4] a sum certain in money to or for the order of a specified person [B1], or to bearer [B2] (s 3(1)). However, where the bill contains words prohibiting transfer, it is valid between the parties but not negotiable (s 8). A forged signature on a bill is a nullity.[5]

2   *A cheque* is defined as 'a bill of exchange drawn on a banker [C] payable on demand' (s 73) and is generally subject to the same provisions as bills of exchange,[6] except where the 1992 Act applies (see post, para 7.28).

3   *A promissory note* is an unconditional promise in writing made by one person [C] to another [A] signed by the maker [C], engaging to pay, on demand or at a fixed or determinable future time, a sum certain in money, to, or to the order of, a specified

---

5   For the relationship of this rule to the doctrine of *non est factum* (see post, para 10.16), see Geva, *op cit*, note 1, pp 54–58.

6   *Graham v Johnson* (1869) LR 8 Eq 36 (no consideration). As to why C cannot recover sums mistakenly paid to B, see Geva, *op cit*, note 1, pp 72–80.

7   See generally Goode, *Legal Problems of Credit and Security*, Chapter 5; Oditah, *op cit*, note 1, pp 227–31. But see cut-off clauses (see post, para 7.25); and distinguish counter-claims, eg, under the SGA, s 53(1) (see post, para 29.26), and running-account credit (see ante, para 7.08).

8   *Roxburghe v Cox* (1881) 17 Ch D 520 (before); *Laurence v Hayes* [19271 2 KB 511 (after).

9   *Young v Kitchen* (1878) 3 Ex D 127.

10   *Government of Newfoundland v Newfoundland Railway* (1888) 13 App Cas 199, PC.

11   *Bennett v White* [1910] 2 KB 643, CA.

12   For the non-assignability of the burden of a contract, see post, para 7.27.

[7.24]

1   Unless otherwise stated, all subsequent references are to the 1882 Act, which (like the SGA 1893) was drafted by Sir MacKenzie Chalmers (see ante, para 1.02).

2   Distinguish travellers' cheques, which are conditional: see Paget, *Law of Banking* (11th edn), p 256.

3   If the drawee signifies his acceptance of the order, he becomes the 'acceptor' (s 17) and incurs the special liability of an acceptor (s 54).

4   A 'time bill' is one which the drawee/acceptor must pay at the time stipulated, eg, a 90-day bill (s 11). The holder of a time bill may always discount it (ie, sell it at less than its face value) to obtain payment before due date. And see further post, para 23.14.

5   1882 Act, s 24. Distinguish fraudulent alteration in the body of the bill, which is dealt with by s 64.

6   It has special rules as to crossings (1882 Act, ss 76–81) and the protection of the paying and collecting banker (Cheques Act 1957). As to payment by cheque, see post, para 23.14.

person [B1] or bearer [B2] (s 83). Generally speaking, a promissory note is subject to the same rules as a bill of exchange.[7]

4   *A bank note* is a promissory note made by the Bank of England [C] payable to the bearer [B2] on demand.[8] It amounts to legal tender (see post, para 23.14).

Besides having special rules as to consideration (ss 27–30), negotiable instruments have two important characteristics:

(a) *Transfer.* The manner in which a negotiable instrument may be transferred (negotiated) from A to B depends on the manner in which it is currently expressed to be payable:[9] if it is payable to order, it may be transferred by indorsement on the back and delivery by the transferor [A]; whereas, if it is payable to bearer [B2], it may be transferred by his mere delivery.[10]

(b) *Defects of title.* Whilst an ordinary assignee [B] takes subject to the equities (see ante, para 7.23), under certain conditions the transferee (B: holder) of a negotiable instrument takes free from any defect of title of prior parties,[11] as well as from more personal defences available to prior parties amongst themselves (s 38(2)). B will take free of such equities and is termed a 'holder in due course': every holder is presumed to be a holder in due course unless the instrument is affected by fraud, duress or illegality.[12]

[7.25] Cut-off devices. The rule (see ante, para 7.23) that claims by the debtor [C] against the assignor [A] arising before notice of the assignment can be set off against the assignee [B], may *prima facie* be excluded in either of two ways:

1   *By negotiation.* As payment for the supply of goods could easily be made by the supplier [A] taking a cheque or other bill of exchange (see post, paras 23.14; 24.03), an obvious means by which A might both finance the transaction and shake off C's equities would be for A to negotiate the bill to a holder in due course (see ante, para 7.24). To combat this, the CCA has introduced special rules to restrict the circumstances in which a bill taken in a regulated supply can come into the hands of a holder in due course (ss 123–25: see post, paras 25.09–10).

2   *By cut-off clause.* At common law, C's equities could be excluded by the express provisions of the contract creating the debt, eg, credit card contracts (see ante, para 7.09). Such provisions are already common form in English debentures.[1] In North America cut-off clauses have appeared in instalment credit contracts in terms that the

---

7   1882 Act, s 89, with the modifications necessary because the maker who is promising to pay (ss 83–89).

8   Currency and Bank Notes Act 1954, s 3.

9   Section 31. Compare assignments of choses in action (see ante, para 7.17) and delivery orders (see post, para 23.03). As no notice to C is required, negotiations are free of the rule in *Dearle v Hall*: as to which, see ante, para 7.19.

10   Compare gifts of chattels (see ante, para 2.08), sales of goods (post, para 19.01) and hp (post, para 15.22). Transfer may not in practice be possible where the cheque is crossed 'a/c pay' (see above), which may cause problems to payees who do not have bank accounts (see post, para 7.28).

11   Eg, misrepresentation, breach of contract, or total failure of consideration. Except where a party's signature to the instrument is wholly void under the doctrine of *non est factum* (see post, para 10.16) or under statute. See further Geva, *Financing Consumer Sales and Product Defences*, pp 88–93.

12   Sections 29–30. For the position of a holder not in due course, see Geva, *ibid*, Chapters 5 and 6; *Lipkin Gorman v Karpnale Ltd* [1991] AC 548, HL.

[7.25]

1   See Pennington, *Company Law* (7th edn), pp 612–13.

buyer [C] agrees not to raise against an assignee [B] of the seller [A] any defences he may have under the agreement,[2] so seeking to confer on B something approaching the status of a holder in due course.[3] However, where a UK transaction is regulated, it would appear that s 113(1) of the CCA will prevent the enforcement of such cut-off clauses.[4]

[7.26] Non-assignable rights. Notwithstanding the general rule that contractual rights are *prima facie* assignable (see ante, para 1.23), there are the following exceptions:

1   *A bare right of action*. At common law,[1] a chose in action was not assignable if it savoured of maintenance or champerty: maintenance is supporting litigation in which one has no legitimate interest; and champerty is financing litigation in which one has no legitimate interest in return for a share in the proceeds. However, this rule did not apply to assignment of a debt, nor where the assignee [B] had a legitimate interest in the rights assigned, nor to an agreement to assign the proceeds of litigation.[2] Notwithstanding the abolition of the crimes and torts of maintenance and champerty,[3] these rules against trafficking in litigation may still attack the assignment of a bare right of action, that is, a claim for unliquidated damages; but they do not preclude the assignment of a liquidated debt, even if the assignment is of a bad debt at a heavy discount.[4]

2   *Personal contracts*. A contractual right cannot be assigned if it is clear that the intention was to grant a purely personal right.[5] This principle has been applied to contracts for the sale of goods so as to save a supplier [C] from having to give his buyer's [A's] business successor [B] either credit[6] or enough goods to satisfy all needs.[7] On the

---

2   For ways in which such clauses may surmount the privity problem, see Geva, *Financing Consumer Sales and Product Defences*, pp 93–103.

3   Goode and Ziegel, *Hire Purchase and Conditional Sale*, 111–12; Geva, *ibid*, p 103 *et seq*. Often they include a title retention clause (see post, para 25.29), which causes considerable difficulty as to whether the expressed promissory notes are sufficiently unconditional to amount to bills of exchange: see now UCC, Arts 9-206(1), 318(1); and Geva, Chapter 6.

4   See post, para 25.11. It would seem to have this effect by reason of the wide definition of security: see post, para 25.10.

[7.26]

1   A bare right of action may be made assignable by statute: see *Ramsey v Hartley* [1977] 2 All ER 673, CA (now Insolvency Act 1986, s 314).

2   *Fitzroy v Cave* [1905] 2 KB 364, CA (for conditional fees, see ante, para 3.18); *Glegg v Bromley* [1912] 3 KB 474, CA. See also *Giles v Thompson* [1994] 1 AC 142, HL (credit hire; as to the CCA, see ante, para 5.13; and as to hiring a replacement, see generally post, para 27.28); *Stocznia Gdanska SA v Latvian Shipping Co No 2* [1999] 3 All ER 822 (funder of shipbuilder: for other litigation, see post, para 29.17).

3   By the Criminal Law Act 1967, s 14. It is clear that these restrictions on assignment have survived: *Trendtex Trading Corporation v Credit Suisse* [1982] AC 679, HL; *Brownton Ltd v Edward Moore Inbucon Ltd* [1985] 3 All ER 499, CA; and see generally Tan (1990) 106 LQR 656.

4   *Camdex International Ltd v Bank of Zambia* [1998] QB 22, CA. What about contingent fees (see ante, para 3.15)?

5   Distinguish whether the prohibition is against assigning (a) performance of A's duty, or (b) A's right to payment for that performance: Oditah, *Legal Aspects of Receivables Financing*, 259.

6   *Cooper v Micklefield Coal and Lime Co Ltd* (1912) 107 LT 457 (on the grounds that credit was granted on the basis of business experience).

7   *Kemp v Baerselman* [1906] 2 KB 604 (where the buyer sold his business to a large company).

other hand, any such presumption of non-assignability will be rebuffed where the contractual right is expressly or impliedly made assignable.[8]

3 *Contracts expressed to be not assignable.* Suppose a particular type of contractual right is *prima facie* assignable; for instance, a debt (see ante, para 7.17), hp rights (see ante, para 1.23), a guarantee (see post, para 25.06). Nevertheless, at common law a provision in the contract may render it non-assignable.[9] Thus, an instalment credit contract frequently provides that the rights of the buyer or hirer [A], but not of the supplier, shall not be assignable; and, if the buyer or hirer [A] nevertheless purports to assign them, his assignee [B] cannot enforce the assignment as against the supplier.[10] In this event, it seems that the contract of assignment may nevertheless be effective as between the assignor [A] and assignee [B],[11] with the result that the supplier should logically recover the entire value of the goods. Perhaps not surprisingly, this has caused confusion as to whether the supplier can sue the assignee [B] in conversion for the full value of the goods, this being the seemingly logical answer (see post, para 27.30), or must deduct the value of the hirer's [A's] option, perhaps the fair answer (see post, para 27.31). In a consumer supply agreement (see post, para 11.12A), a prohibition on assignment may be unfair (UTCC, reg 4: see post, para 11.15).

[7.27] The burden of the contract. Whilst the benefit of a contract is *prima facie* assignable (see ante, para 7.17), the position is different in relation to the burden of a contract. Suppose C supplies goods to A under an instalment contract which makes C responsible for their servicing; and subsequently C wishes to retire from business. Can C assign to B both the right to collect the price and the burden of the servicing? It would appear that the servicing obligation can be passed to B in a number of ways, unless the contract expressly or impliedly provides for personal service by C:[1]

1 C may delegate performance to B, though this is not a true assignment because C will remain liable to A for the servicing.[2]

2 A, B and C may by novation agree to discharge the old contract between A and C, replacing it with a new one between B and C.[3] This process may be streamlined by securitisation.[4]

---

8 *Tolhurst v Associated Portland Cement Co* [1903] AC 414, HL (promise to supply); *Re Charge Card Services Ltd* (set out ante, para 2.27; promise to pay); promises to pay under instalment supply contracts (see ante, para 1.23); and generally Treitel, *Law of Contract* (10th edn), p 641.

9 *Linden Gardens Trust Ltd v Lenesta Sludge Disposals Ltd* [1994] 1 AC 805, HL, esp *per* Lord Browne-Wilkinson at 428–29 (110 LQR 42; [1994] JBL 129). See also *Bawejem Ltd v MC Fabrications Ltd* [1999] 1 All ER (Comm) 377, CA. As to assignment of the proceeds of a debt, see McCormack [2000] JBL 422.

10 *United Dominions Trust (Commercial) Ltd v Parkway Motors Ltd* [1955] 2 All ER 557; doubted by two members of the CA in the *Wickham Holdings* case (set out post, para 27.31). As to attempts by vehicle transfer agencies to do this, see ante, para 1.15. Could such an attempt take effect as a declaration of trust under the rule in *Re Turcan* (1888) 40 Ch D 5 (suggestion by JWA Thornely)?

11 *Chitty on Contract* (28th edn), vol 1, para 20-044; and ante, para 1.23.

[7.27]

1 *Robson and Sharpe v Drummond* (1831) 2 B and Ad 303 (hire: C entitled to refuse performance by B). Cf *British Waggon G v Lea* (1880) 5 QBD 149, CA (hiring contract allowed vicarious performance).

2 *Stewart v Reavell's Garage* [1952] 2 QB 545; and see note 7, below.

3 Eg, *Harbinger UK Ltd v GE Information Services Ltd* [2000] 1 All ER (Comm) 166, CA. For the distinction between assignment and novation, see ante, para 7.17.

4 Which removes the need for B's consent on transfer: Goode [1991] LM & CLQ 177 at 187.

3   Payment of the debt may be conditional on performance of the servicing, in which case B may not enforce the debt without seeing that the servicing is performed;[5] and B will in any event take subject to the equities (see ante, para 7.23).

4   C may make the contract an undisclosed principal for B;[6] but the agency must be created before the supply, because an undisclosed principal cannot ratify (see post, para 10.06).

Beyond the foregoing, at common law the burden of a contract cannot be voluntarily assigned.[7] Different rules apply to involuntary assignments[8] and possibly to assignments of regulated agreements.[9]

[7.28] Cheques. Under the scheme contained in the Bills of Exchange Act 1882 (see generally ante, para 7.24), an ordinary cheque would be a document in which the holder of a bank account (A: the drawer) directed his bank to pay a specified sum from that account to a named payee [B] 'or order', this last expression being the authority for the instrument to be transferred by endorsement and delivery (see ante, para 7.24). If the instrument were stolen, the thief could forge the indorsement of the payee and present the cheque for payment: normally, such a forged indorsement would be of no effect (s 24). To protect himself from loss, A was likely to cross the cheque 'not negotiable': the effect of this was that the cheque remained transferable, but could not transfer a good title free of the equities.[1] At common law, the innocent bank [C] would thus be liable to the payee as true owner in the tort of conversion (see post, para 19.04); but, provided he acts in good faith and without negligence, the collecting banker of a cheque 'or other document' is protected by s 4 of the Cheques Act 1957.

The Cheques Act 1992. With the prevalence of the habit of paying debts by posted cheque, there was a wave of theft of cheques in course of post, in which case A or B lost his money. The *Jack Report* recommended that this problem be dealt with by the creation of a new non-transferable 'Bank Payment Order'.[2] Instead of creating a new instrument, the Government preferred to amend the existing law in the Cheques Act 1992 so that the effect of the crossing 'account payee' became that (s 81A(1) of the 1882 Act, as inserted by s 1 of the 1992 Act):

… the cheque shall not be transferable, but shall only be valid as between the parties thereto.

Almost immediately, the clearing banks [C] altered their ordinary printed cheque forms: first, they printed them with an 'account payee' crossing to bring them within the 1992 Act;[3] and second, they deleted the 'or order', so that the cheque was expressed to be

---

5   Diamond (1956) 19 MLR 498 at 500.
6   See Reynolds [1984] JBL 260.
7   See further *Chitty on Contracts* (28th edn), vol 1, paras 20-075/78.
8   Eg, on death or insolvency, where there is statutory provision for automatic assignment.
9   The issue is whether the statutory definition in s 189(1) of 'creditor' and 'owner' includes an assignee of their duties: compare Goode, *Consumer Credit Law and Practice*, para 23.21; Guest and Lloyd, *Encyclopedia of Consumer Credit Law*, para 2-190.

[7.28]
1   1882 Act, s 81; *Sutters v Briggs* [1922] 1 AC 1, HL.
2   *Banking Services* (1989, Cm 622), para 7.35.
3   Bankers collecting for the wrong person bearing the name of the payee still have the protection of s 4 of the Cheques Act (see above): 1992 Act, s 3.

payable to a named payee [A] only.[4] The combined effect of the 1992 Act and the new payee-only cheques seems to be this: not only will a transferee [B] always take subject to the equities,[5] but such cheques cannot be 'negotiated' and can only be assigned.[6] In effect, this has turned the modern cheque into a Bank Payment Order. It is for consideration whether or not the other rules relating to bills of exchange (see ante, para 7.24) apply payment made by such modern cheques, eg, the rules relating to the effect of payment by cheque. Further payment by such an essentially old-fashioned paper-based system may be compared with payment by modern electronic transfer by debit card.[7]

Cheque cashing businesses. Whilst the above 1992 Act safeguards the interests of payees of cheques who have bank accounts, it has created something of a dilemma for those payees who do not have a bank account (up to 9% of the population: see ante, para 2.15). To meet the needs of this group there have sprung up 'cheque cashing' businesses: these cannot take title to an 'account payee' cheque by negotiation (see above); but they may obtain title to the underlying debt by way of assignment.[8]

---

4   It may be that the instrument is then not a bill of exchange within the meaning of s 8 of the 1882 Act: Wheatley (1992) 142 NLJ 607.
5   As to assignment subject to the equities, see ante, para 7.23. For the prohibition on taking a negotiable instrument by way of payment under a regulated agreement, see post, para 25.09.
6   *Plimley v Westley* (1835) 2 Bing NC 249. For assignment, see ante, para 7.17.
7   For payment by debit card, see post, para 23.15. Compare the additional liability of a banker (as card-issuer) where he is a connected lender (see post, para 16.11).
8   Macleod (1997) 113 LQR 133; Cooke (1998) 52 CC 6/35.

PART 3

NEGOTIATING SUPPLY CONTRACTS

CHAPTER 8

SEEKING BUSINESS

ADVERTISING GENERALLY

[8.01] Introduction. This section deals with the legal rules relating to seeking business by advertising as it concerns persons outside the advertising industry.[1] To maximise its effectiveness in promoting the distribution of goods, commercial advertising of products will normally be aimed at a target group (see post, para 8.05 *et seq*). However, such advertising also has a powerful effect on third parties, so that some consideration must also be given to the rules relating to advertising as it affects third parties (see post, para 8.02).

Besides this substantial body of legal rules, in recent years significant attempts have been made at the self-regulation of the advertising industry. Thus, the broadcasting of advertisements is strictly controlled by the IBA Code of Practice, whilst other forms of advertisement fall within the purview of the ASA (see ante, para 3.14). The OFT (see generally ante, para 3.03) has also been active in promoting voluntary codes of practice, eg, mail order advertisements (see ante, para 3.11 *et seq*), recognising that what is needed is a judicious mixture of legal controls[2] and self-regulation;[3] and the OFT's representatives on the ground are the trading standards officers of the local authority (see ante, para 3.05). Some such codes are easier to police than others, as where the code is produced by the advertising medium[4] or approved by it.[5] To the foregoing may be added the effect of numerous EU-generated rules, such as that relating to public procurement,[6] data protection (see ante, paras 3.26–28) and misleading advertisements. There seems to be little general legal control as regards the misleading packaging, as opposed to labelling, of goods.[7]

[8.02/04] Effect on third parties. In the 20th century, the Victorian belief in *laissez-faire* in the field of advertising was substantially eroded. Thus, rules have developed for both the following purposes:

[8.01]

1 For the legal relationships within the industry, see Lawson, *Advertising Law*, Chapters 2 and 3; Circus, *Sales Promotion Law* (2nd edn); Shears (1995) 145 NLJ 1682.

2 See the OFT powers in relation to misleading advertisements: see post, para 8.12A.

3 OFT, 1982-AR, 11. For the OFT sponsored codes, see ante, para 3.13.

4 Eg, the ASA code (above); the ICSTIS code for premium-rate phone services; the codes of British Advertisers and Institute of Purchasing (set out in Circus, *op cit*, note 1, 211 *et seq*).

5 Eg, the schemes applying to the mail order trade, such as MOPS.

6 See Singleton (1994) 13 Tr L 414; Bovis [1994] JBL 615.

7 For examples, see [2001] 5 Which? 6.

(a) To combat false claims that a particular person endorses a product.[1] At common law, this may amount to defamation[2] or passing off.[3] Additionally, the criminal law may offer protection by way of the TDA. Thus, a false trade description may be applied to goods by falsely suggesting the identity of the manufacturer,[4] or the testing or approval by any person,[5] including Royal Approval (ss 12, 13 of the TDA: see ante, para 4.10).

(b) Against unfair competition. Where one party imitates the goods of another, this may amount to the tort of passing off;[3] or unfair trading[6] could be made the subject of a statutory instrument under Part II of the Fair Trading Act 1973 (see ante, paras 6.06–08). One way for an aggrieved trader to overcome the uncertainties of the common law in this field is by invoking the trade mark system,[7] or the TDA,[4] or the misleading pricing rules (see post, paras 8.09–10). Other statutory protection against unfair competition is provided by the copyright laws,[8] as regards regulated agreements[9] and in some cases by EU Regulations.[10]

Effect on target groups

[8.05] The common law of contract. Except in the field of misrepresentation (see post, para 17.10), English law has traditionally seen little need for the imposition of general restrictions upon negotiations leading up to a contract for the supply of goods. However, in the famous case of *Carlill v Carbolic Smoke Ball Co*[1] it was made clear that the manufacturer's advertisement may amount to an offer of a reward to the whole world, which could be accepted so as to complete a binding contract on the basis of its terms by

---

[8.02/04]

1   Eg, as recommended by – see [1995] 10 Which? 30; lookalikes – see brand copies (below); comparative credit advertising – see (1995) 49 CC 5/13; parallel imports – see [1999] 12 Which? 10.

2   *Tolley v JS Fry and Sons Ltd* [1931] AC 333, HL; and see generally Lawson (1993) 143 NLJ 432.

3   Eg, *Morris Motors Ltd v Lilley* [1959] 3 All ER 737 (falsely claiming to be a franchised dealer); *Reckitt and Colman Products Ltd v Borden Inc* [1990] 1 All ER 873, HL (get-up of goods); *Bowater Windows Ltd v Aspen Windows Ltd* [1999] FSR 759 (copied sales literature). The tort extends to switch selling: *Associated Newspapers plc v Insert Media Ltd* [1991] 3 All ER 535. As to use of the OFT's name, see OFT, (1991) 3 Beeline 7. As to injunctions, see post, para 29.39.

4   Sections 2(1)(i), (j): see ante, para 4.06. As to counterfeiting, see Roberts (1993) 10 Tr L 30. As to brand copies, see Smith (1993) 137 Sol J 822; and ante, para 4.09.

5   TDA, s 2(f), (g) (see ante, para 4.07). Because of the false implication of approval under s 3(3), it is arguable that an offence may be committed simply by falsely representing a personality as using goods: see further Lawson, *Advertising Law*, pp 65–66; Bragg, *Trade Descriptions*, p 29.

6   See *Erven Warnick BV v J Townsend and Sons (Hull) Ltd* [1979] AC 731, HL. But see Adams [1985] JBL 26.

7   Trade Marks Act 1994, ss 10, 92: these are strict liability offences (*R v Keane* [2001] 4 CL 135, CA). But the Act does allow mention of a trade mark by way of comparative advertising: see s 10(6); *Barclays Bank Plc v RBS Advanta Ltd* [1996] Tr LR 262, CA (see 51 CC 1/11); *Vodafone Group plc v Orange Personal Communicator Services Ltd* [1997] FSR 34.

8   See Lawson, *op cit*, note 2, pp 104, 113–17. This law cannot be used to inhibit a free market in vehicle spares: *British Leyland Motor Corp v Armstrong Patents Co Ltd* [1986] AC 577, HL (102 LQR 345; 114 LQR 39); but see now the Copyright, Designs and Patents Act 1988, s 171(3). The Act is also used to protect databases (s 56).

9   CCA, s 44 (breach of regulations: see post, para 8.30); CCA, s 46 (false or misleading advertisements: see post, paras 8.27–28).

10 Eg, EU Regulation 1576/89, defining Scotch whisky: see *Scotch Whisky Association v Glen Kella Distillers Ltd (No 2)* [1997] Eu LR 455.

[8.05]

1   [1893] 1 QB 256, [1891–94] All ER Rep 127, CA. For the formation of contracts, see generally post, para 10.01 *et seq.*

any of that target group who knowingly fulfils them. In this case, a consumer purchased the goods to which the advertisement related from a retailer, so that the £100 contract with the manufacturer is what would today be described as collateral to the retail supply contract;[2] but in other cases it may be a question whether a manufacturer's advertisement might also form part of the retail supply contract.[3] Alternatively, the advertisement may be published by the retail supplier; and it may be possible to spell out that he thereby intends only, eg, a personal quotation.[4]

However, not every advertisement amounts to an offer: it is a question of fact whether the advertisement lacks any intention to create legal relations (see post, para 10.01) and is simply an invitation to treat[5] or a mere puff.[6] This may be the case with a manufacturer's advertisement, eg, sales literature.[6] It is also commonly the case with advertisements by or on behalf of a retailer.[7] If the advertisement does not amount to an offer, then it may be a question in civil law whether it is devoid of all contractual effect as being a mere puff;[6] or whether it amounts to a misrepresentation[8] or induces a mistake (see post, paras 10.14 et seq; 17.11), so affording certain remedies to the disappointed reader obtaining goods from the advertiser on the faith of it.[9]

[8.06] Statutory intervention. Against the foregoing background as to the contractual effect of advertisements (see ante, para 8.05), there has also been significant statutory intervention, primarily concerned with ensuring the truthfulness of claims made:[1]

1   *Trade descriptions*. In Chapter 4, the general TDA rules relating to false statements as to goods and services were considered; and it has been shown that these extend to product endorsement (see ante, para 8.02). However, the TDA makes special provision to deal with false trade descriptions when they are found in advertisements for goods (see post, para 8.07), whilst saying nothing specific about the advertisement of services.

---

2   Eg, the Hoover fiasco: see Shears (1995) 145 NLJ 1754. For collateral contracts by manufacturers, see generally post, para 17.09.

3   See *Esso Petroleum Ltd v Commissioners of Customs and Excise* (set out ante, para 2.08). This could be either alternatively, or as well as, making a contract between the manufacturer and consumer; but it has been argued that the case does not represent a change in the attitude of the courts towards advertising (Cranston, *Consumers and the Law* (3rd edn), pp 51–52). For express terms, see generally post, para 11.07; and for counterfeiting, see ante, para 4.06 and post, para 13.11.

4   *Philp and Co v Knoblauch* 1907 SC 994. But see *Boyers v Duke* [1905] 2 IR 617.

5   Eg, circular requesting tenders (*Spencer v Harding* (1870) LR 5 CP 561). For offers and invitations to treat, see generally post, para 10.02.

6   *Lambert v Lewis* (set out post, para 17.06); *Bowerman v ABTA* [1995] Tr LR 246; and see generally Treitel, *Law of Contract* (10th edn), pp 149, 305–07. As to whether a puff can be a false trade description, see ante, para 4.08.

7   It has been so held in the case of advertisements for auctions, catalogues and price lists, displays of goods in a shop window or on a self-service shelf; see further post, para 10.02.

8   Eg, *Moorehouse v Woolfe* (1882) 46 LT 379 (moneylender advertising 'easy terms'; 125% interest charged); *Word v Stevens* [1993] CLY 1993, Cty Ct (car advertised as 'absolutely immaculate'). For misrepresentation, see generally post, para 17.10.

9   *Contra* where the advertiser is not privy to the retail supply and does not make the advertisement as agent of the retail supplier.

[8.06]

1   See generally Harvey, *Consumer Protection and Fair Trading* (6th edn), Chapter 2; Cranston, *Consumers and the Law* (3rd edn), pp 51–55.

2   *Credit advertising* (see post, para 8.20 *et seq*).

3   *Pricing*. Regulations sometimes require the display of prices (see post, para 8.08); and, in any event, there are prohibitions on misleading price indications (see post, para 8.09).

4   *Food and drink* (see post, para 8.11).

5   *Medicines and drugs* (see post, para 8.12).

6   *Community law*. Article 28 [ex 30] of the Treaty of Rome prohibits all restrictions to the free circulation of goods as well as any measure having equivalent effect. This rule has been used to encourage a negative harmonisation[2] by striking down some discriminatory regulation of advertising by Member States.[3] Additionally, the Community has felt the need for a measure of positive harmonisation[2] to control the growing volume of cross-border advertising, notably on television. Accordingly, the Misleading Advertisements Directive was adopted to lay down minimum standards and later amended to include comparative advertising (see post, para 8.12A). Moreover, as part of the 1992 initiative, there has been adopted Art 95 [ex 100A], which for some purposes allows harmonisation by majority vote (instead of the previous rule of unanimity in all cases, eg, the directives on tobacco advertising.[4]

7   *Miscellaneous*. Among the miscellaneous statutory powers concerned with the protection of target groups in the advertising of goods may be included those relating to the following matters: weights and measures (s 23(1) of the 1985 Act: see ante, para 4.25); trading stamps (s 6 of the 1964 Act: see post, para 15.17); mail order transactions and business advertisements (see ante, para 4.22); printed material;[5] indecent or obscene advertisments;[6] petrol consumption;[7] discrimination;[8] 'host mailing', where a trader inserts a third party's leaflet in his mailings;[9] sale of tobacco to children;[10] and the general power to obtain Part III assurances (see ante, para 6.06). Additionally, there are substantial voluntary controls sponsored by the Advertising Standards

---

2   As to positive and negative harmonisation, see ante, para 1.03A.

3   Article 28 (see generally ante, para 2.13) has been applied to strike down national regulations concerning the advertisement of alcoholic beverages: *Cassis de Dijon* case [1979] ECR 649 (liqueurs); *Commission v France* [1980] ECR 2799 (wine); and see Tayleur (2001) 151 NLJ 859. For a table of restrictions on sales promotions in different EU countries, see Circus, *Sales Promotion Law* (2nd edn), Appendix 8. These may be struck down by EU law: *GB-INNO-BM v Confederation du Commerce Luxembourgeois* [1991] 2 CMLR 801, Eu Ct.

4   See Council Directive 89/622 (as amended), implemented in the Tobacco Products Labelling (Safety) Regulations 1991 SI 1530. After a 1998 Directive containing more stringent restrictions was struck down as being made *ultra vires* under the wrong article (see ante, para 1.03A), it has been adopted afresh under Art 95 and is to come into force in 2002.

5   Any paper or book must contain the name and business address of the printer: Newspaper, Printer and Reading Rooms Repeal Act 1869 (as amended).

6   Indecent Displays (Control) Act 1981: see Stone (1982) 45 MLR 62. For indecent advertisements communicated by post or telephone, see post, para 8.17. See generally Lawson, *Advertising Law*, pp 301–04.

7   See the Energy Act 1976, s 15(1), and the Passenger Car Fuel Consumption Order 1996, SI 1132. For the display of petrol prices, see the orders made under the Prices Acts (post, para 8.08).

8   Race Relations Act 1976, s 29(1); Sex Discrimination Act 1975, s 38(1); Disability Discrimination Act 1995. See generally Lawson, *op cit*, note 6, pp 314–17; and ante, para 4.23.

9   See (1994) 49 CC 4/32. This may infringe the DPA (see ante, para 3.27): DPR, *Personal Data Held Within The Finance Industry* (1994), para 19.

10 Children and Young Persons (Protection from Tobacco) Act 1991, s 4. See also the Tobacco Advertising and Promotion Bill 2001.

Authority and the indirect controls of the Broadcasting Authorities (see ante, para 3.14); and there is pressure for control of labelling claims relating to green matters and energy consumption.[11]

[8.07] Trade descriptions by advertising. The Trade Descriptions Act 1968 makes special provision to deal with the situation 'where in an advertisement[1] a trade description[2] is used in relation to any class of goods'. If the advertisement is for a specific item, application of a false trade description may be clear;[3] but, where the reference is to a class of goods, s 5(3) helpfully explains that:

> In determining for the purposes of this section whether any goods are of a class to which a trade description used in an advertisement relates regard shall be had not only to the form and content of the advertisement but also to the time, place, manner and frequency of its publication and all other matters making is likely or unlikely that a person to whom the goods are supplied would think of the goods as belonging to the class in relation to which the trade description is used in the advertisement.

It has been said that this enables a court to take into account **all** the following:[4]

(i) that the advertisement was contained in an out-of-date periodical, eg, the 'shelf-life' prescribed in the Pricing Code (see post, para 8.10A);

(ii) that publication of the advertisement was recent, whilst the goods were supplied and offered as old stock;[5] and

(iii) that the advertisement had not circulated in the area in which the goods were supplied or offered.[6]

In the foregoing circumstances and for the purposes set out in paragraphs (a) and (b) considered below, s 5(2) introduces the presumption that:

> The trade description shall be taken as referring to all goods of the class, whether or not in existence at the time the advertisement is published ...

The effect of s 5 is thus that any trade description contained in an advertisement is 'used' in relation to goods of a class and thus 'applied' to them by virtue of s 4(1)(c).[7] In these circumstances s 5(2) carefully distinguishes according to whether a retailer is advertising his own wares, or a manufacturer is advertising his products to promote sales of them by retailers. Thus, the presumption introduced by s 5(2) distinguishes between the two s 1 offences (see ante, para 4.03) as follows:

---

11 See NCC, *Green Claims* (1996). The EU-inspired energy labelling scheme may be inaccurate: [1996] 6 Which? 6, 31.

[8.07]

1 'Advertisement' includes a catalogue, a circular and a price list: s 39(1). Compare the CCA definition: see post, para 8.29.

2 For trade descriptions, see ante, para 4.07. Section 5 does not apply to the advertisement of services: see ante, para 8.06.

3 Eg, *Rees v Munday* [1974] 3 All ER 506, DC.

4 Current Law Statutes, Annotation to s 5(3). Misleading advertisements as to prices are now dealt with elsewhere: see post, para 8.10.

5 But see Bragg, *Trade Descriptions*, p 17.

6 Is the test subjective (referring to the particular consumer misled) or objective (referring to the generality of consumers)?

7 For s 4(1)(c), see ante, para 4.04. It may be that comparative advertising can be brought within this provision: Lawson, *Advertising Law*, pp 253–54.

Paragraph (a) offences. Section 5(2) presumes application of the trade description for the purpose of deciding whether the person who both manufactures and sells has applied a false trade description.[8] However, it also extends to the person who innocently advertises goods supplied by another, and s 25 therefore contains a special defence for such advertisers (see post, para 28.16) and s 39(2) makes it clear that the s 5 offence does not extend to editorial comment.

Paragraph (b) offences. Section 5(2) presumes application of the trade description contained in, eg, the manufacturer's advertisement, to goods supplied by another, eg, a retailer.[9]

As both the s 1 offences are ones of strict liability, the Act provides a number of defences to them (see post, para 28.13 *et seq*) and contains power to specify the information to be contained in the advertisements (see ante, para 4.10).

[8.08] Price displays. Whilst the presentation of the weight of goods sold is controlled by the Weights and Measures Acts (see ante, para 4.25), there are two different types of control in relation to the **display** of prices, which should both be distinguished from the **level** of prices (see ante, para 2.12):

1   *The Prices Acts 1974 and 1975*. Section 4 of the 1974 Act (as amended)[1] contains wide powers enabling the Secretary of State to make positive regulations as to the display of the prices of goods and services being sold[2] or supplied by retail; and s 7 and the Schedule make contravention a criminal offence and contain wide, almost common-form, powers of enforcement (see post, Chapter 28). In the 1980s, extensive use was made of these powers;[3] and in 1991 it was then decided to utilise the s 4 powers to implement a series of EU Directives (see generally ante, para 3.10). The present powers are to be found in the Price Marking Order 1999 (SI 3042), which reflect an EU Directive (98/6/EC), and contain two distinct strands for the protection of 'consumers'.[4] First, reg 4(1) imposes a general obligation[5] on retailers (which it calls 'traders'[6]) to show a rounded (regs 10–11) 'selling price' (reg 1(2)), unless the product is sold from bulk (see below), or except in the case of a separate 'advertisement'.[7]

---

8   *British Gas Corp v Lubbock* [1974] 1 All ER 188, DC (accessories). It would appear that in some of the cases referred to in note 9 below the charge could have been laid under s 1(1)(a).

9   Eg, *Rees v Munday* (above); *Chidwick v Beer* [1974] RTR 415, DC; *Furniss v Scholes* [1974] RTR 133, DC.

[8.08]

1   As substituted by s 16(1) of the Price Commission Act 1977. Without prejudice to the generality of these powers, s 4(2) of the 1974 Act (as amended) spells out some examples.

2   The expression 'sale of goods' may include any conditional sale or hp agreement: Counter-Inflation Act 1973, s 21(5). Curiously, this provision does not appear to have been amended so as to refer to the CCA.

3   For the statutory instruments for the time being in force, see Thomas and Clarke, *Encyclopedia of Consumer Law*; for the prohibition of false pricing claims, see (post, para 8.09); and for the power to control credit advertisements, see ante, para 8.02.

4   'Consumer' means 'any individual who buys a product for purposes that do not fall within the sphere of his commercial or professional activity' (reg 1(2)).

5   It does not apply to goods supplied during the course of a service, eg, a plumber supplying a new tap (see ante, para 2.05); nor to sales by auction (see post, para 10.10); nor of works of art or antiques (reg 3).

6   'Trader' means 'any person who sells or offers for sale products which fall within his commercial or professional activity' (reg 1(2)).

7   'Advertisement' means 'any form of advertisement which is made in order to promote the sale of a product but does not include any advertisement by means of which the trader intends to encourage a consumer to enter a "distance contract" (also defined in reg 1(2)), a catalogue, a price list, a container or a label' (reg 1(2)).

Second, reg 5 requires most such 'traders' to indicate 'unit prices'[8] for all 'products sold from bulk',[9] or under Parts IV or V of the Weights and Measures Act, or pre-packaged (see ante, para 4.25). However, there are exempted from this unit-pricing rule all the following (reg 5(3)): all advertisements of the type listed in Sched 2, eg, shown on TV, damaged goods sold at a reduced price; goods sold at a unit price identical to the selling price, eg, goods sold in a 1 kilo pack exhibiting a price per kilo; pre-packaged goods in a constant quantity and sold in a 'small shop', by an 'itinerant trader', or from a vending machine (see the definitions in reg 1). In respect of both types of control, the price must *prima facie* be shown in sterling (reg 6) and clearly include VAT (regs 7, 9).

2   *Section 26 of the Consumer Protection Act 1987 (CPA).* Whilst the above provisions are generally positive in flavour, specifying how prices shall be displayed, s 26 contains a power to make regulation which seems rather more **negative**. Section 26 mentions two purposes for which regulations may be made: first, as regards price indications for the retail supply of any goods, services or accommodation; and second, to facilitate enforcement of s 20 (see post, para 8.10). Under s 26, there have been made the Price Indication Regulations 1991 (SI No 199) to deal with traders who choose to charge a different price when the customer pays for goods, services or accommodation by different payment methods, eg, payment by cash, as against cheque or payment card. The Regulations apply whenever such a 'price'[10] is stated generally either orally or in writing by a trader who does not intend that price to apply to all acceptable methods of payments: they do not apply where the price discrimination consists only of a charge made for instalment credit (reg 2(4)); nor to supplies by a club to its members (reg 2(5)); nor to private sales (reg 2(6)); nor to supplies of motor fuel (reg 2(1)). The duty is for that trader to provide before contract a statement in a specified manner either of the difference in price or percentage difference.[11] Regulation 8 makes contravention an offence and also employs the CPA defences, etc, to misleading price indications under ss 24(3), 39, 40 (see post, Chapter 28).

Enforcement of s 26 regulations is placed in the hands of the local weights and measures departments;[12] and compliance with the regulations will be a defence to s 20 proceedings (see post, para 8.09).

---

8   'Unit price' means the final price, including VAT and all other taxes (eg, petrol tax), for one kilogram, etc, or in respect of the products specified in Schedule 1, the final price for the corresponding unit of quantity set out in that Schedule, or, where products are sold by number, the final price for one individual item of the product' (reg 1(2)).

9   'Products sold from bulk' means 'products which are not pre-packaged and are weighed or measured at the request of the consumer' (reg 1(2)). As to pre-packaged solid food presented as a liquid, take the 'net drained weight' (reg 1(2)): see reg 8. As to 'Metric Martyrs', see ante, para 4.24.

10   'Price' is defined (by reg 2(2), (3)) by reference to s 20(6) of the CPA: see post, para 8.09. As to ticket tout regulations, see Clayson (1995) 14 Tr LR 321.

11   Regulation 3; and for the specified manner of price displays, see regs 5–7. Alternatively, the trader can give actual prices to the individual consumer (reg 3(3)); or generally by notice at public entrances, with special provisions for petrol stations and restaurants (reg 4).

12   Weights and Measures Act 1985 (see ante, para 4.24); Prices Act 1974, s 7 and Sched, para 6; CPA, s 27. See further post, Chapter 28. It has been pointed out that the prosecution has a lesser burden of proof under s 26 regulations than as regards misleading price indications: OFT, (1992) 1 Beeline 8.

[8.09] Misleading price indications. Attempts were first made to tackle false or misleading prices in the TDA (s 11) and then the Bargain Offer Orders. These unsatisfactory provisions have now been replaced by Part III of the CPA, of which s 20 creates new offences where a trader 'in the course of any business of his' (see below) gives to any private consumer (see post, para 8.10) a misleading (see post, para 8.09A) indication as to the price at which any goods,[1] services,[2] accommodation,[3] or facilities[4] are available, whether from himself or another.[5] These pricing offences are clearly restricted to trade supplies to consumers,[6] but do extend to both goods and services. The offence concentrates on the 'price', defining this as 'the aggregate of the sums required to be paid by a consumer ... in respect of the supply'.[7] In *R v Kettering Magistrates' Court ex p MRB Insurance Brokers Ltd*:[8]

> M Ltd arranged a contract of motor insurance and also entered into a regulated consumer credit agreement to facilitate payment of the insurance premiums. In making the latter, M Ltd quoted a substantially inaccurate APR (see post, para 8.21). The court held that the fact that the APR became a term of the credit agreement did not preclude its being an 'indication' within s 20(1).

Douglas Brown J pointed out that the inaccurate APR was quoted in the contract and said that 'every term is an indication for the purposes of the Act; not every indication is a term of the contract' (at 356j).

The scope of the offence was considered in *Warwickshire County Council v Johnson*:[9]

> J was employed as a branch manager of Dixons. With Dixons' authority, he placed a notice outside the shop stating – 'We will beat any TV HiFi and Video price by £20 on the spot'. Whilst that notice was displayed, a customer saw a TV offered for sale elsewhere in the area for £159.95. The customer demanded to purchase an identical set from J's shop for £139.95 (£159.95 – £20). J refused to sell it at the reduced price, his normal price being £179.95, but was prepared to sell for £159.95 (£179.95 – £20). J was prosecuted under s 20(1) of the CPA.

[8.09]

1 As to 'goods', see s 45(1); and further ante, para 4.33. For a history of Part III, see Bragg, *Trade Descriptions*, pp 113–15.

2 'Services' includes the provision of credit, banking or insurance services (s 22(1)(a)), but not when provided under a contract of employment (s 22(2)). 'Credit' has the same meaning as in the CCA (s 22(5)): see ante, para 5.21. It does not extend to Euro-services: 1992 SI 3218, Sched 9.

3 As to 'accommodation', see s 23, which excludes from the CPA most disposals of interests in land other than new residential property, whilst keeping within the Act goods, services or facilities supplied as part of the same transaction (s 23(2)). As to 'services, accommodation or facilities', compare TDA, s 14: see ante, para 4.16. As to misdescriptions of real property, see ante, para 4.03.

4 This would catch shopping facilities, eg, a closing-down sale, cf *Westminster CC v Ray Allen (Manshops) Ltd* (set out ante, para 4.16): Bragg, *op cit*, note 1, p 142.

5 Section 20(3)(b). So it is an offence to mis-state the price charged by another trader: *Denard v Burton Retail Ltd* [1997] CLY 973, DC (franchise). Similarly, it is irrelevant whether the indication is misleading to all consumers or only some of them: s 20(3)(c).

6 But not to any particular consumer: *MFI v Hibbert* [1995] CLY 741, DC. As to 'consumers', see post, para 8.10. Cf the TDA, which also protects traders and penalises purchases by traders (see ante, para 4.03A). Regrettably, it is not entirely clear whether there must be an actual supply; and it does not deal expressly with mixed use (cf post, para 18.18).

7 As to price, see s 20(6), including any method to determine an aggregate. What of a manufacturer's advertisement 'up to 50% off'; or an 'estimate'?

8 [2000] 2 All ER (Comm) 353, DC.

9 [1993] AC 583, [1993] 1 All ER 299, HL.

There were only two issues before the House of Lords; namely, (1) whether for the purposes of s 20(1) the notice was misleading (yes: see post, para 8.09A); and (2) whether J could commit a s 20(2) offence. Section 20(2) says that a person shall be guilty of an offence if, 'in the course of any business of his', he gives a misleading price indication.[10] The Divisional Court construed this phrase in the sense of the occupation of J,[11] bearing in mind the CPA definition of 'business' as including 'a trade or profession' (s 45(1): see ante, para 4.33). The court worried that, if an employee could not be convicted under s 20, he could not be convicted under the by-pass provision (s 40: see post, para 28.12). An argument that this could be avoided by construing 'business of his' in s 40 as business of the employer (see below) was rejected by the House (at 303g–304j: see further post, para 28.12). However, the House of Lords unanimously held that J was not guilty of the offence charged for two reasons. First, s 20 was designed to replace s 11 of the TDA, under which both an employer and employee could probably be strictly liable for a pricing offence and this remains the position under s 1 of the TDA (see ante, para 4.03A); whereas the different wording of s 20(1) must refer to a business of which the defendant is 'either the owner or in which he has a controlling interest' (at 304). Second, they found decisive an explanation of the s 20 wording given when the Bill was before Parliament (see ante, para 1.04). Nevertheless, their Lordships found it strange 'that the person actually responsible for what happened, as [J] clearly was, should be immune from conviction' (at 304). But was J 'responsible' when he appears to have been carrying out Dixons' policy? It has been said that the Divisional Court followed the traditional criminal law policy of attributing responsibility to the actor, whereas the House of Lords looked instead to the policy of the legislation.[12]

[8.09A] Misleading. For the purposes of determining whether there has been a misleading price indication within s 20 (see ante, para 8.09), the CPA lays down in s 21 an extensive definition of what is 'misleading'. It provides that (s 21(1)):

> ... an indication given to any consumer is misleading as to a price if what is conveyed by the indication, or what those consumers might reasonably be expected to infer from the indication, includes ...

certain listed matters. It is to be noted that this formula makes it clear that the test of price **given**[1] is objective[2] and extends to omissions;[3] but it does not mention disclaimers and it remains to be seen whether they will be effective.[4] The list is as follows, dealing with both the price itself and any method of determining the price (s 21(1)):

---

10   The certified question from the Divisional Court concerned the same phrase in s 20(2)(a) – presumably because the claim only became misleading after it was given (see post, para 8.09A): but see Scott [1993] JBL at 492, note 6.

11   (1991) 11 Tr LR 76, DC. Popplewell J argued that this must have been the intention of Parliament, bearing in mind the existence of multiple retailers (as here) and the by-pass procedure (see below): Oughton [1993] JBL at 47–48; Holgate (1993) 10 Tr L at 24–25.

12   Scott [1993] JBL at 494.

[8.09A]

1   As to when the price indication is 'given', see *Toys 'R' Us v Gloucestershire CC* (below; where goods displayed on retailer's shelf; see Holgate (1994) 13 Tr LR 410).

2   *Holman v CWS Ltd* [2001] CCLR 2777, DC. Cf TDA, s 3: see ante, para 4.08.

3   Eg, a compulsory extra charge. What about an optional charge? As to VAT, see Bragg, *Trade Descriptions*, pp 127–28. As to the difficulty with mail order catalogues, see Bragg, p 124.

4   See Bragg, *ibid*, p 118. If it can be disclaimed, is the test of disclaimer the same as for the TDA (see ante, para 4.09)?

(a) The price is less that it in fact is, eg, overcharging.[5]

(b) The applicability of the price does not depend on circumstances on which it does depend, eg, quoted price only available to cash customers.[6]

(c) The price covers matters for which an additional charge is in fact made, eg, delivery charges.[7]

(d) That a person expects the price to change when in fact he has no such expectation, eg, that a manufacturer's recommended price is to increase.[8]

(e) The facts upon which a consumer draws a price comparison are not what in fact they are, eg, never knowingly undersold.[9]

Section 21(2) applies the same rules to the method of determining or calculating the price, eg, price per pound, stating a weight, an example which may also fall within the Weights and Measures Act 1985 (see ante, paras 4.25; 8.08).

In *Warwickshire CC v Johnson* (set out ante, para 8.09), the question arose whether promises later dishonoured could be misleading. The Divisional Court treated the statement in the advertisement as a continuing offer[10] and concluded that it was therefore misleading when taken up by a consumer. The House of Lords approved the decision that a notice could be rendered misleading by refusal to honour it without reference to any other provisions, saying that to hold otherwise would restrict the efficacy of this part of the consumer protection legislation (at 302g–j). See further post, para 8.10.

[8.10] Offences. Giving a misleading price indication (see ante, para 8.09A) is only an offence where it is given by a person in the course of his business (see ante, para 8.09) to one or more (s 20(3)(c): see below) consumers. A **consumer** in relation to goods means one who takes 'for his own private use or consumption';[1] and in relation to services, accommodation or facilities one who takes 'otherwise than for the purposes of any

---

5 Section 21(1)(a). Eg, *R v Kettering Justices, ex p MRB Insurance Brokers Ltd* (set out ante, para 8.09). On overcharging: see Bragg, *op cit*, note 3, pp 120–21; *contra* Fidler (1989) 139 NLJ 943. Bar-coding (see ante, para 2.06) may differ from shelf-pricing: see [1996] 6 Which? 20. Discrepancies from bar-coding can be obviated by instructing the cashier always to charge the lower price: *Toys 'R' Us v Gloucester CC* (1994) 13 Tr LR 276, DC.

6 Section 21(1)(b). As to the cash customer example, cf CCA, s 45: set out post, para 8.27. Similarly, if the quoted price does not apply to part-exchange deals (see generally, ante, para 2.09); or misleading 'free' offers (Bragg, *op cit*, note 3, pp 129–30).

7 Section 21(1)(c). Eg, *Toyota (GB) Ltd v North Yorkshire CC* (1998) 162 JP 794, DC. *Cf MFI Warehouses Ltd v Nattrass* (set out ante, para 4.17).

8 Section 21(1)(d). Eg, falsely indicating foreknowledge of a price change to be recommended by the manufacturer on future stock deliveries.

9 Section 21(1)(e). Eg, *MGN Ltd v Ritter* [1997] CLY 974, DC; *DSG Retail Ltd v Oxfordshire CC* [2001] 4 CL 121, DC. See further s 21(3).

10 It clearly is not an offer in the contractual sense (see post, para 10.20). Nor does the CPA contain any provision giving an extended meaning to 'offer'; cf TDA s 6 (see ante, para 4.05). However, the case law on s 14 has developed a similar notion of a continuing statement: see *Wings Ltd v Ellis* (set out ante, para 4.17).

[8.10]

1 Section 20(6)(a). Cf UCTA, s 12(1)(c) (see post, para 18.18), which incorporates a similar test in relation to the goods rather than what a person 'might wish'. *Contra* the TDA, which also protects traders and penalises purchasers: see ante, para 4.03. As to part-exchange, see Bragg, *Trade Descriptions*, p 122. 'Consumer' includes a tso (see post, para 28.03): *Toys 'R' Us v Gloucestershire CC* (1994) 13 Tr LR 276, DC.

business of his'.[2] For the purposes of a s 20 offence, it is immaterial (s 20(3)): whether (a) the person giving the indication is acting as principal or agent, eg, the second-hand shop selling goods as agent for private sellers; (b) he is the person from whom the services, etc, are available (see below); (c) the indication misled some or all consumers, eg, withdrawal of a pensioner discount.

At this point, s 20(1) in laying down the offences distinguishes according to whether or not the price indication was misleading when given (see ante, para 8.09A). Suppose a retailer's advertisement is accurate when published, eg, as to a manufacturer's recommended price, which later becomes inaccurate, eg, because the manufacturer alters his recommendation. Bear in mind that an indication is **given**, according to *Wings Ltd v Ellis* (set out ante, para 4.17) every time the advertisement is read. So, offences may be committed as follows:

1 *Misleading when given.* According to s 20(1):

> Subject to the following provisions of this Part, a person shall be guilty of an offence if, in the course of any business of his, he gives (by any means whatever) to any consumers an indication which is misleading as to the price at which any goods, services, accommodation or facilities are available (whether generally or from particular persons).

If the manufacturer changes his recommendation before a consumer reads the advertisement, there may be a s 20(1) offence.[3] A defendant charged with this offence[4] is granted two special defences not available under s 20(2) (below): he may escape conviction by proving (a) due diligence (ss 24(5), 39(5): see post, para 28.13); or (b) that he was a prior party in the chain of distribution, eg, importer, recommending a price which he reasonable believed 'was for the most part being followed'.[5]

2 *Subsequently misleading.* Section 20(2) provides that a person shall also be guilty of an offence if:

(a) in the course of any business of his, he has given an indication to any consumers which, after it was given, has become misleading as mentioned in subsection (1) above; and

(b) some or all of those consumers might reasonably be expected to rely on the indication at a time after it has become misleading; and

(c) he fails to take all such steps as are reasonable to prevent those consumers from relying on the indication.

It should be noted that there is no due diligence defence available under s 20(2): this is because lack of diligence is part of the offence. So, if the above manufacturer changes his recommended price after the consumer has read the advertisement, but before the

---

2   Section 20(6)(b), (c). Cf UCTA, s 12(1)(a) (see above). What about the businessman who, to the knowledge of the supplier, puts his private purchases through the books of his business, or of the private consumer who shows a trade card to get a trade discount?

3   *DSG Retail Ltd v Oxfordshire CC* [2001] 4 CL 121, DC (display notice did not contain the limitations to which it was subject). See further the Pricing Code, para 1.6: see post, para 8.10A.

4   It may extend to overcharging, by combining s 20(1) with s 21(1)(b): Bragg, *Trade Descriptions*, p 126.

5   Section 24(4). Is the manufacturer precluded from relying on this defence if he knows at the time his advertisement is read of a discount war between retailers of his product? See s 24(4)(d) and Bragg, *ibid*, p 145.

consumer enters the transaction, there may be a s 20(2) offence. This has caused difficulty where a retailer does not honour his price promises. *Warwickshire CC v Johnson* (set out ante, para 8.09) appears to suggest that there might be a s 20(2) offence. However, it has been strenuously argued that s 20(2) refers only to a change of **external** circumstance, not a change of mind; that s 21(1)(d) was not contravened because J always intended the price reduction (which he granted on other goods) right up until the moment of confrontation with this customer; and that the offence should not extend to broken promises.[6] It may be that this issue simply was not considered in *Warwickshire CC v Johnson*; and that on this basis there can be supported later cases denying application of s 20(2) to broken price promises.[7]

Subject to a time limit (s 20(5): see post, para 28.07), a person acting in the course of his business may *prima facie* commit either of the above offences,[8] whatever his function in the chain of distribution (s 20(3): above). However, under s 24 it is a defence for the defendant to show any of the following:[9] he is an advertiser innocently taking an advertisement (s 24(3): see post, para 28.16); or the indication was given through the media but not in an advertisement;[10] or that he complied with pricing regulations.[11] Other provisions make relevant compliance with the price code (see post, para 8.10A).

[8.10A] Pricing codes of practice. To increase the flexibility of the above misleading pricing rules, it was decided to introduce a pricing code with statutory backing.[1] Accordingly, s 25(1) of the CPA lays down that:

> The Secretary of State may, after consulting the Director General of Fair Trading and such other persons as the Secretary of State considers it appropriate to consult, by order approve any code of practice issued (whether by the Secretary of State or another person) for the purpose of –
>
> (a) giving practical guidance with respect to any of the requirements of section 20 above; and
>
> (b) promoting what appear to the Secretary of State to be desirable practices as to the circumstances and manner in which any person gives an indication as to the price at which any goods, services, accommodation or facilities[2] are available or indicates any other matter in respect of which any such indication may be misleading.

---

6 See Oughton [1993] JBL at 45–46, commenting on the DC judgment; and Bragg, *ibid*, p 125, writing in 1990.

7 See *Link Stores Ltd v Harrow LBC* [2001] 3 CL 108.

8 As to offences, see s 20(4): see generally post, para 28.04. They give rise to no civil right of action nor render the contract illegal: see post, para 8.10A.

9 The burden of proof is clearly cast on the defendant. As to the weight of that burden, see post, para 28.13.

10 Section 24(2). Eg, an author mis-stating the price of his book during a TV interview. Even if he did so knowingly?

11 Section 24(1). Unlike the general safety requirement (see ante, para 4.33), compliance is not an automatic defence unless the trader follows the practices designated in the regulations (see ante, para 8.08).

[8.10A]

1 As to such statutory orders, see s 25(4). There is power for the minister to modify or withdraw his authority from a code (s 25(3)).

2 As to 'goods, services, accommodation or facilities', see ante, para 8.09.

The Bill originally envisaged that compliance with the code should be a complete defence, but this was subsequently modified by s 25(2) so that non-compliance with the code 'shall not of itself give rise to any criminal or civil[3] liability', whereas compliance may be relied on by a person charged with a s 20 offence (see ante, para 8.10). Thus, it has a status like that of the Highway Code and has the effect of putting the burden of proof on the defendant, so making it more readily enforceable.

The Code.[4] Addressed to the retailer, the Code gives advice on all the following matters:[5] express comparison with his own previous price;[6] introductory offers and special promotions intended whilst stocks last (para 1.3); comparisons with prices related to different circumstances (para 1.4), eg, special prices for 'seconds' or kit-form; comparisons with other traders' prices (para 1.5), eg, 'If you can buy for less, we will refund the difference'; comparisons with recommended prices;[7] flash, sale and free offers;[8] quoted prices misleading because of other factors;[9] and the price of credit (para 2.2.18), which refers to regulations made under the CCA (see post, para 8.27).

The end result of Part III of the CPA should thus be a flexible, three-tiered scheme as to what constitutes misleading pricing: the general principles are enshrined in the Act (see ante, para 8.09); but more detailed matters are confined to regulations (see ante, para 8.08); and practical guidance for traders set out in plain English (see post, para 11.08) in the codes.

[8.11] Food and drink. Leaving aside the special rules concerning the advertising of alcoholic beverages,[1] the Food Safety Act 1990 (see generally ante, para 4.26) creates several offences connected with the advertising of food or drink for human consumption.[2]

(a) *Food safety requirement*. It being an offence to sell food not complying with the food safety requirement (see ante, para 4.27), the Act prohibits the advertising[3] of food

---

3   Non-compliance gives rise to no civil right of action (s 41(2): see generally ante, para 3.21), nor does it render any contract illegal (s 41(3): see generally post, para 10.19). Cf the food code: see ante, para 4.26.

4   Consumer Protection (Code of Practice for Traders on Price Indications) Approval Order 1988 SI 2078. The Code is to be enforced by Trading Standards Officers (Arts 4, 5). For its effect in court proceedings, see Arts 3, 6. The Code is set out in Thomas, *Encyclopedia of Consumer Law*, para 2-1035. The DTI have set up a committee to monitor the working of the Code: OFT, 1991-AR 19. See criticism of the code in [1994] 5 Which? 20–22.

5   The Code also contains separate sections dealing with Price Indications which have become misleading after being given (Part 3) and Sale of New Houses (Part 4).

6   Paragraph 1.2.2 introduces a test of offering the goods for at least 28 consecutive days during the previous 6 months at the same premises. See *AG Stanley Ltd v Surrey CC* [1996] CLY 1166, DC (Clayson 15 Tr L 229); and generally Bragg, *Trade Descriptions*, pp 136–37.

7   Paragraph 1.6. Where such recommended prices are particularly out of touch with retail prices charged, such comparisons are 'banned'. See Bragg, *ibid*, pp 132–34.

8   As to reductions already printed on packaging ('flash offers') see para 1.7; as to special sale prices, see para 1.9; and as to 'free offers', see para 1.10; and ante, para 2.08.

9   Paragraph 2.2. Eg, prices which do not mention optional extras, postage and packing, VAT, service charges.

[8.11]

1   See the Customs and Excise Act 1952, ss 162–64 (as amended).

2   For offences, see s 35; and for presumptions, see s 3. For offences by corporations (s 36) and the defences of another's default (s 20) and due diligence (s 21), see post, para 28.07 *et seq*.

3   'Advertisement' is defined by s 53(1). Compare the other statutory definitions of advertisement: see post, paras 8.12.

which fails to comply with that requirement (s 8(2)), though providing a special defence of innocent publication (s 22. See further post, para 28.16).

(b) *False descriptions*. Section 15(1) makes it an offence to provide a label in connection with the sale or display of any food which either (i) falsely describes the food[4] or (ii) is likely to mislead the ordinary man[5] as to the nature or substance or quality of the food (see ante, para 4.28). A separate offence is committed by anyone who publishes an advertisement which does either of those things (s 6(2)). Nevertheless many such false descriptions are likely to continue to be prosecuted under the TDA.

(c) *Positive labelling*. Besides not being untruthful, Parliament has also been concerned that labelling should be positively required to state matters connected with food.[6] Besides this, the 1990 Act contains sweeping new regulation-making powers, which extend to, for instance, antibiotic residues in meat, food irradiation, the implementation of EU obligations[7] and novel foods.[8] Under the regulating-making power there have been made the Labelling of Food Regulations.[9] Inevitably, there will always be those who want labels to contain more information;[10] and, if a food label makes a medicinal claim,[11] it is dealt with as a medicine (and post, para 8.12). However, it may be that, rather than increase the foregoing **positive** requirements, it might be more satisfactory to adopt the US **negative** position that nothing may be claimed on a food label without prior official authorisation.

[8.12] Medicines and drugs. Leaving aside the prohibitions of advertisements relating to remedies for certain specific diseases[1] or controlled drugs,[2] Parts V and VI of the Medicines Act 1968 are concerned with the promoting, labelling and packaging of 'medicinal products' (see generally ante, para 4.29). The 1968 Act distinguishes in its treatment of statements between those made (a) on any label attached to the medicine, or

---

4   But see *Cheshire CC v Mornflake* (1993) 157 JP 1011 (can help cut down heart disease: DC acquitted as ambiguous). The statement may also fall within the TDA: see ante, para 4.07.

5   *Concentrating Foods Ltd v Champ* [1944] KB 342, DC, *per* Wrottesley J at 350. The Act expressly states that mere accuracy is not necessarily a defence (s 15(4)) and also extends the section to include misleading presentation (s 15(3)).

6   Eg, *Hackney LBC v Cedar Trading Ltd* [1999] CLY 2603 (Coca-cola labelled in Dutch; DC convicted; see 149 NLJ 1111). Positive labels will have little impact in the absence of consumer education: Cayne and Trebilcock (1973) 23 University of Toronto LJ 396 at 406.

7   See Lawson (1993) 143 NLJ 520 and 557; and note 10, below. For language requirements, see *Geffroy and Casino France SNC's Reference* [2001] All ER (EC) 222, ECJ.

8   Eg, genetically modified foods: see [1999] 3 Which? 8. For new EU measures on GM foods, see (1999) 18 Tr L 322.

9   1996 SI 1499 (as amended), eg, 'use by' and 'best before' dates; Holgate (1995) 14 Tr L 408; [1996] 4 Which? 28. See generally O'Keefe, *Encyclopedia of Food and Drugs*.

10 Eg, as to food claims ([1993] 5 Which? 15; [1995] 8 Which? 14); eco-labels. The government is committed to clear labelling: *Modern Markets: Confident Consumers* (1999, Cm 4410) para 6.8. The Food Standards Agency (see ante, para 4.26) is developing labelling guidelines for industry, eg, 'fresh', 'natural', 'fat-free'.

11 See *Cheshire CC v Mornflake Oats* (1993) 12 Tr LR 111, DC (ambiguous claim that cut down heart disease). There is a voluntary code: see [2001] 2 Which? 4.

[8.12]

1   Eg, Cancer Act 1939, s 4 (as amended); Health and Medicines Act 1988, s 23 (aids test kits).

2   Misuse of Drugs Act 1971, s 4: see generally ante, para 4.29.

its container or package, or leaflet to accompany products[3] and (b) promotions independent of the goods by advertisement or representation:

(a) *Labels*. Part V empowers the minister to make regulations for the purpose of ensuring that medicinal products are correctly described, readily identifiable and contain any appropriate warning or instruction, and to promote safety.[4] The Act makes it an offence[5] in the course of business to have in one's possession for the purposes of sale or supply a medicinal product which contravenes any such regulations (s 85(3)), or which is falsely or misleadingly described by that labelling (s 85(5)).

(b) *Promotions*. Part VI of the Act seeks to control false or misleading advertisements[6] and representations.[7] Section 93 makes it an offence for a 'commercially interested party'[8] to issue or cause to be issued a false or misleading advertisement relating to medicinal products (93(1)); or for a person carrying on a 'relevant business' (s 93(4)) to make a false or misleading[9] representation relating to a medicinal product (s 93(3)). Section 95 contains powers to regulate advertisements and representations; and there are also powers to impose further controls on advertisements directed at practitioners[10] and for the licensing authority to require copies of advertisements (s 97).

More modern regulations tend to be made jointly under the 1968 Act and s 2 of the ECA to implement Directives;[11] and these provisions may be enforceable by Stop Now Orders (see ante, para 6.08).

[8.12A] Misleading advertisements.[1] Pursuant to EU Directives,[2] there has been introduced the Control of Misleading Advertisement Regulations[3] with the object of curbing the following:

---

3 'Label', 'container', 'packet' and 'leaflet' are all defined by s 132(1) of the Medicines Act 1968. Homeopathic medicines are mostly excluded: see [1996] 3 Which? 26.

4 Section 85(1), (2), which have been extensively used. There are special powers to make regulations with regard to leaflets (s 86), containers (ss 87, 88), automated machines (s 89) and medicated animal foodstuffs (s 90). As to instructions generally, see post, para 18.28 *et seq*.

5 For offences, see s 91. For the special defences of default of another (s 121) and warranty (s 122), see post, para 28.13 *et seq*.

6 'Advertisements' are elaborately defined by s 92. Compare the other statutory definitions: see ante, para 8.11 and post, paras 8.12A; 8.29.

7 'Representations' are defined in s 92(5) as meaning 'any statement or undertaking (whether constituting a condition or a warranty or not) which consists of spoken words other than words falling within subsection (2)'. Compare the CCA, s 189(1): see post, para 16.08.

8 A 'commercially interested party' is defined by s 92(4), and includes a manufacturer, wholesaler or retailer.

9 The 1968 Act is really only interested in misleading descriptions of medicinal properties: s 93(7); *R v Rousell* (1989) 88 Cr App R 140.

10 Section 96: as to the effect of such warnings on such liability, see post, paras 17.30; 18.28 *et seq*. This is quite apart from the separate statutory controls over trade publications found in Part VII of the Act.

11 Medicines (Advertising) Regulations 1994, SI No 1932 (as amended).

[8.12A]

1 See generally Lowe and Woodroffe, *Consumer Law and Practice* (5th edn), paras 17.26–33; Moore [1986] JBL 72; Glass (1989) 139 NLJ 1643.

2 Misleading Advertisements Directives 84/450/EEC and 97/55/EC.

3 1988 SI 915 (as amended by 2000 SI 914), made under the ECA, s 2 (see ante, para 1.03A).

1 Most misleading 'advertisements'[4] carried by the media to promote trade in the supply of goods and services. 'Misleading' is defined by reg 2(2) as an advertisement that both (a) 'deceives or is likely to deceive' and (b) therefore affects the economic behaviour of consumers.[5]

2 Some 'comparative' advertising, which is defined thus (reg 2A):

> An advertisement is comparative if in any way, either expressly or by implication, it identifies a competitor or goods or services offered by a competitor.

According to reg 4A, a comparative advertisement shall be permitted only if it does not infringe any of the following: (i) it is not misleading (see above); (ii) 'it compares goods or services meeting the same needs or intended for the same purpose'; (iii) 'it objectively compares one or more material, relevant, verifiable and representative features of those goods and services, which may include price'; (iv) it does not create confusion in the market place; (v) it does not denigrate the trade marks (see ante, para 8.02), or other distinguishing marks, etc, of a competitor; (vi) it does not confuse designations of origin (see ante, para 4.10); (vii) it does not take unfair advantage of a competitor's trade or distinguishing mark; (viii) it does not present goods or services as imitations or replicas of a competitor's goods.

In implementing these Directives, government policy that nothing should hinder the work of the existing procedures for the control of advertising (see below) led to the formulation of the new powers as a long-stop. The regulations divide misleading advertisements as follows (reg 4):

(a) In the case of a 'broadcast advertisement', a duty is cast upon the broadcasting authority, eg, the IBA (see ante, para 3.14), to consider any such complaint (reg 4(2)).

(b) With regard to other advertisements, the complaint must first be considered by the appropriate body, which is likely to be the local trading standards authority (see ante, para 3.05) or the Advertising Standards Authority (ASA: see ante, para 3.14), but could in the last resort be the OFT (see ante, para 3.03), eg, internet advertisements (see post, para 8.17).

Only where the above procedure has failed to deal adequately with the complaint (reg 4(3)) do the regulations require the OFT to consider any reasonable complaint as to misleading advertising;[5] for instance, a complaint by the ASA of repeated publication of a misleading advertisement notwithstanding ASA warnings.[6] As a first resort, the Director has adopted the practice of seeking suitable assurances from the advertiser.[7] However, if

---

4 'Advertisement' is defined in reg 2(1). Cf other statutory definitions referred to ante, para 8.12. The Regulations do not apply to 'investment advertisements': reg 3. Are they wide enough to cover internet advertisements?

5 Regulations 4(1), (2). The Director must have regard to the public interest and to the desirability of encouraging control by self-regulation (reg 4(4)). As to his obtaining and disclosing information, see reg 7.

6 Eg, the activity reported in (1992) 9 Tr LR 39.

7 See OFT, 1994-AR, 31; 1998-AR, 28–29; 1999-AR, 27–29; 2000-AR 37, 44; and generally (2001) 29 Fair Trading 19.

appropriate, the Director[8] may institute High Court proceedings for a Stop Now Order[9] to prohibit that or further publication (regs 6(1), (2), (6)). Thus, only repetition of injuncted advertisements will amount to an offence.[10]

There may be some overlap between these rules and the following: (i) trade descriptions (see ante, para 4.02 *et seq*); (ii) misleading pricing (see ante, para 8.10); (iii) the CCA advertising regulations (see post, para 8.30) and (iv) the UTCC Regulations (see post, para 11.12).

PARTICULAR TYPES OF RESTRICTION

[8.13] Shops. Because so many retail sales take place at the retailer's premises, a significant control of sales is indirectly provided by planning restrictions, especially on the siting of shops and markets (see ante, para 6.02), and discrimination legislation (see ante, para 4.23). Apart from special controls for particular types of business (see ante, para 6.05), general controls were consolidated in the Shops Act 1950, which dealt with two matters within the scope of this work:

1 *Hours of closing*. Part I of the 1950 Act laid down hours of closing and early closing, but has now been repealed.[1]

2 *Sunday closing*. Part IV contained some long-standing restrictions on Sunday closing,[2] but has now been replaced by the Sunday Trading Act 1994, likewise imposing criminal sanctions.[3] Central to the 1994 Act is the definition of a 'shop' as meaning 'any premises where there is carried on a trade or business consisting wholly or mainly of the sale of goods' (Sched 1, para 1). This looks to a number of elements. First, it requires premises on which designated activity is carried on: there is no definition, which may cause difficulty with forecourts, markets, and telephone mail order businesses.[4] Second, on those premises there must be carried on a trade or business.[5] Third, the business activity on those premises must consist wholly or

---

8 In some Member States consumer associations have been given the right to proceed at law against misleading advertisements. For class actions, see generally post, para 17.05.

9 See ante, para 6.08. Except where an interlocutory injunction is concerned, the court must first be satisfied that the advertisement is misleading (reg 6(1)). For a shift of the burden of proof, see regs 6(3)–(5). For injunctions, see post, para 29.39.

10 *Director General of Fair Trading v Tobyward* [1989] 2 All ER 266. *Contra* price indications: see ante, para 8.09.

[8.13]

1 Deregulation Act 1994, s 23: see ante, para 5.10.

2 It has been decided that these restrictions did not infringe Art 28 [ex 30] of the Treaty of Rome (see ante, para 2.13).

3 See generally, Askham, *The Sunday Trading Act 1994*, Chapter 1; Envis (1994) 144 NLJ 1176.

4 Askham, *ibid*, paras 2.56–62.

5 There is no definition in the Act of 'trade or business'. Cf s 1 of the TDA: see ante, para 4.03. Does it extend to outdoor car boot sales (see post, para 8.13A)?

mainly[6] of a sale of goods, eg, auction houses. It does not include the service sector, such as shops specialising in the hiring out of goods or the supply of services, eg, video and equipment hire shops; and this would also exclude travel agents, launderettes, shoe repairers and dry cleaners. Further, there are specific exemptions for shops selling food, whether to be consumed on the premises (eg, restaurant, public house) or taken away (eg, off-licence, take-away shops).

The basic scheme of the 1994 Act is to be found in Sched 1: it is to control only large retail shops,[7] but not small ones. The Schedule defines a 'large shop' by floor area[8] and provides that in general[9] 'a large shop shall not be open on a Sunday for the serving of retail customers' (para 2(1)), breach of this rule being an offence.[10] However, a large shop may trade for up to six hours on a Sunday by giving notice to the Local Authority (para 4), which is responsible for enforcing the Act (see Chapter 28).

Apart from these general restrictions, there are special rules with regard to contracts with minors (see post, para 10.18), sales promotions (see post, paras 8.13A–16) and home sales (see post, para 8.17–19).

Sales promotions

[8.13A] Introduction. Enhancement of the effect of advertising is commonly sought by the use of sales promotion devices such as the following:[1]

1   *Free samples and gifts.* These may either be supplied directly (see post, para 8.14), or indirectly by way of trading stamps (see below). Both these transactions must be carefully distinguished from inertia selling (see post, para 8.18).

2   *Pricing ploys.* Apart from trading stamps, vouchers and loyalty cards (see post, para 15.17), perhaps the most common pricing ploy is the loss leader, whose promotion must avoid contravening the misleading pricing rules (see ante, para 8.09) and the rules relating to pricing displays (see ante, para 8.08). However it must be borne in mind that *prima facie*[2] the mere fact of a price reduction will not deprive the transferee of his ordinary rights with the regard to the goods, eg, the statutory implied terms (see Chapters 12–15), though it may reduce the value of those rights, as where a price reduction or specified defect reduces their weight (see post, para 14.15 *et seq*).

---

6   It has been suggested that this requires at least 50% of the turnover to consist of sales of goods: Askham, *op cit*, note 3, paras 2.32–41.

7   But not wholesalers. This may cause difficulty at the borderline, eg, DIY stores: see Askham, *op cit*, note 3, paras 2.21–23.

8   Eg, *Haskins Garden Centres Ltd v East Dorset DC* [1998] CLY 836, DC. There is no definition of a small shop. For the difficulties of applying this yardstick, see Askham, *op cit*, note 3, paras 3.7–18.

9   Schedule 1 contains two exceptions of large shops which may open on a Sunday without restriction: (a) exempted shops, eg, chemists, filling stations, farm shops, exhibition stands; (b) shops instead closing on the Jewish Sabbath.

10 Schedule 1, para 7. Under the 1950 Act, it has been repeatedly held that the offence consists of the **personal** serving of customers: see Askham, *op cit*, note 3, paras 4.4–15.

[8.13A]

1   See generally Lawson, *Advertising Law*, Chapter 8; Circus, *Sales Promotion Law* (2nd edn, 1995).

2   *Aliter* if the goods are marked, eg, 'shopsoiled', or 'seconds' or 'rejects'.

3   *Games and competitions.* A sale of a chance is unlikely to amount to wagering (see ante, para 2.03), but there must also be examined the issue of whether certain games and competitions are illegal under the Lotteries and Amusements Act 1976 (see post, para 8.16).

4   *Trading representations.* Naturally, these must comply with the TDA, both as regards goods and services (see ante, para 4.02 *et seq*). Additionally, a recurring sharp practice has been the promotion of goods by the false representation that purchase will benefit a charity or particularly deserving class.[3] Accordingly, it has been made an offence[4] for an unregistered person in the course of a business to sell or solicit orders for goods by representing in the course of a visit from house to house that blind or otherwise disabled persons are either employed in the production of the goods or will benefit from the proceeds of sale.[5]

5   *Mail shots.* Advertising material is frequently delivered to the homes of actual or prospective customers. Computerised lists of customers may be obtained from loyalty cards,[6] or obtained by purchasing lists compiled by third parties (usually) for other reasons. In any event, these lists are subject to the data protection rules (see ante, para 3.27); and, if the material is delivered by mail, it is subject to the rules referred to later (see post, para 8.17). A modern version might be to embody the information on a CD-Rom.

6   *Promotional credit*, such as 'interest free credit' and 'buy now, pay later' offers are considered elsewhere (see post, para 8.20 *et seq*).

7   *Car boot sales.* Commonly held at special venues on a Sunday, car boot sales must avoid infringing the territorial rights of local markets (see ante, para 6.02) and may be subject to the Sunday trading laws (see ante, para 8.13). Particular hazards identified are: misdescriptions and fakes;[7] stolen goods;[8] dangerous new goods and shoddy old ones.[9]

8   *Mock auctions* (see post, para 10.11).

9   *Switch selling.* This is where sales staff criticise the advertised product and recommend the purchase of a more expensive alternative. The practice may lead to the commission of a TDA offence (see ante, para 4.05) and is likely to contravene the British Codes of Advertising and Sales Promotion (see ante, para 3.14).

---

3   This requires a licence under the House to House Collections Act 1939 (see ante, para 6.02): *Cooper v Coles* [1987] 1 All ER 91, DC.

4   The enforcement of the provisions is in the hands of local authorities, and there are special rules for offences by corporations: see further post, Chapter 28.

5   Trading Representations (Disabled Persons) Act 1958, s 1 (as amended); regulations made under s 64 of the Charities Act 1992.

6   Plastic identity cards issued by retailers to customers and commonly offering some perk, such as a discount off future purchases.

7   It may be possible to invoke: the TDA, if it can be shown that the supplier is a trader (see ante, para 4.03A); or the misleading advertisements regulations (see ante, para 8.12A).

8   For implied undertakings as to title, see post, para 12.01.

9   For dangerous goods generally, consider criminal and civil claims (see ante, para 4.32; and post, para 17.21); and for food, see ante, para 4.27. For shoddy goods, see the implied terms (see post, Chapters 13, 14 and 15).

10 *Cashbacks*. These schemes are usually offered to the consumer, eg, of furniture or financial services, by a third party.[10] Under them, the retail buyer is provided with a post-dated 'cashback cheque' redeemable in (say) five years, subject to stringent terms and conditions, eg, presentation by post to the third party of the receipt for the retail purchase within a week of the fifth anniversary of purchase. Such conditions may be subject to the UTCC Regulations (see post, para 11.12). If the goods are obtained on credit, this may give rise to additional claims against the creditor under ss 56 or 75 of the CCA (see Chapter 16).

[8.14] Free samples and gifts. The purpose of a free sample is to encourage the transferee subsequently to enter a contract to obtain more of the same sort of goods;[1] whereas in commerce a 'free gift' is more often used as a bait to sell different goods and may actually be supplied under a contract (see ante, para 2.08).

1 *Free samples*. Where a free sample is supplied gratuitously, as in door-to-door promotions,[2] it will amount to a gift in law and thus only be complete on delivery;[3] but, if the transferee is unwilling to accept the goods, he may become an involuntary bailee (see ante, para 1.17). In either case, the donor will escape all those legal obligations which are attached to a supplier under a supply contract;[3] and any action would have to be at common law for the tort of negligence (see post, para 15.25) or under the ASA Code (see ante, para 3.14). However, free samples may fall within particular statutory restrictions if they consist of unfit food given away for the purposes of advertisement[4] or medicines and drugs;[5] and other unsafe goods may contravene the GPS Regulations (see ante, para 4.32).

2 *Free gifts*. Where a so called 'free gift' of goods is in fact supplied under a contract,[6] the transferee is likely to have the benefit of the implied terms imported by the SGA or SGSA (see post, Chapters 13–15); but those provisions have no application where the transfer in fact amounts to a gift,[3] matters then being governed by the law of negligence (see above). Nor may any valid conditions be attached to the completed gift.[7] Subject to the same particular statutory restrictions as free samples in respect of food,[4] medicines or drugs,[5] free gifts supplied by retailers to promote other goods are sometimes objectionable on those grounds to their manufacturer.[8] A 'free offer' with

---

10 See generally (1997) 15 Fair Trading 6; and *Elida Gibbs Ltd v Customs and Excise Comrs* [1996] CLY 5908, Eu Ct (a VAT case).

[8.14]

1 As to the function of a sample, compare contracts by sample: see post, para 15.03.

2 Because the supply is intended to be gratuitous, the unsolicited goods rules are inapplicable: as to these rules, see post, para 8.18.

3 See ante, para 2.08. Gifts are expressly taken outside Part I of the SGSA by s 1(2)(d): see ante, para 2.10. See *The Second Report on Exemption Clauses* (Law Com 69) para 35.

4 Food Safety Act 1990, s 2(2). By this section, the unfit food comes within the s 8 prohibition against sale: as to which, see ante, para 4.27.

5 In the case of both medicines and drugs, 'supply' would seem wide enough to cover free samples and gifts: see ante, para 4.29.

6 Eg, under a credit or charge card agreement 'free' gifts or insurance may be offered on card use (see post, para 15.18).

7 Eg, 'not to be sold': *R v Cording* [1983] Crim LR 175 (selling not theft).

8 Agreements not to supply may be restraints of trade: see ante, para 2.12.

other goods sold may contravene the misleading pricing rules (see ante, para 8.09), whereas an 'extra value pack' may breach the weights and measures rules.[9]

[8.15/16] Games and competitions. In civil law, entry in compliance with its terms into a game or competition for which a prize is offered may constitute the formation of a *prima facie* binding contract.[1] If that is so, and if the prize offered is goods, it maybe that such a transaction amounts to a conditional contract for the sale of goods within the SGA (see ante, para 1.11). However, Parliament has long rendered certain such contracts illegal, in which case the winner cannot enforce his claim to a prize,[2] but any entry contributions may be recoverable from the holder of the fund.[3] The enactments relating to lotteries, prize competitions and amusements with prizes was consolidated in the Lotteries and Amusements Act 1976 (as amended).

1   *Lotteries.* Section 1 lays down that, except as provided by the Act,[4] 'all lotteries which do not constitute gaming (as defined by s 23(1)) are unlawful'.[5] Whilst not defined in the Act, a 'lottery' has been explained as 'any game of total chance in which there is an award of prizes and people pay, directly or indirectly, to contribute'.[6] In practice, the courts have experienced some difficulty in applying that notion, whilst agreeing that a competition is not a lottery if it requires for success the requisite degree of skill,[7] or if it genuinely allows gratuitous entry,[8] or is a genuine pyramid selling scheme.[9]

2   *Prize competitions.* Likewise undefined by the Act, a competition may either allow free entry or amount to a contract.[10] Where the competition requires a degree of skill it cannot amount to a lottery, but may fall within the prohibition contained in s 14(1) of

---

9   This is where a manufacturer increases the size of a pack. It may infringe the weights and measures rules on declarations of quantity (see ante, para 4.25): See Circus, *Sales and Promotion Law* (2nd edn), pp 70–73.

[8.15/16]

1   Eg, *Hall v Cox* [1899] 1 QB 198, CA (competition: but see now s 14 of the 1976 Act, below). Cf *Rooke v Dawson* [1895] 1 Ch 480 (exam); and the case cited in note 8, below. *Contra* if there is insufficient skill to amount to consideration; or if the arrangement is expressed to be binding 'in honour only'; or is discriminatory (see ante, para 4.23). For a consumer satisfaction survey, see OFT, 1996-AR 20.

2   *Blythe v Hulton and Co Ltd* (1908) 72 JP 401, CA. See generally Lawson (1991) 13 Tr L 41.

3   *Barclay v Pearson* [1893] 1 Ch 154. See generally post, para 10.20.

4   There are exemptions for small lotteries (s 3), private lotteries (s 4), societies, lotteries (s 5), local lotteries (s 6) and the National Lottery (1993 Act). The conduct of these permitted lotteries is governed by Part II of the Act.

5   Section 2 deals with offences connected with the unlawful activity, including handling tickets and advertising. Part IV of the Act contains measures relating to enforcement, including in s 21 a standard provision in relation to offences by bodies corporate: as to which, see generally post, para 28.11.

6   Circus, *Sales Promotion Law* (2nd edn), p 25, summarising *per* Widgery LCJ in *Readers Digest Association Ltd v Williams* [1976] 3 All ER 737, DC, at 739e. See also *Imperial Tobacco Ltd v AG* [1981] AC 718, HL (prize tickets included in each cigarette packet).

7   Eg, *News of the World Ltd v Friend* [1973] 1 All ER 422, HL (Spot-the-Ball competition).

8   Eg, *Readers Digest Association Ltd v Williams* [1976] 3 All ER 737, DC (prize entries via the 'No' envelope); *Express Newspapers plc v Liverpool Daily Post and Echo plc* [1985] 3 All ER 680 (newspaper bingo); and see Circus, *op cit*, note 6, pp 28–31. But see Lawson (1996) 15 Tr LR 209; and *Russell v Fulling* [1999] CLY 587 (scratchcards; few free entrants did not save scheme).

9   *Re Vanilla Accumulation Ltd* [1998] CLY 642 (company wound up on grounds that conducting an illegal lottery); *Re Delfin International (SA) Ltd* [1999] CLY 589 (similar). For pyramid selling, see ante, para 1.09.

10 *Express Newspapers plc v Liverpool Daily Post and Echo plc* [1985] 3 All ER 680 (free entry); *Chaplin v Hicks* [1911] 2 KB 786, CA (contract).

the 1976 Act.[11] This provision makes it 'unlawful to conduct in or through any newspaper, or in connection with any trade or business or the sale of any article to the public' any competition in which either:

(a) prizes are offered for forecasts of results, or

(b) which does not depend for success to a substantial degree on the exercise of skill.[12]

Competitions should be run in conformity with the rules set out in the British Code of Sales Promotion Practice (see ante, para 3.14).

Home sales

[8.17] Introduction. In attempting to effect sales to people in their own homes, suppliers may make use of a number of techniques, abuse of which may fall within Part III of the FTA (see ante, para 6.06) and the DPA (see ante, para 3.27). Some of these techniques amount to contracting with minors (see post, para 10.18), or fall within the direct marketing codes (see ante, para 3.13; and post, para 8.19).

1 *Leaflets and circulars.* If the sender is a registered company, they may have to contain prescribed identifying information (Companies Act 1985, ss 349, 351 (correspondence)). Where such matter ('junk mail') is delivered by post, it will usually have been generated by computerised address lists and hence be subject to the DPA (above) and the British Code of Sales Promotion Practice (see ante, para 3.14). Further, the sending by post of noxious items or malicious communications may be an offence; and it is an offence to send by any means any item describing human sexual techniques,[1] or to minors any advertisement as to the availability of credit or hire (see post, para 8.33), or to anyone an unsolicited credit token (see ante, para 7.12).

2 *Canvassing.* Selling goods from door-to-door may amount to peddling within the Pedlars Act 1871 (see ante, para 6.02), or fall within the doorstep selling rules (see post, para 10.21). The CCA makes it an offence to canvass DC agreements in any circumstances (see ante, para 7.07), or to canvass DCS agreements without a special canvassing indorsement (s 23(3): see ante, para 6.14); and a regulated agreement so canvassed may be cancellable (s 67: see post, para 10.29). There are special restrictions where the trader represents that he is selling on behalf of disabled persons (see ante, para 8.13A).

3 *Telephone selling.* Systematic unsolicited telephone calls ('junk calls') is a modern phenomenon, eg, of goods[2] or services.[3] Frequently, the supplier cold-calls, his telephone

---

11   According to s 14(3) offences are governed by s 2: as to which, see note 6, above. There is exempted from s 14 certain bookmaking operations (s 14(2)) and amusements with prizes (ss 15–17).

12   Eg, *Imperial Tobacco Ltd v AG* (above). But see Lawson, *op cit,* note 8.

[8.17]

1   Respectively under the Post Office Act 1953, s 11 (as amended); Malicious Communications Act 1988; and the Unsolicited Goods and Services Act 1971, s 4 (see *DPP v Beate Uhse (UK) Ltd* [1974] QB 158, DC (includes advertising materials for such items).

2   It is possible to buy goods via a premium-rate telephone service with the price debited to the telephone bill: [1999] 10 Which? 6. Pretence at surveys ('sugging') is now curbed by reg 7(4): see post, para 9.05A.

3   Telephone selling of financial services, eg, consumer credit, has become common; and there is a Draft Directive on distance marketing of consumer financial services (Document 598PC0468). It is not yet clear whether it will extend to hp and conditional sales.

lists raising privacy problems (see ante, para 3.27); but sometimes advertisements entice consumers into phoning suppliers. Repeated calls by traders might lead to liability under the general law: there might be criminal responsibility for unlawful harassment (see post, para 24.24) or civil liability in nuisance;[4] and there is a ban on sending to 'individuals' unwanted 'junk' telephone calls and faxes.[5] It is possible for the consumer to complete the transaction during that telephone call (see post, para 10.02); but, in that case any incorporated terms may be unfair, as being hidden terms within the UTCC Regulations (Grey Term 1(i): see post, para 11.17). Payment may be effected by oral direct debit (see post, para 23.14) or by giving a credit card number: the latter form gives the consumer the advantage of s 75 protection (see post, para 16.11); but it does facilitate 'card-not-present' fraud, though this could be reduced by adopting the US practice of dispatching goods only to the card-address.[6] Some such telephone contacts are likely to be followed up by a personal visit, so possibly bringing any resulting transactions within the present CCA definitions of canvassing (s 48) and cancellable agreements (s 67: see above).

4 *Sales parties*. Housewives may be persuaded to sponsor in their own home parties for the sale of goods, the housewife hostess to invite her friends and frequently being rewarded by a commission. Unless the invitation makes it clear that the seller is a trader, an offence may be committed under the Business Advertisements Order (see ante, para 4.22), and where the goods are supplied on credit the agreements might arguably be cancellable (see above). In any event, the transaction will fall within a code of practice (see ante, para 3.13).

5 *Mail order* (see further post, para 8.19). A major problem in this business sector used to be inertia selling (see post, para 8.18); and a continuing difficulty is card-not-present fraud (see above).

6 *Pyramid selling* (multi-level marketing) (see ante, para 1.09).

7 *Internet sales* (see post, para 8.17A).

The Distance Selling Regulations. Following an EU Directive (97/7/EC), additional consumer protection has been introduced under the Distance Selling Regulations;[7] apart from excepted contracts (see below), these generally[8] apply to '**distance contracts**', meaning (reg 3(1)):

> ... any contract concerning goods or services concluded between a supplier and a consumer under an organised distance sales or service provision scheme run by the supplier who, for the purposes of the contract, makes exclusive use of one or more means of distance communication up to and including the moment at which the contract is concluded.

---

4 If the call is indecent or amounts to a false alarm, an offence may be committed under the British Telecommunications Act 1981, s 49, which also contains a provision (s 51) as to offences by bodies corporate (see generally post, para 28.11). As to location-based marketing, see (2001) 56 CC 3/21.

5 Under Directive 97/66/EC, which has been brought into force in the UK by 1998 SI 3170: the present references are to the DPA 1984, but it is intended in due course to update to the DPA 1998 (see ante, para 3.27). There is also a popular fax/telephone preference to stem junk faxes/calls.

6 See Brownsword and MacGowan (1997) 147 NLJ 1806.

7 Consumer Protection (Distance Selling) Regulations 2000, SI 2334.

8 Under reg 6, the regulations do not apply to supplies of certain perishable consumer goods, eg, food, beverages, by a regular roundsman, eg, milk. Nor do they apply to certain types of contract beyond the scope of this work, viz, timeshares and certain service contracts.

This covers consumers buying goods or services (including energy: see ante, para 3.07) at a distance from home, ie, not face-to-face with the seller, whether by telephone, internet or mail order. Excepted contracts are the following (reg 5): sale of an interest in land (see post, para 9.03), other than short-term rentals; financial services, of which a non-exhaustive list (Sched 2) excludes 'banking services';[9] or contracts concluded by means of a 'vending machine or automated commercial premises', or by public payphone (*contra* private phone: see above), or by public auction (see post, para 10.10). In respect of distance contracts made by a business supplier,[10] the Regulations provide some protections to 'consumers', meaning 'any natural person who, in contracts to which these Regulations apply, is acting for purposes which are outside his business'.[11] These compulsory (reg 25) protections in distance contracts are as follows: usually the provision of listed particulars (regs 7–9: see post, para 9.05A); a right of cancellation (regs 10–18: see post, para 10.22A); a requirement that the contract be performed within 30 days (reg 19: see post, para 23.04); protection where the payment has been made by payment card (reg 21: see ante, paras 7.01; 7.07A; 7.13); and some new rules as regards inertia selling (see post, para 8.18). These Regulations are to be enforced (reg 26) by the 'enforcement authorities',[12] who must consider complaints (reg 26), may extract undertakings from errant business suppliers (reg 26(4)) and apply for Stop Now Orders against them (reg 27: see ante, para 6.08).

[8.17A] Internet sales.[1] Attracting customers for goods and services over the Internet (e-commerce) is burgeoning, eg, auctions (see post, para 10.10), particularly as regards products more traditionally bought by mail order (see post, para 8.19), or over the telephone, eg, books, music, banking (see ante, para 8.17). However, e-customers are, of course, for the most part limited to those who have payment cards and computers. In considering the legal position of such English and Welsh customers, a distinction must be drawn according to whether or not the internet trader is within the jurisdiction.

1 *Internet traders within the jurisdiction.* Internet shopping within the jurisdiction would appear to behave legally much like mail order sales (see above), so that it would seem to attract the ordinary rules as to the formation of contract (see post, para 10.01 *et seq*). The transaction will normally be subject to the Distance Selling Regulations (see ante, para 8.17). Payment can be effected by payment card in a manner similar to telephone selling (see above), so enabling the consumer to seek redress from the creditor instead of the internet trader, whether the consumer uses a credit card[2] or other payment card.[3] Under the above Regulations, delivery must be made within 30 days; but delivery risks are subject to the ordinary rules[4] and fraud (a particular problem with internet auctions) minimised in the same way as in mail order (see above). If a document is desired, it may

---

9   Eg, lending (including consumer credit), leasing, credit cards. But an excepted credit card is within reg 21: see text below.

10 'Supplier' means any person who ... is acting in his commercial or professional capacity.

11 Regulation 3(1). See also the definition in the UTCC Regulations: post, para 11.12A.

12 Meaning the OFT (see ante, para 3.03) and Local Authorities (see post, para 28.03): reg 3(1).

[8.17A]

1   See generally, Atiyah, *Sale of Goods* (10th edn), Chapter 5; *Modern Markets: Confident Consumers* (1999, Cm 4410) 7. As to shopping online, see [2000] 11 Which? 6; OFT, 2000-AR 30.

2   Under the CCA, s 75: see post, para 16.11 *et seq*.

3   Under the Distance Selling Regulations, reg 21: see ante, para 7.01.

4   As to risk, see Chapter 22. As to possible applications, see [1999] 10 Credit Today 29.

be obtained by getting the website to generate a hard-copy order, which the consumer signs and posts to the supplier: this would seem to attract the ordinary rules considered elsewhere in this work, including Stop Now Orders (see ante, para 6.08). However, if a document is required by statute (see post, para 9.02), the Electronic Communications Act 2000 introduces two changes relevant to this work: s 7 clarifies that electronic signatures are admissible in court;[5] and ss 8–10 permit the 'appropriate Minister' by statutory order to modify the requirement of any statute or subordinate legislation that certain documents be in writing, replacing it with 'electronic communications or electronic storage'.[6] The maintenance of credit card security, both in terms of identifying the consumer and protecting his credit card details, should be enhanced by smart cards (see ante, para 2.23) and through encryption.[7] Does the website amount to an 'advertisement'? Compare the definitions for trade descriptions (s 39(1) of the TDA: see ante, para 8.07); and for regulated agreements.[8] May the website owner (if different) be engaged in credit brokerage (see ante, para 5.38)?

2 *Internet traders outside the jurisdiction.* The parties may in their transaction agree to be subject to a particular set of courts and system in a choice of laws clause (see post, para 18.13). However, if not, where an English or Welsh consumer deals over the internet with a trader from outside the jurisdiction, the legal position depends on the location of the internet trader, an issue much of which is outside the scope of this work.

(a) Internet trader within the EU, including Scotland and Ireland. Under the Brussels Convention,[8a] enacted here by the Civil Jurisdiction and Judgments Act 1982, the claimant must *prima facie* sue in the courts of the defendant's domicile: but, a contract action may be brought in the place of performance, which is likely to be the place of delivery (see post, para 23.04); and a tort action in the place where the harm occurred, which may be where the consumer examined the goods (see post, para 23.10). That action will be decided according to English law if the contract was made here, which will be the place where acceptance is received:[9] this is likely to depend on whether the website is an invitation to treat or an offer.[10] If that is England or Wales, the substantive rules will be as for trading within the jurisdiction (above).

(b) Internet trader outside the EU. For the consumer to sue in the English courts, he will usually have to show that either the contract was made here, or tortious damage sustained here. The law to be applied was agreed in the Rome Convention, given effect here by the Contracts (Applicable Law) Act 1990. *Prima facie*, this is the law of the country with which the contract is most closely connected, eg, the place of delivery (see above); but, in a consumer contract, it is usually the consumer's habitual

---

5   This would seem to be consistent with the provisions of the EU Electronic Signatures Directive (1999/93/EC). What if an electronic signature is stolen?

6   This could be used to modify, eg, the CCA Agreement Regulations: see post, para 9.10 *et seq.* For discussion of reform, see [2001] 7 Credit Today, Extra.

7   Controlled by the Regulation of Investigatory Powers Act 2000.

8   CCA, s 189(1): see post, para 8.29. As to designing regulated web advertisements, see Patrick [2000] 9 Credit Today 21.

8a   To be replaced by the Brussels Regulation: see (2002) 152 NLJ 26.

9   *Glencore International AG v Metro Trading Inc* [2001] 1 All ER (Comm) 103. See further the Electronic Commerce Directive 2000/31/EC (presently under consideration before UK implementation).

10   Atiyah, *op cit*, note 1, pp 55–56.

residence, which gives rise to problems with ss 26, 27 of the UCTA (see post, para 18.13). Furthermore, if the English consumer using a credit card seeks to circumvent these problems by suing the creditor under s 75 of the CCA, this may raise further problems (see post, para 16.11).

[8.18] Inertia selling. Strictly speaking, at common law the practice of sending unsolicited goods produced this result: the involuntary bailment did not give rise to the usual bailee's duty of care (see ante, para 1.17); and, where delivery amounted to an offer (see post, para 10.02), the bailee/consumer was under no obligation to accept, though his use of the goods might amount to an implied acceptance[1] or conversion (see post, para 19.04). Parliament intervened in both aspects of inertia selling by businesses with the Unsolicited Goods and Service Acts 1971 and 1975.[2] The reference in that title to 'services' is misleading: with one minor exception relating to trade directories,[2a] the Acts only apply to the delivery of goods, not services such as credit insurance (see post, para 8.20) or extended warranties (see post, para 17.09). Furthermore, by reason of the Distance Selling Regulations 2000 (see ante, para 8.17), it is necessary to distinguish according to whether the recipient is a consumer or a business.

1 *Supplies to consumers.* These are now dealt with wholly by the Regulations, which presumably apply to any attempt to make a **distance contract**, whereby (reg 24(1)):

(a) unsolicited goods are sent[3] to a person ('the recipient') with a view to his acquiring[3] them;

(b) the recipient has no reasonable cause to believe that they were sent with a view to their being acquired for the purposes of a business; and

(c) the recipient has neither agreed[4] to acquire nor agreed to return them.[5]

The key notion is that the goods are **'unsolicited'**, an expression whose definition enables the Regulations to be avoided by acting only on a prior request: so a mail order trader may avoid the Act by sending out goods only in response to a returned newspaper reply coupon. Once given, a written request endures until retracted, eg, annual subscriptions, though such a request may be an unfair term (see post, para 11.15).

[8.18]

1 *Felthouse v Bindley* (1862) 11 CBNS 869; *Capital Finance Ltd v Bray* (set out post, para 24.25); and generally post, para 10.02. Could it amount to a sale or return transaction (see post, para 20.24): see Ping-fat (1991) 8 Tr L 207 at 208? For implied acceptance, see *Weatherby v Banham* (1832) 5 C & P 228.

2 The 1975 Act simply strengthened the 1971 Act by adding provisions to it. All subsequent references are to the 1971 Act as amended. For s 4, see ante, para 8.17.

2a Section 3. In December 1999, the DTI consulted on amendments to allow directory entries to be made by e-commerce.

3 'Acquire' includes hire: reg 24(6). As to 'sender', reg 24(6) says that it includes '(a) any person on whose behalf or with whose consent the goods are sent; (b) any other person claiming through or under the sender or any person mentioned in paragraph (a); and (c) any person who delivers the goods'.

4 Does it also include the situation where the recipient so agrees, in ignorance of his legal rights? There is an obligation to draw the recipient's attention to these rights in the documentation (reg 24(7)): see below.

5 Does the recipient have a lien for expenses, even though a rejecting buyer does not (see post, para 24.03)? Does the notice operate from posting or receipt?

(i) The actual delivery. Any rights of the business sender[6] to the goods are immediately[7] extinguished (reg 24(3)) and the recipient may treat the goods as if they were an unconditional gift.[8] For gifts, see ante, para 2.08.

(ii) Any demand for payment. The regulations make criminal any direct demand, provided that 'in the course of business[6] a person[9] makes a demand for payment, or asserts a present or prospective right to payment,[10] for what he knows are' unsolicited goods or services 'sent to another with a view to his acquiring them for purposes other than those of his business' (reg 24(4)). Nor may he indirectly pressure a consumer to pay for unsolicited goods: this too is an offence where he:

(a) threatens to bring any legal proceedings, or

(b) places or causes to be placed the name of any person on a list of defaulters or debtors or threatens to do so, or

(c) invokes or causes to be invoked any other collection procedure, or threatens to do so.

2 *Supplies to businesses.* Whilst the business recipient may no longer treat unsolicited goods as a gift,[11] there continues to exist on the statute book a very similar offence of making a demand for payment in respect of unsolicited goods.[12] So, the business recipient of unsolicited goods is left with an unfettered choice between paying for, or returning, the goods.

The Secretary of State for the purpose of these Acts and the Distance Selling Regulations may make 'regulations as to the contents and form of such notes of agreement, invoices and similar documents' (s 3A; reg 24(8). See the Unsolicited Goods and Services (Invoices etc) Regulations 1975, SI 732).

[8.19] Direct marketing (home shopping). This form of business developed during the Victorian era and at first serviced consumers by way of the post office. Today, it tends also to accept orders by telephone and internet (see ante, paras 8.17–17A). To reach individual consumers by advertisement, direct market suppliers must obtain their names and addresses: as the acquisition of such data can only proceed with the consent of the subject under the DPA, the consumer is in a position to block such direct marketing and is

---

6 See *Eimon v Waltham Forest LBC* (1982) 90 MR 204 (discussed by Bragg, *Trade Descriptions*, 60). For supplies in the course of trade, see generally ante, para 4.03A.

7 Under the now-repealed 1971 Act, this right was suspended for 30 days or six months.

8 Regulation 24(2). Might this provision be struck down as a contravention of human rights: see *Wilson v First County Trust Ltd* (set out post, para 9.20)?

9 See *Reader's Digest Association Ltd v Pirie* 1973 SLT 170 (knowledge of a junior member of staff not to be imputed to the Association: see further, post para 28.10). For offences by corporations, see s 5 of the 1971 Act, but no equivalent in the Regulations; and generally post, para 28.11.

10 'Asserting a right to payment' 'includes any invoice or similar document which (a) states the amount of a payment, and (b) fails to comply with' regulations referred to below: see s 6(2), as substituted, and reg 6(7). See Lawson, *Advertising Law*, 163. Is a pre-payment invoice (see [1996] 5 Which? 6) a 'demand' for payment? There may also be an offence under s 40 of the AJA: see post, para 24.24.

11 Section 1 of the Unsolicited Goods and Services Act 1971, repealed by reg 22(2) of the Regulations.

12 Section 2 of the 1971 Act, as amended by reg 22(3). The offences are not confined to the 'sender' of the goods, so it includes such as a debt-collecting agency or solicitor. Cf unlawful harassment of debtors: see post, para 24.24. As to reasonable cause, see Ping-fat, *op cit*, note 1, at 211.

entitled to compensation in default.[1] Some seek custom via inertia selling (see ante, para 8.18). As direct marketing houses offer delivery direct to the door, typically via an independent carrier, normally the two principles will never meet face-to-face: so, this form of business will be subject to the Distance Selling Regulations (see ante, para 8.17); and, whereas in a shop the consumer will choose and take goods immediately, with direct marketing the consumer will have to choose and await delivery (for delivery rules, see post, para 23.04).

Direct marketing houses tend to fall into one of two categories:

1 *Direct sales houses.* Typically, the business advertises by way of catalogue or the internet (see ante, para 8.17). Most solicit business by advertisements, chiefly in the press; and it is this which makes them particularly susceptible to the voluntary codes of practice.[2] Many such advertisements tend to be on the terms cash-with-order, so avoiding any unpaid seller's transit problems (see post, para 24.17 *et seq*): if sent by post, there are a number of means of effecting payment (see post, para 23.14); but a telephone order will usually be made with a payment card (see ante, para 2.23). Other types of mail order are frequently done by instalment deliveries.[3] To help the public seek redress from mail order traders, under the Regulations the latter must disclose both their business character and address;[4] delivery to the consumer must be made within 30 days;[5] the supplies will be subject to a right of cancellation by the consumer;[6] and there is special protection where payment is made by payment card.[7] However, unless the goods are supplied on sale or return (see post, para 20.23), in the absence of a right of cancellation, the property and risk in them is likely under the *prima facie* rules to pass on posting:[8] this may cause difficulty over pre-payments on the traders' insolvency (see post, para 23.22) or where goods are lost in the post (see post, para 22.01). Despite the consumer's signature on an acceptance note (see post, para 23.10), he retains the right to reject defective goods (see post, para 29.05).

2 *Catalogue houses.* The crucial thing here is the production of an elaborate catalogue,[9] copies of which are distributed either direct to private consumers or via an agent. The agent is commonly a housewife supplying family or friends on commission: if the agent recruits other agents, it may amount to pyramid selling (see ante, para 8.17). Supplies are likely to be on credit sale (see ante, para 1.13): as a form of distance sale, this is likely to attract most of the above sale rules applicable to direct sales houses. Moreover, most such business is conducted with a money-back guarantee; that is, the

---

[8.19]

1 For controls on such lists, see the DPA, s 11 (ante, para 3.27).

2 See the Mail Order Code (ante, para 3.13); the Advertising Standards Authority Code (ante, para 3.14); the British Code of Sales Promotion Practice; and the Code of the Direct Marketing Association.

3 Eg, book or record clubs. For instalment contracts, see post, para 23.23 *et seq*. Consumers should be careful over the minimum obligation, as the small print will usually avoid the inertia selling rules (see ante, para 8.18).

4 Distance Selling Regulations 8 and 9: see post, para 9.02.

5 Regulation 19: see post, para 23.04.

6 Regulations 10–18: see post, para 10.22A.

7 Regulation 21: see ante, paras 7.01; 7.07A; 7.13.

8 These rules may be ousted by a contrary intent: see post, paras 20.06, 22.02. With regard to risk, is a trade custom developing that the trader will bear the risk in course of post? For trade custom, see generally post, para 15.11.

9 Eg, *The Littlewoods Organisation Ltd v Harris* [1978] 1 All ER 1026, CA.

consumer is granted an express right to rescind without cause: this may amount to a sale or return transaction (see above). Further, whether or not a credit sale is used, there will almost certainly be some form of credit, so that there is likely to be a regulated consumer credit agreement (see ante, para 5.19) under which the mail order trader is the creditor (see ante, para 5.25) and his business is susceptible of control by the credit licensing system (see ante, para 6.11 *et seq*). Any housewife agent is specially saved from being a credit-broker or other ancillary credit business (see ante, paras 5.41; 5.43). The industry may have difficulty complying with the CCA documentation rules.[10] Moreover, the agreement will be cancellable: whilst it is unlikely to be cancellable under the CCA,[11] it will be cancellable under the Distance Selling Regulations. However, if payment were made by payment card, the transaction will usually give the consumer rights against the card issuer: if a credit card is used, this will be under the CCA;[12] and if a debit or charge card is used, this will be under the Distance Selling Regulations.

SUPPLIES ON CREDIT OR HIRE

[8.20] Introduction. Parliament has long felt the need to impose statutory restrictions where it is sought to obtain business is by way of credit or hire.[1] Early controls on the advertising of credit are to be found in the Moneylenders Act 1927 (now repealed). Subsequently, there appeared restrictions on advertising instalment credit consolidated in the Advertisements (Hire Purchase) Act 1967 (now repealed).

These two veins of legislation have now been amalgamated and extended in the CCA. The greater part of these provisions are to be found in Part IV of the Act, which restricts both the information which may be supplied to the debtor or hirer (see post, para 8.21 *et seq*) and that which may be obtained about him (see post, para 8.35 *et seq*). Additionally, the compulsory licensing system in Part II enables the Director to curb undesirable advertising practices (see ante, para 6.19), eg, inertia selling of credit insurance; s 26 empowers the minister to control by regulation the conduct of licensees[2] and the canvassing[3] and cancellation (see post, para 10.28 *et seq*) provisions are likely to have a substantial effect on the manner in which a creditor or owner will go about seeking business.[4] Additionally, where any lending is secured on land (see ante, para 7.04A), advertisement of that facility must carry a special warning (see post, para 8.30).

---

10 Consumers are normally sent a credit agreement and asked to return it; but, if they do not, there may be a breach of the documentation rules (CCA, s 62(2)), in which case the agreement would be improperly executed: see (2001) 61 QA 13; and post, para 9.19.

11 Because there are no face-to-face dealings: CCA, s 67 (see post, para 10.29).

12 Section 75: see post, para 16.11 *et seq*.

[8.20]

1 For analysis of the reasons why consumers in credit transactions are particularly in need of protection by way of pre-contract controls, see Goode, *Consumer Credit Law and Practice*, para 28.1.

2 See ante, para 6.17. This power is expressly extended by ss 54, 152(1) to regulations relating to the seeking of business by a licensee.

3 See ante, paras 7.05–07. In commercial terms, the canvassing of consumers (loan financing) and persuading dealers to proffer credit terms at point of sale (direct financing) are alternative ways of attracting business.

4 As to the control of credit-brokers' fees, see s 155; and ante, para 5.37.

Information supplied to the debtor or hirer

[8.21] Introduction. Following the recommendations of the *Crowther Report*,[1] a major feature of the CCA is the importance attached to the disclosure to the consumer of information concerning the terms and cost of credit.[2] An important objective is to enable the consumer to make an informed choice between different credit packages available in the market place.[3] Nowhere is this more obvious than in the rules designed to ensure that the cost of credit is uniformly expressed (see post, para 8.22). The Act provides for pre-contract disclosure of this information at **all** the following stages of consumer credit:[4]

1   In advertisements, which will typically be aimed at a segment of the market (see post, para 8.27).

2   In quotations, which will be directed to a particular potential customer (see post, para 8.32).

3   In the copy of the agreement-form which the consumer must always obtain when he first signs it (see post, para 9.14).

Failure to disclose accurately, or at all, the cost of the credit at **all** the above stages will usually amount to a CCA offence.[5] However, the whole edifice is predicated on rate sensitivity being the crucial thing for consumers,[6] whereas there is persistent evidence that they are more interested in the size of the deposit and repayment.[7] There is also the problem of making rate comparisons in a segmented market (see post, para 8.23).

Expression of credit charge

[8.22] Introduction. The Moneylenders Acts 1900–27 (now repealed) contained some restrictions both as to the rate of interest which might be charged (rate ceilings: see post, para 29.40) and the manner in which that rate might be expressed. Taking over the latter function only, s 20 of the CCA breaks the process down into two stages:

Stage 1. To identify all the items which are to be included in the credit charge – what it termed the 'total charge for credit' (see post, para 8.23).

Stage 2. To turn that total charge for credit from a sum of money into a rate of interest – what it termed the 'annual percentage rate' (APR: see post, para 8.25).

[8.21]

1   Paragraphs 6.5.15–21. For the Report, see generally ante, para 5.03. See also the subsequent White Paper, *Reform of the Law on Consumer Credit* (1973, Cmnd 5427), paras 28–30.

2   What is termed 'truth-in-lending': see generally ante, para 5.08. Contrast the position of the cash seller who does not have to reveal his mark-up.

3   Nevertheless, there continues to be evidence that debtors remain insensitive to the cost of credit: [1986] Which? 449; (1988) 138 NLJ 589, 657; OFT, 1989-AR 102; Howells, *Aspects of Credit and Debt*, pp 36–37, 84.

4   The requirements as to disclosure of cost do not apply to consumer hire agreements.

5   Giving an inaccurate interest rate may also amount to misleading pricing (see ante, para 8.09A); and it may contravene ASA codes (see ante, para 3.14).

6   See OFT, 1994-AR, 22. There is even the suggestion that some consumers think that the crucial notation APR (see post, para 8.25) stands for 'always pay regular'.

7   Eg, Cayne and Trebilcock (1973) 23 Univ Tor LJ at 403, 423–26; Howells, *op cit*, note 3, p 48. Would consumers pay more attention if it was expressed in cash terms?

For greater flexibility, s 20 did not itself set out those two steps in detail, but instead empowered the Secretary of State to make regulations to this end (see post, paras 8.24–26). To simplify and standardise the processes, these regulations make a series of assumptions and allow certain tolerances (see post, para 8.26); and for this purpose, the Regulations (see post, para 8.24) employ two important dates: (i) the agreement date, which is the date upon which the regulated agreement is made (see post, para 9.12); and (ii) 'the relevant date', which is the date upon which the debtor is entitled to begin enjoyment of the contract, eg, delivery of the hp goods, draw upon the credit.[1] Therefore, in approaching those regulations, 'the key point to bear in mind is that the [calculation of the APR is] based on what the consumer credit agreement stipulates is to happen and what ... the regulations deem to happen, not in what in fact happens'.[2]

Before plunging into the CCA details as to the expression of the credit charge, it is worth bearing in mind the potential applicability of certain other branches of the law, as highlighted in the County Court case of *Falco Finance Ltd v Gough*:[3]

> G, a non-status borrower (see post, para 8.35) entered into an unregulated mortgage with FF which contained all the following unusual features contravening the 'Non-Status Guidelines' (see ante, para 7.04A): the interest rate was calculated at a flat rate, rather than an APR (see post, para 8.25); the wording made it difficult for G to avoid defaulting and, if G defaulted by even one day, the interest rate for the remainder of the mortgage rose by a further 5% (the dual interest rate); if G sought to redeem, there was a redemption charge calculated under the 'Rule of 78' (see post, para 26.19A).

The County Court judge refused to apply the terms of the mortgage because: the dual interest rate made the mortgage an extortionate credit bargain (see post, para 29.40); its terms were unfair under the UTCC Regulations (see post, para 11.16); and they amounted to a clog on the equity of redemption (see post, para 25.20) and a penalty at common law (see post, para 27.46). Contrast the treatment of an undeserving debtor pleading technicalities.[4]

[8.23] Total charge for credit. Basically, these are the additional payments which a cash purchaser would not have incurred. In seeking to define what items are to be included as part of the cost of credit, s 20 of the CCA makes it clear that what matters is the cost to the debtor rather than the net return to the lender, thereby disadvantaging those forms of credit which have high administrative costs.[1]

Which items are given statutory recognition as part of the cost of credit is essentially a matter of legislative policy: at the minimum, it could be confined to pure interest; but at the maximum it might embrace everything the debtor has to pay other than the capital sum 'borrowed'.[2] The Act attempts to steer between these two extremes: it starts by naming the items collectively 'total charge for credit' (TCC) and defining this (s 189(1)) by reference to the regulations made under s 20 (see post, para 8.24). Exactly where that

---

[8.22]
1   Regulation 1(2). See Goode, *Consumer Credit Law and Practice*, paras 29.126–39.
2   Goode, *ibid*, para 29.124.
3   (1998) 17 Tr LR 526 (see 115 LQR 360; 52 QA 9; [1999] Credit Today 18).
4   See *Broadwick Financial Services Ltd v Spencer* (2001) 61 QA 21, Cty Ct.
[8.23]
1   Eg, the cost of money to the creditor, something likely to vary greatly as between the different types of lender; home collection costs. See ante, para 2.17.
2   Goode, *Consumer Credit Law and Practice*, para 29.4.

(arbitrary) line is drawn may have implications for the relative fairness of the system as between different sectors of the finance industry.[3] Particularly noticeable are differences produced by the statutory rules as between the following different types of credit: mortgage credit as opposed to (shorter term) personal loans;[4] bank overdrafts;[5] credit cards[6] as opposed to weekly collected credit;[7] small loans for short periods.[8] In *Huntpast v Leadbeater*,[9] the Court of Appeal said that, in construing and applying the regulations, courts should have regard to the substance and reality of the transaction rather than the form, as the whole point of the regulations is the determination of the true cost of the credit to the debtor.

The TCC is significant in a number of contexts (see ante, para 5.08); and the EU is proposing reform (see ante, para 5.12). However, the very complication of the system makes for both loopholes and difficult policing; and the government is trying to plug the gaps with voluntary standards.[10]

[8.24] The TCC Regulations.[1] These simply state which items are to be included and which will be excluded from the TCC.[2]

1   *Items included*. Regulation 4 provides that the TCC is to include items, unless expressly excluded by reg 5 (below), which are either of the following:

(a) interest charges, eg, bank interest.[3] This does not include repayments of the capital sum borrowed (see ante, para 5.22).

(b) premiums for compulsory credit insurance solely against the debtor's death, invalidity, illness or unemployment (see post, para 24.44).

(c) 'other charges':

> ... at any time payable under the transaction by or on behalf of the debtor or a relative of his whether to the creditor of any other person.[4]

---

3   Eg, with credit cards, the low interest rates charged for an initial period in respect of balance transfers.

4   A first mortgage may be fixed rate: see *National Westminster Bank v Devon* CC (1994) 13 Tr L 70, DC (Whisson 14 Tr L 304; 48 CC 4/21; OFT, 1997-AR, 24). A second mortgage is secured (see ante, para 7.04A); and it only has to quote the rate to one decimal place (Goode, *op cit*, note 2, Part VII, para 3027), a concession the more valuable the longer the repayment period.

5   If charges were included, an unauthorised bank overdraft could cost in the order of 9,000% APR. For examples, see CCA (UK) *Mirage or Reality?* 31, 58, 60.

6   As the amount of credit is unknown, the creditor may choose a representative sum (see post, para 8.30). Adroit choice of this sum as compared with any annual fee and interest-free period can allow manipulation of the APR: Goode, *op cit*, note 2, Part VII para 1.68.

7   Which has heavier administration charges and rarely charges for late payment. For the effect of this, see CCA (UK), *op cit*, note 5, pp 28, 30, 57.

8   Whereas a personal loan may have a minimum loan size over which to spread costs, the small lender does not. For the effect of this see CCA (UK), *op cit*, note 5, p 29.

9   [1993] CLY 467, CA (a case on an earlier version of the regulations).

10   Eg, the Treasury's CAT standards announced January 2001.

[8.24]

1   Consumer Credit (Total Charge for Credit) Regulations 1980, SI 51, Part 2 (as amended). There are helpful annotations in Part 3 of Guest and Lloyd, *Encyclopedia of Consumer Credit*.

2   Article 3. For a serious drafting slip, see Goode, *Consumer Credit Law and Practice*, para 29.141.

3   As to interest, see generally ante, para 7.03A. What if the rate of interest is variable, whether automatically or consensually (see post, para 26.21)? See Goode, *Payment Obligations in Commercial and Financial Transactions*, pp 81–82. *Sed quaere?*

4   As to 'debtor', 'creditor' and 'relative', see respectively ante, paras 5.24; 5.25; 5.33.

This latter formula is very wide, extending to charges paid by the debtor or a relative of his under the credit agreement itself, eg, hp finance charges and probably option fees, credit card fees, survey fees, legal fees, stamp duties.[5] It also extends to charges arising under any other contract which the creditor insists on the debtor or his relative making or maintaining as a condition of being granted the credit, which will usually be a linked transaction (see generally ante, para 5.31), eg, compulsory installation or most maintenance contracts in respect of the subject matter of the credit agreement (which may extend beyond the period of the credit agreement). Additionally, it comprehends any security agreement[6] and brokerage fees.[7]

2   *Items excluded.* Even though they may fall within the above rubric, reg 5 excludes from the TCC all the following classes of items: (i) default charges, as for late payment;[8] (ii) charges payable by cash and credit customers alike, eg, car delivery fees, voluntary maintenance contracts; (iii) previously incurred charges for incidental services or benefits, eg, membership fees for an organisation which offers *inter alia* cheap credit facilities, but not brokerage fees; (iv) bank charges, as charges for operating a current account which are unrelated to any overdraft facility, eg, for standing orders; and (v) premiums in respect of most insurances other than compulsory credit insurance (above), which will comprehend most voluntary insurance, compulsory life or motor insurance and any insurance where the debtor can choose the insurer,[9] but seemingly not a payment waiver policy. In *Watchtower Investments Ltd v Payne:*[10]

> Payne applied to WI, a non-status lender, for a loan with which, *inter alia*, to pay off the arrears on his building society mortgage. WI granted the loan, on condition that the building society charge was paid off, and paid off the building society arrears direct. Payne, having fallen into arrears with his WI loan, pleaded that the building society charge was in the documentation improperly described as part of the loan, rather than part of the tcc.

Looking at all the surrounding circumstances, the Court of Appeal said that the test of whether the building society charge fell within reg 4 depended on whether that charge could fairly and in reality be regarded as part of the TCC; and it held that it was not an 'other charge' within reg 4, but part of the credit.

[8.25] Annual percentage rate (APR). Even when the TCC has been fixed (see ante, paras 8.23–24), it is clear that this sum of money may be translated into a percentage rate in a number of different ways having very different mathematical results.[1] The regulations made under s 20 have to cover the many very different types of regulated agreement, including fixed-sum and running-account credit (see ante, para 5.28). Whilst the purposes for which the APR scheme is set up (see ante, para 8.22) requires that the APR be quoted at the outset of a transaction, it will be obvious that many of the factors required to calculate the APR will not be settled at that point; so, with running account credit, it will

---

5   See *Humberclyde Finance Ltd v Thompson* (payment waiver policy: set out ante, para 5.22).

6   See post, para 25.11. It will also include any survey or valuation fees paid by a surety.

7   *Huntpast v Leadbeater* [1993] CLY 467, CA (on an earlier version of the regs).

8   Eg, unauthorised overdraft. If a default is made good, the right to any default charge is avoided (see post, para 24.32); and, if a default is not made good, the default charge may amount to a penalty (see post, para 27.46).

9   This may have encouraged negative option insurance (see generally post, para 24.46).

10   [2001] 9 CL 118, CA. The case was remitted to the county court on other issues.

[8.25]

1   See the *Crowther Report*, paras 6.5.18–21.

then be unknown for how long the agreement is to run and how much will be drawn down. The Regulations take matters in two stages:

1 *Assumptions*. The Regulations make certain assumptions about these factors unknown at the date of contracting.[2] There are two different classes of assumption:

(a) The overriding assumptions to be found in reg 2, which are applicable irrespective of the terms of the consumer credit agreement, include the following: the debtor is not entitled to income tax relief (reg 2(1)(a)); the credit will not accelerate payment under an acceleration clause;[3] if the agreement allows for variation of the rate upon the happening of an uncertain event, eg, the interest rate is linked to FHBR, that the uncertain event, eg, a change in FHBR (see ante, para 2.18), will not occur;[4] where the provision or repayment of credit is to be made 'on or before' a specified date, it is assumed that that date is the 'relevant date' (see ante, para 8.22), so ignoring the fact that payment/repayment may be delayed (reg 2(2)(a)); where the agreement is for running-account credit so that the amount repayable at the end of each billing period is uncertain, eg, an overdraft or credit card, the charge is calculated on the debit balance at the beginning of the billing period, eg, month,[5] and the consumer is left to work out for himself the advantage to him of paying as late as possible in the month; and, if the debtor has a choice as to the amount of payment, eg, under a credit card, he is assumed to make only the minimum payment (reg 2(2)(c)).

(b) The assumptions in Part IV of the regulations are gap-fillers: unlike those above, the Part IV assumptions are to be employed only where the regulated agreement is silent as to some matter relevant to the computation of the APR. These include the following: where the amount of credit is unascertainable, that the debtor will borrow up to the credit-limit if there is one (reg 15), eg, a bank overdraft; where the period of credit is unascertainable, that the credit is provided for one year (reg 14); where the interest rate is index-linked, the prevailing rate at the date of agreement will be taken;[6] where the agreement is of uncertain duration and the rate charged will increase after a specified period, the higher of the two rates is to be taken (reg 16); where the earliest date as to the provision of credit is unascertainable, eg, on delivery, the date of contract is to be taken (reg 17); and where a charge is payable on an uncertain date, it will usually be assumed to be payable on the 'relevant date' (above), eg, date of provision of credit.

2 *Formulae for computation* (see post, para 8.26).

[8.26] Computation of APR. In most situations, complete mathematical accuracy is not achievable; and in any event, the primary objective is that the rate provided by different

---

2 See Goode, *Consumer Credit Law and Practice*, paras 29.207–27.

3 Regulation 2(1)(c). For acceleration clauses operating on the debtor's default, see ante, para 7.03.

4 Regulation 2(1)(d). As to what amounts to uncertainty for this purpose, see *Scarborough BS v East Riding of Yorkshire CC* [1997] CCLR 47, DC (discussing the applicability of reg 2(1)(d) of 1980 SI 51 to a low-start mortgage). As to interpretation, see ante, para 1.05. As to the special rule for land mortgages, see reg 2(1)(e).

5 Regulation 2(2)(b). Thus, the calculation is simplified by ignoring any payments made during the month.

6 Regulation 15. There is a special rule for index-linked mortgages: reg 15A.

creditors be expressed according to a common yardstick so that the consumer may draw comparisons. Under the original version of the regulations, there were three different methods of calculating the APR: (a) published rate tables for the most common cases, which were like a train timetable; (b) two statutory formulae applicable to most, but not all, circumstances; and (c) the universal method of trial and error calculation.[1] With the advent of computers and pocket calculators, it was possible to sweep away this cumbersome system. Accordingly, the revised Consumer Credit Directive[2] prescribes a single equation which will be satisfied if the APR is correctly stated.[3] Regulation 6 provides as follows:

> The rate of the total charge for credit in the case of an actual or prospective agreement shall be the annual percentage rate of charge determined in accordance with the following provisions of this Part of these Regulations and (where it has more than one decimal place) rounded to one decimal place in accordance with regulation 6A below.

Whilst the original regulations disregarded anything after the first decimal place, reg 6A requires a rounding up or down. Regulation 7 embodies the euro-formula for calculating the APR;[4] and this formula is simply programmed into industry calculators so that, together with the programmed statutory assumptions (see above), it should be relatively simple for those within the industry in any given situation to calculate the appropriate APR.[5]

Advertising

[8.27] Introduction. Of course, there are a large number of statutory controls relating to the advertising of goods which apply whether the supply is intended to be on cash terms or credit.[1] However, where the advertising relates to a credit supply, there also existed some pre-CCA statutory controls (see ante, para 8.20), which were eventually supplemented by various voluntary controls, covering broadcasting and the media (see ante, para 3.14).

Following its normal pattern, Part IV of the CCA sought in the main to take the earlier statutory controls and make them systematically applicable across the full range of 'advertising'. As will be seen, s 43 starts from the premise that all 'advertising' of credit or hire facilities is within Part IV, regardless of whether the resulting credit or hire agreements would be within the ambit of the CCA (s 43(1): set out post, para 8.29), eg, credit in excess of the statutory maximum or to a corporate debtor, and then excluding

---

[8.26]
1   See Butterworths edn, 1989, para 8.26.
2   98/7/EC: see ante, para 5.12.
3   See Goode, *Consumer Credit Law and Practice*, para 29.140.
4   See Goode, *ibid*, paras 29.206a–b.
5   Because it determines the ambit of the Act, the APR has to be calculated more strictly in the case of exempt agreements, whereas some tolerances are allowed by the regulations in the other cases: Goode, *ibid*, para 29.123.

[8.27]
1   Eg, trade descriptions (see ante, para 8.07); price displays (see ante, para 8.08); misleading pricing (see ante, para 8.10); misleading advertising (see ante, para 8.12A).

some situations (ss 43(2)–(5): see post, para 8.29). For cases within its ambit, Part IV lays down the following types of restriction in relation to credit or hire businesses:[2]

1 *Detailed stipulations in regulations made under s 44 as to the form and content of advertisements* (see post, para 8.30 *et seq*), which can also be enforced by Stop Now Orders (see ante, para 6.08).

2 *Availability of cash terms*. Section 45 provides that:

> If an advertisement to which this Part applies indicates that the advertiser is willing to provide credit under a restricted-use credit agreement relating to goods or service to be supplied by any person, but at the time when the advertisement is published that person is not holding himself out as prepared to sell the goods or provide the services (as the case may be) for cash, the advertiser commits an offence.

The object is to prevent effective avoidance of s 44 (above) in relation to restricted-use credit (see ante, para 5.29) in the following manner: an 'advertiser' who did not supply the goods for cash[3] could assume an inflated notional cash price,[4] so enabling him to advertise his goods with no credit charge or a very low one in a manner which literally conformed with the rules as to the contents of advertisements.[5] However, this restriction has done little to curb the popularity in financed transactions of 'interest free' credit, often advertised as '0% APR' (see ante, para 2.07). In this class of business, the cash and credit retail customer will both pay the same price for an item, thus satisfying s 45;[6] but the creditor will deduct the cost of the credit from the amount it pays the supplier,[7] which may mean that cash customers unwittingly contribute towards another customer's credit (for the advertising rules as regards 0% finance, see post, para 8.30). Again, it would appear that the traders who deal on both cash and credit terms could seek to avoid s 45 by stocking separate brands/models for cash and credit customers.[8]

3 *False or misleading advertisements* (see post, para 8.28).

Contravention of any of the above advertising rules *prima facie* amounts to a criminal offence;[9] but that fact does not in itself lead to any further sanctions (s 170: see post, para 10.19). The primary offence is committed by the 'advertiser' which expression refers, not to the publisher of the advertisement, but (s 189(1)):

---

2   They are also applicable to credit-brokers: s 151(1); *R v Mumford and Ahearne* [1995] CCLR 16, CA.

3   What about the advertiser who just does not push cash sales? Cash sales will be uncommon for ghetto merchants: Cayne and Trebilcock (1973) 23 Univ of Toronto LJ 396 at 412–13.

4   Eg, *Metsoja v Norman (H) Pitt and Co* (set out post, para 8.28).

5   See Cayne and Trebilcock, *op cit*, note 3, at 398, 405. Some mail order firms (see generally ante, para 8.19) are geared exclusively to credit transactions; but they are saved from this rule by an exemption order under s 43(5): see post, para 8.29.

6   And the advertising regulations (see post, para 8.30). Any brokerage fee charged would fall within the tcc regulations (see ante, para 8.24).

7   The retailer may not be charged VAT (see ante, para 2.06) on that deduction: *Primback Ltd v Customs and Excise Comrs* [1996] STC 757, CA (see 51 CC 2/18).

8   Dobson (1996) 140 Sol Jo 1026.

9   Sections 167(2), 45, 46. For penalties, see s 167(1) and Sched 1; and generally post, Chapter 28. For the defences, see s 168: see post, para 28.13.

> ... means any person indicated by the advertisement as willing to enter into transactions to which the advertisement relates.

Eg, if a car dealer places an advertisement indicating the willingness of XYZ Finance Ltd to enter hp agreements in relation to that dealer's cars, XYZ Finance Ltd is 'the advertiser'; and it has been suggested that there may be more than one 'advertiser' in relation to a single advertisement, so that the car dealer is also the 'advertiser'.[10] Moreover, s 47 extends the scope of the notion of 'advertiser' to the following cases:

Case (a). One who publishes the advertisement in the course of business,[11] eg, a newspaper proprietor, though he is given a special defence (s 47(2): see post, para 28.16).

Case (b). One who in the course of business[11] devised the advertisement, eg, an advertising agency.

Case (c). One who procured the publication of the advertisement. This will cover the situation where a person is the advertiser, not because he placed the advertisement, but because he is named in it as the person willing to enter into a transaction within Part IV of the Act.[12]

[8.28] False or misleading credit advertisements. Section 46(1) provides that:

> If an advertisement to which this Part applies conveys information which in a material respect is false or misleading the advertiser commits an offence.

Although restricted to Part IV advertisements (see post, para 8.29), the offence is widely drawn. Thus, in *Metsoja v Norman H Pitt and Co:*[1]

> A car dealer's advertisement referred to '0% finance deal', 'payments over 24 months without paying a penny in interest' and '0% APR'. In practice, the dealer allowed a higher part exchange allowance to cash customers than to credit customers.

The Court held that, besides infringing the Advertising Regulations (see ante, para 8.27), the advertisement was *prima facie* false in that it clearly indicated that a purchaser using the finance scheme would pay the same as a cash purchaser. The test has been said to be whether the advertisement would mislead an 'ordinary member of the public';[2] but this does not seem to have stemmed the profusion of confusing 'interest free' deals advertised.[3]

Nor is the s 46(1) offence confined to credit information:[4] it extends to **any** information in a Part IV advertisement,[5] including that a broker was providing his own

---

10   By straining the meaning of 'transaction': see Goode, *Consumer Credit Law and Practice*, Part IIB, para 5.87.
11   As to course of business, cf SGA s 14: see post, para 14.04.
12   Goode, *op cit*, note 10, para 28.69.
[8.28]
1   [1990] CLY 620, DC (see 43 CC6/2). See also *National Westminster Bank v Devon CC* (1994) 13 Tr LR 70, DC.
2   *Dudley MBC v Colorvision plc* [1997] CCLR 19, DC.
3   See [1998] 11 Which? 49; [1998] 12 Which? 7. As to 'instant credit', see (1986) 41 CC 1/4.
4   Eg, where the advertisement does not mention that it relates only above a minimum amount of credit (47 CC1/14); nor that in a low-start mortgage the interest shortfall would be capitalised (48 CC5/25); cashbacks with unstated early redemption penalties (51 CC 2/21).
5   *Rover Group Ltd v Sumner* [1995] CCLR 1 (quoted price did not include road tax and other items).

credit.[6] The provision speaks of information which is false or misleading 'in a material respect'. This is reminiscent of the language of the TDA (s 3(1): see ante, para 4.08); and it may be that there is some overlap between the provisions. Whilst at common law a false statement of intention would not amount to an offence,[7] s 46(2) adds that:

> Information stating or implying an intention on the advertiser's part which he has not got is false.

This provision will catch out-of-date sales literature;[8] and, in relation to prices quoted, may overlap with the misleading prices rules (CPA, s 21(1)(d): see ante, para 8.09).

The CCA lays down that breach of one of its requirements attracts no other sanctions (s 170(1): see post, para 10.19). However, it is thought that this does not affect civil liability arising independently of the Act:[9] so the false or misleading statement may amount to a material misrepresentation (see post, para 17.10), or a breach of term of any supply contract thereby induced, whether as an express (see post, para 11.07) or implied term, eg, as to description (see post, para 13.11).

[8.29] Credit advertisements. Part IV of the CCA applies to 'advertisements', which expression is widely defined by s 189(1). However, s 43 proceeds to limit the ambit of Part IV to certain classes of 'advertisement'. Section 43(1) provides that:

> This Part applies to any advertisement, published for the purposes of a business carried on by the advertiser, indicating that he is willing –
>
> (a) to provide credit, or
>
> (b) to enter into an agreement for the bailment ... of goods by him.

Thus, the essence of s 43(1) is that the 'advertisement'[1] must be an indication: (i) 'published';[2] (ii) for the purposes of a credit or hire business, whether regulated or not;[3] (iii) carried on by the 'advertiser';[4] (iv) indicating a willingness to provide credit. In *Jenkins v Lombard North Central plc*:[5]

> The defendant national finance company, LNC, supplied a car dealer with stickers to be placed on cars offered for sale. The stickers were vertically divided: the cash price was to be

---

6 *R v Munford and Ahearne* [1994] CCLR 16, CA (advertisement also false in that it referred to fixed rate loan without disclosing that fixed rate only for 12 months).

7 *R v Dent* [1955] 2 QB 590, CCA. *Contra* civil law: see post, para 17.18.

8 Eg, *Home Insulation v Wadsley* [1988] CCLR 25, DC.

9 Goode, *Consumer Credit Law and Practice*, Part IIB, para 5.86; and see post, para 10.19.

[8.29]

1 There have been attempts to distinguish mere information, eg, notification of interest rate changes, from statements promoting new business: Goode, *Consumer Credit Law & Practice*, para 28.10. See also Jones, *Credit Cards*, pp 38–39.

2 It will be observed that the definition is not confined to visual advertisements but extends to oral ones, and even to sales patter in a shop. Does it include the supply of a complimentary diary or pencil? See generally Goode, *ibid*, para 28.21. Two or more documents may constitute an advertisement: s 189(4).

3 As to which, see Goode, *ibid*, para 28.23. As to reform for unregulated credit cards, see ante, para 5.11.

4 See ante, para 8.27. Or a credit brokerage business (s 151); as to which, see generally ante, para 5.38. For regulated and unregulated agreements, see ante, para 5.13; and for credit and hire businesses, see ante, para 6.12.

5 [1984] 1 All ER 828; [1984] 1 WLR 307, DC.

indicated in ink by the dealer on the right-hand side; and on the left-hand side were printed the name and logo of LNC. The prosecution argued that, because it was well-known that LNC offered credit for the acquisition of motor cars, the stickers amounted to an indication within s 43 that the advertiser (LNC) was willing to provide credit and thus fell within the advertisement regulations.

However, the Divisional Court held that corporate advertising which merely kept LNC's name in the public eye did not amount to such an indication, even if members of the public might infer such a willingness from LNC's reputation. It seems to follow that corporate advertising by itself is not an 'indication' within s 43.[6] On the other hand, service advertising 'indicating' an express willingness to grant credit or hire facilities is within s 43.[7]

Even where an advertisement *prima facie* falls within s 43(1), the Act exempts certain types of advertisement from its provisions (s 43(2), (5)):

1   As regards the business of the advertiser,[8] where either (a) that business does not amount to a consumer credit or consumer hire business (s 43(2)(a)), eg, the advertiser only places such advertisements occasionally; or (b) the advertiser does not provide credit to individuals secured on land (s 43(2)(b)). So, if the advertiser is lending on the security of land, he is caught by Part IV even if the loans are unregulated or the agreement exempt, eg, the loan is by a building society.[8a]

2   Even where the advertiser carries on a business within the scope of Part IV, he can still issue particular advertisements to which the Act does not apply if he makes it plain in that advertisement that:

(a) as to credit facilities, either that the credit must exceed the statutory maxima and only security other than land is required, or that credit is available only to a body corporate (s 43(3)), eg, an advertiser carrying on a consumer credit business who issues an advertisement for credit which must exceed the statutory maximum, or is only available to corporations;

(b) as to hiring facilities, that he is not willing to enter into consumer hire agreements (s 43(4)), eg, an advertiser carrying on a consumer hire business who issues an advertisement for the hiring of commercial plant above the financial limit.

3   Agreements of the following types: mortgages of land which fall within the FSMA;[9] agreements exempt as short-term credit, low cost credit or finance for foreign trade.[10]

[8.30] Form and content. Different detailed controls of both the content (amount and type of information) and form (the way in which the information is presented) of credit advertisements was previously to be found in both the Moneylenders and

---

6   *Quaere* with Mastercard and Visa logos, which appear to guarantee the provision of credit.

7   Goode, *op cit*, note 1, Part III, para 44. Or perhaps the distinction lies in the difference between an express or implied indication: see Goode, Part I, para 28.27.

8   Section 43(2)(c) (as amended) attempts to prevent circumvention of Part IV by the use of ingenious 'off-shore' operations. But is there a drafting slip in that it contains too many negatives? Does the amendment achieve this?

8a   These controls may be transferred to the FSMA (see ante, para 3.02).

9   See ante, para 3.02. These are exempt from the CCA: see ante, para 5.15.

10   Consumer Credit (Exempt Advertisements) Order 1985, SI No 621. As to exempt agreements, see generally ante, paras 5.14–15.

Advertisements (HP) Acts (see ante, para 8.20). However, for flexibility, s 44 of the CCA chose to allow the control of 'advertisements' to be introduced by regulation, breach of which provisions amounts to an offence (s 167(2): see ante, para 8.28). It also gave the following indication of what is expected:[1] the regulations should be designed to ensure that 'an advertisement conveys a fair and reasonably comprehensive indication of the nature of the credit or hire facilities ... and of their true cost to the person using them' (s 44(1)).

The Advertising Regulations[2] apply not only[3] to advertisements within Part IV of the Act in respect of both credit and hire facilities published by the creditor, lessor or credit-broker (see ante, para 8.29). They allow for three alternative types of advertisement (see post, para 8.31) and also contain certain general rules as to any information required or permitted to be included in any advertisement. First, where that information varies from one transaction to another, the advertiser is generally allowed to state 'representative terms'.[4] Secondly, the required information must be 'clear and easily legible' (reg 2(6)): clarity refers to substance, whilst legibility is directed at the ability to read it.[5] Might the legibility requirement prohibit radio advertising? Thirdly, that information must generally[6] be 'shown together as a whole',[7] except for split advertisements, where the statement of cash price may be split off from the other required information in a dealer's catalogue (reg 5) or showroom (reg 6). Fourthly, special prominence must be given to the current APR (reg 8(1)), especially as compared with any other rate statement, eg, flat rate. Fifthly, the use of certain types of statement is restricted.[8] Sixthly, if a mortgage is required there must be a prominent wealth warning in statutory form that the debtor's home is at risk if he defaults.[9]

[8.31] The types of advertisement. The foregoing Regulations require that an advertisement for credit or hire facilities to consumers which falls within Part IV of the CCA must comply with the above general rules (ante, para 8.30); and must be drawn

---

[8.30]

1 The OFT have questioned whether such a highly prescriptive regime is in the consumers' best interest: (1993) 14 CCA News 4/9.

2 Consumer Credit (Advertisement) Regulations 1989, SI 1125. Whilst the Regulations contain some definitions (reg 1), in other cases reference should be made to the CCA definitions (see generally ante, para 5.05).

3 This extends to agreements in excess of the CCA financial limit (reg 1(6)); but there is excluded advertisements of credit or hire facilities for business purposes only (reg 9).

4 Regulation 3; and Sched 3. Eg, for where hp terms vary according to the age of a car; or it is not known how much credit a debtor will draw down under an overdraft or credit card.

5 This may also infringe UTCC reg 7: see post, para 11.13.

6 For convenience, there are special rules for catalogues containing variable information (reg 2(7)) and for seasonal catalogues (reg 4).

7 Regulation 2(6). Unlike the Agreement Regulations (see post, para 9.11), this seems to allow the interspersal of other information: Goode, *Consumer Credit Law and Practice*, para 28.147.

8 Regulation 7. This refers to: 'overdraft' (see regs 1(2), 2(3)); comparative advertising (10 Tr LR 46; cf ante, para 8.06); 'interest free' (see ante, para 8.27); 'no deposit' ('deposit' defined CCA, s 189(1): set out ante, para 5.22). See *Holman v CWS Ltd* [2001] CCLR 2777, DC (co-op divi).

9 Regulation 8(2); *First National Bank plc v Sec of State for Trade and Industry* (1990) 9 Tr LR 184, CA. As to the prominence of this warning, see Goode, *op cit*, note 7, para 9.33. As to refinancing, see ante, para 7.04A.

within one of the following categories,[1] the relevant one being determined by the amount of credit or hire information shown:

1   *Simple advertisements* are designed just to keep the name of a business in the public eye, eg, a brief advertising message at sponsored event; 'give-away' items such as a book of matches. The credit or hire information which can be given is limited to the following (Sched 1, Part I): the name of the creditor[2] and 'a statement of the general nature of his occupation' (Sched 1, Part I, para 5), eg, 'moneylender', 'finance company'. Additionally, there may be included any non-credit information (that does not obscure the clarity of the credit information), eg, 'established 1861', other than the cash price.[3]

2   *Intermediate advertisements* specify most of the **credit** or **hire** information which must be included;[4] but reg 10 lists a small amount of other **credit** or **hire** information which may be included (see below) and makes it clear that there is no restriction as to other types of information, eg, about the goods. The following information **must** be given in an intermediate advertisement: the name[2] and an address or telephone number from which written information may be obtained, eg, 'Post the coupon for written details of our credit terms'; any compulsory security, foreign currency mortgage, deposit,[5] credit broker's fee; or some compulsory insurance, eg, credit insurance. In relation to any specific property or services advertised as available on credit from an 'identified dealer' (reg 1(2)), eg, advertisements of a particular TV as available on hp,[6] usually there must be stated the cash price[3] and APR.[7] Additionally, an intermediate advertisement **may** include certain other specified credit information (para 10), such as advertiser's occupation (see above), or the class of persons to whom the facilities are offered eg, 'householders'. Any further **credit** or **hire** information included will turn it into a full advertisement.

3   *Full advertisements* are the most detailed category, the Regulations drawing a distinction according to whether the advertisement is aimed at prospective debtors,[8] or only at existing debtors (reg 2(i)(d)). Concentrating on the former, the Regulations

---

[8.31]

1   Regulations 2(1) (credit) and 2(2) (hire). See especially the commentary on the whole of the regulations in Guest and Lloyd, *Encyclopedia of Consumer Credit*, para 3-117 *et seq*. For helpful simplified explanations, see the following: OFT, *Advertisements and Quotation Regulations*; Patrick, *A Short Guide to Advertising Regulations*. For simplicity, only the rules for credit, not hire (see Sched 2), are discussed here.

2   The name must be that on any standard licence (reg 1(5)): as to such licences, see generally ante, para 6.14. For a drafting difficulty, see Goode, *Consumer Credit Law and Practice*, para 28.228.

3   The 'cash price' (reg 1(2)) could only be quoted if the (simple) advertisement is not within the regulations. For misleading pricing generally, see ante, para 8.09.

4   Sched I, Part II, paras 1–9. The text is for credit advertisements and there are some variations for hirings: see especially Sched 4.

5   *Ibid*, para 4. It is said that this refers, not to a deposit in hp, but to a special deposit by way of security: Goode, *op cit*, note 2, para 28.221.

6   *Contra* if an electrical retailer just advertises his credit terms for his audio equipment generally. In the case of hiring facilities, the advertisement must state that it is for the hire of goods.

7   Paragraph 7. APR is given (by reg 1(2)) the same meaning as in the tcc regulations (see ante, para 8.25); and detailed rules as to the statement of the APR are found in Sched 3, which permits certain extra tolerances in calculating the APR (see generally ante, para 8.25). For representative APRs, see ante, para 8.30.

8   Apart from a few restrictions (see ante, para 8.30), the advertiser is free to include further information, whether or not about his credit or hire terms.

generally impose only the following minimum requirements in respect of the advertiser's credit facilities:[8] the compulsory information required of all intermediate advertisements (see above); plus, usually most of the information which is optional in such cases (see above), eg, the APR, plus some further information.[9]

Miscellaneous

[8.32] Apart from the extensive control of advertising (see ante, paras 8.27–31), Part IV of the CCA also contains a number of other restrictions upon a creditor or owner seeking business with regard to information that he may supply to the debtor or hirer.

1   *Canvassing dcs credit* (see ante, paras 7.05–07).

2   *Issuing unsolicited credit-tokens* (see ante, para 7.12).

3   *Quotations.* A quotation is a document giving a particular prospective debtor or hirer information about the terms on which any one of the following persons are prepared to do business (s 52(1)(a)): one who carries on a consumer credit or consumer hire business (see ante, para 6.12); or a credit-broking business (s 152(1): see post, para 16.19); or a business in the course of which he provides credit to individuals, even if outside the financial limit of the CCA (see ante, para 5.22). Section 52 allows regulations to be made as to the form and content of any quotations, any breach amounting to a criminal offence.[1] Under the deregulation initiative (see ante, para 5.11) the general regulations were replaced by some restricted to mortgages secured on the customer's home.[2]

4   *Circulars to minors* (see post, para 8.33).

5   *Display of information.* Section 53 empowers the making of regulations requiring the display of prescribed information at his place of business about consumer credit or consumer hire or second mortgage business.[3]

6   *The licensing rules* (see ante, para 6.11 *et seq*).

[8.33/34] Circulars to minors. Besides the civil protection to minors offered by ordinary contract law (see post, para 10.18), there has long been some special criminal protection as regards credit contracts.[1] This policy was continued in the CCA, s 50(1) of which provides as follows:

A person commits an offence[2] who, with a view to financial gain, sends to a minor any document inviting him to–

(a)   borrow money,[3] or

---

9   Schedule 1, Part III. Eg, the total amount payable by the debtor (para 14).

[8.32]

1   Section 167(2) and Sched 1; and see generally post, Chapter 28.

2   Consumer Credit (Content of Quotations) etc Regulations 1999 SI 2725.

3   In 1982, the government announced that they did not for the time being intend to make any regulations under this section.

[8.33/34]

1   The Betting and Loans (Infants) Act 1892 (now repealed).

2   For penalties, see s 167(1) and Sched 1; and see generally post, Chapter 28. As to the effect of minority on any subsequently formed contract, see post, para 10.18.

3   For contracts of loan, see ante, Chapter 7.

(b) obtain goods on credit or hire,[4] or

(c) obtain services on credit, or

(d) apply for information or advice on borrowing money or otherwise obtaining credit, or hiring goods.

The offence consists of the **sending**[5] to the minor of a document inviting him to do any of the four listed things,[6] there being a special exemption for student loans.[7]

Besides the ordinary defences available under ss 168–69 (see Chapter 28), s 50 provides a special defence to s 50(1): the sender is protected if he proves that he did not know and had no reasonable cause to suspect that the recipient was a minor;[8] but, if he sends the document to a minor at an educational establishment for minors, he is deemed to know the recipient was a minor (ss 50(3), 171(5)). Curiously, there would appear to be no offence committed under s 50 when a person **hands** (instead of sends) such a document to a minor,[9] or complies with a request to permit a minor to become an 'additional' credit card holders.[10] The offence has no civil effect on any contract made with the minor (s 170(1): see post, para 10.19).

INFORMATION ABOUT THE DEBTOR OR HIRER

[8.35] Introduction. The consumer has no right to credit; it is a privilege granted by the creditor only when satisfied that the loan is a commercial proposition, provided only that in reviewing the matter the creditor does not indulge in unlawful discrimination (see ante, para 4.23). If credit is refused, lenders' codes of practice (see ante, para 3.13) normally say that the lender should give an indication of any problem; but this is not an obligation. In considering whether to enter agreements, the fundamentals of risk assessment are Character, Capacity and Collateral.[1] To apply these three Cs, creditors or owners will normally seek information about the prospective debtor or hirer from either or both of two sources.[2]

---

4   For credit and hire contracts, see ante, Chapter 5.

5   'Send' may extend beyond sending by post: Guest and Lloyd, *Encyclopedia of Consumer Credit*, para 2-051. What if it is re-addressed to a minor? What if it is not a 'document', but a disc?

6   *Alliance and Leicester BS v Babbs* [1993] CCLR 77, DC (circular stated loans not available to minors). See also the Code of Banking Practice (see ante, para 3.13).

7   Education (Student Loans) Act 1990, Sched 2, para 3(8).

8   Section 50(2). Cf *Tesco Stores Ltd v Brent LBC* [1993] 2 All ER 718, DC (decided under a similar defence in the Video Recordings Act 1984, s 11).

9   It might amount to unlawful canvassing (see generally ante, paras 7.05–07): Guest and Lloyd, *Encyclopedia of Consumer Credit*, para 2-051.

10 The request must come from the adult account holder, be signed by the minor and sent to the adult. See generally ante, para 7.09 *et seq*.

[8.35]

1   See the Chairman of the NCC, reported in (1990) 45 CC 4/4–6; and see also the OFT, in *Credit Scoring* (1992) paras 2.1, 7.7; and see post, para 8.39. Apart from the discrimination and durability rules (see ante, para 4,23), there are no rules requiring the creditors to grant credit, nor even any such provisions in a Code of Practice (see ante, para 3.13). As to giving reasons for refusing credit, see post, paras 8.37; 8.38.

2   These expensive enquiries necessary for new business can be avoided with regard to on-going running-account business: see post, para 8.39.

First, information is likely to be sought from the prospective debtor or hirer himself;[3] and this is commonly done through the device of a signed proposal form for him to complete,[4] together with the production of some identification,[5] upon which a credit check can be run (see below). *Inter alia*, the proposal form is likely to ask about his address (to trace), income and outgoings (to establish capacity to pay), his credit record (to assess willingness to pay) and whether he is a property owner;[6] and it may seek to make all this information the basis of the contract (see post, para 26.08). For the creditor or owner to run an effective credit check, the proposal form must give him effective permission to search for the purposes of the DPA (Sched 3, para 1: see ante, para 3.27).

Second, applications may be made to third parties for information, eg, the Voters' Roll to check the address (see ante, para 3.26). Particularly with a non-status loan secured on a house, a valuation is likely to be important.[7] With regard to any motor vehicle traded in, the financier is likely to have recourse to the private title-register, HP Information Ltd;[8] and, with an eye to the prospective credit or hire agreement, the most significant sources of information about the debtor or hirer, after any county court judgments (CCJs),[9] are likely to be his existing[10] or past creditors.[11] The last can either be approached individually or the information can be sought from credit bureaux (see post, para 8.36). Techniques have been developed for dealing systematically with all the computerised information thus obtained by what are known as credit scoring and behavioural scoring (see post, para 8.39). Since it became common for retailers to have on their premises terminals with on-line connection to credit bureaux, it has been possible for them to offer more safely 'Instant Credit', which is essentially an offer to undertake the above credit-vetting within a few minutes whilst the customer waits.[12]

[8.36/37] Credit reference bureaux. These bureaux are in business to provide information about the financial standing (credit status) of credit-seekers,[1] whether businesses or

---

3   These may amount to unfair terms (see post, para 11.12): Adams [2000] JBL 203. Cf the basis of the contract clauses in insurance policies.

4   For the effect of misrepresentation by the customer in the proposal form, see post, para 17.10.

5   Eg, the production of a photocard driving licence (see ante, para 6.02); Master or Visa card (so relying on the credit-check of that card issuer).

6   Home ownership would indicate the availability in default of a charging order (see post, para 27.04); tenancy suggests possible reliance on distress (see post, para 19.17).

7   Eg, *Platform Home Loans Ltd v Oyston Shipway Ltd* [1996] EGLR 112 (valuer liable in negligent misstatement: see generally post, para 17.19). As to 'non-status loans', see post, para 8.36.

8   As to which, see post, para 21.01. What, if any, redress does the prospective debtor or hirer have if HP Information Ltd (HPI) erroneously state that they have an interest registered against his vehicle?

9   CCJs are held on computer by the Registry Trust Ltd (see post, para 27.03). Unpaid CCJs are one of the main bars to obtaining credit.

10 If the prospective creditor is already the applicant's banker or building society, they will have the advantage of already-available internal information. Similar considerations favour applications to increase revolving credit limits. Not all existing debts are likely to be recorded, eg, water board, student loans.

11 For the lender's contractual duty of confidentiality to the borrower, see post, para 11.10. For the bankers' Code of Practice as to confidentiality, see ante, para 3.13. This is in effect what happens in the CIFAS system: see post, para 8.38.

12 For the problems of offering 'Instant Credit', see (1986) 41 CC 1/4.

[8.36/37]

1   Hence, many offers/advertisements are expressed to be 'subject to status'. For conditional offers, see post, para 10.02.

individuals.[2] Their effectiveness has been enhanced by the advent of major computers,[2a] which has rendered feasible in this field the collection of an enormous amount of information about credit status on a nationwide basis.[3] The capacity to store much fuller information, both favourable and adverse, has led to the development of what are called 'payment profile services' (see post, para 8.39). This has two results. First, credit-seekers are effectively allowed under a single name a maximum of one free bite at the credit industry: the registration of sufficient adverse information with such a bureau will normally ensure that further credit is virtually never granted to that name;[4] and a favourable payment record is likely to have the opposite effect.[5] Second, it enables creditors to stratify applicants according to credit risk: a good credit risk is said to establish credit 'status'; and a bad credit-risk is said to be 'non-status', eg, those with outstanding CCJs and a poor employment history. This status helps determine whether credit will be granted and on what terms.[6]

The consequent power wielded by these credit bureaux was responsible for the inclusion of some special provisions in the CCA (see below) and later for some more generalised controls in the DPA 1984. When the DPA 1998 came into force, the statutory duties to disclose data held on individuals (not corporate bodies) was divided as follows: partnerships and unincorporated bodies will be dealt with under the CCA (see below); private individuals and sole traders will fall under the DPA (see post, para 8.38).

Credit reference agencies. Following the recommendations of the *Crowther Report* (paras 9.1.16–23), the CCA placed some controls on what it termed a 'credit reference agency'.[7] Any agency which satisfies these criteria requires a Category F licence (see ante, para 6.15). Where a credit reference agency is involved in any transaction, ss 157–60 of the CCA (as amended) stipulate a number of steps, whose details are elaborated by regulations:[8]

1 *Discovering the agency.* One of the greatest difficulties of the disappointed individual seeking credit or hire facilities is to discover why he has been turned down. Whilst he has no right to such facilities (see ante, para 8.35), his rejection may be caused by information from the agency. To meet this case, s 157(1) provides the debtor or hirer with a statutory right to know of any credit reference agency consulted during the antecedent negotiations.

---

2   Only non-profit-making bureaux may be protected by qualified privilege: *Clerk and Lindsell on Tort* (18th edn), para 22-128. See further *Crowther Report*, para 9.1.23.

2a As to the DPA rules governing the collection of credit information on individuals, see post, para 8.38.

3   Does the bureaux owe a duty of care to the person being rated? Cf *Ministry of Housing and Local Government v Sharp* [1970] 2 QB 223, CA.

4   Eg, unsatisfied CJJs (see ante, para 3.22). These do not fall within the purview of the Access to Personal Files Act 1987. For credit repair firms, see ante, para 3.23.

5   There seems to be a consensus on the sharing of adverse information to check actual credit applications (but not as a marketing tool – termed 'pre-screening'), though less willingness to share favourable information. See FLA, 1995 AR 16.

6   For non-status loans, see ante, para 7.04A. For the different types of contracts likely to be offered to applicants of different financial status, see post, para 24.49.

7   The complicated expression is defined in ss 145(8), 189(1): for discussion, see Butterworths edn, 1989, para 8.37.

8   Consumer Credit (Conduct of Business)(Credit Reference Agency) Regulations 1977, SI No 330 (as amended); Consumer Credit (Credit Reference Agency) Regulations 2000, SI 290.

2   *File disclosure*. Armed with the foregoing information, the disappointed applicant for credit or hire can approach the identified agency and obtain a copy of the information held on him.[9]

3   *File rectification*. Upon disclosure of the agency's file, the 'objector' may discover that it contains inaccurate information. If the objector considers this to be prejudicial to him, then s 159 affords him a procedure for having the inaccurate information removed or amended.[10]

Failure to comply with these rules amounts to an offence;[11] but otherwise the state of affairs gives rise to no statutory right of action (s 170(1)), though there may sometimes be a possible action in defamation or negligence (see ante, para 8.36).

[8.38] Data Protection Act 1998 (DPA): individuals. Not only has the consumer no right to credit (see ante, para 8.35), it is plainly desirable to minimise over-indebtedness amongst consumers.[1] To do this, the prospective creditor needs to be aware of the prospective debtor's existing commitments, a matter controlled by the DPA where the 'personal data' relates to a 'living individual' (see ante, para 3.27). Under the 1998 Act, data on partnerships, etc, will be dealt with under the CCA provisions (see ante, para 8.37); and the administration of both sets of provisions will be conducted by the Data Protection Commissioner, now the Information Commissioner (IC).

The IC takes the view that both credit reference bureaux and the financiers who use their services are 'data controllers' within the 1998 Act (see ante, para 3.27). Information submitted by creditors and collected by bureaux must comply with the Data Protection Principles.[2] This is particularly relevant to credit scoring (see post, para 8.39). An example of the effectiveness of the DPA concerns the industry practice of filing information by address: because this may result in the disclosure of information about third parties, eg, persons previously living at the address, the Data Protection Tribunal prohibited such practices as breaching the *First Data Protection Principle*.[3] The IC has also forcefully argued that the collection of both favourable and adverse information (see ante, para 8.36) are both within the DPA.[4] But, in practice, these rules are not used against industry systems designed to combat fraud.[5] The following Data Protection Principles also seem particularly relevant to credit bureaux (see ante, para 3.28):

---

9   Under ss 158 (private individuals), 160 (small traders). The latter may not be entitled to know the source of filed information.

10   Section 159 of the CCA was amended by s 62 of the DPA.

11   Sections 157(3), 158(4), 159(6), 160(6), 167 and Sched 1; and see further post, Chapter 28.

[8.38]

1   The Younger Committee concluded that checking creditworthiness prevented reckless or dishonest people from obtaining credit, kept down overheads and prices by reducing bad debts and stimulated trade by facilitating the ready granting of credit in appropriate cases: *Report on the Committee on Privacy* (1972, Cmnd 5012) 78.

2   See ante, para 3.26. On the application of those Principles, see DPC, *Guidance Notes on Default*.

3   The Tribunal amended the enforcement notices issued by the DPR: see *CCN Systems Ltd v DPR* (1992) and the subsequent cases set out in Charlton and Gaskill, *Encyclopedia of Data Protection*, Part 6, para 030 *et seq*.

4   The Registrar argues that both may only be obtained with the subject's consent; and that consent is subject to the UCT Regulations (see post, para 11.12): DPA, *Guidance on Credit Referencing* (1996).

5   The 'Principle of Reciprocity'. Eg, the Gone Away Information Network (GAIN), the Credit Industry Fraud Avoidance System (CIFAS): see (1994) 49 CC 2/23, 31.

The fourth principle requires a bureau to correct any errors in the data held of which it becomes aware.[6]

The sixth principle grants a right of access by the data subject to all personal data held on him.[7]

The seventh principle requires the user or bureau to take appropriate security measures against (a) unauthorised access or (b) accidental loss of the data.[8]

[8.39] Credit scoring.[1] Traditionally, lenders tried to minimise bad debt by finding out as much as they could about individual applicants, concentrating on 'the three C's' (see ante, para 8.35), eg, home credit. This was done on the premise that the behaviour of new applicants will closely resemble that of similar previous applicants (see below). Its weakness was the inability to predict extraneous events closely associated with default, eg, family break-up, redundancy, serious injury.[2] To cope with huge increases in volume, modern lenders have standardised these procedure into a process known as 'credit scoring', which is inevitably more remote and impersonal. Small volume lenders (in modern terms) may conduct this process manually; but large volume lenders usually computerise the process, normally on the back of computer-based accounting and management systems.[3]

The technique. In essence, credit scoring seeks to harness two streams of information as a credit-granting tool:

(a) A statistical analysis of a large number of existing accounts, with numerical values assigned to pieces of information found significant in determining payment record, eg, age of debtor, deposit percentage, householder or tenant.[4] The programme will allocate a positive or negative score to each of those pieces of information. This body of data has the advantage of objectivity. Yet, it only deals in probability, whilst ignoring the applicant's willingness to pay.

(b) Personal information about the applicant. Much of this he will supply on an Application Form (see ante, para 8.35). But more about his personal credit history will be obtained from a credit reference agency (see ante, paras 8.36–38); and lenders of large sums may also run checks with other third parties, eg, bank (see ante, para 7.03), or employer: this will usually be done by the lender's computer automatically and on-line calling up the agency's computer. If accurate,[5] this will say much about the applicant's ability to pay.

---

6   More than one in ten files contained errors: [2000] 9 Which? 9.

7   See DPA 1998, Sched 1, Part 2, para 8. See further ss 7, 10, 11, 12: ante, para 3.27.

8   See DPA 1998, Sched 1, Part 1, para 7. See further ante, para 3.28.

[8.39]

1   See generally the OFT document, *Credit Scoring* (1992), which is currently being reviewed: (1999) 22 Fair Trading 6. For the current version, see Goode, *Consumer Credit Law and Practice*, VIII, Part A, para 7.

2   Some of these risks can be reduced by credit insurance (see post, para 24.48). But this does create a problem in detecting over-indebtedness, as to which see post, para 27.01.

3   See [2000] 9 Credit Today, Extra.

4   For maximum effectiveness, each lender needs to assess his own (unique) lending experience; and then keep that assessment updated (monitoring).

5   The agency file on the applicant may be inaccurate from fraud (despite CIFAS and GAIN) or from innocent input, or insufficient, eg, where a judgment debt was paid, or manipulated, eg, by credit repair (see ante, para 3.22).

The lender's system then constructs a score card for the applicant from the points he achieves in respect of each scoring piece of information and hence whether he attains an overall pass score. Too harsh a scheme leads to rejection of too many good credit risks, whereas too lenient a scheme would tend to produce too many bad debts.

Credit and behaviour scoring. A lender will undertake a credit scoring at the outset of a fixed-sum transaction, eg, direct selling, hp, mail order, personal loan. However, with regard to running-account credit, the lender can also take advantage of the continuing credit characteristics of the debtor, eg, his payment record or average balance in what has become known a 'behaviour scoring', eg, credit cards, charge cards, overdrafts. This is a 'statistically derived assessment of the future risk of a current customer'[6] and have been found to be highly predictive of future performance.

Control of scoring systems. Generally speaking, the law is in favour of such systems because they are so effective in minimising fraud and over-indebtedness.[7] Yet that very effectiveness has led to statutory intervention with regard to the construction and operation of scoring systems. Controls on construction of the system deal with direct or indirect discrimination;[8] and data protection rules control both the lender and credit reference agency whose automatic processing 'significantly' affect the applicant (ss 12(1)(d), 12(1) of the DPA), which expression presumably includes credit-granting. Controls on the operations of the system are aimed as follows: providing individuals with a general description of how the credit-scoring system works;[8a] granting the applicant the right to see, and if necessary correct, his credit record;[9] ensuring that the automatic scoring process is subject to review by a human being;[10] and the entire regime for the storage of personal data on a computer, eg, third party information (see ante, para 8.38). Additionally, the OFT have inspired a code of practice, *The Guide to Credit Scoring*, which covers a large number of other matters in the operation of credit scoring systems.[11]

---

6 OFT, *op cit*, note 1, para 4.10. Thus, it is both a credit granting and management tool, so it can also be used after default to predict the recoverability of judgment (see post, para 27.04) and to detect stolen cards from uncharacteristic spending patterns.

7 As to fraud, see CIFAS and GAIN (ante, para 8.38); and as to over-indebtedness, see post, para 27.01.

8 Eg, red-lining (see OFT, *op cit*, note 1, paras 5.35–47). For a word of caution, see OFT, *Vulnerable Consumers and Financial Services* (1999) para 612. As to discrimination, see ante, para 4.23; and as to the unfitness to hold a credit licence, see ante, para 6.18.

8a DPA, s 7. UK creditors are reluctant to divulge too much information to consumers, eg, application declined for over-indebtedness. For a comparison of the position in the US and UK, see [2001] 10 Credit Today 33.

9 See CCA, ss 157–60 (see ante, paras 8.37–38); and the *Sixth Data Protection Principal* (see ante, para 8.38).

10 DPA, s 12. But the decision whether to grant credit is exempt: ss 12(4)–(7).

11 This 1993 code is set out in Annex C of the OFT *Credit Scoring* (see above).

CHAPTER 9

FORMALITIES OF THE AGREEMENT

[9.01] Introduction. With regard to the formalities required in a simple contract for the supply of goods, a sharp contrast may be observed between the SGA and the CCA. As to ordinary sales within the SGA, required formalities are the exception (see post, para 9.02 *et seq*); but, in the case of regulated transactions, compliance with extensive formalities is seen as an essential measure of consumer protection and is therefore the norm (see post, para 9.06 *et seq*). In the absence of the consideration necessary for a simple contract,[1] ownership of goods may be transferred by gift[2] or deed.

Deeds. Whether or not supported by consideration, a formal promise made in a deed will be enforced by the courts,[3] subject to the defence of *non est factum* (see post, para 10.16). However, the law relating to the formalities required of a deed was amended by statute in 1989. First, the requirement of a seal has been partially abolished: for the execution of a deed by an individual, statute now requires only that the instrument makes it clear on its face that it is intended to be a deed and that it be signed and witnessed,[4] whereas, for execution of a deed by a registered company, another statute requires the deed to be described as such and signed or sealed.[5] Secondly, there has been repealed the famous s 40 of the LPA requiring the sale or other disposition of an interest in land to be evidenced in writing (see post, para 9.03).

ORDINARY SUPPLIES

[9.02] The Sale of Goods Act. The common law required no special formalities in the conclusion of a contract of sale;[1] but the SGA 1893 mentioned two such cases; namely, where one of the parties was a corporation[2] or the price was £10 or more.[3] The modern rule is to be found in s 4(1) of the SGA and provides as follows:

[9.01]

1 See post, para 10.01.
2 As to gifts, see ante, para 2.08.
3 See generally *Chitty on Contracts* (28th edn), vol 1, para 1-042 *et seq*.
4 By the Law of Property (Miscellaneous Provisions) Act 1989, s 1. See (1989) 105 LQR 553–55.
5 Sections 36, 36A of the Companies Act 1985, as substituted by s 130 of the Companies Act 1989.

[9.02]

1 But the parties may seek to impose special formalities, as where one indicates that he will only contract by signature on standard terms: as to standard terms, see generally post, para 11.08; and as to formation by signature, see post, para 10.02.
2 SGA 1893, s 3 itself imposed no formalities whatsoever but simply referred to other legislation which has required no formalities for some time: Companies Act 1948, s 32 (now CA 1985, s 36); Corporate Bodies' Contracts Act 1960 (as amended).
3 SGA 1893, s 4, which embodied the old Statute of Frauds rule requiring such sales to be evidenced in writing. It was repealed by the Law Reform (Enforcement of Contracts) Act 1954, s 1.

Subject to this[4] and any other Act,[5] a contract of sale may be made in writing (either with or without seal), or by word of mouth, or partly in writing and partly by word of mouth, or may be implied from the conduct of the parties.

Certain formalities are, however, required for sales of goods which also fall within the following categories:

1 Regulated conditional or credit sales (see post, para 9.06 *et seq*).

2 Sales of an interest in land (see post, para 9.03).

3 Documentary sales caught by the Bills of Sale Acts must also comply with the rules there laid down, subject to the following distinction (see post, para 9.04):

    (a) ordinary sales, or absolute transfers, fall within the SGA and must also comply with the formalities of the 1878 Act (s 62(3) of the SGA);

    (b) sales by way of mortgages, or non-absolute transfers, are outside the SGA (s 62(4)) but must comply with the 1882 Act.

4 Sales of a ship. Under the Merchant Shipping Act 1995, sale of an interest in a ship must be in the prescribed form and registered, there being a simplified system for small ships.[6]

5 Sale of an aircraft. There are special rules for the sale of an interest in an aircraft, which must be registered with the Civil Aviation Authority.[7]

6 Caravans. Touring caravans are subject only to the ordinary rules but there are special provisions governing licences to park residential caravans.[8]

7 Auctions. Auctioneers are required to display at auctions their name and addresses, and also copies of the Auctions (Bidding Agreements) Acts.[9]

8 Pyramid selling. Regulations made under the FTA require that each distributor enter a written contract and be given a copy of it (see ante, para 8.17).

9 Goods subject to special statutory regimes, such as firearms (see ante, para 4.31) or motor vehicles.[10]

10 Consumer supply contracts (see post, para 11.12A) must be drafted legibly in Plain English (reg 6 of the UTCC: see post, para 11.13) and may be unfair if important terms are given insufficient prominence (Grey Term 1(i): see post, para 11.17).

11 Distance sales (see post, para 9.05A) and doorstep sales (see post, para 10.22).

[9.03] Goods and land. In place of the old rule requiring dispositions of an interest in land (see post, para 19.02) to be **evidenced** in writing (s 40 of the LPA 1925; repealed), the Law

---

4 The reference is otiose: *Benjamin's Sale of Goods* (5th edn), para 2-020.

5 'Nothing in this section affects the law relating to corporations' (s 4(2)); as to which, see note 2, above.

6 Part II. Likewise a mortgage of a ship, so that there is a registration system for ship sales and mortgages. These rules do not apply to small boats, eg, rowing boats.

7 See further Goode, *HP Law and Practice* (2nd edn), p 132D. These rules do not apply to very small aircraft, eg, models.

8 Caravan Sites etc Act 1960 (as amended); Mobile Homes Act 1983 (as amended). Such parking does not constitute a bailment: see ante, para 1.17.

9 Auctioneers Act 1845, s 7; and as to the Auction (Bidding Agreements) Acts: see post, para 10.13.

10 The DVLC (see ante, para 6.02) requires the submission of signed transfer forms.

of Property (Miscellaneous Provisions) Act 1989 now requires that the 'sale or other disposition of an interest in land can only be **made** in writing' and must incorporate or refer to all the terms which the parties have expressly agreed.[1] 'Disposition' extends to contracts to grant a mortgage or charge,[2] so that it is no longer possible to have a valid charge created by a mere deposit of deeds.[3]

As there is now no similar rule in relation to sale of goods (see ante, para 9.02), this requires a line to be drawn between sales of interests in land (within the LPA) and sales of goods (within the SGA).[4] One view is that there is no overlap between the LPA and SGA because a contract in respect of something which is attached to, or part of, the land is always a sale of goods because it is sold with a view to its ultimate severance. Another view is that the word 'goods' may have a different meaning under the SGA from that under the LPA, so that one transaction may be both a sale of goods within the SGA and a sale of an interest in land within the LPA.[5] For the present purposes, the definitions of 'goods' (see ante, para 2.02) give rise to several problems:

1 *Crops, trees, etc.* It is said that, for the purposes of the SGA, sales of such emblements and industrial growing crops will almost always be sales of goods, 'since the agreement between the parties must be that they shall be severed [from the land] either 'before sale' or 'under the contract of sale' as provided by s 61(1)'.[6]

2 *Fixtures.* As will be seen later (see post, para 25.23), where a chattel is annexed to land so as to become a fixture, at common law it generally becomes the property of the owner of the land and the title of its previous owner is extinguished.[7] If the owner of the land agrees with X that X shall build, eg, a wall, or attach a fixture, eg, central heating, on terms that no property is to pass until affixed, for most purposes this is not a sale of goods to the landowner,[8] but a contract for work and materials (see ante, para 2.05) annexed to the land (see above). However, if the landowner subsequently severs either a fixture, or part of the building, which he then sells, it is a sale of goods, eg, an old boiler, or slate roof.

3 *Minerals, gravel, soil, etc.* These are not merely 'attached to' the land, but part of it. If the landowner has himself already severed the minerals, etc, before contracting to sell them, or if he agrees to do so before the property is to pass, there is a sale of goods.[9] However, the courts have had more difficulty if the severance is to be done by the buyer: in the case of trees, it has been held to be a sale of goods;[10] but in the case of

---

[9.03]

1 Section 2. See *Benjamin's Sale of Goods* (5th edn), para 1-091; Annand (1989) 105 LQR at 555–58; Greed (1990) 140 NLJ 296.

2 Section 2(6). As to fittings sold with land, see *Wright v Robert Leonard (Developments)* [1994] NPC 49, CA (lease of show-flat to include furniture and fixtures). For fixtures, see note 7, below.

3 *United Bank of Kuwait v Sahib* [1996] 3 All ER 215, CA (see 113 LQR 533).

4 There is also a difference in the application of UCTA: see post, para 18.17.

5 Atiyah, *Sale of Goods* (10th edn), pp 71–72 .

6 See Benjamin, *op cit*, note 1, para 1.092. Is this the explanation of 'pick-your-own-strawberries'?

7 *Reynolds v Ashby & Son* [1904] AC 446, HL (hirer of machinery fixed it to floor: see further post, para 25.23).

8 See Benjamin, *op cit*, note 1, para 1-095, suggesting that some SGA provisions may nevertheless apply to the transaction.

9 See Benjamin, *op cit*, note 1, para 1-096.

10 *Kursell v Timber Operators Ltd* (set out post, para 20.04).

cinders and slag, there has been held not to be a sale of goods, but a sale of an interest in land.[11]

[9.04] Bills of Sale Acts. The first such Act, passed in 1854, was designed to combat fraud on creditors by use of bills of sale; that is, where a debtor secretly sold (usually in writing) personal chattels to one creditor who thereby acquired the right to those chattels to the exclusion of other creditors who may later advance money to the debtor under the illusion that possession of them indicated the debtor to be a man of substance.[1] The rules governing such transactions were eventually embodied in the Bills of Sale Act 1878, which did not apply to all sales, but only those where **all** the following conditions were satisfied:

(a) There was a transfer of 'personal chattels'. This expression was carefully defined by s 4 to include 'goods',[2] 'other articles capable of complete transfer by delivery'[3] and 'fixtures separately assigned' from land.[4] However, the definition expressly excluded choses in action (see ante, para 7.15/17).

(b) The transfer was recorded in a 'bill of sale', that is, a document recording the sale of an interest in goods.[5] The expression 'bill of sale' was elaborately defined in s 4 as including:

> ... assignments,[6] ... declarations of trust without transfer, inventories of goods with receipt thereto attached,[7] or receipt for the purchase money of goods[8] and other assurances of personal chattels[9] ... or licences to take possession of personal chattels as security for any debt,[10] and also any agreement ... by which a right in equity to any chattels, or to any charge or security thereon, shall be conferred.[10]

Specifically excluded from this definition are assignments for the benefit of creditors (see post, para 19.24), transfers of any ship or vessel,[11] bills of lading and other

---

11 *Morgan v Russell & Sons* [1909] 1 KB 357, DC; *Mills v Stockman* (1966–67) 116 CLR 61, Aus HC (waste dumped from a slate quarry).

[9.04]

1 By such secret transactions, a hard-pressed debtor might avoid precipitating insolvency proceedings and gradually work his way back to solvency.

2 'Goods' is not defined in the Acts. Cf the SGA definition: ante, para 2.02.

3 After-acquired chattels not being capable of complete transfer by delivery are probably not within the definition: Bridge [1992] JBL at 6. Consequently, unless void for uncertainty, absolute transfers of property not yet owned by the grantor will be enforced. But non-absolute transfers of future-acquired chattels are expressly caught by the Acts: see post, para 9.05.

4 The definition carefully excludes fixtures assigned with land. For fixtures, see ss 5 and 7; and see generally post, para 25.23.

5 See *Allsop v Day* (1861) 7 H & N 457.

6 Assignments, declarations of trust and charges are used in indirect financing: see ante, para 2.22.

7 To be within the Act, the inventory or receipt must amount to an assurance: see below.

8 A receipt is only a bill of sale if it is part of the transaction which passes the property in personal chattels: *Ramsey v Margrett* [1894] 2 QB 18, CA.

9 *Coburn v Collins* (1886) 35 Ch D 373 (sale of business, seller to have 'lien' for price). But this rule does not extend to liens arising by operation of law, eg, unpaid seller's lien (see post, para 24.04).

10 Such licences to seize are non-absolute transfers: see post, para 9.05. As to instruments giving a power of distress, see s 6.

11 As to which, see ante, para 9.02. But such transfers are caught by the registration provisions of the Companies Acts: see post, para 25.28A. Also excluded are agricultural charges by farmers within the Agricultural Credits Act 1928 (as amended).

documents used in the ordinary course of business as proof of the possession or control of goods, eg, trust receipts (see post, paras 20.09; 25.16).

(c) The 'personal chattels' must remain in the 'possession or apparent possession' of the grantor (seller).[12]

Where there is such a paper transfer of 'personal chattels' recorded in a 'bill of sale' but the goods remain in the 'possession or apparent possession' of the grantor, the legislation draws a clear distinction according to whether or not the transfer is absolute (see post, para 9.05).

[9.05] Absolute and non-absolute transfers. Where a paper transfer falls within the ambit of the Bills of Sale Acts (see ante, para 9.04), the legislation provides as follows:[1]

1 *Absolute transfers*. If the grantor (seller) transfers his entire interest in the 'personal chattels', the intention of Parliament was to provide an effective registration system for the protection of subsequent creditors. This it achieved in the Bills of Sale Act 1878, which requires that all transfers (originally both absolute and non-absolute: but see below) must be attested and registered. Two or more bills have priority in order of the respective dates of registration, whilst unregistered bills are void as against the grantor's execution creditors and trustee in bankruptcy.[2]

2 *Non-absolute transfers (mortgages)*. Almost immediately upon it coming into force, the 1878 Act proved extremely popular with moneylenders because of the very effective security which it provided for mortgages. To discourage this, Parliament then imposed such severe restrictions on these mortgage bills[3] as would fall little short of a complete prohibition: the 1882 Act is almost commercially unworkable and is relatively little used. This was achieved by an amending Act of 1882, which took over control of all bills of sale under which the grantee (lender) was granted a licence to seize.[4] Any mortgage bill of sale falling within the 1882 Act was declared void as against all persons,[5] unless strictly in the form set out in the Schedule (s 9), which form precludes the granting of charges.[6] Chattel mortgages are considered later (see post, para 25.27).

After-acquired personal property. In *Holroyd v Marshall*,[7] a financially embarrassed mill owner entered into a mortgage which included not only his mill machinery, but also any machinery bought in substitution for it. After the old machinery had been replaced by

---

12 'Personal chattels' are deemed to be in the 'apparent possession' of the grantor whilst in his constructive possession (as to which, see post, para 23.03): s 4.

[9.05]

1 See generally Crossley Vaines, *Personal Property* (5th edn), Chapter 22; Gibson's *Conveyancing* (20th edn), Part 3.

2 1878 Act, ss 8, 10–12. As to execution creditors, see post, para 19.15; and as to insolvency, see post, para 19.18 *et seq*.

3 A mortgage bill will be one where the grantor (borrower) retains an equity of redemption: see generally post, para 25.20.

4 Section 3. Technically, this is the Bills of Sale (1878) Amendment Act 1882.

5 Including the parties: *Maas v Pepper* [1905] AC 102, HL.

6 Because it insisted on transfer of ownership: for the definition of charges, see post, para 25.02. The 1882 Act also makes repossession difficult (s 13).

7 (1862) 10 HLC 191; [1861–73] All ER Rep 414, HL.

new, the mortgagee sought to recover the new machinery from an execution creditor. The House of Lords held that, whilst at common law the conveyance might be void, it was effective in equity to transfer the beneficial interest in property immediately it was acquired and in priority to the execution creditor.

The effect of this decision was to place a most powerful security device in the hands of the creditor;[8] and it may save that property from the debtor's subsequent insolvency, even if acquired after commencement of the insolvency.[9] Whilst absolute transfers of after-acquired personal property escaped the 1878 Act[10] and are anyway dealt with by the SGA (see post, para 20.22 *et seq*), mortgage transfers of after-acquired personal chattels are generally avoided by the 1882 Act except as against the grantor (borrower).[11] Mortgage assignments of choses in action remain outside the 1882 Act,[12] but mortgage transfers of choses in action or possession require registration under the Companies Act (see post, para 25.28A). For priorities in real property, see post, para 25.22.

[9.05A] Distance sales. Whether the private consumer is dealing by phone, internet or mail order, the Distance Selling Regulations (see ante, para 8.17) require that the supplier shall provide to the consumer information divided into two divisions.

First division of information. 'In good time prior to the conclusion of the contract,[1] he will supply the following information' (reg 7(1)(a)) in a medium unspecified (see below):

(i) the identity of the supplier and, where the contract requires payment in advance, the supplier's address;[2]

(ii) a description of the main characteristics of the goods of services;[3]

(iii) the price of all goods or services including all taxes;[4]

(iv) delivery costs where appropriate;[5]

(v) the arrangements for payment, delivery or performance;[6]

---

8   Goode, *Legal Problems of Credit and Security*, p 6. For a limitation in respect of subsequent purchase-money finance, see Goode, pp 55–57.

9   Goode, *ibid*, p 8. For fixed and floating charge, see post, para 25.25.

10   Neither future goods nor choses in action amounted to personal chattels: see ante, para 9.04. The 1882 Act must *pro tanto* amend that definition to include future goods: see ss 3, 15 of the 1882 Act.

11   Section 5. For the exceptions, see s 6: these must be in the statutory form.

12   *Tailby v Official Receiver* (set out ante, para 7.18).

[9.05A]

1   'In the case of a telephone communication, the identity of the supplier and the commercial purpose of the call shall be made clear at the beginning of the conversation with the consumer': reg 7(4).

2   For the problems of advance payment, see post, para 23.22.

3   How, if at all, does this differ from the identity test for the implied term as to description: see post, para 13.13.

4   As to price, see ante, para 2.06. Is it possible for an internet supplier to comply as regards all taxes/countries? 'Services' should include credit.

5   This is because delivery will usually be at the consumer's home. As to the delivery rules, see post, para 23.04.

6   Why only one of these arrangements? Performance must be within 30 days (reg 19: see post, para 23.04). As to payment cards, see reg 21 (see ante, paras 7.01, 7.07A, 7.13/14).

(vi) the existence of a right of cancellation;[7]

(vii) the cost of using the means of distance communication where it is calculated other than at the basic rate;[8]

(viii) the period for which the offer or the price remains valid; and

(ix) where appropriate, the minimum duration of the contract, in the case of a contract for the supply of goods or services to be performed permanently or recurrently.[9]

Further, if the supplier proposes, in the event of non-availability, to supply substitute goods or services, the following is required: the consumer must be informed of this fact (reg 7(1)(b)) and the supplier will bear the return-cost of returning the substitute (reg 7(1)(c)). Moreover, under reg 7(2), all this information must be provided in an appropriate 'clear and comprehensible manner' with due regard to the principles of commercial good faith (see post, para 11.15) and the protection of minors (see post, para 10.18).

Second division of information. Except for the most part as regards the provision of some one-off services (reg 9), usually at a later stage (see below) 'the supplier shall provide to the consumer in writing or in another durable medium which is available and accessible to the consumer' (reg 8(1)) certain stipulated information: *viz* items (i)–(vi) in reg 7(1) above; details of any right of cancellation; the supplier's business address to receive complaints; and information about after-sales service and guarantees (see post, para 17.09).

For instance, if the transaction is by internet, the website must contain the first division information;[10] and the second division information is likely to be provided by fax or letter. Regulation 8(1) provides that the second stage information must be made available to the consumer either:

(a) prior to the conclusion of the contract, or

(b) thereafter, in good time and in any event –

(i) during the performance of the contract, in the case of services; and

(ii) at the latest at the time of delivery where goods not for delivery to third parties are concerned.

So, in the case of goods, the second stage durable-medium information could be supplied either before acceptance (see post, para 10.02), eg, a catalogue, or before delivery, eg, in a posted acceptance or delivery note.

---

7 Under regs 10–18: see post, para 10.22A. The consumer must also be told the conditions and procedures for exercising any statutory right of cancellation; any obligation to return the goods and consequent cost he should bear (reg 8(2)(b)); any conditions for exercising any contractual right of cancellation (reg 8(2)(e)); and in a contract of services that he has no statutory right of cancellation.

8 Eg, premium-rate telephone call.

9 Eg, a book club.

10 An OFT survey in 2001 discovered widespread non-compliance.

REGULATED AGREEMENTS

Introduction

[9.06] The scope of controls. The elaborate safeguards developed by owners ensured that hire purchase (hp) agreements would usually be in writing (see ante, para 1.20 *et seq*); and in respect of hp, credit and conditional sale (see ante, paras 1.13; 1.14) the HP Acts 1938–65 developed a series of consumer safeguards relating to the formalities of the agreement. Most of these ideas now extend to loans as well, are to be found in Part V of the CCA, and may be classified as follows:

1 Pre-contract disclosure (see post, para 9.08).

2 The form and content of regulated agreements (see post, para 9.09).

3 The execution of regulated agreements (see post, para 9.12 *et seq*).

4 Copies of regulated agreements (see post, para 9.14 *et seq*).

5 The withdrawal from prospective regulated agreements and cancellation of actual regulated agreements (see post, para 10.26 *et seq*).

The Act provides some exemptions from the above rules (see post, para 9.07) and makes special provision for the situation where a regulated agreement is subsequently varied: even if the modifying agreement would not be regulated taken by itself, if it is for fixed-sum credit it will always be taken as regulated,[1] whereas this will not necessarily be the case with running-account credit;[2] and, if the earlier agreement was cancellable, any modifying agreement made within the cancellation period will also be cancellable.[3] The effect of non-compliance with all these rules is considered later (post, para 9.19).

[9.07] Exemptions from Part V. According to s 74 of the CCA (as amended), the following categories of regulated agreement (see ante, para 5.13) are not caught by any of the provisions of Part V of the Act except for those as to pre-contract information (s 55: see post, para 9.08) and agency (s 56: see post, para 16.08).

1 *Non-commercial agreements* (s 74(1)(a): see ante, para 5.18).

2 *Small DCS agreements for restricted use (RU) credit.* Thus, regulated transactions such as small credit sales (£50: see ante, para 1.13) may be made wholly orally (s 74(2)); but, insofar as any part of them is expressed in writing, that part must comply with the Part V rules as to form and contents.[1]

3 *Small cancellable agreements.* Whereas the Doorstep-selling Regulations provide for the cancellation of **cash** transactions on the doorstep (see post, para 10.21), s 74(2A) of the

---

[9.06]

1 Section 82(3). Eg, if the amount of a fixed sum loan is increased beyond the ambit of the Act. As to variation of commercial agreements, see further post, para 26.22.

2 See s 82(4): para 9.07. If the credit limit permanently exceeds the ambit of the Act, the agreement is no longer regulated and falls outside Part V; but, if the credit limit is only temporarily exceeded, it remains regulated and within Part V. How temporary is 'temporary'?

3 Section 82(5). But not necessarily otherwise: s 82(6). As to cancellable agreements, see post, para 10.29.

[9.07]

1 Section 74(4) (as amended). Subject to the ordinary dispensing power under s 60(3): see post, para 9.09.

CCA, provides a matching lower limit (£35) for the application to doorstep credit transactions of the CCA cancellation provisions.[2]

4 *Overdrafts*.[3] These will be exempt from Part V only if the Director so determines,[4] though a distinction is now drawn according to whether or not it is a bank overdraft:

(a) Bank overdrafts. There is a presumption in favour of such a determination unless he thinks it would be against the public interest.[5] Further, there is an outright exemption where a bank on one occasion honours a cheque above an agreed overdraft limit (s 82(4)).

(b) Other overdrafts, eg, in-store budget accounts, finance company revolving credit schemes. These may be exempted only if the Director is of the opinion that this is not against the interest of debtors.[6]

5 *Agreements to finance payments on death.* Insofar as made orally,[1] these rather specialised agreements[7] may be exempted from Part V, but only if the Director so determines and it is not against the interest of debtors.

Finally, the effect of this system on modifying agreements[8] and house mortgages should be noted. Unregulated mortgages to secure sums in excess of the CCA are outside most of the Act[9] other than the advertisement rules (see s 43(1): ante, para 8.29); but regulated mortgages can only escape Part V by reason of the rules of this paragraph (see also post, para 10.27).

[9.08] Pre-contract disclosure. In pursuance of the objective of truth-in-lending (see ante, para 5.08), the CCA took steps to make creditors and owners disclose the costs charged for their services at all the following stages:

(a) when seeking business from the public generally (see ante, para 8.21); and

(b) before an individual regulated agreement is made, s 55 allowed the imposition of disclosure requirements by regulation; but none has been made; and

(c) in a regulated agreement (see post, para 9.13).

---

2 See post, para 10.28 *et seq*. There is no lower limit as regards the cancellation of distance contracts (see post, para 10.22A).

3 This term is not defined in the CCA, but should perhaps be read as referring to running account credit (as to which, see ante, para 5.28): Karpinski and Fielding, *Consumer Credit Agreements*, para 7.11. Was this a drafting slip? Some such overdrafts will also fall within the Doorstep-selling Regulations: see post, para 10.21.

4 He may exempt on such conditions as he sees fit: s 74(3)(a). For such determinations, see Goode, *Consumer Credit Law and Practice*, Div IV.

5 Section 74(3A), inserted by the Banking Act 1979, s 38. Even if that contradicts the interests of debtors. The consequent lack of written record of a loan may cause later difficulties: see Banking Ombudsman, *Annual Review 1990/91*, para 4.3.

6 Sections 74(3), 183. Thus, the Act discriminates with regard to test and burden of proof against overdrafts offered by, eg, building societies, department stores and smaller finance companies.

7 Eg, for court fees for probate. For the scope of this exemption, see Goode, *op cit*, note 4, para 30.17.

8 Section 82(3). See also s 82(4) (above). As to the CCA restrictions on modifying agreements, see generally post, para 26 22; and as to cancellation of modifying agreements, see post, para 10.32.

9 They may instead fall within the FSMA: see ante, para 3.02.

Form and content of agreements

[9.09] Introduction. Following its usual strategy, the CCA does not itself spell out any requirements. Instead, s 60(1) enables the Secretary of State to 'make regulations as to the form and contents of documents embodying[1] regulated agreements' (see para 9.10). However, such regulations will not extend to agreements exempted from Part V of the Act (see ante, para 9.07). Additionally, the Director is empowered (s 60(3)) upon application of any consumer credit or consumer hire business (see ante, para 6.12) to relieve[2] by notice[3] that business from any such regulations insofar as it appears to the Director to be impracticable[4] for the applicant to comply with any requirement 'in a particular case'.[5] If a document falling within their ambit does not comply with the regulations, it is not properly executed (s 61(1)(a): set out post, para 9.12), with the effects considered below (post, para 9.19) but no others (s 170: see post, para 10.19).

Additionally, agreements are likely to contain a 'notification' clause, warning consumers that information about them may be registered with a credit reference agency.[6]

[9.10] Agreement Regulations. Section 60(1) provides that the Secretary of State may make regulations as to the form and content of regulated agreements (see ante, para 9.09), which:

> ... shall contain such provisions as appear to him appropriate with a view to ensuring that the debtor or hirer is made aware of –
>
> (a) the rights and duties conferred or imposed on him by the agreement,
>
> (b) the amount and rate of the total charge for credit (in the case of a consumer credit agreement),
>
> (c) the protection and remedies available to him under this Act, and
>
> (d) any other matters which, in the opinion of the Secretary of State, it is desirable for him to know about in connection with the agreement.

These powers have been utilised to introduce Agreement Regulations,[1] which lay down detailed rules to govern the content and form of regulated agreements, subject to any prior waiver by the Director.[2] This rule will also apply indirectly to the documents which

---

[9.09]

1 'A document embodies a provision if the provision is set out either in the document or in another document referred to in it' – s 189(4).

2 The statute speaks of the requirement being 'waived or varied'. This relief only extends to regulations made under s 60, so that the successful applicant must still comply with s 61: as to which, see post, para 9.12.

3 Only if the Director 'is satisfied that to do so would not prejudice the interests of debtors or hirers': s 60(4).

4 As to the meaning of 'impracticable', see Goode, *Consumer Credit Legislation*, para 1221.

5 Not only is this in no sense a general dispensing power, but it can only be exercised on behalf of the applicant to cover specific circumstances.

6 The form of clause has been agreed as complying with the First Data Protection Principle: see ante, para 3.28.

[9.10]

1 Consumer Credit (Agreements) Regulations 1983 (SI 1553) (as amended). There are separate rules covering cancellation notices and copies: see post, para 9.17.

2 Under ss 60(3), (4), 183. A s 60(3) application must be made before an agreement is entered into: *Dimond v Lovell* (set out ante, para 5.13/14); and Macleod [1999] JBL at 462–63.

will become regulated agreements when signed by all parties[3] – what the Act terms 'prospective agreements' (as to which see ante, para 5.20).

1   *Content of agreements.* Section 60(2)(a) explains that the regulations may:

> ... require specified information to be included in the prescribed manner in documents, and other specified material to be excluded.

In fact, the Agreement Regulations specify different rules for different permutations as follows: the two types of regulated agreement, consumer credit and consumer hire agreements (as to which see ante, para 5.13/14); the time at which the agreement becomes executed;[4] and whether or not the agreement is cancellable.[5] Leaving aside multiple agreements,[6] the rules generally speaking[7] require all the different permutations to display prominently at their commencement the type of agreement,[8] to identify the parties,[9] to show the other financial and related particulars (see further post, para 9.11) and to embody any security provided by the debtor or hirer.[10]

2   *Form of agreement.* According to s 60(2)(b), the regulations may:

> ... contain requirements to ensure that specified information is clearly brought to the attention of the debtor or hirer, and that one part of a document is not given insufficient or excessive prominence compared with another.

Usually, the specified information (prescribed terms) is contained together on the signature-side of the document, whilst the desired standard terms (including the required terms) are on the back (see post, para 9.13). The Agreement Regulations simply provide that:[11]

> ... the lettering of the terms of the agreement ... shall, apart from any signature, be easily legible and of a colour which is readily distinguishable from the colour of the paper.

The Regulations also contain specific provisions as to the required prominence of particular items (see post, para 9.11).

Entirely separate from the foregoing rules are those dealing with the information which must be provided by the parties during the continuance of the agreement (ss 77–80: see post, para 15.16) or at its termination.[12]

---

3   See Goode, *Consumer Credit Law and Practice*, para 30.47. The rules also apply to security instruments signed by the debtor or hirer: see post, para 25.12. What is the effect of using CCA documentation for transactions outside the Act?

4   This may or may not be when the document is signed by the debtor or hirer: see further post, para 9.13.

5   As to the prescribed notices in cancellable agreements, see post, para 9.17.

6   As to multiple agreements, see ante, para 5.27; and as to the regulatory requirements for multiple agreements, see Goode, *op cit*, note 3, paras 1312–18.

7   For further details, see Goode, *op cit*, note 3, paras 30.161, 30.260.

8   Schedule 1, para 1; Sched 3, para 1. Eg, 'Hire purchase agreement regulated by the CCA'.

9   Schedule 2, para 2; Sched 3, para 2. The names and postal addresses of the parties. Can the creditor use an accommodation address or PO Box number (see 13 CCA News 1/24)?

10 CCA, s 105(9): Agreement Regulations, reg 2(8). As to 'embody', see post, para 9.12.

11 Regulation 6(2). See also s 61(1)(c): post, para 9.12. The OFT has had cause to make public complaint at the small print used in some credit and charge card applications ((1985) *The Times*, 15 August). Cf *L'Estrange v Graucob Ltd* [1934] 2 KB 394, DC (small print).

12 As to settlement figures (s 97), see post, para 26.19A; as to termination statements (s 103), see post, para 26.04; and as to notices (ss 76, 87, 98), see post, para 24.28.

[9.11] An example. The Agreement Regulations (see ante, para 9.10) provide a set of detailed instructions to the draftsmen of regulated agreements within their ambit as to some of the information which must be included and its layout. For instance, such a conditional sale or hp agreement must always contain the prescribed headings (see ante, para 9.10), the prescribed terms and signature box[1] and the statutory statements of repossession and termination rights,[2] together with the special cancellation notice (see post, para 9.17) if the agreement is cancellable (see post, para 10.29). Additionally, under what has been termed the 'holy ground rule',[3] the agreement must show 'together and as a whole' the following information: a description of the goods,[4] their cash price,[5] any advance payments,[6] the amount of credit,[7] the total amount payable,[8] the timing and amount of repayments (Sched 1, paras 12 and 13, which allow considerable flexibility) and the APR,[9] with special provision for where the rate is variable.[10] This, combined with the requirements of s 61 considered below (post, para 9.12) and of the copies rules (see post, para 9.14), ensures a substantial similarity in appearance between the documentation of different consumer credit businesses as regards documentation which fall within the Agreement Regulations. Which categories of document each business produces will depend on its types of business.[11] In practice, the larger businesses tend to produce their own documentation in most categories, whilst smaller businesses commonly use the CCTA or CCA (UK) documentation, perhaps over-printed with their individual logo.[12]

[9.11]

1 Regulation 2(7) and Sched 5, Part 1. There are similar requirements for consumer hire agreements: Art 3(6) and Sched 5, Part 2. As to signing within such boxes, see post, para 9.13.

2 Regulation 2(3) and Sched 2, Part 1. There are similar rules for consumer hirings: see Art 3(3) and Sched 4. As to rights of termination, see post, paras 26.05–07; and as to protections against repossession, see post, para 24.34.

3 So called because of the requirement to separate it from other information: Goode, *Consumer Credit Law and Practice*, paras 30.223–25.

4 Schedule 1, para 3. There is a similar rule for consumer hire agreements but no such requirement in respect of DC loans (see ante, para 5.35) or running-account credit (see ante, para 5.28), and a special rule where both goods and services are supplied.

5 Schedule 1, para 4, requiring just one cash price in respect of each 'list' of items. 'Cash price' is defined as 'the price or charge at which the goods ... may be purchased by, or supplied to, the debtor for cash': art 1(2); and see *R v Baldwins Garage (Warrington)* [1988] Crim LR 438.

6 Schedule 1, para 5. This rule extends to DC loans and running account credit, and there is a similar rule for consumer hirings (Sched 3, para 4). 'Advance payment' includes any deposit and any part-exchange allowance: see Art 1(2); but for the statutory definition of a 'deposit', see ante, para 5.22.

7 Schedule 1, paras 6 and 7. In the case of running-account credit, the credit **limit** must be shown (para 8); but it seems that the credit **rate** may be unilaterally variable: *Lombard Tricity Finance Ltd v Paton* (set out post, para 26.22); and see generally post, para 10.05.

8 Schedule 1, para 11: as this includes any option fee, it is the same as the 'total price' defined by the CCA (see ante, para 5.22). A separate rule exists for consumer hirings (Sched 3, para 5); and there can be no such requirement for running-account credit, nor for fixed-sum variable rate credit.

9 Schedule 1, paras 15–17. For the APR, see ante, para 8.25. In an interest-free agreement, this could be shown as '0% APR'.

10 Schedule 1, paras 18–19. These have been held to apply only to external varying factors (see post, para 10.05), leaving intact variations at the absolute discretion of one party: *Lombard Tricity Finance Ltd v Paton* (above). For notice of variation, see post, para 26.22.

11 See Goode, *op cit*, note 3, Div XI, Parts D and E.

12 As to financiers, see generally ante, para 2.17. The CCTA and the CCA (UK) are two trade organisations.

Execution of the agreement

[9.12] Section 61(1) embodies the primary requirements[1] as to the execution of all regulated agreements within its ambit.[2] It provides that:

A regulated agreement is not properly executed unless –

(a) a document in the prescribed form itself containing all the prescribed terms and conforming to regulations under section 60(1) is signed in the prescribed manner both by the debtor or hirer and by or on behalf of the creditor or owner, and

(b) the document embodies all the terms of the agreement, other than implied terms; and

(c) the document is, when presented or sent to the debtor or hirer for signature, in such a state that all its terms are readily legible.

Thus, a regulated agreement within Part V (see ante, para 9.07) is not properly executed[3] unless it complies with all the following requirements:

Paragraph (a). See post, para 9.13.

Paragraph (b). It requires that the regulated agreement[4] contains or refers to all the express terms[5] of that agreement.[6] This does not include mere puffs which have no legal significance (see post, para 11.01), nor those which have only non-contractual legal significance.[7] Indeed, the paragraph does not even extend to all contractual statements, omitting both implied terms (see post, para 11.10) and collateral contracts.[8] It is thus confined to the express terms 'embodied' in the regulated agreement:[9] most of these are likely to be in printed standard form. Where the regulated agreement also amounts to a consumer supply contract, the express terms must also comply with the UTCC Regulations as to both legibility and fairness, except insofar as prescribed by the CCA (UTCC, Sched 1, para (e)(i): see post, para 11.12A): so, the UTCC is inapplicable to CCA-prescribed terms (see para 9.13), but may attack express terms which are not CCA-prescribed.

[9.12]

1   As to the additional requirements in respect of land mortgages, see post, para 9.17A.

2   For exemptions from these rules, see ante, para 9.07. For the position where there is more than one debtor or hirer, see post, para 9.18.

3   With the effect considered later (post, para 9.19) but no others (s 170): see post, para 10.19.

4   This will normally be in standard form: as to which, see generally post, para 11.08.

5   As to express terms, see generally post, paras 11.07–11.09. Presumably, parol evidence may be tendered to show that the written terms do not include all the terms expressly agreed: Goode, *Consumer Credit Law and Practice*, para 30.127. As to clerical errors, see Guest and Lloyd, *Encyclopedia of Consumer Credit*, para 2-062.

6   By s 189(4), one document is 'embodied' in another if referred to in it (see ante, para 9.09). But, bear in mind that certain information must be exhibited 'together as a whole' (see ante, paras 9.10–9.11).

7   Such as misrepresentations (see post, para 11.02); or conditions precedent and subsequent which do not acquire promissory status (see post, paras 15.21, 26.01). Eg, that the consumer must furnish a guarantor before the deal is finalised.

8   Collateral contracts (outside the paragraph) should be carefully distinguished from collateral terms (within it): see generally post, para 11.06.

9   It has been claimed that this does not extend to 'mere items of information': Goode, *op cit*, note 5, para 30.125. *Sed quaere?*

Paragraph (c). It has already been pointed out that the other formalities rules are only expressly referrable to actual agreements (see ante, para 9.10). However, paragraph (c) is applicable to prospective agreements. It covers indistinctly printed forms (and see ante, para 9.10) and also requires that the blanks on the form are completed legibly[11] and are not presented in such a way as to hide any information from the consumer.[12]

[9.13] Paragraph (a). This paragraph of s 61(1) (see ante, para 9.12) clearly requires that a regulated agreement, including a credit token agreement (see ante, para 7.10), within its ambit (see ante, para 9.07) be in **writing** and that the documents which constitutes that agreement must comply with all the following requirements:[1]

1   *Prescribed form.* The document must accord with the layout prescribed by the Agreement Regulations (see ante, para 9.10).

2   *Prescribed terms.* On the same side as the signatures, the document **itself** must contain the terms **prescribed** in the Agreement Regulations (reg 6(1)). According to Sched 6, these will vary according to the type of agreement, but broadly deal with the following:[2] the amount of the credit or credit limit; in some cases the rate of interest; and a term stating how the financial obligations of the debtor or hirer are to be discharged. To the extent that these rules refer to information falling into the category of that which must be stated 'together and as a whole' (see ante, para 9.11), that will ensure that the larger list is included in the actual agreement rather than any document referred to in it. The regulation makes it clear that the absence of these terms takes an agreement outside the dispensing power of the court (reg 6(1)), with the results considered later (see s 127(3); and further post, para 9.20).

3   *Required terms.* Commonly on the non-signature side of the form, the agreement must 'embody' (s 189(4)) the terms required by the Agreement Regulations so that they must be included either in the agreement itself or a document referred to in it (see ante, paras 9.10–9.11). It would appear to be a matter of judgment as to whether these rules are so complicated that it would not on balance be more satisfactory to lay down compulsory statutory forms of agreement (see generally post, para 11.08).

4   *Signed by the parties.* Paragraph (a) requires the agreement to be '**signed**[3] ... both by the debtor or hirer and by or on behalf of the creditor or owner': the signatures need not be legible (reg 6(2)). Unlike the common law (see post, para 10.02), the CCA thus requires formation of the agreement by signature of the parties on a document conforming with the requirements of the Act and the Agreement Regulations. So,

---

11   It is therefore normal for the information inserted in such blanks to be carefully printed. Signatures are an exception: see post, para 9.13. For a possible difficulty with dispensers, see ante, para 7.08.

12   In the sense of impede by physical difficulty, eg, by stapling pages together. See Reform of the Law on Consumer Credit (1973, Cmnd 5427), para 47.

[9.13]

1   It is clear that s 61(1)(a) is referring to the prospective regulated agreement, so that its requirements must be fulfilled by that document and not just by another document to which it refers: Goode, *Consumer Credit Law and Practice*, paras 30.102–30.103.

2   Compare the longer list of information required by the Agreement Regulations: see ante, para 9.11.

3   A company seal will suffice: s 189(3).

there is no compliance where the debtor or hirer signs in blank.[4] Absence of personal signature by the debtor or hirer[5] takes an agreement outside the court's dispensing power (s 127(3): see above).

5 *Signed in the prescribed manner.* To protect consumers so far as possible from unwittingly signing hp agreements, the HPA 1964 devised a successful scheme whereby consumers sign in a special signature box. This scheme is adopted by the Agreement Regulations, which require that the debtor or hirer sign within the signature box whilst the creditor or owner signs outside it (reg 6(3)). Furthermore, that signature box must be in the form laid down in Sched 5 appropriate for the type of agreement, including the date of signature by the debtor of hirer, warnings against the binding effect of signature[6] and sometimes resale.[7]

It is for consideration whether a prospective agreement complying with all the above rules contains too much information for optimum effect.

Copies of the agreement

[9.14] Introduction. The hp legislation slowly evolved two principles; and the key to understanding them is to bear in mind that normally in this field a transaction will be effected by document, which will only take legal effect when signed (see post, para 10.08). The first principle was that consumers should be sent a copy of the signed agreement within seven days of the agreement being made (the agreement copy) and subsequently further copies on demand (see post, para 15.16). The second principle, as the first rule might leave a gap of up to seven days between a consumer signing and obtaining a copy of what he signed, it sought to ensure that the consumer was never without a copy of what he signed (the signature copy). The *Crowther Report* gave enthusiastic support to these two principles and recommended that they be extended to all types of transaction within the scope of the legislation (para 6.5.14). The CCA has done just that, adding the gloss that in the case of joint consumers the copies rules must be observed in relation to each of them.[1] The CCA has sought to implement the principles by formulating rules requiring that generally speaking[2] the two copies[3] be dealt with on one of the following bases:

---

4 Goode, *op cit*, note 1, para 30.108. As to the effect at common law of signing documents in blank, see post, para 16.05.
5 Where there is more than one debtor or hirer (see ante, para 5.24), generally speaking all of them must sign personally, eg, spouses (s 185(3)); but signature by agent is allowed where the joint debtors or hirers are either a partnership (s 61(4)) or in respect of the one of them which is a body corporate (s 185(6)) or presumably under a power of attorney.
6 Eg, 'This is a Hire Purchase Agreement regulated by the Consumer Credit Act 1974. Sign it only if you want to be legally bound by its terms'.
7 Eg, for hp 'The goods will not become your property until you have made all the payments. You must not sell them before then'.

[9.14]
1 Section 185(1)(a): see ante, para 5.24. However, in relation to periodic copies of running accounts (s 78(4)), the Act provides a dispensing procedure (s 185(2)): see ante, para 7.08.
2 As to the variations for cancellable agreements, and land mortgages, see post, paras 9.17–9.17A; and as to the situation where there is more than one debtor or hirer, see post, para 9.18.
3 As to the contents of copies and documents referred to therein, see post, para 9.18.

(a) documents **presented personally** to the debtor or hirer for signature (see post, para 9.15); or

(b) documents **sent** to the debtor or hirer for signature (see post, para 9.16).

In each of these two cases the CCA principles usually require that the debtor or hirer obtain two copies as follows: the first copy was of the 'unexecuted agreement';[4] and the second copy was of the 'executed agreement'.[5] However, if the document becomes an executed agreement on the occasion upon which the debtor or hirer signs,[6] it would be pointless to require two copies.[7] Accordingly, the CCA dispenses with the signature copy in some cases as follows (s 63(1)):

> If the unexecuted agreement is presented personally to the debtor or hirer for his signature, and on the occasion when he signs it the document becomes an executed agreement, a copy of the executed agreement, and of any document referred to in it, must be there and then delivered to him.

This will cover vendor credit situations (see ante, para 2.19) where the creditor or owner is prepared to make an instantaneous decision as to whether to supply on credit ('instant credit'); but it is not particularly common, because most creditors or owners will prefer to forward the document signed by the debtor or hirer to their credit department for processing;[8] however, it is commonly employed with weekly collected credit (see post, para 10.17). But, even leaving aside any difficulty over the meaning in s 63(1) of 'there and then' (see post, para 9.15), this rule would appear to leave a hiatus when the debtor does not sign in the presence of the creditor's representative a form already signed by the creditor.[9] A similar position is taken by the Act where the debtor or hirer obtains documents from some impersonal source, eg, from a dispenser or a trade display stand, or by cutting them out from a newspaper, so that it would be impracticable to require the creditor or owner to supply then a first completed copy signed by the debtor or hirer.[10]

Unless it complies with all the applicable copies rules, a regulated agreement is not properly executed (ss 62(3), 63(5), 64(5)), with the effects considered below (post, para 9.19), but no others (s 170: see post, para 10.19).

[9.15] Unsigned document presented personally. This paragraph deals with the common situation where the document is 'presented personally' to the prospective[1] debtor or hirer

---

4   This is defined as 'a document embodying the terms of a prospective regulated agreement, or such of them as it is intended to reduce to writing': s 189(1). As to prospective agreements, see generally ante, para 5.20. For a deficiency in this definition of 'unexecuted agreement', see Goode, *Consumer Credit Law and Practice*, para 30.301.

5   This 'means a document, signed by or on behalf of the parties, embodying the terms of a regulated agreement, or such of them as have been reduced to writing': s 189(1).

6   This formula avoids any difficulty that might arise in deciding whether the document was signed first by the debtor or hirer, or first by the creditor or owner.

7   Any notional delay between the signature of the debtor or hirer on the document and when he obtained a copy of the executed agreement is thus ignored, eg, instant credit.

8   For such enquiries about the debtor or hirer, see ante, para 8.35 *et seq*.

9   How will the creditor know when to supply a s 63(1) copy? If the debtor signs in his home, is this a cancellable agreement so as to require a s 64 notice (see post, para 9.17)?

10 See Goode, *op cit*, note 4, para 30.302. But why should the debtor or hirer not have to be supplied with two copies initially, so that he can complete, sign and return one whilst retaining the other?

[9.15]

1   By s 189(1) 'debtor', 'hirer', 'creditor', 'owner' here mean prospective parties: see ante, para 5.20.

for his signature,[2] but does not on that occasion become a regulated agreement because it is not 'there and then' signed by or on behalf of the prospective creditor or owner.[3] In this situation, the CCA requires that the prospective debtor or hirer obtain two copies as follows:

Signature copy. Section 62(1) provides that:

> If the unexecuted agreement is presented personally to the debtor or hirer for his signature, but on the occasion when he signs it the document does not become an executed agreement, a copy of it, and of any documents referred to in it,[4] must be there and then delivered to him.

It has been persuasively argued that 'there and then' refers to the time of presentation to the debtor or hirer, not of signature by him: otherwise, if the debtor or hirer took the document away for signature, it would be impossible for the creditor or owner to comply with s 62(1).[5] What if the prospective debtor or hirer leaves his copy of his offer behind on trade premises?

Agreement copy. Except in the case of credit tokens (see below), s 63(2) requires that, in the circumstances covered by this paragraph:

> A copy of the executed agreement, and of any other document referred to in it, must be given to the debtor or hirer within the seven days following the making of the agreement.

The agreement is actually made by signature by or on behalf of the creditor or owner (see post, para 10.08). As 'give' means 'deliver or send by post',[6] it is common for the agreement copy to be posted to the debtor or hirer; and in the case of cancellable agreements that second copy must be sent by post.[7] With regard to credit-token agreements (see ante, para 5.30), the creditor can send the second copy by post as above but is alternatively permitted to 'give' it to the debtor before or with the credit-token.[8]

[9.16] Unsigned documents sent by post. This would typically be the case with distance contracts, eg, mail order business (see ante, para 8.19). Unless the signature of the debtor or hirer at home were preceded by oral representations made by the negotiator in his presence (s 67: see post, para 10.29), agreements sent to the consumer by post for his signature no longer automatically give him a right of cancellation. Unless it does so,[1] the copies rules are as follows for documents sent by post.

---

2   Presentation to the prospective debtor or hirer will usually be made by an agent of the creditor: this may be an employee, as in DC loan financing (see ante, para 5.35); but it is more likely to be made by a credit-broker, as with DCS arrangements (see ante, para 5.34).

3   For the situation where it becomes an executed agreement 'there and then', see ante, para 9.14. Does this category extend to dispenser agreements – are they 'presented personally'?

4   As to 'documents referred to in it', see post, para 9.18. Is a photocopy produced quickly enough?

5   Goode, *Consumer Credit Law and Practice*, para 30.304.

6   Section 189(1). Cf *Skuse v Cooper* [1975] 1 All ER 612, CA. Is posting sufficient during a postal strike?

7   Section 63(3). As to the special documentation rules for cancellable agreements, see post, para 9.17.

8   Section 63(4): see ante, para 7.12. As to cancellable credit-token agreements, see post, para 9.17.

[9.16]

1   In the case of cancellable agreements (see above), the second copy must be sent by post (s 63(3)). As to the special documentation rules for cancellable agreements, see post, para 9.17.

Signature copy. Section 62(2) provides that:

> If the unexecuted agreement is sent to the debtor or hirer for his signature, a copy of it, and of any other document referred to in it,[2] must be sent to him at the same time.

So, the initial step required is for the debtor or hirer to receive two copies:[3] one to be signed and returned by him to the creditor or owner; and the other to be retained by him as a record.[4]

Agreement copy. Exceptionally, the creditor or owner may sign the document before sending it to the debtor or hirer, eg, British Telecom telephone rental contract, in which case the signature of the debtor or hirer may be the acceptance[5] and no further copy need be initially supplied to him.[6] However, in the normal case, the posting back of a signed copy by the debtor or hirer will be an offer and a second copy of the document signed by the creditor or owner (now an executed agreement) must be sent to the debtor or hirer within seven days (s 63(2): set out ante, para 9.15). There appears to be nothing to prevent the creditor or owner including advertising material with this copy.

[9.17] Documentation of cancellable agreements. As will be seen later, the debtor or hirer under a regulated agreement in some cases has a statutory right of cancellation (see post, para 10.28 *et seq*). The CCA is usually anxious that the debtor or hirer is aware of this right so that he may exercise it within the statutory time-limit. This s 64 seeks to achieve by two additional steps:[1]

1 *Prescribed notices.* Whilst the original cancellable form signed by the debtor or hirer must contain a short boxed cancellation notice as prescribed by Sched 2 to the Agreement Regulations (see ante, para 9.10), s 64(1) lays down that copies must include:

> ... a notice in the prescribed form indicating the right of the debtor or hirer to cancel the agreement, how and when that right is exercisable, and the name and address of a person to whom notice of cancellation may be given.

These powers have been utilised to introduce the CNC Regulations,[2] specifying in detail the precise type of boxed notice of cancellation rights to be included in each different type of agreement and situation.[3] These boxes should not only alert the

---

2   As to 'documents referred to in it', see ante, para 9.09.
3   It has been suggested that this should be read to include an agent, eg, solicitor or spouse, of the debtor or hirer: Goode, *Consumer Credit Law and Practice*, para 30.305. *Sed quaere?* Cf s 185(1)(a).
4   Suppose the debtor carries his copy to the creditor's premises and signs there. Does the creditor have to comply with s 62(1) as well?
5   For offer and acceptance by signature, see post, para 10.02.
6   Section 63(2)(b). Did the draftsman intend this only to operate where the offeror dispensed with communication of acceptance?

[9.17]
1   The documentation must, of course, otherwise comply with the ordinary rules considered in this chapter: see ante, para 9.06 *et seq*. As to the comparable rules for doorstep and distance selling transactions, see post, paras 10.22; 10.22A.
2   Consumer Credit (Cancellation Notices and Copies of Documents) Regulations 1983 (SI 1557) (as amended).
3   See further Goode, *Consumer Credit Law and Practice*, paras 31.114–31.117.

debtor or hirer to any cancellation rights,[4] but also tell him how he should exercise those rights (see post, para 10.31). To make it easier for the debtor or hirer to exercise this right, the notice must be accompanied by a cancellation form (CNC Regulations, reg 5(2)(b) and Part IV of the Schedule: see further post, para 10.31).

2 *Copies rules.* Under s 64(1)(a), these prescribed notices will usually[5] have to be included in each of the two copies required and the second copy must always be sent to him by post (see ante, paras 9.15–9.16). In those cases where only one statutory copy need be supplied to the debtor or hirer (see ante, paras 9.14–9.15), a separate notice of cancellation must generally be sent by post[6] to the debtor or hirer.[7] To avoid this expense, in the home credit industry (see ante, para 2.18) it is common for the creditor to sign the agreement before the debtor, so bringing the case within s 63(1) (see ante, para 9.14), with the cancellation notice to be delivered on a subsequent visit.[8] However, dispensations from sending this separate notice may be granted under regulations (s 64(4)); and these have been utilised to allow the Director to grant dispensations in respect of certain mail order consumer credit (but not hire) agreements.[9]

[9.17A] Documentation of land mortgages. As will be seen later, the CCA here wished to give the debtor or hirer a special regime of protection (see post, para 10.27). Applying principally to second mortgages, this introduced an additional third tier of copies, applicable where the 'prospective regulated agreement' (see ante, para 5.20) is to be secured[1] on land ('the mortgaged land')[2] other than remortgages or bridging loans (see post, para 10.27). These rules may be simplified under the deregulation initiative (see ante, paras 5.10–5.11):

1 *Advance copy.* According to s 58(1):

> Before sending to the debtor or hirer, for his signature, an unexecuted agreement, the creditor or owner shall give the debtor or hirer a copy of the unexecuted agreement which contains a notice in the prescribed form indicating the right of the debtor or hirer to withdraw from the prospective agreement, and how and when the right is exercisable, together with a copy of any other document referred to in the unexecuted agreement.

---

4 To cover the situation where the creditor or owner gives his customer a contractual right of cancellation, the amended CNC Regulations treat the agreement as if it were cancellable: reg 5(4).

5 In the case of credit-tokens, the notice can be sent by post before or with the credit-tokens: s 64(2).

6 It has been suggested that it is sufficient if the notice be sent by some independent carrier: Goode, *op cit*, note 3, para 30.306.

7 Section 64(1)(b). Section 64(3) allows regulations to require that a further copy of the executed agreement be included; but this power has not been exercised.

8 Does this comply with s 64(1)(b)?

9 Consumer Credit (Notice of Cancellation Rights) (Exemptions) Regulations 1983 (SI 1983/1558). Such dispensations must he individual, not general, and are recorded in the public register (as to which, see ante, para 6.26). See further Goode, *op cit*, note 3, para 31.118.

[9.17A]

1 The test is thus as to the common intention of the parties prior to the formation of the regulated agreement that it will, when concluded, be secured on the mortgaged land. This may give rise to factual disputes: see Goode, *Consumer Credit Law and Practice*, para 31.54.

2 Section 58(1). The rules are applicable whether the land mortgage is to be given by the debtor/hirer or by a third party.

It will be noted that the debtor or hirer must be given[3] copies of both the prospective regulated agreement and any other document referred to in it.[4] These copies must be true copies;[5] and the advance copy of the prospective regulated agreement must also contain a notice of this right to withdraw in statutory form[6] and comply with the copies regulations (see post, para 9.18).

2   *Signature copy.* Section 61(2) provides that:

> In addition,[7] where the agreement is one to which section 58(1) applies, it is not properly executed[8] unless-
>
> (a) the requirements of section 58(1) were complied with, and
>
> (b) the unexecuted agreement was sent, for his signature, to the debtor or hirer by post not less than seven days after a copy of it was given to him under section 58(1).

Thus, service of the advanced copy (above) does not absolve the creditor or owner from his duty to supply separate copies of both the agreement-form and any document referred to in it in accordance with the ordinary rules for documents sent by post.[9] Further, it will be noticed that there is a compulsory time gap between the sending of the advance and signature copies, this being known as the 'consideration period' (see further post, para 10.27). These two copies of the unexecuted agreement will differ in that only the advance copy will contain the notice of right of withdrawal.[10]

3   *Agreement copy.* After the debtor or hirer signs and returns the signature copy,[11] that document must be signed by or on behalf of the creditor or owner (see ante, para 9.12) and a copy of the now-executed agreement, together with any document referred to in it,[4] sent to the debtor or hirer within seven days.[9]

In the normal case within s 58, the agreement-form will refer to the mortgage, so that if the transaction is undertaken by a couple as a joint debtor or hirer, the above rules will require the creditor or owner to serve at least 12 documents![12]

[9.18] Contents and copies. The CCA requires that, when a transaction is set up, the debtor or hirer and any surety obtain not only the required copies of the agreement-form but also copies of 'any other document referred to in it' (ss 62, 63, 105(5): see ante, paras 9.14–9.16; and post, para 25.12). As it was appreciated that some limitation should be

---

3   '"Give" means deliver or send by post': s 189(1). It does not need to be given to the debtor personally: Goode, *op cit*, note 1, para 31.56.

4   Eg, the intended mortgage. However, no copy need be served of documents referred to in the 'other document', eg, referred to in the mortgage. See further post, para 9.18.

5   CNC Regulations (see ante, para 9.17), reg 3(1). It has been reasoned that the copies must therefore be complete, except for execution: Guest and Lloyd, *Encyclopedia of Consumer Credit*, para 2-059.

6   CNC Regulations, reg 4. There is a statutory warning that a debtor's home will be at risk: see ante, para 8.30.

7   This will ensure that land mortgages also comply with the requirements of s 61(1): see ante para 9.12.

8   With the effects considered later (post, paras 9.19; 10.27) but no others (s 170): see post, para 10.19.

9   As to the copies rules for documents sent by post, see generally ante, para 9.16.

10 This should preclude the production of a single document to comply with both ss 58 and 62.

11 What if he mistakenly signs and returns the advance copy?

12 Six on each debtor or hirer. No dispensing notice would appear available under s 185: but see the suggestion in Guest and Lloyd, *op cit*, note 5, para 2-062.

placed on this duty, the CCA provides for derogation by regulation (s 180(3)). Accordingly, the CNC Regulations (see ante, para 9.17) contain a list of excluded classes of documents, such as the following:[1] documents obtained by the debtor or hirer from a third party, eg, a survey report, catalogue or document of title; or to be kept by him under the terms of the agreement, eg, receipts for insurance premiums, rent or rates; entries in public registers, eg, copies of birth certificates or entries in the CCA register (as to which, see ante, para 6.26); enactments, which presumably includes subordinate legislation, both UK and EU; or any earlier agreement being modified (see generally post, para 26.22).

Not content with stipulating the documentation to be supplied, the CCA also requires the creditor or owner to supply copies of it to all the debtor(s) or hirer(s) and any sureties: this applies to copies of the unexecuted agreement (ss 62, 185(1)(a): see generally ante, paras 9.15–9.16), initial copies of the executed agreement (ss 63, 185(1)(a): see generally ante, paras 9.14–9.16), subsequent copies of that agreement[2] and notices.[3] In relation to copies of the unexecuted and executed agreement, the CNC Regulations require that every copy shall be a 'true copy' (reg 3). In relation to the original documentation, it is now common practice for creditors or owners to satisfy this requirement by printing their agreement-forms in three copies.[4] Whilst extra copies can be photocopied, the CNC Regulations in fact permit some information to be omitted from copies.[5]

Effect of non-compliance

[9.19] Improperly executed. The concept of unenforceable contracts has long existed under the Statute of Frauds (see ante, para 9.03). When the documentation rules under the CCA are infringed, the 1974 Act provides that the regulated agreement 'is not properly executed'. This is the sanction expressed in respect of breaches of all the following documentation rules: pre-contract disclosure (s 55(2): see ante, para 9.08); land mortgage rules (ss 58, 61(2): see ante, para 9.17A); signing agreements in proper form (s 61(1): see ante, para 9.12); supply of copies (ss 62(3), 64(5): see ante, para 9.17); and for sureties (s 105(4) and (5): see post, para 25.12). The key provision is s 65, which gives the following explanation:

(1) An improperly-executed regulated agreement is enforceable against the debtor or hirer on an order of the court only.

(2) A retaking of goods or land to which a regulated agreement relates is an enforcement of the agreement.

[9.18]

1   See further Goode, *Consumer Credit Law and Practice*, paras 30.309–30.326.

2   Sections 77–79, 107–10, 185(1)(a). See generally post, paras 15.17, 25.12.

3   Sections 64, 76, 87, 98, 111, 185(1)(a). See ante, para 9.17 and post, para 24.28.

4   An original (for retention by the creditor or owner); a first copy (to be handed or sent to the debtor or hirer as the unexecuted agreement); and a second copy (to be sent to the debtor or hirer as the executed agreement). Carbonising or photocopying will ensure that most of the blanks will be identically completed and required printed variations between first and second copies can be ensured. An extra copy may be needed for land mortgages: see ante, para 9.17A.

5   Eg, material in the section 'For Office Use Only'. See further Goode, *op cit*, note 1, para 1338.

It follows that an improperly executed agreement will still exist:[1] on ordinary principles, it can be enforced by the debtor or hirer if he so wishes as against anybody;[2] or by the creditor or owner as against a third party.[3] On the other hand, the agreement cannot be enforced by the creditor or owner by judicial process[4] or self-help (see post, para 24.33), except by court order (see post, para 9.20) or with the consent of the debtor or hirer (s 173(3): see post, para 18.11). This position is reinforced by s 142(1), which allows parties other than the creditor or owner[5] to seek a declaration of unenforceability in the following circumstances,[6] unless the agreement is unenforceable 'on technical grounds only':[7] where either the court dismisses an application for an enforcement order[8] or on application by 'an interested party':[9]

> the court may if it thinks just make a declaration that the creditor or owner is not entitled to do that thing, and ... thereafter no application for an enforcement order in respect of it shall be entertained.

Whilst the creditor is not subject to any further sanctions (s 170: see post, para 10.19), he cannot avoid the above rules by the devices of either a preliminary agreement (s 59(1): see ante, para 5.20) or taking security.[10]

[9.20] Enforcement orders. In a number of cases, the CCA provides that a regulated agreement can be enforced 'on an order of the court only', whether because that agreement was improperly executed (see ante, para 9.19) or otherwise (see post, para 24.33); and the same result follows as regards any security (s 113: see post, para 25.14). Section 127 then deals with applications to the court for an 'enforcement order' (defined in s 189(1)). Save in the cases mentioned below, s 127(1) instructs the court to grant an enforcement order unless it considers it just to refuse such an order, having regard only to the following of its powers:

(a) *Prejudice.* 'Prejudice caused to any person by the contravention in question and the degree of culpability for it.'[1]

[9.19]

1   It is not void, or even voidable (as to which, see post, para 10.14); nor is it illegal (as to which, see post, para 10.19): *Carlyle Finance Ltd v Pallas Industrial Finance Ltd* (set out post, para 10.08).

2   See *R v Modupe* [1991] CCLR 29, CA (criminal case, where debtor prosecuted for deception).

3   *Wilson v First County Trust Ltd* (set out post, para 9.20), *obiter* at 144g.

4   *Dimond v Lovell* (set out ante, para 5.13); [1999] JBL 452 at 464. For enforcement by judicial process, see post, para 24.27 *et seq*.

5   Guest and Lloyd, *Encyclopedia of Consumer Credit*, para 2-143; Goode, *Consumer Credit Law and Practice*, Div IIB, para 5.282.

6   Section 142(2) also makes provision for declarations of cancellation (s 69(1) and (2): see post, para 10.32) or termination (s 91: see post, para 24.38), though in these cases the creditor or owner may, as 'an interested party', be seeking the declaration. Outside s 142, the power to seek a declaration rests on the ordinary procedure under the rules of court.

7   See s 189(5); post, para 25.13; and the discussion of 'technical grounds' by Goode, *op cit*, note 5, para 37.222.

8   As where the creditor or owner seeks to enforce the agreement by judicial process: see above.

9   Eg, a party standing in the shoes of the debtor or hirer, such as a personal representative or trustee in bankruptcy, afraid that the creditor or owner will resort to self-help: as to which see above.

10 See post, para 25.11. Do the above rules also apply to s 124 (see post, para 25.09)?

[9.20]

1   Section 127(1)(i). Note the extension beyond prejudice to the debtor or hirer to 'any person', eg, surety.

(b) *Reduction of debt.* The power contained in s 127(2) that:[2]

> ... if it appears to the court just to do so, it may in any enforcement order reduce or discharge any sum payable by the debtor or hirer, or any surety, so as to compensate him for prejudice suffered as a result of the contravention in question.

(c) *Condition or suspension.* The powers contained in s 135(1) that the court may, if it considers it just to do so, include in its order provisions:

(a) making the operation of any term of the order conditional on the doing of specified acts by any party to the proceedings;[3]

(b) suspending the operation of any term of the order either –

(i) until such time as the court order subsequently directs, or

(ii) until the occurrence of a specified act or omission.[4]

The court may feel inclined to exercise this power if, for instance, the infringement is technical only (as to 'technical grounds', see ante, para 9.19); or the consumer parties can be safeguarded by varying or suspending the agreement. It may subsequently vary such an order (s 135(4)). There are two qualifications to the suspending power in s 135(1)(b): the court shall not suspend an order for the return of the goods (see post, para 24.26) by any person, unless satisfied that the goods are in his possession (s 135(2)); nor may the power be used to extend the period of a consumer hiring (s 135(3)).

(d) *Amendment.* Under s 136, the court has the following power to amend any agreement:

> The court may in an order made by it under this Act include such provision as it considers just for amending any agreement or security in consequence of a term of the order.

Provided only that it is 'in consequence of a term' of an order, s 136 empowers the court to vary the contractual rate of interest.[5] Thus, in cases falling within s 127(1), the court is instructed to refuse an enforcement order only if it cannot do justice as between the parties under one of the powers (a)–(d) above.

However, in the following cases only, the Act deems the infringement to be so prejudicial to the debtor, hirer or surety that the court is given no discretion to order enforcement, so that the agreement remains permanently unenforceable:

1 *An unsigned document.* A regulated agreement remains perpetually unenforceable if either it did not contain the prescribed terms or it was not signed by the debtor or hirer.[6] Where there are more than one debtor or hirer, this rule applies to all of them

---

2 Compare *Nissan Finance UK v Lockhart* [1993] CCLR 39, CA with *National Guardian Mortgage Corp v Wilkes* [1993] CCLR 1.

3 Eg, the return of certain property to the debtor or hirer.

4 Eg, an order to return goods to the creditor or owner (see post, para 24.43) can be made conditional on further default by the debtor or hirer. But see s 135(2).

5 *Southern and District Finance plc v Barnes* (set out post, para 24.41).

6 Section 127(3): *Wilson v First County Trust Ltd* [2001] QB 407, CA (see Dobson (2000) 150 NLJ 1815). For further proceedings, see below.

(s 185(3)). On the other hand, the court does have a dispensing discretion with regard to other breaches of s 61(1)(a), eg, where the debtor signed outside the signature box, or the document was not in the prescribed form, or did not contain the required terms (see s 127(5)), or (except as below) in relation to breaches of the copies rules (ss 62–63: see ante, paras 9.14–9.16).

2   *A cancellable agreement.* Under s 127(4), the court has no dispensing power where a cancellable agreement either does not comply with the copies rules (ss 62–63: see above) or contain the prescribed notices of the right of cancellation (s 64: see ante, para 9.17). However, in the former case this rule may be avoided by giving the debtor or hirer the requisite copy at any time before the commencement of proceedings, in which case he can then exercise his right of cancellation (see post, para 10.31); and, in any event, it may be that voluntary payments made under that agreement cannot be recovered.[7]

3   *Any security.* This is enforceable to no greater extent than the regulated agreement (s 113(1): see post, para 25.11).

In *Wilson v First County Trust Ltd:*[8]

> In 1999, W borrowed £5,000 from FCT, a pawnbroker, pledging her car as security (see post, para 25.15). The loan was properly documented, except that the £250 documentation fee was misstated as part of the credit (stated at £5,250), rather than of the tcc (see ante, para 5.22). W defaulted and FCT sought to sell the car. In an interim judgment, the Court of Appeal held that the documentation therefore did not correctly state the amount of credit, one of the prescribed terms (see ante, para 9.13); and it followed that the agreement was not properly executed under s 61(1)(a), so that both the agreement and the pledge were permanently unenforceable under ss 127(3), 113(2).[6] The court then adjourned the case, indicating that the effect of s 127(3) appeared to have the effect of depriving FCT of its legal rights without a hearing, contrary to the European Convention on Human Rights (see ante, para 3.09).

At the resumed hearing, the Court of Appeal unanimously held as follows: whenever the agreement was made, the Convention rights applied in any proceedings after the Human Rights Act 1998 came into force;[8a] in weighing those Convention rights as against the impugned Act, consideration must be given to the policy of the impugned Act (see ante, para 1.04); and, in the absence of such extraneous assistance, the Court identified the policy aims of s 127(3) and held that the means used to achieve those aims (total prohibition on action) was not legitimate because 'disproportionate to the policy aim' (at 149–50). As s 3 of the 1998 Act requires, the court considered whether it was possible to interpret s 127(3) of the CCA in a manner compatible with Convention rights and held that it was not;[9] and the court therefore made a declaration under s 4(2) of the 1998 Act that s 127(3) was incompatible with FCT's human rights (at 151–52). The declaration did

---

7   *Barclays Bank v Lee* [1993] CLY 474, Cty Ct.

8   [2001] 2 All ER (Comm) 134; [2001] 3 All ER 229, CA (see Livesey (2001) 56 CC 2/4).

8a   At 142c–h. Would it follow that, even though the court had refused an enforcement order before the HRA came into force, another application to court (this time under the HRA) is now possible?

9   At 150. Nor did the court think (at 151) that this could be done in relation to s 113(2) on the grounds that dismissal was 'on technical grounds only' within s 106: see post, para 24.14. The HL have given leave to appeal.

not affect the rights of the parties in the case: so s 127(3) defeated FCT; but s 127(3) may be excised from the CCA in the future.[10]

---

10 Similarly inflexible would appear to be CCA, s 127(4) (cancellable agreements: see above); s 91 (protected goods: see post, para 24.38); s 125(1) (negotiable instruments: see post, para 25.09). See also the Doorstep and Distance Selling Regulations (see post, paras 10.22–22A); and Lawson (2001) 151 NLJ 882.

CHAPTER 10

FORMATION OF THE AGREEMENT

GENERAL PRINCIPLES

[10.01] Introduction. This book is concerned for the most part with contracts for the supply of goods[1] and loans taken out to finance such acquisitions.[2] Apart from the special rules for auctions (see post, para 10.10), in the fundamentals of contract the SGA simply refers back to general contractual principles (s 62(2)); related Acts do not even bother to include such a cross-reference, eg, SOGIT; CCA; UCTA; SGSA; and unregulated loans,[2] hp and bailments are largely governed by the common law anyway. The general rules as to the formation of contract will be found in the standard works[3] but their application in the present context requires mention as follows:

1 *Agreement*. There will be considered below the process of agreeing (see post, para 10.02 *et seq*), mistake (see post, para 10.14) and invalidity (see post, para 10.18). Into that agreement, written terms may be incorporated (see post, para 18.04): if a party is foolish enough to accept (say) harsh standard terms (see post, para 11.08), *prima facie* at common law he is bound by them;[4] but he may be able to escape those terms under the Unfair Terms in Consumer Contracts (UTCC) Regulations (see post, para 11.12 *et seq*). In a supermarket, where the contract is usually made at the check-out,[5] the price is likely to be charged according to a bar code (see ante, para 2.06). As to advertisements, see ante, para 8.05.

2 *Consideration*. Whilst consideration is not required for a deed,[6] in the case of a simple contract to supply goods, consideration is likely to take the form of price, rent or goods taken in part exchange (see respectively ante, paras 2.06, 1.18, 2.09). At common law, only one who provides that consideration will be privy to the contract. This rule has two aspects:

  (a) *The burden of the contract*. Only a person who is a party to the contract is subject to its burdens, a rule which will be relevant as regards restrictions on the use of goods which purport to bind a sub-buyer (see ante, para 2.14) and exemptions (see post, para 18.05).

  (b) *The benefit of the contract*. Whilst at common law, disregarding agency (see post, para 10.06) and assignment (see ante, para 7.15/17), the promisee can usually only

---

[10.01]

1 The principal forms of contract for the supply of goods (sale, hiring and hp) are explained in Chapter 1.

2 For contracts of loan, see generally ante, paras 7.02–03A.

3 *Chitty on Contract* (28th edn), vol I, Chapters 2–3; *Halsbury's Laws* (4th edn, reissue), vol 9, para 601 *et seq*; Treitel, *Law of Contract* (10th edn), Chapters 2–4; Goode, *Hire Purchase Law and Practice* (2nd edn), Chapter 7. As to the planned European civil code on contract law, see Jack (2001) 151 NLJ 1602.

4 *Per* MacKinnon LJ in *South Bedfordshire Electrical Finance Ltd v Bryant* [1938] 3 All ER 580, at 584, CA. On 'sugging', see (1992) 142 NLJ 888.

5 *Pharmaceutical Society of GB v Boots* [1953] 1 QB 401, CA.

6 See *Chitty on Contract* (28th edn), vol 1, para 1-052. For the formalities required of deeds, see ante, para 9.01. Compare gifts: see ante, para 2.08.

enforce the benefit of a contract against the promisor, for our purposes there are three important statutory exceptions: (i) deemed agents (see post, para 10.24); (ii) connected lenders (see post, para 16.11); and (iii) named beneficiaries (see post, para 17.08A).

3 *Intent to create legal relations.* Where an agreement is made between businessmen, it is presumed that they intend to enter a binding contract,[7] though this may be negatived,[8] as in the case of a letter of comfort.[9] At the other end of the scale, a domestic arrangement to exchange goods for cash is more likely to constitute reciprocal gifts (as to gifts, see ante, para 2.08). Advertisements may fall either side of the line.[10] Further, goods supplied under a statutory obligation may not give rise to contractual obligations, eg, drugs dispensed under the NHS (see ante, paras 1.07; 4.29–4.30).

4 *Governed by English law.* The ordinary rules governing (i) the courts and (ii) the law applicable where one of the parties is outside the jurisdiction have already been out outlined (see ante, para 8.17A). However, this rule may be ousted where the parties show a contrary intention (see post, para 18.13).

The process of agreeing

[10.02] Offer and acceptance. Generally speaking, for the formation of a contract between A and C what the law is looking for is a declaration of their willingness to be bound to each other on identical terms.[1] Leaving aside those unusual cases where it is difficult to identify the offer and acceptance,[2] the first such declaration will be the offer and the second the acceptance, it being possible for either A or C to act through an agent (see post, para 10.06).

The offer. The first question which arises is whether the statement by A is intended as a declaration of willingness to be bound (an offer),[3] or only an invitation to make an offer

---

7 *Rose & Frank Co v Crompton & Bros Ltd* [1925] AC 445, HL (sales contract).

8 *Ibid* (franchise contract); *Orion Insurance Co v Sphere Drake Insurance* [1990] 1 Lloyd's Rep 465 (discharge of insurance contract).

9 *Kleinwort Benson Ltd v Malaysia Mining Corp Bbd* [1989] 1 All ER 785, CA; *Re Atlantic Computers plc* (set out post, para 19.19; and see 105 LQR 346; [1990] JBL 281). As to letters of intent, see Ball (1988) 99 LQR 572; Chitty, *op cit*, para 2-089.

10 Compare *Carlill v Carbolic Smoke Ball Co* (ante, para 8.05) and *Bowerman v ABTA* [1995] Tr LR 246 (113 LQR 47).

[10.02]

1 See the texts referred to ante, para 10.01. For auctions, see post, para 10.10. For offer and acceptance by computer, see Nicoll [1998] JBL 35, esp at 42–49. For pre-incorporation contracts, see Treitel, *Law of Contract* (10th edn), p 679 *et seq*.

2 Eg, where the parties continue to negotiate terms during performance (see post, para 10.03); in a battle of forms (see post, para 10.04).

3 Eg, *Great Northern Railway Co v Witham* (1873) LR 9 CP 16 (standing offer); *Financings Ltd v Stimson* (set out post, para 10.08; hp proposal form). For advertisements and quotations, see ante, para 8.05.

(an invitation to treat).[4] Any offer may be absolute or conditional,[5] eg, 'subject to availability', 'subject to credit status', 'whilst stocks last'; and all the express terms of an offer must either be stated expressly in the offer or incorporated by reference.[6] These may be standard form terms (see post, para 11.08). For instance, if the terms expressly granted the consumer an initial period for reflection, whether by way of warming up or cooling off (cf post, para 10.23), that might assist in equalising the relative bargaining position of the parties for the purposes of the UTCC Regulations (reg 4(1): see post, para 11.15).

The acceptance. An offer may only be accepted before its termination, eg, by revocation by the offeror, rejection by the offeree, lapse of time, occurrence of condition, impossibility.

Assuming an existing offer by A, the next question is whether C has accepted it. Of course, C can only accept where the offer is made to him (see post, paras 10.15) and acceptance by C is then his declaration of willingness to be bound on identical terms: if C attempts to introduce any new or different terms or conditions, he will be making a counter-offer.[7] Usually, the offer will require communication of acceptance by C to A before a binding contract is made.[8] The precise moment of formation is *prima facie* when C's acceptance is communicated to A;[9] but the parties may dispense with communication of acceptance and provide that some act is to constitute the acceptance.[10] The resulting contract may be absolute or conditional; and the latter may be subject to conditions precedent or subsequent (see ante, para 1.11). Moreover, leaving aside agency (see above), there may be more than three separate principals involved in what appears to be a single transaction, as where the transaction is financed (see post, Chapter 16).

[10.03] Incomplete agreements. 'To be a good contract, there must be a concluded bargain; and a concluded contract is one which settles everything that is necessary to be

---

4 Eg, *Spencer v Harding* (1870) LR 5 CP 561 (circular requesting tenders); *Pharmaceutical Society of GB v Boots Cash Chemists (Southern) Ltd* [1952] 2 QB 795, CA (self-service shop); *Fisher v Bell* [1961] 1 QB 394, DC (shop window display); *Partridge v Crittenden* [1968] 2 All ER 421, DC (magazine classified advert); *Esso Petroleum Ltd v Comrs of Customs and Excise* (set out ante, para 2.08; petrol station promotion). For the difficulty of classifying 'quotations' and 'estimates' in respect of the supply of services, see Woodroffe, *Goods and Services – The New Law*, paras 3.06–3.09; [1984] Which? 166; OFT, *A Buyer's Guide*, pp 21, 43 (defining a quotation as a firm price; and an estimate as an informed guess).

5 Distinguish promissory conditions: see post, para 11.04.

6 Eg, price adjustment clauses (see post, para 10.05). See also the battle of the forms (post, para 10.04). For the incorporation of exclusion clauses, see post, para 18.04; and for express and implied terms, see post, paras 11.07 and 11.10.

7 *Hyde v Wrench* (1840) 3 Beav 334 (not a goods case). Distinguish attempts to put additional terms in A's mouth: *Stevenson v Maclean* (1880) 5 QBD 346. See also the battle of the forms: post, para 10.04.

8 *Felthouse v Bindley* (1872) 11 CBNS 869; and as to inertia selling, see further ante, para 8.18. What about internet shopping (see ante, para 8.17A)? It would seem that the offeror may waive his right to communication of acceptance: *Robophone Facilities Ltd v Blank* [1966] 3 All ER 128, CA; and for direct financing, see post, para 10.08.

9 *Brinkibon Ltd v Stahag Stahl etc mbH* [1983] 2 AC 34, HL (telex); *Holwell Securities Ltd v Hughes* [1974] 1 All ER 161, CA (post; manner of communication specified). An offer cannot be revoked after acceptance: *Byrne v Van Tienhoven* (1880) 5 CPD 344.

10 Eg, *Carlill's* case (above; unilateral contract); *Financings Ltd v Stimson* (above; bilateral contract); *Byrne v Van Tienhoven* (above; the *prima facie* postal rule of acceptance on posting); *Re Charge Card Services Ltd* (set out ante, para 7.09). See also CCA, s 66 (ante, para 7.11).

settled and leaves nothing to be settled by agreement between the parties.'[1] Thus, in *Scammell & Nephew Ltd v Ousten*:[2]

> O, a businessman, was negotiating with S, a dealer, to trade in his Bedford van for a Commer lorry, it being envisaged that the transaction would be directly financed. On 8 December 1937, O placed a written order for a Commer lorry from S 'on the understanding that the balance of the purchase price can be had on hp terms over a two year period'. Notwithstanding that the hp terms had yet to be settled, the CA held that there was a concluded agreement;[3] but this decision was reversed by the HL on the grounds that the phrase 'on hp terms' was too vague.

The objection is that the parties only agreed in outline, whilst showing that they still intended to negotiate the detail.[4] Similar decisions have been reached where the following remained to be settled: price and delivery;[1] detailed written terms to be supplied,[5] 'subject to *force majeure* conditions (see ante, para 22.13A); or there was a contract to negotiate.[6]

On the other hand, the agreement between the parties may be completed, although not worked out in meticulous detail,[7] and the SGA itself provides for the price 'to be fixed in a manner agreed by the contract'.[8] Thus, the parties have been held to have finished agreeing in the following cases: where a contract was made on auction particulars;[9] where the missing detail was left to be supplied by the law, as by way of implied terms (see post, para 11.10); or on the basis of what is reasonable, eg, s 8(2) of the SGA (see ante, para 2.06); or supplied by a third party, eg, agreements to sell at a valuation (see s 9 of the SGA: see post, para 10.05); or where the apparently uncertain terms were meaningless.[10] Indeed, the courts are normally anxious to uphold agreements made between

---

[10.03]

1 *May and Butcher Ltd v R* (1929) [1934] 2 KB 17 at 21, HL, *per* Lord Dunedin.

2 [1941] AC 251; [1941] 1 All ER 14, HL.

3 Following *Hillas & Co Ltd v Arcos Ltd* (1932) 147 LT 503, HL. Where this might amount to a prospective regulated agreement, the issue is now academic because of the requirement that the regulated agreement be made in signed writing (see ante, para 9.12) and the prohibition on preliminary agreements (CCA, s 59: see ante, para 5.20).

4 The result is the same where the agreement itself is subject to a condition precedent: *Astra Trust v Adams & Williams* [1969] 1 Lloyd's Rep 81 (purchase of ship 'subject to a satisfactory survey'); and see generally post, para 15.21. Similarly, mere standing orders: see ante, para 10.02.

5 *JH Saphir (Merchants) Ltd v Zissimos* [1960] 1 Lloyd's Rep 490. See also *Manatee Towing Co v Oceanbulk Maritime SA* [1999] 2 All ER (Comm) 306 ('subject to details').

6 *Walford v Miles* [1992] 1 All ER 453, HL (sale of business). For argument that this decision is wrong and that there is a duty to negotiate in good faith see: Brown [1992] JBL 353; Neill (1992) 108 LQR 405; Jamieson [1992] LMCLQ 186.

7 They may intend a binding provisional agreement to be later replaced by more elaborate terms negotiated between them: *Brogden v Metropolitan Railway Co* (1877) 2 App Cas 666, HL; *The Blankenstein* [1985] 1 All ER 475, CA; *Pagnan SpA v Feed Products* [1987] 2 Lloyd's Rep 601, CA. Eg, an open credit card contract (see ante, para 7.09A).

8 SGA, s 8(1): set out ante, para 2.06; *Masport Ltd v Morrison Industries Ltd* [1996] CLY 1252, PC. For argument as to whether the 'manner' might include subsequent agreement between the parties, see Atiyah, *Sale of Goods* (10th edn), p 31. This would not appear to be what Parliament intended: see the amendment to the Bill referred to ante, para 2.06. What is the effect of 'Our offer is made on the basis of our current price list'?

9 *Filby v Hounsell* [1896] 2 Ch 737 (not a goods case; as to auctions, see post, para 10.10).

10 *Nicolene Ltd v Simmonds* [1953] 1 QB 543, CA ('usual conditions of acceptance').

businessmen despite imprecision and omission;[11] and this is particularly the case where the agreement is partially executed.[12]

Whilst everything therefore turns upon the attitude of the courts to whether the parties have shown they have finished agreeing, this has not obviated difficulties such as the 'battle of the forms' (see post, para 10.04), price escalation formulae (see post, para 10.05), letters of intent (see ante, para 10.01) or forms signed in blank (see post, para 16.05).

[10.04] The battle of the forms.[1] Suppose that during the negotiating process leading towards a contract (see ante, para 10.02), an attempt is made to introduce into it standard terms (see post, para 11.08). If only one party proffers such terms, the question will be whether those terms are incorporated in their contract.[2] However, each party may repeatedly put forward his own standard terms, which are most unlikely to coincide. On classical theory, the second and each subsequent proffering of standard terms is a counter-offer: the last such document proffered embodies the final offer ('the last shot'); and the recipient accepts by acting on it.[3] The matter was litigated in *Butler Tool Co Ltd v Ex-Cell-O Corp (England) Ltd*:[4]

> In response to an enquiry from B, S quoted for the supply of machine tools under a quotation which included a price escalation clause (see post, para 10.05) and provided that these conditions 'shall prevail over any terms and conditions in the Buyer's order'. B responded by placing an order on terms which contained no price escalation clause and included a tear-off slip stating 'We [S] accept your order on the Terms and Conditions stated thereon'. S returned that slip, together with a covering letter stating that B's order was being placed in accordance with S's quotation. The goods were delivered and S subsequently claimed a price increase under the escalation clause.

Looked at objectively, the parties had never reached agreement and there could only be liability to pay a reasonable price (*quantum meruit*) in quasi-contract.[5] A similar answer could have been reached in contract if only the parties had remained silent as to price (s 8(2) of the SGA). However, whilst these two avenues remained closed, the parties had (as is common in such situations) proceeded as if there were a contract between them and the court, of course, wished to uphold an executed agreement (see ante, para 10.03). The majority of the Court of Appeal, applying classical doctrine, held that S had contracted on B's terms because returning the tear-off slip amounted to acceptance of B's counter-offer

---

11   *Hillas & Co Ltd v Arcos Ltd* (above); *Stratton Motor Co v Mattimoe* (1994) 138 SJ 528. But see Atiyah, *op cit*, note 8.

12   *Foley v Classique Coaches Ltd* [1934] 2 KB 1, CA; *F & G Sykes Ltd v Fine Fare Ltd* [1967] 1 Lloyd's Rep 53; *Mack & Edwards (Sales) v McPhail Bros* (1968) 112 SJ 211, CA; *Mamidoil-Jetoil Greek Petroleum Co SA v Okta Crude Oil* [2001] 2 All ER (Comm) 193, CA.

[10.04]

1   See generally *Benjamin's Sale of Goods* (5th edn), para 2-013; Treitel, *Law of Contract* (9th edn), pp 19–20; Hoggett (1970) 33 MLR 518.

2   *British Crane Hire Corp Ltd v Ipswich Plant Hire Ltd* [1975] QB 303, CA (by reference); *Financings Ltd v Stimson* (set out post, para 10.08; by signature); and see generally post, para 18.04.

3   *British Road Services Ltd v A Crutchley & Co Ltd* [1968] 1 All ER 811, CA.

4   [1979] 1 All ER 965; [1979] 1 WLR 401, CA (discussed Adams 95 LQR 481; Rawlings 42 MLR 715; Parris, *Retention of Title on Sale of Goods*, pp 18–21).

5   *Sumpter v Hedges* [1898] 1 QB 673, CA (loose materials on site); *British Steel Corp v Cleveland Bridge and Engineering Co Ltd* [1984] 1 All ER 504. But there must be a voluntary retention: *The Liddesdale* [1900] AC 190, PC.

of a fixed price contract.[6] The case was therefore lost on S's tactical error in returning B's tear-off slip.[7] At common law, it may be possible to avoid losing the battle of the forms by careful handling of adequate documentation: if nothing is said by the counter-offeree, his performance might constitute an implied acceptance of the counter offer;[8] but in a consumer supply contract (see post, para 11.12A), such a term might be unfair (Grey Term 1(i): see post, para 11.17). However, if both sides are equally careful, it would appear that there would be a stalemate with no contract at all,[9] an inconvenient solution which may need statutory intervention.[10]

[10.05] Price adjustment formulae. Particularly if there is likely to be any significant delay between formation of a supply contract and delivery/payment, it is common to find that the supplier seeks to include in his contract a price escalation clause.[1] A similar position is likely to obtain in respect of loans of substantial sums of money and 'big ticket' leases.[2] In such cases, suppliers of goods or money frequently embody their price/rate escalation clause in standard form contracts (see generally post, para 11.08). Particularly in the case of commercial buyers, resistance to the introduction of such clauses may lead at common law to a battle of forms (see ante, para 10.04).

Even if such an adjustment clause is accepted by the buyer, hirer or borrower and does not amount to the offence of misleading pricing (see ante, para 8.10), there is the danger that it will result in a court finding that the clause negatives the existence of any contract on the grounds that the parties have not finished agreeing.[3] Even if the clause is part of the contract, there may be an implied term that the interest rate adjustment clause should not be exercised for an improper purpose, dishonestly, capriciously, arbitrarily or unreasonably;[3a] and, in a consumer supply it may not be binding on the consumer because it is an unfair term (UCT Regulations, Sched 3, para 1(j): see post, para 11.17). It is common for a loan agreement to contain a variable rate of interest clause (see ante, para 7.03A). To reduce these dangers, such a clause will usually provide for the price/rent/interest rate to be fixed by some third party or objective formula.

1   *Third party pricing.* Agreements to sell at a valuation are dealt with by s 9 of the SGA:

---

6   *Per* Lawton and Bridge LJJ. Lord Denning MR preferred to reach the same answer by the broader approach of construing all the documents together. See also *Muirhead v Industrial Tank Specialities Ltd* [1986] QB 507, CA, *per* Robert Goff LJ at 530.

7   But how can acceptance be implied from S's conduct when that implication is flatly contradicted by an express term of S's repeated original offer? See *Rimeco Rigglsen & Metal Co v Queensborough Rolling Mill* [1995] CLY 798, CA.

8   *Sauter Automation v Goodman (Mechanical Services) (In Liq)* (1986) 34 Build LR 881? Cf the *British Steel Corp* Case (above).

9   Treitel, *op cit,* note 1, p 20; and see generally post, para 10.16.

10 Cf UCC Art 2-207, criticised for attempting to separate the acceptance of terms from their content: Waddams, *Contracts* (1977), pp 47–55. For suggested common law solutions, see Howarth [1987] JBL 122; Bradgate [1988] JBL 477 at 478–80.

[10.05]

1   With the almost continuous inflation of modern times, these clauses have become common in commercial contracts, eg, *Hillas & Co Ltd v Arcos Ltd* (1932) 147 LT 503, HL. Mistaken beliefs that a contract contains a price escalation clause will not necessarily amount to a repudiation: see post, para 26.15. For VAT charges, see the Value Added Tax Act 1994, s 89.

2   See Soper and Munro, *The Leasing Handbook,* p 70 *et seq.*

3   *May & Butcher Ltd v R* (1929) [1934] 2 KB 17, HL. It may be evidence that the terms are just an invitation to treat: see ante, para 10.03. Compare *Queensland Electricity GB v New Hope Collieries* [1989] 1 Lloyd's Rep 205, PC.

3a *Paragon Finance plc v Staunton* (set out post, para 11.10) *per* Dyson LJ at para 36, *obiter.*

(1) Where there is an agreement to sell goods on the terms that the price is to be fixed by the valuation of a third party,[4] and such third party cannot or does not make such valuation, the agreement is avoided; provided that if the goods or any part thereof have been delivered to and appropriated by the buyer he must pay a reasonable price for them.

(2) Where such third party is prevented from making the valuation by the fault of the seller or buyer, the party not in fault may maintain an action for damages against the party in fault.[5]

Section 9(1) assumes that the contract is void in the circumstances there set out, though it is conceivable that the seller or buyer may **promise** that the third party will make the valuation.[6] Do the same rules apply by analogy to quasi-sales, hp and simple hiring agreements?[7]

2 *Objective formula.* The clause may only give the supplier/lender **power** in designated circumstances to vary the price/rent/rate;[8] but more commonly it provides for **automatic** variation by reference to some outside criteria of price[9] or interest rate.[2] Assuming the variation is not so great in relation to market value as to turn the transaction into a wager,[10] an automatic variation clause will generally be effective.[11] In respect of regulated agreements, see the CCA rules as to documentation (ante, para 9.11) and variation (post, para 26.22).

[10.06] Agency. Under the ordinary common law rules of agency, which are expressly saved by the SGA (s 62(2)), any party (A) who makes a contract personally with C in the manner considered above (paras 10.01–10.05) may alternatively make that contract through his agent (B) in a number of ways:[1]

(1) *Actual authority.* Where A confers actual authority on B, whether expressly or by implication,[2] and whether disclosed or undisclosed.[3]

---

4   For the effect of an erroneous valuation, see *Burgess v Purchase & Sons (Farm) Ltd* [1983] Ch 216 (sale of shares). Cf auctions: post, para 10.11.

5   Does the action sound in contract or tort? 'Fault' is rather unhelpfully defined by the SGA as 'wrongful act or default' (s 61(1)), but presumably comprehends breach of contract or tort. Cf 'fault' in another statute: post, para 27.40.

6   See Atiyah, *Sale of Goods* (10th edn), p 34. Compare the discussion on s 6 of the SGA (post, para 22.10) and on s 22(2) of the SGA (post, para 22.03).

7   What, if any, is the relevance here of *Scammell & Nephew Ltd v Ousten* (set out ante, para 10.03)?

8   *Vitol BV v Compagnie Europeane* [1988] 1 Lloyd's Rep 574; *Lombard Tricity Finance Ltd v Paton* (set out post, para 26.22). For the effect of the CCA on such powers, see post, para 26.22.

9   Eg, *Motor Agents Association Retail New Vehicle Order Form* (1979 edn), cl 1.3(d) of which provides for price changes in line with changes in the manufacturer's recommended price; and, in the event of a consequent price increase, the buyer is given a right of cancellation. within 14 days (as to rights of cancellation, see further post, para 10.28).

10 *Brogden v Marriott* (1836) 5 LJCP 302 (horse sold for £200 if within a month it trotted 18 miles in an hour; but for 1 shilling if it failed to do so).

11 Under the doctrine *certum est quod certum reddi potest*: see per Viscount Dunedin in *May & Butcher Ltd v R* (above).

[10.06]

1   For the ways in which an agent may bind his principal, see generally Treitel, *Law of Contract* (10th edn), Chapter 17.

2   *Lloyds and Scottish Finance Ltd v Williamson* [1965] 1 All ER 641, CA; *SMC Electronics Ltd v Akhter Computers Ltd* [2001] 6 CL 11, CA.

3   An undisclosed principal cannot ratify: *Keighley Maxted & Co v Durant* [1901] AC 240, HL; *Secured Residential Funding plc v Douglas Hendeles & Co* [2000] CLY 2607, CA (loan on house mortgage). But an unnamed principal can: *Sui Yin Kwan v Eastern Insurance Co Ltd* [1994] JBL 260.

(2) *Apparent authority*. Notwithstanding that there is no actual authority, where A clothes B with the appearance of authority.[4] This rule requires a representation from A to C[5] that B has A's authority to act as A's agent.[6] It is closely related to estoppel,[7] and shares with it a number of rules, including the rule that a mere handing over of possession of goods to B generally will not, without more, confer an apparent authority on B to dispose of them (see post, para 21.13).

(3) *Usual authority and ratification*. Notwithstanding that there is no actual or apparent authority, where it is in the usual course of B's business to make such a disposition,[8] or A subsequently ratifies that transaction.

(4) *Necessity*. Notwithstanding that there is no actual, apparent or usual authority, there may be an agency of necessity, though the courts are today reluctant to find such an agency.[9] The principle has been applied in the case of the sale of perishable goods by a carrier,[10] but not to a sale of furniture by a voluntary bailee;[11] and Parliament has extended the list of bailees who have authority to sell by reason of the bailor's failure to collect the goods (ss 12, 13 and Sched 1 of the Torts Act 1977).

For the CCA provisions as to how the agent (B) may affect relations between the principal (A) and third party (C), see post, para 10.24. The relationship between A and B is governed by the common law (see s 62(2) of the SGA: set out post, para 10.18) as amended.[12]

Direct financing

[10.07] The effect of the foregoing principles must now be examined in those circumstances where a third party provides the finance. The first question is: to whom does the supplier sell? In loan financing, there is a simple sale from supplier to consumer with the price provided by the financier lending that sum to the consumer.[1] Alternatively, the transaction may be directly financed, in that the supplier sells the goods to the

---

4   As to where an employee/agent changes employers, see *Discount Kitchens v Crawford* [1989] CLY 51, CA. See also *Charrington Fuel Oil v Parvant Co* [1989] CLY 58, CA (order by new owner of property).

5   Distinguish the consent exception (post, paras 21.04–21.05) where A tells B that B may dispose of the goods on his own account.

6   This overlaps with the estoppel exception, where A may represent to C either (i) that B has A's authority to sell on behalf of A, or (ii) that B is the owner: see post, para 21.10.

7   For the rules of common law estoppel, see post, para 21.10 *et seq*. For further comment on the relationship of this form of agency to estoppel, see post, para 16.06A.

8   *Watteau v Fenwick* [1893] 1 QB 346; *Kinahan Ltd v Parry* [1910] 2 KB 389, CA. It has been argued that this rule may extend to all agents exceeding their actual authority whilst acting within the scope of their employment as agent: the *Albright and Wilson* case (set out post, para 13.01) at para 17; and Atiyah, *Sale of Goods* (10th edn), pp 381–82. But see *Chitty on Contracts* (28th edn), vol 2, para 32-063.

9   See *Prager v Blatspiel, Stamp and Heacock Ltd* [1924] 1 KB 566.

10   *Springer v Great Western Rly Co* [1921] 1 KB 257, CA.

11   *Sachs v Miklos* [1948] 2 KB 23, CA. See post, para 21.06.

12   See Commercial Agents (Council Directive) Regulations 1993 (SI 3053) (see Singleton (1994) 13 Tr LR 26); and generally Fridman, *Agency* (7th edn), Part 3.

[10.07]

1   See *Edmond Murray v BSP International Foundations* [1994] CLY 548, CA. For loan financing, see ante, para 2.23.

financier, who himself supplies them to the consumer under an instalment contract (see ante, para 2.21), in which case there will be two supply contracts as follows:[2]

1 *Dealer/financier.* The three parties will envisage the dealer selling the goods chosen by the consumer to the financier. In *North West Securities Ltd v Alexander Breckon Ltd:*[3]

> On 10 May 1977, the consumer (C) completed negotiations with the dealer (D) for the supply on hp terms of a Ford truck. C signed an hp proposal form and was allowed to drive the truck away. That same day, D sent the financier (NWS) an invoice which stated 'we agree to sell the goods to you ... upon your acceptance of the [hp] agreement'. On 27 May 1977, C fraudulently sold the Ford truck to a bona fide purchaser (bfp). NWS paid D on 31 May 1977 and signed the hp agreement on 3 June 1977. NWS successfully sued the bfp for conversion of the truck.

No doubt it would have been safer for NWS if the truck had not been delivered until their acceptance of the hp agreement,[4] as envisaged by the invoice which, as usual in such cases, was in fact drafted by NWS. Thus, the bfp relied upon the invoice, arguing that its effect was to suspend the sale from D to NWS until 3 June 1977 so that NWS had no title to sue in conversion on 27 May 1977.[5] However, the Court of Appeal unanimously held as follows: (a) the envisaged two supply contracts were entirely separate;[6] and (b) as a matter of fact D and NWS had varied their contract from the terms set out in the invoice to provide for an oral sale on 27 May 1977.[7]

2 *Financier/consumer.* Between the financier and consumer, it is envisaged that there will be an entirely separate instalment contract (see ante, para 1.03). The formation of that contract must be examined (see post, para 10.08), together with the effect of a prior delivery of the goods to the consumer (see post, para 10.09).

[10.08] The financier/consumer contract. 'The conventional manner in which offer and acceptance takes place ... is for the proposed ... (retail customer), as offeror, to sign the agreement for forwarding to the finance company and for the finance company to accept it by signing the agreement itself, subsequently communicating that acceptance to the offeror, usually by post.'[1] Where the CCA applies, that procedure will satisfy the rules as to copies (see ante, paras 9.14–9.18). At any moment before then, the consumer can back out of the transaction and recover his deposit (see post, para 16.05) or perhaps any part-exchange goods (see post, para 10.09); but the position may be significantly different if the agreement is regulated.[2]

---

2 For collateral contracts between dealer and consumer, see post, para 16.18.

3 [1981] RTR 518, CA.

4 For similar advance deliveries, see *Financings Ltd v Stimson* (set out post, para 10.08); *R & B Brokers Ltd v United Dominions Trust Ltd* [1988] 1 All ER 847, CA.

5 Purchase by the bfp on 27 May 1977 would be an act of conversion: see post, para 19.05.

6 Viz a contract of sale from D to NWS and a contract of hp from NWS to C: at 522H–K; 523J; 524G.

7 The CA obviously thought the case close to the borderline, but accepted the trial judge's finding of fact: at 523G–H; 524C; 524G. Cf *Financings Ltd v Stimson* (above). As to variation of contract, see generally post, para 26.21.

[10.08]

1 *Carlyle Finance Ltd v Pallas Industrial Finance Ltd* (below), *per* Potter LJ at para 35, accepting the analysis of counsel at para 21.

2 If the debtor or hirer exercises either of his statutory rights of withdrawal or cancellation (see respectively post, paras 10.26, 10.29), the CCA then allows him certain cancellation rights (ss 57(1), 69); these rights are discussed post, para 10.31.

(a) *The offer.* In *Financings Ltd v Stimson*,[3] the parties were intending to set up a directly financed transaction (see ante, para 10.07) and the facts were as follows:

> On 16 March S signed an hp proposal form produced by a dealer; and two days later the dealer allowed him to take away the car to which that document related. On 20 March, S returned the car to the dealer, saying that he did not want it and (believing himself to be bound by a contract) offered to forfeit his deposit. During the night of 24/25 March, the car was stolen from the dealer's premises and recovered badly damaged. On 25 March, the finance company (not having been informed that S had returned the car to the dealer) signed the agreement.

The finance company's action against S for breach of the hp agreement failed before the Court of Appeal. Their Lordships unanimously took the view that S's completed proposal form constituted an offer (see ante, para 10.02), but that offer had come to an end before the finance company purported to accept it on 25 March for the following reasons:

(i) (*per* Pearson LJ, dissenting) the return of the car by S to the dealer on 20 March amounted to a revocation of his offer (see generally ante, para 10.02) as the dealer had an ostensible authority to accept the revocation of the offer on behalf of the finance company;[4]

(ii) (unanimously) the offer was conditional on the car being in substantially the same condition at the time of acceptance as at the time of offer, and therefore the offer terminated on the night of 24/25 March.[5]

(b) *The acceptance.* To try to ensure that the contract is made in the manner outlined at the beginning of this paragraph, the proposal form will usually contain some clause such as the following to be found in *Financings Ltd v Stimson*:

> This agreement shall become binding on the (finance company) only upon acceptance by signature on behalf of the (company) and the hiring shall be deemed to commence on such date of acceptance.

Their Lordships therefore took the view that the offer contained in the proposal form had not been accepted before 25 March;[6] and they also rejected the argument that there was a preliminary oral contract containing most of the terms embodied in the proposal form.[7] The early release of the goods by the dealer to the retail customer 'does not in the ordinary way amount to more than a preliminary bailment pending formal acceptance'. Whether or not the transaction is regulated, the common motor

---

3   [1962] 3 All ER 386; [1962] 1 WLR 1184, CA. Distinguished *Hitchens v General Guarantee Corp Ltd* [2001] 4 CL 291, CA (directly financed agreement made orally).

4   As to an agent's ostensible authority generally, see ante, para 10.06; and as to variations in the authority of an agent to accept communications on behalf of the financier, see post, para 10.24. As to regulated agreements, see post, para 10.25.

5   An alternative view is that there is a contract breached by delivery of goods in a different condition from that obtaining on the consumer's prior inspection: *Karsales (Harrow) Ltd v Wallis* (set out post, para 18.07); *Bentworth Finance Ltd v Lubert* (set out post, para 15.23).

6   Can the offeree stipulate that he need not communicate his acceptance? See ante, para 10.02.

7   Presumably because of the clause cited above. Alternatively, acceptance may be implied at common law from delivery of the goods: *Carlyle Finance* case (see below). Cf *NWS Ltd v Alexander Breckon Ltd* (set out ante, para 10.07).

trade practice of delivering new cars against a mere offer seems dangerous (see post, para 10.09). In *Carlyle Finance Ltd v Pallas Industrial Finance Ltd*:[8]

> The customer (V) and dealer agreed that V should purchase a car under a directly finance regulated conditional sale agreement with a finance company (C). C approved the transaction in principle, paid the price to the dealer and authorised delivery of the car to V. Before C could sign the conditional sale, V sold the car, which eventually passed to P, another finance company. It was accepted that P would obtain a good Part III title if, at the time of V's sale, a conditional sale existed between C and V (see post, para 21.55).

The Court of Appeal distinguished *Financings Ltd v Stimson* on the basis that the Carlyle (C) contract contained no such acceptance provision (at para 32) and ascertained that, whilst the agreement envisaged the normal formal signed acceptance,[9] C had made up its mind to accept the proposal and authorised the dealer to deliver the goods (at para 27). On the basis that V had no reason to suppose that the delivery of the car was not an acceptance by the dealer on behalf of C (see ante, para 10.06) of V's offer to enter a conditional sale, the court held that at common law the dealer on behalf of C had accepted that offer by conduct[10] in delivering the car to V (at para 33: see post, para 16.06). The court said that the fact that the regulated agreement was not properly executed (see ante, para 9.19) for breach of s 61 (see ante, para 9.12) did not prevent that unenforceable agreement passing title (*per* Potter LJ at para 30).

As to the situation where a consumer signs a proposal form in blank and the dealer subsequently completes the form and forwards it to the financier for acceptance, see post, para 16.05.

[10.09] Delivery before acceptance. This paragraph is concerned with the situation where the parties are negotiating a directly financed transaction (see ante, para 2.21) but the dealer delivers the 'new' goods[1] to the consumer before the financier accepts the transaction, seemingly a fairly common situation (see ante, paras 10.07–10.08), perhaps in return for delivery to the dealer of part-exchange goods (see ante, para 2.09).

1   **The new goods.** Generally speaking, in the period before the financier accepts the proposal the consumer is likely to hold the new goods as a bailee at will from the dealer;[2] but it is possible that an agreement between the consumer and financier may be inferred, so that the consumer may pass a Part III title to a bfp.[3] On the other hand, it is possible that the parties intend a provisional contract of sale between dealer and

---

8   [1999] 1 All ER (Comm) 659, CA.

9   Potter LJ argued that the formal provision for acceptance by signature had been waived under the rule that a party inserting a provision for his own benefit may do so: at para 34.

10   *Aliter* where either (i) C had not already bought the car from the dealer, or (ii) the dealer made delivery to V on his own account without C's authority: *per* Potter LJ at paras 31, 33.

[10.09]

1   The expression 'new' is used only to identify the goods the consumer is acquiring (which may be new or second hand) from those traded in by him.

2   Will the consumer have to pay for that use? What if the consumer is injured by the defective state of the goods? See generally ante, para 1.17; and further Goode, *Hire Purchase Law and Practice* (2nd edn), pp 146–48.

3   *Carlyle Finance Ltd v Pallas Industrial Finance Ltd* (set out ante, para 10.08). *Hitchens v General Guarantee Corp Ltd* [2001] 4 CL 291, CA; and see post, para 21.55.

consumer, to be set aside if the financier subsequently accepts the proposal.[4] In the latter event, if the financier subsequently declines the proposal, the consumer may have a better right to the new goods than the dealer.[5] Whether the consumer initially holds as bailee or buyer, consideration will be given later to the liability of the financier after his acceptance of the proposal for any misrepresentations by the dealer (see post, para 16.03 *et seq*) or breach of implied terms (see post, para 14.13).

2   *The part-exchange goods.* In effect, the consumer sells the part-exchange goods to the dealer for the amount of the part-exchange allowance, which sum the dealer holds as the deposit payable in respect of the new goods.[6] Suppose the financier declines the proposal. It is conceivable that there is an independent unconditional sale of the part-exchange goods,[7] but much more likely that the parties intended the two transactions to be interdependent. However, there would appear to be several possible analyses of the nature of that interdependence:[7] in relation to the transfer of the part-exchange goods to the dealer, formation of the contract to supply the new goods was a condition precedent either to its formation[8] or performance;[9] or that there is an immediate sale of the part-exchange goods to the dealer, subject to a condition subsequent that it is determinable if the financier does not accept the transaction in respect of the new goods. Which analysis is adopted might be important, as where the part-exchange goods are damaged in the meantime,[10] or the consumer has only a defective title to them,[11] or the part-exchange goods are defective.[12] A standard form contract may well seek to deal with these matters (see post, para 11.08).

---

4   The sale between dealer and consumer may thus be subject to a condition subsequent (see generally ante, para 1.11); but it may infringe the Bills of Sale Acts: *Polsky v S & A Services Ltd* (set out post, para 25.34).

5   *City Motors v Southern etc Service* (1961) 106 CLR 477, HC (criticised Goode, *op cit*, note 2, pp 148–49).

6   Goode, *op cit*, note 2, pp 309–10.

7   Goode, *op cit*, note 2, pp 311–13.

8   It would follow that the dealer had not agreed to buy the goods (see note 10, below). But what if the dealer had meanwhile settled any outstanding balance due to a fourth party in respect of the part-exchange goods?

9   The dealer would have agreed to buy the goods (see note 11, below). Does it also follow that the consumer has conditionally agreed to take the new goods in breach of CCA, s 59 (set out ante, para 5.20)?

10 Eg, *Clarke v Reilly* (1962) 96 ILTR 96. For the passing of property, see further post, Chapter 20.

11 Has the dealer 'agreed to buy' them within s 9 of the Factors Act 1899 (as to which see post, para 21.45)? See Goode, *op cit*, note 2, pp 305–06. For the position as between the contracting parties, see below.

12 Does the supply attract the implied terms from ss 12–15 of the SGA or ss 2–5 of the SGSA (see post, Chapters 12–15)? See, generally, Law Com 95, paras 52–53.

Auctions[1]

[10.10] Introduction. An auction normally involves a sale to the highest bidder by public[2] competition,[3] conducted on behalf of the seller by an agent, the auctioneer (see post, para 10.11). Even if the auction is advertised in advance, the auctioneer is *prima facie* not bound to hold the auction;[4] and, if he is commissioned to sell a number of items, the SGA provides that (s 57(1)):

> Where the goods are put up for sale by auction in lots, each lot is *prima facie* deemed to be the subject of separate contract of sale.

Almost inevitably, an auctioneer will apply some sort of description to each lot, perhaps in a catalogue and/or when he puts each lot up: as to the incorporation of such terms into the contract, see post, para 18.04. In a trade auction he may seek to exclude any liability of himself or the seller for any misdescription in either civil[5] or criminal[6] law by means of conditions of sale;[7] and it may be possible, eg, in the auction conditions of sale, for the seller to deny the auctioneer any actual or apparent authority to make representations on his behalf.[8]

However, where a consumer supply contract is made, the express terms will be subject to the UTCC rules with regard to legibility and fairness, eg, events when commission payable (OFT, *Bulletin No 15*, case 6); and any attempt to deny the auctioneer authority to make representations an unfair term (UTCC Grey Term 1(n): see post, para 11.18).

Once the bidding on a particular lot has commenced, s 57(2) describes how a contract for its sale comes into existence:

> A sale by auction is complete when the auctioneer announces its completion by the fall of the hammer, or in other customary manner; and until the announcement is made any bidder may retract his bid.

[10.10]

1   See generally Harvey and Meisel, *Auctions* (2nd edn, 1995). In relation to goods, auctions are frequency used to achieve sales at market value of commodities, plant and machinery and motor vehicles: see Harvey and Meisel, pp 9–12.

2   Distinguish competing for a contract by sealed bid: see *Harvela Investments Ltd v Royal Trust Co of Canada (CI) Ltd* [1986] AC 207, HL, *per* Lord Templeman (at 230).

3   The concept of an auction is not defined by the SGA. Does s 57 extend to the descending-price system (Dutch Auction)? As to the different types of auction, see Harvey and Meisel, *op cit*, note 1, pp 1–4.

4   *Harris v Nickerson* (1873) LR 8 QB 286.

5   Express terms or misrepresentations (see post, Chapter 11). As the buyer is not 'dealing as consumer' (UCTA, s 12(2): see post, para 18.18), any exclusion of the undertakings as to description or quality need only be reasonable: see *Spriggs v Sotheby Parke Bernet & Co* (1986) 278 EG 969, CA; and post, para 18.19.

6   *Derbyshire CC v Vincent* (1991) 8 Tr LR 63, DC. Whether or not inserted in the conditions of sale, it may be that a disclaimer can only be effective if apt words are used as the lot is put up: see Harvey and Meisel, *op cit*, note 1, pp 222–24; and generally ante, para 4.09.

7   For some auctioneers' conditions of sale, see Harvey and Meisel, *op cit*, note 1, p 173 *et seq*, App 1; and for standard form contracts generally, see post, para 11.08. Some of these are standardised and registered as restrictive practices (see generally ante, para 2.13): Harvey and Meisel, p 289.

8   See Harvey and Meisel, *op cit*, note 1, pp 37–38; Harvey (1995) 14 Tr LR 190; and generally post, paras 17.10; 17.20.

Thus, the auctioneer's request on behalf of the seller for bids amounts only to an invitation to treat;[9] each successive bid is an offer,[10] revocable until acceptance;[11] and the auctioneer is, on behalf of the seller, *prima facie* free to accept or reject that bid. Bidders sometimes go to some lengths to conceal their bid from other bidders.[12]

There may be attempts to manipulate the system of selling by auction to their own advantage by any of the three parties involved: the seller may or may not reserve a price or right to bid (see post, para 10.12); the seller/auctioneer may conduct a mock auction (see post, para 10.11); and the bidders may form a ring (see post, para 10.13). Goods unsold in an auction may be sold by the auctioneer privately thereafter, in which case the ordinary rules of offer and acceptance apply (see ante, para 10.02).

[10.11] Auctioneers. In selling goods,[1] the auctioneer acts primarily as the agent of the seller,[2] *prima facie* having a lien over the goods sold[3] and a right to sue the purchaser for the price.[4] As he is not normally a party to the sale, the auctioneer is not usually himself liable for the statutory implied conditions (see post, para 14.04); but he may be liable to the buyer in respect of statements at the auction, either on the basis of negligent misstatements[5] or collateral contract (see post, para 11.06). If, in selling the goods, an auctioneer exceeds his authority, as a mercantile agent he may nevertheless pass a good title (see post, para 21.24 *et seq*). Suppose an auctioneer's principal (the seller) is not the true owner of goods sent for auction: in knocking down those goods to the highest bidder, the auctioneer (albeit innocently) commits conversion of the goods[6] and is then in difficulty as to the proceeds.[7]

Mock auctions.[8] These are a form of elaborate and long-established confidence trick which Parliament has sought to contain by the Mock Auctions Act 1961. The major

---

9   *British Car Auctions Ltd v Wright* [1972] 3 All ER 462, DC (criminal case: see ante, para 4.37).

10 Perhaps each bid falls when superseded by a valid higher bid: Treitel, *Law of Contract* (10th edn), p 11.

11 *Payne v Cave* (1789) 3 Term 148. It seems to follow that in 'taking' a bid, the auctioneer is not accepting that offer, but merely indicating that he has no objection to treating with that bidder (suggestion by JWA Thornely).

12 See Harvey and Meisel, *op cit*, note 1, pp 129–30. In the event of a disputed bid, the conditions frequently allow the lot to be put up again, eg, *Richards v Phillips* [1969] 1 Ch 39 (sale of land).

[10.11]

1   Whether he actually knocks the goods down in the auction (see ante, para 10.10) or sells them privately (perhaps because the goods have failed to find a buyer at auction). The agency contract may contain an implied term that the auctioneer will carefully value the goods: *Luxmoore-May v Messenger, May, Baverstock* [1990] 1 All ER 1067, CA (see 107 LQR 28) (painting).

2   For the circumstances in which, and the extent to which, he may also act as the agent of the buyer, see Harvey and Meisel, *Auctions* (2nd edn), pp 115–18. For the auctioneer's authority as agent of the seller, see Harvey and Meisel, pp 24–26, 36–38. For a situation in which the auctioneer buys and resells as principal, see Harvey and Meisel, pp 294–96.

3   The lien is good against both seller and buyer and is for the auctioneer's charges and the price respectively; see Harvey and Meisel, *ibid*, pp 62–67. The lien is free of any claim for distress by the seller's landlord (as to distress, see generally post, para 19.18): Harvey and Meisel, *ibid*, pp 77–79.

4   *Chelmsford Auctions Ltd v Poole* [1973] QB 542, CA; *Pollway Ltd v Abdullah* [1974] 2 All ER 381, CA. As to actions for the price, see post, paras 27.16–27.18.

5   *McAnarney v Hanrahan* [1993] 3 IR 492; and see generally post, para 17.20.

6   *Hollins v Fowler* (1875) LR 7 HL 757 (goods obtained by fraud); *Unicorn Transport Finance Ltd v British Car Auctions Ltd* [1978] 2 All ER 385, CA (car on hp); and post, para 19.05. As to where the auctioneer acts in some lesser capacity, see Harvey and Meisel, *op cit*, note 2, pp 136–39; and as to goods sold with foreign title acquired abroad, see post, para 21.05.

7   See Harvey and Meisel, *op cit*, note 2, pp 104–08. The safest course may be to interplead.

8   See generally Harvey and Meisel, *op cit*, pp 206–09; and Cranston, *Consumers and the Law* (3rd edn), pp 418–19. For a list of convictions see Thomas, *Encyclopedia of Consumer Law*, para 1-334.

difficulty faced by the draftsman was to catch all such mischievous activities whilst not hindering genuine auctions. The Act makes it a criminal offence to sell or 'to promote or conduct or to assist in the conduct of, a mock auction'[9] by way of competitive bidding[10] any lot which includes prescribed articles, eg, plate, linens, china, jewellery (s 3(2)), using any of the following techniques, there being provisions to lighten the burden of proof on the prosecution (s 3(3)–(5)): the goods are knocked down to a person at a price less than his highest bid or part of the price is repaid to him (s 1(3)(a)), there being an exemption if the reduction in price/repayment was on account of a 'defect' or 'damage sustained after the bid was made' (s 1(4)); or the right to bid is restricted to persons buying more than one article;[11] or there are free gifts (s 1(3)(c): for 'free gifts', see generally ante, para 2 08). The OFT have sought to discourage such offences by utilising their powers under Part III of the FTA (see ante, para 6.07).

[10.12] Seller's reserve/right to bid. There are several permutations as to whether the seller may impose a minimum price.[1]

1   *Express reserve/right to bid.* The SGA expressly recognises that (s 57(3)):

> A sale by auction may be notified to be subject to a reserve or upset price, and a right to bid may also be reserved expressly by or on behalf of the seller.

Notification will usually be by way of announcement in the conditions of sale and/or auctioneer's oral announcement before opening the bidding. Both types of notification are means of informing bidders that the authority of the auctioneer is limited to selling at above a (usually undisclosed) figure, so limiting the auctioneer's actual, apparent and usual authority (as to which, see generally ante, para 10.06). The Act also explains that (s 57(6)):

> Where, in respect of a sale by auction, a right to bid is expressly reserved (but not otherwise) the seller or any one person on his behalf may bid at the auction.

The effect is to convert each bid into a conditional offer. It follows that, if by mistake the auctioneer knocks the goods down to the highest bidder below the reserve price, there is no contract of sale and the auctioneer is not liable for breach of warranty of authority.[2] However, assuming that the auctioneer remembers his reserve, or the highest bid is made by the **one** person authorised to do so on behalf of the seller,[3] that seller has failed in his objective of disposal of the goods by way of public auction. In such a situation, the auctioneer will frequently be able to negotiate a subsequent private sale below the reserve between the seller and highest *bona fide* bidder.[4]

---

9   Section 1(1). For offences, see s 1(2) and post, para 28.01. For offences by corporate officers, see s 2 and post, para 28.11. Other criminal proceedings, eg, theft, or civil actions are expressly saved (s 3(6)): see ante, para 3.21.

10 See s 3(1). It will extend to English and Dutch auctions (see ante, para 10.10): see *Allens v Simmons* [1978] 3 All ER 662, DC; *R v Pollard* [1984] CLY 664, CA.

11 Section 1(3)(b). Eg, *Clements v Rydehead* [1978] 3 All ER 658, DC.

[10.12]

1   Or a modern practice is for the auctioneer to guarantee a minimum price. As to guarantees, see post, para 25.06.

2   *McManus v Fortescue* [1907] 2 KB 2, CA.

3   It has been argued that, where the auctioneer accepts bids by more than one person on behalf of the seller, the transaction is invalid: *Benjamin's Sale of Goods* (5th edn), para 3-009.

4   Eg, *RH Willis & Son v British Car Auction Ltd* [1978] 2 All ER 392, CA (discussed Harvey and Meisel, *Auctions* (2nd edn), pp 278–79).

2   *Seller's instruction unannounced.* Where the seller instructs the auctioneer to place a reserve on his goods but that instruction is unannounced, the auctioneer may still execute the seller's wishes by refusing to accept any bid below the reserve, because bids are only offers (see ante, para 10.10). However, he may not do so by accepting a bid on behalf of the seller. Section 57 lays down that:

> (4) Where a sale by auction is not notified to be subject to a right to bid by or on behalf of the seller, it is not lawful for the seller to bid himself or to employ any person to bid at the sale, or for the auctioneer knowingly to take any bid from the seller or any such person.

> (5) A sale contravening subsection (4) above may be treated as fraudulent by the buyer.

The effects are as follows: (a) to prohibit the seller or his agent from bidding or the auctioneer from accepting any such bid;[5] and (b) if he does so, to enable the buyer to rescind the contract of sale *ab initio*, claim damages for deceit[6] and perhaps treat the contract as illegal.[7]

3   *Sale announced without reserve.* Notwithstanding the announcement, the auctioneer is not bound to put the goods up; but if he does so the auction may be completed by his knocking the goods down to the highest *bona fide* bidder (see ante, para 10.10). However, the SGA leaves obscure what is to happen if, in contravention of the announcement, the seller intervenes after the auction has started either to revoke the auctioneer's authority or buy in the goods;[8] or if the auctioneer seeks to promote the bidding by taking an imaginary bid 'off the wall'.[9] In *Barry v Davies*:[10]

> Two new condensing engines worth about £14,000 were put up for sale 'without reserve'. The auctioneer refused to accept P's bid of £200 each, because he considered it far too low. Presumably because he felt that the owner could not be compelled to accept his bid and enter a contract of sale (see ante, para 10.10), P sued the auctioneer for damages.

The Court of Appeal held the auctioneer liable for damages under a separate collateral contract for breach of warranty of authority, awarding P the same measure of damages as if the seller had been sued for non-delivery (see post, para 29.19 *et seq*). Could any attendee or bidder sue?

[10.13] Buyer's bidding ring.[1] Whilst a seller will normally auction his goods with a view to obtaining their market price (see ante, para 10.10), this expectation may be defeated if prospective buyers form a ring to operate as follows: before the auction a group of prospective buyers agree not to compete against each other but appoint one of their

---

5   The seller and/or auctioneer may be liable in tort (see below). But is the auctioneer strictly liable for breach of warranty of authority? Are they both liable for breach of statutory duty (see generally ante, para 3.21)? What if the auction conditions expressly permit such a bid?

6   As to rescission *ab initio*, see post, para 26.12; and as to the tort of deceit, see post, para 17.18.

7   Benjamin, *op cit*, note 3. As to illegality, see generally post, para 10.19.

8   US law will not permit this: Uniform Commercial Code, Art 2-328(3).

9   As to the criminality of such behaviour, see Harvey and Meisel, *op cit*, note 4, 219 *et seq*.

10 [2001] 1 All ER 944, CA. See further *Benjamin's Sale of Goods* (5th edn), para 2-005; Harvey and Meisel, *op cit*, note 4, pp 29–33.

[10.13]

1   See generally Harvey and Meisel, *Auctions* (2nd edn), p 209 *et seq*.

number to bid for the goods on behalf of the ring; and, if successful, the ring subsequently hold their own private auction ('knockout') for the goods, the difference between the two prices then being divided between members of the ring. This practice is not illegal at common law[2] but may fall within the Auction (Bidding Agreements) Acts 1927 and 1969.[3] These Acts apply only where one or more of the members of a 'ring' are 'dealers',[4] in which case the conduct is made criminal[5] unless the prior agreement between the prospective buyers was to purchase at the auction on *bona fide* joint account and a copy of that agreement was deposited with the auctioneer. In practice, it may be difficult to distinguish an illegal ring from a genuine joint account, hence the requirement that a copy of the latter agreement be deposited with the auctioneer. However, whilst safeguarding ad hoc joint agreements, the proviso may pose a trap for genuine long term partnerships. Not only are persons convicted of belonging to rings (an infrequent occurrence) banned from subsequently attending auctions for a stipulated time[6] but the seller has the right to treat the auction sale as voidable,[7] the parties to the ring then being jointly and severally liable for any loss to the seller (1969 Act, s 3(2)). The major difficulty in enforcing the Acts has been found to be proving the existence of a ring. It has been argued that the Acts should be repealed, leaving the seller to the protection of his reserve (see ante, para 10.12) and trade self-regulation (see generally ante, para 3.11); or that it would be more effective to require registration of ring agreements with the auctioneer (what if he participated in the ring?). Dealers' rings may also be impugned under Art 81 [ex 85] of the EC Treaty.[8]

Mistake

[10.14] Introduction. Apart from the circumstance where mistake raises the question of impossibility of performance (see post, para 22.09 *et seq*), s 62(2) of the SGA expressly saves the common law rules relating to the effect of mistake which includes the rules of equity (see ante, para 1.02); and the other major statutes regulating the supply of goods are entirely silent on the matter, eg, SOGIT; CCA; SGSA; CPA. If mistake operates at common law at all, it operates so as to negative or in some cases nullify consent to a contract.[1] Mistake negatives consent when it prevents the parties from reaching agreement, eg, mistake as to person (see post, para 10.15), mistake as to terms (see post, para 10.16); and it nullifies consent where the parties reach agreement, but that agreement has no legal effect because it is based on a fundamental mistaken assumption, eg, mistake

---

2   *Cohen v Roche* [1927] 1 KB 169.

3   The auctioneer's name and copies of these Acts must be exhibited at auction sales: 1927 Act, s 3; 1969 Act, s 4.

4   '"Dealer" means a person who in the normal course of his business attends sales by auction for the purposes of purchasing goods with a view to reselling them': 1927 Act, s 1(2); 1969 Act, s 3(5).

5   Triable summarily or on indictment (1927 Act, s 1(1)); 1969 Act, s 1), but only with the consent of the Attorney General (1927 Act, s 1(3)).

6   1969 Act, s 2, under which contravention of such a ban is itself an offence.

7   1969 Act, s 3(1): as to voidable contracts, see post, para 10.15. The 1927 Act had made such sales 'fraudulent' (cf SGA, s 57(5): see ante, para 10.12); but this provision was repealed by the 1969 Act, s 3(4).

8   *Per* Webster J (*obiter*) in *Shearson Lehman Bros v Maclaine Watson & Co Ltd* [1989] 2 Lloyd's Rep 570, at 621. For Art 81 (ex Art 85), see ante, para 2.13.

[10.14]

1   *Per* Lord Atkin in *Bell v Lever Bros Ltd* [1932] AC 161 at 217, HL.

as to quality (see post, para 10.17). The general rules on mistake can safely be left to the standard works on contract[2] and what follows is only a summary of those rules which are particularly important for our purposes. They should be distinguished from the recovery in quasi-contract of money paid under mistake[3] and mistakes in operating contractual arbitration machinery.[4]

[10.15] Mistake as to person.[1] Leaving aside the rules of agency,[2] *prima facie*, an offer can only be accepted by the person to whom it is made.[3] To determine that person, the offer is normally construed objectively;[4] but, where the person receiving the offer is aware that the offeror is mistaken and did not intend to contract with him, the test is subjective — with whom did the offeror actually intend to contract?[5] In the latter case, there is said to be a 'void contract', though this is really a contradiction in terms.[6]

In many of those cases where the offeree is aware that the offeror has mistakenly directed an offer to him, the offeree will have fraudulently induced the offer, it being the essence of the fraud that the offeror does not realise that his offer was internally contradictory. If the alleged contract is in writing, it will be a matter of interpretation for the court to decide which of the two contradictory intentions predominates;[5] but where the parties are dealing face to face it is helped by a presumption that the offeror intended to deal with the person in front of him.[7] In modern case law, this issue has given rise to disputes as to whether the mistake of the offeror relates to:

(a) the **identity** of the person addressed, in which case the alleged contract between them is wholly void;[8] or

(b) the **attributes** of that person, in which case the contract is only voidable,[9] that is, valid at common law, but in equity capable of being rescinded *ab initio*.[10] As will be seen later (see post, para 21.19), in the interim the apparent purchaser can pass a good title to a *bona fide* purchaser (bfp), because of the ordinary equitable rule that the innocent party's equitable right to rescind gives way to the rights of a bfp.

---

2 See *Benjamin's Sale of Goods* (5th edn), para 3-012 *et seq* and the authorities cited at the outset of that section.

3 *Kleinwort Benson Ltd v Lincoln CC* [1999] 2 AC 349, HL (not a goods case).

4 *Soules CAF v Louis Dreyfus Negoce SA* [2000] 2 All ER (Comm) 154.

[10.15]

1 See generally *Halsbury's Laws of England* (4th edn, reissue), vol 9, paras 704–06; *Benjamin's Sale of Goods* (5th edn), paras 3.012–3.015.

2 An undisclosed principal cannot ratify; and see generally ante, para 10.06.

3 *Newborne v Sensolid (Great Britain) Ltd* [1954] QB 45, CA (non-existent company). As to pre-incorporation contracts, see Gower, *Company Law* (6th edn), pp 141–44.

4 *Boulton v Jones* (1857) 2 H & N 564 (sale of business). As to the difficulties inherent in this test, see post, para 10.16.

5 *Cundy v Lindsay* (1878) 3 App Cas 459, HL (whether to sell to Blenkiron (the genuine firm) or the addressee (the rogue Blenkarn)).

6 *Per* Gresson P in *Fawcett v Star Car Sales Ltd* [1960] NZLR 406 at 412; and *per* Devlin LJ in *Ingram v Little* [1961] 1 QB 31, CA at 63–64.

7 *Phillips v Brooks Ltd* [1919] 2 KB 243 (shop sale where rogue purported to be Sir GB); *Lewis v Averay* (see below).

8 *Cundy v Lindsay* (above: written negotiations); *Ingram v Little* [1961] 1 QB 31, CA (three old ladies deal face-to-face with rogue).

9 *King's Norton Metal Co Ltd v Edridge, Merrett Co Ltd* (1897) 14 TLR 98, CA (written negotiations); *Lewis v Averay* [1972] 1 QB 198, CA (face to face dealings).

10 As to rescission *ab initio*, see post, para 26.12. See also *Citibank NA v Brown Shipley & Co Ltd* [1991] 2 All ER 690 (mistake as to bailee).

In *Shogun Finance Ltd v Hudson*:[11]

> A rogue went to showrooms and selected a Shogun car he wished to acquire on directly financed hp. He told the dealer that he was Mr Patel and produced a stolen driving licence in the name of Patel. The dealer faxed to the finance company an hp proposal form in the name of Patel and a copy of the stolen driving licence. Having conducted credit searches in the name of Patel, the company accepted the proposal; and the car was released to the rogue. The rogue then sold the car to H, a bfp. The company sought to recover the car as owner and H pleaded a Part III title (see post, para 21.55).

At common law, everything depended on whether the company had contracted with the rogue: H argued that there was only a mistake as to identity, because the company intended to contract with the rogue in front of the dealer (case (b), above), the dealer acting as agent of the company.[12] However, the majority of the Court of Appeal held that there was a mistake as to identity, because it only intended to contract with the genuine Mr Patel (case (a), above).

[10.16] Mistake as to terms. Whilst there is no agreement without the assent of both parties, in most cases each party will look as though he is assenting to the proposed terms; and on the objective test[1] will therefore be precluded from denying the formation of an agreement on terms which an objective bystander would have thought the parties were agreeing.[2] Whilst the agreement may purport to enable the supplier to cancel the contract if his quotation contains an arithmetical or clerical error (see post, para 10.28), in a consumer supply this may amount to an unfair term (OFT, *Bulletin No 15*, case 9). On the other hand, there are bound to be a few cases where the objective bystander would conclude that the parties had never reached agreement, so that there was no contract between them, as where they are genuinely at cross-purposes as to the subject matter,[3] or in a battle of the forms (see ante, para 10.04) or where the agreed terms are ambiguous.[4]

The situation is entirely different where one party (A) is aware that the intentions of the other party (B) are not the same as his own. There will then be no justification for imposing an agreement in an objective sense or, if different, in the sense understood by A: the cases do not distinguish whether in this situation there is an agreement in the sense understood by B or no agreement at all.[5] If a dealer mistakenly completes a non-Act form in respect of a regulated agreement, it would seem safer to start again with CCA documentation.[6] But it is another matter where an Act form is completed in respect of an unregulated agreement, as it is usually thought that the effect is that the financier has

---

11 [2001] 8 CL 108, CA.

12 As to agency generally, see ante, para 10.06. As to the agency of a dealer for a finance company, see post, para 16.06 *et seq*.

[10.16]

1 This test is also applied in mistake as to person: see ante, para 10.15. For the difficulties inherent in this test, see Howarth (1984) 100 LQR 265; Vorster (1987) 104 LQR 274.

2 *Tamplin v James* (1880) 15 Ch D 215 (not a goods case). Distinguish mistake as to quality: see post, para 10.17.

3 *Scriven v Hindley* [1913] 3 KB 564 (auction). As where there is a mistake at a supermarket check-out as to the item sold: see [1996] 6 Which? 20.

4 *Falck v Williams* [1900] AC 176, PC (patent ambiguity); *Raffles v Wichelhaus* (1864) 2 H & C 906 (latent ambiguity).

5 *Smith v Hughes* (set out post, para 10.17); *Hartog v Colin & Shields* [1939] 3 All ER 566 (price per piece/pound).

6 Because the agreement will be not properly executed under s 61(1): see ante, para 9.12.

contracted to give his customer all the CCA protections;[7] or where the dealer and consumer collude to defraud the financier.[8]

Non est factum. The ancient common law defence of *non est factum* (literally – 'it is not my deed') originally developed as a defence by one who could not read (whether through blindness or illiteracy) to a claim based on a promise made by him in a deed under seal (see ante, para 9.01); but by the 19th century it had been extended to persons who could read and to all kinds of signed contract.[9] Whilst the general common law rule remains that a man is bound by his signature, the basis of this defence is that the signatory is mistaken as to the nature of the document he signed, so that his signature is a nullity and cannot be relied upon by anyone into whose hands the document may have come, though it is not normally applicable to documents mistakenly signed in blank (see post, para 16.05). The modern ambit of the plea of *non est factum* was laid down by the House of Lords in 1970: it is an exceptional defence in which the burden of proof falls on the signatory to show that in signing he acted with reasonable care in making a fundamental mistake as to the nature of what he signed.[10] If the plea was successful in relation to a regulated agreement, it would presumably render that agreement not properly executed (see ante, para 9.13) under the CCA and void at common law. What if a credit card slip signed in blank is subsequently completed in an unauthorised manner (see ante, para 7.09)? If regulated, the position depends on ss 83 and 171(4)(b) of the CCA (see ante, para 7.13).

[10.17] Mistake as to quality. It has long been recognised that a common mistake as to the **existence** of the subject matter of a sale at the time of contracting will normally render the contract void.[1] In *Bell v Lever Bros Ltd*,[2] Lord Atkin accepted that the doctrine of mistake was not limited to the foregoing and that a contract is void if there is a mistake such as to nullify 'a foundation essential to its existence' (at 225–26). However, where the mistake relied upon is as to the quality of goods bought, Lord Atkin said that 'such a mistake will not affect assent unless it is the mistake of both parties, and is as to the existence of some quality which makes the thing without the quality essentially different from the thing as it is believed to be'.[3] Whilst this doctrine is clearly a very narrow one, the different opinions as to its precise scope in the light of modern cases is beyond the scope of this work.[4] Nevertheless, its existence gives rise to the rule *caveat emptor* (see post, para 15.22) and makes it important to distinguish carefully between mistakes as to (i) quality and (ii) warranties as to quality. In *Smith v Hughes*:[5]

---

7   See (1991) 46 CC 4/30.

8   Eg, by inflating a deposit or trade-in: see (1992) 46 CC 5/5.

9   *Foster v Mckinnon* (1869) LR 4 CP 704 (not a sale of goods case).

10   *Saunders v Anglia Building Society* [1971] AC 1004, HL (not a sale of goods case). Doctrine applied in *Lloyds Bank v Waterhouse* (1991) 10 Tr LR 161, CA (guarantee: see post, para 25.06).

[10.17]

1   *Res extincta*: see post, para 22.10. A similar view is taken where a man mistakenly purports to buy his own goods (*res sua*).

2   [1932] AC 161; [1931] All ER Rep 1, HL (not a goods case).

3   At 218. For the narrow range of such operative mistakes, see *Harrison and Jones Ltd v Bunten and Lancaster Ltd* (set out post, para 17.11); *Great Peace Shipping Ltd v Tsavliris Salvage Ltd* (2001) 151 NLJ 1696 (see Pavlowski (2001) 152 NLJ 132); and generally *Benjamin's Sale of Goods* (5th edn), para 3-020.

4   See Benjamin, *ibid*, para 3-021. Distinguish where A's mistake is caused at least in part by the misrepresentation of B: A will then have a right to rescind (see post, para 26.12) and/or claim damages for misrepresentation (see post, paras 17.10; 26.12).

5   (1871) LR 6 QB 597; [1861–73] All ER Rep 632.

B, a farmer, invited A, a trainer of racehorses, to buy some oats from him, and showed a sample to A. A wrote to say he would take the whole quantity but later complained that the oats were useless to him because they were new, whereas he needed old oats to feed his racehorse. B knew they were new oats – he had no old oats – but refused to take them back and sued for the price. There was a crucial conflict of evidence as to how B described the oats at their meeting: B said he described them as 'good oats'; but A said B described them as 'good old oats'.

As the court pointed out, assuming B had not in fact used the word 'old',[6] the difference in A's perception of what B had said was crucial:

(i) If A had actually realised that B had described them as 'good oats' but A had mistakenly thought them old, then A's unilateral mistake as to quality would not avoid the contract (see above) for 'good oats'.[7]

(ii) If A had thought mistakenly that B had described them as 'good **old** oats', then the contract would be void because A would be mistaken as to the terms of the offer, believing them to include a warranty of quality (see ante, para 10.16).

Invalidity

[10.18] Introduction. Leaving aside insolvency (see post, para 19.18 *et seq*) and restraint of trade (see ante, para 2.13 *et seq*), this paragraph attempts to draw together the various rules which may invalidate a contract for the supply of goods. Where a transaction falls within s 62(2) of the SGA lays down that:

> The rules of the common law, including the law merchant,[1] except in so far as they are inconsistent with the provisions of this Act,[2] and in particular the rules relating to the law of principal and agent[3] and the effect of fraud,[4] misrepresentation,[5] duress or coercion,[6] mistake,[7] or other invalidating cause,[8] apply to contracts for the sale of goods.

No counterpart to this section is to be found in the other major statutes governing the supply of goods, eg, the CCA; but the position is presumably the same. In addition, there

---

6   If he had, B would have given an express warranty of quality. As to express promises, see generally post, para 11.07.

7   B's 'passive acquiescence' in the 'self-deception' of A will not entitle A to avoid the contract: *per* Cockburn CJ at 603.

[10.18]

1   As to the rules of equity and law merchant, see ante, para 1.02; and generally Goode, *Commercial Law* (2nd edn), p 197.

2   Whilst Chalmers attempted to capture the spirit of the common law in his draft Bill of 1890, some substantive changes were made during its passage through Parliament (see below; and ante, para 1.02).

3   As to the common law rules of agency, see ante, para 10.06.

4   As to the action in tort for deceit, see post, para 17.18; and as to rescission *ab initio*, see post, para 26.12.

5   As to actions for damages for misrepresentation, see post, paras 17.10, 26.12.

6   'Coercion' was added when the 1890 Bill was extended to Scotland. As to duress and undue influence, see generally Treitel, *Law of Contract* (10th edn), Chapter 10; and as to economic duress, see *CTN Cash & Carry Ltd v Gallagher* [1994] 4 All ER 714, CA.

7   As to mistake, see ante, para 10.14 *et seq*.

8   'Invalidating causes' has been said to cover illegality (*Benjamin's Sale of Goods* (5th edn), para 3-027); and it presumably also extends to contracts void on grounds of public policy; fraudulent auctions (s 57(5): see ante, para 10.12); and contracts with minors (see below). What about sales of human body parts by live persons (see 139 NLJ 159)? Or a credit card used to obtain the services of a prostitute?

are a number of offences, mostly statutory, which may be committed in the course of completing a contract for the supply of goods, eg, the offences referred to in Chapters 4 and 5. The difficulty is to know what is the effect of transgression on the supply agreement (see post, para 10.19). There must be distinguished from illegal contracts those made unenforceable by statute. This category includes all the following: unevidenced guarantees (see post, para 25.06 *et seq*); improperly executed regulated agreements (see ante, para 9.06 *et seq*); and supplies made in contravention of the distance or doorstep selling rules (see ante, para 8.17; post, para 10.21).

Contracts with minors.[9] Capacity to buy and sell is governed by the general law concerning contracts to transfer and acquire property (s 3(1) of the SGA): the general rule was that a contract made by a minor was voidable at his option; but he was liable to pay a reasonable price for necessaries actually supplied.[10] Contracts under which a minor acquires property with obligations are voidable by the minor during minority, but bind him whilst he retains the property.[11] Loans which a minor uses to obtain necessaries would seem to be recoverable, though possibly involving criminal offences (see ante, para 8.33); but other loans do not bind a minor, though any agreement by the minor after achieving his majority to repay the loan (and any negotiable instrument made in connection with it) is now enforceable (s 1(b) of the Minors' Contracts Act 1987). A minor is not liable in tort for obtaining goods or a loan by fraudulently misrepresenting his age;[12] but under the Minors' Contracts Act 1987 he may be liable to restore the property obtained where he refuses to pay for it (s 3) and a guarantee of the minor's contractual obligations is enforceable, whether or not the minor's contract was regulated (s 2 of the 1987 Act). For guarantees of unregulated agreements, see post, para 25.06; for guarantees of regulated agreements, see post, para 25.11; and for student loans, see ante, para 3.15. The foregoing special rules for minors would not appear to inhibit contracts for those forms of payment card which do not include credit (see ante, paras 2.24–2.25); but, combined with the data protection rules against searching parents' credit records (see ante, para 3.28), may inhibit the granting of credit to minors without an adult co-debtor.

[10.19] Illegality. Where a contract for the supply of goods gives rise to a criminal offence (see ante, para 10.18), attention must first be turned to the statute creating the offence. Sometimes the statute spells out the effect of that offence on the supply contract, eg, the Discrimination Acts.[1] Conversely, the TDA provides that:[2]

---

9   Minors are persons under 18 years of age (formerly 'infants' until 21): Family Law Reform Act 1969. For the law relating to contracts with minors, see generally Treitel, *Law of Contract* (10th edn), Chapter 13. For co-principals, see post, para 25.05.

10 SGA, s 3(2). For the definition of 'necessaries', see s 3(3); and *Nash v Inman* [1908] 2 KB 1, CA. It is presumed that the same rule applies to hp and hiring of necessaries: Goode, *Hire Purchase Law and Practice* (2nd edn), p 134, note 10. It is not clear whether or not a minor is liable on an executory contract for necessaries.

11 There are cases on leases of land; and it is thought that similar principles apply to non-necessary leases and hp of goods. See Goode, *ibid*, pp 135–37.

12 *Leslie Ltd v Sheill* [1914] 3 KB 607, CA.

[10.19]

1   See ante, para 4.23. See also the Prices Act 1974, Sched, para 5(2); Auctions (Bidding Agreements) Act 1969 (see ante, para 10.13); Scotch Whisky Act 1988.

2   Section 35. See also the Weights and Measures Act 1985, s 72; Road Traffic Act 1988, s 75(7); Courts and Legal Services Act 1990, s 106(7); Property Misdescription Act 1991, s 1(4).

A contract for the supply of any goods[3] shall not be void or unenforceable by reason only of a contravention of any provision of this Act.

The effect is that a civil action does not lie merely for breach of the TDA. However, where (as will commonly be the case) the breach **also** amounts to a civil wrong, eg, for misrepresentation or breach of contract, or for the return of goods subject to a cancelled agreement (see post, para 10.34), the injured party may institute proceedings in respect of that separate civil wrong. Even more far-reaching, the CCA lays down that (s 170(1)):

A breach of any requirement[4] made (otherwise than by any court) by or under this Act shall incur no civil or criminal sanction as being such a breach, except to the extent (if any) expressly provided by or under this Act.

Apart from expressly preserving the functions of the Director[5] and any judicial controls thereon,[6] the intention of s 170 might appear to be to deprive breaches of the CCA of any legal consequences[7] other than those provided by the Act itself,[8] except where the actions contravening the CCA give rise to separate civil[9] or criminal[10] wrongs; but it has been decided that s 170 should be restricted to common law wrongs, so that s 170(1) does not preclude reliance on statutory offences.[11] Finally, the CPA provides different rules for its separate criminal parts:[12] breach of safety rules or regulations (Part II) does not render any agreement void or unenforceable (s 41(3): see ante, paras 4.34–4.35) and only infringement of the regulations gives rise to an action for breach of statutory duty (s 41(1), (5), (6): see ante, para 4.35); whereas contravention of the misleading pricing provisions (Part III) has none of these civil effects (s 41(2), (3): see ante, para 8.10A).

Where statute does not spell out the effect of the offence on a supply contract, recourse must be had to common law principles (see post, para 10.20).

[10.20] Illegality at common law. The standard works consider contracts rendered illegal at common law. Insofar as statutory offences arising during the supply of goods do not spell out the extent (if any) to which that offence taints the supply contract (see ante, para 10.19), recourse must be had to common law principles. Now, these criminal offences may

---

3   What about a supply of services in contravention of s 14 (as to which, see ante, para 4.15 *et seq*)? See the annotation in Current Law Statutes.

4   Presumably, 'requirement' does not extend to provisions conferring enforceable rights on debtors or creditors, eg, ss 69, 70(1), 71(2), 73(2), 75, 94, 95, 99, 100, 101. Exclusion of these rights is prevented by s 173(1): see post, para 18.11. But what of the following sections: s 81(2) (see post, para 23.13); s 113(1) (see post, para 25.14)?

5   CCA, s 170(2). In particular, in relation to his licensing function (s 25): see ante, para 6.18.

6   CCA, s 170(3). This leaves open the question of which functions of the Director are judicial acts amenable to judicial review.

7   See s 39(2) (see ante, para 6.20); ss 44–46 (see ante, para 8.28); s 78(4) (see ante, para 7.08); s 105(7) (see post, para 25.12); s 126 (see post, para 24.33); s 91 (see post, para 24.38).

8   Eg, the further penalty for unlicensed trading (s 39) is limited to unenforceability under s 40 (see ante, para 6.20); there is no action for breach of statutory duty (see ante, para 3.21), except where the Act so provides (eg, s 92(3): see post, para 24.34); and repossession of protected goods (s 90) gives rise only to the sanctions in s 91 (see post, para 24.38). What if the party subject to the duty finds it profitable to ignore the duty and pay any statutory penalty? See Goode, *Consumer Credit Legislation*, Part III, para 171.

9   'Civil sanction' includes unjust enrichment: *Dimond v Lovell* (set out ante, para 5.13); and Macleod [2000] JBL 14.

10 *Hicks v Walker* [1984] Crim LR 495, DC; *Brookes v Retail Credit Cards Ltd* [1986] Crim LR 327, DC.

11 *R v Kettering Justices ex p MRB Insurance Brokers Ltd* [2000] 2 All ER 353, DC (CPA, Part III).

12 The statutory product liability (Part I) imposes only civil sanctions: see post, para 17.24.

be committed at the following different stages in the life of the transaction for the supply of goods:

(i) the offence may occur prior to the formation of contract;[1] or

(ii) the formation of the contract may constitute the criminal offence, examples being found elsewhere in this work,[2] or otherwise;[3] or

(iii) the contract may be legal in its formation, but the illegality occur subsequently in performance[4] or use.[5]

Leaving aside the question of severance of an illegal contract and illegality of performance (case (iii)), which are adequately dealt with in the ordinary contract books, we must consider the effect of the illegality in cases (i) and (ii). Whilst it is clear that the illegality taints the contract in case (ii), this is by no means so clear in case (i): the illegality may be totally unconnected with the contract, in which event the contract presumably may not be tainted; but, where the statute is intended to protect one party in his entering into such transactions, it is arguable that the illegality should taint the transaction.

The effect of illegality.[6] Assuming that a contract is tainted with illegality, the effect may be as follows:

(a) As a general rule, to prevent either party relying on the illegal contract in any litigation,[7] though it may be that a party who entered into the transaction under an innocent mistake as to the facts which constitute the offence can sue on the contract or in tort[8] or under a collateral contract[9] or where there is no affront to public conscience.[10]

[10.20]

1 Eg, under the Business Advertisements Order (see ante, para 4.22); Wildlife and Countryside Act 1981, s 6(1)(b); Children and Young Persons (Harmful Publications) Act 1955 (as amended); Highways Act 1980, Part IX (as amended: obstruction); Knives Act 1997, s 1.

2 Eg, the sale of some kinds of wildlife (see ante, para 4.23); sales which contravene the Misuse of Drugs Act 1971 (see ante, para 4.29); supplying unsafe goods, such as crossbow bows and other offensive weapons (see ante, para 4.31); intoxicating liquor (see ante, para 6.05); out of hours and Sunday sales (see ante, para 8.13); unsolicited goods (see, ante, para 8.18).

3 Eg, the tobacco products (see Children and Young Persons Act 1933, s 7 (as amended)); sales only by approved persons (Pharmacy and Poisons Act 1933, s 17; Opticians Act 1989, s 27); sale of pet animals in street (Pet Animals Act 1951, s 2 (as amended)); gaming machines (Gaming Act 1968, ss 26–28); video-nasties (Video Recordings Act 1984, ss 9, 11–14); Motor Cycle Noise Act 1987; supplies of aids test kits (Health and Medicines Act 1988, s 23); human organs (Human Organ Transplants Act 1989, s 1(1) and (2)); tobacco to children (Children and Young Persons (Protection from Tobacco) Act 1991); Breeding and Sale of Dogs Act 1999, s 8.

4 Eg, the supply of an unroadworthy vehicle which the supplier had promised to put in good order before delivery (see ante, para 4.37); sale of a solvent-based product. Does this category include sales contravening the Anatomy Act 1984, s 5(2), and cocaine-snorting kits? Does a recaption which amounts to a contravention of s 40 of the AJA 1970 (discussed post, para 24.24) fall within this category?

5 Eg, Wireless Telegraphy Act 1949, Part II (surveillance equipment); Powers of Criminal Courts Act 1973, s 43, as amended by Road Traffic Act 1991, s 36 (property used for purposes of crime); inflated invoice to make insurance claim (112 LQR 545).

6 See *Benjamin's Sale of Goods* (5th edn), paras 3-028–3-033.

7 *Pearce v Brooks* (1866) LR 1 Ex 213; *Snell v Unity Finance Ltd* [1964] 2 QB 203, CA; *Birkett v Acorn Business Machines Ltd* [1999] 2 All ER (Comm) 429, CA.

8 *Archbolds Ltd v Spanglett Ltd* [1961] 1 QB 374, CA (contract); *Belvoir Finance Co Ltd v Stapleton* [1971] 1 QB 210, CA (tort).

9 *Strongman (1915) Ltd v Sincock* [1955] 2 QB 525, CA; *Southern Industrial Trust v Brooke House Motors* (1968) 112 SJ 798, CA.

10 *Howard v Shirlstar Container Transport Ltd* [1990] 3 All ER 366, CA.

(b) By way of exception, to allow a claim in respect of transferred money or other property, notwithstanding the illegality. Usually that title passes under an illegal contract notwithstanding the illegality, so that goods or money[11] transferred cannot be recovered by the transferor from the transferee; but exceptionally property may be recovered, either by one who belongs to a class that the statute infringed was intended to protect (for lotteries, see ante, para 8.16), or that the illegal transfer was for a limited interest which has expired.[12]

[10.21] Doorstep-selling. The government has chosen to implement the EU Doorstep-selling Directive[1] by statutory instrument.[2] The intention of the Directive is to neutralise the element of surprise available to a trader who knocks on the door of the consumer's home and to allow the consumer time to make a comparison between the trader's offer and other offers available elsewhere. The ambit of the regulations is generally[3] restricted by reg 3(1) to a doorstep supply[4] for cash by a trader[5] of goods[6] or services[7] to a consumer[8] which is made during an unsolicited visit (see below) to the consumer's home for a VAT inclusive price of £35 or more: if the goods or services are supplied on credit, the transaction escapes these Regulations (reg 3(2)(g)), but will usually fall within the cancellation rules of the CCA (see post, para 10.28 *et seq*). However, it would seem that the remainder of reg 3(1) is to be read disjunctively, so that the regulations also extend to the following: a solicited visit which is used for switch-selling (reg 3(1)(b)); or a visit made after an order is placed by a consumer (reg 3(1)(c)); or a sale made during an excursion organised by the trader.[9] For distance selling, see post, para 10.22A.

---

11 *Kingsley v Stirling Industrial Securities Ltd* [1967] 2 QB 747, CA (goods); *Belvoir Finance Co Ltd v Stapleton* (above; goods; see Treitel, *Law of Contract* (10th edn), pp 462–63); *Berg v Sadler and Moore* [1937] 2 KB 158, CA (money).

12 *Bowmakers Ltd v Barnet Instruments Ltd* [1945] KB 65, CA: followed *Belvoir Finance Co Ltd v Harold Cole & Co Ltd* [1969] 2 All ER 904; *Belvoir Finance Co Ltd v Stapleton* (above). The 1945 case has been severely criticised by academic writers seeking to maintain a rule that such an action can only be supported where recovery can be made without reference to the illegality: Treitel, *ibid*, pp 458–59. For another view, see Enonchong (1995) 111 LQR 135.

[10.21]

1 Council Directive 85/577/EEC. As to the text of this Directive, see Guest and Lloyd, *Encyclopedia of Consumer Credit*, para 9024 *et seq*; Thomas, *Encyclopedia of Consumer Law*, para 5-184 *et seq*; Goode, *Consumer Credit Legislation*, X, para 22.01. As to the background to this Directive, see *Consumer Law in the EEC* (ed Woodroffe), pp 73–74. As to Directives generally, see ante, para 1.03A.

2 Consumer Protection (Cancellation of Contracts Concluded away from Business Premises) Regulations 1987 (SI 2117) (as amended).

3 Under reg 3(2), the following classes of contract are excepted: (a) those concerned with the purchase of land; (b) such as milk or bread delivery; (c) mail order business (see post, para 10.22A); (d) insurance contracts; (e) investment agreements.

4 'Supply' is not defined by the regulations, but presumably covers any contract under which the possession and/or property in goods is transferred, eg, sale, hp or simple hiring.

5 '"Trader" means a person who, in making a contract to which these regulations apply, is acting for the purpose of his business, and anyone acting in the name or on behalf of such a person': reg 2.

6 'Goods' has the same meaning as in the SGA (reg 2): see ante, para 2.02.

7 'Service' includes a guarantee, but only of a private debt: *Bayerische Hypotheken-und Wechselbank AG v Dietzinger* [1998] All ER (EC) 332.

8 '"Consumer" means a person, other than a body corporate, who, in making a contract to which these regulations apply, is acting for purposes which can be regarded as outside his business': reg 2. *Contra* the CCA, applicable to 'individuals': see ante, para 5.24.

9 Regulation 3(1)(d). This follows the Directive and is apparently aimed at malpractices more familiar on the Continent. However, it could catch UK timeshare operators and also act as an anti-avoidance device. See *Travel-Vac SL v Sanchis* [1999] All ER (EC) 656.

In relation to a doorstep supply for cash, the Regulations apply where the transaction is conducted during an **unsolicited visit** to the consumer's home[10] or place of work (reg 3(1)(a)). According to reg 3(3), '**unsolicited visit**':

> ... means a visit by a trader, whether or not he is a trader who supplies goods or services, which does not take place at the express request of the consumer;[11]

and this basic definition has subsequently been enhanced as an anti-avoidance device to include a visit which is arranged by telephone or during another unsolicited visit.[12] The likely effect of the regulations is this: *prima facie*, they will catch cash doorstep supplies of goods, such as vacuum cleaners, and building services, such as burglar alarms, double-glazing, roof repairs and tarmacking; and to avoid the regulations these businesses will have to solicit business by such as newspaper advertisements and leaflet drops.

[10.22] Where a transaction falls within the ambit of the Doorstep Selling Regulations (see ante, para 10.21), reg 4 provides the consumer with a compulsory[1] seven day right of cancellation, which must be notified to him in the prescribed form[2] at the time of the offer or contract (reg 4(4)). The regulations also seek to deal with potential overlap with other rights of cancellation by excluding them from the present regulations as follows (reg 4(2)):

(a) An agreement which is a cancellable regulated agreement within the CCA (see post, para 10.29). The effect of this is to leave within the present regulations both unregulated consumer credit,[3] and also most regulated non-cancellable agreements where the total payments exceed £35.[4]

(b) 'An agreement which may be cancelled by the consumer in accordance with terms of the agreement conferring upon him similar rights as if the agreement were such a cancellable agreement.' The test seems to be whether the contractual cancellation rights are 'similar' to those for regulated agreements.[5]

The doorstep selling provisions. The regulations now contain both civil and criminal provisions.

---

10 The extension by reg 3(1)(a)(i) to 'the home of another person' will bring in sales parties (see ante, para 8.17).

11 *Havair Ltd v Vile* [2000] CLY 848, Cty Ct (leafleting). For telephone sales pitches, see ante, para 8.17. An example of an 'express request' may be returning an advertising coupon. What of a letter informing a consumer he has 'won a prize' and inviting him to phone?

12 Holgate (1999) 18 Tr LR 33.

[10.22]

1 Regulation 10. For contracting out prohibitions, see generally post, paras 18.09 *et seq*.

2 As to the contents of the notice, see reg 4(3), (4) and the Schedule; and as to service of the notice, see regs 4(7), 11; and the Interpretation Act 1978, s 7. Compare the different requirement for notices of cancellation under the CCA: see post, para 10.31.

3 Eg, credit agreements above the financial limit; or exempt from the CCA; regulated agreements signed on trade premises after a home visit by the trader (reg 3(1)(c)). See further Guest and Lloyd, *Encyclopedia of Consumer Credit*, para 2-068.

4 Regulation 3(2)(f), unless under an hp or conditional sale agreement (reg 3(2)(g)). The minimum figure for the CCA cancellation provisions is reduced to the same figure: see post, para 10.29.

5 For express contractual rights of cancellation, see post, para 10.28. Does this extend to other statutory rights of cancellation, eg, under the Timeshare Act 1992?

Civil provisions. Regulation 4(1)) provides that:

> No contract to which these Regulations apply shall be enforceable against the consumer unless the trader has delivered to the consumer notice in writing [of his right of cancellation and a Cancellation Form].

There is an express prohibition on contracting out (reg 10) and no dispensing power, unlike the CCA (see ante, para 9.20). It should be observed that such transactions remain fully enforceable **against** the trader; but, within seven days of the making of the contract,[6] the consumer may give notice of cancellation 'however expressed' which 'shall operate to cancel the contract' (reg 4(5)), in which event it 'shall be treated as if it had never been entered into by the consumer'.[7] The regulations then proceed to deal with the civil consequences of such a cancellation in a manner which closely resembles that of the CCA: they provide for the recovery by the consumer of money paid by him[8] or goods given in part-exchange (reg 8. Cf s 73 of the CCA: see post, para 10.34); and his subsequent redelivery of the goods subject to the cancelled contract (reg 7. Cf s 72 of the CCA,: see post, para 10.34) and repayment by the consumer of any credit (reg 6, as amended. Cf s 71 of the CCA: see post, para 10.33).

Criminal provisions. Under the amended regulations, a trader commits an offence if he fails to deliver to the consumer a cancellation notice[9] and a duty to enforce the regulations is placed upon the local authority,[10] who may apply for a Stop Now Order (see ante, para 6.08).

[10.22A] Distance selling. The government has chosen to implement the EU Distance Selling Directive[1] by statutory instrument.[2] As has already been seen (ante, para 8.17), these regulations grant a consumer certain rights when he enters a distance contract; for instance, one made by telephone, internet or mail order. Among these rights is a right of cancellation. Even if the transaction is regulated by the CCA, the consumer will not have a CCA right of cancellation, because there are no face-to-face negotiations (see post, para 10.29); but he may have such a right under these regulations in respect of both regulated and unregulated distance contracts.

The right of cancellation. Starting with a requirement that the consumer receives at an appropriate time notice of his right to cancellation (reg 8(2)(b): see ante, para 9.05A) and a

---

6   Compare the time limit for cancelling cancellable agreements: see post, para 10.30. Will it lead to much difference in practice? And is it sensible to have slightly differently worded rules?

7   Regulation 4(6). Unlike the CCA (see post, para 10.32), this would leave any linked transaction standing. Is this satisfactory?

8   Regulation 5, which gives the consumer a lien on goods delivered to him as well as cancelling any security. Cf CCA, s 70: see post, para 10.33.

9   Regulation 4A. For the liability of other persons, see reg 4C; and post, paras 28.11–28.12. This is subject to an offence of due diligence: reg 4B; see post, para 28.13.

10 The duty is cast upon the local Weights and Measure Authorities (regs 4D, 2(1); and see post, para 28.02), who have powers of investigation (regs 4E; 4F; and see post, para 28.05) and duties of confidentiality (reg 4G; and see post, para 28.06).

[10.22A]

1   Council Directive 97/7/EEC. As to the text of this Directive, see Thomas, *Encyclopedia of Consumer Law*, para 5-495/1 *et seq*.

2   Consumer Protection (Distance Selling) Regulations 2000 (SI 2334).

prohibition on contracting out (reg 25(1): see post, para 18.10), reg 10(1) generally[3] grants the consumer a right of cancellation within a cancellation period, exercisable by giving 'a notice of cancellation[4] to the supplier, or any other person' to whom a notice of cancellation may be given (see reg 8: ante). The cancellation period begins when the contract is concluded (regs 11(1), 12(1)) and ends at times which differ according to whether there is supplied goods or services:[5] in the case of goods, if the supplier complies with the documentation rules in reg 8 (see above), it ends on the expiry of seven working days of goods-delivery (reg 11(2)); if within a three month period of goods delivery the supplier complies late with reg 8, it ends seven working days after the consumer received the information (reg 11(3)); otherwise, it expires three months plus seven working days after goods-delivery (reg 11(4), (5)). When due notice of cancellation is given,[6] that notice 'shall operate to cancel the contract' (reg 10(1)) and any 'related credit agreement',[7] upon which 'the contract shall be treated as if it had not been made' (reg 10(2)) and any security given 'treated as never having had effect' (regs 14(4); 15(4)). The regulations then proceed to deal with the civil consequences of such a cancellation in a manner which closely resembles that of the CCA: they provide for the recovery by the consumer of almost all[8] money paid by him[9] or goods given in part-exchange (reg 18. Cf s 73 of the CCA: see post, para 10.34); and his subsequent redelivery of the goods subject to the cancelled contract (reg 17. Cf s 72 of the CCA: see post, para 10.34) and repayment by the consumer of any credit (reg 16. Cf s 71 of the CCA: see post, para 10.33).

REGULATED AGREEMENTS

[10.23] Introduction. Generally speaking, all the rules as to the formation of contract previously considered in this chapter apply to the formation of a regulated agreement (see ante, para 5.13 *et seq*). However, over the years it was found that, if the formation of agreement was left to the common law rules, these would be manipulated by the stronger party to his advantage. Particularly in the field of what are now regulated agreements, this was thought to be undesirable. The common law rules have therefore been statutorily

---

3   *Prima facie*, the consumer has no right to cancel in any of the following cases (reg 13(1)): (a) supply of services begun with the consumer's consent before expiry of the cancellation period; (b) goods or services supplied at a price fluctuating with the financial market; (c) customised goods; (d) audio or video recordings or computer software unsealed by the consumer; (e) newspapers, periodicals or magazines; (f) gaming, betting or lottery services.

4   The notice may be given in writing or 'another durable medium' and takes effect however expressed: reg 10(3).

5   On a supply of services, there are similar expiry rules in reg 12(2)–(4).

6   A notice may be treated as properly given if it complies with reg 10(4) and (5).

7   Regulation 15(1). 'Related credit agreement' is defined by s 15(5) and (6). In lender credit (reg 14(8)), the supplier must notify the creditor of the cancellation (reg 15(2)), upon which charges paid under the credit agreement must usually be returned to the consumer (reg 15(3)).

8   Except that, if previously agreed by a term which is not unfair (reg 14(6)(b): see post, para 11.12 *et seq*), the supplier is entitled to make a re-delivery charge for the goods supplied, but not substitutes (reg 14(5), (7)). The re-delivery charge is not available where the consumer is exercising a right to reject defective goods (reg 14(6)(a)).

9   Regulation 14(1). This includes sums paid by the consumer under any 'personal credit agreement' (reg 14(2), (8)).

amended in the following areas concerned with the formation of such agreements:[1] (1) agency (see post, para 10.24); (2) withdrawal by debtor: a warming up period (see post, para 10.26); (3) right of cancellation: a cooling off period (see post, para 10.28).

Deemed agency

[10.24] It will be seen later (post, para 16.06) that it is sometimes a difficult question at common law whether a dealer in a directly financed transaction is the agent of either the financier, or the consumer, or both of them.[1] Between the two World Wars, it therefore became common for the proposal form to provide expressly that the dealer was to be regarded as the agent of the consumer. This was thought to be unfair,[2] and such deemed agency clauses were avoided by the HPA 1938 in a provision now re-enacted in s 56(3) of the CCA (set out post, para 16.05). This section introduces the wide concept of the 'antecedent negotiations' which precede the making of a regulated agreement and of the 'negotiator' who conducts them; but for the time being, it is sufficient to think of the 'negotiator' as the dealer setting up a financed transaction.

The effect of what is now s 56(3) is simply to avoid any deemed agency clause and to allow the court to apply the common law to the true facts. However, the HPA 1964 went further and actually **increased** the liability of the financier by making the dealer (negotiator) the agent of the financier for certain purposes. These compulsory[3] deemed agency provisions are now to be found in the CCA and cover the following purposes:

(a) to receive notices from the consumer of withdrawal of his offer contained in the proposal form or, where that offer has been accepted, the cancellation or rescission of the agreement (see post, para 10.25); and

(b) to receive notice from the consumer of the particular purpose for which the goods were required so that the consumer might invoke the implied undertaking as to fitness (see post, para 14.12); and

(c) for any representations made by the dealer to the consumer in the course of negotiating the transaction (see post, para 16.06).

[10.25] To receive notices. As part of its general deemed agency provisions (see ante, para 10.24), the CCA deems the 'negotiator' (dealer) to be the agent of the creditor or owner for the purpose of receiving notices from the debtor or hirer in all the following respects:

(1) The debtor or hirer is withdrawing his offer to enter a regulated agreement. Where the debtor or hirer has such a right of withdrawal (see post, para 10.26), s 57(3) provides that each of the following shall be deemed to be the agent of the creditor or owner for the purposes of receiving such notice of withdrawal:

[10.23]

1 The Act takes special measures to deal with the situation where there is more than one creditor/owner (s 186: see ante, para 5.25) and/or debtor/hirer (s 185: see post, para 25.08).

[10.24]

1 As to basic common law agency, see generally ante, para 10.06.

2 It might now amount to an unfair term under the UTCC Regulations: see post, para 11.18.

3 The parties cannot contract out of these provisions (s 173(1)): see further post, para 18.11.

(a) a credit-broker or supplier[1] who is the negotiator in antecedent negotiations,[2] and

(b) any person who, in the course of a business carried on by him, acts on behalf of the debtor or hirer in any negotiations for the agreement.[3]

Apparently to protect the creditor or owner in circumstance (b),[4] s 175 places that deemed agent 'under a contractual duty to the creditor or owner to transmit the notice ... to him forthwith'.[5]

(2) The debtor or hirer is cancelling a cancellable agreement. Where the debtor or hirer has such a right of cancellation (see post, para 10.29), s 69(6) deems exactly the same persons to be the agent of the creditor or owner as in the case of withdrawal (see above).

(3) The debtor or hirer is exercising any common law right of rescission. Where the debtor or hirer has such a right (see post, paras 26.11–26.16), s 102(1) deems exactly the same persons to be the agent of the creditor or owner as in the case of withdrawal (see above).

Withdrawal of offer (a warming up period)

[10.26] The ordinary case. Except in the case of those regulated agreements exempted from Part V of the Act (see ante, para 9.07) and the special rules for land mortgages (see post, para 10.27), s 57 enables either side to withdraw from a 'prospective regulated agreement', wherever made.[1] At common law, an offer may ordinarily be revoked or rejected at any time before acceptance (see ante, para 10.02); and this rule achieves statutory confirmation in s 57(2), which provides that:

The giving to a party of a written or oral[2] notice which, however expressed, indicates the intention of the other party to withdraw from a prospective regulated agreement operates as a withdrawal from it.

The Act thus does not mind which party made the offer to enter a regulated agreement,[3] nor whether the withdrawal is technically a revocation or rejection of offer; but it does make three alterations in the common law rules. First, whilst at common law a revocation

---

[10.25]

1 As to 'credit-broker', see ante, para 5.41; and as to 'supplier', see ante, para 5.34.

2 This effectively enacts the decision in *Financings Ltd v Stimson* (set out ante, para 10.08).

3 So a debtor can effectively serve a notice on his creditor by physically sending it to his (the debtor's) own agent, eg, spouse or solicitor!

4 As to whether this affects service of notice of cancellation, see post, para 10.31.

5 'Forthwith' presumably means at the earliest available moment: Goode, *Consumer Credit Law and Practice*, para 52.5.

[10.26]

1 *Contra* cancellable agreements, which depend on the place of negotiation (s 67): see post, para 10.29. As to 'prospective regulated agreements', see generally ante, para 5.20; but as to the earliest moment when such an agreement exists, see below.

2 This ousts the s 189(1) definition of 'notice'. Compare notices of cancellation under s 69(1): see post, para 10.31.

3 Or even whether the parties have got as far as either of them making an offer. Goode, *Consumer Credit Law and Practice*, Div IIB, para 5.107, suggests that s 57 does not apply to conditional offers which lapse under the condition.

or rejection is generally[4] ineffective unless and until communicated,[5] withdrawal from a prospective regulated agreement probably takes effect on posting.[6] Secondly, in favour of the debtor or hirer only, the common law rule that one may contract not to revoke an offer (= an option) is generally void (see ante, para 5.20). Thirdly, in favour of the debtor or hirer only, an extension is made of the deemed agents upon whom such notice may be served (see ante, para 10.25), though no steps are taken to ensure that the debtor or hirer is aware of this right of withdrawal. Compare the case of a cancellable contract, where the debtor or hirer is entitled to a statutory notice of his right of cancellation (s 64: see ante, para 9.17).

Turning to the effect of withdrawal, because of the above alterations to the common law rules, the right of withdrawal may sometimes be exercisable where on common law principles there is a binding contract; and so in some cases the CCA recognises that a prospective agreement in respect of which both sides have a right of withdrawal may also be cancellable by the debtor or hirer (see post, para 10.29). Even where that is not the case, the Act directs that the **effect** of withdrawal shall be as if the prospective agreement were cancellable (s 57(4)). Section 57(1) explains that:

> The withdrawal of a party from a prospective regulated agreement shall operate to apply this Part[7] to the agreement, any linked transaction and any other thing done in anticipation of the making of the agreement as it would apply if the agreement were made and then cancelled under section 69.

The effect of withdrawal is summarised as cancelling (see post, para 10.32) all the following: (a) the prospective regulated agreement;[8] and (b) any linked transaction, eg, maintenance contracts, which in any event have no effect until the regulated agreement is made (s 19(3): see ante, para 5.31);[9] and (c) any other thing done in anticipation of the making of the agreement, eg, paying survey or brokerage or legal fees. Any security given is rendered ineffective (s 113(6): see post, para 25.13).

[10.27] Land mortgages. It was felt that special protection was needed by householders who entered into second mortgages of their homes to secure regulated agreements, eg, credit agreements to finance home improvements such as central heating, double-glazing or kitchen refits, or refinancing agreements. However, application to such transactions of

---

4   Except in the case of revocation of offers to the whole world, or unilateral contracts, or perhaps where reliable indirect evidence of revocation is acquired.

5   This rule extends to the revocation of offers made by post: *Byrne v Van Tienhoven* (1880) 5 CPD 334.

6   By s 189(1), which defines 'give' as 'delivers or sends by post': cf s 69(7) (see post, para 10.31). See Guest and Lloyd, *Encyclopedia of Consumer Credit* para 2-058; Goode, Div IIB, para 5.107.

7   The effect of this reference would seem to be that, if the creditor or owner breaches s 57, the agreement will also be improperly executed with the effects described in s 65: see ante, para 9.19. For what purpose is this extra protection necessary?

8   How soon will negotiations amount to a 'prospective regulated agreement'? It is suggested that this concept is narrower than 'antecedent negotiations' (see post, para 16.08) and requires a 'clear prospect' that a regulated agreement will ensue: Goode, *op cit*, note 3, para 31.31.

9   Suppose after the apparent conclusion of a cash sale contract a customer inquires about the possibility of paying by credit card? When (if ever) does that enquiry become a prospective regulated agreement (see above), so turning the cash sale into a linked transaction? It has been suggested that a communicated offer is required: Goode, *op cit*, note 3, Div IIB, para 5.107. *Sed quaere?*

the cancellation provisions (see post, para 10.29) was ruled out[1] on grounds of administrative difficulty.[2] Accordingly, it was decided to protect this group by re-enforcing the ordinary withdrawal provisions (see ante, para 10.26) with the introduction of an advance copy procedure together with its 'consideration period' (see below). The following categories of transaction were excluded from this procedure: (a) totally exempt agreements (see ante, para 5.15); (b) those agreements exempt from Part V of the Act (see ante, para 9.07); and (c) agreements specially exempted from these rules by s 58(2), effectively remortgages and bridging loans.[3]

Where a land mortgage falls within s 58(1), the Act provides the debtor or hirer with the following three additional protections against undue pressure to commit himself, which makes the whole procedure extremely long-winded:

(1) An additional 'advance copy' notifying him of his right of withdrawal (see ante, para 9.17A).

(2) Thereafter, an isolation period. Section 61(2)(c) stipulates that:

> ... during the consideration period,[4] the creditor or owner refrained from approaching the debtor or hirer (whether in person, by telephone or letter, or in any other way)[5] except in response to a specific request made by the debtor or hirer after the beginning of the consideration period.[6]

It has been suggested that, if the creditor or owner does break this rule, he can save himself by starting the procedure again and sending a new advance copy.[7]

(3) Subsequent pestering. The creditor or owner may not send the signature copy after he has received notice of withdrawal (s 61(2)(d)).

Breach of any of these requirements will render an agreement not properly executed (s 61(2)). This has the effects considered above (see ante, para 9.19) but no others (s 170: see ante, para 10.19), which may be useful if the creditor or owner has thereby inveigled the debtor or hirer into completing a regulated agreement. Presumably, the creditor or owner is entitled to start the whole procedure all over again.

Cancellation of agreement (a cooling-off period)

[10.28] Introduction. At common law, there is nothing to prevent a contract from expressly allowing one side a unilateral right of cancellation subsequent to its formation

---

[10.27]

1   Section 67(a): see post, para 10.29. As s 67(a) repeats the exemptions contained in s 58(2), it would appear that the transactions falling within s 58(2) escape the controls of both ss 58 and 67.

2   Goode, *Consumer Credit Law and Practice*, para 31.53. What about additional secured home improvement loans?

3   See further Goode, *ibid*, para 31.57.

4   This is defined by s 61(3)(a) as effectively a minimum seven day period between service of the advance and first copies. For the possible meanings of s 61(3)(b), see Goode, *ibid*, Div IIB, para 5.121.

5   Is the prohibition restricted to matters related to the prospective regulated agreement and to the debtor/hirer personally? See Guest and Lloyd, *Encyclopedia of Consumer Credit Law*, para 2-059.

6   As to the practice of obtaining the written request of the debtor/hirer to such an approach, see Guest and Lloyd, *ibid*.

7   Goode, *op cit*, note 2, para 31.59.

and before it is fully executed, with[1] or without cause,[2] possibly on terms.[3] If unbalanced, in a consumer supply contract (see post, para 11.12A) such an express right of cancellation may nowadays be unfair under the UTCC, eg, a cancellation fee (Grey Term 1(e): see post, para 11.16); but, if there are 'hidden terms', an express right of cancellation, eg, in a telephone sale (see ante, para 8.17) might avoid the supplier's standard terms being unfair (Grey Term 1(i): see post, para 11.17).

However, whilst the matter remained voluntary, such a right was seldom accorded to the consumer. For this reason, the Molony Report recommended that, in order to protect the consumer from unfair selling practices exercised against him in his home, a person signing consumer instalment credit documents otherwise than at a retail establishment should be allowed a compulsory 'cooling-off period' of 72 hours within which he could withdraw from the transaction.[4] This idea was taken up in the HPA, but limited by the CCA to those circumstances where there is personal contact between the salesman and consumer, though enlarging its scope comprehends a wider range of credit and hire transactions.[5] On the other hand, it has not proved possible to escape the place-of-signature test which first appeared in the HPA, even though this allowed an unscrupulous salesman to escape the cancellation rules by enticing the customer to return to trade premises to sign the relevant documents.[6] But at least a positive act is required of the consumer before the restrictions are avoided: he has the journey time to business premises to repent. Reputable traders should keep two sets of documentation (applicable where the transaction is/is not cancellable) and ensure the correct documentation is used (see ante, paras 9.10, 9.17). Nevertheless, for the scrupulous trader the cancellation rules amount to a serious restriction on trade. Indeed, it is a common precaution for traders not to deliver goods until the cooling-off period has expired,[7] nor to customise them,[8] though the home credit trade tends to be an exception.[9]

The cancellation device has been so effective that it has also been adopted as a consumer protection measure in other statutory provisions,[10] including the Distance

---

[10.28]

1   Eg, *Hyundai Heavy Industries Co Ltd v Papadopoulos* [1980] 2 All ER 29, HL. In such cases, the express right to cancel tends to merge with the common law right to rescind for breach: see post, para 26.15.

2   This may be the explanation of sale or return transactions: see post, para 20.23. See also price adjustment clauses: ante, para 10.05. Does this extend to where a CCA cancellable agreement form is mistakenly used? See (1991) 46 CC 4/30.

3   Eg, as to proof of purchase, exchange, credit voucher. For a table of the policy of retailers, see [1996] 1 Which? 17.

4   *Final Report of the Committee on Consumer Protection* (Cmnd 1781, 1962), paras 525–29. Eg, *Code of Practice of the Direct Selling Association* (see generally ante, para 3.13).

5   See post, para 10.29. Adherence to the letter and spirit of these rules is reinforced by the licensing powers of the OFT: see ante, para 6.19. For modified agreements, see ante, para 9.06.

6   To some extent, the OFT can overcome this inflexibility by utilising their powers under Part III of the FTA: see ante, para 6.07.

7   Would it not have been simpler if, instead of the complicated provisions as to the effect of cancellation described in the following paragraphs, the Act had merely forbidden delivery until after expiry of the cooling-off period?

8   What is the trader to do with a fitted garment or furniture?

9   Whatever the risks (see post, paras 10.33–10.34), such suppliers tend to take the view that commercially they need to hand over the goods/money immediately.

10 Eg, Insurance Companies Act 1982, ss 75–77; Timeshare Act 1992 (as amended) (which extends to both timeshare and timeshare credit agreements: see Goode, *Consumer Credit Law and Practice*, para 31.241 *et seq*); FSMA (see ante, para 3.02).

Selling Regulations (see ante, para 8.19) and the Doorstep-selling Regulations (see ante, para 10.21).

[10.29] Cancellable agreements. Following the recommendations of the *Crowther Report* (paras 6.7.1–6.7.4), the CCA provides that a 'cancellable agreement' is one which may be cancelled by the debtor or hirer by virtue of s 67 (s 189(1)). Section 67 lays down that, with the exceptions set out below:

> A regulated agreement may be cancelled by the debtor or hirer in accordance with this Part if the antecedent negotiations included oral representation made when in the presence of the debtor or hirer by an individual acting as, or on behalf of, the negotiator.

Part V thus grants the debtor or hirer (as to 'debtor' and 'hirer', see respectively ante, paras 5.24; 1.19) a compulsory (s 173: see post, para 18.11) statutory right of cancellation (see post, para 10.31) during a cooling-off period (see post, para 10.30) where the regulated agreement (see ante, para 5.13) was preceded by a face-to-face sales pitch which satisfies all the following requirements:

1 it was made during antecedent negotiations,[1] a formula which appears to exclude agreements solicited by the army of housewives acting as catalogue agent, because of the combined effect of ss 56(1)(b) and 146(5) (see ante, para 5.41);

2 by an individual salesman acting 'as, or on behalf of, the negotiator';[1]

3 which included oral representations before contracting (see below); and

4 those representations were made (anywhere) in the presence of the debtor or hirer.[2]

Thus, in *Moorgate Services Ltd v Kabir*:[3]

> K and M wished to obtain a refrigerated cabinet from their food business. A directly financed regulated credit sale was arranged by the supplier's employee, Fowler. When the financier (MS) sued for unpaid instalments, K pleaded that the agreement was cancellable and should therefore have been made on cancellable documentation (see ante, para 9.17).

Everything turned on whether the statements uttered by Fowler at the business premises of K and M amounted to 'representations' within s 67, this expression being defined by s 189(1) as including:

> ... any condition or warranty, and any other statement or undertaking, whether oral or in writing.

The Court of Appeal thought that this apparently wide definition must be restricted to statements 'of fact or opinion or an undertaking as to the future which is capable of inducing the proposed borrower to enter into the agreement', though it does not need to actually induce K's entry into the agreement (*per* Staughton LJ). Nevertheless, the court unanimously held that Fowler's statements did include representations: the statement

---

[10.29]

1 As to 'antecedent negotiations' and 'negotiator', see s 56, discussed post, para 16.08.

2 The representation does not need to be addressed to the debtor/hirer so long as it was made his presence, eg, to a spouse: see Goode, *Consumer Credit Law and Practice*, para 31.96. It follows that distance selling is normally outside the cancellation provisions.

3 [1995] GCCR 1947; [1995] CLY 722, CA (Lawson (1995) 14 Tr LR 525).

that the amount of credit would be £7,000 was a 'representation', whereas the statement that Fowler would have to phone his office for the APR was not.

Exceptions. Even where an otherwise regulated agreement satisfies all of the above four requirements, it will **not** be cancellable if it falls within any of the following categories:

(a) Exempt (see ante, para 5.14) or some small agreements.[4]

(b) Agreements outside Part V of the Act (see ante, para 9.07).

(c) Agreements secured on land,[5] or remortgages or bridging loans.[6]

(d) Unexecuted agreements signed by the debtor or hirer at 'business premises',[7] which are (s 67(b)):

> ... premises at which any of the following is carrying on any business (whether on a permanent or temporary basis):[8]

> (i)   the creditor or owner;

> (ii) any party to a linked transaction (other than the debtor or hirer or a relative of his);[9]

> (iii) the negotiator in any antecedent negotiations.

It should be noted that the foregoing list does not include the business premises of the debtor or hirer, eg, a partnership, nor unconnected trade premises, eg, a public house; and that, where there are joint debtors or hirers, eg, spouses, the exception at first sight appears confined to the situation where both sign at the listed 'business premises'.[10] Further, the formula may cause difficulty where there is a directly financed consumer hire transaction signed at the premises of the dealer, in which case it is arguable that such a transaction is cancellable, which seems surprising,[11] or where a consumer credit agreement is signed by the debtor at the premises of an agent of the creditor, because s 56(1) may not include such business agent within the term 'negotiator' (see post, para 16.08); or if the debtor takes the form home to sign, though there may then be trouble with the copies rules (see ante, para 9.14) and cancellation notice (see ante, para 9.17).

Agreements not within the above rules may be caught by the Doorstep-selling or Distance Selling rules (see ante, paras 10.21, 10.22A).

---

4   This will exclude small credit sales and unsecured loans where the credit in either case does not exceed £35: s 74(2)(A), inserted by reg 9 of the Doorstep-selling Regulations (see ante, para 10.21). Hp and conditional sales remain within these rules without bottom limit.

5   These may instead be subject to the mortgage withdrawal rules: see ante, para 10.27.

6   Section 67(a). Remortgage and bridging loans are also outside the withdrawal rules: see ante, para 10.27.

7   As s 67(b) refers to the signing by the debtor or hirer of an 'unexecuted agreement' (see ante para 9.14), does it follow that, if the creditor or owner signs first, an agreement signed by the debtor or hirer on business premises remains cancellable?

8   Temporary business premises would include a stand at an exhibition, a mobile sales caravan. What of a company car in a car park; or even the car parked outside the consumer's house?

9   As to 'linked transactions', see generally ante, para 5.31; and as to 'relative', see ante, para 5.33.

10 Cf canvassing: see ante, para 7.06. But what if the spouse signing at home was **not present** during the face-to-face sales pitch?

11 See Dobson [1983] JBL at 317–18; Goode, *op cit*, note 2, para 31.111 and Div IIB, para 5.106.

[10.30] Cooling-off period. Where there is a cancellable regulated agreement (see ante, para 10.29), the debtor or hirer has a right of cancellation (see post, para 10.31) only during the statutory cooling-off period. This period is defined by s 68 as the applicable one of the following, each of which runs from the date of signature by the debtor or hirer on the agreement form:

(a) Where the unexecuted agreement does not become executed on the occasion when the debtor or hirer signs it then he must normally receive two copies, whether the agreement form was presented to him personally (see ante, para 9.15) or sent by post,[1] each copy containing the prescribed notice of cancellation.[2] This will be the usual case and s 68(a) then gears the cooling-off period to the date upon which the debtor or hirer received the signature copy, providing that the agreement may be cancelled 'until the end of the fifth day following the day on which he receives' the signature copy.[3]

(b) Where the agreement is executed on the occasion when the debtor or hirer signs it, then he need only receive one copy of the agreement, whether it was presented to him personally (see ante, para 9.14) or sent to him by post.[1] In this situation, a separate notice of cancellation must normally within seven days be sent to the debtor or hirer[2] and s 68(a) sets the five days running from receipt of that notice.[3] However, in those cases where the Director has dispensed with that notice,[2] the cooling-off period runs until 'the end of the fourteenth day following the day on which he signed the unexecuted agreement'.[4]

Except where the Director has dispensed with a notice of cancellation,[4] it will be observed that time runs from receipt by the debtor or hirer of a second copy or notice. Suppose that copy or notice is never received.[5] Unless a fresh copy or notice can be served within the seven days, it would appear that the agreements remains binding[6] and enforceable[7] but perpetually cancellable.[8]

[10.30]

1 See ante, para 9.16.

2 See ante, para 9.17.

3 Eg, signature copies/notice **received** on Monday, agreement may be cancelled until end of following Saturday. Note that time does not start running whilst the notice is detained or lost in the post.

4 Section 68(b). For those cases where the Director has dispensed with a notice of cancellation, see ante, para 9.17.

5 The evidential problems this may cause for the creditor/owner are examined later (post, para 10.31). However, it would seem possible to avoid them in the case of a cancellable credit-token agreement by sending the token with the second copy/notice: use of the token then proves receipt.

6 For the definition of agreement, the CCA relies on the common law (see ante, para 5.20). As to the common law rules for formation of agreement, see ante, para 10.02 et seq. To this extent, the cancellation rules are not as advantageous to the consumer as those on inertia selling (see ante, para 8.18).

7 It is properly executed since 'service' by post does not require receipt (see s 176 and the s 189(1) definition of 'service') so that posting complies with ss 63 and 64. Even during a postal strike?

8 Because the plain words of s 68 override the s 189(1) definition of 'serve' and the court has no dispensing power (see ante, para 9.20): Goode, *Consumer Credit Law and Practice*, para 31.135; *contra* Howells, *Consumer Debt*, 4.42–4.43. How can the creditor or owner counter a simple denial by the debtor or hirer that he ever received the second copy/notice, bearing in mind s 173(1) (see post, para 18.11)?

[10.31] The right of cancellation. According to s 69(1):

> If within the period specified in s 68 the debtor or hirer under a cancellable agreement serves on:
>
> (a) the creditor or owner, or
>
> (b) the person specified in the notice under section 64(1), or
>
> (c) a person who (whether by virtue of subsection (6) or otherwise) is the agent of the creditor or owner,
>
> a notice (a 'notice of cancellation') which, however expressed and whether or not conforming to the notice given under section 64(1), indicates the intention of the debtor or hirer to withdraw from the agreement,

that notice shall take effect (see post, para 10.32). The provision thus contains the following requirements, which must **all** be satisfied before the right of cancellation can be exercised in respect of a cancellable agreement (see ante, para 10.29) during the cancellation period (see ante, para 10.30):

1   *Form of notice of cancellation.* The Act is here unclear, although a Cancellation Form is provided in the regulations (see ante, para 9.17). Whilst it explicitly allows the debtor or hirer to use any form of words to indicate his[1] intention,[2] that notice must be in writing (s 189(1)). A posted notice must be properly addressed and stamped;[3] but s 69(7) adds that:[4]

    > Whether or not it is actually received by him, a notice of cancellation sent by post to a person shall be deemed to be served on him at the time of posting.

2   *On whom served.* Section 69(1) provides that a notice of cancellation (as above) may be served on[5] any of the following:

    (a) the creditor or owner (see respectively ante, paras 5.25; 1.19); or

    (b) the person specified in the cancellation notice (see ante, para 9.17); or

    (c) any person who is the agent of the creditor or owner, being either their statutory agent (s 69(6): see further ante, para 10.25), or common law agent (see post, para 16.06).

In the common case,[6] this will enable service of a notice of cancellation on the dealer[7] or financier by post, which will take effect immediately on posting, even if never received. It

---

[10.31]

1   In the case of joint debtors or hirers, it would appear that one of them may give a cancellation notice which will then bind both (s 185(1)(b): set out post, para 25.08). So a spouse who signs at business premises can give notice of cancellation even though his/her spouse who signed at home does not.

2   Compare the tightly controlled form of words which the creditor or owner must use to give the debtor or hirer notice of his right of cancellation: see ante, para 9.17.

3   Interpretation Act 1978, s 7. What if there is a postal strike? Compare creditors' notices, which must arrive: see ante, para 10.29.

4   How does the creditor or owner rebut a claim by the debtor or hirer that he posted such a notice in due form or time? See further below.

5   Even to an address known to be vacated ((1975) 38 MLR 728)?

6   For the position with regard to check-trading, see Goode, *Consumer Credit Law & Practice*, para 31.120.

7   Even if the agent is known to have severed his connection with the creditor; or to be worthless, so nullifying the statutory indemnity under s 175 (see ante, para 10 25): Adler (1975) 38 MLR 8.

has been said to be 'scarcely conceivable' that s 69(7) would be confined to the creditor/owner, not applying to notices posted to his agent.[8] But would not such a construction avoid the dilemma posed above, confining deemed receipt to the situation where a creditor/owner could himself arrange for mail to be forwarded, though it would have the drawback of not then covering genuine loss in course of post to dealer?

[10.32] The effect of cancellation. Where a debtor or hirer properly exercises a right of cancellation (see ante, para 10.31), s 69(1) lays down the general rule that the notice shall operate:

    (i) to cancel the agreement, and any linked transaction, and

    (ii) to withdraw any offer by the debtor or hirer, or his relative, to enter into a linked transaction.

The general effect[1] of cancellation thus extends over all the following matters:

(a) *The regulated agreement.* Since a notice of cancellation may be sent by the debtor or hirer at any time after he has signed the unexecuted agreement (see ante, para 10.30), its effect depends on whether or not a contract then exists:[2]

    (i) if not, s 57(1) operates to withdraw any offer (see ante, para 10.26);

    (ii) if so, s 69(1)(i) cancels the agreement and s 69(4) adds that:

        Except as otherwise provided by or under this Act, an agreement or transaction cancelled under subsection (1) shall be treated as if it had never been entered into.

The exercise of this right of cancellation makes the regulated contract void *ab initio*[3] and is in addition to any common law right of rescission[4] or statutory right of termination (see post, paras 26.05–26.07). The cancellation also cancels any modifying agreement made during[5] the cooling-off period.[6] For the further effects of cancellation on money and goods, see post, paras 10.33–10.34.

(b) *Any linked transaction.* The meaning of the expression 'linked transaction' has already been examined (see ante para 5.31), where it was seen that a linked transaction has no effect until the principal agreement is made (s 19(3)). If the principal agreement is

---

8   Goode, *op cit,* note 6, para 52.5.

[10.32]

1   The ordinary rules as to the effect of cancellation are ousted (s 69(3)) and some special ones applied in the following cases (s 69(2)): (a) goods or work supplied under a DCS agreement for RU credit to meet an emergency, eg, gas cooker in winter; or (b) goods supplied which the debtor or hirer has incorporated in any land or unassociated thing, eg, new engine for car, washing machine plumbed in. As to an unfortunate omission from (a), see Goode, *Consumer Credit Law and Practice,* para 31.138.

2   Any interested party may apply to the court for a declaration to this effect: s 142(2)(a); and generally see ante, para 9.19.

3   *Colesworthy v Collman Services* [1993] CCLR 4, Cty Ct.

4   By either side either *ab initio* or *de futuro*: see post, paras 26.12–26.16. Exactly the same persons are made deemed agents for this purpose (s 102): see post, para 26.04. What if the agreement is frustrated?

5   But the cancellation provisions do not apply to modifying agreements (see post, para 26.22) made **after** expiry of the cooling-off period: s 82(6).

6   Even if the modifying agreement would not otherwise be cancellable, eg, because signed on business premises: s 82(5).

cancelled, the linked transaction generally[7] falls as well: if still an offer, it is withdrawn; or, if an agreement, it is cancelled; for instance in loan financing the contract for the supply of goods; or in a second mortgage, the life insurance cover. Whilst applying to a consumer sale which is loan financed, this rule does not apply to the sale to a financier in a directly financed transaction.[8]

(c) *Any security.* Security given by the debtor or hirer entering a regulated agreement is not a linked transaction (s 19(1)), but it is elsewhere provided (s 113(3)(a)) that the security shall automatically be invalidated under s 106 (see post, para 25.13) and that any duty to return, eg, property lodged by the debtor or hirer, must be completed before the debtor or hirer has to repay any credit or restore any goods (s 113(5)). As to these duties, see post, paras 10.33–10.34.

[10.33] Further effects. Where an agreement is cancellable (see ante, para 10.29), it may be that the parties prudently defer performance of any part of the transaction until after expiry of the cooling-off period (see ante, para 10.30): if the agreement is cancelled, it will then have only the effects above-mentioned (ante, para 10.32). However, the Act also seeks to deal with the possibility that before cancellation the parties may have transferred money or goods thereunder.

1 *Money paid.* Under the cancelled agreement, money may have been paid by either side as follows:

(a) If the debtor or hirer or any relative[1] has **paid** any money under the cancelled agreement, eg, deposit, s 70 generally makes it recoverable[2] from the person to whom it was paid.[3] Thus, in direct financing the deposit will under the CCA normally be recoverable from the supplier whilst subsequent instalments are recoverable from the creditor. If the debtor or hirer has any goods in his possession under the terms of the cancelled agreement, the debtor or hirer has a lien on them for that repayment (s 70(2). For liens, see generally post, para 25.02). But there are special provisions for loan financing,[4] credit-tokens,[5] brokerage fees[6]

---

7 There is power to save classes of linked transaction by regulation (s 69(5)). It has been used to save, eg, vehicle insurance, product guarantee insurance. See further Bone and Rutherford [1985] JBL 209; and Goode, *op cit*, note 1, paras 31.177–31.179.

8 So cancellation of a directly financed transaction will leave the sale from dealer to financier standing (see ante, para 5.31); and the best way for the financier to divest himself of the goods would appear to be under a repurchase provision (see post, para 16.21).

[10.33]

1 As to 'debtor', see ante, para 5.24; as to 'hirer', see ante, para 1.19; and as to 'relative', see ante, paras 5.31, 5.33.

2 Section 70(1)(a); but see s 113(5) (ante, para 10.32). And any sum payable ceases to be payable: s 70(1)(b).

3 Section 70(3); *Colesworthy v Collmain Services* [1993] CCLR 4.

4 Section 70 does not apply to credit already extended to the debtor under a cancelled loan falling within s 71 (s 70(5): see below). In other cases, both the creditor and supplier are liable to repay such sum (s 70(3)), eg, the deposit in loan financing is recoverable from either creditor or supplier. If the sum is recovered from the creditor, he has a right of indemnity against the supplier (s 70(4)).

5 The token must be returned before money payable for its issue is recoverable (s 70(5)), eg, some charge cards and trading checks.

6 As the Act restricts the broker's commission to a nominal figure, if no credit or hire agreement results from his introduction (see post, para 16.19), a similar ceiling is imposed in respect of brokerage fees for cancelled agreements (s 70(6)) or sums so deemed (s 70(7)).

and cases falling within s 69(2),[7] whilst the common law deals with deposits in direct financing (see post, para 16.05).

(b) As regards any credit **received** by the debtor, the Act is deliberately designed to discourage the creditor from making any cash loan to the debtor before either expiry of the cooling-off period for cancellation or time for withdrawal of offer (see ante, para 10.26), because of the likelihood that it will be immediately spent so making repayment difficult.[8] Accordingly, s 71(1) provides that such a cancelled agreement 'shall continue in force so far as relates to repayment of credit and payment of interest'; but any obligations with respect to future advances, linked transactions or security are extinguished (see ante, para 10.32). In making these payments,[9] the debtor is given a choice:

(i) Take one month's free credit before repaying without interest the whole or any part of the credit already advanced.[10]

(ii) Insofar as he cannot repay the capital as above, repay it with interest as follows: if the loan was repayable in a lump sum, repay with the contract interest provisions; if the loan was repayable by instalments, repay the capital with an advantageous pro-rating rule as to interest.[11]

2   *Property transferred* (see post, para 10.34).

[10.34] Property transferred. Under a cancelled agreement (see ante, para 10.32), property may have been transferred either way as follows:

1   *Part-exchange goods*. In some cases the debtor or hirer[1] will at an early stage have tendered to the negotiator goods in part-exchange (see generally ante, para 2.09) in respect of a transaction which is subsequently cancelled[2] or from which he has withdrawn (see ante, para 10.26). Under s 73(2) the primary entitlement of the debtor or hirer is to recover the 'part-exchange allowance[3] from the negotiator, eg, dealer, except in the case of loan financing;[4] and, where that allowance is recovered by the debtor or hirer, his title to the part-exchange goods vests in the negotiator (s 73(6)). This will be so regardless of from whom the allowance is recovered, so a loan financier paying the allowance will need the above indemnity. However, within a

---

7   Section 70(8). For cases falling within s 69(2), see ante, para 10.32.

8   Goode, *Consumer Credit Law and Practice*, para 31.180.

9   Payments may be made to any person upon whom a notice of cancellation could have been served (see ante, para 10.31), except one who was the agent of the debtor (s 71(4)).

10   Section 71(2). Insofar as the debtor has not spent the advance, he can therefore return it without further obligation.

11   Section 71(3). Eg, under a personal loan. See explanation in Goode, *op cit*, note 8, paras 31.95–98; and also Howells, *Consumer Debt*, para 4.51.

[10.34]

1   As to 'debtor', 'hirer' and 'relative', see respectively ante, paras 5.24, 1.19, 5.33. To the extent that the dealer in a directly financed consumer hire transaction is not the 'negotiator' (see ante, para 10.29), s 72 covers the agreement goods but the part-exchange goods are outside s 73 (see s 73(1): below).

2   Section 73(1). See further the definition of when goods are taken in part-exchange in s 73(7)(a). What rules are to govern consumer hirings (see above)?

3   The part-exchange allowance is defined in s 73(7)(b). It assumes the part-exchange goods are not supplied under a linked transaction (see ante, para 5.31).

4   When the dealer and financier will be jointly and severally liable for payment of the part-exchange allowance (s 73(3), (8)). But in this case the creditor is entitled to an indemnity from the dealer (s 73(4)).

period of 10 days from the date of cancellation, the above duty to pay the part-exchange allowance may be discharged by the return of the part-exchange goods to the debtor or hirer in a condition substantially as good as when they were delivered to the negotiator.[5] For the foregoing purposes, the debtor or hirer is given a lien over any goods (s 73(5)) to which the cancelled agreement relates (see below).

2   *Agreement goods.* If the debtor, hirer or any relative has acquired possession of goods under a cancelled transaction, eg, under a credit sale, but not otherwise,[6] s 72 generally[7] places him under a legal duty, actionable as a breach of statutory duty,[8] to re-deliver[9] those goods,[10] subject to his lien for any part-exchange goods (see above) and the recovery of any security (see ante, para 10.32). Meantime, the debtor, hirer or any relative is under the following duties:[11]

(a) To retain possession of the goods. Whilst the consumer need ordinarily only hold the goods awaiting collection (see above), what if he moves house?

(b) To take reasonable care of the goods for 21 days after cancellation,[12] thereafter usually becoming an involuntary bailee, with a duty only to refrain from wilful damage. This is designed to encourage the other side to collect the goods and hence relieve the consumer of their inconvenience.

---

5   Section 73(2). As to attempts by the debtor or hirer to insist on return of the part-exchange goods, see Goode, *Consumer Credit Law & Practice*, Div IIB, para 5.143. If both sides agree, any deterioration or delay can be ignored (s 173(3): see post, para 18.11).

6   So, if DC credit is used to buy goods, the sale contract continues despite the cancellation of the credit: Howells, *Consumer Debt*, para 4.55.

7   Except in the case of perishable or consumable goods or those supplied to meet an emergency or incorporated in land (s 72(9)) and subject to s 113(5) (see ante, para 10.32). See further Goode, *op cit*, note 5, paras 31.157–31.171.

8   Section 72(11). For such duties, see generally ante, para 3.21.

9   Redelivery is to the 'other party' (s 72(4)), meaning the person from who the consumer acquired possession (s 72(2)(b)). Physical possession will usually have been acquired from the dealer; but it has been argued that the required redelivery is to the financier: Goode, *op cit*, note 5, para 1460. *Sed quaere?*

10 Section 72(4). Goods can actually be taken or posted back; but redelivery need only be made at the address of the debtor/hirer (s 72(5), (10)); and it may be made to anyone upon whom a notice of cancellation could have been served (see ante, para 10.31), except one who is the agent of the debtor (s 72(6)).

11 Section 72(3). This makes the duties retrospective to include the period before cancellation, and is to deal with the time when, eg, the buyer under a credit sale, had a perfect common law right to damage or sell goods. It then links up with s 72(11): see above.

12 Section 72(8). This obligation ceases on redelivery (s 72(7)) but may be indefinitely extended by unreasonable failure to redeliver (s 72(8)). As to the duty of a bailee to take reasonable care of goods, see generally ante, para 1.17. What if the debtor drives, eg, 3,000 miles before redelivery?

PART 4

THE CONTENTS OF A CONTRACT
FOR THE SUPPLY OF GOODS

CHAPTER 11

CONTRACTUAL TERMS

REPRESENTATIONS AND TERMS

[11.01] Pre-contractual statements. In the course of the negotiations which precede a contract, it is common for the parties to make some statements either by words or conduct, or occasionally by silence. Sometimes those statements are of no legal significance to that contract, as where the 'statement' says nothing of relevance or is not intended seriously (mere puffs: see ante, para 8.05); but at other times they may amount to representations – statements of fact inducing the contract.[1] The common law refused to grant damages for innocent misrepresentation,[2] but would do so in the tort of deceit if the representation were fraudulent (see post, para 17.17), or in contract if the representation became a term of a contract between the parties.[3] Whilst deceit required the plaintiff to discharge the heavy burden of proving that the defendant did not honestly believe his statement to be true (always a difficult matter), liability in contract was strict, and fraud need not be proved (see post, para 17.18). This relative attractiveness of the contractual action led litigants to frame actions based on misrepresentation in contract rather than tort, so that the vital question was frequently whether the representation had attained contractual status (see post, para 11.02). However, modern reform has widened the scope of actions for innocent misrepresentation: not only are more such actions now available, either in tort (see post, para 17.19) or under the Misrepresentation Act 1967 (see post, para 17.10); but the list of potential defendants extends beyond the scope of the doctrine of privity of contract, either by suing in tort (see above) or under s 56 of the CCA (see post, para 16.08). Attempts to exclude liability for misrepresentation may be both unfair (UTCC, reg 4: see post, para 11.15) and unreasonable (s 3, Misrepresentation Act 1967: see post, para 18.27).

Further, there may now also be criminal liability under the TDA (see ante, paras 4.07–08) or other statutes.[4]

[11.02] Misrepresentation or contractual term. The courts had to decide whether a statement remained a mere representation, in which case it attracted only the remedies for misrepresentation (see post, para 17.10); or became a contractual term, in which case it also attracted the remedies for breach of contract (see post, Chapter 26), though without any double recovery (see post, para 27.39–40). This issue turned on the intention of the parties.[1] Where it was expressly stated that the defendant warranted the truth of the

---

[11.01]

1   Eg, *Watford Electronics Ltd v Sanderson CFL Ltd* (set out post, para 18.24A; unappealed point). See further Treitel, *Law of Contract* (10th edn), pp 305–16.

2   *Hopkins v Tanqueray* (1854) 15 CB 130 (auction: see ante, para 10.10); *Oscar Chess Ltd v Williams* [1957] 1 All ER 325, CA (car log book misled parties); *Humming Bird Motors v Hobbs* [1986] RTR 276, CA (seller's statement to best of knowledge and belief).

3   *Harling v Eddy* [1951] 2 KB 739, CA (auction: see ante, para 10.10).

4   Eg, Weights and Measures Act 1985, s 29 (see ante, para 4.25).

[11.02]

1   See Burrows (1983) 99 LQR 251.

statement, then it was easy to infer such an intention,[2] but in many other cases the enquiry led the courts into considerable difficulty, because the parties may not have adverted their minds to the question. Alternatively they may not have exhibited any clear intention, or may have exhibited contrary intentions.[3] In view of such possibilities, the criterion of the intention of the parties may be criticised as elusive, artificial and almost useless. However, the persistence of the litigants has forced the courts to return to the question time and again, though the amount of light shed has been slight.[4] All that can be said is that, in the field of consumer transactions,[5] the courts in modern times appear to be making a determined effort to impose on a dealer contractual liability for the representations he makes[6] to private consumers. Fortunately, it may be that the extension of liability for misrepresentation (see ante, para 11.01) will shift attention away from the dichotomy of contractual term and mere representation.

THE NATURE OF THE TERMS

[11.03] **Introduction**. Having distinguished contractual terms from mere representations (see ante, para 11.02), this section concentrates on the promissory effect of the former. The nature of contractual terms is subject to considerable confusion, largely because of the nomenclature involved: the appellations 'condition' and 'warranty' have been used by the courts without any precise definition and the same expressions have been used to explain different phenomena.[1]

(a) *Warranty*. Whilst starting life as an action in tort for deceit (see post, para 17.18), towards the end of the 18th century the action began to be declared *in assumpsit*, and soon came to be thought of in a contractual rather than a tortious context.[2] This process had particular repercussions in the law relating to the sale of goods, then fast developing; and the legacy is to be seen in Chalmers' definition of a 'warranty' in what is now s 61(1) of the Sale of Goods Act 1979 (SGA) as:

> ... an agreement with reference to goods which are the subject of a contract of sale, but collateral to the main purpose of such contract, the breach of which gives rise to a claim for damages, but not to a right to reject the goods and treat the contract as repudiated.

Leaving aside for the moment the meaning of collateral (see post, para 11.06), it will be observed that Chalmers in part defined a warranty according to the effect of its breach (see post, para 11.04).

(b) *Condition*. By the 19th century, English courts were familiar with the notion of what are today known as conditions precedent: namely, non-promissory conditions to which a contractual promise by B to A might be made subject (see ante, para 1.11).

---

2   Eg, *Liverpool and County Discount Co Ltd v AB Motor Co (Kilburn) Ltd* [1963] 2 All ER 396, CA.
3   See Gilmore and Axelrod (1948) 57 Yale LJ 517, p 518, n 3.
4   See *Heilbut, Symonds & Co v Buckleton* [1913] AC 30, HL.
5   As to where both parties are in the same trade, see *Harlingdon & Leinster Enterprises Ltd v Christopher Hull Fine Art Ltd* (set out post, para 13.11A).
6   Eg, *Dick Bentley Ltd v Harold Smith (Motors) Ltd* [1965] 2 All ER 65, CA. *Contra* a private supplier to a trade buyer: *Oscar Chess Ltd v Williams* [1957] 1 All ER 325, CA.
[11.03]
1   Stoljar (1952) 15 MLR 425; (1953) 16 MLR 174.
2   See post, para 17.18. As to criminal proceedings in respect of breach of warranty, see ante, para 4.24.

However, reflecting recognition by the courts that B may sometimes promise that that condition will occur, Chalmers in the SGA 1893 employed the expression 'condition' in both its promissory and non-promissory senses.[3] In s 2 it is utilised in the sense of condition precedent,[4] whereas in ss 11–15 it means an important contractual promise. In the latter sense, 'condition' is also defined in terms of the effect of its breach (see post, para 11.04).

[11.04] Conditions and warranties. After a breach of warranty by the seller, a buyer might, in theory, wish to reject the goods tendered and affirm the contract; but it would seem that the meaning of the Act (see ante, para 11.03) is that he may neither reject nor rescind,[1] no matter how serious the effects of the breach of warranty.[2] On the other hand, the SGA defines a promissory condition in s 11(3) as a term, breach of which will give rise not only to the right to damages, but also to reject goods and repudiate the contract. Thus, under the scheme adopted by the SGA a condition in the sense of an essential stipulation is clearly superior to a warranty, the relationship between them being partly explained by s 11(2) (set out post, para 26.24). In view of the rigid distinction between the two types of term, it may therefore be important to determine whether a particular term is a condition or a warranty. Section 11(3) of the SGA says that in each case it depends on the construction of the contract, and adds unhelpfully that[3] 'A stipulation may be a condition, though called a warranty in the contract'. In many cases, the SGA avoids the problem by expressly assigning a status to a particular term; and this approach has been continued in those later statutes which imply terms into other types of contract for the supply of goods: namely, the Supply of Goods (Implied Terms) Act 1973 (SOGIT); and the Supply of Goods and Services Act 1982 (SGSA).

However, in the absence of such statutory specification the question can only be determined on common law principles. Perhaps the most widely accepted test is that laid down by Fletcher Moulton LJ in *Wallis, Son and Wells v Pratt and Haynes*:[4]

> There was a sale by sample of quantity of seed described as 'common English sainfoin'. Seed equal to sample was delivered and planted by a sub-buyer. When it came up, it was found to be not common English, but giant sainfoin, a seed which is indistinguishable but of inferior quality. Reliance was placed on a clause 'Sellers give no warranty ... as to description'.

Notwithstanding that the seed was equal to sample, the House of Lords held that there was **also** an undertaking that the goods complied with their description (see post, para 15.06); that the undertaking was an implied condition of the contract (see post, para 13.11); that the implied condition did not lose this status simply because the buyer was

---

3   It has been convincingly demonstrated that the 19th century common law development was itself based on a misconception: see Stoljar (1954) 69 LQR 485. See further Montrose (1937) 15 Can BR 303, p 323; Treitel (1990) 106 LQR 185; Goode, *Commercial Law* (2nd edn), pp 290–94.

4   See ante, para 1.11. Conditions precedent are further discussed post, paras 15.21, 26.01.

[11.04]

1   For rejection, see post, para 29.03; and for repudiation for breach, see further post, para 26.15. In contracts for the supply of services, as opposed to goods, the courts have been willing to temper this right to rescind by the doctrine of substantial performance: as to which, see post, para 26.02.

2   See *Benjamin on Sale* (8th edn), p 983.

3   Perhaps in recognition of the lack of consistency in nomenclature used by the courts. Was it also designed to enable the courts to restrict exemption clauses (see post, para 18.06)?

4   [1911] AC 394; [1911–13] All ER Rep 989, HL.

reduced to claiming damages, by reason of the subsale under s 11(4) (see post, para 29.04); and that the sellers were therefore not protected by a clause excluding liability for breach of warranty (see post, para 18.06). In drawing the vital distinction between a condition and a warranty, the House adopted the dictum of Fletcher Moulton LJ in the Court of Appeal that the issue turned on whether the term went to the substance of the contract, or was:[5]

> ... so essential to its very nature that [its] non-performance may fairly be considered by the other party as a substantial failure to perform the contract at all.

So classifying terms as conditions or warranties has the advantage of certainty, but that certainty is obtained at the expense of rigidity. Modern English law offers two methods by which a court can escape having to classify the term as a condition and hence give the innocent party the excessive right of treating the contract as repudiated for slight breach of condition:

(1) Classify the breach instead of the term (see post, para 11.05).

(2) Allow only damage for slight breach of condition (see post, para 11.05A).

(3) In a consumer supply, any such term may be unfair.[6]

[11.05] Innominate terms. It was at one time thought that the distinction between conditions and warranties (see ante, para 11.04) was the main criterion for determining the effect of breach of contract in general.[1] However, a new approach to the question of remedies available for breach of contract was made by Diplock LJ in *Hong Kong Fir Shipping Co v Kawasaki Kisen Kaisha*:[2] whilst agreeing that some simple terms could be categorised as conditions or warranties, his Lordship argued that there were other more complex contractual undertakings:

> ... and the legal consequences of a breach of such an undertaking ... depend on the nature of the event to which the breach gives rise and do not follow from a prior classification of the undertakings as a 'condition' or 'warranty'.

Obviously, this new approach allowed for a greater flexibility; and it was extended to the law of sale in *Cehave v Bremer*:[3]

> There was a sale of 12,000 tons of US citrus pulp pellets cif Rotterdam for use as animal feed, the goods then being in Florida. Shipments arrived at Rotterdam after a fall in their market price, and the buyers purported to reject on the grounds that the goods had not been shipped in good condition. The buyers having claimed repayment of the purchase price (£100,000), the Rotterdam County Court ordered the cargo to be sold: it was bought for £30,000 by the original buyers, who proceeded to use it (as originally envisaged) as an ingredient in cattle food, but at a lower concentration than would have been normal for sound goods.

---

5   [1910] 2 KB 1003 at 1012, CA. Compare this test with that for innominate terms (see post, para 11.05) and for the doctrine of frustration (see post, para 22.14).

6   Under the UTCC Regulations: see OFT, *Bulletin No 16*, case 11; and see post, para 11.12 *et seq*.

[11.05]

1   *Benjamin's Sale of Goods* (4th edn), para 10.029.

2   [1962] 2 QB 26 at 70, CA (not a sale case).

3   *The Hansa Nord* [1976] QB 44; [1975] 3 All ER 739, CA. See also *Rubicon Computer Systems Ltd v United Paints Ltd* [2000] CLY 899, CA.

The Court of Appeal rejected the buyer's claim to rescind on the grounds that, although the goods were defective,[4] because they were used for that intended purpose they were merchantable (see post, para 14.17); but it held that the buyers were entitled to damages for breach of the express warranty that the goods should be 'in good condition' (see post, para 11.07). Whilst the latter point is correct, the decision overall looks like an attempt to classify the breached term in accordance with the effect of breach. At the time of decision, it is difficult to see how this could be justified;[5] but statutory authority to do so has subsequently become available (see post, para 11.05A).[6]

[11.05A] Slight breaches of condition. Suppose a contract for the sale of a new motor vehicle which on delivery has a defective trafficator bulb. Such a minor defect would cause the vehicle to be unroadworthy (see ante, para 4.37) and hence breach undertakings as to fitness and quality (see post, Chapter 14). Under the SGA 1979, these broken terms were implied conditions, which necessarily gave the buyer a *prima facie* right to reject the goods and rescind the contract (see ante, para 11.04), except possibly where there has been a substantial performance (see post, para 26.02). However, the Law Commission thought that this may cause unfairness to the seller, whose loss on rejection may far exceed the cost of replacing the defective bulb.[1] On the other hand, the Commission argued that such obvious unfairness may lead a court to deny that there is any breach at all, so leaving the buyer without a remedy.[2] Accordingly, the Commission proposed to draw a distinction according to whether or not the buyer was a consumer: a consumer would almost always be buying for domestic use or consumption and want perfect goods rather than compensation;[3] whereas a business buyer would normally be buying for profitable resale, would be in a position to resell defective goods and so could be satisfied with compensation.[4] Acting on this recommendation, the Sale and Supply of Goods Act 1994 introduced a new rule. The new s 15A(1) of the SGA now provides as follows (s 4(1) of the 1994 Act):

Where in the case of a contract of sale –

(a) the buyer would, apart from this subsection, have the right to reject the goods by reason of a breach on the part of the seller of a term implied by section 13, 14 or 15 above, but

(b) the breach is so slight that it would be unreasonable for him to reject them,

then, if the buyer does not deal as consumer, the breach is not to be treated as a breach of condition but may be treated as a breach of warranty.

The following points arise:

---

4 The arbitrator found that the goods were only saleable at a 60% allowance and only usable for compounding at smaller percentages than normal.

5 For support for this approach on a common law basis, see Benjamin, *op cit*, note 1, para 10-031.

6 Under the UTCC Regulations: see OFT, *Bulletin No 16*, case 11; and post, para 11.12 *et seq*.

[11.05A]

1 *Sale and Supply of Goods* (1987, Law Com 160), para 4.1. Cf *Arcos Ltd v Ronaasen & Sons Ltd* (set out post, para 13.12) and *Re Moore Ltd* (set out post, para 13.14).

2 Cf *Cehave v Bremer* (set out ante, para 11.05).

3 *Sale and Supply of Goods*, para 4.5. The Commission also cited the likely stronger bargaining position of the business seller and the reluctance of the consumer-buyer to litigate.

4 *Ibid*. The Commission also cited the differing motive of the commercial buyer, who may seek to reject just because of a fall in the market.

1   As recommended by the Law Commission (para 4.7), this reduction of remedy for breach of condition applies only to a buyer who does not 'deal as consumer', which expression is given the same meaning as in UCTA.[5] The consumer buyer retains his *prima facie* right to reject for even slight breaches.

2   This reduction of remedy does not apply to a non-consumer (business) buyer where the contract expressly or impliedly evinces a contrary intention.[6]

3   Even where the contract is silent on the matter, the business buyer only loses his *prima facie* right to reject for breach of the specified implied conditions (new s 15A(1)(a)): he retains his right for breach of express condition, or any other implied condition.[7]

4   Notwithstanding that a business buyer relies on one of the designated implied conditions, he only loses his right to reject if 'the breach is so slight that it would be unreasonable' for him to reject the goods;[8] and it is for the seller to show this (new s 15A(3)). It might be thought that this category is likely to include many minor or cosmetic defects (see post, paras 14.23–24).

The 1994 Act imports provisions virtually identical to the above into quasi-sales,[9] simple hirings[10] and hire purchase agreements.[11]

[11.06] Warranties and collateral contracts. Returning to the warranty, it will be recalled that the SGA defines the warranty as being 'collateral to the main purpose of' a contract of sale (see ante, para 11.03). No doubt, this formula faithfully reflects case law developments in the 19th century; and it still reasonably describes the common situation where the agent makes a promise to a customer to induce him to contract with the agent's principal.[1] However, it has been pointed out that the ordinary warranty in the contract of sale certainly is not a separate agreement as distinct from the rest of the contract, since no further consideration is required.[2] Indeed, we must carefully distinguish the collateral term from the collateral contract, the latter being supported by its own consideration. The collateral contract may be of one of the following types:

(1) A makes a representation to B, as a result of which B enters into a contract with C;[3] or

(2) A makes a representation to B, as a result of which B enters into a contract with A.[4]

---

5   New s 61(5A) of the SGA (as inserted by the 1994 Act, Sched 2, para 9(c)), which likewise puts the burden of proving that the buyer does not deal as consumer on the seller.

6   New s 15A(2) (as inserted by the 1994 Act, s 4(1)).

7   As to the effect of designation of an express term as a 'condition', see post, para 18.06. As to the difficulty of distinguishing express from implied conditions as to description (see post, para 13.11), see Bridge [1995] JBL at 404.

8   New s 15A(1)(b). There is no definition of 'slight' or 'unreasonable'. Presumably, 'slight' means more than '*de minimis*' (see post, para 13.12). For 'unreasonable', cf UCTA, s 11 (see post, para 18.20).

9   SGSA, new s 5A (as inserted by the 1994 Act, Sched 2, para 6(5)).

10 *Ibid*, new s 10A (as inserted by the 1994 Act, Sched 2, para 6(9)).

11 SOGIT, new s 11A (as inserted by the 1994 Act, Sched 2, para 4(6)).

[11.06]

1   Eg, *Barnett v Peter Cox Group Ltd* [1996] CLY 3406, CA.

2   Stoljar (1952) 15 MLR 425, 430–32.

3   Eg, *Andrews v Hopkinson* (set out post, para 16.18); *Wake v Renault* UK Ltd [1996] CLY 1250.

4   Eg, *Webster v Higgin* [1948] 2 All ER 127, CA; *Esso Petroleum Ltd v Comrs of Customs and Excise* (discussed ante, para 2.08).

In *Wells (Merstham) Ltd v Buckland Sand and Silica Co Ltd,*[5] the facts fell within case (1) and Edmund Davies J said:

> As between A ... and B ... two ingredients, and only two, are ... required in order to bring about a collateral contract containing a warranty: (1) a promise or assertion by A as to the nature, quality or quantity of the goods which B may reasonably regard as being made *animo contrahendi*, and (2) acquisition by B of the goods in reliance on that promise or assertion.

It is submitted that this *dictum* should also be applied to case (2), and the cases treated in the same manner, though case (2) does involve an additional factor in that it may circumvent the parol evidence rule.[6]

In our context, the collateral contract has been particularly useful in respect of statements by a dealer in a directly financed transaction (see post, para 16.18); but has been less successful when pleaded by consumers against manufacturers (see post, para 17.09). As to the formalities required of a contract collateral to the sale of an interest in land, see ante, para 9.03.

EXPRESS AND IMPLIED TERMS

[11.07] Express terms. Where express stipulations are put forward, some statements are designed to prevent any contract coming into existence at that stage, perhaps by making them only an invitation to treat (see ante, para 10.02); or to preclude particular words becoming part of that contract, eg, mere puffs (see ante, para 8.05). Where words spoken[1] or written are intended to be contractual,[2] they may range from the barest essentials to an elaborate written contract. Examples include express warranties,[3] conditional offers, eg, 'whilst stocks last' (see ante, para 10.02), price statements,[4] limitations on supplier's liability,[5] performance by words, eg, instructions for use (see post, para 18.28 *et seq*), provisions assigning to terms the status of conditions or warranties (see ante, para 11.04), eg, making time of the essence (see post, para 23.20), and restrictions on remedies.[6] Particularly significant in this context may be the implied terms imposed by law.[7] For

---

5   [1965] 2 QB 170, at 180. Contrast *Inntrepreneur Pub Co Ltd v East Crown Ltd* [2000] CLY 869 (entire agreement clause).

6   See Treitel, *Law of Contract* (10th edn), pp 175–83.

[11.07]

1   The spoken word inevitably raises problems of proof and possibly also the parol evidence rule (see ante, para 11.06).

2   For the common law rules concerning the incorporation of terms in any contract, see post, para 18.04. For a review of the intentions of businessmen in negotiating contractual clauses, see Livermore [1986] JBL 90.

3   Eg, *Cehave v Bremer* (set out ante, para 11.05); *Harling v Eddy* [1951] 2 KB 739, CA (see ante, para 11.01); *Mendelssohn v Normand Ltd* [1970] 1 QB 177, CA (see post, para 18.05); *Thomas Witter Ltd v TBP Industries Ltd* (set out post, para 26.14). A forged MOT certificate (see ante, para 4.37) might amount to false trade description (see TDA, s 2(1)(f): see ante, para 4.06).

4   Eg, 'guaranteed lowest prices – or we will refund the difference'. Does 'never knowingly undersold' give a contractual right to the refund of any difference (see [2000] 12 Which? 9)? For offences, see ante, para 8.10.

5   Eg, 'bought as seen' (limiting description: see post, para 13.16); 'E & OE' (but see UCTA, ss 6, 7: see post, para 18.19); express guarantees for a finite period (see post, paras 14.06, 17.09).

6   Eg, 'no cash refunds' (but see the Restrictions on Statements Order 1976 (SI 1813): ante, para 4.22).

7   For the distinction between terms implied in fact and those implied in law, see post, para 11.10.

instance, an express warranty as to description may be converted by statute into an implied condition (see post, para 13.11).

At the other end of the scale, there may be elaborate written contracts (see post, para 11.08) and terms incorporated by reference,[8] both of whose construction may involve the factual implication of terms. These may be freshly drafted for the particular contract or standard terms, the latter usually being printed beforehand.[9] There may even be the rules of a trade association (as subsequently amended) incorporated into a contract by reference;[10] and these may be registrable as a restrictive practice (see ante, para 2.12). Commercial documents and contracts should be construed in a manner which makes good commercial sense and not by a detailed semantic and syntactical analysis if that would defeat the commercial purpose of the document.[11] The rules for interpreting exclusion clauses, disclaimers and indemnities are considered later (see post, para 18.06), though more flexibility may be obtainable by treating them as unfair terms (see post, para 11.12).

In all cases, any promises are only worthwhile to the consumer whilst the promisor-supplier continues in existence/business, or is insured. However, his promises may sometimes give rise to criminal liability, eg, it may amount to a false statement as to services (see ante, para 4.15), or save from that liability, eg, a defence of words of another person (see post, para 28.18).

[11.08] Standard form contracts. If both parties try to impose their own, different, standard terms on a transaction, this may give rise to the 'battle of the forms' (see ante, para 10.04); and the expression 'written standard terms' has now received statutory recognition.[1] They have considerable advantages to a party engaged in numerous transactions. First, this saves the cost of individual drafting and hence time and money. Where documents commonly used contain particular phrases and expressions which have a clear and well-established meaning among commercial lawyers, it is important that those expressions should be construed consistently with that meaning, unless there are compulsive surrounding circumstances or a context strongly suggestive of some other meaning.[2] It may be extremely convenient to businessmen to be able to make a contract, perhaps orally, merely by reference to one of the standard forms well known in their particular trade.[3] Thus, the standard form contract is a useful device for allocating the many risks of a transaction between the parties.[4] Secondly, the standard form contract has

---

8   *The Varenna* [1984] QB 599, CA (charterparty/bill of lading); and see further post, para 18.04.

9   For standard terms, see post, para 11.08. If there are both written and standard terms, the written terms may give rise to criminal liability, eg, it may amount to a false statement as to services (*Indian Oil Corp v Vanol Inc* [1991] 2 Lloyd's Rep 634).

10   *Shearson Lehman Hutton Inc v Maclaine Watson & Co Ltd* [1989] 2 Lloyd's Rep 570 (see [1990] LMCLQ at 308–09); *Brondeis (Brokers) Ltd v Black* [2001] 2 All ER (Comm) 980.

11   *The Antaios* [1985] AC 191, HL (not a sale case); *Sinochem International Oil (London) Co Ltd v Mobil Sales and Supply Corp* [2000] CLY 761, CA. See also *per* Lord Hoffman in *Investor's Compensation Scheme Ltd v West Bromwich BS* [1998] 1 All ER 98 at 114–15, HL (not a sale case).

[11.08]

1   UCTA, s 3 (see post, para 18.24). For general discussion of standard form contracts, see Treitel, *Law of Contract* (10th edn), Chapter 7.

2   *The Varenna* [1984] QB 599, CA (charterparty).

3   Eg, *British Crane Hire Corp Ltd v Ipswich Plant Hire Ltd* [1975] QB 303, CA (operating lease).

4   Eg, price variation clauses (see ante, para 10.05); *Romalpa* clauses (see post, para 25.29); acceleration clauses (see ante, para 7.03); risk in transfer of the goods (see post, para 22.02) or payment (see post, para 23.14). See generally *Encyclopedia of Forms and Precedents* (5th edn, 1991), vol 34.

been used to exploit economic advantage, eg, *Romalpa* clauses (see post, para 25.29). This is particularly the case in respect of those enterprises doing business with the consumer: the terms and price are rigidly laid down, and the only choice available to the individual consumer is whether or not to contract at all.[5] A good example is provided by instalment credit contracts,[6] and the maintenance of security clauses many of them contain (see post, para 11.09).

At common law standard form contracts are made under the incorporation and *contra proferentem* rules (see post, paras 18.04–06); and by statute are subject to the reasonableness test in s 3 of UCTA (see post, para 18.22) and the notices required by the DPA (see ante, para 3.28).

Consumer contracts.[7] Reaction to consumer standard form contracts has included criticism of their incomprehensibility to the public.[8] Besides all of the above general common law and statutory rules, if the contract is regulated by the CCA,[9] it must contain the prescribed terms and notices (see ante, para 9.11). Moreover, if it amounts to a consumer supply contract it is subject to the UTCC test of fairness (see post, para 11.15): for instance, struck down as unfair may be terms which use small print or jargon (reg 7: see post, para 11.13); or grant the supplier automatic extensions (Grey Term 1(h): see post, para 11.17); or deny the salesman's representations any effect unless embodied in writing, what are termed 'entire agreement' clauses (Grey Term 1(n): see post, para 11.18).

[11.09] Maintenance of goods clauses. A modern conditional sale or hp agreement will usually take three steps designed to ensure that the supplier does not lose his right to look to the goods in default.

1   *Notification of address.* The agreement will usually contain a provision requiring the consumer to keep the owner informed as to the whereabouts of the goods; and, where the agreement is regulated, there is a statutory duty to do so (s 80, CCA: see post, para 15.16).

2   *Repossession value.* The agreement may spell out the circumstances in which the supplier becomes entitled to repossess the goods,[1] whose value is meanwhile preserved by imposing on the buyer or hirer a personal duty[2] to bear the risk,[3] look after the goods[4] and keep them insured[5] for the benefit of the supplier.[6]

---

5   Eg, motor trade sales of new or used cars; loans (see ante, para 7.03); credit card contracts (see ante, para 7.09); auction conditions of sale (see ante, para 10.10).

6   Eg, deemed agency clauses (see ante, para 10.24); snatch-back clauses (see post, para 24.25); prescribed terms (see ante, para 9.12). As to model forms of instalment credit contract, see Goode, *Consumer Credit Law and Practice*, Part XIII; Guest and Lloyd, *Encyclopedia of Consumer Credit*, Part 8.

7   See Cranston, *Consumers and the Law* (3rd edn), pp 74–78.

8   Since 1984, such considerations have figured prominently in the Plain English Campaign by the NCC, eg, the 'Fog Index' and the 'Golden Bull Awards'. See also NCC, Language on Trial (1996).

9   In which case, the OFT may use its licensing powers (see ante, Chapter 6): (1997) 16 Fair Trading 1.

[11.09]

1   For termination provisions, see post, paras 26.08–09; and for actions for repossession, see post, para 24.25.

2   For provisions rendering contractual rights non-assignable, see ante, paras 1.23, 7.26.

3   For the rules as to risk of loss of goods, see post, para 22.02.

4   Normally, the duty is to keep them at a designated place, eg, the consumer's home.

5   The agreement usually requires the goods to be comprehensively insured and for a note of the financier's interest to be indorsed on the insurance policy.

6   For the extent of the supplier's interest in the repossessed goods, see post, para 24.22. For entitlement to the insurance monies, see Adams [1992] JBL 291; (1998) 53 CC 2/31.

3   *Minimum payments.* The agreement may be designed to ensure that the buyer or hirer effectively promises to make good any loss sustained by the supplier, by requiring the buyer or hirer on termination of the agreement to make the following types of payment under a 'minimum payments clause': (a) the expenses of repossession; (b) sums paid by the supplier on behalf of the buyer or hirer, eg, insurance premiums; (c) arrears of instalments to the date of termination; (d) damages for breach of contract; and (e) 'compensation' for depreciations or loss of profit. The effect of such clauses is to narrow the gap between conditional sale and hp (see ante, para 1.22); and the courts have in both situations sought to control them by the rule against penalties (see post, para 27.25). Nowadays, if they are in consumer contracts, such clauses may be struck down by the UTCC Regulations (see reg 4(4); Sched 3, para (e): post, para 11.16).

[11.10] Implied terms. It has been pointed out that the expression 'implied terms' covers two distinct categories:[1]

1   *Logically implied terms* are those terms which, though unenunciated by the parties, may be logically deduced from the terms expressly agreed,[2] as where there is no delivery date for the supply of goods or services and the law will imply a reasonable one (s 29(3) of the SGA; s 14 of the SGSA).

2   *Non-logically implied terms.* At one end of the scale are terms implied by custom,[3] course of dealings (see post, para 18.04) or trade usage (see post, para 15.11), such as the banker's duty of confidentiality.[4] From there, the expression 'implied terms' extends to those necessary give business efficacy to a transaction,[5] sometimes said to be based on the more modern test of reasonableness.[6] At the other extreme are the situations where the terms are said to be 'implied' whatever the actual intention of the parties, as with the statutory implied terms imported into contracts for the supply of goods (see post, para 11.11). Indeed, in consumer supplies UCTA makes such implication compulsory (ss 6 and 7: see further post, para 18.19): in such circumstances, the 'implied terms' cannot be grounded in the intention of the parties at all.

In *Paragon Finance plc v Staunton:*[7]

A mortgagee specialising in non-status loans claimed possession for arrears due under two agreements containing variable interest rate clauses. The mortgagee was committed to charging above market rates to retrieve a serious financial position. The mortgagors

---

[11.10]

1   See Glanville Williams (1945) 61 LQR 384, pp 401–06.

2   Eg, where a seller tenders non-conforming goods, he may be deemed to offer the goods actually tendered (SGA, s 30): see post, para 13.02. See generally Treitel, *Law of Contract* (9th edn), pp 185–88.

3   There are two types of customary term: (i) common law customs, which are supposed to date back to 1189, eg, market overt (now repealed: see post, para 21.05); and (ii) commercial customs or trade usage, eg, *Goodwin v Robarts* (1875) LR 10 Ex 337 (Ex Ch) (see ante, para 7.24; and post, paras 15.11, 18.09).

4   See ante, para 7.03. This rule probably extends to any borrower/lender relationship: Ferran, *Mortgage Securitisation,* pp 130–34; and see ante, paras 3.13, 8.35.

5   The *Moorcock* (see post, para 15.22).

6   See Peden (2001) 117 LQR 459.

7   [2002] 2 All ER 248, CA (discussed 62 QA 9).

admitted the arrears, but unsuccessfully claimed relief on the following grounds: breach of an implied term (see below); s 3 of UCTA (see post, para 18.24A); and the extortionate credit bargain rules (see post, para 29.40A).

In delivering the judgment of the Court of Appeal, Dyson LJ held that the right of the mortgagee to vary interest rates from time to time was not completely unfettered, saying that there was in the mortgage an implied term (not breached here) that the mortgagee would not set interest rates 'dishonestly, for an improper purpose, capriciously or arbitrarily';[8] nor do so unreasonably.[9]

[11.11] Statutorily implied terms.[1] There must first be identified the type of transaction to determine which statute is applicable, eg, for sales, look in the SGA. The major obligations[2] imposed on the parties to a contract for the supply of goods by common law or statute[3] are as follows:

1 *Identification of the goods.*[3] The law imports a condition that the goods delivered will correspond with their contract description. This undertaking will be examined in Chapter 13.

2 *Title to goods.*[3] Recognising that the object of the transferee is normally to acquire title to the goods, the law imports certain undertakings by the supplier as to title. These will be examined in Chapter 12.

3 *Quality and fitness.*[3] As the 'use-value' of goods is perhaps the most important aspect of the transaction to the buyer or hirer, English law imports certain obligations designed to ensure the usability of the goods. These will be examined in Chapters 14 and 15.

4 *Delivery and payment.* As the primary object for the supplier is the transfer of goods for a sum of money, the obligation to deliver will be considered together with payment of the price in Chapter 23.

5 *Risk.* Because of the association of risk of loss of goods with the property in them, it is convenient to deal with it in that context. The passing of risk will be discussed in Chapter 22.

On behalf of consumers, these may now be enforceable by Stop Now Orders (see ante, para 6.08).

---

8 At para 32. For reasons, see paras 34–35. The implication seems to be on the *Moorcock* basis (para 36).

9 In the *Wednesbury* sense (a well known administrative law test): see paras 38–41. The CA found the rates reasonable because the mortgage was committed to paying high rates of interest on the loan capital employed (para 2)

[11.11]

1 These were first codified in the SGA 1893 (now re-codified in the SGA 1979). Similar terms were implied into hp agreements by SOGIT 1973; and into quasi-sales and simple hirings by the SGSA 1982.

2 It will be noted that categories 1–3 are called 'implied terms' whereas categories 4–5 are not. This probably accurately reflects 1893 usage derived from their common law origins. But does it accurately reflect the modern position?

3 As will be seen, the supplier is strictly liable for breach of these implied terms (Chapters 12–14). Some commercial suppliers have adopted the practice of insuring this liability under group insurance – and even sometimes the performance of express promises, eg, extended guarantees.

UNFAIR TERMS

[11.12] Unfair Terms Regulations.[1] Whilst our (inaccurately named) Unfair Contract Terms Act 1977 primarily deals with exclusion clauses (UCTA: see post, para 18.12), the Unfair Contract Terms Directive[2] has initiated substantial changes to the effectiveness of a wide range of express (and possibly some implied) terms, though without prejudice to more stringent national rules.[3] Unfortunately, the Directive was implemented in 1994 without any change to the overlapping s 3 of UCTA (see post, para 18.24); and this point was still not met when the provisions were re-enacted 'to reflect more closely the wording of the Directive' in the Unfair Terms in Consumer Contracts (UTCC) Regulations 1999.[4] Further, in some places the UTCC Regulations follow the Directive verbatim ('copying-out'),[5] despite the fact that the latter is expressed in the continental form of drafting, perhaps clouding its meaning for English lawyers.[6] In the *First National Bank* case (set out ante, para 7.03A), Lord Steyn noted that the Directive was the 'dominant text' (para 31) and continued:

> The purpose of the Directive is twofold, viz, the promotion of fair standard contract forms to improve the functioning of the European market place and the protection of consumers throughout the European Community. The directive is aimed at contracts of adhesion, viz, 'take it or leave it' contracts. It treats consumers as presumptively weaker parties and therefore fit for protection from abuses by stronger contracting parties. This is an objective which must throughout guide the interpretation of the directive as well as the implementing regulations.

The Regulations are enforced by the OFT and other bodies (see post, para 11.19); and the OFT publishes frequent detailed *Bulletins* on their operation.[7] The purpose of the *Bulletins* is to: (i) provide a systematic record of all cases taken up under the Regulations; (ii) enable the OFT to set out its views and procedures (*Bulletin* No 4, p 5); and (iii) enable the monitoring of whether businesses are honouring agreed changes (*Bulletin* No 12). The 1993 Directive committed the Commission to report within five years on its operation;[8] and the DTI have consequently produced a Consultation Paper (July 2000) raising the following issues with regard to the Directive: (a) scope, which includes its ambit and individually negotiated terms;[9] (b) transparency;[10] and (c) sanctions (see post, para 11.21).

[11.12]

1 See generally, Treitel, *Law of Contract* (10th edn), p 244 *et seq*; Goode, *Consumer Credit Law and Practice*, Part IJ, para 124.31 *et seq*; *Chitty on Contract* (28th edn), Chapter 15.

2 93/13/EEC, based on Art 100A of the Treaty of Rome. For the text of the Directive, see Goode, *ibid*, Part X, para 1.181.

3 Article 8. Eg, the Restrictions on Statements Order (see ante, para 4.22); UCTA, s 2 (see post, para 11.16).

4 1999 (SI 2083) (as amended), made under s 2(2) of the ECA 1992 (see ante, para 1.03A). For an explanation of the intention of the sponsoring Department, see DTI, *Guidance Notes* (1995: set out in Goode, *op cit*, note 1, Part VIII, para 1006 *et seq*).

5 For a discussion on copying-out, see Bright (2000) 20 LS 330 at 338–39.

6 As to interpretation, see the *Guidance Notes*, para 2.

7 OFT, 1998 AR 29–30.

8 Article 9. The Commission reported on 27 April 2000 (COM (2000) 248 final), the main part of which is set out as an annexe to the DTI Paper referred to in the text below.

9 See post, paras 11.12A, 11.14.

10 See post, para 11.13.

In 1999, the OFT examined 1,228 cases, in 525 of which businesses took action to remove or amend unfair terms. So, for transactions within its ambit (see post, para 11.12A), the Regulations in a sense represent the death of freedom of contract (see ante, para 1.02). Henceforth, lawyers drafting contracts for such suppliers may best serve the interests of their client not by maximising his position (the traditional objective), but by producing a balanced draft in Plain English (see post, para 11.13).

[11.12A] The ambit of the Regulations. This is confined to **consumer supply contracts**, which may be analysed into the following requirements:[1]

(1) There must be a contract for 'sale or supply'. In relation to goods (see ante, para 2.01), this presumably covers sales of goods (see ante, para 1.07), quasi-sales (see ante, para 2.10) and other supplies, as on simple hiring or hp (see ante, paras 1.18; 1.20). The expression also seems apt to extend to supplies of services.[2]

(2) That contract must be governed by the law of a Member State (see ante, para 10.01), and this requirement cannot be side-stepped by a choice of non-EU law clause (reg 9. See DTI, *Guidance Notes*, para 8). Do the Regulations apply to a contract governed by English law under a choice of laws clause (see post, para 18.13) where the parties have no other connection with the EU?

(3) There must be a 'seller or supplier', which expression means (reg 3(1)):

> ... any natural or legal person who, in contracts covered by these Regulations, is acting for purposes relating to[3] his trade, business or profession, whether publicly owned or privately owned.

So contracts between two private persons are outside the Regulations, as may be contracts with unincorporated associations, eg, Clubs.[4] However, so long as the 'seller or supplier' is conducting a trade, etc, it matters not whether it is a natural person, a business corporation or a public authority.[5]

(4) The person obtaining the goods or services must be a 'consumer'; that is, 'a natural person who, in making a contract ... is acting for purposes which are outside his trade, business or profession' (reg 3(1)). So, contracts between two businessmen are outside the Regulations.[5] What if a car is being bought for a mixture of business and pleasure?

(5) Exemptions. From the above, reg 4(2) excludes altogether contractual terms which reflect:

[11.12A]

1 See DTI, *Guidance Notes* (Goode, *Consumer Credit Law and Practice*, para 1009). Cf the definition of 'dealing as consumer' within s 12 of UCTA: see post, para 18.18. As to whether it is possible to contract out of the Regulations, see Brownsword and Howells [1995] JBL at 244–45.

2 See ante, para 2.05. The Regulations seem to apply to insurance contracts. (*Contra* UCTA: see post, para 18.17). *Quaere* whether the Regulations apply to sale and mortgage of land? See Bright and Bright (1995) 111 LQR 655; Bright (1999) 115 LQR 361.

3 'Purposes related to' in reg 2(1) may be wider than 'dealing in the course of' in UCTA, s 12: Beatson [1994] CLJ 236.

4 Because of the difficulty of distinguishing the consumer from the supplier: *Bulletin No 5*, p 18. But see ante, para 1.09.

5 See *R & B Customs* case (set out post, para 18.18). The same formula of a business seller and private buyer is to be found in the Doorstep and Distance Selling Regulations: see ante, paras 10.21, 10.22A.

(a) mandatory[6] statutory[7] or regulatory[8] provisions (including such provisions under the law of any Member State or in Community legislation having effect in the United Kingdom without further enactment);[9]

(b) the provisions or principles of international conventions to which the member States or the Community are party.[10]

On the other hand, the Regulations may catch terms which **mislead** consumers as to their rights under that other legislation, eg, the right of cancellation under the Doorstep-selling Regulations (as to which, see ante, para 10.21).

In respect of such **consumer supply contracts** as satisfy the above requirements, the Regulations contain two classes of rule protective of the consumer, irrespective of whether or not he had legal advice before entering the transaction. Most transactions are likely to fall within both; but it is not clear whether the Regulations are so confined.

A *Written terms* (see post, para 11.13).

B *Terms which have not been individually negotiated* (see post, para 11.14).

[11.13] Any written terms: transparency. Regulation 7 provides two rules applicable to any 'written terms' in a consumer supply contract (see ante, para 11.12A), designed to enhance their transparency in content, style and presentation. It does not apply to statutory implied terms (reg 4(2)(a): see ante, para 11.12A) but does not appear to be restricted to terms 'not individually negotiated' (see post, para 11.14).

A   According to reg 7(1):

> A seller or supplier shall ensure that any written term of a contract is expressed in plain intelligible language.

The effect would appear to be to encourage the Plain English Campaign (see ante, para 11.08). First, the OFT have interpreted 'plain ... language' to mean that a consumer supply contract must be intelligible to ordinary consumers without recourse to legal advice.[1] Thus, a contract drafted in technical language must, under reg 7, at the very least contain a definition clause explaining technical terms in plain English;[2] and it may be safer not to use technical terms at all. Secondly, the contract must be expressed in 'intelligible language'. So, it would seem insufficient to say 'this does not affect your statutory rights', as these may be unfamiliar to the average

---

6   Three different interpretations of 'mandatory' have been identified: DTI, Consultation Paper (July 2000), paras 3.11–3.13.

7   Eg, the statutory implied terms made mandatory by s 6 or 7 of UCTA: see post, para 18.19. What about other implied terms (see ante, para 11.10)? The OFT suggests that, in casting future statutory implied terms, the government must ensure that they comply with the Directive: OFT, *Bulletin No 1*, para 1.21. The DTI have asked whether this exemption should be removed: Consultation Paper (July 2000), para 3.14.

8   Eg, contractual provisions reflecting the Doorstep Selling Regulations (see ante, para 10.21); *Bulletin No 13*, case 23 (Parcelforce terms when trading under s 28 of the Post Office Act 1969); services supplied by utilities (see ante, para 3.07).

9   The words in brackets refer to such EU provisions as have direct effect in the UK: see ante, para 1.03A.

10 This would cover international conventions which have not (yet) become part of national law.

[11.13]

1   OFT, *Bulletin No 2*, 2.19–2.20; *Bulletin No 3*, paras 12.2–12.5; DTI, Consultation Paper (July 2000), para 5.3. But plain and intelligible to whom – lawyer or lay person? See Dean (1995) 145 NLJ 153.

2   Eg, 'bailee', 'consequential loss', *'force majeure'*, 'indemnify', 'joint and several', 'liquidation', 'of the essence of the agreement', 'representations and warranties', 'passing of title', 'waiver', 'without prejudice'. See OFT, *Bulletin No 2*, 2.14–2.18; *Bulletin No 5*, Part 6, Group 19.

consumer.[3] This rule should also attack unreadably small print.[4] Moreover, if a core term (see post, para 11.14) is hidden away in small print as if it were unimportant when in fact it is potentially burdensome, then it is considered as potentially unfair (*Bulletin No 6*, para 1.25). Thirdly, the foregoing are of little value to consumers unless they have a **real** opportunity to read and understand the terms before contracting.[5] The Regulations have to be interpreted so as to achieve the purpose of the ... Directive they implement. Recital 20 of the ... Directive makes clear that the aim is not just the substitution of plain words for legal jargon but rather that consumers are given a real chance to read and understand contracts before becoming bound by them. So, this regulation links up with the requirement that consumers be given a pre-contract opportunity to examine all contractual terms;[6] small wonder, then, that the OFT claims that the demands of the Regulations will displace the long-standing precedents and that the very process of re-writing a standard form in intelligible language in itself helps to make contracts fairer (*Bulletin No 4*, p 26).

B Regulation 7(2) says that:

> If there is doubt about the meaning of a written term, the interpretation which is most favourable to the consumer shall prevail but this rule shall not apply in proceedings brought under regulation 12.

The objective is to give the consumer the benefit of the doubt in respect of language of doubtful meaning: it seems to invite the mischief rule of interpretation[7] and appears to mirror the English *contra proferentem* rule (see post, para 18.06). Not only will this provide a sanction that may be deployed in any consumer litigation relying on the principles in A (above), but the OFT also claim that it entitles them to consider any ambiguous clause according to its least favourable meaning.[8] However, the concluding phrase excludes proceedings for an injunction (reg 12: see post, para 11.20) from reg 7(2): in such a case, the plaintiff, eg, the Director, will have to prove according to the ordinary rules of interpretation the meaning for which he contends; but this would appear to make little difference in the light of the common law *contra proferentem* rule.

Whilst the Regulations mention no direct sanction for breach of reg 7, it may be that breach will bring any term within the sanctions regarding an 'unfair term' (see post, para 11.15A). The DTI have questioned whether it should be possible for the enforcement authorities to act against terms breaching reg 7 regardless of fairness.[9]

[11.14] Terms not individually negotiated. The Regulations apply to 'unfair terms' (see post, para 11.15) in consumer supply contracts (see ante, para 11.12A) 'which have not been individually negotiated' (regs 2(1), 5). The rationale seems to be that the consumer

---

3   DTI, Consultation Paper (July 2000), para 5.4; *Bulletin No 15*, cases 1, 19. Some of these rights will be non-excludable (see post, para 18.19) and to purport to exclude them may be an offence (see ante, para 4.22).

4   OFT, *Bulletin No 1*, para 1.16; *Bulletin No 2*, 2.27–2.28; DTI, Consultation Paper (July 2000), para 5.6. Cf *L'Estrange v Graucob Ltd* [1934] 2 KB 394. See also Grey Term 1(i): see post, para 11.17.

5   Compare the frequently only theoretical opportunity available at common law: see post, para 18.04.

6   Grey List (i) (see post, para 11.17): see OFT, *Bulletin No 2*, 2.6 and example at p 31.

7   See Reeves (1997) 147 NLJ 576; and generally ante, para 1.04.

8   *Bulletin No 2*, 2.9–2.10; *Bulletin No 7*, case 7 (consumer declaration that terms have been fully understood).

9   Consultation Paper (July 2000), para 2.7.

should have a genuine opportunity to influence the substance of contract terms: that this rarely happens with the small print, but that the consumer is likely to address the core of the contract. The Regulations address both notions:

1   *The small print*, which is described in reg 5 as 'terms not individually negotiated'. Typically, such a term will be found in a signed standard form contract (see ante, para 11.08); but the Regulations do not require such terms to be in writing, let alone signed[1] and reg 5(2) presumes that:

> A term shall always be regarded as not having been individually negotiated where it has been drafted in advance and the consumer has not been able to influence the substance of the term.

Thus, reg 5(2) is drawing a distinction familiar to English law in respect of written contracts between **standard terms** printed in advance (see ante, para 11.08) and **customised terms;**[2] that is, those blanks which are filled in when the contract is made, eg, a proposal form for a regulated agreement.[3] The distinction refers to **terms**, not contracts, because it will frequently be the case that a written (mixed) contract will contain some of each; and the burden of proving that a term has been individually negotiated lies on the seller or supplier.[4] Where there is a mixture of standard and 'individually negotiated' terms, reg 5(3) provides that:

> Notwithstanding that a specific term or certain aspects of it in a contract have been individually negotiated, these Regulations shall apply to the rest of a contract if an overall assessment of the contract indicates that it is a pre-formulated standard contract.

Whilst reg 5 does not apply to individually negotiated terms in a mixed contract, the effect of reg 5(3) is that the Regulations will usually apply to the standard terms,[5] for which purpose the contract must be considered **as a whole**, including the individually negotiated terms.[6]

2   *The core terms.* As regards such standard terms, reg 6(2) provides that, 'insofar as it is expressed in plain intelligible language', ie, in accordance with reg 7(1) (see ante, para 11.13), 'the assessment of fairness of a term shall not relate' to terms which in effect encompass the vital interests of the trader and may be described as 'the substance of the bargain' (*per* Lord Bingham, see below); for the Regulations are not intended to operate as a mechanism of quality or price control.[6a] The effect of these opening words is that, insofar as a core term itself satisfies reg 7 (see ante, para 11.13) and is fairly brought to the notice of the consumer (see Grey Term 1(i): see post, para 11.17),

---

[11.14]

1   Regulation 3 does not stipulate that the agreement must be signed; and the recitals to the Directive clearly include an oral contract. For the incorporation of standard terms by notice or signature, see post, para 18.04.

2   Both standard and customised terms will have to satisfy the statutory test of reasonableness in s 3 of UCTA: see post, para 18.24A.

3   As to the formalities and formation of which, see ante, Chapters 9 and 10. The European Commission is worried that this dichotomy can be circumvented by a business never printing standard terms, the whole contract being computer-generated each time: see DTI, Consultation Paper (July 2000), p 14.

4   Regulation 3(5). See further DTI, *Guidance Notes*, para 5 (Goode, *Consumer Credit Legislation*, Part VIII, para 1010).

5   Unless on 'an overall assessment' it is not a standard form contract, in which case the effect of reg 3(4) seems to be that the Regulations will not apply to any standard terms. *Quaere?*

6   This seems to be pointing to the interaction of terms: Dean (1995) 145 NLJ 28 at 29.

6a   Treitel, *Law of Contract* (10th edn) p 248; quoted with approval by Lord Bingham in the *First National Bank* case (see below), at para 12. See also Lord Steyn, at para 34.

the court cannot interfere with it on grounds of unfairness (see post, para 11.15). According to reg 6(2), core terms are those which relate:

(a) to the definition of the main subject matter of the contract, or

(b) to the adequacy of the price or remuneration, as against the goods or services sold or supplied.

So, core terms would appear to be those 'central to how the consumer perceived the bargain' (OFT, *Bulletin No 2*, 2.26); for instance, terms in our context stating the description of the product (colour, model, etc), the price or the delivery date.

Paragraph (a).[7] Of the two classes of core terms, these may give rise to the greater difficulty: as the Regulations do not extend to the statutory implied terms (reg 4(2)(a): see ante, para 11.12A), will this category be limited to the ambit of the statutory implied condition as to descriptive quality; or does it extend to descriptive quantity, title and fitness (see generally ante, para 11.11)? Moreover, para (a) seems to require a distinction to be drawn between those terms which **define** the contract and those which do not;[8] and the OFT argue that this must be viewed from the perception of the consumer.[9] What is the effect of a clause purporting to make any term part of the basis of the contract (see ante, para 8.35)?

Paragraph (b) is the 'value-for-money' equation.[10] This dovetails with the English law dismissal of the adequacy of the consideration (see ante, para 10.01), so that the Regulations should not touch the bad bargain cases (see post, para 27.28); but it should be remembered that the are circumstances where statute imports an obligation to pay a reasonable sum, eg, s 8(2) of the SGA; s 15 of the SGSA (see ante, para 2.06; post, para 15.15), or the sum stipulated extortionate (see post, para 29.40). However, the UTCC Regulations may defeat interest rate variations and price escalation clauses (see Grey List, paras j, l: post, para 11.17) and perhaps dual interest rates (see ante, para 8.22).

The meaning of both these categories of core term were considered in *DG v First National Bank plc* (set out ante, para 7.03A), where the House of Lords had to decide whether cl 8 was unfair, or escaped the Regulations as being a core term. The first instance judge, the Court of Appeal and the House of Lords all agreed that cl 8 was not a core term: its effect was only to deprive a defaulting borrower of the statutory prohibition on interest from judgment until payment (see ante, para 7.03A); and this was not amongst the important terms which a borrower would have under consideration when deciding whether or not to accept an advance. After pointing out that the Regulation gives effect almost verbatim to the words of Art 4(2) of the Directive, Lord Bingham explained that cl 8 (para 12):

... does not concern the adequacy of the interest earned by the bank as its remuneration but is designed to ensure that the bank's entitlement to interest does not come to an end on the entry of judgment.

---

7 Eg, the expiry date on gift vouchers; OFT, *Bulletin No 6*, case 56. As to gift vouchers, see post, para 15.18.

8 For the difficulty of identifying terms which 'define the main subject matter of the contract', see Macdonald [1994] JBL at 460–62; Brownsword and Howells [1995] JBL 248–52.

9 *Bulletin No 2*, para 2.26 and example at p 26.

10 What Lord Rodger in the *First National Bank* case termed the 'appropriateness' of the price (at para 64).

[11.15] Unfair terms. It has been seen that the UTCC Regulations strike at non-core standard terms in consumer supply contracts (see ante, para 11.13) which are 'unfair'. This last concept the Regulations derive from Art 3 of the Directive and explain as follows (reg 5(1)):

> A contractual term which has not been individually negotiated shall be regarded as unfair if, contrary to the requirement of good faith, it causes a significant imbalance in the parties' rights and obligations arising under the contract, to the detriment of the consumer.

As Lord Bingham (at para 17) in the *First National Bank* case (set out ante, para 7.03A):

> The member states have no common concept of fairness or good faith, and the directive does not purport to state the law of any single member state. It lays down a test to be applied, whatever their pre-existing law, by all member states. If the meaning of the test were doubtful, or vulnerable to the possibility of differing interpretations in differing member states, it might be desirable or necessary to seek a ruling from the European Court of Justice on its interpretation.

Under United Kingdom law, a non-core standard form term is 'unfair' if it satisfies **all** the three following tests,[1] which are to be read in the light of the Directive (see ante, para 11.12).

A *Lack of good faith*. Now, an English lawyer will already be familiar with the concept of good faith, both at common law[2] and under statute (SGA, s 61(3): see post, para 21.19). Whilst the cynical common law largely confines good faith to lack of proved dishonesty, ignoring further protestations as likely to be self-serving, civil law starts from the idealistic standpoint that all contracting parties will do their utmost to make, perform and break their contract in an even-handed manner.[3] In the *First National* case (above) Lord Bingham said:[4]

> The requirement of good faith in this context is one of fair and open dealing. Openness requires that the term should be expressed fully, clearly and legibly, containing no concealed pitfalls or traps. Appropriate prominence should be given to terms which might operate disadvantageously to the customer. Fair dealing requires that a supplier should not, whether deliberately or unconsciously, take advantage of the consumer's necessity, indigence, lack of experience, unfamiliarity with the subject matter of the contract, weak bargaining position or any other factor listed in Sched 2 of the regulations. Good faith in this context is not an artificial or technical concept; nor, since Lord Mansfield was its champion, is it a concept wholly unfamiliar to British lawyers.

[11.15]

1   It has been suggested that a term does not have to satisfy all three criteria to be 'unfair', so long as it fails the good faith test: DTI, *Guidance Notes*, para 7.2. The OFT look at the term itself, any balancing provision, the context and good faith: *Bulletin No 4*, pp 22–23.

2   Eg, in applying the exceptions to the *nemo dat* rule (see post, Chapter 21); or the rules for the incorporation of terms (see post, para 18.04); or the notion of contracts *uberrime fidei* (see ante, para 11.01). See *per* Bingham LJ in *Interfoto Picture Library Ltd v Stiletto Visual Programmes Ltd* [1988] 1 All ER 348, CA, at 352–53, 357. As to the common law position, see Mason (2000) 116 LQR 66.

3   As developed by the European Court, it seems good faith is required 'at all times': see DTI, *Guidance Notes*, para 7 and Annex 2; McNeil [1995] JR 148; *Halsbury's Laws* (4th edn (revised)), *Contract*, paras 612–14.

4   At para 17. See also Lord Steyn, at para 36.

The Directive may lead to a dichotomy in English law: consumer contracts to be governed by good faith,[5] whilst commercial contracts are subject to reasonableness (s 2 of the UCTA: see post, para 18.22). It would seem to have both a substantive and a procedural aspect: that is, it may relate to (i) the substance of a term, in which respect it may overlap with the imbalance of rights (see below); and (ii) procedural matters, such as whether the consumer has notice of the term.[6]

Is this EU concept of 'good faith' in fact wide enough to comprehend also both the following factors?

B   A significant imbalance of rights. Regulation 5(1) says that an 'unfair term' is one which 'causes a significant imbalance in the parties' rights and obligations'. At the substantive level, this is obviously aimed at contractual terms under which the supplier has a **right** to do something, but the consumer does not, eg, the seller has a price escalation clause (see ante, para 10.05), whereas the consumer has no counter-balancing right to cancel the contract without penalty (OFT, *Bulletin No 1*, para 1.05; No 5, p 34), or the two sides have uneven rights of cancellation or assignment (*Bulletin No 15*, cases 1, 17); and also terms which impose an **obligation** on the consumer but not on the supplier. No doubt, many such instances will involve clauses which embody an important interest of the supplier, but are simply drafted too widely. Regulation 5(5) provides that Sched 2 contains a list of the terms which may be regarded as unfair and is known as the Grey List (see post, paras 11.16–18). But all this is to be done without taking into account the price (see ante, para 11.14). On the other hand, whilst the Regulations do not formally transfer the burden of proof to the trader, the OFT consider that this requirement produces a similar effect (*Bulletin No 4*, pp 24–26). Further, at the procedural level, it would seem that this requirement extends to clauses which may be fair in substance, but tucked away in the small print so that they are not drawn to the attention of the consumer.[7]

C   *To the detriment of the consumer.* At the obvious level, this requirement excludes from the Regulations contracts where the imbalance of rights is to the detriment of the supplier.[8] However, in determining whether a non-core term in a consumer contract contrary to the requirement of good faith causes such a significant disadvantage to the consumer, reg 6(1) lays down that, without prejudice to reg 12 (see post, para 11.19):

> An assessment of the unfair nature of a term shall be made taking into account the nature of the goods or services for which the contract was concluded and referring, as at the time of the conclusion of the contract, to all circumstances attending the conclusion of the contract and to all the other terms of the contract or of another contract on which it is dependent.

Notice the emphasis in reg 6(1) on surveying matters 'as at the time of the conclusion of the contract': like s 11(1) of UCTA (see post, para 18.20), it would seem that the

---

5   The 1994 version of the Regulations contained a definition of 'good faith' (Sched 2): the first three factors bore a considerable resemblance to three of the reasonableness factors in Sched 2 to UCTA (see post, para 18.21); and the last factor read '(d) the extent to which the seller or supplier has dealt fairly and equitably with the consumer'. See Treitel, *Law of Contract* (10th edn), p 250.

6   See *per* Peter Gibson LJ in *DG v First National Bank plc* (above) at 769, paras 28–30.

7   Bright (2000) 20 LS 331, at 348–49.

8   It has been suggested that the detriment requirement has the further purpose of allowing recourse to *de facto* detriment to consumers outside the scope of the contract: Brownsword and Howells [1995] JBL 243, at 254.

Regulations do not bite on terms fair as made, but which are, or may be, applied unjustly, though the OFT disagrees.[9] On the other hand, reg 6(1) is wider than s 11(1) in that 'it places emphasis on the interaction of terms, both in the particular contract and any related to it'.[10] The reference to 'all circumstances attending the conclusion of the contract' seems to direct the emphasis more towards procedural matters,[11] such as drawing core and other important terms to the attention of the consumer (OFT, *Bulletin No 3*, para 13); and it may also focus attention on any applicable Code of Practice (see ante, para 3.13). Within that context, a consumer pleading the Regulations must show actual detriment arising from the unfair term.

The first reported judicial consideration of the above concept of a unfair term occurred in *DG v First National Bank plc* (set out ante, para 7.03A), where the disputed and widely used cl 8 was neither mentioned in the Grey List, nor within UCTA. The Bank argued that, as with a regulated loan the court has jurisdiction under s 136 of the CCA to adjust cl 8 to prevent interest accruing after judgment (see ante, para 9.20), cl 8 was not unfair just because the court had not exercised that jurisdiction and the debtor was unaware of it. Whilst the Court of Appeal disagreed, the House of Lords unanimously agreed with the first instance judge that cl 8 was fair, noting that it did not violate or undermine the statutory scheme for the protection of consumers (at para 22) and taking into account the following factors: cl 8 was not within the Grey List (at para 13); lenders would not lend unless satisfied that borrowers could repay (paras 19–20); neither did the *Crowther Report* recommend (see ante, para 5.03), nor the CCA forbid post-judgment interest (para 22); the CCA gives the courts discretion to distinguish between can't pays and won't pays (para 23) and does not require prior notification of its default provisions (para 24); and that a provision such as cl 8 is common in commercial agreements (para 54).

[11.15A] The effect of unfair non-core provisions. The primary thrust of the UTCC Regulations is to strike at non-core standard terms which are 'unfair' (see ante, para 11.15). Thus, reg 8(1) lays down that:

> A unfair term in a contract concluded with a consumer by a seller or supplier shall not be binding on the consumer.

This postulates that, *prima facie*, the contract will remain binding on both sides, even in respect of unfair terms imposing burdens on the seller or supplier. However, insofar as the unfair term burdens the consumer, 'it shall not be binding on him', cf unregulated guarantees (see post, para 25.06). At first, the DTI interpreted this neutral phrase to mean 'voidable'.[1]

However, the effect seems more like that of improperly executed regulated agreements (s 5 of the CCA: see ante, para 9.19); and it has been likened to the English blue pencil rule.[2] The effect of this is spelt out in reg 8(2):

---

9   *Bulletin No 4*, p 21. The OFT thinks the test of unfairness is whether the term could be used unfairly: *Bulletin No 3*, p 7.
10 Dean (1995) 145 NLJ 30.
11 Such as fraud, duress, undue influence, misrepresentation, non-disclosure and sharp practice: Beatson [1995] CLJ 237.

[11.15A]
1   DTI, *Consultation Document on the UTCC Directive* (October 1993). As to voidable contracts, see ante, para 10.15.
2   Bright (2000) 20 LS 331, at 350.

... the contract shall continue to bind the parties if it is capable of continuing in existence without the unfair term.

Clearly, two situations are envisaged; and in practice there may be scope for argument as to which side a particular term falls. First, perhaps in the majority of cases, the standard form contract can continue without the unfair term. Secondly, if the contract is not capable of continuing in existence without the unfair term, the contract falls[3] and the position of the parties is presumably governed by quasi-contract.[4] Suppose the consumer suffers financial loss as a direct result of the supplier's use of the unfair term: are damages recoverable?[5]

[11.16] The Grey List (1). To help decide whether a non-core standard term in a consumer contract is unfair (see ante, para 11.14), Sched 2 to the UTCC Regulations 1999 contains what it terms an '**indicative and non-exhaustive** list of terms which may be regarded as unfair'.[1] So, Sched 2 (which repeats verbatim the Annexe to the Directive and Sched 3 to the 1994 Regulations) is not a black-list, but 'simply illustrates a selection of overlapping types of term whose use might cause unfairness':[2] whether they do so or not is a matter of substance, not form (*Bulletin No 5*, p 10). Absence from the list does not indicate that a term is fair;[3] and appearance on the list does not necessarily mean that it is unfair, though it raises a substantial suspicion (*Bulletin No 4*, p 22). A list of specimen terms for each Grey List category is to be found in the Bulletins.[4] Subject to some savings (Sched 2(2)), Sched 2 lists some (overlapping) 'terms which have the object or effect of' the following:[5]

(a) *No liability for death or injury.* These are terms 'excluding or limiting the legal liability of a seller or supplier in the event of the death of a consumer or personal injury to the latter resulting from an act or omission of that seller or supplier'. Unlike UCTA (s 2: see post, para 18.17), this rule is not limited to injury caused by negligence.[6]

(b) *No liability for breaches of contract.* These are terms '**inappropriately** excluding or limiting the legal rights of the consumer vis à vis the seller or supplier or another party in the event of total or partial non-performance or inadequate performance by the seller or supplier of any of the contractual obligations, including the option of offsetting a debt owed to the seller or supplier against any claim which the consumer

---

3 Is it discharged *ab initio* or *de futuro* (see post, para 26.11)?
4 Is there a total failure of consideration (see post, para 29.15)?
5 Consultation Paper (July 2000), para 2.9.

[11.16]

1 The EU has some doubt as to the wisdom of the List approach: see Report on Implications of UTCC Directive (April 1993), para 3 (set out in DTI, Consultation Paper (July 2000)).
2 DTI, *Guidance Notes*, para 6; OFT, *Briefing – Unfair Standard Terms* (1995) 4. For example, see OFT, *Bulletin No 2*, Part 4.
3 For examples of unfair terms not in Sched 2, see OFT, *Bulletin No 3*, para 11: indemnification; unfair enforcement; signed statements; instalment deliveries.
4 The OFT have found the following gaps in the list (DTI, Consultation Paper (July 2000), para 4.7): allowing a supplier to impose an unfair financial burden; transferring unfair risks (eg, by indemnities) to consumers; onerous enforcement clauses; excluding consumer's right to assign; consumer's declarations about financial circumstances; excluding consumer's non-contractual rights; delivery at supplier's discretion.
5 The '**object**' is the intention behind the wording; the '**effect**' is the practical outcome of inclusion of the term as worded, even if different from what was intended: OFT, *ibid*. This analysis is used to limit the operation of restrictions: *Bulletin No 5*, p 10.
6 Eg, OFT, *Bulletin No 1*, case studies 7, 13 (cl 6); No 4, pp 9–10. Cf product liability (CPA, s 7: see post, para 17.30). Any more stringent liability in UCTA, s 2, is saved by Art 8 (see ante, para 11.12: DTI, *Guidance Notes*, para 6.3).

may have against him'. For instance, it may be applicable where a business tries to ensure that the consumer has no redress for a delivery of goods which is late, eg, a deemed delivery clause, or the goods delivered are defective; or there is a time limit for a consumer of running account credit to challenging his regular statement, eg, 30 days; or a swingeing *force majeure* clause (as to which, see post, para 22.13A). Unlike s 3 of UCTA (see post, para 18.24), this category is confined to consumer contracts, but explicitly refers to set-offs, as where a business tries to prevent the consumer offsetting the balance of the price against a defective delivery.[7] It clearly extends to attempts to exclude implied terms;[8] deny the ordinary remedy for breach of condition (see ante, para 11.04), eg, 'no refunds', 'credit notes only', 'colour shading excluded'; limiting damages, eg, by excluding consequential loss (see post, paras 29.23, 29.31, 29.35); or deeming any notice by the consumer only to be served on the supplier if complying with certain formalities, eg, by recorded delivery letter; or by requiring the consumer to pay the return carriage on defective goods (but see s 36, SGA: post, para 23.09).

(c) *Right not to provide goods or services.* These are terms 'making an agreement binding on the consumer whereas provision of services by the seller or supplier is subject to a condition whose realisation depends on his own will alone', eg, that the trader may on whim cancel the contract or will repair any goods he deems defective.

(d) *Retention of pre-payments.* These are terms 'permitting the seller or supplier to retain sums paid by the consumer where the latter decides not to conclude or perform the contract, without providing for the consumer to receive compensation of an equivalent amount from the seller or supplier where the latter is the party cancelling the contract'.[9]

(e) *Penalty clauses.* These are terms 'requiring any consumer who fails to fulfill his obligation to pay a disproportionately high sum in compensation',[10] eg, excessively harsh minimum payment clauses (see ante, para 11.09); clogs on the equity of redemption (see post, para 25.20); retention of title clauses (see post, para 25.29); default clauses (see post, para 26.19); penalties (see post, para 27.25). A good example of the application of this clause is *Falco Finance Ltd v Gough.*[11]

(f) *General opt-out clauses.* These are terms 'authorising the seller or supplier to dissolve the contract on a discretionary basis where the same facility is not granted to the consumer, or permitting the seller or supplier to retain the sums paid for services not yet supplied by him where it is the seller or supplier himself who dissolves the

---

7 So depriving the consumer of a lever to secure performance and requiring him to take court action: see *Bulletin No 3*, paras 2.13–2.16. As to the right to set off claims, see post, para 29.26.

8 For the major implied terms, see ante, para 11.11. Attempts to exclude any of these may be void under UCTA, ss 6 and 7 (see post, para 18.19), in which case the purported exclusion is a criminal offence (see ante, para 4.22).

9 Eg, a non-returnable deposit (see *Bulletin No 3*, para 3; and post, para 23.27); *Hartman v P & O Cruises Ltd* [1998] CLY 3732, Cty Ct.

10 For the common law rule against penalties, see post, paras 27.25–26A.

11 Set out ante, para 8.22: dual interest rates; the rule of 78: see OFT, 1998-AR 30–31; Bright (1999) 115 LQR 360. See also *Bulletin No 13*, case 15.

contract',[12] eg, under a supplier's right to cancel for minor breaches (*Bulletin No 15*, cases 4, 8), refund of deposit discretionary (*Bulletin No 15*, case 8).

[11.17] The Grey List (2). Further to the foregoing paragraph, the Grey List continues:

(g) *Right to terminate.* Except in the case of financial services contracts,[1] these are terms 'enabling the seller or supplier to terminate a contract of indeterminate duration without **reasonable notice**,[2] except where there are serious grounds for so doing', eg, to terminate a periodic hiring or running account credit without notice where there are no serious grounds for doing so; snatchback clauses (see post, para 26.08).

(h) *Automatic renewal.* These are terms 'automatically extending a contract of fixed duration where the consumer does not indicate otherwise, when the deadline fixed for the consumer to express this desire not to extend the contract is unreasonably early'.[3]

(i) *Hidden terms.* These are terms 'irrevocably binding the consumer to terms with which he had no real opportunity of becoming acquainted before conclusion of the contract'. This covers two principal areas: first, where terms are not physically available to the consumer at the time he enters a contract, which would appear to impinge on the common law rule of incorporation of terms by reference;[4] and second, the phrase 'no real opportunity' may extend to vital terms 'buried' in small print of even signed contracts,[5] including core terms and the lack of plain language (*Bulletin No 4*, pp 21–22). The OFT consider that this extends to rendering unfair a declaration that the consumer's signature signified his acceptance of the terms of the document;[6] but it does suggest that a trader may be able to avoid such a result by giving the consumer an express right to cancel the contract (see ante, para 10.28) when he discovers the terms (*Bulletin No 7*, para 1.12).

(j) *Variation clauses.* Except in the case of financial services contracts,[1] these are terms 'enabling the seller or supplier to alter the terms of the contract unilaterally without a valid reason,[2] which is specified in the contract'. This strikes at a business power of arbitrary alteration (*Bulletin No 15*, case 22), including changes to core terms (see ante, para 11.14), price increases (see *Bulletin No 16*, case 4; and ante, para 10.05) and retrospective early redemption penalties. Not only must there be a valid reason for the

---

12 Eg, termination provisions in instalment contracts (see post, para 26.08); retention of sums paid in advance for installation or services not supplied; *Bulletin No 2*, 18; home improvement contracts (*Bulletin No 3*, para 5).

[11.17]

1 By Sched 2, para 2(a), there is then saved the supplier's 'right to terminate unilaterally a contract of indeterminate duration without notice where there is a valid reason, provided that the supplier is required to inform the other contracting party or parties thereof immediately', eg, termination of an overdraft facility. See also para 2(c)). For an explanation of the purpose of Sched 2, para 2, see DTI, *Guidance Notes*, para 6.7.

2 It has been suggested that 'the practical effect' of this reasonableness test is similar to the UCTA reasonableness test (see post, para 18.20): DTI, *Guidance Notes*, para 6.6.

3 As where an annual service agreement provides for automatic renewal unless the consumer cancels 'unreasonably early'; and see *Bulletin No 2*, 18. Cf inertia selling (see ante, paras 8.18; post, para 24.44); *Interfoto Picture Ltd v Stiletto Ltd* [1988] 1 All ER 348, CA.

4 See post, para 18.04, eg, other written terms held elsewhere, eg, lodged at head office of the business (OFT, *Bulletin No 2*, 25).

5 See reg 6 (ante, para 11.13); OFT, 1995-AR 10. Eg, *Bulletin No 2*, 16–17; No 15, case 19; set out only in a Code of Practice (*Bulletin No 16*, case 11).

6 Bulletin No 13, case 8. This will substantially reverse the rule in *L'Estrange v Graucob Ltd* [1934] 2 KB 394, DC (see post, para 18.04).

alteration, eg, the manufacturer has altered the specification, but this reason must be 'specified in the contract'. It does not apply to variation by the consumer, eg, early settlement (see post, para 26.19A). However, the special treatment of financial services is here extended in the following circumstances, provided the consumer is subsequently given notice and 'is free to dissolve the contract':[7] to variations of interest rate and other charges;[8] and to unilateral alterations to 'the conditions of contracts of indeterminate duration'.[9]

(k) *Switch sales.* These are terms 'enabling the seller or supplier to alter unilaterally without a valid reason any characteristics of the product or service to be provided'. This obviously covers not just criminal switch-selling, but also sales by sample in which the goods do not comply with the sample (see post, para 15.07: OFT, *Bulletin No 2*, 17, 21), eg, where there is significant product development between contract and delivery (*Bulletin No 3*, para 6; *No 5*, p 38; *No 13*, case 1; *No 15*, cases 1, 4, 8).

(l) *Price increases.* Except in the case of price indexation clauses,[10] these are terms 'providing for the price of goods to be determined at the time of delivery or allowing a seller of goods or supplier of services to increase their price without in both cases giving the consumer the corresponding right to cancel the contract if the final price is too high in relation to the price agreed when the contract was concluded'. This refers to two types of term: sales of goods where the price is left to be settled on delivery;[11] and price escalation clauses.[12] In both cases, it requires that the consumer have a contractual right of cancellation (see ante, para 10.28).

[11.18] The Grey List (3). Further to the foregoing two paragraphs, the Grey List continues:

(m) *Exclusive jurisdiction.* These are terms 'giving the seller or supplier the right to determine whether the goods or services supplied are in conformity with the contract, or giving him the exclusive right to interpret any term of the contract'. This deals with two ways in which the supplier may seek exclusive jurisdiction over the contract: first, by controlling the evidence;[1] and secondly, having the final say in the meaning of any term, which, being a matter of law, would anyway be void at common law (see ante, para 3.23).

---

7   As to whether this is consistent with the CCA Regulations permitting variation by newspaper advertisement (see post, para 26.22), see Guest and Lloyd, *Encyclopedia of Consumer Credit Law*, para 2-083.

8   Provided the supplier gives notice 'at the earliest opportunity' (Sched 2, para 2(b)). Eg, changes of interest rate or other charges on a personal loan, eg, OFT, 1999-AR 31. Distinguish the power to vary a regulated agreement by notice (CCA, s 82(1): see post, para 26.22).

9   'On reasonable notice' (Sched 2, para 2(b)). Eg, unilateral variation of terms of an overdraft, such as the credit limit. As to whether the 'reasonable' notice requirement is consistent with the CCA procedure under s 82, see Guest and Lloyd, *op cit*, note 7.

10 This 'is without hindrance to price indexation clauses, where lawful, provided that the method by which prices vary is explicitly described' (Sched 2, para 2(d): see also para 2(c)).

11 Eg, a term in a double-glazing contract that the price will be determined when the assembled windows are delivered (DTI); OFT *Bulletin No 2*, 28, 32. *Contra* supplies of services: see SGSA, s 15(1): see post, para 15.15.

12 See ante, para 10.05. Evidently, this is not to be a core term (see ante, para 11.14). See OFT, *Bulletin No 2*, 27; *No 3*, para 7; *No 15*, cases 4, 16.

[11.18]

1   *Bulletin No 3*, para 8.2. Cf *Lowe v Lombank Ltd* (set out post, para 18.06).

(n) *Agents and formality.* These are terms 'limiting the seller's or supplier's obligation to respect commitments undertaken by his agents or making his commitments subject to compliance with a particular formality'. The first part attacks clauses saving the supplier from the acts of his agents, eg, denying the agent power to make any representations on the part of the supplier.[2] Such 'entire agreement' clauses have already been the subject of careful OFT scrutiny, on the grounds that they encourage salesmen to increase sales by misrepresentations (*Bulletin No 1*, paras 2.5–2.6; 2.7–2.21; *No 3*, paras 9.2–9.6; *No 13*, case 2; *No 15*, cases 16, 17, 20; *No 16*, case 21); and it is for consideration whether this will avoid limitations on the agent's power to contract.[3] Moreover, the prohibition may also extend to clauses deeming, eg, a salesman to be the agent of the consumer (see post, para 16.07). The second part deals with the supplier's attempt to make his liability dependant on difficult conditions, as where the consumer must comply with onerous formalities before the supplier becomes liable to perform one of his promises, eg, give notice in a particular manner or within a certain time.[4]

(o) *Unequal obligations.* These are terms 'obliging the consumer to fulfill all his obligations where the seller or supplier does not perform his', eg, obligations to pay a service charge, but with exclusion of the service-provider's liability for interruptions of the service.[5]

(p) *Assignability.* These are 'terms giving the seller or supplier the possibility of transferring his rights and obligations under the contract, where this may serve to reduce the guarantees for the consumer, without the latter's agreement', eg, where the supplier subcontracted the installation of goods; or gives a non-assignable guarantee.[6] As to non-assignability by consumers, see ante, para 11.15.

(q) *Restrictions on remedies.* These are terms 'excluding or hindering the consumer's right to take legal action or exercise any other legal remedy, particularly by requiring the consumer to take disputes exclusively to arbitration not covered by legal provisions, unduly restricting the evidence available to him or imposing on him a burden of proof which, according to the applicable law, should lie with another party to the contract'. This provision attacks a number of restrictions on the consumer's legal remedies: starting with impediments of the right to sue, eg, setting a short time limit for complaints.[7] It also covers exclusive jurisdiction clauses,[8] compulsory

---

2   Eg, *Watford Electronics Ltd v Sanderson CFL Ltd* (set out post, para 18.24A). See OFT, *Bulletin No 2*, 37; *No 15*, case 4; and see Beatson [1995] CLJ 236; and ante, para 10.24.

3   Cf *Overbrooke Estates Ltd v Glencombe Properties Ltd* [1974] 3 All ER 511 (not a goods case: see post, para 18.17).

4   *Bulletin No 3*, para 9.7; *No 13*, case 13; *No 14*, case 23; *No 15*, case 4. Cf UCTA, s 13(1)(a): see post, para 18.16.

5   Newstead [1994] *Lawyers' Europe* at 4. Also restrictions on the borrower's power to pay off a loan, including clogs on the equity of redemption (see post, para 25.20); demands for full payment before supply (OFT (1999) 22 *Fair Trading* 3; 1999-AR 30).

6   Obligations cannot be assigned (see ante, para 7.27); but rights under an instalment contract are *prima facie* assignable (see ante, paras 1.23, 7.26).

7   Cf UCTA, s 13(1)(b): see post, para 18.16. See also examination clauses (post, para 18.06).

8   If there is no international element in the transaction, the clause may fall within UCTA (see post, para 18.13; but, if it is a genuine cross-border transaction, the clause may be unfair: *Bulletin No 5*, p 35; *No 15*, cases 17, 21.

arbitration,[9] increasing his burden of proof[10] and delivery acknowledgments (*Bulletin No 15*, cases 15, 21).

[11.19] Enforcement of UTCC Regulations. Following the usual English pattern, the individual consumer can plead the Regulations in an action concerning a consumer contract (see ante, para 11.12); but, of course, his supplier cannot do so. Further, it may be that the court has power to evaluate the fairness of terms of its own motion.[1]

Now, there has already been pointed out (see ante, para 3.15) the difficulties caused by consumer inertia and aversion to costs. However, this problem is reduced by the Directive, which follows the continental pattern of designating a public official as able to litigate on behalf of consumers generally. In responding to this lead, the DTI drafted the UTCC Regulations so as to confer the enforcement powers on the Director General of the Office of Fair Trading (the Director):[2] this allows pre-emptive challenges of clauses before any dispute has arisen, which has been described as 'a more effective way of preventing the continuing use of unfair terms';[2a] or for a 'qualifying body' to take up the cudgels on behalf of a consumer in dispute.[3] Whilst the Directive makes provision for representative actions, all reference to such actions[4] was omitted from the 1994 version of the Regulations. However, the 1999 Regulations have given a subsidiary enforcement power to the 'qualifying bodies' set out in Sched 1 (as amended),[5] including the Local Authorities (see post, para 28.03) and the Consumers' Association (see ante, para 3.08). To streamline the administration, the OFT has entered into concordats with these qualifying bodies (*Bulletins 12* and *13*).

The powers of the OFT and the qualifying bodies under the Regulations are as follows:

(i) *Consider complaints*. The Director **must** consider any complaint made to him that any contract term drawn up for general use is unfair, unless (a) the complaint appears to him to be frivolous or vexatious, or (b) a qualifying body has agreed to consider it.[6] The qualifying bodies would appear to have a **discretion** as to whether or not to consider complaints; but, if they so notify the Director, they must do so (reg 11(1)). To help them consider complaints, the Director and qualifying bodies have been given a new power to require any person, eg, the trader, to produce copies of their standard contracts and give information about their use (reg 13). The purpose of considering **complaints** is for the Director or qualifying body to consider whether to take injunctive action (see (iii) below).

---

9   Eg, OFT, *Bulletin No 2*, 24; *No 15*, case 9. As to arbitration agreements, see ante, paras 3.23–24.
10 Cf UCTA, s 13(1)(c): see post, para 18.16.
[11.19]
1   See *Oceano Grupo Editorial SA v Quintero* [2000] C-240/98 to 244/98, European Ct. *Contra* DTI, Consultation Paper (July 2000), para 6.8.
2   See the definition of 'Director' in reg 2(1); and as to the Director, see generally ante, para 3.03. In practice, matters are considered within the OFT by the Unfair Contract Terms Unit.
2a See Lord Steyn in the *First National Bank* case (set out ante, para 7.03A), at para 33.
3   The OFT believe that the Director must wait until a complaint is made to him: *Briefing – Unfair Standard Terms* (1995), p 3. As to complaints by consumers in other Member States, see Brownsword and Howells [1995] JBL 243, at 262–63.
4   Article 7(2) refers to this power being granted to 'persons or organisations having a legitimate interest under national law ... in protecting consumers'.
5   Regulation 3(1). These also include the following: the Data Protection Commissioner (see ante, para 3.27); the utilities regulators (see ante, para 3.07); the Financial Services Authority (see ante, para 3.02).
6   Regulation 10(1). For summaries and analysis of the level and origin of complaints, see the *Bulletins*.

(ii) *Obtain undertakings*. In deciding whether or not to apply for an injunction (see below) in respect of a term considered unfair, the Director or qualifying body (regs 10(3), 11(2)):

> ... may, if he considers it appropriate to do so, have regard to any undertakings given to him by or on behalf of any person as to the continued use of such a term in contracts concluded with consumers.

So, ignoring any continued use of the unfair term in contracts with business consumers, the Director or qualifying body **may** accept a suitable **undertaking**;[7] and, if a qualifying body accepts such an undertaking, it must so notify the Director (reg 14(a)). Both the Director and any qualifying body must give reasons for applying or not applying for an injunction (regs 10(2), 11(2)). This is the OFT's preferred course of action. There is now a very considerable number of informal undertakings,[8] and a few formal ones:[9] their terms are set out for the guidance of traders, trade associations and local authorities in Bulletins.[10] However, the Director has always made it clear that he has no power to give formal 'clearance' of replacement terms (*Bulletin No 1*, paras 1.8–1.10; 1.12–1.13). Nor would he wish to do so: he must and does reserve the freedom to take further action against any term shown as having been revised, in the light of complaints and experience (*Bulletin No 5*, p 51). Nor may a business receiving OFT clearance claim OFT approval for his term (*Bulletin No 12*, paras 1.9; 2.2; *No 16*, paras 1.4; 2.2); and such a claim may amount to a misleading advertisement (see ante, para 8.12A).

(iii) *Seek injunctions*. See post, para 11.20.

Besides the above powers, the Director may arrange for the dissemination of information and advice to the public concerning the operation of these Regulations (reg 15(3). The OFT attach considerable importance to this (*Bulletin No 1*, paras 1.22–1.23): besides issuing **guidance** for the general public and answering **enquiries**, the Director **negotiates** extensively with traders to 'improve' their contracts[7] and with trade associations over the production of model terms.[10] Additionally, the 1999 Regulations require the Director to arrange for publication of all undertakings given to him or a qualifying body, or to the court in injunction proceedings (reg 15(1)); and he must inform any person upon request whether any particular term has been the subject of an undertaking or court order (reg 15(2)).

[11.20] Court action. If judged by him to be unfair, the Director or qualifying body:[1]

> ... may apply for an injunction (including an interim injunction) against any person appearing to the Director or that body to be using or recommending use of, an unfair term drawn up for general use in contracts concluded with consumers.

---

7 Eg, *DG v First National Bank plc* (set out ante, para 7.03A); undertaking set out in *Bulletin No 9*, Appendix A.

8 The OFT have reported that over 2,000 unfair terms have been dropped/improved so far: (2000) 28 *Fair Trading* 10.

9 Under reg 13(6). Eg, *Bulletin No 12*, Appendix C; *No 13*, Annexes; *No 15*, para 1.7.

10 *Bulletins No 5*, p 13; *No 6*, paras 1.16–1.18; *No 7*, para 1.11. For accounts of the OFT process, see *Bulletin No 4*, p 20 *et seq*; 1999 AR 31.

[11.20]

1 Regulation 12(1), (2). If the practice was sufficiently widespread in a trade, could the Director use this as a basis for a new trade Code of Practice (see ante, para 3.11)?

Notice that there is no duty to apply for an injunction; but that one **may** be applied for against 'any person': this will include not just the trader using the unfair clause, but also the trade organisation recommending it, eg, in a code of practice (see ante, paras 3.11–3.14).

Reasons must be given for applying, or not applying, for any such injunction (see above). The OFT consider this power to be exercisable not only where there is **actual** detriment, but also where the term has the **potential** to be unfair to consumers; but it sees this power very much as one of the last resort.[2]

Upon application by the Director or a qualifying body (see ante, para 11.19), the court is empowered to grant an injunction[3] on such terms as it thinks fit,[4] and (reg 12(4)):

> An injunction may relate not only to the use of a particular contract term drawn up for general use but to any similar term, or a term having like effect, used or recommended for use by any party to the proceedings.

So, whilst the injunction need not be confined to the precise formula of words used by the supplier, it can only be granted against 'any party to the proceedings'; and consequently, the injunction can have no effect against any third party using similar provisions in his contract. Further, the OFT takes the view that it is not intended that the OFT should litigate for the purpose of obtaining a direct civil law remedy for a particular aggrieved consumer, but rather that action will only be taken in the more general interests of consumers and competitors (DTI, *Guidance Notes*, para 9.2). This presumably means that, when seeking an injunction, the OFT will not also claim damages on behalf of the aggrieved consumer. But could the consumer intervene in the proceedings himself to request damages?

[11.21] Reform. Besides the suggestions already noted, the DTI are canvassing a number of other suggested changes to the Regulations.[1] These relate to problems encountered with the judicial system which the European Commission believes may thwart the goal of the Directive.[2]

1 *Paucity of sanctions*. The Commission argues that the existing sanctions leave business virtually free to trade with unfair terms until injuncted; and that what is needed are strengthened sanctions, eg, punitive damages or fines (Chapter 6).

2 *Slowness of judicial process*. The Commission's desire for an accelerated procedure (para 7.3) would seem to be satisfied by Stop Now Orders (see ante, para 6.08).

3 *Injunctions bind only the parties*, not other traders using identical terms. The Commission suggests a new special procedure to apply injunctions industry-wide (para 7.6).

---

2 OFT, *Bulletin No 1*, paras 1.2, 1.7.
3 The first High Court action, the *First National Bank* case (set out ante, para 11.14), was unsuccessful. For injunctions, see generally post, para 29.39. Cf Part III of the FTA: see ante, para 6.06.
4 Regulation 8(5); eg, *Bulletin No 15*, case 13. As to possible difficulties with the jurisdiction of the court, see Brownsword and Howells [1995] JBL 243, at 261–62.

[11.21]
1 *Consultation Paper on the UTCC Directive* (July 2000).
2 Paragraph 2.10. The goal is to be seen in the Recitals to the Directive.

CHAPTER 12

UNDERTAKINGS AS TO TITLE

[12.01] Introduction. Section 12 of the SGA 1893 provided for an implied condition as to the seller's title to the goods sold, and two implied warranties by him of quiet possession and freedom from encumbrances. It seems probable that these three implied undertakings were largely declaratory of the common law;[1] and, subsequently, the courts implied similar undertakings in hp agreements. To do so, they rejected the (now abolished) common law rule of bailment that a bailee was estopped from denying his bailor's title,[2] and introduced a presumption to the opposite effect.[3]

In modern times, these three undertakings have been re-enacted for sales in s 12 of the SGA 1979, for quasi-sales (see ante, para 2.10) in s 2 of the SGSA and for hp[4] in s 8 of SOGIT (as amended). A necessarily different version for simple hiring agreements has been embodied in s 7 of the SGSA (see post, para 12.01A). In 1973, a further statutory refinement was introduced by SOGIT to limit the supplier's power to exclude the undertakings as to title; and this has made it necessary to distinguish those contracts where there is no attempt to limit the supplier's statutory obligations to transfer title (clean contracts: see post, para 12.02) from those which contain such an exclusion clause (see post, para 12.17). The Sale and Supply of Goods Act 1994 rechristens each of the undertakings in s 12 of the SGA 'terms' and then provides:[5]

> As regards England and Wales and Northern Ireland, the term implied by subsection (1) above is a condition and the terms implied by subsections (2), (4) and (5) above are warranties.

Similar amendments have been made for hp,[6] but not quasi-sales.[7]

This is the first time there has been encountered the difficulty that the statutory terms implied in favour of the transferee as to title, identification, quality and fitness, and sample (see generally ante, para 11.11) are to be found in different statutes according to the legal nature of the supply contract. So to apply these statutory implied terms, the type of supply contract must first be identified: if it is a sale, these implied terms must be found in the SGA; if it is hp, they must be found in SOGIT; and if it is a quasi-sale or simple hiring, they must be found in the appropriate part of the SGSA. Remember, it is now possible to obtain Stop Now Orders in respect of these breaches (see post, para 28.03).

[12.01]

1 Section 12 largely followed s 7 of the Conveyancing Act 1881. For conditions and warranties generally, see ante, para 11.04; and for implied terms, see generally ante, para 11.10.
2 Abolished by the Torts Act 1977, s 8: see post, para 19.06.
3 *Karflex Ltd v Poole* [1933] 2 KB 251, DC.
4 For a statutory definition of hp, see ante, para 1.24.
5 Section 12(5A) of the SGA 1979 (as inserted by SSGA 1994, Sched 2, para 5(3)).
6 See SSGA 1994, Sched 2, para 4(1).
7 *Sed quaere?*

[12.01A] Contracts of simple hiring. In 1973, Parliament imported into hp agreements by SOGIT implied undertakings closely modelled on those in sales,[1] as for example in the undertakings as to title (see ante, para 12.01). The next step was taken in 1982, when Part I of the SGSA attempted to import into simple hirings undertakings as closely modelled on sale as the circumstances permitted:[2] with regard to the undertakings as to description, quality and fitness, the similarity is very great;[3] and such undertakings are considered together with those of sale in Chapters 13–15. However, the undertakings as to title are necessarily different (see post, para 12.04A).

The ambit of the statutory implied terms in hirings is fixed by s 6(1) of the SGSA, which provides that:

> In this Act a 'contract for the hire of goods' means a contract under which one person bails or agrees to bail goods[4] to another by way of hire, other than an excepted contract.

The essence of this category is a bailment for value, which will include some of the common law transactions termed here simple hirings (see ante, para 1.18) and all regulated consumer hire agreements (see ante, para 1.19). As with quasi-sales,[5] the category 'contract for the hiring of goods' includes (by reason of s 6(3)) both transactions under which services are also supplied[6] and whatever the nature of the consideration.[7] But this time, there is excluded under the title 'excepted contracts' hp agreements, trading stamp transactions (s 6(2)) and non-contractual bailments.[8]

CLEAN CONTRACTS

Implied conditions as to title

[12.02] The rule. Where there is a sale of goods, the amended s 12(1) of the SGA provides that, unless a contrary intention appears,[1] there is:

[12.01A]

1 This gave effect to the proposals of the Law Commission: see its *First Report on Exemption Clauses* (1969, Law Com No 24).

2 This gives effect to Law Com No 95: see post, para 15.02. See generally Palmer [1983] 3 LMCLQ 377.

3 But do ss 6–10 extend to replacement parts added to leased chattels by the lessor under a repair obligation?

4 Section 18 defines 'goods' in terms identical to those employed in the SGA: as to which, see ante, para 2.01.

5 See ante, para 2.10. Does the present category extend to sales whilst there is a reservation of property, eg, conditional sale, sale or return.

6 Does this category include use of a washing machine at a launderette? For terms imported by the SGSA as regards the service element, see post, para 15.15.

7 For examples see Woodroffe, *Goods and Services – the New Law*, para 5.05.

8 Could this result in the exclusion from this Act of meters supplied by the gas, electricity, telephone and water authorities, on the grounds that they are supplied under statutory authority rather than contract (as to the utilities, see ante, para 3.07)?

[12.02]

1 Section 12(3), emphasis supplied. As to where there is a contrary intention, see post, para 12.17 *et seq.*

An implied **term** on the part of the seller that in the case of a sale he has a right to sell the goods, and that in the case of an agreement to sell he will have a right to sell the goods at the time when the property is to pass.

This implied term is designated as a condition (new s 12(5A) of the SGA: see ante, para 12.01).

In respect of quasi-sales, there is an almost identical provision, except that the supplier is there described as the 'transferor'[2] and his duty is to have 'the right to transfer the property'.[3] However, in the case of hp the supplier will, by definition (see ante, para 1.21), never transfer his title immediately the contract is made, so s 8(1)(a) of SOGIT simply provides that there is:[4]

... an implied **term**,[5] on the part of the creditor[6] that he will have a right to sell the goods at the time when the property is to pass.

On the other hand, SOGIT also saves the common law undertaking that the supplier is capable of conferring a good title at the time the hiring commences (see post, para 12.04).

Two matters must be considered: first, what right must be transferred (see post, para 12.03, *et seq*); and second, the effect of a breach of this obligation (see post, para 12.05 *et seq*).

[12.03] The 'right to sell'. It is clear that, leaving aside simple hirings (see post, para 12.04A), the nub of the implied condition, both at common law and under the statutory formulations is a 'right to sell' (see ante, para 12.02). In 1895, Lord Russell CJ drew the (apparently logical) deduction that the duty was merely to pass the general property in the goods;[1] but a more extended view of the transferor's obligations has since been taken by the Court of Appeal. In *Niblett v Confectioners' Materials Co*,[2] the facts were as follows:

The seller agreed to sell 3,000 tins of condensed milk, to be shipped from America to England. The price was paid on tender of the shipping documents; but, what those documents did not reveal, was that the tins were labelled 'Nissly' brand, which was a colourable imitation of Nestle's trade mark, and gave the latter company the right to restrain their sale in England by injunction. The buyer therefore had to strip off the labels, and sell the tins of milk unbranded for the best price obtainable. He then sued the seller to recover the difference between the price obtained, and that which the milk would have

---

2   'Transferor' is defined by s 18(1) and (2) of the SGSA as '(depending on the context) a person who transfers the property in the goods under the contract, or a person who agrees to do so or a person to whom the duties under the contract of either of those persons have passed [by assignment, operation of law or otherwise]'.

3   SGSA, s 2(1). For the situations where the undertaking is implied, see post, para 15.12.

4   As amended and set out in para 35 of Sched 4 of the CCA, emphasis supplied. Does the amended version apply even to unregulated agreements?

5   This term is designated a condition (SOGIT, new s 8(3)): see ante, para 12.01.

6   By s 15(1) of SOGIT (as amended), 'creditor' means – 'the person by whom the goods are bailed ... under a hire-purchase agreement or the person to whom his rights and duties under the agreement have passed by assignment or operation of law'. Cf ante, para 5.25.

[12.03]

1   *Montforts v Marsden* [1895] 12 RPC 266, at 269. This could be done by a principal himself, or by an agent on his behalf (see generally ante, para 10.06).

2   [1921] 3 KB 387; [1921] All ER Rep 459, CA. Compare *Lloyds and Scottish Finance Ltd v Modern Cars and Caravans Ltd* (set out post, para 12.14).

fetched as a branded article, alleging breach of the implied undertakings of (1) the right to sell, (2) quiet enjoyment and (3) merchantable quality.

At this point, we are only interested in the right to sell (the other pleas are considered post, paras 12.14; 14.16). Upon this matter, the trial judge followed Lord Russell's view. However, his decision was unanimously reversed by the Court of Appeal and Atkin LJ commented (at 402):

> The Lord Chief Justice is using the right to sell in two different senses. The right to pass the property is one thing, and no doubt the [seller] could have passed the property in the milk but for the intervention of the Nestle Company; but the existence of a title superior to that of the vendor, so that the possession of the vendee [buyer] may be disturbed is another thing ... The owners of the patent had no right or ability to pass the property, but they had a right to disturb the possession of the [vendee/buyer] in that case.

It would appear from this decision that 'right to sell' must be read as meaning 'power' or 'ability' to sell: as the vendors could have been prevented by injunction from selling, they had no power or ability to sell.[3]

Plainly, if the vendor does not possess the unencumbered general property in the goods and cannot pass it,[4] there is a breach of both the undertakings of a right to sell or transfer the property.[5] What if the supplier can pass a good title under one of the exceptions to the *nemo dat* rule (see Chapter 21)? From the viewpoint of what the buyer obtains, it might seem that, as the buyer has lost nothing, there is likely to be no breach,[6] or an insignificant one.[7] However, it was decided in *Barber v NWS Bank plc* that a buyer who obtained a Part III title could still plead breach of an express condition as to title.[8]

Further, does the rule in the *Niblett* case extend to the undertaking to 'transfer the property' in goods?[9]

The position with regard to sale, quasi-sale and hp may be contrasted with that for simple hirings, where the obligation is just to transfer rightful possession (see post, para 12.04A).

---

3 Does this rule extend to any common law or statutory prohibition on selling? What of sale of a book published in breach of copyright?

4 In some cases it will be possible to check whether or not any third party owns the goods or has a security interest in them: if the supplier is a natural person such interest may be registrable as a bill of sale (see ante, para 9.05); if he is a registered company, it may be registrable under the Companies Acts (see post, para 25.28); and in the case of a motor vehicle a financier's interest may be registered with HPI (see ante, para 3.26).

5 What if he can pass the general property, but subject to the special property of, eg, a pledgee? As to the situation where title is doubtful, see Goode, *Commercial Law* (2nd edn), p 297.

6 See *per* Atkin LJ in the *Niblett* case (above), at 401; and *per* Mustill J in *The Elafi* (set out post, para 20.05A) at 215; *Benjamin's Sale of Goods* (5th edn) para 4-004. Compare Atiyah, *Sale of Goods* (10th edn), pp 104–05; the *Crowther Report*, para 5.7.32; Goode, *ibid*, p 298; Brown (1992) 108 LQR 221; and post, para 21.58.

7 Even in a sale to a business buyer, that would not reduce the claim to one for breach of warranty: see ante, para 11.05A.

8 See post, para 12.04. Is this justifiable on the grounds that the bfp can only prove title by the expense and uncertainty of litigation?

9 SGSA, s 2(1). The actual language might appear closer to *Montforts v Marsden* (above); if so, the SGSA undertaking would not be as extensive as the SGA one.

[12.04] The time factor. When must the supplier have the right to sell? In *Barber v NWS Bank plc*:[1]

> CC was the hirer on hp of a Honda car owned by Mercantile. In breach of the hp agreement, CC disposed of the car, which subsequently came into the hands of NWS under a directly financed conditional sale to Barber. When Barber some twenty months later sought to trade-in the Honda, HPI (see ante, para 3.26) was consulted, revealing Mercantile's title. Barber sought to rescind the conditional sale and recover all monies paid on grounds of total failure of consideration.

The Court of Appeal unanimously held that there was an **express** condition that NWS was the owner of the car at the time it contracted with Barber; that this condition had been broken, *prima facie* entitling Barber to rescind;[2] and that this right had not been lost by Barber's acceptance of the goods[3] or Part III title (see post, para 21.58).

Implied title terms. In the case of a sale of goods or quasi-sale, statute provides that the crucial time is when the property in the goods is to pass.[4] However, when a similar obligation was imported by the courts into hp agreements, they rejected the existing rule as to time, and decided that the transferor must have a right to sell at the time of delivery.[5] Statute restored the test of the time when the property is to pass (see now s 8(1)(c) of the SOGIT); but it also preserved the common law rule (see now s 15(4) of the SOGIT). Thus, unless the hp agreement effectively ousts the common law term, the result will be that in a hp agreement the supplier must have a right to sell both at the time of delivery and when the property is to pass.[6] The position is similar with regard to contracts of hiring (s 7(1) of the SGSA: see post, para 12.04A).

[12.04A] The right to transfer possession. In the case of a simple hiring agreement (see ante, para 1.18), it would be inconsistent with the nature of the transaction to introduce statutory implied terms that the bailor impliedly undertook to make an out-and-out transfer of a good title to the bailee in the manner of the undertakings in sale (see ante, para 12.03). To the contrary, it has been necessary to modify the sale undertakings in two important respects before analogous terms could be imported into a 'contract for the hire of goods' (see ante, para 12.01A) by s 7 of the SGSA:

(a) The undertakings had to be limited to the period of the hiring contract; and

---

[12.04]

1 [1996] 1 All ER 906, CA (Macleod 15 Tr L 223 (pages transposed)).

2 NWS paid out Mercantile at some unspecified time. If this had been before Barber rescinded, Barber should have thereby lost his right to rescind by the feeding of title to him: see *Butterworth's* case (set out post, para 12.06).

3 It would appear that a *prima facie* right to rescind for breach of s 12(1) is not lost by acceptance of the goods (s 11(4)): see post, para 12.06A.

4 SGA s 12(1); SGSA, s 2(1): see ante, para 12.02. However, in practice this rule may be displaced in effect where the supplier can subsequently make good the defect, as by cure (see post, para 29.03), or where the title is fed (see post, para 12.06).

5 *Mercantile Union Guarantee Corporation Ltd v Wheatley* [1938] 1 KB 490.

6 If the impediment to title arises only after the passing of property, there will be no breach of the implied condition, but there may be a breach of the implied warranty of quiet possession: see *Microbeads A G v Vinhurst Road Markings Ltd* [1975] 1 All ER 529, CA. But there will be no breach of the warranty of freedom from encumbrances: see post, para 12.13 *et seq*.

(b) There had to be an express saving of the contractual right of the bailor to repossess the goods under the express or implied terms of the hiring contract.[1]

Subject to this, s 7 of the SGSA follows the model of sale and imports into contracts for the hiring of goods undertakings as follows, though allowing their reasonable exclusion (see post, para 18.19):

1   *Implied condition as to title.* Section 7(1) provides that:

> In a contract for the hire of goods there is an implied condition[2] on the part of the bailor that in the case of a bailment he has the right to transfer possession of the goods by way of hire for the period of the bailment and that in the case of an agreement to bail he will have such a right at the time of the bailment.

Just as in relation to sales, there is a distinction drawn on the basis of when the transaction is executed: if there is to be an immediate transfer of possession, the undertaking is to be tested at once; whereas, if there is only an agreement to bail goods in the future, it is tested when possession is transferred.[3] However, it will be noted that, whereas in the case of sales the implied condition is of a 'right to sell' (see ante, para 12.03), here it is only a 'right to transfer possession'. It has been suggested that the rule in *Rowland v Divall* (set out post, para 12.05) is here inapplicable,[4] from which it would follow that a hirer who has to relinquish possession to a third party with a better title has to bring into account the use obtained with regard to both the claims for rescission and damages.[5]

2   *Implied warranties as to title* (see post, para 12.13).

Breach of the undertaking

Where the supplier is in breach of the undertaking/condition that he has the right to sell the goods, the buyer or hirer *prima facie* has two courses of action open to him: he may elect either to rescind or affirm the agreement.[1]

[12.05] Rescission. *Prima facie*, the transferee under a contract of sale, quasi-sale or hp agreement has a right to rescind where his supplier has no 'right to sell' (see ante, para 12.03). If the buyer or hirer takes this course, it has been said that the proper method of recovering the price is by an action in quasi-contract on the grounds of total failure of consideration (see post, para 29.12). Ordinarily, a party who brings such a claim will not have obtained any benefit at all; but, in the present context, it would seem that the buyer

---

[12.04A]

1   Section 7(3). For contractual termination of the bailment, see post, para 26.09; and for actions to repossess the goods bailed, see post, para 24.25. What if such repossession breached the CCA provisions (see post, para 24.27)?

2   Compare the modern two-stage process in sale for making the terms conditions.

3   Eg, if a leasing contract is made in respect of goods not at the moment owned by the lessor, as where there is a directly financed transaction. Cf hp, where the implied term does not have this second leg: see ante, para 12.02.

4   *Sed quaere?* See Woodroffe, *Goods and Services – the New Law*, para 5.23.

5   See the criticism by Palmer (1983) 46 MLR at 624–25.

[12.05]

1   These remedies are considered further in Chapter 26.

or hirer may sometimes have his cake and eat it as well. Thus, in the leading case of *Rowland v Divall*:[2]

> The plaintiff dealer bought a car from the defendant for £334, repainted it and two months later sold it to X for £400. After a further two months, it was discovered that the car had been stolen by the person who sold it to the defendant. The plaintiff refunded the £400 to X,[3] and then sought to rescind his contract with the defendant, and to recover his price (£334) on the grounds of total failure of consideration.

Bray J found that there had not been a total failure of consideration (see post, para 29.15) because the plaintiff had had the use of the car for a considerable time, so that there was a deemed acceptance (see post, para 29.07) and the breach of condition could only be treated as a breach of warranty. This decision was unanimously reversed by the Court of Appeal, who held that, as the buyer had not received any part of that for which he bargained, his use of the car was immaterial[4] and there had been a total failure of consideration, so that he could recover the £334 price.[5] The majority ignored the problem of whether the condition was converted into a warranty by the plaintiff's resale and delivery (see post, para 12.06A). On the facts of this case rough justice may have been done in favour of the plaintiff dealer.[6]

[12.06] The effect. The implications of *Rowland v Divall* (see ante, para 12.05) were spelt out in *Butterworth v Kingsway Motors Ltd*,[1] where the plaintiff was not a dealer, but a consumer:

> X let a car to Miss R under an hp agreement. Mistakenly thinking that she had a right to sell the car subject to her continuing to pay the instalments, Miss R sold the car to K before she had completed payments. K resold to H; H resold to the Kingsway Motors; and the latter resold the car to Butterworth for £1,275. After making full use of the car for 11 months, Butterworth was notified by X of his title, and immediately wrote to the Kingsway Motors claiming the return of his price. About a week later, Miss R paid the remaining instalment due to X and exercised her option to purchase, upon which X notified Butterworth that he, X, had no further interest in the car. Nevertheless, Butterworth continued his action against the Kingsway Motors; and H, K and Miss R were joined in the action. Owing to the fall in the market values, the car which Butterworth had bought for £1,275 was only worth about £800 when he repudiated, and £400 by the date of the hearing.

---

2   [1923] 2 KB 500; [1923] All ER Rep 270, CA. See also *Karflex Ltd v Poole* [1933] 2 KB 251, DC. It has been argued that this rule also applies to quasi-sales: Woodroffe, *Goods and Services – the New Law*, para 3.14.

3   It has been suggested that the plaintiff could now reduce his liability to X by an increase in value attributable to the repainting under the Torts (Interference with Goods) Act 1977, s 6(3) (see post, para 27.30): Treitel, *Law of Contract* (10th edn), p 981, note 83. But are there 'proceedings for wrongful interference with goods'?

4   This might have been material if he had held onto the car with knowledge of the facts, and thereby affirmed: see post, para 29.13.

5   A reasonable outcome as the plaintiff was a dealer buying for resale: Treitel, *op cit*, note 3, p 981, n 11.

6   But, in fact, the plaintiff acquired the car for £260: Atiyah, *Sale of Goods* (10th edn), p 106. Cf the reasons given in note 5 with those of Bridge, *Sale of Goods*, 393.

[12.06]

1   [1954] 2 All ER 694; [1954] 1 WLR 1286.

Pearson J held that the sale by Miss R to K was a clear breach of s 12(1), as was each succeeding sale in the chain,[2] but observed that a great deal of trouble would have been saved if Butterworth had merely bought off X, and recovered the sum from Miss R.[3] His Lordship agreed that the Kingsway Motors, H and K were reduced to claiming damages for breach of warranty, but held, on the authority of *Rowland v Divall* (set out ante, para 12.05), that Butterworth was entitled to rescind notwithstanding his use of the car for 11 months, because the issue of total failure of consideration (see post, para 29.15) was to be tested at the date Butterworth purported to rescind. Pearson J further held that, in assessing the value of what Kingsway Motors received for the purposes of mitigating their loss as against H, the material date was when Miss R exercised her option and her newly-acquired title thereupon 'fed down the line' to Kingsway Motors (see post, para 12.10). Accordingly, Butterworth recovered his £1,275 from Kingsway Motors; and the latter recovered £475 from H.[4] Thus, Kingsway Motors, as owners, lost £400.[5] The other £475 was the amount of damages arising from the breach of warranty of title; and this was passed back up the line to Miss R, together with cumulative costs (see post, para 29.36). The decision has subsequently been followed in a line of cases involving defective title to goods supplied on hp,[6] but has been restricted to lack of title: once a valid option to purchase has been conferred, there is no total failure of consideration where the hirer is for some reason prevented from exercising the option,[7] or where defects make the goods virtually unusable.[8] Presumably the rule in *Rowland v Divall* has no application to simple hirings (see ante, para 12.04A), because it is not a title-transferring transaction.[9]

[12.06A] The right to rescind. There is an obvious injustice (see post, para 12.11) in allowing the plaintiff consumers in *Butterworth* (see ante, para 12.06) and *Barber* (see ante, para 12.04) 11 and 20 months' free use of the car respectively. Further, there is also an illogicality in applying the quasi-contractual rule in *Rowland v Divall* (see ante, para 12.05) in the *Butterworth* case to a person who bought for use rather than resale: the prime motive of a dealer-buyer is presumably resale, so that he has lost that prime objective if he cannot sell because he has no title; but a consumer-buyer presumably buys for enjoyment, which Butterworth achieved, although the court ignored this by treating enjoyment as confined to lawful enjoyment.[1]

---

2   Nowadays, it would seem that Butterworth would get a good Part III title: see post, para 21.59. As to whether there would nevertheless be a breach of s 12, see ante, para 12.03.

3   As in *Whiteley Ltd v Hilt* [1928] 2 KB 808, CA. In fact, X offered to allow Butterworth to acquire for a settlement figure of £175: for settlement figures, see post, para 26.19A.

4   The price repaid to Butterworth (£1,275) less the value of the goods when Kingsway Motors acquired title to them (£800).

5   The depreciation of the car from the moment Kingsway Motors acquired title to the judgment on grounds of *res perit domino*: as to which, see further post, para 22.01.

6   Eg, *Karflex Ltd v Poole* [1933] 2 KB 251, DC; *Warman v Southern Counties Finance Corp Ltd* (set out post, para 12.07; where the point arose on a counter-claim against the hirer); *Barber v NWS Bank plc* (set out ante, para 12.04: see Treitel, *Law of Contract* (10th edn), pp 981–82).

7   *Kelly v Lombard Banking* [1958] 3 All ER 713, CA: see post, para 29.15.

8   *Yeoman Credit Ltd v Apps* (set out post, para 29.25).

9   But Atiyah seems to suggest otherwise: *Sale of Goods* (10th edn), p 106, note 16.

[12.06A]

1   See the cases cited by Bridge, *Sale of Goods*, p 392, note 28.

Even leaving these issues aside, the immediate problem is to know why a buyer is not in these circumstances reduced to claiming damages by his acceptance of the goods. As will be seen later (see post, para 29.04), acceptance of goods by the buyer will usually have such a result by reason of s 11(4) of the SGA.[2] In *Rowland v Divall*, Bray J would seem to have based his decision at least in part on the application of the forerunner of s 11(4); but, in the Court of Appeal, only Atkin LJ referred to this provision, and he merely said that it had no application to breaches of the implied condition as to title, without offering any convincing reason (at 506–07).

On the other hand, it has since been accepted that, if the buyer were to take delivery with knowledge of the seller's lack of title, he would be reduced to claiming damages;[3] and in *Butterworth* none of the intermediate parties was allowed to rescind.[4] Whilst there would appear to be no logical reason why s 11(4) should never apply to breaches of the implied condition as to title,[5] a similar view has unanimously been taken by the Court of Appeal as regards breach of an express condition as to title.[6] As s 11(4) only applies to some sales as opposed to other types of disposition (see post, para 29.04), this position at least has the merit of avoiding distinctions between, eg, cash sale and hp.

[12.07] Affirmation. The buyer or hirer may elect, with knowledge of the breach, to affirm the agreement,[1] as occurred in *Warman v Southern Counties Finance Corp Ltd*:[2]

> In pursuance of a directly financed hp transaction, the plaintiff agreed to hire a Hillman car from the defendants. Before payments were completed, the plaintiff received notice from the true owner, X, of his claim to the hired car. Nevertheless the plaintiff continued to pay the instalments due and eventually exercised the option to purchase on the very day that X served a writ on him claiming the return of the car. The plaintiff returned the car to X, and sued the defendants for damages for breach of the implied term as to title, claiming all the sums paid under the hp agreement, together with the cost of insurance, repairs and legal expenses.[3]

Following *Karflex Ltd v Poole* (see post, para 12.17), Finnemore J held that there was an express condition that the defendants were the owners of the car. He added that that condition was to be tested on delivery (see ante, para 12.04), and that any knowledge gained by the hirer thereafter was therefore irrelevant.[4] By way of damages, the court awarded the sum claimed.[5]

---

2   But not a hirer under a hp agreement. Nor would this provision have been applicable if Butterworth had been a conditional buyer within SOGIT, s 14(1) (as amended): see post, para 29.04.

3   See *per* Devlin J in the *Kwei Tek Chao* case, as reported in [1954] 1 All ER 779, at 788. See also the *Warman* case (post, para 12.07).

4   But the plaintiff in *Rowland v Divall* was an intermediate party.

5   See Atiyah, *Sale of Goods* (10th edn), p 110; Samek (1960) 33 ALJ 392; Bridge, *Sale of Goods*, p 393.

6   *Barber v NWS Bank plc* (set out ante, para 12.04).

[12.07]

1   As to whether it is more advantageous to rescind and reclaim the price (see ante, para 12.05), a claim in debt, or to affirm and claim damages, see Treitel, *Law of Contract* (10th edn), p 984; and generally post, para 27.15A.

2   [1949] 2 KB 576; [1949] 1 All ER 711. see also *Bowmaker (Commercial) Ltd v Day* [1965] 2 All ER 856; *Rubicon Computer Systems Ltd v United Paints Ltd* [2000] CLY 899, CA.

3   The action for damages is further considered post, para 29.27.

4   The answer might have been different if the plaintiff had made the agreement with knowledge of the defect in the defendants' title.

5   Criticised by Bridge, *Sale of Goods*, p 394; Treitel, *op cit*, note 1, p 984.

The defendants, however, counter-claimed for a reasonable sum for hire of the vehicle for the seven months during which the plaintiff hirer had had the use of it, and thereby raised a point which Goddard J had expressly left open in *Karflex Ltd v Poole*. The counter-claim was rejected by Finnemore J, who said:[6]

> If [the plaintiff] wanted to make an agreement merely to hire a car he would make it, but he enters into a hire purchase agreement because he wants to have the right to purchase the car; that is the whole basis of the agreement ... I should have thought that, even on broad principle, if the defendants break their contract or are unable to carry it out they are not entitled to claim on a sort of *quantum meruit*.

Actually, the loss in this case did not fall on the defendant finance company, because the company brought in the dealer as third party, pleading breach of warranty of title; and Finnemore J held that the dealer must indemnify the company for all loss arising from the breach.[7]

The effect of the undertaking

[12.08] Let us take a typical example, where the goods are stolen from O by a thief (X), who sells them to A, who resells to B, who resells to C, who resells or lets on hp to D:

O

X _____ A _____ B _____ C _____ D

In the normal case, there will be at least three innocent parties involved in breach of the undertaking as to title: namely, the original owner (O), the intermediate buyer (A) and the ultimate buyer or hirer (D). Besides the complication necessarily arising from the number of parties involved, certain other factors must be borne in mind. First, the value of the goods may rise, fall or fluctuate as they pass down the chain. Second, O may, though he will not necessarily, sue any or all of the parties in the chain in conversion because any of the acts of selling, buying, letting or hiring is sufficient ground for such actions.[1] Third, depending on the circumstances and the actions taken by the parties, the property in the goods may at the end of the day still reside in O, eg, *Rowland v Divall* (set out ante, para 12.05); or it may be found in any one of the subsequent innocent parties, eg, *Butterworth* (set out ante, para 12.06). Fourth, in addition to the ordinary remedies of rescission and damages for breach, the transferee may be able to reclaim all monies paid in quasi-contract on grounds of total failure of consideration (see post, para 29.12); but, because the last claim can only be made where the failure of consideration is total (see post, para 29.15) this will not normally lead to his unjust enrichment, except insofar as the quasi-contractual claim is obtainable notwithstanding that the transferee has obtained a benefit (see post, para 12.11).

---

6   At 582. The language reported in the All ER is slightly different (at 714a–b).
7   For such recourse provisions, see further post, para 16.22.
[12.08]
1   For the statutory tort of wrongful interference with goods, see post, para 19.05. The effect of breach of the undertaking does not appear to be circumscribed by the doctrine of acceptance (SGA, s 35): see post, para 29.05.

In a typical case, the owner (O) will be suing in the tort of conversion (see post, para 19.04) any of the later parties in the chain of dispositions of the goods (A, B, C, D: see post, para 12.09); and we must then consider the position of both the intermediate parties (A, B, C: see post, para 12.10) and the ultimate buyer or hirer (D: see post, para 12.11).

[12.09] The original owner (O). Assuming that at the beginning O has the property in the goods, it may be that he will recover possession and still have the best title to the goods.[1] On the other hand, it may be that either A or B or C or D has acquired the best title either by buying off O[2] or by satisfying a judgment in conversion obtained by O (see post, para 26.17); and, on acquisition, such title is immediately fed down the chain to each party in succession, stopping only when and where the chain has been broken by rescission.[3] On principle, it would seem that the risk of any change in the value of the goods should be borne by the transferee in whom the title is vested.[4]

[12.10] The innocent intermediate parties (A, B or C). Each may complain that his seller is in breach of the undertaking as to title, and recover damages on this ground, such damages being passed back up the chain, so that the loss is suffered by the first innocent party, eg, *Warman's* case (set out ante, para 12.07). Such a result follows the normal pattern of the law that the party (A), who bought from the thief (X), should be left to seek his remedy from X; but it is a little harsh when X is instead an innocent hirer under a hp agreement, eg, Miss R in *Butterworth's* case (set out ante, para 12.06). Three particular problems arise with the intermediate parties:

(1) Can they be made to pay for any use of the goods which they may have had? It has been shown that at common law whoever is sued by O in conversion, the loss is passed back up the line from that person, no allowance being made for any use of the goods by the intermediate parties, eg, *Butterworth's* case (above). However, whilst, the common law has no power to apportion, the person sued in conversion can always claim a contribution from any other tortfeasor under the Civil Liability (Contribution) Act 1978:[1] whether or not they are joint tortfeasors,[2] each defendant[3] 'liable in respect

---

[12.09]

1   Eg, *Rowland v Divall* (set out ante, para 12.05); *Warman's* case (set out ante, para 12.07).

2   Eg, *Karflex Ltd v Poole* (see post, para 12.17); *Butterworth's* case (set out ante, para 12.06).

3   Eg, *Butterworth's* case (above), sale by Kingsway Motors to B.

4   It is on this ground that the Kingsway Motors had to bear the loss of £400 in the *Butterworth* case. On risk, see generally post, Chapter 22.

[12.10]

1   Following the recommendations of the Law Commission, *Report on Contribution* (1977, Law Com 79), the 1978 Act replaced the contribution rules previously found in the Law Reform (Married Women and Tortfeasors) Act 1935, s 6. The 1978 Act is wider than s 6 in that it is not restricted to the situation where both parties are joint tortfeasors (eg, see post, para 17.04); but the 1978 Act does not seek tc deal with the apportionment rules on contributory negligence (as to which, see post, para 27.40).

2   This will depend on whether they committed the same or different acts of conversion. For separate acts of negligence, see post, paras 17.15.

3   Compare the situation where the claims for 'apportionment' is between plaintiff and defendant: eg, post, paras 12.12; 27.30; 27.40.

of the same damage'[4] is *prima facie*[5] liable to make a contribution[6] because he has converted the goods;[7] and that contribution may reflect any use made of the goods.[8]

(2) Can each intermediate party rescind and claim the price he has paid as on total failure of consideration? Such a possibility would seem to follow from *Rowland v Divall*[9] but gives rise to a number of legal problems. Can a contract be rescinded after resale and delivery (see post, para 29.06)? Is the quasi-contractual claim dependent on the ability to rescind (see post, para 29.13)? Must a breach of the condition as to title necessarily amount to a total failure of consideration (see post, para 12.11)?

(3) There may be difficulty in applying the notion of feeding title propounded in *Butterworth* (see ante, para 12.06) where the person in the position of Miss R makes two successive dispositions to K1 and K2 and then acquires title.[10]

[12.11] The ultimate buyer or hirer (D). The major problem here is whether D can be made to pay for his use of the goods. At common law, this involves the issues of his right to rescind, and the relationship of the quasi-contractual claim to rescission (see post, respectively paras 29.06 and 29.13). However, sometimes such dilemmas can be avoided by use of the Civil Liability (Contribution) Act 1978 (see ante, para 12.10), as in the famous problem where the goods consumed are whisky rather than a car.[1]

The ordinary rule in quasi-contract is that he who seeks the return of any benefit given, must *prima facie* restore any benefit gained (see post, para 29.16). In *Rowland v Divall*[2] the car had been returned to the true owner, and the defendant therefore argued that the plaintiff could not maintain his claim because he could not return the car to the defendant; but this argument was rejected by the Court of Appeal, which pointed out that the very reason for the plaintiff's inability to return the car to the defendant was that of which he was complaining, namely, the defendant's lack of title. The defendant also argued unsuccessfully that the plaintiff's use and enjoyment of the car made restitution impossible; but Atkin LJ replied (at 507):

> To my mind [the use] makes no difference at all ... The buyer has not received any part of that which he contracted to receive namely, the property and right to possession – and, that being so, there has been a total failure of consideration.

---

4 See *Eastgroup Ltd v Lindsey Morden Group Inc* [2001] 2 All ER (Comm) 1050, CA (not a goods case). But not where one was liable in contract and the other in tort: *Howkins & Harrison v Tyler* [2000] CLY 1448, CA.

5 Subject to any effective contractual arrangement between them for exclusion or indemnity (s 7(3)). As to exclusion, see UCTA, ss 6(1), 7(4): post, para 18.19.

6 Even after the other tortfeasor has settled: s 1(3) and see *Logan v Uttlesford DC* (1986) 136 NLJ 541, CA.

7 Section 1(1): see Treitel, *Law of Contract* (10th edn), p 983. For discussion of the 1977 Act, see generally *Street on Torts* (10th edn), pp 594–601.

8 Section 2. It could even amount to a complete indemnity if, say, one of the parties had enjoyed possession of the goods for virtually the whole of their useful life.

9 Set out ante, para 12.05. But see the *Butterworth* case (above).

10 Compare *West Ltd v McBlain* [1950] NI 144 (buyer after title fed prevailed) with *Patten v Thomas* (1965) 66 SR (NSW) 458 (first in time prevailed). The latter solution may be defeated by SGA, s 24: see post, para 21.38.

[12.11]

1 The problem was invented by Atiyah: see his *Sale of Goods* (10th edn), p 107. It has been argued that a fair result can be achieved by using the 1978 Act: Treitel, *Law of Contract* (10th edn), pp 983–84.

2 Set out ante, para 12.05. See generally Goff and Jones, *Law of Restitution* (5th edn), pp 527–30.

This might be considered a reasonable argument on the facts because, although the plaintiff dealer had had four months' use of the car, he had purchased for resale (see ante, para 12.05); but it would appear unrealistic as applied to the consumer Butterworth, who thereby obtained 11 months' free use of the goods.[3] It came about because the court confined enjoyment to lawful enjoyment (see ante, para 12.06A).

Now, it is well settled that the quasi-contractual remedy requires that the failure of consideration be total, not partial (see post, paras 29.15–16). Yet, despite the fact that the transferee in these circumstances will be bargaining for title **and** possession, it has been held that if he gets possession but **not** title there is a total failure of consideration, eg, *Rowland v Divall* (above); *Butterworth* case (above). It is difficult to know how far this principle extends. First, does it apply to any breach of the undertaking as to title, eg, such as occurred in the *Niblett* case, (set out ante, para 12.03); or merely to inability to transfer the property in the goods? Second, would the answer be the same if the buyer or hirer acquired a good title, but the goods were never delivered to him?[4] Third, suppose the transferor does not initially pass a good title, but the transferee subsequently acquires one: he may buy off the true owner;[5] or an intermediate party may do so, eg, *Butterworth* case (above). It has been held that D could still claim total failure of consideration.[6] Would it make any difference if D did not discover the defect in title until after it had been cured by an intermediate party?[7] A Commonwealth court has held that it would then be too late to rescind.[8]

[12.12] Reform proposals and conclusions. Many of the difficulties outlined above flow from the disregard of substantial enjoyment of tortious possession in an action for the return of the price.[1] If the action were merely for damages for breach of the implied condition as to title, any net benefit obtained could be taken into account in assessing the overall position,[2] though that might sometimes be outweighed by expenses incurred[3] and consequential loss.[4] In 1975 the Law Commission proposed that the innocent party should be entitled to rescind and get his money back, subject to a deduction for his use and possession of the goods.[5] Certain problems were shown to arise from this approach;[6] so in 1983 the Commission canvassed opinion on the merits of restricting a claim to

---

3   Treitel, *Law of Contract* (10th edn), p 981. *A fortiori Barber* (set out ante, para 12.04), who had had 20 months' free use.
4   It has been suggested that it follows from *Rowland v Divall* (above) that there will be no total failure of consideration – Atiyah, *Sale of Goods* (3rd edn), p 39 (point dropped from later editions). *Contra* Samek (1959) 33 ALJ 392, 397.
5   Eg, *Whiteley Ltd v Hilt* [1918] 2 KB 808, CA.
6   *Barber v NWS Bank plc* (above; Part III title).
7   In the *Butterworth* case (above) Pearson J felt some difficulty on this point. Cf Samek (1959) 33 ALJ 392, 398; Treitel, *op cit*, note 3, p 949; Atiyah, *op cit*, note 4, p 81, note 16; Goode, *HP Law and Practice* (2nd edn), p 590.
8   See *Patten v Thomas Motors Pty Ltd* [1965] NSWR 1457; and Bridge, *Sale of Goods*, pp 397, 398.
[12.12]
1   *Karflex Ltd v Poole* [1933] 2 KB 251, DC: see ante, para 12.07.
2   Eg, *Charterhouse Credit Co Ltd v Tolly* [1963] 2 QB 683, CA (hirer's net benefit valued at only £5 in view of serious defects in car).
3   Eg, *Mason v Burningham* [1949] 2 KB 545.
4   Eg, *Farnworth Finance Facilities Ltd v Attryde* [1970] 2 All ER 774, CA (inconvenience).
5   *Pecuniary Restitution on Breach of Contract* (1975, Law Com WP No 65), para 78.
6   See Treitel, *Law of Contract* (10th edn), pp 982–83.

damages;[7] but in 1987 they concluded that it was so difficult to devise a satisfactory scheme to preclude the buyer's unjustified enrichment that matters were best left as they are.[8] This unsatisfactory result has been characterised as 'title obsession'.[9] Apparently despairing of finding a precise solution fair in all circumstances, Atiyah has suggested that 'the answer may well lie, not in abandoning all attempt at reform, but rather in abandoning the attempt to reform the law by working out detailed rules in advance'.[10] Bridge proposes that the problem may be mitigated by utilising the proposed right of the contract-breaker to effect a cure (see post, para 29.03A), perhaps combined with the statutory right to make early payment (see post, para 26.19A), to prevent the transferee from exercising contractual rights of rescission, and hence quasi-contract.[11]

In view of these many difficulties, it is sometimes suggested that *Rowland v Divall* was wrongly decided (see ante, para 12.06A): if s 12(1) were made subject to the acceptance rule (s 11(4): see post, para 29.04), the disappointed buyer after that acceptance would be left to rely on *Warman* (set out ante, para 12.07). More radically, it has been suggested that the implied condition as to title should be excised from this branch of the law.[12] A third possibility would be to allow the ultimate buyer a common law right to reclaim his price on grounds of total failure of consideration, but make this subject to the statutory contribution rules as regards his use of the goods (see ante, para 12.11).

Implied warranties as to title

[12.13] The rules. Where there is a clean sale of goods, amended s 12(2) of the SGA provides that, unless a contrary intention appears,[1] there are implied **terms**[2] that:

(a) the goods are free, and will remain free until the time when the property is to pass, from any charge or encumbrance not disclosed or known to the buyer before the contract is made; and

(b) the buyer will enjoy quiet possession of the goods except so far as it may be disturbed by the owner or other person entitled to the benefit of any charge of encumbrance so disclosed or known.

These implied terms are designated as warranties.[3] In the case of quasi-sales, virtually identical undertakings are to be found in s 2(2) of the SGSA.[4] Similarly, almost identical

---

7   *Sale and Supply of Goods* (1983, Law Com WP No 85), para 6.12. See also the further possibility canvassed in that Paper at para 6.13.

8   *Sale and Supply of Goods* (1987, Law Com 160) para 6.5.

9   Bridge [1991] LMCLQ 52 at 66.

10   *Sale of Goods* (10th edn), p 109.

11   *Ibid*, p 397.

12   Atiyah, *Sale of Goods* (3rd edn), p 40 (point dropped from later editions); *Law Reform Committee, Twelfth Report* (1966) Cmnd 2958, para 36.

[12.13]

1   Section 12(3): as to where a contrary intention appears, see post, para 12.17.

2   As amended by SSGA 1994, Sched 2, para 5(3)(a).

3   SGA, new s 12(5A): see ante, para 12.01.

4   Substituting 'transfer' for 'sale'. 'Transferor' is defined in s 18 of the SGSA: see ante, para 12.02. Why did the 1994 Act not substitute 'term' for 'warranty'?

undertakings[5] are imported into hp agreements by s 8(1)(b) of SOGIT. However, as regards contracts for the hiring of goods (see ante, para 12.01A), s 7(2) of the SGSA provides that:

> In a contract for the hire of goods there is also an implied warranty that the bailee will enjoy quiet possession of the goods for the period of the bailment except so far as the possession may be disturbed by the owner or other person entitled to the benefit of any charge or encumbrance disclosed or known to the bailee before the contract is made.

This limited implied warranty in hire is similar to that found in sales (see post, para 12.20); but it will be noted that there is no implied warranty of freedom from encumbrances – that is because the essence of the transaction is a transfer only of possession.[6]

It will be observed that all these implied warranties are expressed *de futuro*, from which it would follow that the limitation period does not begin to run until breach.[7] Leaving aside for the moment the precise details of the two separate warranties (see post, paras 12.15–16), it must first be asked to what extent the warranties overlap with the implied condition (see post, para 12.14), and whether they should only be warranties however serious the breach.[8]

[12.14] Relationship of undertakings. Not only will a breach of the implied condition as to title frequently involve a breach of one or both of these warranties,[1] but it has sometimes been doubted whether the warranties cover any cases which do not also amount to breaches of the implied condition as to title. However, the usefulness of the warranties was demonstrated in *Lloyds and Scottish Finance Ltd v Modern Cars Ltd*:[2]

> In pursuance of a writ of execution, a sheriff took 'walking possession' of a caravan occupied by the judgment debtor.[3] But subsequently, the debtor sold the caravan to the defendant dealer, who removed it, and resold it to the plaintiff finance company as part of a directly financed hp transaction with W. By the dealer's invoice to the finance company, he expressly warranted that 'the goods are ... our sole property unencumbered and that we have the right to sell such goods free from any lien'. Later, the sheriff seized the caravan, and W repudiated the hp agreement. The plaintiffs claimed damages from the defendant for breach of warranty of title.

Edmund Davies J held that the sheriff had effectively seized the caravan by taking 'walking possession'[4] of it and he concluded that (at 781):

---

5   But substituting the language of bailment for that of sale. The SSGA 1994 also substituted 'term' for 'warranty' and added a new provision designating them warranties (Sched 2, para 4).

6   See the criticism by Palmer (1983) 46 MLR at 624–25.

7   See Atiyah, *Sale of Goods* (10th edn), p 112.

8   *Sale and Supply of Goods* (1983, Law Com WP No 85) para 6.22. As to conditions and warranties generally, see ante, para 11.04. The suggestion was not repeated by the Law Commission in their *Final Report* (Law Com 160).

[12.14]

1   Eg, *Niblett* case (set out ante, para 12.03). The buyer pleaded ss 12(1) and (2): only Atkin LJ referred to s 12(2) and he thought that there had been a breach of that subsection.

2   [1966] 1 QB 764; [1964] 2 All ER 732. It has been suggested that there was also a breach of s 12(1) in this case: *Benjamin's Sale of Goods* (5th edn), para 4-029, note 78.

3   For 'walking possession', see post, para 19.16.

4   For seizure by a sheriff in execution, see post, para 19.15.

... although the defendants transferred a good title in the caravan to the plaintiffs, they did so in breach of the express warranty in their dealer's invoice that it was unencumbered, and also in breach of the warranties as to quiet possession and freedom from encumbrance implied by s 12 of the [SGA].

He therefore held that the plaintiffs were entitled to recover the price they paid for the caravan, the hp charges that were irrecoverable from the hirer, and also the expenses to which they had been put in asserting title to the caravan.[5]

[12.15] Freedom from encumbrances. It would seem probable that this warranty was originally derived from land law, but differs therefrom in that it is broken by the mere existence of an encumbrance over the goods supplied.[1] However, in practice, this warranty is likely to be of limited utility because of the comparatively rare circumstances in which a third person not in possession can have an encumbrance binding on a purchaser,[2] eg, a sheriff taking walking possession,[3] a pledgee taking a trust receipt.[4]

The implied undertaking is not absolute, but only that there are no encumbrances 'not disclosed or known' to the transferee **before** the supply contract was made:[5] it follows that, if the supplier knows of any such encumbrance, it would be prudent to disclose it – and preferably to record this fact in any written supply agreement. How specific should the disclosure be?

Insofar as the supplier does not make disclosure of encumbrances unknown to the transferee,[6] the implied undertaking covers not just encumbrances existing at the time the supply contract is made, but also amounts to a promise that none will attach at any time after contract and before the property is to pass.[7] It does not apply to encumbrances arising thereafter.[8]

[12.16] Quiet possession. Normally, this warranty will be broken where the transferee suffers some physical interference with his possession either by his supplier,[1] eg, a computer installer secretly fitting a 'time-lock' to ensure payment;[2] or some third party acting lawfully, as where wrongfully sold goods are repossessed by a third party who has

---

5   The measure and mitigation of damages are discussed post, paras 29.27 and 27.44.

[12.15]

1   *Benjamin's Sale of Goods* (5th edn), para 4-022.

2   Atiyah, *Sale of Goods* (10th edn), p 112. But a third party in possession may have an encumbrance, eg, the lien of a prior unpaid seller or of an unpaid warehousekeeper.

3   Cf the *Lloyds and Scottish* case (set out ante, para 12.14).

4   Cf *Mercantile Bank of India Ltd v Central Bank of India Ltd* (discussed post, para 25.16).

5   Any disclosure after the moment of contracting is mere evidence of breach.

6   It would be unwise to rely on the knowledge of the transferee unless he signs a written acknowledgment to this effect.

7   See Yates [1973] JBL 136, at 137.

8   *Contra* quiet possession: see post, para 12.16.

[12.16]

1   *Industria Azucarera Nacional SA v Cubazucar, The Playa Larga* [1982] Com LR 171 (first instance). He would also have a right of action in tort: see post, para 19.05.

2   *Rubicon Computer Systems Ltd v United Paints Ltd* [2000] CLY 899, CA.

a better title,[3] or where the transferee's use and enjoyment of goods could be restricted by virtue of a right vested in a third party such as a copyright, design, patent or trade mark.[4] In *Microbeads AG v Vinhurst Road Markings Ltd*:[5]

> In spring 1970, the English buyer (VRM) bought from a Swiss seller (Microbeads) some machinery for marking white lines on roads. Unbeknown to the parties, at that time, a third party had already applied for a patent which would cover such machinery: such applications were confidential; but, when the patent specification was granted in 1972, statute back-dated the patent-holder's rights to cover the Spring sale, so that he was able to claim patent infringement against VRM.

The Court of Appeal held that the Swiss seller had unwittingly breached the undertaking as to quiet enjoyment, so establishing that the undertaking includes events occurring after the supply contract is made. Two questions arise:

(1) For how long after the supply contract does the supplier's obligation last? It has been suggested that, unless and until he resold or the goods cease to exist, the transferee should be entitled to the benefit of the undertaking for the entire limitation period.[6]

(2) Is the supplier liable for all third party interference? Clearly, the supplier is liable where a private third party is entitled to interfere under the law of the supply contract; but perhaps this does not extend to private third party rights under other systems of law.[7] Further difficulties arise where the interference is by lawful act of state.[8] What about a third party who unlawfully but foreseeably interferes, eg, a third party owner defeated by one of the exceptions to the *nemo dat* rule (see post, Chapter 21)?[9]

Once more the implied warranty is not absolute; there is no undertaking in respect of any disturbance of the transferee by 'any person entitled to the benefit of any charge or encumbrance ... disclosed or known' **before** the contract was made (see ante, para 12.15).

CONTRACTS CONTAINING EXCLUSION CLAUSES

[12.17] The problem. Can the implied undertakings as to title be excluded at common law? Obviously, such a result could only be achieved by an unmistakable contractual intention and even clear words to this effect may be struck out on grounds of repugnancy (see post, para 18.06) if a supplier also gives an express guarantee as to title. Thus, in

---

3   *Mason v Burningham* [1949] 2 KB 545; *Lloyds and Scottish Finance Ltd v Modern Cars Ltd* (set out ante, para 12.14).

4   Eg, *Niblett* case (trade mark: set out ante, para 12.03); *Microbeads AG v Vinhurst Road Markings Ltd* (see below; patent).

5   [1975] 1 All ER 529; [1975] 1 WLR 218, CA.

6   Bridge, *Sale of Goods*, p 407.

7   *Time-Life International (Netherlands) BV v Interstate Parcel Express Co Pty Ltd* (1976) 12 ALR 1, Aust (Aust supply contract; US copyright); and see Chandran [1999] Tr L 14.

8   See *The Playa Larga* (below); and Chandran [1999] Tr L 14.

9   *Empresa Exportadora de Azucar v Iansa, The Playa Larga* [1983] Com LR 58, CA. See Bridge, *Sale of Goods*, pp 408–09.

Karflex Ltd v Poole[1] the courts were able to ignore such an exclusion clause on the grounds that the references in the hp agreement to 'the owner' amounted to an express term that the person named as 'the owner' was the true owner. For this reason, it is unlikely that a purported exclusion of all the undertakings as to title in an hp agreement will be effective at common law.[2]

In relation to sales, one view was that, despite the fact that the 1893 Act allowed contracting out, a contract of sale without any express or implied undertakings as to title would amount to a sale of a chance, and not to a sale of goods within the SGA on the grounds that such a sale cannot be brought within the then statutory definition of sale of goods.[3] On the other hand, it was argued that that definition (see ante, para 1.08) did not require an absolute promise to transfer the general property in the goods, and a conditional promise to do so would be sufficient.[4] Certainly, the language of the 1893 Act would appear to favour the latter view[5] and it seems likely that the position was as follows: there was a sale within the meaning of the SGA 1893 where the seller agreed to transfer such title as he had; but not where he did not promise to transfer even such title as he had.[6] The Law Commission accepted this, but recommended that the implied condition as to title should only be excludable where it was clear that this is what was intended, and that the implied warranties as to title should never be totally excludable.[7] These recommendations have been implemented (see post, para 12.18) and should facilitate dealings with such as abandoned vehicles and rebuilt insurance write-offs.

Has UCTA made any difference in those circumstances where the supplier does not even promise to convey such title as he has? At first sight, this looks like a breach of UCTA's prohibition on a supplier denying title (ss 6(1), 7(3A): see post, para 18.19). However, it is submitted that the reality is that the transaction is one of bailment with the appropriate *prima facie* implied terms (see ante, para 12.04A), in which case UCTA only makes the exclusion of title subject to the reasonableness test (ss 7(1), (4)).

[12.18] The rules. Nowadays, the statutory provisions dealing with the undertakings as to title expressly make provision for the situation where:[1]

[12.17]

1   [1933] 2 KB 251, DC. Followed in *Warman v Southern Counties Finance Ltd* (set out ante, para 12.07).

2   Should the new CCA terminology of 'creditor' and 'debtor' make any difference to this argument? Cf *Barber v NWS Bank plc* (set out ante, para 12.04).

3   Eg, Atiyah, *Sale of Goods* (3rd edn), p 40; Cheshire and Fifoot, *Law of Contract* (7th edn), pp 149–50; Guest (1961) 77 LQR 98. Whilst these authors placed reliance on *Rowland v Divall* (set out ante, para 12.05), the plea was not raised therein, and it does not appear that the decision necessarily supports their conclusion.

4   Eg, Hudson (1957) 20 MLR 236 and (1961) 24 MLR 690; Samek (1959) 33 ALJ 392 and (1961) 35 ALJ 437; Reynolds (1963) 79 LQR 534; Coote, *Exception Clauses*, 61–69; Battersby and Preston (1972) 35 MLR 268 at 272–75.

5   See ss 1(2), 5(2) and the opening words of s 12 of the 1893 Act. See also *per* Atkin LJ in *Niblett v Confectioners Materials Co* (set out ante, para 12.03) at 401.

6   See Thornely (1958) CLJ 123, at 125; Reynolds (1963) 79 LQR 534, 542; Yates and Hawkins, *Standard Business Contracts*, p 179.

7   *The First Report on Exemption Clauses in Contracts* (1969, Law Com No 24), paras 16–18.

[12.18]

1   SGA, s 12(3). See also SOGIT, s 8(2); and SGSA, s 2(3).

... there appears from the contract or is to be inferred from its circumstances an intention that the [supplier] should transfer only such title as he or a third person may have.

In such cases, statute will import no implied condition as to title, but only two qualified warranties as to freedom from encumbrances and quiet possession (see post, paras 12.19–20). Thus, it has been clearly spelt out that a supplier may explicitly or impliedly promise to supply goods subject to all or any defects of title, a state of affairs necessary if the law is to encourage dealing in those very many situations where title is uncertain. It has been said that the true consideration would seem to be the assignment of the right, whatever it is, that the supplier or the third party has at the time of the supply.[2] In all such cases, the combined effect of the statutory undertakings and the prohibition on contracting out seems to be this: the supplier may contract to transfer only such title as he or a third party may have; but he may not enter into a sale, quasi-sale or hp agreement promising less than that.[3] If the supplier contracts to transfer possession only, the contract is one of simple bailment, whose statutory implied terms as to were considered above (see ante, para 12.17).

[12.19] Freedom from encumbrances. Except in the case of simple hirings, in supply contracts containing an appropriate exclusion clause (see ante, para 12.18), there is:[1]

... an implied warranty that all charges and encumbrances known to the seller and not known to the buyer have been disclosed to the buyer before the contract is made.

The concept of encumbrances has already been explained, where it was seen that the warranty was broken by the mere existence of such an encumbrance (see ante, para 12.15). However, where the contract contains an appropriate exclusion clause, there is no such absolute promise in respect of all encumbrances not disclosed or known to the transferee: the promise is only to disclose[2] such encumbrances existing at the time of contracting which are **both** known[3] to the supplier[4] **and** not known to his transferee.[5] In practice, there is thus likely to be a substantial area where, notwithstanding the existence of an encumbrance, the supplier is not in breach, and this will certainly be the case with regard to all encumbrances coming into existence after formation of the supply contract.

[12.20] Quiet possession. In supply contracts containing an appropriate exclusion clause (see ante, para 12.18), there is an implied warranty that none of the following will disturb the buyer or hirer's quiet possession of the goods; namely:[1]

---

2   *Benjamin's Sale of Goods* (5th edn), para 4-031.
3   *Contra* Yates [1973] JBL 136, 137.
[12.19]
1   SGA, s 12(4). See also SGSA, s 2(4); and SOGIT, s 8(2)(a).
2   How specific must disclosure be?
3   What has to be known: the facts or the law or both?
4   Will stupid ignorance be a sufficient defence?
5   For argument that the buyer's knowledge should be irrelevant, see Goode, *Commercial Law* (2nd edn), pp 301–02.
[12.20]
1   SGA, s 12(5). See also SGSA, s 2(5); SOGIT, s 8(2)(b).

(a) the seller;

(b) in a case where the parties to the contract intend that the seller should transfer only such title as a third person may have, that person;

(c) anyone claiming through or under the seller or that third person otherwise than under a charge or encumbrance disclosed or known to the buyer before the contract is made.

The concept of quiet possession has already been explained, together with the fact that in a clean contract the warranty of quiet possession was only as against interference by encumbrancers not disclosed or known to the transferee (see ante, para 12.16). However, where the contract contains an appropriate exclusion clause, there is no such absolute promise in respect of all encumbrancers not disclosed or known to the transferee: the warranty is only in respect of such disturbance by the supplier, or other person whose title is being transferred or any person claiming 'through or under' either of them; and there is no undertaking that quiet possession will not be disturbed by any other person.[2]

---

2   Even where the supplier knows that such a person has a right to disturb the transferee's quiet possession?

CHAPTER 13

UNDERTAKINGS AS TO QUANTITY AND QUALITY

INTRODUCTION

[13.01] Suppose the supplier tenders goods which do not comply with the contract description in a manner which is not *de minimis*; that is, 'microscopic deviations which businessmen and therefore lawyers will ignore'.[1] Two explanations of his conduct may be possible. First, his act may suggest that he has no intention of performing the existing contract, but is offering to enter into a new contract to deliver the goods tendered, this new contract to discharge the old one.[2] The supplier is then making an entirely new offer, which the offeree has complete freedom to accept or reject:[3] If he accepts it, the old contract is at an end; but, if he rejects that offer, he may sue for breach of the existing contract.[4] Second, it may be clear that in tendering goods which do not comply with the contract description the supplier does not intend to make a new offer, but is merely trying to perform, albeit defectively, the existing supply contract. In such a case, acceptance of the goods tendered will neither create a new supply contract nor discharge the old one: it will merely limit the remedies available to the transferee for breach of contract, for it will operate as an election to forego the right to repudiate so that he can thereafter only claim damages in respect of that breach (see post, para 29.04). Thus, in *Albright & Wilson UK Ltd v Biochem Ltd*:[5]

> A Ltd, a chemical producer, placed two orders with two different suppliers as follows: (i) with Berk for 23 tonnes of sodium chlorate for delivery to their plant A; and (ii) with X for 23 tonnes of EPI for delivery to their plant B. Both sellers engaged the same delivery agent, who mixed up the two orders.[6] As a result, 23 tonnes of sodium chlorate was delivered by tanker to plant B, together with a delivery order saying that it was EPI from X. The tanker discharged into existing stocks of EPI, causing an explosion.

On a trial of preliminary issues and confirming the decision of Eady J, the Court of Appeal held as follows: in a case giving rise to potential claims in contract or tort, A Ltd may elect to sue in contract;[7] A Ltd was entitled to assume the delivery documents presented are relevant to the load to which they purported to relate (see post, para 23.03), so that the misdelivery objectively amounted to a purported performance by the two sellers;[8] this amounted to a breach of the undertakings as to description,[9] quality and fitness, the delivery note being part of those undertakings (see post, para 14.02); and the

[13.01]
1 *Per* Lord Atkin in *Arcos Ltd v Ronaasen & Son* (set out post, para 13.12). See further post, para 13.03.
2 For discharge by subsequent agreement, see post, para 26.18.
3 At common law, it has been held that a buyer cannot exercise such an option until he knows the true facts: see post, para 13.05. However, by statute, he may be able to treat it as a unsolicited gift: see ante, para 8.18.
4 For the transferee's remedies, see post, Chapter 29.
5 [2001] 2 All ER (Comm) 537, CA.
6 The CA held that the delivery firm was acting as agent (see ante, para 10.06).
7 See post, para 26.17. So the Law Reform (Contributory Negligence) Act 1945 (see post, para 27.39) was not applicable: at para 13.
8 At paras 30; 37: by X (at para 22); and by Berk (at paras 24; 29).
9 See post, para 13.12. There may also be hybrid terms which escape SGA, s 14 (see post, para 15.22).

contract incorporated A Ltd's terms (see ante, para 10.06), those of X being proffered too late (see post, para 18.04).

[13.02] Quantity and quality. Where the supplier tenders a different quantity of goods from that stipulated by the contract,[1] the ordinary inference is likely to be that he is offering to enter into a new contract; whereas, if he tenders goods which only deviate from the contract description in quality, the inference is more likely to be that this is merely a defective performance of the existing contract. Whilst the difference between these two situations is merely one of degree, in practice it is sufficiently marked to merit separate treatment.[2]

In respect of transactions falling within the SGA, undertakings as to descriptive quality are to be found in s 13, located within Part II of the Act headed *'Formation of the Contract'*, whereas delivery of the wrong quantity is dealt with by s 30, located within Part IV of the Act headed *'Performance of the Contract'*; and it was one of the oddities of the SGA 1893 and 1979 that these headings appeared to suggest exactly the opposite inference on offer and acceptance from that suggested by the facts and set out above. Under those two Acts, the only area of overlap between ss 13 and 30 was to be found in the now repealed s 30(4), which purported to deal with the situation where there was a delivery of the contract goods 'mixed with' goods of a different description.[3]

Moreover, the SSGA 1994 has further lessened the gap between ss 13 and 30 by reducing the remedy available to a non-consumer buyer in both cases. As in the case of breach of s 13 (see new s 15A: set out ante, para 11.05A) and following the recommendations of the Law Commission,[4] for breaches of s 30 new s 30(2A) provides (new s 30(2A) was inserted by s 4(2) of the SSGA):

> (2A) A buyer who does not deal as consumer may not –
>
> (a) where the seller delivers a quantity of goods less than he contracted to sell, reject the goods under subsection (1) above, or
>
> (b) where the seller delivers a quantity of goods larger than he contracted to sell, reject the whole under subsection (2) above,
>
> if the shortfall or, as the case may be, excess is so slight that it would be unreasonable for him to do so.

References to **dealing as consumer** are to be construed in accordance with Part I of UCTA.[5] It is for the seller to show both that the buyer does not deal as consumer[5] and that the shortfall or excess falls within the above rule.[6] 'Slight' must logically mean a breach more than *de minimis* (see ante, para 13.01).

[13.02]

1 Unless the excess is obviously delivered in error. As to mistake, see generally ante, para 10.16.

2 Is 'acceptance' in s 30 to be taken in the offer and acceptance sense (see ante, para 10.02), or does it have the s 35 meaning (see post, para 29.05)? The latter view has been suggested: *Benjamin's Sale of Goods* (5th edn), para 8-043.

3 Compare *Barker Ltd v Agius Ltd* (1927) 33 Com Cas 120 with *Re Moore Ltd* at [1921] 1 KB 73 (affd on other grounds). For an explanation of the difficulties caused by s 30(4), see Atiyah, *Sale of Goods* (9th edn), pp 473–75.

4 *Sale and Supply of Goods* (1987) Law Com 160, para 6.21.

5 SGA, new s 61(5A), was inserted by SSGA 1994, Sched 2, para 5(9). For the UCTA concept of dealing as consumer, see post, para 18.18.

6 SGA, new s 30(2B), was inserted by SSGA 1994, s 4.

UNDERTAKINGS AS TO QUANTITY

[13.03] Introduction. Neither in relation to quasi-sales, hp or simple hiring agreements are there any provisions dealing with delivery of the wrong quantity (see SGSA, Part I and SOGIT respectively). However, in relation to sales, s 30 of the SGA makes it clear that it is the seller's duty to deliver the exact quantity of the goods specified and, as regards breaches which are more than slight, spells out the results of his failure to do so in a manner which suggests that delivery of the wrong quantity is being treated as a new offer (see ante, para 13.02). Insofar as this is simply a formulation of the common law rules of offer and acceptance, then it presumably applies by analogy in the case of quasi-sales, hp and simple hiring agreements; and insofar as the scheme is not all-embracing even for sales, then it may be complemented by reference to the common law.

Section 30 of the SGA thus insists on strict compliance, but subject to the following exceptions. First, s 30(5) lays down that:

> The provisions of this section are subject to any usage of trade, special agreement, or course of dealing between the parties.

Whilst allowing for the importation of a special trade meaning (see post, para 13.11) or an agreed tolerance,[1] this provision also envisages that the parties may contract beforehand as to what is to happen if the seller is in breach of his duty under s 30.[2] Second, the strict duty of performance is qualified by the *de minimis* rule in a manner similar to that of s 13.[3] Third, it should be borne in mind that the strict rules of s 30 will not be applicable where the seller elects to treat the contract as repudiated by reason of the buyer's breach before the time for delivery arrives.[4] Fourth, the effect of the rules in s 30 may be varied where the contract is severable or divisible (see post, paras 23.24–25). Fifth, where the wrong quantity is delivered, it may sometimes be possible to construe this as a new offer allowing the buyer to accept just part of the goods delivered.[5]

Subject to the foregoing, s 30 deals separately with the following situations: delivery of too little (see post, para 13.04); and delivery of too much (see post, para 13.05). However, in respect of some retail sales, there are also special provisions to ensure minimum quantity enforced by criminal law.[6]

[13.04] Delivery of too little. Section 30(1) provides that:

> ... where the seller delivers to the buyer a quantity of goods less than he contracted to sell, the buyer may reject them, but if the buyer accepts the goods so delivered he must pay for them at the contract rate.

[13.03]

1 Eg, *Shipton Anderson & Co v Weil Brothers* [1912] 1 KB 574; *The Elafi* (set out post, para 20.05A).

2 Such clauses are outside ss 6 and 7 of UCTA (see post, para 18.19) but may be within s 3 of UCTA (see post, para 18.24).

3 Compare *Shipton Anderson & Co v Weil Brothers* (above) with *Wilensko Slasko Towarcy Stwo Drewno v Fenwick & Co Ltd* [1938] 2 All ER 429. And see *per* Diplock LJ in *Margaronis Navigation Agency v Peabody & Co of London Ltd* [1965] 2 QB 430, CA, at 448. See further *Benjamin's Sale of Goods* (5th edn), paras 8-050/58. Cf TDA, s 3(1): see ante, para 4.08.

4 *Gill & Duffus SA v Berger & Co Inc* (set out post, para 23.06). As to repudiation, see post, para 26.15.

5 *Hart v Mills* (1846) 15 M&W 85; and Hudson (1976) 92 LQR 506.

6 Eg, Weight and Measures Acts; alcoholic beverages, food; and under the TDA: see ante, Chapter 4.

In *Behrend & Co v Produce Brokers Co*:[1]

> There was a contract for the sale of 700 tons of cotton seed ex the Port Inglis. The ship discharged 37 tons in London, and then left for Hull in order to discharge there other goods which had been loaded on top of the remainder of the seed.

Bailhache J held that the buyer was entitled to keep the part actually delivered and pay for it at the contract rate,[2] and to reject the balance of the goods and reclaim the remainder of the price as on total failure of consideration.[3] This rule has been subject to a number of refinements. First, in a subsequent case, Wright J held that the buyer could not be taken to have exercised the option conferred on him by s 30 unless and until he knew the true facts.[4] Second, the strict duty of performance is slightly relaxed in respect of microscopic deviations under what is known as the *de minimis* principle (see ante, para 13.01). Third, a seller accused of short delivery cannot usually justify himself by claiming that he will deliver the remainder later, because *prima facie* the buyer is not bound to accept delivery by instalments (s 31(1): see post, para 23.24). However, where there is a short delivery of one instalment in an instalment contract (see post, para 23.24), s 30(1) is inconsistent with s 31(2): here the more flexible s 31(2) is to be preferred on the issue of repudiation,[5] whilst a claim for damages may lead the buyer to accept the balance in mitigation.[6]

In 1994, the foregoing pattern was amended by new s 30(2A) (set out ante, para 13.02) to vary his remedy according to whether or not the buyer 'deals as consumer' (see ante, para 13.02). Thus, a buyer who 'deals as consumer'[7] may still choose to reject the entire delivery on grounds of **short** measure;[8] whereas, if the seller satisfies the requisite burden of proof, a commercial buyer may be restricted to only so doing if it is reasonable within the new provision (see ante, para 13.02).

[13.05/06] Delivery of too much. Section 30 provides that:

> (2) Where the seller delivers to the buyer a quantity of goods larger than he contracted to sell, the buyer may accept the goods delivered in the contract and reject the rest, or he may reject the whole.

> (3) Where the seller delivers to the buyer a quantity of goods larger than he contracted to sell and the buyer accepts the whole of the goods so delivered he must pay for them at the contract rate.

Thus, if the seller sends too many goods of the contract type, this rule saves the buyer from the trouble and expense of separating the contract goods from the others, whilst

---

[13.04]

1 [1920] 3 KB 530; [1920] All ER Rep 125.

2 He cannot accept only part of that which is delivered: Hudson (1976) 92 LQR 506.

3 See post, para 29.12. An alternative explanation is that recovery was made on the basis of money had and received.

4 *Barrow, Lane and Ballard Ltd v Phillips & Co Ltd* (set out post, para 22.12). Compare rescission: post, para 29.06.

5 *Regent OHG Aisenstadt Und Barig v Jermyn St Ltd* [1981] 3 All ER 327: see further post, para 23.25.

6 Goode, *Commercial Law* (2nd edn), p 383. See generally post, para 27.44.

7 This phrase is to be construed in accordance with Part I of UCTA (see post, para 18.18): SGA, s 61(5A), inserted by Sched 2, para 5(9)(c) of the 1994 Act.

8 Any attempt to exclude such liability may be an unfair term (OFT, *Bulletin No 16*, case 11). Delivery of short measure is also likely to be an offence under s 28 of the Weights and Measures Act 1985 (see ante, para 4.25).

allowing him to do so if he wishes.[1] Alternatively, s 30(3) allows the buyer to accept the whole and pay *pro rata*; but, presumably on the basis that this is a counter-offer, it has been argued that this is not the case where it is obvious that the seller did not mean to supply the excess.[2]

In 1994, the foregoing pattern was amended by the new s 30(2A) (set out ante, para 13.02) to vary his remedy according to whether or not the buyer 'deals as consumer'.[3] Thus, a buyer who 'deals as consumer' may still choose to reject the entire delivery on grounds of **excess** measure; whereas, if the seller satisfies the requisite burden of proof, a commercial buyer may be restricted to only so doing if it is reasonable within the new provision.

[13.07] Conclusion. It has already been observed that in one sense s 30 merely deals with an aspect of the undertaking to be found in s 13. Yet there is good reason for distinguishing between the two situations. The availability of the right to reject may vary according to whether the goods tendered constitute merely a defective performance or a counter-offer: if the latter, the 'buyer' must always have a right to reject the offer; but, in the former situation, the availability of the right to reject the goods and rescind the contract may be restricted by the terms of the contract or the general law.[1] Since 1994, matters have been further complicated by the need to distinguish according to whether or not the buyer deals as consumer:

(1) *Consumer buyers.* By expressly giving the buyer a right to accept or reject the whole of the goods delivered, s 30 seems to envisage that the delivery will constitute a counter-offer. Unlike many other provisions of the SGA, the rules contained in s 30 are not expressed to give way to a contrary intention;[2] but neither is s 30 subject to the UCTA prohibition on exclusion (s 6: see post, para 18.19). Can it be inferred that breaches of s 30 will **always** constitute a counter-offer (but see below)?

(2) *Commercial buyers.* The buyer who does not deal as consumer nowadays only retains his s 30 right to accept or reject the goods delivered where the amount delivered is more than a 'slight' deviation from the contract quantity. If there is only a slight deviation, but more than *de minimis* (see ante, para 13.01), the matter is treated as a defective performance and the buyer must accept the amount delivered and claim damages.

Despite the apparently mandatory wording of ss 30(1) and (2) (see above), the SGA does contain a general rule that its provisions give way to a contrary intention,[3] which might point to the conclusion that s 30 does, after all, only embody a *prima facie* rule.

[13.05/06]

1   Eg, *The Elafi* (set out post, para 20.05A). Even if he is not asked to pay for the excess?

2   See *Sale and Supply of Goods* (1987, Law Com 160), para 6.23. For mistake as to terms, see ante, para 10.16.

3   This phrase is to be construed in accordance with Part I of UCTA (see post, para 18.18): SGA, s 61(5A), inserted by Sched 2, para 5(9)(c), of the 1994 Act.

[13.07]

1   For the restrictions imposed by law, see post, para 29.04.

2   But could the reference in s 30(5) to 'special agreement' (see generally ante, para 13.03) be used to achieve such a result? Cf the problem in SGA, ss 6 and 7, where the omission also causes uncertainty: see post, para 22.11.

3   Section 55(1): set out post, para 18.09.

UNDERTAKINGS AS TO DESCRIPTIVE QUALITY

[13.08] Introduction. In a sense, the SGA 1893 marked the beginning of the movement away from *caveat emptor*.[1] It is true that the common law had to some extent modified its attitude where this was found to be excessively inconvenient or unfair; but the SGA as subsequently amended may have taken the process somewhat further when it laid down a number of implied terms. Sections 13 and 14 of the SGA 1979 now include three major implied conditions:[2] that in all sales the goods are as described (s 13); and that in a 'trade sale'[3] they are of satisfactory (previously merchantable) quality under that description (s 14(2)); and are fit for the particular purpose for which they are supplied (s 14(3)).[4] These provisions have since been more or less consistently interpreted by the courts in favour of the buyer. Particularly important has been the gradual extension of the scope of 'sales by description'. Today it covers most if not all contracts for the supply of goods, with the result that all three implied conditions may today apply to almost any 'trade sale', though of course the undertaking as to compliance with description alone of the three extends to private sales.[5] This development of the concept of supplies by description is dealt with first.

Supplies by description[1]

[13.09] History. The common law attempted to draw a sharp distinction between sales of specific goods and sales by description, and this dichotomy was adopted by Chalmers when he drafted the SGA 1893.[2] At its simplest, the dichotomy depended on the idea that a buyer would know the subject matter of his contract either by acquaintance or by description. However, perhaps because there are many cases which do not fall neatly into one or other of the two categories, the ambit of each of them was never clearly defined. The two categories were these:[3]

(1) Sales 'of unascertained or future goods, as being of a certain kind or class, or to which otherwise a "description" is applied'. Here, it is essential that the contract is by description, for in no other way can the parties achieve certainty of subject matter.[4]

[13.08]

1   Let the buyer beware. For the modern extent of the doctrine *caveat emptor*, see post, para 15.22. It does not apply where the supplier fraudulently induces the contract: *Gordon v Selico* [1986] CLY 1877, CA.

2   For conditions generally, see ante, para 11.04; and for implied terms generally, see ante, para 11.10.

3   Where goods are supplied in the course of a business: see post, para 14.04.

4   For the basic undertaking as to description, see post, para 13.11; but for the undertaking in respect of goods supplied as in accordance with both description and sample, see post, para 15.06. The undertakings as to fitness and suitability will be considered in Chapter 14, but for samples, see also, post, para 15.10.

5   Eg, *Varley v Whipp* (set out post, para 13.14). *Contra* the undertakings as to fitness and quality: see above.

[13.09]

1   See generally, Montrose (1937) 15 Can BR 760; Stoljar (1952) 15 MLR 425, at 441–45; and (1953) 16 MLR 174; Feltham [1969] JBL 16.

2   In respect of sales by description, Chalmers also separated the common law undertaking into two separate statutory terms: (1) the goods must comply with their description; and (2) they must be merchantable under it. For the two modern implied terms, see respectively post, paras 13.11; 14.15.

3   *Benjamin's Sale of Goods* (8th edn, 1950), p 615. This dichotomy was approved in *Harlingdon & Leinster Enterprises Ltd v Christopher Hull Fine Arts Ltd* (set out post, para 13.11A).

4   See *per* Channell J in *Varley v Whipp* (set out post, para 13.14), at 516.

(2) Sales 'of specific goods, bought by the buyer in reliance, at least in some part, upon the description given or to be tacitly inferred from the circumstances, and which identifies the goods'. The law had already recognised that sales by sample fitted within this category (see post, para 15.03).

Category (2) does not fit easily into any simple dichotomy of goods known **either** by acquaintance **or** by description; and it has been within this category that the crucial developments have taken place. The first step was to interpret the concept of sales by description to cover all sales of specific goods where the buyer had not seen the goods either before or at the time of contracting, but was relying on the description alone.[5] Then, the concept was extended to cover those situations where the buyer was contracting in the presence of goods which he had no opportunity to inspect before purchase, such as beer bought in a public house.[6] From this point, it broadened to cover virtually all retail sales (see post para 13.10). However, the fact that a sale of specific goods may be a sale by description does not prove that it must be so (see post, para 13.11).

[13.10] Retail sales. With the gradual erosion of the restrictions on the concept of sales by description (see ante, para 13.09), the courts soon became indifferent as to whether or not the parties were negotiating in the presence of the goods. Thus, in *Grant v Australian Knitting Mills Ltd* Lord Wright said:[1]

> It may also be pointed out that there is a sale by description even though the buyer is buying something displayed before him on the counter: a thing is sold by description, though it is specific, so long as it is sold not merely as the specific thing but as a thing corresponding to a description, eg, woollen undergarments, a hot-water bottle, a second-hand reaping machine, to select a few obvious illustrations.

In that case, the Privy Council decided that a retail sale of undergarments conducted across a shop-counter was a sale by description.[2] A striking case is *Beale v Taylor*:[3]

> The seller advertised a 1961 Herald car for sale. The buyer inspected the car and agreed to buy it, but subsequently discovered something the seller had never realised all the time he had owned the car: that the rear half of the car was a 1961 Herald but the front half was part of an earlier model, the two halves having been welded together.

The buyer succeeded before the Court of Appeal in his claim for damages for breach of the implied condition that the goods correspond with their description (see post, para 13.11). In delivering the judgment of the Court, Sellers LJ said that, even if there were no other terms as to the state of the goods, fundamentally the seller was selling a 1961 Herald car. However, his Lordship did adopt one limitation to be found in *Chalmers*,[4] namely that the rule be confined to non-apparent defects (see post, para 13.11).

---

5 *Varley v Whipp* (above). See Goode, *Commercial Law* (2nd edn), p 305.
6 *Wren v Holt* [1903] 1 KB 610, CA. See also *Thornett v Beers* [1919] 1 KB 486 (buyer declined invitation to inspect contents).
[13.10]
1 [1936] AC 85, at 1001, PC.
2 In *Godley v Perry* [1960] 1 All ER 36, Edmund Davies J accepted that a retail sale of a plastic catapult by a newsagent to a six year old boy was a sale by description.
3 [1967] 3 All ER 253; [1967] 1 WLR 1193, CA.
4 *Sale of Goods* (15th edn, 1967), p 57; but cf the 18th edn, p 120. See further post, para 13.11, fifth point.

Today, the position would appear to be that almost every sale, whether of specific or unascertained goods, can be a sale by description. Even if the seller does not himself describe the goods to the buyer, either orally or in writing, it may be that any label attached to the goods may form part of the description and that the physical shape of the goods may itself amount to a description.[5] Just to clarify matters, statute now provides that the supply or hiring may be by description, notwithstanding that the goods are selected by the buyer or bailee (s 13(3) of the SGA; ss 3(3), 8(4) of the SGSA; s 9(2) of the SOGIT): this will cover retail outlets using the self-service system[6] and auctions.[7]

Undertakings as to the description

[13.11] The undertakings. The new s 13(1) of the SGA lays down that:[1]

> Where there is a contract for the sale of goods by description, there is an implied term that the goods will correspond with the description.

In English law, this implied term is a condition.[2] A virtually identical undertaking is implied into quasi-sales, except that the supplier is there described as the 'transferor'.[3] Similarly, where goods are bailed by description, there is an implied condition that the goods will correspond with their description, whether the contract be one of simple bailment[4] or hp.[5]

Several points may be made at the outset. First, the nature of the supply contract must be identified in order to apply the appropriate implied term (see ante, para 12.01). Second, it is rather misleading of the Act to speak of **implying** such conditions when the condition will often be an express term of the contract,[6] eg, as to a motor vehicle, the model, its mileage (odometer), previous ownership or use. Third, whilst it is not possible to challenge the unfairness of the statutory implied term itself,[7] there are limitations on the supplier's ability to exclude or restrict this undertaking (see post, para 13.16), though it is questionable whether these limitations extend to certificates of compliance.[8] Fourth, unlike the major conditions as to the state of the goods (see post, para 14.04), the

---

5   Eg, the rear of the car in *Beale v Taylor* bore the inscription '1200'; but compare the monogrammed painting in the *Harlingdon* case (see post, para 13.11A). See also Diamond (1960) 23 MLR 200; Feltham [1969] JBL 16, at 21.

6   As to the manner in which the contract is made in a self-service store, see Treitel, *Law of Contract* (10th edn), pp 12–13; and generally ante, para 10.02.

7   This brings in any catalogue description: Harvey and Meisel, *Auctions* (2nd edn), p 162. As to the manner in which the contract is made by auction, see ante, para 10.10.

[13.11]

1   As amended by the SSGA 1994, Sched 2, para 5(4)(a). See generally ante, para 11.11. For EU proposed changes, see post, para 14.01.

2   New SGA, s 13(1A): see SSGA 1994, Sched 2, para 5(4)(b).

3   SGSA, s 3(1) For 'transferor', see ante, para 12.02. The SSGA does not amend the status of the term as in the SGA.

4   SGSA, ss 8(1), (2). See Woodroffe, *Goods and Services – the New Law*, para 5.15. The SSGA does not amend the status of the term as in the SGSA.

5   SOGIT, s 9(1), as amended: see ante, para 12.02. The SSGA here amends the status of the implied term as in the SGA: see SSGA, Sched 2, para 4(3).

6   Eg, goods counterfeiting (see ante, paras 4.06; 8.05); *Wallis, Son & Wells v Pratt and Haynes* (set out ante, para 11.04); *Andrew Brothers, Ltd v Singer Ltd* [1934] 1 KB 17, CA. Compare the *First Report on Exemption Clauses* (1969, Law Com No 24) paras 21–22.

7   UTCC Regulations, Sched 1, para (e)(i): see ante, para 11.12.

8   Eg, *Toepfer v Continental Grain Co* [1974] 1 Lloyd's Rep 11. See generally post, para 14.02.

undertaking as to correspondence with description is implied whether or not the supplier is a dealer; but, like those conditions, a business transferee will only be able to treat a 'slight breach' as a breach of warranty (see ante, para 11.05A). Fifth, if the description has a special trade usage, the goods may have to comply with that specialised meaning, rather than the ordinary one, but only if it possible to spell out an agreement by the parties to the term being used in the sense ascribed to it by the trade usage,[9] as perhaps where it is a requirement of the criminal law that the goods are of a certain description (see ante, para 4.23 et seq). However, particularly if the trade usage was not known to one of the parties, it may be that there is no contract because the parties were never ad idem as to the description of the goods;[10] or that they are actually using the description in a general sense.[11] Sixth, in a sample contract (see post, para 15.04), the goods also have to comply with the sample (see post, para 15.06). Seventh, notwithstanding that a description has been used, it is another question whether the contract is by description (see post, para 13.11A) or sample (see post, para 15.04). Eighth, for consumer sales (see post, para 14.01), another version of this undertaking is to be found in an EU Directive (Arts 2(1), (2)(a), (5)). Ninth, it is now possible to obtain Stop Now Orders in respect of these breaches (see post, para 28.03).

[13.11A] The description. Suppose that in negotiating the supply contract, the supplier describes the goods. Leaving aside any criminal law liability for misdescription,[1] the descriptive words may give rise to civil liability in ascending order of legal significance: (1) for mistake;[2] (2) for misrepresentation;[3] (3) for breach of contract. Concentrating on the last possibility, there may be liability for breach of an express promise as to description (see ante, para 11.07) or an implied condition (see ante, para 13.11), eg, a sale of counterfeit goods.

Attention has already been drawn to the ordinary rules by which a representation becomes a contractual term and in particular the attitude of the courts where one party was in trade, whereas the other was not (see ante, para 11.02). However, in a later case between two private parties, Sellers LJ seemed to suggest that s 13 of the SGA somehow converted all descriptive statements into contractual terms.[4] However, this view was impliedly rejected in *Harlingdon & Leinster Enterprises Ltd v Christopher Hull Fine Art Ltd*:[5]

---

9   Eg, *Grenfell v EB Meyrowitz Ltd* [1936] 2 All ER 1313, CA. Compare *Andrews Ltd v Singer & Co Ltd* (above) and *Morris Motors Ltd v Lilley* [1959] 3 All ER 737 (new cars). See also an auctioneer's system of painting attribution: Harvey and Meisel, *Auctions* (2nd edn), p 341. What is the effect of dealers registering new cars as sold by them simply to qualify for a manufacturer's bonus? Or when he has already contracted to supply the goods to another on sale or return? See also OFT, 1992-AR, 13. As to implied terms annexed by trade usage, see post, para 15.11.

10 See *Peter Darlington Ltd v Gosho Ltd* [1964] 1 Lloyd's Rep 149. What of 'low alcohol beer' supplied in response to a request for 'alcohol-free' drink? See further, the discussion on mistake, post, para 17.11.

11 Eg, hoover (for vacuum cleaner); biro (for ball point pen). What about 'woollies' as a mere description of knitted garments, regardless of fibre?

[13.11A]

1   As to when words may amount to a trade description for the purpose of criminal liability under the TDA, see ante, para 4.07.

2   For mistake as to identity of subject matter, see ante, para 10.16; and for mistake as to quality, see ante, para 10.17 and post, para 17.11.

3   Eg, *Harrison v Knowles and Foster* [1918] 1 KB 608, CA. For misrepresentation, see post, para 17.10.

4   *Beale v Taylor* (set out ante, para 13.10) It has even been suggested that all express statements which 'constitute a substantial ingredient in identity' are conditions: *per* Scott LJ delivering the unanimous judgment of the CA in *Couchman v Hill* [1947] KB 554 at 559. *Sed quaere?*

5   [1991] 1 QB 564; [1990] 1 All ER 737, CA (see Brown 106 LQR 561; Snaith 140 NLJ 1672; Bentil 8 Tr L 25; Adams [1990] JBL 433.

D was an art dealer. In 1984, he was asked to sell two monogrammed oil paintings which had been described in a 1980 auction catalogue as being by Münter, an artist of the German expressionist school. As D specialised in British contemporary art, he took the paintings to P, who ran a gallery specialising in the German expressionist school. D made it clear to P that he was not an expert in this class of painting. P bought them for £6,000 without further enquiries, D's invoice describing the paintings as by Münter. The paintings were subsequently discovered to be forgeries. P sought to recover the price on grounds of breach of ss 13(1) and 14(2).

On the s 13(1) issue[6] the Court of Appeal found for D, holding that for a s 13 undertaking to arise, the parties had first to evince a common intention that the description was part of the contract under the ordinary rules,[7] whereas here D's disclaimer of expert knowledge helped to show that P was not relying upon him and hence did not intend the seller's description[8] to become part of the contract.[9] *A fortiori*, a patent misdescription by a seller of goods which are in the presence of the parties will not normally become part of the contract because the parties will have evinced an intention to contract for *those* goods, regardless of description, eg, goods sold 'as seen'.[10]

[13.12] The extent of the duty. Assuming the descriptive words amount to a contractual promise, the extent of that duty is dependent on the degree of precision of description:[1] if the description is vague, the duty may be minimal;[2] and the better the description,[3] the more onerous the duty.[4] Thus, in *Arcos Ltd v Ronaasen & Son*:[5]

There was a contract for the sale of a quantity of staves of half inch thickness. The buyer purported to reject the staves delivered on the grounds that they did not comply with the contract description. The arbitrator found that only 5% of the staves were of half inch thickness, but that the rest were nearly all less than 9/16 inch thick. Moreover, the staves

---

6   As to the s 14(2) issue, see post, paras 14.19; 14.21. As to *caveat emptor*, see post, para 15.22. No claims for misrepresentation was possible because (i) D reasonably believed the paintings were by Munter and (ii) P had resold them.

7   See ante, para 11.03. Is this another facet of the identity test (see post, para 13.13)? See Brown, *op cit*. If so, then presumably the description amounted to a mere puff (see ante, para 11.01). As to mistakes as to quality (see post, para 17.11), see Snaith, *op cit*, note 5.

8   The CA do not seem to have addressed the point that the monogram described the painting. Nor did they mention *Beale v Taylor*, when the goods also described themselves (see ante, para 13.10).

9   Stuart Smith LJ dissented on the inference of intention to be drawn from the facts (QB at 580 D–F). It follows from the majority rules (supported by Adams, *op cit*, note 5; Bentil, *op cit*, note 5, p 30) that there could be no question of any misrepresentation (see ante, para 11.02) because of the absence of reliance by P, nor of an express warranty as to description. Cf the apparently much more easily satisfied reliance test in the undertaking as to fitness: see post, para 14.13.

10 See *Benjamin's Sale of Goods* (5th edn), para 11-011 ('as such').

[13.12]

1   This may particularly be the case with contracts for work and materials, eg, servicing a car, as it may not be known in advance what needs to be done: Woodroffe, *Goods and Services – the New Law*, para 3.18.

2   A statutory minimum description has been suggested for used cars: Borrie [1987] JBL at 440. As to where a supplier offered to supply his choice from a list, see [1995] 11 Which? 6.

3   Eg, auction catalogues (see ante, para 10.10). Many commercial sales are made against detailed specifications or according to elaborate definitions, eg, of chemical composition or engineering characteristics.

4   Eg, 'new car': see *Andrews Bros Ltd v Singer & Co Ltd* [1934] 1 KB 17, CA; *Raynham Farm Co Ltd v Symbol Motor Corp Ltd* [1987] CLY 447; and cf TDA, s 2 (see ante, para 4.08). The contract itself may expressly provide for changes in description, eg, 'subject to alterations in our supplier's specifications'.

5   [1933] AC 470; [1933] All ER Rep 646, HL.

were required to the knowledge of the seller, to make cement barrels; and the arbitrator found that they were fit for this purpose, and that they were commercially within and merchantable under the contract description. He therefore held that the buyer was not entitled to reject.

The decision was reversed by Wright J, who was unanimously upheld by the Court of Appeal and the House of Lords. Lord Atkin said (at 479–80):

> It was contended that in all commercial contracts the question was whether there was 'substantial' compliance with the contract: there must always be some margin; and it is for the tribunal of fact to determine whether the margin is exceeded or not. I cannot agree. If the written contract specifies conditions of weight, measurement and the like, those conditions must be complied with. A ton does not mean about a ton, or a yard about a yard. Still less when you descend to minute measurements does half an inch mean about 1/2 inch. If the seller wants a margin he must, and in my experience does, stipulate for it ...

> No doubt there may be microscopic deviations which businessmen and therefore lawyers will ignore ... But, apart from this consideration, the right view is that the conditions of the contract must be strictly performed.

The net effect is that, in relation to contractual descriptions (see ante, para 13.11A), there are now three classes of misdescription:

1 De minimis *rule (microscopic deviations)* which the courts will ignore (see above). Whilst primarily used in relation to undertakings as to quantity (see ante, para 13.04), in principle the law ought to be willing to ignore microscopic deviations as to descriptive quality,[6] though much should depend on the degree of accuracy reasonable in that contract.[7]

2 *'Slight breaches'* can only be treated by a commercial buyer as grounds a claim in damages (see ante, para 11.05A): this might reverse the actual decision in the *Arcos* case (see above). A similar result may be achievable at common law by the doctrine of substantial performance (see post, para 26.02).

3 *Other cases.* The implied condition that goods comply with their description may well in practice overlap with the undertakings as to fitness and quality (as to which, see Chapter 14)[8] and any relevant sample provisions (see post, para 15.06). However it is likely to be particularly important where there is no such overlap, as where there is a private supplier;[9] or the desired quality is not within the undertakings of fitness or quality;[10] or where those undertakings are excluded whilst the implied condition as to description is not (see post, para 13.16). In practice, the misdescription cases tend to fall into one of two categories: (a) where the misdescription alters the identity of the goods (see post, para 13.13); (b) non-identifying misdescriptions (see post, para 13.15).

---

6 *Steels & Busks Ltd v Bleeker Bike Co Ltd* [1956] 1 Lloyd's Rep 228 (sale of crepe rubber; preservation chemical ignored). In the consumer context, this might apply to small discrepancies in the size of vegetables or garments. See generally Atiyah, *Sale of Goods* (10th edn), pp 133, 153–55.

7 *The Troll Park* [1988] 2 Lloyd's Rep 423, CA. In this a test of fitness for the purpose supplied?

8 Eg, the *Albright and Wilson* case (set out ante, para 13.01), at para 32. Examples given by *Benjamin's Sale of Goods* (5th edn), para 11.017 include unsuitable 'baby food', 'cough mixture', 'cold cure'.

9 Eg, *Beale v Taylor* (set out ante, para 13.10).

10 Eg, *Arcos Ltd v Ronaasen & Son* (above). Atiyah, *Sale of Goods* (9th edn), p 124 gives the example of a suit sold as 'pure wool'.

[13.13] The identity test. The leading case on the scope of the implied statutory condition that the goods comply with their description is *Ashington Piggeries Ltd v Christopher Hill Ltd*:[1]

> The plaintiff manufacturers habitually undertook the compounding of animal feedstuffs to customers' formulae. The defendants asked the plaintiffs to compound a vitamin-fortified mink food, to be called King Size, in accordance with a formula to be supplied by the defendants. The plaintiffs made it clear that they knew nothing about mink, but did suggest that herring meal should be substituted for one of the other ingredients. After making satisfactory deliveries for about 12 months, the plaintiffs began to make up the compound with herring meal purchased from N, under a contract which stipulated that it was 'fair average quality of the season' and was to be taken 'with all faults and defects ... at a valuation'. Unknown to any of the parties, that meal contained DMNA, a chemical produced in the meal by chemical reaction. DMNA was found to be harmful in some degree to all animals but particularly toxic to mink. The plaintiffs sued for the price, the defendants counter-claimed for breach of what is now the SGA, ss 13(1), 14(2) and (3) and the plaintiffs brought in N.

At this stage, we need consider only the argument on s 13.[2] The decision of Milmo J that each seller was liable to his buyer under s 13 was reversed by the Court of Appeal,[3] whose judgment was affirmed by the House of Lords.

1   *King Size*. As between the plaintiffs and defendants, their Lordships held that the compound did correspond with its description, the contract description being 'King Size, meaning thereby a food compounded in accordance with an agreed formula'. Davies LJ delivering the judgment of the Court of Appeal made the following points: first, the description did not include the suitability of the compound as a food for mink; and second, that DMNA was a condition of the herring meal, and not an additional unauthorised ingredient.[4] This view was followed by the majority of the House of Lords,[5] who contrasted this case with those where so much of a different ingredient was added as to make the goods a different commodity.[6] As Lord Wilberforce put it, the defendant's formula for King Size was commercial, not chemical.

2   *Norwegian Herring Meal*. Nor did the Court of Appeal think that there was a breach of the undertaking as to description as between the plaintiff and N: they held that the contract description was 'Norwegian Herring Meal, fair average quality of the season'; and that the goods complied therewith, because that description related only 'to such qualities as are apparent on an ordinary examination or analysis of the goods, such as is usually done in the trade in relation to such goods' (at 1519–22). The House of Lords agreed, explaining that the goods complied with their description

---

[13.13]

1   [1972] AC 441; [1971] 1 All ER 847, HL.

2   These other issues are considered post, Chapter 14, especially at paras 14.04; 14.09; 14.14.

3   [1969] 3 All ER 1496, CA.

4   At 1510–13. But see Patient (1970) 33 MLR 565, at 566.

5   Lords Hodson (at 853), Guest (at 858), Wilberforce (at 872), Diplock (at 884). Lord Dilhorne, dissenting, agreed that the matter was one of degree, but thought that the facts had crossed the line (at 868).

6   *Pinnock Bros v Lewis and Peat* [1923] 1 KB 690 (castor oil added to copra cake); *Munro & Co Ltd v Meyer* [1930] 2 KB 312 (cocoa husks added to meat and bone meal).

'Norwegian Herring Meal', whereas the contractual description 'fair average quality of the season' was not part of the s 13 implied condition because it was not needed to identify the goods.[7] Lord Guest distinguished *Arcos Ltd v Ronaasen & Son* (discussed post, paras 13.14–15), where he explained that the full description was necessary to identify the contract goods.[8]

[13.14] It is interesting to consider the *Ashington* case (set out ante, para 13.13) in the light of Benjamin's two categories of sales of goods by description (see ante, para 13.09):

(1) *Sales of unascertained or future goods.* The courts had previously applied the strict test of breach of the undertaking as exemplified in *Arcos Ltd v Ronaasen & Son* (see ante, para 13.12) to contracts for the supply of goods to consumers and trade buyers: as in a sale of 'common English sainfoin grass seed';[1] or a 'new Singer car'.[2] Further, in the case of trade buyers, the courts had previously shown themselves willing to extend the undertaking beyond the physical state of the goods: as to the size of bags containing goods;[3] the average weight of parcels;[4] the date of the arrival of a ship in which the goods were being transported;[5] and that the goods have been shipped under-deck[6] or packed in the wrong multiples.[7]

(2) *Sales of specific goods.* In *Varley v Whipp*:[8]

> The defendant agreed to buy a second-hand reaping machine then owned by a third party, which the defendant had never seen, but which the plaintiff seller stated to have been 'new the previous year' and very little used. On discovering that the machine did not comply with this description, the defendant returned the reaper to the plaintiff. Channell J held that there was a breach of s 13.

A similar approach was taken with an advertised '1961 Triumph Herald'[9] and is presumably applicable to such mundane consumer matters as the sizing of clothing, domestic equipment or furniture.[10]

---

7 Lords Hodson (at 856), Guest (at 860), Wilberforce (at 877), Diplock (at 890). Lord Dilhorne, dissenting, agreed that for the purposes of the undertaking, the description was only 'Norwegian Herring Meal', but thought that the goods did not comply with that description by reason of the presence of DMNA (at 869).

8 He expressly agreed that a qualitative description could be within the undertaking, as in *Varley v Whipp* (set out post, para 13.14).

[13.14]

1 *Wallis Son & Wells v Pratt and Haynes* (set out ante, para 11.04).

2 *Andrews Brothers (Bournemouth) Ltd v Singer & Co Ltd* [1934] 1 KB 17, CA.

3 *Manbre Saccharine Co Ltd v Corn Products Ltd* [1919] 1 KB 198.

4 *Ballantine & Co v Cramp and Bosman* [1923] 129 LT 502.

5 *Macpherson Train & Co Ltd v Ross & Co Ltd* [1955] 2 All ER 445.

6 *White Sea Trust Timber Ltd v North Ltd* [1933] 148 LT 263. See also *Fisher, Reeves & Co v Armour Co* [1920] 3 KB 614, CA (ex-store).

7 *Re Moore Ltd* [1921] 2 KB 519, CA.

8 [1900] 1 QB 513. It is difficult to reconcile this decision with ss 11(4) and 18 of the SGA: see post, para 20.08. For other points raised by this case, see post, paras 20.02; 20.03.

9 *Beale v Taylor* (set out ante, para 13.10)

10 Cf TDA, s 2(1)(a): see ante, para 4.06.

In the light of the *Ashington* case, the difficulty is to judge the extent to which the foregoing cases are still good law (see post, para 13.15).

[13.15] Of course, a contractual description may always amount to an **express condition** under the ordinary rules for classifying terms (see ante, para 11.04). However, where this is not the case, the *Ashington Piggeries* case (set out ante, para 13.13) clearly establishes an identity test as to whether or not an **express term** amounts to an **implied condition** (see ante, para 13.11).

Descriptive words may identify the contract goods with different degrees of precision (see ante, para 13.12), though it does seem from that case that the test is a commercial one,[1] with the courts ignoring an obscure chemical reaction, albeit a disastrous one.[2] On the one hand, it might be argued that only those elements in the description which delineate the **commercial class or kind** within which the goods belong should be within the undertaking (eg, a garment with a wrong size label), in which case a small amount of another ingredient would not breach it.[3] On the other hand, **any matter** delineating the contract goods might be within the undertaking, so that even a small amount of another ingredient would, unless *de minimis*, breach the undertaking.[4] A third possibility is that the former test applies to specific goods, whilst the latter is apposite to unascertained goods.[5] Yet this last distinction seems undermined by the wide view of identity taken by Stuart-Smith LJ:[6]

> Every item in a description which constitutes a substantial ingredient in the 'identity' of the thing being sold is a condition ... That the identity of the artist who painted a picture can be a substantial ingredient in the identity of the thing sold seems to be beyond question.

Even if the former, narrow view, of the undertaking is taken, this does not necessarily deprive other descriptive statements of all effect.[7] The words may amount to an express condition or warranty as to description;[8] or an express or implied undertaking as to fitness or quality;[9] or a remedy may be available on grounds of misrepresentation.[10]

[13.15]

1 Eg, the way the courts approach samples: see post, para 15.06.

2 Atiyah, *Sale of Goods* (10th edn), p 154.

3 This narrower test seems to be supported by *Benjamin's Sale of Goods* (5th edn), para 11.018, citing *Reardon Smith Line Ltd v Hansen-Tangen* [1976] 3 All ER 570, HL, *per* Lord Wilberforce at 576f (describing some of the authorities as 'excessively technical and due for fresh examination in this House'). See also *Tradex Export SA v European Grain & Shipping Ltd* [1983] 2 Lloyd's Rep 100.

4 This wider test seems to be supported by Atiyah, *Sale of Goods* (6th edn), pp 94–95; but compare his 10th edn, p 152.

5 See further Goode, *Commercial Law* (2nd edn), p 304 *et seq*. As to specific goods, see generally post, para 20.02.

6 In *Harlingdon & Leinster Enterprises Ltd v Christopher Hull Fine Arts Ltd* (set out ante, para 13.11A) at AER 747b.

7 See Atiyah, *op cit*, note 2 (10th edn), p 147.

8 Eg, the statement 'fair average quality of the season' in the contract between the plaintiff and N in the *Ashington Piggeries* case (above); *Trasimex Holdings SA v Addex BV, The Red Sea* [1991] 1 Lloyd's Rep 28, CA.

9 See Atiyah, *op cit*, note 2, p 151; Benjamin, *op cit*, note 3, para 11-016 *et seq*.

10 Eg, *Harrison v Knowles and Foster* [1918] 1 KB 608, CA; *Howard Marine & Dredging Co v Ogden (Excavations) Ltd* (set out post, para 17.10); and see ante, para 13.11.

[13.16] Exclusion. In the case of supplies falling within Part I of UCTA, there are severe statutory limitations on the supplier's power to exclude or restrict undertakings as to compliance with description: where the transferee deals as consumer, any exclusion or restriction is void; and in other cases the clause is subject to the test of reasonableness.[1] Suppose the contract labels express terms as to description as only being warranties in the technical sense. Insofar as that express description is within both the statutory undertakings as going to the identity of the subject matter (see ante, para 13.13) and UCTA (see above), the foregoing statutory consequences obviously apply,[2] though there remains the issue of the effect of designating other parts of the contractual description as a warranty. In a consumer contract, it might be possible to ignore such a non-core express provision as being an unfair term;[3] but in a non-consumer contract the position is as follows. Where there is a slight breach, the express provision merely re-enforces the amended SGA (new s 15A: see ante, para 11.05A); and, in other cases matters seem to be left to the common law.[4] Thus, the clause will be construed strictly as against the proferens;[5] but a distinction must also be drawn between those clauses which exclude and those which limit liability: the clause may either prevent any obligation from arising or merely limit liability for breach of an obligation once it has arisen (see post, para 18.03). If the contract goods are unascertained, an attempt to exclude all undertakings as to description would destroy any certainty of subject matter;[6] but this argument would not obtain where the contract goods are specific.[7] Thus, if the only objection to clauses excluding undertakings as to description was on grounds of certainty of subject matter,[8] the position would appear to be as follows: the seller could always limit his liability; he could exclude it where the contract was for the sale of specific goods;[9] and, even where the contract was for the sale of unascertained goods, he could probably exclude liability for such trivial breaches as those which occurred in *Arcos Ltd v Ronaasen & Son*.[10]

[13.16]

1 UCTA, ss 6(2)(3), 7(2), (3): see further post, para 18.19.

2 Because the designation as 'warranty' is intended to 'restrict ... a remedy' (s 13(1)(b)): see post, para 18.16.

3 UTCC Regulations, reg 5 (see ante, para 11.14) and Grey List terms (b) and (q) (see ante, paras 11.16; 11.18).

4 The general common law rules for dealing with exclusion clauses are considered post, para 18.02 *et seq*.

5 See *Munro & Co v Meyer* [1930] 2 KB 312; *Harrison v Knowles and Foster* [1918] 1 KB 608, CA; *Nicholson and Venn v Smith-Marriott* [1947] 177 LT 189; *Christopher Hill Ltd v Ashington Piggeries Ltd* [1969] 3 All ER 1496, CA, at 1522–23 (the exclusion clause in the contract between the plaintiffs and N). For the *proferens*, see post, para 18.06.

6 See *Benjamin on Sale* (8th edn), pp 622–23. *Contra* Yates and Hawkins, *Standard Business Contracts* 231.

7 *Hughes v Hall* [1981] RTR 430 at 437F, *per* Donaldson LJ (sold as seen and inspected); *Cavendish-Woodhouse v Manley* (1984) 82 LGR 376, DC (bought as seen).

8 See *First Report on Exclusion Clauses in Contracts* (1969, Law Com No 24) para 21: see further post, para 18.07.

9 Goode, *Commercial Law* (2nd edn), p 311.

10 See Atiyah, *Sale of Goods* (10th edn), p 148. As to the manner in which auction houses deal with deliberate forgeries, see Harvey and Meisel, *Auctions* (2nd edn), p 163 *et seq*.

CHAPTER 14

UNDERTAKINGS AS TO FITNESS AND SATISFACTORY QUALITY

SCOPE OF UNDERTAKINGS

[14.01] Introduction. There has never been anything to prevent the parties from inserting in their contract express promises as to fitness and quality **more** onerous than the statutory implied terms.[1] But any attempt to insert **less** onerous terms is likely to amount to an exclusion clause (see post, para 14.02. As to criminal liability in relation to trade descriptions, see ante, para 4.02 *et seq*).

The SGA 1893 probably narrowed the scope of the common law maxim *caveat emptor* (see ante, para 13.08) by providing that, subject to a contrary intention and leaving aside sales by sample (see post, paras 15.03–10), there shall be implied into a contract of sale three conditions[2] – as to description, merchantable quality and fitness for the purposes supplied[3] – and an implied warranty as to trade usage (see post, para 15.11). It has been pointed out that these three implied conditions represent a series of graduated duties.[4] The undertaking as to correspondence with description offers the buyer only minimal statutory protection, but applies to almost all sales (see ante, paras 13.09–10), whereas the other two undertakings apply only to trade sales (see post, para 14.04). Thus, the undertaking as to quality (now termed 'satisfactory quality') affords a greater degree of protection to the buyer, though it does not cover such a wide area: trade sold goods may correspond with their description and still not be of a high enough quality.[5] The greatest degree of protection is that afforded by the undertaking as to fitness, which applies in still more limited circumstances: this undertaking may be broken even though trade sold goods correspond with their description and are of a high enough quality.[6] Even within the foregoing restrictions, all three implied undertakings leave open some issues of policy. Thus, the level at which each of them should be pitched is a matter of judgment,[7] including such factors as nationally desired standards of quality control by manufacturers.[8]

[14.01]

1   Eg, a scheme run for classified advertisements (see [1999] 8 Which? 6). Express detailed specifications are common in large engineering contracts. For express terms, see generally ante, para 11.07, *et seq*; post, para 15.22; and Atiyah, *Sale of Goods* (10th edn), p 140.

2   As to the content of the conditions (as opposed to when they were applicable) it would seem that the SGA 1893 largely reproduced the common law: where there was a sale by description (see ante, para 13.09), there was an implied condition that the goods were merchantable under their description; and where there was a sale of specific goods there might be an undertaking as to fitness.

3   See *per* Lord Buckmaster in *Manchester Liners Ltd v Rea Ltd* [1922] 2 AC 74, HL, at 79. For conditions generally, see ante, para 11.04; and for implied terms, see generally ante, para 11.10.

4   Atiyah, *op cit*, note 1, 138.

5   Eg, the *Ashington Piggeries* case (set out ante, para 13.13), the contract between P and D.

6   Eg, the *Ashington Piggeries* case (above), the contract between N and P.

7   The undertakings cover both new and second-hand goods: *Bartlett v Sidney Marcus Ltd* [1965] 2 All ER 753, CA.

8   See *Sale and Supply of Goods* (1983, Law Com Working Paper No 85), para 3.3.

At a later date, these undertakings were re-enacted for sale in an amended form; and similar undertakings have been imported by statute into quasi-sales, simple hirings and hp (see ante, para 12.01). The EU have adopted a Directive designed to harmonise the laws of Member States by giving additional protections to consumers over and above the ordinary national ones.[9] This is to be implemented in the UK by Regulations[10] made under the ECA (see ante, para 1.03A). These Regulations will make a substantial difference as follows:

(1) *Statutory implied promises.* Largely confirming the above major statutory implied terms in supply contracts,[11] the Regulations will amend those statutes as from 2002 to give the following: special provisions as to the durability of the undertakings; suing back up the chain of distribution (see post, paras 14.06; 17.07); exclusion clauses (see post, paras 18.10; 18.15); and additional remedies (see post, para 29.03A) to a 'consumer'.[12]

(2) *Express statements.* As regards non-conformity of goods supplied to a 'consumer'[12] with express statements made by the manufacturer, the Regulations will enhance the remedies available to the consumer as against (a) his supplier (see post, para 29.01) or (b) that manufacturer ('guarantees': see post, para 17.09A).

Besides the ordinary remedies (see Chapter 29), it is now possible to obtain Stop Now Orders in respect of these breaches (see post, para 28.03).

[14.02] Scope of the undertakings: common limitations. In this chapter, the two undertakings as to fitness and quality will be considered separately below. However, before so doing, it is convenient to mention several points which they have in common:

(1) *Exclusivity of undertakings.* Apart from undertakings mentioned (see ante, para 14.01), there are no other statutory implied undertakings applicable to any supply of goods (see post, para 15.22), though there is nothing to prevent the supplier giving an express promise to similar effect (see ante, para 14.01).

(2) *Goods supplied.* This phrase in the statutory implied terms extends beyond the subject-matter of the contract to include any goods supplied under the contract (see post, para 14.03) and any label[1] or instructions for use (see below).

(3) *Trade suppliers.* The undertakings are limited to contracts made by trade suppliers (see post, para 14.04), but indifferent as to whether or not their customers are in business –

---

9   Directive on the Sale of Goods and Associated Guarantees 99/44/EC, Arts 1(1), 8. As to publicity, see Art 9.

10   Sale of Goods to Consumers Regulations 2002. The UK has already passed the implementation date: see ante, para 1.03A.

11   As to the implied terms as to conformity with description (see ante, para 13.11); as to fitness (see post, para 14.07); and as to satisfactory quality (see post, para 14.15).

12   '"Consumer" means any natural person who in the contracts covered by this Directive, is acting for purposes which are not directly related to his trade, business or profession' (Art 1(2)(a)); 'seller' covers any trade seller, whether a natural or legal person (Art 1(2)(c); and 'consumer goods' includes any tangible moveable goods, present or future (unless sold by way of execution), except wholesales of water or gas or electricity, or perhaps some sales of second-hand goods by auction (Art 1(2)(b), (3), (4)). Cf the UTCC Regulation definition of 'consumer': see ante, para 11.12A.

[14.02]

1   *Niblett v Confectioners' Materials Co* (set out ante, para 12.03); the *Albright and Wilson* case (set out ante, para 13.01), at para 35.

a matter relevant to exclusion clauses (see below) and remedies (see new s 15A: set out ante, para 11.05A).

(4) *Unprepared goods.* If it is contemplated that something be done to the goods by the transferee before use, eg, assembly, the goods must conform with the statutory undertakings after, though not necessarily before, this has been done.[2] However, in that circumstance, it may be that any instructions for preparation or assembly of the goods themselves become part of the goods for the purposes of the undertakings, eg, cooking or assembly instructions (see further post, para 18.28, *et seq*).

(5) *Partial non-compliance* (see post, para 14.05).

(6) *Congeries of defects.* In the Scottish case of *Pollock v Macrae*[3] the marine engine supplied was held to have 'such a congeries of defects as to destroy the workable character of the machine' and took the goods outside the ambit of an exclusion clause.[4] This notion that minor defects each in themselves insubstantial may be taken together and the effect of the total considered was subsequently imported into English law to support the development of the doctrine of fundamental breach.[5] This last doctrine having been subsequently set aside (see post, para 18.07), the concept of a congeries of defects ought for English law to be relevant only as follows: bearing in mind that partial non-compliance breaches the undertakings (see post, para 14.05), whereas any matters *de minimis* are to be ignored (see ante, para 13.12), presumably a congeries of defects can only be a collection of minor matters, individually *de minimis*, but cumulatively amounting to a partial breach,[6] perhaps outside the construction of any exclusion clause (see below).

(7) *Durability* (see post, para 14.06).

(8) *Consumer contracts.* In a consumer supply contract, it is possible to challenge the fairness of **express terms**;[7] and there may be some enhancement of the statutory **implied terms** (see ante, para 14.01).

(9) *Exclusion.* Restrictions on the power of the supplier to exclude or limit his liability under these implied statutory undertakings by UCTA will be considered later (Chapter 18), though in a consumer supply contract such exclusions will also be unfair (Grey Term 1(b): see ante, para 11.16). It is doubtful whether the UCTA restrictions extend to certificates of compliance.[8]

(10) *Different statutes.* Remember to apply the statute appropriate for the particular type of supply contract (see ante, para 12.01).

---

2   *Heil v Hedges* [1951] 1 TLR 512 (sale of partly-cooked pork chops). As to the possible overlap with SGSA, s 13, see post, para 15.15.

3   1922 SC (HL) 192. In Scots, but not English law, there is a rule preserved by SGA, s 11(5) that the right of the innocent buyer to treat the contract as repudiated depends on whether or not there is a failure by the seller to perform any 'material part' of the contract.

4   See *Benjamin's Sale of Goods* (5th edn), para 13-049.

5   Eg, *Yeoman Credit Ltd v Apps* (set out post, para 29.25).

6   This argument may be relevant in relation to the undertaking as to satisfactory quality: see post, para 14.23.

7   See ante, para 11.12. *Contra* the statutory implied terms: UTCC Regulations, Sched 1, para (e)(i).

8   Eg, *Galaxy Energy International Ltd v Eurobunker SpA* [2001] 2 All ER (Comm) 912. See generally Schmitthoff, *Export Trade* (10th edn), 4-012/4. Distinguish arbitration agreements: see ante, para 3.23.

[14.03] Goods supplied. The two implied conditions are expressed to be applicable not just to the contract goods, but also any other goods **supplied under** the contract.[1] Thus, in *Geddling v Marsh*:[2]

> The plaintiff shopkeeper purchased bottles of mineral water from the defendant manufacturer on the basis that one penny was refundable on every bottle the shopkeeper returned to the manufacturer. Whilst the plaintiff was handling a bottle, it burst and injured her.

Despite the fact that the contract in respect of the bottles seems to have been one of hire rather than sale, the plaintiffs successfully claimed damages before the Divisional Court: Bailhache J pointed out that the goods could not be supplied except in some sort of container; and Bray J found support in the fact that the opening words of the relevant provision of the SGA (s 14) speak of 'goods supplied under the contract of sale'. A spectacular application of those statutory words by the Court of Appeal is to be found in *Wilson v Rickett Cockerell Ltd*:[3]

> The plaintiff purchased a ton of coalite from the defendant coal merchant. Subsequently, the plaintiff was injured when there was an explosion in the grate by reason of the inclusion of an explosive substance (a detonator) in the consignment.

The Court of Appeal unanimously rejected the defendant's plea that there was nothing wrong with the Coalite as Coalite. If the rules apply to (presumably) unintended extras, perhaps it also applies to 'free gifts' supplied under a contract of supply (see ante, para 2.08), in which case they too would attract the benefit of the implied undertakings as to fitness and quality under the SGA[4] or SGSA.[5]

[14.04] Trade suppliers. The two statutory undertakings now apply only to goods supplied 'in the course of a business'[1] and provide a definition of 'business'.[2] In relation to sales, this represented an extension in the ambit of the undertakings. The apparently restrictive wording of the SGA 1893 (suggesting just supplies of stock-in-trade) had already been extended in the *Ashington Piggeries* case[3] to any across-the-counter supply.[4]

[14.03]

1   SGA, ss 14(2) and (3). Identical language is employed in the other enactments applicable to supplies of goods: see SOGIT, ss 10(2) and (3); SGSA, ss 4(2) and (5), 9(2) and (5). Cf CPA, s 46(1): see ante, para 4.34.

2   [1920] 1 KB 668; [1920] All ER Rep 631, DC. See also *Niblett's* case (set out ante, para 12.03).

3   [1954] 1 QB 598; [1954] 1 All ER 868, CA.

4   See the *Second Report on Exemption Clauses* (1975, Law Com No 69) para 35.

5   It could amount to a quasi-sale (see post, para 15.12) or be left to the common law (see post, para 15.25).

[14.04]

1   This phrase is also found in UCTA s 12(1)(b): see post, para 18.18. Cf the TDA, FTA, CCA: see respectively ante, paras 4.03; 4.19; 5.18; and Lunn and Miles (1996) 15 Tr LR 120. *Contra* trade usage: see post, para 15.11.

2   'Business' is defined so that it 'includes a profession and any activities of any government department or local public authority': SGA, s 61(1); SOGIT, s 15(1); SGSA, s 18(1). See further *Benjamin's Sale of Goods* (5th edn), para 11-046. Is the effect that the SGSA now extends to faulty devices fitted by a surgeon?

3   Set out ante, para 13.13: the supply of King Size by P.

4   Benjamin, *op cit*, note 2, para 11-045.

It would seem that trade supplies include both the last sale in a business[5] and supplies by part-time traders.[6] Indeed, it has since been held that the present statutory formulation has extended the ambit still further to any goods which go through a dealer's business books.[7] In *Stevenson v Rogers*:[8]

> R had been a fisherman for some 20 years. In 1988, he sold his sea-going fishing boat, the *Jelle*, which he had owned for some three years. Finding the *Jelle* defective, the buyer (S), as a preliminary issue, had to show that the sale was a sale 'in the course of a business' within s 14(2) of the SGA. The trial judge held that the *Jelle* was not sold 'in the course of a business', relying on *Davies v Sumner* (set out ante, para 4.03A) and the *R & B Customs Brokers* case (set out post, para 18.18).

In the Court of Appeal, the leading judgment allowing S's appeal was delivered by Potter LJ. Having reviewed the legislative history of s 14(2), his Lordship applied the mischief rule (at 624e: see ante, para 1.04) to find that the words were simply used 'to distinguish between a sale made in the course of the seller's business and a purely private sale of goods outside the confines of the business (if any) carried on by the seller' (at 623j). He explained the narrower interpretation of sales of stock in *Davies v Sumner* as being appropriate in a criminal case (at 624h); and he distinguished the civil *R & B Customs* case as involving another statute, UCTA (at 625d). He explained (at 625–26):

> As to the proper construction of s 14(2), given the clear view which I have formed, I do not consider it right to displace that construction simply to achieve harmony with a decision upon the meaning of s 12 of UCTA 1977. Section 14(2) ... was itself a piece of consumer protection intended to afford wider protection to a buyer than that provided in the 1893 Act. Indeed, there is a sense in which the decision in *R & B Customs* case can be said to be in harmony with that intention. It dealt with the position of consumer **buyers** and the effect of adopting the construction propounded in *Davies'* case in relation to s 12(1)(a) of UCTA 1977 was to further such buyers' protection.

As to sales by a private seller through a trade agent, see post, para 14.04A.

[14.04A] Trade agents. It is clear that the undertakings as to fitness and quality will not normally attach to a supply by a person in his private capacity (see ante, para 14.04), though it should be remembered that it is an offence to disguise a business sale as a private one.[1] By way of exception to that trade-supplies-only rule, the undertakings are applicable if a private supplier-principal chooses to use a business agent, eg, an auctioneer, to find a client. Thus, s 14(5) of the SGA provides:

> The preceding provisions of this section apply to a sale by a person who in the course of a business is acting as agent for another as they apply to a sale by a principal in the course of a business, except where that other is not selling in the course of a business and either the buyer knows that fact or reasonable steps are taken to bring it to the notice of the buyer before the contract is made.

---

5   *Buchanan-Jardine v Hamlink* 1983 SLT 149 (stock sold off as part of a sale of business).
6   For moonlighters, see Woodroffe, *Goods and Services – the New Law*, para 3.23.
7   *Contra* the test under UCTA, s 12(1)(a): see post, para 18.18.
8   [1999] 2 QB 1028; [1999] 1 All ER 613, CA (Brown (1999) 115 LQR 384, who asks whether this case extends to some amateur sellers, eg, a car-boot sale, a bring-and-buy sale?).

[14.04A]
1   Eg, a business selling bankrupt stock at a car-boot sale (see ante, para 4.22).

A similar provision is to be found in the case of quasi-sales, hp and simple hirings.[2] It has been argued that, in the above provision, the phrase 'sale by a person' makes the agent liable for breach of the implied terms in the supply contract;[3] but this view was rejected in *Boyter v Thomson*:[4]

> T was the owner of a cabin cruiser. T instructed HML to sell the cruiser under their brokerage scheme. The cruiser was sold by HML in the course of their business to B, but was found to be unseaworthy and the parties agreed she was unfit for the purpose for which she was purchased. It was found as a fact that B thought HML was the seller, so that it was a sale by an undisclosed private principal (T: see ante, para 10.06) through a business agent (HML).

Now, if the private seller (T) had sold the cruiser himself, he could not be liable under s 14; but the House of Lords held T liable by reason of the above s 14(5).[5] In delivering the judgment of the court, Lord Jauncy said:[6]

> In my view, sub-s (5) is applicable to any sale by an agent on behalf of a principal, whether disclosed or undisclosed, where the circumstances giving rise to the exception do not exist.

Thus, the fact that the supplier-principal putting his goods up for auction is acting as a private person will not relieve him from the undertakings, except where

(a) he is not in fact supplying in the course of business; **and**

(b) prior to contracting the transferee knows this fact or reasonable steps have been taken to bring it to his notice.[7]

In view of the uncertainty as to what will amount to sufficient notice to take a case outside s 14(5), it has been argued that, at least for a consumer-buyer, it would be preferable if an auctioneer were liable on the statutory implied terms.[8]

[14.05] Partial non-compliance. The buyer will *prima facie* be able to reject the goods where only part of them do not comply with the undertakings, except in the following circumstances: (a) the contract is severable; or (b) the *de minimis* rule applies. Both exceptions were considered in *Jackson v Rotax Motor and Cycle Co*:[1]

> A contract for the sale of about 600 motor horns allowed for delivery in 19 cases at varying dates over a period of two months. Upon delivery of the last case, the buyer inspected the goods, and he thereupon determined to reject the whole of them, except for one case which he had legally accepted by reason of his having resold it. The buyer alleged that 364 horns

---

2   SOGIT, s 10(5); SGSA, ss 4(8), 9(8). The SOGIT amended provision refers to 'credit-broker'. Does the amended version apply even to unregulated agreements?

3   Atiyah, *Sale of Goods* (10th edn), p 160.

4   [1995] 2 AC 629; [1995] 3 All ER 135, HL(s) (see Brown (1996) 112 LQR 225).

5   On the basis that T had given express authority to sell to HML: see generally ante, para 10.06.

6   At 138d. Because HML was contracting for an undisclosed principal, B could have sued HML under s 14 of the SGA. *Contra*, if T had been disclosed, but unnamed. See generally Fridman, *Law of Agency* (7th edn), p 253 *et seq*.

7   As to the extent to which auctioneers do this, see Harvey and Meisel, *Auctions* (2nd edn), p 153. As to where the private seller forbids the agent from disclosing his status, see Brown (1996) 112 LQR at 228–29.

8   Brown (1996) 112 LQR at 229. As to auctioneers, see generally ante, para 10.11.

[14.05]

1   [1910] 2 KB 937, CA.

were defective; but the official referee found that the horns were substantially in accordance with the contract, and that 'most if not all ... could at a very slight cost have been made merchantable'.

The Court of Appeal unanimously held that the contract was divisible (set post, para 23.24), so that acceptance of one case did not bar rejection of the others (see post, para 29.08), and that the goods were not of merchantable quality so that the buyer might reject them. Their Lordships rejected the attempt to apply the *de minimis* rule (see ante, para 13.12) and said that if the buyer had to expend money on the goods to make them saleable, albeit a trifling amount, there was a breach of the undertaking.[2] Subsequently, doubt would appear to have been cast on this last finding.[3]

[14.06] Durability. There is the question of for how long after delivery the goods must continue to comply with the undertaking. The common law took the view that the goods ought to comply with the undertaking for long enough for the buyer to deal with them in the ordinary way of business;[1] but, for some time after the passage of the SGA 1893, it was thought that this rule might have been abrogated by s 33 of that Act.[2] In *Mash and Murrell Ltd v Joseph I Emmanuel Ltd*:[3]

> The plaintiff dealer contracted to buy c & f from the defendant 2,000 half-bags of Cyprus Spring potatoes then afloat the SS Ionian bound for Liverpool. The seller knew that the potatoes were required for human consumption. After a normal voyage, the goods were found on arrival to be unfit for human consumption; and the buyer alleged breach of the undertakings as to fitness and merchantability.

Having held as a fact that the potatoes were not fit to travel to Liverpool when they were loaded in Cyprus (inherent vice), Diplock J decided that there had been a breach of both undertakings. His Lordship explained (at 493):

> A necessarily and inevitable deterioration during transit which will render [the goods] unmerchantable upon arrival is normally one for which the seller is liable.

This decision concerns natural produce[4] and was reversed by the Court of Appeal simply on the grounds that there was insufficient evidence on which Diplock J could have based his finding of fact.[5]

Whilst some thought that this and subsequent decisions demonstrate a clear requirement of durability in the undertakings,[6] it was recommended that the matter be

---

2   See Cozens Hardy MR at 943. The contract price was £450 and the repairs cost £35 (= 7.7%).
3   *Cehave v Bremer* (set out ante, para 11.05). The issue would appear to need HL resolution.
[14.06]
1   *Beer v Walker* (1877) 46 LJQB 677.
2   This section deals with risk of deterioration during ordinary transit, but not inherent vice: see post, para 22.05.
3   [1961] 1 All ER 485; rev [1962] 1 All ER 77, CA.
4   Where manufactured goods are concerned, the issue may occur somewhat differently, eg, whether there is a design or manufacturing defect rendering the goods insufficiently durable; but in some such cases it may be possible to show that the goods were thereby rendered defective at the moment of retail delivery.
5   The burden of proof is discussed by Sassoon (1965) 28 MLR 180, 191–92; and see further below.
6   *Lambert v Lewis* (set out post, para 17.06); *Crowther v Shannon Motor Co* [1975] 1 All ER 139, CA; and see Atiyah, *Sale of Goods* (10th edn), pp 181–82. *Contra* Hudson (1978) 94 LQR 566.

put beyond doubt by statute.[7] Accordingly, in 1994 it was enacted that, *inter alia*, the quality of the goods includes their durability.[8] Two issues arise:

(1) At what moment in time should the undertakings be tested? A test of the time when property passes might suit sale and quasi-sale, whilst relating the test to the time of delivery would suit also hp and simply hirings.[9]

(2) For how long must the goods last? According to Benjamin:[10]

> In principle durability is an aspect of quality on delivery: goods are not of satisfactory quality at that time unless they are capable of enduring for a period reasonable in the circumstances, and the fact that they seriously deteriorate or (for example) break down during such a period is evidence that they were not of satisfactory quality.

Plainly, this is a question of fact, which will vary from one circumstance to another, eg, it may depend on the price of the goods, whether or not they are second-hand, a declared 'shelf-life'. Moreover, in some cases further uncertainty may be caused by the supplier arguing that the lack of durability is due to the way in which the goods have been treated after delivery.

These uncertainties in the issue of durability have been thought to be inimical to the consumer interest. In an attempt to reduce them, an EU Directive provides that in a consumer supply:[11]

> The seller shall be liable for any lack of conformity which exists when the goods are delivered to the consumer and which becomes manifest within a period of two years unless, at the moment of conclusion of the contract of sale, the consumer knew or could not have been unaware of the lack of conformity.

Unless proved otherwise, any lack of conformity which becomes apparent within six months of delivery will usually be presumed to have existed at the time of delivery (Art 5(3)); and to take advantage of these durability rules, the consumer will probably have to notify his supplier within two months of discovering the defect.[12]

Additionally, there may sometimes be offered optional product insurance for an extended period (see post, para 17.09). Further, there must be distinguished from the durability of the implied terms the length of time during which the transferee may rescind for breach (see post, paras 29.04–29.10).

---

7   *Implied Terms in Contracts for the Supply of Goods* (1979, Law Com No 95) paras 113–14; *Sale and Supply of Goods* (1987, Law Com No 160), paras 3.47–3.61.

8   SGA 1979, s 14(2B)(e), as inserted by the SSGA 1994, s 1: set out post, para 14.20. In respect of hp, quasi-sales and simple hirings, the 1994 Act also inserted identical provisions in SOGIT, s 10(2B)(e); and the SGSA, s 18(3)(3).

9   See *Benjamin's Sale of Goods* (5th edn), para 11.062. Cf *Vikase Ltd v Paul Kiefel GmbH* [1999] 3 All ER 362, CA, esp *per* Chadwick LJ at paras 16 and 20 (case on Civil Jurisdiction and Judgments Act 1982, Sched 1, Art 5(2)).

10 Benjamin, *ibid*, para 11.052; [2001] 2 Which? 6.

11 Sale of Goods and Associated Guarantees 99/44/EC (see ante, para 14.01), Arts 2(3), 3(1), 5(1), 7(1) proviso.

12 Art 2(2). The Commission is going to monitor and report on this rule.

UNDERTAKINGS AS TO FITNESS

[14.07] The undertakings. In the absence of any express undertaking as to the fitness of goods supplied, such an undertaking may only be imported by operation of law. In the case of sales, s 14(3) (as amended) of the SGA provides as follows:[1]

> Where the seller sells goods in the course of a business and the buyer, expressly or by implication, makes known –
>
> (a) to the seller, or
>
> (b) where the purchase price or part of it is payable by instalments and the goods were previously sold by a credit-broker to the seller, to that credit-broker,[2]
>
> any particular purpose for which the goods are being bought, there is an implied term that the goods supplied under the contract are reasonably fit for that purpose, whether or not that is a purpose for which such goods are commonly supplied, except where the circumstances show that the buyer does not rely, or that it is unreasonable for him to rely, on the skill or judgment of the seller or credit-broker.

In English law, this implied term is a condition.[3] Similar obligations are imported into quasi-sales,[4] hp[5] and simple hiring.[6] Certain common limitations have already been considered (see ante, para 14.02); and, in the next two subsections, there will be explained: (a) the content of the undertakings (see post, paras 14.08–09) and (b) the further special limitations on them (see post, paras 14.10–14). The requirements of the criminal law as to the fitness of goods supplied are dealt with elsewhere.[7] For consumer sales (see ante, para 14.01), a simpler version of this undertaking is to be found in an EU Directive (Art 2(2)(b), (5)).

Content of the undertakings

[14.08] Strict liability. The foregoing statutory undertakings (see ante, para 14.07) all require that the goods be 'reasonably fit for the purpose for which they are supplied'. This is not to say that the supplier's liability is founded on carelessness. On the contrary, his liability is strict, as may be seem from *Frost v Aylesbury Dairy Co*:[1]

[14.07]

1 As amended by the SSGA 1994, Sched 2, para 5(5)(a). See generally ante, para 11.11.

2 As to the meaning of 'credit broker', see post, para 14.12.

3 New SGA, s 14(6): see SSGA 1994, Sched 2, para 5(5)(b).

4 SGSA 1982, s 4(4), (5) and (6). The SSGA 1994 does not amend the status of the term as in the SGA. Section 4 of the SGSA makes use of the expression 'transfer' instead of seller (see ante, para 12.02).

5 SOGIT 1973, s 10(3). The SSGA 1994 here amends the status of the implied term as in the SGA: SSGA, Sched 2, para 4(4)(b) and (c). Section 10 of SOGIT uses the expression 'creditor', which it defines as including any assignee therefrom (s 15(1)).

6 SGSA 1982, s 9(4), (5) and (6). The SSGA 1994 does not amend the status of the term as in the SGA. Section 9 of the SGSA uses the term 'bailor' and is said to represent a significant tightening of the previous law: Woodroffe, *Goods and Services – the New Law*, paras 5.14–19; 5.27.

7 Eg, TDA (see ante, para 4.07); Food Act 1984 (see ante, para 4.28); Construction and Use Regulations (see ante, para 4.37).

[14.08]

1 [1905] 1 KB 608, [1904–07] All ER 132, CA. See also *Preist v Last* [1903] 2 KB 148, CA; *Henry Kendall & Sons Ltd v William Lillico & Sons Ltd* (set out post, para 14.10).

Typhoid germs were found in milk sold by a dairy for 'family use'. As these germs could only be discovered by prolonged scientific investigation, the sellers argued that they could not reasonably have discovered the defect by the exercise of reasonable care.

Notwithstanding this, the Court of Appeal unanimously held the dairy liable for breach of the undertaking as fitness. Nor is it any answer for the seller to plead that he promised two contradictory things, so that in *Baldry v Marshall Ltd*[2] the seller was held liable for breach of the undertaking in promising to sell (1) a Bugatti car that (2) was suitable for touring.[3] Nor is it even any answer that the transferee was himself unaware of the possibility of harm. Thus, in the *Ashington Piggeries* case (set out ante, para 13.13) there was no dispute that the meal was toxic to mink, and the House of Lords found that each buyer had made known to his seller that he required the goods as animal feeding stuffs, rather than as fertiliser (see post, para 14.10). Accordingly, their Lordships held each seller liable to his buyer for breach of the undertaking as to fitness because, not only was DMNA highly toxic to mink, but it was in some degree toxic to all other domestic animals and poultry.[3a] It would seem the answer would have been otherwise if DMNA had only been toxic to mink – because neither buyer had asked for food suitable to feed to mink.[4]

The result is that, in the law of contract,[5] the supplier is under a strict liability[6] to ensure that the goods are 'reasonably fit' (see post, para 14.09) for the purpose supplied (see post, para 14.10).

[14.09] Reasonably fit. Whilst strict (see ante, para 14.08), the statutory undertaking that the goods be 'reasonably fit' is not absolute: it must be tested in relation to the purpose for which the goods are supplied and must depend on the degree of precision with which that purpose is specified. In *Griffiths v Peter Conway Ltd*:[1]

P contracted dermatitis from a Harris Tweed coat which she had bought from D. It was found as a fact that P had an unusually sensitive skin and that the coat would not have harmed an ordinary person.

In finding the seller not liable for the unfitness of the coat for P, Lord Greene MR explained that, if a person suffering from such an abnormality desires to obtain the benefit of the implied condition:[2]

---

2   [1925] 1 KB 260; [1924] All ER Rep 155, CA. Cf *Lynch v Thorne* [1956] 1 All ER 744, CA.

3   Greer J held that the Bugatti car ordered was not suitable for touring. Perhaps a modern equivalent might be a car to be suitable for motorway driving.

3a   Actually, it was held that once it was proved that DMNA was toxic to mink, the onus (which they had not discharged) was on the sellers to show that the meal could have been fed with impunity to all other types of livestock. See further post, para 14.10.

4   See also *Henry Kendall & Sons Ltd v William Lillico & Sons Ltd* (above); *Sumner, Permain & Co v Webb* (set out post, para 14.16), where the CA decided against the buyer on other grounds.

5   Compare the supplier's liability in tort, which is substantially based on negligence: see post, para 17.12 *et seq*.

6   In the case of hp and simple hiring, this would appear to represent a clear increase in the supplier's liability beyond the common law position: as to which, see Macleod, *Sale and HP*, p 86.

[14.09]

1   [1939] 1 All ER 685, CA.

2   At 691. But could the buyer realistically expect the seller to know about the effect of the garment on her skin? Compare the cases in note 5 with the discussion of reliance post, paras 14.13–14.

The essential matter for the seller to know ... consists in the particular abnormality or idiosyncrasy from which the buyer suffers. It is only when he has that knowledge that he is in a position to exercise his skill or judgment ... The fact that those essential characteristics are not known ... to the buyer does not seem to me to affect the question.

Certainly, if the buyer does make clear to the seller the **particular purpose** for which he requires the goods, the seller **may** be strictly liable,[3] notwithstanding that he could not reasonably have prevented the harm.[4] A case where neither party was aware that a particular characteristic was needed was *Slater v Finning Ltd*:[5]

The owner of a fishing vessel engaged a marine engineer to repair the vessel's engine, including replacing the camshaft. Neither party was aware that the vessel had an abnormal tendency to produce excessive torsional resonance. The engineer fitted a new type of camshaft, which failed.

The House of Lords unanimously held that there was no breach of the implied condition as to fitness, Lord Keith saying that in the course of argument there was (405j–406a):

... put the illustration of a new front wheel tyre being purchased for a car which, unknown to the buyer or seller, had a defect in the steering mechanism as a result of which the tyre wore out after a few hundred miles of use, instead of the many thousands which would normally be expected. In these circumstances it would be totally unreasonable that the seller should be liable for breach of s 14(3).

This links up with the presumption that, if nothing is said, the implication is that the goods are required for an ordinary purpose (see post, para 14.11); but it seemingly makes no allowance for those circumstances where an inexpert buyer presents the circumstances in which the goods are to be used to an expert seller so that the latter may exercise his expertise in advising what goods should be supplied as suitable for the buyer's purpose.[6] Alternatively, it may be that in the circumstances the seller's duty is merely to warn the buyer of possible hazards connected with the purpose for which the goods are required.[7]

What is the ambit of strict liability? According to Lord Greene in *Griffiths v Peter Conway Ltd*, it might seem that the seller should be liable for any injury to the buyer which flows from the range of 'essential characteristics' made known. Yet it is submitted that there must be some limitation on the rule. The burden of the rule ought to be limited by the circumstances of the transaction: A, who buys a 30 year old car for £150 cannot expect it to be as fit for driving as the three-year-old car purchased by B for £5,500;[8] and B cannot expect his car to be as fit as the new car purchased by C for £15,500.[9] It may be that

---

3   But that might amount to unreasonable reliance: as to which, see post, para 14.13.

4   Eg, *Frost v Aylesbury Dairy Co* (set out ante, para 14.08); *Henry Kendall & Sons Ltd v William Lillico & Sons Ltd* (set out post, para 14.10).

5   [1996] 3 All ER 398; 15 Tr LR 458, HL(s).

6   Eg, a parent buying shoes for a child expecting the shop assistant to measure the child's foot: see Gullifer (1997) 16 Tr LR 29.

7   Eg, *Vacwell Engineering Co Ltd v BDH Chemicals Ltd* (set out post, para 18.32).

8   Distinguish cars purchased as vintage or for scrap. Would an MOT test certificate affect the position?

9   Compare *Bartlett v Sidney Marcus Ltd* [1965] 2 All ER 753, CA (second-hand) and *Rogers v Parish Ltd* (set out post, para 14.23: new car).

this is the proper meaning of the words 'reasonably fit': the goods must be as fit for the purpose supplied as goods of that description and in those circumstances usually are.[10]

Qualification of the undertakings

Knowledge of particular purpose

[14.10] The undertakings as to fitness (see ante, para 14.07) are expressed to apply only where the transferee, expressly or by implication, makes known to certain stipulated persons (see post, para 14.12) the 'particular purpose for which the goods are being' bought or hired. Since the SGA 1893 where they first appeared, the quoted words have consistently been interpreted by the courts in favour of the buyer: first, they refused to read 'particular' in the sense of special, as opposed to ordinary, purpose;[1] second, they did not insist that the buyer gave the information as to his purpose to the seller, but held it to be sufficient that the seller was aware of the purpose for which the goods were required;[2] and third, that purpose might be made known either expressly[3] or impliedly. For instance, in *Kendall v Lillico*:[4]

> K and G Ltd were both wholesale dealers and members of the London Cattle Food Trade Association. K sold to G Ltd a quantity of 'Brazilian ground nut extraction' knowing that G Ltd required the goods for resale for compounding as food for cattle and poultry. However, the goods contained a toxic substance (unsuspected at this time) which resulted in their being fit for use as food for cattle, but not for poultry. G Ltd orally agreed to sell part of the goods to one of their long-standing customers, SAPPA Ltd, a dealer, and subsequently sent SAPPA Ltd one of their ordinary 'sold notes' which stated that the buyer took liability for latent defects.[5] SAPPA Ltd made known to G Ltd that the goods were required for compounding into food for pigs and poultry. SAPPA Ltd then compounded the goods bought from G Ltd into food for birds, and sold some to the Hardwick Game Farm. Many of their pheasants having died as a consequence of being fed the compound, the farmers sued SAPPA Ltd for breach of the undertakings as to fitness and quality (see post, para 14.19), who brought in G Ltd, and G Ltd brought in K, each buyer alleging similar breaches of s 14 against his seller.[6]

---

10 And see Lord Pearce in *Henry Kendall & Sons Ltd v William Lillico & Sons Ltd* (above) at 115. For the possible relevance of instructions for use, see post, para 18.34.

[14.10]

1 Eg, *Frost v Aylesbury Dairy Co* (set out ante, para 14.08; milk). See also *Wallis v Russell* [1902] 2 IR 585 (crabs 'for tea').

2 *Ashington Piggeries Ltd v Christopher Hill Ltd* (set out ante, para 13.13) as between N and P. CA decision reversed by HL, who held that N was aware that the herring meal was required for compounding for animal feedstuffs: see Lords Hodson (at 857), Guest (at 862–63), Dilhorne (at 869–70), Wilberforce (at 877–78); and Diplock dissenting (at 891).

3 *Ashington Piggeries Ltd v Christopher Hill Ltd* (above) as between P and D. The decision of the CA on this point was not in dispute before the HL.

4 *Henry Kendall & Sons Ltd v William Lillico & Sons Ltd* [1969] 2 AC 31; [1968] 2 All ER 444, HL. See generally Davies (1969) 85 LQR 74.

5 The CA explained that, whilst the 'sold note' became part of the contract between G Ltd and SAPPA Ltd (see post, para 18.04), it did not protect G Ltd from liability for breach of the undertaking as to fitness (see post, para 18.06).

6 The CA held that there had been no breach of the undertaking as to merchantability (see post, para 14.20): *sub nom Hardwick Game Farm v Suffolk Agricultural Poultry Producers Association* [1966] 1 All ER 309, CA.

The House of Lords agreed with the Court of Appeal that the purpose for which each buyer required the goods, even though their normal and obvious purpose, was a sufficient particular purpose made known to the seller. Lord Morris said:[7]

> The degree of precision or definition which makes a purpose a particular purpose depends entirely on the facts and circumstances of a purchase and sale transaction. No need arises to define or limit the word 'particular' ... There is no magic in the word 'particular'. A communicated purpose, if stated with reasonably sufficient precision, will be a particular purpose ...

> The next question that arises is whether that particular purpose was made known so as to show that the buyers relied on the skill and judgment of the sellers ... Again, there is no magic in any particular word in the section.

[14.11] Single and multi-purpose goods. It has long been settled that the undertaking as fitness (see ante, para 14.07) applies to goods which have only one ordinary purpose.[1] The difference between goods capable of ordinary use for many purposes and those ordinarily used for only one purpose was explained by Collins MR in *Priest v Last*,[2] where he said that in the multi-purpose case:

> ... in order to give rise to the implication of a warranty, it is necessary to show that, though the article sold was capable of general use for many purposes, in the particular case it was sold with reference to a particular purpose. But in a case where the discussion begins with the fact that the description of the goods by which they were sold points to one particular purpose only, it seems to me that the first requirement of the sub-section is satisfied ... The sale is of goods which, by the very description under which they are sold, appear to be sold for a particular purpose.

The effect of the cases would appear to be as follows: if the goods have only one ordinary use, the supplier is impliedly promising that the goods are fit for that use;[3] whereas, if the goods have more than one ordinary use, there is no implication that they fit for any particular of their ordinary uses[4] unless the buyer specifies for which ordinary use he requires the goods,[5] though there will be a breach of the undertaking unless the supplier proves that the goods are fit for at least one of their ordinary uses.[6] Whilst the

---

7   At 93–94. See also *per* Lord Pearce, at 114–15.

[14.11]

1   Eg, *Priest v Last* [1903] 2 KB 148, CA (hot-water bottle); *Grant v Australian Knitting Mills Ltd* [1936] AC 85, PC (underpants); *Griffiths v Peter Conway Ltd* (set out ante, para 14.09; clothing); *Wilson v Rickett Cockerell Ltd* (set out ante, para 14.03; Coalite); *Lowe v Lombank Ltd* (set out post, para 18.06; car); and the cases cited in para 14.10, note 1.

2   [1903] 2 KB 148, CA at 153.

3   Eg, *Wilson v Rickett Cockerell Ltd* (above; Coalite is bought for burning); *Lowe v Lombank Ltd* (above; car for driving).

4   Eg, *Sumner, Permain & Co v Webb* (set out post, para 14.16; sale in particular country).

5   Eg, *Kendall v Lillico* (set out ante, para 14.10); *Baldry v Marshall Ltd* [1925] 1 KB 260, CA (Bugatti car suitable for touring). In the *Ashington Piggeries* case (set out ante, para 13.13), it was made clear meal required for animal feed rather than fertiliser (see ante, para 14.08).

6   The *Ashington Piggeries* case (above): although the meal could have been intended for a range of animals, it was toxic to all of them (see ante, para 14.08). See further Goode, *Commercial Law* (2nd edn), pp 335–36.

undertakings are expressly made applicable to extraordinary use,[7] if the transferee wishes to obtain the benefit of the undertaking in relation to an extraordinary use, he must specify that use.[8]

[14.12] Recipient of knowledge. The modern statutes have solved one particular problem which arose from the form of directly financed transactions (see ante, para 2.21): at common law, it was sometimes difficult to say that a particular purpose made known by the consumer to the dealer was necessarily communicated to the financier, who in law supplied the goods to the consumer.[1] The HPA 1965 sought to overcome this difficulty by allowing the consumer to make his purpose known to **either** of the two following parties; and this formula was adopted (with suitable amendment) by the CCA:

(a) the supplier (the financier); **or**

(b) the dealer, which the CCA termed the 'credit-broker' (Sched 4, paras 3, 35).

The solution was accepted by s 14(3) of the SGA (set out ante, para 14.07), s 61(1) of which appears to have lifted, without acknowledgment,[2] the definition of 'credit-broker' from the CCA.[3] A similar approach is to be found in relation to the undertakings as to fitness in relation to quasi-sales,[4] hp[5] and simple hiring.[6] Where the consumer is an 'individual' within the meaning of the CCA (see ante, para 5.24), the effect would appear to be similar to that first introduced by the HPA 1965. However, it has been pointed out that, where the sole consumer is a registered company (and hence not within the CCA category of 'individual'),[7] it might appear that such a transferee-company has unintentionally been put back in the pre-1965 position of having to show that he has made his purpose known to his supplier (the financier);[8] but such a result could be avoided by saying the CCA definition of 'individual' does not apply here.

---

7 'Whether or not that is a purpose for which such goods are commonly supplied': SGA, s 14(3); SOGIT, s 10(3); SGSA, ss 4(5), 9(5).

8 *Griffiths v Peter Conway Ltd* (see above); *BS Brown Ltd v Craiks Ltd* 1969 SLT 107 and 357 (the subsequent appeal to the HL was only based on the undertaking as to merchantable quality: as to which, see post, para 14.21).

[14.12]

1 Eg, the householder's special requirements will obviously be made known to a double-glazing contractor, but not necessarily to the financier; a finance lease (see ante, para 1.18A); and see generally post, para 16.03.

2 Does this mean that the CCA requirement that the transferee is an individual (see ante, para 5.24) does not apply here?

3 For a 'credit-broker' within the CCA, see ante, para 5.38. Presumably the effect is to apply that learning to both regulated sales, eg, credit sales and unregulated sales, eg, cash sales.

4 SGSA, s 4(4), 'credit-broker' being defined in s 18(1).

5 SOGIT, s 10(3), 'credit-broker' being defined in s 10(6).

6 SGSA, s 9(4), 'credit-broker' being defined in s 18(1).

7 *Contra* where the company is joint consumer with an individual: see ante, para 5.24.

8 Dobson [1983] JBL 312 at 313–15. The CCA has put the corporate consumer in a similarly disadvantageous position. But see his greater protection under UCTA: post, para 18.18.

Reliance

[14.13] At common law, the undertaking as to fitness was ousted by the mere opportunity on the part of the buyer to inspect the goods;[1] the undertaking in the SGA 1893 did not apply where the goods were sold under a trade name[2] and required the buyer to show that he relied on the seller's skill and judgment. However, the courts decided that such reliance might be in part only. In *Cammell Laird Ltd v Manganese Bronze and Brass Ltd:*[3]

> The buyer of ship's propellers stipulated for certain specifications. The propellers supplied were found to be unfit for the purpose supplied because they were not thick enough, a matter not covered by the specifications. The House of Lords held that in respect of matters not specified the buyer was relying on the seller's skill and judgment.

The next step was taken in 1973, when statute appeared to shift the burden of proof to the supplier;[4] once the transferee showed that he had made his purpose known, the undertaking was imported unless the supplier could show either non-reliance (see post, para 14.14) or unreasonable reliance[5] on the supplier or credit-broker.[6]

These 1973 changes were reproduced in the present legislation. Where the transferee can show that he expressly or impliedly made known to the supplier or credit-broker the purpose for which the goods were required (see ante, paras 14.10–12), there is an implied undertaking that the goods are reasonably fit for that purpose except where the circumstances show that the transferee 'does not rely, or that it is unreasonable for him to rely, on the skill or judgment of' the supplier or credit-broker (see ante, para 14.07). This provision represents a further step in the statutory protection of the transferee (see post, para 14.14).

Ousting the undertaking. Not only are there restrictions on the ability of the supplier to exclude the undertaking (see post, para 18.19), but it is clear that the mere recitation in a standard-form agreement that the transferee does not rely on the supplier's skill and judgment will not necessarily oust the undertaking:[7] and such a term may also be attacked under the UTCC Regulations (see ante, para 11.12) and the UCTA (s 3: see post, para 18.24). Nor will even the fact that the goods have been delivered and the defect discovered before the contract is made necessarily do so.[8] On the other hand, if the

---

[14.13]

1 Compare the present position in relation to the suitability of goods supplied by reference to a sample: see post, para 15.10.

2 Eg, *Webb's* case (set out post, para 14.16).

3 [1934] AC 402; [1934] All ER Rep 1, HL. See also the *Ashington Piggeries* case (set out ante, para 13.13), where all the parties had different areas of expertise: if the DMNA had been toxic only to mink, D would have relied on his own skill and the CA would have been correct (see post, para 14.14).

4 SOGIT, ss 3, 10(3). Did this transfer the legal or only factual burden of proof?

5 Consider the extent to which this requirement may have reversed the previous decisions mentioned ante, para 14.09. The change was based on the *First Report on Exemption Clauses in Contracts* (1969, Law Com No 24), para 37. But see the *Aswan Engineering* case (set out post, para 14.14).

6 This formula was first introduced in SOGIT, s 10(3), to deal with directly financed hp transactions, where the dealer was likely to be an expert in the type of goods supplied.

7 *Lowe v Lombank Ltd* (set out post, para 18.06). See Goode, *Commercial Law* (2nd edn), pp 341–42.

8 *R & B Customs Brokers Co Ltd v UDT Ltd* (set out post, para 18.18). *Sed quaere?*

transferee insists on the supply of unsuitable goods, there remains the obligation that those goods must be of satisfactory quality.[9]

[14.14] Reliance. Even under the SGA 1893, it had been held that, merely because the buyer inspected the goods, this did not necessarily prevent there being any implication of reliance.[1] In the *Ashington Piggeries* case (set out ante, para 13.13), the House of Lords held as follows:

(1) *As between P and D*. The Court of Appeal had held that D did not rely on the manufacturer (P) in respect of the suitability of any of the ingredients of King Size for feeding to mink, but D relied on his own skill. This was reversed by the House of Lords on the following grounds: even though D had relied on his own skill and judgment to ensure that the formula King Size was suitable for feeding to mink, D relied on P's skill to ensure that the ingredients were of a quality suitable for compounding into animal foodstuffs.[2]

(2) *As between P and N*. The Court of Appeal did not have to consider the question of reliance,[3] whereas the House of Lords held that there had been reliance[4] and Lord Guest commented that, once knowledge of particular purpose had been shown, it was an 'easy step' to infer reliance.[5]

With this case may be compared *Aswan Engineering Establishment Co v Lupdine Ltd*:[6]

A was a construction company carrying on business in Kuwait. A bought from L a quantity of liquid waterproofing packed in heavy duty plastic pails manufactured and supplied by TB. On arrival at Kuwait, the pails were stacked in the sun on the quayside. The pails collapsed in the heat and the compound was lost, though if the pails had been stacked in a particular way they would not have done so. Neill J's decision that L was liable to A for breach of s 14(3) of the SGA was not appealed.

As between L and TB,[7] the Court of Appeal held that there was no liability for breach of the undertaking as to fitness in supplying the pails because 'the circumstances showed

---

9   *Young & Marten Ltd v McManus Childs Ltd* [1969] 1 AC 454, HL. As to satisfactory quality, see post, para 14.15 *et seq*.

[14.14]

1   *Wallis v Russell* [1902] 2 IR 585, CA.

2   *Per* Lords Hodson (at 468–69), Guest (at 473), Dilhorne (at 485), Wilberforce (at 490), Diplock (at 507–08). Lord Diplock appeared to be saying that, at least where there was partial reliance, it was for the supplier to prove that the defect lay within the transferee's area of responsibility.

3   Because the CA had held that N had no knowledge of the particular purpose for which P required the herring meal; but they were reversed on this point by the HL: see ante, para 14.10.

4   *Per* Lords Hodson (at 471), Guest (at 477), Dilhorne (at 486–87), Wilberforce (at 496); Lord Diplock dissenting on the grounds that it is not sufficient for the buyer to show that the seller knew only that the goods may be used for such a purpose before the inference can be drawn (at 513).

5   See also *Manchester Liners Ltd v Rea* [1922] AC 74, HL; *Henry Kendall & Sons Ltd v William Lillico & Sons Ltd* (set out ante, para 14.10).

6   [1987] 1 All ER 135; [1987] 1 WLR 1, CA.

7   For the merchantability chain between A and L, see post, para 14.21; and for the product liability claim between A and TB, see post, para 17.14. L being insolvent, for A's claim against L's insurers, see post, para 17.02.

positively that the buyers did not rely on the seller's skill or judgment in any relevant sense'.[8]

A number of other examples may be given of factors which may be taken into account in deciding whether to infer reliance. First, there is the relative expertise of the parties, though this is not conclusive;[9] and, bearing in mind the introduction of the supplier's defence of unreasonable reliance (see ante, para 14.13), it remains to be seen whether this consideration will play any significant part in relation to goods supplied for consumption.[10] For instance, might it oust the undertaking where the transferee probably knows more about the suitability of the goods for his purpose than the supplier, as in *Griffiths v Peter Conway Ltd* (set out ante, para 14.09); or perhaps from a self-declared know-all? Second, there may be relevant any instructions which the supplier may have provided as to the use of the goods (see post, para 18.32). Third, there is the situation where the transferee is bound under contract with a third party to obtain goods fit for that contract: in this event, there would appear to be a breach of the undertaking if the goods supplied are defective,[11] but not if they are unsuitable.[12]

UNDERTAKINGS AS TO SATISFACTORY QUALITY

[14.15] **The undertakings.** In the absence of any express undertakings as to the quality of goods supplied, an undertaking as to quality may be imported at common law: this required that goods sold by description be merchantable under that description; and in 1815 Lord Ellenborough defined 'merchantable' as meaning that the goods:[1]

> ... shall be saleable in the market under the denomination mentioned in the contract.

In codifying the subject, Chalmers wrote into s 14(2) of the SGA 1893 the requirement that the goods must be of 'merchantable quality', thus introducing the word 'quality' (see post, para 14.16), but not defining 'merchantable'.[2] Following the recommendation of the Law Commission,[3] 'merchantability' has been replaced by a new undertaking of 'satisfactory quality'. Accordingly, new s 14(2) provides:[4]

---

8   After the supply of both a sample and a trial order: *per* Lloyd and Fox LJJ at 149d, 159f. See also *per* Nicholls LJ (at 157f), who held that the fitness claim failed because the merchantability claim failed. Where is the evidence here of a burden of proof on TB (see ante, para 14.13)?

9   Thus, reliance has been found even as between two wholesale-dealer members of the same trade association: *Henry Kendall & Sons Ltd v William Lillico & Sons Ltd* (above). But see post, para 14.26.

10 Cf *Priest v Last* [1903] 2 KB 148, CA; *Grant v Australian Knitting Mills Ltd* [1936] AC 85, PC; *Ashford Shire Council v Dependable Motors Ltd* [1961] AC 336, PC.

11 *Young & Martin Ltd v McManus Childs Ltd* [1969] 1 AC 454, HL.

12 *Comyn Ching & Co (London) v Oriental Tube Co Ltd* [1981] Com LR 67, CA.

[14.15]

1   *Gardiner v Gray* (1815) 4 Camp 144 at 145. For the development of the notion in 19th century common law, see Mitchell (2001) 117 LQR at 645–56.

2   In the 19th century, there was no need to define this commercial man's notion, which would be readily understandable to commercial courts and juries: *Benjamin's Sale of Goods* (3rd edn), para 800.

3   *Sale and Supply of Goods* (1987, Law Com 160), Part 3.

4   As inserted by the SSGA 1994, s 1. See generally Bridge [1995] JBL 398.

... where the seller sells[5] goods in the course of a business, there is an implied term that the goods supplied under the contract are of satisfactory quality.

In English law, this implied term is a condition.[6] Similar obligations are imported into quasi-sales,[7] hp,[8] and simple hiring.[9] Certain limitations have already been considered (see ante, para 14.02); and, in the next two subsections, there will be explained (a) the content of the undertaking (see post, paras 14.16–24) and (b) the limitations on them (see post, paras 14.25–26).

For consumer sales (see ante, para 14.01), another version of this undertaking is to be found in an EU Directive (Art 2(2)(c), (d), (4)).

Content of the undertakings

[14.16] Quality. Section 61(1) of the SGA 1893 provided that the **quality of goods** 'includes their state or condition'. Unfortunately, in the two leading cases on the point, the same Court of Appeal appears to have come to opposite conclusions as to the meaning of the word quality. In *Niblett's* case (set out ante, para 12.03), the majority held that there had been a breach of s 14(2), as well as of the implied condition as to title, and Bankes LJ said (at 395):

> Quality includes the state or condition of the goods. The state of this condensed milk was that it was packed in tins bearing labels. The labels were as much a part of the state or condition of the goods as the tins were. The state of the packing affected the merchantable quality of the goods.

On the other hand, in *Sumner, Permain & Co v Webb*[1] the same Court of Appeal found that there had been no breach of s 14(2):

> The defendant was the manufacturer of a product known as 'Webb's Indian Tonic Water'. As the defendant knew, the plaintiff purchased some of this tonic water from him for the purpose of shipment to the Argentine. However, the defendant was unaware of two vital facts: (1) his product contained a small quantity of salicylic acid; and (2) the sale of any article of food or drink containing salicylic acid was prohibited in the Argentine. After the Argentine authorities had seized and condemned his tonic water, the plaintiff claimed damages for breach of the undertakings as to fitness and quality.

In respect of s 14(2),[2] the Court of Appeal were clear that the fact that the goods were unsaleable in the Argentine did not prevent their being of merchantable quality: a

---

5   'Sells' presumably includes agreement to sell (see ante, para 1.10): Goode, *Commercial Law* (2nd edn), p 314.

6   New SGA, s 14(6): see SSGA 1994, Sched 2, para 5(5)(b).

7   SGSA 1982, s 4(2). The SSGA 1994 does not amend the status of the term as in the SGA. Section 4 of the SGSA makes use of the expression 'transferor' instead of seller (see ante, para 12.02).

8   SOGIT 1973, s 10(2). The SSGA 1994 here amends the status of the implied term as in the SGA: SSGA Sched 2, para 4(4)(b), (c).

9   SGSA 1982, s 9(2). The SSGA 1994 does not amend the status of the term as in the SGA. Section 9 of the SGSA uses the term 'bailor'.

[14.16]

1   [1922] 1 KB 55; [1921] All ER Rep 680, CA.

2   In relation to the undertaking as to fitness, the argument turned on what significance should be attached to the use of the trade name, a matter specifically mentioned in the 1893 Act, but now dropped: see ante, para 14.13.

subsequent change in the law would now reverse that decision (see post, para 14.21). Very naturally, the buyer in *Webb's* case relied on *Niblett's* case, which he alleged turned on the fact that the milk could not be sold in this country because of the law of registered trade marks. Scrutton LJ, who had ventured no opinion on the matter in *Niblett's* case, was clear that merchantable quality did not cover 'the legal title to goods or the legal right to sell them' (at 63) and Atkin LJ sought to explain his decision in the earlier case as follows:[3]

> ... nobody would buy those tins, because, if they did, they would probably be buying a law-suit, and the tins in that state and condition were unsaleable, not merely in this country by reason of a law peculiar to this country, but unsaleable anywhere.

Logically, it might be thought that the above decisions should be the other way round if a distinction is to be drawn between them.[4] But perhaps some satisfaction is to be gained from the distinction suggested by Atkin LJ: the condensed milk with those labels was treated as not being saleable anywhere, and not merely by reason of the law peculiar to this country;[5] but the tonic water could be sold almost anywhere as such, except in the Argentine.[6] Yet it would be unfortunate if too much emphasis were attached to the word **quality**.[7] The same definition of 'quality' now appears as part of a much larger definition in new s 14(2B): see post, para 14.20.

[14.17] Merchantability. This concept was not defined in the SGA 1893.[1] However, over the course of time the persistence of litigants repeatedly forced the courts to examine the meaning of 'merchantable'[2] and two distinct judge-made formulations of the concept appeared:

(1) *Acceptability*. The formulation of Farewell LJ in *Bristol Tramways Carriage Co v Fiat Motors Ltd* stressed whether the goods were **acceptable** to the buyer.[3] This test addressed itself to the needs of a commercial buyer. However, not only was it

---

3   At 65–66. See also Banks LJ at 61. In *Buchanan-Jardine v Hamilink* 1983 SLT 149 (cattle sold held of merchantable quality, even though subject to a Ministry 'stop notice' because another cow not subject to the sale reacted positively to a tuberculosis test).

4   In *Niblett's* case there was no complaint as to the quality of the actual milk, whilst in *Webb's* case it is the contents which were criticised. Benjamin plays down the disagreement: *Sale of Goods* (5th edn), para 11-032, note 55.

5   Is this so? Did Atkin LJ have in mind the conflict rule that, if no evidence of foreign law is produced, it is assumed to be the same as English law? Does this rule apply to statute law? See Dicey and Morris, *Conflict of Laws* (8th edn), pp 1118–19. Would there have been a reasonable distinction if Atkin LJ had said 'not saleable anywhere by reason of English law'?

6   This would fit in with the general maxim that the undertaking as to merchantability is not usually an undertaking that the goods will be fit for any particular purpose – see post, para 14.21.

7   This word does not appear in the similar statutory undertaking where goods are supplied by reference to a sample (see post, para 15.10); and supplies by sample are only a specialised form of supply by description (see ante, para 13.09). Continued use of the expression was, however recommended: *Sale and Supply of Goods* (1987, Law Com No 160), para 3.37.

[14.17]

1   As with the undertaking as to fitness (see ante, para 14.08), liability is strict: *Daniels and Daniels v White & Sons Ltd* (set out post, para 17.13).

2   Whilst a 19th century term of general use (see ante, para 14.15), in the 20th century it fell into disuse: *Cehave v Bremer* (set out ante, para 11.05) at 80.

3   [1910] 2 KB 831, CA, at 841, as elaborated by Dixon J in *Australian Knitting Mills Ltd v Grant* (1993) 50 CLR 387, HL (affd [1936] AC 85, PC).

circular,[4] but the test also assumed a particular level of demand for the goods in question.[5]

(2) **Usability**. Particularly to meet the situation where goods were bought for consumption rather then resale, there was developed the test of **usability** of the goods based on a *dictum* of Lord Wright in *Cammell Laird Ltd v Manganese Bronze and Brass Ltd*.[6]

Usually, whichever of the above tests was selected was entirely suitable for the circumstances in which it was applied. The trouble was that it seemed inconsistent with the other test. By 1970, an impasse appeared to have been reached[7] and attention switched to statutory reform.

Unfortunately, the Law Commission assumed that, given the desirability of introducing a statutory definition of merchantability, a choice had to be made between the **acceptability** and **usability** tests: their working paper favoured the **acceptability** test,[8] whereas their 1973 Final Report plumped for the **usability** test.[9] Not surprisingly, therefore, the statutory definition was something of a disappointment.[10] Accordingly, the Law Commission returned to the subject and resolved to make a fresh start. First, the Commission proposed the introduction of a brand new concept to replace merchantability (see post, para 14.18). Second, the commission recommended a multiple definition to meet the different circumstances in which the concept would have to be used (see post, para 14.20).

[14.18] The statutory definition of *satisfactory*. In 1987, the Law Commission recommended that the old concept of 'merchantability' should be replaced by a positive adjective,[1] whilst retaining much of the rest of the definition;[2] and the draftsman chose in new s 14(2) to employ the expression 'satisfactory' (see ante, para 14.15). This notion he explained in new s 14(2A), which provides as follows:[3]

> For the purposes of this Act, goods are of satisfactory quality if they meet the standard that a reasonable person would regard as satisfactory, taking into account any description of the goods, the price (if relevant) and all the other relevant circumstances.

Similar provisions are to be found in quasi-sales, hp and simple hirings.[4]

---

4   A reasonable buyer would only accept the goods if he were legally bound to do so: *per* Salmond J in *Taylor v Combined Buyers Ltd* [1924] NZLR 627, at 646. *Contra* Benjamin, *Sale of Goods* (5th edn), para 11-035, speaking of the amended version.

5   *Per* Scrutton LJ in *Webb's* case [1922] 1 KB 55, CA at 63.

6   [1934] AC at 430, case set out ante, para 14.13.

7   *BS Brown & Sons Ltd v Craiks Ltd* (above) at 825, *per* Lord Reid. See Benjamin, *op cit*, note 4, para 11-037.

8   1986, Working Paper No 18, para 23.

9   *First Report on Exemption Clauses in Contract* (1969, Law Com No 24), para 43.

10   See old s 14(6) of the SGA 1979 (now repealed).

[14.18]

1   *Sale and Supply of Goods* (1987, Law Com 160), paras 3.14–3.18.

2   *Ibid*, para 3.12. See, post, para 14.19.

3   As supplied by the SSGA 1994, s 1.

4   As supplied by Sched 2 of the SSGA 1994: see respectively SOGIT, new s 10(2A) (hp); SGSA 1982, new s 4(2A) (quasi-sale); SGSA 1982, new s 9(2A) (hiring).

The essence of the new definition is the standard of the reasonable man. The Commission recommended (para 3.25) that the definition should ask 'not whether a reasonable person who had already bought the goods might be tempted to keep them simply through inertia'; but rather it should be 'an objective comparison of the state of the goods with the standard which a reasonable person would find acceptable'. 'This is intended to require a full comparison of the goods with the standard, not merely a comparison limited to what was visible at the time of sale' (para 3.25). 'We do not think, however, that the buyer's expectations should form the basis of the test ... [T]he fear is that reliance on the buyer's expectations would allow the required standard of quality to decline, because, if the seller was able to establish that goods of a particular type could reasonably be expected to possess a number of minor defects on delivery, it could then also be argued that such defects were not breaches of contract' (para 3.26). In short, the Commission intended that the test should be whether the goods would be acceptable to the reasonable man with hypothetical knowledge of the defects, from which should be distinguished both the following situations where the buyer himself knows of the defects: (i) because he has actually examined the goods (see post, para 14.26); and (ii) where he is assumed to know of the defects because the sale is by sample, which he is presumed to have examined (see post, para 15.10). Earlier decisions on defective goods may provide some guidance (see below).

Defective goods held unmerchantable. Examples of one major defect rendering goods unmerchantable are beer contaminated with arsenic,[5] lemonade contaminated with acid,[6] underpants impregnated with sulphate,[7] a power-boat going into self-destruct within 27 days of delivery[8] and coalite packed with a detonator.[9] Alternatively, the single major defect may be a legal one, as where labels contain an infringing trade mark,[10] or a motor vehicle contravenes the construction and use regulations[11] or does not carry a rust warranty.[12]

[14.19] *Satisfactory:* **the specified factors.** The new statutory notion of when goods are satisfactory (see ante, para 14.18), like the definition of merchantability it replaces, includes express reference to the following factors:

---

5   *Wren v Holt* [1903] 1 KB 610, CA. Not every contaminant would necessarily render goods unmerchantable: there might be permitted and even desirable levels of what may in higher concentration be toxic.

6   *Daniels and Daniels v White & Son Ltd* (set out post, para 17.13).

7   *Grant v Australian Knitting Mills Ltd* [1936] AC 85, PC.

8   *Rasbora Ltd v JCL Marine Ltd* [1977] 1 Lloyd's Rep 645. See also *Bernstein v Pamson Motors Ltd* (set out post, para 29.07).

9   *Wilson v Rickett Cockerell Ltd* (set out ante, para 14.03).

10 *Niblett's* case (set out ante, para 12.03).

11 *Farnworth Finance Ltd v Attryde* [1970] 2 All ER 774, CA; *Yeoman Credit Ltd v Apps* (set out post, para 29.25); *Charterhouse Credit Ltd v Tolly* [1963] 2 QB 683, CA; *Lee v York Coach and Marine* [1977] RTR 35, CA. As to the Construction and Use Regulations, see ante, para 4.37. *Aliter,* if the vehicle is bought only for scrap.

12 *Shine v General Guarantee Corp* [1988] 1 All ER 911, CA (mistakenly referring to SGA instead of SOGIT).

1   *Any description of the goods.*[1] The Law Commission argued that 'goods of a different description may well be expected to be of different quality'.[2] Thus, the quality of goods must usually be judged in the light of the contractual description. For instance, in *Harlingdon* (set out ante, para 13.11A), the majority of the Court of Appeal decided that a miss-attributed painting was merchantable, though they disagreed as to whether a non-contractual description could be taken into account in assessing merchantability.[3] Another example would be the retail sale of goods described as 'new',[4] an expression which may presumably be subject to any trade usage (cf ante, para 13.11).

2   *The price (if relevant).* In *Kendall v Lillico*, Lord Pearce argued that the price could be a relevant factor in assessing merchantability, eg, the regular retail market for 'seconds' with a price discounted to reflect the defect;[5] and the same may be true of inferior quality.[6] Whilst a useful indicator of standards in some circumstances,[7] care is required in the inference to be drawn from the price, which might instead reflect market price fluctuations,[8] or that the supplier is a discount store, or errors of judgment. Thus, in *Harlingdon* the majority thought that, although the painting was bought by a dealer for resale and its price depended on its attribution, it was still merchantable as not unfit for 'aesthetic appreciation'.[9] What if the price reduction reflects that the goods are unsafe?[10]

3   *All the other relevant circumstances.* The Commission suggested (para 2.12) that the 'relevant circumstances' may include any inadequate instructions as to the use of the goods (see post, paras 18.32–33) and perhaps any manufacturer's repair warranties (see post, para 17.09). Whilst the undertaking obviously applies to second-hand goods, even in the absence of specified defects (see post, para 14.25), goods described as 'second-hand' or 'demonstration model' only have to reach a lower standard,[11] both as to major defects[12] and minor or cosmetic ones (see post, paras 14.23–14.24).

[14.19]

1   As to substantive errors in books, see [1993] JBL at 48–49.
2   *Sale and Supply of Goods* (1987, Law Com 160), para 3.27.
3   Of the majority, Slade LJ (at QB 586F) said that a non-contractual description should be ignored, whilst Norse LJ conceded (at QB 576F) that the description was 'applied to' the painting within the definition of merchantability (old s 14(6)). Stuart-Smith LJ (dissenting) held that the court was 'entitled and required' to take that description into account (at QB 583A).
4   See *Andrews Ltd v Singer & Co Ltd* [1934] 1 KB 17, CA. Cf TDA s 2(1)(j): see ante, paras 4.06–07.
5   [1969] AC, at 118; set out ante, para 14.10. The Law Commission enthusiastically endorsed this suggestion: *First Report on Exemption Clauses* (1969, Law Com No 24), para 42.
6   *Feast Contractors Ltd v Ray Vincent Ltd* [1974] 1 NZLR 212.
7   Eg, *Rogers v Parish* (set out post, para 14.23); *Shine v General Guarantee Corp Ltd* [1988] 1 All ER 911, CA.
8   Eg, *Cehave v Bremer* (set out ante, para 11.05); seasonal sales.
9   Even though it could only have been resold for £50–100 as against the contract price of £6,000 (see Norse LJ at QB 576D). See criticism by Brown (1990) 106 LQR at 563–64; and post, para 14.20.
10 Cf *Godley v Perry* [1960] 1 All ER 36. Safety is now an expressed feature of quality: see post, para 14.20.
11 *Benjamin's Sale of Goods* (5th edn), para 11.061.
12 *Thain v Anniesland Trade Centre* 1997 SLT 102, Sh Ct (5-year-old automatic car, the buyer accepted the risk that the gearbox might fail at any time).

[14.20] Statutory definition of quality. Following the recommendation of the Law Commission,[1] the hitherto largely statutorily undefined[2] notion of 'quality' has been expanded by the Sale and Supply of Goods Act 1994 (SSGA). New s 14(2B) of the SGA provides as follows:[3]

> For the purposes of this Act, the quality of goods includes their state and condition and the following (among others) are in appropriate cases aspects of the quality of goods –
>
> (a) fitness for all the purposes for which goods of the kind in question are commonly supplied,
>
> (b) appearance and finish,
>
> (c) freedom from minor defects,
>
> (d) safety, and
>
> (e) durability.

A similar provision is introduced as regards hp,[4] quasi-sale and simple hiring.[5] Besides rendering more prominent the 'state or condition' of the goods (see ante, para 14.16), the provision also draws attention to a non-exhaustive list of factors to be taken into account in assessing the quality of the goods.

(a) *Fitness for purpose.*[5a]

(b) *Appearance and finish* (see post, para 14.24).

(c) *Freedom from minor defects* (see post, para 14.23).

(d) *Safety.* It is already a criminal offence where goods do not comply with the general safety requirement or safety regulations;[6] or as regards food which is unsafe to eat or motor vehicles to drive.[7] Whilst breach of such provisions might already sometimes give rise to a civil right of action, whether under the supply contract[8] or otherwise,[9] the Law Commission recommended that this aspect should constitute a clear breach of the supply contract.[10] It remains to be seen whether the criminal and civil law will prove co-extensive in this respect. As to the safety aspects of work by the Design Council, see ante, para 3.08.

(e) *Durability* (see ante, para 14.06).

[14.21/22] Fitness for purposes. Where the goods are not in any way defective, the real complaint may be that the goods delivered comply with the contract description but do

---

[14.20]

1   *Sale and Supply of Goods* (1987, Law Com 160), para 3.37 *et seq.*

2   The short definition of 'quality' (see ante, para 14.16) was previously found in SGA, s 61. That definition was repealed by the SSGA 1994, Sched 2, para 5(9)(a): this follows the recommendation of the Commission (*ibid*, para 3.37).

3   Inserted by s 1 of the SSGA 1994.

4   SOGIT, new s 10(2B): see SSGA 1994, Sched 2, para 4(4)(a).

5   SGSA 1982, new s 18(3): as inserted by the SSGA 1994, Sched 2, para 6(10).

5a See post, para 14.21. For the common law as to the fitness of goods supplied, see ante, para 14.07, note 7.

6   See ante, paras 4.32–35.

7   See ante, paras 4.27; 4.37. As to genetically modified organisms, see Waldron [1999] JBL 395.

8   *Bernstein v Pamson Motors Ltd* (set out post, para 29.07): see 145 NLJ 687.

9   It directly does so as regards breach of the safety regulations (see ante, para 4.35), but not for breach of the general safety requirements or GPS regulations (see above).

10 *Op cit*, note 1, paras 3.44–3.46.

not have the specific qualities required. However, if the transferee has not expressly or impliedly specified the required qualities and therefore cannot plead the undertaking as to fitness (see ante, para 14.10), he may attempt to frame his complaint in terms of quality. This raises the issue of the relationship of the undertakings as to fitness and quality.[1] The extent of the overlap depends on the number of ordinary uses to which the goods may be put.

1   *Single-user goods.* Where the goods have only a single ordinary use, the undertaking as to satisfactory quality requires that the goods be fit for the purpose 'for which goods of the kind in question are **commonly** supplied'.[2] At its simplest, the difference between the two undertakings is this: the undertaking as to quality requires that the goods be fit for their **common** purpose;[3] whereas only the undertaking as to fitness demands that the goods be fit for any particular (**in the sense of special**) purpose made known.[4] However, it has already been seen that the courts extended the notion of 'particular purpose' to include ordinary purpose (see ante, para 14.10), so establishing an overlap between the two undertakings. The extent of the overlap depends on the number of ordinary uses to which the goods may be put (see below). Thus, the courts have accepted that, if single-user goods are not so usable, they are neither fit for the purpose supplied nor of the requisite quality.

2   *Multi-user goods.* Where the goods have more than one ordinary use, it would seem that the SSGA 1994 has changed the law. The pre-1994 position is exemplified in *Kendall v Lillico* (set out ante, para 14.10). The evidence showed that buyers who only compounded poultry food would not be prepared to buy the contaminated goods at any price; but that compounders of cattle food would be prepared (with complaints) to pay the full price, test the goods and use the less highly contaminated groundnuts in their cattle feedstuffs. The majority of the House of Lords held that, if the goods were fit for **any** ordinary purpose, they were merchantable.[5] This decision may be contrasted with the post-1994 position, which requires that, to be of satisfactory quality, the goods must be fit for '**all** the purposes for which goods of the kind in question are commonly supplied'. So, if feeding to poultry was **one** of the ordinary purposes for which groundnuts were ordinarily sold, presumably a court would now find that the groundnuts were not of satisfactory quality.[6] Similarly, an aesthetically pleasing fake painting would presumably now fail the undertaking as genuine paintings are bought at least in part as an investment.[7]

[14.21/22]

1   Eg, *Amstrad plc v Seagate Technology Inc* [1988] CLY 4384 (agreement by correspondence not reduced to formal contract: disc drives should not be subject to random and unpredictable failure).

2   SGA, new s 14(2B)(a): set out ante, para 14.20.

3   *Rogers v Parish* (set out post, para 14.23); *Danka Rentals Ltd v Xi Software Ltd* (1998) 17 Tr LR 74.

4   *Brown v Craiks* [1970] 1 All ER 823, HL (s) (sacking required for unusual purpose not unmerchantable); *Slater v Finning* (set out ante, para 14.09).

5   Lords Reid (at 76–79), Morris (at 96–98) and Guest (at 108). It is worth noting that Lords Reid and Morris applied the usability test whilst the majority preferred the acceptability test (see ante, para 4.17).

6   Similarly reversed would be: *Sumner, Permain & Co v Webb* (set out ante, para 14.16); *Aswan Engineering Establishment Co v Lupdine Ltd* (set out ante, para 14.14).

7   Cf the *Harlingdon* case (set out ante, para 13.11A).

[14.23] Minor defects. Bringing the text of the statute into line with case law development, the new expanded definition of 'quality' now explicitly includes 'freedom from minor defects' (see ante, para 14.20), so expanding the notion of 'satisfactory quality' (see ante, para 14.15).

Suppose new goods supplied have a congeries of minor defects (see ante, para 14.02) collectively too great to be dismissed as *de minimis* (see ante, para 13.12), eg, the Monday morning car (the first manufactured on a Monday). In *Rogers v Parish*:[1]

> The parties treated the issue as concerning the sale of a 'new' yellow Range Rover by the dealer for a price of £16,000.[2] The vehicle was found to be unsatisfactory and underwent a series of repairs by the dealer. However, after driving 5,500 miles in some 6 months, the consumer-buyer gave notice of rejection.[3] The judge found that the car was merchantable because it was roadworthy and the defects had been repaired under the manufacturer's warranty.

However, the Court of Appeal unanimously held the dealer in breach of old s 14(2) and explained that the judge had applied the wrong test.[4] The fact that the defects were repairable did not prevent the car being unmerchantable on delivery;[5] the presence of the manufacturer's warranty did not assist the dealer;[6] and the fact that the car was safely driveable did not necessarily suffice. Mustill LJ explained the statutory definition of merchantable (old s 14(6)) as follows:[7]

> Starting with the purpose for which 'goods of that kind' are commonly bought, one would include in respect of any passenger vehicle not merely the buyer's purpose of driving the car from one place to another but of doing so with the appropriate degree of comfort, ease of handling and reliability and, one may add, of pride in the vehicle's outward and interior appearance. What is the appropriate degree and what relative weight is to be attached to one characteristic of the car rather than another will depend on the market at which the car is aimed.

[14.23]

1　[1987] QB 933; [1987] 2 All ER 232, CA (discussed 138 NLJ 6). See also *Danka Rentals Ltd v Xi Software Ltd* (1998) 17 Tr LR 74 at 83B.

2　The facts were actually more complicated in all the following respects, none of which the parties relied on: the original supply was of a green Range Rover by way of a directly financed conditional sale; but after a few weeks' use, the green car proved unsatisfactory and was replaced by the yellow one; and no issue of lack of privity was taken.

3　The dealer did not plead that the buyer was precluded by his conduct from rejecting the car. See further post, para 29.04.

4　Compare the decision in *Cehave v Bremer* (set out ante, para 11.05), which was cited to the court. *Rogers* would also appear consistent with the decision as to merchantability (if not some of the *dicta* thereon) in the also cited *Bernstein v Pamson Motors Ltd* (set out, post, para 29.07).

5　The CA dismissed as irrelevant to the issue of merchantability the normal post-delivery adjustments: see below; and post, para 15.11.

6　Mustill LJ suggested that, insofar as the manufacturer's warranty was advanced to exclude the contractual liability of the retail supplier, it would infringe s 6 of UCTA (see post, para 18.19); and he denied that that warranty could be a 'relevant circumstance' under s 14(6) such as should reduce the reasonable expectations of the buyer (see ante, para 14.19).

7　At 237a. His Lordship actually thought there might have been an express undertaking as to merchantability but noted that the parties were content to rely on s 14 of the SGA.

His Lordship noted that the buyer of a new Range Rover was entitled to expect a standard in all respects higher than that of a second-hand Range Rover or of a new ordinary family saloon, and to what the judge termed 'value for money'.[8]

Of course, this case was argued on a rather artificial basis. Whilst irrelevant to the issue of merchantability, retention and use of the car might go to the right to reject;[3] and in any claim for damages, submission or otherwise of the car to post-delivery adjustments might go both to the measure of damages[9] and acceptance (see post, para 29.05). Moreover, the case suggests a test for new goods which is plainly more onerous for the supplier than would be the case with second-hand goods: whilst the latter must *prima facie* be free of major defects,[10] minor ones are to be expected 'sooner or later'.[11]

Finally, the effect of the 1994 statutory definition of quality is to make minor defects part of the implied condition (see ante, para 14.20). Taken together with other changes in the remedies available for breach of slight breaches of these conditions (see ante, para 11.05A), this may produce the following results: a consumer may *prima facie* be able to rescind for minor defects and cosmetic defects (see post, para 14.24), whilst a business buyer or hirer may be reduced to claiming damages.

[14.24] Appearance and finish. In *Jackson v Rotax Cycles* (set out ante, para 14.05), the Court of Appeal held unmerchantable motor horns bought for resale which were slightly dented and discoloured; and this would seem correct, because the goods in that condition were unsaleable by the buyer under the contract description. This case involved goods bought for resale and, it may be that the courts had already reached a similar position in respect of goods bought for consumption.[1] However, the Law Commission recommended that the matter be put on a clear statutory footing.[2] Accordingly the new expanded definition of 'quality' now explicitly includes 'appearance and finish' (see ante, para 14.20), so expanding the notion of 'satisfactory quality' (see ante, para 14.15).

There may now be a breach of the undertaking where goods, with a cosmetic defect are obtained for consumption, eg, the stained fur coat or consumer durable with chipped or discoloured paint.[3] As to the Design Council, see ante, para 3.08.

---

8 As to the relevance of price, see generally ante, para 14.19.

9 Submission of the car for cure might amount to a variation or waiver of claim (see post, para 26.21 *et seq*), whilst non-submission might breach the duty to mitigate (see post, para 27.44).

10 *Shine v General Guarantee Corp* [1988] 1 All ER 911, CA (second-hand car insurance write-off because submerged in water for over 24 hours. See 104 LQR at 522–23).

11 *Business Application Specialists Ltd v Nationwide Credit Corp Ltd* [1988] CLY 3169, CA, applying a *dictum* by Lord Denning MR in a 1965 case. See also *Benjamin's Sale of Goods* (5th edn), para 11-061; Stephenson (1988) 6 Tr L 172.

[14.24]

1 *Rogers v Parish* (set out ante, para 14.23): the judge found the bodywork of the yellow car defective; and Mustill LJ expressly included this in the items rendering the goods unmerchantable in his reference to 'appearance' in the *dicta* quoted ante, para 14.23.

2 *Sale and Supply of Goods* (1987, Law Com), para 3.39.

3 But compare supplies of services: see post, para 15.15.

Qualification of the undertakings

[14.25] Specified defects. The Sale and Supply of Goods Act 1994 transfers the previous qualifications on the undertaking as to merchantability to the new one as to 'satisfactory quality' (see ante, para 14.15). Thus, new s 14(2C) of the Sale of Goods Act provides as follows (as supplied by s 1 of the 1994 Act):

> The term implied by subsection (2) above does not extend to any matter making the quality of goods unsatisfactory –
>
> (a) which is specifically drawn to the buyer's attention before the contract is made,
>
> (b) where the buyer examines the goods before the contract is made, which that examination ought to reveal, or
>
> (c) in the case of a contract for sale by sample, which would have been apparent on a reasonable examination of the sample.

These are similar qualifications as regards the undertaking as to satisfactory quality in contracts of hp, quasi-sale and simple hiring (1994 Act, Sched 2, paras 4(4), 6(3), 6(7)).

1 *Specified defects*, eg, goods marked 'shop soiled' or 'seconds'.[1] As the Law Commission pointed out on an earlier occasion,[2] in one sense this defence was already comprehended within the statutory definition of the undertaking; but this mode of expressing it makes available to the supplier a clear-cut defence in law, even in those circumstances where he is prohibited from contracting out of his liability for breach of the implied terms.[3] *Prima facie*, a supplier may save himself by specifically drawing the attention of the transferee to enumerated defects before the contract is concluded,[4] as for instance in a warning as to use (see post, para 18.32). How effective such a defence is to the supplier perhaps depends on how precisely he specifies the defect: it is presumably not enough for the supplier to use some general phrase such as 'bought as seen',[5] though the matter would seem one of degree; and any attempt to utilise this provision to achieve a blanket exclusion of the undertaking is likely to meet a fate similar to that of clauses 8 and 9 in *Lowe v Lombank Ltd*.[6] Where goods are supplied by a trader to a consumer, it is for consideration whether such specified defects are saved from the UTCC Regulations by its provisions.[7]

2 *Examination* (see post, para 14.26).

3 *Sample* (see post, para 15.10).

[14.25]

1 Cf *Crowther v Shannon Motor Co* [1975] 1 All ER 139, CA. Examples might be goods expressly sold as 'seconds' or 'damaged' or 'imperfect', or 'display models'.

2 *First Report on Exemption Clauses* (1969, Law Com No 24), para 49.

3 UCTA, ss 6 and 7: see post, para 18.19.

4 SGA, s 14(2)(a); SOGIT, s 10(2)(a); SGSA, ss 4(3)(a), 9(3)(a). It would be a wise precaution to note these defects on the invoice.

5 *Cavendish-Woodhouse v Manley* (1984) 82 LGR 376, DC. See also Woodroffe, *Goods and Services – the New Law*, para 3.30; OFT, UCT *Bulletin No 4*, 32, 37; *Bulletin No 5*, 47.

6 Set out post, para 18.06. See also Goode, *Commercial Law* (2nd edn), pp 317–18.

7 Sched 1, para (e)(i): set out ante, para 11.12A.

[14.26] Examination. At common law, the undertaking as to merchantability was excluded from a sale by the mere opportunity for pre-contract examination. Whilst this rule was retained for sales by sample (see post, para 15.08), the SGA 1893 brought about two changes: (1) the exclusion of the undertaking was made to rest on an examination in fact; and (2) even if there was an examination, the undertaking was only ousted in respect of defects which such examination ought to have revealed. After difficulties with a case where a buyer, pressed for time, wrongly told the seller that he had made an examination,[1] the Law Commission recommended a verbal alteration of the qualification with the following object:[2] to put beyond doubt that this qualification will only exclude the undertaking in respect of such defects as the examination actually made ought to have revealed.[3] That change was made in 1973 by SOGIT (ss 3(2)(b), 10(2)(b)) and is now to be found in all the current undertakings:[4] a thorough examination or a cursory examination will each oust the undertaking as regards defects they respectively would have revealed,[5] possibly making something of a trap for the consumer who takes possession before contract and discovers the defect before contract without realising its gravity.[6] Indeed, the provision would seem to both reward the careless buyer who does not examine the goods before contract and penalise the careful buyer (who perhaps obtains an expert pre-contract report), not to mention one who brags as to his expertise when making an examination.[7]

[14.26]

1 *Thornett v Beers* [1919] 1 KB 486. It may be that in such circumstances the buyer would be estopped from denying he had made the examination represented, and that the undertaking is ousted in respect of defects which that represented would have revealed. Alternatively, the case has been explained on grounds of waiver: Goode, *Commercial Law* (2nd edn), p 318.

2 *First Report on Exemption Clauses* (1969, Law Com No 24), para 48.

3 But see Yates [1973] JBL at 139, n 12.

4 SGA, s 14(2)(c), as supplied by the Sale and Supply of Goods Act 1994, s 1. For similar undertakings, see the 1994 Act, Sched 2, paras 4(4), 6(3), 6(7).

5 But might deliberate failure to inspect be a 'relevant circumstance' within the definition of satisfactory quality (see ante, para 14.19) making the goods merchantable?

6 *Per* Dillon LJ in *R & B Customs Brokers Co Ltd v UDT Ltd* (set out post, para 18.18), at 851c, CA.

7 See generally Atiyah, *Sale of Goods* (10th edn), p 165.

CHAPTER 15

OTHER IMPLIED TERMS, TRANSACTIONS AND OBLIGATIONS

[15.01] Introduction. The statutory obligations as to delivery and payments will be dealt with in Chapter 23; and it remains to consider here the residue of undertakings[1] as to the character and quality of goods implied by statute (see post, para 15.02) or common law (see post, para 15.21). Furthermore, discussion of all the express and implied terms and obligations considered in Chapters 11–15 for the most part assume a two party transaction. In Chapter 16 there will be considered the effect upon these terms and obligations of the fact that the transaction is financed by lender credit. The wider ramifications of liability back up the chain of distribution will be discussed in Chapter 17. Lastly, attempts to avoid or reduce this liability by suitable wording is the subject of Chapter 18.

TERMS AND OBLIGATIONS DERIVED FROM STATUTE

[15.02] Chapters 12–14 considered the major terms implied into contracts for the supply of goods. The original statutory formulation of these undertakings was to be found in the SGA 1893. A series of Hire Purchase Acts gradually introduced increasingly similar undertakings in respect of hp agreements;[1] and the undertakings reached almost common form in respect of sale and hp agreements with the enactment of SOGIT in 1973.[2] The provisions in relation to sales were subsequently re-enacted in the SGA 1979, whilst those in respect of hp are still to be found in SOGIT. As a result of further recommendations of the Law Commission,[3] Part I of the SGSA[4] imported similar undertakings into quasi-sales (see ante, para 2.10) and simple hiring agreements (see ante, para 12.01A); and modification of the remedies was made by SSGA 1994 (see ante, para 11.05A). It remains to consider here the following types of special case: the undertakings as to sample and trade usage imported into all four types of contract for the supply of goods (see respectively post, paras 15.03; 15.11); the undertakings in supplies of services (see post, para 15.15) embodied in Part II of the SGSA;[4] the undertakings in regulated agreements (see post, para 15.16); the variations with regard to other sorts of transaction

---

[15.01]

1 Some are implied conditions and some are implied warranties. For conditions and warranties see generally ante, para 11.04; and for implied terms, see generally ante, para 11.10.

[15.02]

1 These provisions of the HPA 1938 and HPA 1964 were consolidated in the HPA 1965, ss 17, 19.

2 SOGIT gave effect, with modifications, to the *First Report of the Law Commission on Exemption Clauses in Contracts* (1969, Law Com No 24).

3 *Implied Terms in Contracts for the Supply of Goods* (1979, Law Com No 95).

4 Whereas Part I of the SGSA gives effect, with minor modifications, to the proposals in Law Com No 95 (see note 3, above), Part II of the SGSA has its origins in the NCC publication, *Service Please* (1981). On the SGSA generally, see Palmer (1983) 46 MLR 619; James [1982] JBL 10; Woodroffe, *Goods and Services – The New Law* (1982); and for an annotated text, see Thomas, *Encyclopedia of Consumer Law*.

(see post, paras 15.17–20); and terms derived from the common law (see post, paras 15.21–26).

Undertakings in contracts by sample

[15.03] Background. The classic exposition of the legal function of a sample is that of Lord Macnaghten in *Drummond v Van Ingen*,[1] where he said:

> The office of a sample is to present to the eye the real meaning and intention of the parties with regard to the subject matter of the contract which, owing to the imperfections of language, it may be difficult or impossible to express in words. The sample speaks for itself.

A sample may be utilised in the supply of specific or unascertained goods, in which case the sample will be taken respectively from the contract goods, or bulk from which it is to be drawn; or there may be a supply of future goods as corresponding with a particular sample.[2] In either case, the function of the sample is similar to that of the description of the goods supplied, and might almost be regarded as a special type of supply by non-verbal description. Yet it is normal to distinguish between the two, because statute makes separate provision for supplies by sample,[3] and even contemplates that supply may be both by description and by sample (see post, para 15.06).

[15.04] Sample contracts. When does a sample become part of the contract? Just as with supplies by description (see ante, para 13.11), it is a question of intention whether the sample (non-verbal description) becomes part of the contract.[1] Therefore, s 15(1) provides:

> A contract of sale is a contract for sale by sample where there is an express or implied term to that effect in the contract.

Of course, the provision as to a sample may be express.[2] However, s 15(1) may cause more difficulty where such a term is to be implied, as it would appear to import all the pre-1893 learning on the matter. The position at common law seems to have been that, just because a sample is exhibited at the time of sale,[3] there is not necessarily a sale by sample: the seller may decline to sell by sample, and require the buyer to inspect the bulk; or the parties may in some other way show that in their contract they are not relying on

---

[15.03]

1 (1887) 12 App Cas 284, HL at 297.

2 If the contract goods are yet to be manufactured, the contract may provide that they are to be manufactured according to a model. If the contract is for goods yet to be grown, notorious variations in crops of different seasons may affect the legal significance of the sample: Murdoch (1981) 44 MLR 388, at 389–90.

3 It has been argued that this separate treatment is of little practical value and could be abolished: Murdoch, *ibid*, at 388.

[15.04]

1 If the sample does not become part of the contract, it has been suggested that it may nevertheless take effect as a misrepresentation: Murdoch (1981) 44 MLR 388, at 392–93. As to the effect of misrepresentation, see post, para 17.10.

2 Eg, *Re Walkers, Winser & Hamm and Shaw Son & Co* [1904] 2 KB 152 (barley: 'as per sample'); *Champanhac & Co Ltd v Waller & Co Ltd* (set out post, para 15.07).

3 It has been argued there may also be a sale by sample where, in accordance with the contract, the sample is to be exhibited only after the formation of the contract: Hudson [1982] JBL 485. But see *Benjamin's Sale of Goods* (5th edn), para 11-094.

the sample.[4] On the other hand, there are many retail sales where the customer closely inspects a 'demonstration model', eg, a new car, a household appliance; and in some cases the consumer has no realistic opportunity to inspect the purchased item until some time after its delivery, eg, shrink-wrapped electronic appliances. It therefore seems puzzling that it has been said to be 'less likely' that a consumer sale is by sample.[5]

On the other hand, the more modern provisions dealing with quasi-sales, hp and simple hiring speak rather of goods being supplied 'by reference to a sample'.[6] It has been said that goods will be let or sold by reference to a sample:[7]

> ... where a sample is exhibited or supplied ... during the negotiations for the contract, and there need be no term in the contract, express or implied to this effect.

For example, if a car dealer takes a customer for a demonstration run in a new car, it would seem that if a similar new car is subsequently let to the customer it may be let by reference to the demonstration car, even if the transaction is directly financed. If so, the effect of the difference in terminology in the Acts would appear to be that a sample is more likely to become part of a transaction which falls within the other statutes than part of one which is within the SGA.[8]

[15.05] Title. Section 15 of the SGA, which sets out the terms which are to be implied into sales by sample, makes no mention of undertakings as to title, but presumably s 12 is wide enough to cover such transactions (see Chapter 12). A similar omission is to be found in those statutes dealing with the terms to be implied into sample contracts by way of quasi-sale, hp and simple hiring (SOGIT; SGSA).

[15.06] Correspondence with sample. In the case of a sale by sample, s 15(2)(a) of the SGA provides that there is an implied condition that:[1]

> ... the bulk will correspond with the sample in quality.

Identical provisions are to be found in relation to quasi-sales, hp and simple hirings,[2] except for the following: the SGA contains a definition of 'bulk', introduced in 1995 for another purpose, and thought inapplicable here.[3] None of the enactments specifically refers to the question of quantity; and the rules concerning quantity have been considered above (see ante, paras 13.03–07). The position in relation to exclusions is examined below (see post, para 15.07).

---

4   Benjamin, *ibid*, para 11-091.
5   Benjamin, *ibid*, para 11-092.
6   SOGIT, s 11; SGSA, ss 5(1), 10(1). See the warning about applying the appropriate statute: see ante, para 12.01.
7   Guest, *Law of HP*, para 302. It has been argued that a transaction is unlikely to be by sample unless the sample is released to the transferee: Goode, *Commercial Law* (2nd edn), pp 342–43. *Sed quaere?*
8   Does it make any difference whether (a) there is being supplied more than one of the item, (b) the contract goods include the sample?

[15.06]
1   As with the other implied terms, s 15(2) reduces the undertaking to an implied 'term', but a new provision (here new s 15(3)) gives it the status of a condition for English law: SSGA 1994, Sched 2, para 6.
2   SOGIT, s 11(a); SGSA, ss 5(2)(a), 10(2)(a). In the case of SOGIT, all subsequent references are to s 11(a) as amended by the CCA: see further ante, para 12.02.
3   SGA, new s 61(1), introduced by the SGAA 1995: see post, para 20.22B.

The undertaking that the goods will correspond with the contract sample in quality is closely related to the undertaking that goods shall correspond with their description (see ante, paras 13.08 *et seq*). A strict attitude used to be taken to compliance with the undertaking: for instance, it has been held insufficient that it might be possible to make the bulk conform with the sample by a simple process.[4] However, even where a contract sample is involved,[5] compliance will be subject to the *de minimis* rule[6] and the following: if the normal trade practice is that a sample be subjected only to a visual examination, there is no breach of the undertaking if the bulk does not correspond with the sample in some manner not discoverable by such examination;[7] a trade certificate of compliance may be conclusive;[8] and there may also be a breach of the undertaking as to satisfactory quality (see post, para 15.10).

The obvious close similarity of this undertaking with that as to compliance with description raises the question of whether to apply to the former the *Ashington* rule (see ante, para 13.14): if so, there would only be a breach where the non-compliance of the bulk with the sample amounts to a difference in kind.[9] On the other hand, both the SGA and the other statutory undertakings stipulate in almost identical terms that in this situation:[10]

> ... it is not sufficient that the bulk of the goods correspond with the sample if the goods do not also correspond with the description.

These would appear to reflect the common law,[11] where the undertaking of compliance with description appears to have been paramount.[12] However, it may suggest that s 15(2)(a) is wider than s 13 and extends to non-identifying contractual description (see ante, para 13.12), which would give some separate meaning to each provision.

[15.07] Exclusion clauses. Where a transaction falls within Part I of UCTA, there are substantial restrictions on the power of the supplier to exclude the statutory undertakings implied in supplies by sample (see post, para 18.19); but no further restrictions are imposed by the UTCC Regulations (see Sched 1, para (e)(i): see ante, para 11.12A).

---

4   *F & S Ruben Ltd v Faire Brothers & Co Ltd* [1949] 1 KB 254. Has this survived the rule in the *Ashington Piggeries* case (see below)?

5   Not every sample will be a contract sample: see ante, para 15.04.

6   *Joe Lowe Food Products Ltd v JA and P Holland Ltd* [1954] 2 Lloyd's Rep 70. As to the *de minimis* rule, see ante, para 13.12.

7   *Hookway v Isaac* [1954] 1 Lloyd's Rep 491; *Steels & Busks Ltd v Bleeker Bik & Co Ltd* [1956] 1 Lloyd's Rep 228.

8   *Gill & Duffus SA v Berger & Co Inc* (set out post, para 23.06). For certificates of inspection, see generally ante, para 14.02.

9   *Polenghi Brothers v Dried Milk Co* (1904) 92 LT 64.

10 SGA, s 13(2). See also SOGIT, s 9(1); SGSA, ss 3(3), 8(3). Eg, *Wallis, Son & Wells v Pratt & Haynes* (set out ante, para 11.04).

11 See *Nichol v Godts* (1854) 10 Exch 191.

12 For what appears to be an exceptional case, see *Joseph Travers & Sons Ltd v Longel Ltd* (1947) 64 TLR 150.

Outside those provisions, the problem was illustrated in *Champanhac & Co Ltd v Waller & Co Ltd:*[1]

> There was a sale of a quantity of government surplus balloons under a contract in which the seller stipulated that the goods were sold 'as sample taken away' and 'it is distinctly understood that these are government surplus goods and we sell them to you with all faults and imperfections'. On delivery, the goods were found to be perished and unmerchantable.

Slade J held that there was a sale by sample; and that the goods did not correspond with their sample, which was neither perished nor unmerchantable. In considering the exclusion clause, his Lordship thought that the cases under s 13 of the SGA were *in pari materia*, and held that the seller was not protected in respect of breach of the undertaking that the goods should correspond with their sample.[2] In this case, the undertaking was express, so that it may be that any exclusion clause must be otiose; but it has been suggested on the basis of this case that the undertaking as to correspondence with sample can never be excluded.[3] The problem would seem to be the same as that considered in relation to attempts to exclude the undertaking that the goods comply with their description (see ante, para 13.16).

[15.08/09] Opportunity for inspection. By s 15(2)(b) of the SGA, there was an implied condition that the buyer shall have 'a reasonable opportunity of comparing the bulk with the sample'. The result would appear to have been that, where there was a sale by sample the buyer had two rights to examine the goods: he had the ordinary right to examine under s 34 (see post, para 23.10) and the special right now under discussion. These two rights imposed on the buyer different duties; and attempts to exclude this special right were subject to UCTA (ss 6, 7: see post, para 18.19).

Whilst similar statutory rights of inspection were introduced into hp, quasi-sale and simple hirings,[1] it was difficult to justify two statutory rights of inspection. Accordingly, such a right was deleted for sales by the SSGA 1994,[2] though the Act inexplicably left standing the parallel rights in hp, quasi-sale and simple hiring.[3]

[15.10] Satisfactory quality and fitness.

1   *Satisfactory quality.* In *Drummond v Van Ingen*,[1] the House of Lords accepted that there was ordinarily a presumption that if the bulk corresponded with the sample it satisfied the contract, but that this presumption was rebutted by proving that the goods contained a latent defect rendering them unmerchantable. For sales, this rule

---

[15.07]

1   [1948] 2 All ER 724.

2   He suggested *obiter* that the clause might have protected the seller if there were latent defects in the goods and sample which rendered the goods unmerchantable.

3   Chalmers, *Sale of Goods* (15th edn), p 57, note (t) – suggestion dropped from subsequent editions.

[15.08/09]

1   SOGIT, s 11(b); SGSA 1982, ss 5(2)(b), 10(2)(b).

2   SSGA 1994, Sched 2, para 5(6)(a).

3   Presumably, such deletion should have been listed in Sched 2, paras 4(5) and 6(8).

[15.10]

1   (1887) 12 App Cas 284, HL.

was embodied in s 15(2)(c) of the SGA,[2] which provided that there is an implied condition:[3]

> ... that the goods will be free from any defect, making their quality unsatisfactory, which would not be apparent on reasonable examination of the sample.

A virtually identical provision is to be found in relation to quasi-sales, hp and simple hiring.[4] In all cases, the expression 'satisfactory' is to be construed in accordance with the concept of satisfactory quality already considered.[5] However, it will be observed that the provisions currently being discussed differ from the ordinary undertakings as to satisfactory quality in **all** the following respects: there is no requirement as to supply in course of business (see ante, para 14.04); there is no express defence of specified defects (see ante, para 14.25); and the undertaking is ousted in respect of defects which would be apparent on reasonable examination of the sample (see ante, para 14.26), so the undertaking is thus confined to latent defects.[6] What should happen, therefore, if the supply is both by description and by sample? It is submitted that in those circumstances the ordinary undertaking as to satisfactory quality can have no application: this would appear to reach an answer consistent with the common law; and, if the latter were applicable in these circumstances, the more severe limitations of the undertakings applicable to supplies by sample would be pointless.[7]

2 *Fitness.* Neither the SGA nor the other statutes applicable to supplies of goods makes any special reference to an undertaking that the goods are fit for the purpose for which they are supplied where the transaction is by sample;[8] and in all cases the statutory language of the ordinary undertaking appears to be wide enough to cover this situation.[9] Support for the application of the ordinary undertakings as to fitness to transactions by sample is to be found in the common law.[10]

For exclusion of these two undertakings, see post, para 18.19.

---

2   As supplied by the SSGA 1994, s 1(2). There is an identical limitation in new s 14 of the SGA: see ante, para 14.25.

3   As with the other implied terms, s 15(2) reduces the undertaking to an implied 'term', but a new provision (here new s 15(3)) gives it the status of a condition for English law: SSGA 1994, Sched 2, para 6.

4   SOGIT, s 11(c); SGSA, ss 5(1)(c), 10(1)(c).

5   SGA, s 15(3); SOGIT, s 15(2); SGSA, ss 5(3), 10(3): see ante, para 14.19.

6   The latent defect may be in the sample, or in the bulk, or in both: see Goode, *Commercial Law* (2nd edn), p 344.

7   But see Murdoch (1981) 44 MLR 388, at 398–99. It has been recommended that the law should be so clarified: *Sale and Supplies of Goods* (1987, Law Com No 160), para 6.27.

8   SGA, s 15; SOGIT, s 11; SGSA, ss 5, 10.

9   SGA, s 14(3); SOGIT, s 10(3); SGSA, ss 4(4)–(6), 9(4)–(6): see further ante, para 14.07.

10   *Drummond v Van Ingen* (1887) 12 App Cas 284, HL. See especially *per* Lords Macnaghten and Herschell, at 295, 293.

OTHER STATUTORY UNDERTAKINGS

[15.11/13] Trade usage. Section 14(4) of the SGA provides that:[1]

> An implied term as to quality or fitness for a particular purpose may be annexed to a contract of sale by usage.

This undertaking is not limited to trade sales (compare the undertakings as to quality and fitness: see ante, para 14.04). A virtually identical undertaking is imported into quasi-sales, hp agreements and simple hirings.[2] These rules are statutory formulations of what is perhaps the best-known example of implied terms at common law.[3] The alleged usage must fulfill all the normal tests of a commercial[4] custom;[5] but, provided that it does so,[6] it will become part of the contract so long as it is reconcilable with the express or implied terms of that contract.[7]

Hitherto, most of the cases on trade usage have involved contracts between businessmen; but there would appear to be no reason why the rule should not also apply to retail sales to private consumers, given that the consumer has the requisite degree of knowledge of the trade custom, cf undertakings as to description (see ante, para 13.11). Thus, in respect of a retail sale of a new car this undertaking may be used to import the following obligations:

(a) the retailer will make the pre-delivery checks and adjustments as per the manufacturer's specifications; and

(b) the retailer is entitled to make reasonable post-delivery adjustments **before** it is decided whether the vehicle meets the statutory implied obligations,[8] or under the cure rule (see post, para 29.03A).

Similarly, it may be possible to import by means of this undertaking common-form warnings and instructions as to the use of goods supplied after the contract is made (see post, para 18.33), and possibly trade voluntary codes of practice (see ante, para 3.12).

[15.11/13]

1   As amended by the SSGA 1994, Sched 2, para 5(a). As the term could be a condition or warranty, there would appear to be no substantive change.

2   See SOGIT, s 10(4) (as amended by the 1994 Act, Sched 2, para 4(4)(b); SGSA, ss 4(7); 9(7). Inexplicably, the terms implied by the SGSA were not amended by the 1994 Act.

3   See *per* Lord Blackburn in *Tucker v Linger* (1883) 8 App Cas 508, at 511. See Allen, *Law in the Making* (7th edn), Chapters 1 and 2.

4   Distinguish common law customs: see ante, para 11.10.

5   Eg, *Peter Darlington Ltd v Gosho Ltd* [1964] 1 Lloyd's Rep 149; *Three Rivers Trading Co v Gwinear and District Farmers* (1967) 111 Sol Jo 831, CA. That which is insufficiently established to amount to a trade custom may become part of the contract by reason of the course of dealings between the parties: see post, para 18.04.

6   If the custom extends to private sales, so may the implied term. Cf the restriction of the undertakings of quality and fitness to trade sales (see ante, para 14.04).

7   See *Produce Brokers Co Ltd v Olympia Oil and Cake Co Ltd* [1916] 1 AC 314, HL; and further litigation under the same name, [1917] 1 KB 320, CA. See generally ante, para 13.11.

8   But see *Rogers v Parish* (set out ante, para 14.23).

[15.14] Supplies of services. Part 2 of the SGSA[1] applies where there is a 'contract[2] for the supply of services',[3] whether or not goods are also transferred or bailed under that contract.[4] In such a case, unless the contract is one of employment (s 12(2)), or of a type exempted by the Secretary of State,[5] there are implied the following innominate[6] statutory terms (see post, para 15.15), subject to the usual restrictions on exclusions (s 16: see post, para 18.09).

[15.15] Undertakings in supplies of services. Where there is a supply of services (see ante, para 15.14), there are the following implied terms:

1   *Care and skill.* Where the supplier is acting in the course of a business,[1] it is implied that 'the supplier will carry out the service with reasonable care and skill'.[2] Thus, if a plumber supplies and fits a tap which thereafter leaks, the position is probably this: if the defect is in the tap, the householder must look to the implied undertakings as to quality and fitness (is this to be under the SGA (s 14) or the SGSA (s 4)?); whereas if the defect is in the fitting he must look to the present rule. Whilst the common law only required the supplier of the service to carry it out with reasonable care and skill,[3] it has been claimed that s 13 requires the contractor to achieve a satisfactory result,[4] an argument which might be useful where the supplier fails to collect an instalment of his fee by direct debit (see post, para 23.13); or a restaurant prepares an inedible meal.[5] At all event s 16(3) of the SGSA saves any stricter duty imposed by the contract, common law or statute, eg, s 14 of the TDA (see ante, para 14.15).

[15.14]

1   As to Part II, see generally ante, para 15.02, note 4; and Thomas, *Encyclopedia of Consumer Law*, para 1-1269. As to codes of conduct in relation to the supply of services, see ante, paras 3.11–14; and as to criminal offences, see ante, paras 4.15–17. See generally Murdoch [1983] 4 LMCLQ 652.

2   Part II will not apply where liability in respect of the provision of a service lies only in tort (eg, negligence: see post, para 17.13 *et seq*). *Contra* where the action lies in contract or tort: Woodroffe, *Goods and Services – The New Law*, paras 6.09–10.

3   SGSA, ss 12(1) and (3): see generally ante, para 2.05. Does Part II extend to the provision of facilities for self-service, eg, launderette, petrol, supermarket (cf ante, para 4.16)? What of the provision of computer software?

4   Section 12(3). Examples of contracts of service frequently linked with a supply of goods are the following trades: plumbing; building; electrician; roofing; installation of double-glazing, central heating and cavity-wall insulation.

5   For exemptions, see s 12(4) and (5); and see Thomas, *op cit*, note 1. Note that the reference is only to implied terms, without any attempt to classify them as conditions or warranties: see further ante, para 11.04.

6   They are all described simply as 'implied terms'. For innominate terms, see generally ante, para 11.05.

[15.15]

1   For supply in the course of business, see ante, para 14.04; and for a survey, see [1992] Which? 492. Does this extend to 'foreigners' and 'moonlighting'?

2   SGSA, s 13; and see Bell, *Personal Property*, 104. This does not appear to extend to cosmetic defects: *CRC Flooring v Heaton* (1984) Tr L 33, CA; but compare supplies of goods (see ante, para 14.24). For other criticisms, see Borrie, *The Development of Consumer Law and Policy*, 22; and Palmer (1983) 46 MLR at 628–30.

3   Eg, *Eyre v Measday* [1986] 1 All ER 488, CA (sterilisation); *Wilson v Best Travel Ltd* [1993] 1 All ER 353 (travel operator). There are also some relevant provisions in codes of practice: see ante, para 3.13.

4   *John Lelliott (Contracts) Ltd v Byrne Bros Ltd* (1995) 31 Con LR 89, Cty Ct. See Bragg and Lowe, *The Business of Licensing*, p 55. Cf the right of cure: see post, para 29.03A.

5   *Aliter*, where the food is unfit for human consumption: see SGA, s 14(2B)(d), ante, para 14.20.

2   *Time for performance*. Where the supplier is acting in the course of a business, and no time is specified, that 'the supplier will carry out the service within a reasonable time', which is a question of fact (s 14). This provision could be applicable both to simple service contracts, eg, of repair,[6] and also where the service was linked with a supply of goods, eg, a supply of goods upon which a service is to be performed before delivery.[7] It has been suggested that in the case of supplies to consumers time will be of the essence,[8] but even where it is not, an action for damages will lie (cf post, para 29.28).

3   *Consideration*. Whether or not the supplier is in business, if no consideration is agreed, 'there is an implied term that the party contracting with the other party will pay a reasonable charge'.[9] The drafting here appears to follow the provisions as to price in s 8 of the SGA (see ante, para 2.06): it only applies where there is a contract between the parties,[10] in which case it in effect directs the court to apply the industry standard. It does not preclude express agreement to a charge which proves exorbitant.[11]

Thus, where a consumer orders a meal in a restaurant, in the absence of sufficient express terms, there may be implied terms that the meal is produced with reasonable skill (s 13), within a reasonable time (s 14) at a reasonable charge (s 15). To complement the Directive on Product Liability (see post, para 17.23), there has been proposed a Draft Directive on the liability of suppliers of services.[12] In a consumer supply contract, exclusion of any of the above terms may be unfair (UTCC Regulations, reg 4: see ante, para 11.15).

[15.16] Undertakings in regulated agreements. The major terms implied in favour of a debtor or hirer are to be found elsewhere (see Chapters 12–14), the CCA having little to say on the subject. It remains to draw together here those few other obligations arising under regulated agreements (see ante, para 5.13).

The common law right of the creditor or owner to refuse to accept instalments of price or rent tendered after a breach by the debtor or hirer is modified in relation to regulated agreements by the default notice procedure considered later (see post, para 24.30); and, where there is more than one debt due from the debtor or hirer to one person under two or more regulated agreements, the common law right of the supplier to appropriate payments to a particular debt is excluded (see post, para 23.13). On the other hand, the

---

6   Cf *Charnock v Liverpool Corp* [1968] 3 All ER 473, CA.

7   As with the pre-delivery inspection of a motor vehicle (see generally ante, para 15.11). Cf *McDougal v Aeromarine of Emsworth Ltd* [1958] 3 All ER 431 (contract to build and supply yacht).

8   Thomas, *Encyclopedia of Consumer Law*, para 1-1273, citing *Charles Rickards Ltd v Oppenheim* (set out post, para 26.25). Cf the SGA delivery rule: see post, para 23.04. See also Woodroffe, *Goods and Services – The New Law*, paras 6.33–36.

9   SGSA, s 15(1). 'What is a reasonable charge is a question of fact': s 15(2). Cf SGA, s 8(2), (3): see ante, para 2.06. If the consumer wished the service to be performed under the terms of a guarantee (see post, para 17.09), it would thus be safer to say so.

10   *Russell Brothers (Paddington) Ltd v John Lelliott Management Ltd* (1996) 11 Const LJ 377 (OR).

11   It is exempt from the UTCC Regulations as being a core term: see ante, para 11.14. It has been argued that there should be a statutory power to re-open such charges: Woodroffe, *op cit*, para 6.39, citing the extortionate credit bargain provisions (see post, para 29.40).

12   This would shift to the supplier the burden of showing that he was not at fault: see (1991) 8 Tr LR 190; 135 Sol Jo 318; Geddes, *Product and Service Liability in the EEC*. For continuing problems with motor vehicle servicing, see (2000) 28 *Fair Trading* 12.

common law duty of a bailee to take reasonable care of the goods bailed receives statutory reinforcement under the termination provisions (see post, para 27.49).

The CCA also seeks to avoid a fertile source of misunderstanding and even oppression by ensuring that both parties can ascertain their rights and duties under a regulated consumer credit agreement at any time during its currency. Most such information provisions are in favour of the debtor or hirer and any surety:[1]

(1) At the outset, ie before and at entry into the agreement (ss 44, 52, 62–63: see ante, para 8.21).

(2) Periodically, in the case of running account credit (s 78(4)–(7): see ante, para 7.08).

(3) Upon request. During the currency of most regulated agreements, the debtor or hirer is entitled to receive from the creditor or owner[2] at minimum intervals and upon tender of the prescribed fee a copy of the executed agreement;[3] and a statement setting out the prescribed information appropriate to that type of agreement.[4] If the creditor or owner fails to supply such a statement, he commits a criminal offence;[5] and the agreement is **unenforceable** whilst default continues.[6] Any statement he supplies is *prima facie* binding on him (s 172). Thus, if the creditor or owner understates the amount owed, the debtor or hirer is then entitled to a termination statement at that figure (see below).

(4) Settlement figure to discharge the agreement (s 97: see post, para 26.19A).

(5) Termination statement that agreement has been discharged (s 103: see post, para 26.04).

Almost as a *quid pro quo* for the creditor, s 80 requires the debtor or hirer to inform the creditor or owner of the whereabouts of any goods supplied under the agreement.[7]

Other transactions

[15.17] Loan financing. Where the goods-supplier (dealer) makes a cash sale to the consumer with the price of those goods being loaned to the consumer by the financier (see ante, para 2.20), the lender credit may take any of the following forms:

1 *Ordinary loan*. Since the 1960s, the clearing banks, finance companies and building societies have undertaken a substantial amount of lending by way of overdraft and

---

[15.16]

1 As to the rights of any surety to similar statements, see ss 105–10: see post, para 25.12.

2 Sections 77 (fixed sum credit); 78(1)–(3) (running-account credit); 79 (consumer hire). The rules do not apply to non-commercial agreements (see ante, para 5.18): ss 77(5), 78(7), 79(4).

3 This has implications for the credit/owner as to the storage of agreements, eg, microfilming, computerising.

4 The detailed information required by the Regulations is set out in Goode, *Consumer Credit Law and Practice*, para 34.11 *et seq*.

5 Sections 77(4)(b); 78(6)(b); 79(3)(b). For offences, see Sched 1. But the offence in itself gives rise to no further sanctions: s 170, set out ante, para 10.19.

6 Sections 77(4)(a); 78(6)(a); 79(3)(a). As to the effect of a more permanent type of unenforceability, see ante, para 9.19.

7 A removal of the goods by the debtor from a nominated place may amount to a breach of an express term of the agreement: see further ante, para 11.09. Perhaps this provision could also be used to get the debtor to admit he has sold the goods.

personal loan to finance the acquisition of goods for consumption (see ante, para 2.17). Retailers have developed their budget accounts.[1] At the same time, the business of the 18th century tallyman (see post, para 5.02) has developed into the modern weekly collected credit trade for the bottom end of the market (see ante, para 2.18).

2   *Check or voucher trading.*[2] Developing about 1880, the traditional check-trader (financier) issues a 'trading check' to the consumer,[3] which check will be accepted in lieu of payment to its face value by any retailer with whom the check-trader has an arrangement: the retailer can redeem (at a discount) these checks with the check-trader; and the consumer will subsequently pay the face value of the check (plus a service charge) to the check trader by subsequent instalments.[4] It seems clear that check trading is a form of lending.[5] A modern variant are vouchers carrying the name of the retailer. Where they are issued to the consumer by the retailer, the position may be as follows: if the consumer pays at issue the face-value of the voucher to the retailer and that voucher is subsequently 'cashed' in return for goods, the consumer is lending money to the retailer, as in a Christmas Club (see ante, para 7.02); whereas, it is a form of vendor credit (see ante, para 2.19) if the consumer takes delivery of the goods before completing the payments.[5] Another variant is for a financier to buy the voucher at face-value (less discount) from the retailer and then 'sell' it to a consumer either for cash,[6] or on credit, which will usually be for weekly collected credit (above).

3   *Pawnbroking.* This is making a business of lending money on the security of the transfer of possession (pledge) of goods (see post, para 25.15). Flourishing from the 17th century, traditional pawnbrokers have recently seen revival, partly on a weekly collected credit basis.

4   *Trading stamps.* This scheme of sales promotion basically works as follows: a retailer enters into a 'franchise' agreement with the trading stamp company, which agreement will not itself fall within the SGA (see ante, para 1.09); the retailer will supply to each consumer a number of 'stamps' in proportion to 'purchases' made;[7] and the consumer, normally after collecting these stamps in a book, can exchange the stamps

---

[15.17]

1   See ante, para 2.20. For the converse situation, where the consumer in effect lends money to the supplier, see post, para 15.18.

2   See *Mason v Provident Clothing* [1913] AC 724, HL; and generally the *Report on Consumer Credit* (1971, Cmnd 4596) paras 2.4.1–7; Goode, *HP Law and Practice* (2nd edn), pp 898–900; *Chitty on Contracts* (28th edn), vol 2, para 38-442; Rowlingson, *Money Lenders*, pp 25–26. The expression 'voucher' is sometimes used for respect of larger amounts over longer periods: see Goode, *Consumer Credit Law and Practice*, para 2.35.

3   This amounts to a promise by the check-issuer to pay the face-value of the check on behalf of the presenter/consumer to the retailer: it is thus a form of chose in action; as to which, see post, para 7.15.

4   A home collection agent may also use the opportunity to sell new checks: as to the restrictions on such canvassing, see CCA, ss 48–49, considered ante, para 7.05.

5   Chitty, *op cit*, note 2, para 38-225, note 9.

6   See (1990) 11 CCA News 6/11; (1992) 13 CCA News 1/7; Griffiths and Howells (1991) 42 NILQ 199. It then acts like a gift stamp: see ante, para 2.11.

7   The retail franchise-holder is supposed to benefit from increased sales to consumers addicted to collecting the stamps: for sales promotions generally, see ante, para 8.13. Insofar as a consumer purchasing for a principal retains stamps, he is extracting from his principal a commission on purchasers, eg, commercial traveller buying petrol. Could this amount to a secret profit?

for goods, usually at one of the stamp company's distribution centres. Sometimes services are offered instead of stock, eg, holiday stamps, air miles. It is not clear whether the exchange of trading stamps for goods is a form of barter,[8] or a sale of goods;[9] but it cannot amount to a quasi-sale (s 1(2)(e), SGSA: see ante, para 2.10). At all events, this form of transaction has received separate treatment by the legislature in the Trading Stamps Act 1964 as amended (TSA). Trading stamps are no longer issued as a promotional device and the TSA rules governing them are to be found elsewhere.[10] However, there remains the question of whether the various vouchers, stamps and other perks next considered (see ante, para 15.18) fall within the above definition of a 'trading stamp', because the provisions of the TSA are not usually observed in such cases. It is submitted that Christmas Club stamps and petrol stamps may be within the definition because they are supplied 'in connection with' the purchase of goods, whereas gift stamps and vouchers are not because they are not to be redeemed by the stamp-purchaser; and money-off coupons are expressly excluded, whether printed on the goods or in newspapers, whereas such paper coupons, 'points' or 'cash-back' vouchers are caught if issued by a multiple retailer.[11] As to whether such schemes are within the TSA when operated via smart cards or other plastic cards depends on whether such cards are within the definition of a 'stamp' as being a 'similar device'.[11]

5   *Credit unions* (see post, para 15.19).

6   *Other forms.* These include loans by friendly and loan societies, life assurance offices and building societies.[12]

[15.18] Vouchers, stamps and other perks. Some such items may be part of promotion competitions,[1] or are methods of financing the price (see post ante 2.16), or are simply receipts for payment, as with payment in advance of delivery, eg, Co-op milk tokens. Leaving these aside, any of the following types of item may be connected with a supply of goods:

(1) A stamp or voucher separately purchased from, eg, a retailer, whereunder the stamp-supplier (retailer) undertakes to exchange the stamp for goods to its face value on subsequent presentation. Such schemes would appear to sub-divide as follows:

   (a) 'Christmas Club' stamps (see ante, para 15.17).

   (b) 'Gift' stamps, where it is contemplated that the stamp purchaser will donate the stamp (frequently mounted on a fancy card) to a third party.[2] Such a stamp would

---

8   *Benjamin's Sale of Goods* (5th edn), para 1-040. *Quaere* whether there could be a barter in these circumstances?

9   *Davies v Customs and Excise Comrs* [1975] 1 All ER 309, DC. See also ante, para 2.06. Could the transaction be split into (1) a notional redemption of stamps for cash and (2) a sale of goods?

10   See Butterworths edn, 1989, paras 2.10; 15.18; 15.19.

11   See Lawson (1992) 142 NLJ 1273; Circus, *Sales Promotion Law* (2nd edn), pp 87–88. It is intended that a revised TSA deal with Loyalty Schemes: DTI, *Modern Markets: Confident Consumers* (1999), para 6.16.

12   See Goode, *op cit*, note 2, paras 2.37–39.

[15.18]

1   Eg, in newspapers or magazines, or on products (see generally [1975] Which? 32). Prize competitions are governed by the Betting, Gaming and Lotteries Act 1963 (see ante, para 8.16).

2   There is also a variation whereunder the voucher is provided by a third party, being sold to the public and redeemed from them by any participating retailer, eg, book tokens. Cf check-trading (see ante, para 15.17).

appear to be a credit note transferable by delivery.[3] It is for consideration whether the donee's redemption of this stamp for goods from a retailer amounts to a quasi-sale by the retailer (see ante, para 2.10).

(2) By way of promotional scheme, a retailer or manufacturer[4] may promise a consumer a reduced price in respect of his next purchase from that retailer or of that manufacturer's goods.[5] When the coupon is supplied free to the consumer, it is simply an advertisement of price reduction and may fall within the CPA (see ante, para 8.10). However, where the consumer gives value for the coupon, eg, coupons printed on product or in newspapers purchased, he may also have a collateral contract with the coupon issuer.[6] What is the effect where retailer A accepts for value the vouchers issued by retailer B; or where A accepts vouchers issued by manufacturer X against supplies of goods manufactured by Y?[7]

(3) Stamps, vouchers, etc, issued by the supplier at the time of supply and to be exchanged for goods or services at a later date so that value is given for the stamp, voucher, etc. Usually, the stamp, voucher, etc is of small face-value and is meant to be collected over repeated purchases. The original versions of such an idea were Co-op Dividend stamps and then Trading stamps, both forms of promotion which fell into disuse. Instead modern promotions tend to offer for collection 'points' on a payment card, eg, 'loyalty cards;[8] or 'cashback' vouchers on goods (see ante, para 8.13A). Can a stamp-supplier *bona fide* redeeming a stolen stamp, voucher, points, etc, take free of the equities (see post, para 7.24), perhaps on the basis that it is 'negotiable by estoppel?'[9] Some of the above promotions fall within the Trading stamp legislation (see ante, para 15.17).

The foregoing schemes may be subject to the Sales Promotion Code (see ante, para 3.14) and their terms may be subject to the Unfair Terms Regulations (see ante, para 11.15).

[15.19] Credit unions. In essence, a credit union is a non-profit-making loan society formed on a co-operative basis.[1] This concept has flourished abroad, but has been more

---

3 This would be a form of chose in action: as to which, see generally ante, para 7.17. It is neither a bill of exchange within the Bills of Exchange Act 1882 (s 3), nor a promissory note (s 83): see generally *Chitty on Contract* (28th edn), vol 2, para 34-020.

4 Eg, retailers' coupons delivered from door-to-door, or in a 'newspaper'; manufacturer's coupons printed on goods, in newspapers or magazines, or delivered from door-to-door. Sometimes these are just promotional schemes, eg, by two manufacturers.

5 See the Institute of Sales Promotion, *Recommended Best Practice*, set out in Circus, *Sales Promotion Law*, Appendix 3.

6 *Taylor v Smetten* (1883) 11 QBD 207 (illegal lottery); *Scott & Co Ltd v Soloman* [1905] 1 KB 577 (statutory licence). Cf the Esso promotion scheme discussed ante, para 2.08. *Quaere* whether a coupon 'issued' by a manufacturer will bind the retailer?

7 Have the vouchers then become transferable, as with some gift vouchers (above)? As to whether such actions by A infringe the British Code of Advertising Practice (see ante, para 3.14), see Lawson, (1992) 142 NLJ at 1274.

8 Eg, Tesco Clubcard. See [1998] 1 Which? 16. What is the point if customers hold multiple loyalty cards?

9 *Easton v London Joint Stock Bank* (1886) 34 Ch D 95 at 113–14; see *Paget on Banking* (11th edn), p 579; and Jacobs, *Bills of Exchange*, Chapter 6. Cf travellers cheques, as to which see Chitty, *op cit*, note 3, para 34-173.

[15.19]

1 The 1971 *Crowther Report* (see ante, para 5.03), para 2.4.28(v).

reluctant to take root in the UK.[2] Here, they have mutual status like building societies (see ante, para 2.17) and are developing within the framework of the Credit Unions Act 1979.[3] They have two basic functions: (i) they act as savings clubs, in which capacity they typically pay rates of interest which exceed the commercial rate for size of savings and are now controlled by the FSA (see ante, para 3.02); and (ii) make loans to members (usually with free life insurance), which because of their low interest charges have been exempted from the CCA (see ante, para 5.15). The essence of credit unions is the common bond between members, eg, neighbourhood, association, or workplace;[4] but experience saw a divergence between the more successful industry-based unions and the less successful area-based unions.[5] However, from the viewpoint of low-income groups, the crucial potential for development is neighbourhood credit unions in areas from which commercial banks have withdrawn; but for some reason these proved particularly reluctant to develop, despite Government support.[6] Accordingly, the 1979 Act has been substantially amended through Deregulation Orders (see ante, para 5.10), principally to relax the common bond requirement[7] and ease loan conditions,[8] which has led to an increase in the popularity of credit unions. The Government has plans to support these local unions by the introduction of a Central Service Organisation:[9] this should help unions to offer current accounts with access to the clearing system (see ante, para 2.15), with cash machines, direct debits and standing orders.

[15.20] Miscellaneous cases. Apart from the cases above considered, there are a number of other statutes which impose obligations on the contracting parties. Often these provisions are aimed at a particular type of transaction or a transaction involving a specified type of goods, or both.

In imposing such an obligation, three techniques are available to the legislature. First, terms may be imported into a contract, breach of which will give the innocent party civil law rights by statute[1] or statutory instrument.[2] Second, the agreement may be rendered

---

2   The *Crowther Report,* paras 9.2.12–13.

3   (As amended). See generally Griffiths and Howells (1991) 42 NILQ 199 at 204–15; (1992) 142 NLJ 235; Howells, Aspects of Credit and Debt, pp 15–17, 51, Chapter 8; (1993) 14 CCA News 4/12. As to how to set up a credit union, see the Open University, *An Introduction to Credit Unions;* NCC, *Saving for Credit: The Future of Credit Unions in Britain* (1994).

4   Area-based unions lack confidentiality and the resources to institute the (frequently) desired weekly collected credit: (1990) 11 CCA News 2/17; *Mirage or Reality,* Appendix C. Griffiths and Howells, *ibid,* pp 48–49. Compare commercially-based weekly collected credit: see ante, para 5.01.

5   Industry-based unions have the advantages of payroll deduction repayments and employer discipline.

6   There are concerns with the size of unions, their administration, economic viability and the inflexibility of the legislation. See OFT, *Vulnerable Consumers and Financial Services* (Jan 1999); Liverpool JMU Report for Joseph Rowntree, *Keep Out or Opted Out* (Mar 1999); Social Exclusion Unit, *Access to Financial Services* (Nov 1999); [1999] CCA News, Winter, 3.

7   Section 1(4), as amended by the Deregulation (Credit Unions) Order 1996, SI 1189, Art 3.

8   Sections 11 (as amended), 11A–D.

9   See Ryder [2001] JBL 510. Cf the Michigan Credit Union League, USA.

[15.20]

1   Eg, Hops (Prevention of Frauds) Act 1866, s 18; Anchors and Chain Cables Act 1899, s 2; Agriculture Act 1970, s 72; Plants and Seeds Act 1964, s 17.

2   Remember that English statutes can be amended by regulations made under the ECA or Deregulation Acts (see ante, para 1.03A; 5.10).

unenforceable or terminated in the event of non-compliance.[3] Third, a statute may refuse[4] or impose (see the statutes considered in Chapter 4) criminal sanctions in respect of the prohibited act. This last course tends to be more favoured nowadays as it is more likely to be effectively enforced, but it does give rise to certain problems: (1) does it render the agreement illegal?[5] (2) If so, to what extent does this prevent the parties from relying on the agreement;[5] and (3) does contravention give rise to an action for breach of statutory duty?[6]

TERMS AND OBLIGATIONS DERIVED FROM COMMON LAW

[15.21] There is nothing in any of the Acts relating to supply contracts to oust any express or implied condition precedent, eg, s 2(3), SGA (ante, para 1.11). Conditions in the sense of essential stipulations have already been distinguished from conditions precedent (see ante, para 11.04); and in relation to conditions precedent it is further necessary to distinguish between those precedent to the existence of a contract[1] and those precedent only to performance of some or all of its obligations.[2]

We are now in a position to consider the terms implied by common law into supply transactions, whether they are terms within the contract, or conditions precedent of one sort or the other.

As to quality and fitness

[15.22] *Caveat emptor.* Where a transaction falls within the SGA (see ante, para 1.07 *et seq*), then amended s 14(1) appears to re-affirm the basic rule of freedom of contract (see ante, para 1.02) by re-stating the old *caveat emptor* rule, that (as amended by Sched 2, para 5(5) of the SSGA 1994):

> Except as provided by this section[1] and by section 15 below[2] and subject to any other enactment,[3] there is no implied term about the quality or fitness for any particular purpose of goods supplied under a contract of sale.[4]

---

3   Eg, CCA, s 65 (see ante, para 9.19); CCA, s 90 (see post, para 24.35).
4   This may be the effect of the obscurely worded SGA, s 60: see Chalmers, *Sale of Goods* (18th edn), p 261. What then is the effect of SGA, s 57(5)?
5   See generally ante, para 10.20.
6   See generally ante, para 3.21.
[15.21]
1   Ie, the offer may be conditional, eg, *Financings Ltd v Stimson* (set out ante, para 10.08).
2   Eg, *Marten v Whale* (set out ante, para 1.11); *Bentworth Finance Ltd v Lubert* (set out post, para 15.23); and post, para 26.01.
[15.22]
1   For the terms implied by s 14, see ante, Chapter 14, and ante, para 15.11. For a summary of the historical development of the implied terms, see Goode, *Commercial Law* (2nd edn), pp 192–93.
2   For the terms implied by s 15, see ante, paras 15.03–10.
3   See the examples referred to ante, para 15.20.
4   For discussion of the phrase 'goods supplied under a contract of sale', see ante, para 14.04.

There is a very similar provision in respect of hp, quasi-sales and simple hirings.[5] These words might appear to confirm the full severity of the common law attitude of *caveat emptor*,[6] but they have been said not to prevent any implication of terms as to quality or fitness under the doctrine of the *Moorcock*.[7] In the *Harlingdon* case, the disclaimer by the seller of any expert knowledge was held by the majority of the Court of Appeal to rule out any implied promise by him as to the description or merchantability of the goods.[8]

However, there are a number of ways in which the full severity of this rule may be mitigated. First, the section says 'there is no warranty or condition', which seems to imply that 'condition' is here used in the sense of essential stipulation. If so, the sections do not prevent the implication of conditions precedent (see ante, para 15.21). Second, the sections do not prevent the prudent buyer or hirer from securing an express contractual promise by the seller or owner as to the quality or fitness of the goods supplied (see ante, para 11.07) or as to some related matter.[9] Does such an express promise oust the terms which would ordinarily be implied? At common law this turned on whether the parties intended the term to be in addition to the implied term or to replace it;[10] and statute now provides (s 55(2) of the SGA. See also s 12 of SOGIT; s 11(2) of the SGSA, with a slight variation in wording):

> An express warranty or condition does not negative a warranty or condition implied by this Act unless inconsistent therewith.

This subsection would appear to be merely an example of the ordinary rule as to the exclusion of implied terms set out elsewhere (see post, para 18.09). Third, it may be possible for the buyer to bring an action in tort, though such an action will not usually be as likely to succeed as a claim in contract (see post, para 17.12 *et seq*). Fourth, it has been suggested that a person who buys (or hires?) goods with a latent defect may be able to rescind the contract on the grounds of non-disclosure.[11] Fifth, there may be particular statutory offences concerning the quality of goods supplied, eg, motor vehicles, where the provisions extend to private sales (see ante, para 4.37). Bear in mind compensation orders (see ante, para 3.20). Sixth, there may be other implied terms which are not exclusively about quality and fitness.[12]

---

5   See respectively: SOGIT, s 10(1) as amended by SSGA 1994, Sched 2, para 4(4)(a); SGSA, s 4(1); SGSA, s 9(1). In the case of the SGSA, the 1994 Act has not replaced 'condition or warranty' by 'term' – is this a mistake?

6   See *Smith v Hughes* (set out ante, para 10.17). But have the implied terms now developed so far that this traditional introduction is now misleading? See Goode, *op cit*, note 1, p 313; and compare Brown (2000) 116 LQR 537; Hedley [2001] JBL 114.

7   (1889) 14 PD 64, CA. See *St Albans DC v International Computers Ltd* (set out post, para 18.24), *per* Glidewell LJ at 494b–d; *Watford Electronics Ltd v Sanderson Ltd* (set out post, para 18.24A; unappealed point). This may be important in relation to the common law terms in bailment and hp: see post, paras 15.23–24.

8   The first instance judge had rejected evidence of a custom that sales in the art market are on a *caveat emptor* basis. But the CA achieved the same result, thereby depriving the buyer of the protection of the implied terms by way of UCTA (see post, para 18.12 *et seq*). See Smith (1990) 140 NLJ at 1675. Thus, the ruling may not apply to a private art buyer: see Bentil (1991) 8 Tr LR at 32–33, 36.

9   Such as that the goods would be supplied with any necessary warning: *Vacwell Engineering Ltd v BDH Chemicals Ltd* (set out post, para 18.29). See also ante, para 14.01.

10 See *Bigge v Parkinson* (1862) 7 H & N 955.

11 Atiyah (1968) 2 Ottawa LR 337 at 339–44.

12 The *Albright and Wilson* case (set out ante, para 13.01), at paras 34; 35.

Other terms in hire purchase

[15.23] In contrast to the situation with regard to sales, the courts have been able to import into hp agreements a considerable number of implied terms for the benefit of both owners and hirers: there is express permission to do so contained in SOGIT, s 15(4). Many of these implied terms obviously owe their inspiration to the law of bailment (see generally ante, para 1.17).

For the benefit of the hirer, it has been decided that the hiring does not commence until delivery,[1] and that the goods have not been delivered until they have been accepted by the hirer so as to pass into his possession.[2] Furthermore, the courts have implied conditions that the goods should remain in substantially the same condition from the time when the offer is made up to the time of acceptance;[3] and from then until the time of delivery.[2] In *Bentworth Finance Ltd v Lubert*:[4]

> ... the plaintiff finance company agreed to let a car to L under a directly financed hp transaction under which M agreed to act as surety for L. The dealers left the car unlicensed and untaxed, outside L's house, and L neither used the car nor paid any instalments.

The Court of Appeal unanimously dismissed the plaintiff's action against L and M for arrears of instalments on the following grounds:

(1) it was an implied condition of the hp agreement that the log-book should be supplied, and until it was supplied 'there was no contract of hp at all', and no instalments fell due;[5]

(2) M was not liable because the plaintiff's loss did not arise from the contract of hp being unenforceable, but from the 'plaintiff's allowing the dealers to hand over the car without the log-book' (see further post, para 25.06).

Now, in all the cases so far cited in this paragraph the owner was suing the hirer, and the courts did no more than hold that performance of a particular act by the owner was a condition precedent to his enforcement of the agreement.[6] It is, however, usually thought that the owner impliedly promises to deliver the goods, and to deliver them in substantially the same condition as they were when inspected by the hirer. In *Karsales (Harrow) Ltd v Wallis*:[7]

> ... the consumer (C) entered into a directly financed transaction in respect of a Buick car. Prior to signing the agreement, C had inspected the car, and found it to be in good order. Shortly after the date of the agreement, the 'car' was (apparently) towed into position outside C's premises at night; and on inspection the following morning it was found to be in a deplorable condition, and incapable of self-propulsion.

[15.23]

1. *National Cash Register Co v Stanley* [1921] 3 KB 292, DC.
2. *Karsales Ltd v Wallis* (set out below). As to what amounts to a delivery, see generally post, para 23.03.
3. *Financings Ltd v Stimson* (set out ante, para 10.08).
4. [1968] 1 QB 680; [1967] 2 All ER 810, CA.
5. For conditions precedent, see generally ante, para 15.21.
6. Were they conditions precedent to contract or performance? See Lord Denning MR in *Lubert's* case (above), at 685; and *Financings Ltd v Stimson* (above).
7. [1956] 2 All ER 866; [1956] 1 WLR 936, CA. See Goode, *HP Law and Practice* (2nd edn), p 227.

The Court of Appeal unanimously found for C on the grounds that the object delivered was not the car contracted for, and that such a breach disentitled the plaintiff[8] from relying on the exclusion clause. Alternatively, the majority were prepared to decide the case on the further ground that delivery of the car had not been accepted.[9]

[15.24] In favour of the owner. The terms which the common law will imply into simple bailments in favour of the owner have already been considered (ante, para 1.17). Similarly, the courts have implied in favour of the owner under a hp agreement obligations that the hirer will accept delivery of goods tendered in performance of the contract;[1] that he will take reasonable care of them during the currency of the agreement;[2] that he will not do any act in relation to the goods which is totally repugnant to the terms of the bailment (see post, para 26.09); and that he will pay the sums stipulated in the agreement subject to the ordinary common law rules of payment (see post, para 23.26 *et seq*). Furthermore, where the agreement is determined, the hirer is under a common law duty[3] to redeliver the goods;[4] but, should redelivery become impossible through no fault of his own, the hirer is *prima facie* discharged from this duty (see post, para 22.10 *et seq*).

Analogous transactions[1]

[15.25] Goods are sometimes supplied on a commercial or quasi-commercial basis under transactions which do not fit easily within the established categories of contract for the supply of goods. Of course, the supplier will be subject to the obligations of the law of tort applicable to such circumstances; but this will normally mean only liability towards his transferee in the tort of negligence (see post, paras 17.13; 17.20). The question is this: in view of the business basis of the transaction, can the supplier be subjected to the more onerous strict liability of contract? To the extent that there is statutory strict civil product liability (see Chapter 17), this question may *pro tanto* be rendered otiose.

At the outset, a distinction must be drawn according to whether or not there is any contractual basis to the supply.[2] Transactions where there is **no** such basis are outside the SGSA[3] and may fall into one of the following categories:

---

8   The finance company assigned their rights to the plaintiff dealer under a repurchase provision: see post, para 16.21.

9   It would follow that the plaintiff's only possible remedy would be for damages for non-acceptance (see post, para 27.24), which right had not been assigned to him (see ante, para 7.17).

[15.24]

1   *National Cash Register Co v Stanley* [1921] 3 KB 292 DC.

2   The extent of this common law duty is uncertain; and it is unlikely to be settled as the agreement will almost always impose strict liability on the hirer. See ante, paras 1.14; 1.15.

3   In the absence of any contractual provision to the contrary, the common law duty is merely to hold the goods ready for the owner to fetch them: see post, para 24.25.

4   Failure to comply with his duty to redeliver will render the hirer liable to an action for breach of contract or in tort for conversion (see post, para 19.05).

[15.25]

1   See generally Miller and Lovell, *Product Liability*, pp 115–22; Waddams, *Product Liability*, pp 87–100; Cranston, *Consumers and the Law* (3rd edn), Chapter 6.

2   For transactions where there is a contractual basis to the supply, see post, para 15.26.

3   Because of the absence of a contract: see the SGSA, s 1(1), considered ante, para 2.10.

(1) Where there is a simple transfer of possession, the supplier retaining the property in the goods. This will amount to a bailment at will, and the obligations of such transactions have already been examined (ante, para 1.14), the bailor probably only being liable to the bailee in the tort of negligence.[3a] If there were liability at common law for negligence, does s 2 of the Unfair Contract Terms Act 1977 (see post, para 18.17) prevent its exclusion?

(2) Where there is a transfer of possession and property with the requisite intent, this will amount to a gift (see ante, para 2.09), the donor's only liability being in the tort of negligence. Leaving aside drugs supplied under the NHS (see ante, para 1.07), perhaps the most obvious difficulty here concerns 'free gifts'. Some transactions so described are clearly sales of goods, eg, 'three for the price of two'; whilst in others the 'free' goods are in fact supplied under a quasi-sale (see ante, para 2.10), as where goods are supplied in return for coupons, wrappers or points, with[4] or without[5] some additional monetary consideration.[6] On the other hand, some free gifts or samples are clearly gifts, probably attracting to the supplier only liability towards the donee in the tort of negligence (see post, para 17.13).

(3) Where the intending purchaser is injured by the goods before the formation of the contract for their supply.[7] If the parties envisage an instalment transaction which will fall within the ambit of the CCA, it is described as a 'prospective regulated agreement' and the transaction even in the precontract stage attracts some of the restrictions of the CCA.[8] On the other hand, there is no contract, and hence no possibility of any express or implied promises, so that the tort of negligence is the supplier's only other possible liability to the injured consumer.[9]

[15.26] Contract basis. Where goods are supplied on a commercial or quasi-commercial basis under a contract, before the SGSA it was sometimes difficult to decide how to treat such transactions. Some transactions were found on closer inspection to fall within the SGA (see ante, para 1.06 et seq): for instance, goods sold in a hired container;[1] or a 'three for the price of two' constitutes a sale of all three units; or where an apparent barter turns out to amount rather to reciprocal sales;[2] or a sale of goods-to-be-fitted.[3] On other occasions, there may be found to be two contracts within one transaction, a contract for the sale of goods supplied plus an installation or fitting contract (see ante, para 2.05); and in these cases the rules of sale or hp or hiring can clearly be applied to the supply of

---

3a See ante, para 8.14, note 3.
4   *Chappell & Co Ltd v Nestle Co Ltd* [1960] AC 87, HL.
5   *Esso Petroleum Ltd v Comrs of Customs and Excise* (see ante, para 2.08).
6   Or the transferee may supply some consideration in kind, eg, by submitting an entry to a competition for a prize.
7   Eg, a supermarket customer injured by goods before reaching the check-out; or where goods are at the time of injury being demonstrated to, or examined by, a customer before purchase. Does this category include goods on sale or return before purchase (see post, para 20.23)?
8   Eg, Parts IV and V of the CCA, discussed ante, Chapters 8, 9 and 10.
9   *Lasky v Economy Grocery Stores* (1946) 65 NE (2nd) 305; 163 ALR 235.
[15.26]
1   See *Geddling v Marsh* (set out ante, para 14.03).
2   See ante, para 2.09. But what if the supplier agrees to replace defective goods 'free of charge'?
3   Eg, *Phillip Head and Sons Ltd v Showfronts Ltd* [1970] 1 Lloyd's Rep 140 (fitted carpets).

goods, and Part II of the SGSA to the supply of services (see ante, para 15.15). However, there remained the difficult cases where goods were supplied under a collateral contract (is this the proper analysis of the sale of a fully furnished house?); or where there was only one hybrid contract under which there was a supply in part of goods and in part of services.[4] Presumably, the fact that the details of a pure contract to provide services are set out in writing and that document handed to the other party does not make the contract a hybrid one.[5]

In some hybrid contracts, the courts applied the rules of sale by analogy.[6] However, s 1(3) of the SGSA provides that:

> For the purposes of the Act a contract is a contract for the transfer of goods whether or not services are also provided or to be provided under the contract, and (subject to subsection (2) above) whatever is the nature of the consideration for the transfer or agreement to transfer.

It follows that the category of quasi-sales within Part I of the SGSA (see ante, para 2.10) clearly includes both the following categories:

(a) the first limb of s 1(3) brings in hybrid contracts;[7] and

(b) the second limb extends the category to barter or exchange,[8] some 'free gifts'[9] and other title transferring transactions,[10] including perhaps collateral contracts.[11]

In a consumer supply contract, any exclusion clause may be an unfair term.[12]

---

4   Eg, *Young and Marten Ltd v McManus Childs Ltd* [1969] 1 AC 454, HL (roofing sub-contractor supplying defective tiles); *Watson v Buckley Ltd* [1940] 1 All ER 174 (hairdresser applying dye); *Dodd v Wilson* [1946] 2 All ER 691 (vet inoculating with defective serum); *Samuels v Davis* [1943] 1 KB 526 (dentist supplying dentures). See Greig, *Sale of Goods*, p 8.

5   What about the provision of computer software? See *per* Norse and Glidewell LJJ in *St Albans DC v International Computers Ltd* (set out post, para 18.24), at 487j, 494a.

6   *Per* Lord Diplock in the *Ashington Piggeries* case (set out ante, para 13.13) at 501. Eg, *Ingham v Emes* [1956] 2 QB 366, CA (hairdresser applying dye); *Andrews v Hopkinson* (set out post, para 16.18). See further ante, para 1.04.

7   Eg, *Stewart Gill Ltd v Horatio Meyer & Co Ltd* [1992] 2 All ER 257, CA (decided on another point: see post, para 18.16); *Watford Electronics Ltd v Sanderson CFL Ltd* (set out post, para 18.24A; unappealed point).

8   This includes part-exchange. For contracts of barter or exchange, see generally ante, para 2.09.

9   Notwithstanding the terminology, the 'free gift' of goods may amount to a collateral contract (see ante, para 15.25), under which goods are supplied subject to all the ordinary implied terms. But see Law Com No 95, para 32; and further Woodroffe, *Goods and Services – The New Law*, paras 2.11–15.

10   Eg, prizes award in competitions. See further Palmer (1983) 46 MLR at 621–22.

11   Distinguish collateral contracts which do not transfer the property in goods: see post, paras 16.14; 17.09.

12   OFT, UCT *Bulletin No 13*, case 8: for Grey Term 1(b), see ante, para 11.16.

CHAPTER 16

FINANCED TRANSACTIONS

[16.01] Introduction. The express and implied terms which may be found in contracts for the supply of goods have been examined in Chapters 11–15, together with the effect of any misrepresentation inducing entry into the supply contract. In the present chapter, the extent to which that scheme may be amended where the retail supply is financed is considered, whilst product liability and exclusion clauses are respectively left over until Chapters 17 and 18. Particularly important in lender credit are the rules concerned with the financier's liability for the dealer's acts (see post, para 16.04 *et seq*) and the liability of the dealer to the financier and consumer (see post, para 16.18 *et seq*).

However, before embarking on these topics, it may be helpful to summarise the circumstances in which the SGA, the SOGIT, the CCA and the SGSA are applicable to the various forms of vendor and lender credit (see respectively post, paras 16.02–03).

STATUTORY ANALYSIS

[16.02] Vendor credit (see ante, para 2.19). This involves the retail-supplier himself financing the transaction and may take either of the following forms:

(a) *A single instalment credit contract* (see ante, para 1.03), to which all the rules previously considered in Chapters 11–15 apply. Which statutes are applicable will vary according to the form of instalment credit contract utilised as follows:

   (i) a credit[1] or conditional[2] sale, whose 'supply' element will be **within** the SGA[3] or SGSA,[4] and whose 'credit' element may also amount to a regulated DCS agreement **within** the CCA;[5] or

   (ii) a hp agreement,[6] whose 'supply' element falls **outside** the SGA,[3] but within SOGIT,[7] and which may have a 'credit' element which amounts to a regulated DCS agreement **within** the CCA;[5] or

   (iii) a simple hiring agreement,[8] whose 'supply' element falls **outside** both the SGA[3] and SOGIT,[7] but **within** the SGSA,[4] and which may amount to a regulated consumer hire agreement **within** the CCA.[9]

[16.02]

1   For credit sales, see ante, para 1.13.
2   For conditional sales, see ante, paras 1.14–15.
3   For the ambit of the SGA, see ante, 1.07. For the implied terms, see ante, Chapters 12–15.
4   The SGSA introduced some new implied terms for quasi-sales and simple hirings: see ante, Chapters 12–15.
5   For DCS agreements, see ante, para 5.34.
6   For hp agreements, see ante, para 1.20 *et seq*.
7   The SOGIT introduced some new implied terms for hp agreements: see ante, Chapters 12–15.
8   For simple hiring agreements, see ante, paras 1.18–19.
9   For consumer hiring agreement, see ante, para 1.19.

(b) *Two associated transactions* as follows:

   (i) a contract of loan (see ante, para 7.02), which may amount to a regulated DCS agreement **within** the CCA;[5] **and**

   (ii) a cash sale, whose 'supply' element will fall within the SGA[3] or SGSA,[4] and which may amount to a linked transaction **within** the CCA (see ante, para 5.31).

[16.03] Lender credit. This involves a third party financing the transaction and may take either of the following forms, each of which requires **two** major contracts:

(a) *Direct financing* (see ante, para 2.21), where there is **both** –

   (i) A cash sale of the goods **within** the SGA[1] or SGSA[2] from the dealer to the financier;[3] **and**

   (ii) An instalment contract between the financier and consumer, which contract will follow the same analysis as in the case of vendor credit (see ante, para 16.02).

(b) *Loan financing* (see ante, paras 2.23–24), where there is **both** –

   (i) A cash sale of the goods **within** the SGA[1] or SGSA[2] from the dealer to the consumer; **and**

   (ii) A loan by the financier to the consumer, which loan may amount to a regulated consumer credit agreement **within** the CCA.[4]

If the regulated loan is independent of the sale,[5] the loan will then be a DC agreement;[6] but, if the loan and sale are both part of a single package,[7] the loan will be a DCS agreement[8] and the sale a linked transaction (see ante, para 5.31).

FINANCIER'S LIABILITY FOR THE DEALER'S ACTS

[16.04] Introduction. The matter to be considered here is the effect which the form of the financing may have on the personal obligations of the parties.[1] Where a binding transaction is financed by the dealer – vendor credit (see ante, para 2.19) – there will

---

[16.03]

1   For the ambit of the SGA, see ante, para 1.07. For the implied terms, see ante, Chapters 12–15.

2   The SGSA introduced some new implied terms for transactions analogous to sales: see ante, Chapters 12–15.

3   This is not a linked transaction: see ante, paras 5.31; 10.32.

4   For regulated consumer credit agreements, see ante, para 5.13.

5   Because the statutory definitions of 'creditor' and 'owner' in s 189(1) include their assignees: see ante, paras 5.25; 1.19.

6   For DC agreements, see ante, para 5.35.

7   See the CCA, s 187: discussed ante, para 5.33.

8   For DCS agreements, see ante, para 5.34.

[16.04]

1   The security element of instalment credit transactions will be considered later: post, Chapters 24 and 25.

always be a contract for the supply of goods between the dealer and consumer, so that all the rules previously considered in Chapters 11–15 will apply to the dealer's conduct. The same will be true if the transaction is loan financed (see ante, para 2.23). However, if the transaction is directly financed (see ante, para 2.21), there will be no primary contractual relationship between the dealer and consumer;[2] and, if the transaction is financed by way of loan of the price to the consumer, there will be no contract for the supply of goods from the financier to the consumer.

For these reasons, the insolvency of the dealer in a directly financed or loan financed transaction has caused problems; and the feeling has developed that some attempt must be made to help the consumer to find a solvent defendant by giving him rights against the financier in respect of wrongdoing by the dealer,[3] on the basis that the financier should in some way be 'responsible' for the dealer.[4] This has led to three different (overlapping) veins of statutory intervention:[5]

(a) interference with the common law rules of agency as between the dealer and financier;[6]

(b) the dealer in directly financed transactions has been made the agent of the financier as regards his misrepresentations;[7]

(c) the financier in loan financing has been made liable for misrepresentations and breaches of the supply contract by the dealer.[8]

[16.05] Direct financing. The absence of any primary contractual relationship between dealer and consumer in direct financing (see ante, para 16.04) has caused some special difficulties at common law.

(1) *The deposit*. On signing the proposal form, the consumer will usually hand over a deposit to the dealer. This deposit may be either cash or goods taken in part-exchange (see ante, para 2.10).

(a) If the financier does not accept the proposal or the agreement is void *ab initio*, it is a question of intention whether the deposit is recoverable by the consumer from the dealer: normally, it is intended simply to form part of the consideration for the contemplated contract,[1] in which case it is recoverable by the consumer from the dealer on grounds of total failure of consideration;[2] but, if it is intended to be by

---

2   Though there may be a collateral contract between them (see post, para 16.18). For some special difficulties caused by this absence of any primary contractual relationship, see post, para 16.05.

3   This has given financiers a real sense of grievance: see, eg, *Instalment Credit* (ed Diamond), pp 27–29.

4   At common law, this 'responsibility' argument is usually conducted in terms of whether the dealer is participating in the transaction as agent of the financier: as to which, see below.

5   Whilst (a) leads into (b), it is perhaps unfortunate that (b) and (c) have been drafted in ss 56 and 75 of the CCA so that there may be considerable overlap between them. But in loan financing, liability under (b) and (c) is not co-extensive: Jones, *Credit Cards*, pp 215–17.

6   This intervention is now to be found in s 56(3) of the CCA: see post, para 16.07.

7   This rule is now to be found in s 56(2) of the CCA: see post, para 16.10.

8   This liability has been introduced by s 75 of the CCA: see post, para 16.11.

[16.05]

1   *Chillingworth v Esche* [1924] 1 Ch 97, CA – a real property case cited in an old edition of *Benjamin on Sale* (8th edn), p 947, note (e).

2   As to which, see generally post, para 29.13. Is the deposit alternatively recoverable from the financier under s 56(2) of the CCA? See post, para 16.10.

way of security for completion of the transaction by the consumer, then in the event of his default it cannot be recovered at common law, though equity may offer relief against forfeiture (see post, para 27.20), or that agreement may be avoided by the CCA (s 59: see further ante, para 5.20), or the UTCC Regulations may offer relief.[3]

(b) Where the financier accepts the proposal, the dealer will credit the financier with the amount of the deposit or part-exchange allowance, in which case that amount will be regarded as being given by the consumer indirectly to the financier. In *Branwhite v Worcester Finance Ltd*[4] the majority of the House of Lords decided that the dealer was not the agent of the financier;[5] but their Lordships unanimously held that, as the dealer had credited the financier with the deposit as against the price to be paid by the financier to him, this was equivalent to an actual payment of the deposit to the financier on behalf of the consumer in respect of a transaction which had wholly failed so far as the consumer was concerned; and so the financier must return the deposit to the consumer (at 572, 582, 590). This rule will apply wherever the consumer elects to treat as discharged for breach his instalment credit contract with the financier (as to which, see post, para 26.15).

(2) *Documents signed in blank.* Particular difficulty has arisen where the consumer has signed the proposal in blank and then the dealer has subsequently fraudulently completed and forwarded the documents to the financier.[6] In *Mercantile Credit Co Ltd v Hamblin:*[7]

> The defendant (A) asked a motor dealer (B) if he could obtain for her a loan of £1,000 on the security of her Jaguar car, and B agreed to make enquiries of a finance company. In the meantime, B suggested that it would expedite matters if he were to give A blank cheques and she were to sign the necessary documents in blank. Accordingly, A signed three documents, which were in fact those appropriate for a directly financed hp transaction, though she did not realise this. B later fraudulently completed the forms and tendered them to the plaintiff finance company (C), who accepted them and paid B and the latter pocketed the money. A, who thought the transaction had fallen through, refused to pay C any instalments, and C therefore claimed the car.

Against C's claim to title in the car, A pleaded that she was not bound by the hp proposal she had signed in blank on the following grounds:

(i) A unsuccessfully claimed that she could deny her signature on grounds of *non est factum*,[8] though nowadays, if regulated, she would be able to plead that the agreement was not properly executed;[9] but

---

3 See the Grey List, term 1(0): see ante, para 11.18.
4 [1969] 1 AC 552; [1968] 3 All ER 104, HL. In this litigation, it had been decided in previous proceedings (and was so binding by issue estoppel) that the hp agreement was void *ab initio*, the customer having signed in blank: but it has now been shown that this may be wrong – see below.
5 *Per* Lords Morris, Guest and Upjohn, at 573, 578. Lords Reid and Wilberforce dissented, at 589. See further post, para 16.06.
6 See generally Allcock (1982) 45 MLR 18.
7 [1965] 2 QB 242; [1964] 3 All ER 592, CA.
8 See also *United Dominions Trust Ltd v Western* [1976] QB 51, CA; and generally ante, para 10.16.
9 *PB Leasing Ltd v Patel and Patel* [1995] CCLR 82, Cty Ct; and generally ante, para 9.13.

(ii) She did convince the court that she should not be estopped by her negligence from setting up her title to the car.[10]

(3) *Defective goods.* Whilst the goods are physically supplied to the consumer by the dealer (see ante, para 2.21), in law they are supplied to him by the financier (see post, para 16.11). Statutory alteration to this pattern has made the financier additionally liable for the dealer's representations (see post, para 16.07); but the dealer may alternatively be liable as 'supplier' under the safety legislation.[11]

Agency of the dealer

[16.06] Common law. The question of whether the financier can be made 'responsible' for the acts of the dealer on the basis that the latter acted as the former's agent has caused particular difficulty in relation to directly financed transactions.[1] The are two diametrically opposed judicial views of the matter. On the one hand, it is argued that the dealer is the financier's agent on the basis of ostensible authority (see ante, para 10.06). For instance, in *Financings Ltd v Stimson*[2] Lord Denning MR argued:

> The dealer holds the necessary forms; he hands them over to the hirer to sign; he forwards them to the finance company; he receives the deposit as agent for the finance company; he receives from the finance company information that they are willing to accept the transaction; and he is authorised to pass on that communication to the hirer .... It seems to me that, if we take, as we should, a realistic view of the position, the dealer is in many respects and for many purposes the agent of the finance company.

On the other hand, there is considerable authority for the rejection of any general proposition that the dealer is the agent of the financier. Thus, in *Mercantile Credit Ltd v Hamblin*[3] Pearson LJ said:

> There is no rule of law that in a hire-purchase transaction the dealer never is, or always is, acting as agent for the finance company or as agent for the customer. In a typical hire-purchase transaction the dealer is a party in his own right, selling his car to the finance company, and he is acting primarily on his own behalf and not as general agent for either of the other two parties. There is no need to attribute to him an agency in order to account for his participation in the transaction.

No doubt, the above two *dicta* are strictly reconcilable; but they were accepted as involving rival views in *Branwhite v Worcester Finance Ltd,*[4] a case involving a directly financed hp transaction. Three members of the House of Lords there expressly adopted the *dicta* cited from the judgment of Pearson LJ,[5] whereas the other two expressly rejected

---

10   However, the court did allow the argument a theoretical possibility of success: see post, para 21.15.
11   CPA, s 46(2): see further ante, para 4.34 and post, para 17.27.
[16.06]
1   As to directly financed transactions, see generally ante, para 2.21. For further discussion of the agency issue, see Goode, *HP Law and Practice* (2nd edn), pp 286–96.
2   [1962] 3 All ER 386, CA, at 388. He was supported in this case by Donovan LJ (at 389); but Pearson LJ disagreed (at 392).
3   [1965] 2 QB 242, CA, at 269. See also Holroyd Pearce LJ in *Campbell Discount Co Ltd v Gall* [1961] 1 QB 431, at 441, CA.
4   [1969] 1 AC 552; [1968] 3 All ER 104, HL.
5   *Per* Lords Morris, Upjohn and Guest, at 573, 576.

it in favour of the argument put forward by Lord Denning MR.[6] In practice, the courts seem to be very reluctant to accept that at common law the dealer has acted as agent of the financier: for instance, it has been held that the dealer had authority neither to accept the consumer's offer contained in the proposal form;[7] nor to receive instalments of hire rent;[8] nor to fix the financier with knowledge that the transaction was a disguised bill of sale;[9] nor that the dealer's title to the goods was defective;[10] nor probably for the purposes of making representations,[11] nor paying a settlement figure (see post, para 26.19A). In *Woodchester Leasing Equipment Ltd v BACFID*:[12]

> Black was employed as a salesman by Magnum, an office equipment supplier. Black persuaded BACFID, a trade association, to sign a hp agreement for a fax machine, leaving the supplier's name blank. Black then changed employers and submitted the proposal to a financier in the name of his new employers. Meanwhile, Magnum sent another salesman, Marco, to retrieve the business: by misrepresentation, Marco persuaded BACFID to complete a separate proposal to lease from Woodchester. When two fax machines were delivered, BACFID declined to continue with the transaction.

Woodchester sued BACFID for breach of the lease and the latter sought to rely on Marco's misrepresentation. Following the *Branwhite* case (above), the Court of Appeal held that Woodchester were not responsible for the misrepresentation of Marco. Contrast the position of eponymous subsidiaries (see post para 16.06A); and for statutory intervention, see post, para 16.07.

[16.06A] Equipment leasing. This paragraph is concerned with the problems which have arisen with directly financed equipment leases (see ante, para 1.18), particularly office equipment such as photocopiers, personal computers, computer printers, mobile telephones, fax and vending machines. The common scenario, whereby the photocopier-supplier sells the equipment to a leasing company which in turn leases it to a business consumer, led to such a close relationship between the supplier and lessor as to attract the appellation 'sales-aid leasing'. In the 1980s, this kind of business generated so much abuse as to prompt an OFT enquiry,[1] which *inter alia* noted the following complaints: eponymous subsidiaries as lessors (see below); misrepresentations by the supplier's commission-paid salesman;[2] inappropriate machines supplied;[3] lease periods which

---

6 *Per* Lords Wilberforce and Reid at 585. The relationship is not governed by the Commercial Agents (Council Directive) Regulations 1993, SI 3053 (as amended): 48 CC 6/22.

7 *Financings Ltd v Stimson* (set out ante, para 10.08). But compare *Carlyle Finance Ltd v Pallas Industrial Finance Ltd* (set out ante, para 10.08).

8 *Bentworth Finance Ltd v White* (1962) 112 LJ 140, Cty Ct. For actions for arrears of rentals, see generally post, para 27.21.

9 *Spencer v North County Finance Ltd* [1963] CLY 212, CA.

10 *Car and Universal Finance Ltd v Caldwell* (set out post, para 21.22).

11 *Williams & Co v McCauley* [1994] CCLR 78, CA.

12 [1995] CCLR 51; CLY 1193, 49 CC6/2, CA.

[16.06A]

1 OFT, *Photocopier Selling Practices* (March 1994).

2 Eg, *Woodchester Leasing Equipment Ltd v BACFID* (set out ante, para 16.06).

3 Where the machine was inappropriate, the lessee may want to rely on the implied term as to fitness in s 9(5) of the SGSA 1982 (see ante, para 14.07), the supplier being a credit broker for the purpose (see ante, para 14.12).

exceed the likely life of the goods combined with Draconian settlement terms,[4] standard form leases which hide the price,[5] as by combining the lease price with a service charge, or requiring the lessee to pay for a monthly minimum number of copies, or inserting a price escalator clause (see ante, para 10.05), or salesman-encouraged early termination and replacement (churning).[6] Initially, the OFT threatened to curb such practices by use of the following statutory powers: monopolies, misleading advertisements and CCA licensing.[7] However, the OFT Report preferred to sponsor an appropriate code of practice and argue that the salesman was the agent of the lessor.[8]

Eponymous subsidiaries. In *Lease Management Services Ltd v Purnell Secretarial Services:*[9]

> P carried on a printing business and for many years had been a customer of Canon (South West) Ltd, a supplier of photocopying machines. In 1986, P was using a Canon 400, of which an important feature to P was that the machine would produce 'photo plates'. When P was looking for a replacement photocopier, Canon's representative (B) supplied a demonstration 3525 model so that she could see if it made 'photo plates'. Convinced, P agreed to lease a new 3525 model, on a document produced by B. The new 3525 model turned out to be unable to make 'photo plates'.

The lease was prominently headed 'Canon (South West) Ltd', with that company's logo, whereas the small print described the lessor as LMS, 'trading as Canon (South West) Finance': this formula had been agreed by Canon (South West) Ltd to finance its business. P therefore wrote to Canon purporting to terminate the unregulated lease, in the reasonable belief that it had leased the machine from Canon. In fact, P had leased the photocopier from LMS.[10] LMS denied liability for any representation made by B and sought to rely on an exclusion clause in the lease. Leaving aside the latter point (see post, para 18.20), the Court of Appeal unanimously held that, as the lease gave the impression that P was contracting with Canon, LMS was estopped from asserting that it was a different body and that Canon's representative (B) had no authority to speak for it.[11] Under pressure in respect of this and other misleading practices,[12] the industry has agreed to adopt a new code of practice in respect of sales aid leasing (see ante, para 3.13), which is, after all, just a form of equipment leasing (see ante, para 1.18A).

---

4   By tying the lessee in to the supplier this may amount to a restrictive practice (see ante, para 2.12). In so far as it is not a genuine pre-estimate of damage, it may be void as being a penalty (see post, para 27.46).

5   Eg, price-per-copy contracts (see the OFT Report, Chapter 8), which may still be equipment leases: *Eurocopy (Scotland) v Lothian Health Board* [1995] CLY 5578 (S).

6   The lessee being encouraged to break the earlier agreement, upon which the lessor may seek to claim under the above settlement terms. As to whether the lessor can so claim where he encouraged the breach, see post, para 26.02.

7   So the OFT Report, Chapter 13. As to these statutory powers, see respectively ante, paras 2.12; 8.12A; 6.18.

8   OFT Report, para 2.24, arguing on the (above) close connection between the supplier and lessor. But see the leasing cases cited ante, para 16.06. The FLA Code of Practice is set out in Guest and Lloyd, *Encyclopedia of Consumer Credit Law*, Part 10, para 10-043.

9   (1994) 13 Tr LR 337, CA.

10 The use of such eponymous subsidiaries was common in the finance industry, but criticised by Nicholls VC as a 'misleading trade practice' (at 341B). Cf 'private label cards' (see ante, para 2.24).

11 At 341D–343A. It has been doubted (unconvincingly?) whether such apparent or ostensible authority is really just an application of estoppel (see ante, para 10.06): Phang [1995] JBL 378 at 380.

12 See OFT (1994) 7 Fair Trading 13; *Photocopier Selling Practices* (1994); 1993-AR, 9–10, 17.

[16.07] Statutory intervention. To obviate the difficulties at common law described above (see ante, paras 16.06–06A) of determining whether or not the dealer has acted as agent of the financier, the financier in an instalment credit transaction governed wholly by the common law will usually expressly deny the dealer any authority to commit him by acting as his agent, so preventing any possibility of actual authority; and he will normally take steps to notify the consumer of this fact,[1] so as to preclude any apparent authority.[2] If so, it follows that at common law the financier can normally only be rendered contractually liable on the basis that he has done something which overrides the disclaimer and clothes the dealer with some apparent or ostensible authority to act as his agent.[3] However, where the transaction falls within one or both of the following statutory protections it is a different matter altogether.

1 *The CCA.* Following the precedent in the HPA 1965, where such deemed agency clauses occur in regulated agreements, they may be attacked under s 56 of the CCA. This provision christens the dealer the 'negotiator' in the 'antecedent negotiations' (see post, para 16.08). Section 56(3) provides as follows:[4]

> An agreement[5] is void, if and to the extent that, it purports in relation to an actual or prospective regulated agreement:[6]
>
> (a) to provide that a person acting as, or on behalf of, a negotiator is to be treated as the agent of the debtor or hirer, or
>
> (b) to relieve a person from liability for acts or omissions or any person acting as, or on behalf of, a negotiator.

It will be observed that this provision is entirely **negative**: it does not make the dealer the agent of the financier for any purpose, but simply precludes the parties from ousting the ordinary common law rules for determining the extent, if any, to which the negotiator[7] is the agent of the financier, or the latter vicariously liable for the former.[8] However, other CCA provisions do **positively** deem the dealer to be the agent of the financier for certain purposes (see ante, para 10.24), including for the purpose of making representations during the 'antecedent negotiations' (see post, para 16.08).

2 *The UTCC regulations.* Where there is a 'consumer supply contract' (see ante, para 11.13), the deemed agency clause may be an 'unfair term' and hence not binding on

---

[16.07]

1 The instalment contract will usually recite that the dealer is not the agent of the financier making it difficult to advance an ostensible authority argument on the basis put forward by Lord Denning MR in para 16.06. See generally, Goode, *HP Law and Practice* (2nd edn), pp 283–85.

2 *Overbrooke Estates Ltd v Glencombe Properties Ltd* [1974] 3 All ER 511 (see further post, para 17.10); and generally ante, para 10.06.

3 *Mendelssohn v Normand Ltd* [1970] 1 QB 177, CA.

4 The parties cannot contract out of this provision (s 173(1)): see further post, para 18.11.

5 This 'agreement' may or may not be the regulated agreement. The CCA provides that 'agreement' here means agreement whenever made: Sched 3, para 12(2), eg, a Master Agreement (as to which see ante, para 2.21) entered into before the CCA was enacted.

6 For actual and prospective regulated agreements, see ante, para 5.20; and post, para 16.12.

7 Because of the drafting of s 56(1), s 56(3) will not usually extend to a directly financed lease: see post, para 16.08.

8 See further Goode, *Consumer Credit Law and Practice*, para 32.32.

the consumer (see ante, paras 11.14–15). This is because such deemed agency provisions are probably within the Grey List (Sched 3, para 1(n): see ante, para 11.18).

[16.08] Antecedent negotiations. According to s 56(1) of the CCA:

In this Act 'antecedent negotiations' mean any negotiations with the debtor or hirer –

(a) conducted by the creditor or owner in relation to the making of any regulated agreement, or

(b) conducted by a credit broker in relation to goods sold or proposed to be sold by the credit broker to the creditor before forming the subject matter of a debtor-creditor-supplier agreement within section 12(a), or

(c) conducted by the supplier in relation to a transaction financed or proposed to be financed by a debtor-creditor-supplier agreement within section 12(b) or (c), and 'negotiator' means the person by whom negotiations are so conducted with the debtor or hirer.

This provision concentrates on the 'negotiator' (including his servant or agent), meaning the person who conducts the 'antecedent negotiations' leading towards a regulated agreement in any one of three scenarios:

Para (a): creditor or owner as negotiator. Negotiations conducted by the creditor or owner[1] in relation to the making of any regulated agreement, eg, a moneylender's employee negotiating a DC loan, or a dealer negotiating a directly financed transaction as agent of the financier.[2]

Para (b): dealer as negotiator. Negotiations conducted by the credit broker[3] in relation to a directly financed consumer credit agreement: in the appropriate circumstances, these may render the agreement cancellable, eg, Sched 2, Example 4; and see generally ante, para 10.29. Two problems have arisen. First, the consumer may arrange with the credit broker to trade-in an existing model upon which there is outstanding finance which the credit broker undertakes to discharge; and whether the second finance company (the creditor) can be made liable under s 56 for any such undischarged finance: the issue turns on whether the credit broker's undertaking is made 'in relation to the goods sold or proposed to be sold'.[4] Second, because of the reference to s 12(a), category (b) cannot include directly financed leases, which are consequently unlikely to be cancellable (see ante, para 10.29), or leave the financier liable for the dealer's misrepresentations.[5]

[16.08]

1. By the s 189(1) definitions, this expressly includes any prospective creditor or owner (see ante, para 5.25), which is important here because the negotiations must take place before formation of the regulated agreement.

2. See respectively CCA, Sched 2, Example 1; and for the exceptional agency case ante, para 16.04. For reasons explained below, this is the only way that a directly financed lease can be brought within s 56.

3. Eg, Sched 2, Example 2. As to 'credit broker', see ante, para 5.38. As this category does not include a housewife acting as a part-time agent for a mail-order house (see ante, para 5.41), she will not be a 'negotiator': Goode, *Consumer Credit Law and Practice*, para 31.91. It is suggested that he does not need to be acting as a credit broker in that particular transaction: Guest and Lloyd, *Encyclopedia of Consumer Credit*, para 2-057.

4. The matter was settled in the affirmative in *Forthright Finance Ltd v Ingate* (set out post, para 16.10).

5. *Moorgate Mercantile Leasing v Isobel Gell* [1986] CLY 371, Cty Ct; *Contra Woodchester Leasing Equipment v Clayton* [1994] CLY 500, Cty Ct. *Aliter*, in respect of the implied undertakings as to fitness: see ante, para 14.12.

Para (c): supplier as negotiator. Negotiations conducted by the supplier[6] in a financed transaction,[7] as where it is loan financed.[8] Note that this paragraph overlaps with s 75 (see post, para 16.12): so, by using s 56(1)(c) it may be possible to avoid the limitations in s 75(3) (see post, para 16.13).

As all regulated agreements must inevitably be preceded by some prior communications between the parties, they must always be preceded by 'antecedent negotiations', and the effect of s 56(1) is that a wide variety of persons may amount to the 'negotiator'. Further, s 56(4) provides that:

> For the purposes of this Act, antecedent negotiations shall be taken to begin when the negotiator and the debtor or hirer first enter into communication (including communication by advertisement), and to include any representations made by the negotiator to the debtor or hirer and any other dealings between them.

The effect of s 56(4) is twofold. First, negotiations are made to include (a) any 'representation', which expression is widely defined to include 'any condition or warranty, and any other statement or undertaking, whether oral or in writing' (s 189(1); see further ante, para 10.29) and (b) 'other dealings'.[9] Second, s 56(4) extends back in time the commencement of 'antecedent negotiations' to the time when the debtor or hirer reads any 'advertisement'[10] put out by the 'negotiator', eg, point-of-sale advertising poster by dealer, such as a windscreen sticker, or a newspaper advertisement placed on the dealer's behalf by an advertising agency; or a manufacturer's advertisement adopted by the dealer, as on packaged goods. What if the advertiser is independent of the dealer and the advertisement is not adopted by the dealer? Whilst the Act is silent on the point, it would appear that 'antecedent negotiations' terminate on formation of the regulated agreement: this may have different effects according to whether the agreement is for fixed-sum credit[11] or running-account credit.[12]

Misrepresentation by the dealer

[16.09] Where a dealer induces a consumer to enter into a financed transaction by means of a misrepresentation,[1] the common law position of the financier[2] would appear to be

---

6   This will in effect be the dealer who in law and fact supplies the goods to the consumer: see ante, para 5.34.

7   Section 56(1)(c). It is here unlikely to matter that leases are excluded (see above).

8   See s 12(b). Eg, goods bought with a credit card (Sched 2, Example 3). As to an example within s 12(c), see Goode, *op cit*, note 3, para 31.92.

9   Eg, installation maintenance or insurance contracts – Goode, *op cit*, note 3, para 32.19. What of part-exchange goods?

10 As to 'advertisement', see ante, para 8.29. Does the advertisement have to play any part in inducing the debtor or hirer to enter into the transaction? Cf the common law misrepresentation rule.

11 It would follow that oral statements after formation, eg, during fitting or on delivery, are not within s 56 and hence will not attract s 67: see Goode, *op cit*, note 3, para 31.93.

12 If there is a fresh contract each time the card is used (see ante, para 7.11), oral statements preceding each use will be part of the 'antecedent negotiations': Goode, *op cit*, note 3, Div IIB, para 5.106.

[16.09]

1   For the effect of misrepresentations at common law on contracts induced thereby, see post, para 26.12 *et seq*; and for statutory intervention, see post, 17.10.

2   For the liability of the dealer in respect of such misrepresentations, see post, para 16.18.

weakened by the fact that the primary contractual relationship is between the financier and the consumer: in a directly financed transaction,[3] there is an instalment supply contract[4] made between them; and in loan financing, there is a loan contract made between them. Now, we are postulating a case where the misrepresentation inducing the consumer to enter the financed transaction is made by a third party, the dealer. Leaving aside any rights which this may give the consumer against the dealer, it can only affect the relationship between the financier and consumer if the dealer made the misrepresentation as agent of the financier.[5]

The problem first arose in connection with directly financed transactions, where the common law position was probably that the dealer was not the agent of the financier for the purposes of affecting the financier with liability in respect of misrepresentations made by the dealer in the course of negotiating the transaction with the customer.[6] In their Tenth Report (on *Innocent Misrepresentation*), the Law Reform Committee thought that this was unjust, and recommended that the dealer should be deemed to be the agent of the financier for such purposes.[7] This proposal was adopted by the HPA 1965 (s 16); but its formulation was thought defective in that it concentrated on direct financing. Hence, this deemed agency provision was extended by the CCA to ensure coverage of both direct and loan financing. Moreover, whilst s 16 was restricted to 'representations with respect to the goods', the comparable s 56 of the CCA was not so restricted (see post, para 16.10).

[16.10] Statutory agency. Having carefully defined 'antecedent negotiations' (see ante, para 16.08), the CCA provides that (s 56(2)):

> Negotiations with the debtor in a case falling within subsection (1)(b) or (c) shall be deemed to be conducted by the negotiator in the capacity of agent of the creditor as well as in his actual capacity.

Two points must be borne in mind in relation to this compulsory[1] deemed agency. First, s 56(2) does not apply to **all** those 'antecedent negotiations' within s 56(1) which lead to any two- or three-party transaction involving a regulated agreement: s 56(2) probably does not touch consumer hirings;[2] nor does it extend to vendor credit;[3] nor does it apply in favour of persons other that the debtor.[4] What s 56(2) clearly does cover is direct and loan financed consumer credit transactions, where the dealer/negotiator and financier/creditor are engaged in a joint operation in financing the supply of goods or

---

3   As to the forms of financing, see ante, paras 2.21–24.
4   As to the various forms of instalment contract, see ante, para 1.03.
5   *Lease Management Services Ltd v Purnell Secretarial Services* (set out ante, para 16.06A).
6   See Guest, *Law of HP*, para 384; Goode, *HP Law and Practice* (2nd edn), p 289, and ante, para 16.06.
7   Cmnd 1782, paras 19–20.
[16.10]
1   By s 173(1): see further post, para 18.11.
2   Because they remain outside ss 56(1)(b) and (c): see ante, para 16.08.
3   Whilst not needed in vendor credit, s 56(2) would have been useful to a debtor in an indirectly financed transaction.
4   *Lombard North Central plc v Gate* [1998] CLY 2491, Cty Ct (guarantor).

services on credit to the consumer:[5] direct financing is within s 56(1)(b) and loan financing within s 56(1)(c) (see ante, para 16.08).

Second, provided only the negotiations are made, in the words of s 56(1), 'in relation' to the above transactions (presumably including any trade-in), the words 'in the capacity of' would seem to import a deemed authority whether or not the common law would regard the dealer as acting within the scope of his actual or apparent authority (see ante, para 16.06). The result has been said to be that 'provided the debtor to whom the representations are made acts in good faith, he can treat the negotiator's representations as those of the creditor himself, however fanciful and extravagant they may be and whether or not they are of a kind which a person in the position of the negotiator would ordinarily be authorised to make by a person in the position of the creditor'.[6] It would seem that this will be so even where the agent making the representation does so overseas.[7] Indeed, the generosity with which the courts have interpreted this statutory deemed agency is exemplified in *Forthright Finance Ltd v Ingate*:[8]

> The consumer was the conditional buyer of an Austin Metro under and agreement made with F Ltd. Before she had completed the payments due under that agreement, the consumer decided to change the car for a Fiat Panda owned by a dealer. The dealer ascertained that the settlement figure on the Metro was £1,9929 and offered her £2,000 for it.[9] That leaving virtually no surplus, the consumer put down a £1,000 deposit and entered a directly financed transaction, under which she agreed to buy the Panda under a regulated conditional sale from C Ltd. The dealer became insolvent without having paid the settlement figure to F Ltd; and F Ltd sued the consumer to recover that sum. The consumer bought in C Ltd as third party, arguing that anything said by the dealer was, under s 56, said as agent for C Ltd.

The Court of Appeal unanimously held as follows: the negotiations conducted by the dealer over the Metro and the Fiat were part of a single package within s 56(1)(b),[10] relating to the regulated supply of the Fiat;[11] s 56(4) made it clear that a wide construction should be given to the words 'negotiations ... in relation to' in s 56(1)(b);[12] so that under s 56(2) C Ltd was liable to discharge the dealer's debt in relation to the settlement figure. As to the effect of this deemed agency, see post, para 16.10A.

---

5   Within s 187: as to which, see ante, para 5.33. Is the wording of s 56(1)(b) wide enough to produce the same result even where the consumer chooses and introduces the financier into the transaction?
6   Goode, *Consumer Credit Law and Practice*, para 32.12.
7   *Jarrett v Barclays Bank plc* [1997] 2 All ER 484, CA (timeshare).
8   [1997] 4 All ER 99, CA.
9   The 'settlement figure' is the amount needed to complete the payments due under the regulated conditional sale with F Ltd, less any statutory rebate: see post, para 26.19A.
10 Set out ante, para 16.08.
11 *Per* Staughton LJ at 102. This is despite the fact that the part-exchange was only worth a net £8 (£2,000–£1,992) and seems to have been ignored by the parties and the court. As to part-exchanges, see ante, para 2.09.
12 Because s 56(4) was wide enough to comprehend the customer's discussions with the dealer, which the subsection described as 'other dealings': *per* Henry LJ at 106.

[16.10A] The effect of the statutory agency. Where there is such a statutory deemed agency (see ante, para 16.10), it has a number of effects.

First, the effect of s 56(2) is that **both** the financier/creditor and the dealer/negotiator will be liable to the consumer/debtor for those acts or omissions of the dealer/negotiator as 'relate' to, and are made in the course of, 'antecedent negotiations'. Thus, the dealer/negotiator will remain liable at common law to the consumer/debtor in tort or under any collateral contract (see post, para 16.18); whilst by s 56(2) the dealer/negotiator is also deemed to be acting in these respects as agent of the financier/creditor, so that the latter takes on the – normally additional[1] – liability.[2] Such liability may 'relate' to the consumer credit agreement, as where the consumer/debtor is enabled by s 56(2) to invoke against the financier/creditor the remedies for misrepresentation (see post, para 26.12). Or that liability may be independent of the consumer credit agreement, as in the torts of negligence, negligent misstatement or deceit (see Chapter 17).

Second, there is the question whether the financier/creditor may be fixed with s 56(2) liability where, after the dealer has completed the negotiations with the consumer, the creditor declines to accept the proposal: s 56(1) speaks of actual and proposed transactions:[3] but it may be that 'proposed' refers here only to those cases where a consumer credit agreement is subsequently made.[4]

Third, the wide definition of 'representations' (see ante, para 16.08) extends their scope far beyond the goods or credit supplied.[5] Building on this, the financier's s 56(2) liability comprehends not just the dealer's mere representations, but also those misrepresentations of the dealer which become express[6] contractual promises:[7] the latter may amount to, or be part of, a contract between the dealer and consumer at common law;[8] and by virtue of s 56(2) they may also become a term of an agreement between the financier and consumer.[9] This leads as regards loan financing to a very substantial overlap between s 56(2) and s 75 (see post, para 16.14).

[16.10A]

1 Additional, because at common law the dealer would not normally be the agent of the financier. It will thus be prudent for the financier to create full dealer recourse in respect of this liability (see post, para 16.22).

2 Does the imputed knowledge extend beyond this to the dealer's knowledge, eg, that the transaction is a disguised bill of sale, that the dealer's title to the goods is defective, or that an agreement signed in blank has been wrongly completed by the dealer, or that the agreement is to be conditional on settlement of a trade-in? See Guest and Lloyd, *Encyclopedia of Consumer Credit*, para 2-057.

3 See Bennion, *Consumer Credit Manual* (3rd edn), pp 25–27, 48–49, suggesting that this is only possible where the dealer is a connected-lender. *Sed quaere* in respect of his category (1)? This view could be significant also in relation to deposits.

4 Guest and Lloyd, *op cit*, note 2, para 2-057.

5 Jones, *Credit Cards*, p 198. *Contra*, s 75: see post, para 16.14.

6 But not the statutorily implied terms: see ante, Chapters 12–15. *Contra* s 75 liability: see post, para 16.14.

7 A misrepresentation becomes a contractual promise when the parties so intend: see ante, para 11.02. But how can the parties to a deemed agency have any intention? See Goode, *Consumer Credit Law and Practice*, para 32.12.

8 Where there is a contract between them for the supply of goods (ie loan financing), it may become a term of that contract; and in the case of both loan and direct financing, it may become part of a collateral contract between them.

9 It may become a term of the regulated agreement, or of a collateral contract between them. In the former case, does it make the contract improperly executed (see ante, para 9.12)?

Fourth, the creditor has no special right of indemnity in respect of the liability over against the dealer (cf s 75(2): see post, para 16.17), but is left to his ordinary remedies.[10]

Connected lender liability

[16.11] Introduction. The purpose of this section is to consider the liability of the financier for the financed supply of defective goods or services, or related misrepresentations.

1   *Direct financing.*[1] Where there is a directly financed transaction, the financier will, on the basis of principles already discussed, be liable to the consumer for misrepresentations and breaches of contract: as there is an instalment credit contract between them, the financier will as supplier be liable for breaches of express or implied terms of the supply contract or misrepresentations made by him.[2] Further, by reason of s 56(2) the financier has a deemed agency liability for any misrepresentation or express promise which the negotiator (dealer) might make during the antecedent negotiations (see ante, para 16.10).

2   *Loan financing.* As there is no initial supply contract between the financier and consumer, the financier will not on ordinary principles be liable for misrepresentations and breaches of the supply contract by the dealer, though there may be some liability under s 56(2) (see ante, para 16.10). Accordingly, the *Crowther Report* recommended that, where the financier was 'connected with' the dealer, the financier should be made so liable (para 6.6.28). This recommendation was adopted by s 75 of the CCA (see post, para 16.12). A threatened s 75 claim against the creditor may give the consumer/debtor a potent lever against a solvent supplier.

Section 75 does not create any new cause of action. Rather, it establishes a new defendant (the financier) for an existing cause of action against the dealer by introducing a new limited exception to the privity rule (see ante, para 10.01). When first introduced, s 75 was primarily used with personal loans (usually fixed-sum) taken out to finance the purchase of a motor vehicle from a connected dealer.[3] However, more recently, its principal application has been in connection with credit cards (running-accounts) used to obtain goods or services within the United Kingdom, eg, Master and Visa cards (see generally ante, para 2.28). The OFT have argued that the effect of s 75 is to spread the risk[4] and so act as a sort of insurance for card-users;[5] but the card issuers in particular have been so

---

10   See the Civil Liability (Contribution) Act 1978.

[16.11]

1   For direct, indirect and loan financing, see ante, paras 2.20–22.

2   *Renton v Hendersons Garage* [1994] CCLR 29 (S).

3   OFT, *Second Report on Connected Lender Liability* (1995), para 6. It also applies to trading checks (see ante, para 2.23) and store cards (see ante, para 2.24).

4   Because s 75 liability is passed back up the payment chain towards the original supplier (see post, para 16.17) and forms an element in the annual fee (see ante, para 7.11): OFT, *Connected Lender Liability* 1994) paras 3.18; 4.4(8).

5   OFT, *Second Report on Connected Lender Liability* (1995) recommends the following limitations to the s 75 liability of creditors: (a) second-in-line (see below); (b) limited to amount of credit (see post, para 16.15); (c) subrogation (see post, para 16.17). For criticism by LACOTS (see post, para 28.02). See (1995) 16 CCA News 4/8.

apprehensive as to their potential s 75 liability,[6] that they have taken every opportunity to deny or restrict that liability.[7] Reviewing these worries, the OFT have come to the following conclusions:[8] there was no case for amending s 75 in relation to traditional loan financing;[9] but that, in relation to credit cards, it might be appropriate to restrict s 75 liability to the amount paid by credit card.[10]

Nor has any change to a financier's s 75 liability been made by the 1987 EC Consumer Credit Directive: whilst that Directive only makes the financier second-in-line liable after the consumer has first pursued the supplier,[11] the Directive allows the UK to retain the greater first-in-line liability of the financier under s 75 (see post, para 16.17), a provision which could be enforced by Stop Now Orders (see ante, para 6.08). On the other hand, the OFT have recommended (above) early reduction of the credit card issuer's liability.[12]

[16.12] Ambit of s 75. Section 75(1) of the CCA extended the liability of financiers for the acts of dealers with whom they were 'connected' in the following compulsory[1] guarantee:

> If the debtor under a debtor-creditor-supplier agreement falling within section 12(b) or (c) has, in relation to a transaction financed by the agreement, any claim against the supplier in respect of a misrepresentation or breach of contract, he shall have a like claim against the creditor, who, with the supplier, shall accordingly be jointly and severally liable to the debtor.

Section 75(1) can come into operation **only** where **all** the following requirements are satisfied in relation to a supply of goods:[2]

(1) **There must be a regulated agreement** (see ante, para 5.13). This requirement will exclude the following:[3]

   (a) All payment cards where there is no credit, which will exclude most cash cards, cheque guarantee cards and debit cards (see ante, para 5.33).

   (b) All unregulated credit cards, as where the amount of credit exceeds the credit limit or the debtor is a limited company (see ante, paras 5.23; 5.24).

---

6 Eg, for failure of a cashback insurer (see ante, 8.13A); internet usage (see ante, para 8.17A).

7 Eg, arguing that in the use of credit cards to obtain goods and services abroad there is no privity (see post, para 16.14) and no 'like claim' (see post, para 16.16).

8 OFT, *Second Report on Connected Lender Liability* (1995).

9 Paragraph 6. The OFT is believed to include store cards in this category: (1995) 50 CC2/20. Criticised: 50 CC4/19.

10 Paragraphs 13–18. The OFT also recommended (paras 19–22) removing the cash price limits (s 75(3): see post, para 16.13); and granting card issuers paying s 75 claims subrogation to any rights the debtor may have against fourth parties eg, insurers (paras 22–25: see post, para 16.17).

11 (1987/102/EEC, as amended) Art 11: set out in Goode, *Consumer Credit Law and Practice*, Part X, para 2312. As to the effect of this on EU supplies; see Gidney (1996) 146 NLJ 762.

12 By implementation by way of delegated legislation under s 2(2) of the ECA (see ante, para 1.03A) and repeal of the present s 75 under the Deregulation Acts (see ante, para 5.10). See further (2001) 30 Credit Finance 2.

[16.12]

1 By s 173(1): see further post, para 18.11.

2 Our concern is primarily with financing the supply of goods. However, it should be noticed that s 75 is also apt to cover the financing of supplies of services, eg, holidays, or mixed goods and services, eg, installation of double-glazing.

3 Insofar as payment cards fall outside s 75, there is no obligation under the Banking code of practice (see ante, para 3.13) for card issuers voluntarily to apply similar rules.

    (c) All exempt credit cards, eg, charge cards (see ante, para 5.13).

    (d) All credit agreements made before 1 July 1977, when the section came into force.[4]

(2) **The claim must be by a debtor under that regulated agreement.** It seems that this extends the ambit of s 75 to joint debtors, but not to authorised users, because s 75(1) says 'if the debtor ... has [a] claim'.

(3) **The transaction must fall outside the special exemptions** contained in s 75(3) (see post, para 16.13).

(4) **There must be a DCS agreement falling within ss 12(b) or (c):**

    (a) As s 12 only refers to consumer credit agreements (see ante, para 5.34), this must exclude from s 75 all consumer hirings.

    (b) As s 12 requires a s 187 connection between creditor and supplier, this will exclude from s 75 all DC loans.

    (c) As s 75 deliberately excludes DCS agreements falling within s 12(a), this seems to shut out any form of vendor credit.[5] Furthermore, s 75(1) seems to envisage that the creditor and supplier must be different persons, as does the definition of 'supplier' in s 189(1).

Where the transaction is loan financed (see ante, para 2.23), this requirement is clearly satisfied; and this will be the normal case where s 75 is invoked. However, difficulty has arisen with directly financed transactions (see ante, para 2.21): whilst the goods originate so far as the three parties are concerned with the dealer and are physically supplied by him to the consumer, it has been pointed out that in law the goods are supplied to the consumer by the financier; and, on the assumption that 'supplier' in s 75 means supplier in the eyes of the law to the consumer,[6] it has therefore been concluded that s 75 has no application to direct financing.[7]

(5) **The particular types of claim** which the debtor may have against the supplier falls within the section (see post, para 16.14).

[16.13] Special exemptions. Section 75(3) contains a special regime of exemptions, laying down that s 75(1) (as to which, see ante, para 16.12) does not apply to a claim:

    (a) under a non-commercial agreement, or

    (b) so far as the claim relates to any single item to which the supplier has attached a cash price not exceeding [£x] or more than [£y].

Paragraph (a) will save from s 75 liability a creditor in respect of an agreement entered into by him which is not made by him 'in the course of a business carried on by him'.[1]

---

4   See Macleod, *Consumer Sales Law* (Butterworths edn, 1989), para 7.14; Goode, *Consumer Credit Law and Practice*, para 51.3.

5   As to vendor credit, see ante, para 2.19. For discussion of s 12(a), see ante, para 5.34; and as to pleading such claims as against the dealer, see post, para 16.18.

6   See ante, para 5.34. *Sed quaere?* Alternatively, it could mean (i) in fact to the consumer, or (ii) supplier into the transaction, ie, seller to the financier = dealer.

7   *Renton v Hendersons Garage* [1994] CCLR 29 (S). Goode, *op cit*, note 4, para 33.147. But see *Porter v General Guarantee Corp Ltd* [1982] RTR 384, criticised by MacQueen 1984 SLT 65. See also Guest and Lloyd, *Encyclopedia of Consumer Credit*, para 2-076; and post, paras 16.17; 16.21.

[16.13]

1   See s 189(1): see ante, para 5.16.

Paragraph (b) does not disturb the ordinary financial limit within which a personal credit agreement may be a consumer credit agreement:[2] instead, it exempts from the attentions of s 75 those regulated consumer credit agreements where the cash price[3] of 'any single item' (see below) is either:

(1) **very small**, which is now defined as 'not exceeding £100', which will save from s 75(1) many credit card and check trading transactions; or

(2) **very large**, which is now defined as 'more that £30,000', eg, the purchase of industrial plant priced over £30,000 with a loan of less than £25,000.

Typically, transactions likely to fall within the scope of s 75 may involve larger consumer durables and more expensive travel, entertainment and other services. However, it is anticipated that the phrase 'any single item' may cause difficulty.[4] Even supposing it means any single item due under a single contract, eg, a set of golf clubs, can the effect of s 75 be avoided by assigning separate prices of less than £100 to various parts of the goods?[5] Or what if some parts are priced less than £100, some more than £100, the loss being caused by defects in some of each class?[6] In respect of misrepresentations, it may be that these limitations can be avoided by suing under s 56 (see ante, para 16.10).

As the effect of s 75 is to make the creditor liable co-extensively with the supplier (see post, para 16.15), however great the claim asserted (including consequential loss), there may be advantages to the debtor in taking out a minimum regulated DCS loan regardless of his financial needs, eg, to pay a deposit by credit card (see ante, para 7.12): presently, this may fall within s 75 however small the amount of credit, provided the cash price is within s 75(3)(b);[7] but the OFT have recommended that the liability of a card issuer be limited to the amount of the credit (see ante, para 16.11).

[16.14] The debtor's claim against the supplier. Section 75(1) (see ante, para 16.12) is applicable only where the debtor has a particular sort of claim.

(1) The section only applies where the debtor has a 'claim against the supplier'. Card issuers sometimes argue that this category does not extend to overseas suppliers where the card is used abroad on the grounds that they have no s 187 connection (see ante, para 5.33) with such suppliers, because there is no **agreement** between the English creditor and the overseas supplier;[1] but the OFT argue that there is an

---

2   Section 8(2): see ante, para 5.22.

3   For a general discussion of 'price', see ante, para 2.07. The power to increase these limits was included in s 181; and the level as stated in the text was introduced by the Consumer Credit (Increase in Monetary Limits) Order 1983, SI No 1878. For a recommendation that the limit should be expressed in terms of the amount of credit, see OFT, *Second Report on Connected Lender Liability* (1995) paras 19–21.

4   See generally Goode, *Consumer Credit Law and Practice*, para 33.183; Campbell (1994) 13 Tr LR 18 at 20–21. Cf the concept of a 'commercial unit' in the SGA, new s 35(7): see post, para 29.08.

5   As to the ordinary test of when there are either (a) separate contracts or (b) a single severable contract, see post, para 23.23. Are those tests apposite here, when s 75(3) talks of the supplier having 'attached a cash price'?

6   The exception is only 'so far as' the claim relates to items below £100. How is the loss to be apportioned?

7   The s 75 protection continues even after the credit has been paid off: Campbell, *op cit*, note 4, 24.

[16.14]

1   Because the English card issuer did not recruit the overseas supplier (see ante, para 2.28), there is no privity of contract between them.

arrangement between them[2] and obtained the temporary *ex gratia* concession of card issuers to honour such claims.[3] Again, it is sometimes argued that, in relation to the travel trade, card issuers will be under no s 75 liability where the travel agent is the agent of the consumer/card holder.[4]

(2) 'In respect of a misrepresentation or breach of contract'.[5] In a loan financed transaction (see ante, paras 2.23–25), it is clear that this expression comprehends breaches by the dealer/supplier of express or implied terms of his supply contract with the consumer: this will include express guarantees by the supplier, eg, a 10 year guarantee on double glazing; and the statutory implied terms (see Chapters 12–15). Further, a s 75 claim would also lie on the grounds that the consumer was induced to enter that sale contract by the misrepresentation of the dealer/supplier – which will include actions for deceit or negligent misstatement (see generally post, para 17.18 *et seq*); and in this context there is a substantial overlap as regards loan financing with s 56(2) (see ante, para 16.10). However, it would seem that s 75 does not comprehend other torts committed by the dealer/supplier in the course of negotiating the transaction, eg, negligent acts,[6] or statutory product liability.[7] On the other hand, it would appear to extend to a quasi-contractual claim by a buyer who has rightly rescinded the sale contract to recover his price on grounds of total failure of consideration.[8]

(3) The claim referred to above must be made 'in relation to a transaction financed by the [regulated] agreement'. Accordingly, s 75 does not extend to claims made in relation to ancillary contracts, eg, maintenance, extended warranties, unless that ancillary contract is also financed by the creditor, eg, free gifts.[9] It is not clear what is the position in relation to cashbacks (see ante, para 8.13A) or replacements (see post, para 29.03).

For the effect of s 75, see post, para 16.15.

[16.15] The effect of s 75. Where the conditions for the application of s 75 are all satisfied (as set out above), s 75(1) provides that the debtor:

> … shall have a like claim against the creditor, who, with the supplier, shall accordingly be jointly and severally liable to the debtor.

---

2 OFT, *Second Report on Corrected Lender Liability* (1995) para 2. See also Goode, *Consumer Credit Law and Practice*, para 33.185; Gidney (1996) 146 NLJ 762.

3 OFT, 1995-AR, 19. The concession expired 31 December 1996.

4 If the misrepresentation was made by a professional agent, there may be difficulty in showing that he was the supplier in law: see Samuels (1993) 10 Tr LR at 92; OFT, *op cit*, note 2, paras 5.11; 5.14; Rutherford (1994) 144 NLJ 668.

5 What if the debtor is making a contract on behalf of a club?

6 Goode, *Consumer Credit Law and Practice*, para 33.161. What of torts committed in performing the contracts, eg, wrongful refusal to deliver the goods, or wrongful recaption?

7 Under Part I of the CPA (see post, para 17.24): Guest and Lloyd, *Encyclopedia of Consumer Credit*, para 2-076.

8 For this claim, see post, para 16.16. For quasi-contractual remedies generally, see post, para 29.12 *et seq*.

9 Goode, *op cit*, note 6, para 33.161. Is his test whether the transaction is a linked one (see ante, para 5.31)?

Leaving aside what amounts to 'a like claim' (see post, para 16.16), it will be observed that the effect of s 75(1) is to create another statutory exception to the privity rule.[1] This liability in the creditor towards the debtor is co-terminous with the liability of the supplier to the debtor,[2] and may far exceed the amount of the credit (see ante, para 16.13), or perhaps its duration.[3] Most such claims are made against the credit card issuers when the supplier is insolvent; and card issuers have argued that the extent of the liability is unreasonable particularly when consequential loss is taken into account, eg, air travel, where claims arise from death or injury in a major crash. The OFT have recommended that the liability of the card issuer should be limited to the amount charged to the card account (see ante, para 16.11).

To the extent only that the supplier effectively excludes or restricts his liability towards the debtor (see Chapter 18), that exclusion or restriction enures for the protection of the creditor facing a s 75 claim; but the creditor cannot rely as against a s 75 claim[4] on any term in the consumer credit agreement excluding or restricting his liability.[5] Moreover, the debtor may pursue his s 75 claim against either or both the supplier and creditor;[6] an unsatisfied judgment against one does not bar proceedings against the other;[7] nor does the CCA require the debtor to pursue first his remedies against the supplier (see ante, para 16.11). Further, s 75(4) would appear to be intended to extend the scope of the creditor's s 75(1) liability, for it provides that:

> This section applies notwithstanding that the debtor, in entering into the transaction, exceeded the credit limit or otherwise contravened any term of the agreement.

This is probably aimed at revolving credit agreements, eg, credit cards, and refers to the 'credit limit' fixed by such agreements.[8] If so, then the draftsman would seem to have intended that a debtor should be able to take advantage of s 75 even in respect of a

---

[16.15]

1 See ante, para 10.01. For the effect of limitation periods, see Guest and Lloyd, *Encyclopedia of Consumer Credit*, para 2-076.

2 It would seem to follow that the creditor can be under no s 75 liability in respect of items for which the supplier incurs no liability, eg, where the supplier 'sells' a maintenance contract or 'extended warranty' by a third party who subsequently becomes insolvent (see generally post, para 17.09).

3 What if a supplier's express guarantee is only repudiated by him after the term of the credit has expired? See Guest and Lloyd, *op cit*, note 1, para 2-076.

4 *Aliter*, where the creditor is being sued for breach of a term of the credit agreement which the CCA does not make compulsory.

5 UCTA, s 10 (see post, para 18.16); CCA, s 173(1) (see post, para 18.11); UTCC Regulations, reg 8 (see ante, para 11.15A). What is the effect of the differing scope of these sections?

6 Suppose the creditor factors the debt (see ante, para 7.28). It has been argued that, notwithstanding s 189(1), 'creditor' does not here include his assignee: Goode, *Consumer Credit Law and Practice*, para 33.181. *Sed quaere?*

7 Civil Liability (Contribution) Act 1978, s 3; Guest and Lloyd, *op cit*, note 1, para 2-076. As to this Act see generally ante, para 12.10.

8 See the definition of 'credit limit' in ss 189(1), 10(2): for an explanation of such credit limits and of revolving credit generally, see ante, para 5.28. The alternative would seem to be to say that 'credit limit' in s 75 refers to the upper financial limit of regulated agreements (as to which see ante, para 5.22) – which would produce a far wider range of liability.

transaction which took his debit balance above his agreed credit limit,[9] and hence amounted to a breach of the revolving credit agreement.[10]

Finally, if the creditor is liable under s 75(1), he is given a subsidiary claim against the supplier (see post, para 16.17).

[16.16] 'A like claim'. Section 75 of the CCA does not create any additional ground of complaint: it simply adds a third party[1] against whom an existing complaint can be made. Where a transaction falls within the ambit of the section and the debtor has on ordinary principles a claim against his supplier (see ante, paras 16.13–14), s 75 grants the debtor 'a like claim' against the creditor.[2] The obvious example is where the debtor has a claim for damages against the supplier on grounds of misrepresentation or breach of contract: s 75(1) will there enable the debtor to claim that sum from the creditor, eg, a 10 year warranty on a double glazing installation; and this even extends to where the UK 'like claim' is as regards a complaint in respect of a foreign supply.[3]

However, suppose the debtor's claim against the supplier is for rescission *ab initio* or *de futuro* of the supply contract (see post, para 26.11). If the debtor in a loan financed transaction rescinds the linked **sale** agreement with the supplier,[4] then the creditor is jointly and severally liable in respect of any restitutionary claim which the debtor may have against the supplier in respect of any sums paid by the debtor to the supplier under the rescinded **sale** agreement, eg, for the return of part of the price. On the other hand, the fact that the debtor in a loan financed transaction is entitled to rescind the sale agreement would not by a combination of s 75 and ordinary principles give the debtor a right to rescind the **credit** agreement,[5] because the words 'a like claim' refer back to the transaction financed by the agreement (the **sale**).[6] However, such a result may be achievable by praying in aid s 56(2) (see ante, para 16.10) as well:[7] by s 56(2) the supplier is deemed to make any representation as agent of the creditor, so enabling the debtor to rescind the regulated **credit** agreement on grounds, eg, of a misrepresentation inducing entry into the linked sale.[8]

---

9 Goode, *op cit*, note 6, para 33.167.
10 Does s 75(4) prevent the creditor suing the debtor for this breach? And if not, do the creditor's damages for breach of the revolving credit agreement include the sums he has to pay the debtor by reason of s 75(4) – thus nullifying the effect of s 75(4)? See Goode, *op cit*, note 6, Div IIB, annotation to s 75(4).

[16.16]

1 What if a debtor uses two different cards to effect payment under a single transaction?
2 As to the position where the creditor has assigned his rights under the credit agreement, eg, *Re Charge Card Services Ltd* (set out ante, para 2.27), see Guest and Lloyd, *Encyclopedia of Consumer Credit*, para 2-076.
3 *Jarrett v Barclays Bank plc* [1997] 2 All ER 484, CA (timeshare).
4 The sale agreement will be a linked transaction within s 19(1)(b): see ante, para 5.31. As to who is entitled to the goods (supplier or creditor?), see Jones, *Credit Cards*, p 208.
5 Davidson (1980) 96 LQR 343, criticising *UDT v Taylor* 1980 SLT 28 (Sh Ct). Of course, the debtor could recover his price from the supplier, and then exercise his statutory right to make early payment of sums due under the credit agreement: as to early payment, see post, para 26.19A. See also Guest and Lloyd, *op cit*, note 2.
6 Goode, *Consumer Credit Law and Practice*, para 33.165.
7 As to which, see ante, para 16.10. For an alternative argument via a claim for damages see Lowe (1981) 97 LQR 532, Dobson [1981] JBL 179.
8 Goode, *op cit*, note 6, para 33.165. *Contra* Guest and Lloyd, *op cit*, note 2. Cf the rule that withdrawal or cancellation of the regulated agreement has the same effect on the linked transaction.

It seems likely that s 75 does not interfere with the ordinary common law right of set-off (see generally post, para 23.14). Thus, a creditor sued under s 75 can reduce his liability by exercising any right of set-off vested in the supplier.[9] Likewise, a debtor sued under the consumer credit agreement may set off by way of s 75 any sum owed to him by the supplier which he could have set off against a claim by the supplier. So, reliance on s 75 by a debtor may be either offensive or defensive: he may sue on the section to recover a sum of money from the creditor; or he may wait until sued by the creditor and then plead a s 75 set-off by way of a defence.[10]

[16.17] Statutory recourse. Because it is recognised that the real fault in cases falling within s 75(1) lies in the supplier, s 75(2) allows the financier/creditor full statutory recourse[1] to the supplier in the following terms:

> Subject to any agreement between them, the creditor shall be entitled to be indemnified by the supplier for loss suffered by the creditor in satisfying his liability under subsection (1), including costs reasonably incurred by him in defending proceedings instituted by the debtor.

And so that the creditor may obtain judgment against the supplier in the same proceedings, s 75(5) enables the creditor sued under s 75(1)[2] to make the supplier a party to those proceeding.[3] In practice, that liability may be enhanced by chargeback arrangements, particularly where the card issuer and merchant acquirer are separate businesses.[4] There remains the danger that the supplier may be insolvent, or recourse liability excluded,[5] in which case the creditor is left to foot the bill,[6] even where the supplier is insured.[7]

The justification for imposing this risk on a creditor is that the creditor and supplier are engaged in a joint business enterprise within the meaning of s 187 (see ante, para 5.33). However it may be that the supplier has put the consumer's deposit in a trust account or insured it.[8] Will this allow a creditor to claim on that fund in the hands of a third party?[9]

---

9   Goode, *op cit*, note 6, para 33.163; Guest and Lloyd, *op cit*, note 2.

10   Goode, *op cit*, note 6, paras 33.169–70; Lowe (1981) 97 LQR 533. This would indirectly produce the same result as *UDT v Taylor* (above).

[16.17]

1   For recourse agreements, see post, para 16.22.

2   *Quaere* whether s 75(2) is applicable where the liability of the financier/creditor is otherwise than under s 75(1): see post, 16.22.

3   Eg, *Porter v General Guarantee Corp Ltd* [1982] RTR 384 (a directly financed transaction: see note 2, above; and ante, para 16.12). For third party proceedings, see Guest and Lloyd, *Encyclopedia of Consumer Credit*, para 2-076.

4   OFT, *Connected Lender Liability* (1994), para 4.4(d). See generally ante, para 2.28.

5   Such exclusion is not prohibited by CCA s 173 (see post, para 18.11); nor will it fall within the ambit of the UTCC Regulations because both parties are in business (see ante, para 11.12). But it might be subject to UCTA, s 3 (see post, para 18.24).

6   Unless he has a right of contribution against another party; eg, manufacturer, under the Civil Liability (Contribution) Act 1978.

7   The OFT has recommended that the creditor have a right of subrogation, so that he may claim under the insurance policy: *Second Report on Connected Lender Liability* (1995), paras 22–25.

8   See post, para 23.22. Can the creditor get at trust funds?

9   See post, para 23.22. Can the creditor get at an insurance fund?

LIABILITY OF THE DEALER

To the consumer

[16.18] Where there is a loan financed transaction, the primary contract in respect of the goods is between the dealer and the consumer; and the fact that a finance company may be involved does not alter this. The position is very different in a directly financed transaction, where there is ordinarily no primary contractual relationship between the dealer and consumer.[1] Frequently, the consumer will allege that he was induced to enter into the directly financed transaction by some misrepresentation on the part of the dealer, eg, deceit (see post, para 17.18). The question arises whether the consumer has any redress against the dealer.[2] The leading case is *Andrews v Hopkinson*:[3]

> The dealer said to the consumer in respect of one of his vehicles: 'it is a good little bus; I would stake my life on it.' The following day, the consumer signed a hp proposal form in respect of a directly financed transaction for the vehicle; and he subsequently took delivery of it. About a week later, the steering failed, and the consumer was involved in an accident. The consumer's action against the dealer succeeded before McNair J.

The grounds of the consumer's claim were as follows:

(1) Express warranty. 'For breach of an express warranty that the car was in good condition ... whereby he was induced to enter into a hire purchase agreement in respect thereof.' In finding the dealer liable under this head of claim, McNair J said:[4]

> There may be an enforceable warranty between A, the intended purchase of a car, and B the motor dealer, supported by the consideration that B should cause the hire purchase finance company to enter into a hire purchase agreement with A.

In practice, of course, it is usually the signature of the consumer on the proposal form that is induced by the misrepresentation.[5] Furthermore, it has rightly been pointed out that the term 'warranty' is a misnomer in this context:[6] that the allegation must be of a collateral contract of warranty (see ante, para 11.06); and the representation made by the dealer is at most evidence of such a collateral contract.[7]

(2) Implied warranty. 'For breach of an implied warranty that the car was reasonably fit for driving on the public highway.' Whilst preferring to rest his decision on the first ground, McNair J said:[8]

[16.18]

1. *Drury v Victor Buckland Ltd* [1941] 1 All ER 269, CA. But see *Polsky v S & A Services Ltd* [1951] 1 All ER 1062, CA. But for use of the Contracts Act 1999, see post, para 16.22.

2. For causes of action which this may give the consumer as against the financier, see CCA, ss 56; 75: discussed ante, para 16.06 *et seq*.

3. [1957] 1 QB 229, [1956] 3 All ER 422. See also *MacKenzie Patten & Co v British Olivetti Ltd* (1984), reported in 48 MLR 344.

4. At 235. For the measure of damages, see *Yeoman Credit Ltd v Odgers* [1962] 1 All ER 789, CA; *Wells Merstham Ltd v Buckland Sand and Silica Co Ltd* [1965] 2 QB 170, and post, para 29.34.

5. Eg, *Astley industrial Trust Ltd v Grimley* [1963] 2 All ER 33, CA: see Goode, *HP Law and Practice* (2nd edn), p 639, note 3.

6. Wild, *HP* (2nd edn), pp 195–99; Goode, *HP Law and Practice* (2nd edn), p 640.

7. See *per* Pearson LJ *Astley Industrial Trust Ltd v Grimley* (above) at 45.

8. At 237. His Lordship distinguished earlier cases refusing an implied warranty on the grounds that the point was not argued in them.

> Bearing in mind that the statutory implied warranty now embodied in [s 14(3) of the SGA] was merely a modification of the long-existing common law in relation to sales, I feel that there is much to be said for the view that in a transaction such as the present, which, though not in law a transaction of sale between the parties, is closely akin to such a transaction, the court ought to imply such a condition or warranty if any contractual relationship between the parties can in fact be established.

There appears to be few subsequent cases where this idea has been taken up (see ante, para 15.26); and it has been doubted whether an intention to contract would be inferred where there was no express representation.[9]

(3) Negligence. 'For negligence in that the defendant knew or ought to have known that the car was dangerous.' In *Herschtal v Stewart and Arden Ltd*,[10] the dealer in a directly financed transaction was held liable in tort to the consumer for the negligent repair of the vehicle which was the subject matter of the transaction; and McNair J relied on that decision in finding the dealer in the present transaction liable for negligence by omission, saying:[11]

> I have no hesitation in holding that the defendant in the circumstances was guilty of negligence in failing to make the necessary examination, or at least in failing to warn the plaintiff that no such examination has been carried out.

[16.19] CCA controls. A credit broker (see ante, paras 5.38–41) is subject to a number of restrictions.

1 *Licensing.* A credit broker needs a category C licence, together (if he so requires) with special permission to canvass.[1]

2 *Seeking business.* It was seen in Chapter 8 that the Act places a considerable number of restrictions on the creditor or owner with regard to his seeking business; and the Act also imposes these restrictions on credit brokers,[2] including in relation to credit status enquiries.[3]

3 *Entry into agreements.* It was seen in Chapters 9 and 10 that there are considerable powers to make regulations controlling the entry into credit or hire agreements. Section 156 contains similar powers in relation to credit brokerage.[4]

4 *Brokerage fees.* One of the complaints considered by the *Crowther Report* concerned brokers' fees (para 6.4.22) and this led to the following restrictions:

(a) No fees can be charged by an unlicensed ancillary credit business (see ante, para 6.27), though this provision may be under-enforced.

(b) Section 155 provides that, where no credit or hire agreement results from the introduction by the licensed credit broker, brokerage fees chargeable to the

---

9 Cf Goode, *op cit*, note 5 (1st edn), p 198 and (2nd edn), p 640. But for analogous terms, see generally ante, para 15.26. A statutory warranty has been suggested: ELA, 1988-AR 19.
10 [1940] 1 KB 155; [1939] 4 All ER 123.
11 At 237. As failure to act, see post, para 17.14; and as to failure to warn, see post, para 18.29.
[16.19]
1 As to licences, see ante, para 6.15; and as to canvassing indorsements, see ante, para 6.14.
2 See ss 151–52. Moreover, even though licensed to canvass credit or hire agreements (see above), s 154 forbids the credit broker from canvassing his own services (see ante, para 7.07).
3 Section 157 actually casts the duty on 'the negotiator': see ante, para 8.37.
4 The power also extends to debt-adjusting and debt-counselling (see ante, para 5.43). No regulations have yet been made.

individual must in most cases be kept to a purely nominal amount,[5] whatever the costs incurred. Attempts to circumvent this rule, eg, by mortgage brokers, are more likely to be dealt with under the CCA licensing provisions (see ante, para 6.11 *et seq*) than as an unfair term.[6] Further, the debtor will usually be the debtor's agent, so that any commission paid to the broker by the creditor may amount to a secret commission.[7]

(c) If any regulated agreement is validly cancelled by the debtor or hirer, the maximum fee is similarly limited (see ante, para 10.33).

To the financier

The liability of the dealer to the company financing his retail trade may arise in two separate and distinct phases of that trade:

(1) *Stocking plans* when the dealer is acquiring his stock (see post, para 16.20).

(2) *Dealer recourse* when he is disposing of it by retail (see post, para 16.22).

[16.20] Stocking plans.[1] These are most common in the motor trade; and their economic purpose is to 'loan' the retailer the value of the stock he must keep in his showroom, especially to meet seasonal fluctuations in retail demand. At its simplest, such financial accommodation may be provided by the person supplying the goods to the retailer – be that supplier a manufacturer, importer or wholesaler – just delaying his demand for payment of the price, a situation normally described as 'trade credit'[2] and falling outside the CCA.[3] However, particularly where items of a larger unit value are involved (typically motor vehicles), that supplier will normally insist on early payment and the transaction is likely to be financed by a third party (financier).[4] Such loans are normally provided by financiers on favourable terms to encourage retailers to introduce to them proposals from consumers for credit:[5] they are usually outside the ambit of the CCA[6] and may include dealer recourse (see post, para 16.22).

Because of the large sums of money likely to be involved, the person providing stocking finance would normally prefer to take security. Theoretically, real security may be available in the form of a mortgage or charge over the dealer's land (see post, para

---

5 There is power to increase the £1 of the original provision by statutory order (s 181); and this has been exercised to increase it to £5: Consumer Credit (Further Increase in Monetary Limits) Order 1998, SI No 997.

6 OFT, *Bulletin No 6*, para 1.21; AR-2000 109, eg, (2001) Fair Trading 4.

7 *Industries & General Mortgage Co Ltd v Lewis* [1949] 2 All ER 573 (see (2001) 61 QA 11).

[16.20]

1 See generally Goode, *HP Law and Practice* (2nd edn), pp 670–74; *Commercial Law* (2nd edn), pp 794–800.

2 For vendor credit, see generally ante, para 2.19.

3 The agreement is likely to fall within the trade credit exemption: see ante, para 5.15. See also below, note 6.

4 For lender credit, see generally ante, para 2.20 *et seq*. Stocking business has now been freed of the dangers of the Moneylenders Acts (ante, para 6.10).

5 This enables financiers to offer profitable point-of-sale credit and is one way in which financiers overcome the difficulty of contacting consumers.

6 Even if the dealer is an 'individual' (see ante, para 5.24), the amounts of credit involved are normally too substantial for the agreement to be regulated (see ante, para 5.22). In the unlikely event of a stocking plan being regulated, the dealer would enjoy the CCA protections primarily designed for domestic consumers.

25.21) or sale of accounts receivable (see ante, para 2.22). However, in practice the dealer seeking stocking finance is likely to have already fully charged his land and accounts receivable for other purposes, in which case the only available security will be the goods which are the subject of the stocking plan (see post, para 16.21).

[16.21] Security in stocking plans. This paragraph is concerned with attempts by providers of stocking finance to take security in the stock financed, whether before or after the delivery of that stock.

1 *Security after delivery*. Apart from a chattel mortgage granted by a dealer who is a registered company,[1] there would not seem to be any way in which the financier can obtain effective security rights over these goods. If the financier attempts to 'advance' the retailer the price by way of purchase and letting back on hp to the retailer, the transaction may be caught by the chattel mortgage legislation (see post, para 25.27). If the financier tries to escape this danger by a purchase and simple letting back (leaseback), the dealer may be able to pass on a good title to a bfp, either because he has actual or ostensible authority to sell,[2] or under the Factors Act 1889.[3] If a financier desires to extend a stocking loan to a dealer in those circumstances, he will therefore normally resign himself to making straightforward loans: where the transaction falls outside the CCA,[4] this will sometimes be on short-term bills of exchange.[5]

2 *Security before delivery*. Besides a chattel mortgage granted by a dealer who is a registered company, a common method of conducting stocking operations is by way of unit-financing, utilising the sale or return type of contract (see post, para 20.23 *et seq*). As between financier and retailer, the sale or return transaction may provide that, if the retailer re-sells,[6] the proceeds are to be impressed with a trust in favour of the financier.[7] *Prima facie*, on resale by the retailer the property in the goods will pass to the sub-buyer (see post, para 20.24); and, even, where there is a reservation of property clause in the agreement between financier and retailer (see post, para 25.29), it is arguable that the retailer may still pass a good title under one of the exceptions to the *nemo dat* rule.[8]

[16.22] Dealer recourse. The techniques used to achieve dealer recourse in financed transaction (see ante, para 16.20) are as follows:

[16.21]

1 The transaction will fall within the registration provisions of s 395 of the Companies Act: see post, para 25.28. If the dealer is not a registered company, the agreement will be avoided by the Bills of Sale Act 1882: see post, para 25.27.

2 For these two exceptions to the *nemo dat* rule, see ante, para 10.06.

3 Eg, *Pacific Motor Auctions Ltd v Motor Credits Ltd* [1965] AC 867, PC. See generally ss 2 and 8 of the FA: these provisions are considered post, paras 21.24; 21.38.

4 Some such transactions may fall within the CCA (see ante, para 16.20) in which case the taking of a bill of exchange is prohibited: CCA, s 123 (discussed post, para 25.09).

5 Eg, *Premor Ltd v Shaw Bros* [1964] 2 All ER 583, CA.

6 When the dealer sells, the property in the vehicle passes to him (see post, para 20.23). This helps his cash-flow, as only then does he need to pay car tax and VAT: *Benjamin's Sale of Goods* (5th edn), para 5-050.

7 There is often no right to trace in such circumstances: see Goode (1976) 92 LQR at 375–76, 387. For the right to trace proceeds of sale, see post, para 27.14.

8 Section 9 of the Factors Act 1889: see post, para 20.27. Finance companies dispute this.

(1) *Directly financed transactions.* The contract of sale from the dealer to the finance company will, of course, subject the dealer to all the implied undertakings discussed in Part 4;[1] and, in addition, that contract may provide that the dealer warrants the truth of all the information contained in the proposal form,[2] or is liable for any misrepresentation it contains.[3] Apart from these types of liability, dealer recourse is usually achieved in one of three ways. First, the dealer may be required, as part of the consideration for the finance company agreeing to accept the transaction and purchase the goods, to promise that in the event of default by the consumer he will repurchase the goods at a price which covers the finance company's 'loss'.[4] In the event of repurchase, the finance company will usually have promised to assign all its rights against the consumer and the goods to the dealer,[5] so that the latter is left to enforce the supply agreement against the consumer.[6] This form of recourse provision suffers from the disadvantage that it cannot be enforced against the dealer unless all the conditions of the repurchase clause are satisfied to the letter[7] and the company is able to redeliver the goods to the dealer.[8] Second, as the primary vehicle for achieving recourse,[9] the dealer may simply agree to indemnify the finance company against all loss it may incur in the transaction,[10] in return for which the dealer has the option of calling for an assignment of the finance company's rights against the consumer and the goods. Whilst such recourse provisions are usually expressed as indemnities, they have often been interpreted by the courts as being in reality contracts of guarantee, in which case the finance company can have no greater rights against the dealer than it has against the consumer and the dealer will be discharged if the company impairs the security (see post, para 25.06). Further, it may even be possible in these

---

[16.22]

1   Eg, *Karflex Ltd v Poole* [1933] 2 KB 251, DC; *Warman v Southern Counties Finance Corp Ltd* (set out ante, para 12.07); *United Dominions Trust (Ireland) Ltd v Shannon Caravans Ltd* [1976] IR 225.

2   Eg, *Liverpool and County Discount Ltd v AB Motors Ltd* [1963] 2 All ER 396, CA. Alternatively, an action may lie for deceit: *United Motor Finance Co v Addison & Co Ltd* [1937] 1 All ER 425, PC.

3   *Royscot Trust Ltd v Rogerson* (set out post, para 27.28).

4   Is this such a case that it would be reasonable for the seller (finance company) to exclude the implied terms: see Sched 2 of the Unfair Contract Terms Act 1977 (see post, para 18.21)? As the repurchase is for money or moneys worth, there will be no question of the CCA treating it as a consumer credit agreement.

5   This assignment is unlikely to savour of maintenance: see ante, para 7.26. If the finance company is in breach of the reassignment provision, the measure of damages is the value of the goods: *Bowmaker (Commercial) Ltd v Smith* [1965] 2 All ER 304, CA.

6   Eg, *Karsales (Harrow) Ltd v Wallis* (set out ante, para 15.23). It would seem that the dealer does not in those circumstances have to be a licensed debt-collector: see ante, para 5.42.

7   See *United Dominions Trust (Commercial) Ltd v Eagle Aircraft Ltd* [1968] 1 All ER 104; [1968] 1 WLR 74, CA.

8   Because non-delivery will lead to a total failure of consideration: *Watling Trust Ltd v Briffault Range Co Ltd* [1938] 1 All ER 525, CA; and generally post, para 29.13.

9   There may also be an auxiliary right of repurchase exercisable by the dealer (at his own expense) if and when the financier has achieved full recourse, but without any obligation on the financier of either delivery or implied terms.

10 Eg, *Southern Industrial Ltd v Brooke House Motors Ltd* (1968) 112 Sol Jo 798, CA (retailer and hirer conspired to enter false figures, the agreement being illegal).

circumstances to invoke the statutory recourse provision to be found in s 75 of the CCA.[11] Third, the consumer may be encouraged to sue the dealer direct by introducing an aptly granted right in the contract under which the dealer supplies the goods to the financier: whereas at common law there would normally be no privity of supply contract between dealer and consumer (see ante, para 16.18), that problem can be overcome by use of the Contracts Act 1999 (see post, para 17.08A).

(2) *Loan financed transactions.* Whilst there will be no question of any repurchase clause because the financier is not the legal supplier of the goods, there may be an express recourse provision similar to that found in direct financing (above). Furthermore, where the loan is a regulated DCS agreement, then the financier may have the advantage of a statutory right of recourse where the financier (creditor) has been held liable to the consumer (debtor) under s 75 of the CCA (see ante, para 16.17).

---

11 *Porter v General Guarantee Corp Ltd* [1982] RTR 384, criticised by MacQueen 1984 SLT 65. For consideration of the issue of whether s 75 is applicable to directly financed transactions, see ante, para 16.12.

CHAPTER 17

PRODUCT LIABILITY[1]

INTRODUCTION

[17.01] The chain of distribution. This chapter is concerned with the legal position of parties in the chain of distribution of goods in this country to their eventual consumption. The goods may be imported;[2] or they may commence their existence in this country by growth or by manufacture such as to create a new identity.[3] Further, in relation to the last category, already-created goods may lose their separate identity by alteration, accession or intermixture.[4] Take the typical case of manufactured consumer durables, such as a motor car: the person who in common parlance is described as the 'manufacturer' (Z)[5] will actually create some parts of the vehicle, eg, the body shell; but he will buy some components, eg, electrical, from a components manufacturer or grower (X) or component wholesaler/importer (Y); and Z will wholly or in part act as an assembler or canner of those products.[6] The assembled goods will then be supplied by Z to the retail seller (B),[7] either directly, eg, own brand goods, or by way of one or more wholesalers (A1, A2, A3).[8] The retail buyer (C)[9] may use or consume the goods himself, or he may donate (see ante, para 2.08) them to a donee/consumer (D). If the goods prove defective, the donee (D) may have a right of action against B or C in the tort of negligence (see post, para 17.14), or perhaps in contract against B on the basis of agency or assignment (see post, para 17.12). This whole sequence of events may be rendered diagrammatically as follows:[10]

[17.01]

1   See generally Miller, *Product Liability Encyclopedia*; Waddams, *Product Liability*; Mildred, *Products Liability: Law and Insurance* (2000).

2   International trade is beyond the scope of this work: see ante, para 1.01.

3   Eg, *Borden (UK) Ltd v Scottish Timber Products* (manufacture of chipboard: set out post, para 25.31).

4   See generally Crossley Vaines, *Personal Property* (5th edn), Chapter 9.

5   It is Z's name and brand which will normally appear on assembled goods. In other cases, the retailer may be sufficiently strong commercially to insist that the goods are supplied for retail sale under the retailer's name and own or exclusive brand (= own brand goods).

6   In some cases, Z will seal the goods in such a manner that they are obviously intended to be unsealed only by their end-consumer. In other cases, trade usage may require inspection and adjustment by some intermediate trade party in the chain of distribution (A, B) or member of the public (C, D).

7   A 'retailer' is the common description of the person who is usually intended to be the last business purchaser for resale unused: his sale will therefore be the one that effectively bears VAT and any car tax (see ante, para 2.06). Cf *Chappell & Co Ltd v Nestle & Co Ltd* [1960] AC 87, HL.

8   The expression 'wholesaler' is usually reserved for those who make a business of purchasing goods for resale in their purchased form in bulk.

9   For legislative attempts to distinguish retail (C) from trade (Z, A, B) purchasers, see post, paras 18.18; 21.56.

10 Each of the contracting parties may act in person, or via an agent who may be disclosed, eg, trader's employee, or undisclosed, eg, many retail purchases (see post, para 17.07).

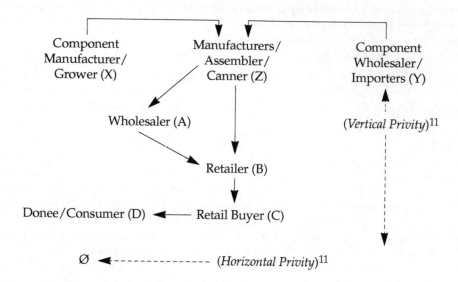

[17.02] Product liability. The rationale of what the Americans term 'products liability' is to allocate within the chain of distribution (see ante, para 17.01) any loss caused by using a defective product, presumably with the following inter-related objectives:[1]

(a) To achieve the optimum balance between the interests of the person injured in recovering compensation and that of other uninjured consumers in minimising the price of the product.[2]

(b) To encourage accident prevention by good design and quality control in production,[3] clear warning labels[4] and an effective recall system where dangers subsequently appear.[5] Failure to do so may amount to negligence (see post, para 17.14).

---

11   For the notions of 'horizontal' and 'vertical' privity, see post, para 17.08.
[17.02]

1   See generally Harris, *Compensation and Support for Illness and Injury*, pp 17–25; Winfield and Jolowicz, *Tort* (15th edn), pp 1–4; *The Royal Commission on Civil Liability and Compensation for Personal Injury* (1978, Cmnd 7054), paras 1199–1204; Clark, *Product Liability*, p 183; Mildred, *Product Liability: Law and Insurance*, Chapter 7.

2   As to the risk-benefit analysis of tort, see Clark, *op cit*, note 1, 30–34; Harvey, *Consumer Protection and Fair Trading* (6th edn), pp 23–28. As to welfare weighting, see OFT, 1999-AR 103.

3   What about goods which are inherently dangerous to the consumer or others, eg, medicine, motor vehicles? Does it make any difference if the goods are regarded as of little social utility, eg, alcoholic beverages, tobacco, cannabis? What if a manufacturer is warned that a criminal has poisoned his products? But see [1995] 2 Which? 14 (cars).

4   This is part of the general product safety requirement: see ante, para 4.34. Warnings may not always be effective: see (1992) 142 NLJ 83. It has been argued that it is undesirable for warnings to be effective as a substitute for redesign, and that warnings should be reserved for those circumstances where it is not possible to eliminate risk: Clark, *op cit*, note 1, p 103.

5   Under a code of practice (see ante, para 3.13), which will be monitored by the DTI: see DTI, *Consumer Product Recall: a Good Practice Guide* (1999). For the 2000 vehicle recall figures, see [2001] 7 Which? 17; [2001] Which Car? 66. Cf *Carroll v Fearon* (set out post, para 17.16). As to tracing ownership of motor vehicles, see post, para 21.60.

(c) To minimise loss to the economy, whether in the form of junked defective products, personal or property loss to purchasers and users, or loss of productive labour occasioned by injury to the consumer or others.[6]

(d) To institute a morally and politically acceptable form of compensation for injury.[7]

(e) To achieve all this in as cost-efficient manner as possible,[8] both as regards the cost of the compensation system to the parties[9] and any effect which the consequently enhanced price of the product may have on its circulation,[10] perhaps through higher product liability insurance premiums.[11]

[17.03] Criminal proceedings. Some types of behaviour connected with the distribution of products and some defects in products are covered by statutes imposing strict criminal liability (see Chapter 4), further enhanced by vicarious criminal liability (see post, para 28.09). Theoretically, a conviction under one of these statutes could be used to achieve civil compensation under the Powers of Criminal Courts Act 1973.[1] However, there would appear to have been a conscious decision to make this route difficult as follows: by statutory limitation;[1] by judicial caution in using even the power granted; and by the reluctance of prosecuting authorities.[2] Nevertheless, such convictions may still be of interest to the injured user. From his personal viewpoint, not only is there the emotional element,[3] but the conviction is useful evidence in any subsequent civil litigation.[4] From the viewpoint of society, prosecution under central guidance is more likely to achieve uniform enforcement free from the vagaries of private litigation.[5] However, in relation to safety, the (criminal) general safety requirement (see ante, para 4.33) plus safety regulations and (civil) strict product liability (see post, para 17.24) are seen as complementary: the former can be used as a preventative device, aimed at keeping very

---

6   See Abbott, *Safe Enough to Sell?* (1980, Design Council). For BSI standards, see ante, para 3.08.

7   If any new form of product liability were uninsurable, it might be better to opt for a state social security system to cover it. However, for the foreseeable future it looks unlikely that any such State system will appear.

8   For group actions, see Mildred, *op cit*, note 1, Chapter 10; and see generally ante, para 3.18.

9   In some cases, product liability insurance will be taken out by some parties in the chain of distribution, eg, *Zurich Insurance Co v FW Martin & Son* (1984) 134 NLJ 38. If the insured then becomes insolvent, his rights under the policy are 'transferred' to any claimant whose injury falls within the terms of that policy: Third Parties (Rights Against Insurers) Act 1930, s 1; *M/S Aswan Engineering Establishment Co v Iron Trader Mutual Insurance Co* [1987] 1 Lloyd's Rep 289. But this procedure cannot be used after the insured company is dissolved: see (1989) 139 NLJ 571.

10 Cf the approach to contractual allocation of loss by Milner in (1979) 42 MLR 508. It has long been claimed that a no-fault liability system would be far more cost effective than any tort-based system: Brahams (1988) 138 NLJ 678.

11 This is unlikely to be significant: Clark, *op cit*, note 1, p 74. *Sed quaere?* See generally Mildred, *op cit*, note 1, Chapter 5.

[17.03]

1   However, the 1973 Act provision is itself hedged around with restrictions (see ante, para 3.20). Moreover, many of the statutes imposing criminal liability expressly deny any action for breach of statutory duty (see ante, para 3.21): does that deny use of the 1973 Act?

2   There is a reluctance to prosecute simply to facilitate civil compensation for what is really product liability: see ante, para 3.19.

3   Besides the element of retribution, he will be saved the emotional (and financial) cost of enforcement.

4   Under s 11 of the Civil Evidence Act 1968: see ante, para 3.21.

5   For enforcement by the public authorities of the strict liability offences considered in Chapter 4, see post, Chapter 28.

unsafe goods off the market;[6] whereas the latter provides compensation in respect of items which are not necessarily all that unsafe.[7]

[17.04] Substantive civil law. This chapter is chiefly concerned with the substantive rules of civil law applicable to product liability in the possibly lengthy chain of distribution (see ante, paras 17.01–02) further extended by financing (see ante, Chapter 16), whilst leaving aside any complication arising from the presence of exclusion clauses or instructions for use (see post, Chapter 18).

From the late 16th century, the common law began to make consideration the touchstone of an enforceable promise (*assumpsit*), with these results:

(a) The distinction between contract and tort developed on the basis of whether or not a cause of action was supported by consideration.[1]

(b) The doctrine of privity was treated as a logically inevitable outcome from the requirement of consideration in contract.[2]

(c) The development of strict liability in contracts for the supply of goods[3] versus *mens rea* liability in tort, the latter chiefly through the all pervasive tort of negligence.[4]

All these developments may be seen in the English common law tests of product liability,[5] which in modern times have begun to blur once more the contract/tort dichotomy.[6] First, the courts have allowed an action from a single set of facts to succeed in both contract and tort.[7] Second, they have permitted an action in tort for failure to provide a benefit promised under a contract to which the plaintiff was not a party.[8] Third, there are the statutory contribution rules.[9] Fourth, to supplement the common law rules of privity,[10] there has been introduced statutory extensions of privity to third parties

---

6   Eg, the statutory instrument requiring consumer durables to be fitted with electrical plugs by manufacturers. As to safety regulations, see generally ante, para 4.35.

7   See Wright, *Product Liability*, p 90.

[17.04]

1   It would seem that NHS drugs are not supplied to the consumer under contract (see ante para 1.07), which enhances the importance of the non-contractual remedies.

2   It follows that warranties do not run with the goods: see ante, para 2.13. For the effect of privity on exclusion clauses, see post, para 18.05.

3   See Chapters 12–14. *Quaere* contracts for the supply of services (see ante, para 15.15)?

4   There may also be difficulty in determining whether liability is in contract or tort in respect of matters ancillary to the supply of goods, eg, a cloakroom in a restaurant, though this may be obscured if there is a contractual duty of care, eg, under a bailment.

5   The contract (suitability) test concerns consumer expectations, whereas the tort (negligence) test is about 'social standards of acceptable safety': Clark (1985) 48 MLR at 338. See also the development of the writ of deceit (see post, para 17.18); and generally Goode, *Commercial Law* (2nd edn), pp 189–91.

6   In the United States, this process has been taken much further by deleting the requirement of consideration from the action for breach of warranty (see post, para 17.08) and by making tort liability strict (see post, para 17.22).

7   *Esso Petroleum Co Ltd v Mardon* [1975] QB 819, CA. And perhaps by allowing recovery for economic loss in actions for negligence (see post, para 17.14): Holyoak (1983) 99 LQR 591.

8   See post, para 17.14; and the interesting argument by Jaffey (1985) 5 LS 77, especially at 89 *et seq*.

9   As between defendants, it may be possible to claim a contribution regardless of whether their respective liability to the plaintiff is in contract or tort: see generally ante, para 12.10.

10   For the extent to which contract-based liability can be extended without breaching the privity rules, see post, para 17.07 *et seq*; and for the scope of common law tort liability, see post, para 17.12 *et seq*.

expressly named in the contract (see post, para 17.08). Fifth, statute has introduced strict civil liability for unsafe goods (CPA: see post, para 17.24).

The result is to draw a sharp distinction for civil law purposes between shoddy and unsafe goods: there is strict statutory liability with regard to unsafe goods, whether by way of an implied term under the supply contract (see ante, Chapter 14) or the CPA (see above); but with regard to shoddy goods outside the privity rule, there is only common law negligence liability (see post, para 17.13).

[17.05] Problems. The major problems faced by the injured product user in obtaining compensation in civil proceedings within the jurisdiction of the English courts[1] are as follows:

1   *The state-of-the-art issue.* Whereas it is no defence in a contract-based action that the state of scientific knowledge at the relevant time did not allow of any possibility of precautions,[2] such a defence is normally available outside the contractual nexus.[3] Such a defence has been criticised as making consumers guinea pigs.[4]

2   *Burden of proof.* The difficulties of proving that an injury was caused by a defect in a product include the following: obtaining expert evidence,[5] including the lack of access to substantial government information acquired from indigenous producers[6] and importers;[7] but the Freedom of Information Act 2000 is unlikely to help in this regard.[8] The multiplicity of parties involved in the chain of distribution (see ante, para 17.01) itself exacerbates the problem.[9]

3   *The cost of civil litigation.* Notwithstanding modern improvements in redress systems (see ante, para 3.15 *et seq*), the sheer cost of litigation at both the High Court and County Court level will tend to raise the stakes so high that most injured private consumers are likely to be deterred from litigation. First, there is the apparently conscious restriction in our courts of trial by paper (see ante, para 3.23). Second, there is the propensity of the present substantive law of product liability to inflate costs, in

---

[17.05]

1   Especially in the case of personal injury caused in circumstances with an international flavour, eg, crash of a foreign manufactured aircraft, there may be attempts to bring civil proceedings in the jurisdiction likely to award the largest damages (forum shopping): see *SNI Aerospatale v Lee Kui Jak* [1987] 3 All ER 510, PC; and Geddes (1988) NLJ 542.

2   Eg, the *Ashington Piggeries* case (set out ante, para 13.13); *Frost v Aylesbury Dairy* (set out ante, para 14.08).

3   As in the tort of negligence: see post, paras 17.14; 17.19. For the position in relation to statutory product liability, see post, para 17.24 *et seq*.

4   For the significance of this defence to the pharmaceutical industry, see Newdick (1985) 101 LQR 405, and post, para 17.30.

5   See Harris, *Compensation and Support for Illness and Injury*, pp 110–12.

6   Eg, Medicines Act 1968, s 118; Deregulation Act 1994, s 75 and Sched 15 (see post, para 28.06).

7   There is now power for HM Customs to transmit information on a confidential basis to LAs: see ante, para 4.36. For discussion of the issue of public access to Government information, see Baxter [1997] JBL 199.

8   Section 43. See also ss 29, 40, 41; and generally Johnson (2001) 151 NLJ 1030; [2001] 10 Which? 10. The LCD has announced that the Act will not be implemented until 2005.

9   For the difficulties this has caused in tort claims, see post, para 17.16. But note the burden of proof in negligent representation: see post, para 17.10.

particular by reason of its complexity and uncertainty;[10] and the advantage which the foregoing gives to economically powerful litigants.

4 *Liability for acts of another.* As the transaction will frequently be arranged by a salesman on behalf of a stockist of goods, there may well be involved the different rules as to the latter's liability for the former: if the transferee's action is in contract, it will introduce the rules of agency, whereas in tort vicarious liability is involved;[11] and, if criminal proceedings are undertaken, yet another set of rules are involved (see post, para 28.12).

5 *The international dimension* (see ante, para 10.01).

[17.06] Many of the legal problems in this area are neatly exemplified in the case of *Lambert v Lewis*:[1]

> The plaintiff family were travelling along the highway in a car. Coming the other way was a Landrover, owned by a farmer (C) and driven by his employee, towing a trailer. The trailer became detached, slewed across the road and crashed into the plaintiffs' car, killing two of them and injuring the other two. The unhitching occurred by reason of a defective coupling between the Landrover and trailer: it had a defectively designed locking mechanism allowing the spindle to sheer; but C must have known about this for some months. The coupling had been supplied and fitted by a retailer (B), who had indirectly obtained it from the manufacturer (Z).

The plaintiff's claim for negligence. The plaintiff sued all the identified parties in the chain of distribution in the tort of negligence. Stocker J found that the coupling was of an unsafe design, that C was negligent in not noticing this and he apportioned liability 25% to C and 75% to Z; but he dismissed the plaintiff's claim against B, on the grounds that B had not been negligent in obtaining the coupling with no apparent defects from a reputable dealer.[2]

Third party proceedings. The farmer (C) sought to recover his share of the damages from B for breach of the undertaking as to fitness (see ante, para 14.07). The Court of Appeal held B liable for all the damage which flowed from his undoubted breach of the undertaking,[3] but this was unanimously reversed by the House of Lords on the grounds that the loss was caused, not by B's breach, but by C's failure to remedy the breach.[4]

Fourth party proceedings. The retailer (B) could not prove from which of two wholesalers (A1 or A2) he had obtained the offending coupling and therefore could not

---

10 See post, para 17.12. Bear in mind also the complexity which may arise simply from the length of the chain of distribution (as to which, see ante, para 17.01).

11 See post, para 17.12. For the possibility of a contribution, see the Civil Liability (Contribution) Act 1978.

[17.06]

1 [1982] AC 225; [1981] 1 All ER 1185, HL (discussed by Harvey and Parry, *The Law of Consumer Protection and Fair Trading* (6th edn), pp 165–70. It has been pointed out that the incidence of loss depends on the inability to identify A and the plaintiff's choice of defendant: Schofield [1981] JBL at 213.

2 [1978] 1 Lloyd's Rep 810; [1979] RTR 61. The events occurred before the Civil Liability (Contribution) Act 1978 came into force.

3 [1980] 1 All ER 978; [1980] 2 WLR 299, CA.

4 For discussion of the causation issue, see post, paras 27.29; 29.37.

sue either of them in contract. Accordingly, he chose to sue Z, and lost in the Court of Appeal on all the following grounds:

(1) There was no express collateral warranty on the basis of statements made in Z's sales literature,[5] because the claims it contained were not intended to be acted upon.[6]

(2) There was no negligent misstatement because there was no special relationship between the parties (see generally post, para 17.20).

(3) There was no liability for the negligent act of design because B's loss was wholly financial (see post, para 17.14). Though in the House of Lords, Lord Diplock *obiter* cast serious doubts on this argument (at 278), it has subsequently been affirmed.[7]

WITHIN THE CONTRACTUAL NEXUS

Where there is a contractual nexus between the parties, it is important to distinguish whether or not there are any contractual promises between the parties as to the state of the product. If not, other remedies must be sought (see post, para 17.10 *et seq*).

Assuming that there is such a contractual promise, the discussion may be conveniently sub-divided according to whether that promise became: (1) a term of a supply contract, (2) under an extension of the privity doctrine, or (3) a term of a collateral or other contract.

[17.07] A supply contract. Within the privity rule (see post, para 17.08), there should first be considered the identity of the person who is in law the supplier of the goods to the retail customer. The retail supplier may act through a servant or agent (see ante, para 10.06); the salesman will not necessarily be an employee of the occupier of the premises, as may happen where there is a franchise system (sometimes termed 'a shop-within-a-shop': see ante, para 1.07) or the salesman is the manufacturer's representative;[1] that apparent retailer may not even be the person who in law contracts to supply the goods to the retail cash customer, as where the salesman acts for an undisclosed principal, eg, where the salesman is simply taking orders subsequently fulfilled by supply direct from the manufacturer to the retail consumer; and the picture is further altered where the transaction is directly financed, in which case the financier will in law be the supplier to the retail consumer (see ante, para 2.21).

---

5   'Requires no maintenance, it is foolproof, once pin home – locked absolutely.' Cf *Baxter v Motor Co* (1934) 179 Wash 123. See generally ante, para 8.05.

6   The CA explicitly distinguished the cases cited post, para 17.09, notes 4 and 5. But see *E Hobbs (Farms) v The Baxenden Chemical Co* [1992] 1 Lloyd's Rep 54; and generally ante, para 8.05.

7   *Murphy v Brentwood DC* [1991] AC 398, HL (not a goods case).

[17.07]

1   Eg, the beauty preparations counter in a retail store. But the representative might only be a demonstrator, so that the store is the retail supplier.

Assuming that the identity of the supplier in law of the goods to the retail customer is established, there are two possible types of promise in that supply contract upon which the retail customer[2] may *prima facie*[3] sue:[4]

1 *Express promises.* The supplier's express promises[5] may be termed 'guarantees'[6] or 'warranties';[7] and there may sometimes be difficult questions of fact involved in determining whether a supplier has adopted a promise made by a prior party in the chain of distribution, eg, the manufacturer or importer. Sometimes, the benefit of the promise is expressed to be transferable,[8] and sometimes not; but a prohibition on assignment by the consumer may be an unfair term (OFT, *Bulletin No 12*, case 19).

2 *Implied promises.* In the previous chapters of Part 4, the various implied undertakings which may be imported into contracts for the supply of goods were considered, and it was seen that the major protection of the buyer or hirer rests on the undertakings as to title, description, fitness and quality. No doubt, the effect of these strict liability provisions may in practice be to force an element of disclosure on the supplier, shifting (in a non-technical sense) a burden of proof onto him. However, the very complicated route by which this is achieved may itself work against the interests of the consumer, not only at the level of ascertaining his rights, but also with regards to the cost of enforcement imposed by the complexity of the issues and multiplicity of the parties (see ante, para 17.05).

A chain of supply contracts. Where a chain of supply contracts can be traced (see ante, para 17.01), it may be possible for each buyer to bring a similar action for breach of express or implied terms (see above) against his supplier, all the actions being joined together in a single set of proceedings;[9] and this technique may even be available where there is an impecunious intermediate buyer.[9a] In such a case, the last transferee will *prima facie* have a right to rescind for breach of condition; but previous transferees are less likely to be able to rescind (see s 35 of the SGA, which is discussed post, para 29.05). To the extent that any previous transferee can only claim damages, as under an express indemnity, eg, in a recourse provision (see ante, para 16.22), his position is similar to that of a person suing under a collateral contract (see post, para 17.09). Yet the two situations must be carefully

---

2   As to the position of the family of the retail purchaser, see post, paras 17.12; 17.22.

3   Even if the retail consumer enters into a product insurance increasing his rights in respect of defective goods (see post, para 17.09), UCTA would prevent the retail supplier excluding his liability: see post, para 18.19. *Contra*, where subsequent to breach, the retail consumer enters into a contract of compromise: see post, para 26.18.

4   What if the retail consumer has in fact donated the goods to another? Will he thereupon lose any right to rescind (see post, para 29.06); and what damages will he suffer?

5   Eg, *Parker v Oloxo Ltd* [1937] 3 All ER 524; *Carlill v Carbolic Smoke Ball Co* [1893] QB 256, CA (discussed by Simpson (1985) Jo of Legal Studies 345). See generally ante, para 11.07.

6   Eg 'money-back guarantees': see post, para 20.24. Distinguish contracts of guarantee: see post, para 17.09.

7   As against the suppliers, the label 'warranty', will not necessarily be given its technical meaning: see post, para 18.06. For warranties, see generally ante, para 11.04.

8   As to where a transferable express promise is purportedly transferred to a donee, see equitable assignments (see ante, para 7.18); or transferred to one expressly mentioned in the contract (see post, para 17.08). For the effect of the assignment of rights and duties, see generally ante, para 7.23 *et seq*.

9   Eg, *Kasler and Cohen v Slavouski* [1928] 1 KB 78 (see post, para 29.36); *Parker v Oloxo Ltd* (above); *Butterworth v Kingsway Motors Ltd* (set out ante, para 12.06); *Lambert v Lewis* (set out ante, para 17.06); and see further Macleod, *Consumer Sales Law* (Butterworths edn), para 17.08.

9a   He may assign his rights to his sub-buyer: *Total Liban SA v Vitol Energy SA* [2000] 1 All ER 267.

distinguished because only[10] a contract for the supply of goods will attract the whole of the paraphernalia of implied terms discussed in Chapters 12–16, including the extra persons made liable under CCA, ss 56, 75. Finally, it should be borne in mind that any person in the chain of distribution found liable may claim a contribution from any other person in that chain 'liable in respect of the same damage', whether the latter's liability be in contract or tort;[11] and that, where there is a 'consumer supply' (see ante, para 14.01), an EU Directive reinforces the rights of suppliers to sue back up the chain (Art 4).

On the other hand, even supposing there is a chain of *prima facie* contractual liability, there are several weaknesses in that chain from the viewpoint of a consumer (say) pursuing an original substantial supplier. An intermediate contract may contain a valid exclusion clause (see post, Chapter 18). An intermediate party may be insolvent (see post, Chapter 20), or his identity uncertain. In any event, such chain litigation may be protracted and expensive.

[17.08] Extension of privity. No doubt, the common law has already blurred the edges of the privity doctrine in the field of product liability by both the device of the collateral contract (see post, para 17.09) and 'astute manipulation' of the rules of the agency or assignment (see post, para 17.12). *Inter alia*, the latter will include the undisclosed principal doctrine, though development here is limited by the rule that an undisclosed principal cannot ratify (see ante, para 10.06). Additionally, important extensions have been made by the CCA, with the making of further defendants liable for misrepresentation or on the basis of being a connected lender (ss 56, 75 of the CCA,: see ante, Chapter 16). However, in the United States there has been developed two new exceptions to the privity doctrine specifically to impose strict contractual liability in favour of consumers.

1 '*Horizontal privity*'.[1] To obviate the artificial arguments as to whether the retail buyer (C) purchased as agent for the injured consumer (D), the United States have come up with the idea of a limited waiver of the privity rule in favour of all in the household of the retail buyer (Uniform Commercial Code, article 2-318, alternative c).

2 '*Vertical privity*': a 'leapfrog' action. At common law, instead of a chain of supply contract actions (see ante, para 17.07), in some US jurisdictions an injured retail consumer (C or D) has been allowed to 'leapfrog' the 'innocent' retailer (B) and sue the 'guilty' producer (X, Y, Z) in just the same way as if the consumer had purchased the goods direct from the producer: this has particularly been the case where unsafe goods caused physical damage.[2]

---

10 But see the suggestion (2) by McNair J in *Andrews v Hopkinson* (ante, para 16.18).

11 Civil Liability (Contribution) Act 1978, s 6(1). For this Act, see generally ante, para 12.10.

[17.08]

1 For a diagrammatic portrayal of the ambit of this concept and the 'vertical privity' concept, see ante, para 17.01. For an excellent exposition, see the Law Commission Working Paper on *Liability for Defective Products* (1975, WP No 64), paras 119–33.

2 *Henningsen v Bloomfield Motors Inc* 161 A 2d 69 (1960) New Jersey (car with defective steering).

The extension of English privity.[3] Besides his rights under all the other exceptions to the privity rule,[4] s 1 of the Contracts (Rights of Third Parties) Act 1999 introduces a new general[5] statutory right for a third party (T) to enforce a contractual term in a contract to which he is not a party (see below): T is then entitled to exercise all those remedies which would have been available to him in an action for breach of contract had he been a contracting party;[6] and he may also take advantage of any exclusion or limitation clause in his favour (s 1(6)), eg, excluding liability for negligently caused personal injury. However, T is to be in no better position than if he had been a party to the contract (s 1(4)), eg, as to time limits; and his rights will therefore be subject to all defences and set-offs that the promisor may have against the other contracting party (s 3). The promisor's duty shall be owed to both the other contracting party (s 4) and the third party, though he is protected from double jeopardy (s 5). The Act does not make T a party to the contract (s 7(4)), nor alter the limitation rules (s 7(3); and see generally post, para 26.17); nor does it impose on T the burdens of that contract (s 3(4)(b); and see generally ante, para 10.01). T cannot usually be deprived of this new statutory right by subsequent agreement between the contracting parties (s 2; and see generally post, para 26.18); and s 1 extends to commercial arbitrations (s 8; and see generally ante, para 3.23).

The above section 1 right is expressed in general terms, but is likely to have considerable significance for product liability, where it would appear capable of extending both horizontal and vertical privity (see above). For T to take advantage of this provision (s 1(3)), he:

> ... must be expressly identified in the contract by name, as a member of a class or as answering a particular description but need not be in existence when the contract is entered into.

Where he falls within s 1(3), T may enforce a term of the contract in either of the following situations (s 1(1)):

(1) The contract expressly provides that T, which it identifies by 'name, class or description', may enforce the promise,[7] eg, where C purchases a gift for D and explicitly agrees with B that D shall be able to enforce the contract, or in a directly financed transaction the dealer's contract with the financier so provides (see ante, para 16.22). This situation should be distinguished from that where the contract is made as agent for T (see ante, para 10.06).

---

3   The Act is largely based upon the Report of the Law Commission, *Privity of Contract: Contracts for the Benefit of Third Parties* (1996, Law Com 242). See generally Treitel, *Law of Contract* (10th edn), p 600 *et seq*.

4   Section 7(1): see ante, para 10.01. Exempt from this Act is the right of a victim of negligent property damage under s 2(2) of UCTA to subject an exclusion clause to the reasonableness test (s 7(2)): see Dean [2000] JBL 143 at 148–49; and post, para 18.17.

5   Of the exceptional cases excluded from the Act by s 6, the only one likely to be relevant here are bills of exchange (s 6(1)).

6   Section 1(5): 'action' would rule out use the self-help remedies, eg, recaption (see post, para 24.23); 'breach of contract' would preclude T's use of tort actions, eg, wrongful interference with goods (see post, para 19.04) and restitutionary remedies (see post, para 29.12). Section 1(5) also explicitly makes T's action subject to the ordinary rules relating to 'damages, injunctions, specific performance and other relief' (see post, para 27.27 *et seq*).

7   Section 1(1)(a). Cf *Tweddle v Atkinson* (1861) 1 B & S 393; *The Eurymedon* [1975] AC 300, PC (not sale cases).

(2) The contract purports to confer a benefit on T.[8] Here, the fact that T is identified by 'name, class or description' merely creates a rebuttable presumption that he may enforce the contract (s 1(2)); so, the ordinary retail purchaser of defective goods (C) would not, without more, normally have the right to sue under the contract between the retailer (B) and the wholesaler or manufacturer (A, Z);[9] but it would be quite possible to frame, eg, a manufacturer's guarantee (see post, para 17.09A), so that it extended to C and D. Thus, where C directs B to send a purchased gift direct to D and the gift is defective, D will have the benefit of the statutory implied terms in the SGA.[10]

[17.09] Collateral or other contracts. Whether there is a single contract for the supply of goods or a chain of such contracts (see ante, para 17.07), there may also be one or more collateral[1] or other contracts. In this field of product liability, there are four particular situations where this device of a collateral contract has been used to impose liability as between remote parties in the chain of distribution.[2]

1 *In direct financing.* To impose contractual liability on the dealer to the consumer (see ante, para 16.18) and financier (see ante, para 16.21).

2 *On manufacturers.*[3] The promise may be made personally to the consumer by the representative of the manufacturer,[4] distributor or wholesaler.[5] It is more likely, however, that the promise will be made to the consumer in a less personal way by sales literature,[6] or other advertisement, whether distributed at the point of retail sale, directly mailed or carried in newspapers or on television.[7] One particular device which requires special mention here is the manufacturer's 'guarantee' against defects (see post, para 17.09A). Further problems arise with network guarantees; ie where a manufacturer sets up a system that any accredited outlet will do warranty work, regardless of from which outlet the consumer obtained the goods.[8]

---

8 Section 1(1)(b). Cf *Jackson v Horizon Holidays Ltd* [1975] 3 All ER 92, CA (package holiday).

9 The above Law Commission Report, para 7.18.

10 The above Law Commission Report, paras 7.41; 7.54; and as to remedies, see generally Chapter 29.

[17.09]

1 For collateral contracts, see generally ante, para 11.06. For cases where the necessary *animus contrahendi* was absent, see the *Howard Marine* case (set out post, para 17.10); *Jonathan Wren & Co Ltd v Microdec plc* [2000] CLY 876.

2 For the chain of distribution, see ante, para 17.01. Distinguish title-transferring collateral contracts: see ante, para 15.26.

3 See generally, Atiyah, *Sale of Goods* (10th edn), pp 266–67. Several industry codes of practice deal with such guarantees: see generally ante, para 3.13. For concern that Art 85 of the Treaty of Rome (see ante, para 2.13) may require such a warranty to be honoured community-wide, see Fine (1989) 10 ECLR 233.

4 Eg, *Shanklin Pier Ltd v Detel Products Ltd* [1951] 2 KB 854; *Comyn Ching & Co (London) Ltd v Oriental Tube Co Ltd* [1981] Com LR 67, CA.

5 Eg, *Wells (Merstham) Ltd v Buckland Sand and Silica Ltd* [1965] 2 QB 170.

6 Which may be a separate document, or printed on packaging, eg, chocolates. For EU avoidance of restrictions on guarantees see ante, para 2.13.

7 Liability is, perhaps, less likely here, because the advertising industry is usually very careful not to make any material representations of fact, eg, *Lambert v Lewis* (set out ante, para 17.06). See Bradgate (1991) 20 Anglo-Am LR 334.

8 Twigg-Flesner [1999] JBL 568.

3 *After-sales service.* Outside their legal liability for defects (see post, para 29.03A), manufacturers or retailers may offer after-sales service, perhaps with an extended warranty (see below). As regards the promised after-sales service, whilst its absence might amount to an offence under s 14 of the TDA (see ante, para 4.15), all too often the service is available, but at a seemingly disproportionate cost (but see s 15 of the SGSA: see ante, para 15.15).

4 *Insurance.*[9] In some cases, B and Z arrange to increase C's rights if the goods prove defective by offering a (say five year) optional 'extended warranty'.[10] This amounts to a product insurance for the stated period beyond the ordinary express (say for one year) manufacturer's guarantee. It is often cast in the form of a contract of insurance provided by a separate insurance company,[11] which may offer a significant commission to the retailer on such business and may be 'covered' by a special code of practice (see ante, para 3.13). A second range of risk is covered by the consumer's product loss insurance.[12] A third example is the cashback insurer (see ante, para 8.13A), where any regulated financier may incur liability under ss 56 or 75 of the CCA (see Chapter 16).

[17.09A] Manufacturers' guarantees. At common law, a manufacturer's guarantee could only take effect as a collateral contract (see generally ante, para 17.09). Such a device[1] used normally to contain two elements: it would probably purport to confer limited rights on the consumer (C) as against the manufacturer (Z) or retailer (B) in respect of defects in the goods, in consideration for which C agreed to forgo his ordinary legal rights against Z and also possibly against B. However, the legal effect of such guarantees is substantially affected by statute: as between B and C, B cannot adopt the words of the guarantee so as to exclude or restrict his statutory liability under the implied undertakings;[2] and, where the 'guarantee' refers to B, it must state positively that it does not affect C's statutory rights against B.[3] As between Z and C, Z cannot employ such

---

9 Even where there is a regulated supply, these insurance contracts are exempt from the linked transaction rules: see ante, para 5.31. These extended warranties may be extremely profitable to retailers (see 144 NLJ 401); and to deal with abuses the OFT recommended codes of practice: (1994/5) 9 Fair Trading, 10; 14 Tr LR 136; [1995] 4 Which? 22.

10 For the duration of the statutory implied terms and retailer-promoted insurance, see ante, para 14.06; and as to insolvency see post, para 19.13 *et seq.* Such insurances do not always cover maintenance and are sometimes offered 'free' where purchases are made with a plastic card. As to whether these insurances are worthwhile to consumers, see [2000] 4 Which? 35. Cf prior payment insurance (see post, para 23.22).

11 Recovery under the policy may be subject to onerous conditions: see [1998] 11 Which? 4. Moreover, if offered by B to C, the 'guarantee' may contravene insurance legislation: Twigg-Flesner [1999] JBL 279.

12 Long-term cover should normally be taken out via a household insurance policy; but interim cover may be automatically available where items are obtained by credit or charge card.

[17.09A]

1 Distinguish a supplier's guarantee (see ante, para 17.07); and note whether any guarantee is transferable (see ante, para 17.07). Some manufacturers' guarantees purport to allow subsequent unilateral variation by the manufacturer: see [1991] Which? 63. For a summary of reliability of electrical appliances, see [1995] 3 Which? 8.

2 For the implied undertakings, see ante, para 17.07; for the prohibition on exclusion, see UCTA, ss 6, 7 (see post, para 18.19); and for the OFT guidelines, see ante, para 3.11.

3 Consumer Transactions (Restrictions on Statements) Order 1976, Art 4: see ante, para 4.22. Does this requirement produce sufficient clarity?

words to exclude or restrict his liability in the tort of negligence.[4] For the private consumer, the result of the foregoing is frequently this: whilst the statutes prevent his losing his general rights, they may also remove the consideration which may support any promise (albeit limited) by Z, so rendering the 'guarantee' without legal effect, a matter for which a new remedy has been sought (see below). However, sometimes C cannot claim the benefit of the foregoing statutory provisions, as where C is a business consumer, or the guarantee refers only to after-sales servicing; but even here, Z may still face the difficulty that, if the 'guarantee' is only brought to the attention of C after purchase, it may be that any consideration is past, whether the promise is in respect of the goods or their servicing.[5]

Consumer guarantees. In addition to the above English law on the subject, there is an EU Directive which applies to any **express** 'guarantee' which is given by a 'producer',[6] providing that (Art 1(2)(e)):[7]

> ... any undertaking given by a seller or producer to the consumer, given without extra charge, to reimburse the price paid or to replace, repair or handle consumer goods in any way if they do not meet the specifications set out in the guarantee statement or in the relevant advertising.

It will be noted that this definition is not restricted to an 'undertaking' given by manufacturers to private consumers, but extends to any 'seller or producer', a phrase which seems apt to extend to any business 'seller or producer' in the chain of distribution who gives an express 'undertaking' to a private consumer. The Directive does not force that 'seller or producer' to make any express promises whatsoever; but, of course, he may voluntarily do so as part of his marketing effort. Where he does so, the Directive lays down that the (Art 6(1)):

> ... guarantee shall be legally binding on the offeror under the conditions laid down in the guarantee statement and the associated advertising.

The Directive goes on to state the following requirements for such guarantees:[8]

(1) It must state that it is in addition to the consumer's rights under the supply contract.

(2) It must set out 'in plain intelligible language the contents of the guarantee', its duration, etc.

(3) On request, the consumer must be provided with a written copy.

---

4   For Z's liability in the tort of negligence, see post, paras 17.14, 17.19; and for the prohibition on exclusion, see UCTA, s 5 (see post, para 18.26). If there is an agreement between traders to offer similar guarantees, this might be a restrictive trade practice: see ante, para 2.12.

5   Eg, *Roscorla v Thomas* (1842) 3 QB 234 (goods); *Stewart v Reavell's Garage* [1952] 2 QB 545 (servicing). For another argument, see Howells and Bryant [1993] Consum LJ 6.

6   '"Producer" shall mean the manufacturer of consumer goods, the importer of consumer goods into the territory of the Community or any person purporting to be a producer by placing his name, trademark or other distinctive sign on the consumer goods': Art 1(2)(d).

7   For the Directive definitions of 'seller', 'consumer' and 'consumer goods', see ante, para 14.01. The UK has already passed the implementation date: see ante, para 1.03A.

8   Arts 6(2), (3). More than one language may be required (Art 6(4)). Infringement of these requirements shall not affect the validity of the guarantee (Art 6(5)).

Other remedies

Even though there is no breach of any contractual promise made to a party, **as against the other contracting party only** he may be able to rely on the law relating to misrepresentation, illegality, unenforceability or mistake (see ante, para 10.18).

[17.10] Misrepresentation. At common law, a misstatement of fact which induced a contract is termed a 'misrepresentation' (see ante, para 11.01). Of course, at a later stage, that misrepresentation may become a term of the contract (see ante, para 11.02); but, even where it does not, that 'mere representation' gives rise in the representee to a right to rescind (see post, paras 26.12–14), though at common law only an inferior right to damages: if fraudulent, damages will lie in the torts of deceit or negligent misstatement (see post, para 17.18–19); but otherwise there is only the possibility of an indemnity. However, the Misrepresentation Act 1967 may enable the representee to recover damages from the other contracting party[1] in two extra situations (see below), though only where that party has made or authorised the representation.[2] There is no statutory definition of 'misrepresentation', so the common law definition presumably applies (see ante, para 11.01); and the measure of those damages is tortious (see post, para 27.24).

1   *Careless misrepresentations*. Where there is an innocent but careless misrepresentation, s 2(1) provides:

> Where a person has entered into a contract after a misrepresentation has been made to him by another party thereto and as a result thereof he has suffered loss, then, if the person making the misrepresentation would be liable to damages in respect thereof had the misrepresentation been made fraudulently,[3] that person shall be so liable notwithstanding that the misrepresentation was not made fraudulently, unless he proves that he had reasonable ground to believe and did believe up to the time the contract was made that the facts represented were true.

The effect of s 2(1) is thus to cast upon the **representor** the (legal?) burden of proof as to his state of mind: this should be compared with the representor's much lighter onus in the tort of deceit, where the legal and evidential burden is on the representee. The last phrase of s 2(1) spells out the state of mind which he must disprove, making him liable if he has either of the following states of mind:

(i)   **The unreasonable believer** will refer to the, more common, careless man.[4] In *Howard Marine & Dredging Co Ltd v A Ogden & Sons (Excavations) Ltd:*[5]

---

1   But not against an agent authorised to make the representation: *The Skopas* [1983] 2 All ER 1. If the agent were acting outside his authority, he might instead be liable for breach of warranty of authority. But see *Gran Gelato Ltd v Richcliff (Group) Ltd* [1992] 1 All ER 865 (criticised 109 LQR 539).

2   *Overbrooke Estates Ltd v Glencombe Properties Ltd* [1974] 3 All ER 511; *SW General Properties v Marton* [1983] 2 Tr LR 14. For a case where a retail supplier may adopt the misrepresentation of a manufacturer, see ante, para 17.07; and for auctioneers, see ante, para 10.10.

3   The effect of this would appear to be to incorporate by reference the law of deceit, including the Statute of Frauds Amendment Act 1818 (as to which, see generally post, para 17.18). The difficult question of how much of that law is so incorporated is discussed by Atiyah and Treitel (1967) 30 MLR 369 at 374–75.

4   See also *Thomas Witter Ltd v TBP Industries Ltd* (set out post para 26.14). By suing under s 2(1), P will gain the deceit test of remoteness rather than that applicable for common law negligence (see post, para 27.41).

5   [1978] QB 574; [1978] 2 All ER 1134, CA. See also the *Gran Gelato* case (above).

In order to tender for a contract to dump oil at sea, D were negotiating to hire suitable barges from P, their tender price depending in part on the carrying capacity of the barges. P innocently, misrepresented the carrying capacity of the barges prior to the conclusion of a charter. On discovering the truth, D refused to pay the hire; P withdrew the barges; and D counter-claimed for damages.

Notwithstanding the exclusion clause,[6] the majority of the Court of Appeal held P liable for damages for breach of s 2(1) on the grounds that P had failed to prove that they had reasonable grounds for believing the truth of the statement. However, the Court refused to allow D's claim on the basis of a collateral contract (see ante, para 17.09) and disagreed over the tort of negligent misstatement.[7]

(ii) **The non-believer**. There may here be an overlap with the tort of deceit (see post, para 17.18), though failure by the representor to prove his innocence does not make him liable for deceit.[8]

2 *Non-fraudulent misrepresentations*. Where there is an innocent misrepresentation, whether careless or not,[9] s 2(2) gives the court a discretion in a claim for rescission to award damages in lieu of rescission (see post, para 26.12).

[17.11] Other vitiating factors. These include the following:

1 *Illegality and unenforceability*. There are a number of statutory provisions which may taint a contract with illegality or render it unenforceable; and many of these were specifically designed for the protection of a particular group of persons (see ante, Chapter 4). The effect of these on the contract has already been considered (see ante, para 10.19).

2 *Mistake*.[1] Frequently as a line of last resort, the buyer or hirer may claim to avoid his contractual liability on grounds of mistake. Immediately, it is vital to decide whether or not the parties have reached agreement. If they have, but are both labouring under the same fundamental mistake, such as where the goods have been destroyed, this raises the question of impossibility (see post, para 22.10). On the other hand, it may be denied that the parties were ever *ad idem*, so that the alleged contract was void *ab initio*;[2] or alternatively, that a written contract should be rectified because it does not accurately represent the mutual intention of the parties.[3] It has been pointed out that such a plea is particularly likely to be raised by the buyer or hirer who finds that the

---

6   The majority (Lord Denning MR dissenting) affirmed the decision of Bristow J that it would not be 'fair or reasonable' within the meaning of the unamended s 3 of the Misrepresentation Act 1967 to allow P to rely on his exclusion clause (see post, para 18.17).

7   Shaw LJ for liability; Lord Denning MR against; and Bridge LJ *dubitante*.

8   Distinguish s 2(1) from actual claims for fraud, because under s 2(1), D is liable simply for lack of proof of innocence: Hooley (1991) 107 LQR 31.

9   Section 2(3) enables the court to award damages under both ss 2(1) and (2), provided that there is no element of double recovery: see generally post, para 27.39.

[17.11]

1   See generally Treitel, *Law of Contract* (10th edn), Chapter 8.

2   Eg, *Scriven Bros & Co v Hindley & Co* [1913] 3 KB 564; *Hartog v Colin and Shields* [1939] 3 All ER 566. And see *Henkel v Pape* (1870) LR Ex 7, discussed by Treitel, *op cit*, 27.

3   See *Frederick E Rose (London) Ltd v William H Pim Jnr Co Ltd* [1953] 2 QB 450, CA (rectification refused).

contract goods are defective.[4] Within the English law of contract, there are only two possible solutions in such a case of mistake of quality:

(1) The goods are at the risk of the buyer or hirer, that is, the rule *caveat emptor* (see ante, para 15.22) applies; or

(2) the goods are at the risk of the supplier for one of the following reasons:

(a) there is a breach of an express or implied term which puts responsibility on the supplier (see ante, Chapters 13–15), or

(b) the contract is void, in which case the supplier as owner bears the risk in the sense of the reduced worth of the goods due to any defect (see post, para 22.01).

On this basis, it is clear that the plea by a buyer or hirer of mistake of quality is really an alternative method of trying to place the risk on the supplier.[5] Such a plea was raised for this purpose by the buyer in *Harrison and Jones Ltd v Bunten and Lancaster Ltd*:[6]

> There was a contract for the sale by sample of Calcutta Kapok, 'Sree' brand. Neither party was aware that this brand of kapok contained an admixture of cotton, which rendered it unsuitable for use by the buyer on his machines.

Pilcher J rejected the buyer's plea of mistake, pointing out that there was no finding of fact that the parties directed their minds towards the question of whether the goods contained an admixture of cotton (at 657). Nevertheless, his Lordship did consider what the position would have been had they done so. He denied that the mistake would be such as to make the goods 'essentially different', so that the contract would be void at common law under the doctrine in *Bell v Lever Brothers Ltd*.[7] Nor did he think that the buyer should be able to rescind in equity under the rule in *Solle v Butcher*.[8] Of course, there is a strong argument for saying that it is undesirable that the law should too frequently allow a buyer or hirer escape from his supply contract on a plea of mistake, on the grounds that this would unduly interfere with the interests of finality. Indeed, there is only one reported case where a contract for the sale of goods has been held void on grounds of such a mistake.[9]

---

4   Where he has lost the right to reject for breach of contract: Atiyah, *Sale of Goods* (10th edn), p 210. See generally ante, paras 10.16–17.

5   Eg, *Smith v Hughes* (set out ante, para 10.17); *Oscar Chess Ltd v Williams* [1957] 1 All ER 325, CA.

6   [1953] 1 QB 646; [1953] 1 All ER 903.

7   [1932] AC 161, HL (not a sale case).

8   [1950] 1 KB 671, CA (not a sale case). Cf *Associated Japanese Bank (International) Ltd v Credit du Nord* [1988] 3 All ER 902.

9   *Nicholson and Venn v Smith-Marriott* (1947) 177 LT 189: but see the criticisms of that case in Atiyah, *Sale of Goods* (10th edn), p 211, note 335; Treitel, *Law of Contract* (10th edn), p 267, note 55.

OUTSIDE THE CONTRACTUAL NEXUS

[17.12] With a few limited exceptions, the common law takes an extremely strict view of contractual promises, the promisor being almost regarded as guaranteeing his promise (see post, para 26.02). Yet this strict contractual liability is limited by the doctrine of privity (see ante, para 17.04), albeit extended by statute (see ante, para 17.08); and those who are not privy can only be civilly liable in tort, where liability at common law usually depends on fault,[1] except in the case of vicarious civil liability, eg, that of an employer for the acts of his employee.[2]

It has already been noted how the courts have sought to avoid this limitation of strict liability[3] by tracing breach back along the chain of distribution, by the collateral contract of warranty (see ante, paras 17.07–09A) and by the action for breach of statutory duty (see ante, para 3.21); and it has been pointed out that the courts have also sought to mitigate the effects of the doctrine of privity by astute manipulation of the agency concept and a husband's or parent's claim in the case of injury or death to his wife or child.[4] For such a contractual claim, the argument must be within the laws of agency (see ante, para 10.06), not vicarious liability.[5] Alternatively, it might be possible for a donor to assign his contractual rights to a sub-buyer[6] or donee,[7] or to find an implied contract[8] or joint purchase.[9]

However, because there are so many claims that cannot be fitted within the framework of contract, we must consider, albeit briefly, the grounds of product liability in tort. In this discussion, it is convenient to distinguish product liability as between the following: (1) common law liability for acts and omissions, which will be relevant as regards both design and production defects; (2) common law liability for statements (see post, para 17.17), which will include sales literature; and (3) statutory product liability for unsafe goods (see post, para 17.24). There should also be borne in mind any relevant instructions for use (see post, para 18.28 *et seq*).

[17.12]

1 See post, paras 17.13; 17.18. Cf *Balsamo v Medici* [1984] 2 All ER 304.

2 For vicarious criminal liability, see post, para 28.09.

3 To the extent that it may now be possible to impose strict statutory product liability such motivation will be lessened.

4 Eg, *Lockett v Charles* (below); *Jackson v Horizon Holidays* (above). See also the comments of the Law Commission in the *First Report on Exemption Clauses in Contracts* (Law Com No 24), paras 60–63. For the rules as to when an agent may bind his principal, see generally ante, para 10.06.

5 *Director General of Fair Trading v Smiths Concrete Ltd* [1991] 4 All ER 150, CA.

6 *Total Liban SA v Vitol Energy SA* [2000] 1 All ER 267.

7 As to assignment of choses in action, see ante, para 7.16 *et seq*. For a transmissible warranty of safety, see (1991) 107 LQR at 270–75.

8 *Lockett v AM Charles Ltd* [1938] 4 All ER 170.

9 Why is this not an answer when purchases are by spouses? Cf *Daniels v White* (set out post, para 17.13).

Common law liability for acts and omissions[1]

[17.13] Introduction. Outside the contractual nexus, the supplier of goods will seldom be under any strict liability at common law in relation to defects in the goods causing physical loss:[2] the doctrine of *Rylands v Fletcher* (see post, para 17.21) probably has no application in this context;[3] except in respect of breach of safety regulations, an action for breach of statutory duty is seldom available;[4] and the possibility of an action in trespass will usually be ruled out because the act or omission of the supplier on which the complaint is based will generally have occurred whilst the goods were in the supplier's ownership or control.[5] Thus, recovery in tort will usually depend on the tort of negligence.[6] The difference between liability in contract, and that in the tort of negligence was neatly exemplified by *Daniels and Daniels v White & Sons Ltd*:[7]

> The male plaintiff sued the retailer in contract and his wife sued the manufacturer in tort when they both suffered injury by reason of the fact that the sealed bottle of lemonade sold to them included a large element of carbolic acid.

Notwithstanding that it seemed extremely likely that the acid was introduced into the bottle whilst at the manufacturer's plant, Lewis J held that the manufacturer was not liable in negligence on the grounds that his process was foolproof,[8] but that the innocent retailer was liable for breach of the undertaking as to merchantability (see ante, para 14.18). Indeed, it was only with the decision of the House of Lords in *Donoghue v Stevenson*,[9] to the effect that a manufacturer owed a duty of care to the ultimate consumer, that it became clear that participation in the chain of distribution might involve a general liability in the tort of negligence (see post, para 17.14) and now also termed 'wrongful interference with goods'.[10]

Nowadays, this sharp dichotomy between strict and negligence liability is only likely to obtain as regards **safe** but shoddy goods: this is because contract liability for shoddy goods is strict (see ante, para 14.08), whereas tort liability usually depends on proof of negligence (see above). As regards **unsafe** goods, the position is otherwise: whilst contract liability continues to be strict, outside the contractual nexus there is frequently a sort of strict civil liability under the CPA (see post, para 17.21 *et seq*); and there may also be strict criminal liability under the GPS Regulations (see ante, para 4.32 *et seq*).

[17.13]

1 Fleming, *Torts* (9th edn), Chapter 23; *Street on Torts* (10th edn), p 340 *et seq*; Winfield and Jolowicz, *Tort* (12th edn), Chapter 10; Clark, *Product Liability*, 1–8.

2 Possibly, an action on the case for physical injury might lie on the analogy of *Wilkinson v Downton* [1897] 2 QB 57. Cf *Beaudesert Shire Council v Smith* (1966) 40 ALJR 211, HC: see Dworkin and Harari 40 ALJ 296, 347.

3 See the judgment of Scott LJ in *Read v Lyons Ltd* [1945] 1 KB 216, CA, decision affd [1947] AC 156, HL.

4 For breach of safety regulations, see ante, para 4.35. As to actions for breach of statutory duty, see generally ante, para 3.21.

5 Now termed 'wrongful interference with goods': Torts (Interference with Goods) Act 1977, s 1(b) (see post, para 19.04).

6 For negligent loss of credit cards, see ante, para 7.13.

7 [1938] 4 All ER 258. See also Street, *op cit*, note 1, p 346, note 14.

8 But there might still be vicarious liability: see post, para 17.16.

9 [1932] AC 562; [1932] All ER Rep 1, HL (see Rodger (1992) 108 LQR 236).

10 Torts (Interference with Goods) Act 1977, s 1(c): see post, para 19.04.

[17.14] The scope of negligence liability. Leaving aside the possibility of an intermediate examination (see post, para 17.15) and the burden of proof (see post, para 17.16), the scope of the rule in *Donoghue v Stevenson* (see ante, para 17.13), as developed in subsequent cases, may be analysed as follows:

1   *The subject matter.* In *Donoghue v Stevenson*, the court was dealing with a bottle of ginger beer and referred to a 'manufacturer of products'. Subsequently, the principle has been extended to other manufactured products,[1] and probably now includes not only the goods sold, but also damage caused by any other goods transferred under the contract (cf ante, para 14.03).

2   *The plaintiff.* In *Donoghue v Stevenson*, the court was prepared to contemplate that a donee of goods (her donor having purchased them from the retailer) might recover, and the court spoke in terms of the 'ultimate consumer'. Is this right limited by the rule that a buyer can sue in negligence only after the property in goods has passed to him (see post, para 22.08)?

3   *The defendant.* In *Donoghue v Stevenson*, the defendant was a manufacturer, but the rule has subsequently been extended to cover manufacturers of components, assemblers, distributors and retailers.[2] Thus, it would seem that any business person who forms a link in the chain of distribution (see ante, para 17.01) may potentially be liable to any later link, though the manifestation of the duty may vary according to the defendant's place in the chain:[3] the manufacturer or assembler may be liable for negligent design or manufacture or failure to warn,[4] whereas distributors are more likely to be liable only for negligent handling, eg, examination (see post, para 17.15), or failure to warn.[5] Moreover, it has now been settled that, where there is liability in contract, then a fortiori a duty of care is owed in tort,[6] though the extent of the duty of care which any of these defendants owes to a donee is still open.[7]

4   *The defendant's duty to the plaintiff.* The duty owed by each above business party in the chain of distribution to every subsequent party in the chain is merely to exercise reasonable care so as not to cause damage:[8] this could be to get it right in the first place, ie the design or manufacturing defects; or to recall the product when a defect is subsequently discovered (see ante, para 17.02). Moreover, a defendant may be

---

[17.14]

1   Eg, *Grant v Australian Knitting Mills Ltd* [1936] AC 85, PC (underpants); *Parker v Oloxo Ltd* [1937] 3 All ER 524 (hair dye); *Herschtal v Stewart and Arden Ltd* (motor car: set out ante, para 16.18).

2   *Evans v Triplex Ltd* [1936] 2 All ER 283 (component manufacturer); *Howard v Furness Ltd* [1936] 2 All ER 781 (assembler); *Parker v Oloxo Ltd* (distributor; above); *Fisher v Harrods Ltd* [1966] 1 Lloyd's Rep 500 (retailer).

3   For a contribution between defendants, see the Civil Liability (Contribution) Act 1978, s 1(1). For this Act, see generally ante, para 12.10.

4   *Vacwell Engineering Ltd v BDH Chemicals Ltd* (set out post, para 18.29); *E Hobbs v The Baxenden Chemical Co* [1992] 1 Lloyd's Rep 54. In the case of a motor manufacturer, the duty may be to recall vehicles: see Harvey and Parry, *Consumer Protection and Fair Trading* (6th edn), pp 162–64.

5   Eg, *Clarke v Army and Navy Co-operative Society* [1903] 1 KB 155; *Andrews v Hopkinson* (set out ante, para 16.18).

6   *White v John Warwick & Co* [1953] 2 All ER 1021, at 1026; and see post, para 17.19.

7   See *Street on Torts* (10th edn), p 343, note 9.

8   The *Aswan Engineering* case (set out ante, para 14.14). Compare the strict liability in contract (see ante, para 17.13) and under statutory product liability (see post, para 17.24).

exonerated from liability, or that liability reduced, where the plaintiff himself knows of the danger and disregards it; or where the defect is due to wear and tear, inadequate maintenance, repair or warning;[9] or the plaintiff uses the goods for a purpose which is materially different from that for which it is designed, although it may be doubted whether this is so as regards a very young child who drinks furniture polish or sniffs solvent.[10]

5   *The damage.*[11] The liability clearly comprehends physical damage done by the defective product, particularly personal injury. However, if the product is merely shoddy, rather than unsafe, liability is likely to be only in contract; and the same is likely to be true if a dangerous defect is discovered before it causes an injury. The reason is that, where the goods are shoddy or the defect discovered, the loss is then purely economic and the courts are reluctant to impose liability in the tort of negligence to do the work of a warranty of quality (see ante, para 11.03 *et seq*), as it would amount to a transmissible warranty of quality.[12]

[17.15] Intermediate examination.[1] In *Donoghue v Stevenson*, the court stressed that there was 'no reasonable opportunity of intermediate inspection' of the sealed bottle.[2] Conversely, the liability of the manufacturer may be reduced or cancelled by the failure of some later party in the chain of distribution to inspect the goods: the test would not seem to be whether there is any possibility of examination, but whether that party is foreseeably likely to examine the goods for that particular defect.[3] Where the intermediate party is foreseeably likely to examine the goods, he is liable to anybody further along the chain of distribution injured by his negligent discharge of that duty,[4] though such liability will not necessarily exonerate persons through whose hands the goods have earlier passed,[5] and liability may be apportioned.[6] It has been suggested that similar principles should apply where the ultimate purchaser might reasonably be expected to inspect the goods and discover the fault;[7] but a manufacturer cannot exclude that liability by way of a guarantee[8] or as regards personal injury.[9]

---

9   For warnings, see post, paras 18.04; 18.29. What of the dilemma that such a warning may suggest a new form of misuse to some, eg, glue or aerosol spray sniffing?

10 *Evans v Souls Garages Ltd* [2001] 2 CL 458 (petrol to a 13 year old).

11 See Clark, *Product Liability*, 107–26; Street, *op cit*, note 7, pp 344–45.

12 Per Lord Keith in *Murphy v Brentwood DC* [1990] 2 All ER 908 at 921b, HL (not a goods case). Eg, *Lambert v Lewis* (set out ante, para 17.06; third party proceedings); *Hamble Fisheries Ltd v L Gardner & Sons Ltd* [1999] CLY 3960, CA.

[17.15]

1   See generally *Street on Torts* (10th edn), pp 343–44; Mildred, *Product Liability: Law and Insurance*, p 128 *et seq*.

2   But the retailer may be liable in contract: see *Daniels and Daniels v White & Sons Ltd* (set out ante, para 17.13).

3   Eg, *Grant v Australian Knitting Mills Ltd* [1936] AC 85, PC; *Watson v Buckley, Osborne, Garrett & Co Ltd* [1940] 1 KB 155. Cf *Clay v Crump Ltd* [1964] 1 QB 533, CA.

4   Eg, *Herschtal v Stewart and Arden Ltd* (set out ante, para 16.18).

5   See *Kubach v Hollands* [1937] 3 All ER 907; *Lambert v Lewis* (set out ante, para 17.06).

6   This will be under the Civil Liability (Contribution) Act 1978, s 1. See generally ante, para 12.10.

7   Fleming, *Torts* (9th edn), p 542.

8   UCTA, s 5: see post, para 18.26.

9   UCTA, s 2(1): see post, para 18.17.

[17.16] The burden of proof. Frequently, the most vital matter in a product liability claim is proof of causation, a matter which become more difficult to prove as more links exist in the chain of distribution between plaintiff and defendant (see ante, para 17.01). Whilst the burden of proving liability on the balance of probabilities is then a formidable task,[1] it is not impossible (see post, para 17.24). Theoretically, it might be lightened by the doctrine of *res ipsa loquitur*;[2] but there have been suggestions that that doctrine is expiring.[3]

However, even without the benefit of that doctrine, a negligence action for product liability may succeed. In *Carroll v Fearon*:[4]

> In 1988, there was a fatal collision between two cars, seemingly caused by a sudden and complete tread strip of a rear tyre of one of them. The tyre was manufactured in 1981 by Dunlop; and it was proved that Dunlop's manufacturing process had been defective as the radial tyre contained inadequate rubber penetration of the cords. The judge decided that Dunlop had been negligent, but apportioned 20% of the blame to the driver/owner. On appeal, Dunlop argued that no particular act of negligence by itself had been established.

Nevertheless, the Court of Appeal unanimously held Dunlop wholly liable at common law,[5] saying that the particular individual responsible for the manufacturing defect need not be identified, nor need the particular act of negligence be specified.[6] Judge LJ pointed out that the tyre had burst many years after it had left the factory and had been regularly used, so that its failure might have resulted from any one of a number of possible causes. Ignoring speculative considerations, eg, that the driver was negligent, and focusing on the evidence, the judge was entitled to decide on the balance of probabilities negligence had been established against Dunlop;[7] and there was no evidence upon which the drivers could have been held partly to blame.

However, it is in the nature of this type of situation that the defect may be caused by the default of any one of a number of people in the chain of distribution, so that it is very difficult to prove that only one person was at fault. As it will normally be impossible to say whose fault caused the defect, he who bears the burden of proof will normally lose.[8] On the other hand, it is sometimes possible to escape this dilemma by apportioning loss,[9] or because the evidence clearly establishes the innocence of all but one of the parties in the chain of distribution.

These problems will also arise with statutory product liability (see post, para 17.24).

[17.16]

1 See *Daniels and Daniels v White & Sons Ltd* (set out ante, para 17.13); and *Street on Torts* (10th edn), pp 345–47.

2 See Street, *ibid*, pp 258–63; Mildred, *Product Liability: Law and Insurance*, pp 127–28.

3 See McInnes (1998) 114 LQR 547; Witting (2001) 117 LQR 392.

4 [1998] CLY 3995, CA; discussed by Slapper (1998) 148 NLJ 345.

5 The CPA Part I (see post, para 17.24 *et seq*) did not apply to goods manufactured in 1981.

6 Relying on a *dictum* by Lord Wright in *Grant v Australian Knitting Mills Ltd* [1936] AC 85 at 101.

7 In part, this was because, knowing of the manufacturing defect, Dunlop had decided not to institute a recall 'for commercial reasons'.

8 Normally the plaintiff: *Ng Chun Pui v Lee Chuen Tat* [1988] CLY 1582, PC.

9 Civil Liability (Contribution) Act 1978, s 1(1) (see generally ante, para 12.10); Law Reform (Contributory Negligence) Act 1945 (see post, para 27.39).

Common law liability for statements

[17.17] Introduction. Irrespective of any contractual nexus, there are a number of torts giving a partial, sometimes overlapping, protection against loss arising by reason of the untrue statement of another. First, the law of torts offers some protection in respect of injury to the person or goods by way of defamation,[1] injurious falsehood[2] and passing off.[3] Second, statements calculated to cause injury to the person may be actionable: for instance, there may be liability for inducing breach of contract.[4] Third, where reliance on a statement causes injury, it may be possible to bring an action in deceit or negligence (see below).

Each tort is subject to its own rules and limited in its scope; and for the details reference must be made to the standard works on tort. However, some comments about the third category may be apposite here in relation to both the torts of deceit (see post, para 17.18) and negligent misstatement (see post, para 17.19), though attempts at exclusion will be left until later (see post, paras 18.17).

[17.18] Deceit. Where the defendant knowingly[1] or recklessly makes a false statement with the intention that the plaintiff should act on it,[2] then the plaintiff may at common law recover in respect of any loss caused by his reliance on it,[3] irrespective of whether or not the statement was made directly to him.[4] The independent tort of deceit is a relatively modern one, but its basis may be traced back to the writ of deceit in the 13th century.[5] This writ was the origin of two separate lines of development: the modern tort of deceit itself;[6] and, quite separately, the old writ, which had been used to give a remedy for breach of warranty, was absorbed into the action of assumpsit, as may be seen from the modern definition of a warranty (see ante, para 11.03). With the passage of time, the two developments became quite distinct: so that liability for breach of warranty became strict, subject only to the privity rule (see ante, para 17.04); but liability in deceit required proof

---

[17.17]

1 See Kidner [1992] JBL 570.

2 As distinguished from a mere puff (see ante, para 8.05): *De Beers Abrasive Products Ltd v International General Electric Co* [1975] 2 All ER 599.

3 *Associated Newspapers plc v Insert Media Ltd* [1991] 3 All ER 535, CA. See also Copyright etc Act 1988, s 300. As to injurious falsehood (slander of title), see *Street on Torts* (10th edn), p 137 *et seq*; and as to passing off, see ante, paras 4.07, 8.03–04.

4 See *Street on Torts* (10th edn), p 148 *et seq*. Cf *Shearson Lehman Hutton Inc v Maclaine Watson & Co Inc* [1989] 2 Lloyd's Rep 570 ([1990] LMCLQ at 308).

[17.18]

1 What if the representation is made innocently, but its falsity is later discovered? See Fleming, *Torts* (9th edn), p 696. Cf *Wings Ltd v Ellis* (set out ante, para 4.17).

2 *Goose v Wilson Sandford & Co (No 2)* [2001] 5 CL 738, CA.

3 To stop litigants avoiding the statute of Frauds by suing in deceit, it was enacted that only written false statements as to creditworthiness were actionable: Statute of Frauds Amendment Act 1828, s 6. This provision does not apply to actions for negligent misstatement (see post, para 17.19): *Anderson v Rhodes* [1967] 2 All ER 850.

4 *Derry v Peek* (1889) 14 App Cas 337, HL. Cf CCA, s 46: see ante, para 8.27. For damages, see *Archer v Brown* [1985] QB 401.

5 For the effect of this on product liability generally, see ante, para 17.04.

6 See *Pasley v Freeman* (1789) 3 Term Rep 51.

of a fraudulent intent,[7] but no privity of contract between representor and representee, so that a deceitful company director might be personally liable to a person contracting with his company.[8]

Where there is no contractual liability and fraud cannot be proved, there may be a remedy in the tort of negligent misstatement (see post, para 17.19). However, where fraud can be shown, by suing instead under s 2(1) of the 1967 Act (see ante, para 17.10) the plaintiff can not only reduce the burden of proof[9] whilst recovering the same measure of damages as for fraud, but also leave open the possibility of summary judgment.[10] Nevertheless, it seems likely there remain a number of distinct benefits for a victim of fraud in pleading a claim in deceit,[11] such as that no defence of contributory negligence (see post, para 27.39) is available.[12]

[17.19] Negligent misstatement. For some considerable time, at common law there has been liability for negligent misstatements which caused harm to the person.[1] However, in the absence of a fiduciary relationship, the courts were unwilling to impose liability where the loss was purely financial. *Hedley Byrne & Co Ltd v Heller Ltd*[2] appears to mark a change of heart in this respect, though their Lordships were there impressed by the need to confine liability for negligent misstatements within fairly narrow limits and said that normally the only duty should be to give an honest answer.[3] See further post, para 17.20.

Insofar as it results in damage to goods, the tort must now be termed 'wrongful interference with goods'.[4] It has since been held that the mere fact that there was a contract between the parties under which there was an implied term to exercise due care did not preclude the existence of a tortious duty of care between the same parties;[5] and that the tort liability was not necessarily co-extensive with the contract liability.[6]

[17.20] The scope of the action. In *Smith v Bush*:[1]

Surveyors commissioned by the mortgagees carelessly gave favourable reports on properties about to be purchased, those reports containing express disclaimers. The

---

7 *Hornal v Neuberger Products* [1957] 1 QB 247, CA.; *Thomas Witter Ltd v TBP Industries Ltd* (set out post, para 26.14). For the measure of damages, see post, para 27.24.
8 *Thomas Saunders Partnership v Harvey* (1990) 9 Tr LR 78, DC. This avoids the *Salomon* rule (see post, para 19.25).
9 *Garden Neptune Shipping v Occidental etc Corp* [1990] 1 Lloyd's Rep 330, CA (see 107 LQR 31).
10 *Newton Chemical v Arsenis* [1989] 1 WLR 1297, CA (for summary judgment, see post, para 27.03). See Hooley (1992) 142 NLJ 60.
11 Hooley, *ibid*.
12 *Corporacion Nacional del Cobre de Chapter ile v Sogemin Metals Ltd* [1997] 2 All ER 917.

[17.19]
1 Eg, *Parker v Oloxo Ltd* [1937] 3 All ER 524.
2 [1964] AC 465; [1963] 2 All ER 575, HL (not a goods case; liability disclaimed). See further *Street on Torts* (10th edn), p 215 *et seq*.
3 Per Lords Reid, Morris, Hodson, and Devlin, at 483, 504, 513, 514. But see *Intervention Board for Agricultural Products v Leidig* [2000] Lloyd's Rep PN 144, CA.
4 Torts (Interference with Goods) Act 1977, s 1(c): see post, para 19.04.
5 *Henderson v Merrett Syndicates Ltd* [1995] 2 A C 145, HL (not a goods case).
6 *Holt v Payne Skillington* [1996] PNLR 179, CA (not a goods case).

[17.20]
1 [1990] 1 AC 831; [1989] 2 All ER 514, HL (see 105 LQR at 511–13; 52 MLR at 845).

mortgagors relied on those reports to purchase the properties. The properties contained overlooked defects.

The House of Lords unanimously held that the surveyors owed a duty of care to the mortgagors, which could not be disclaimed (see post, para 18.17). In other cases a defendant has been held liable for a negligent misstatement as to creditworthiness;[2] or as seller's agent (see ante, para 10.11) or buyer's agent;[3] or sometimes where the parties were in the process of contract negotiation;[4] or by piercing the corporate veil;[5] or the giving of a mortgage valuation[6] or loan advice; or where a local authority erroneously stipulated that expenditure must be incurred under the Food Safety Act 1990;[7] or where the originator fails to implement a direct debit mandate.[8] On the other hand, the courts have held a manufacturer was not liable for negligent misstatement contained in his sales literature to a retailer because there was no special relationship between them;[9] nor a finance company in respect of erroneous statements issued by HPI;[10] nor as against a commodity market in amending it rules;[11] nor a Lloyd's shipping classification.[12]

Where the negligent misrepresentation induces a contract between the parties, it may be more advantageous to the representee to proceed under s 2(1) of the Misrepresentation Act 1967, rather than at common law for negligent misstatement, because of the reversal of the burden of proof (see ante, para 17.10). In any event, the representor is only liable for loss caused by the misrepresentation (see post, para 27.29).

Statutory product liability[1]

[17.21/22] Introduction. The sharp distinction between contract and tort is clearly logical once it is settled that a contract requires consideration; and it may not have mattered

---

2   *Anderson Ltd v Rhodes Ltd* [1967] 2 All ER 850. Why did the plaintiff not plead a collateral contract?

3   *Chaudhry v Prabhakar* [1988] 3 All ER 718, CA. *Contra Gran Gelato Ltd v Richcliff (Group) Ltd* [1992] 1 All ER 865 (criticised 109 LQR 539).

4   *Esso Petroleum Co Ltd v Marden* [1976] QB 801, CA; *Howard Marine & Dredging Co Ltd v A Ogden & Sons (Excavations) Ltd* (set out ante, para 17.10). As to whether there could be liability in contract on the basis of a contract to negotiate, see ante, para 10.03.

5   *Thomas Saunders Partnership v Harvey* (1990) 9 Tr LR 78, DC. This avoids the *Salomon* rule (see post, para 19.25).

6   *Smith v Bush* (above); *South Australia Asset Management Corp v York Montague Ltd* (1996) 146 NLJ 956, HL. Cf *Luxmoore-May v Messenger May Baverstock* [1990] 1 All ER 1067, CA; *Thomas Witter Ltd v TBP Industries Ltd* (set out post, para 26.14). As to advice to a lender, see Ross (2001) 151 NLJ 960.

7   *Welton v North Cornwall DC* [1997] 1 WLR 570, CA.

8   *Weldon v GRE Linked Life Assurance Ltd* [2000] 2 All ER (Comm) 914 (not a goods case). For direct debits, see post, para 23.14.

9   *Lambert v Lewis* (set out ante, para 17.06): this is *a fortiori* from a negligent act: see ante, para 17.14.

10 *Moorgate Mercantile Co Ltd v Twitchings* (set out post, para 21.17). Only Lord Denning MR in the CA made a clear finding of such liability: [1976] QB 225, CA; *contra* Geoffrey Lane LJ, with Browne LJ *dubitante*. In the HL, liability was expressly rejected by Lord Fraser (924, 663).

11 *Shearson Lehman Hutton Inc v Maclaine Watson & Co Inc* [1989] 2 Lloyd's Rep 570 (see [1990] LMCLQ at 308). Cf *Punjab National Bank v de Boinville* [1992] 3 All ER 104, CA.

12 *The Nicholas H* [1995] 3 All ER 307, HL.

[7.21/22]

1   Clark, *Product Liability*; Stapleton, *Product Liability*; Mildred, *Product Liability: Law and Insurance*, Chapters 2, 9.

much when the chain of distribution was short. However, with the modern application of the techniques of mass production to an increasingly sophisticated range of products and greatly increased chains of distribution (see ante, para 17.01), problems were bound to occur: they appeared to indicate the need for stricter product liability which reached beyond the doctrine of privity of contract.[2] Analytically, this might appear achievable in either of the following ways:

(1) By extending the ambit of the privity doctrine (see ante, para 17.08).

(2) By increasing strict liability in tort. Whilst in English common law there have been few extensions of strict tort liability beyond the doctrine of *Rylands v Fletcher*,[3] such a development occurred in the EU, spurred on by the Thalidomide tragedy of the 1960s. Following the tort rather than the contract route, the EU developed a Directive relating to liability for defective products. Eventually, the more important disagreements between Members were solved by making certain provisions optional[4] and the Directive was promulgated in 1985.[5] Its major impact seemed likely to be in relation to unsafe design defects, shifting the focus from (negligence-based) fault to strict liability founded on causation.[6]

The foregoing product liability regime extends Europe-wide: the Directive should be implemented in all EU countries; and its reach has later been extended to much of the rest of Europe.[7] However, it does not require the manufacturer to take out compulsory product insurance, cf compulsory road traffic insurance, so it is possible for the manufacturer to avoid liability by going into liquidation (see post, para 19.21).

[17.23] Consumer Protection Act 1987, Part I.[1] The Directive (see ante, para 17.22) was enacted into English law by Part I of the Consumer Protection Act 1987 (CPA), which for the first time ever provides that:[2]

> This part shall have effect for the purpose of making such provision as is necessary in order to comply with the product liability Directive and shall be construed accordingly.

---

2 Cf the strict criminal liability introduced to protect the consumer: see the rules of liability in Chapter 4 and the defences in Chapter 28.

3 (1868) LR 3 HL 330, a doctrine beyond the scope of this work: see ante, para 17.13.

4 The areas of disagreement included: (i) the state-of-the-art defence (see post, para 17.30); (ii) whether the Directive should extend to primary agricultural products (see post, para 17.26); (iii) whether there should he an overall financial limit in respect of identically defective items (the UK Government decided not to introduce an overall financial limit for damage caused by identical items).

5 85/374. For the text of the Directive see Thomas and Clark, *Encyclopedia of Consumer Law*, para 5-163; Guest and Lloyd, *Encyclopedia of Consumer Credit*, para 9-001. For argument as to the legality of the Directive, see Stapleton, *op cit*, note 1, p 52 *et seq*.

6 Clark, *op cit*, note 1, p 215; (1991) 135 Sol J 245.

7 By Treaty: see the European Economic Area Act 1993. For a general discussion of Europe-wide product liability claims, see Cromie (1992) 142 NLJ 14 and 1423.

[17.23]

1 See generally *Street on Torts* (10th edn), p 348 *et seq*; Clark, *Product Liability*; *Clerk and Lindsell on Tort* (16th edn), paras 12–19 *et seq*; Stoppa (1992) 12 Legal Studies at 225; Howells (1990) 51 NILQ 22; Stapleton, *Product Liability*; Mildred, *Product Liability: Law and Insurance*, Chapter 2.

2 Section 1(1). Suppose a Part 1 provision is clear but flatly contradicts the Directive: as to whether an individual disadvantaged by that contradiction could sue in the European Court, see ante, para 1.03A; and for an attempt to avoid such a contradictory construction, see ECA, s 3(1) and Von Colson [1984] ECR 1891.

It has already been seen that in the event of conflict, EU law prevails over national law (see ante, para 1.03A); and this provision is simply explicit Westminster recognition of that fact. It has considerable practical importance: in interpreting Part I of the CPA, one should always cross-check for consistency with the Directive.[3]

Following the Directive, Part I makes it clear that the liability it contains cannot be excluded (s 7: see post, para 17.30), is additional to any other contract or tort-based product liability[4] and binds the Crown (s 9): this last provision will bring within the scheme medicine supplied under the NHS and may hence sidestep an SGA problem (see ante, para 1.07). In the hope that the disagreements which led to the optional provisions will be resolved with the passage of time, s 8 provides that the whole scheme may be modified at a later date by the authorities.[5] On the other hand, Part I introduced a special limitation period[6] to deal with difficulties caused by the number of hands through which a product is likely to pass and the length of time it may retain the capacity to damage:[7] the rules contain an ordinary limitation period of three years, with a long-stop of ten years.[8]

[17.24] The ambit of Part I. The key lies in s 2(1) of the CPA, which provides that:

Subject to the following provisions of this Part, where any damage is caused wholly or partly by a defect in a product, every person to whom subsection (2) below applies shall be liable for the damage.

The effect is that, even in the absence of fault, s 2(1) casts a new civil[1] liability:[2]

(1) in respect of any '**product**' (see post, para 17.25)

(2) on the '**producer**' (see post, para 17.26) or other party in the supply chain (see post, para 17.27)

(3) as regards any **defect** (see post, para 17.28) in that product which

(4) the complainant must prove **causes** (see below) within the special limitation period (see ante, para 17.23)

(5) **damage** (see post, para 17.29).

---

3   *A v National Blood Authority* (set out post, para 17.28); and Mildred, *op cit*, note 1, para 2.5.

4   Section 2(6). *Contra* breaches of statutory duty (s 41(2)): see ante, para 10.19.

5   Section 8. The operation of the Directive is being monitored by the EU Commission.

6   Section 6(6) and Sched 1, Part 1, introducing a new s 11A to the Limitation Act 1980. See Street, *op cit*, note 1, p 356; McGee, *Limitation Periods*, Chapter 7; Clerk and Lindsell, *op cit*, note 1, paras 12-25, 12-26. For the ordinary limitation periods, see post, para 26.17.

7   In respect of property damage, time begins to run when such loss 'occurred', which is defined as 'the earliest time at which a person with an interest in the property had knowledge of the material defect (s 5(5)); and see further s 5(6), (7).

8   Schedule I, para 4. Part 4 stipulates a normal limitation period of three years from whenever is the later: (a) the date on which the cause of action accrued; and (b) the date of knowledge of the defect.

[17.24]

1   Contrast Parts II and III of the CPA which primarily impose strict criminal liability: see ante, paras 4.32; 8.09A–10A.

2   Part I applies only to goods put into circulation by their producer after it comes into force (s 50(7)), which was a day to be appointed (s 50(2)), later fixed at 1 March 1989.

To mount such an action, the person injured[3] must prove all the matters listed above,[4] upon which the defendant becomes strictly liable, unless he proves one of the defences.[5]

Causation. This is perhaps the single most important practical issue facing a claimant alleging product liability, especially in the field of allegedly defective drugs and drug abuse. It requires the claimant to prove on the civil burden of proof (the balance of probabilities) that the product for which the defendant producer was responsible 'wholly or partly' caused the claimant's non-remote (see post, para 27.41) damage.[6] Even where the damage was caused wholly by the defendant, this link of causation may be a very difficult thing to prove and involves a two-part test:[7] first, was the damage caused by the product;[8] and second, would the damage have happened in any event?[9] But, where the damage is caused partly by a defect in the product and partly by the fault of the person suffering the damage, the rules dealing with contributory negligence 'shall have effect as if the defect were the fault of every person liable by virtue of this Part', a rule which may cause some difficulty in practice.[10] However, the burden of proof is reversed for the defences (s 4: see post, para 17.30). It is for consideration as to the extent to which the rules of remoteness (see post, para 27.41) apply to this statutory tort.[11] As to joint liability, see post, para 17.26.

[17.25] A product. Under Part I of the CPA (see ante, para 17.24), a producer (see post, para 17.26) is only liable in respect of a 'product', which last expression means (s 1(2)):

> ... any goods or electricity and (subject to subsection (3) ...) includes a product which is comprised in another product, whether by virtue of being a component part or raw material or otherwise.

The definition of 'product' thus embraces,[1] but is wider than, the notion of goods within the SGA (see ante, para 2.02): electricity and components (see s 1(3): post, para 17.26) are specifically mentioned in s 1(2); the expression 'goods' is defined in s 45(1)[2] to include

---

3   The claimant does not need to be a consumer in the restricted sense employed by the CCA (see ante, para 5.24), or UCTA (see post, para 18.18), or at all; he may be a mere bystander injured by the defective product.

4   On the balance of probabilities: see ante, para 17.16. Contrast the criminal burden (beyond all reasonable doubt) applicable to Parts II and III of the CPA. As to the civil burden, see the following note.

5   Section 4: see post, para 17.30. Cf the standard form criminal defences (see post, para 28.13). Insofar as any of the defences only require the defendant to be careful, the effect of Part I is to shift the burden of proof, so that the defendant must prove that he took care.

6   Section 2(1). Presumably the ordinary rules of causation apply? As to which, see Clark, *op cit*, note 1, pp 194–96; *Street on Torts* (10th edn), p 355; and post, para 27.29.

7   Mildred, *Product Liability: Law and Insurance*, para 1.91; and see also para 1.185 *et seq*. See generally post, para 27.29.

8   *F v Bosil* [2001] 9 CL 120 (see (2000) 150 NLJ 1780).

9   *Richardson v LRC Products Ltd* [2000] 8 CL 101 (condom burst in use).

10   Section 6(4), (5), eg, the goods-owner who carelessly fails to submit goods to a manufacturer's recall. See Street, *op cit*, note 6, p 354. As to contributory negligence, see generally post, para 27.40.

11   See Bell (1991) 20 Anglo-Am LR 371 at 380–81.

[17.25]

1   For an unconvincing attempt to argue that some 'goods' are not 'products', see Stapleton, *Product Liability*, p 309.

2   '"Goods" includes substances, growing crops and things comprised in land by virtue of being attached to it and any ship, aircraft or vehicle'. 'Ships', 'aircraft' and 'motor vehicles' are themselves defined by s 45(1).

'substances'; and 'substance' is itself defined in s 45(1) to include water and 'gas'.[3] The overall effect is to extend the scope of 'products' beyond what might be described as consumer goods, eg, asbestos, train door locks.[4] However, it does not extend to those producing services,[5] eg, advice,[6] as opposed to supplying services produced by another,[7] or where the service includes the provision of a defective spare part, eg, a plumber replacing a tap; but the position of information products, eg, a recipe book, software, is unclear.[8] The Act makes two special cases, one an extension, the other a restriction.

Buildings. Whilst the CPA does not extend to a defective building itself,[9] Part I does apply to goods incorporated into land: it does not apply to goods incorporated by their installer into his own land (s 46(4)); so a 'spec' builder erecting a building on his own land (contra on a developer's land) is not liable under Part I of the CPA with regard to defects in any building materials, but rather under the Defective Premises Act 1972. However, as regards land not owned by the installer, s 46(3) provides that:

> ... the performance of any contract by the erection of any building or structure on any land or by the carrying out of any other building work shall be treated for the purposes of this Act as a supply in so far as, but only in so far as, it involves the provision of any goods to any person by means of their incorporation into the building, structure or works.

Thus, whilst the SGA applies only to property severed from land under the sale (see ante, para 9.03), Part I of the CPA extends not just to fixtures, eg, child's swing or roundabout (for fixtures, see generally post, para 25.23), but also to materials incorporated in a building,[10] whether initially[11] or subsequently. So, in relation to later-fitted double glazing, the injured house occupier can proceed under Part I against the producer of the units or perhaps the installer.

Agriculture. In sharp contrast, Part I of the CPA was particularly restrictive over agriculture: following the 1985 Directive, it exempted 'game or agricultural produce'

---

3   'Gas' is itself defined by s 45(1). As to electricity, gas and water, see ante, para 3.07. As to environmental products, eg, chemical waste, see Mildred, *Product Liability: Law and Insurance*, para 2.19.

4   This wide definition will help extend the ambit of Part I to some major disasters: Clark, *Product Liability*, p 52. Human blood and organs may be products: in *A v National Blood Authority* [2001] 3 All ER 289 the point was conceded (at 307a).

5   They remain liable to the ordinary negligence rules (see ante, para 17.12 *et seq*). *Contra* supplies of goods and services, which are both subject to strict liability under the SGA and SGSA.

6   Clerk and Lindsell, *Torts* (16th edn) para 12–22. 7. Clark, *op cit*, note 4, p 64.

7   Clark, *op cit*, note 4, p 64.

8   As to intellectual products, eg, books, see Whittaker (1989) 105 LQR 125. As to misstatements in books, see Clark, *Product Liability*, p 53. As to software, see (1989) 5 Comp L & P 154; (1990), 6 Comp L & P 2.

9   For an explanation of why builders and building-owners remain free of liability, see Stapleton, *op cit*, note 1, pp 305–09.

10   Does s 46(3) extend Part I liability to a builder erecting a 'building, structure or works' on his customer's green-field site? Or does s 46(3) imply that there must already be a 'building structure or works' on the site to which the complained of item is added? The Directive was intended to apply only to movables; and the building is already within the Defective Premises Act 1972. See further the Current Law annotation to 'product' in s 1(2).

11   Part I thus applies to the sub-contractor's installation in a new building being erected on the consumer's land, eg, wiring, plumbing, tiling. Such materials will also be covered by the SGA and SGSA.

(s 2(4)). However, a 1999 amendment to the Directive repealed this exemption and both s 2(4) and the definition of 'agricultural produce' have been duly repealed.[12]

[17.26] A producer. The basic liability under s 2(1) is laid upon 'the producer of the product' (s 2(1)(a)). 'Producer' is widely defined by s 1(2) to include the following categories of persons involved in the production and marketing of goods:

(a) *'The person who manufactured it'.* Leaving aside imports and own-brands,[1] this establishes the primary liability on the manufacturer of the defective product (Z).[2] However, to meet the case where the injured consumer (D) cannot identify the manufacturer, the Act allows D to treat any identifiable party in the chain of distribution as the producer, unless he in turn identifies his supplier (s 2(3)). That aside, perhaps the most difficult issue concerns bought-in components. Suppose the retail purchase from B by C as a gift for D of a new car with a defective tyre which injures D, that tyre having been supplied to the car manufacturer (Z) by a component-supplier (X). For the case where the real complaint is about a defective component manufactured by a third party (X), s 1(2) assumes by its wide definition of product (see ante, para 17.25) that both the manufactured goods, eg, car, and its bought-in components, eg, tyres, are 'products', so that X is liable under s 2 for his defective component, eg, tyre.[3] However, s 1(3) provides that:

> For the purposes of this Part a person who supplies any product in which products are comprised, whether by virtue of being component parts or raw materials or otherwise, shall not be treated by reason only of his supply of that product as supplying any of the products so comprised.

The obvious effect of s 1(3) is that Z is not the 'supplier' of the tyre he fitted on the car: so that as against the injured claimant, Z cannot off-load the liability under s 2(3) to X (see above); and Z is also liable under s 2 as 'producer'.

(b) *Unmanufactured, unprocessed goods.* According to s 1(2)(b), 'producer' means:

> ... in the case of a substance which has not been manufactured but has been won or abstracted, the person who won or abstracted it.

'Won' perhaps includes gold panned, rubber tapped, root crops harvested and salt mined; and 'abstracted' obviously refers to raw materials which are the products of mines or quarries, eg, diamonds mined, slate quarried. In the original version of the CPA, liability of the farmer for primary agricultural produce was excluded; but, as this exclusion has now been repealed (see ante, para 17.25), this s 1(2)(b) category presumably now extends to agricultural produce.

(c) *Unmanufactured, processed goods.* In a cumbersome provision designed to mesh with the now-repealed exemption of primary agricultural products (see above), s 1(2)(c) lays down that:

---

12 Directive 1999/34; enacted in the UK by 2000 SI 2771.

[17.26]

1 Section 2: see post, para 17.27.

2 Eg, the manufacturer of proprietary medicines, motor vehicles, machinery. But not a mere designer, researcher, tester or repairer: see Mildred, *Product Liability: Law and Insurance*, para 2.42.

3 For joint liability, see below.

... in the case of a product which has not been manufactured, won or abstracted but essential characteristics of which are attributable to an industrial or other process having been carried out (for example, in relation agricultural produce), the person who carried out that process.

Whilst 'essential characteristics' are not defined, the sense would appear to embrace goods whose characteristics are changed by an industrial or other process,[4] eg, canning, freezing, crushing, filleting:[5] in which case, s 1(2)(c) covers both the processor of agricultural produce[6] and the industrialist subjecting any other goods to a non-manufacturing industrial process.[7] The effect of s 1(2)(c) seems to be to make the 'producer' liable even if the defect is traceable back to the farm. Whilst already within the Food Safety Act (see ante, para 4.27–28), there would appear to be some doubt as to the position under the CPA of processed foodstuffs. What of cooked foods, eg, cooked ham, pork pies, pickled onions?

Joint liability. Whilst the usual scheme of the CPA is to enable liability to D to be passed back up the chain to a single manufacturer (s 2(3): see above), in the case of components the effect of the Act is that there may be more than one 'producer' liable under s 2: the justification for this has been said to be to give the injured claimant a solvent defendant.[8] Where this results in two or more persons being liable under s 2, the Act provides that they shall be jointly and severally liable. This will be likely to increase the cost of insurance and litigation;[9] but the Act is silent as to how that liability is to be shared between the defendants.[10] However, as between X and Z, if the root cause of the problem is a defective component, Z will on ordinary principles be able to sue X under his supply contract (see ante, para 17.07); whereas, wrongful design by Z will give X a CPA defence (s 4(1)(f): see post, para 17.30) leaving Z to carry the CPA liability to D.

[17.27] The supply chain. Under s 2, the primary liability for breach of s 2(2) (see ante, para 17.24) is laid upon the producer of the product (s 2(2)(a)), that is, the manufacturer (Z) or component manufacturer (X) (as to 'product', see ante, para 17.25; and as to 'producer', see ante, para 17.26). However, the Act is anxious to ensure that persons injured can easily find a defendant within the jurisdiction and therefore extends the liability to three additional categories of persons (as to joint liability, see ante, para 17.26).

1   *Own-branders.* According to s 2(2)(b), the **producer's** liability applies to:

---

4   The Directive refers to 'initial process': insofar as they may differ from the CPA, see Clerk and Lindsell, *Torts* (16th edn),para 12-21; Merkin, *Guide to the CPA*, para 2.2.3.

5   *Contra* harvesting, picking, grading, slaughtering, packaging. What of mixing produce, eg, muesli, or processes which do not change the characteristics of a product, eg, bottled herbal medicines, sawn timber?

6   '"Agricultural produce" means any produce of the soil, of stock farming or of fisheries' (s 1(2)). Eg, tinned or frozen foods, milled flour, granulated sugar. What about muesli? For criticism of the phrase, see Tiplady (1988) 132 Sol Jo 430 at 434.

7   Eg, smelted ore, refined oil. *Contra* Merkin, *op cit*, note 4, para 2.2.1.2. Does the phrase extend to bulking of agriculture produce from several farms?

8   Stapleton, *Product Liability*, p 295 *et seq.*

9   Section 2(5)). See also the Civil Liability Act 1978, s 1. As contributory negligence, see post, para 27.39.

10   Clark (1987) 50 MLR at 616. As to concurrent liability, see Merkin, *op cit*, note 4, para 2.6. As to piercing the corporate veil, see post, para 19.25.

... any person who by putting his name on the product or using a trade mark or other distinguishing mark in relation to the product, has held himself out to be the producer of the product.

This rule will cover both own-branders and sub-branders[1] and appears to be grounded in estoppel (cf post, para 21.10). The own-brander will typically be the retailer (B): whilst B is already strictly liable in contract to C,[2] except in those cases where it is well known that he does not do his own manufacturing, s 2(2)(b) will make him strictly liable to the donee/consumer (D). What if the goods carry a logo of both a retailer (B) and manufacturer (Z)? Or if B or Z use the logo of manufacturer M under a licensing or franchising agreement (but see s 4(1)(b): post, para 17.30)? What of 'exclusive' brands?

2   *Importers.* Section 2(2)(c) also extends producer's liability to:

... any person who has imported the product into a member State from a place outside the member States in order, in the course of any business of his, to supply it to another.

It should be noticed that liability is here confined to the first importer[3] into any 'Member State' from outside the EU, so that an injured UK consumer may have to sue a foreign EU national (Y) before a UK court and have any favourable judgment enforced in Y's country under the Civil Jurisdiction and Judgments Act 1982.[4]

3   *Suppliers.*[5] In potentially the most far-reaching extension of **producer's** liability, designed to combat the uncertainties of long distribution chains (see ante, para 17.01), s 2(3) enables the person injured (D) to hold an effective supplier[6] liable where all the following conditions are satisfied:

(a)   D requests that supplier to identify any prior supplier in the distribution chain;[7] and

(b)   D's request is made within a reasonable time and whilst it is not reasonably practicable for D to identify all such suppliers;[8] and

---

[17.27]

1   Own-branders are retailers who put their own trading name on goods sold (see ante, para 17.01); whereas sub-branders use a different label of their own: see [1996] 3 Which? 10. For the borderline between manufacturer and own-brander, see Mildred, *Product Liability: Law and Insurance*, paras 2.47–48.

2   See ante, para 17.07. As to chemists, see Merkin, *Guide to the CPA*, para 2.3. For a suggestion that this liability is avoidable by apt packaging, see Howells (1991) 20 Anglo-Am LR 204 at 208.

3   As to whether 'importer' includes both the transport agent and the person who instructs him, see Mildred, *op cit*, note 1, paras 2.50–51.

4   Surprisingly, 'Member State' is not defined, but presumably refers to members of the EU for the time being. What about re-imports into the EU of goods manufactured within it? See the Civil Jurisdiction and Judgments Act 1991, which creates a virtually uniform system of civil jurisdiction and enforcement of judgments throughout Western Europe (EU & EFTA); and see ante, para 8.17A.

5   Eg, dangerous hire tools (see 7 Tr LR 227). For this Part of the CPA only, 'supplier' is not confined to a business supplier (s 46(5)). *Contra* for Parts II and III: see ante, para 4.34.

6   In a directly financed transaction, this will be the dealer rather than the financier (s 46(2)): see ante, para 4.34.

7   If D makes the request to B, B could identify Z, A or Y 'whether still in existence or not' (s 2(3)(a)). B could not identify a financier (see above), nor possibly X (see below).

8   Under s 2(3)(b), the reasonable time runs from damage to D, subject to the special limitation period (see ante, para 17.24). As to ambiguities of when damage occurs, see Merkin, *op cit*, note 2, para 2.5.2. For criticism of the drafting, see Tiplady (1988) 132 Sol Jo at 432.

(c) The supplier to whom D's request is addressed fails within a reasonable time to identify at least one supplier.[9]

If, in response to a s 2(3) request by D, B identifies A, then D may repeat the procedure to make A identify manufacturer (Z):[10] if B cannot make any such identification, the policy of the Act is to make B liable, even if it is not his fault that he cannot identify his source;[11] but, if that process identifies an insolvent Z, it seems that A and B escape liability under the Act. This whole s 2(3) procedure is a powerful incentive to good record-keeping by all commercial parties in the chain of distribution.

[17.28] Defect. Loosely following the Directive (Art 6(1)), Part I of the CPA is confined to **dangerous** goods, where there may also be criminal liability under Part II of the CPA and the GPS Regulations (see ante, paras 4.32–35). Thus, if the real complaint is of **shoddiness** or **unsuitability** of the goods, the usual remedy will remain an action for breach of contract.[1] Section 3(1) provides as follows:

> Subject to the following provisions of this section, there is a defect in a product for the purposes of this Part if the safety of the product is not such as persons generally are entitled to expect; and for those purposes 'safety', in relation to a product, shall include safety with respect to products comprised in that product and safety in the context of risks of damage to property, as well as in the context of risks of death or personal injury.

Without distinguishing between manufacturing and design defects,[2] s 3(1) insists that, for the purposes of s 2(1) (see ante, para 17.24), the goods contain a 'defect' only if the safety of the product, or its components, 'is not such as persons generally are entitled to expect'[3] as regards both personal injury (such as in *Daniels v White*[4]) and limited property damage (see post, para 17.29); and there is a special defence for Z in respect of defective components (s 4(1)(f)): see post, para 17.30). However, s 3(2)(c) makes it clear that this test is to be applied at 'the time when the product is supplied by its producer' (see below),

---

9   Under s 2(3)(c). This makes it important for suppliers to preserve for the relevant time adequate records, so that they can at least identify their own supplier: see Bradgate and Savage (1987) 137 NLJ at 953–54. Will this cause difficulty, eg, for chemists as regards generic drugs? Compare *Street on Torts* (10th edn), p 356 and ante, para 17.16.

10   Bearing in mind s 1(3), can this procedure be used to require Z to identify X? Does s 2(3) apply to own-branders?

11   This is not vicarious liability because B can escape liability by identifying Z, whether or not Z is still in existence (see above). This will be so regardless of whether Z is liable to B, perhaps because there is some exclusion clause in the contract between them. It is thus a sort of secondary liability: Merkin, *op cit*, note 2, paras 2.1; 2.5.4.

[17.28]

1   Clark, *Product Liability*, pp 28–30. As to express and implied terms, see ante, para 11.07; and as to statutorily implied terms, see ante, Chapters 13–15. What of inherently dangerous goods, eg, arsenic?

2   In practice, Part I may operate quite differently in relation to manufacturing and design defects: see the Dobson annotation to s 3 in *Current Law Statutes*; Stoppa (1992) 12 LS 211-8. As to the Design Council, see ante, para 3.08.

3   Defectiveness is to be determined, not by fitness for use, but by the lack of safety to which the public at large were entitled to expect: *Abouzaid v Mothercare (UK) Ltd* [2001] 3 CL 109, CA (Cosytoes sleeping bag: see Hodges 151 NLJ 424). Does it matter whether 'generally' is read with 'persons' or 'entitled to expect'? Are they entitled to expect more than reasonable care, which would change the law hardly at all for design defects? See generally Clark (1987) 50 MLR at 617; *Product Liability*, pp 40–41, 45, 213; Howells (1992) 20 Anglo-Am LR 211-8.

4   Set out ante, para 17.13. But s 3(1) may rule out those suffering from some specific sensitivity or allergy: Lawson (1991) 141 NLJ 1103.

which for goods with a long shelf-life may be some time before they are supplied to the consumer.[5] Without such a rule, producers might be liable for fair wear and tear; and they could also be discouraged from making safety improvements in the light of experience or increased knowledge; and Parliament did not want a hindsight test to discourage recalls or redesigns by manufacturers of unsafe goods, eg, vehicles, cigarettes. In *A v National Blood Authority*:[6]

> The claimants were infected with Hepatitis C virus through blood transfusions with blood which NBA had obtained from infected donors. This risk with 1–3% of bags was known to the medical profession, but at the time undetectable; but the risk was unknown to consumers. On a trial of preliminary issues in a test case, Burton J held that (a) the blood was defective, (b) the NBA were not protected by the state-of the-art defence (see post, para 17.30) and (c) explained what damages were recoverable (see post, para 17.29).

On the first point and placing heavy reliance on the text of the underlying Directive (see ante, para, 17.23), Burton J held that, whilst the NBA was not liable in negligence because the defect was unavoidable (see ante, para 17.14), the blood used on the claimants was from the 1–3% defective (or non-standard) blood-bags amounted to a defect within s 3 (paras 66, 79), because the NBA had not taken all steps legitimately expectable by the public to be free from infection as a standard product (the other 97–99%; para 80). In respect of such non-standard products,[7] Burton J made the following points: the fact that the risk was known to doctors is irrelevant because unknown to consumers (paras 56, 65); 'all circumstances' in s 3(2) meant all relevant circumstances (para 57: see below) and did not include the fact that the defect was unavoidable at the relevant time (para 63); the CPA liability should be distinguished from contract liability founded on fitness for use (see ante, para 14.07) because the CPA liability emphasises safety (para 66); and that the primary issue was 'whether the public at large accepted the non-standard nature of the product' (para 68).

There is no explicit reference in s 3 to the cost of safety measures; but to assist in the application of the above criteria at this time, s 3(2) also contains a number of non-exclusive factors which may be considered, but only insofar as relevant (see above):

(a) *Marketing circumstances.* Section 3(2)(a) refers to 'the manner in which, and purposes for which, the product has been marketed' and 'its get-up', eg, styling. This would cover advertising and distribution, eg, in a manner likely to attract children, drugs on prescription only. The reference to 'purposes' would appear to allow a cost-benefit analysis (see ante, para 17.02), so that harmful side-effects may be tolerated in a life-saving medicine but not in something marketed exclusively for pleasure.[8]

---

5   As to the burden of proof, see s 4(1)(d) (see post, para 17.30). Safety improvements on later models are expressly disregarded (see below).

6   [2001] 3 All ER 289 (see McAdams 151 NLJ 647; Hodges 117 LQR 528).

7   As regards standard products (see para 67), Burton J thought that the defective product should be compared with products from other manufacturers and their prices (para 71).

8   Cf *Watson v Buckley Ltd* [1940] 1 All ER 174. What of contraceptives; or cigarettes; or alcoholic drinks? See *Street on Torts* (10th edn), p 352.

(b) *Marks*. The reference to 'the use of any mark in relation to the product' would give a civil remedy for an improperly used mark,[9] whereas mere compliance with the mark would not of itself be a defence under this Act, though it may avert the commission of a safety offence (see ante, paras 4.33; 4.35).

(c) *Instructions*. The provision also refers to 'any instructions for, or warnings with respect to, doing or refraining from doing anything with or in relation to the product' (s 3(2)(a)). This will allow any such instructions (see generally post, para 18.28 *et seq*) to be taken into account in the absence of privity. They are already relevant in discharging the common law duty of care (see ante, para 17.14). Can Z rely on instructions being given by B? Can an adequate instruction ignored break the chain of causation or amount to contributory negligence?[10] It is to be hoped that extra warnings will not be used as a substitute for producing safer goods.

(d) *Use*. Section 3(2)(b) directs attention to 'what might reasonably be expected to be done with or in relation to the product'. Whilst the test may have been intended to refer to reasonable use it would in fact appear to deal with reasonable expectation (even of unreasonable) use, eg, glue sniffing. Is the expectation that of a supplier or consumer?[11] The subsection may involve a risk/benefit analysis (see ante, para 17.02) and may also link up with marketing circumstances and instructions for use; but it could cause difficulty where adequate instructions are foreseeably ignored, eg, a toddler suffocated by instant glue or a polythene bag, or a bad car driver.[12]

(e) *Time of supply*. The section not only refers to the actual time of supply by the producer (above), but goes on explicitly to refute the inference of defect from the fact that at a later date safer goods are supplied (ss 3(2)(c), 3(2)), eg, new car supplied without seat belts before their fitting became compulsory. This offers no incentive to manufacturers to recall products found to be unsafe. See also the state-of-the-art of defence (post, para 17.30). What of a later supply of an earlier unsafe version?

[17.29] Damage. One of the constituent requirements of s 2 is that, in respect of any 'defect' which comes to light,[1] a party shall suffer 'damage' (see ante, para 17.24). So 'damage' is an essential part of a cause of action under Part I of the CPA, just as in the tort of negligence (see ante, para 17.14). 'Damage' is defined by s 5(1) to mean 'death or personal injury' or any loss of or damage[2] to any property (including land[3])'. In *A v National Blood Authority* (set out ante, para 17.28), Burton J rejected the NBA's attempt to assess damages on the basis of a breach of duty and said that 'the damage to be compensated to the claimant is the damage caused by the defect in a product' (para 178).

---

9   Section 3(2)(a). Eg, BSI or Kite Mark (see ante, para 3.08).

10   See post, para 17.29. See generally Clark (1987) 50 MLR at 618; Merkin, *Guide to the CPA*, para 4.2.2.1; Clark, *Product Liability*, pp 98–100.

11   See Clark, *ibid*, p 93; Clerk and Lindsell, *Torts* (18th edn), para 9.48.

12   As to where there are component manufacturers, see Clerk and Lindsell, *ibid*.

[17.29]

1   Section 5(5)–(7). So a buyer of already-damaged goods is not covered: Tiplady (1988) 132 Sol Jo at 480.

2   The special rules for nuclear accidents are preserved (s 6(8)). But does this preclude action under the CPA in respect of irradiated food?

3   Because 'property' includes land, liability would extend to soil damaged by a defective weed killer: Clark, *Product Liability*, 127.

His Lordship went on to discuss the available heads of damage in detail, a matter far too detailed for this work.[4]

Whilst consequential financial loss is not here mentioned, it is submitted that it is recoverable as follows. First, as regards death or personal injury,[5] it will be recoverable as usual: claims for loss of earnings will frequently be a large part of any personal injuries claim;[6] and the Act expressly preserves such claims after death (s 6(1)–(5)). Second, whilst pure financial loss is probably not recoverable,[7] claims for consequential loss damage to property are allowed,[8] subject to the rules considered below. However, the foregoing definition of 'damage' is expressly made subject to all the following limitations:

(a) *The product itself.* If the product goes into self-destruct, s 5(2) provides that there will be no s 2 liability:

> ... for the loss of or any damage to the product itself or for the loss of or any damage to the whole or any part of any product which has been supplied with the product in question comprised in it.

Thus, if a new car contains a defective electrical component which causes the car to catch fire, the position is as follows:[9] the burnt driver (D) can under s 2 sue the manufacturer and component manufacturer (Z, X) in respect of burns to his person or clothing caused even before he had the opportunity to use the car; but Z and X will not be liable under s 2 in respect of damage to the car or defective component. What about optional extras fitted to a car, eg, an expensive stereo?

(b) *Private property only.* The CPA intends to exclude business property. Thus, under s 5(3) there will be no liability in the above example for property loss unless **both** the following conditions are fulfilled: (i) the property[10] is of description ordinarily intended for private use, occupation or consumption, eg, D's clothing (unless a uniform of his business), *contra* equipment supplied by D's employer, eg, a commercial traveller's samples or stock; **and** (ii) mainly so intended by the person suffering the loss, eg, D's cigarettes, even though he occasionally offers one to a customer. *Contra* D's tools, where he is a self-employed plumber.

(c) *Trivial property damage.* Under s 5(4), no damages shall be awarded in respect of property damage where the total capital loss does not exceed £275; but, if the total property loss does exceed £275, then that first £275 worth is also recoverable. So, if D in the above example lost only his clothing and cigarettes, he would probably have no s 2 claim (because below the financial limit); whereas he would do so if he lost a

---

4 At paras 211, 214–16, 219–25, 226–31.

5 'Personal injury' is defined by s 45(1). Does it extend to a temporary rash? As to congenital disabilities, see s 6(3). What about fear of contracting asbestosis?

6 *A v National Blood Authority* (set out ante, para 17.28).

7 See ante, para 17.14; and Clark, *Product Liability*, 127; Clerk and Lindsell, *Torts* (16th edn), para 12-24.

8 It seems such claims are generally permissible on ordinary principles: Bradgate and Savage (1987) 137 NLJ at 1026. *Contra* Dobson in the *Current Law Annotation to s 5*.

9 The retail purchaser (C) could sue the retailer (B) under the supply contract (see ante, para 17.07); but C and D could only sue X and/or Z in negligence where C's loss may be purely economic (see ante, para 17.14). See Owles (1988) 138 NLJ 771; Tiplady, *op cit*, note 1, p 480; Clark, *op cit*, note 3, pp 127–28; Clerk and Lindsell, *op cit*, note 7. *Contra* a second-hand car with a replacement battery: Howells (1991) 20 Anglo-Am LR 204 at 222.

10 Because 'property' includes land (s 5(1)), this would extend to land damaged by a defective weed killer: Clark, *op cit*, note 3, p 127.

valuable fur coat (eg, worth £300) as well. What if D, instead of losing the fur coat, had personal injuries and minor property damage?

[17.30] Defences. In a **reversal** of the ordinary burden of proof (see ante, para 17.16), the CPA provides that, 'in any civil proceedings by virtue of this Part against any person (the 'person proceeded against') in respect of a defect in a product it shall be a defence for him to show' any of the following (s 4(1)):

(a) *Legal requirements*. This defence will only save him if the defect was the inevitable result of compliance with mandatory[1] domestic or EU law (s 4(1)(a), eg, safety regulations (see ante, para 4.35); food regulations (see ante, para 4.27).

(b) *No supply*. Complete absence of 'supply' (see ss 45, 46) to any person is a defence (s 4(1)(b)), which appears to cover both a franchiser specifying an approved supplier and a producer from whom goods are stolen.[2] The corresponding terminology of the Directive is if the defendant 'did not put the product into circulation' (Art 7(a)) and 'supply' is likely to be so read.

(c) *Non-profit activities*. Section 4(1)(c) protects a person where any 'supply' (see above) by him was **both** otherwise than in the course of his business, eg, grandfather making toy for grandchild; private sale of home-made wine to a guest (cf trade suppliers: see ante, para 14.04) **and** not done with a view to profit, eg, mother making batch of cakes for village fête.[3]

(d) *Subsequent defects*. It is a defence under s 4(1)(d) to show that the defect did not exist in the goods at the 'relevant time':[4] if the person proceeded against is the producer or importer, this will be the time he supplied the goods to another;[5] whereas it is the time of last business supply in other cases (s 4(2)(b), which actually refers to s 2(3): see ante, para 17.27). Even in the exceptional case where B can use this defence, he remains liable to C under the supply contract (see ante para 14.08).

(e) *Components*. Whereas a component manufacturer (X) may *prima facie* be liable as producer of a defective product (see ante, para 17.26), X will escape if he can show that the problem arose wholly from Z's fault in designing his own goods or specifying the design of the component (s 4(1)(f)). Presumably, if the fault is wholly attributable to Z's assembly of the product X will also escape because he has not 'caused' the defect (see ante, para 17.29); but perhaps it might have been wiser if this had been spelt out.

[17.30]

1 Mere compliance with any rule of law, code of practice (see ante, para 3.11) or private standard (eg, BSI standard: see ante, para 3.08) is insufficient: see Mildred, *Product Liability: Law and Insurance*, paras 2.64–65.

2 Also toxic waste dumped or omitted: Clark, *Product Liability*, p 189.

3 *Contra* promotional gifts: see ante, para 2.08. What about charity shops; or the fatal jam supplied to a Women's Institute sale of work? Note the different wording of the Directive, Art 7(c): instead of 'view to profit', it says 'in the course of his business'.

4 Eg, third party removes safety features or instructions, or poorly fits or services: Clark, *op cit*, note 2, pp 191–92.

5 Section 4(2)(a), which actually refers to s 2(2) (see ante, para 17.27). Eg, sale of old stock by retailer will not render producer liable, as where the goods carry a 'sell by' date. If a blackmailer tampers with products of X whilst on a supermarket shelf (B), both X and Z can use this defence when sued by C or D. The hoax blackmailer may commit an offence under s 5 of the Public Order Act 1986.

(f) *State-of-the-art*. According to s 4(1)(e), it is a good defence:

> ... that the state of scientific and technical knowledge at the relevant time was not such that a producer of products of the same description as the product in question might be expected to have discovered the defect if it had existed in his products while they were under his control.

This seemingly legally permissible[6] but politically controversial defence of development risks known at the 'relevant time' (see above) seems likely to have greatest significance as regards unexpected side-effects of new drugs,[7] eg, Thalidomide, the drug which prompted the Directive in the first place (see ante, para 17.23). Producers argued that, in the absence of such a defence, product innovation would be stifled,[8] whilst consumers pleaded that such a defence would re-introduce negligence by the back door.[9] However, it has been held that accident reports are not 'technical knowledge for this purpose;[10] and that, once a defect is known, the defence is no longer available, even though that defect might remain unavoidable.[11]

However, if a defendant cannot bring himself within any of the above defences, he cannot escape liability to consumers by reliance on the printed word. Section 7 lays down that:

> The liability of a person by virtue of this Part to a person who has suffered damage caused wholly or partly by a defect in a product, or to a dependant or relative of such a person, shall not be limited or excluded by any contract term, by any notice or by any other provision.

As with some UCTA restrictions (s 1(3): see post, para 18.17), s 7 enures only for the benefit of an injured consumer, or his 'dependent relative' (see s 1(2)); but it may be confined to written 'notices' (s 45(1)). On the other hand, a businessman or his workmen suffering personal injury may find his action blocked by a written or oral exclusion clause (s 5(3): see ante, para 17.29). Nor does s 7 interfere with the freedom of parties prior to the retail supply regulating their rights *inter se* by contract, perhaps for use if they are found jointly and severally liable to the injured consumer.[12] If not so blocked, redress on behalf of consumers may be obtainable by Stop Now Orders (see ante, para 6.08).

---

6   *European Commission v UK* [1997] All ER (EC) 481; discussed by Miller [1997] All ER LR Annual Review 81.

7   See generally Clark, *op cit*, note 2, Chapter 6; *Street on Torts* (10th edn), pp 354–55; Tiplady (1988) 132 Sol Jo at 482. For its parliamentary history, see Merkin, *Guide to the CPA*, para 4.5.11. As to whether s 4(1)(e) complies with the Directive, see Crossick (1988) 138 NLJ 233; Clark, *op cit*, note 2, pp 152–53.

8   Yet most of our major trading competitors seem unlikely to introduce such a defence. Might this tend to make the UK a guinea pig market (see ante, para 17.05) and be discriminatory (see [1985] JBL at 437)? But does it add anything to s 3(2) (see ante para 17.28)?

9   See Bradgate and Savage (1987) 137 NLJ at 1049–50; Clark, *op cit*, note 2, pp 182–85, 215–16. This fear was shown to be groundless in *A v National Blood Authority* (set out ante, para 17.28).

10 So that the absence of such reports was no defence: *Abouzaid v Mothercare (UK) Ltd* [2001] 3 CL 109, CA.

11 *A v National Blood Authority* (set out ante, para 17.28; para 74), where Burton J observed that a non-standard product might qualify once for such a defence (para 77).

12 But might the exclusion be unreasonable within s 3 of UCTA (see post, para 18.24) or be avoided by s 2(1) of UCTA (see above)?

CHAPTER 18

EXCLUSIONS AND DISCLAIMERS

[18.01] It is common, particularly in standard form contracts,[1] to find that one of the parties (the *proferens*) has introduced into a transaction words purporting to avoid or restrict any liability that would otherwise accrue to him.[2] The *proferens* may purport to do so either by excluding or restricting his obligations, or by inserting a formula of words to discharge that obligation. Leaving the latter case of discharge by words (para 18.28 *et seq*), there must first be examined the effect of words designed to exclude or restrict either the obligation, or the liability of the *proferens* for failure to fulfill it.[3] This will begin with an examination of the effect of such clauses at common law (para 18.02 *et seq*) and then deal with statutory control of such clauses (para 18.09 *et seq*).

EFFECT AT COMMON LAW[1]

[18.02] Introduction. In considering how the common law deals with attempts to avoid liability by way of disclaimer or exclusion clause, two questions arise in any action: first, what in fact happened; and second, is the defendant liable to the plaintiff in view of the facts which are proved to have occurred? The first question has very great practical significance: it may be extremely difficult to prove what happened;[2] but the problem of who bears the burden of proof is beyond the scope of this work.[3] The present discussion will concentrate on the second question, which involves the effectiveness of any disclaimer. The disclaimer may be oral, though a written form is usually favoured by those seeking to rely on it, because it is easier to prove, and may be drafted more comprehensively.[4] The disclaimer may originate from the seller, or from any prior party in the chain of distribution;[5] it is frequently printed on the goods, their packaging, or in a supply agreement; and it may purport to protect either the immediate supplier or any prior party in the chain of distribution – or even all of them.

[18.01]

1   As to which, see ante, para 11.08. As to exclusion clauses in such contracts, see generally Yates and Hawkins, *Standard Business Contracts*.

2   Distinguish penalty clauses, which attempt to increase the obligations of the other party, and are subject to different considerations: see post, para 27.25.

3   Clauses which achieve this object have been described by judges and text-writers as 'exemption', 'exclusion' or 'exception' clauses. These terms are used interchangeably; and this usage will be adopted here. See further *Benjamin's Sale of Goods* (5th edn), para 13-001; and post, para 18.03.

[18.02]

1   See generally Coote, *Exception Clauses*; Yates, *Exclusion Clauses in Contracts* (2nd edn); Macdonald, *Exemption Clauses and Unfair Terms*. For the *res ipsa loquitur* doctrine, see ante, para 17.16.

2   As to the burden of proof, see ante, paras 17.05; 17.16.

3   See Treitel, *Law of Contract* (10th edn), pp 220–21.

4   See the strictures of Lord Reid in the *Suisse Atlantique Societe D'Armement Maritime SA v NV Rotterdamsche Kolen Central* [1967] 1 AC 361, HL at 406.

5   For a description of chains of distribution, see ante, para 17.01.

[18.03] Nature and effect of exclusion clauses. Whether the attempt is to exclude tortious or contractual liability, the clause may or may not be embodied in a contract.

1   *Non-contractual disclaimers.*[1] These clauses are termed disclaimers[2] to distinguish them from contractual exclusion clauses (see below). A disclaimer cannot affect contractual liability, except by way of the doctrine of waiver (see post, para 26.23) or instructions (see post, para 18.28 *et seq*), but may well defeat an action in tort.[3] Perhaps the most obvious example of the operation of a disclaimer in tort is where it either expressly or impliedly ousts liability in negligence, because the other party voluntarily assumes the risk,[4] or the disclaimer discharges a duty of care.[5] Here, however, the courts may try to restrict the ambit of the disclaimer so as to be free to apportion loss under the Law Reform (Contributory Negligence) Act 1945 (see post, para 27.40).

2   *Contractual exclusion clauses.* A party may seek by incorporation of an exclusion clause in a contract (see post, para 18.04) to exclude either his contractual or tortious liability, or both. The clause may be effective to exclude tortious liability by its express terms;[6] or it may do so impliedly, as where it purports to exclude an equivalent duty in contract;[7] or it may act as a sufficient warning to discharge or reduce tort liability in any of the ways suggested above.[8]

[18.04] Incorporation. Suppose that packaged goods descending a typical distribution chain (ante, para 17.01) bear a notice purporting to exempt the manufacturer and retailer from any liability (whether in contract or tort), the position is as follows: if the retailer is sued by the person to whom he sold the goods (C), the issue will probably be the effect of the exclusion clause on the supply contract; but, if the manufacturer is sued by C, or by any person to whom C transfers the goods, the problem is more likely to be a tortious one. The question whether the exclusion clause is incorporated into the transaction may therefore arise both inside and outside the contractual context (see ante, para 17.12).

Prima facie, an exclusion clause may become incorporated in a contract in either of the following ways:[1]

1   *Incorporation by notice.* The incorporation of a clause excluding liability into a contract between two parties is a matter of intention: such an exclusion will become part of a contract so as to bind one of the parties (irrespective of whether he listened to, or read

---

[18.03]
1   See generally, Yates and Hawkins, *Standard Business Contracts*, pp 193–95, 198.
2   For disclaimers of strict criminal liability, see ante, para 4.09.
3   Eg, *Hurley v Dyke* [1979] RTR 265, HL. Subject to s 2 of UCTA: as to which, see post, para 18.17.
4   Eg, see *per* Lord Denning (dissenting) in *Scruttons Ltd v Midland Silicones Ltd* [1962] AC 446, HL at 488–89. See generally Yates and Hawkins, *op cit*, note 1, 201–03.
5   Eg, *Southern Water Authority v Carey* [1985] 2 All ER 1007. See generally ante, para 17.13 *et seq*.
6   Eg, *Hedley Byrne & Co Ltd v Heller Ltd* (see ante, para 17.19).
7   Cf *White v John Warwick & Co* [1953] 2 All ER 1021, CA; *Humming Bird Motors v Hobbs* [1986] CLY 2283, CA.
8   However, in relation to the application of UCTA, it has been held that the court must first establish *prima facie* liability in the absence of the exclusion clause: see post, para 18.12.
[18.04]
1   Eg, *Apioil Ltd v Kuwait Petroleum Italia SpA* [1995] 1 Lloyd's Rep 124 (variation). See generally Yates and Hawkins, *Standard Business Contracts*, Chapter 3.3.

it) provided that, at the time of contacting,[2] he realised that the other party intended it to form part of the contract between them.[3] Alternatively,[3] in the absence of actual knowledge, a party may be bound where he ought to have realised that it was intended to have contractual force because the other party took reasonable steps to bring it to his attention,[4] as where there is a consistent course of dealings between the parties[5] or a trade usage,[6] or the incorporation of club rules for the time being.[7] Where an exclusion of liability does not become incorporated in a contract between the parties, it can usually only operate on adequate notice as a disclaimer of liability in tort.[8] Thus, in the example above, the disclaimer on the package may save the manufacturer from liability in the tort of negligence by 'discharging' the duty of care;[9] or, where C ignores the warning, it may give rise to a voluntary assumption of risk[10] or contributory negligence on C's part. As to contributory negligence, see post, para 27.39. As to warnings, see post, para 18.29.

2 *Incorporation by signed document.* Where the exclusion clause is embodied in a signed contract, the general common law rule is that the signatory is bound by the contents of the document regardless of whether he has read or understood them.[11] On the other hand, the signed document may neither amount to, nor evidence, a contract: possibly, a disclaimer in that document will become binding on the signatory merely by signature, rather than only by notice.[12]

In respect of consumer supply contracts (see ante, para 11.12A), terms so incorporated by notice or signature may be unfair simply because the consumer has not actually seen them (see Grey Term 1(i): see ante, para 11.17).

---

2 *Contra* where he did not realise the intention of the *proferens* in that regard until after the contract was made: *Olley v Marlborough Court* [1949] 1 KB 532, CA (not a sale case); the *Albright and Wilson* case (set out ante, para 13.01), at paras 44, 48.

3 *Parker v South Eastern Railway Co* (1877) 2 CPD 416, CA; and see also post, para 18.30. For the battle of the forms, see ante, para 10.04.

4 *Interfoto Picture Library Ltd v Stiletto Ltd* [1988] 1 All ER 348, CA (Macdonald [1988] JBL 375); *Grogan v Robin Meredith Plant Hire* [1996] 15 Tr LR 371, CA; *Ocean Chemical Transport Inc v Exnor Craggs Ltd* [2000] 1 All ER (Comm) 519, CA; *O'Brien v MGN Ltd* [2001] 9 CL 124, CA. In respect of consumer transactions, the 1994 Regulations might apply: see ante, para 11.17.

5 *Kendall v Lillico* (set out ante, para 14.10: the sold notes); the *Vacwell Engineering* case (set out post, para 18.29); *George Mitchell (Cheshire) Ltd v Finney Lock Seeds Ltd* (set out post, para 18.08); and post, para 18.09. See Macdonald (1988) 8 Legal Studies 48.

6 See ante, para 15.11. When does a course of dealing (see above) become a trade custom (see ante, para 11.10)?

7 *Shearson Lehman Hutton Inc v Maclaine Watson & Co Inc* [1989] 2 Lloyd's Rep 570 ([1990] LMCLQ at 308); and see ante, para 11.07.

8 Adequate notice here is the same as in contract: *Ashdown v Samuel Williams Ltd* [1957] 1 QB 409, CA.

9 See *Hedley Byrne & Co Ltd v Heller Ltd* [1964] AC 465, where the HL thought that the effect of the disclaimer was to prevent the duty of care from arising; and generally John (1985–86) 5 Litigation 91.

10 *Ashdown v Samuel Williams Ltd* (above). There is considerable dispute as to the basis of the decision in this case: see Winfield and Jolowicz, *Tort* (15th edn), pp 306–08).

11 *L'Estrange v Graucob Ltd* [1934] 2 KB 394, DC. *Contra* if he can plead *non est factum* (see ante, para 10.16); or the additional term on the back was unannounced (*Harvey v Ventilatorenfabrik Oelde GmbH* [1988] CLY 463, CA). As to unreasonable terms, see *Danka Rentals Ltd v Xi Software Ltd* (1998) 17 Tr LR 74 at 84–85. As unusual terms, see *Montgomery Litho Ltd v Maxwell* 2000 SC 56.

12 Cf *Ashdown v Samuel Williams Ltd* (above).

[18.05] Attitude of the courts to exclusion clauses. There are a number of legal rules[1] which will render an exclusion clause ineffective, even though the clause be incorporated in the transaction (see ante, para 18.04) and whatever its meaning (see post, para 18.06):

(1) Where the exclusion of liability is contrary to statute[2] or unfair (see ante, para 11.12 *et seq*).

(2) Where the object of the clause is contrary to public policy, as where it purports to exclude liability for fraud.[3]

(3) Where the *proferens* gives an overriding oral undertaking[4] or misrepresents the contents of the clause.[5] Paradoxically, a clause in a consumer supply contract giving effect to these decisions may be unfair.[6]

(4) Where in a contractual action there is no privity of contract between the parties, whether the clause purports to confer a benefit[7] or a burden.[8] However, it should be borne in mind that the effect of the privity doctrine is mitigated in a number of statutory[9] and common law[10] rules.

[18.06] The *contra proferentem* rule. Where an exclusion clause cannot be struck down on one of the above grounds, at common law its effect will be a matter of construction. In seeking to ascertain the intention of the parties, the courts will, if the clause was inserted merely for the benefit of the *proferens*, construe the words against him (the *contra proferentem* rule). This common law rule is a general one,[1] but has achieved special prominence in the field of contractual exclusion clauses and tortious disclaimers, which the courts have consistently construed strictly against the *proferens*,[2] eg, to prevent a party taking advantage of his own wrong.[3] Thus, where it is to the disadvantage of the *proferens*,[4] they have attributed precise legal meanings to technical terms, regardless of

---

[18.05]

1 These rules are generally framed in the law of contract, but there would appear to be no reason why they should be so confined.

2 See the provisions considered later in this chapter post, para 18.09 *et seq*.

3 See also post, para 18.27. Cf *Gordon v Selico* [1986] CLY 53, CA; ante, para 4.09. Can a clause be struck down at common law purely on grounds of unreasonableness?

4 *Mendelssohn v Normand Ltd* [1970] 1 QB 177, CA; *Harling v Eddy* [1951] 2 KB 739, CA. Cf *Pagnan Sp A v Tradex Ocean Transportation* [1987] 1 All ER 81 (overriding written provision).

5 *Curtis v Chemical Cleaning Co* [1951] 1 KB 805, CA; *Harvey v Ventilatorenfabrik Oelde* [1989] Tr LR 138, CA.

6 Grey Term 1(i): OFT, UTCC *Bulletin No 4*, p 51; and see generally ante, para 11.17.

7 *Scruttons Ltd v Midland Silicones Ltd* [1962] AC 446, HL. See generally Yates and Hawkins, *Standard Business Contracts*, pp 246–56.

8 *Dunlop Pneumatic Tyre Co Ltd v Selfridge & Co Ltd* [1915] AC 847, HL.

9 Eg, the statutory deemed agency provisions (see ante, para 16.04); Contracts (Rights of Third Parties) Act 1999 (see ante, para 17.08).

10 Eg, the doctrines of agency and collateral contract (see respectively ante, paras 10.06 and 17.09).

[18.06]

1 Where there is a consumer supply, cf UTCC, reg 7(2): see ante, para 11.13.

2 Eg, *Henry Kendall & Sons Ltd v William Lillico & Sons Ltd* (set out ante, para 14.10). But see post, para 18.08. As to statutory formulations, see ante, para 15.22.

3 *Alghussein Establishment v Eton College* [1991] 1 All ER 267, HL (not a goods case).

4 *Contra* where a strict construction would advantage the *proferens*: *Schuler AG v Wickman Machine Tool Sales Ltd* [1974] AC 235, HL.

whether the parties understood the technicalities: clauses excluding warranties have been held ineffective to exclude conditions;[5] clauses excluding implied terms have been held not to affect liability for breach of express conditions;[6] and plain words are needed to exclude liability for negligence.[7] A striking illustration of the effectiveness of the *contra proferentem* rule is to be found in *Lowe v Lombank Ltd*:[8]

> P, a widow of 65, agreed to enter a directly financed hp transaction, and signed a proposal form at her home without reading it. Clause 8 purported to exclude all warranties; and clause 9 read as follows:
>
> > The hirer acknowledges that he has examined the goods and that there are no defects in the goods which such examination ought to have revealed and that the goods are of merchantable quality. The hirer further acknowledges and agrees that he has not made known to the owners expressly or by implication the particular purpose for which the goods are required, and that the goods are reasonably fit for the purpose for which they are in fact required.
>
> On delivery, P signed a 'delivery receipt', in which she acknowledged that the goods were in good order; but the car was, in fact, completely unroadworthy owing to a number of serious, but latent, defects.

The Court of Appeal held that P was entitled to damages against the finance company for breach of the implied condition as to fitness in the HPA 1938 because:

(1) P impliedly made known that she required the car as a means of transport (see ante, para 14.10).

(2) Clause 8 did not purport to exclude conditions; nor had it been brought to P's attention and its effect made plain to her as the 1938 Act required. Nowadays, assuming P were found to be dealing as consumer, such a clause would be avoided by UCTA (s 6(2)(b): see post, para 18.19).

(3) Clause 9 was merely a statement of past facts, not a contractual promise, and at common law[9] could, at most, give rise to an estoppel; but that there was no estoppel here because (a) the clause did not unambiguously cover the latent defects and (b) there was no evidence either that P intended the statements to be acted upon, nor that the company signed the agreement on the basis of the truth of the statement.[10] The position might have been otherwise with regard to visible external defects.[11]

---

5   Eg, *Wallis Sons and Wells v Pratt and Haynes* (set out ante, para 11.04); *Baldry v Marshall Ltd* [1925] 1 KB 260, CA; *Harling v Eddy* [1951] 2 KB 739, CA; *Lowe v Lombank Ltd* (below).

6   Eg, *Andrews Brothers (Bournemouth) Ltd v Singer & Co Ltd* [1934] 1 KB 17, CA.

7   *Dorset CC v Southern Felt Roofing Co* [1990] Tr LR 96, CA (words could refer to other events which did not include negligence); *Thomas Witter Ltd v T B P Industries Ltd* (set out post, para 26.14), at 167E–170A (111 LQR at 389).

8   [1960] 1 All ER 611, [1960] 1 WLR 196, CA. As to delivery notes, see generally post, para 23.02. On the facts of the case, see now post, para 18.16.

9   But such clauses may be relevant in relation to the UCTA reasonableness test: see the *Photoprint* case (set out post, para 18.21); the *Watford Electronics* case (set out post, para 18.24A).

10 For a discussion of the common law doctrine of estoppel, see post, para 21.10 *et seq*; and for acceptance notes, see post, para 23.10. The statement in the agreement that clause 8 had been brought to the hirer's notice, and its effect made plain to her, was not relied on in this action: see Goode, *HP Law and Practice* (2nd edn), pp 201–02, 252. Cf certificate of quality: see ante, para 14.02.

11 *Astley Industrial Trust Ltd v Grimley* [1963] 2 All ER 33, at 44–45, CA. Cf *Farnworth Finance Facilities Ltd v Attryde* [1970] 2 All ER 774, CA; *Coastal (Bermuda) v Esso Petroleum* [1984] 1 Lloyd's Rep 11, CA; *Gill & Duffus SA v Berger & Co Inc* (set out post, para 23.06).

Similar rules apply to the interpretation of indemnities.[12] Moreover, in respect of consumer supply contracts such as that in *Lowe* (above), the Unfair Terms Regulations seem likely to produce the same result: clause 8 would be unfair (Grey Terms 1(b), 1(m): see ante, paras 11.16; 11.18); clause 9 would be read *contra proferentem* (reg 7(2): see ante, para 11.18); and the delivery receipt attacked as an unfair term (Grey Term, 1(q): see ante, para 11.18).

[18.07] The doctrine of fundamental breach.[1] Particularly in the period after 1945, there was an almost continuous battle of wits between the draftsmen of standard form contracts (see ante, para 11.08) and the Court of Appeal: the draftsmen devised exclusion clauses on behalf of the *proferens* which were ever-more sweeping; whereas the Court of Appeal defeated the draftsman's intention by applying the *contra proferentem* doctrine (see ante, para 18.06) to such clauses with increasing severity.[2] Eventually, this begun to lead to the doctrine of fundamental breach, the notion that there may be some terms which are so fundamental to a contract that, as a matter of law, no exclusion clause can offer protection against breach.[3] In *Karsales (Harrow) Ltd v Wallis*[4] the Court of Appeal did this on the basis that the object delivered was not the car contracted for. Two years later, in *Yeoman Credit Ltd v Apps* (set out post, para 29.25) a bolder court went further and held that in respect of a defective car:

(1) there was implied into the hp agreement a common law condition that the goods are reasonably fit for the purpose for which they were required;[5] and

(2) the accumulation (congeries) of defects when added together amounted to such a fundamental breach of contract as to disentitle the plaintiffs from relying on the exemption clause.[6]

[18.08] A matter of construction. Before 1977, Lord Denning MR in particular[1] maintained a judicial campaign that there was a rule of law that an exemption clause, no matter how widely drafted, could not protect the *proferens* against a fundamental breach by him (see ante, para 18.07). However, few of the cases unambiguously sought to raise the *contra proferentem* rule (see ante para 18.06) into a rule of law concerning fundamental breaches (see ante, para 18.07). With the enactment of UCTA in 1977 (see post, para 18.12 *et seq*), not only were the courts freed from any such rule of law (s 9), but they were also

---

12   *Smith v South Wales Switchgear Ltd* [1978] 1 All ER 18, HL; *EE Caledonia Ltd v Orbit Valve Co* [1993] 4 All ER 165 (service contracts).

[18.07]

1   The history of the doctrine is traced by Coote (1967) 40 ALJ 336. See also Treitel, *Law of Contract* (10th edn), p 205 *et seq*.

2   See eg, the cases on the exclusion of liability for negligence – *Alderslade v Hendon Laundry Ltd* [1945] KB 189, CA; *White v John Warwick Ltd* [1953] 2 All ER 1021, CA.

3   *Per* Devlin J in *Smeaton Hanscomb & Co Ltd v Sassoon Setty Son & Co* [1953] 2 All ER 1471 at 1473.

4   Set out ante, para 15.23.

5   For the statutory undertaking as to fitness, see now ante, para 14.07.

6   It was so applied in *Farnworth Finance Facilities Ltd v Attryde* [1970] 2 All ER 33, CA; *Charterhouse Credit Ltd v Tolly* (set out post, para 29.34). But see further ante, para 14.02 and post, para 18.08.

[18.08]

1   Eg, *Harbutt's Plasticine Ltd v Wayne Tank Ltd* [1970] 1 QB 447, CA (not a sale case). A position he later revised: see below.

given a statutory weapon for controlling exclusion clauses in general;[2] and, when the other party dealt as consumer, many such clauses were deprived of all effect.[3] With the prime motivation for this line of development removed, the attitude of the courts, led by the House of Lords, began to change: not only did they deny that there was a rule of law concerning fundamental breaches, but they also began to apply the *contra proferentem* rule in a much more even-handed manner.[4] A striking case is *George Mitchell (Chesterhall) Ltd v Finney Lock Seeds Ltd*:[5]

> The plaintiffs were farmers in one of the few places in the country where Dutch winter cabbage can be grown successfully; and, being harvested in February, it captures the market at a time when very little other green stuff is available. About Christmas 1973, the plaintiffs orally ordered 30lbs of Late Dutch Spring Cabbage seed from the defendant seed merchants, from whom they had purchased seed for many years. The seed was delivered together with the defendant's customary invoice, which contained many conditions. The seed looked alright; but six months after planting there sprouted from the plaintiff's 63 acres a lot of loose green leaves, which were not cabbage in common parlance because there were no hearts: the growth was found to be commercially useless. The price of the seed was £192, but the loss to the plaintiffs was over £61,000.

The sellers sought to protect themselves by relying on a wide-ranging exclusion clause of long-standing in the seed trade, which purported to limit their liability to refund of the price. The Court of Appeal held that the exclusion clause formed part of the contract by course of dealings;[6] but their decision in favour of the buyers was confirmed by the House of Lords on partially different grounds.

(1) Whilst a majority of the Court of Appeal held that, as a matter of construction, the limitation clause did not protect the sellers against the event which occurred,[7] the House of Lords held that it was apt to do so. In delivering the unanimous judgment of their Lordships, Lord Bridge declined to 'read an ambiguity into it by the process of strained construction', adding that 'the very strict principles ... applicable to exclusion and indemnity clauses cannot be applied in their full rigour to limitation clauses'.[8]

(2) Although enforceable at common law, their Lordships affirmed the unanimous judgment of the Court of Appeal that the clause was rendered unenforceable by statute, because it would not be 'fair or reasonable to allow reliance' on it.[9]

---

2   See especially UCTA, s 3(2)(b)(i): see post, para 18.24.
3   See especially UCTA, ss 6–7: see post, para 18.19.
4   Eg, *Photo Production Ltd v Securicor Transport Ltd* [1980] AC 827, HL; *Ailsa Craig Fishing Co Ltd v Malvern Fishing Co Ltd* [1983] 1 All ER 101, HL(s) (not sale cases).
5   [1983] 2 AC 803; [1983] 2 All ER 737, HL.
6   [1983] QB 284, CA: see generally ante, para 18.04.
7   Oliver and Kerr LJJ, with a powerful dissent by Lord Denning MR.
8   At 742: his Lordship expressly agreed with Lord Denning MR on this point. See also *British Fermentation Products Ltd v Compair Reavell Ltd* (set out post, para 18.24), at 395–97; Atiyah, *Sale of Goods* (9th edn), pp 210–11; and also ante, para 1.04.
9   Under s 55 of the Sale of Goods Act as set out in para 11 of Sched 1 to the SGA 1979. This transitional provision is now replaced by that found in UCTA, ss 6(3), 11(2); as to the latter see post, para 18.21.

STATUTORY CONTROLS

Introduction

[18.09] Contracts for the supply of goods. The SGA 1893 allowed almost complete freedom of contract. Apart from the half-hearted limitation that express terms did not negative implied terms unless inconsistent,[1] many of its provisions were expressed to give way to a contrary intention.[2] Furthermore, s 55 (now replaced by s 55(1) of the SGA 1979) provides:

> Where any right, duty or liability would arise under a contract of sale of goods by implication of law, it may (subject to the Unfair Contract Terms Act 1977) be negatived or varied by express agreement, or by the course of dealing between the parties, or by usage if the usage is such as to bind both parties to the contract.

Whilst SOGIT contains no counterpart to this provision for hp agreements, the SGSA does include a virtually identical provision for quasi-sales, simple hiring agreements and service contracts (ss 11(1), 16(1)). The provision envisages three ways in which any 'right, duty, or liability' might be 'negatived or varied' at common law. First, it might be ousted by express agreement; and the rules for interpreting that express agreement are considered above (paras 18.06–08). Second, it might be impliedly displaced by the course of dealings between the parties, even though no term to such effect could be implied in any single contract standing alone.[3] Third, even where there was neither such an express term nor a course of dealings, it might be negatived by a trade usage to that effect.[4]

[18.10] Because it was thought that the dominant party had frequently taken unfair advantage of this freedom of contract, Parliament sometimes sought to modify it.[1] In relation to instalment credit contracts, the HPA specified a detailed list of provisions which were avoided and this function has now been taken over by the CCA (see post, para 18.11). With regard to misrepresentations which induce entry into any type of contract, some restriction on contracting out was introduced by the Misrepresentation Act 1967 (see post, para 18.17). Subsequently, more generalised controls on attempts to exclude contractual and tortious liability were introduced by the Unfair Contract Terms Act 1977 (see post, para 18.12); powers to deal with more particular abuses were taken in Part II of the Fair Trading Act 1973 (see ante, para 4.22); and the CPA introduced restrictions on contracting out of product liability or safety regulations.[2]

[18.09]

1   For this rule, see now SGA, s 55(2), and its counterparts in SOGIT, s 12(1) as amended and SGSA, s 11(2).

2   For reinforcement of the *caveat emptor* rule, see ante, para 15.22.

3   *Henry Kendall & Sons Ltd v William Lillico & Sons Ltd* (set out ante, para 14.10), *per* Lords Morris, Guest, and Pearce, at 90, 105, 113, affirming the unanimous decision of the CA on this point; [1966] 1 All ER 309, CA, *per* Sellers, Davies and Diplock LJJ, at 322, 331. See generally ante, para 18.04.

4   *Cointat v Myhan* (1914) 84 LJKB 2253, CA; and see generally ante, para 15.11.

[18.10]

1   As to trading stamp transactions, see ante, para 15.17.

2   As to product liability, see CPA, s 7 (see ante, para 17.30); and as to safety regulations, see CPA, s 41(4) (see ante, para 4.35).

To this must be added EU-inspired interventions. The Unfair Terms Regulations have granted a court wide powers to interfere with unfair standard terms in consumer supply contracts (see ante, para 11.12): just one of its Grey Terms is attempts to exclude or restrict the consumer's rights against his supplier other than the implied terms (para 1(b): see ante, para 11.16); and this may be used to reinforce those provisions.[3] Further, it is not possible to contract out of some other specific protections, eg, Doorstep selling (reg 10: see ante, para 10.22), Distance selling (reg 25(1): see ante, para 8.17), implied terms and guarantees in consumer supplies (Art 7(1): see ante, para 14.01).

[18.11] The Consumer Credit Act. Whilst the HPA sought to achieve its object by avoiding certain specifically listed provisions (consolidated list in s 29 of the HPA 1965), the CCA adopted a new technique – a blanket prohibition on contracting out. Thus, s 173(1) provides:

> A term contained in a regulated agreement or linked transaction, or in any other agreement relating to an actual or prospective regulated agreement or linked transaction, is void if, and to the extent that, it is inconsistent with a provision for the protection of the debtor or hirer or his relative or any surety contained in this Act or in any regulation made under this Act.

This does not of itself prevent the regulated agreement containing any clause inconsistent with the CCA,[1] but only denies such clause effect.[2] Nor does s 173(1) render void all provisions inconsistent with the CCA: it only strikes down those inconsistent with such CCA provisions as are 'for the protection of the debtor or hirer or his relative or any surety'.[3] However, s 173(2) makes it clear that this avoidance refers to both sides of the coin: whilst s 173(1) avoids attempts by the creditor or owner to cut down his duties, s 173(2) similarly avoids any attempt by the creditor or owner to increase the duties of the debtor or hirer above any CCA duty 'in those circumstances'.

On the other hand, s 173(3) provides:

> Notwithstanding subsection (1), a provision of this Act under which a thing may be done in relation to any person on an order of the court or the Director only shall not be taken to prevent its being done at any time with that person's consent given at that time, but the refusal of such consent shall not give rise to any liability.

This is quite consistent with the policy of the Act: whilst the creditor or owner may not by clever language in the documentation of the transaction increase his rights, or reduce those of the debtor or hirer, he can do so if he can persuade the debtor or hirer to give consent thereto at the time. Thus, the debtor may waive his right to treat as unenforceable a regulated agreement entered into by an unlicensed trader,[4] or an improperly executed

---

3   OFT, UCT *Bulletins, No 4*, pp 29, 30; *No 5*, pp 43, 46.

[18.11]

1   Nor is such a statement prohibited by the Consumer Transactions Order: see ante, para 4.22. But in a consumer supply it might be an unfair term (OFT, *Bulletin No 15*, case 8).

2   What would be the effect (if any) of a change in a creditor's employment contracts prohibiting his employees from contravening the CCA?

3   Eg, on the death of the debtor or hirer – s 86(1): see post, para 24.47. Does this protection extend to a dealer acting as surety under a recourse provision?

4   Section 40: see ante, para 6.20. See also ante, para 6.27.

agreement,[5] or a regulated land mortgage;[6] or he may waive his right to resist repossession of protected goods,[7] or entry into his premises for the purposes of recapting them.[8] But the consent must be informed (see post, para 24.37).

THE UNFAIR CONTRACT TERMS ACT[1]

Introduction

[18.12] History. Sweeping limitations on attempts by suppliers to exclude liability in sale and hp contracts were first introduced in 1973 by SOGIT, on the recommendations of the Law Commission.[2] Partly as a result of subsequent recommendations of the Law Commission,[3] these and other limitations were later embodied in the Unfair Contract Terms Act 1977 (UCTA) and have since been extended by the SGSA (ss 11(1), 17(2), (3)) to quasi-sale and simple hirings (see ante, paras 2.10; 12.01A). The title 'Unfair Contract Terms Act' is a misnomer: unlike the UTCC Regulations (see ante, para 11.12 *et seq*), the Act does not deal with unfair contract terms generally, but mostly with exclusion clauses in particular types of contract.

The UCTA (as amended) does not render it unlawful[4] to purport to incorporate an invalid exclusion clause in a contract, but simply avoids in some circumstances exclusion clauses within its ambit. Thus, the Act does not prevent the drafting of contracts in such a manner that no promise is ever made nor duty arise;[5] and it is questionable whether UCTA touches liquidated damages clauses.[6] On the other hand, in *Phillips Products Ltd v Hyland* (set out post, para 18.16) the Court of Appeal decided that, in considering whether there had been a breach of obligation, the court 'has first to leave out of account, at this stage, the contract term which is relied upon by the defence as defeating the plaintiff's

---

5   Section 65: see ante, para 9.19.
6   Section 126: see post, para 25.24.
7   Section 90: see post, para 24.34.
8   Section 92: see post, para 24.34.

[18.12]

1   See generally *Benjamin's Sale of Goods* (5th edn), para 13-051 *et seq*; Treitel, *Law of Contract* (10th edn), pp 226–44; Mildred, *Product Liability: Law and Insurance*, para 3.231 *et seq*.

2   *First Report on Exemption Clauses in Contracts* (1969, Law Com 24).

3   *Second Report on Exemption Clauses* (1975, Law Com 69). This Report (paras 290–314) rejected any system of prior validation of standard terms: as to which, see ante, para 11.08.

4   But inclusion of the exclusion clause may amount to an offence under the Restrictions on Statements Order: see ante, para 4.22. Further, it may sometimes infringe one of the codes of practice (see ante, paras 3.11–14).

5   *The Casper Trader* [1991] 2 Lloyd's Rep 550; and see ante, para 18.03. As to tortious duties, see post, para 18.17. What of contracts of compromise made after breach (see post, para 26.18)? For a contrary view, employing s 13, see post, para 18.16.

6   Treitel, *op cit*, note 1, p 227; and as to liquidated damages clauses, see generally post, para 27.24. UCTA expressly saves arbitration clauses: see post, para 18.16.

claim'.[7] But how does one distinguish the clause defining the duty[8] (outside UCTA) from the one excluding liability for breach of that duty (inside UCTA)?[9] Or the apparent contradiction where ss 3 and 6 overlap (see post, para 18.24)?

The scheme set up by UCTA draws a sharp distinction between those contracts with an international flavour (see post, para 18.13) and wholly domestic contracts, confining its restrictions substantially to the latter.[10] Restrictions on 'exemption clauses'[11] in domestic contracts governed by English law are to be found in Part I of UCTA.[12]

[18.13/15] International contracts. The basic principle by which English law decides which system of law applies to a contract with an international flavour is to look for the proper or applicable law of the contract (see ante, para 10.01). However, these rules give way to any contrary intention expressed by the parties in their agreement;[1] and many foreigners making contracts which have little or nothing to do with England have included in their contract a provision that English law shall be the proper law of the contract. It is therefore common in commercial contracts to find that the parties have so provided in what has become known as a choice laws clause;[2] and this may be enforced by an anti-suit injunction.[3] To safeguard this lucrative jurisdiction, UCTA excludes from its ambit those contracts which are only governed by English law by reason of a choice of laws clause (s 27(1), as amended by Sched 4 of the 1990 Act). At the same time, Parliament did not wish to allow parties to escape from the restrictions of UCTA simply by dressing up what was really a domestic contract as a foreign one. Accordingly, s 27(2) seeks to bring such sham transactions[4] within the rules for domestic contracts discussed below (see post, para 18.16 *et seq*).

Where a contract with an international flavour is governed by English law by reason of the above rules, Part III of UCTA saves it from the restrictive rules which Part I makes applicable to domestic contracts (see post, para 18.16 *et seq*). Thus, Part III makes special provision for both the carriage of passengers by sea (s 28) and contracts for the

---

7   *Per* Slade LJ at 625c, delivering the judgment of the court; and in *Smith v Bush* [1990] 1 AC 831 HL, Lord Griffiths described this as the 'but for' test. However, this view appears to be inconsistent with some academic views as to the manner in which exclusion clauses operate at common law: see ante, para 18.03.

8   Eg, an instruction to use goods only in a specified manner is impliedly saying do not use them in any other manner (see further post, para 18.31); 'sold as seen' (see Tiplady (1987) 137 NLJ at 428).

9   See Macdonald (1991) 107 LQR at 557–58; and *Photoprint Ltd v Forward Trust Ltd* (see post, para 18.21).

10   Nor does the Act affect contractual provisions authorised by statute or made with a view to compliance with international obligations (s 29(1)).

11   For a discussion of the expression 'exemption clauses', see the *Second Report on Exemption Clauses* (above) paras 160–68.

12   Part II of UCTA lays down separate rules for Scots law.

[18.13/15]

1   *Centrax Ltd v Citibank NA* [1999] 1 All ER (Comm) 557, CA (proper law); Contracts (Applicable Law) Act 1990, Sched 1, Art 3.

2   Eg, *Indian Oil Corp v Vanol Inc* [1991] 2 Lloyd's Rep 634.

3   *Donohue v Armco Inc* [2000] 1 All ER (Comm) 641, CA; and see generally post, para 29.39.

4   Section 27(2) operates in either or both the following circumstances: (a) the contract contains a choice of laws clause 'wholly or mainly for the purpose' of evading UCTA; (b) one party to that contract dealt as consumer (see post, para 18.18) and was 'habitually resident' in the UK. This rule still stands after the 1990 Act (below): [1991] JBL at 214.

international supply of goods.[5] However, the effect of this statutory scheme is to put foreign commercial buyers from an English seller at a considerable disadvantage as compared with English buyers, because any exclusion clause in the supply contract is not subject to the constraints of UCTA. If the commercial buyer is within the EU, an exclusion clause in the supply contract may contravene Art 25 [ex-12] of the Treaty of Rome, in which case an English court would have to 'disapply' the exclusion clause.[6] Of course, if the EU buyer is a consumer, eg, in an e-mail contract, the exclusion clause may be an unfair term[7] and perhaps contravene the E-commerce Directive (see ante, para 8.17A). The conclusion is likely to be that s 26 of UCTA can nowadays only apply to foreign non-EU business buyers; and, in any event, it is beyond the scope of this work. As to 'consumer supplies', there is a similar provision in an EU Directive (Art 7(2): see ante, para 14.01).

Domestic contracts

[18.16] Scope. Generally speaking (see ante, para 18.12), in domestic contracts[1] governed by English law (see ante, para 18.13), Part I of UCTA precludes or restricts reliance on certain exclusion clauses and clauses of similar effect. In fact, UCTA does not comprehensively define exclusion clauses, a common law notion (see ante, para 18.06). However, in *Phillips Products Ltd v Hyland*:[2]

> X ran a business hiring out JCBs with a driver under a contract which provided (cl 8) that the drivers were 'for all purposes to be regarded as the servants or agents of the Hirer'. Under such a contract, X hired out a JCB and driver (H) to PP. An accident occurred as a result of H's negligence, causing considerable damage to PP's factory. PP claimed that X was vicariously liable for H's negligence.

The Court of Appeal first looked at the contract without the exclusion clause to determine whether H had been 'negligent' within the meaning of s 1(1) (see post, para 18.17). Turning to the exclusion clause, they held that the matter was one of substance, not form: whilst the form of clause 8 was a transfer of vicarious liability, its effect was to exclude X's vicarious liability,[3] so that the clause fell within s 2(2) (see post, para 18.17).

An extension to the concept of exclusion clauses is to be found in s 13(1), which provides as follows:

> To the extent that this Part of this Act prevents the exclusion[4] or restriction[5] of any liability it also prevents –

---

5   *Ocean Chemical Transport Inc v Exnor Craggs Ltd* [2000] 1 All ER (Comm) 519, CA.

6   See *Econoler v GEC Alsthom* [1999] unreported (Burbridge 150 NLJ 1544).

7   *Oceano Grupo Editorial SA v Quintero* (2000) C240-244/98 (Whittaker 117 LQR 215).

[18.16]

1   Are pre-payment meters supplied by gas and electricity undertakings supplied under contract or statutory obligation? See Fairest (1985) 135 NLJ 238.

2   [1987] 2 All ER 620; [1987] 1 WLR 659, CA (see 108 LQR at 109–11).

3   See also *Thompson v T Lohan (Plant Hire) Ltd* (set out post, para 18.25) and the discussion by Macdonald [1994] JBL 441, at 447–49.

4   Eg, *Andrews Bros Ltd v Singer & Co Ltd* [1934] 1 KB 17, CA. There is no objection to clauses preventing the duty from arising: see ante, para 18.12.

5   Eg, *George Mitchell (Chesterhall) Ltd v Finney Lock Seeds Ltd* (set out ante, para 18.08).

(a) making the liability or its enforcement subject to restrictive or onerous conditions;

(b) excluding or restricting any right or remedy in respect of liability, or subjecting a person to any prejudice in consequence of his pursuing any such right or remedy;[6]

(c) excluding or restricting rules or evidence or procedure;

and (to that extent) sections 2 and 5 to 7 also prevent excluding or restricting liability by reference to terms and notices which exclude or restrict the relevant obligation or duty.

Examples would be as follows:

Para (a): a term requiring notification of loss within a specified time or in a specified manner. What of a clause allowing the supplier to substitute any later model? Or onerous instructions for use (see post, para 18.31)? Or *force majeure* clauses (see post, para 22.13A)?

Para (b): as to exclusion of a remedy, a term denying the right to rescind for breach of a condition, or limiting liability to a specified amount. Does it extend to the right of examination under s 34 of the SGA (as to which, see post, para 23.10)?

Para (c): *Lowe v Lombank Ltd* (set out ante, para 18.06). Does s 13(1)(c) also cover certificates of compliance (as to which see ante, paras 13.11; 14.02; 14.04; 15.06).

In *Stewart Gill Ltd v Horatio Meyer & Co Ltd*:[7]

> There was a contract for the supply and installation of an overhead conveyor system which provided for stage payments, including 5% on completion and 5% thirty days thereafter. On completion of the installation, the buyer (B) refused to pay the final 10% on the grounds that the goods and installation were defective. The seller (S) applied for summary judgment, seeking to avoid (B's) claim by relying on a provision (cl 12(4)) that B should not be able to withhold any payment by reason of any 'set off, counterclaim, allegation of incorrect or defective goods ...'

The Court of Appeal agreed with B that cl 12(4) was struck down by s 3 (see post, para 18.24). Whilst it was not a clause 'excluding or restricting liability', the Court thought that cl 12(4) fell within both s 13(1)(b) – by suppressing B's right of set-off[8] – and s 13(1)(c) – by making B pay the price in full and then mount a separate action. Lord Donaldson MR[9] found the closing words of s 13(1) obscure, but thought that they were not intended to cover contractual exclusion clauses within paragraphs (a), (b) or (c), but instead to deal with non-contractual disclaimers (see ante, para 18.03; and post, para 18.23). This is except in relation to ss 3 and 4, which deal with exclusions of strict contractual promises (see post, paras 18.24 and 18.25).

On the other hand, the scope of s 13(1) is narrowed by s 13(2): this expressly saves from s 13(1) arbitration clauses (see further ante, paras 3.23–24). But it is regrettably unclear whether s 13(1)(b) extends to any compromise a consumer makes with regard to a claim;[10] nor to instructions for use (see post, para 18.28 *et seq*); nor to 'card-not-present' transactions (see ante, para 7.09). For secondary contracts, see post, para 18.16A.

---

6   Eg, *British Crane Hire Corp Ltd v Ipswich Plant Hire Ltd* [1975] QB 303, CA (hired equipment at hirer's risk); commercial indemnities (see post, para 18.17).

7   [1992] QB 600; [1992] 2 All ER 257, CA (see (1993) LQR 41; Macdonald [1994] JBL 441–44).

8   Such suppression is not at common law contrary to public policy: *Coca-Cola Financial Corp v Finsat International Ltd* [1998] QB 43, CA.

9   At 260j. See also *Smith v Bush* (set out ante, para 17.20) (Kaye 52 MLR at 845–46).

10 The point is clarified (it does not) for Scots Law by s 15(1).

[18.16A] Secondary contracts. Section 10 makes it clear that the Act cannot be evaded by means of a secondary contract:

> A person is not bound by any contract term prejudicing or taking away rights of his which arise under, or in connection with the performance of, another contract, so far as those rights extend to the enforcement of another's liability which this Part of this Act prevents that other from excluding or restricting.

This section applies where a consumer contracting with X and Y in separate contracts agrees with X that he will not sue Y[1] in respect of future claims:[2] it has no application where both parties to the contract are the same (such cases fall within s 13: see ante, para 18.16), or with regard to compromises of existing claims.[3] Instances within s 10 are where the consumer is entering a directly financed transaction and agrees with the dealer that he will not sue the financier;[4] or where the consumer agrees with a retailer that he will not sue a prior party in the chain of distribution for product liability;[5] or agrees with a servicer under a maintenance contract that he will not sue the retailer.[6]

[18.17] Part I of UCTA. This applies to exclusion clauses as above explained (see ante, para 18.16), with the following limitations (s 1(2)): contracts with an international flavour (see ante, paras 18.13–15) are wholly outside the Act; whereas those within Sched 1 fall outside only some of its provisions. *Inter alia*, the latter category includes contracts for sale of land.[1]

Subject to this, Part I proceeds by dealing separately with every sort of transaction within its ambit. Unlike the UTCC Regulations (see ante, para 11.12 *et seq*), Part I does not start with generally applicable rules, but instead has a separate primary provision applicable to each of the following types of business liability:[2]

(a) **implied terms in domestic supply contracts** (ss 6–7: see post, paras 18.18–19);

(b) **against negligence liability**.[3] Where a business purports to exclude or restrict (see ante, para 18.16) liability for 'negligence', defined by s 1(1) to include contractual or tortious negligence, s 2 carefully distinguishes the following **consequences** of that negligence.

[18.16A]

1 At common law, such a clause could only be effective where X has agreed to indemnify Y: cf *Gore v Van Der Lann* [1967] 2 QB 31, CA (not a sale case).

2 Could the ambit of s 10 be confined to indirect attempts to exclude ('prevent'), rather than restrict, liability (see Brown (1992) 108 LQR 223–24)?

3 *Tudor Grange Holdings Ltd v Citibank NA* [1991] 4 All ER 1, CA (108 LQR 223); [1994] JBL at 450–55.

4 *Quaere* whether such a provision would anyway contravene paras 16.10; 18.11?

5 Does this overlap with s 5 of UCTA (see post, para 18.26)? On s 10, see generally Yates and Hawkins, *Standard Business Contracts*, pp 314–16.

6 *Per* Browne-Wilkinson VC in the *Tudor Grange* case (above) at 13 (*obiter*).

[18.17]

1 Eg, *Electricity Supply Nominees Ltd v IAF Group plc* [1993] 3 All ER 372. As to the distinction between sales of goods and sales of an interest in land, see ante, para 9.03.

2 Except in the case of s 6(4) (see post, para 18.19), Part I is limited to attempts to exclude 'business liability' (s 1(3)). 'Business' includes a profession and the activities of any government department or local or public authority (s 14).

3 Detailed discussion of these provisions is beyond the scope of this work. See further the specialist works on contract and tort.

1   *Death or personal injury.* Section 2(1) provides:

> A person cannot by reference to any contract term or to a notice[4] given to persons generally or to particular persons exclude or restrict his liability for death or personal injury[5] resulting from negligence.

The phrase 'contract term or notice' obviates any difficulty which might arise in deciding whether or not the exclusion clause was apt to exclude or restrict liability to the person injured for breach of either a contractual or tortious duty of care[6] or a disclaimer apt only to exclude or restrict tort liability (see ante, para 18.03). However, s 2(1) is directed to protecting only the injured person:[7] it has nothing to say about arrangements made by the person liable for negligence to re-coup his loss from a third party;[8] but the Contracts (Rights of Third Parties) Act 1999 may enable a third party to rely on the above s 2(1) rule (see ante, para 17.08). Regardless of negligence, where such death or personal injury arises in connection with a 'consumer supply' contract for goods or services, any such exclusion clause may be an 'unfair term' (UTCC Regulations, Sched 2, para 1a: see ante, para 11.16).

2   *Other loss or damage.* 'In the case of other loss or damage, a person cannot so exclude or restrict his liability for negligence except in so far as the term or notice[4] satisfies the requirement of reasonableness.'[9] A third party cannot take advantage of this rule under the above 1999 Act (s 7(2)).

As regards indemnity clauses in commercial contracts, but not consumer contracts (s 4: see below), it seems probable that they are 'exclusion clauses' within s 13(1)(b) (see ante, para 18.16) and fall within s 2 at least sometimes. Whilst common law product liability is usually based on negligence (see ante, paras 17.14; 17.19), presumably Parliament intended attempts to exclude or restrict that liability by product guarantees to fall, not within s 2 (above), but s 5 (see below):

(c) **express terms in contract** (s 3: see post, para 18.24);

(d) **indemnity clauses** (s 4: see post, para 18.25);

(e) **for misrepresentation.** Where a contract is induced by a misrepresentation (see ante, para 11.01), *prima facie* that will give the contracting party representee certain rights in respect of the contract as against the contracting representor (see ante, para 17.10). However, where that contract purports to exclude or restrict the representor's foregoing liability, new s 3 of the Misrepresentation Act 1967[10] makes that exclusion subject to UCTA's requirement of reasonableness (see post, para 18.20). The effect of new s 3 was considered in *Thomas Witter Ltd v TBP Industries Ltd* (set out post, para 26.14). The parties to this contract were both businessmen, but new s 3: (i) applies

---

4   '"Notice" includes an announcement, whether or not in writing, and any other communication or pretended communication' (s 14): *Smith v Bush* (below).

5   '"Personal injury" includes any disease and any impairment of physical or mental condition' (s 14).

6   Section 2(3) prevents circumvention of the foregoing rule by reliance on the *volenti* principle.

7   *Phillips Products Ltd v Hyland* (see below). Compare the *Thompson* case (below).

8   *Thompson v T Lohan (Plant Hire) Ltd* (set out post, para 18.25).

9   Section 2(2). Eg, *Phillips Products Ltd v Hyland* (set out ante, para 18.16); *Smith v Bush* (set out ante, para 17.20).

10   As amended by s 8 of UCTA, which is not confined to business liability (s 1(3)).

regardless of whether representor or representee is in business; (ii) in supply contracts does not distinguish whether or not the misrepresentation is made by the supplier; and (iii) applies to contracts which are not for the supply of goods, eg, loan. There is no definition of the s 3 words 'misrepresentation made by him', which throws one back to the common law, including the law of agency (see ante, para 10.06). The common law allowed the representor to exclude liability for misrepresentations made by his servants or agents. It would therefore appear to be a simple matter for a party to exclude liability for misrepresentations made on his behalf by denying the speaker any actual or apparent authority to make the representation.[11] However, where the misrepresentation induces a 'consumer supply' (see ante, para 11.12) such a clause may be a an 'unfair term' (UTCC Regulations, Sched 3, para 1(n): see ante, para 11.18).

Domestic supply contracts

[18.18] Dealing as consumer.[1] Section 12(1) provides that a party to a contract for the supply of goods 'deals as consumer' only where all the following criteria are satisfied:

1   *The supplier* makes the contract 'in the course of a business'.[2] This does not cover any sales by a private supplier (cf offences under the TDA, ss 1, 14: see ante, paras 4.03; 4.15); nor is there any extension here to sales conducted on behalf of a private supplier by a business agent (cf the implied undertakings as to fitness and quality: see ante, para 14.04). Even where the supplier is involved in a business supplying goods, there must clearly be a connection between that business and the supply, as where items are turned over in the course of that business as stock-in-trade. But does s 12 comprehend any sales which go through the books of that business, including dispositions of its plant and equipment, eg, of an electrician selling his van? In the *R & B Customs* case (see below) the Court of Appeal restricted the notion to stock-in-trade; but in *Stevenson v Rogers* (set out ante, para 14.04) a later Court of Appeal construed the same phrase in s 14(2) of the SGA to include such sales of plant (AER at 625–26).

2   *The other party* does not take the goods 'in the course of a business'.[3] It has been held that the same construction should be used for s 12(1)(a) and s 12(1)(b); and that this phrase should be interpreted in the same narrow manner as the House of Lords had employed in *Davies v Sumner* in relation to the criminal law (TDA: see ante, para 4.03A). Thus, in *R & B Customs Brokers Ltd v United Dominions Trust Ltd*:[4]

---

11   In the *Watford Electronics* case (set out post, para 18.24A), the efficacy of an entire agreement clause was explicitly put on grounds of estoppel (supported by 117 LQR at 549).

[18.18]

1   The concept of 'dealing as consumer', is relevant not only for domestic supply contracts (see post, para 18.19), but also within UCTA for standard form contracts (see post, para 18.24) and indemnities (see post para 18.25). Compare the scheme in UCC, Art 109.

2   Section 12(1)(b). '"Business" includes a profession and the activities of any government department or local or public authority': s 14. Does 'business' comprehend a co-operative society, Oxfam, a students' union (see Kidner (1987) 38 NILQ 46 at 53–54)? Cf CPA, s 45(1): see ante, para 4.33.

3   Section 12(1)(a). Eg, *Lease Management Services Ltd v Purnell Secretarial Services Ltd* (set out ante, para 16.06A).

4   [1988] 1 All ER 847, CA (Price 52 MLR 245; Pearce (1989) LMCLQ 371). Cf the following definitions: 'debtor' in the CCA (see ante, para 5.24); 'trade or finance purchaser' in Part III of the HPA 1964 (see post, para 21.56).

Freight Forwarders, R & B Ltd, by way of a directly financed transaction, obtained a car from UDT Ltd under a conditional sale which purported to exclude any implied conditions as to fitness or quality where the buyer did not deal as consumer within s 12. This was the second or third such credit purchase by R & B Ltd and the car was intended for use by two of the directors. The contract on this occasion was not signed by R & B until some weeks after delivery, by which time R & B Ltd had discovered the roof leaked and returned the car to the dealer for repairs.

The Court of Appeal held that, as the purchase was only incidental to R & B Ltd's business activity, there was insufficient regularity of car purchase to make that purchase an integral part of R & B Ltd's business,[5] so that they dealt as consumers and the exclusion clause did not preclude their claim for breach of s 14(3) of the SGA.[6] Neill LJ suggested, *obiter*, that the same meaning should be given to the phrase 'in the course of a business' in both ss 12(1)(a) and (b) (AER at 859g): if this were the case and R & B Customs were selling the car to a private buyer, it would produce the surprising result that the latter would not be 'dealing as consumer' so as to have the full protection of UCTA in respect of the implied terms; and it appears inconsistent with *Stevenson v Rogers* (above). In any event, it is for consideration whether this treatment is confined to small limited companies. However, the Act does expressly take outside the concept of 'dealing as consumer' two particular cases: (1) sales by auction or competitive tender;[7] and (2) supply to a person who holds himself out as acquiring in the course of business, eg, to get a trade discount. What if the supplier knows that the other party is really a private buyer?

3   *The goods* must be of 'a type[8] ordinarily supplied[9] for private use or consumption':[10] perhaps a saloon car as opposed to a van. Does 'use or consumption' include all categories of private enjoyment? Does it comprehend items collected for enjoyment and as investment, eg, a painting, stamps, coins? (cf s 10(7) of the CPA: see ante, para 4.33).

Notwithstanding the foregoing, the essence of 'dealing as consumer' is relatively easy to grasp; and any difficulties as the borderline may be eased by s 12(3), which enacts that 'it is for those claiming that a party does not deal as consumer to show that he does not'.

Subsequently, this concept of 'dealing as consumer' has also been employed in the Sale and Supply of Goods Act 1994 (see ante, paras 11.05A; 13.02; and post, para 29.05).

---

5   *Per* Dillon LJ at 854g–h, treating a one-off sale as integral; and see Neil LJ at 859.

6   See ante, para 14.13. Note that R & B Ltd would not be a 'consumer' for the purposes of the Unfair Terms Regulations: see ante, para 11.12A.

7   Section 12(2). As to sale by auction, see ante, para 10.10 *et seq*. If the goods fail to reach their reserve price and are subsequently sold by the auctioneer by private treaty, the position is unclear: *D & M Trailers (Halifax) v Sterling* [1978] RTR 468, CA.

8   How specific a connotation does this bear, see Kidner, *op cit*, note 2, pp 54–55.

9   What of goods sometimes bought for business use and sometimes for private use? Does 'ordinarily' connote 'frequent', 'usual', 'the norm', or 'the majority of cases'? See *Benjamin's Sale of Goods* (5th edn), para 13-0691.

10   Section 12(1)(c). This phrase is also to be found in relation to the restrictions on product liability in s 5: see post, para 18.26. What, if any, is the effect of the goods bearing a legend 'industrial strength'?

[18.19] Exclusion of statutory undertakings. In relation to domestic contracts (see ante, para 18.16) for the supply of goods,[1] UCTA deals with attempts to exclude or restrict the undertakings implied by statute in favour of the transferee as follows:

1 *Undertakings as to title*.[2] Whilst those provisions themselves envisage that the undertakings in contracts for the supply of goods by way of sale, hp or quasi-sale[3] may be limited (see ante, para 12.18), UCTA provides that, except in the case of trading stamp transactions,[4] those (possibly limited) undertakings cannot be excluded or restricted by reference to any contract term.[5] However, the SGSA makes separate provision for simple hiring agreements (see ante, para 12.01A); and UCTA lays down that these cannot be excluded or restricted by any term 'except insofar as it satisfies the requirement of reasonableness' (s 7(4)),[5a] a concept considered later (see post, para 18.20).

2 *Undertakings as to description, quality, fitness and sample*. These implied undertakings are considered in Chapters 13–15.[6] Bear in mind that some of these undertakings themselves envisage a limited degree of contracting out, eg, as regards specified defects,[7] and UCTA does not affect this.[8] In relation to attempts to exclude or restrict them, UCTA leaves aside trading stamp transactions, but otherwise draws a distinction according to whether or not the transferee 'deals as consumer' (see ante, para 18.18):

(a) Where he does, then in respect of sales, quasi-sales, hp and simple hiring agreements these undertakings 'cannot be excluded or restricted by reference to any contract term' (ss 6(2), 7(2).[5a] But see post, para 18.24B).

(b) Where the transferee deals otherwise than as consumer, these undertakings 'can be excluded or restricted by reference to a contract term, but only in so far as the term satisfies the requirement of reasonableness' (ss 6(3), 7(3):[5a] see post, para 18.20). This category will comprehend those situations where the supplier does

---

[18.19]

1 'Goods' has the same meaning as in the SGA: UCTA, s 14 (as to which, see ante, para 2.01). For the reasons why the blanket prohibition was not extended to services and the effect of this, see Woodroffe, *Goods and Services – The New Law*, paras 7.07–10. Exclusion clauses in service contracts are now controlled by ss 2 and 3 of UCTA (see post, paras 18.23; 18.24) and the UTCC Regulations (see ante, para 11.12 *et seq*).

2 Whilst for the most purposes Part I of UCTA only applies to 'business liability' (see post, para 18.22), ss 6(4), 7(3A) expressly extend to private suppliers by way of sale or hp the restrictions on contracting out. What about quasi-sales?

3 Hp is defined simply by reference to the CCA (UCTA, s 14): see ante, para 1.24.

4 Section 7(5). The implied undertakings in trading stamp transactions are considered ante, para 15.17.

5 Sections 6(1), 7(3A), inserted by s 17(2) of the SGSA. As to the reason, see Woodroffe, *op cit*, note 1, 7.04.

5a UCTA, s 6, applies to the exclusion of implied terms in sale or hp; and UCTA, s 7, applies to exclusion in quasi-sale and simple hiring.

6 The undertaking as to description (but not fitness/quality) applies to sales by a private seller. In the case of sale and hp, s 6(4) applies to it the UCTA provisions in this paragraph. But there is no comparable provision for quasi-sales and simple hirings in s 7 of UCTA: so it seems s 7 does not apply to exclusions of the implied terms in SGSA, ss 3 and 8, in the case of private sales. Section 17(2) of the SGSA would seem to this extent defective.

7 See ante, para 14.25. For attempts to invoke such limitations by standard terms, see ante, para 18.06; and generally Yates and Hawkins, *Standard Business Contracts*, pp 181–84.

8 For the effect of this in relation to instructions for use, see post, para 18.31.

not supply in the course of a business,[9] or where the transferee acquires the goods in the course of business,[10] or insofar as the contract is one for services,[11] or the goods are not of a type ordinarily supplied for private use or consumption (see ante, para 18.18).

[18.20] The requirement of reasonableness (1).[1] Part I of UCTA permits a party to exclude or restrict his liability by a term which satisfies the requirement of reasonableness in all the following cases: (a) negligent damage to property;[2] (b) standard form contracts (see post, para 18.24); (c) indemnities (see post, para 18.25); (d) some domestic contracts for the supply of goods (see ante, para 18.19); and (e) liability for misrepresentation.[2] Whilst expressly deeming reasonable any contractual term put forward by a competent authority exercising any statutory jurisdiction,[3] in all other cases s 11(1) explains that the requirement of reasonableness:

> ... is that the term shall have been a fair and reasonable one to be included having regard to the circumstances which were, or ought reasonably to have been, known to or in the contemplation of the parties when the contract was made.

Whereas under the previous law the issue was whether **reliance** on the clause was reasonable, eg, the *George Mitchell* case (set out ante, para 18.08), the s 11(1) test concentrates on the reasonableness of the **term** in that particular contract rather than in general.[4] Further, in testing reasonableness, reference cannot be made to circumstances arising **after** the making of the contract,[5] but is confined to matters existing **at the time of contracting**.[6] In the *Stewart Gill* case (set out ante, para 18.16) S argued that, if cl 12(4) did fall within s 13, the effect of s 3 (see post, para 18.24) was only to cut out the objectionable words from cl 12(4). The Court of Appeal disagreed, holding that the reasonableness test must be applied to the whole of cl 12(4): it failed,[7] so that the wider the clause the more

---

9   Section 6(4). Eg, breaches of undertakings as to the description of goods supplied, which apply to private supplies: see ante, para 13.11. But see note 2, above.

10   Eg, the *Stewart Gill* case (set out ante, para 18.16); *Knight Machinery (Holdings) v Rennie* 1993 SLT 65. All the implied undertakings considered in Chapters 13–15 are then applicable.

11   Even in instances in favour of one who 'deals as consumer'. See s 3, discussed post, para 18.24.

[18.20]

1   See generally Yates and Hawkins, *Standard Business Contracts*, Chapter 2; Adams and Brownsword (1988) 104 LQR 94.

2   See ante, para 18.17.

3   Section 29(2),(3). Eg, terms approved by the Regulator (see ante, para 3.06) under s 56 of the Water Industry Act 1991. But see *Timeload Ltd v British Telecommunications plc* [1995] EMLR 459, CA.

4   So an identical clause may be unreasonable in one contract (*Philips Products Ltd v Hyland* [1987] 2 All ER 620, CA) but not in another (*Thompson v T Lohan (Plant Hire) Ltd* [1987] 2 All ER 631, CA). See Adams and Brownsword, *op cit*, note 1, at 114–16.

5   Eg, the *George Mitchell* case (above). Further examples may include a later unexpected event insufficiently serious to frustrate the contract, or situations where the doctrine of frustration cannot be pleaded because self-induced. See further *per* Slade LJ in the *Phillips* case (above), at 628. For frustration, see post, para 22.09 *et seq*.

6   Eg, how the *proferens* had used the clause in previous disputes with other buyers; or the blameworthiness of either party: the *George Mitchell* case (see post, para 18.21). What about codes of practice (see generally ante, para 3.13) prohibiting the exclusion, eg, Motor Industry Code, para 5.6?

7   Lord Donaldson MR at 261e; Stuart-Smith LJ at 262e (see 109 LQR 41). See also *Thomas Witter Ltd v TBP Industries Ltd* (set out post, para 26.14). Whilst s 11(4) deliberately says that this is to be without prejudice to the guidelines for supply contracts, does s 11(4) in any other respect restrict consideration of other factors which might otherwise fall within s 11(1)? Cf the *George Mitchell* case (see post, para 18.21).

likely it is to fail.[8] Nor does the mere longevity of an exclusion clause or disclaimer appear to be any defence,[9] though widespread usage within an industry may indicate that it has been accepted as fair and reasonable by those in the trade.[10] In *Lease Management Services Ltd v Purnell Secretarial Services Ltd* (set out ante, para 16.06A) the Court of Appeal unanimously held that the wide exclusion clause in a directly financed lease did not satisfy the test of reasonableness. Nicholls VC made the following points (at 344F–346E): (a) it cannot be fair and reasonable to exclude liability for breach of an express promise; nor, as here, for LMS to exclude liability for breach of an implied term which was fundamental to the contract; (b) an exclusion clause which would be unreasonable if put forward by a supplier (Cannon) cannot be reasonable just because put forward by a financier (LMS) on the basis of their non-inspection of the goods. More recently, in *Overseas Medical Supplies Ltd v Orient Transport Services Ltd*:[11]

> The plaintiff (P) wished to transport some of their equipment to an exhibition in Teheran and so employed a freight forwarder, OTS. OTS's order form required P to insure and also contained a clause limiting OTS's liability to £600. Despite P instructing OTS to arrange the insurance, OTS omitted to do so; the goods were lost; and OTS sought to limit their liability to £600. The judge held that OTS's limitation clause was subject to the requirement of reasonableness by s 3 of UCTA (see post, para 18.24) and failed the test.

This decision was confirmed; and, in delivering the judgment of the Court of Appeal, Potter LJ set out the following propositions as relevant to the question of reasonableness arising from previous authorities (at 986–87, his numeration):

> (1) The way in which the relevant conditions came into being and are used generally – here the trade association standard terms.

> (2),(3), (8) The UCTA Schedule 2 guidelines are relevant (see post, para 18.21).

> (4) Reasonableness must be assessed having regard to the relevant clause viewed as a whole; it is not right to take any particular part of the clause in isolation.

> (5) A significant consideration is the reality of the plaintiff's consent to OTS's clause, which he here doubted (at 991).

> (6) In the case of a limitation clause rather than an exclusion clause (here £600), the size of the limit as compared with other limits in widely used standard terms.

> (7) Whilst relevant, the availability of insurance is not conclusive (see post, para 18.20A).

Of considerable practical importance is likely to be s 11(5), which shifts the burden of proof to the supplier in the following terms:[12]

---

8   Eg, *Miljus v Yamazaki Machinery UK Ltd* [1997] CLY 992; *South West Water Services Ltd v ICL* [2000] CLY 870.

9   Eg, the *Thompson* case (set out post, para 18.25); *First National Commercial Bank plc v Loxleys* [1997] PNLR 211, CA (not a goods case).

10 *Overland Shoes Ltd v Schenkers Ltd* [1998] 1 Lloyd's Rep 498, CA.

11 [1999] 1 All ER (Comm) 981, CA.

12 Reversing the *George Mitchell* case (see below). In consumer cases, there may be a trend indicating that suppliers will have considerable difficulty overcoming this presumption: the *Phillips* case (above), at 628. As to the pleading of reasonableness, see *Kristina Sheffield v Pickfords Ltd* (1997) 16 Tr LR 337, CA (not a goods case).

It is for those claiming that a contract term or notice satisfies the requirement of reasonableness to show that it does.

In the *Lease Management* case (see above), it was held that the burden of proof on the *proferens* (LMS) was not to be lightly discharged and certainly not by standard terms purporting to negative an express oral assurance. Similarly, in the *Overseas Medical Supplies* case (see above) the court likewise held that the *proferens* had not discharged the burden of proof of reasonableness (at 992).

[18.20A] The requirement of reasonableness (2). Further to the foregoing paragraph, s 11 of UCTA deals explicitly with certain special cases.

(1) *Restrictions to a specified sum.* Section 11(4) provides that:

> Where by reference to a contract term or notice a person seeks to restrict liability to a specified sum of money, and the question arises (under this or any other Act) whether the term or notice satisfies the requirement of reasonableness, regard shall be had in particular (but without prejudice to subsection (2) above in the case of contract terms) to –
>
> (a) the resources which he could expect to be available to him for the purpose of meeting the liability should it arise; and
>
> (b) how far it was open to him to cover himself by insurance.

For instance, in *St Albans City and District Council v International Computers Ltd* Scott Baker J used this provision to find that a clause limiting ICL's liability for breach of an express contractual term to £100,000 was unreasonable;[1] and this decision was unanimously affirmed by the Court of Appeal.[2] In relation to s 11(4)(b), in the *Overseas Medical* case (set out ante, para 18.20), Potter LJ commented that, as there (at AER 989e; 992g), the availability of insurance 'is by no means a decisive factor'.[3] By comparison, both limbs of s 11(4) were applied in the *Watford Electronics* case (para 53) in finding the exclusions reasonable.[4]

(2) *Non-contractual disclaimers.* Section 11(3) provides:

> In relation to a notice (not being a notice having contractual effect),[5] the requirement of reasonableness under this Act is that it should be fair and reasonable to allow reliance on it, having regard to all the circumstances obtaining when the liability arose or (but for the notice) would have arisen.

In *Smith v Bush*, the House of Lords applied this provision in finding a clause unreasonable (see ante, para 18.17).

(3) *Guidelines for supply contracts.* Section 11(2) provides:

[18.20A]

1   [1995] FSR 686. See the discussion in Atiyah, *Sale of Goods* (10th edn), pp 251–52.

2   [1996] 4 All ER 481, CA, at pp 492a, 492c, 492e. The case is set out post, para 18.24.

3   At AER 987f. Compare the *George Mitchell* case (set out ante, para 18.08) where the HL thought the supplier could have insured (see post, para 18.21) with the *Photo Production* case [1980] AC 827, HL, discussed by Adams and Brownsword (1988) 104 LQR at 101–02.

4   *Watford Electronics Ltd v Sanderson CFL Ltd* (set out post, para 18.24B).

5   As to the definition of 'notice', eg, disclaiming negligence liability in tort, see ante, para 18.17. Is a 'swing ticket' within ss 11(1) or (3) where the consumer purports to relinquish common law rights in return for promise, eg, of free replacement parts?

In determining for the purposes of section 6 or 7 above whether a contract term satisfies the requirement of reasonableness, regard shall be had in particular to the matters specified in Schedule 2 to this Act; but this subsection does not prevent the court or arbitrator from holding, in accordance with any rule of law, that a term which purports to exclude or restrict any relevant liability is not a term of the contract.

These guidelines, which are expressed to be applicable in respect of contracts for the supply of goods,[6] will be considered later (see post, para 18.21). The latter part of s 11(2) makes it clear that these guidelines have no place in determining the issue of whether the exclusion clause was ever incorporated in the transaction, a matter still governed by the common law (see ante, para 18.04).

It has already been suggested that the pre-1977 approach of the courts to exclusion clauses has begun to change from open hostility to greater even-handedness as the court realised they could achieve most of their objectives under the 1977 Act (see ante, para 18.08). Indeed, it has been pointed out that in the *Photo Production* case[7] the House of Lords in upholding the exclusion clause even seemed to suggest that in commercial contracts there was a presumption in favour of exclusion clauses; whereas, in the (later) *George Mitchell* case (set out ante, para 18.08), the House in rejecting the clause took a much more neutral position[8] and Lord Bridge said that an appellate court should refrain from interfering with the original decision on this point unless satisfied that it proceeded on some erroneous principle or was plainly and obviously wrong.[9] However, an appellate court has interfered on sufficient grounds.[4]

[18.21] The guidelines. Acting on the recommendation of the Law Commission,[1] SOGIT introduced a set of guidelines as to the reasonableness of clauses purporting to exclude or restrict the liability of the supplier in respect of the statutorily implied undertakings (ss 4, 12(4)). These provisions have been re-enacted by s 11(2) of UCTA (see ante, para 18.20) and are expressed by the Act to be relevant for the purposes of ss 6(3), 7(3), 7(4). The guidelines for the application of the reasonableness test must be applied to the whole of the exclusion clause (see ante, para 18.20) and are now set out in Sched 2 of UCTA as follows:

(a) the strength of the bargaining positions of the parties relative to each other, taking into account (among other things) alternative means by which the customer's requirements could have been met;[2]

---

6   Eg, *Shearson Lehman Hutton Inc v Maclaine Watson & Co Inc* [1989] 2 Lloyd's Rep 570 (see [1990] LM & CLQ at 309). They have been applied beyond that context: see Adams and Brownsword, *op cit*, note 3, p 113.
7   [1980] AC 827, HL (not a goods case).
8   See Adams and Brownsword, *op cit*, note 3, pp 103–04, 114.
9   At 816, 743f. See also the *Phillips* case (above), at 629; *St Albans DC v International Computers Ltd* (above), *per* Norse LJ at 491j–492b; the *Overseas Medical Supplies* case (set out ante, para 18.20), *per* Potter LJ at 986g. See also Adams and Brownsword, *op cit*, note 3, pp 99, 113, 116–19.

[18.21]
1   *First Report on Exemption Clauses* (1969, Law Com 24), para 113.
2   Eg, a two tier pricing system; or a monopoly supplier. Does paragraph (a) clearly enable the court to take into account the terms on which the goods were supplied to the supplier?

(b) whether the customer received an inducement to agree to the term, or in accepting it had an opportunity of entering into a similar contract with other persons, but without having to accept a similar term;[3]

(c) whether the customer knew or ought reasonably to have known of the existence and extent of the term (having regard, among other things, to any custom of the trade and any previous course of dealing between the parties);[4]

(d) where the term excludes or restricts any relevant liability if some condition is not complied with, whether it was reasonable at the time of the contract to expect that compliance with that condition would be practicable;[5]

(e) whether the goods were manufactured, processed or adapted to the special order of the customer.[6]

Plainly, in any particular case, various of these factors may come into play at varying strengths on one side or the other. What the court has to do is weigh the factors and strike a balance. Thus, in *George Mitchell (Chesterhall) Ltd v Finney Lock Seeds Ltd*, the House of Lords unanimously held that, whilst the limitation clause as a matter of construction was apt to protect the seller in respect of the event which occurred (see ante, para 18.08), it would not be 'fair or reasonable to allow reliance' on it. Affirming a unanimous Court of Appeal on this point, Lord Bridge in delivering the judgment of the House identified the following factors (at 817): (a) in other cases of seed failure, the seed merchants had recognised that reliance on the clause was unreasonable and had negotiated settlements of farmers' claims for damages rather than seeking to rely on the limitation clause;[7] (b) the supply of defective seed was due to the carelessness of the seed merchant's associate company; and (c) the seed merchants could have insured against claims arising from the supply of defective seed (see ante, para 18.20).

An illustration of the reasonableness issue in the context of direct financing, concerns the situation where there is a business consumer who is a relative expert in relation to the goods financed as compared with the financier. In *Photoprint Ltd v Forward Trust Ltd*:[8]

> The business hirer was a well established photographic and processing services business with a turnover of nearly £2m in 1989 and which over the previous decade entered into over 80 hp agreements with the defendant finance company (FT). This time, the hirer himself selected the a defective prototype machine from the manufacturer and only later arranged the finance.

---

3   Cf the *Overseas Medical* case (set out ante, para 18.20), *per* Potter LJ in observation (2) at 986–87.

4   Cf the pre-UCTA cases: *RW Green Ltd v Cade Bros Farms* [1978] 1 Lloyds Rep 602; the *George Mitchell* case (below).

5   Eg, notification of complaint within a reasonable time. It has been suggested para (d) extends to whether a motor dealer carried out any pre-delivery check (see ante, para 15.11).

6   Eg, factory-fitted options; adaptions for a handicapped buyer. See generally Yates and Hawkins, *Standard Business Contracts*, p 236.

7   What has been described as the 'estoppel argument': see Adams and Brownsword (1988) 104 LQR at 100, 107. The moral appears to be that it is safer to be hard-nosed: Adams (1983) 46 MLR at 774. Might such a frequent relaxation take an exclusion clause outside s 3 (see post, para 18.24)?

8   (1993) 12 Tr LR 146 (145 NLJ 697; 13 Tr LR 95). See also *Knight Machinery (Holdings) v Rennie* 1995 SLT 166.

The judge held that the financier's exclusion clause was fair and reasonable for the following reasons:[9] the parties were of relatively equal bargaining power for guideline (a); exclusion of consequential loss was not unreasonable; P was in a position to judge the efficacy of the machine, whereas, FT was not; and there was a sufficient course of dealings for guideline (c). This case may be compared with *Danka Rentals Ltd v Xi Software Ltd*:[10]

> It was critical to the defendant's business to have a working photocopier so that they could copy detailed computer software manuals for clients. It entered into a sales-aid lease (see ante, para 16.06A) of a replacement photocopier which turned out to be a complete disaster.

The judge held that the plaintiff lessor was unable to rely on his exclusion clause to protect him from such a breach of the implied undertakings as to fitness and quality on grounds of unreasonableness as follows: the plaintiff had chosen to finance the transaction by becoming the owner of the goods and could not be dissociated from the obligations of ownership (at 92C); the transaction had been made to enable the parties to avoid litigation over a previous defective photocopier; and guideline (c) favoured the plaintiff while guideline (d) favoured the defendant. A major difference between the two case would appear to be that in the one the hirer selected a prototype, whereas in the other sought a standard model.

In the *Stewart Gill* case concerning exclusion of a set-off (set out ante, para 18.16), there was both a quasi-sale within s 7 (see ante, para 18.19) and a standard form contract within s 3 (see post, para 18.24). Stuart-Smith LJ said that, although the Sched 2 guidelines were not strictly applicable to s 3, 'they are usually regarded as being of general application to the question of reasonableness'.[11] In the *British Fermentation* case (set out post, para 18.24) the judge applied the statutory guidelines set out in Sched 2 (see ante, para 18.21); he did not derive much assistance from precedents, as he said the matter was one of fact (at 403g); but he drew attention to the good commercial sense of the IME terms (at 403j) and held the contract reasonable.

Other cases

[18.22/24] Liability in standard form contracts. Where a transaction falls within the ambit of Part I (see ante, para 18.22), s 3 introduces restrictions on attempts to exclude or restrict (see ante, para 18.16) contractual liability. It applies only as between contracting parties and in favour of the weaker party in one or both the following (sometimes overlapping) circumstances:

(a) *One party 'deals as consumer'*, where the protection will basically be offered to a private individual dealing with a business.[1] It will be noted that this does not require the contract to be on standard terms, nor that it be for the supply of goods, so that s 3

---

9   See Macleod (1993) 13 Tr LR 96; Lawson (1993) 13 Tr LR 495, at 498.

10 (1998) 17 Tr LR 74. See also the *Lease Management Services* case (set out ante, para 16.06A); *Sovereign Finance Ltd v Silver Crest Furniture Ltd* [1998] CLY 852.

11 At 262h. Applied in the *British Fermentation* (at 402–03) (set out post, para 18.24) and *Watford Electronics Ltd* (set out post, para 18.24A) cases.

[18.22/24]

1   For 'dealing as consumer', see *Brigden v American Express Bank Ltd* [2000] IRLR 94 (not a goods case); and ante, para 18.18. Note that if the contract is for the supply of goods, those goods must be of 'a type ordinarily supplied for private use or consumption': s 12(1)(c).

would extend to eg, consumer loans (see ante, Chapter 7). However, the normal case is likely to involve a standard form contract for the supply of goods to a consumer; and, here, the transaction may also amount to a 'consumer supply contract' and attract the UTCC Regulations (see ante, para 11.12).

(b) *One party deals 'on another's written standard terms'*,[2] which will protect anybody (business or private) contracting on standard **written** terms produced by another (the *proferens*), eg, the merchant acquirer's franchise contract (see ante, para 7.09). Following the advice of the Law Commission,[3] the Act made no attempt either to apply the protection as against oral terms; nor to define standard terms.[4] It is to be noted that the provision refers to **terms**, not **contracts**: this would appear to extend the ambit of the category to those situations where a standard form contract contains customised parts, eg, blanks completed at the time,[5] and even where the standard terms were only altered 'without material variation'.[6] Broadly speaking, there would appear to be two possibilities:

(1) The *proferens* refers to his own standard terms. In *St Albans DC v International Computers Ltd*:[7]

The LA entered into a contract with ICL for the supply of computer software designed to administer the collection of the community charge. Notwithstanding that ICL had £50 million of insurance worldwide, the contract purported to limit ICL's liability to £100,000. The software contained an error which led to the LA collecting less revenue then it should have done. When the LA sued for breach of contract, ICL sought to rely on the limitation clause.

The Court of Appeal unanimously confirmed that there was a breach of an express term[8] of ICL's standard terms: they held that the LA had **dealt on** ICL's standard terms within s 3(1)(b) because, notwithstanding the prior negotiations, the LA had entered into the contract on those terms.[9] The Court then proceeded to confirm the decision of Scott Baker J that the limitation clause failed to satisfy the requirement of reasonableness (see ante, para 18.20A) in s 3(2) (see post, para 18.24A).

(2) The *proferens* refers to the standard terms of a third party. In *British Fermentation Products Ltd v Compair Reavell Ltd*:[10]

There was a contract to supply and install for a business buyer an air compressor. The supplier's (S's) quotation said: 'Our offer is based on the Model Form ... as

---

2   *McCrone v Boots Farm Sales Ltd* 1981 SLT 103 (see [1983] JBL 226); *Shearson Lehman Hutton Inc v Maclaine Watson & Co Inc* [1989] 2 Lloyd's Rep 570 (see [1990] LMCLQ at 309); the *Stewart Gill* case (below), *per* Lord Donaldson MR at 259g; *Lease Management Services Ltd v Purnell Secretarial Services Ltd* (set out ante, para 16.06A); the *Overseas Medical Services* case (set out ante, para 18.20).

3   *Second Report on Exemption Clauses* (1975, Law Com No 69) para 157.

4   Eg, the *Overseas Medical Services* case (above).

5   Cf UTCC Reg 5(3): see ante, para 11.14.

6   *Watford Electronics Ltd v Sanderson CFL Ltd* (set out post, para 18.24A; unappealed point, at 1016a–c).

7   [1996] 4 All ER 481, CA. See also Lawson (1998) 17 Tr LR 487–88.

8   Glidewell LJ also found there to be a breach of an implied term, being expressly supported by Norse LJ (at 487j): whilst the SGA did not apply because the software was not 'goods' (see ante, para 2.02), there was a common law implied term as to fitness (see ante, para 15.22).

9   At 491. This was despite the fact that the negotiations began with the LA's formal invitation to tender.

10 [1999] 2 All ER (Comm) 389.

recommended by the Institution of Mechanical Engineers' (IME). The Model Form gave the buyer (B) two rights to reject the goods for failure to meet the expressly agreed performance criteria and buy a replacement at S's expense; but clause 11(ii) provided that S should 'not be under any liability to' to B for 'any damage' ... 'resulting from such defects'. When the compressor failed to meet its performance standards, B chose not to reject it, but instead operate it for its useful life and claim consequential loss.

On a trial of preliminary issues and assuming that the IME terms were incorporated in the contract (see ante, para 18.04), the judge held as follows:

(i)   Applying an even-handed business common sense approach to construction (at 395j: see ante, para 11.07), he held that the IME terms were intended to give a disappointed buyer a clear right to reject; but, if he instead chose to keep the defective goods he was not to be entitled to damages for consequential loss.

(ii) Section 3(1)(b) may be wide enough to cover third party terms (here IME's), but only on 'proof that the model form is invariably or at least usually used by the party in question' (at 401b), that is, S; that, in the absence of an express statutory provision, it was for the party alleging that the statute applied, ie B, to prove that it applied (at 402b); but that he failed to do so.

(iii) In case he was wrong and s 3 was applicable, the judge considered whether clause 11 was reasonable (see post, para 18.24A); and in so doing he applied the statutory guidelines (see ante, para 18.21).

[18.24A] The effect of s 3. Where a case falls within s 3(1) (see ante, para 18.24), s 3(2) provides that, as against the weaker party, the business or *proferens*:

cannot by reference to any contract term –

(a) when himself in breach of contract, exclude or restrict any liability of his in respect of the breach; or

(b) claim to be entitled –

(i)   to render a contractual performance substantially different from that which was reasonably expected of him, or

(ii) in respect of the whole or any part of his contractual obligation, to render no performance at all,

except in so far as (in any of the cases mentioned above in this subsection) the contract term satisfies the requirement of reasonableness.

Thus, s 3(2) applies to contractual terms having either of the following two effects:

Section 3(2)(a). This refers to clauses which 'exclude or restrict liability', a phrase given an extended meaning by s 13.[1] According to the Law Commission, 'this paragraph does not impose any control over terms which lay down whether a breach of contract occurs'.[2]

Section 3(2)(b). It is to be noted that s 3(2)(b) does not refer to clauses which exclude or restrict liability or fall within s 13[1] and is not limited thereto.[3] However, it is seemingly confined to attempted **reductions** in the duties of the business or *proferens* in either of two

---

[18.24A]
1   See ante, para 18.16.
2   *Second Report on Exemption Clauses* (1975, Law Com No 69) para 119.
3   Does it extend to clauses in meter hiring contracts making the hirer liable for loss of coins inserted?

ways; and so presumably it could not touch clauses **increasing** the obligations of the other party, eg, consumer. The two ways of **reducing** liability are:

(i) Render a substantially different contractual performance.[4] So, where the supplier of a computer system supplied defective software, it was no answer for him to plead that there was nothing wrong with the hardware, which could not be used without the software.[5] On the other hand, unilateral variation of interest rates under the term of the loan would not appear to be 'a contractual performance'.[5a] Perhaps this clause is likely to take over much of the work of the now defunct doctrine of fundamental breach (as to which, see ante, para 18.08). How far beyond the express terms will the courts be prepared to look? Will the courts look to the normal terms in that trade, the relative bargaining power of parties, the extent to which the weaker party understood the term?

(ii) Render no performance at all, eg, a *force majeure* clause (see post, para 22.13A). Does it apply to stipulations for a tolerance as to quality or quantity? What of provisions denying all contractual promises on one side, and so appearing to translate the arrangement into a unilateral contract?

[18.24B] In *Watford Electronics Ltd v Sanderson CFL Ltd*:[1]

After lengthy negotiations and the provision of brochures, three contractual documents were signed for the supply to W of a bespoke integrated software system, containing an 'entire agreement' clause and some other exclusion clauses. The standard terms provided for use of the software on licence, defined 'software' as the computer package and its storage medium and provided that the property in the software did not pass. An additional term provided for the supplier (S) to use his best endeavours, etc. After W found the system unsatisfactory, S supplied new hardware and bespoke software. The system still being unsatisfactory, W obtained a new system from different suppliers and sued S for damages; and a trial of preliminary issues was ordered.

At first instance and on unappealed points, the judge held as follows:[2] the brochures contained misrepresentations (see ante, para 11.01); that in their contract the parties had defined the software as goods (see ante, para 2.02); that there was a single contractual package of goods and services (see ante, para 2.05); that, as the software had been supplied on licence, it had been bailed (see ante, para 1.17); that a hybrid of implied terms as to merchantability and fitness were implied by virtue of ss 9 and 13 of the SGSA and s 14 of the SGA (see ante, para 15.26), together with a common law duty to exercise all care and skill in giving professional advice (see ante, para 15.22); that on their true construction the exclusion clauses were apt to exclude liability for the losses claimed (but see below); that both the Misrepresentation Act 1967 (s 3: see ante, para 18.17) and UCTA (s 3: see ante, para 18.24) were applicable to the contracts; and that those clauses were struck down by the reasonableness test. Only on this last point was the decision appealed and overturned. In the leading judgment, Chadwick LJ held as follows: whilst an

---

4   As to the possible application to card-not-present transactions, see ante, para 7.09, note 11. As to whether the provision might apply to 'all monies' *Romalpa* clauses (see post, para 20.29), see Lawson (1998) 17 Tr LR 487 at 490.

5   *South West Water Services Ltd v ICL* [1999] BLR 420.

5a *Paragon Finance plc v Nash* [2001] 2 All ER (Comm) 1025, CA (see also ante, para 10.05).

[18.24B]

1   [2001] 1 All ER (Comm) 696, CA (see 117 LQR 545).

2   [2000] 2 All ER (Comm) 984, CA.

appellate court should normally refrain from interfering with the trial judge's assessment of reasonableness (see ante, para 18.20), here the first instance judge had misconstrued the legal effect of the exclusions (at paras 32; 37; 40; 42–48). His Lordship thought the different parts of different exclusion clauses in the contract were each to be considered separately and were reasonable as follows:

(1) The entire agreement clause was simply an acknowledgment by the parties that their entire agreement was contained in the contract and they could not rely on anything said during their extensive prior negotiations.[3] His Lordship described this as a 'common feature of professionally drawn commercial contracts' (at para 39); said that it may operate by giving rise to an estoppel (at para 40: see ante, para 18.06); and found nothing unreasonable in it within the Misrepresentation Act 1967 (at para 41: see ante, para 18.17).

(2) Limitation of direct loss for breach of contract to the contract price would *prima facie* fall within the first rule in *Hadley v Baxendale*.[4] His Lordship pointed out that the starting point for assessing this loss was the *prima facie* rule contained in s 53(3) of the SGA (see post, para 29.33), and the limitation clauses simply pegged that value (at para 34); in other words, it was just a liquidated damages clause (see post, para 27.24).

(3) Exclusion of indirect loss for breach of contract would *prima facie* fall within the second rule in *Hadley v Baxendale*. His Lordship (at paras 52–54) applied the guidelines set out in Sched 2 of the 1977 Act (see ante, para 18.21) and also s 11(4) (see ante, para 18.20A), adding that two experienced businessmen 'should be taken to be the best judge on the question whether the terms of the agreement are reasonable' (at para 55).

Statutory overlap. Where the contract is one for the supply of goods, there appears to be a considerable overlap between the present provision and two others:

(a) *The UTCC Regulations.* Where one party deals as consumer on the other's standard terms (s 3(i)(a) of UCTA: see ante, para 18.25A), it may be that the contract is a 'consumer supply', in which case the claim by the business supplier to do one of the things listed in s 3(2) of UCTA (see ante, para 18.24A) may also be an 'unfair term' within the UTCC Regulations (Sched 3, paras 1(c), (f): see ante, para 11.16). To this extent, it may be sensible for the courts not to strive to find a clause unreasonable under UCTA, which also applies to supplies between businesses, eg, the *Watford* case.

(b) *Sections 6 and 7 of UCTA* (see ante, para 18.19). Where the transferee deals as consumer, the two sets of provisions appear inconsistent: s 3 subjects the terms to the reasonableness test, whereas ss 6 and 7 make them void. However, in *Photoprint Ltd v Forward Trust Ltd* (set out ante, para 18.21), the judge suggested that the financier's exclusion clause fell outside s 3(2) because its effect was that the statutory implied terms did not become part of FT's 'contractual obligation' (at 156F). Whilst this approach appears at variance with *Phillips Products Ltd v Hyland* (set out ante, para 18.12), it would avoid any clash with ss 6 and 7 by taking the statutory implied terms outside s 3.[5] The result would be that exclusion of **express** terms would be dealt with by s 3, but exclusion of **implied** terms by ss 6 and 7.

---

3   If that had been a consumer supply contract, such a clause would probably have been unfair: see Grey Term 1(n); ante, para 11.18.
4   See post, para 27.41.
5   See Macleod (1993) 13 Tr L 96 at 99–100.

Where applicable, s 3(2) subjects an express contractual term to the reasonableness test (see ante, para 18.20 *et seq*).

[18.25] Consumer indemnity clauses.[1] Where a transaction falls within the ambit of Part I (see ante, para 18.22), s 4(1) provides that:

> A person dealing as consumer[2] cannot by reference to any contract term be made to indemnify another person (whether a party to the contract or not) in respect of liability that may be incurred by the other for negligence or breach of contract, except in so far as the contract term satisfies the requirement of reasonableness.

Whereas an exemption clause in respect of business liability for death or personal injury may be void,[3] a clause requiring a consumer to indemnify another against such business liability[4] is only by s 4 subject to the test of reasonableness (see ante, para 18.20); and it may be that an important factor here will be the relative ability of the parties to insure against the risk (see s 11(4)(b): set out ante, para 18.20).

Where the indemnity is in a commercial contract between two businesses, the position was considered in *Thompson v T Lohan (Plant Hire) Ltd*:[5]

> The deceased (D) worked for a plant hire company (PH), which hired out his services and those of a fellow employee (Hill) to a quarry, along with the excavators under a similar standard form contract to that in the *Hyland* case (set out ante, para 18.16). D was killed by the negligence of Hill. D's widow obtained judgment against PH, who on ordinary principles was vicariously liable for Hill's negligence. PH claimed to be indemnified by the quarry under clauses 8 and 13.

The Court of Appeal unanimously held:

(i)   At common law, cl 8 was effective to transfer the vicarious liability from PH to the quarry;

(ii) Clause 8 was not struck down by s 2(1), which was only designed to protect D (see ante, para 18.17); and

(iii) Under cl 13 the quarry was required to indemnify PH and this commercial indemnity was not within s 4.[6] Nor did the Court appear to think that cl 13 should be judged in accordance with s 2(2): if this is correct, commercial indemnities are subject only to s 3 (see ante, para 18.24), or perhaps s 10 (see ante, para 18.16A).

[18.25]

1   See generally Adams and Brownsword [1982] JBL 200; Yates and Hawkins, *Standard Business Contracts*, Chapter 8; and post, para 25.05. As to the interpretation of indemnity clauses, see ante, para 18.06.

2   As to which, see ante, para 18.18.

3   Section 2(1): see ante, para 18.17.

4   The section applies whether the liability in question (a) is directly that of the person to be indemnified or is to be incurred by him vicariously (see s 1(4)) or (b) is to the person dealing as a consumer or to someone else (s 4(2)). Note that s 4 does not apply to indemnity contracts between two consumers.

5   [1987] 2 All ER 631; [1987] 1 WLR 649, CA.

6   See further Macdonald [1994] JBL 441 at 449–50.

[18.26/27] Product guarantees. Where a transaction falls within Part I (see ante, para 18.22), s 5 strikes at clauses purporting to exclude or restrict (see ante, para 18.16) product liability (see ante, Chapter 17) between remote parties in the chain of distribution (see ante, para 17.01): that is, as between persons who are not 'parties to a contract under or in pursuance of which possession or ownership of goods passes'.[1] Typically, this will be the manufacturer (Z) and the retail purchaser (C) and consumer (D); and the obvious examples within s 5 are disclaimers on packaging, the 'guarantee card' packed with goods, and the manufacturer's instruction booklet (see post, para 18.28). Section 5(1) provides:

(1) In the case of goods[2] of a type ordinarily supplied for private use or consumption,[3] where loss or damage –

   (a) arises from goods proving defective while in consumer use; and

   (b) results from the negligence of a person concerned in the manufacture or distribution of the goods,[4]

liability for the loss or damage cannot be excluded or restricted by reference to any contract term or notice[5] contained in or operating by reference to a guarantee of the goods.

The following points arise. First, 'loss or damage' extends beyond death or personal injury to all types of loss.[6] Second, 'defective' covers design and production defects, shoddy as well as dangerous goods (cf s 3 of the CPA: see ante, para 17.28). Third, s 5(2)(a) lays down that:[7]

... goods are to be regarded as 'in consumer use' when a person is using them, or has them in his possession for use, otherwise than exclusively for the purposes of a business.

Leaving aside *de minimis* use, what length of time is to be taken in deciding whether the goods are exclusively for business use? Fourth, s 5(2)(b) explains that:[8]

... anything in writing is a guarantee if it contains or purports to contain some promise or assurance (however worded or presented) that defects will be made good by complete or partial replacement, or by repair, monetary compensation or otherwise.

Where the above requirements are satisfied, the effect of s 5 is to render void any provision in the 'guarantee' excluding or restricting the consumer's rights.[9] A

[18.26/27]

1 Section 5(3). Insofar as a case falls within s 5(3), any guarantee should be considered under s 6 or 7: as to which, see ante, paras 18.19.

2 'Goods' has the same meaning as in the SGA (s 14): as to which, see ante, para 2.02.

3 Cf s 12(1)(c): see ante, para 18.18.

4 For negligence liability in tort, see ante, para 17.14 *et seq*. Distinguish strict product liability: see ante, para 17.24 *et seq*.

5 As to the definition of 'notice', see s 14 (see ante, para 18.23).

6 See further ante, para 18.23. Cf CPA, s 5: see ante, para 17.29.

7 If for exclusive business use, any guarantee will be dealt with under ss 2 or 3: as to which, see ante, paras 18.23; 18.24.

8 Distinguish the completely different surety contract termed a 'guarantee': see post, para 25.05.

9 Is s 5(1) contradicted by s 2(2) (see ante, para 18.17)?

(presumably unintended?) result may be to deprive any promise by the manufacturer in the guarantee of any contractual effect (see ante, para 17.09A). The ambit of s 5 is almost wholly duplicated by a Directive (see ante, para 17.09A).

DISCHARGE BY WORDS[1]

[18.28] Introduction. In modern times, many goods are supplied together with instructions or warnings as to their use or consumption. Such instructions may prescribe procedures for any one or more of the following purposes: (a) using the goods;[2] (b) maintaining the goods;[3] (c) constructing, erecting or preparing the goods;[4] (d) avoiding hazards in relation to, or emanating from, the goods.[5] They may be addressed to the generality of UK consumers;[6] or they may be customised.[7] And they may originate from any prior party in the chain of distribution (see ante, para 17.01); or they may be introduced in pursuance of an industry-wide voluntary code.[8] Sometimes warnings will be addressed to the consumer himself, whilst on other occasions they may be addressed to an 'informed intermediary'.[9] Thus, in the case of medicines (see ante, para 4.29), it has been argued that for prescription drugs the warning should be given to the prescriber, whereas for other products it should be given to the consumer.[10] Notwithstanding that there may be little evidence that warnings do change behaviour,[11] they are sometimes vested with legal effect (see post, para 18.29).

[18.29] Legal effect. Particularly where it can be shown that the dangerous nature of the goods gives rise to personal injuries, there are a number of criminal offences to which instructions may be relevant, mostly imposing strict liability, eg, as to consumer safety,[1] or a medicine labels (see ante, para 8.12) or labelling of dangerous goods[2] or trade

---

[18.28]

1　See generally Macleod (1981) 97 LQR 550; Clark [1983] JBL 130; Brown [1988] LMCLQ 502; HMSO, *Instructions for Consumer Products* (1988).

2　Besides the implied terms as to fitness and quality (see post, para 18.32), there may also be instructions as to the time-span within which goods should be used, eg, 'use by' or 'best before' dates for food (see ante, para 8.11), labels on medicines (see ante, para 8.12).

3　Eg, *Wormell v RHM Agriculture (East) Ltd* (set out post, para 18.34).

4　For the position of unprepared goods, see ante, para 14.02. As to unsafe goods, see ante, paras 4.32; 4.35.

5　Does this make them more or less objectionable or effective? How far should warnings go in stating the obvious – eg, on microwaveable food 'Take care – product will be hot after heating'?

6　So that little account is taken of the foibles of particular classes of consumer, eg, minors, elderly, illiterates, foreigners. For some examples, see [1987] Which? 242.

7　Eg, a retailer's verbal instruction, directions for use on medicines, manufacturer's letter to particular consumer.

8　Eg, categorising foods for microwave cooking. For voluntary codes, see generally ante, para 3.11 *et seq*.

9　Eg, *Holmes v Ashford* [1950] 2 All ER 76, CA.

10　See Ferguson (1992) 12 OJ LS 59.

11　See Robinson and Brickle (1992) 142 NLJ 83. Yet the Government invests labels with significance: see DTI, *Modern Markets: Confident Consumers* (1999), paras 3.4; 3.5.

[18.29]

1　See the General Product Safety Regulations (ante, para 4.34); *Janbo Trading v Dudley MBC* [1994] 12 Tr LR 190, DC.

2　There are Directives on the labelling of dangerous substances, eg, 1999/45; 1999/77 (see 18 Tr LR 276).

description for such as an out-of-date instruction book (see ante, paras 4.06–07). In civil law, the first issue will be the interpretation of the instructions,[3] which are presumably to be read *contra proferentem*.[4] Thus, in *Vacwell Engineering Ltd v BDH Chemicals Ltd*:[5]

> The plaintiff manufacturers of plant were accustomed to obtain supplies of chemicals from the defendant manufacturers of chemicals, which products normally contained an appropriate warning of industrial hazards. The plaintiffs devised a new method of manufacturing plant utilising the chemical, X, and requested that the defendants supply X to them, making known the purpose for which it was required. X was supplied in glass ampoules bearing the legend 'Harmful Vapour'. Unknown to either party, X was uniquely dangerous in that it exploded violently on contact with water. There having been such an explosion whilst the plaintiff's servant was washing some of the ampoules, the plaintiff claimed for damage to his premises and for loss of profit. Rees J held the defendants liable because their failure to warn of the explosive risk constituted (1) a breach of the undertakings implied (a) by s 14 of the SGA, and (b) from the course of dealings between the parties (see generally ante, para 15.22); and (2) the tort of negligence (see generally ante, para 17.13).

However, it would seem that liability was on the basis that the danger had been pointed out in scientific literature. Without that factor, there could have been liability in contract;[6] but not in the tort of negligence,[7] or under the CPA.[8]

As regards the tort of negligence, insofar as the action is based on a negligent act, eg, design or production defects (see ante, para 17.14 *et seq*), the duty of care may be adequately discharged by an aptly worded warning[9] or because the defect was in some way discoverable on reasonable inspection (which might give rise to contributory negligence: see post, para 27.40); and, if the action is based on negligently drafted instructions, there are the usual difficulties attendant on actions for negligent misstatement, eg, misleading wiring instructions on an electrical appliance (see generally ante, para 17.17 *et seq*).

Alternatively, where the statutory strict product liability is being considered, it will be relevant in deciding whether a product is defective to have regard to any instructions.[10] Is there a duty to warn of known dangers, either at common law or under the CPA?[11]

---

3   Can instructions in a foreign language have any relevance to retail supply within the UK? What of Welsh?

4   For the *contra proferentem* rule, see ante, para 18.06. Does it make any difference if the person seeking to rely on the instructions is not their trade originator? Cf *Wormell v RHM Agriculture (East) Ltd* (set out post, para 18.34). See generally Yates and Hawkins, *Standard Business Contracts*, pp 295–98; Clark, *Product Liability*, Chapter 4.

5   [1971] 1 QB 88; [1969] 3 All ER 1681. This case was settled during appeal [1970] 3 All ER 553. See Weaver (1970), 33 MLR 446.

6   What is now s 14(3): see *Frost v Aylesbury Dairy* (set out, para 14.08).

7   See ante, para 17.09. Eg, *Lambert v Lewis* (set out ante, para 17.06). As to manufacturers' guarantees, see ante, para 17.09A.

8   Section 4(1)(e): see ante, para 17.30.

9   *Holmes v Ashford* [1950] 2 All ER 76, CA; the *Vacwell Engineering* case (above); *Hurley v Dyke* [1979] RTR 265, HL. For the effect of such disclaimers, see generally ante, para 18.04.

10   CPA, s 3(2)(a): see ante, para 17.28. But see the state-of-the-art defence (ante, para 17.30).

11   See *Herschtal v Stewart & Arden Ltd* (set out ante, para 16.18); and Clark, *op cit*, note 4, 85–89. As to the ineffectiveness in fact of warnings, see (1992) 142 NLJ 83.

If there is a contractual relationship between the parties, this may be by reason of a supply contract, where it has been seen as a duty to inform,[12] or a collateral contract: the effects of a collateral contract have already been explored (see ante, para 17.09); and the impact on these of s 5 of UCTA considered above (see ante, para 18.26).

Contracts for the supply of goods

[18.30] Incorporation. Where there is a contract for the supply of goods between the party injured and the person seeking to rely on the instructions, the first question in determining civil liability[1] is whether the instructions have been incorporated in the contract (see ante, para 18.04). If there is a signed supply contract, the instructions may be incorporated therein expressly,[2] or impliedly (see ante, para 11.08), provided that this is done before the contract was made.[3] If there is no signed supply contract, then the instructions could be incorporated by actual or reasonable notice;[4] but, the more unusual the instructions, the more steps have to be taken to give such notice.[5] However, if the instructions have not been incorporated in either of these ways, then it would seem that they can only take effect as part of the goods supplied (see post, para 18.33). In the case of a consumer supply contract, the common law rules may be unfair.[6]

Pre-contract instructions

[18.31] Where the instructions as to the use of goods supplied are served before formation of the supply contract (see ante, para 18.30), they may *prima facie* amount to a promise (express or implied) by the transferee to use the goods in conformity with those instructions, eg, 'Do not spray aerosol on naked flame or burn container'. Suppose those instructions are inconsistent with other terms of the contract. If the instructions and other inconsistent terms are both express, the position would appear to be this: insofar as both terms are embodied in a contractual document, it would presumably be read *contra proferentem* the supplier;[1] whereas, if one is embodied in the writing and the other in an oral undertaking, the latter may override the former at common law[2] or the whole fall within the UTCC Regulations (see UTCC Grey Term (b): see ante, para 11.16).

---

12 Hedley [2001] JBL 114, at 117, 122–24: see post, para 18.32.

[18.30]

1 An incorrect statement or instructions supplied with goods may amount to an offence under the TDA if the instructions can be said to induce entry into the supply contract: see ante, para 4.03.

2 Express incorporation may be either directly (where the instructions form part of the signed contract) or by reference (see ante, para 11.07).

3 *Olley v Marlborough Court* [1949] 1 KB 532, CA (not a sale case).

4 Eg, the *Vacwell Engineering* case (incorporation by course of dealings): set out ante, para 18.29.

5 *Interfoto Picture Library Ltd v Stiletto Ltd* [1988] 1 All ER 348, CA (Macdonald [1988] JBL 375).

6 Grey Term 1(i): see ante, para 11.17.

[18.31]

1 Eg, the *Vacwell Engineering* case (set out ante, para 18.29). For the *contra proferentem* rule, see ante, para 18.06.

2 *J Evans & Sons (Portsmouth) Ltd v Andrea Mezario Ltd* [1976] 2 All ER 930, CA (not a sale case).

Leaving aside the special provisions in contracts by sample (see ante, paras 15.03–10), it will be recalled that the major terms implied into contracts for the supply of goods are as to their description,[3] fitness[4] and satisfactory quality (see ante, para 14.15 *et seq*). Furthermore, under the provisions of UCTA, the extent to which these terms may be 'excluded or restricted' (see ante, para 18.16) depends on whether or not the transferee is 'dealing as consumer' (see ante, para 18.18): if he does, then the instructions will be void to the extent that they 'exclude or restrict' the statutory implied terms (see ante, para 18.19); whereas, if the transferee does not 'deal as consumer', the instructions may only take effect insofar as they satisfy the requirement of reasonableness.[5] The extent to which instructions for use may be compatible with these statutory implied terms is considered below (see post, para 18.32).

[18.32] Compatibility with statutory terms. The instructions are clearly part of the goods supplied.[1] There must now be considered the extent to which pre-contract instructions for use may be compatible with the statutory undertakings as to the goods supplied.

1   *Undertakings as to description*. Pre-contract instructions may render obvious the contractual identity of the goods,[2] eg, dismantling instructions may show that a machine was only supplied for scrap.

2   *Undertakings as to fitness*. Insofar as the instructions originate from a remote party in the chain of distribution (see ante, para 17.01), that may show that the transferee did not rely on the skill and judgment of his immediate supplier as regards matters falling within the ambit of the instructions;[3] or reasonable fitness may be judged in the light of the instructions,[4] eg, a 'Dry Clean Only' label on a garment whose fabrics shrink at different rates if washed.

3   *Undertakings as to satisfactory quality*. In relation to this undertaking (see ante, para 14.18), it may be 'reasonable' to fix the characteristics required of the goods by the statutory definition in the light of the instructions for their use: like any other label, instructions affixed to goods are to be taken into consideration in assessing their quality.[5] Further, it may be possible to construe pre-contract instructions as a specified defect (see ante, para 14.25), eg, where there is a warning printed on glass ampoules against careless submersion in water.[6]

---

3   See ante, para 13.11 *et seq*.

4   See ante, para 14.07 *et seq*.

5   See ante, para 18.20. Alternatively, the instructions may be subject to the reasonableness test by reason of s 3 of UCTA: see generally ante, para 18.24.

[18.32]

1   *Per* Glidewell LJ in *St Albans DC v ICL* (set out ante, para 18.24), at 493f.

2   The test for this undertaking probably turns on any difference in the identity of the goods: see ante, para 13.13.

3   For this limitation on the undertakings as to fitness, see ante, paras 14.13–14.

4   *Wormell v RHM Agriculture Ltd* (set out post, para 18.34).

5   *Niblett's* case (set out ante, para 12.03); and see generally ante, para 14.16–17. Alternatively, instructions may be considered as a relevant circumstance: see ante, para 14.19.

6   *Vacwell Engineering Ltd v BDH Chemicals Ltd* (set out ante, para 18.29), *obiter*, at 104C–G.

Post-contract instructions

[18.33] Where instructions as to the use of goods supplied are only communicated *after* formation of the supply contract (see ante, para 18.30), it would not usually seem possible for them to affect the formulation of the supplier's contractual duties in the manner above considered.[1] Nor can post-contract instructions have any effect as modifying the supply contract,[2] except in the (perhaps unlikely) event that they are supported by fresh consideration.[3] On the other hand, such post-contractual instructions, eg, as part of a manufacturer's product recall, might have a legal effect as part of the goods supplied[4] in either of the following ways:

(a) to discharge by performance the supplier's duties (see post, para 18.34); or

(b) by reducing or extinguishing the damages flowing from the supplier's breach of those duties (see post, para 18.35).

[18.34] Instructions performing duties. Whilst post-contractual instructions cannot affect the **formulation** of the supplier's contractual duties (see ante, para 18.33) they may be relevant to the **performance** of those duties, either in whole or in part. Thus, in *Wormall v RHM Agriculture (East) Ltd*:[1]

> The plaintiff farmer (P) telephoned the defendant dealer in agricultural produce (D) and enquired whether he had any herbicide designed to kill wild oats in fields of wheat so late in the 1983 season. D recommended Commando, which P duly ordered. The copious manufacturer's instructions on the canisters inter alia directed that Commando was to be applied only between particular stages of crop growth and during particular weather conditions and added 'Damage may occur to crops sprayed after the recommended growth stage'. Unfortunately, weather conditions were not suitable for application until the recommended growth stage had passed, when Commando was applied but had very little effect on either the wild oats or wheat. P sued for breach of SGA, s 14(3).

The first instance judge held that these instructions were part of the contract goods; that the whole package of chemicals with instructions must be looked at the determine whether it was fit; that P believed the instructions meant merely that there was a risk of damage to the wheat crop from late application (a risk he was prepared to take); and that Commando was not fit because P had interpreted the instructions as a reasonable farmer.[2] On the last point, he was unanimously reversed by the Court of Appeal[3] because P had ignored the clear warning. The judge had found the instructions misleading as to the

---

[18.33]

1 See ante, paras 18.31–32. Except perhaps by trade custom: see *Shearson Lehman Hutton Inc v Maclaine Watson & Co Ltd* [1989] 2 Lloyd's Rep 570 (see [1990] LMCLQ at 309); and generally ante, para 15.11.

2 *Roscorla v Thomas* (1842) 3 QB 234.

3 For variation by subsequent contract, see post, para 26.18.

4 As to goods supplied under the contract, see further ante, para 14.03.

[18.34]

1 [1987] 3 All ER 75; [1987] 1 WLR 1091, CA.

2 [1986] 1 All ER 769 at 778. As to goods supplied for the purpose of these undertakings, see ante, para 14.03.

3 During the 1983 season, there never was a time in P's locality when the weather conditions and crop development would have allowed application (*per* Dillon LJ at 77).

effect of disregarding the warning; but the CA held that this was irrelevant (at 80g; 82b). Whilst the goods were not absolutely fit, they were reasonably fit (see below).

The effect of post-contract instructions would therefore appear to be as follows:

1   *Undertakings as to fitness*. Suppose the post-contract instructions specify the manner in which the goods are to be used, eg, a garment to be dry cleaned only. As the requirement of the undertakings is that the goods must be 'reasonably fit' (see ante, para 14.09), the instructions are to be approached as evidence of what constitutes reasonable use.[4]

2   *Undertakings as to satisfactory quality*. Likewise, in relation to this statutory undertaking (see ante, para 14.19), post-contract instructions may be a 'relevant circumstance' (as to multi-purpose goods, see ante, para 14.21).

In the case of pre-contract instructions, the law does not require actual notice, so long as the *supplier* does what is reasonably necessary to bring them to the attention of the transferee (see ante, para 18.04). Similarly, in the case of post-contract instructions, it seems likely from the *Wormell* case that constructive notice to the transferee could amount to performance of the supplier's contractual duties.[5] Does the matter now turn upon what a reasonable consumer should anticipate by way of instructions?[6] Even if post-contractual instructions do not prevent liability arising, they may reduce or extinguish damages (see post, para 18.35).

[18.35] Instructions reducing or extinguishing damage. The damages flowing from a breach by the supplier of his duties under the supply contract is limited by the chain of causation (see post, para 27.29) and the doctrine of mitigation of damage (see post, para 27.44). Suppose a transferee discovers, but ignores, post-contract instructions. In *Dobell & Co Ltd v Barber & Garrett*:[1]

> Goods were sold with a compulsory warranty of quality,[2] but the seller expressly disclaimed responsibility for the defect in question. The majority of the Court of Appeal nevertheless held that the buyer was entitled to resell the goods in reliance on the statutory warranty, and recover damages paid to his sub-buyers.

Lawrence LJ pointed out that, were it otherwise, the seller could always protect himself against the full consequences naturally flowing from his breach of warranty by stating that he did not accept the responsibility which the Act cast upon him.[3] Greer LJ dissented on the grounds that, in the light of the seller's attempted disclaimer, it was 'unreasonable'

---

4   The *Wormell* case (see above). See also *Vacwell Engineering* case (set out ante, para 18.29), where the instructions suggested only precautions against inhaling the vapour.

5   Dillon LJ pointed out that both P and D knew that the goods would be supplied with detailed instructions (at 77e). Contrast *Feuer Leather Corp v Frank Johnstone & Sons* [1981] Com LR 251 (appealed on another point). But see generally Reynolds [1984] JBL 14; Goode (1983) 3 LS at 292. Cf disclaimers as a defence to strict criminal liability: see ante, para 4.09.

6   Is this to import a sort of constructive notice into commercial transactions, notwithstanding the general prohibition against so doing (see 109 LQR at 369–70).

[18.35]

1   [1931] 1 KB 219, CA. See also *Kendall v Lillico* (set out ante, para 14.10).

2   Under s 2 of the Fertilisers and Feeding Stuffs Act 1926 (now replaced by s 72 of the Agriculture Act 1970: see ante, para 15.20).

3   At 237. Cited with approval by *McGregor on Damages* (16th edn), para 887.

for the buyer to resell the goods without having them analysed;[4] and it has subsequently been held by the House of Lords in another case that the chain of causation is broken where the buyer continued to use the goods with actual knowledge of the remediable breach as regards subsequent consequential loss.[5]

The position of post-contractual instructions which identify a defect in the goods but do not oust the implied undertakings[6] would appear to be this: in respect of the *prima facie* measure of damages flowing from the reduced value of the goods in the defective state,[7] the instructions appear to be no more than advance notice of breach; but, as regards consequential loss,[8] the supplier is under no liability for such loss occurring subsequent to the transferee's discovery of the defect, whether or not such discovery arises from the instructions. The difficult area seems to concern consequential loss arising before discovery of the defects.[9] The current view would appear to be that the supplier cannot plead the contributory negligence of his transferee in not discovering that instruction (see post, para 27.40), though the effect of such a defence is canvassed elsewhere.[10]

---

4   At 247. See also Roche J at first instance. Cf the *Wormell* case (set out ante, para 18.34).

5   *Lambert v Lewis* (set out ante, para 17.06). See also *Worsley v Tambrands Ltd* [2000] CLY 548, CA.

6   In the *Wormell* case (above), the CA do not appear to have addressed the issue of how, in a contract made by phone, unmentioned instructions can oust the undertakings. At any rate, it is submitted that the ruling cannot apply to totally unexpected instructions.

7   See post, paras 29.30; 29.33.

8   See post, paras 29.23; 29.36.

9   Eg, washing instructions on clothes; assembly instructions on goods supplied in kit-form.

10   Macleod (1981) 97 LQR 550, at 572–73.

PART 5

THE CONVEYANCE IN SUPPLY CONTRACTS:

THE EFFECTS OF THE CONTRACT

CHAPTER 19

CONTRACT AND CONVEYANCE

[19.01] Leaving aside most simple bailments (see ante, para 1.17), the object of the parties to the transaction of sale, quasi-sale or hp is normally to transfer the proprietary rights in the subject matter of the contract, and the conveyancing aspect of the transaction must now be examined. The difference between contractual and proprietary rights (rights *in rem*) is traditionally this: a contractual right merely gives the party entitled a right against the other contracting party, whereas a proprietary right gives an interest in the goods which can be asserted against third parties.

At a fairly early stage, the English law of sale rejected the idea that proprietary rights in goods sold automatically passed at the time of either contract or delivery:[1] instead, it was settled that the matter should be left to the agreement between the parties.[2] The SGA lays down rules as to the passing of proprietary rights where the parties do not evince any specific intent in this respect: these rules will be considered in Chapter 20 and are presumably also applicable to quasi-sales[3] and to hp upon exercise of the option to purchase.[4]

Whilst, therefore, the actual conveyance may, but need not, take place at the time the contract is made, it remains true that the contract suffices to effect the conveyance.[5] Unlike certain other systems of laws, and even certain other branches of our own law,[6] the English law of sale of goods does not require some legal act distinct from the contract to effect the conveyance. An apparently similar position is to be found in contracts of hp, though here the agreement usually provides that the option cannot be exercised – and the contract of sale made – until all the instalments of hire rent have been paid (see ante, para 1.25).

Possession and ownership

[19.02] Having separated the contract from the conveyance, it is necessary to examine what is conveyed by the transaction. In common parlance, it is usually said that the parties intend to transfer the 'ownership' in the goods; but this is not a term of art and

---

[19.01]

1   For the permutations of the passing of property and delivery, see post, para 23.02.

2   See now the SGA, ss 2(6), 17. For alternative solutions, see TB Smith, *Property Problems in Sale*, p 53 *et seq*.

3   Because the common law rules were largely codified in the SGA 1893: see Chapter 20. What should happen where there was a change, eg the requirement of notice in rr 2 and 3 of s 18 (see post, para 20.13).

4   Because the exercise of the option completes the sale: see ante, para 1.22.

5   This is recognised by the statutory definition of sale to be found in the SGA, s 61(1). See also the distinction between 'sale' and 'agreement to sell', ante, para 1.10.

6   A delivery, deed or special statutory form may be required in the case of all gifts, transfers for value of choses in action, mortgages or pledges of chattels.

merely obscures the true position.[1] Early law tended to concentrate on possession,[2] which was protected largely for two reasons, the one proprietary and the other tortious (delictual). During the Middle Ages, the actions in respect of land developed their proprietary side almost exclusively, particularly with the evolution of the real actions in the protection of seizen ('ownership'?).[3] On the other hand, in the case of chattels the law concentrated on the tortious element.[4] The long term effect of this development was the evolution of the dichotomy between real and personal property at common law: the former was governed by the law of 'real property', but the latter mostly developed through the law of crime and tort,[5] the proprietary rules remaining rudimentary (see post, para 19.03) until the efforts of Blackburn.[6] It logically follows that, in the absence of a better title, even a receiver of stolen goods can succeed in an action of conversion.[7]

[19.03] Personal property. At the outset of the consideration of the notion of personal property, three points must be made.[1] First, whatever be the effect of the doctrine of seizin in the law of real property, our common law probably does not recognise any theory of absolute ownership in the case of personal property;[2] and, whilst ss 16–20 of the SGA would appear to recognise an absolute right,[3] when a remedy is sought the courts are only concerned with the relative question of which of the two parties before the court has the better right to the goods.[4] Secondly, the doctrine of estates in real property has no application to personal property:[5] generally speaking, successive interests, eg, life interests, in personal property can only exist behind a trust;[6] and a mortgagor of personalty has only an equity of redemption (see post, paras 25.20, 25.25). Thus, in one sense, the 'ownership' of personalty is indivisible;[7] but there may be concurrent legal

---

[19.02]

1 See Crossley Vaines, *Personal Property* (5th edn), Chapter 4; Bell, *Personal Property*, Chapter 1.

2 Indeed, it may be that no sharp distinction was drawn between 'property', 'possession' and 'seizen': Ibbetson (1991) 107 LQR 480 at 498.

3 Holdsworth, *History of English Law* (3rd edn) vii, p 465.

4 Holdsworth, *ibid*, vii, pp 466–68; TB Smith, *Property Problems in Sale*, p 38; Bridge [1991] LMCLQ 52 at 63 *et seq*.

5 For tortious developments, see post, para 19.04.

6 See *Blackburn on Sale*. Was this work partly responsible for Chalmers assigning such a central place to 'property' in his SGA 1893 (see post, para 19.08)?

7 *Costello v Chief Constable of Derbyshire Constabulary* [2001] 3 All ER 150, CA (see 117 LQR 565).

[19.03]

1 See further Crossley Vaines, *Personal Property* (5th edn), Chapter 4; *Oxford Essays in Jurisprudence*, Chapter V Ownership (by Honore); Goode, *Property Rights and Insolvency in Sale Transactions*, Chapter 1; Bell, *Personal Property*, Chapter 2.

2 But see Maitland (1885) 1 LQR 324; Hudson (1984) 100 LQR at 118, n 60; and post, para 19.08.

3 But see post, Chapter 20. It has been argued that the SGA concept of the property in goods should be expanded into an absolute legal interest analogous to the fee simple in land: see post, para 19.08.

4 See the action in conversion (wrongful interference with goods) considered post, para 19.04. For situations where a plaintiff in conversion may be entitled only to something less than the market value of goods, see post, para 27.30.

5 See Bell, *op cit*, note 1, p 75. Hence the need to develop special rules in the pre-1925 law whereby on intestacy heirlooms devolved with the realty: see Megarry and Wade, *Law of Real Property* (4th edn), pp 343, 388–89, 522–23 (material dropped from later editions).

6 Eg LPA 1925, s 130 (entailed interests in real and personal property); and as to conversion, see post, para 19.05. As to trusts of chattels, see post, para 19.23; and generally Crossley Vaines, *op cit*, note 1, pp 30–32.

7 See the explanations in Crossley Vaines, *op cit*, note 1, p 41; Bell, *op cit*, note 1, p 67.

rights in personal property,[8] as for instance between a bailor and bailee[9] or co-owners,[10] though this rule does not seem to have been extended to instalment sales (see post, para 24.22). Thirdly, the distinction between ownership and possession of goods is not always apparent, because the courts will normally accept possession as *prima facie* proof of ownership; and this lends some substance to the maxim that 'possession is nine-tenths of the law'.[11] This maxim may, for instance, conceal some nice problems in relation to motor vehicles.[12]

The title to goods

[19.04] Wrongful interference with goods.[1] At common law, the buyer or hirer might wrongfully deprive the supplier of the goods supplied in various different ways, which amount to a number of separate and overlapping torts. However, the Torts (Interference With Goods) Act 1977 has made a welcome (albeit modest) start on the long overdue simplification of this excessively technical branch of the law, subsuming all the following different actions under one new statutory tort, termed 'wrongful interference with goods' (s 1):[2]

1 *Conversion.* The Act refers to any act that would have amounted to an act of conversion (trover) at common law (s 1(a)), thus incorporating rather than replacing all the old learning (see further post, paras 19.05–19.06). At common law, a wrongful detention of goods,[3] evidenced by a refusal to deliver them up on demand, amounted to both the torts of detinue[4] and conversion;[5] but the tort of detinue has been abolished by the 1977 Act (s 2(1)), the one area where the two torts might not overlap[6] now being brought within the purview of conversion (s 2(2)).

2 *Trespass.* It is provided that the statutory tort extends to any taking of the goods out of the actual or constructive possession of the supplier (s 1(b)), which at common law would have amounted to trespass to goods.[7]

---

8 For examples of co-ownership, see *Lloyds Bank Ltd v Bank of America* [1938] 2 KB 147, CA; *The Ypatianna* [1987] 3 All ER 893 (inseparably mixed goods); and Goode, *Commercial Law* (2nd edn), pp 228–29. To transfer a good title to personal property, all persons with a concurrent interest must act together: see the *Lloyds Bank* case (above). What if one co-owner murdered the other?

9 As to simple bailment, see ante, para 1.17; as to hp, see ante, para 1.20; as to pledges, see post, para 25.15 *et seq*. The rule does not apply to liens, which create no proprietary interest: see post, para 25.02.

10 See Bell, *op cit*, note 1, pp 74–75; and see post, para 20.22A.

11 See Bell, *op cit*, note 1, pp 76–77. But matters of proof aside, the common law has long preferred ownership to possession: see *Hartrop v Hoare* (1743) Atk 44 (see 103 LQR 182); and post, para 21.13.

12 Eg the accession or intermixture of spare parts (see post, para 19.05); the fixture of accessories (see post, para 25.23); the title to abandoned vehicles (see ante, para 12.17).

[19.04]

1 See generally Winfield and Jolowicz, *Tort* (15th edn), Chapter 17; *Street on Torts* (10th edn), Chapter 4.

2 It should be borne in mind that some such tortious liability may be modified or excluded by the terms of any agreement between the parties: see ante, para 18.03.

3 But there may be no duty on the bailee to return the goods to the bailor: see post, para 24.25.

4 *Strand Electric and Engineering Co Ltd v Brisford Entertainment Ltd* (set out post, para 27.33). But see note 6, below.

5 *Henderson & Co v Williams* (set out post, paras 21.11–12).

6 Where the refusal to return the goods did not amount to a denial of title, as where the bailee had negligently lost the bailed goods, it had never been decided whether there was a conversion.

7 *Wilson v Lombank Ltd* [1963] 1 All ER 740.

3 *Negligence.* The 1977 Act comprehends the tort of negligence (see ante, para 17.13) 'so far as it results in damage to goods or an interest in goods' (s 1(c)). For instance, a bailee in possession of goods will owe a duty of care to his bailor (see ante, para 1.17); and as to product liability, see ante, paras 17.15, 17.19.

4 *Residual torts.* The section also encompasses other torts so far as they result in damage to goods (s 1(d)). This category will include damage by a third party to a bailor's residuary interest in goods,[8] which it has been suggested includes in some circumstances the bailor under an instalment credit contract.[9] It has been expressly extended to product liability claims.[10] Where a bailor at will has recovered in full for the loss from the third party, his bailee may not subsequently recover from that third party.[11]

[19.05] Acts of conversion. These have been summarised as any 'dealing with the goods which amounts to an unjustifiable denial of [P's] rights [in goods] or the assertion of rights inconsistent therewith',[1] and include the following:

1 *Wrongfully taking possession.* This comprehends taking possession in such a manner as to question P's title, as by taking possession under a contract to purchase the goods from a third party,[2] or wrongful seizure by a sheriff in purported execution.[3] On the other hand, the mere receipt of goods as an involuntary bailee is not conversion; and this rule has been extended by statute to the retention of unsolicited goods (see ante, para 8.18). Wrongful repossession by the supplier from his transferee is conversion,[4] as is withholding of goods by an administrator.[5]

2 *Abusing possession.* This may take many forms, such as the sale and delivery to a third party of P's goods or documents of title;[6] or the use of a borrowed car to carry contraband;[7] or a negligent loss of goods by their bailee (see ante, para 19.04); or where D's possession is adverse to P, as where D wrongfully refuses to return goods to P (see post, para 24.25), though this will depend upon the bailee being in breach of

---

8 *Mears v London & South Western Railway Co* (1862) 11 CB (NS) 859.

9 See Street, *op cit*, note 1, p 72; Goode, *Hire Purchase Law and Practice* (2nd edn), pp 775–76.

10 CPA, Sched 4, para 5. See generally ante, para 17.24 *et seq.*

11 *O'Sullivan v Williams* [1992] 3 All ER 385, CA.

[19.05]

1 Winfield and Jolowicz, *Tort* (15th edn), p 588.

2 *Ingram v Little* [1961] 1 QB 31, CA. Taking possession of goods by way of pledge was not a conversion at common law; but it has been made so by the 1977 Act (s 11(2)); see further post, para 25.15.

3 *Neumann v Bakeway Ltd* [1983] 2 All ER 935, CA. *Contra* if the seizure is within the terms of the writ: see post, para 19.16. As to wheelclamping, see *Arthur v Anker* [1996] 3 All ER 783, CA.

4 *The Playa Larga* [1983] 2 Lloyd's Rep 171, CA; recaption (see post, para 24.23). It is also a breach of the undertaking as to quiet possession: see ante, para 12.16.

5 *Barclays Mercantile Business Finance Ltd v Sibee Developments Ltd* [1993] 2 All ER 195 (see further post, para 19.19).

6 *Hollins v Fowler* (1875) LR 7 HL 757; *Union Transport Finance Ltd v British Car Auctions Ltd* [1978] 2 All ER 385, CA; *North West Securities Ltd v Alexander Breckon Ltd* (set out ante, para 10.07); *Long v Jones* [1990] CLY 4033, DC. There is an exception in favour of a bailee of uncollected goods: Torts Act 1977, ss 12–13; *Jerry Juhan Developments SA v Avon Tyres Ltd* [1999] CLY 834.

7 *Moorgate Mercantile Co Ltd v Finch* [1962] 1 QB 701, CA (see Customs and Excise Management Act 1979, s 152(b)).

a duty to return the goods (see post, para 24.45; and also CCA, s 134: see post, para 24.42). On the other hand, a mere contract to sell P's goods to a third party without any transfer of possession does not amount to conversion,[8] though it might amount to an injurious falsehood (see ante, para 17.17).

3   *Residual acts.* Any other action inconsistent with P's rights to the goods may be conversion: this may include signing a delivery order for goods which are delivered under that order;[9] or refusing to hand over the log-book of a car;[10] or deprivation of title by reason of unauthorised accession[11] or intermixture.[12] However, it has now been settled by the Torts Act 1977 that a mere denial of P's title by a person who is not in possession will not without more amount to a conversion (s 11(3)). The Act also confirmed the rules for co-owners, who broadly must act together in dealing with goods (s 10); and, where there is disagreement, there should be application to the court (s 188 of the LPA 1925). For the exception as regards co-owners of an undivided bulk, see post, para 20.22C.

[19.06] Some rules of conversion. Whilst detailed discussion of the requirements of the tort of conversion – in its new statutory guise of 'wrongful interference with goods' (see ante, para 19.04) – is beyond the scope of this work, several of the rules of this very technical tort must be borne in mind, for it is not enough that D has committed an act of conversion (see ante, para 19.05). First, the action is not necessarily available to the owner:[1] it lies only at the suit of one who at the time of D's act of conversion either is in possession of the goods[2] or who at the time of the act of conversion has an immediate right to possess them;[3] and a person who has only an equitable interest is liable to be defeated by a *bona fide* purchaser of the legal title.[4] Secondly, even where P has a legal title, in all cases D may now plead that a third party has a better title to the goods than P (s 8 of the Torts Act 1977), which rule is intended to allow the court power to settle

---

8   *Lancashire Wagon Co v Fitzhugh* (1861) 6 H & N 592.

9   *Smith v Bridgend CBC* [2002] 1 All ER 292, HL, *per* Lord Scott at para 70; and see Winfield and Jolowicz, *op cit*, note 1, 595, n 99.

10 *Bryanston Leasing Ltd v Principality Finance Ltd* [1977] RTR 45. Cf *Douglas Valley Finance Co Ltd v S Hughes (Hirers) Ltd* [1969] 1 QB 738 (special transferable commercial vehicle licences).

11 *Glencore International AG v Metro Trading Inc* [2001] 1 All ER (Comm) 103. Alternatively, consider the removal of items attached to goods, eg severing fixtures (see post, para 25.23). As to cherished vehicle registration numbers, see *Naylor v Hutson* [1994] FSR 63.

12 Eg, fixtures (see post, para 25.23), the mixture of woodchips and resin to make chipboard in *Borden's* case (set out post, para 25.31). See generally Crossley Vaines, *Personal Property* (5th edn), Chapter 19; TB Smith, *Property Problems in Sale*, pp 197–213; Guest (1964) 27 MLR 505; McCormack (1990) 10 LS 293; 12 LS at 203. As to ownership, see ante, para 19.03.

[19.06]

1   *Lord v Price* (1874) LR 9 Exch 54 (auction sale, goods neither removed nor paid for; so unpaid seller entitled to his lien (see post, para 24.10) and the buyer had no immediate right to possession, and thus could not sue a third party in conversion).

2   Eg, *The Winkfield* [1902] P 42, CA (Postmaster General as bailee of mail); *The Jag-Shakti* [1986] 1 All ER 480, PC (pledgee); attornee (1989) 112 Law Com WP 17, n 48; *Costello v Chief Constable of Derbyshire Constabulary* [2001] 3 All ER 150, CA (receiver of stolen goods); and post, para 23.03. Is the explanation of *North West Securities Ltd v Alexander Breckon Ltd* (set out ante, para 10.07; hp) that the financier under the intended transaction was in constructive possession?

3   *Smith v Bridgend CBC* [2002] 1 All ER 292, HL, at para 39. Eg, a bailor where the bailment is at will, either under the terms of the bailment (*Manders v Williams* (1849) 4 Exch 339) or because the bailment has been terminated (see post, para 26.09); one who acquires title under one of the exceptions to the *nemo dat* rule (see post, Chapter 21); and see post, para 25.15, n 3.

4   *MCC Proceeds Inc v Lehman Bros International (Europe)* [1998] 4 All ER 675, CA (not a goods case).

competing claims in one set of proceedings. Thirdly, liability for an act of conversion is strict:[5] it is immaterial that D acted by mistake, or in good faith;[6] and P's contributory negligence is no defence (Torts Act, s 11(1). For contributory negligence, see post, para 27.40). Fourthly, at common law, the only remedy available in an action in conversion was damages, and this remains the general rule:[7] only where D is in 'possession or control of goods' does s 3 of the Torts Act give the court power to order delivery of the goods to P;[8] and in other cases, whether within or outside s 3, D will normally have the choice (see post, para 24.26) of either returning the goods or paying their assessed value (see post, para 27.30). Fifthly, s 9 of the Torts Act makes provision for concurrent actions, so that proceedings may be heard together, whether they arise from concurrent interests in goods[9] or from successive acts of conversion. There may be concurrent actions of conversions for any or all of the following reasons: there are successive acts of conversion in respect of the same goods, eg, a chain of sales; or there are concurrent interests in goods in respect of the same act of conversion; or there are one or more claims for an improvement allowance under s 6 (see post, para 27.30).

Property and title

[19.07] Originally, the common law failed to distinguish between the property in and possession of chattels.[1] As it began to draw such a distinction, the notion of the ownership (or 'general property' in goods) developed, perhaps for the following reasons: (a) in contradistinction to the 'special property' of a pledgee (see post, para 19.08); (b) with an eye to the developing bankruptcy law;[2] (c) the rule *res perit domino* now embodied in s 20(1) of the SGA (see post, para 22.01); and (d) (perhaps?) equitable rights, eg, successive interests in goods (see ante, para 19.03), mortgages and charges of goods (see post, para 25.02). However, in practice the courts tended to concentrate on the availability of remedies rather than any *a priori* theory of rights, so that the concept of 'ownership' has

---

5   At common law, conversion did not lie for negligent loss of goods by a bailee; but such conduct is now within the statutory tort: see ante, para 19.04, n 6; and the Torts Act, s 2(2).

6   *Hollins v Fowler* [1875] LR 7 HL 757 (innocent buyer from thief); *Consolidated Co v Curtis & Son* [1892] 1 QB 495 (innocent auctioneer); wrongful seizure in execution (see ante, para 19.05; n 3); *RH Willis & Son v British Car Auctions Ltd* [1978] 2 All ER 392, CA (innocent auctioneer); *Motis Exports Ltd v Dampskibsselstabet AF 1912, A/S* [1999] 1 All ER (Comm) 571 (carrier misdelivered goods against a forged bill of lading).

7   For the value of the goods and any consequential loss. As to consequential loss, see claims for loss of profit by a supplier (post, para 27.33) or buyer (post, para 29.36).

8   Section 3(1), (2)(a). As to the circumstances where an order for specific delivery is likely to be made, see post, para 24.26.

9   Where more than one person would be entitled to sue in respect of a single act of wrongful interference with goods by D, s 7 attempts to ensure that D does not have to pay out in total more than one *prima facie* measure of damage ('double liability'). *Quaere* whether s 7 applies to bailment: see Bell, *op cit*, pp 83–84. For the relationship between ss 7 and 8, see Winfield and Jolowicz, *Tort* (12th edn), pp 490–92; and for the measure of damages available to the owner of goods let on hp, see post, para 27.30.

[19.07]

1   See ante, para 19.02. The term 'chattel' appears to have developed from the Latin '*capitale*' meaning property. In modern law, it has been largely displaced by the expression 'goods': as to which, see ante, para 2.02.

2   The early bankruptcy statutes, eg, the Act of 1570, did not spell out the different types of matter which fall into an insolvency, but later Acts used the convenient and compendious term 'property' to describe them: see now post, para 19.23.

tended to follow the remedies rather than lead them. In the field of personal property, possession has been protected by the action of trespass,[3] and title by the actions of conversion[4] and detinue,[5] these torts now all being subsumed into the statutory tort of 'wrongful interference with goods' (see ante, para 19.04). However, none of these actions necessarily protect ownership (see ante, para 19.06); and the expression 'owner', used by the SGA on a number of occasions, itself causes trouble.[6]

The SGA also uses two other concepts involving 'ownership': those of 'property' and 'title' (see post, paras 19.08–19.09) and carefully explains the relationship between property and contract (see ante, para 1.10). It insists that the objective of a sale is to transfer the property in goods[7] and makes the seller impliedly promise to do so.[8] As between the seller and buyer, the right to maintain an action for wrongful interference with goods (Torts Act 1977, s 1: see ante, para 19.04) turns not on the whereabouts of the general property in them, but upon having a right to immediate possession (see ante, para 19.06). Indeed, under the SGA, this in turn *prima facie* depends on payment of the price,[9] unless the seller assents to a subsale (see post, para 21.02).

[19.08] The general property in goods. 'Property' is defined by s 61(1) as *prima facie* meaning:

> ... the general property in goods, and not merely a special property.

Perhaps because of its ambiguous origins (see ante, para 19.07), it is difficult to grasp the concept of the general property in goods. However, the 'general property' in goods may be thought of as the ownership of goods; and it has already been pointed out that this ownership is indivisible (see ante, para 19.03). On the other hand, the Act also allows that there may exist at the same time a 'special property' in the same goods. One theoretical view seeks to equate 'general property' with ownership and 'special property' with possession.[1] However, this 'special property' of a pledgee (see ante, para 19.07) is the right of the pledgee-creditor to retain possession of goods as security for his loan and sell them in default (see post, para 25.02); and it is also appears to be an ownership right in property,[2] albeit one inferior to the general property, because the pledgee has the right to sue in conversion anybody who interferes with his right to possess.[3] The explanation has been said to be that the concept of property is like an onion, coming in many layers: when

---

3   *Wilson v Lombank Ltd* [1963] 1 All ER 740.

4   *The Winkfield* [1902] P 42.

5   *Kahler v Midland Bank Ltd* [1950] AC 24, HL.

6   Sections 2(2), 5(1), 21, 24, 25. See also the Factors Act 1889, s 2. For the difficulties to which the expression 'owner' gives rise in relation to the transfer of title, see post, Chapter 21.

7   SGA, s 2(1): see ante, paras 1.07–1.08.

8   SGA, s 12(1): see ante, paras 12.02–12.03.

9   *Lord v Price* (1874) LR 9 Ex 54.

[19.08]

1   See the authorities cited in Curwen (2000) 20 LS 181 at 183.

2   See the discussion in *Donald v Suckling* (1866) LR 1 QB 585; and post, para 25.15. Cf *Lee v Atkinson* (1609) 1 Yelv 172 (speaking of the 'special interest' of a bailee for reward).

3   *Gordon v Harper* (1796) 7 TR 9 (where sheriff wrongfully seizes hired goods, it is the hirer, not the owner, who can sue the sheriff in conversion). *Aliter*, where the bailment is at will: see ante, para 19.06.

the owner holding the general property pledges those goods, what he is doing is stripping off a layer of ownership and passing it to the pledgee; but the owner/pledgor is retaining the central core of the onion.[4] If this analogy is right, the general property is the central core of the onion – that which the owner retains after parting with some lesser rights ownership rights. It may be this core which is indivisible.

[19.09] The concepts of 'property' and 'title'. The notion of 'title' was built upon the availability of an action in conversion or detinue; but the concept of the 'property' in goods is peculiar in that there is no action upon which it is obviously founded.[1] A layman might be forgiven for asking whether it is necessary for our law of personal property to have two concepts of 'property' and 'title'. Yet the SGA draws a clear distinction between them. Part III of the Act is entitled 'Effects of the contract', and is further sub-divided into sections entitled 'Transfer of property as between seller and buyer' (ss 16–20A) and 'Transfer of title' (ss 21–26). 'Title' is nowhere defined in the Act, but at first sight, it is perhaps difficult to see what the Act intended to be the relationship between 'property' and 'title', though it is reasonably clear when the provisions of the two sub-divisions of the Act are to operate: the sections under the heading 'transfer of property as between seller and buyer' (ss 16–20A) are concerned with the very many situations where the dispute is solely between the seller and buyer, or persons standing in their shoes, eg, trustee in bankruptcy or liquidator (see post, para 19.18); whereas the sections under the heading 'Transfer of title' (ss 21–26) provide for the cases where the title to goods is effectively transferred by a person who has no property in them.[2]

What is the relationship of property and title? It is clear that 'property' is the residual notion,[3] and that the basic premise is that he who has the property in goods can usually pass the best title to them (see the *nemo dat* rule: post, para 19.10). However, once having adopted the rule that property passes merely by the contract, the demands of mercantile convenience made it essential to introduce exceptions to the *nemo dat* rule in favour of the *bona fide* purchaser for value (hereafter called the bfp) from the person in possession. In fact, so many such exceptions have been introduced (see Chapter 21) that the basic rule is substantially reversed in practice.[4] It is clear that title is a relative concept: a number of persons may have a title to goods, and it will be a question of which litigant has the better title.[5] Because of the basic rule that title passes with property, it is usually unnecessary to make an enquiry into title as between the immediate parties to a contract of sale. However, where a third party enters the picture, the existence of the exceptions makes an enquiry into title necessary; and, if one of the exceptions operates, then the property in the goods might be regarded as being attracted from the original owner to the bfp to whom the law gives best title. In this sense, title is either superior to property, or the

---

4   Curwen (2000) 20 LS 181 at 192.

[19.09]

1   See Kiralfy (1949) 12 MLR 424. Nevertheless it has been suggested that the two concepts bear a similar (but undefined) meaning: Davies (1987) 7 LS 1 at 7.

2   See Thornely [1958] CLJ 349.

3   *Mischief v Springett* [1942] 2 KB 331.

4   See Chapter 21. On terminology, see Lawson (1949) 65 LQR 352.

5   Whilst it is customary to speak of 'best title', it would presumably usually be more accurate to refer to which of the litigants has the better title because the court only decides the issues as between the parties before it.

exceptions should be read as transferring the best of the competing titles and the general property in the goods.

Two different theoretical views have been adopted on the relationship of property and title.

First view. The chief feature of all proprietary rights is that they are rights in rem and that they bind third parties.[6] It is said to follow from this that it is contradictory for the SGA to speak of a transfer of property as between seller and buyer.[7]

Second view. There is a clear parallel between the title to transfer an estate in land and a title to transfer an interest in goods: according to this view, the concept of 'property' defines the interest in the goods which is being transferred[8] and is analogous to the legal fee simple in land;[9] and the Act's sub-title really just means 'Transfer of property **from** seller to buyer'.[10]

Whilst the latter view has a tempting logical symmetry, the explanation may be rather simpler: that Chalmers adopted this terminology from the common law because he felt that it was not the place of a codifying statute to reverse completely the theoretical basis of the existing law (see ante, para 1.02). The significance of the property in goods is discussed below (see post, para 19.10 *et seq*).

THE INCIDENTS OF PROPERTY

[19.10] From the practical point of view, perhaps the best way of looking at the concept of the general property in goods is as a bundle of legal consequences.[1] Amongst the consequences which follow the general property in goods, the more important are as follows:

1   *Property as the core of the contract.* As the transfer of the property in goods is regarded as the core of a contract of sale (s 2(1) of the SGA: set out ante, para 1.07), a failure to transfer that property is regarded as a breach of the undertaking of a right to sell, regardless of any transfer of possession (see ante, para 12.06). Further, it is a general rule that the buyer acquires no common law real rights in the goods short of his obtaining property or possession of them, as may be seen in regard to sales of a share in an undivided bulk (see post, para 20.22).

2   *Nemo dat quod non habet.* The general rule is that only the person with the general property in the goods can pass a good title to them (see post, para 19.11). It follows that, where an owner makes successive sales of goods, the property *prima facie* passes

---

6   Lawson (1949) 65 LQR 352, especially 359–60.

7   Atiyah, *Sale of Goods* (10th edn), p 309; TB Smith, *Property Problems in Sale*, pp 39–52.

8   The actual definition of a sale in s 2(1) of the SGA speaks of a transfer of the property in goods (see ante, para 1.07), meaning 'general property'; elsewhere the Act allows the seller to limit the title to that general property which he is to pass (SGA, s 12: see ante, para 12.17); and it creates exceptions to the *nemo dat* rule (see post, para 19.10).

9   See Llewellyn (1939) 15 New York LR 159; Battersby and Preston (1972) 35 MLR 268; Lawson, *Introduction to the Law of Property*.

10 See Battersby and Preston, *ibid*, p 277; Battersby [2001] JBL 1.

[19.10]

1   Atiyah, *Sale of Goods* (10th edn), p 313. See also Goode, *Commercial Law* (2nd edn), pp 224–27.

under the first purported conveyance,[2] so that first buyer will have sufficient title to recover the value of the goods in an action in conversion (see post, para 27.30). However, there are many exceptional cases where an innocent person in possession of goods may, regardless of whether he has the property in goods, have a good title to them (see Chapter 21).

3   Res perit domino. Generally speaking, the risk of accidental loss or injury to goods lies upon the person with the general property in them (see post, para 22.01). There is a special rule for some co-owners: see post, para 20.22C. However, property and risk will often be separated where the sale involves a sea transit (see post, para 22.07) and modern commercial codes have tended to divorce the two issues.[3] Risk itself may be relevant to frustration (see post, para 22.17).

4   *Action in tort for damage to goods.* As between the seller and buyer, where one has the property and the other possession of the goods, liability in tort is determined by the law of bailment.[4] However, as against third parties, an action for negligent damage to goods normally lies only at the suit of the owner[4] or possessor,[5] but not both.[6]

5   *Specific relief.* Generally, the seller can only sue for the price when the property has passed[7] and is otherwise left to claim damages (see post, para 27.34). Moreover, the buyer's chance of obtaining specific relief seems to be greater if the property has passed to him.[8]

6   *Debtors and creditors.* The general rule of insolvency is that all goods of which the insolvent has the general property will fall into his insolvency (see post, para 19.23). As against an insolvent buyer, it may be possible for his supplier to avoid this rule by employing a reservation of title clause (see post, para 20.29). However, the buyer from an insolvent seller usually acquires no interest in the goods prior to the passing of property.[9] There is a special rule for some co-owners (see post, para 20.22A).

It is clear, therefore, that there are important results which flow from the passing of property. On the other hand, some other common law jurisdictions, eg, the United States,[10] have taken the view that it is too confusing to have so many of the above-listed issues turning on the passing of property and have instead introduced separate provisions to deal with them. However, the drawback to such a 'specific issue' approach

---

2   *Johnson v Credit Lyonnais* (1877) 3 CPD 32. This rule was substantially reversed by what is now s 8 of the Factors Act 1889: see post, para 21.38.
3   *Benjamin's Sale of Goods* (5th edn), para 5-002. For treatment of the issue in other legal systems, see Smith, *Property Problems in Sale,* pp 23–35.
4   Atiyah, *op cit,* note 1, p 312; and post, para 22.08.
5   Whether the bailee is in possession under a conditional sale, hp or simple hiring. See Goode, *Hire Purchase Law and Practice* (2nd edn), p 776. For negligence, see generally ante, paras 17.13, 17.17.
6   *O'Sullivan v Williams* [1992] 3 All ER 385, CA.
7   See post, para 27.16. *Contra* a bailor for value claiming hire rent: see post, para 27.26.
8   Atiyah, *op cit,* note 1, p 311; and see generally post, para 29.38.
9   *Re Wait* (set out post, para 20.22). For the position with regard to part of a bulk on insolvency, see post, paras 20.22B, 20.22C.
10   See the Uniform Commercial Code, Art 2-105(4). See the account by Burns (1996) 59 MLR 260 at 264–66.

lies in its inability to deal with new problems,[11] leaving some English commentators to cast doubts on the advantages which might be gained by such a change.[12]

[19.11] The *nemo dat* rule. The basic rule of common law is that nobody can transfer a better common law title than he himself possesses, a rule which is conveniently expressed by the Latin maxim *nemo dat quod non habet*:[1] in the context of priorities, this is usually expressed as 'the first in time prevails';[2] and it must be distinguished from the rule that a bfp will defeat one with an equitable interest, eg, right to trace (see post, para 27.14). The operation of the *nemo dat* rule may be illustrated by the following example: suppose a chain of sales from A through B to C, where the title of B is defective in that he did not obtain the property in the goods from A. B can only pass a defective title to C; and A may successfully sue C in tort because he (A) has a better title than C.[3]

The *nemo dat* rule is embodied in s 21(1) of the SGA, which provides that, subject to certain exceptions (see Chapter 21):

> ... where goods are sold by a person who is not the owner thereof..., the buyer acquires no better title to the goods than the seller had.

This section speaks of goods being 'sold' by B and it has been decided that this does not include a mere agreement to sell. In *Shaw v Commissioner of Police*:[4]

> The owner of a Porsche car (A) entrusted it to B to find a buyer, but also signed a letter stating that the had sold the car to B. Relying on that letter, C, a bfp, agreed to buy the car under a contract which did not pass property until B was paid. B never having been paid, the court held that C did not get a good title under the *nemo dat* rule[5] or one of its exceptions.

These exceptions did not apply as follows: (a) the estoppel rule was inapplicable; (b) the buyer in possession rule did not apply because B had not agreed to buy (see further post, para 21.44).

However, assuming a disposition of the property in goods by B, the common law rule would appear to be wider than s 21(1) in respect of both the disposition and the defect of title. Any disposition recognised by law may bring the principle into play, so that it is enough that the goods be pledged or given. As regards the defect of title, it is clear that the principle applies where B has no title whatsoever, or has merely a possessory title;[6]

---

11   Eg, *The Span Terza (No 2)* [1984] 1 WLR 27, HL (ownership of ship's bunkers as between charterer and mortgagee).

12   Atiyah, *op cit*, note 1, p 315.

[19.11]

1   Eg, *Re St Mary's Barton-on-Humber* [1987] Fam 41; [1987] 2 All ER 861. See *per* Lord Cairns LC in *Cundy v Lindsay* (1878) 3 App Cas 459, HL at 463–64.

2   See Bell, *Personal Property*, p 459; and ante, para 7.21.

3   See *National Employers Mutual etc Ltd v Jones* (set out post, para 21.54), where a longer chain included a thief.

4   [1987] 3 All ER 405; [1987] 1 WLR 1332, CA.

5   The reason was 'more fundamental' than the *nemo dat* rule in that B never purported to transfer the property in the goods to C: *per* Lloyd LJ at 410d.

6   *Cundy v Lindsay* (1878) 3 App Cas 459, HL (no title); *North West Securities Ltd v Alexander Breckon Ltd* (set out ante, para 10.07: possessory title in thief).

but it has been taken even beyond this. In the *Mercantile Bank of India Ltd v Central Bank of India Ltd:*[7]

> B pledged some groundnuts to A, acquired custody of them by giving a trust receipt to A (see post, para 25.16) and then pledged the same goods to C. A successfully sued C for conversion.

Whilst it is true that A would not have succeeded if he had given B authority to sell on its behalf,[8] nor if B were a mercantile agent and could pass a good title under the Factors Act,[9] the decision has been severely criticised[10] on the grounds both that it is most unfair that an owner of goods who is in physical possession of them cannot pass a good title and that it is most unusual that an encumbrance should run with goods.[11] Of course, the decision depends on the technicality that A retained legal possession, and B only obtained custody; but the case would appear to create difficulties for the commercial community.

DEBTORS AND CREDITORS[1]

[19.12] It has been pointed out that the whole body of English law could be contained in comparatively few rules had everyone sufficient money to meet the debts and obligations incurred by him.[2] Nowhere is this more obvious than in relation to the rules relating to the passing of property in goods. In principle, an unsatisfied creditor has available to him, since the Insolvency Act 1986, as amended (IA), the following strategies:

(a) To go after particular property owned by the debtor (see post, paras 19.13–19.17).

(b) To go against the debtor himself by way of insolvency proceedings (see post, paras 19.18–19.23). But he cannot so petition whilst goods are included in a county court administration order (see post, para 27.04).

Actions against property

[19.13] If the unsatisfied creditor is considering recouping his loss by action against the property of the debtor, his position depends on whether his debt is secured, meaning whether he has taken the precaution of 'reserving' a proprietary interest in the property of the debtor by way of security for repayment of that debt. Upon default by the debtor, the creditor's position is thus as follows:

---

7   [1938] AC 287; [1938] 1 All ER 52, PC.
8   *Babcock v Lawson* (1880) QBD 284, CA.
9   *Lloyds Bank Ltd v Bank of America* [1938] 2 KB 147, CA.
10 Atiyah, *Sale of Goods* (10th edn), pp 370–71.
11 The decision appears to run counter to *Dunlop Pneumatic Tyre Co Ltd v Selfridge & Co Ltd* [1915] AC 847, HL. Perhaps the two cases can be distinguished on the grounds that the one is concerned with contractual rights and the other with possessory rights.
[19.12]
1   See generally Goode, *Commercial Law*, Chapter 34; Fletcher, *Law of Insolvency* (2nd edn).
2   See Crossley Vaines, *Personal Property* (5th edn), p 465.

(a) If the debt is secured, eg, the creditor is the owner under a conditional sale, hp or simple hiring agreement, or an execution creditor,[1] he may look to that security to recoup the debt (see post, para 19.14), in which case he must hand over to the trustee or liquidator any surplus (see post, para 19.23), but may prove like any other unsecured creditor[2] for any balance due to him (see below). Alternatively,[3] he may surrender his security and prove for his whole debt,[4] just like the unsecured creditors (see below).

(b) If the debt is unsecured, he can obtain a judgment for that debt[5] and then as a judgment creditor levy execution on the property of the judgment debtor (see post, para 19.15). Exceptionally, some categories of creditor have a special right to seize (distrain) goods of the debtor without first obtaining a judgment, eg, a landlord distraining for rent (see post, para 19.17). Where there are multiple debts, the law takes a 'devil-take-the-hindmost' attitude: in the absence of insolvency (see post, para 19.18), the greatest advantage usually accrues to the creditor who first enforces his debt: so, it is no answer to garnishee proceedings (see post, para 27.04) that the debtor is insolvent.[6]

[19.14] Realisation of security. A loan may be secured against a particular piece of property[1] by way of mortgage,[2] fixed charge[2] or pledge (see post, paras 25.15–25.18); or a supplier may seek to reserve title in the goods supplied.[3] In all these cases, an unpaid creditor may seek to recoup his loss by selling that property and repaying himself out of the proceeds.[4]

Administrative receiver. However, where a debtor company instead grants his creditor a floating charge (see post, para 25.02), that charge will normally give the chargee the power in default to appoint a receiver and manager of property within the scope of that charge:[5] such a person may well come within the statutory definition of an 'administrative receiver',[6] in which case he has the powers and duties designated in Part II of the IA (see ss 28–49); but he does not have the power (as does a trustee in

---

[19.13]

1 *Peck v Craighead* [1995] CLY 2847; and see generally post, para 19.15.

2 In the case of realty, any such deficiency is termed 'negative equity'. For the effect of negative equity on the mortgagee's proprietary remedies, see post, para 25.20.

3 Eg, a conditional seller may either seize the goods or sue for their price (see post, para 27.19).

4 *Alliance and Leicester plc v Slayford* [2001] 1 All ER (Comm) 1, CA.

5 Distinguish an action for debt from one for damages (see post, para 27.21).

6 *Reed v Oury* (2001) unreported, High Ct.

[19.14]

1 Distinguish personal security: see post, paras 25.04–25.14.

2 This will create in the debtor an equity of redemption: see post, para 25.20.

3 A supplier may achieve this by a reservation of a right of disposal (see post, para 20.28) or a reservation of the property in goods (see post, para 24.22).

4 If such a realisation produces a surplus after satisfaction of the debt, the right to that surplus depends on the type of security (see post, para 24.22).

5 If a chargee issues instructions to the directors of the debtor company that subsequently becomes insolvent, could the chargee be liable as a 'shadow director' for wrongful trading under s 214 of the Insolvency Act 1986? See ss 214(7), 251; and generally Oditah, *Receivables Financing*, pp 67–68; 102–03.

6 Insolvency Act 1986, s 29(2). The powers of an English receiver and manager are regulated by ss 28–49: see further Oditah [1991] JBL 49.

bankruptcy: see post, para 19.23) to disclaim onerous property.[7] Thus, the receiver may chose to keep the debtor company trading to try to recoup the debts.[8] However, even if the debt is secured by a general charge over all the property of the debtor, this will not normally give the receiver the power to seize and sell property supplied on hp or lease to the debtor,[9] though the position is otherwise in respect of an administrator (see post, para 19.19). There are Government proposals to abolish the right of a secured creditor to appoint an administrative receiver.

[19.15] Levying execution. Where court judgment is handed down for payment of a sum of money, it becomes a judgment debt (see ante, para 3.22), upon which interest normally runs (see ante, para 7.03A). The formal means to enforce this judgment of the law is termed 'levying execution' and may take different forms (see post, para 27.04) according to the nature of the property of the judgment debtor out of which the judgment creditor seeks to satisfy the judgment debt.[1]

The most common forms of execution are seizure and sale of goods (see below) and attachment of debts and earnings,[2] though all forms of execution may be suspended by the insolvency of the judgment debtor.[3] Executing judgment on the goods belonging to the judgment debtor will involve their seizure and sale:[4] this is usually effected by the sheriff or bailiff, who are officers of the High Court and county court respectively; but certain prescribed property cannot be seized (s 15 of the Courts and Legal Services Act 1990). In earlier times, this unpleasant procedure was more commonly used against business debtors; but more recently, there has been a growth of executions against private debtors, whether for public debts, eg, taxes; or commercial debts, eg, mortgages or instalment credit. This has led to demands for the reform of this antiquated law, which needs to balance the needs of creditors, eg, for quick action, with those of debtors, eg, delay.[5]

Execution involves two stages:

1   *Seizure of the goods from the judgment debtor.* The sheriff or bailiff has a limited right of entry into the debtor's premises. Once entered, he is directed to find such of the debtor's goods as might be sold (see below) for the amount stipulated in the writ. In principle, he should seize and immediately physically remove those goods; but in practice, he may with the debtor's co-operation take only legal ('walking') possession, leaving the goods in the physical possession of the debtor (see post, para 19.16). In relation to the seized goods, the fundamental principle is that the judgment creditor is

---

7   See Oditah, *ibid*, pp 192–95.

8   Eg, *Transag Haulage Ltd v Leyland Daf Finance plc* (set out post, para 27.22).

9   Aliter in respect of the reservation of title (see generally post, para 25.29): *Lipe Ltd v Leyland DAF Ltd* [1993] BCC 385, CA. (Criticised by Giddins (1993) BJIBFL 263.)

[19.15]

1   Crossley Vaines, *Personal Property* (5th edn), p 485.

2   See post, paras 27.04–05. As to the effect of an earnings order on other forms of execution, see Administration of Justice Act 1970, s 17(2).

3   Insolvency Act 1986, ss 10(1)(c), 11(3)(d) (administration order: see post, para 19.19); s 128 (liquidation); s 285 (bankruptcy).

4   As to the priority of writs of execution, see *Bankers Trust Co v Galadari* [1987] QB 222, CA.

5   In 1999, the Lord Chancellor commissioned a review of the procedure by Professor Beatson; and, following the latter's report, a Green Paper was produced in July 2001, *inter alia*, on the creation of a single enforcement agency.

in no better position than the judgment debtor so far as the rights of third parties are concerned.[6] Thus, the execution creditor seizing goods held by the judgment debtor on conditional sale,[7] hp or simple hiring has no greater rights as against the supplier than the buyer or hirer has (see ante, para 1.21).

2 *Sale of the seized goods.* Normally, the sale will be by public auction. However, the execution creditor will not necessarily be entitled to retain the benefit of the execution if the debtor becomes insolvent before the execution is completed.[8]

The effect of the above process on the title to goods seized and sold is considered below (post, para 19.16). Even where completed, this process tends to produce very small sums (see post, para 27.04).

[19.16] The title in executed goods. Where goods are seized and sold in execution (see ante, para 19.15), the effect of that process on the title to the goods seized may be divided into three stages:

(a) A writ, or warrant of execution, binds the general property in the goods:[1] in the case of a High Court writ, from the moment it is delivered to the sheriff to be executed;[2] and in the case of a county court warrant, from the moment application is made for the warrant to the registrar.[3] The title of the execution debtor does not at this stage transfer to the court officer, the effect of the provision being to create a sort of charge over the goods;[4] and special arrangements are made to deal with the situation where the execution debtor becomes insolvent at this point.[5] Moreover, at this stage the execution debtor can still transfer such title as he has to a third party[6] and can pass a good title to a bfp without notice of the writ or warrant.[7]

(b) The execution of the writ. Once the sheriff takes possession of goods under a writ of execution, the writ becomes executed and the foregoing exception in favour of the bfp can no longer operate. It has been decided that this will be so even where the sheriff merely takes 'walking possession'.[8]

(c) The sale by the sheriff. Where goods belonging to a third party, but in the possession of the execution debtor, are seized by the sheriff, the interest of the third party is not

---

6   *Holroyd v Marshall* (set out ante, para 9.05). What of co-owned goods? See *Sale and Supply of Goods* (Law Com 215, 1993), para 4.35.

7   Including where there is a *Romalpa* clause (see post, para 25.30).

8   See the Insolvency Act 1986, ss 183, 346. For completion of execution, see IA, ss 183(3), 346(5). For criticism of the incomplete execution rule, see Oditah, *Receivables Financing*, pp 147–49.

[19.16]

1   These statutory rules used to be found in s 26 of the SGA 1893. However, it was considered more appropriate to transfer them to statutes dealing with the administration of justice as follows: for High Court proceedings, they are to be found in the Supreme Court Act 1981, s 138 (as amended); and for county court proceedings in s 99 of the County Courts Act 1984.

2   Supreme Court Act 1981, s 138(1), (3). For definitions, see s 138(4).

3   County Courts Act 1984, ss 99(1), (2), 103(2). For definitions, see s 199(4).

4   *Woodland v Fuller* (1840) 11 Ad & El 859.

5   Insolvency Act 1986, ss 184, 346. See further Evans (2001) 151 NLJ 1882.

6   See *per* Danckwerts J in *Re Cooper* [1958] Ch 922, at 928–29.

7   Supreme Court Act 1981, s 138(2); County Courts Act 1984, s 99(2).

8   *Lloyds and Scottish Finance Ltd v Modern Cars Ltd* (set out ante, para 12.14). As to 'walking possession', see ante, para 19.15.

thereby overridden.[9] However, the sheriff is protected in his seizure and sale of the goods;[10] and a bfp from the sheriff is protected as against the execution debtor's trustee in bankruptcy.[11]

[19.17] Distress.[1] Originally a form of self-help, distress has survived as a statutory remedy by which, *inter alia*, a landlord letting unfurnished premises might without taking court action recover arrears of rent from his tenant. The levying of distress for rent entails the landlord (or his bailiff) seizing from the rented premises personal property found there, provided that it is owned by the tenant;[2] and, in the event that the tenant does not pay off the arrears, there is a statutory right to sell the goods, usually exercised by auction.[3] Certain goods are privileged from distress;[4] and the Law of Distress Amendment Act 1908 lays down a procedure by which a third party whose goods are distrained whilst in the possession of the tenant might extricate those goods from the distress by serving a statutory declaration on the distrainor, assuming the goods-owner who supplied them learns of the distress in time.[5]

The goods supplier. In respect of goods comprised in any hp, conditional sale, consumer hiring or bill of sale, the position is as follows: whilst the agreement is running, the goods can usually be distrained by the landlord,[6] after which any repossession by any third party (eg, goods supplier) is tortious; but once the goods agreement has been terminated (see post, para 26.09), the supplier of the goods has the protection of the 1908 Act.[7] In any event, where the buyer, hirer, debtor or grantor of the bill of sale becomes insolvent, distress proceedings must by stayed;[8] and, even where the process has been completed, the distrainor will not necessarily be able to retain the proceeds.[9]

---

9 The third party can claim the proceeds of sale from the execution creditor. As to interpleader by the sheriff, see post, para 21.06.

10 In his seizure by the writ; and in his sale by statute (see *Benjamin's Sale of Goods* (5th edn), para 7-107, fn 81). *Contra* if the seizure is outside the terms of the writ (see ante, para 19.05); or if the sheriff might 'by making reasonable enquiry have ascertained' the third party's interest, eg, by consulting HPI (see post, para 21.01).

11 Insolvency Act 1986, ss 183(2)(b), 346(7).

[19.17]

1 See generally Howells, *Consumer Debt*, paras 9.52–9.58; *Money Advice, Court Procedure*, p 121; Evans (2001) 151 NLJ 1882. In 2001, the Lord Chancellor issued a Consultation Paper on reform of the process: see [2001] 6 Credit Today 21.

2 Sometimes, it is possible for a third party owner to avoid a seizure either by obtaining in advance a 'landlord's waiver', or by affixing a notice of ownership to goods.

3 Law of Distress Act 1689, s 1 (as amended). Provided there is a 'true sale', this will pass a good title to a bfp: see post, para 21.06. However, there is no true sale where the landlord himself purchases the goods: *Moore, Nettlefold & Co v Sugar Manufacturing Co* [1904] 1 KB 820.

4 Eg, fixtures: *Crossley v Lee* [1908] 1 KB 86, DC (gas engine on hp bolted to floor); and see generally post, para 25.23.

5 Eg, *Lawrence Chemical Co Ltd v Rubenstein* [1982] 1 All ER 653, CA.

6 Except whilst goods the subject of a regulated agreement are subject to default notice: as to which, see post, para 24.30.

7 1908 Act, ss 4, 4A: see CCA, Sched 4, para 5 and Sched 5. It is for this reason that attempts are made to draft agreements so that as the insolvency of the buyer or hirer approaches the agreement is terminated: see post, para 26.09.

8 IA 1986, ss 10(1)(c), 11(3)(d) (administration order: see post, para 19.19); s 128 (liquidation); s 285 (bankruptcy).

9 IA 1986, ss 176, 347. Cf *Re Memco Engineering Ltd* [1986] Ch 86.

Actions against the insolvent debtor

[19.18] Insolvency. The notion of bankruptcy is almost entirely the creature of statute law.[1] First introduced by statute in respect of insolvent traders, by the time of the 1571 Act the law of bankruptcy had a twofold purpose. First, it was to prevent fraud on creditors and secure an equal distribution of the bankrupt's property between them, rather than a devil-take-the-hindmost rule (see ante, para 19.13). Secondly, to allow the person who had become insolvent due to genuine misfortune to make a fresh start by assigning his entire estate to his creditors,[2] after which he will usually be discharged from all debts provable in the insolvency ('bankruptcy debts').[2a] In essence, these remain the rules for personal insolvency:[3] they are untouched by the SGA (s 62(1)) and continue to cause controversy as to the extent to which the system ought to release the debtor from his debts.[4] In Victorian times, the provisions of the bankruptcy legislation were extended to non-traders and a not dissimilar procedure was introduced for the liquidation of insolvent companies registered under the Companies Acts. However, the latter procedures differed in that, whilst a bankrupt's property vests in his trustee and the bankrupt eventually walks free, a liquidator simply assumes the functions of the directors of a company, administers its assets and eventually kills off the company. Considerable disquiet having been expressed at the parallel development of the insolvency rules for natural persons (the Bankruptcy Acts) and registered companies (in the Companies Acts), the two branches of the law were deliberately brought together in the Insolvency Act 1985[5] and consolidated in the Insolvency Act 1986, as amended (IA).[6]

Another innovation by the IA allows the unsatisfied creditor to take a view as to whether the insolvency of his debtor is temporary or permanent:

(a) If he judges the embarrassment to be temporary, the creditor may institute the Administration or Individual Voluntary Arrangement procedures, which are designed to take over the running of the debtor's affairs until the debt is repaid (see post, paras 19.19–19.20), with a fall-back position as below.

(b) If he judges the case hopeless, the creditor may proceed to make the debtor formally insolvent (see post, para 19.21). In this case, he should bear in mind all the following:

   (i)   the position of secured and unsecured creditors (see post, para 19.22);

   (ii) the property available to the insolvency (see post, para 19.24);

   (iii) rogue company directors (see post, para 19.25).

To the consumer-debtor, the above proceedings have the disadvantage that they will be registered with a credit bureau, upon which the debtor is unlikely to be able to obtain

---

[19.18]

1   The policy behind the legislation is traced in *Halsbuy's Statutes* (2nd edn), Vol 2, p 284.

2   The procedure was adapted to deal with criminal bankruptcy in the Powers of Criminal Courts Act 1973, ss 39–41 (as amended): see further ante, para 3.20.

2a Non-proveable debts include parking offences, but not parking charges: (2001) 61 QA 18.

3   In 2001, the Government announced in a White Paper that they propose for most cases to reduce the bankruptcy period to 12 months: see [2001] 2 Credit Today 8.

4   It is not quite true today: some liabilities remain with the insolvent, eg non-proveable debts (see above); and there are restrictions on his obtaining credit (see post, para 19.21).

5   This is particularly relevant as to the circumstances under which the debtor should be allowed to initiate his own insolvency (see post, para 19.21): see Rees (1993) 14 CCA News 4/13–4/14.

6   Except for the provisions relating to the disqualification of directors: see post, para 19.25.

fresh credit, except upon the disadvantageous terms available to 'non-status' debtors (see ante, para 8.36).

For the spring of 2002, the DTI is planning an Enterprise Bible, *inter alia*, to introduce (see ante, para 5.11): 12 month automatic release for non-culpable bankrupts; relinquishment of Crown Preference; and generally to streamline procedure.

[19.19] Administration of registered companies. Besides the little used informal arrangements,[1] the IA offers more formal temporary arrangements under the Administrative Order procedure (ss 8–27, as amended). The latter procedure was created by adapting for a different purpose the model of the receiver appointed by a floating chargee (see ante, para 19.14). Whereas a receiver appointed by the chargee will be operating only for the benefit of that chargee, the Administration Order will enable the creditors generally, including unsecured creditors (s 9(1)), to apply to the court for the appointment of an administrator[2] to run the company and allow it breathing space to attempt to restore it to economic health for the benefit of all interested parties (s 8(2), (3)). During this period, there is frozen (without leave of the court (s 10(2)) all the following: any attempt to procure a winding up resolution (ss 10(1)(a), 11(1)(a)); or of a secured creditor who has consented to the administration (s 9(3)) to enforce any security over the company's property (ss 10(1)(b), 11(3)(c)); or of an owner to repossess without consent goods in the debtor company's possession under any instalment credit agreement (see ante, para 1.03); or to initiate any other proceedings, execution, legal process or distress (ss 10(1)(c), 11(3)(d)). The administrator is also given power to deal with and dispose[3] of property of the company which is subject to a fixed or floating charge (s 248(b): see post, para 19.22), or in the possession of the debtor company under any instalment credit agreement:[4] the protection of the secured creditor is that the administrator must pay for his use of the goods;[5] and that the minimum of the net proceeds of any disposal must be applied towards the over-reached debts according to the ordinary priorities (s 15(4), (5), (6)). The effect of these provisions is illustrated by *Re Atlantic Computer Systems plc*:[6]

> ACS conducted a leasing business for end-users as follows: the end-user would select a computer from a manufacturer; the computer would be sold to a funder who would then supply it at variable rates of interest for a fixed period on hp or lease (head-lease) to ACS and ACS would then sublease it at a fixed rate for a variable period to the end-user. There

---

[19.19]

1 IA, ss 2–7, as amended. These may become more popular with the moratorium scheme introduced by the IA 2000, s 1.

2 Generally speaking, an administrator will not be appointed if the secured creditors have already appointed an administrative receiver (see ante, para 19.14) unless those secured creditors consent (s 9(3)). Administrators and administrative receivers have identical statutory powers (ss 14(1)(a), 42, Sched 1).

3 Section 15. This enables depreciating assets to be dealt with at an early date to maximise value, eg, motor vehicles. But unlike a liquidator (see post, para 19.23), the administrator has no power to disclaim onerous property. See generally Oditah, *Receivable Financing*, pp 201–06.

4 Sections 10(1)(b), 11(3)(c). Eg, *Re David Meek Ltd* [1993] BCC 175, Cty Ct. The sections expressly refer only to hp; but s 10(4) extends this to conditional sales, retention of title agreements (s 251: see post, para 25.29) and chattel leases exceeding three months (s 251).

5 *Barclays Mercantile Business Finance Ltd v Sibec Developments Ltd* [1993] 2 All ER 195 (payment of hire charges).

6 [1992] 1 All ER 476, CA (see 107 LQR 394; 108 LQR 488–90; [1992] JBL at 18–20). For the trade background, see Soper and Munro, *The Leasing Handbook*, pp 309–15.

was an assignment of sub-rentals to a funder.[7] ACS got into financial difficulties and an administration order was made. The administrators of ACS received £1.7m rentals from end-users but made no payments due under headleases to the funders. The funders applied to the court for relief.

The Court of Appeal held in a unanimous judgment:

(a) The court had a **discretion** to treat the head rents as an expense of the administration: the funders had no automatic right to the head rents;[8] but, as a matter of discretion, the funders would be granted an order for payment.[9]

(b) Although the computers were mainly on the premises of end-users, they remained (at 492f) in ACS's 'possession for the purpose of s 11(3)(c)', so that funders were prohibited from taking steps to repossess them without leave of the administrators or the court; but the court would exercise its discretion to grant a repossession order.[10]

Sadly, most administration orders eventually lead to either a compulsory or voluntary liquidation, having just been used as a more flexible way of realising the company's assets.[11]

[19.20] Individual Voluntary Arrangements for natural persons. In practice, many consumer debt situations are resolved informally, perhaps by a refinancing of debts, debt consolidation or further advance (see ante, para 7.04A) and often with the aid of a debt-counsellor.[1] Such arrangements with creditors are only binding on participating creditors if there is a common law composition.[2] However, if it is desired to bind the debtor and all his creditors, the IA offers the fairly popular formal system of Individual Voluntary Arrangements[3] as a measure short of bankruptcy:[4] this system is more expensive than a County Court Administration order (see post, para 27.03), and for that reason less suitable for consumer debts.[5] The procedure establishes a new form of Interim Order, under the protection of which an insolvent individual may negotiate a 'voluntary arrangement' of his affairs with his unsecured creditors (ss 252–63): the debtor must be in a position to petition for his own bankruptcy (see post, para 19.21), so he cannot seek the protection of

---

7   The court thought this was a fixed charge: *per* Nicholls LJ at 492–94. See further post, para 25.02.

8   At 491d–e. In the case of an administrative receiver, such head rents would be automatically payable to the funders; but the CA thought the effect of s 11 was rather to put the administrator in a similar position to a liquidator, except with a rather greater degree of discretion.

9   At 489b–g; 499h. The amount of sub-rent handed over was not to exceed the amount due under the respective head-leases (at 500a). As to how the courts should exercise such discretion in general, see 500h–503a.

10 At 492e–g; 498h–g. Eg, *Re David Meek Ltd* (above). As s 11(3)(c) was never intended to so strengthen the administrators' position in negotiations with funders (at 499c) and because the sub-rents were insufficient to enable the administrators to pay all the outgoings under the head leases (at 499d).

11 Brown [1998] JBL 75; and see post, para 19.21.

[19.20]

1   These are usually a type of ancillary credit business (see ante, para 5.43), which will require a CCA licence (see ante, para 6.27). They may be based in a Money Advice Centre (see ante, para 3.08).

2   As to doubts as to whether such a composition is binding at common law, see Treitel, *Law of Contract* (8th edn), p 118.

3   IA, ss 252–63, as amended. This procedure is to be in addition to, rather than instead of, the rarely used Deeds of Arrangement Act 1914.

4   For simple descriptions, see *Money Advice Services, Court Procedures* (2nd edn), pp 62–64; Howells, Consumer Debt, Chapter 10; Griffiths (1992) 46 CC 5 at 25. See further Pond [1995] JBL 118.

5   And it is usually only suitable where about 50% or more of the total debts is available: (1992) *The Times*, 15 February.

an Interim Order simply to avoid paying debts he could meet. Whilst the Interim Order is in effect, no bankruptcy petition relating to the debtor may be progressed (s 252(2)(a)); nor may any other proceedings, execution or other legal process[6] be progressed except with leave of the court.[7] However, there is no provision comparable to s 11(1)(c), whereby in respect of a company debtor holding goods under an instalment credit contract there is frozen any attempt to repossess the goods without consent (see ante, para 19.19). This would seem to leave intact the effect of any *Smart v Holt* clauses (see post, para 26.09).

If the negotiations are successful, the court may replace the Interim Order by giving approval to an Individual Voluntary Arrangement (IVA): this will bind all unsecured creditors who are parties to it,[8] but may not interfere with the rights of any secured or preferential creditors.[9] It has been said that the key to a successful IVA is a compromise between the interests of the debtor and creditors:[10] if this is unsuccessful, the likely result is bankruptcy proceedings (see post, para 19.21). Notwithstanding the cost (see above) and concomitant non-status (see ante, para 19.18), IVAs have in recent years become relatively popular with consumer-debtors.[11]

[19.21] Insolvency.[1] Under the Insolvency Act 1986 (as amended) (IA), a debtor company may be wound up (ss 73–251) or an individual made bankrupt (ss 264–385) broadly on the petition of creditor or debtor before either the High Court or a designated county court (IA, s 374). If there are insufficient assets in the insolvency to attract a private trustee or liquidator ('insolvency practitioner'), his place will be taken by the Official Receiver (IA, ss 399–401) on payment of the latter's fees.[2]

1 *Creditor's petition.* In the case of an individual debtor, a creditor's bankruptcy petition may be presented only where all the following are satisfied:[3]

(a) The amount of his undisputed net debt exceeds a minimum level, termed the 'bankruptcy level'.[4] A single creditor below this level may take steps to reach this threshold;[5] or instead of bankruptcy consider the alternative county court administration procedure (see post, para 27.04).

---

6 'Legal process' means court actions (see ante, para 19.19); and it has since been extended to include distress (see ante, para 19.17) by s 3 of the IA 2000. But it does not include re-caption (see post, para 24.23).

7 Sections 252(2)(b), 254. For execution and distress, see ante, paras 19.15–17.

8 Section 260(2). But not unsecured creditors who were not: *Re A Debtor* [1994] 1 WLR 264.

9 Without their consent: s 258(4), (5). As to the rights of secured and preferential creditors, see post, para 19.21.

10 Pond (1999) 54 CC4/4.

11 (2001) 30 Credit Finance 4.

[19.21]

1 See generally, Fletcher, *Law of Insolvency* (2nd edn). For a layman's outline, see *Money Advice, Court Procedures* (2nd edn), pp 64–69; Howells, *Consumer Debt*, Chapters 10–13.

2 A petitioning debtor is not entitled to a waiver of the compulsory deposit (£250) against fees: *R v Lord Chancellor ex p Lightfoot* [1999] 4 All ER 583, CA (income support claimant).

3 Section 267. The court has a general power to dismiss or stay the proceedings where appropriate (s 266(3)), eg, where the creditor has behaved improperly.

4 The figure has initially been fixed at £750, which may be increased by statutory order. The gross debt may be reduced by any set-off or counterclaim (see post, para 29.26). The petition should not be founded in any debt(s) bf disputed on substantial grounds. See further Fletcher, *op cit*, note 1, p 102.

5 By acting jointly with other creditors whose debts aggregate to the bankruptcy level; or by buying other debts up to that level (for assignment, see generally ante, para 7.16 *et seq*).

(b) That debt remains payable to the petitioning creditor(s). So the debtor can always avoid the bankruptcy by paying off before service of the petition so much of the debt as exceeds the bankruptcy threshold.[6]

(c) That debt is liquidated (see post, para 27.24), any security being surrendered (see ante, para 19.13).

(d) The debtor appears to have no reasonable prospect of being able to pay that debt as it falls due (s 267(2)).

To make the creditor's task easier by saving him from first having to obtain a judgment for debt (see ante, para 3.22), the IA says that a debtor is deemed to be unable to pay his debts in either of the following circumstances: there has been an unsatisfied execution;[7] or non-compliance with a 'statutory demand'.[8] Further, it had been decided that the statutory demand procedure may be used in respect of debts due under regulated agreements, thereby avoiding the CCA protections for defaulting debtors under regulated agreements.[9] In respect of a debtor company, a similar procedure is available by way of compulsory liquidation by the court (ss 122(1)(f), 123, 221(5)(b), 222–24). Alternatively, the creditors of an insolvent company may oust the directors and wind up the company under the creditors' voluntary winding up procedure (s 97).

2 *Debtor's petition*. Especially in the absence of personal sureties (see post, para 25.05), a debtor may choose to petition for his own bankruptcy (s 272) in order to relieve himself of pressure from his creditors, a proposal which has special attractions where the costs are met by the State.[10] Such an action will usually be undertaken in the county court. The court is first enjoined (ss 273–74 of the IA) to see whether it might be possible to conclude instead an Individual Voluntary Arrangement (see ante, para 19.20); or, failing that, whether to issue a certificate invoking the summary bankruptcy procedure under s 275, initially under the responsibility of the Official Receiver.[10a] In respect of a debtor company, a similar procedure is available by way of a members' voluntary winding up (ss 91–96). Instead of bankruptcy, the debtor may consider the alternative county court administration procedure (see post, para 27.04).

Where a court grants one of the above insolvency petitions, control of the debtor's assets passes to a liquidator or trustee (ss 91, 103, 144–45, 306). The extent of those available assets is considered below (post, paras 19.23–24), together with the system of entitlement to claim on them (see post, para 19.22). Whilst the debtor thus loses control of his assets, he is at the same time protected from most creditors' proceedings (ss 126, 128, 285, 345–47), in respect of provable debts (see ante, para 19.18). However, any malpractice by

---

6 Section 271 (as amended); *Re Marr* [1990] 2 All ER 880, CA.

7 Section 268(1)(b); and see ante, para 19.15. As to what amounts to an unsatisfied execution, see *Re A Debtor* [1996] 2 All ER 211, CA.

8 Section 268(1)(a). The matter is one of substance: *Re A Debtor* [1992] 2 All ER 664. On statutory demands, see generally Fletcher, *op cit*, note 1, p 110 *et seq*; [1991] JBL 70; (1992) 142 NLJ 1452. Cf SGA, s 61(4): see post, para 24.04.

9 *Enid Mills v Grove Securities Ltd* [1996] CCLR 74, CA (see Lawson (1997) 16 Tr LR 34). As to the CCA protections of the debtor following the service of a default notice, see post, para 24.39 *et seq*.

10 As used to be the case under the Bankruptcy (Scotland) Act 1985: see (1990) 45 CC2/17; (1992) 13 CCA News 6/14; 14 CCA News 1/12. But see now the 1993 Act; summarised 48 CC1/15.

10a Fletcher, *op cit*, note 1, pp 138–40; and see further post, para 27.04.

the debtor before or during the insolvency may amount to a criminal offence;[11] there is a specially strengthened system in respect of company directors (see post, para 19.25); and it is expressly made an offence for an undischarged bankrupt to obtain credit without disclosing his status.[12]

[19.22] Secured and unsecured creditors. At the outset, a distinction must be drawn between these two classes of creditors because secured creditors can frequently chose to remain outside the statutory scheme imposed by the IA (s 107).

1   *Secured creditors.* The debt may be secured by the grant of rights over the property of the debtor by way of 'mortgage, charge, lien or other security'.[1] In such a situation, as between themselves, secured creditors normally rank in order of creation of their security (see post, para 25.22). However, as against the liquidator (representing unsecured creditors), the secured creditor may take any of the courses of action above outlined (see ante, para 19.13). Thus, provided only that a secured creditor has taken adequate security, he can normally ensure that he is paid in full regardless of the plight of unsecured creditors (see post, para 19.25). This has caused some problems. First, it has led to reprehensibly secret attempts by creditors to achieve for themselves the status of secured creditors, eg, by a secret sale or mortgage from the debtor. The reply of the law has been to require such transactions to be registered: where the transferor is an individual, under the Bills of Sale Acts (see ante, paras 9.04–9.05); and, where the transferor is a registered company, under the Companies Acts (see post, paras 25.28–25.29). Secondly, a floating charge is normally more vulnerable to unsecured creditors than a fixed charge,[2] which has led to attempts to convert the one into the other.[3] Thirdly, there is the question of whether a set-off (see generally ante, para 7.23) is an 'other security', and is hence preserved from the insolvency.[4]

2   *Unsecured creditors.* Whereas secured creditors usually take in order of priority of creation (see above), unsecured creditors are divided into the following three classes of descending priority. Generally, unsecured creditors take available property rateably within those classes:

(a)   *Preferential creditors.* An IA Schedule lists certain types of debt as preferential.[5] It provides that these shall have priority over all other debts, including any floating charge created by an insolvent company (ss 40(2), 175(2)(b), 251 of the IA); and it

---

11   For bankruptcy offences, see ss 350–62. For offences by an insolvent company and its officers, see ss 206–19. Such offences will usually become apparent during the investigation of the insolvent's affairs: ss 131–34; 288–91, 366–71.

12   Section 360: see generally Goode, *Consumer Credit Law and Practice,* paras 71.110–122. As to credit within the CCA, see ante, para 5.21.

[19.22]

1   IA, ss 248, 383(2). Presumably, 'security' thus includes the rights under a pledge (see post, para 25.15). For mortgages, charges and liens, see generally post, Chapter 25; and for the unpaid seller's lien, see post, para 24.10. For *Romalpa* clauses, see post, para 25.29.

2   See Berg [1995] JBL 433. Eg, a floating, but not a fixed, charge is postponed to preferential creditors (see below).

3   See Goode (1994) 110 LQR 592; criticised by Berg, *ibid.*

4   See Oditah, *Receivables Financing,* p 200.

5   Preferential debts are listed in Sched 6, eg, PAYE, VAT, remuneration of employees. An unsuccessful attempt was made to add consumer prepayments: NCC, 1985/6 Annual Report, p 10.

lays down that, after payment of the expenses of insolvency, these preferential debts shall rank equally amongst themselves (ss 175, 328, 386 of the IA).

(b) *Ordinary creditors*. Apart from the special position of preferential creditors (above), distraining landlords, execution creditors[6] and those with a right of set-off,[7] ordinary creditors rank equally and are paid in equal proportions between themselves.[8] The normal result is payment of a small proportion of his debt to each ordinary creditor, this usually being expressed as a 'dividend' of so-much-per-pound of debt.[9] As a matter of public policy, it may not be possible to contract out of this rule,[10] though there are said to be exceptions to it.[11]

(c) *Deferred debts*. Only when all the preferential and ordinary creditors have been paid in full is any surplus distributed equally between the insolvent's deferred creditors, eg, spouses or company members (ss 329, 107 of the IA).

Finally, it is important to remember that, in the case of personal bankruptcy, only debts which can be proved ('bankruptcy debts': s 382) may take the benefit of the above scheme and that the bankrupt's discharge will only expunge all bankruptcy debts: so, other unprovable debts, eg, fines and security rights (see ante, para 19.18), continue to subsist (s 281(5), (2)), whereas unproven bankruptcy debts are extinguished,[12] eg, the secured debt itself. As to the position of any surety, see post, para 25.04 *et seq*.

[19.23/24] Available property. Insofar as a creditor is not a supplier able to rely on an effective reservation of title clause (see post, para 25.29), or is otherwise unsecured (see ante, para 19.22), it may be vital for him to determine what property has fallen into the insolvency. Thus, an unpaid seller will be reduced to claiming a dividend on his price if he cannot lay claim to the goods supplied,[1] as by exercising his seller's lien or right of stoppage (as to which see post, paras 24.08, 24.17).

The general rule is that the person administering the insolvent estate (trustee or liquidator) steps into the shoes of the insolvent person or company and takes control[2] of whatever interest the insolvent had in real or personal property: in the case of an insolvent natural person, the property actually vests in the trustee (s 306 of the IA); including where the bankrupt has died (s 421), eg, as regards joint tenancies;[2a] whereas

---

6   See respectively, ante, paras 19.17, 19.15.

7   IA, s 323. As to set-offs, see generally ante, para 7.23. See comment by Goode [1986] JBL 431; and generally Derham (1992) 108 LQR 99.

8   IA, ss 107, 328(3). If there is any surplus, there are provisions as to payment of interest (ss 189, 328(4)). As to the payment of interest on debts generally, see ante, para 7.03A.

9   IA, s 324. It has been argued that the position of unsecured creditors should be improved generally rather than adjusted by *Romalpa* clauses (above): see Goodhart and Jones (1980) 43 MLR 489, p 511. But does not a purchase-money security deserve some preference?

10 *British Eagle International Airlines Ltd v Compagnie Nationale Air France* [1975] 2 All ER 390, HL.

11 Oditah, *op cit*, note 4, pp 172–77. See also *Re Charge Card Services Ltd* (set out ante, para 2.27); and Nolan [1995] JBL 485.

12 Where a regulated agreement is improperly executed (see ante, para 9.19), is there a 'bankrupt debt' (s 382(3) – contingent); and is that debt so extinguished? See Howells, *Consumer Debt*, para 12.40.

[19.23/24]

1   Including any *Mareva* injunction (see post, para 29.39).

2   Eg, hire rent due under leases: (*Re Atlantic Computer Systems plc (No 2)* [1990] BCC 454); surplus on any security (see ante, para 19.13). As to the rule for the passing of property, see post, Chapter 20.

2a IA, s 421A (as inserted by IA 2000, s 12). This may require a surviving spouse to vacate the matrimonial home or pay the debts: see (2002) 62 QA 20.

the liquidator of an insolvent company *prima facie* simply takes control of the company (s 145). However, this is subject to any legal or equitable rights that any third party might have in the property.[3] The last-mentioned principle covers the SGA rules governing the passing of property (see post, Chapter 20). The latter rule extends to 'mere equities'[3] and to the important equitable principle that equity regards as complete an assignment of after-acquired property, because of the rule in *Holroyd v Marshall* (set out ante, para 9.05). But an exception is provided by the SGA in respect of sales of unascertained goods by description, which, apart from the legal property in goods (see above), *prima facie* pass no interest: *Re Goldcorp Exchange Ltd* (set out post, para 20.22).

However, if that property is impressed with a trust, the trustee or liquidator *prima facie* takes subject to that trust (ss 144; 283(3)(a) of the IA). For instance, in *Re Kayford Ltd*:[4]

> A mail order business was anxious, in the event of its insolvency, to protect customers who might have sent in money for goods. Their accountants advised the opening of a separate 'Customers' Trust Deposit Account' but the company instead instructed its bank to utilise a dormant deposit account for that purpose. The company subsequently being put into liquidation, it was held that a trust had been created and that the moneys were held in trust for those customers who had sent them.

Megarry J explained:[5]

> No doubt the general rule is that if you send money to a company for goods which are not delivered, you are merely a creditor of the company unless a trust has been created. The sender may create a trust by using appropriate words when he sends the money ... or the company may do it by taking suitable steps on or before receiving the money.

These cautionary words refer to the heavy burden of proof required to show the existence of an express trust:[6] it has been suggested that this is more easily achieved in respect of consumers than trade creditors;[7] and that this could be done by codes of conduct.[8]

Thus, the general rule is that there falls into the insolvency all property beneficially owned by the insolvent at the moment of insolvency (ss 144, 283(1)(a) of the IA) or acquired thereafter.[9] This rule is subject to a number of qualifications:

1   *Subsequent dispositions.* Subject to the consent of the court, any disposition of property owned by the insolvent made after the relevant date is *prima facie* void.[10]

---

3   *Tilley v Bowmans Ltd* [1916] 1 KB 745 (right to rescind for misrepresentation: see generally post, para 26.12). See generally Goode (1987) 103 LQR 433, at 438–47.

4   [1975] 1 All ER 604 (discussed [1985] JBL 456). See also *Carreras Rothmans Ltd v Freeman Matthews Treasure Ltd (In Liq)* [1985] 1 All ER 155 (not a sale case); *Re EVTR* (1987) 3 BCC 389, C.A.

5   At 607. Why is it not a registrable charge (see post, para 27.14)? It is insufficient if the debtor fails to fulfill his promise to set up a trust: *MacJordan Construction v Brookmount Erostin* [1992] BCLC 350, CA ([1992] JBL at 420–21). As to prior payment, see post, para 23.22.

6   Ulph [1996] JBL 482, at 486–87. But such a trust may be struck down by statute as amounting to an undue preference: see below.

7   Ulph, *ibid*, pp 491–93.

8   Suggestion by DTI: see (1996) 14 Fair Trading 2.

9   Section 307. There are also powers under which the liquidator or trustee may disclaim onerous property: IA 1986, ss 178–83, 315–21.

10 IA, ss 127, 284. But remember the rule in *Tailby v Official Receiver* (set out ante, para 7.18). See further Oditah, *Receivables Financing*, pp 63–65.

2 *Statutory registration.* In order to prevent one creditor secretly obtaining the status of secured creditor, statute provides compulsory registration systems (see ante, para 19.22).

3 *Incomplete executions* (see ante, para 19.16).

4 *Swelling the assets.* Besides allowing the trustee or liquidator to avoid executions (see ante, para 19.15), the IA also recognises certain actions which can be brought to swell the assets of a liquidation (ss 112, 213–14 of the IA: see post, para 19.25).

5 Ultra vires *contracts.* Like any other third party dealing with a debtor company in good faith, a creditor can enforce a debt against the company 'free of any limitation under the company's constitution' (s 35A(1) of the Companies Act 1985 (as inserted)).

6 *Avoidable transactions.* The property available to the unsecured creditors on insolvency is increased by setting aside for their benefit a number of types of unsecured transaction thought to have potential for causing inequality. These include transactions defrauding creditors (ss 238–41, 245, 339–42, 423(2) of the IA); transactions at an undervalue (ss 238(2), 340(2) of the IA); general assignments of book debts by a natural person (s 344(2) of the IA); and extortionate credit transactions. Where, in the three years before insolvency, the insolvent company or natural person borrowed money, the liquidator or trustee may claim that the transaction is, or was, extortionate.[11] Unless the creditor disproves this, the court has power to set aside or vary the transaction, recover any money paid to the creditor, or any security held by him, or to direct a taking of accounts (ss 244(4), 343(4) of the IA). In the case of a natural person, the provision dovetails with the general rules relating to extortionate credit bargains in the CCA,[12] though lacking an equivalent set of guidelines (cf s 138 of the CCA).

[19.25] Rogue company directors. Many of the problems which the law has encountered in this respect may be traced back to the decision of the House of Lords in *Salomon v Salomon*:[1]

> S was the sole proprietor of a boot manufacturing business. In 1892, after some 30 years' trading, he decided to incorporate the business as a limited liability company under the Companies Acts. He sold the business to the company, the purchase price being partly satisfied by the issue of paid up shares and partly left on loan secured by a floating charge over the business. The company became insolvent in 1893, S having three roles: director of a liquidated company; principal shareholder and secured creditor. It was held that on incorporation the business became in law an independent person; that S was liable for the debts of the business neither as director nor shareholder; and that his secured loan ranked before the unsecured creditors.

It will be observed that the decision to benefit S follows logically from the effects of incorporation and basically still stands with regard to the position of shareholders and

---

11 The IA defines extortionate (ss 244(3), 343(3)) in terms which are very similar to the CCA definition (s 138(1)): as to the latter, see post, para 29.41.

12 IA, s 343(5), (6). For similar provisions operating in the absence of the debtor's insolvency, see CCA, ss 137–40: see post, para 29.40.

[19.25]

1 [1897] AC 22; [1895–96] All ER Rep 33, HL.

fixed (but not floating) charges (see ante, para 19.21). Exceptionally, the courts have been willing to 'pierce the corporate veil' and look to the person behind the registered company,[2] eg, fraudulent or negligent misstatement (see ante, paras 17.18, 17.20), pre-incorporation contracts (see ante, para 10.15), on insolvency (see ante, para 19.18 et seq). Take the example of a small one-man company: normally, the acts or words of even the dominant director will have been on behalf of the corporate entity, so that only the company will be liable for them;[3] but exceptionally that director may have so acted as to give rise to his personal liability in either tort[4] or contract.[5]

Another example is the so called 'phoenix business', where an unscrupulous businessmen sets up a company, incurring substantial debts and obligations in the name of the company, and then walks away to incorporate a new company to carry on a sometimes almost identical business.[6] It was thought unfair that the moving spirit behind such a business should so triumph: not only have the courts been willing in these circumstances to lift the corporate veil;[7] but there is also a statutory prohibition on a director resuming trading under a new company with a similar name.[8] The IA 1986 also allows for a director to be penalised with regard to the previous business: first, there may be a misfeasance action against a delinquent director to remedy a breach of a duty that director owes to the company (s 112); and secondly, he may be sued for fraudulent or wrongful trading (ss 213, 214). Other statutes allow for the possibility of disqualification of the director;[9] control may be exercised over such individuals by way of personal assurances under Pt III of the FTA (see ante, para 6.08); and there are some strict liability offences (see post, para 28.11). There have been calls for more effort to record serial fraudsters.[10]

---

2   Eg, *Trustor AB v Smallbone (No 2)* [2001] 3 All ER 987; *Noel v Poland* [2002] unreported (deceit). See generally Gower, *Company Law* (6th edn), Chapter 8, esp p 124 *et seq*.

3   *Williams v Natural Life Health Foods Ltd* [1998] 2 All ER 577, HL (not liable for negligent misstatement: see Griffin 115 LQR 36).

4   The director must so act as to create the clear impression that he was holding himself personally answerable: *Williams v Natural Life Health Foods Ltd* [1998] 2 All ER 577 at 583a, HL, *per* Lord Steyn (*obiter*). See Watson and Willekes [2001] JBL 217.

5   *Ojjeh v Waller* [1999] CLY 4405 (making a director personally liable for warranties in respect of goods sold by his company).

6   Fletcher [1989] JBL at 368.

7   Eg, *Creasey v Breachwood Motors* [1993] CLY 383 (making the new company liable for the obligations of the old company; but perhaps overruled in *Ord v Belhaven Pubs Ltd* [1998] CLY 377, CA); Clark, *Product Liability*, pp 67–70.

8   Insolvency Act 1986, s 216. Contravention is both an offence (s 216(4)) and leads to his personal responsibility for any debts incurred by the new company (s 217). These provisions have not been altogether effective: Brickman (1993) 143 NLJ 1614. See also Milman [1997] JBL 224.

9   See the Company Directors Disqualification Act 1986 (as amended). A list of disqualified directors is available.

10   (1999) 54 CC3/32.

CHAPTER 20

THE PASSING OF PROPERTY

INTRODUCTION

[20.01] There are a number of circumstances in which it may be important to determine whether the property in goods has passed from the seller to the buyer (see ante, para 19.10). In such cases, the first question to ask is whether, under the contract, the goods are specific or unascertained (see post, para 20.02); because this important question will determine in relation to the diagram set out below on which side of the bold vertical line the contract falls. Once that issue is determined, except by novation a contract will never cross the bold vertical line in the diagram below.[1] That issue being settled, the rules for the passing of property provide for carefully defined stages. Stage 1 is that the legislature has laid down in s 16 of the SGA the earliest moment at which a contract for the sale of unascertained goods may pass the property in goods (see post, para 20.05).[2] However, the s 16 rule is cast in such a manner that it is automatically satisfied with regard to specific goods. Stage 2 is that, once the previous requirement is met, the property in the goods will pass when the parties so intend (s 17 of the SGA: see post, para 20.06). Stage 3 is that, where the parties do not provide for the passing of property in their contract, s 18 of the SGA lays down a number of different rules, basically according to whether the goods are specific (see post, para 20.08 *et seq*) or unascertained (see post, para 20.15 *et seq*). This pattern may be represented diagrammatically as follows:[3]

	Specific Goods	**Unascertained Goods**
Stage 1		s 16 (unascertained)
Stage 2	s 17	s 17 (ascertained)
Stage 3	s 18, rr 1–4	s 18, r 5

Special rules are laid down for the passing of property in (a) sale or return transactions, where the goods may be specific[4] or unascertained[5] and (b) sales of an unascertained part of a specific bulk (see post, para 20.22).

[20.01]
1. Thus, unascertained goods do **not** become specific when later identified: they become ascertained at Stage 2.
2. As to the special rules for sale or return transactions, see post, para 20.23 *et seq*.
3. There cannot be appropriation before ascertainment (see post, para 20.05); but there may be ascertainment before appropriation (see post, para 20.21).
4. Eg, supply of an item of clothing on sale or return.
5. Eg, supply of cans of beer for a party on sale or return.

Specific and unascertained or future goods

[20.02] Specific/unascertained dichotomy. Section 18 carefully distinguishes between sales of specific and unascertained goods, applying different rules as to the passing of property in the two situations:

(1) Sales of specific goods (see post, paras 20.08–14).

(2) Sales of unascertained goods (see post, paras 20.15–22).

Leaving aside sale or return transactions (see post, paras 20.23–27), the position is this: the term 'specific goods' occurs in the first three rules of s 18 and it presumably has the same meaning in each of them; whereas 'unascertained goods' are dealt with by rule 5. It has already been seen (see ante, para 2.04) that the SGA expressly defines 'specific goods', subject to a contrary intention and leaving aside sales of an undivided share, as:

... goods identified and agreed upon at the time a contract of sale is made;

and inferentially defines 'unascertained goods' as those which are not specific. Several points may be made at the outset:

(a) The expression 'specific goods' is employed in several sections of the SGA;[1] and, especially in view of the express disclaimer, it does not necessarily have precisely the same meaning in all of those contexts.[2]

(b) In the context of the passing of property, it is clear that the test of whether or not the goods are 'specific' is to be applied at the moment of contracting.[3] Goods which do not meet the test are initially unascertained, but may thereafter become 'identified and agreed upon' – at which point they are said to become 'ascertained'.[4]

(c) At the precise moment of contracting, the SGA directs one to see if the goods are 'identified and agreed upon'; that is, whether only those particular goods will satisfy the contract, so that there is no room under the contract for further selection or substitution.[5] Thus, the test of specific goods is not whether the goods are within eye-shot of the contracting parties:[6] the retail purchase of 'one of those widgets on the shelf' may be a sale of unascertained goods; but a buyer who takes one widget from the self-service shelf to the checkout is buying specific goods. Nor do the goods fail to be specific simply because they are not within eye-shot of the parties at the time of their contracting: the upstairs sale of 'the only bottle of wine in my cellar' is specific;[7] whereas the upstairs sale of 'any one of the six identical bottles of wine in my cellar' is a sale of unascertained goods.

[20.02]

1 Sections 6 and 7 (see post, paras 22.10–16); ss 17 and 18; s 19 (see post, para 20.28–29); s 29(2) (see post, para 23.04); s 52(1) (see post, para 29.38).

2 The substance of the test may differ for some other purposes, eg, ss 6 and 7 (see post, para 22.15).

3 As to present and future goods, see post, para 20.03.

4 Under ordinary circumstances, unascertained goods never become specific: see ante, para 20.01.

5 *Benjamin's Sale of Goods* (5th edn), para 1-113; Goode, *Commercial Law* (2nd edn), p 215, the suit example.

6 So, a tin with a label saying baked beans may be sold as specific goods, notwithstanding that the tin may contain rhubarb.

7 Benjamin, *op cit*, note 5, para 1-113, the black horse example.

(d) The matter is one of substance, not form: where what the parties say differs from reality, the test of specificity follows substance rather than form.[8] Thus, to continue with the example of the upstairs sale of a bottle of wine in the cellar, if the parties mistakenly think there is only one bottle when there are several identical ones, the contract is not for the sale of specific goods; whereas, if they think there are several when there is in fact only one, the contract is for specific goods.[9]

[20.03] Section 5. Thinking about the foregoing dichotomy for the passing of property between specific and unascertained goods, it has been seen (see ante, para 2.03) that the poorly drafted s 5(1) establishes the following categories of goods:[1]

1　*Existing goods.* Section 5(1) defines these as either:[2]

(a) Goods owned, but not possessed, by the seller. These would seem to be capable of being either specific or unascertained (see ante, para 20.02) and the s 5 category appears to add nothing to the passing of property in them.

(b) Goods possessed, but not owned, by the seller. It would seem impossible for the seller to pass the property in goods he does not own; and this group would seem to fall also within the definition of future goods (see below).

2　*Future goods.* Section 5(3) recognises that the property cannot pass immediately in such goods; and s 5(1) defines the category as either:[3]

(a) *Goods to be manufactured by the seller.*[4] As such goods do not exist at the time of contracting, it is argued that such goods cannot be specific, because they cannot be identified.[5]

(b) *Goods to be acquired by the seller.* In *Varley v Whipp* (set out ante, para 13.14), all parties proceeded upon the assumption that there was a sale of specific goods within the meaning of s 18, notwithstanding that at the time of contract the reaper was owned by a third party. Certainly, some future goods do fall literally within the wording of the s 61 definition of 'specific goods'.[6] On the other hand, as regards s 18 future goods are expressly referred to only in rule 5 dealing with unascertained goods; and it has been suggested that future goods must always be

---

8　Goode, *op cit*, note 5, 215–16, the cellar wine example.

9　For the application of the rules to identifiable goods, see post, para 20.04.

[20.03]

1　The text sets out the traditional interpretation, though the drafting is infelicitous. Did Chalmers really mean to classify goods only possessed by the seller as 'future goods'?

2　Logically, there should be a third category, goods owned and possessed by the seller; but, as far as the passing of property is concerned, this seems to follow the same pattern as goods owned, but not possessed, by the seller. Or did Chalmers mean to bracket together goods owned by the seller, whether or not possessed by him?

3　Presumably, the position here is the same for the sale of a chance (as to which, see s 5(2); and ante, para 2.03).

4　In view of the pre-SGA cases (see post, para 20.18), why did not Chalmers also mention goods to be grown by the seller?

5　So, all goods 'bought off the drawing board', eg, a suit to be made, a custom-made machine tool, must be unascertained goods. *Contra* where the item is substantially complete at the time of contracting, perhaps only needing some small adjustment.

6　It has been suggested that the property in such goods could not pass under rule 1: *Benjamin's Sale of Goods*, para 1.13. Why not under rule 2, the contract being conditional on the seller being able to buy the goods?

unascertained.[7] Should the concept of specific goods be confined to those identified and owned by the seller at the time of contracting (see post, para 20.04)?

[20.04] Identifiable goods. This issue was considered by the Court of Appeal in *Kursell v Timber Operators Ltd*:[1]

> A contract for the sale of uncut timber then standing in a Latvian forest provided that the buyer might cut and remove all timber of certain minimum specifications within the period of the next 15 years. The buyer paid a first instalment of the price, £30,000.00; but before the buyer could cut much timber, the forest was nationalised, and thereafter performance of the contract became illegal. The arbitrator found that the contract had been frustrated, so that no further part of the price was payable.

This finding was unanimously affirmed by the Court of Appeal, who held that the property in the timber had not passed to the buyer, and that the risk remained in the seller. Several reasons were given for the decision:

(1) The trees were *fructus naturales*, so that the property did not pass until severance.[2]

(2) Notwithstanding a clause in the contract that, if the buyer were prevented by the Latvian Government from cutting any timber, the 15 years was to be extended by the length of the interruption, the commercial object of the contract was frustrated (see the judgment, at 306–12, 314–15. See further post, para 22.14).

(3) Section 18, r 1 did not apply to this case. Lord Hanworth MR was content to find a contrary intention (at 309–310. See further post, para 20.06); but his brethren examined the matter in rather more detail, and concluded that, for two reasons, there was not a sale of specific goods. First, they thought that it was really a contract for the sale of a right of severance, that the trees did not become 'specific or ascertained' for the purposes of s 17 until put in a deliverable state (see post, para 20.12), and that they were not in a deliverable state until cut.[3] Second, they thought that the trees were not specific goods because the contract intended the trees to be measured at the date of cutting, rather than at the date of contracting;[4] but, even if the requisite date was the date of contracting, Sargant LJ said (at 314):

> I cannot think that the timber sold was at the date of the contract identified, or more than identifiable; and in order that the goods may be specific they must ... be identified and not merely identifiable ... For the purpose of the passing of the actual property in goods as distinguished from a right to ultimately claim a title to the goods as against the vendor or volunteers under him, a present identification of the goods as specific goods appears to be required by the statute.

---

7   Atiyah, *Sale of Goods* (10th edn), p 318. Chalmers, *Sale of Goods* (18th edn), p 271 does not go quite so far, saying only that such contracts 'for most purposes would be subject to the same considerations as unascertained goods'.

[20.04]

1   [1927] 1 KB 298, CA.

2   *Per* Lord Hanworth MR at 309–10; and Sargant LJ at 314. As to *fructus naturales*, see ante para 2.02. Another example might be *PYO strawberries*.

3   *Per* Scrutton and Sargant LJJ at 312, 314, who both expressly adopted the reasoning in the Scots case of *Morison v Lockhart* 1912, SC 1017. 'Deliverable state' is considered further post, para 20.12.

4   *Per* Scrutton and Sargant LJJ at 311, 313–14. See also Lord Hanworth MR at 307–08.

The last view that the goods are not specific where only identifiable at the moment of contracting is difficult to reconcile with some of the other cases.[5] The better view may be that, where **all** the contract goods are then owned by the seller and also identified or identifiable[6] at the time of contracting,[7] they are specific;[8] but not where measurement is at the date of cutting.[9]

Stages in the passing of property

[20.05] Stage 1: ascertainment. The basic thesis of the law in respect of the passing of property is to be found in s 16 of the SGA, which provides that, subject to s 20A:[a]

> Where there is a contract for the sale of unascertained goods no property in goods is transferred to the buyer unless and until the goods are ascertained.

This section is concerned with the single issue of the passing of the sole general property in the goods. In form negative[1] and mandatory,[2] its justification is that otherwise there is no method of identifying (ascertaining) the contract goods.[3] In fact, s 16 deals with two possibilities with regard to goods which are unascertained at the time of contracting, eg, a sale of 500 tons of wheat of a certain description:[4]

(1) The goods are purely generic, eg, a contract for the sale of any 500 tons of such wheat.[5] Lacking identification, section 16 continues to prevent the passing of property in such generic goods. Distinguish the sale of an undivided share of specific goods eg, sale of half a race horse, which can amount to a sale of specific goods: see ante, para 2.02.

(2) There is a contract for the sale of 500 tons of wheat out of a cargo of 1,000 tons on a particular ship. Before the cargo is made up, the contract is for the sale of generic goods as in (1) above.[6] However, once the cargo is made up, the source of the contract

---

5   Eg, *Varley v Whipp* (set out ante, para 13.14); *Lord Eldon v Hedley Brothers* [1935] 2 KB 1, CA.
6   Eg, a contract to sell all the black-faced lambs in the seller's flock, that number then being unknown to the parties; the single bottle of wine now in the seller's cellar, the parties not then being in the cellar.
7   Even if the goods cease to be identifiable thereafter: see *Re Stapylton Fletcher Ltd* (set out post, para 20.05A; ESV).
8   As to goods not owned by the seller, see ante, para 20.02.
9   Because at least 15 years would have to be awaited before all the contract goods could be identified: see note 4, above. Compare post, para 22.15.

[20.05]
a   SSGA, s 1(1): see post, para 20.22B.
1   This is not to say that the property in the goods will pass when they are specific or ascertained, for this depends on the intention of the parties: see Stage 2 (post, para 20.06).
2   The ascertainment of the goods is thus a condition precedent to the passing of property: SGA s 2(4)–(6); *Mischeff v Springett* [1942] 2 KB 331.
3   Section 18, rule 5: see post, para 20.15. If the bulk is possessed by a third party, eg, a warehouseman, his mere attornment (see post, para 23.03) to the part-buyer is insufficient to pass the property in the part: *Laurie & Morewood v Dudin & Sons* [1926] 1 KB 223, CA. As to where the part is then separated from the bulk and sub-sold with consent, see post, para 21.02.
4   As to future goods (see ante, para 20.03), eg, goods to be manufactured or grown by the seller, see post, para 20.18.
5   As to generic goods and an unascertained part of a specific whole, see ante, para 2.04.
6   *Re Goldcorp Exchange Ltd* (set out post, para 20.22). See also Goode, *Proprietary Rights and Insolvency in Sales Transactions* (2nd edn), p 17.

goods is agreed, even if the particular grains of wheat due to our buyer are not. Nevertheless, the earlier versions of s 16 not only prevented the property passing,[7] it also prevented the purchaser from acquiring any interest in the contract goods. As this is thought sometimes to work unfairly, the law has been amended to allow for both positive and negative ascertainment (see post, paras 20.05A and 20.05B).

[20.05A] Positive ascertainment. The seller may, after making his contract of sale, do some act in relation to some goods which comply with the contract which clearly shows that he intends to use those goods to fulfill his contract. So he may ascertain the contract goods by physically setting them aside.[1] However, there may also be situations where the contract goods are fleetingly parted from a bulk and then merged back into a bulk. Thus, in *Re Stapylton Fletcher Ltd*:[2]

> ESV and SFL were for many years two entirely separate wine merchant companies who both sold wines to customers and after payment held stocks of wine for them. Shortly before insolvency, the shares in both companies passed to a single owner, but this had not affected their different systems for dealing with wine stocks. Administrative receivers (see ante, para 19.14), appointed by the bank under longstanding debentures securing overdrafts, claimed the stock.

The judge dealt with the receivers claims as against stocks held by the two companies as follows:

(a) ESV traded from two adjoining industrial units: the trading stock was put into unit 13; but, when (say) one case of a particular vintage was sold to a customer on the basis that ESV would store it for him, ESV would take a case of that description out of their stock in unit 13 and put it into the customer reserve in unit 12, where it would be stored unmarked together with identical wine held for other customers. The court held that, on such a removal from unit 13, a case became ascertained as that contracted to a particular buyer and appropriated, even though not delivered to him (see post, para 20.19); and, when merged in the bulk in unit 12, that buyer became an owner in common of a proportion of that bulk.[3]

(b) SFL had sold various quantities of wine held in a bonded warehouse to different buyers, but made no attempt to allocate that wine as between different customers. The court held that at common law this gave the individual buyers no proprietary rights in the wine.[4]

[20.05B] Negative ascertainment (by exhaustion). In one case, S agreed to sell to B 200 quarters of maize out of a parcel of 618 quarters then owned by him and lodged at a certain warehouse. Although S gave B a delivery order,[1] this was held to be a sale of

---

7   Eg, *Re Wait* (set out post, para 20.22). But not risk: *Sterns Ltd v Vickers Ltd* (set out post, para 22.04).
[20.05A]

1   *Pignatoro v Gilroy* (set out post, para 20.19).
2   [1995] 1 All ER 192 (see 110 LQR 509; [1996] JBL 199).
3   See also *Aldridge v Johnson* (set out post, para 20.16).
4   See post, para 20.20. However, this has been achieved by adding two new sections to the SGA (see post, para 20.22B).
[20.05B]

1   The delivery order was held not to be a document of title: see post, para 23.03. If it had been, B could have passed a good title: see post, para 21.49.

unascertained goods, because the buyer could not point to any particular grain and say 'S agreed to sell that to me'.[2] On the other hand, if S had subsequently sold and delivered the remainder of the grain to a third party, it would have become clear which grains were to be delivered to B, so that they would become ascertained by being the only grains left. Following the recommendation of the Law Commission,[3] statutory effect was given to the latter rule by new s 18, rules 5(3) and (4),[4] which are subject to a contrary intention (see post, para 20.07). These new rules are restricted to the situation (new s 18, rule 5(3)):

> Where there is a contract for the sale of a specified quantity of unascertained goods in a deliverable state forming part of a bulk which is identified either in the contract or by subsequent agreement between the parties and the bulk is reduced to (or to less than) that quantity ...

Thus, the new rules do not apply where the goods are specific (as to where parties jointly buy specific goods, see ante, para 2.02); nor where unascertained goods are later delivered (the property may pass on delivery under rule 5(2): see post, para 20.17); nor where there are other separate purchases without delivery from the undivided bulk;[5] nor where the bulk remains greater than the contract amount; nor where the goods are not in a deliverable state (as to when goods are in a deliverable state, see post, para 20.12). However, where there is a contract to sell a specified quantity of unascertained undelivered goods and the bulk is reduced to at most that quantity of deliverable goods, these new rules distinguish according to whether the single buyer is due the goods under one or more contracts.

1   *A single contract buyer.* Confirming the common law,[6] where the single buyer is due all the remaining goods under a single contract, new s 18 rule 5(3)[4] provides that, in the above circumstances, *prima facie:*[7]

> ... if the buyer under that contract is the only buyer to whom goods are then due out of the bulk –
>
> (a) the remaining goods are to be taken as appropriated to that contract at the time when the bulk is so reduced; and
>
> (b) the property in those goods then passes to that buyer.

2   *A multi-contract buyer.* Largely confirming the common law, where the single buyer is due all the remaining goods under more than one contract, new s 18 rule 5(4), provides that, in the above circumstances, *prima facie:*[7]

> Paragraph (3) above applies also (with necessary modifications) where a bulk is reduced to (or to less than) the aggregate of the quantities due to a single buyer under separate contracts relating to that bulk and he is the only buyer to whom goods are then due out of that bulk.

---

2   *Laurie & Morewood v Dudin & Sons* [1926] 1 KB 223, CA. See also *Healy v Howlett* (set out post, para 22.06); and generally Nicol (1979) 42 MLR 129.

3   *Sale of Goods Forming Part of a Bulk* (1993, Law Com No 215), para 4.11.

4   As supplied by the Sale of Goods (Amendment) Act 1995, s 1(2).

5   As to unascertained rights in an undivided share, see post, para 20.22B.

6   See *Wait and James v Midland Bank* (1926) 31 Com Cas 172.

7   See post, para 20.06.

Thus, in the pre-Act case of *The Elafi*:[8]

> A cargo of copra was being shipped from the Philippines, part to Germany and the remainder to Sweden, under a number of bills of lading. Before the ship reached Europe, the material bills, each acknowledging receipt of 500 tons 5% more or less[9] were sold on cif terms to X who resold them to the claimants for delivery in Sweden. Subsequently, it was discovered that more copra had been loaded onto the vessel than that for which bills of lading had been issued: 500 tons of that excess was sold to FF, who resold it to the claimants.[10] In Germany, the vessel discharged all the copra which had been sold to third parties, and the vessel then proceeded to Sweden, where part of the cargo was damaged during the discharge.

Mustill J held that the cargo was ascertained by process of exhaustion when discharge of all the copra sold to third parties was completed in Germany; that the parties had evinced an overriding intention that the property in the remainder of the cargo should pass to the claimants (see post, para 20.06); and that it followed that the claimants had sufficient title to sue the shipowner in tort (see post, para 22.08). His Lordship noted that in this case the ascertainment of the claimants' copra 'had been dealt with automatically by the facts, in the sense that the goods had become ascertained by process of exhaustion'.[11] Whilst *The Elafi* may have been confined to the situation where all the goods due to the buyer remained in the undelivered bulk, new rule 5(4) explicitly extends to the situation where a lesser quantity of goods remain and confirms that the buyer is entitled to the entire bulk.

[20.06] Stage 2: actual intention. Subject to Stage 1, the Act confirms that the passing of property is a question of intention. Section 17(1) provides:

> Where there is a contract for the sale of specific or ascertained goods the property in them is transferred to the buyer at such time as the parties to the contract intend it to be transferred.

Specific and ascertained goods are here coupled together, which seems to suggest that ascertained goods are those which are agreed upon[1] at some time **after** the contract is made.[2] Assuming that the goods are specific or ascertained, s 17(2) reiterates the common law rule[3] that:

> For the purpose of ascertaining the intention of the parties regard shall be had to the terms of the contract, the conduct of the parties, and the circumstances of the case.

---

8   [1982] 1 All ER 208; [1981] 2 Lloyd's Rep 679.

9   Deliveries in excess of 102% were to be accepted at the lower of the contract or market price for tolerances, see further ante, para 13.03.

10   The delivery was in excess of 105% and hence above the contract maximum. It was not challenged that the claimants were entitled to accept the entire delivery: as to which, see ante, para 13.05.

11   At 213. Nor did it matter that the claimants acquired title to part of the goods from X and part from FF, acquisition rather than disposition being the important thing (at 215). See further ante, para 12.03.

[20.06]

1   See ante, para 20.04; and further post, para 20.22.

2   *Per* Atkin LJ in *Re Wait* (set out post, para 20.22), at 630. See also Lord Blackburn in *Seath v Moore* (1886) 11 App Cas 350, HL, at 370.

3   See *Ogg v Shuter* (1875) LR 10 CP 159, CA at 162.

In the case of a written contract, the intention of the parties may become a matter of construction, as in *Re Anchor Line Ltd*:[4]

> There was a contract for the sale of a crane, the price to be paid by instalments subsequent to delivery. Eve J held that the property passed when the contract was made under s 18, r 1 (see post, para 20.09); but the Court of Appeal pointed out that s 18 gives way to a contrary intention, and held that on a true construction of the written contract the parties had shown an intention that the property should not pass until the full price had been paid.

Similarly, the charterparty of a ship (a form of hiring: see ante, para 1.18) may provide that, in relation to the oil on board for the operation of that ship (= bunkers), at the commencement of the charter the property in that oil shall pass under a sale from the shipowner to the charterer, whilst at the end of the charter the remaining bunkers shall be 'resold' to the shipowner.[5] Again, in *The Elafi* (set out ante, para 20.05B) where there was a sale of unascertained goods, Mustill J found that the contract goods had become ascertained,[6] but that s 18 had been ousted (for s 18, r 5, see post, para 20.15). As regards the goods purchased cif from X, the judge could see nothing to displace the ordinary presumption that the property is intended to pass on negotiation of the documents, with the result that intention was fulfilled immediately the claimants' goods were ascertained; whilst in respect of the copra bought from FF, the arbitrators had found a similar intention as a matter of fact.[7] Subsequent conduct may also provide evidence of intention.[8]

One example of an implied contrary intention to oust s 18 receives separate treatment in the SGA, namely where there is a reservation of a right of disposal (see post, para 20.28); and is the basis of *Romalpa* clauses (see post, para 25.30). This attitude has even been extended to an 'all monies' reservation in *Armour v Thyssen* (set out post, para 20.29).

In the case of a consumer supply contract, an express provision as to the passing of property may be an unfair and unreasonable term; whereas in a business contract it may be merely an unreasonable term.[9]

[20.07] Stage 3: deemed intention. Whilst it may be possible in some cases to find a common intention, express[1] or implied,[2] as to the passing of property, most laymen do not act so as deliberately to satisfy such esoteric legal criteria; and, because the common law rejected any other objective test as to the passing of property (see ante, para 19.01), the courts therefore had to lay down a series of more or less arbitrary rules for attributing

---

4   [1937] 1 Ch 1; [1936] 2 All ER 941, CA; *Davy Offshore v Emerald Field Contracting* [1992] 2 Lloyd's Rep 142, CA.

5   See *The Span Terza (No 2)* [1984] 1 WLR 27, HL; *The Saetta* [1994] 1 All ER 851.

6   For a discussion of cif contracts, see post, para 22.07. Of course, the property could not pass when the documents were negotiated because the claimant's goods were not then identified: see post, para 20.19.

7   For appropriation before delivery, see further post, para 20.17.

8   *The Filiatra Legacy* [1991] 2 Lloyd's Rep 337, CA.

9   For unfair terms, see ante, para 11.12 *et seq*; and for unreasonable terms, see ante, para 18.22 *et seq*.

[20.07]

1   Many standard form contracts expressly deal with the point: for standard form contracts, see generally ante, para 11.08.

2   Eg, trade custom: *Lord Eldon v Hedley Brothers* [1935] 2 KB 1, CA, especially *per* Greer LJ at 16–19.

such an intention (usually fictitious) to the parties. These rules have been embodied in s 18 of the SGA; and, in practice, they are very important simply because the parties so seldom evince any intention on this point. On the other hand, s 18 does make it clear that the intention of the parties is paramount, for the opening words of the section are as follows:[3]

> Unless a different intention appears, the following are rules for ascertaining the intention of the parties as to the time at which the property in the goods is to pass to the buyer.

The rules that the section contains will apply not just to sales, but also to quasi-sales and hp transactions. As regards the latter, when the hirer exercises his option, a contract of sale comes into existence and the property passes in accordance with the intention of the parties or under the rules laid down in s 18.

THE PASSING OF PROPERTY IN SPECIFIC GOODS

[20.08] Leaving aside sales on approval, which receive special treatment (see post, para 20.23 *et seq*), the rules of s 18 with respect to the passing of property in specific goods differentiate between conditional and unconditional contracts, making special provision in r 1 for 'unconditional contracts'. The two major uses of the term 'condition' in the law of contract are that of conditions precedent (see ante, para 1.11) and essential stipulations (see ante, para 11.04); and, at first sight, it appears too obvious for argument that 'unconditional contract' in r 1 means a contract not subject to any conditions precedent as to the passing of property. This was the common law position;[1] but the courts have in several cases since 1893 suggested that 'unconditional contract' in r 1 means one without any essential stipulations.[2] Their motive for this apparently illogical attitude seems to have been to avoid the unfortunate effect of the combination of s 11(1)(c) and s 18, r 1 of the SGA 1893, which might in some circumstances have denied a buyer any right of rejection at all.[3] However, this undesirable result has been removed from the law;[4] and it is submitted that it is now safe to regard 'unconditional' in r 1 as meaning 'without conditions precedent' as to the passing of property (see further post, para 20.10).

Unconditional contracts

[20.09] Section 18, rule 1 provides:

> Where there is an unconditional contract for the sale of specific goods in a deliverable state, the property in the goods passes to the buyer when the contract is made, and it is immaterial whether the time of payment or the time of delivery, or both, be postponed.

---

3   Are these 'rules' in fact implied terms? See Bradgate [1988] JBL at 482.
[20.08]
1   See *Street v Blay* (1831) 2 B & Ad 456.
2   Only *Varley v Whipp* (set out ante, para 13.14) seems to have been decided on these grounds.
3   Where there was a contract for the sale of specific goods, the property in which passed to the buyer on formation of the contract: see further my 1st edn, para 20.08.
4   By s 4 of the Misrepresentation Act 1967. The modern version of the limitation on the right to reject is to be found in s 11(4) of the SGA 1979: set out post, para 29.04.

It is usually said that this rule reiterates the position at common law;[1] and an example of the operation of the rule is to be found in *Dennant v Skinner*:[2]

> A rogue, X, attended an auction, and successfully bid for a van. Afterwards, he told the plaintiff auctioneer that his name was King and that he was the son of the proprietor of a well-known firm, King's of Oxford. The plaintiff then knocked down five more vehicles to X, including a Standard car. Afterwards, X went to the auctioneer's office, and asked to be allowed to pay by cheque, repeating that he was from King's of Oxford. The auctioneer allowed him to take the Standard away after he had signed a memorandum in the following terms: 'I agree that the ownership of the vehicles will not pass to me until such time as ... my cheque ... [is honoured]'. X disappeared, and the Standard found its way into the hands of the defendant, a bfp.

Hallett J held that there was a contract of sale between the auctioneer and X made 'by the fall of the hammer' under s 57(2) of the SGA, (set out ante, para 10.10), the identity of X being at that time irrelevant; and that the property passed under s 18, r 1 to X at the time the contract was made, this case being indistinguishable from *Phillips v Brooks*.[3] Nor did his Lordship think the memorandum aided the auctioneer: he pointed out that it merely stated a legal error. This case has given rise to controversy on several grounds not directly relevant to r 1. First, did the auctioneer's mistake as to the identity of X prevent there ever being a contract between the two of them in relation to the five vehicles (see post, para 21.19)? Second, assuming that there was a contract, why did the defendant not plead title under the SGA, s 25 (see post, para 21.43)? Third, why did the memorandum not impliedly revest the property in the auctioneer?[4]

[20.10] So far as the actual wording of r 1 is concerned, the meaning of the terms 'unconditional contract' and 'specific goods' have already been discussed (see respectively ante, paras 20.08; 20.02–04); and the meaning of 'deliverable state' will be dealt with later (see post, para 20.12). It only remains to consider the final words of the rule:

> ... it is immaterial whether the time of payment or the time of delivery, or both, be postponed.

Though immaterial as such, these events are clearly relevant as possibly giving some indication of a contrary intention which may exclude the operation of s 18 altogether. Thus, in *Ward Ltd v Bignall*[1] Diplock LJ commented:

> The governing rule ... is in s 17, and in modern times very little is needed to give rise to the inference that the property in specific goods is to pass only on delivery or payment.

[20.09]

1   *Tarling v Baxter* (1827) 6 B & C 360 (sale of stacked hay. Payment 4 February; delivery 1 May. Held property passed on contracting). See criticism by Grieg, *Sale of Goods*, p 32.

2   [1948] 2 KB 164; [1984] 2 All ER 29.

3   [1919] 2 KB 243 (the rogue North obtained a ring from a jeweller by misrepresenting his identity, and Horridge J held that the rogue obtained a voidable title to the ring).

4   Hallett J merely said that it had not revested the property, but it has been suggested (it is submitted wrongly) that even by appropriate wording it could not have done so. See Atiyah *Sale of Goods* (10th edn), p 315. Cf *The Elafi* (set out ante, para 20.05B).

[20.10]

1   Set out post, para 27.10; [1967] 1 QB 534 at 545.

In *Lacis v Cashmarts*, moreover, the Divisional Court held that in a supermarket or 'cash and carry' shop 'the intention ... is that the property shall not pass until the price is paid';[2] and it may indeed be that s 18 is particularly likely to be ousted in consumer sales and auctions.[3]

Finally, another factor sometimes looked at by the courts in order to ascertain the intention of the parties is any special agreement with respect to the passing of risk, because of the presumption that risk passes with property (s 20(1): see post, para 22.01). However, an agreement with regard to risk is at best an ambiguous indication of the intention of the parties with regard to the passing of property.[4]

Conditional contracts

[20.11] Rules 2 and 3 of s 18 deal with the passing of property in conditional contracts for the sale of specific goods;[1] and, apart from the question of notice (see post, para 20.13), they appear to embody the common law.[2]

Rule 2 provides as follows:

> Where there is a contract for sale of specific goods and the seller is bound to do something to the goods, for the purpose of putting them into a deliverable state,[3] the property does not pass until such thing be done, and the buyer has notice thereof.

This rule seems to be based on *Rugg v Minett*:[4]

> There was a sale by auction as separate lots[5] of a number of casks containing different quantities of turpentine. The agreement provided that, before delivery, the seller was to top up the casks from two of their number, and the price was to be computed at so much for each full cask and a *pro rata* payment for the remainder. Halfway through the process of topping up, the seller stopped for the night, during which all the casks were destroyed by a fire which occurred without fault on the part of either seller or buyer. The court held that the property did not pass until the barrels were topped up; and hence the property and risk only passed to the buyer in respect of the barrels which had been topped up.

Rule 3 provides as follows:

> Where there is a contract for the sale of specific goods in a deliverable state, but the seller is bound to weigh, measure, test, or do some other act or thing with reference to the goods for the purpose of ascertaining the price, the property does not pass until such act or thing be done, and the buyer has notice thereof.

---

2   At 407. Compare *Clarke v Reilly* (1962) 96 ILTR 96.
3   Harvey and Meisel, *Auctions* (2nd edn), p 172.
4   See *Re Anchor Line Ltd* (set out ante, para 20.06); and *Federspiel & Co Ltd v Twigg & Co Ltd* (set out post, para 20.16).

[20.11]
1   The conditions in rr 2 and 3 would appear to be both promissory on the part of the seller and conditional as to the obligations of the buyer: see generally post, para 26.01.
2   As to whether reliance can be placed on pre-Act cases, see ante, para 1.04.
3   For 'deliverable state', see post, para 20.12.
4   (1809) 11 East 210.
5   See now s 57(1), discussed ante, para 10.10. The fact that there were separate lots is important for the doctrine of total failure of consideration: see post, para 29.15.

This rule appears to be founded on *Hanson v Meyer*:[6]

> There was a contract for the sale of all the starch then lying in a certain warehouse at £6 per hundredweight, though the exact weight was unknown to the parties at the time of contracting. The seller gave a note to the buyer which directed the warehousekeeper to weigh and deliver the starch to the buyer. Part of the starch was weighed and delivered, but the buyer became bankrupt; and the rest remained in the warehouse unweighed, and at the seller's expense. The assignees of the buyer unsuccessfully sued in trover for the remainder of the starch.

It would seem that Lord Ellenborough carefully worded his judgment so as to decide no more than that the contract made the weighing a condition precedent to delivery (at 626–27); but the case was taken as an indication of the opinion of the Court of Kings Bench as to the vesting of the general property in the goods:[7] it was so adopted in a number of cases, and subsequently embodied in the SGA.

[20.12] Deliverable state. It will be observed that under r 2 the property in goods does not pass until the goods are put in a 'deliverable state' by the seller, whereas rr 1 and 3 deal with situations where the goods are already in a deliverable state.[1] Presumably, the phrase 'deliverable state' means the same in each case, and is defined by s 61(5) as follows:

> Goods are in a 'deliverable state', within the meaning of this Act when they are in such a state that the buyer would under the contract be bound to take delivery of them.

The expression does not refer to the seller's duty of delivery under s 29 (as to which, see post, para 23.04), but to the state in which the contract requires those goods to be upon delivery. It meaning was considered by the courts in *Underwood Ltd v Burgh Castle Brick and Cement Syndicate*:[2]

> There was a contract for the sale 'free on rail' of a condensing engine weighing over 30 tons, then cemented to the floor of the seller's premises. It was envisaged by the parties that the process of detaching and loading the engine onto a railway truck would take about two weeks and cost about £100; and the contract provided that this was to be done by the seller at his own expense. The seller subsequently detached the engine; but it was severely damaged whilst being loaded, without any fault on the part of the seller, and, apparently, before the buyer had notice that it had been detached. The buyer refused to accept the damaged engine, and the seller argued that the property and risk had passed to the buyer at the time of the accident.

Rowlatt J thought that the parties intended the sale of a chattel, the severed engine, not of a fixture.[3] His decision in favour of the buyer was unanimously affirmed by the Court of Appeal, who stressed the time and money involved in the operation of loading. Bankes and Atkin LJJ were prepared to find a contractual intention that the property should not

---

6   (1805) 6 East 614.
7   See *Blackburn on Sale* (3rd edn), p 187.
[20.12]
1   As to whether this refers only to the whole of the goods, see post, para 20.14.
2   [1922] 1 KB 343; [1921] All ER Rep 515, CA.
3   In a subsequent case, a contract was interpreted as a sale of a right of severance by two members of the CA: *Kursell v Timber Operators Ltd* (set out ante, para 20.04).

pass until the engine was loaded on rail;[4] but all three judges agreed that the engine was not in a deliverable state at the time of the accident because the contract was for the sale on an engine-loaded-on-rail. Bankes LJ explained (at 345):

> A 'deliverable state' does not depend upon the mere completeness of the subject matter in all its parts. It depends on the actual state of the goods at the date of the contract, and the state in which they are to be delivered by the terms of the contract.

It would seem then that 'deliverable state' does not refer to whether or not the goods are deliverable in any literal sense.[5] Thus, if the buyer is not bound to take delivery, that does not necessarily show that the goods are not in a deliverable state, because the contract may contain conditions precedent to the passing of property other than the state of the goods, eg, r 3.[6]

[20.13] Notice. Where r 2 or 3 are applicable (see ante, para 20.11), they are subject to the requirement that something is done, and that the buyer have notice thereof, this last stipulation being an addition to the common law (see ante, para 1.02). The Act does not provide that the seller shall give notice, merely that the buyer shall have notice;[1] and it may be that such notice is to be contrasted with the assent required under r 5.[2] This requirement of notice may provide another explanation of *Underwood's* case (set out ante, para 20.12): even if the engine was in a deliverable state at the time of the accident, the buyer did not know this.[3]

[20.14] Effect of rr 2 and 3. It should be noticed that both rr 2 and 3 are expressed in the negative, and are only applicable where something is to be done by the seller. Thus, it does not follow that once the rule is satisfied the property will pass, as there may be other conditions precedent to the passing of property: for instance, suppose A agrees to buy a second-hand car from B provided that (i) B executes certain repairs and (ii) A's wife likes the colour; when the car is repaired it is put in a deliverable state,[1] but the property will not pass until A's wife approves.[2] Even the negative effect of the rules has a fairly narrow scope: they do not apply where the act is to be done by the buyer;[3] and it has been suggested that they are only applicable where the act in relation to the goods is to be done by the seller before delivery.[4] Moreover, even where it is applicable, the presumption

---

4   At 345, 346. See also *Young v Matthews* (1866) LR 2 CP 127.
5   See *Phillip Head & Sons Ltd v Showfronts Ltd* [1970] 1 Lloyd's Rep 140 (a case under s 18, r 5).
6   Smith (1957–58) JSPTL, at 192; Thornely (1958) CLJ, at 126; and also Atiyah, *Sale of Goods* (3rd edn), p 108, note 7. Thereafter, Atiyah changed his mind: see now *Sale of Goods* (10th edn), p 319, note 48, criticised by Goode, *Commercial Law*, p 183, note 83 (dropped from next edition).

[20.13]
1   It is suggested that 'notice' is here equivalent of 'knowledge': *Benjamin's Sale of Goods* (5th edn), para 5-033.
2   This passive requirement of 'notice' may be compared with the active requirement of 'assent' needed in respect of ascertained goods: see post, para 20.22.
3   Cf *Aldridge v Johnson* (set out post, para 20.16).

[20.14]
1   *Contra* Atiyah, *Sale of Goods* (10th edn), p 322.
2   Insofar as the wife's approval is a condition precedent to contract, this raises other issues: see ante, para 1.11.
3   Even if done on behalf of the seller?
4   *Benjamin's Sale of Goods* (5th edn), para 5-031.

contained in rule 3 would appear to be weaker than that in r 2,[5] and has seldom been applied.[6]

Finally, there is the question whether rr 2 and 3 can operate to pass the property in part of the contract goods. At common law, the property could be passed in part only of the contract goods.[7] But s 18 would appear to be ambiguous on this point.[8] In *Underwood's* case (set out ante, para 20.12), the fact that small part of the engine had already been delivered does not seem to have been considered significant. Even assuming that the property can pass in part of the contract goods, it would appear that this will not of itself prevent the buyer rejecting the goods under s 30(1) on the grounds that the contract quantity has not been delivered.[9]

THE PASSING OF PROPERTY IN UNASCERTAINED GOODS

The rule

[20.15] If the contract is for the sale of unascertained goods, then it must initially be an agreement to sell, because s 16 prevents the property passing until the contract goods have been ascertained (see ante, para 20.05). Once the goods have become ascertained, s 17 states that the property will pass when the parties so intend (see ante, para 20.06); and, in the absence of a contrary intention, the property will pass according to r 5 of s 18, paragraph (1) of which states the general rule as follows:

> Where there is a contract for the sale of unascertained or future goods by description, and goods of that description and in a deliverable state are unconditionally appropriated to the contract, either by the seller with the assent of the buyer, or by the buyer with the assent of the seller, the property in the goods thereupon passes to the buyer. Such assent may be express or implied, and may be given either before or after the appropriation is made.

Unlike rr 2 and 3 (see ante, para 20.11), r 5 is expressed in positive terms: it says that the property **will** pass when **all** the following requirements are fulfilled:

(1) The contract is for the sale of 'unascertained or future goods[1] by description'. It has already been suggested that today most sales will be by description (see ante, para

---

5   Atiyah, *op cit*, note 1, p 323; *Blackburn on Sale* (3rd edn), p 194.

6   *Eldon (Lord) v Hedley Bros* [1935] 2 KB 1, CA; *Nanka Bruce v Commonwealth Trust* [1926] AC 77, PC. Indeed, *The Napoli* (1898) 15 TLR 56 would appear to be the only reported post-1893 case where r 3 has been applied; and it is difficult to see why the buyer's action in conversion in that case should have depended on the passing of property.

7   See *Hanson v Meyer; Rugg v Minett* (both set out ante, para 20.11).

8   Can goods be in a 'deliverable state' where only part of them are in the contract state? Before the amendment of s 11(1)(c) of the SGA 1893 by the Misrepresentation Act 1967, s 4(1) (as to which see ante, para 20.08), the operation of that subsection and s 18, r 2 appeared to conflict with s 30(1). Is this a reason for deducing that the Act did not intend to pass the property in part of the goods?

9   See *Barrow, Lane and Ballard Ltd v Phillip Phillips & Co Ltd* [1929] 1 KB 574 (discussed post, para 22.12); and post, para 20.15, item 2.

[20.15]

1   As to future goods, see ante, para 2.03. The inclusion of future goods here amends the common law by adopting the equitable rule in *Holroyd v Marshall* (see ante, para 9.05) that the buyer may automatically became the owner upon acquisition of the goods by the seller: Goode (1987) 103 LQR at 437, note 5.

13.09); and the concepts of unascertained and future goods have also been considered. It may therefore be that the passing of property in future specific goods (see ante, para 2.03) is governed by this rule.[2]

(2) The goods appropriated to the contract are of the contract description and in a deliverable state. The latter expression presumably has the same meaning as under the other rules.[3] 'Contract description' certainly deals with (all?) matters of quality:[4] no purported appropriation, however, can pass the property in goods which do not comply with the contract description.[5] Nevertheless, it has been held that the property passed where there was appropriated to the contract less (*Aldridge v Johnson* (set out post, para 20.16)) or more than the contract quantity of goods of the contract description (*The Elafi* (set out ante, para 20.05B)), though in the last case it would seem that it is always open to the buyer to reject for breach of s 30.[6]

(3) The appropriation is unconditional. As in the case of the other rules, it is submitted that this refers to the absence of any condition precedent:[7] it may be that such a condition precedent evinces an intention to oust s 18 altogether.[8] On the other hand, it has been suggested[9] that the position is analogous to that in relation to r 3 (see ante, para 20.11): whilst the goods remain to be weighed, etc, by the seller, the property does not pass;[10] but, once that measuring has taken place, the property will pass.[11] An appropriation may be on terms (s 19: see post, para 20.28).

(4) There is appropriation with assent. It is this requirement which usually gives rise to the greatest difficulty; and the two constituent parts, 'appropriation' and 'assent' will be considered separately below (see post, paras 20.16–21). However, it must be remembered that there is little point in searching for an act of appropriation if there is no evidence of assent; and vice versa: both are required before the property will pass.

Appropriation

[20.16] In a contract for the sale of unascertained goods, an act done by one party in relation to certain goods which evinces an intention that the property in those goods

---

2   Goode, *Commercial Law* (2nd edn), p 238. But see ante, para 20.04.

3   See ante, para 20.12. For another view, see Goode, *ibid*, p 238.

4   *Healy v Howlett & Sons* (set out post, para 22.06).

5   *Vigers Brothers v Sanderson Brothers* [1901] 1 KB 608. For comparison of the buyer's rights to reject appropriation and delivery in breach of s 13, see Goode, *op cit*, note 2, p 221, note 32. For appropriation by mistake, see *Benjamin's Sale of Goods* (5th edn), para 5-086.

6   This would give the same answer as in the case of specific goods: see ante, para 20.14. But it may be difficult to reconcile with the old cases such as: *Cunliffe v Harrison* (1851) 6 Exch 903; *Levy v Green* (1859) 1 E & E 969.

7   See ante, para 20.08. *Contra Polar Refrigeration Ltd v Moldenhauer* (1967) 61 DLR (2d) 462; *Ollett v Jordan* [1918] 2 KB 41 (criminal case, said by *Benjamin's Sale of Goods* (5th edn), para 5-072 to be wrong).

8   Eg, *Stein, Forbes & Co v County Tailoring Co* (1916) 86 LJ KB 448.

9   Atiyah, *Sale of Goods* (10th edn), p 336.

10   *National Coal Board v Gamble* [1959] 1 QB 11, DC (prosecution in respect of coal loaded onto a lorry by hopper, priced by weighbridge).

11   *Edwards v Ddin* [1976] 3 All ER 705, DC (prosecution for theft in driving away without paying for petrol).

should pass in pursuance of the contract is termed an 'appropriation'.[1] Two cases may be cited to illustrate the difficulty of determining whether there has been a sufficient appropriation. In *Aldridge v Johnson*:[2]

> There was a contract for the sale 'free on rail' of 100 quarters of barley from a larger bulk then situated in the seller's granary, the price of £215 to be paid as to £23 in cash and the rest in cattle.[3] It was agreed that the buyer was to send his own sacks, which the seller was to fill. The cattle were delivered, and the sacks sent to the seller. The seller filled most of the sacks, but emptied the barley back onto the pile of grain just before he became bankrupt. The buyer sued the seller's assignees in bankruptcy in conversion and detinue to recover the sacks and the barley.

The court held that the buyer was entitled to his sacks,[4] and also to so much of the barley as had been put into sacks,[5] because the property had passed when it was put into the sacks.[6] It has now been made clear that, when the barley was emptied back onto the pile, the buyer became an owner in common of part of that pile.[7]

On the other hand, in *Federspiel v Twigg Ltd*[8] the court came to the opposite conclusion:

> There was a contract for the sale of cycles by a British manufacturer to a foreign buyer, fob a British port (for fob sales, see post, para 22.07). The seller packed and marked the goods in preparation for shipment, and the buyer paid the price. Before the goods could be dispatched to the port of shipment, the seller went into liquidation. The buyer sued the liquidator for conversion of the cycles, alleging that they had been appropriated to the contract and that the property had passed to him.

In rejecting this contention, Pearson J said (at 255–56):

> ... usually, but not necessarily, the appropriating act is the last act to be performed by the seller ... If there is a further act, an important and decisive act to be done by the seller, then there is *prima facie* evidence that probably the property does not pass until the final act is done.

His Lordship was of the opinion that the emphasis throughout was on shipment as the decisive act to be done by the seller, so that *prima facie* it appeared that the earliest time when the parties intended that the property should pass would be on shipment.[9] Nor could his Lordship find anything to displace this presumption.

[20.16]

1   *Per* Pearson J in *Federspiel v Twigg* [1957] 1 Lloyd's Rep 240, at 255. See also *Denny v Skelton* (1916) 86 LJKB 280.

2   (1857) 26 LJQB 296.

3   See ante, para 2.09.

4   But the supplier could not identify which grains were his. This would not matter for conversion (see ante, para 19.05); but was the detinue action therefore misplaced?

5   Cf *Underwood Ltd v Burgh Castle Brick and Cement Syndicate* (set out ante, para 20.12).

6   It has been suggested that such an action will always result in specific recovery: *Williams on Bankruptcy* (18th edn), p 273. This is because the buyer is the co-owner of the bulk (see below), so that he may sue for wrongful interference with goods (see ante, para 19.06).

7   See *Re Stapylton Fletcher Ltd* (set out ante, para 20.05A).

8   [1957] 1 Lloyd's Rep 240.

9   On the question of assent, see post, para 20.20.

[20.17] Delivery. Perhaps the most obvious example of appropriation (see ante, para 20.16) is delivery,[1] a matter which receives special mention in paragraph (2) of r 5:

> Where, in pursuance of the contract, the seller delivers the goods to the buyer or to a carrier or other bailee ... (whether named by the buyer or not) for the purpose of transmission to the buyer, and does not reserve the right of disposal,[2] he is deemed to have unconditionally appropriated the goods to the contract.

Thus, in *Wardar's (Import and Export) Co Ltd v W Norwood & Sons Ltd:*[3]

> There was a sale of 600 out of 6,500 cartons of frozen kidneys then stored in a cold store belonging to the seller's agent. When the buyer's carrier arrived to collect the goods, he found them already stacked on the pavement outside the coldstore. The loading took some four hours, towards the end of which the carrier noticed that the last cartons on the pavement were dripping. The goods were found unfit for human consumption.

The Court of Appeal held that, where a third person in possession of goods sold acknowledges them as the buyer's, there is an attornment which amounts to a delivery in law;[4] that upon such delivery the property passes to the buyer; and that the risk passed with the property.[5]

To satisfy r 5(2), the delivery must be made 'in pursuance of the contract', which implies that the goods must be of the contract description and in a deliverable state (see ante, para 20.15); and, as we shall see later, 'delivery' is defined by the SGA in such a way as to include actual and constructive delivery (see post, para 23.03). Whilst r 5(2) seems to be couched as if it were merely an example of r 5(1), there has been a tendency on the part of the courts to treat appropriation as being synonymous with an actual or constructive delivery. Chalmers concludes that:[6]

> If the term 'delivery' had been substituted for 'appropriation', probably less difficulty would have arisen.

But would this be so? It may be that an actual delivery would clearly show when the property had passed;[7] but it is equally clear that there may be an appropriation notwithstanding that there has not been an actual delivery.[8] Thus, in *Aldridge v Johnson* (set out ante, para 20.16) it was held that the property passed when the grain was put into the buyer's sacks. To say that the difference between this case and *Federspiel v Twigg Ltd* is that in the former case there has been a constructive change of possession does not seem to advance matters much further, because this issue too turns on the intention of the parties.

[20.17]

1   *Per* Parke B in *Wait v Baker* (1848) 2 Ex 1, at 7–8.

2   As to reservation of a right of disposal, see post, para 20.28.

3   [1968] 2 QB 663; [1968] 2 All ER 602, CA.

4   Attornment took place when the third party accepted the carrier's note and indicated the cartons on the pavement: see post, para 23.03.

5   See post, para 22.01. *Contra* if the seller had contracted to deliver the goods to the destination of the carrier's journey instead of its commencement: *Healey v Howlett & Sons* (set out post, para 22.06). As to a sea transit, see *The Elafi* (set out ante, para 20.05B).

6   See Chalmers, *Sale of Goods* (18th edn), p 151.

7   Eg, *Edwards v Ddin* [1976] 3 All ER 705 (a criminal case).

8   Eg, the goods sold to FF in *The Elafi* (above): see ante, para 20.06.

As the position may vary according to the type of unascertained goods involved,[9] the cases on appropriation may usefully be considered according to whether the goods are: (1) to be manufactured or grown by the seller (see post, para 20.18); or (2) generic goods or an unascertained part of a specific whole (see post, para 20.19).

[20.18] Goods to be manufactured or grown by the seller. These will be future goods; and s 5(3) provides that the contract must initially operate as an agreement to sell, though it says nothing about when the property is to pass (see ante, para 20.03). The two types of future goods will be considered separately:

(a) *Goods to be manufactured by the seller*. According to Benjamin:[1]

> Such a contract is *prima facie* a contract for the sale of goods when finished. Normally, therefore, no appropriation will be held to have been made until the goods are completed and ready for delivery; and the buyer must then assent to the appropriation before the property can pass.

Thus, in *Federspiel v Twigg Ltd*[2] Pearson J thought that there had not been a sufficient appropriation, notwithstanding that the goods were packed and marked ready for shipment. A similar reluctance on the part of the courts to find an appropriation in any act by the manufacturer short of delivery is to be seen in the shipbuilding cases.[3] One explanation for this attitude may be that the courts wish to leave the manufacturer a reasonable amount of freedom to allocate his products between different buyers;[4] another possibility might be that there is a special rule for fob contracts (as to which, see post, para 22.07).

(b) *Goods to be grown by the seller*. In *Langton v Higgins*:[5]

> The parties made a contract in January 1858 for the sale at a price per pound of the whole of a crop of peppermint to be grown by the seller in that year. In September 1858, the buyer sent bottles to the seller; and the latter, having weighed the oil, poured it into these bottles. The Court of Exchequer followed *Aldridge v Johnson* (set out ante, para 20.16): it held that the property passed when the oil was poured into the bottles, and that the buyer might sue for conversion of the oil.

It has been suggested that the considerations of flexibility obtaining in the case of a manufacturing seller 'do not apply in the case of goods to be grown by the seller, and here it might well be held that the property in the goods, if sufficiently designated, passes as soon as they come into existence'.[6] However, whilst it is true that there

---

9 A similar variation may be noticed in relation to the cases on the passing of risk, though there is no necessary connection between the two.

[20.18]

1 *Benjamin's Sale of Goods* (5th edn), para 5-090.

2 Set out ante, para 20.16. See also *Hendy Lennox Ltd v Grahame Puttick Ltd* [1984] 2 All ER 152 at 155f. Cf *Donaghey's Rope and Twine Co Ltd v Wright Stevenson & Co* (1906) 25 NZLR 641.

3 See *Mucklow v Mangles* (1808) 1 Taunt 318; *Laing & Sons Ltd v Barclay, Curle & Co Ltd* [1908] AC 35, HL; *Re Blythe Shipbuilding Co and Dry Docks Co Ltd* [1926] Ch 494, CA.

4 Atiyah, *Sale of Goods* (7th edn), p 239: point dropped from later editions. Cf Benjamin, *op cit*, note 1, para 5-091.

5 (1859) 4 H & N 402.

6 Atiyah, *op cit*, note 4, p 239: point dropped from later editions. But should the comparison not be between the manufacturer's distribution (not manufacture) and the farmer's distribution?

cannot be a sale of goods[7] until they come into existence,[8] it does not follow that the property should pass at that moment. Why should the grower not have a similar flexibility in allocating his crop between buyers? Such an argument was suggested in *Langton v Higgins* by Bramwell J, who said *obiter* that he thought the property in the goods did not pass when the oil was made up, notwithstanding that the one buyer had contracted for the entire crop.

It is just possible that there may be one exceptional case, the common law category of 'potential property',[9] where the property passes automatically when the goods come into existence;[10] but it maybe that this is now subsumed into new s 20A (see post, para 20.22B).

[20.19] Generic goods, or an unascertained part of a specific whole. In *Aldridge v Johnson* (set out ante, para 20.16) the property was held to have passed when the seller put goods which conformed with the contract into containers supplied by the buyer.[1] Moreover, just as the goods may become ascertained by process of exhaustion (see ante, para 20.05B), so they may become appropriated by being physically set aside.[2] Thus, in *Pignatoro v Gilroy*:[3]

> There was a contract for the sale by sample of 140 bags of rice to be delivered within 14 days in two lots – 125 bags at a certain wharf, and 15 bags at the seller's premises. In response to the buyer's request, the seller sent the buyer a deliver order for the 125 bags, and also notified him that the 15 bags had been set aside ready for delivery. When the buyer eventually sent for the 15 bags nearly a month after the contractual delivery date, it was found that they had been stolen. The buyer's action to recover part of the price paid was dismissed on the grounds that the property and risk had passed to him.

A common situation which may cause some difficulty is the cash mail order business. Where the seller posts goods of the type ordered, this would seem to be an act of appropriation.[4] But can any act prior to posting amount to an appropriation? Clearly, where the customer's order constitutes an offer and the posting an acceptance,[4a] posting is the earliest moment at which there may be an appropriation: the property may well pass when the contract is made.[5] But if the contract is made at some prior stage,[6] then it is arguable that the buyer may have conferred on the seller a power of selection (see post,

---

7 Where the contract is for the sale of an undivided whole, eg, a cargo, it has been suggested that 'goods' means the whole cargo, and that the property cannot pass until the cargo be made up: Benjamin, *op cit*, note 1, para 21-032.

8 Eg, *Langton v Higgins* (above); *Kursell v Timber Operators Ltd* (set out ante, para 20.04).

9 'Potential goods' have been defined as goods which 'grow naturally out of anything already owned by the seller': Chalmers, *Sale of Goods* (18th edn), p 97.

10 It is debatable whether 'potential property' has survived the Act as a separate category: see Benjamin, *op cit*, note 1, para 5-094.

[20.19]

1 As where petrol is irretrievably mixed with that already in the buyer's car: *Edwards v Ddin* [1976] 3 All ER 705 (criminal case).

2 Provided they conform with the contract description: *Healey v Howlett* (set out post, para 22.06).

3 [1919] 1 KB 459, DC.

4 See *Badische Anilin und Soda-Fabrik v Basle Chemical Works, Bindschedler* [1898] AC 200, HL, which demonstrates the difficulty of trying to consider this in terms of constructive possession.

4a But could cashing the consumer's cheque be an implied acceptance? Cf *IRC v Fry* [2002] 1 CL 101.

5 Compare s 18, r 1, considered ante, para 20.09.

6 Could such goods be in a deliverable state (see generally ante, para 20.12) before packaging is completed?

para 20.20); and it would seem that the same considerations obtain with regard to appropriation as in the case of goods manufactured by the seller (see ante, para 20.18).

[20.20] Assent. Section 18, r 5(1) infers that an act of appropriation by one party cannot pass the property in the goods without the assent of the other (see ante, para 20.15) and adds:

> ... the assent may be express or implied, and may be given either before or after the appropriation is made.

Thus, the rule requires a common intention to pass the property;[1] but in one case Lord Wright observed that this is generally to be inferred from the terms of the contract or the practice of the trade.[2] This, in *Pignatoro v Gilroy*[3] Rowlatt J thought that, by asking for a delivery order, the buyer had assented in advance to the seller's appropriation; but he was also prepared to find a subsequent assent in the fact that the buyer did nothing for a whole month in response to an appropriation made in consequence of his own request.

In considering the problem of implied assent, two situations have to be distinguished:

(1) Where the buyer appropriates with the assent of the seller. In these circumstances, the goods will usually be in the actual or constructive possession of the seller, in which case it will normally be fairly easy to see whether there has been a sufficient appropriation by the buyer and assent by the seller.

(2) Where the seller appropriates with the assent of the buyer. Because the goods will usually be in the actual or constructive possession of the seller, it may be rather more difficult in these circumstances to find an appropriation by the seller and assent by the buyer, as for instance in the mail order business (see ante, para 20.19). It is submitted that the buyer may impliedly assent in advance,[4] by conferring on the seller a power of selection, notwithstanding that the buyer has not seen the stock from which the goods are selected.[5]

This would confirm that the *prima facie* risk in course of post is on the mail order cash buyer;[6] but, on the other hand, it might offer some protection against the insolvency of the mail order trader,[7] who too frequently appears to utilise the customer's advance payments as risk capital.[8]

[20.20]

1 Eg, *Federspiel v Twigg* (set out ante, para 20.16). This active requirement of 'assent' may be compared with the passive requirement of notice required in respect of specific goods: see ante, para 20.13.

2 *Ross T Smyth & Co Ltd v Bailey, Son & Co* [1940] 3 All ER 60, HL, at 66.

3 Set out ante, para 20.19. See also *Aldridge v Johnson* (set out ante, para 20.16).

4 Contra where unsolicited goods are supplied: for the formation of contract in such cases, see ante, para 8.18.

5 Eg, *Pignatoro v Gilroy* (set out ante, para 20.19); *Healey v Howlett* (set out post, para 22.06. *Contra* Atiyah, *Sale of Goods* (10th edn), p 338.

6 See post, para 22.01, and generally ante, para 8.19. Cf where the goods are supplied on sale or return: see post, para 20.23. Distinguish supplies on credit, where there is usually a standard form contract.

7 As to the difficulties, see *Prepayments: Protecting Consumers' Deposits* (1984, National Federation of Consumer Groups); and further post, paras 23.22; 23.27.

8 For other schemes to protect the consumer against the trader's insolvency see: (i) trusts (post, paras 23.22; 27.14); (ii) the Newspaper Mail Order Protection Scheme (ante, para 3.13). Payment by credit card may avoid the insolvency problem: CCA, s 75; see ante, para 16.11.

[20.21] Ascertainment and appropriation. Neither of these processes is defined by the SGA; but appropriation is an act showing an intention that the property in certain goods should pass under the contract. It has been suggested above that ascertained goods are those identified and agreed upon after the contract is made (see ante, para 20.04): this implies that ascertainment is the process of identification of the goods as being the contract goods.[1] Thus, both the acts of ascertainment and appropriation are acts evidencing an intention of a party to a contract of sale. However, an ascertainment shows an intention that certain goods be earmarked as the contract goods;[2] but appropriation evinces an intention that the property should pass in those goods under that contract. Of course, the distinction is rarely considered by the parties,[3] and the one act usually fulfils both purposes,[4] in which case the 'ascertainment' and 'appropriation' take place at the same moment.[5] It is for this reason sometimes erroneously assumed that the two words, ascertainment and appropriation, are interchangeable; and confusion is worse confounded by the fact that the courts sometimes, understandably, use the two terms synonymously.

It would seem there cannot be appropriation before ascertainment; but this rule has been altered as regards the undivided share in a bulk (see post, para 20.22 *et seq*).

Undivided share in bulk

[20.22] The effect of appropriation in equity. At very least, the general effect of the cases seems to be that under the SGA 1893 the goods should be identified before they could be regarded as sufficiently appropriated for the property to pass.[1] Thus, in *Re Wait*:[2]

> W contracted on 20 November to buy a cargo of 10,000 tons of wheat *ex Challenger,* the cargo to be made up the following month. On 21 November, W agreed to sell 500 tons of this cargo to X. The cargo was duly shipped, and, whilst the *Challenger* was at sea, X paid the price to W, who shortly afterwards became insolvent. W's trustee succeeded in claiming the entire cargo.

It was common ground that there had been no appropriation sufficient at law to pass the legal title in 500 tons of the wheat to X; and that X could not acquire any interest in the goods on 21 November, because the goods were then future goods (see ante, para 20.03). However, the majority thought that, before the SGA 1893, when the cargo was made up the buyer would have acquired an equitable lien which floated over the entire cargo.[3]

[20.21]

1 Once ascertained, is it necessarily a breach of contract for the seller to dispose of the goods elsewhere?
2 *The Elafi* (set out ante, para 20.05B).
3 But it will be crucial where the contract evinces an intention as to the passing of property (s 17): see ante, para 20.06.
4 *Per* Mustill J in *The Elafi* (set out ante, para 20.05B), at 215.
5 But see, eg, cif contracts, post, para 22.07.

[20.22]

1 This was the common law, even in the case of potential property (as to which, see ante, para 20.18).
2 [1927] 1 Ch 606; [1926] All ER Rep 433, CA.
3 At 645, 649. But Lord Hanworth MR took the view that such a right could not attach unless and until the contract goods became identifiable, which these never did (at 621–25). Cf *Holroyd v Marshall* (pre-Act case; set out ante, para 9.05); and Worthington [1999] JBL 1.

Atkin LJ responded that, even if there had been such an equitable right, it could not have survived the SGA, arguing as follows (at 635–36):

> It would have been futile in a code of intended for commercial men to have created an elaborate structure of rules dealing with rights at law, if at the same time it was intended to leave, subsisting with the legal rights, equitable rights inconsistent with, more extensive, and coming into existence earlier than the rights so carefully set out in the various sections of the Code.

At the same time, Atkin LJ argued that this did not preclude what he termed rights coming into existence 'dehors' the contract of sale for the following reason (at 636):

> A seller or a purchaser may ... create any equity he pleases by way of charge, equitable assignment or any other dealing with or disposition of the goods, the subject matter of the sale; and he may, of course, create such an equity as one of the terms expressed in the contract of sale.[4] But the mere sale or agreement to sell or the acts in pursuance of such a contract mentioned in the Code will only produce the legal effects which the Code states.

The views of Atkin LJ as to the effect of the sale itself appear to have been confirmed by the Privy Council in *Re Goldcorp Exchange Ltd*:[5]

> G Ltd were dealers in gold and other precious metals. They advertised that they would purchase bullion on behalf of investors on terms that it would be stored and insured free of charge by G Ltd and investors would receive a certificate of ownership and the right to take physical possession of their bullion on giving seven days notice. G Ltd became hopelessly insolvent, the bullion in its possession was claimed by the bank under a debenture and receivers were appointed in 1988 (see ante, para 19.14).

This action was brought by two classes of investor, both of whom had paid G Ltd to purchase gold for them and would as unsecured creditors lose their money unless they could make a proprietary claim on some of the gold (see ante, para 19.22):

1   *Allocated claimants*.[6] Until about 1983, bullion purchased for customers was stored and recorded separately, but thereafter it was pooled. The New Zealand judge held that the effect was this: before 1983, bullion was ascertained and appropriated to individual customers; and thereafter, each pre-1983 customer had a shared interest in the pooled bullion.[7] As there was nothing left for the claimants to demand in specie and very little to trace, they unsuccessfully sought before the Privy Council an equitable lien on all the property of G Ltd at the time of receivership.

2   *Unallocated claimants*.[8] In respect of post-1983 investors, the Privy Council held that in this case there was a mere sale of generic goods so that there was no question of the property passing (see ante, para 20.05), the case being in this respect even stronger than *Re Wait*. As regards the above *dictum* of Atkin LJ concerning proprietary rights arising *dehors* the contract, the Privy Council held that G Ltd's collateral promise in

---

4   As to the creation of such equities as part of the financing of instalment supplies, see post, Chapter 25.

5   [1994] 2 All ER 806, PC (See McKendrick 110 LQR 509).

6   Subsequent English statutory changes (see post, para 20.20A) would, for us, reverse this result for allocated claimants (if they bought from 'bulk'), but not for the unallocated claimants.

7   See also *Re Stapylton Fletcher Ltd* (set out ante, para 20.05A), ESV.

8   It is simply to promise to maintain a fund of bullion to meet commitments to customers, whilst reserving freedom to use the bullion for other purposes. This attitude is supported by Ulph [1996] JBL 482, at 486.

respect of such generic goods could not amount to declaration of trust, nor title by estoppel, nor give rise to a fiduciary relationship. Nor did G Ltd's simple breach of contract impress the price paid with a beneficial interest in favour of the customer.[9]

[20.22A] Co-owners. In its Part entitled 'Transfer of Property as between Seller and Buyer', the SGA 1893 dealt with the transfer of the general property in the goods from one seller to one buyer (see ante, para 19.08). However, it did envisage that ownership of the goods might be divided between more than one person, for it provided that one part owner might sell to another.[1] More recently, the Law Commission sought to clarify the law as to sales and purchases by co-owners;[2] and its recommendations have been enacted in the Sale of Goods (Amendment) Act 1995 (SGAA):

1 *Sale by co-owner.* The SGAA has made clear that the sale of an undivided share by one co-owner to a third party is a sale of goods (see ante, para 2.02). Moreover, the Commission thought that the law already allowed the sale of an undivided share in a larger bulk where that share was stated as a proportion,[3] rather than as a specified quantity (para 2.5): the buyer became a tenant in common of the bulk. Accordingly, the SGAA provides that, if the undivided share is 'specified as a fraction (eg, 1/2) or percentage (eg, 50%)', this is a sale of specific goods (see ante, para 2.04); and hence, it may pass a share in the general property in the goods under the ordinary rules for specific goods (see ante, para 20.08).

2 *Purchases by a co-owner.* Similarly, a purchase of an undivided share 'by fraction or percentage' may pass the property in goods, the buyers becoming owners in common.[4] The SGAA has confirmed that, where there is a sale of a specified quantity of unascertained goods, the goods may subsequently become ascertained by exhaustion (see ante, para 20.05B), so that the property in the remaining bulk may thereupon pass to the buyer.[5] Additionally, case law has decided that, where goods are fleetingly parted from bulk and then merged back into the bulk, the buyer becomes a co-owner of the general property in that bulk.[6]

It is thus clear that the general property in the goods may be divided between several owners. On the other hand, the basic thrust of s 16 is to prevent the general property in the goods passing until the contract goods have become ascertained; and the effect of this was to prevent a buyer of part of a bulk from acquiring any part of the general property in the goods (see ante, para 20.05). The unfair result was that a pre-paying buyer of a specified quantity (not expressed by fraction or percentage) of an identified of a bulk might be reduced to the position of unsecured creditor in the event of his seller's

---

9   See also *Re Stapylton Fletcher Ltd* (above), SFL. See further Ulph, *ibid*, at 488–89, 493–96.

[20.22A]

1   See now, SGA 1979, s 2(2): see ante, para 1.09.

2   In its Report *Sale of Goods Forming Part of a Bulk* (1993, Law Com No 215). For actions in tort, see ante, para 19.05.

3   Para 2.5. See *Benjamin's Sale of Goods* (5th edn), paras 1.080; 1.120.

4   Eg, *Re Goldcorp Exchange Ltd* (set out ante, para 20.22), pre-1983 position of allocated claimants; Goode, *Commercial Law* (2nd edn), pp 229–31.

5   The (above) Commission Report, para 2.4. Eg, goods bought jointly by spouses or a business consortium.

6   *Re Stapylton Fletcher Ltd* (set out ante, para 20.05A), ESV.

insolvency, even where the buyer had obtained a delivery order.[7] Accordingly, the above Law Commission Report recommended (para 4.1) that such a pre-paying buyer should be given an 'undivided share' in the bulk (see post para 20.20B). If all went well with the transaction, in due course the goods would become ascertained (see ante, para 20.05) and that rule would be superseded by the passing of property in the goods themselves under the rules previously considered.[8]

[20.22B] Undivided share in bulk. The problem just elicited (see above, para 20.22A) is primarily likely to arise in certain commodity trades, eg, the facts of *Re Wait* (set out ante, para 20.22), but it could involve private consumers.[1] To meet it, new ss 20A and 20B of the SGA provide a new set of rules applicable in the following circumstances (s 20A(1):[2]

> This section applies to a contract for the sale of a specified quantity of unascertained goods if the following conditions are met –
>
> (a) the goods or some of them form part of a bulk which is identified either in the contract or by subsequent agreement between the parties; and
>
> (b) the buyer has paid the price for some or all of the goods which are the subject of the contract and form part of the bulk.

The new provisions introduced by the SGAA to deal with this situation are carefully restricted by **all** the following requirements:

(1) There is a sale of 'a specified quantity of unascertained goods'. This will exclude a sale of specific goods,[3] such as a sale of a share by 'fraction or percentage' (see ante, para 20.22A).

(2) The unascertained goods are not generic, but form an identified 'bulk'.[4] According to new s 61(1):

> 'bulk' means a mass or collection of goods of the same kind which –
>
> (a) is contained in a defined space or area; and
>
> (b) is such that any goods in the bulk are interchangeable with any other goods therein of the same number or quantity.

For the provision to operate, not only must there be a contractual bulk,[5] but the goods which compose it must be interchangeable (fungible), eg, a cargo of wheat in a named ship (new s 20A(1)(a)). The bulk may be future goods (see ante, para 20.03) or ever-changing, eg, oil being drawn off from a tank and replenished.

---

7   *Laurie Morewood v Dudin* [1926] 1 KB 223, CA; *Re Goldcorp Exchange Ltd* (set out ante, para 20.22). See *Goods Forming Part of a Bulk* (above) paras 2.8; 3.2–4; 3.6.

8   So the buyer's co-ownership under new s 20A (see below) would merely be an interim stage: (above) Commission Report, para 4.9.

[20.22B]

1   Eg, a buyer of a length of carpet from an identified roll. See *Sale of Goods Forming Part of a Bulk* (1993), Law Com No 215, para 4.3.

2   Introduced by s 1(3) of the SGAA 1995.

3   As to specific and generic goods, see ante, para 2.04. See further *Benjamin's Sale of Goods* (5th edn), para 5.111.

4   It is intended that this concept should not extend to the seller's general stock, but be limited to an identified bulk within that stock: see the (above) Commission Report, para 4.3.

5   See also the other examples set out in the (above) Commission Report, 4.3; Benjamin, *op cit*, note 3, para 5.112.

(3) The contract 'goods or some part of them form part of a bulk'; that is, the seller is contractually obliged to derive them from the bulk. This formula should also bring within new s 20A the situation where the buyer has obtained a part-delivery.[6]

(4) That bulk 'is identified either in the contract or by subsequent agreement between the parties'. The reference to 'subsequent agreement' will meet, for example, the case of the sale of a cargo yet to be made up.[6]

(5) The buyer had paid the price.[7] This obviated some insolvency problems: as ordinarily a buyer cannot be forced to pay in advance of delivery (s 28 of the SGA: see post, para 23.16), new s 20A is restricted to the pre-paying buyer,[8] including part-payment.[9]

Where all the above conditions are satisfied, new s 20A may confer on the buyer an undivided share in the bulk (see post, para 20.22C). However, new s 20A(2) gives the parties the freedom to contract out of this rule, in which case the proprietary rights will only pass according to the traditional rules.[10]

[20.22C] The buyer's undivided share. As soon as the conditions specified in new s 20A(1) are met (see ante, para 20.22B), 'or at such later time as the parties may agree',[1] new s 20A(2) provides that:

(a) property in an undivided share in the bulk is transferred to the buyer, and

(b) the buyer becomes an owner in common of the bulk.

So, the buyer does not at that point become the legal owner of the goods themselves, the passing of the property in which remains governed by the ordinary rules (see ante, para 20.15 et seq). Instead, under new s 20A(1) the buyer becomes a proportionate owner of the bulk: para (a) describes the interest (see ante, para 19.10) and risk[1a] that is passed to the buyer, whilst para (b) explains how that interest is in principle to be reconciled to that of other co-owners in the bulk, including as to risk (see post, para 22.01). In quantifying that interest, 'the basic idea is that the buyer's share is the share which the quantity bought and paid for bears to the quantity in the bulk'.[2] Suppose part sale(s) of a bulk of 90 widgets owned by S:

(1) The buyer's undivided share 'shall be such share as the quantity of goods paid for and due to the buyer out of the bulk bear to the quantity of goods in the bulk at the time' (s 20A(3)). For instance, if B agrees to buy 20 widgets from the bulk and pays S

---

6 Eg, *Re Wait* (set out ante, para 20.22). See further the (above) Commission Report, para 4.5.

7 New s 20A(1)(b). As to what amounts to payment of the price, see post, para 23.14.

8 See the (above) Commission Report, para 4.6. As to an argument for extending this right to a buyer who has not pre-paid, see Goode, *Commercial Law* (2nd edn), p 246, note 143.

9 Section 20A(6). Thus, a 10% pre-payment was intended to be treated as payment for 10% of the goods agreed to be purchased: (above) Commission Report, para 4.7.

10 The (above) Commission Report, para 4.8. As to the traditional rules for the passing of property, see ante, para 20.15–21.

[20.22C]

1 Section 20A. Eg, on a later exchange of documents: see *Sale of Goods Forming Part of a Bulk* (1993, Law Com No 215) para 4.8; *Benjamin's Sale of Goods* (5th edn), para 5.115.

1a Notwithstanding s 20A(3), it is argued that the effect of s 20A(2) is to pass the risk to the buyer: see Benjamin, *op cit*, note 1, para 6-006. Cf *Sterns Ltd v Vickers Ltd* (set out post, para 22.04).

2 The (above) Law Commission Report (see ante, para 20.22B), para 4.10; Benjamin, *op cit*, note 1, para 5.117.

for 10, B owns an undivided 1/9 share in the bulk (= 9), whilst property and risk in the remaining 8/9 share (= 80) stays in S.[3]

(2) If the bulk is insufficient to meet in full the claims of all buyers from the bulk, *prima facie* the seller's claim is *pro tanto* ignored.[4] For example, if out of the bulk of 90 widgets, S sells 30 to B1 and 20 to B2, who each pay the full price: at first, B1 owns a 3/9 undivided share in the bulk (= 30), B2 owns a 2/9 share (= 20) and S a 4/9 share (40); if 40 are destroyed that is S's loss and the shares of B1 and B2 remain the same; and if B2 removes his 20, the remaining 30 are appropriated by exhaustion to B1 (s 18, rule 5(3): see ante, para 20.05B).

Section 20A also deals with the following special cases:

(a) *Further reductions.* If, even leaving aside the seller's claim (see above), the bulk is insufficient to meet in full the claims of all the co-buyers of the bulk, the effect of s 20A(4) is that the claims of the co-buyer are 'reduced proportionally so that the total of their shares in the undivided bulk is equal to the whole bulk'.[5] Thus, if in the above example 50 are destroyed, of the remaining 40, B1 owns a 3/5 share (= 24) and B2 owns a 2/5 share (= 16).

(b) *Part deliveries.* As s 20A only applies to undelivered pre-paid goods, any part delivery[6] is first ascribed to the part-payment.[7]

Rules to facilitate normal trading. Whilst the ordinary rule is that co-owners must act in agreement (see ante, para 19.05), the Law Commission recommended that both the seller and co-**owning** buyers should remain free to deal with their undivided share in the bulk by way of normal trading.[8] Accordingly, new s 20B(1) provides:

A person who has become an owner in common of a bulk by virtue of s 20A above shall be deemed to have consented to –

(a) any delivery of goods out of the bulk to any other owner in common of the bulk, being goods which are due to him under his contract;

(b) any dealing with or removal, delivery or disposal of goods in the bulk by any other person who is an owner in common of the bulk in so far as the goods fall within that co-owner's undivided share in the bulk at the time of the dealing, removal, delivery or disposal.

---

3 If the bulk is actually 95 widgets, the remaining 85 belong to S: the (above) Commission Report, para 4.14.

4 Section 20A(4), which does not mention any seller's share.

5 See the (above) Commission Report, para 4.11; and the example there set out.

6 For the purposes of new ss 20A and 20B, the meaning of 'deliver' (see generally post, para 23.03) has been extended by the SGAA, s 2(b).

7 Section 20A(5). For the effect of this, see the (above) Commission Report, paras 4.7; 4.12; Benjamin, *op cit*, note 1, para 5.119.

8 Para 4.16. Distinguish co-buyers: see ante, para 20.22A.

Thus, new s 20B(1)(b) gives the seller and co-owning buyers the right to deal with their own undivided shares without any third party raising the non-consent of co-owners;[9] whereas, as between co-owning buyers themselves, new s 20B(1)(a) allows any one of their number to withdraw his full share without regard to the others,[10] so establishing a first-come-first-served rule: subject to the obligations of the seller, or any contract arrangement between co-owning buyers, that buyer is under no duty to compensate those other buyers.[11] If such a seller sells more than his remaining co-share, he may still pass a good title on delivery under SGA, s 24 (see post, para 21.38). If such a co-owning buyer takes delivery of more than his co-share, then, without liability to his co-buyers, he may exercise his s 30 rights (see ante, para 13.05). The foregoing scheme is not meant to interfere with the contractual rights of each buyer against the seller (s 20B(3)(c)); nor with the position of a trustee or liquidator.[12]

'SALE OR RETURN' TRANSACTIONS[1]

[20.23] Rule 4 of s 18 seeks to deal with the passing of property in sale or return transactions, eg, retailers obtaining vehicles or books from manufacturers (see ante, para 16.21) or publishers; or supplying goods by cash mail order (see ante, para 8.19). However, the formation of a contract of sale must necessarily precede the passing of property, and there would appear to be two possible interpretations of the time of contracting.[2] First, the parties may intend to enter into a contract of sale immediately, but to give the buyer a unilateral right to discharge the contract if he does not approve of the goods after trial:[3] this may explain the decision in *P Edwards Ltd v Vaughan;*[4] but it might enable a supplier to side-step the unsolicited goods rules (see ante, para 8.18). Second, the goods may be delivered to the potential buyer only as bailee, in which case the bailor has merely made an offer to sell, and some later act of acceptance is required.[5] Thus, in *Atari Corp (UK) Ltd v Electronics Boutique Stores (UK):*[6]

> Atari supplied a quantity of Atari Jaguar computer games on sale or return to EB, a multiple retailer, which contract provided for payment by November 1995 and return until 31 January 1996. In mid-January, EB wrote to Atari to say that the goods were selling too

---

9   As he would otherwise be entitled to do: see ante, para 19.05.

10 Section 20B(2). This rule is justified on grounds of commercial convenience: the (above) Commission Report, para 4.17.

11 Section 20B(3)(a) and (b)): see the (above) Commission Report, para 4.20.

12 The Law Commission considered, and rejected, further alterations to spread the loss between co-buyers on the insolvency of a party: see Burns (1996) 59 MLR 260 at 269–70.

[20.23]

1   See generally the essay by Adams in *Essays for Clive Schmitthoff* (1983) 1–13; *Benjamin's Sale of Goods* (5th edn), para 5.039 *et seq.*

2   Is it relevant whether or not the person taking the goods on 'sale or return' upon delivery of the goods to him (a) pays the price, or (b) pays a sum expressed to be a 'deposit'? For other views, see Taylor [1985] JBL at 394–95.

3   *Mackay v Dick* (1881) 6 App Cas 251, HL(S). Is this an example of a condition subsequent (see ante, para 1.11)? It must, in any event, be distinguished from the ordinary right of the buyer to rescind for breach: compare post, paras 26.02; 26.15; and 29.03. See also Taylor, *op cit*, note 2, at 396.

4   (1910) 26 TLR 545, CA: see post, para 20.27.

5   Alternatively, it might be argued that there is a contract of bailment plus an option to buy: see post, para 20.27.

6   [1998] QB 539; [1998] 1 All ER 1010; (1997) Tr LR 529, CA (see 114 LQR 198).

slowly; that EB had decided to withdraw all such stock from its branches; and that, when all stock had been returned to EB's central warehouse, EB would notify Atari of the precise stock to be returned.

The Court of Appeal held that this was a good notice by EB of rejection of unsold Atari Jaguar stock, notwithstanding that EB was not at that moment in a position to identify precisely the unsold stock, nor to return that stock to Atari. As from that notice, Waller LJ said that EB would commit conversion in selling any further stock within the notice (at 535B). Phillips LJ characterised the transaction as a contract of bailment with an irrevocable option in EB to buy (per Phillips LJ at 536C; 537B).

The distinction between the two alternatives is, of course, crucial in the period after delivery and before the transferee approves the purchase. If there is a contract of sale, the position is governed by the SGA; but, if there is merely a bailment, then the common law rules of bailment will apply (see ante, para 1.17). The distinction may have important effects in the following respects:[7]

(1) *Risk*. If there is a mere bailment, the underlying risk is on the bailor,[8] and the bailee is *prima facie*[9] only liable for breach of the duty of care he owes under the bailment.[10] The incidence of risk generally in the case of sale is considered below (see s 20(3) of the SGA: see post, para 22.08), and in relation to the transferee above (para 15.24).

(2) *Rejection*. Whereas a buyer's right to reject if he does not approve may be restricted by the terms of the agreement (s 34 of the SGA; see post, para 23.10), the bailee has an unrestricted right to reject,[11] in which case he becomes a bailee for custody only.[12]

(3) *Resale*. As a bailee has no general property in the goods, before he accepts the bailor may sell to a third party: the bailee may bring an action against his bailor for breach of any collateral contract, eg, option, but he cannot thereafter by that transaction acquire for himself the property in the goods. On the other hand, a buyer in possession has an indefeasible right to the goods. The effect of a resale by a buyer or bailee in possession is considered below (see post, paras 20.27; 21.43).

(4) *Insolvency of the transferee*. As his trustee or liquidator only steps into the shoes of the transferee (see ante, para 19.23), his rights to the goods held on sale or return but not yet accepted differ: if the transferee is merely a bailee, his supplier may recover the goods as there is in English law no obligation for the supplier to register his interest under either the Bills of Sale or Companies Acts (see post, para 25.25 *et seq*. Cf US Uniform Commercial Code, Art 2-326); whereas, if he has bought the goods, they fall into his insolvency (see ante, para 19.23).

---

7   If defective goods cause damage before approval, it would appear less likely to cause much difference because of the virtual uniformity of the implied terms as to description and quality in the SGA and SGSA, and at common law (see ante, para 15.26). See further Adams in *Essays for Clive Schmitthoff*, at 9–13.

8   *Elphick v Barnes* (1808) 5 CPD 321; *Alexander v Glenbroome Ltd* [1957] 1 Lloyd's Rep 157.

9   But in many cases there may be an express or implied term that goods may only be returned in good condition, so effectively throwing risk on the transferee: Benjamin, *op cit*, note 1, para 6.010.

10 *Per* Vaughan Williams, LJ in *Genn v Winkel* (set out post, para 20.25) at 437; and *per* Willmer LJ in *Poole v Smith's Car Sales Ltd* [1962] 2 All ER 482, CA, at 489. See generally Goode, *Commercial Law* (2nd edn), p 268.

11 *Berry & Son v Star Brush Co* (1915) 31 TLR 603, CA.

12 But see *Bradley & Cohn Ltd v Ramsey & Co* (1912) 106 LT 771: affd at 773, CA on other grounds.

(5) *Negligence.* The right to sue a third party in negligence is available only to the owner: if there is a sale, the buyer may be able to bring such a transaction, whilst a mere bailee could not do so (see post, para 22.08. As to negligence, see ante, para 17.14).

The passing of property

[20.24] The next difficulty is to ascertain the scope of r 4, which is expressed to take effect where a person takes possession of goods 'on approval', or 'on sale or return',[1] or 'other similar terms'. What are 'other similar terms'? There is some authority that it includes deliveries 'on free trial' or 'on approbation'.[2] But does it include hp agreements (see post, para 20.27) or unsolicited goods,[3] or money back guarantees?[4]

As in the case of all the other rules of s 18, r 4 only applies in the absence of a contrary intention. Thus, in *Weiner v Gill:*[5]

> Jewellery was delivered to X, together with a memorandum which stated: 'On approbation. On sale for cash only or return ... Goods had on approbation or on sale or return remain the property of [the transferor] until such goods are settled for or charged'. Without paying for the goods, X pledged them; but the Court held that X acquired no property in the goods, and could therefore transfer none to the pledgee.

However, assuming that a transaction falls within r 4 and that there is no contrary intention, that rule provides that the property passes to the transferee as follows:

(a) When he signifies his approval or acceptance to the seller or does any other act adopting the transaction.

(b) If he does not signify his approval or acceptance to the seller but retains the goods without giving notice of rejection, then, if a time has been fixed for the return of the goods, on the expiration of such time, and, if no time has been fixed, on the expiration of a reasonable time.

Thus, assuming that a transaction falls within r 4 and that there is no contrary intention, r 4 provides that the property passes to the transferee as follows:

1 *Approval or acceptance.* This appears to connote a making known of intention to the supplier.[6] Normally, this will present few problems; but difficult questions of fact may occur where the trial involves a partial consumption or destruction.

2 *Adoption* (see post, para 20.25).

3 *Retention* (see post, para 20.26).

[20.24]

1 It has been suggested by Taylor [1985] JBL at 393, that there is a distinction in usage as follows: supply on 'approval' is usually to a consumer to try the goods; supply on 'sale or return' is usually to a businessman for resale. But what of drinks obtained for a party? See also Goode, *Commercial Law* (2nd edn), pp 242–43.

2 See the list of authorities collected in *Benjamin's Sale of Goods* (5th edn), para 5.040.

3 Rule 4 has been said to apply only to consensual arrangements and thus to be inapplicable to unsolicited goods (see ante, para 8.18): Goode, *op cit*, note 1, 243.

4 Eg, 'Your money returned if not absolutely satisfied'.

5 [1906] 2 KB 574; [1904–07] All ER Rep 773, CA. See also *Manders v Williams* (1849) 4 Exch 339.

6 Compare the definition of acceptance for a normal sale in s 35 of the SGA: see post, para 29.05.

[20.25] Adoption. In *Kirkham v Attenborough*:[1]

A manufacturing jeweller [P] entrusted some jewellery to W on sale or return. W pledged the goods with the defendant pawnbroker, and P claimed the return of the goods or their value.

The action was dismissed by the Court of Appeal, who held that in pledging the goods W had done an 'act adopting the transaction' within r 4, so that the property passed to him, and he passed a good title to the defendant. Lord Esher MR explained that the phrase 'act adopting the transaction' (at 203):

... cannot mean the delivery of the goods on sale or return, because that had been already done, and it must mean that part of the transaction which makes the buyer the purchaser of the goods ... There must be some act which shews that he adopts the transaction; but any act which is consistent only with his being the purchaser is sufficient.

He held that pawning was such an act, because it was 'inconsistent with his free power to return [the goods]'.[2] Presumably, the position is the same with regard to sales by the person in possession, eg, stocking plans (see ante, para 16.21).

However, the concept of an act adopting the transaction may become unworkable if pushed too far. In *Genn v Winkel*:[3]

The plaintiff diamond merchant delivered stones to the defendant on sale or return on Tuesday, 4 January; and the same day the defendant entrusted them on sale or return to G. On 6 January G handed the diamonds, probably on sale or return, to X, who lost them.

In view of the prevalence in the diamond trade of the practice that persons taking stones on sale or return immediately handed them to other people on similar terms, the majority of the Court of Appeal were not prepared to find that such an act was of itself necessarily an act adopting the transaction; but they held that the act of G in handing the stones to X was an 'act adopting the transaction'.[4] The difference, they thought, lay in this: the defendant was entitled to demand the stones from G just as soon as the original owner, the plaintiff, was entitled to demand them from him; whereas, by handing the stones to X on similar terms two days later, G had 'done an act which limits and impedes his power of returning the goods'.[5] What are the implications of this case? First, it is submitted that the Court of Appeal did not decide that the accidental[6] loss of the goods by X was an 'act adopting the transaction'.[7] Second, in one sense, any handing over of the goods to a third party impedes the power of return; but the majority of the Court of Appeal did not think

---

[20.25]

1   [1897] 1 QB 201; [1895–99] All ER Rep 450, CA. See also *London Jewellers Ltd v Attenborough* [1934] 2 KB 206, CA.

2   Would a gift be an act adopting the transaction because it passed the property in the goods (see ante, para 2.08)? And what of a conditional gift, eg, of a garment, provided it fitted?

3   (1912) 107 LT 434; [1911–13] All ER Rep 910, CA.

4   Scrutton J (at first instance) and Vaughan Williams LJ thought that any voluntary parting with possession was sufficient.

5   *Per* Fletcher Moulton LJ at 437. What if 4 January had been a Saturday? G's act of adoption was held to be an act of adoption by the defendant.

6   A fraudulent misappropriation is an act adopting the transaction.

7   Yet Fletcher Moulton LJ did suggest that, after handing the goods on, a bailee 'could no longer plead that he merely held them as bailee and had not been guilty of negligence' (at 437).

that this was necessarily[8] sufficient[9] and seemed more interested in whether it was consistent with the terms of the transaction for the goods to be held over beyond the time-limit.[10]

[20.26] Retention. Rule 4(b) provides that the property will pass to the buyer if he 'retains the goods without giving notice of rejection'. This rule substantially reflects the common law position,[1] except that, whereas the common law probably required the transferee to return the goods, the Act only requires him to give notice of rejection.[2] Rule 4(b) assumes that, even without approval or acceptance on the part of the transferee, the property may pass in either of the following circumstances:

(a) The transferee retains the goods beyond any stipulated time limit. Even though the transferee retains the goods beyond the stipulated time, he will not be deemed to have accepted the goods where the transferor induced him to prolong the trial,[3] or his retention was involuntary.[4]

(b) Where there is no time limit laid down, but the transferee retains the goods beyond a reasonable time. What is a reasonable time is a question of fact (s 59), and may depend on trade usage.[5]

The property/title borderline

[20.27] The effect of the operation of r 4 may well be to pass the property in the goods without the supplier realising it. This poses an obvious danger for the supplier, and he may there oust the operation of r 4 altogether by reserving the property in the goods until the price is paid.[1] Such a precaution will usually be effective in the event of the transferee's insolvency; but it is less likely to defeat the bfp, who may, in particular, acquire a good title under one of the following exceptions to the *nemo dat* rule:

(1) *Estoppel.* Whilst the mere transfer of possession to the transferee will not of itself give rise to an estoppel,[2] there may be other circumstances which would do so (see post, para 21.14).

---

8   Would the answer have been different if it had not been the practice for such bailees to hand on the goods on similar terms?

9   Is this consistent with the reasoning in *Kirkham v Attenborough* (above)?

10 Even if it were contractually possible for G to have demanded the return of the goods from X two days earlier than agreed?

[20.26]

1   See *Humphries v Carvalho* (1812) 6 East 45; *Moss v Sweet* (1851) 16 QB 493.

2   Though the agreement may show an intention that the goods actually be returned: *Ornstein v Alexandra Furnishing Co* (1895) 12 TLR 128; *Atari Corp (UK) Ltd v Electronics Boutique Stores (UK)* (set out ante, para 20.23).

3   *Per* Bovill CJ in *Heilbutt v Hickson* (1872) LR 7 CP 438, at 452.

4   *Re Ferrier, ex p Trustee v Donald* [1944] Ch 295.

5   Eg, *Poole v Smith's Car Sales Ltd* [1962] 2 All ER 482, CA. Cf s 35: see post, para 29.07.

[20.27]

1   Eg, *Weiner v Gill* (set out ante, para 20.24).

2   *Per* Bray J in *Weiner v Gill* (above) at 182. And see *Kempler v Bravingtons Ltd* (1925) 133 LT 680, CA.

(2) *Agency*. It may be that the transferor goes further than merely reserving the property in the goods, and evinces an intention that the transferee is never to become the owner of them; that is, the transferee is not a buyer, but an agent with a power to sell on his principal's account. Thus, in *Weiner v Harris*:[3]

> A manufacturing jeweller sent jewellery to a retailer under a standing agreement whereby the property was to remain in the manufacturer until the goods were sold or paid for. The retailer pledged some of the jewellery.

The Court of Appeal unanimously held that the pledgee obtained a good title because the parties only intended the retailer to be an agent for sale, not a buyer:[4] their Lordships distinguished *Weiner v Gill* on the grounds that in that case the property was only to pass to X when the goods were paid for, whereas in the present case the retailer was precluded by the terms of the agreement from ever becoming the owner of the goods under the transaction.

(3) *Buyers in possession*. As we shall see in the next chapter, a person who has agreed to buy goods and is in possession of them may be able to pass a good title (see post, para 21.43). Whilst a mere bailee is not in such a position, one who has agreed to buy subject to a right to rescind after trial clearly could do so.[5] An analogous problem is whether a hp agreement falls within the ambit of r 4. There is a clear difference in function between the two types of transaction, which will be mirrored in the terms of the bailments. Perhaps the biggest difference concerns the effect of an act inconsistent with the ownership of the bailor: in a sale or return, such an act will usually cause the property to pass to the erstwhile bailee; whereas, in a hp agreement it will usually amount to an act of conversion, and prevent the bailee from becoming the owner of the goods.[6] Most commentators accept that hp agreements are not sale or return transactions; and vice versa.[7]

RESERVATION OF A RIGHT OF DISPOSAL

[20.28] Section 19 of the SGA seems designed to deal with the situation where the parties are negotiating at a distance, and the unpaid seller wishes to safeguard himself against the insolvency of the buyer. The general rule is laid down in s 19(1) in the following terms:

> Where there is a contract for the sale of specific goods or where goods are subsequently appropriated to the contract, the seller may, by the terms of the contract or appropriation, reserve the right of disposal of the goods until certain conditions are fulfilled; and in such a case, notwithstanding the delivery of the goods to the buyer, or to a carrier or other bailee ...

---

3   [1910] 1 KB 285; [1908–10] All ER Rep 405, CA.

4   The retailer passed a good title as a mercantile agent: see post, para 21.24.

5   This may be the explanation of *P Edwards Ltd v Vaughan* (1910) 26 TLR 545, CA. See also *London Jewellers Ltd v Attenborough* [1934] 2 KB 206, CA, where the point may have been *obiter*. See the discussion by Adams in *Essays for Clive Schmitthoff* at 506.

6   *Helby v Matthews* (set out ante, para 1.22).

7   See Guest, *Law of HP*, p 51; Goode, *HP Law and Practice* (2nd edn), p 60. It should follow that the CCA does not apply to sale or return transactions because there is no element of 'financial accommodation': see ante, para 5.21.

for the purposes of transmission to the buyer, the property in the goods does not pass to the buyer until the conditions imposed by the seller are fulfilled.

It would seem that this poorly-drafted provision enables the seller to reserve a right of disposal (see below) in two circumstances,[1] which will both be examples of the operation of s 17 (see ante, para 20.06): (1) in the case of specific goods, by the terms of the contract; and (2) as regards unascertained goods, by the terms of the contract or appropriation, so derogating from s 18, r 5(2).[2] Section 19 itself dealt expressly with two uses of the rule common in 19th century international trade (s 19(2), (3)); but the most common modern use concerns *Romalpa* clauses (see post, para 20.29).

The meaning of 'reservation of a right of disposal'. Section 19(1) says that it will have the effect of reserving the property in the goods, eg, a conditional sale (see ante, para 1.14); and whether there has been such a reservation is a question of intention.[3] It might, therefore, be objected that, as s 18 is always subject to a contrary intention, s 19(1) seems superfluous. However, the explanation may be that businessmen do not usually think in terms of the passing of property in goods, but tend to express themselves with regard to risk (which is inconclusive as to the passing of property)[4] and the retention of control.[5] This retention of control must not be confused with the unpaid seller's real rights: the two sets of rights only overlap in the one case where goods are delivered to a carrier for the purposes of transmission to the buyer, and then the phrase 'reservation of a right of disposal' is used by the Act to describe both situations.[6] Nor must it be confused with the power of disposal.[7]

[20.29] *Romalpa* clauses. When *Romalpa* clauses were imported into English law (see post, para 25.29), it was found that their reservation of title in the goods supplied usually satisfied the 'conditions' referred to in s 19(1) (see ante, para 20.28). In such a situation, it has been argued that there are two possible outcomes, depending on whether or not the seller has accepted the buyer's repudiation by non-payment:[1]

(1) If the contract remained on foot, the seller would only be able to sell so much of the goods as was necessary to pay the outstanding balance of the purchase price; and, if the seller resold more, he would be accountable to the buyer for the surplus (see post, para 27.10).

[20.28]

1   *Benjamin's Sale of Goods* (5th edn), para 5.127.

2   See ante, para 20.17: see Benjamin, *ibid*, paras 128–29. *Semble*, even if the reservation is a breach of contract: Benjamin, para 5.127; Bradgate [1988] JBL 477.

3   *Re Shipton Anderson & Co and Harrison Brothers & Co* [1915] 3 KB 676, DC; *The Aliakmon* [1985] 2 All ER 44, CA (affirmed on other grounds).

4   *Per* Lords Westbury and Cairns in *Shepherd v Harrison* (1871) LR 5 HL 116, at 129, 131. See also ante, paras 20.06; 20.10.

5   The reservation cannot be effective where the goods are no longer identifiable, eg, petrol put in a motorist's tank – *Edwards v Ddin* [1976] 3 All ER 705 (criminal case).

6   SGA, ss 19(1), 43(1)(a): see further post, para 24.13. The reservation of a right of disposal also acts as a deemed delivery to the buyer: s 32(1) (see post, para 23.03).

7   The buyer may be able to pass a good title, eg, *Cahn v Pockett's Channel Ltd* (set out post, para 21.50).

[20.29]

1   *Benjamin's Sale of Goods* (5th edn), para 5.141. But see Bridge, *Sale of Goods*, 107–08.

(2) If the contract was discharged, the seller could sell all the goods on his own account, keeping any surplus (see post, para 27.10), but having to restore any part-payment (see post, para 27.19).

However, the operation of s 19 has been extended to where the reservation of title clause was expressed to secure sums **greater** than that necessary to secure payment of the price of goods supplied under that contract. The attraction of this is that a supplier can bring forward past indebtedness and attach it to goods in the buyer's possession, even when paid for; but the ploy can only work when a similar clause is inserted in all supply contracts, because the seller will not know in what order the buyer will consume supplies.[2] In *Armour v Thyssen Edelstahlwerke AG*:[3]

> A German manufacturer (T) sold to a Scottish engineering company (C Ltd) quantities of steel strip for use in C Ltd's manufacturing process. The contracts of sale were each subject to a condition that the property in the goods would not pass to C Ltd until all debts due from C Ltd to T under all contracts had been paid (the 'all monies' clause). At the time a receiver was appointed to C Ltd, part of the steel had been cut into sheets and part was in the course of being so cut, but most of it remained in the state in which it had been delivered by T. T successfully claimed ownership of all this steel, for which C Ltd had made no payment.

The House of Lords expressly applied s 19. It held that in Scottish law an all monies clause did not create a security in favour of T, but rather reserved the property in the goods to T under a genuine sale,[4] even in respect of the cut steel[5] and for debts due under other contracts.[6] Thus, their Lordships allowed T to avoid the problem of identifying which steel was supplied under which contract[7] and also the registration provisions for company charges (see post, para 25.28 *et seq*). It is for consideration whether such all monies clauses should require registration for the protection of the buyer's other creditors, especially if it can be shown that the seller has thereby made a substantial windfall beyond the contract price(s) (see post, para 25.34).

---

2 Bridge, *ibid*, 107.
3 [1991] 2 AC 339; [1990] 3 All ER 481, HL(S).
4 It has been suggested that all monies clauses securing liabilities to third parties, eg, associated companies, may be registrable: Hicks [1992] JBL 398 at 404–05.
5 Compare *Re Peachdart Ltd* [1984] Ch 131: see post, para 25.30.
6 It had previously been argued that reservation of title until payment due under other contracts amounted to a charge: Goode, *Commercial Law*, 718.
7 This may generate a surplus for the seller over the contract payments by reason of (a) previous part-payment by the buyer and (b) the proceeds of resale. The seller would not have to account for any surplus to the buyer, save in the unlikely event of a total failure of consideration: *per* Lord Keith at 485h. See Hicks [1992] JBL 398 at 404; and post, paras 24.22; 27.19.

CHAPTER 21

TRANSFER OF TITLE

NEMO DAT QUOD NON HABET

[21.01] The importance of good title. The relationship between property and title was discussed in Chapter 19; and this chapter will deal with the situation where goods belonging to A are transferred by B to C. Both the original owner (A) and the transferee (C) may be entirely blameless; and the problem is to determine which of the two is entitled to the goods. In theory, this should not make any difference, because the other will usually have the right to look to B for recompense: A could sue B in tort for wrongful interference with goods;[1] C could sue B for breach of the implied undertakings as to title.[2]

However, in practice a right of action against B may be worthless, so that the party left to seek recompense from B may himself have to bear the loss. Thus, the right to the goods may be of vital importance, and will usually be determined through the tort action for wrongful interference with goods. A will argue that, as B had no title, he could pass none to C: this is known as the *nemo dat* rule (see ante, para 19.11). C will argue that by way of one of the exceptions to that rule he has obtained a better title than B or A (see post, para 21.02). The burden of proof on the plaintiff to identify the disputed property should not be underestimated, few types of goods apart from motor vehicles being readily identifiable.[3]

Hire Purchase Information Ltd (HPI).[3a] Incorporated in 1938 as a company limited by guarantee, HPI was established to prevent financing fraud in the motor industry by a simple register of finance agreements on motor vehicles.[4] Subsequently, its service has been extended to other high value identifiable mobile assets, eg, caravans, boats, other types of instalment contract (see ante, para 1.03) and insurance write offs;[5] and the company itself has been taken over by a credit reference agency and the idea taken up by other agencies. As to Certificates of Title, see post, para 21.60.

[21.02] Exceptions. Leaving aside the special rules for sales from a bulk (see ante, para 20.22 *et seq*) and all forms of bailment,[1] the SGA concentrates on the transfer of the general

---

[21.01]

1 Torts Act 1977, ss 1, 2: see further ante, para 19.04 *et seq*.

2 See ante, Chapter 12. Or money handed to B may be traceable (see post, para 27.13). See generally Goode, *Commercial Law* (2nd edn), p 483–84.

3 This may lead to a battle between A and C to secure possession, and hence be defendant in any action: for recaption, see post, para 24.23. If the goods are in the physical possession of the police, their safest course may be to apply to the court under the Police (Property) Act 1897 (as amended). Any other third party in possession, eg a sheriff, should interplead (see post, para 21.06).

3a See further, Goode, *Consumer Credit Law and Practice*, para 2.85.

4 In recent years, the DVLC have offered a number plate transfer to facilitate the trade in cherished number plates. This has engendered some plate transfer fraud (see (1992) 47 CC 2/2) and led to some system changes at HPI. One in three used cars checked had a 'hidden history': (1995) 50 CC 3/14; 50 CC5/21.

5 Vehicles written off by insurance companies have been rebuilt, or their identity transferred to stolen vehicles.

[21.02]

1 SGA, s 62(4): set out ante, para 1.08.

property in goods and the title to that property (see ante, para 19.08). In fact, the SGA deals only with the title at law to goods, saying nothing about equitable titles:[2] a person with an equitable title to goods cannot sue in conversion (see ante, para 19.06); and, under general principles any equitable title to goods gives way to a *bona fide* purchaser (bfp) of a legal interest in them in circumstances where A has parted with the property in the goods, but has an equitable right to rescind the contract and so recover that property, eg, the voidable title rule (see post, paras 2.19–23).

So, let us concentrate on that title in law. In setting out the *nemo dat* rule (see ante, para 19.11), s 21(1) of the SGA expressly makes it 'subject to the provisions of this Act' and also provides that it shall not apply where goods are sold by B 'under the authority or with the consent of the owner'. These reservations refer to the following cases:

1   *Agency.* Section 21(1) recites that the *nemo dat* rule does not apply to a person (B) who sells 'under the authority' of the owner (A); and the common law rules of agency are expressly preserved by the SGA (s 62(2)). Those situations where the common law would allow B to act as agent of A, contracting on A's behalf to transfer A's title to C, have already been outlined (see ante, para 10.06); and their extension in the Factors Acts[3] in respect of mercantile agents is dealt with below (see post, para 21.24 *et seq*).

2   *Consent.* Whereas the agency exception (above) recognises that B will never become the owner of the goods, the present exception envisages that B will do so and resell to C 'with the consent of' A. In these circumstances, A would normally be secure in his unpaid seller's real rights because he has retained possession;[4] but s 47(1) provides that A loses those real rights if he assents to a sub-sale by B to C, presumably by way of waiver (see s 43(1)(c), considered post, para 24 15). Section 47(1) would appear to go somewhat further than the common law,[5] in that it only requires A in some manner to communicate to B[6] his assent,[7] either expressly or impliedly (see post, para 21.03).

3   *The SGA provisions.* The phrase 'subject to the provisions of this Act' in s 21(1) refers to the major SGA exceptions to the *nemo dat* rule (see post, para 21.05) and to s 21(2)(a), which lays down that:

> The provisions of the Factors Acts, or any enactment enabling the apparent owner of goods to dispose of them as if he were the true owner thereof.

---

2   Any underlying policy behind these exceptions will be considered post, para 21.07.

3   For the unpaid seller's rights of lien and stoppage, see post, para 24.04. For the overriding of these rights in favour of a bfp in possession, see post, para 21.43.

4   For the major FA exceptions to the *nemo dat* rule, see post, para 21.05.

5   A could not be estopped on ordinary principles from setting up his real rights where he represents that he will not exercise these: see post, para 26.24. However, the courts were prepared to allow a delivery warrant to have such an effect, eg, *Merchant Banking Co v Phoenix Bessemer Steel Co* (1877) 5 Ch D 205. Was this because the warrant was a negotiable instrument; or because of some rule of equitable estoppel?

6   *DF Mount Ltd v Jay* (set out post, para 21.03). In the pre-Act cases, knowledge of assent was obtained by B and C, and the courts sometimes talked in terms of estoppel: see *Benjamin on Sale* (8th edn), p 872, proposition 3a.

7   It is suggested that 'assent' here means actual assent, notwithstanding that it was obtained by fraud; cf post, paras 21.19; 21.31; 21.47.

Apart from the provisions of the FA, which for many purposes must be treated with the SGA as a single code,[8] it is difficult to see to what s 21(2)(a) is referring.[9] Section 21(2)(b) refers to some miscellaneous powers of sale (see post, para 21.06).

[21.03/04] Implied consent. In applying the consent exception to the *nemo dat* rule (see ante, para 21.02), the courts have experienced some difficulty. Thus, in two cases A agreed to sell part of a larger quantity of goods to B, and B agreed to resell that part to C; B received the price from C, who claimed title; but B neglected to pay A, who stopped delivery.[1] In *Mordaunt v British Oil and Cake Mills Ltd*:[1a]

> B sent C a delivery order,[2] which order directed A to deliver the goods to C, and C forwarded the delivery order to A, who acknowledged that it was 'in order'.

Pickford J decided that neither party regarded the acknowledgment as an assent, pointing out that C paid B before receiving the acknowledgement, so that there could be no question of estoppel (see post, para 21.10). His Lordship added (at 507):

> The assent contemplated by section 47 ... means ... an assent given in such circumstances as to shew that the unpaid seller intends that the sub-contract shall be carried out irrespective of the terms of the original contract.

Compare *Mount Ltd v Jay Ltd*:[3]

> A and B agreed that B should pay A out of the proceeds of resale, and A gave B a delivery order addressed to the wharfingers who held the goods. B forwarded the orders to the wharfingers indorsed 'please transfer to our sub-buyer'. Salmond J held that C had obtained a good title on the grounds that:
>
> (1) A had assented to the resale; and
>
> (2) C obtained a good title under the SGA, s 25, but not s 47(2) (see post, para 21.49).

As regards (1), his Lordship distinguished *Mordaunt v British Oil and Cake Mills Ltd* on the grounds that A was there anxious to get rid of the goods on a falling market and knew that B could only pay for them out of the resale price; the inference was, therefore, that A intended to renounce his rights against the goods and take the risk of B's dishonesty (at 169). Both these cases were concerned with an unascertained part of a specific whole,[4] and in both it was suggested by the court that the inference of assent would be more readily drawn if the goods were specific.[5]

---

8   *Per* Clarke J in *Forsythe International (UK) Ltd v Silver Shipping Co Ltd* [1994] 1 All ER 851, at 862.

9   Perhaps it includes the following: the Bills of Sale Act 1878 (see ante, para 9.05); Part III of the HPA (see post, para 21.55); the annexation of fixtures (see post, para 25.23).

[21.03/04]

1   Nowadays, C might have an undivided share in the bulk under SGA, s 20A: see ante, paras 20B–20C.

1a   [1910] 2 KB 502. *A fortiori Laurie and Morwood v Dudin* [1926] 1 KB 223, CA.

2   The answer would be otherwise if the delivery order were a document of title: Atiyah, *Sale of Goods* (10th edn), p 369, note 7.

3   [1960] 1 QB 159; [1959] 3 All ER 307.

4   So that the property in the goods could not have passed from A to B by reason of SGA, s 16 (see ante, para 20.05). Whilst title may be claimed without ownership (see ante, para 19.06), allowing C to claim title in these circumstances causes problems: see Nicol (1979) 42 MLR 129, especially 133–36.

5   Pickford J (at 506) even went so far as to say that 'no such inference could be drawn if the goods were not in existence'.

[21.05] The major SGA, FA and HPA exceptions.[1] The major exceptions to the *nemo dat* rule (see ante, para 21.01) which are relevant to the disposition of goods to a *bona fide* transferee (C) are as follows:

(1) *Estoppel*. A may be estopped from denying to C that B may pass a good title to C (see post, para 21.08).

(2) *Voidable title*. If B obtains a voidable title from A, B may pass a good title to C at any time before A avoids B's title (see post, para 21.19).

(3) *Mercantile agency*. If A entrusts his goods to B as mercantile agent, B may be able to pass a good title to C under the Factors Act 1889 (see post, para 21.24).

(4) *Seller in possession*. If B has sold goods to A but retained possession of them, B may by statute pass a good title to C (see post, para 21.38).

(5) *Buyer in possession*. If B has agreed to buy goods from A and obtained possession of them, B may by statute pass a good title to C (see post, para 21.43).

(6) *Private sales of motor vehicles*. Under the HPA 1964, if B is in possession of a vehicle under an hp or conditional sale agreement, B may pass a good title to a private purchaser (see post, para 21.57).

Sales in market overt. This oldest exception to the *nemo dat* rule was part of the Law Merchant and incorporated into the law of many Western European States.[1] As developed by Elizabethan lawyers, it was a sensible attempt to balance the conflicting interests of the owner and the bfp. Notwithstanding that subsequent developments left it a curious anomaly in English law,[2] Chalmers embodied it in the SGA,[3] whence it has now been abolished.[4] Nevertheless, for higher value goods eg, cars, antiques, the rule remains in a European context: where the value of the goods makes the cost of transit worthwhile, stolen goods can still be taken to the Continent, passed through say a Parisian market overt and then subsequently sold with a good title in England.[5]

[21.06] Miscellaneous powers of sale. Section 21(2)(b) of the SGA provides that 'nothing in this Act shall affect the validity of an contract of sale under any special common law or statutory power of sale or under the order of a court of competent jurisdiction'.

1 *Common law powers of sale*. Where these powers have not been absorbed by statute (see below), they are expressly preserved by the Act, eg, the power of sale of a pledgee (see post, para 25.15) or of an agent (see ante, para 10.06).

2 *Statutory powers*. From the very considerable list of statutory powers of sale,[1] several are worthy of mention:

[21.05]

1 See Murray (1960) 9 ICLQ 24.

2 See (1994) 114 NLJ 1014. *Contra* European law.

3 It was most recently to be found in s 22 of the SGA 1979. Eg, *Bishopsgate Motor Finance Corp Ltd v Transport Brakes Ltd* [1949] 1 KB 322, CA.

4 Sale of Goods (Amendment) Act 1994 (see Shears 14 Tr L 30).

5 Eg, *Winkworth v Christie Manson and Woods Ltd* [1980] Ch 496.

[21.06]

1 See further *Benjamin's Sale of Goods* (5th edn), para 7.107. Eg, *Bulbruin Ltd v Romanyszyn* [1994] RTR 273, CA.

(a) *Creditor's power of sale*. Unpaid sellers (see post, para 27.08 *et seq*), distraining landlords (see ante, para 19.17), pawnbrokers (see post, para 25.18), innkeepers,[2] and repairers[3] all have varying statutory powers of sale.

(b) *Insolvency*. The trustee in bankruptcy or liquidator has a statutory power of sale; but neither can normally pass a better title than the insolvent person has (see ante, para 19.23), though an administrator may do so.[4]

(c) *Execution*.[5] The effect on the title to goods of execution and sale by a sheriff has already been considered (see ante, para 19.16).

3   *Court orders*. There are a number of powers conferred on the courts to make an order for the sale of property. Particularly worthy of note are the power to order a sale or division of goods owned by co-owners who cannot reach agreement *inter se* with respect to the co-owned goods;[5] the effect of satisfaction of a judgment in an action in conversion (see post, para 26.17); the power to order a sale under the Rules of Court where the sheriff interpleads because of a dispute as to the title of goods taken in execution;[6] or where the subject matter of any litigation is perishable, or is likely to deteriorate if kept, or which 'for any other reason it is desirable to sell forthwith';[7] and the powers of the court to authorise sale by a bailee.[8]

[21.07] The underlying policy. It may be helpful at this point to consider the policy of the law in granting exceptions to the *nemo dat* rule. Generally speaking, the courts have tended to favour ownership and to uphold the *nemo dat* rule; and the history of this area of the law has largely been one where the pressure of the mercantile community has secured the adoption of statutory exceptions to the rule, and the courts have consistently interpreted those exceptions against C and in favour of A. As long ago as 1787, an attempt was made to ascribe a pattern to the rule and the counterbalancing exceptions by Ashhurst J in *Lickbarrow v Mason*,[1] where he said:

> We may lay it down as a broad general principle, that, wherever one of two innocent persons must suffer by the acts of a third, he who has enabled such a third person to occasion the loss must sustain it.

This *dictum* was applied by the Privy Council in *Commonwealth Trust Ltd v Akotey*,[2] where that court appeared to hold that the mere handing over of possession of goods by A to B is sufficient to estop A from setting up his title against C. However, such a view was rejected by the Privy Council in the *Mercantile Bank of India Ltd* case (set out ante, para

---

2   See Crossley Vaines, *Personal Property* (5th edn), pp 135–36.
3   Torts Act 1977, s 12. If in doubt, the bailee may apply to the court see below, note 8.
4   Insolvency Act, 1986, s 15: see ante, para 19.12; and generally ante, para 19.22.
5   See the explanation in Chalmers, *Sale of Goods* (18th edn), p 161.
6   See *Caldwell's* case (set out post, para 21.22); and ante, 19.05, 19.20.
7   *Larner v Fawcett* [1950] 2 All ER 727, CA. See also post, para 27.08.
8   Torts Act 1977, s 13.

[21.07]
1   (1787) 2 Term Rep 63, HL at 70.
2   [1926] AC 72, [1925] All ER Rep 270, PC. See also the dissenting judgment of Lord Denning MR in *Beverley Acceptances Ltd v Oakley* [1982] RTR 417, CA, at 425E–F.

19.11).[3] Perhaps unfortunately, the latter case would seem to be correct: the issue between A and C does not turn on fault, but on the strict application of the *nemo dat* rule and the exceptions thereto; and the *dictum* by Ashhurst J remains no more than an aspiration. Moreover, Ashhurst J was talking about the common law, where there is, of course, no power to apportion. It has been judicially suggested that the courts should have a statutory power to apportion in these circumstances;[4] but this view was rejected by the Twelfth Report of the Law Reform Committee as 'unworkable'.[5] The position therefore remains that, unless C can bring his case within one (or more – for they overlap) of the exceptions, he will lose. Curiously, even if C can bring his case within one of the exceptions, the title he will obtain may vary because he will normally get only such title as A has (see post, paras 21.09; 21.23; 21.37; 21.54; 21.58).

ESTOPPEL[1]

The rule

[21.08] According to the latter part of s 21(1) of the SGA, where A's goods are sold by B to C,[2] the *nemo dat* rule will apply:

> … unless the owner of the goods is by his conduct precluded from denying the seller's authority to sell.

Perhaps the leading case where this provision was applied is *Eastern Distributors Ltd v Goldring*:[3]

> Murphy (A) was the owner of a Bedford van; and he wished to purchase a car as well, but had no money to pay for it, not even enough for the deposit under an hp agreement. Dealer (B) suggested to A that he should raise the deposit in the following manner, and A acquiesced: B would pretend to the plaintiff finance company (C) that he (B) was letting on hp to A both the van and the car, so that the company would send B the balance of the price due to both vehicles. In pursuance of this scheme, A signed a blank hp proposal form in respect of both vehicles. B then filled in his own name as owner of both vehicles and submitted the proposals to C who rejected that in respect of the car. Nevertheless, B proceeded with that in respect of the van – which was really owned by A. C sent a memorandum of the agreement to A, who promptly told B that the whole transaction was cancelled, and shortly afterwards sold the van to the defendant, a bfp. Upon discovering the

---

3   *Per* Lord Wright at 298. See also *per* Cairns LJ in *J Sargent (Garages) Ltd v Motor Auctions (West Bromwich) Ltd* [1977] RTR 121, CA, at 128.

4   *Per* Devlin LJ in *Ingram v Little* [1961] 1 QB 31, CA at 74.

5   1966, Cmnd 2958, paras 12, 40(1). For criticism of this Report, see Atiyah (1966) 29 MLR 541; Diamond 29 MLR 413.

[21.08]

1   See generally Spencer Bower, *Estoppel* (2nd edn); Pickering (1939) 55 LQR 400; *Cross & Tapper on Evidence* (9th edn), p 77 *et seq.*

2   So passing the property from B to C (see ante, para 1.10). *Contra* where there is a mere agreement to sell from B to C so that this exception is inapplicable: *Shaw v Commissioner of Police* (set out ante, para 19.11).

3   [1957] 2 QB 600; [1957] 2 All ER 525, CA; app *Stoneleigh Finance Ltd v Phillips* (set out post, para 25.27).

true state of affairs, C sued the defendants for conversion of the van, alleging title by estoppel,[4] and A was joined as third party.

The defendant pleaded that A had only given B a limited authority to sell, and that anyway they were not privy to the estoppel and were not bound by it. Alternatively, they pleaded that, even if C acquired title by estoppel, C could not recover the van because (i) A had conferred a good title on the defendants under what is now s 24 of the SGA (see post, para 21.39), and (ii) A had not signed the memorandum of the hp agreement as the HPA required;[5] and that that Act did not permit an action in conversion.[6] The Court of Appeal unanimously found that C had acquired a good title by estoppel, and rejected both defences.[7]

[21.09] Effect of statutory exception. *Prima facie*, the statutory formula in s 21(1) would appear to refer to the common law doctrine of estoppel, though that doctrine is nowhere defined by the SGA. However, in *Goldring's* case (set out ante, para 21.08), this assumption was rejected as regards the title transferred, though it would appear that the Court of Appeal thought that the other rules of common law estoppel applied to this exception (see post, para 21.10 *et seq*). The Court was clear that Murphy (A) was estopped and Devlin J explained the effect of a common law estoppel as follows:[1]

> An estoppel affects others besides and representor. The way it has always been put is that the estoppel binds the representor and his privies. But it is not easy to determine exactly who, for this purpose, is a privy. There can be no doubt that, although the representation was actually made by [B], [A] on the facts of this case was privy to the making and bound by it ... It would also appear that anyone whose title is obtained from the representor as a volunteer is a privy for this purpose. But it is very doubtful whether a purchaser for value without notice is bound by the estoppel.

The defendant in this case was a bfp to whom A had purported to sell the van, so that, if s 21(1) merely embodied the common law of estoppel, it would seem that C's title could be defeated by a subsequent sale to a bfp.[2] Whatever the position with regard to the common law of estoppel, however, the Court of Appeal thought that s 21(1) referred rather to the wider common law doctrine of apparent authority resting on mercantile convenience.[3] Devlin J said (at 610–611):

> We doubt whether this principle ought really to be regarded as part of the law of estoppel ... The effect of its application is to transfer a real title and not merely a metaphorical title by estoppel ... The result is that [A] is, in the words of [the SGA, s 21(1)], precluded from

---

4   The Factors Act, s 2(1), did not apply because the dealer was not in possession: see post, para 21.28. What if the hp documents had indicated that B was in possession?
5   For the modern rule contained in the CCA, s 61(1)(a): see ante, para 9.18.
6   For the tort of conversion, now wrongful interference with goods, see ante, para 19.04. For adverse possession, see the CCA, s 134: see post, para 24.42.
7   What effect, if any, would s 56 of the CCA have on this decision? For discussion of this section, see ante, para 16.10.

[21.09]
1   At 606–07. Cf *Henderson & Co Ltd v Williams* (set out post, para 21.11).
2   With or without delivery? Cf Powell (1957) 20 MLR 650, 652.
3   See the criticism by Goodhart (1957) 73 LQR 455, 457; and the discussion in Powell, *Agency* (2nd edn), pp 68–72.

denying [B's] authority to sell,[4] and consequently [C] acquired the title of the goods which [A] himself had and [A] has no title left to pass to the defendant.

Of course, C could get no better title than A: if A had merely stolen the van from O, the plaintiff's title could still have been defeated by O.

The common law doctrine of estoppel[1]

[21.10] The common law doctrine of estoppel requires an unambiguous[2] representation made **by** the person to be estopped (A),[3] or his privy,[4] **to** the person seeking to set it up (C).[5] In our context, this means that the representation relied upon to estop A from setting up his title to goods may be to the effect that another (B) is; (1) the owner of goods;[6] or (2) has A's authority to dispose of them.[7] It makes little difference whether the representation gives rise to apparent ownership or agency,[8] though in the latter situation this exception overlaps with that in respect of the apparent authority of an agent (see ante, para 10.06).

However, before the requirements of this rule are examined (see post, para 21.12), there should be noted the difficulty in applying the doctrine (see post, para 21.11) and the words of caution sounded by Lord Wright in the *Mercantile Bank of India Ltd* case,[9] where his Lordship pointed out:

> There are very few cases of actions for conversion in which a plea of estoppel by representation has succeeded.

[21.11] The operation of common law estoppel may be illustrated by two similar cases, in which the courts contrived to reach different results.[1] In both cases, the owner (A) of goods lying in a warehouse instructed the warehousekeeper to transfer the goods to the order of a rogue (B), and B then sold the goods to a bfp (C), who paid the price to B in return for a delivery order made out to B. In *Henderson & Co v Williams*:[2]

> C distrusted B and before paying him obtained confirmation from the warehousekeeper that the sugar was held to the B's order. C sued the warehousekeeper in conversion, and the

---

4 Is this rule confined to dispositions by the agent by way of sale?

[21.10]

1 See generally *Benjamin's Sale of Goods* (5th edn), para 7-008 *et seq.*

2 Or one which may reasonably be taken as such: *Woodhouse AC Israel Cocoa SA v Nigerian Produce Marketing Co* [1972] AC 741, HL.

3 *Moorgate Mercantile Co Ltd* case (set out post, para 21.16).

4 Eg, B in *Eastern Distributors Ltd v Goldring* (set out ante, para 21.08).

5 Distinguish the situation where A makes the representation only to B: see ante, para 21.04.

6 Eg, *Eastern Distributors Ltd v Goldring* (above). Cf *Mercantile Credit Co Ltd v Hamblin* (set out ante, para 16.05); and further post, para 21.15.

7 See Goode, *Commercial Law* (2nd edn), pp 458–60; and the cases cited in Stoljar, *Agency* 26, note 20. In *Pacific Motor Auctions Pty Ltd v Motor Credits (Hire Finance) Ltd* [1965] AC 867, the Australian courts held that the finance company was estopped; but the point was expressly reserved by the PC.

8 Compare liens, ante, para 1.23.

9 [1938] AC 287, PC, at 302.

[21.11]

1 The following judges sat at different stages in both cases: Lords Halsbury and Lindley reached different conclusions in each case; AL Smith LJ decided that there was an estoppel in both.

2 [1895] 1 QB 521, CA. See also *Woodley v Coventry* (1863) 32 LJ Ex 185.

Court of Appeal held that, although the property in the goods remained in A, the warehousekeeper was estopped as against C from denying C's title.[3]

However, in *Farquharson Brothers & Co v King & Co*:[4]

B, a confidential clerk of A perpetrated a series of frauds over a period of about four years in the following manner: he instructed the warehousekeeper to transfer some of A's timber to the order of Brown; and, under the name of Brown, sold this timber to C and gave him delivery orders. C obtained delivery, and A sued him in conversion. The majority of the Court of Appeal held that A was estopped from setting up his title because he had enabled B to commit the fraud.[5] Sterling LJ dissented on the grounds that there had never been any holding out by A or the warehousekeeper to C as to B's authority; and the House of Lords adopted this dissenting opinion without hesitation.

It will be observed that in both cases the warehousekeeper was justified as far as A was concerned in delivering the goods to the order of B; and in both, B gave C a delivery order which at that moment the warehousekeeper was prepared to honour. However, in *Henderson v Williams* C took the precaution of getting the warehousekeeper to confirm that he would honour the delivery order, which amounted to a representation by A (see post, para 21.13); but in *Farquharson v King* C did not take such a precaution.

[21.12] Requirements. Leaving aside the nature of the representation required (see post, para 21.13 *et seq*), a common law estoppel will only operate where all the following requirements are present.

1 *The representation by A must concern an existing state of facts.* It is fundamental to the common law doctrine of estoppel that the representation must be as to existing facts, and not future intention.[1] A representation of future intention can only[2] take effect under the principles of equitable estoppel and waiver (see post, para 26.23 *et seq*).

2 *The representation must be made to C.* The difficulties inherent in this are neatly illustrated by *Farquharson v King* (set out ante, para 21.11). The decision is intelligible, but makes no allowance for the carelessness of A over a four year period (see post, para 21.15).

3 *The representation must be made with the intention that it be acted upon.* The test is objective. Thus, in *Eastern Distributors Ltd v Goldring* (set out ante, para 21.08) A was estopped from denying B's title to the van because he had signed documents which made it appear as if B were the owner of the van. On the other hand, in *Lowe v Lombank Ltd* (set out ante, para 18.06) one of the reasons given by the Court of Appeal for finding that the hirer was not estopped was that there was no evidence that the hirer intended her representations to be acted on.[3]

---

3 In this sort of situation, the safest course for the warehousekeeper is to interplead, though Lord Halsbury thought A would also be estopped as against the warehousekeeper from denying B's right of disposal.

4 [1902] AC 325; [1900–03] All ER Rep 120, HL. See also *Laurie and Morwood v Dudin* [1926] 1 KB 223, CA; *Moorgate Mercantile Co Ltd v Twitchings* (set out post, para 21.16).

5 [1901] 2 KB 697, CA.

[21.12]

1 *Jorden v Money* (1854) 5 HL Cas 185.

2 Unless it is that the representor has such an intention at the time of making the representation.

3 See also *Debs v Sibec Developments* [1990] RTR 91 ([1989] JBL 284); and settlement figures (see post, para 26.19A).

4   *The representee (C) must have a genuine belief in its truthfulness.* Another ground on which the Court of Appeal refused to find the hirer estopped in *Lowe v Lombank Ltd* was that there was no evidence that the finance company had a genuine belief in the truthfulness of the hirer's representation. On the other hand, in *Eastern Distributors Ltd v Goldring* the Court of Appeal held that the finance company did in fact act on the implied representation of ownership contained in the proposal form.[4]

5   *The representee (C) must act on the representation to his detriment.* In *Farquharson v King*[5] Lord Lindley said that A was not estopped because C was misled, not by anything done by or under the authority of A, but by B's fraud; and in *Lowe v Lombank Ltd* the Court of Appeal thought that the finance company inserted the relevant clause in the proposal form, not so that they might rely on the representation contained therein, but simply to preclude the hirer from invoking the implied undertakings of the HPA as to quality and fitness.[6]

Representations, omissions and negligence

[21.13] The conduct relied upon as amounting to a representation of ownership or authority (see ante, para 21.10) sufficient to found such an estoppel may itself make the representation,[1] or it may allow another to make a representation;[2] and, whilst there will usually be some active conduct, there may be a representation by omission.[3] However, once it is settled that there does not have to be active conduct on the part of the representor himself, it is difficult to decide what is necessary before there will be a representation sufficient to found an estoppel.[4] The *dictum* of Ashhurst J in *Lickbarrow v Mason* (set out ante, para 21.07) suggests that whenever the owner (A) has 'enabled' the rogue (B) to occasion the loss, he should be estopped. Thus, in handing possession of his goods to a B, A in one sense enables B to dispose of them. However, it has been settled since *Johnson v Credit Lyonnais Co*[5] that the mere transfer of possession of goods to another will not generally raise an estoppel. No doubt, this rule is convenient to owners: they would be in a difficult position if any repairer, cleaner, etc, with whom they deposited goods could pass a good title. Yet the rule obviously runs counter to the interests of the mercantile community, who have therefore secured a number of statutory exceptions, where a person in possession can pass a good title if he is either a seller, buyer or mercantile agent (see post, respectively paras 21.38; 21.43; 21.34).

---

4   Perhaps the cases may be distinguished on the basis that the representation is in the very act of signing as opposed to being in the small print.

5   See also *Carr v L & NW Railway* (1875) LR 10 CP 307.

6   See now SOGIT, ss 9–11: see ante, Chapters 13–15.

[21.13]

1   Eg, *Henderson & Co v Williams* (set out ante, para 21.11); *Eastern Distributors Ltd v Goldring* (set out ante, para 21.08).

2   *Coventry v GE Rail Co* (1883) 11 QBD 776, CA.

3   Eg, *Pickard v Sears* (1837) 6 Ad & El 469.

4   For an examination of whether possession plus or carelessness could raise an estoppel see post, para 21.14 *et seq.*

5   (1877) 3 CPD 32, CA. See also *Jerome v Bentley* (set out post, para 21.27); and generally Goode, *Commercial Law* (2nd edn), pp 457–58.

[21.14] Possession plus. If the mere possession of goods will not raise an estoppel (see ante, para 21.13), what more is required? The issue was canvassed in *Central Newbury Car Auctions Ltd v Unity Finance Ltd*:[1]

> The Plaintiff dealer (A) purchased a car, in the log book of which the previous registered owner, Ashley, had not signed his name. A did not register himself owner because he intended to resell the car. Subsequently, a rogue (B) tricked A into parting with possession of the car and log book and then offered the car to C giving the name Ashley. By this time, B had signed the log book in the name of Ashley. C compared the signature in the log book with that which the rogue provided in his presence, and then completed the purchase. C sold the car to the defendant. The defendants pleaded that A was estopped by his negligence from denying B's authority to sell; and the County Court Judge agreed.

However, the decision was reversed by the Court of Appeal, where the majority thought that the result should turn, not upon fault, but upon whether the handing over of the log book was sufficient to take the case outside the general rule. In deciding in favour of A, the majority pointed out that the log book was not a document of title;[2] but in a strong dissenting judgment, Denning LJ adopted Ashhurst J's *dictum*, and pointed out that the log book was best evidence of title.[3] On the other hand, in *Goldring's* case (set out ante, para 21.08), the Court of Appeal unanimously decided that the owner was estopped where he signed a document stating that the dealer was the owner of the vehicle. No doubt, there is an intelligible distinction between a positive statement of ownership and a mere careless transfer of possession, but it makes no allowance for the owner's culpability (see post, para 21.15).

[21.15/18] Carelessness. Suppose an owner (A) has carelessly signed a document which appears to divest him of his property, and this document is utilised by a rogue (B) to enter into a transaction purporting to transfer the property to a bfp (C). In a contest between A and C as to the ownership of the goods, A may advance two separate lines of argument to escape from the effect of the document: a plea of *non est factum* (see ante, para 10.16); and a denial of estoppel. As to the second point, in *Mercantile Credit Co Ltd v Hamblin* (set out ante, para 16.05) the Court of Appeal denied estoppel by representation because A had given B no actual or ostensible authority to sell (see ante, para 21.10). Whilst also denying estoppel by negligence on the facts, Pearson LJ did allow of such a possibility in a suitable case.[1] The point arose again in *Moorgate Mercantile Co Ltd v Twitchings*:[2]

> The plaintiff finance company (A) was a member of HPI (see ante, para 8.35). However, in letting a car on hp to B, A failed to inform HPI of the transaction. During the continuance of the hiring, B offered the car for sale to the defendant motor dealer (C), who was also a

---

[21.14]

1 [1957] 1 QB 371; [1956] 3 All ER 903, CA. Following *Sargent Ltd v Motor Auctions Ltd* (set out post, para 27.30).

2 The log book stated on every page 'The person in whose name a vehicle is registered may or may not be the legal owner of the vehicle'. There might have been an estoppel if it had been a document of title (see post para 21.60).

3 Whilst the majority thought A's negligence irrelevant, Denning LJ was prepared to find a breach of a duty of care giving rise to an estoppel (at 385). But see post, para 21.15.

[21.15/18]

1 At 271. Cf Blackburn J in *Swan v North British Australasian Co* (1863) 2 H & C 175 at 182.

2 [1977] AC 890; [1976] 2 All ER 641, HL.

member of HPI. B falsely told C that he was the owner of the car and that it was not subject to any hp agreement. C contacted HPI, who informed him that the car was not registered with them. In consequence, C bought the car.

A's action for conversion succeeded before the House of Lords, who rejected C's argument of title by estoppel on the following grounds:

(1) HPI's communication to C did not amount to a representation on behalf of A that there was no outstanding agreement on the car: first, it was merely an assertion as to the state of HPI's records and not a positive assertion as to ownership; and second, in answering C's enquiry, HPI was not acting as agents for A, but in their own capacity.[3] It followed that it was not open to C to plead estoppel by representation (Lord Salmon dissenting).

(2) A bare majority[4] held that there was no legal duty owed by A to C to register or to take reasonable care in registering their hp agreements with HPI,[5] noting that the rules of HPI did not impose on members any contractual duty to register and that the search form sent to C expressly disclaimed any pretence that it was a complete record.[6] It followed that C could not plead estoppel by negligence.[7]

As a result of this case, the continued existence of the estoppel by negligence principle must be doubtful.[8] The *Twitchings* decision has subsequently been confirmed by the Court of Appeal.[9] However, if the minority view on above issue (2) in the House had prevailed, that might have established a sort of common law title registration system on HPI rules; and a similar result could be achieved by statutory reversal of *Twitchings* (see post, para 21.60).

VOIDABLE TITLE

[21.19/20] The exception. Suppose A enters a title-transferring contract, proposing to sell, pledge or exchange[1] his car to B, that offer being induced by B's misrepresentation. The distinction has already been drawn according to whether the outcome is a void or voidable contract between A and B (see ante, para 10.15). If the contract is void, B will

---

3   Mr Twitchings seems to have been well aware of this fact: see *per* Lord Edmund-Davies 917. Even if HPI had been acting as an agent for A (see ante, para 16.06), see *Freeman v Cooke* (1848) 2 Exch 654.

4   Lords Edmund-Davies, Fraser and Russell, affirming the dissenting judgment of Geoffrey Lane LJ in the CA. See also Atiyah, *Sale of Goods* (10th edn), p 379.

5   In the CA, Lord Denning MR would have extended such a duty to non-members, so apparently elevating the obligation into the tort of negligence: as to which, see ante, para 17.20.

6   The rules of HPI have subsequently been changed so that members are now obliged to register. Does this strengthen the argument for a collateral contract between A and C (see Phillips (1976) 92 LQR 499) or an estoppel? HPI also offers a guarantee to searchers that the register is accurate: (1996) 51 CC1/10.

7   This attitude has even been taken where the owner of an aircraft let on hp was in breach of a statutory duty to register his title (see ante, para 9.02): *Cadogan Finance Ltd v Lavery* [1982] Com LR 248. Compare Goode, *Commercial Law* (2nd), pp 452–53.

8   See also *Beverley Acceptances Ltd v Oakley* [1982] RTR 417, CA, *per* Donaldson and Slade LJJ at 434K–435D. *Contra* Lord Denning MR at 427.

9   *Dominion Credit & Finance Ltd v Marshall (Cambridge) Ltd* (1993) Lexis, CA. (A test case supported by RMI.)

[21.19/20]

1   *Anderson v Ryan* [1967] IR 34. Or quasi-sale?

acquire no proprietary interest in the car; but, if the contract is merely voidable, he will acquire a defeasible proprietary interest in it. Suppose further, that B purports to dispose of the car to C. If the contract between A and B is void, B acquires no title to the goods, and under the *nemo dat* rule (see ante, para 19.11) can therefore pass none,[2] though C might acquires a good title under one of the other exceptions to that rule, eg, *Eastern Distributors Ltd v Goldring* (set out ante, para 21.08). Leaving aside this last possibility, the position is the same if the contract between A and B is voidable, and has been avoided by A before B purports to dispose of the goods.[3] On the other hand, if the voidable contract between A and B has not been avoided at the time of the disposition by B to C, C will at very least acquire that voidable title, eg, if C is B's trustee in bankruptcy (see ante, para 19.23), or a purchaser with notice (see X in *Caldwell's* case: set out post, para 21.21). However, if C is a *bona fide* transferee for value without notice, he may acquire a good title indefeasible by A.[4] This common law rule only applies to title-transferring transactions:[1] it has no application to bailments.

As to where the disposition by B to C is by way of **sale**,[5] the exception has been encapsulated in s 23 of the SGA as follows:

> Where the seller of goods has a voidable title thereto, but his title has not been avoided at the time of the sale, the buyer acquires a good title to the goods, provided he buys them in good faith and without notice of the seller's defect of title.

'Notice' is not defined in the SGA, but refers to C's knowledge of the defect in B's title.[6] According to s 61(3):

> A thing is deemed to be done 'in good faith' within the meaning of the Act when it is in fact done honestly, whether it be done negligently or not.

To the cynical common law, 'good faith' is only the absence of proven dishonesty,[7] though it does extends beyond C's participation in B's wrongdoing (see post, para 21.36) to his own independent wrongdoing, eg, C tries to defraud B. It is to be compared with the much wider continental concept of 'good faith' (see ante, para 11.15).

The courts do not seem to regard s 23 as having made any changes in the common law. In *Whitehorn Brothers v Davison*[8] the Court of Appeal were of the opinion that the common law exception still stands in respect of pledges by B to C;[9] and that, under both

---

2   *Cundy v Lindsay* (1878) 3 App Cas 459, HL; *Ingram v Little* [1961] 1 QB 31, CA.
3   *Car and Universal Finance Co Ltd v Caldwell* (set out post, para 21.22); *Newtons of Wembley Ltd v Williams* (set out post, para 21.51).
4   This rule in respect of a bfp of goods does not apply in favour of a bfp of a chose in action: see ante, para 7.23.
5   Presumably, s 23 does not apply where B has only agreed to sell to C: cf *Shaw v Commissioner of Police* (set out ante, para 19.11). See *Benjamin's Sale of Goods* (5th edn), para 7.026.
6   It is discussed in the context of another exception to the *nemo dat* rule, post, para 21.49.
7   The *Dodds* case (set out post, para 21.57). See Chalmers, *Sale of Goods* (18th edn), pp 272–73; Benjamin, *op cit*, note 5, para 7.044.
8   [1911] 1 KB 463; [1908–10] All ER Rep 885, CA.
9   See also *Phillips v Brooks* [1919] 2 KB 243. And what if the disposition by A to B is by way of pledge? Or if there is only an agreement to pledge between B and C (see note 5, above)?

statute and common law, if A seeks to recover the goods from C, the onus is on A to show that C did not purchase in good faith and without notice.[10] However, the onus is on C to show that his purchase was made before avoidance.[11]

[21.21/22] Effect of the exception. Assuming that the contract between A and B is voidable under the foregoing rules (see ante, para 21.19), it is necessary to consider how A may rescind or avoid it.[1] Plainly, where A communicates his intention to rescind to B, that will be sufficient; but, for a long time it was thought that A could not effectively rescind by any means short of 'going to court',[2] except by actual communication with B[3] or recaption of the property (see post, para 24.23). Such a rule was perfectly adequate where B was innocent, but not if B was fraudulent. In the latter case, B would usually effectively dispose of the goods before A found him or the goods, with the result that it was assumed that B would usually be able to pass a good title to a bfp (C). However, this assumption was confounded by *Car and Universal Finance Co Ltd v Caldwell*:[4]

> On 12 January, Caldwell (A), contracted to sell his car to a rogue (B) for £975 and allowed B to take the car away in return for payment made as to £965 by cheque. The cheque was dishonoured the next morning; and A immediately went to the police, and also asked the AA to try to find his car. On 15 January, B sold the car to X, a *mala fide* purchaser, who immediately resold to C, a *bona fide* purchaser. On 29 January, A demanded the return of his car from X. In August, C sold the car to the plaintiff (D). Subsequently the car was seized by the sheriff, and the case arose on an interpleader summons. It was conceded that A had taken adequate steps to avoid the contract by 29 January, so that D could have no better title than C. The judge held best title was vested in A.

The Court of Appeal found that X was not the agent of C, so that C was not affected by X's *male fides*;[5] but they unanimously dismissed the appeal on the grounds that A had effectively avoided B's title on 13 January.[6] At first sight, *Caldwell's* case would appear to make substantial inroads into one of the principal exceptions to the *nemo dat* rule:[7] whereas the previous rule left very little chance of avoidance, the new one makes it a real possibility. Yet, it would seem that the Court of Appeal were careful to restrict themselves to cases where a contract was voidable by reason of B's fraud and B deliberately hides from A. Does the rule depend on (a) fraud in the sale, or (b) deliberate evasion, or both?

---

10 Is the position the same if A seizes possession, so that C is the plaintiff? The *Twelfth Report of the Law Reform Committee* (1966, Cmnd 2958), para 25, recommended that the rule be reversed to achieve uniformity with the other exceptions to the *nemo dat* rule: see below and post, para 21.36.

11 *Thomas v Heelas* [1988] C & FLR 211, CA, distinguishing *Whitehorn Brothers v Davison* (above).

[21.21/22]

1 This will be rescission *ab initio*: see post, para 26.12.

2 See *per* Lord Pearson in *Garnac Grain Co Inc v HMF Faure and Fairclough Ltd* [1968] AC 1130 at 1140, HL.

3 *Per* Lord Clyde in *Macleod v Kerr* 1965 SLT 358, at 363.

4 [1965] 1 QB 525; [1964] 1 All ER 290, CA: see Cornish (1964) 27 MLR 472. *Contra Macleod v Kerr* (above).

5 The possible agency relationship between a finance company and dealer is considered ante, para 16.06.

6 '[B] would not expect to be communicated with as a matter of right or requirement ... [A only] has to establish clearly and unequivocally that he terminates the contract' (*per* Sellers LJ at 550–51). See also Upjohn and Davies LJJ at 555, 558.

7 Atiyah [1965] JBL 130, 131.

Furthermore, another limitation on the effect of this case became apparent with the decision in *Newtons of Wembley Ltd v Williams* (set out post, para 21.53). In somewhat similar circumstances to those in *Caldwell*, in *Newtons* it was accepted that A had avoided by doing all in his power to communicate with B; but the Court of Appeal nevertheless held that B had passed a good title as a buyer in possession: *Caldwell* was distinguished on the grounds that X was *male fide*.

[21.23] The implications of *Caldwell* (set out ante, para 21.22) may be illustrated by way of an example. Suppose X steals goods from O, and sells them to A; A resells to B under a contract voidable by A; B resells to C, who resells to D, who resells to E.

voidable

O

X_____A__[voidable]__B_____C_____D_____E

Several questions arise.

(1) Suppose B sells to C before A avoids the contract. Is the effect of the exception to confer on C the title of O or A? It is submitted that C will only obtain A's title, with any defects it contains.[1]

(2) Suppose B sells to C and C resells to D before A avoids his contract with B, but C is *male fide*. In *Caldwell*, the Court of Appeal seem to have thought that D would obtain a good title as being a bfp[2] before avoidance, cf *Williams* case (set out post, para 21.53).

(3) Suppose further that the sale by D to E took place after A's avoidance of his contract with X. It was conceded in *Caldwell* that E had no better title than D. If this is correct, the effect of the exception is that E will only succeed where he, or a prior party,[3] took *bona fide* and for value **before** A rescinds his contract with B.

Finally, it should be noted that the Law Reform Committee in 1966 recommended that the rule as to avoidance laid down in *Caldwell* should be reversed, and actual communication required:[4] if enacted, the recommendation would have reversed the result in *Caldwell*, but not that in *Williams*, that is, the bfp in the *Williams* case would succeed on the basis of s 23 and would not need to rely on s 25. Nothing has been done.[5]

[21.23]

1 Battersby and Preston (1972) 35 MLR at 280–81. This is the usual result: see ante, para 21.07.

2 Is it important that he is the first bfp? See further post, para 21.54. Cf post, para 21.59.

3 *Peirce v London Horse and Carriage Repository Ltd* [1922] WN 170, CA.

4 *Twelfth Report* (1966, Cmnd 2958), paras 16, 40(4).

5 Whilst judicial reform may be dependent on the HL having the opportunity to compare the English and Scots rules, commentators are reduced to minimising the scope of *Caldwell*: see Atiyah, *Sale of Goods* (10th edn), p 392; Treitel, *Law of Contract* (10th edn), p 345; *Benjamin's Sale of Goods* (5th edn), para 7.023.

MERCANTILE AGENCY[1]

Introduction

[21.24] In the series of 19th century Factors Acts, Parliament attempted to increase the protection of the bf purchasers and pledgees (C) who obtained goods from factors (B), to whom the goods had been entrusted by their owners (A). Begun in 1823, the history of the Acts is one of legislation in favour of the bfp followed by the courts adopting a restrictive interpretation in favour of the owner, followed by further legislation in favour of the bfp.[2] Curiously, the SGA then proceeded to repeat some of the more important provisions of the consolidating Factors Act 1889 (FA) in almost identical terms.[3] There are two major themes running through the FA: both are attempts to modify the common law rule that possession by B does not usually give rise to an apparent authority from A to dispose of the goods (see ante, para 21.13).

(1) An intention to increase the power of professional agents, which the 19th century draftsman termed 'mercantile agents'. The object of the Act is not to derogate from the powers of an amateur agent,[4] but to increase the **powers** of the professional agent for the benefit of his transferee (C).[5] At the same time, the Act is careful not to increase the **rights** of the agent vis à vis his principal (A).[6]

(2) The Act lays down that a buyer or seller in possession may in certain circumstances pass a good title. These provisions will be considered later.[7]

Both these themes have certain similarities to the doctrine of estoppel (see post, para 21.54); and they do in fact cover some of the ground covered by estoppel in those situations where a person in possession (B) has an apparent or usual authority to dispose of goods. But there the similarity ends: estoppel demands a representation made by A to C, whereas the FA requires instead that C's transferor (B) should be a mercantile agent, or a seller or a buyer in possession.

[21.25] The mercantile agency exception. The key is to be found in s 2(1) of the FA, which provides:

> Where a mercantile agent[1] is with the consent of the owner,[2] in possession of goods or of documents of title to goods,[3] any sale, pledge, or other disposition of the goods, made by

---

[21.24]

1 See Powell, *Agency* (2nd edn), pp 216–36.
2 See Stoljar, *Agency*, 116–21.
3 Even whilst expressly preserving the Factors Acts: see SGA, s 21(2)(a). There are even discrepancies between the two: see post, paras 21.38; 21.43.
4 The powers of an ordinary agent are outlined ante, paras 10.06; 21.02.
5 Section 13. If the transferee has not paid the price, the 'owner' may be able to recover it from him: s 12(3).
6 Section 12(1). Nor of the agent's trustee in bankruptcy: s 12(2). Or liquidator?
7 See respectively post, para 21.38 *et seq* and para 21.43 *et seq*.

[21.25]

1 See post, para 21.26 *et seq*.
2 See post, para 21.31 *et seq*.
3 See post, para 21.28 *et seq*.

him when acting in the ordinary course of business of a mercantile agent,[4] shall, subject to the provisions of this Act, be as valid as if he were expressly authorised by the owner of the goods to make the same,[5] provided that the person taking under the disposition acts in good faith, and has not at the time of the disposition notice that the person making the disposition has not authority to make the same.[6]

Since 1889, this sub-section has become so encrusted with case law, that each phrase of it must be considered with some care. Indeed, the extent of the case law perhaps suggests the advisability of further statutory reform (see post, para 21.37).

A mercantile agent

[21.26] The FA requires that B should be a mercantile agent (ma):

1 *An agent*. The first requirement is that in acquiring the goods B must be acting as, or on behalf of, an agent: it is not sufficient if he acts as owner,[1] nor as any other type of custodian. Difficult questions may arise where he acts in more than one capacity as, for instance, where he is both a servant and an agent, eg, a commercial traveller.

2 *A 'mercantile agent'*. Before 1889, the Acts merely used the term 'agent'; but this had been judicially interpreted to cover only those professional agents which were termed factors in the normal language of the time. The term 'mercantile agent' appeared for the first time in the 1889 Act. According to s 1(1) of the 1889 Act, the expression 'mercantile agent' shall mean (see also s 26 of the the SGA 1979):

> ... a mercantile agent having in the customary course of his business as such agent authority either to sell goods, or to consign goods for the purpose of sale, or to buy goods, or to raise money on the security of goods.

Thus, a 'mercantile agent' is one who by way of business is customarily entrusted with goods as agent for one of the purposes listed in s 1(1). This is commonly assumed to include a motor dealer: but, in the normal case, he will buy and sell on his own account; and the proposition would only seem to be true where he (perhaps unusually?) takes possession as agent for sale, etc.[2] On the other hand, the courts did somewhat stretch the notion of a mercantile agent in *Lowther v Harris*:[3]

> A installed some antiques he wished to sell in a house. He arranged with an antique dealer, B that B should take a flat in the house and sell the items on commission, but should first obtain the sanction of A. B fraudulently sold and delivered two tapestries to a bfp. As to one, there had clearly been no consent to its removal by a misrepresentation. A's action in conversion against the bfp succeeded in respect of the first tapestry (see post, para 21.31),

---

4 See post, para 21.33 *et seq*.
5 See post, para 21.37 *et seq*.
6 See post, para 21.36.
[21.26]
1 *Belvoir Finance Co Ltd v Cole Ltd* [1969] 2 All ER 904.
2 Eg, *Pearson v Rose & Young Ltd* (set out post, para 21.35); *Stadium Finance Ltd v Robbins* (set out post, para 21.31).
3 [1927] 1 KB 393; [19261 All ER Rep 352. See also *Weiner v Harris* (set out, ante, para 20.27).

but failed as to the second on the grounds that B was a mercantile agent and had passed a good title under the FA.

As B's function was not merely to deliver the goods, but also to collect the price and account for it to A, Wright J concluded that B was acting in the usual course of business of a fine art dealer,[4] albeit for one principal only.[5] It would seem to be uncertain whether the entrusting of goods to another for the purposes of obtaining offers would fall within s 1(1).[6]

[21.27] Commission. It has been pointed out that:[1]

> The kind of factor who today agitates the law is not the factor of old, but is the more casual agent such as the traveller or salesman.

In this situation, it will, of course, be far more difficult to determine whether or not the rogue is an ma. Now, in most of the cases where it has been held that the FA applied, the rogue has been working on a commission basis. This point was seized upon by Macnaughten J in *Budberg v Jerwood and Ward*,[2] where he held that the Act did not apply to defeat the title of the owner who had entrusted her jewellery to a friend for the purposes of sale, and relied upon the absence of any commission to negative any suggestion of a business relationship. However, *Jerome v Bentley*[3] would appear to deny that the presence or absence of commission is decisive:

> B fraudulently induced the plaintiff (A) to hand a diamond ring to him to sell or return within seven days under an agreement which stipulated that B was to try to sell the ring either in his own name or A's and that if he sold it he was to pay A £550, and retain any surplus for himself. After the expiration of the seven days, B sold the ring to a bfp and absconded. A admitted that B was his agent[4] and successfully sued the bfp for conversion. Donovan J held that, at the time of sale, B had no actual, apparent or usual authority to sell.

It has been suggested that B was not an ma;[5] but it would appear that the FA was not pleaded in this case.[6] It maybe that the presence of commission does not conclusively show that an agent is an ma, but the cases other than *Jerome v Bentley* certainly seem to show that it is strong evidence to that effect.

---

4   Would the answer have been the same if B had not already been an antique dealer?

5   Is this the effect of the word 'customary' in s 1(1)? And how is this reconcilable with the view of s 1(1) as a subjective test taken in *Oppenheimer v Attenborough* (above)?

6   Accepted without argument in: *Pearson v Rose and Young Ltd* (set out post, para 21.35); *Stadium Finance Ltd v Robbins* (set out post, para 21.31). But see *per* Salmon LJ in *Lloyds and Scottish Finance Ltd v Williamson* [1965] 1 All ER 641, CA at 644.

[21.27]

1   Stoljar, *Agency* 124. Is every sales assistant a mercantile agent? And what of the manufacturer's representative stationed in a franchised retail store?

2   (1935) 51 TLR 99.

3   [1952] 2 All ER 114.

4   If the case had been argued on the basis that B was a principal, it would have turned on s 18, r 4: see *Kirkham v Attenborough* (set out ante, para 20.25).

5   Atiyah, *Sale of Goods* (10th edn), p 384 says the case is authority for the proposition that 'a person who induces another to let him have goods on a representation that he knows a third party will buy them is not without more an ma'.

6   If it had been, the issue might well have turned on whether B was acting as an agent or principal because, if he were an agent, the commission arrangement would seem to indicate that he was an ma: see Parker (1952) 15 MLR 503; Powell, *Agency* (2nd edn), p 83, note 6.

Possession with consent

[21.28/30] Possession. For the operation of this exception, B must be in possession of goods or documents of title. Under the FA, 'goods' are defined by s 1(3) to 'include wares and merchandise',[1] and documents of title by s 1(4).[2] However, not only must B be in possession with A's knowledge that B is an ma,[3] but it has been held that B must also be in possession in his capacity as (qua) ma. In *Staffs Motor Guarantee Ltd v British Wagon Ltd:*[4]

> B, a dealer in motor lorries, agreed to sell a lorry to the defendant finance company (A) and to rehire it from them under a hp agreement with a view to sub-letting it to X. B then fraudulently sold the lorry, of which he had never relinquished possession, to C, a bfp. When B fell into arrears, A repossessed the lorry. In their action to recover the lorry, C pleaded that: (1) the hp agreement was void under the Bills of Sale Acts (see post, para 25.26), (2) B could pass a good title under what is now s 24 of the SGA (see post, para 21.40); and (3) B could pass a good title under s 2(1) of the FA. The action failed.

Mackinnon J rejected C's plea under s 2(1) of the FA on the grounds that, after B sold the lorry to A, it was entrusted by A to B, not in his capacity as ma, but as hirer (at 313). This view has been expressly accepted by the English courts.[5] However, such a distinction in capacity will obviously, if taken too far, nullify the effect of s 2(1); and it has been rejected by the courts in the somewhat similar context of the exception relating to sellers in possession.[6]

Further, it must be remembered that s 2(1) only applies where a person is an ma at the time he is entrusted with the goods:[7] the mere fact that he later becomes an ma does not bring s 2(1) into operation,[8] unless the owner consents to his possession in that capacity (but see s 2(4): discussed post, para 21.31).

[21.31/32] Consent. The ma (see ante, paras 21.26–27) must be in possession (see ante, para 2.28) with the consent (see below) of the owner. It has been decided that:[1]

> Where the right of ownership has become divided among two or more persons in such a way that the acts which the section is contemplating can never be authorised save by both or all of them, these persons together constitute the owner.

[21.28/30]

1   Compare the definition of goods in the SGA: ante, para 2.02.

2   For the extended meaning given by s 1(4), see post, para 23.03.

3   *Lowther v Harris* (set out ante, para 21.26), the first tapestry; *Henderson v Prosser* [1982] CLY 21. As to the meaning of possession, see post, para 23.03.

4   [1934] 2 KB 305; [1934] All ER Rep 322.

5   See *per* Denning LJ in *Pearson v Rose and Young Ltd* (set out post, para 21.35), at 288; *per* Willmer LJ in *Stadium Finance Ltd v Robbins* (set out post, para 21.31) at 674.

6   Post, para 21.40. But see *per* Chapman J in *Astley Industrial Trust Ltd v Miller* [1968] 2 All ER 36, at 41–42.

7   *Per* Lush J in *Heap v Motorists' Advisory Agency Ltd* [1923] 1 KB 577, at 588–89.

8   *Beverley Acceptances Ltd v Oakley* [1982] RTR 417, CA. See further Butterworths edn, 1989, at para 21.28.

[21.31]

1   *Lloyds Bank Ltd v Bank of America* [1938] 2 KB 147, CA, *per* Lord Greene MR at 162.

The requirement of consent is also to be found in s 25 of the SGA (see post, para 21.47). The FA nowhere defines 'consent', but perhaps the sense of the term is conveyed by the word used in the previous FA, namely '**entrusts**'. It is clear that only consent to the fact of possession need be shown and any secret restrictions on the power of the ma are for this purpose irrelevant.[2] Whilst there must be actual consent to the ma's possession,[3] it is irrelevant that consent was obtained by trick.[4] Moreover, the legislature obviously intended to lessen the burden of the person seeking to prove consent by providing in s 2 as follows:

(2) Where a mercantile agent has, with the consent of the owner, been in possession of goods or of documents of title to goods, any sale, pledge, or other disposition, which would have been valid if the consent had continued, shall be valid notwithstanding the determination[5] of the consent: provided that the person taking under the disposition has not at the time thereof notice that the consent has been determined.[6]

(3) Where a mercantile agent has obtained possession of any documents of title to goods by reason of his being, or having been, with the consent of the owner, in possession of the goods represented thereby, or of any other documents of title to the goods, his possession of the first-mentioned documents shall, for the purposes of this Act, be deemed to be with the consent of the owner.

(4) For the purposes of this Act the consent of the owner shall be presumed in the absence of evidence to the contrary.

However, the courts have shown some reluctance to apply these provisions, except, curiously, in the context of sales by a buyer in possession (see post, para 21.47). Thus, it is difficult to see why the transfer of possession of the log book to the dealer in *Pearson v Rose and Young Ltd* (set out post, para 21.35) was not connected with the business of obtaining offers for sale;[7] or why this was not presumed under s 2(4); and, if it were so connected, why s 2(2) did not prevent such consent being withdrawn. Similarly, in *Stadium Finance Ltd v Robbins*:[8]

The owner (A) of a Jaguar car left it with a car dealer (B) to see what offers to buy it B could obtain. A took away the ignition key, but accidentally left the log book locked in the glove compartment. B opened the glove compartment with a duplicate key and found the log book. B subsequently sold the car to the plaintiff finance company (C). A retook possession of the car and C's claim under s 2(1) failed on the grounds that the resale to C was not made in the ordinary course of business (see post, para 21.35).

The majority were of the opinion that the inference under s 2(4), that the owner had consented to possession by the dealer, had been rebutted as to the log book, but not as to the car.[9] Willmer LJ went even further, and argued that (at 674):

---

2   *Weiner v Harris* (set out ante, para 20.27); *Stadium Finance Ltd v Robbins* (see below).
3   *Lowther v Harris* (set out ante, para 21.26), the first tapestry: see ante, para 21.26.
4   *Folkes v King* [1923] 1 KB 282, CA.
5   Whether that determination be by act of the owner or rule of law, eg, his death?
6   Eg, *Newtons of Wembley Ltd v Williams* (set out post, para 21.53).
7   Powell, *Agency* (2nd edn), p 228, note 4.
8   [1962] 2 QB 664; [1962] 2 All ER 633, CA.
9   Ormerod and Danckwerts LJJ, at 670–71, 676–77.

... without either key or registration book, [the dealer] was not ... in possession of the car in his capacity of [ma].

It is submitted that it would be undesirable if the view of Willmer LJ were to prevail, as it would unduly restrict the operation of s 2.[10]

Dispositions in the ordinary course of business to a *bona fide* purchaser (bfp)

[21.33] The requirements. The section requires all the following:

1   *A disposition.* Section 2(1) refers to 'a sale,[1] pledge[2] or other disposition'.[3] One of the major purposes of the FA was to deal with unauthorised pledges by an ma; and it tackles this subject in considerable detail. Section 5 provides that the pledgee's security extends only to the value of the consideration he gives;[4] and s 4 restricts this to consideration given by the pledgee at the time of the pledge (or subsequently?). However, leaving aside the question of pledges, the implication of s 5 seems to be that the disposition referred to in s 2(1) must be for valuable consideration.[5] But must there also be a delivery?[6]

2   *By a mercantile agent.* The FA envisages the possibility that the disposition may be made on behalf of an ma by his servant or agent. Section 6 provides that:[7]

> For the purposes of this Act an agreement made with a mercantile agent through a clerk or other person authorised in the ordinary course of business to make contracts of sale or pledge on his behalf shall be deemed to be an agreement with the agent.

3   *In the ordinary course of business* (see post, para 21.34).

4   *To a bf transferee* (see post, para 21.36).

[21.34] In the ordinary course of business. Plainly, this requirement cannot be taken literally, because it is never in the ordinary course of business (ocb) for any ma to dispose of goods contrary to his authority. This dilemma is present in the wording of the statute: according to s 1(1), an ma is one who in the ordinary course of his business has authority

---

10   See Hornby (1962) 25 MLR 719.

[21.33]

1   The definition of 'sale' is discussed ante, para 1.06 *et seq.*

2   Pledges are defined in FA, s 1(5). For liens, pledges and mortgages, see generally post, para 25.02. For another point, see post, para 21.41, note 5.

3   Presumably, this includes hp. It has been doubted whether this includes a mortgage bill of sale (*Beverley Acceptances Ltd v Oakley* [1982] RTR 417, CA) or a mere agreement to dispose of goods (Goode, *Commercial Law* (2nd edn), p 466, note 76).

4   The effect of the words 'pecuniary liability' in s 1(5) would appear to be that this covers antecedent liabilities.

5   See Powell, *Agency* (2nd edn), pp 233–34; Goode, *op cit*, note 3, note 74. Cf *Thomas Graham Ltd v Glenrothes Development Corp* [1968] SLT 2.

6   Delivery is required for a pledge (see post, para 25.15), but not for a sale (see ante, para 1.07). Compare s 8 of the FA, which expressly requires a delivery: see post, para 21.41.

7   See the criticism of s 6 in Powell, *op cit*, note 5, p 230.

to sell, etc; but s 2(1) provides that an ma can pass a good title only when acting in the ocb of an ma (see ante, para 21.25). In *Oppenheimer v Attenborough*:[1]

> The plaintiff (A) was induced to entrust a parcel of diamonds to a diamond broker (B) upon the representation that B could sell the diamonds to X at an agreed minimum price. Instead, the broker pledged the diamonds with C who took *bona fide* and for value. Evidence was given that a diamond broker (an ma) employed to sell diamonds and no authority to pledge them. A argued that an ma could only pass a good title under s 2(1) when acting in the ordinary course of his business, and that it was not in the ordinary course of a diamond broker's business to pledge diamonds.

Nevertheless, the Court of Appeal found in favour of C. The Court thought that it was irrelevant that C did not know that his pledgor (B) was not acting as a principal;[2] and it was further irrelevant that the broker (B) had brought the transaction within s 2(1) by acting in the ocb of **an** ma. Buckley LJ explained:[3]

> Section 1(1) is speaking of the arrangement made between the owner of the goods and his agent ... It deals with the circumstances under which the agent gets his authority; to satisfy the definition he must get [the goods] in the customary course of his business as a mercantile agent. Section 2(1) deals with another matter. It has to do with the stage at which the agent is going to deal with the goods in his possession with reference to some other person, and the form of the expression is here altered ... [to mean] 'acting in such a way as a mercantile agent acting in the ordinary course of business of a mercantile agent would act'; that is to say, within business hours,[4] at a proper place of business, and in other respects in the ordinary way in which a mercantile agent would act so that there is nothing to lead the pledgee to suppose that anything wrong is being done, or to give him notice that the disposition is one which the mercantile agent had no authority to make.

This decision clearly accords with the purpose of the Act, namely, to reverse the rule that an apparent owner or factor cannot pledge goods;[5] but the courts have been careful not to extend s 2(1) too far (see post, para 21.35). Thus, it has been held that it is not in the ocb for an ma to ask a friend to pledge goods for him;[6] nor to ask his buyer to pay the price in part to a third party in satisfaction of a judgment debt against the ma;[7] nor where the operation was characterised as 'a very peculiar transaction'.[8]

[21.35] The question of whether a disposition for value of a motor vehicle by an ma has been in the ocb has caused the courts considerable difficulty. In *Pearson v Rose and Young Ltd*:[1]

[21.34]

1 [1908] 1 KB 221; [1904–07] All ER Rep 1016, CA. Cf *Waddington & Son v Neale & Sons* (1907) 97 LT 786, DC.

2 *Per* Lord Alverstone CJ and Kennedy LJ, at 228, 232. But see post, para 21.52.

3 At 230–31. But see criticisms in Powell, *Agency* (2nd edn), p 219.

4 See the *Pacific Motor Auctions* case [1965] AC 867, PC.

5 See ante, paras 21.24; 21.33. Would the decision have been otherwise if C had known (or suspected?) that B was a diamond broker? Would it be relevant to the ocb whether C was aware of the ordinary powers of a diamond broker; or does this last point rather go to *bona fides* (see post, para 21.36)?

6 *De Gorter v Attenborough* (1904) 21 TLR 19. But see s 6 of the FA.

7 *Biggs v Evans* [1894] 1 QB 88. But see *Lloyds and Scottish Finances Ltd v Williamson* [1965] 1 All ER 641, CA at 644.

8 *Heap v Motorists' Agency* [1923] 1 KB 577, at 589.

[21.35]

1 [1951] 1 KB 275; [1950] 2 All ER 1057, CA.

The owner (A) of a Morris car left it with a car dealer (B) to see if the latter could obtain any offers to buy it. At the same time, B tricked A into leaving the log book with him. B sold the car plus log book to C1, who resold the C2, who resold to C3. The owner sued C3 to recover the car, and Devlin J held that C3 obtained a good title by reason of s 2(1). His decision was reversed by the Court of Appeal.

Whilst the case was argued on the issue of whether B, an ma, obtained possession of the goods with the consent of the owner (see ante, para 21.29), it also raised questions as to whether the sale by B to C1 was made in the ocb and whether C1 was a bfp (see post, para 21.36). The Court of Appeal unanimously held that a disposition of a car with its log book was not in the ocb because the ma was in possession of the log book without the consent of the owner, and the log book must therefore be ignored for the purposes of the disposition.[2] It is difficult to accept this reasoning:

(1) It ignores the distinction drawn in *Oppenheimer v Attenborough* between the circumstances of (a) acquisition and (b) disposition by the ma: whilst the test of the owner's consent on acquisition is subjective, that of the ocb on disposition is objective.[3]

(2) Even assuming that the disposition was without the log book, it is difficult to see why such a disposition was necessarily not in the ocb. Somervell LJ suggested that the price would be substantially reduced by the absence of the log book;[4] Vaisey J argued that the reason is that a car without a log book is like a car with only three wheels (at 291), though many cars sold in the ocb are defective[5] or without some parts;[6] and Denning LJ pointed out that it is not in the ocb to sell a second hand car without a log book.[7] In *Astley Industrial Trust Ltd v Miller*[8] Chapman J indicated that he thought that the two Court of Appeal decisions were wrong on this point; but he was prepared if necessary to distinguish the two cases on the grounds that it is in the ocb to buy a new car without a log book. It is submitted that, on the principle laid down in *Oppenheimer v Attenborough*, what should matter is how the transaction ought to appear to the transferee (C): if the ma can supply either a genuine, or a genuine looking, vehicle registration document, or a good reason for its absence, or if that document is not ordinarily handed over, the transaction should be in the ocb.[9]

---

2   See also *Stadium Finance Ltd v Robbins* (set out ante, para 21.31), with respect to both log book and ignition key.

3   See *per* Chapman J in *Astley Industrial Trust Ltd v Miller* (see below) at 42. See also Goodhart (1951) 67 LQR 6; Hornby (1962) 25 MLR 722; Schofield [1963] JBL 344, 350; Powell, *Agency* (2nd edn), p 232.

4   At 283. Cf *Janesich v Attenborough* (1910) 102 LT 605, at 606. But there was no such reduction in Pearson; and, even if there were, this may only go to *bona fides* (see post, para 21.36).

5   See Powell, *op cit*, note 3, 231; Lanerolle [1967] JBL 329, 331–32.

6   The easy availability of replacement parts renders their absence of little significance: Schofield [1963] JBL 344 at 349.

7   At 290. This argument was adopted *Stadium Finance Ltd v Robbins* (above), where C never asked for the log book. They do not normally do so, it being understood that the hirer will take care of such matters. Does it follow, that *prima facie* the ocb is that the hirer will take possession of the log book?

8   [1968] 2 All ER 36.

9   See *Dreverton v Regal Garage Ltd* [1998] CLY 4382, Cty Ct. Does the present illogical position simply reflect a common law bias in favour of ownership that is likely to continue?

[21.36] A *bona fide* transferee. Neither good faith nor notice is defined by the FA;[1] but in *Heap v Motorists' Advisory Agency Ltd*,[2] Lush J held that the burden of proof in these matters lay on the transferee (C). Perhaps the most important issue here is the relationship between the ocb and the present requirement. It is clear from the decision in *Oppenheimer v Attenborough* that, if C thinks he is dealing with a principal, the fact that he is actually dealing with an ma who is not acting in the ocb is irrelevant.[3] However, if C realises that he is dealing with a particular type of ma, the fact that it is notorious that that type of ma never has authority to engage in the kind of transfer undertaken, eg, a pledge, will usually destroy C's *bona fides*.[4] Similarly, the fact that the goods were bought at a gross undervaluation should not prevent the transaction being in the ocb, but may go to C's *bona fides*.[5] Again, the absence of the registration document or ignition key on the sale of a car should not necessarily prevent the transaction from being in the ocb, but may indicate that C is not acting *bona fide*.[6] It is submitted that there are sound reasons for the dual requirements that the transfer be in the ocb and that C act *bona fide* and without notice.[7]

Effect of the exception

[21.37] Where the requirements of s 2(1) are satisfied (see ante, paras 21.26–36), that subsection provides that the disposition by the ma:

> ... shall, subject to the provisions of this Act, be as valid as if he were expressly authorised by the owner of the goods to make the same.

Whilst s 2(1) uses the term 'owner', it is submitted that its effect is to transfer only such title as the ma's transferor (A) has.[1] Even this rule is subject to certain qualifications in the Act. First, it has already been seen how the FA restricts the rights of a pledgee to the extent of the value given by him at the time of the pledge (see ante, para 21.33). Second, the FA enables the ma to create a lien over goods which he consigns to another in respect of 'advances made to or for the use of' the ma by the consignee (s 7).

In their *Twelfth Report*, the Law Reform Committee did not recommend any changes in this exception to the *nemo dat* rule;[2] but the changes they did recommend would

---

[21.36]

1   See the discussions of good faith, ante, para 21.20; and notice, post, para 21.49. The two requirements are not synonymous: Goode, *Commercial Law* (2nd edn), p 467.

2   [1923] 1 KB 577, especially at 590.

3   See also *Lloyds and Scottish Finance Ltd v Williamson* [1965] 1 All ER 641, CA; *Pacific Motor Auctions Ltd v Motor Credit Ltd* [1965] AC 867, PC.

4   *Per* Kennedy LJ in *Oppenheimer v Attenborough & Sons* [1908] 1 KB 221, CA, at 231.

5   This may be the explanation of *Pearson v Rose and Young Ltd* (set out ante, para 21.35): see Thornely [1962] CLJ 139, 141.

6   The crucial factor may often be failure on the part of the transferee to ask for the item: *per* Scrutton LJ in *Folkes v King* [1923] 1 KB 282, CA at 300. But see *per* Ormerod and Willmer LJJ in *Stadium Finance Ltd v Robbins* (set out ante, para 21.31) at 672–76.

7   *Contra* Atiyah, *Sale of Goods* (10th edn), p 388.

[21.37]

1   *National Employers Mutual etc Ltd v Jones* (set out post, para 21.54), *obiter per* Lord Goff at 431e, delivering the unanimous judgment of the HL and relying on the history of the section.

2   Cmnd 2958 (1966), paras 18; 40(5).

appear to offer protection to transferees in the position of the buyers in both *Pearson* and *Robbins* (see post, para 21.52).

SELLER IN POSSESSION[1]

[21.38] The exception. The policy behind the provision about to be discussed is as follows: where the seller (B) has sold the same goods to a number of people in succession, the first buyer to get physical possession of the goods or documents of title (C) is to be preferred to the others, even though he may immediately part with possession again.[2] This new exception to the *nemo dat* rule was embodied in s 8 of the FA 1889 (see ante, para 21.24). Unfortunately, the provision was repeated in the SGA 1893 in almost identical language, no attempt being made to repeal the earlier formulation. This provision, with the extra words of the FA italicised,[3] is now to be found in s 24 of the SGA 1979:

> Where a person, having sold goods, continues, or is, in possession of the goods or of the documents of title[4] to the goods, the delivery or transfer by that person, or by a mercantile agent[5] acting for him of the goods or documents of title under any sale, pledge[6] or other disposition[7] thereof, or *under any agreement for sale, pledge or other disposition thereof,* to any person receiving the same in good faith and without notice of the previous sale, shall have the same effect as if the person making the delivery or transfer were expressly authorised by the owner of the goods to make the same.

Once again, the statutory wording, and its judicial interpretation, needs careful analysis. In particular, the provision requires:

(1) A seller in possession (see post, para 21.39); and

(2) A delivery and disposition by him to a bf transferee (see post, para 21.41). However, if none of the successive transferees so qualifies, the first transferee (A) obtains title under the *nemo dat* rule.[8]

[21.39] Seller in possession. This exception to the *nemo dat* rule only applies where a seller is in possession.[1] Notice, first, the provision says 'sold', not 'agreed to sell': in the latter case, the seller could still pass a good title by virtue of his property in the goods.[2]

[21.38]

1 Compare the unpaid seller's powers and rights of resale: post, para 27.11.
2 See the diagram post, para 21.42. This is effectively to reverse the decision in *Johnson v Credit Lyonnais* (see ante, paras 19.10; 21.13).
3 The extra words still stand by reason of the SGA, s 21(2)(a), which is set out ante, para 21.02; and note the difference in punctuation. See also sales by a buyer: post, para 21.43.
4 See the discussions of 'goods' and 'documents of title': post, para 23.03.
5 For the definition of ma, see SGA, s 26; and ante, para 21.26.
6 For 'pledge' see ante, para 21.33 and post, para 21.41.
7 The phrase 'sale, pledge, or other disposition' is considered in relation to s 2(1) of the FA: see ante, para 21.33; and see post, para 21.49.
8 *Nicholson v Harper* [1895] 2 Ch 415.

[21.39]

1 *Anglo-Irish Asset Finance v DSG Financial Services* [1995] CLY 4491. For this purpose, there must be a contract of sale, so that a mortgage is insufficient: see SGA, s 62(4), ante, para 1.08.
2 Even if the second buyer took with notice of the earlier agreement to sell: Goode, *Commercial Law* (2nd edn), p 468. Compare buyers in possession post, paras 21.44–46.

Second, 'possession' here has its ordinary commercial meaning, so that a seller may be in possession by an agent.[3] Third, the provision does not say that the seller need be in possession with the buyer's consent.[4]

Most of the litigation involving this provision has centred on the meaning of the phrase 'continues, or is, in possession'. In *Mitchell v Jones*:[5]

> B sold and delivered a horse to the appellant (A). Thirteen days later, B leased the horse from A and then sold and delivered it to C, a bfp. The New Zealand Supreme Court held that C was not protected by their equivalent of s 24.

Stout CJ explained that the meaning of the phrase is (at 935):

> ... first, that if a person sells goods and continues in possession, even though he has made a valid contract of sale, provided that he has not delivered them, he may to a *bona fide* buyer make a good title; and, secondly, the putting-in of the words 'or is in possession of the goods' was meant to apply to a case of this character. If a vendor had not the goods when he sold them, but they came into his possession afterwards, then he would have possession of goods, and if he sold them to a *bona fide* purchaser he could make good title to them.

The English courts have similarly insisted that the provision will only operate where the seller (B) remains in possession **qua** seller: but they extended this rule to cover the situation where there has been no actual delivery by the seller, merely a change in the nature of his possession. In *Staffs Motor Guarantee Ltd v British Wagon Co Ltd*[6] Mackinnon LJ held that the dealer (B) who had remained in physical possession, could not pass a good title under what is now s 24 because he was no longer in possession **qua** seller, but in the capacity of hirer. This development received the approval of the Court of Appeal in *Eastern Distributors Ltd v Goldring*.[7] Later, the courts had second thoughts on this matter (see post, para 21.40).

[21.40] Whilst paying lip service to *Mitchell v Jones* (set out ante, para 21.39), the English decisions clearly went far beyond that case; and it would appear that they almost interpreted this exception to the *nemo dat* rule out of existence.[1] However, the Privy Council subsequently rejected the English case law on this point, and held that the disputed words refer, not to the nature of the seller's possession, but to the fact of his possession. In *Pacific Motor Auctions Ltd v Motor Credits Ltd*[2] a dealer unsuccessfully attempted to achieve a stocking plan by way of a sale and rehiring (see ante, para 16.20).

---

3   See s 1(2) of the FA (set out post, para 23.03) and *per* Branson J in *City Fur Manufacturing Co Ltd v Fureenbond (Brokers) London Ltd* [1937] 1 All ER 799, at 802 (see Bell, *Personal Property*, 56–57).

4   Cf ss 2(1) and 9 of the FA: see ante, para 21.31 and post, para 21.47.

5   (1905) 24 NZLR 932, SC.

6   Set out ante, para 21.28. See also *Olds Discount Ltd v Krett* [1940] 2 KB 117.

7   Set out ante, para 21.08, where the court accepted without question that A could not pass a good title under this exception because the character of his possession had changed from that of seller to bailee. See Goodhart (1957) 73 LQR 455, 459.

[21.40]

1   The only reported successful plea was a most unusual case: *Union Transport Finance Ltd v Ballardie* [1937] 1 KB 510.

2   [1965] AC 867; [1965] 2 All ER 105, PC.

Lord Pearce argued that what mattered was the dealer's physical possession.[3] His Lordship therefore concluded that the *Staffs Motor* case (set out ante, para 21.28), and *Goldring's* case (set out ante, para 21.08) *pro tanto*, were wrongly decided.[4] This lead was followed by the English Court of Appeal in *Worcester Works Finance Ltd v Cooden Engineering Co Ltd*:[5]

> The defendants (C) sold a car to B for £525, which was paid by cheque. B took delivery of the car and was registered as owner. Subsequently, B arranged a directly financed transaction whereunder the car was to be sold to the plaintiff finance company (A) who were to let it on hp terms to M. Whilst M signed a delivery receipt, he neither took delivery of the car nor paid any instalments. In the meantime, B's cheque to C had been dishonoured, and B relinquished possession of the car to C. To conceal his fraud from A, B for some time kept up payment of M's hire instalments.

The Court of Appeal unanimously agreed that B was a person who, having sold the car to A, *continued in possession* of it within the meaning of what is now s 24 of the SGA, because the italicised words referred to the **continuity of physical possession**, it being irrelevant that B remained in possession as bailee or trespasser; and the retaking of the car constituted a 'delivery' of it to C under a bf disposition (see post, para 21.41), so that C re-acquired a good title under this exception to the *nemo dat* rule. This new criterion of continuity of physical possession would seem both simpler and fairer, and will restore some worthwhile content to the provision; and it has been applied to a sale and rehiring transaction,[6] on the grounds that, as the sale and rehiring were a single transaction (para 17), there was under the sale a constructive transfer of possession from B to C1[7] and hence a constructive delivery to C1 within the SGA.[8]

[21.41] Delivery and disposition to be a bf transferee. The provision insists on all three of the following requirements:

(1) *Delivery or transfer*. As the intention of the legislature was to protect the first transferee to take possession (see ante, para 21.38), the exception is only expressed to protect a person to whom there is a 'delivery or transfer'.[1] Thus, if the seller in possession (B) makes successive dispositions to different persons, the first to obtain physical possession obtains title under the exception:[2] for instance, the *Worcester Works* case

---

3 'The object of the section is to protect an innocent purchaser who is deceived by the vendor's physical possession of the goods or documents and who is inevitably unaware of legal rights which follow the apparent power to dispose' (at 886). Part of this reasoning was cited with approval in the *Twelfth Report of the Law Reform Committee* (1966, Cmnd 2958), para 20.

4 At 889. See also Atiyah, *Sale of Goods* (10th edn), p 393.

5 [1972] 1 QB 210; [1971] 3 All ER 708, CA (Goode 35 MLR 186).

6 *Michael Gerson (Leasing) Ltd v Wilkinson* (set out post, para 21.41). A accepted that s 24 includes constructive delivery (at para 10).

7 So that B had a right to transfer possession to C1 under s 7(1) of the SGSA (para 20): see ante, para 12.04A.

8 *Per* Clarke LJ at paras 21–31: see post, para 23.03. His Lordship expressly rejected the argument that, unless the case came within the definition of possession in s 1(2) of the FA (set out, post, para 23.03), there cannot have been a delivery within the SGA (paras 34–36). See also *per* Pill LJ at para 92.

[21.41]

1 'Delivery' seems to refer to goods, and 'transfer' to document of title: see post, para 21.49. It is doubtful whether a transfer of goods by deed falls within these expressions: *Kitto v Bilbie* (1895) 72 LT 266. See further *Benjamin's Sale of Goods* (5th edn), paras 7.060; 7.074.

2 If acting for the seller, must an ma have actual authority? Or is it sufficient that the ma is acting within the ocb within s 2(1) of FA (see ante, para 21.25)?

(see ante, para 21.40), where C took physical possession of the car. However, the range of persons protected was extended in *Michael Gerson (Leasing) Ltd v Wilkinson*:[3]

> In March, B1 sought to raise money by a sale and leaseback of its plant and machinery, including the scheduled goods, to A; but B did not keep up the lease payments, though all the time retained physical possession of the goods. Subsequently, the goods were dealt with as follows:
>
> (1) In August, B sold and leased back the scheduled goods to C1; but, as B did not keep up the payments under this lease, C1 terminated the lease and sold the scheduled goods to C2. C1 and 2 successfully claimed title under s 24 of the SGA (see below).
>
> (2) Later, A terminated B1's lease of all the goods, including the scheduled ones, and purported to sell them to B2, who resold them to C2. C2 unsuccessfully claimed title under s 25 of the SGA (see post, para 21.44).
>
> A claimed as owner all the plant and machinery in conversion. C1 and C2 were bf purchasers without notice.

As to the scheduled goods, the Court of Appeal unanimously agreed as follows: under the August sale and leaseback, there had been a constructive delivery of the goods to C1 (see ante, para 21.40); and the result was that C1 obtained a good title under s 24 to the scheduled goods.

(2) *Disposition.* It is clear from the *Worcester Works* case (set out ante, para 21.40) that 'disposition' refers not to a transfer of legal possession, but of a proprietary interest in goods: B's transfer of legal (but not physical) possession to M was ignored, whilst his transfer of a proprietary interest to C satisfied this requirement. However, it would seem from the extra words in the FA that a mere agreement to dispose of the goods to C is sufficient for this purpose.[4] Four questions remain. First, since the formula 'under any sale, pledge or other disposition' is also found in ss 2(1) and 8 of the FA, does the formula have the same meaning in all three cases?[5] Second, does the express reference here to any 'pledge or other disposition' oust the general provision saving from the Act any transaction 'intended to operate by way of mortgage, pledge, charge or other security'?[6] Third, the rule requires a delivery under the disposition.[7] Fourth, by reason of the additional words in the FA referring to any agreement to sell etc, it may be that a conditional sub-buyer may obtain a good title provided his contract has matured into a sale, etc.[8]

(3) Bona fide *transferee*. Both ss 8 and 24 are only expressed to operate in favour of:

---

3 [2001] 1 All ER 148, CA.

4 See also ss 9 and 25(1) considered post, para 21.49. *Contra* the estoppel exception: see ante, para 21.08.

5 See ante, para 21.33. Does it make any difference that ss 2–7 of the FA may not be applicable here? See post, para 21.47.

6 Section 62(4): see further ante, para 1.08. *Contra Ladbroke Leasing (South West) Ltd v Reikie Plant Ltd* 1983 SLT 155.

7 Would a bailment for some other purpose be sufficient? Compare s 2(1) of the FA, which does not expressly require a delivery: see ante, para 21.33.

8 Eg, a *Romalpa* clause (see post, para 25.29) whose terms have been satisfied. *Aliter* if they have not: see the *Mills and Lawrence* case (set out post, para 21.51).

... any[9] person receiving[10] the [goods] in good faith and without notice of the previous sale.

A similar requirement was discussed in relation to mercantile agency, and here too raises questions as to the onus of proof (see ante, para 21.36). Furthermore, in the *Worcester Works* case, where the Court of Appeal unanimously held that C had retaken the car 'in good faith and without notice',[11] Lord Denning MR said that the word 'notice' here meant actual notice, by which he meant actual knowledge on the part of C of the sale by B to A, or deliberately turning a blind eye to it.[12]

[21.42] The effect of the exception. Where the requirements of ss 8 and 24 are satisfied, it is provided that the disposition with delivery to a bfp (C):

... shall have the same effect as if the person making the delivery or transfer were expressly authorised by the owner of the goods to make the same.

Suppose B steals goods from O and sells them successively to A, C and D; and then B delivers them to C.

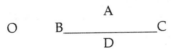

On ordinary common law principles (the first-in-time rule), B would pass his title to his first buyer (A: see ante, para 21.38), retaining nothing to transfer to subsequent innocent buyers (C, D).[1] However, the effect of ss 8 and 24 is to transfer B's best title to his first purchaser to obtain possession (C).[2] Presumably, the term 'owner' refers to the person with the property in the goods under the disposition from B to A,[3] so that C acquires no better title than B had, and best title remains in O.[4]

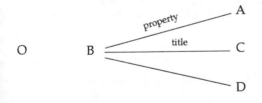

---

9 To whom does 'any person' refer? See Rutherford and Todd [1979] CLJ 346, at 355–58.

10 It is submitted that C's state of mind is to be tested at the time of purported disposal of the goods to him, not delivery to him, so as to make sense of the reference to A's lien. *Contra* Goode, *Commercial Law* (2nd edn), p 470.

11 *Per* Megaw LJ, at 221, upholding the conclusion of the trial judge. See also the comments in the *Pacific Motor Auctions* case [1965] AC 867, PC.

12 Because 'our commercial law does not like constructive notice': *per* Lord Denning MR at 218E.

[21.42]

1 See Goode, *Commercial Law* (2nd edn), p 468.

2 Does it matter in what capacity C acquires possession? Or whether C acquires notice of the previous sales after his purchase but before taking delivery? See generally Rutherford and Todd [1979] CLJ 346.

3 *National Employers Mutual etc Ltd v Jones* (set out post, para 21.54), *obiter per* Lord Goff at 432g– 433a, delivering the unanimous judgment of the HL and relying on the history of the section.

4 Compare ante, para 21.37 and post, para 21.54.

BUYER IN POSSESSION

[21.43] The exception. The converse situation to that of a seller in possession (see ante, para 21.38) is covered by s 9 of the FA and s 25(1) of the SGA.[1] The provision, with the extra words of the FA italicised,[2] is as follows:

> Where a person, having bought or agreed to buy goods, obtains with the consent of the seller possession[3] of the goods or the documents of title to the goods,[4] the delivery or transfer by that person or by a mercantile agent[5] acting for him, of the goods or documents of title,[6] under any sale, pledge, or other disposition thereof,[7] *or under any agreement for sale, pledge, or other disposition thereof*, to any person receiving the same in good faith and without notice of any lien or other right of the original seller in respect of the goods, shall have the same effect as if the person making the delivery or transfer were a mercantile agent in possession of the goods or documents of title with the consent of the owner.

Amazingly, the bfp (C) taking a transfer of a document of title receives further statutory protection under both s 10 of the FA and s 47(2) of the SGA,[8] in terms which differ markedly from ss 9 and 25 and from each other as to effect.[9]

This extraordinary duplication of statutory provisions, which have been restrictively interpreted,[10] require the following:

(1) B to be in possession as buyer (see post, para 21.44);

(2) With the consent of the seller (A) (see post, para 21.47); and

(3) B to make a delivery and disposition to a bfp (C) (see post, para 21.49).

Bought or agreed to buy

[21.44] Sections 9 and 25 are only expressed to be applicable where a person in possession (B) has 'bought or agreed to buy'.[1] In *Michael Gerson (Leasing) Ltd v Wilkinson* (set out ante,

---

[21.43]

1   Care is required with cases, since under the SGA 1893 this provision was numbered as s 25(2).
2   See ante, para 21.38, note 3.
3   See ante, para 21.39.
4   See the discussion of 'goods' and 'documents of title' ante, paras 21.29–30.
5   For the definition of ma, see SGA, s 26 and ante, para 21.26.
6   For the transfer of documents of title, see s 10 of the FA and s 47(2) of the SGA; and further my 1st edn, para 21.48.
7   For 'pledge or other disposition,' see ante, para 21.41.
8   Even the ambit of ss 10 and 47 contain a small verbal discrepancy – 'any' and 'a'. Does this matter?
9   Both are expressed to override A's rights of lien and stoppage, defeating them where B sells to C; but s 47(2) also expressly refers to a pledge by B to C. Does this make any difference? For a case where all four exceptions applied, see post, para 21.50.
10 They may even be confined to those circumstances where the true owner at least entered into a voidable contract to dispose of the goods: see post, para 21.54; and generally Goode, *Commercial Law* (2nd edn), p 472.

[21.44]

1   It is claimed that this emphasis on sale may cause anomalies where there is a contract to supply and fix: Atiyah, *Sale of Goods* (10th edn), p 398. But could not those difficulties be avoided by finding a hybrid contract: see ante, para 2.05?

para 21.41), C2 claimed all the plant and machinery on the basis that A had sold it to B2, who had resold it to C2: whilst the Court of Appeal were clear that there must at very least be a contract between A and B2 before s 25 can operate,[2] the majority were prepared to find such a contract[3] under which B2 had agreed to buy (see post, para 21.45); but C2 seems to have failed at the following hurdle. By virtue of that contract, whilst B must obtain **possession** of the goods or documents of title to them,[4] such possession of goods may be actual or constructive (see post, para 23.03): it includes a temporary loan[5] and has even been held to extend to the situation where A delivers goods direct to C at the request of B.[6] The essence of the provision is that B, being in possession,[7] must as purchaser[8] satisfy one of the following criteria:[9]

(1) *'Bought'*. If B has bought goods, and obtained possession of them with the consent of the seller (A), then at first sight it seems that B should be able to pass a good title by virtue of his property and possession, no exception to the *nemo dat* rule being required. However, it has been suggested that the effect of the exception is that the buyer (B) in possession of his own goods can only pass a good title in conformity with the terms of the exception.[10] Such a result would be startling; and there are two other possible explanations. First, just because a good title is passed under the exception where its terms are complied with, it does not follow that, where its terms are not complied with, a good title cannot be passed in any other way.[11] Second, it may be that the words 'bought or' are redundant, though it has been shown that there may be circumstances where these words are required to pass a good title under ss 9 and 25(1).[12]

(2) *'Agreed to buy'*. (See post, para 21.45.)

[21.45/46] 'Agreed to buy'. The phrase obviously comprehends ordinary conditional sales.[1] Now, it is tempting to assume that, where the seller (A) has agreed to sell, the buyer (B) must have agreed to buy; but this will not necessarily be so, because there can clearly be an agreement to sell without any agreement to buy, as where B purchases an

---

2 The s 25 plea failed on a lack of consent to B2's possession: see post, para 21.47.

3 *Per* Bennett J at para 85, Pill LJ concurring at 93. Clarke LJ dissented on this point (para 57).

4 *Michael Gerson (Leasing) Ltd v Wilkinson* (above), *per* Clarke LJ at para 66, the other two judges agreeing (paras 82, 88). As to the constructive delivery of goods, see ante, para 21.40; and as to delivery of goods and transfer of documents of title, see generally post, para 23.03.

5 *Marten v Whale* (set out ante, para 1.11).

6 *Four Point Garage Ltd v Carter* [1985] 3 All ER 12.

7 Must the possession be *qua* buyer, etc? Cf ante, para 21.40.

8 *Contra* if B only obtains the goods from A as agent for sale: *Shaw v Commissioner of Police* (set out ante, para 19.11).

9 The distinction between 'bought' and 'agreed to buy' is broadly whether the property in the goods has passed to the buyer: see ante, para 1.10.

10 Atiyah, *Sale of Goods* (3rd edn), p 158; but see note 11 below.

11 See Atiyah, *Sale of Goods* (10th edn), p 397.

12 Smith (1963) 7 SPTL 225–226; Rutherford and Todd [1976] JBL 262; *Benjamin's Sale of Goods* (5th edn), para 7.068; Goode, *Commercial Law* (2nd edn), p 472.

[21.45/46]

1 Eg, *Lee v Butler* (set out ante, para 1.15); *Marten v Whale* (set out ante, para 1.11); *Michael Gerson (Leasing) Ltd v Wilkinson* (see ante, para 21.44).

option to buy.[2] The effect of this last distinction was to draw a sharp line between two very similar transactions on the basis of whether or not B has agreed to buy: if he has, there is a conditional sale within s 2(3) of the SGA, and B may therefore pass a good title to C under s 25(1) of the SGA; but, if B has not agreed to buy,[3] the transaction is not a conditional sale and B cannot pass a good title under this exception to the *nemo dat* rule.[4]

Statute has settled doubts as to whether hp legislation applied to conditional sales by making express provision for such transactions.[5] However, in the course of a partial assimilation of conditional sales and hp transactions, s 25(2) of the SGA now provides that, for the purposes of s 25(1),[6] buyers under regulated conditional sales are not to be taken to be persons who have agreed to buy.[7] The effect of s 25(2) would appear to be that only the following contracts for the sale of goods are left within s 25(1): those under which the buyer has bought the goods (see ante, para 21.44); or contracts where there is a reservation of property, but **either** the price is not payable by instalments,[8] **or** the transaction does not amount to a consumer credit agreement.[9]

Whilst it is true that the HPA 1964 did introduce an entirely new exception to the *nemo dat* rule (see post, para, 21.55 *et seq*), the effect of s 25(2) is to reduce the statutory protection of the bfp by denying him the protection of the much wider exception in s 25(1). Not only does this run counter to the general trend of legislation, but it adds further complication to an already unduly difficult branch of the law.[10]

The seller's consent to disposal

[21.47/48] Consent. Unlike the provisions in respect of sellers in possession (see ante, para 21.39), the present exception to the *nemo dat* rule is only expressed to operate where the buyer (B) obtains possession with the **consent** of the seller (A).[1] Leaving aside possession (see ante, para 21.44), two questions arise:

(1) *What is the meaning of consent?* It will be recalled that consent to possession is similarly required in the case of the mercantile agency exception (see ante, para 21.31). On the

---

2   But see *Forthright Finance Ltd v Carlyle Finance Ltd* (set out ante, para 1.22). The question of whether 'sale or return' transactions fall within s 25(1) is discussed ante, para 20.27.

3   Or if his agreement to buy is void *ab initio*: see ante, para 21.19.

4   Eg, *Helby v Matthews* (set out ante, para 1.22).

5   The development was to be found in the HP Acts, is now embodied in the CCA and expressly excludes conditional sales from the definition of hp: see ante, para 1.24.

6   A similar limitation was introduced into s 9 of the FA by para 2 of Sched 4 of the CCA.

7   For conditional sales within the CCA, see ante, paras 1.16; 5.19. The result is to take outside s 25 of the SGA cases like *Lee v Butler* (above), the very decision which appeared to render necessary the invention of hp (see ante, para 1.22).

8   Eg, *Cahn v Pockett's Channel Ltd* (set out post, para 21.50); *Marten v Whale* (above); *Newtons of Wembley Ltd v Williams* (set out post, para 21.53); *Mount Ltd v Jay* (set out ante, para 21.04).

9   Eg, because the credit is outside the financial ambit (see ante, para 5.22) or B is a corporate buyer (see ante, para 5.24) or the agreement exempt (see ante, para 5.14).

10   *The Twelfth Report of the Law Reform Committee* (1966, Cmnd 2958) para 28, thought it inappropriate for the Report to recommend any changes in this area.

[21.47/48]

1   Goode, *Commercial Law* (2nd edn), p 473.

other hand, ss 2 and 9 do not fall under the same sub-heading of the FA,[2] which might imply that the provisions of s 2 do not apply to buyers in possession. This point was taken by the House of Lords in *Inglis v Robertson*,[3] an appeal from Scotland:[4]

> Wine merchant (B) contracted to buy from A whisky then lying in a bonded warehouse.[5] Afterwards, B had the whisky transferred to his own name in the books of the warehousekeeper, and obtained a delivery order from the latter. B then pledged the delivery order to C; but A subsequently claimed the goods as unpaid seller. C admitted that the pledge of the goods was defeated by his failure to notify the warehousekeeper,[6] but pleaded title under ss 3 and 9 of the FA.

Their Lordships found for the unpaid seller (A) on the following grounds:

(a) that the pledge of the documents of title did not amount to a pledge of the goods under FA, s 3, because ss 2–7 of the FA were only applicable where the transferor was a ma (which the wine merchant was not);[7] and

(b) that B had not obtained the goods 'with consent' within s 9 (see below).

However, the English Court of Appeal has twice held that the issue of consent in ss 9 and 25(1) is subject to ss 2(2), (3) and (4) of the FA;[8] and it is submitted that these decisions will probably be followed in England.[9]

(2) *What is meant by 'obtains'?* Sections 9 and 25(1) are expressed to cover only those situations where the buyer:

> ... *obtains* with the consent of the seller possession of the goods or the documents of title to the goods.

The meaning of these words was considered by the House of Lords in *Inglis v Robertson*, where their Lordships concluded that s 9 did not confer on the pledgee (C) a title free from the rights of the unpaid seller (A), because B did not obtain the documents of title either from A or with his consent, but 'in his own right and in his own name'.[10]

[21.49] Disposition by B. The provision insists on all three of the following requirements:

---

2 Sections 2–7 are sub-headed 'Dispositions by Mercantile Agents', whilst ss 8–10 are sub-headed 'Dispositions by Sellers and Buyers of Goods'.

3 [1898] AC 616, HL.

4 The HL held that Scots law applied, but that the FA 1889 was applicable to Scotland by virtue of the Factors (Scotland) Act 1890.

5 The property in the whisky would appear to have passed to the wine merchant: see *per* Lord Watson, at 626. But that would not defeat the unpaid seller's lien: see post, para 24.04.

6 Section 29(4) of the SGA: set out post, para 23.03.

7 At 624, 628, 630; and post, para 25.15. This result has been characterised as 'bizarre', because it allows an ma greater rights of disposal than an owner: Bell, *Personal Property*, pp 59–60.

8 *Cahn v Pockett's Channel Ltd* (set out post, para 21.50); *Newtons of Wembley Ltd v Williams* (set out post, para 21.53). See also *per* Sellers J in *Du Jardin v Beadman Bros Ltd* [1952] 2 QB 712 at 716.

9 *Benjamin's Sale of Goods* (5th edn), para 7.071. But see the recommendations of the Law Reform Committee: post, para 21.52.

10 *Per* Lord Watson at 629. See also *per* Lord Herschel, at 630. Why was the warehousekeeper not treated as the agent of A to issue the documents, in which case it could be said that the documents were issued by and with the consent of A?

(1) *Delivery or transfer*. Where C seeks to rely upon a delivery (see post, para 23.03) of the goods, or part of them,[1] he must show that B has voluntarily transferred possession of them to C. Thus, in *The Saetta*:[2]

> The charterparty of the ship provided (cl 15) that on termination of the charterparty the shipowner (C) shall 'accept and pay for all bunkers remaining on board' (see ante, para 20.06). However, some of those bunkers were claimed by A, who had supplied them to the charterer (B) and claimed to be an unpaid seller acting under a retention of title clause (see ante, para 20.28). C claimed that he had obtained a good title to the bunkers under s 25(1) of the SGA.

Clarke J held that B had agreed to buy the bunkers and obtained possession of them with the consent of A (see ante, para 21.44), but denied that the constructive transfer of possession of them to C under clause 15 amounted to the voluntary delivery required by s 25(1).[3]

(2) *Disposition*. Similar to the requirements in respect of dispositions, or agreements to dispose, by sellers in possession (see ante, para 21.41), there is here the additional factor that ss 10 and 47(2) specifically require that the disposition by B should be for valuable consideration, but it is not clear that ss 9 and 25(1) impose a similar requirement.[4]

(3) *A 'bona fide' transferee*. Sections 9 and 25(1) speak of the goods or documents of title being delivered or transferred to:[5]

> ... any person receiving the same in good faith and without notice of any lien or other right of the original seller in respect of the goods.

As in the cases of sellers in possession and mercantile agency, this raises the same issue as to the burden of proof (see ante, paras 21.36; 21.41). Neither the FA or the SGA defines notice, so this matter is left to the common law.[6] In *The Saetta*, Clarke J said *obiter*[7] that 'notice' means actual notice and not constructive notice; that the issue is objective; that a person is deemed to have notice if he deliberately turns a blind eye, but that a commercial man has no general duty to make enquiries; and that the burden of proof lies on C. Whereas ss 9 and 25(1) require that C should take *bona fide* and without notice of A's rights, ss 10 and 47(2) do not require an absence of such notice;[8] and it has been accepted by the courts that *bona fides* may, but will not necessarily, be defeated by notice.[9] Thus, it

---

[21.49]

1   As to the effect of a sub-sale of an individual bulk, see Nicol (1979) 42 MLR 129; and ante, para 20.22B.

2   [1994] 1 All ER 851; [1994] 1 WLR 1334.

3   Cf *Michael Gerson (Leasing) Ltd v Wilkinson* (see ante, para 21.41), *per* Clarke LJ at para 15.

4   See *Thomas Graham Ltd v Glenrothes Corporation* 1968 SLT 2; and also ante, para 21.33.

5   As to good faith, see SGA, s 61(3). As to liens, see post, para 25.02. As to 'other rights', eg, *Romalpa* clauses, see post, para 25.30; rights analogous to liens under SGA, s 39(2), see post, para 24.06. As to 'original seller', it is argued below that this refers to A (see post, para 21.54).

6   See *per* Tenterden LCJ in *Evans v Truman* (1831) 1 Mood & R 10.

7   The principles were laid down by Neill J in *Feuer Leather Corp v Frank Johnstone & Sons* [1981] Com LR 251 at 253. They were accepted by the parties, and seem to have been applied by Clarke J in *The Saetta* (above).

8   See the explanation in Chalmers, *Sale of Goods* (18th edn), p 309.

9   *Pacific Motor Auctions Ltd v Motor Credits Ltd* [1965] AC 867, PC.

would appear that ss 10 and 47(2) are wider than ss 9 and 25(1) in that a bfp **with** notice may acquire a good title under the former, but not the latter, provisions.[10]

The effect of the exception

[21.50] Introduction. The effect of all four statutory provisions is neatly illustrated by *Cahn v Pockett's Channel Ltd*:[1]

> A contracted to sell 10 tons of copper to B, delivery to be made at Rotterdam, and payment to be by B's acceptance of a bill of exchange. After shipping the copper, A forwarded to B the bill of lading and an acceptance. Meanwhile, B had contracted to sell 10 tons of copper to the plaintiff (C), and had then become insolvent. On the arrival of the documents, B did not accept the draft, but transferred the bill of lading to C who took bf and without notice of A's rights. A stopped the copper in transit, and C claimed title under ss 9 and 10[2] of the FA and ss 25(1) and 47 of the SGA.

The Court of Appeal agreed with Matthew J that the delivery of the bill of lading was conditional on acceptance of the draft, and that therefore s 19(3) of the SGA prevented the property passing from A to B (see ante, para 20.28). However, Matthew J had further held that such a conditional consent by A to B's possession of the bill of lading did not fall within s 25(1) of the SGA; and on this point he was unanimously reversed by the Court of Appeal, who held that C had obtained a good title under all four of the provisions.[3] Their Lordships argued that it was sufficient if there was actual consent, which could not be withdrawn (see ante, para 21.31), and rejected the argument that s 47 contains the only circumstances in which the seller's rights of lien and stoppage could be defeated.[4] It would therefore seem that s 47 merely repeats in part the effect of ss 9 and 25(1),[5] making it clear that the rights of the owner (A) are overridden *pro tanto* by the disposition (see post, para 24.16).

[21.51] Agreement to sell, etc, from B to C. As regards the effect of the exception, the extra words of s 9 of FA seem to bring within the provision those transactions where the second disposition is only an agreement 'for the sale, pledge or other disposition'. It might be thought that the effect of these words is that C can acquire a good title where he has only agreed to buy.[1] But this was denied in *Mills and Lawrence v Harris (Wholesale Meat) Ltd*:[2]

---

10 See Schmitthoff, *Sale of Goods* (2nd edn), p 168. Doubted by Atiyah, *Sale of Goods* (10th edn), p 402.

[21.50]

1 [1899] 1 QB 643, CA.

2 Presumably, the legislature intended s 10 to override the vendor's rights of lien and stoppage. See also FA, s 12(2). Was this expectation defeated by *Lyons v Hoffnung* (1890) 15 App Cas 391, PC?

3 As to the effect of ss 9 and 25(1), see post, para 21.51.

4 *Per* AL Smith and Collins LJJ at 657, 665.

5 But ss 9 and 25(1) refer to the 'owner', whereas, ss 10 and 47(2) refer to the 'seller'; and the seller may not be the owner: see Rutherford and Todd [1976] JBL 262, 264.

[21.51]

1 *Benjamin's Sale of Goods* (5th edn), para 5-151, note 22.

2 (1995) 14 Tr LR 273; *sub nom Re Highway Foods International Ltd* [1994] CLY 4029.

Wholesaler (A) agreed to sell meat (which turned out to be defective) to Highway Food Ltd (B), who in turn agreed to sub-sell and delivered it to a meat processor (C). Each contract contained a *Romalpa* clause (see post, para 25.29), reserving property until payment. Before payment under either contract, B's secured creditors appointed administrative receivers (see ante, para 19.14). A contacted C, who had already processed some 10% of the meat, and they made the following arrangement: C returned the unprocessed meat directly to A who removed the defect and then sold that meat direct to C.

The judge held that the property in the goods never passed from A to B because of the retention of title clause (see ante, para 20.28), so that the position with regard to the contract of sale from B to C was as follows:

(i) *The unprocessed meat.* As between A and B, s 9 of the FA was satisfied, because B had 'agreed to buy' (see post, para 21.44). However, as between B and C, ss 9 and 25(1) are drafted so that, where they operate, the disposition by B 'shall have the same effect as if [B] were an ma in possession ... with the consent of [A]';[3] that is, as if B were expressly authorised by A to dispose of the goods (see post, para 21.52). This last seems to require that B must actually sell the goods (as opposed to agree to see them) to C: as C had not paid the price to B, this had not happened; and so the judge argued that s 9 did not operate (at 279D). Accordingly, A retained title to the unprocessed meat which it repossessed (at 280D): this, it resold directly to C after removing the defect, so that A was entitled to the price due under the resale contract (at 280F). If the judge is correct, the extra italicised words in s 9 would seem to be of no effect whatever.

(ii) *The processed meat.* See post, para 25.30A.

[21.52/53] Sections 9 and 25(1). Where the conditions laid down by ss 9 and 25(1) are satisfied, it is provided thereby that the disposition by the buyer (B):

> ... shall have the same effect as if the person making the delivery or transfer were a mercantile agent in possession of the goods or documents of title with the consent of the owner.

This is an obvious reference back to s 2(1) of the FA (set out ante, para 21.25), but gives no indication how much of that provision was being incorporated, a point left open in *Cahn's* case (set out ante, para 21.50). There are at least two possibilities:

(1) *The lesser incorporation.* The effect might be to incorporate merely the result of s 2(1), so that the disposition by B:

> ... shall be as valid as if he were expressly authorised by the owner of the goods to make the same.

If so, the result would be the same as in the case of sales by a seller in possession (see ante, para 21.42).

(2) *The greater incorporation.* It might be read so that a disposition by B:

> ... made by him when acting in the ordinary course of business of a mercantile agent shall ... be as valid as if he were expressly authorised by the owner of the goods to make the same.

---

3 Atiyah, *Sale of Goods* (10th edn), pp 404, 471.

This would recognise the difference in wording from the exception in respect of sellers in possession (above).

The vital difference between the two is whether B is required to dispose of the goods in the ocb of an ma; and the Court of Appeal seems to have changed its mind on this point. In *Lee v Butler* (set out ante, para 1.15), the court appeared to take the first (lesser) view, there being no hint in that case of such a requirement. But in *Newtons of Wembley Ltd v Williams*[1] the court took the second (greater) view:

> On 15 June, the plaintiff (A) sold and delivered a Sunbeam car to rogue B in return for a cheque, it being agreed that the property should not pass until B's cheque was cleared. On 18 June, A found that B's cheque would not be met, and immediately took steps to try to recover the car. In July, C *bona fide* agreed to buy the car from B in the Warren Street car market; and thereafter C sold the car to D. In A's action to recover the car, the issue thus turned on whether C had a good title to transfer to D.

It was held that B had only obtained a voidable title, which had been avoided within a few days of 18 June (see ante, para 21.22); but the court nevertheless decided that C had acquired a good title under the FA. In the course of examining ss 2, 8 and 9 of that Act, Pearson LJ pointed out that B in possession might or might not be an ma and continued:[2]

> When the provisions of s 2 are applied to the s 9 position of [B] this is the *prima facie* result: if the transaction is made by the person concerned when acting in the ordinary course of the business of a mercantile agent, the transaction is validated: on the other hand, if the transaction is made by him when not acting in the ordinary course of business of a mercantile agent, the transaction is not validated.

On this basis, the Court of Appeal agreed that the determination of A's consent was irrelevant under s 9 by reason of s 2(2) of the FA (set out ante, para 21.31); that the test of whether a disposition (see ante, paras 21.34–35) was made in the ocb for the purposes of s 9 was the same as that under s 2 (see ante, paras 21.34–35); and that the sale by B in Warren St, where there was an established second hand car market, was made in the ocb.[3] In *The Saetta* (set out ante, para 21.49), Clarke J indicated that, had the matter been of first impression, he would not have introduced such a further requirement; but, feeling bound by *Newtons*, he found that B was acting in the ocb of ma.

There is no doubt that, if B is an ma disposing of the goods in the ocb he can pass a good title under this exception.[4] However, if B is not an ma, are the courts required to ask what would have been the situation if he had been? This difficult task has been attempted by an English court;[5] and in *Newtons* the court were saved from the issue by the accident

---

[21.52/53]

1   [1965] 1 QB 560; [1964] 3 All ER 532, CA. Affirming the first instance decision of Davies LJ.

2   At 578. He argued that the difference in wording between ss 8 and 9 must have been intended to bring about some difference in result because the difference was repeated in s 25 of the SGA. See also *per* Sellers LJ, at 574–75.

3   *Per* Sellers and Pearson LJJ, at 575, 580. Why was it not pleaded as a sale in market overt (as to which, see ante, para 21.05)?

4   *Forthright Finance Ltd v Carlyle Finance Ltd* (set out ante, para 1.22).

5   *Lambert v G & C Finance Corp* (1963) 107 SJ 666 (private seller B sold second hand car without the log book); but see ante, para 21.35.

that B happened to dispose of the car in the Warren St car market, hence looking like an ma. However, *Newtons* has been rejected in the Commonwealth in favour of the above lesser incorporation.[6] *Newtons* would appear incompatible with *Oppenheimer v Attenborough*.[7] It would also severely restrict the operation of ss 9 and 25(1),[8] and would appear to have rendered unnecessary the development of hp on the basis of the device sanctioned in *Helby v Matthews* (set out ante, para 1.22).

[21.54] The title transferred. The range of operation of this exception came before the English courts in *National Employers Mutual etc Ltd v Jones*:[1]

> A Fiesta car owned by Miss H was stolen and sold down a chain of buyers to L, to T, to A, to B, to C. Standing in the shoes of Miss H,[2] her insurer sued to recover from C the value of the car. C pleaded title under ss 9 and 25. It was agreed that C was completely honest.

The Court of Appeal decided that title remained in H under the *nemo dat* rule (see ante, para 19.11); and this decision was unanimously affirmed by the House of Lords on different grounds.[3] In delivering the judgment of the House, Lord Goff traced the history of ss 9 and 25, arguing as follows (at 432C): the FA 1877 referred to the transaction taking effect as if B were entrusted by the 'vendor' (A) with the documents of title; whereas s 9 of the FA 1889 spoke instead of the 'consent of the owner'. He reasoned that, for this change in expression to entail an alteration in meaning so that 'owner' referred to Miss H[4] instead of A:[5]

> ... would constitute a change in policy of a fundamental kind, of which there is no evidence whatsoever in the remainder of the 1889 Act.

The result is to reaffirm the estoppel basis of the FA exceptions to the *nemo data* rule (see ante, para 21.24): A, who has done the entrusting to B, has his title barred as against C; and because title to goods is not normally traceable very far, this will often determine such a title dispute.[6]

---

6 See Atiyah, *Sale of Goods* (10th edn), p 407.

7 Set out ante, para 21.34. The bfp thought that the broker was acting as principal, so that even if ss 9 and 25(1) do require the disposition to be in the ocb as in s 2(1), this should not unduly restrict the scope of the exception.

8 For arguments why this (surely *obiter*?) conclusion was wrong, see Goode, *HP Law and Practice* (2nd edn), pp 613–14. For its reversal, see the recommendation of the *Twelfth Report of the Law Reform Committee* (1966) Cmnd 2958, paras 23, 24; and *Benjamin's Sale of Goods* (5th edn), para 7.078.

[21.54]

1 [1990] AC 24; [1988] 2 All ER 425, HL (see Brown 104 LQR 516; Tiplady [1988] LMCLQ 297).

2 Having paid out Miss H, her insurer acquired her rights in the Fiesta by subrogation (cf post, para 25.07).

3 For trenchant criticism of the majority reasoning of the CA, see Tiplady (1988) 51 MLR 240.

4 This was the dissenting CA view of Buckley LJ (at 440f).

5 At 432e. For academic support, see Atiyah, *Sale of Goods* (10th edn), p 408; Goode, *Commercial Law* (2nd edn), pp 475–76; Dobson; [1987] JBL at 306.

6 Unless a case is taken outside this exception as being a consumer credit agreement: see ante, para 21.45.

SUPPLIES OF MOTOR VEHICLES[1]

The exception

[21.55] The decision in *Helby v Matthews* (set out ante, para 1.22) to the effect that a hirer under a hp agreement could not pass a good title under ss 9 and 25(1) (see ante, para 21.43) is particularly likely to work hardship on a bfp of a motor vehicle from the hirer. Accordingly, there was introduced a new exception to the *nemo dat* rule in Part III of the HPA 1964.[2] Unfortunately, in order to keep this new exception within the ambit of the mischief at which it was aimed, it proved necessary to draft it in extremely complex language, running to some four pages of the Statute Book.[3]

The exception is expressed to override the *nemo dat* rule but to be without prejudice to the FA or any other Act enabling the apparent owner to dispose of goods (s 27(5)). Its scope is set out in s 27(1), which says that:

> This section applies where a motor vehicle has been bailed under a hire-purchase agreement, or has been agreed to be sold under a conditional sale agreement, and, before the property in the vehicle has become vested in the debtor, he disposes of the vehicle to another person.

Whilst the terms **hire-purchase** and **conditional sale** are to have the meanings assigned to them by the CCA,[4] the other restrictions of the CCA are not applicable: so, it does not matter whether the agreement is exempt (see ante, para 5.14); nor whether the buyer or hirer is a body corporate (see ante, para 5.24); nor what the value of the goods is (see ante, para 5.22). Further, it should be noticed that s 27(1) is only expressed to operate where a motor vehicle[5] is disposed of by a debtor (hirer or buyer)[6] under a hp or conditional sale agreement:[7] it does not extend to leasing/simple hiring (see ante, para 1.18); and it is not needed in the case of credit sales (see ante, para 1.13). The insistence on an **agreement** means that s 27 can have no application if the proposal form put forward by the hirer or

---

[21.55]

1   See generally Goode, *HP Law and Practice* (2nd edn), pp 617–30; Guest, *Law of HP*, paras 757–71; *Benjamin's Sale of Goods* (5th edn), para 7.083 *et seq*.

2   As amended and set out in Sched 4 of the CCA. All subsequent references are to this amended version. Does the CCA version apply where the transaction is unregulated; or does the original version then apply?

3   The *Twelfth Report of the Law Reform Committee* (1966, Cmnd 2958), para 27, asks whether it is necessary to distinguish between motor vehicles and other goods. One might go further, and ask whether it is necessary to have an exception of this complexity at all.

4   Section 29 does this by setting out definitions of 'conditional sale' and 'hp' in terms identical (except as regards omission of any reference to land with regard to the former) to those in the CCA: as to which, see respectively ante, paras 1.16; 1.24.

5   As defined by s 29(1): 'a mechanically propelled vehicle intended or adapted for use on roads to which the public have access'. For instance, it is not likely to extend to contractors' plant. What about mobile cranes, earth moving equipment, combine harvesters? Cf Road Traffic Act 1988, s 185(1) (ante, para 4.37).

6   *Keeble v Combined Lease Finance plc* [1998] CLY 5656; [1998] GCCR 2065, CA (disposition by one joint debtor).

7   Eg, *Carlyle Finance Ltd v Pallas Industrial Finance Ltd* (set out ante, para 10.08). It obviously does not apply to a disposal by a person who has stolen the goods from the hirer or buyer: see Atiyah, *Sale of Goods* (10th edn), p 411; Guest, *Law of HP*, 760. As to dispositions by an employee or director of the hirer, see (1992) 47 CC2/27.

buyer is not accepted (see ante, para 10.02); nor where that agreement is illegal or void *ab initio*, as where the hirer gives a false identity to the finance company;[8] but that it can apply where the agreement is merely voidable,[9] or unenforceable under the CCA.[10]

It is unclear for how long a person is to be deemed a **debtor** for the purposes of s 27. Whilst s 29(4) seems to suggest that once a person has become a **debtor**, he is always deemed to be one for the purposes of s 27,[11] it has been argued that s 27 should no longer be applicable once the owner has resumed possession of the motor vehicle.[12]

[21.56] Trade or finance purchaser. Within the ambit of Part III (see ante, para 21.55), Parliament intended to protect consumers ('private purchasers'), but not persons in the motor trade.[1] The latter category, it termed **'trade or finance purchasers'**, defined in s 29(2) as 'a purchaser who, at the time of the disposition to him, carries on a business[2] which consists, wholly or partly of' (a) dealing in motor vehicles[3] or (b) directly financing such business.[4] Any other purchaser is a private purchaser (s 29(2): see post, para 21.57), which distinction was considered in *Stevenson v Beverley Bentinck Ltd*:[5]

> A was the owner of a car let on hp to B. Before completing the payments, B purported to sell the car to C, who took bf and without notice of the hp agreement. At the time of the purchase, C was employed full time as a tool room inspector, but in his spare time bought and sold cars: in the previous 18 months he had some 37 dealings in cars, some on his own account and some on account of a principal. When A sued for conversion of the car, C pleaded title as a 'private purchaser' within Part III of the HPA.

Notwithstanding that C bought this car for his own personal use, the Court of Appeal unanimously held that he was a **trade or finance purchaser** within the foregoing provision, pointing out that the provision contains no such qualification as 'in the course of business',[6] so that the courts were concerned with status rather than capacity.[7] Thus, C

---

8   *Shogun Finance Ltd v Hudson* (set out ante, para 10.15; criticised Finucane 151 NLJ 1217 on the grounds that the contract should only be voidable, because made face to face with the dealer who acted as the financier's agent. But on agency, see ante, paras 16.06; 16.10). For void contracts, see generally ante, paras 10.15; 21.19.

9   *Hitchens v General Guarantee Corp Ltd* [2001] 4 CL 291, CA (directly financed agreement made orally; distinguishing *Financings Ltd v Stimson* (set out ante, para 10.08)).

10   *Majid v TMV Finance Ltd* [1999] 5 CL 293, Cty Ct. What if the agreement has been avoided (see ante, para 21.19)?

11   *Chartered Trust plc v Conlay* [1998] CLY 2516, Cty Ct.

12   See Goode, *op cit*, note 1, p 620; Guest, *Law of HP*, para 759.

[21.56]

1   Persons in the motor trade were expected to protect themselves by prior checks with HPI: see ante, para 21.01. It has been suggested that fresh attention should be given to the need to protect bf 'trade or finance purchasers': *per* Lord Edmund-Davies in *Moorgate Mercantile Co Ltd v Twitchings* (set out ante, para 21.16), 922C.

2   As to carrying on a business, cf CCA 189(2): see ante, paras 5.36, 6.12.

3   What if he only repairs cars? Or is a scrap dealer?

4   For finance companies, see ante, para 2.17; and for direct financing, see ante, para 2.20.

5   [1976] 2 All ER 606; [1976] 1 WLR 483, CA.

6   Cf the undertakings as to fitness and quality (see ante, para 14.04) and exemption clauses (see ante, para 18.18).

7   Is this confined to those who deal as principal rather than as agent or employee?

could not acquire a Part III title (see post, para 21.58), though a multinational corporation outside the motor trade could qualify as a private purchaser.[8]

Dispositions to 'private purchasers'

[21.57] Where the disposition within s 27(1) (see ante, para 21.55) is to a **private purchaser** (see ante, para 21.56), s 27(2) provides that, if:

> ... he is a purchaser of the motor vehicle in good faith without notice of the hire-purchase or conditional sale agreement (the 'relevant agreement') that disposition shall have effect as if the creditor's title to the vehicle has been vested in the debtor immediately before that disposition.

1   *The disposition.* In carefully defining the term 'disposition',[1] the Act gives s 27 an effect which is both wider than s 25(1) of the SGA in that it does not require delivery, and narrower in that it does not cover pledges and liens (see ante, paras 21.43–54).

2   *To a private purchaser.* Section 27(2) only operates where the disposition is to a **private purchaser** and s 29(3) explains that:

> ... a person becomes a purchaser of a motor vehicle if, and at the time when, a disposition of the vehicle is made to him.

Moreover, it should be noted that **disposition** is defined in s 29(1) in such a way that there may be two dispositions in the case of a hp agreement with a **private purchaser**: (a) when the contract is made; and (b) when the option is exercised.[2]

3   *In good faith and without notice.* A private purchaser cannot obtain the benefit of s 27 unless he takes in good faith **and** without notice of the prior agreement. There are two separate requirement which must both be satisfied. So, a suspicious buyer who refrains from asking obvious questions (and thereby does not acquire notice) probably will not be in good faith.

It would appear that the underlying burden of proof of these two requirements is on the purchaser;[3] but the Act helps him by laying down certain presumptions in s 28 (see post, para 21.59). 'Notice' is defined by s 29(3) as actual notice at the time of disposition to him. It would therefore appear that constructive notice does not prevent a person claiming the benefit of s 27.[4] Further, in *Barker v Bell*[5] it was held that the agreement referred to in s 29(3) was only a **relevant** agreement,[6] meaning one to

---

8   Nor is the provision confined to regulated agreements: see ante, para 21.55.

[21.57]

1   Section 29(1) includes ordinary and conditional sales and hp. Does it extend to the situation where goods are taken in part exchange or swapped (see ante, para 2.09)? See the unusual conditional sale in the *Dodds* case (below).

2   What is the position if the purchaser is a motor dealer at the time he signs the agreement but not when he exercises his option; or vice versa? See Goode, *HP Law and Practice* (2nd edn), p 623.

3   See *Benjamin's Sale of Goods* (5th edn), para 7-095.

4   Eg, where a hp agreement is registered with HPI (see ante, para 21.01). There is no duty to search HPI (see ante, para 21.15).

5   [1971] 2 All ER 867; [1971] 1 WLR 983, CA (private purchaser falsely informed that all hp instalments had been paid; obtained Part III title).

6   'Or was' in s 27(3) was restricted to a relevant agreement which had automatically terminated on disposition (see post, para 26.09): *per* Lord Denning MR at 869d.

which the goods were subject at the time of the disposition.[7] The effect of these provisions was considered in *Dodds v Yorkshire Bank Finance Ltd*:[8]

> A let a Porsche car on hp to a builder (B). When his business got into financial difficulties, B sought to raise money from X. X arranged for Miss Dodds (C) to purchase the Porsche from B. As C was suspicious, B gave her a receipt saying 'I confirm that there is no hp agreement on this vehicle'. A having repossessed the Porsche, C claimed a Part III title. It was accepted that she had no notice of the hp agreement.

The Court of Appeal unanimously held that the transaction with C was an unusual type of conditional sale. However, A argued that, as a suspicious purchaser, C was not in good faith: whilst good faith was not defined in Part III, A conceded that it had the same meaning as in the SGA (see ante, para 21.20). Neill LJ commented:

> That means that good faith is equated with honesty and bad faith with dishonesty.

His Lordship pointed out that C's suspicions were allayed by the receipt and that she was therefore acting in good faith and acquired a Part III title.[9]

4   *Creditor and debtor.* Under s 27(2), the title of the 'creditor' (A)[10] will vest in the 'debtor'(C).[11]

[21.58] Effect. Section 27(2) provides that a disposition within its ambit:

> ... shall have effect as if the creditor's title to the vehicle had been vested in the debtor immediately before that disposition.

However, s 29(5) explains that:

> ... any reference to the title of the creditor to a motor vehicle which has been bailed under a hire-purchase agreement, or agreed to be sold under a conditional sale agreement, and is disposed of by the debtor, is a reference to such title (if any) to the vehicle as, immediately before that disposition, was vested in the person who then was the creditor in relation to the agreement.

Suppose A is in possession of a motor vehicle which has been stolen from O; A lets it on hp to B; B wrongfully sells it to C during the currency of the agreement; and C resells it to D:

O

A_____hp_____B_____sale_____C_____sale_____D

---

7   See s 27(2). As to the burden of proof, see *Benjamin's Sale of Goods* (5th edn), para 7.095.
8   [1992] CCLR 92; [1992] GCCR 1621, CA (see 47 CC1/7).
9   Miss Dodds gave evidence that she thought the builder would not sign the receipt if untrue. Would a business-buyer (a private purchaser within Part III) likewise be in good faith when insisting on such a receipt?
10   'Creditor' is defined in s 29(1) as the bailor in hp or the seller in sale or his assignee. Cf the CCA definitions: see ante, para 5.25.
11   'Debtor' is defined in s 29(4) as the bailee under a hp agreement or the buyer in a sale (but not his assignee). Cf the CCA definition: see ante, para 5.24. As to s 29(4), see further ante, para 21.55.

If C acts *bona fide*,[1] the effect of ss 27 and 29(5) is to confer on him A's title (usually called a Part III title[2]), though best title remains in O.[3] Suppose A can claim title under one of the other exceptions to the *nemo dat* rule: does this imply that C may, if he wishes, affirm the supply to him and stand in A's shoes and similarly claim title under that exception?[4] If C acts *mala fide*, neither C nor D can claim the benefit of s 27, which is only expressed to apply where the first purchaser from B acts *bona fide*; but, provided C does act *bona fide*, D will have the benefit of s 27 even though he acts *mala fide*[5] or is a dealer.[6] Finally, it should be noticed that s 27(6) explicitly saves any civil or criminal liability of A.[7] In *Barber v NWS Bank plc* (set out ante, para 12.04), the judge ignored C's Part III title on the basis that, even so, the effect of s 27(6) was to preserve C's action against the innocent finance company.[8]

Dispositions to trade or finance purchasers

[21.59] Suppose A is in possession of a motor vehicle which has been stolen from O; A lets it on hp to B and during the currency of the agreement B wrongfully sells it to C, a bf *trade or finance purchaser*; and C later resells to D, a bf *private purchaser*, who resells to E:[1]

O

A____hp____B____sale____C (op)____sale____D (fpp)____sale____E

Section 27(3) terms C the original purchaser, and provides that, where C is a *trade or finance purchaser*:

> ... then if the person who is the first private purchaser of the motor vehicle after that disposition (the 'first private purchaser') is a purchaser of the vehicle in good faith without notice of the relevant agreement, the disposition of the vehicle to the first private purchaser shall have effect as if the title of the creditor to the vehicle had been vested in the debtor immediately before he disposed of it to the original purchaser.

The effect of s 27(3) on the above example is that the title of A ('the creditor') is deemed to have vested in B ('the debtor') immediately before he disposed of the vehicle to C ('the original purchaser'), with the result that, utilising this fiction, C can pass A's title to D ('the first private purchaser': s 29(5): set out ante, para 21.58). So long as D acts *bona fide*, D obtains, and can pass to E, A's title irrespective of whether E takes *bona fide*; but best title remains in O. Notwithstanding that A's title passes through B and C to D, s 27(6) makes it

---

[21.58]

1 For the remainder of this section, the term *bona fide* purchaser is used to mean one who takes in good faith and without notice, and the term *mala fide* purchaser for one who does not.
2 See *Royscot Trust Ltd v Rogerson* (set out post, para 27.28).
3 Under the *nemo dat* rule: see ante, para 19.11. Cf ante, para 21.54.
4 See Goode, *HP Law and Practice* (2nd edn), p 624.
5 D will not then be guilty of handling stolen goods: Theft Act 1968, s 24(3).
6 D will as a dealer commonly discover that C has tendered him a Part III title through a search of HPI (see ante, para 21.01). As to whether this will amount to a breach by C of the SGA, s 12(1), see Goode, *Commercial Law* (2nd edn), pp 479–80; and generally ante, para 12.03.
7 Eg, the tort of conversion (see ante, para 19.04) or crime of theft.
8 This seems to beg the question. Does C have an action against NWS where C acquires a Part III title? See Macleod (1996) 15 Tr LR 223 (pages transposed).

[21.59]

1 Cf *Butterworth's case* (set out ante, para 12.06).

clear that B and C are to remain both civilly and criminally liable.[2] Where the disposition to D is by way of a financed hp transaction,[3] s 27(4) provides that, when the property in the vehicle is transferred to D or E under the terms of the hp agreement,[4] D or E, as the case may be, will obtain A's title.[5]

Particularly where some trade or finance purchasers are involved, it is obvious that the chain of title may be lengthy. In such circumstances, it may be difficult to prove those requirements necessary for the operation of s 27. Parliament therefore enacted in s 28 an elaborate series of presumptions in favour of the person seeking to rely on s 27. They are applicable where a purchaser proves that in a chain of dispositions he[6] is a *bona fide* private purchaser of a vehicle previously supplied on hp or conditional sale.[7] In such circumstances, the effect of s 28 is that that purchaser will get a Part III title unless A can show that there is no bf first private purchaser in the chain.[8]

[21.60] Certificates of title. Because so many suppliers of motor vehicles (see ante, para 4.37) on hp or conditional sale are being deprived of their ownership by Part III titles, their trade organisations (the FLA) sponsored a failed Private Members Bill.[1] A second opportunity for statutory reform has appeared with an EU Directive aiming at a common vehicle registration scheme.[2] The Directive is in two parts:

Part 1 is mandatory for all Member States and lays down that in each an authority will issue certificates containing information as to first registration when the vehicle is new.[3]

Part 2 is voluntary and designed to facilitate the checking of rightful ownership of a motor vehicle for the time being. The issue is whether the UK will adopt this title registration system.[4]

---

2 See ante, para 21.58.

3 Why did the draftsman not provide as well for the case where D takes under a conditional sale agreement?

4 The person exercising the option does not have to be bf at that moment also. What if D sells the motor vehicle to E during the currency of his agreement?

5 Why was it necessary for the draftsman to insert both s 27(4) and the definition of 'disposition' in s 29(1)?

6 Or a party through whom he is claiming (X); the purchaser or X (as the case may be) is described as the 'relevant purchaser'.

7 Section 28(1). *Contra* where all the dispositions are known: *Soneco Ltd v Barcross Finance Ltd* [1978] RTR 444, CA (presumably supportable on the grounds that C, D and E were all shown to be *mala fide*?).

8 See further Goode, *HP Law and Practice* (2nd edn), pp 628–30.

[21.60]

1 The Vehicles (Ownership) Bill 1994. See Davies [1995] JBL 36; 15 Legal Studies 14.

2 1999/37/EC (see Davies [2001] JBL 489). It is due for implementation June 2004.

3 In the UK, the DVLC will presumably satisfy this requirement.

4 For a discussion of the effect of so doing, see Davies, *op cit*, note 1, 499 *et seq*.

CHAPTER 22

RISK AND IMPOSSIBILITY

RISK

General rules

[22.01] Risk. Logically, the term 'risk' ought to cover both losses and gains as regards the goods which are the subject matter of the supply contract; but the pessimistic lawyer will usually use 'risk' solely in the sense of risk of loss.[1] In this sense, the ordinary rule of risk is summed up by the Latin maxim *res perit domino* (risk falls on the owner): it refers to the physical deterioration or destruction,[2] or fall in financial value of, goods supplied happening without breach of the supply contract;[3] and its operation may *pro tanto* override other contractual obligations.[4] Whilst also relating to the subject matter of the contract, the foregoing rule is to be distinguished from both the *nemo dat* rule (see ante, para 19.11) and the rules applicable where one of the parties becomes insolvent (see ante, para 19.22–23).

In the case of sales,[5] the general assumption of the common law is that any risk of loss or chance of gain accrued to the owner, and thus depended on the passing of property.[6] This rule is embodied in s 20(1) of the SGA, which provides that, unless otherwise agreed (see post, para 22.02):

> ... the goods remain at the seller's risk until the property therein is transferred to the buyer, but when then property therein is transferred to the buyer, the goods are at the buyer's risk whether delivery has been made or not.

It has already been seen that delivery is the most obvious act of appropriation of unascertained goods (see ante, para 20.17), so that in sales of unascertained goods the property and risk will usually pass on delivery.[7] However, if property and possession are separated, s 20 is a reminder that risk will follow property, not possession,[8] and may

---

[22.01]

1   See Sealey [1972B] 31 CLJ 225, especially 227–37.
2   The owner will thus remain liable to perform his side of the bargain, notwithstanding any deterioration in the goods, that would otherwise discharge both parties under the doctrine of frustration: see Goode, *Commercial Law* (2nd edn), p 249, and further post, para 22.17.
3   Compare the situation where the loss is due to breach by the supplier of his contractual promises: see post, para 23.09.
4   Thus, an unpaid seller bearing the risk cannot after destruction of the goods sue for the price (*Healy v Howlett*: set out post, para 22.06); but, unless the contract is frustrated (see post, para 22.14), he remains liable for non-delivery (see post, para 29.17).
5   Do these sale rules apply to the supply and fixing of goods (see ante, para 1.08) and other quasi-sales (see ante, para 2.10)?
6   See ante, Chapter 20. Does it matter that property will not necessarily pass at delivery, which is the moment at which the implied terms are to be tested (see ante, para 14.06)?
7   Eg, *Warden's Import and Export Co Ltd v Norwood* (set out ante, para 20.17). For mail order sales, see ante, paras 8.19; 20.22.
8   Eg, *Pignatoro v Gilroy* (set out ante, para 20.19). The rule is criticised by Atiyah, *Sale of Goods* (10th edn), p 350; and see the other solutions referred to ante, para 19.10.

determine the contractual rights of the parties.[9] In the case of co-owners, the risk is divided between them in proportion to their proprietary interest (new s 20A(2)(b) of the SGA: see ante, para 20.22C).

The position in respect of sales may be compared with that in bailment and hp transactions. In both the latter cases, the maxim *res perit domino* also applies: risk of loss *prima facie* falls on the bailor. However, it is a well established rule in bailment that any gains *prima facie* accrue to the bailee, on the grounds that the bailor should not be allowed the double benefit of rent and gains; and, in *Tucker v Farm and General Investments Trust Ltd*,[10] the Court of Appeal decided that this rule should apply to hp agreements, notwithstanding the element of sale they contained, so that the hirer could sue for conversion of the lambs (see generally ante, para 19.05).

[22.02] Contrary intention. It is clear that the presumption outlined above may give way to a contrary intention. It will be recalled that the same is the case with the rules relating to the passing of property (see ante, para 20.06). But there is a practical difference between the two situations: the concept of risk is easier for a layman to understand, so that it is, perhaps, more common for a contract to make special provision as to risk,[1] than to deal expressly with the passing of property.[2] As with a provision as to the passing of property (see ante, para 20.10), the obligation to insure is at best an ambiguous indication of the intention of the parties:[3] it may or may not show where the risk is to lie.[4] Of course, if the contract is a standard form one (see ante, para 11.08), then it is likely to make express provision for risk, property and insurance; and it will do so in the manner most advantageous to the *proferens*.[5] It is, therefore, unlikely that the ordinary standard form instalment contract will leave the matter to the ordinary law. On the other hand, where there is a consumer supply contract (see ante, para 11.12A), an express provision as to risk which favours the supplier may amount to an unfair term.[6]

However, ordinary sales, including retail sales, may well make no provision as to risk of loss, in which case the basic presumption is that *res perit domino*, though there are certain special cases where this presumption is qualified[7] and these special cases must now be examined.[8]

---

9   Eg, if the property and risk is in the buyer, even destruction of the goods will probably not frustrate the contract (see post para 22.17), so that the seller can sue for the price (see post, para 27.35), whilst the buyer cannot sue for non-delivery of those goods (see post, para 29.19).

10   [1966] 2 QB 421; [1966] 2 All ER 508, CA.

[22.02]

1   Eg, to pass on delivery: *Re Bond Worth Ltd* (set out post, para 25.32); *Borden (UK) Ltd v Scottish Timber Products Ltd* (set out post, para 25.31); Harvey and Meisel, *Auctions* (2nd edn), p 219.

2   For the situation where the parties split the risk, see Sealy [1972B] 31 CLJ 225, at 246–47.

3   The existence of insurance does not eliminate issues of risk, but merely shifts them from insured to insurer: Goode, *Commercial Law* (2nd edn), p 270.

4   See Atiyah, *Sale of Goods* (10th edn), p 321.

5   Eg, *Romalpa* clauses (see the cases cited in note 1 above); cif contracts (see post, para 22.07); maintenance of security clauses (see ante, para 11.09).

6   OFT, *Bulletin No 13*, case 1; *No 15*, case 3.

7   Do s 20(2) and (3) give way to a contrary intention? The matter appears to have been rather clearer in the 1893 Act.

8   These may either cause the risk to remain in the supplier, or to revert to him upon some particular occurrence.

Delay in delivery

A distinction must immediately be drawn according to whether or not the delay in delivery amounts to a breach of the supply contract. The contractual duties relating to delivery will be considered later (see post, para 23.05 *et seq*).

[22.03] Delay amounting to breach of contract. For this situation, s 20(2) provides as follows:

> But where a delivery has been delayed through the fault[1] of either buyer or seller the goods are at the risk of the party in fault as regards any loss which might not have occurred but for such fault.

In *Demby Hamilton Ltd v Barden*:[2]

> There was a contract for the sale of 30 tons of apple juice by sample, the juice to be delivered in weekly instalments. The seller crushed all 30 tons at once in order to ensure correspondence with the sample. After some instalments had been delivered, the buyer in breach of contract gave no further delivery instructions; and the juice went putrid. Sellers J decided that the property remained in the seller, but that the loss fell on the buyer under what is now s 20(2).

His Lordship found some difficulty construing the provision, but eventually concluded that it applied because it would have been difficult for the seller (a) to ensure correspondence with sample unless he crushed all 30 tons at once, or (b) to replace the juice with other juice equal to sample if he had sold the juice in his possession.[3] Moreover, the provision clearly requires a causal connection between the fault and the loss, and the test which the judge seems to have applied was whether the seller acted reasonably after the default of the buyer. The implication seems to be that, if the seller had not acted reasonably, what is now s 20(2) would not have applied.[4] Further, it should be noted that s 20(2) does not operate in respect of any breach of contract, but only those breaches relating to delivery, and that it seems to assume that the property passes on delivery.[5]

If s 20(2) is invoked upon default by the buyer, the risk affected by that delay passes to the buyer: the effect is that the contract probably cannot be frustrated by the occurrence of that risk (see post, para 22.17) and the buyer is liable for the price or damages for non-acceptance.[6] If s 20(2) is invoked upon default by the seller, that risk remains with the seller: the seller cannot plead frustration where self-induced (see post, para 22.14), but remains liable for damages for non-delivery.[7]

[22.03]

1 Section 61(1) provides that 'fault' means 'wrongful act of default'. See also ante, para 2.06. 'Fault' seems to be confined in s 20(2) to delay-causing fault: Goode, *Commercial Law* (2nd edn), p 255.

2 [1949] 1 All ER 435; [1949] WN 73.

3 If he could have done, the buyer should have resold the goods elsewhere, in which case the responsibility is on him (at 438A). This ties in with the duty to mitigate: see post, para 27.44.

4 As to the position then, see Goode, *op cit*, note 1, pp 257–58.

5 As under s 18, r 5(2): set out ante, para 20.17. Can s 20(2) apply where property has already passed (as it might under s 18, r 5(1) before delivery: see ante, para 20.16)?

6 See respectively post, paras 27.17–18 and 27.35. Eg, the *Borden* case (above: it is not clear from the reports whether the seller recovered part of the price or damage). See generally Goode, *op cit*, note 1, p 205.

7 See post, para 29.20; and generally Goode, *op cit*, note 1, pp 202–03.

[22.04] Delay which is not a breach of contract. Where the buyer is entitled to, and does, delay in taking delivery, it may sometimes be inferred that the parties intend the risk to pass notwithstanding that property remains in the seller. In *Sterns Ltd v Vickers Ltd*:[1]

> On 3 January, the defendants (D) bought from X 200,000 gallons of white spirit then lying in the tanks of Y on terms that they should have free storage until 31 January. On 17 January, D sold by sample to P 120,000 gallons of that spirit, and it was agreed that P should make their own arrangement for storage after 31 January. On 23 January P resold by sample the 120,000 gallons to Z on terms that Z should pay the storage charges. On 28 January, D obtained a delivery warrant from Y and handed it to P, who endorsed it to Z. Z did not take delivery for some months; but when he did so found that the spirit had deteriorated in quality, mainly due to the fact that Y had topped up the tank with other, slightly different, consignments of spirits in order to save space.[2] Z claimed damages from P who in turn claimed from D. On the only point on which the dispute is reported, the Court of Appeal unanimously found in favour of D as against P.

Scrutton LJ thought that the property in the 120,000 gallons remained in the defendants,[3] but that this did not preclude the plaintiff from having an insurable interest in an undivided share and bearing the risk;[4] and he concluded that the risk passed to the plaintiff because, in handing over the delivery warrant, the defendants had performed their duty to deliver (constructively) and had put it out of their power to control the goods. This decision has subsequently received the approval of the House of Lords, though their Lordships stressed the exceptional nature of the case;[5] and it also seems to accord with the subsequently enacted s 20A of the SGA.[6]

However, *Sterns Ltd v Vickers Ltd* gives rise to a number of problems. Did the risk pass on 28 January with constructive delivery; or only subsequently on the delay in taking actual delivery?[7] Second, would the decision have been the same if the spirit had deteriorated before 28 January? It does not appear from the reports when the spirit was adulterated: but, if it were before 28 January, then the case would appear to conflict with *Healy v Howlett* (set out post, para 22.06). Assuming the spirit was adulterated after 28 January, it is arguable that contractual permission to delay in taking delivery shows an intention that the goods should remain at the seller's risk.[8] Third, could the Court of Appeal have reached this decision if the goods had been any other than an unascertained

---

[22.04]

1   [1923] 1 KB 78; [1922] All ER Rep 126, CA (see the discussions in *Benjamin's Sale of Goods* (5th edn), paras 6-004; 18-240–45).

2   The real complaint is against Y, the bailee. For the situation where the bailee is acting as a carrier, see post, para 22.05.

3   The other two judges expressed no opinion on this point: see now ante, para 20.22A.

4   If the spirit had been stored in two tanks, and Y had only adulterated one, it follows that the buyer should get the contents of the good tank, and a proportion of the bad: see Atiyah, *Sale of Goods* (10th edn), p 351.

5   *Per* Lords Porter and Normand in *Comptoir D'Achat v Luis de Ridder Limitada* [1949] AC 293, HL at 312, 319. But see Goode, *Commercial Law* (2nd edn), p 254.

6   The facts of *Sterns v Vickers* may fall within s 20A of the SGA; and that section, introduced in 1995, may transfer the risk: see ante, para 20.22C.

7   Is the important thing Z's delay in taking actual delivery, or the fact that P made a contract under which Z might, and did, legitimately delay in taking delivery?

8   From the position that, if delay had been a breach of contract on the part of P, the risk would have been on him: see ante, para 22.03.

part of a specific whole?[9] Whilst the rule could apply to specific goods,[10] it is submitted that it could not operate in respect of generic or future goods.[11]

Transit

[22.05] The rule. Where under a contract of sale the goods are subject to a transit from seller to buyer,[1] we have already seen that the implied undertakings as to fitness and quality are tested at the end of the transit, so that the seller is impliedly promising that the goods will stand up to an ordinary transit (see ante, para 14.06). Subject to this understanding that the goods are travelworthy, the SGA makes special provision for risks materialising during the course of transit.[2] Section 33 provides:

> Where the seller of goods agrees to deliver them at his own risk at a place other than that where they are when sold, the buyer must, nevertheless, unless otherwise agreed, take any risk of deterioration in the goods necessarily incident to the course of transit.

This section is expressed to give way to a contrary intention. Moreover, it can only operate where (a) the contract ousts the ordinary assumption that delivery is to be at the seller's place of business,[3] **and** (b) the seller agrees to deliver at his own risk. The section is not expressed very clearly, but was probably intended to reflect the common law, where a distinction was drawn between an ordinary and an extraordinary deterioration.[4] In those circumstances where it operates, s 33 would appear to assume that the parties have agreed to allocate the risk of deterioration because of the contemplated transit as follows:

1. *Normal transit.* The buyer is to bear the risk under s 33 of any deterioration which all goods of the contract description would ordinarily suffer during that transit;[5] but the seller is to bear the risk of any deterioration due to some inherent vice peculiar to the contract goods which precludes their being travelworthy (see ante, para 14.06).

2. *Abnormal transit.* The owner – whether seller or buyer – bears the risk of any deterioration due to any abnormality of the transit under the ordinary principle *res perit domino* (see post, para 22.06).

[22.06] Abnormal transits. The principle *res perit domino* (see ante, para 22.01) applies to abnormal transits. Thus, in *Healy v Howlett*:[1]

---

9 Were the goods unascertained under the contract between P and D? See Nicol (1979) 42 MLR at 134.

10 Eg, a conditional sale (see ante, para 1.14).

11 See Atiyah, *Sale of Goods* (10th edn), 352.

[22.05]

1 Distinguish where the third party has possession of goods but not *qua* carrier: see ante, para 22.04.

2 Delivery to the carrier (see post, para 23.03) *prima facie* marks the commencement of the transit (s 45(1)): see post, para 24.18) and appropriation of the goods (s 18, r 5(2): see ante, para 20.17).

3 As in ex-ship contracts (see post, para 22.07). For the ordinary rule, see s 29(1): discussed post, para 23.04.

4 See *per* Alderson B in *Bull v Robinson* (1854) 10 Exch 342, at 346.

5 Section 33. Is this section redundant? Compare Greig, *Sale of Goods*, pp 217–18 with Goode, *Commercial Law* (2nd edn), p 265.

[22.06]

1 [1917] 1 KB 337, DC.

The plaintiff fish exporter (P), who carried on business in Ireland, contracted to sell 20 boxes of mackerel to the defendant (D), a Billingsgate fish salesman, this being the first transaction between the parties. P consigned by railway 190 boxes of mackerel. He wired instructions to the railway officials at Holyhead to apportion the boxes between three of his customers, including D, and notified D by invoice that the fish was at his risk from the moment it was put on rail. Owing to delays in Ireland, the fish was no longer in a merchantable state by the time it reached D, and he refused to accept it. P's action for the price[2] failed before the Divisional Court, which held that the invoice could not transfer the risk because it was subsequent to the agreement,[3] that risk therefore went with property, and that the property had not passed.

The Court decided that the property had not passed because there had not been any effective appropriation: they argued that the earmarking took place after the delay, when the fish had already begun to deteriorate, and that the railway officials at Holyhead were then in the impossible position of having to decide who would get the deteriorated fish. Whilst it may be that there cannot be any appropriation sufficient to pass the property in these circumstances (see ante, para 20.15), *Sterns Ltd v Vickers Ltd* (set out ante, para 22.04) demonstrates that this does not of itself prevent the risk passing. However, it may be that the two cases can be distinguished on the following grounds: in *Sterns Ltd v Vickers Ltd* the seller had probably discharged his duty of delivery before the deterioration of the spirit;[4] but in *Healy v Howlett* the deterioration had set in before delivery.[5] In the latter case, the delay in transit took it outside s 33.

[22.07] Delivery to a carrier: export sales. Section 32 makes provision for those cases where the contract envisages delivery to a carrier for transmission to the buyer; and s 32(1) provides that delivery to the carrier shall *prima facie* be deemed delivery to the buyer (see post, para 23.03). The importance of ss 32(2) and (3) is primarily in relation to export sales, which are beyond the scope of this work (see ante, para 1.01); but it may be convenient if the major types of such contract are listed:[1]

1   *Ex-works or ex-store contracts.* The designation primarily refers to the place of delivery (see post, para 23.04), and all the ordinary rules as to the passing of property and risk apply.

2   *Free on board (fob) contracts.* The expense of delivering the goods on board ship *prima facie* lies on the seller, who must have a cargo available.[2] It is unusual in an fob contract for the property to pass before shipment;[3] and it may not even pass on shipment, as where an unascertained part of a specific whole is sold (see *Re Wait* (set out ante, para 20.22)), or there is a reservation of a right of disposal (see ante, para

---

2   As to actions for the price, see post, para 27.16.
3   It might be otherwise if this were not the first transaction between the parties: see ante, para 18.04.
4   For the duty to deliver, see post, para 23.05 *et seq.*
5   Presumably delivery was to take place in London, thus ousting s 32(1): as to which, see post, para 23.03.

[22.07]
1   The question of the type to which a particular contract belongs is a matter of construing the intention of the parties: *Couturier v Hastie* (set out post, para 22.10).
2   *The Naxos* [1990] 3 All ER 641, HL.
3   See *Federspiel & Co v Twigg & Co Ltd* (set out ante, para 20.16).

20.28), or the whole of the price has not yet been paid.[4] Although the property may not pass on shipment, the risk will usually do so;[5] subject to the following exceptions:

(a) *Carriage.* To try to ensure that, if the goods are damaged in transit, the buyer has an effective claim against the carrier (see post, para 22.08), s 32(2) requires that, *prima facie,* the seller must make a reasonable contract of carriage on behalf of the buyer. The effect of non-compliance with s 32(2) is that risk does not pass on shipment;[6] and the buyer may recover from the seller in respect of any loss in transit, whether or not this loss is due to the breach of s 32(2) (cf s 20(1): see ante, para 22.01). Where the seller complies with s 32(2), the ordinary rule of risk applies (see above).

(b) *Insurance.* Sometimes, the contract of sale provides that the seller is to ship the goods and pay the freight, but the buyer is left to take out and pay for any marine insurance: these are described as 'C(ost) and F(reight)' contracts. In such cases, the seller must give the buyer sufficient notice to enable the buyer to take out such insurance; and failure to do so leaves the sea transit at the seller's risk (s 32(3)).

3 *Cost, insurance and freight (cif) contracts.* Under this type of contract, the seller undertakes the following duties:

(a) To deliver the goods to the port and to ship them under a contract for their carriage to the agreed destination; and

(b) To insure the goods for the transit; and

(c) To tender the buyer an invoice, bill of lading[7] and insurance policy.

In law, these documents together represent the goods, a rule which has several important effects on cif contracts. First, the seller's duty is to tender the documents, so that s 32(1) is ousted; and delivery of the documents amounts to delivery of the goods (see post, para 23.03). Second, because the seller is under an express obligation to insure, s 32(3) is inapplicable. Third, the risk usually passes on shipment,[8] unless the seller is in breach of s 32(2). Fourth, it is the transfer of the bill of lading (not delivery) which will usually transfer the property in the goods, once they are ascertained.[9] Fifth, the buyer has two rights to reject: he may reject the documents if they do not comply with the contract;[10] and reject subsequently arriving goods that do not comply with the contract (see post, para 29.03). Sixth, destruction of the goods after shipment cannot frustrate a cif contract.[11]

4 *Arrival or ex-ship contracts.* The seller's obligation is to deliver the goods from a ship on arrival at a named port, and not merely to ship goods for transit to that port, as in the

---

4   *Mitsui & Co v Flota Mercante Etc SA* [1989] 1 All ER 951, CA.
5   *Inglis v Stock* (1885) 10 App Cas 263, HL.
6   *Thomas Young Ltd v Hobson* (1949) 65 TLR 365.
7   If the seller is entitled to substitute a delivery order for a bill of lading, it is not a cif contract, but an arrival contract.
8   *Tsakiroglou & Co Ltd v Noblee Thorl GmbH* [1962] AC 93, HL.
9   *Cheetham & Co Ltd v Thornham Spinning Co Ltd* [1964] 2 Lloyd's Rep 17. *Contra* arrival contracts: see below.
10   *Kwei Tek Chao v British Traders Ltd* (set out post, para 29.30). *Contra* where the documents conform with the contract: *Gill & Duffus SA v Berger & Co Inc* (set out post, para 23.06).
11   *Manbre Saccharine Co Ltd v Corn Products Ltd* [1919] 1 KB 198.

case of fob and cif contracts. Section 32 can have no application to arrival contracts. The bill of lading only operates as a delivery order, so that its transfer does not pass the property in the goods; and the risk remains in the seller until arrival.[12]

Bailment during course of a sale

[22.08] It may be that the subject matter of the contract of supply is for some time in the possession of someone other than the owner of the goods; and that someone may be either one of the parties to the supply contract or a third party. Where the loss is not due to any breach of duty by that bailee,[1] the loss will *prima facie* fall on the owner; but, it is otherwise if the loss is due to a breach of duty by the bailee.[2]

1 *A contracting party bailee.* Either the seller or buyer may be in possession as bailee whilst the property in the goods belongs to the other party; and in either case s 20(3) of the SGA enacts that:

> Nothing in this section shall affect the duties or liabilities or either seller or buyer as a bailee ... of the goods of the other party.

This simply preserves the common law rules of bailment and allows of two possibilities:

(a) Property passes before delivery, in which case the seller may be in possession under a contract for value (the supply contract): unless otherwise agreed, his duty is to exercise reasonable care.[3] If the buyer fails to take delivery at the contract time, the supplier becomes either an involuntary or gratuitous bailee, with correspondingly lower duties of care.[4]

(b) Property passes after delivery, in which case the buyer may be a bailee for value (see ante, para 1.14) and *prima facie*[5] under a duty to exercise reasonable care during the continuance of the bailment.[6]

2 *A third party bailee.* Where the goods are damaged or lost by the act of an independent third party, either of the parties to the contract for the supply of the goods may wish to maintain an action against the third party in contract or tort:

(a) In tort. An action in negligence will be available to the buyer when the property in the goods has passed to him (*The Elafi*: set out ante, para 20.05B); but it is unlikely

---

12 *Comptoir D'Achat v Luis de Ridder Limitada* [1949] AC 293, HL. Subject to s 33: see ante, para 22.05.
[22.08]
1 The duties of a bailee are discussed in Crossley Vaines, *Personal Property* (5th edn), p 85 *et seq*; and see ante, para 1.17.
2 If both bailee and owner are negligent, does the Law Reform (Contributory Negligence) Act 1945 apply? As to this Act see post, para 27.40.
3 *Wiehe v Dennis Brothers* (1913) 29 TLR 250; *Nelson v Raphael* [1979] RTR 437, CA.
4 *Benjamin's Sale of Goods* (5th edn), para 6-022. See ante, para 1.17.
5 The typical conditional sale will probably specify the buyer's duties as bailee.
6 Presumably the position is the same in respect of a transferee under a sale or return transaction: see ante, para 20.23.

to succeed prior to that event[7] whilst he is out of (actual?) possession (see ante, para 19.10).

(b) In contract. Whilst an action in contract under the terms of the bill of lading may be available to the seller,[8] the buyer to whom the bill is transferred is prevented by his lack of privity from suing on the bill at common law[9] but was given such a statutory right of action under s 1 of the Bills of Lading Act 1855. This statutory exception to the privity rule having proved to be too narrow, it was replaced by the Carriage of Goods by Sea Act 1992.[10] The central provision of the 1992 Act allows the lawful holder of a bill of lading to assert contractual rights of suit against the carrier of the goods, whether or not the property in the goods has passed to him.[11] It does not cure his lack of privity as against any other third party handling the goods, eg, a stevedore.[12] Nor does it deal with purchase out of a bulk (see SGA, new s 20B: see ante, para 20.22C).

IMPOSSIBILITY

[22.09] Assuming that the parties to a contract for the supply of goods have reached an agreement,[1] that agreement may be, or become, impossible of performance in the manner envisaged in the contract. This impossibility may be caused by any number of events, ranging from the death, insolvency or imprisonment of a contracting party to the destruction of the subject matter or illegality of the contract. The question to be discussed in this section is whether the impossibility of performance will discharge either or both the parties from their contractual obligations; or whether the non-performance caused by the impossibility will constitute a breach of contract actionable by the other party.[2] Leaving aside void and illegal contracts,[3] the supply contract may *prima facie* be open to any one of the following interpretations in respect of a particular type of impossibility:

(1) The supplier promises that the particular type of impossibility has not occurred or will not occur, but the obligations of the other party (the buyer or hirer) will lapse by reason of the impossibility; or

---

7   *The Aliakmon* [1986] 1 AC 785, HL, discussed by Schmitthoff, *Export Trade* (10th edn), 2-030; Goode (1987) 103 LQR 433, at 453–60; [1990] JBL 23; 107 LQR 264–66. As to claims in negligence for economic loss, see Markensis 103 LQR 354, at 384–95; and generally ante, para 17.14. Does this ruling extend to claims for wrongful interference with goods (see ante, para 19.04)?

8   Once the property has passed, the seller suing a bailee in contract may recover only nominal damages: *The Albazero* [1977] AC 774, HL.

9   *Scruttons Ltd v Midland Silicones Ltd* [1962] AC 446, HL. But the bailee may enter into a separate contract of carriage with the buyer: *The Albazero* (above).

10 This is based on the recommendations of the Law Commission Report, *Rights of Suit in Respect of Carriage of Goods by Sea* (1991, Law Com 196).

11 Section 2(1). Section 3 breaks the link in the 1855 Act between the acquisition of contractual rights and the transfer of the property in goods.

12 *Scruttons Ltd v Midland Silicones Ltd* (above); *The Aliakmon* (above).

[22.09]

1   For the rules as to formation of a supply contract, see ante, para 10.02 *et seq.*

2   'Nothing in this section affects a condition or warranty whose fulfilment is excused by law by reason of impossibility or otherwise': SGA, s 11(6).

3   As to which, see respectively ante, paras 10.14–17; 10.18–20.

(2) The buyer or hirer promises that the particular type of impossibility has not occurred or will not occur, but the obligations of the supplier will lapse by reason of the impossibility; or

(3) The obligations of both parties will lapse by reason of the impossibility; or

(4) The obligations of both parties are to remain binding despite the impossibility of performing the primary obligations,[4] because the contract stipulates in these circumstances for an alternative method of performance, eg, *force majeure* (see post, para 22.13A).

At this point, it is necessary to distinguish between initial and subsequent impossibility: the contract may be impossible of performance at the time when it is made; or it may become impossible of performance at some later stage.

Initial impossibility

[22.10] The supply contract may be initially impossible of performance owing to the act or omission of a contracting party, eg, where the contract contemplates that the goods be obtained by the supplier from a third party, and he makes no attempt to obtain them from the third party; or by reason of the conduct of some third party, eg, where the contract contemplates that the goods be obtained by the supplier from a third party who refuses to supply them; or because of the happening or non-happening of some event, eg, the destruction or non-arrival of the goods respectively. The effect of such impossibility should *prima facie* be a question of interpretation; but in one case the matter is apparently dealt with prescriptively by statute. Section 6 of the SGA provides:

> Where there is a contract for the sale of specific goods,[1] and the goods without the knowledge of the seller have perished[1] at the time when the contract is made, the contract is void.

Within its ambit,[2] s 6 would appear to admit of only one interpretation of the contract; namely, that neither party will be under any contractual liability, ie option (3) in para 22.09. The section was always thought to embody the House of Lords decision in *Couturier v Hastie*:[3]

> The seller shipped a cargo of corn at Salonica for delivery in England, and then employed a London corn-factor to sell it on a *del credere* commission. However, owing to inclement weather the cargo became unfit for further transit and was sold by the ship's master in Tunis. Unaware of this sale, the corn-factor shortly afterwards negotiated a sale of the cargo 'free on board, and including freight and insurance to a safe port in the United Kingdom'. On discovering the previous sale by the ship's master the buyer repudiated the contract.[4]

---

4   *The Safeer* [1994] 1 Lloyd's Rep 637. Distinguish secondary obligations: see post, para 26.16.

[22.10]

1   As to 'specific goods' and 'perished', see post, para 22.13.

2   The expression 'contract of sale' is apt to cover the situation whether or not that contract has purported to pass the property in the goods.

3   (1856) 5 HL Cas 673; [1843–60] All ER Rep 280.

4   Because the insurance policy did not cover the loss: Treitel, *Law of Contract* (10th edn), p 271, note 79.

As a *del credere* agent guarantees performance by the party he introduces, the seller sued the corn-factor for the price.

The liability of the corn-factor depended on that of his buyer; and accordingly the argument turned on whether the repudiation by the buyer had been wrongful. The Court of Exchequer held that the true meaning of the contract was that there was a sale of an adventure,[5] **the goods or documents**, so that the buyer, and therefore the corn-factor, remained liable for the price.[6] However, the Court of Exchequer Chamber[7] and the House of Lords took the contrary view; namely, that there was an fob contract for the sale of **goods** alone (see ante, para 22.07), and the buyer, and therefore the corn-factor, was not liable for the price. Not only was this decision reached as a matter of construction, but strictly it only decided that the buyer was not liable for the price in the absence of delivery.[8] Thus, it did not decide whether the seller was liable for non-delivery, or whether both parties were discharged; but it seems to have been taken by Chalmers to have decided the latter.[9]

[22.11] More recently, the issue of *res extincta* has been canvassed in *McRae v The Commonwealth Disposals Commission*:[1]

> The Commission was charged with the task of disposing of the various wrecks lying abandoned in the Pacific at the end of World War Two. By accident, they offered for sale a non-existent tanker on a non-existent reef. The plaintiff, who had submitted the successful tender, incurred considerable expenditure in undertaking an abortive salvage expedition. The plaintiff's action for breach of contract, deceit and negligence succeeded before the High Court of Australia on the first ground.

The Court decided that the equivalent of s 6 in the State of Victoria did not apply because the goods had never existed; that the question was primarily one of construction; and that the Commission had impliedly warranted that the tanker existed, that is, option (1) in para 22.09. On the basis of the cases, there are a number of possible interpretations of English law.[2]

(1) *Couturier v Hastie* (set out ante, para 22.10) indicates that the contract is void for mistake; and this rule is embodied in s 6. This implies that *McRae's* case does not represent English law, and that a contract falling within the ambit of s 6 is always void for mistake.[3]

(2) *Couturier v Hastie* may be distinguished from *McRae's* case on the basis that in the latter the goods never existed, whereas in the former case the goods did have an existence once. If this view is adopted, then it may be that s 6 only applies where the

---

5   Compare cif contracts (ante, para 22.07); and the explanation by Treitel, *ibid*, p 270.
6   (1852) 8 Ex 40.
7   (1853) 9 Ex 102.
8   Slade (1954), 70 LQR 385, 396–97.
9   See Chalmers, *Sale of Goods* (18th edn), p 98.
[22.11]
1   (1951) 84 CLR 377.
2   See *Benjamin's Sale of Goods* (5th edn), paras 1.128–33.
3   Ie, option (3) in para 22.09. See Glanville Williams (1954) 17 MLR 154, 155.

goods once had an existence, which was the view taken by the High Court of Australia.

(3) *Couturier v Hastie* does not show that the contract is void for mistake; and s 6 embodies a mere presumption to that effect.[4] Such an argument may be bolstered by reference to ss 49 and 51(1) of the SGA.[5] On the other hand, s 6 is one of the few which is not expressed to give way to a contrary intention,[6] and the terminology of s 55(1) is difficult to reconcile with its application here.[7]

(4) The contract of supply will always be rendered void by the non-existence of the subject matter, but that there may be a collateral contract whereby the seller warrants the existence of the goods.[8] Such a device would be of no avail if the contract of sale remained purely executory on both sides.[6] Alternatively, it may be that there is liability in tort for deceit or negligent misstatement.[9]

[22.12] Effect of s 6. The effect of the operation of s 6 of the SGA is illustrated by *Barrow, Lane & Ballard Ltd v Phillips & Co Ltd*:[1]

On 7 October, the plaintiff (P) purchased one lot of 700 bags of ground nuts then in the possession of a warehousekeeper (W), and inspected but did not count the bags. On 11 October, P agreed to sell the 700 bags to the defendant (D), and the next day handed D a delivery order, which D immediately presented to W. D agreed to resell the goods; but when D attempted to take delivery six weeks later it was discovered that W only had 150 bags in his warehouse. It was found that 109 bags had been stolen from, or irregularly delivered by, W before 11 October, and that 441 bags had similarly disappeared after that date. W being insolvent, P sued for the price of (150+441=) 591 bags, arguing that the property had passed in the goods then in store on contract (11 October).

Wright J held that the 700 bags was an indivisible parcel;[2] that the present situation fell within s 6, and that the contract was therefore void; but that the seller was entitled to the 'price' of the 150 bags actually received.[3] His Lordship denied that the acceptance of the delivery order by W constituted an appropriation of the 591 bags, on the grounds that the parties only intended to appropriate the 700 bags (see ante, para 20.14). The seller (P) further argued that the case was to be treated as a tender of the wrong quantity within s 30, and that the buyer (D) had accepted the offer of 591 bags; but Wright J disagreed with this on the grounds that (1) s 30 gives the buyer an option to reject and rescind when he knows the true facts (see ante, para 13.04), and (2) the contract was void under s 6. Nor did his Lordship think that the property passed to D by reason of their sub-sale or delay

---

4   See *Bell v Lever Bros* [1932] AC 161, HL, *per* Lord Atkin at 217.
5   As to whether s 49 gives way to a contrary intent, see post, para 27.16. Section 55(1) is set out ante, para 18.09. See Atiyah, *Sale of Goods* (10th edn), p 96; *Chalmers' Sale of Goods* (18th edn), pp 98–99.
6   Treitel, *Law of Contract* (10th edn), p 272.
7   Smith (1963) JSPTL 227.
8   Cheshire and Fifoot, *Law of Contract* (11th edn), p 223; but see 13th edn at 241.
9   See Treitel, *Law of Contract*, *op cit*, note 6; and generally ante, para 17.19 *et seq*.
[22.12]
1   [1929] 1 KB 575; [1928] All ER Rep 74.
2   The answer might have been different if the contract had been divisible: see post, para 23.24.
3   Presumably in quasi-contract. But the buyer had already resold, so how could the quasi-contractual remedy be available? See post, para 29.15.

in taking delivery, and pointed out that there was no contract under which the property could pass.[4]

[22.13] Ambit of s 6. In view of the apparently restricting effect which s 6 has on the ability of the courts to interpret the intention of the parties, it is important to delimit the ambit of the section, which is only expressed to be applicable where 'specific goods' have 'perished' under a contract of sale. Does s 6 apply to quasi-sales, sale or return, or hp?

1   *Specific goods.* Both ss 6 and 7 are limited to sales of 'specific goods'. This term presumably means the same in each case, and will be considered in connection with s 7 (see post, para 22.15).

2   *Perish.* Both ss 6 and 7 are only expressed to be applicable where the contract goods have 'perished'. Presumably, this term means the same in each case, though it is nowhere defined in the SGA. The term obviously covers physical destruction; and it would also seem to include those situations[1] where the goods are unavailable to the parties for completion of the contract for some reason which is beyond the control of the parties.[2] Can the goods be said to 'perish' whilst they remain identifiable in the hands of the parties? According to Benjamin,[3] goods have 'perished' where they have 'ceased to exist in a commercial sense', as where a cargo of cement is submerged, or dates saturated in sewage.[4] But can this be taken further? Can those situations be included where the goods have never existed,[5] or where they are requisitioned,[6] or where the contract is illegal?[7] What if only part of the goods suffer such a calamity?[8] Is it going too far to suggest that the goods have 'perished' where, subject to the *de minimis* rule, any part of them are commercially unavailable to the parties for the performance of the contract?

Subsequent impossibility

[22.13A] The supply contract may become impossible of performance subsequent to its formation. In this situation, the rules of risk decide who bears the loss of the goods (see ante, paras 22.01–08); but they will not determine whether the supervening impossibility from causes not expressly or impliedly dealt with by the allocation of risk (see above)

---

4   Therefore the risk could not pass under *Sterns Ltd v Vickers Ltd* (set out ante, para 22.04).

[22.13]

1   Eg, *Couturier v Hastie* (set out ante, para 22.10); *Barrow, Lane and Ballard Ltd v Phillips & Co Ltd* (set out ante, para 22.12).

2   Eg, lawful sale to third party – *Couturier v Hastie* (above). *Contra* where the supplier caused the non-availability, as by selling and delivering the goods to a third party: *Goode v Garriock* [1972] 2 Lloyd's Rep 369, at 372. What if the seller causes the unavailability, but is protected by an exclusion clause? Compare self-induced frustration: see post, para 22.14.

3   *Sale of Goods* (5th edn), para 1-126.

4   Cf *Asfar & Co v Blundell* [1896] 1 QB 123, CA. But see *obiter* to the contrary in *Horn v Minister of Food* [1948] 2 All ER 1036, which is usually thought to be wrong (Atiyah, *Sale of Goods* (10th edn), 101; Chalmers, *Sale of Goods* (18th edn), p 99) but would provide another method of escaping ss 6 and 7. See also *Rendell v Turnbull* (1908) 27 NZLR 1067.

5   Eg, *McRae's case* (set out ante, para 22.11).

6   Cf *Re Shipton Anderson & Co* [1915] 3 KB 676, DC.

7   Cf *Re Badische Co Ltd* [1921] 2 Ch 331.

8   See the *Barrow, Lane* case (above); *Benjamin's Sale of Goods* (5th edn), para 1-126.

discharges both parties from their obligations under the contract. The parties will only be so discharged where the contract is frustrated. As with a breach discharging a contract (see post, para 26.16), it is thought that the effect of frustration is to bring to an end all the remaining indivisible executory obligations in a contract.[1] Particularly in international trade, the parties sometimes seek to deal with such difficulties by what have become known as *force majeure* clauses.[2] Whilst a simple provision that a contract shall be subject to '*force majeure* conditions' is void for uncertainty,[3] clauses spelling out the events causing difficulty in performance may lead to frustration of the contract (see below) by reason of impossibility.[4] In a commercial contract, such a clause may be subject to the reasonableness test (s 3 of UCTA: see ante, para 18.24); and in consumer contracts it may also be an unfair term (see ante, para 11.12 *et seq*).

When a contract may be frustrated

[22.14] *Prima facie*, a contract for the supply of goods may be frustrated by the destruction of the person or thing essential for its performance,[1] by legal impossibility[2] or illegality,[3] by serious delay inconsistent with the terms of the contract,[4] or by the disappearance of the purpose of the contract;[5] but it is clear that a party cannot rely on a self-induced frustrating event[6] or moral duties.[7]

Suppose the parties make specific provision in their contract for the *prima facie* frustrating event, eg, *force majeure* clauses (see ante, para 22.13A). Can reliance be placed on the possible interpretation of contractual intention analysed above (ante, para 22.09); or does the doctrine of frustration prevent this? In part, the answer may depend on the theoretical basis of the doctrine of frustration;[8] but in one situation there has been statutory intervention. Section 7 of the SGA provides:

[22.13A]

1   As to the implications of this, see post, para 22.17.

2   As to which see Schmitthoff, *Export Trade* (10th edn), 6-017–21; Atiyah, *Sale of Goods* (10th edn), pp 359–60.

3   *British Electrical etc Ltd v Patley Pressings Ltd* [1953] 1 All ER 94; see generally *Benjamin's Sale of Goods* (5th edn), para 8-084 *et seq*; and ante, para 10.03.

4   See further Schmitthoff, *Export Trade* (10th edn), 6-016; Benjamin, *op cit*, note 3, paras 6-050; 18-294 *et seq*.

[22.14]

1   Eg, *Taylor v Caldwell* (1863) 32 LJQB 164. But see cif contracts: ante, para 22.07. As to the situation where there is part destruction of goods promised to several buyers, see post, para 22.16.

2   Eg, *Re Shipton Anderson & Co* [1915] 3 KB 676, DC.

3   *Re Badische* [1921] 2 331; *Kursell v Timber Operators Ltd* (set out ante, para 20.04).

4   Eg, *Jackson v Union Marine Insurance Co Ltd* (1874) LR 10 CP 125. Distinguish non-frustrating delays eg, *Shearson Lehman Hutton Inc v Maclaine Watson & Co Inc* [1989] 2 Lloyd's Rep 570 (see [1990] LMCLQ at 308). For the effect of a non-frustrating delay on risk, see ante, paras 22.03–04.

5   Eg, *Krell v Henry* [1903] 2 KB 740, CA (not a goods case).

6   *Maritime National Fish Ltd v Ocean Trawlers Ltd* [1935] AC 524, PC. Does this rule cover all events falling within ss 20(2), (3) of the SGA (see ante, paras 22.03; 22.08)? See also *Goodey v Garriock* [1972] 2 Lloyd's Rep 369.

7   *Pancommerce SA v Veeckeema BV* [1983] 2 Lloyd's Rep 304, CA. Cf the US Uniform Commercial Code, Art 2-615.

8   See Treitel, *Law of Contract* (10th edn), 858–62. And see *Clarke v Bates* [1913] LJCR 63, Cty Ct; affd by DC at 114.

Where there is an agreement to sell specific goods, and subsequently the goods, without any fault on the part of the seller or buyer,[9] perish before the risk passes to the buyer, the agreement is thereby avoided.

This section expressly refers only to contracts for the sale of goods; and it is then restricted in that it is only applicable where the contract is for the sale of 'specific goods' (see post, para 22.15), the frustrating event is the 'perishing' of those goods (see ante, para 22.13) and neither the property nor risk have passed (see further, post, para 22.18). In all other cases,[10] it is arguable that the matter should depend on the contractual intention of the parties. Even where s 7 is applicable, it is arguable that both ss 6 and 7 give way to a contrary intention (see ante, para 22.11).

[22.15] Specific goods. It will be recalled that s 61(1) says that, 'unless the context or subject matter otherwise requires', specific goods 'means goods identified and agreed upon at the time a contract of sale is made ...' (see generally ante, para 2.04). This concept has already caused difficulty in relation to the passing of property in identifiable goods (see ante, para 20.03); and, with regard to the issue of risk, it has led to litigation in respect of future goods. There have been two cases, in both of which a farmer has agreed before his crops were grown to sell for delivery after harvest the estimated yield of his acreage; but the actual yield has, without fault on the part of either party, fallen substantially below the estimate. In the pre-1893 case of *Howell v Coupland*:[1]

> The contract was made in March for delivery the following autumn of 200 tons of potatoes. In August, the crop was ravaged by potato blight. The buyer accepted the 80 tons actually harvested and sued for non-delivery of the remainder. The Court of Appeal unanimously held that there was an implied term that both parties be excused performance in such an event.

In *Sainsbury Ltd v Street*:[2]

> The contract was made in July for the delivery to a corn merchant the following autumn of 275 tons of barley. The unexpectedly poor harvest produced only 140 tons which the seller sold for a higher price elsewhere. The corn merchant claimed damages for non-delivery, and the farmer pleaded there was a condition precedent that the land would yield 275 tons.

McKenna J held the farmer liable for damages for non-delivery of the 140 tons,[3] holding his duty to deliver 275 tons was *prima facie* subject to an implied condition precedent that the farmer should *pro tanto* be discharged with regard to the shortfall (135 tons). His Lordship put his decision on the following grounds:

(1) He applied the rule in *Howell v Coupland*, which was either embodied in s 5(2) of the SGA, or preserved by the general saving of the common law.[4]

---

9   It has been suggested that 'fault' here means the same as in s 20 (see ante, para 22.03): Goode, *Commercial Law* (2nd edn), p 271, note 115.

10 Ie, other types of supply contract, eg, hp, quasi-sales and sales outside the ambit of s 7, eg, of unascertained goods (see post, para 22.16).

[22.15]

1   (1876) 1 QBD 258; [1874–80] All ER Rep 878, CA.

2   [1972] 3 All ER 1127; [1972] 1 WLR 834.

3   For the action for non-delivery, see generally post, para 29.18.

4   Section 5(2) is set out ante, para 2.03. The common law is expressly preserved by SGA, s 62(2).

(2) The case fell outside s 7, because ss 6 and 7 were dealing only with 'existing goods',[5] whereas a crop which had not yet grown does not fall within that category.[6]

[22.16] Unascertained goods. In *Blackburn Bobbin Ltd v TW Allen Ltd*:[1]

There was a contract for the sale free on rail Hull of 70 standards of Finland birch timber. Unknown to the buyer, the seller was following the usual trade practice, namely, to then load timber in Finland for shipment to England. Before delivery commenced, the outbreak of war made such shipment impossible. The buyer's claim for damages succeeded before McCardie J who saw no reason why such 'a bare and unqualified contract for the sale of unascertained goods' should be frustrated by the outbreak of war; and the Court of Appeal agreed.[2]

This decision must be compared with the failed harvest cases already considered (see ante, para 22.15). The explanation is that everything turns on the precise nature of the allegedly frustrating event in relation to the terms of the contract: in the harvest cases, it was impossible to perform the contracts from the contemplated sources; but in the *Allen* case, there was no source contemplated in the contract and performance could be from any such timber in the world.[3] Such a distinction has sometimes erroneously led to the conclusion that it is not possible to frustrate a contract for the sale of generic goods by their non-availability.[4]

Assuming the contract is frustratable, a further problem concerns the case where there are multiple buyers. Suppose the supplier without fault obtains sufficient goods to satisfy less than the contractual requirements of all his buyers. Subject to the express terms of the supply contracts, are they all frustrated, do they rank in delivery date order, should they be pro-rated, or what?[5]

[22.17] Relationship of risk and frustration. Assuming that it is frustratable and leaving aside the effect of frustration (see post, para 22.18), this issue of the relationship of risk and frustration can only arise where the alleged frustrating event is the damage or destruction of the contract goods occurring whilst some of the promises under that contract remain executory, eg, delivery and payment. Once all promises made under a contract have been performed there remains nothing that could be frustrated (see ante,

---

5   This varies from what Chalmers seems to have assumed was the law: see his *Sale of Goods* (18th edn), p 100. Such future goods are outside s 7 (Goode, *Commercial Law* (2nd edn), p 271), perhaps because the type of future goods are unascertained (see ante, para 20.15).

6   Presumably he thought they were 'future goods' (as to which see ante, para 2.03), and unascertained at the time of contracting. Compare ante, para 20.04, and post, para 22.18.

[22.16]

1   [19181 1 KB 540; affirmed [1918] 2 KB 467, CA.

2   It has been suggested that the CA decision seems to envisage a slightly wider field of operation for the doctrine of frustration: Atiyah, *Sale of Goods* (10th edn), p 358. *Sed quaere?*

3   *Aliter*, if performance of the contract were rendered illegal by the outbreak of war (see generally ante, para 10.20): *Benjamin's Sale of Goods* (5th edn), para 6-036 *et seq*.

4   But see Benjamin, *ibid*, para 6-035.

5   See Hudson (1968) 31 MLR 535; and also the discussion of supervening prohibition of export and import in Benjamin, *ibid*, para 18-248 *et seq*.

para 22.13A). Prior to that point, at simplest[1] and leaving aside any proprietary interest in the undivided share in a bulk (see ante, para 20.22 *et seq*), there are four possible permutations as to the incidence of property and risk.

	Seller	Buyer
Case 1	P + R	
Case 2		P + R
Case 3	P	R
Case 4	R	P

Case 1: the property and risk are in the seller, eg, s 7 of the SGA (set out ante, para 22.14). This is, perhaps, the most obvious case where the contract may be frustrated by the destruction of the goods,[2] in which case the seller ceases to be liable for non-delivery,[3] and the buyer ceases to be liable for the price.[4]

Case 2: the property and risk are in the buyer. If we were to say that this contract were frustrated by the destruction of the goods,[5] the effect would be that the buyer would no longer be liable for the price, thereby effectively throwing the risk back on the seller. Does this show that such a contract cannot be frustrated by the destruction of the goods?

Case 3: the property is in the seller and the risk is in the buyer. A sale contract cannot be executed before the passing of property.[6] But can it be frustrated by the destruction of the goods if the risk has passed, so saving the buyer from liability for the price?

Case 4: the risk is in the seller and the property is in the buyer. It has been argued that the contract cannot be frustrated by the destruction of the goods because its object, the transfer of property, has been carried out.[7] Yet, if the buyer is held liable for the price, this is in effect to put the risk on him. Does it therefore follow that the contract can be frustrated?

It is tempting to simplify this rather difficult pattern by saying that, whether the contract can be frustrated by the destruction of the goods, depends on whether the risk has

---

[22.17]

1 However, it would be possible for the contract to divide the incidents of property and risk and allocate parts of each of them as between the parties.

2 Under the rules of risk the buyer is no longer liable for the price though the seller remains liable for non-delivery: see *Healy v Howlett* (set out ante, para 22.06).

3 For actions against a seller for non-delivery, see post, para 29.19.

4 For actions against a buyer for the price, see post, paras 27.16–18. If he has already paid the price, the buyer may be able to recover it on grounds of total failure of consideration: see post, para 29.13.

5 If the destruction took place before delivery, the incidence of risk will save the seller from liability for non-delivery: see ante, para 22.01.

6 The rules of risk will prevent the seller being liable for non-delivery: *Sterns Ltd v Vickers Ltd* (set out ante, para 22.04).

7 Atiyah, *Sale of Goods* (10th edn), p 356.

passed,[8] perhaps on the basis of the implied term theory of frustration: it would follow that it is possible to frustrate in *Cases 1* and *4*, but not in *Cases 2* and *3*. Yet this view assumes that a provision in the contract passing risk ousts the doctrine of frustration[9] and that frustration affects all the terms of the contract.[10] No doubt it is ordinarily true that only in *Cases 1* and *4* will the contract be frustrated; but this may not simply reflect the incidence of risk so much as the fact that within *Cases 2* and *3* there will rarely be any outstanding contractual obligations which survive the frustrating event. If there were such a survival of terms, it would seem that at very least the contract could be frustrated where it fell within *Case 3*.[11] But is it possible to go further and say that a contract can be frustrated whilst any duty remains to be performed thereunder, in which case it would follow that even contracts within *Case 2* could be frustrated?[12] For instance, where goods have not yet been delivered.

The effect of frustration

[22.18] Assuming that the contract is frustrated, the effect of frustration is governed by the common law, as amended by the Law Reform (Frustrated Contracts) Act 1943 (FCA). That Act is expressed to be applicable to all contracts which have:

> ... become impossible of performance or been otherwise frustrated ... subject to the provisions of s 2 of this Act (s 1(1)).

The only important exception for our purposes is that contained in s 2(5)(c), which excludes from the operation of the FCA:

> ... any contract to which s 7 of the Sale of Goods Act 1979 ... applies, or ... any other contract for the sale, or for the sale and delivery, of specific goods, where the contract is frustrated by reason of the fact that the goods have perished.

In cases falling within s 2(5)(c), only the unamended common law rules apply; and it is therefore necessary to determine the scope of this provision. The first part of s 2(5)(c) refers to contracts falling within s 7 of the SGA (set out ante, para 22.14); and it is often said that the second part of s 2(5)(c) does not add anything to the first part.[1] However, on the basis of the analysis set out above (para 22.17), it is submitted that the first part refers to contracts falling within *Case 1*, and the second part refers to contracts falling within *Cases 3* and *4*, and probably even *Case 2*. Both parts will only apply where there is a contract for the sale of 'specific goods' frustrated by reason of the fact that the goods have 'perished', both of which expressions appear in ss 6 and 7 of the SGA and s 2(5)(c) of the FCA; and they presumably mean the same in all three cases.[2] But what of the requirement

---

8   See Goff and Jones, *The Law of Restitution* (5th edn), pp 575–76; Goode, *Commercial Law* (2nd edn), p 272. *Contra* Glanville Williams, *The Frustrated Contracts Act* 82, note 30.

9   This is consistent with the implied term theory, but not the just solution approach.

10   Atiyah, *op cit*, note 7, p 312. But see Glanville Williams, *op cit*, note 8.

11   See Glanville Williams, *op cit*, note 8, pp 84–85, and especially note 35.

12   Doubted by Atiyah, *op cit*, note 7, p 361.

[22.18]

1   See Atiyah, *Sale of Goods* (10th edn), p 361; Treitel, *Law of Contract* (10th edn), p 857; Goff and Jones, *The Law of Restitution* (5th edn), p 575.

2   As to 'specific goods', see ante, para 22.15; and as to 'perish', see ante, para 22.13.

of s 7 that the goods should perish without fault on the part of either party, and the absence of any such requirement from s 6 of the SGA and s 2(5)(c) of the FCA?[3]

[22.19] The Frustrated Contracts Act. The effect of frustration on contracts falling inside and outside s 2(5)(c) of the FCA is adequately discussed elsewhere;[1] but there would only seem to be any practical difference between the two situations in respect of advance payments and part delivery.

1 *Advance payments.* Two situations must be distinguished:

(a) Where the buyer has paid part or all of the price before the frustrating event. If there has been a total failure of consideration, the buyer may recover that sum at common law[2] or under the FCA. However, where the failure of consideration is only partial (see post, para 29.16), the buyer cannot recover at common law; but he may do so under the FCA (s 1(2)), subject to 1(b) below.

(b) Where the contract provides for payment of part or all of the price before the frustrating event and the seller has incurred expenses before that event. The FCA allows the seller to claim reasonable expenses out of the sums paid or payable (s 1(2)); but he has no such right at common law.

2 *Part delivery.* Again, a distinction must be drawn:

(a) Where the buyer has paid the price and received part of the goods. At common law the buyer could not recover the price because there had been no total failure of consideration;[3] but under the FCA the seller can only claim to retain so much of the price as is attributable to any gain which has accrued to the buyer (s 1(3)) or any expenses incurred by the seller (s 1(2)) as above.

(b) Where the seller has delivered part of the goods, but been paid nothing. Under the FCA the seller may be compensated for any benefit which has accrued to the buyer (s 1(3)), or may claim his expenses out of any sum payable by the buyer before the frustrating event (s 1(2)).[4] However, the seller cannot recover anything from the buyer at common law, unless he can show an implied contract from the fact that the buyer has voluntarily retained the goods after the frustrating event.[5]

---

3 See Glanville Williams, *The Frustrated Contracts Act*, p 83, note 30.

[22.19]

1 See Atiyah, *Sale of Goods* (10th edn), pp 361–67; Treitel, *Law of Contract* (10th edn), pp 847–58. See also *Clarke v Bates* [1913] LJCCR 63 and 114 DC; *British Berna Motor Lorries Ltd v Inter-Transport Co Ltd* (1915) 31 TLR 200; *Shepherd v Ready Mix Concrete (London)* (1968) 112 SJ 518; *BP (Exploration) Libya Ltd v Hunt* [1979] 1 WLR 232, substantially affirmed [1983] 2 AC 352, HL.

2 *Fibrosa Spolka Akcyjna v Fairbairn etc Ltd* [1943] AC 32, HL.

3 But he might recover a proportionate amount of the price on the grounds that the goods were still at the seller's risk: Atiyah, *Sale of Goods* (10th edn), p 363.

4 For an examination of the basis of the rules, see Haycroft and Waksman [1984] JBL 207.

5 The claim is quasi-contractual; and it is difficult to fit in with the requirement that the buyer's retention of the benefit be voluntary the decision in *Barrow, Lane and Ballard Ltd v Phillips & Co Ltd* (set out ante, para 22.12).

[22.20] Summary. In order to decide whether a contract for the supply of goods[1] is affected by impossibility of performance,[2] attention should be directed to those promises under that contract which remain executory at the time of the impossibility.[3] Assuming some executory promises remain, in determining the effect of that impossibility on both the executory[4] and executed[5] promises of the contract, it may be helpful to ask in order a series of questions set out below. If the issue is determined by any one of these questions, there is no need to continue further:

1   *Contract*. At the moment of impossibility, is there a supply contract between the parties? If there is not, the matter is one of initial impossibility;[6] and it is a question of whether or not the subsequent contract is rendered void by that impossibility (see ante, paras 22.10–13). However, if there is such a contract, the matter is one of subsequent impossibility; and attention must be turned to the next question.

2   *Property*. At the moment of subsequent impossibility, has the property passed in the goods subject to the supply contract?[7]

3   *Risk*. At the moment of subsequent impossibility, has the risk passed in the goods subject to the supply contract (see ante, paras 22.01–08)?

4   *Frustration*. Assuming subsequent impossibility, can that frustrating event frustrate the remaining executory obligations under the supply contract?[8] The issue of whether a contract can be frustrated after the risk has passed is discussed above (see ante, para 22.17).

5   *Effect of frustration*. A significant issue here may be whether or not the FCA is applicable (see ante, para 22.19).

[22.20]

1   Sale (including conditional and credit), quasi-sale, hp or simple hiring.

2   For what events might make such a supply contract impossible of performance, see ante, paras 22.10; 22.14.

3   If none of the promises of either party remain executory, there can logically be no question of any impossibility precluding performance of the contract (see ante, para 22.13A); and then risk lies on the owner under the rule *res perit domino* (see ante, para 22.01).

4   Typically the supplier's contractual duty to deliver (see post, para 23.05) and the transferee's duty to pay the price or rent (see post, para 27.16 *et seq*).

5   Insofar as any particular contractual duty has been performed, any benefit conferred may have to be returned on grounds of total failure of consideration (see generally post, para 29.12).

6   As to the distinction between initial and subsequent impossibility, see ante, para 22.09.

7   Unless the goods are specific (see ante, para 20.08 *et seq*), the property will typically pass on delivery (see ante, para 20.17).

8   Not, eg, if the *prima facie* frustrating event is self-induced (see ante, para 22.14), nor sometimes where the goods are unascertained (see ante, para 22.16).

PART 6

PAYMENT IN SUPPLY CONTRACTS

CHAPTER 23

DELIVERY AND PAYMENT

[23.01] Introduction. Under the contract of sale, it is normally envisaged that there will be a delivery of goods (see ante, para 2.01) in exchange for the price (see ante, para 2.06); and, leaving aside all questions of what must be delivered and what must be paid,[1] this chapter is concerned with the acts of delivery and payment. As s 27 of the SGA states:

> It is the duty of the seller to deliver the goods, and of the buyer to accept and pay for them, in accordance with the terms of the contract of sale.

Whilst this section is subject to a contrary intention (s 55: set out ante, para 18.09), it plainly expresses the normal expectation of the parties to a contract of sale.[2] By comparison, hp and simple hiring agreements are both forms of bailment (see ante, para 1.17): the essence of the transaction is a transfer of possession for the payment of rent (see ante, para 1.18).

The duties of delivery and payment will now be separately analysed (post, paras 23.02–15); and the time of performance of those duties, and performance by instalments, is reserved until later (post, para 23.16 *et seq*). However, it should be noted that some retail sales on payment cards (see ante, para 2.24), eg, by supermarkets, also involve a payment of cash to the consumer (cashback),[3] which is in effect a loan by the retailer to the consumer (see ante, para 7.02 *et seq*).

Delivery

[23.02] English law differentiates between the passing of **property** in, and **delivery** of, the contract goods (see ante, para 19.01) and, because of the different incidents attached to the two, they must be carefully distinguished.[1] Four situations are possible:

(1) Property may pass after delivery, as in a conditional sale or hp agreement.[2]

(2) Property may pass at the moment of delivery, as where a delivery of unascertained goods to the buyer or a carrier constitutes an appropriation of them.[3]

(3) Property may pass before delivery, at the earliest when the contract is made.[4]

(4) The property is never to pass under the contract, as with a simple hiring.[5]

[23.01]
1 It is one of the oddities of the SGA (and of the common law?) that delivery and payment are expressed as duties, whereas many other provisions are expressed as implied terms: Goode, *Commercial Law* (2nd edn), pp 274–76.
2 Would there be a similar rule for quasi-sales?
3 About 20%: (2001) 55 CC6/10. For third party cashbacks, see ante, para 8.13A.
[23.02]
1 The incidents of property are analysed ante, para 19.10 *et seq* and those of delivery below.
2 See respectively ante, paras 1.14; 1.20.
3 Section 18, r 5(2): see ante, para 20.17.
4 Section 18, r 1; see ante, para 20.09.
5 See ante, para 1.18.

In all cases, the cautious supplier may require his transferee to sign a delivery note acknowledging that he is satisfied with the delivery.[6] Any contractual provision to this effect may fail as being unreasonable[7] or unfair.[8]

Meaning and rules of delivery

[23.03] The meaning of delivery. The CCA nowhere defines delivery; but the SGA provides that, unless the context otherwise requires:[1]

> 'Delivery' means voluntary transfer of possession from one person to another.

The most obvious example of 'delivery' is the physical transfer of actual possession of goods; but 'possession' clearly includes constructive possession. Section 1(2) of the FA explains that:

> A person shall be deemed to be in possession of goods or of the documents of title to goods, where the goods, or documents are in his actual custody or are held by any other person subject to his control or for him or on his behalf.

Whilst detailed discussion of the common law concept of 'possession' is beyond the scope of this works,[2] certain common instances of a constructive transfer of possession may be noticed:

(1) *Symbolic delivery*; that is, the handing over of the means of control, eg, the keys to a room, or a left-luggage locker.[3]

(2) *Delivery of the documents of title*. Whilst the general rule is that a transfer of documents of title is not a transfer of possession,[4] there are exceptions. One exception encompasses 'documents of title' within the SGA, which for a definition cross-refers (s 61(1) of the SGA) to the FA 1889 and s 1(4) of the latter provides that:

> The expression 'document of title' shall include any bill of lading, dock warrant, warehousekeeper's certificate, and warrant or order for the delivery of goods, and any other document used in the ordinary course of business as proof of the possession or control of goods, or authorising or purporting to authorise, either by endorsement or by delivery, the possessor of the document to transfer or receive goods thereby represented.

---

6   There may be two reasons for this procedure: to protect the supplier (see post, para 23.08) and to protect any carrier. For a possible limitation on the efficacy of delivery notes, see ante, para 18.06; and for their effect on the buyer's right to rescind, see post, para 29.05.

7   Under UCTA, s 3: see ante, para 18.22 *et seq*.

8   Under the UTCC Regulations: see ante, para 11.12 *et seq*.

[23.03]

1   Section 61(1). Note that the concept of delivery is specially extended with regard to sales from a bulk: see ante, para 20.22C.

2   See generally Crossley Vaines, *Personal Property* (5th edn), p 4. Compare possession for the purposes of the exceptions to the *nemo dat* rule (see ante, paras 21.28; 21.39) with loss of possession on terminating the unpaid seller's lien (see post, para 24.14).

3   *Benjamin's Sale of Goods* (5th edn), para 8-008; Bell, *Personal Property*, pp 57–61. But for criticism of the expression 'symbolic', see Crossley Vaines, *ibid*, p 307.

4   Bell, *ibid*, p 58.

But how far are FA 'documents of title' also treated as such for SGA purposes; and to what extent does this remain a common law issue, eg, delivery orders?[5] Even where the goods are unascertained,[6] the transfer of the documents of title may itself amount to a sort of symbolic delivery of the goods,[7] though not usually for the purpose of pledging the goods (see post, para 25.15).

(3) *Delivery to the buyer's agent.* This may amount at common law to a transfer of possession,[8] but special provision is made for one particular case only by s 32(1) of the SGA as follows:

> Where, in pursuance of a contract of sale, the seller is authorised or required to send the goods to the buyer, delivery of the goods to a carrier, whether named by the buyer or not, for the purpose of transmission to the buyer is *prima facie* deemed to be a delivery of the goods to the buyer.

This presumption gives way to a contrary intention, as where the carrier is the agent of the seller.[9] Delivery to a carrier may also pass the property in goods (see ante, para 23.02).

(4) *Attornment;* that is, acknowledgment by the person in physical possession of goods that he is holding the goods on behalf of another, upon which the law regards the former as having merely custody and the other as being in legal possession.[10] Attornment to the buyer or hirer could be by either of the following:

(a) the supplier, as where he agrees to retain possession as agent of the buyer or hirer;[11]

(b) a third party, eg, a warehouseman or carrier. In such a case, s 29(4) of the SGA provides as follows:[12]

> Where the goods at the time of sale are in the possession of a third person, there is no delivery by seller to buyer unless and until the third person acknowledges to the buyer that he holds the goods on his behalf; but nothing in this section affects the operation of the issue or transfer of any document of title to goods.

---

5   Benjamin, *op cit*, note 3, para 8-013. Documents of title are expressly excluded from the definition of bills of sale: s 4, Bills of Sale Act 1878 (see ante, para 9.04). Nor do they include all delivery orders: see Nicol (1979) 42 MLR at 130, note 7, and see further ante, para 20.05.

6   See Benjamin, *op cit*, note 3, para 7-069. *Contra* Nicol (1979) 42 MLR 129 at 138–40.

7   *Per* Bowen LJ in *Saunders v Maclean* (1883) 11 QBD 327, CA, at 341. See, eg, cif and arrival contracts: ante, para 22.07.

8   *The Saetta* (set out ante, para 21.49); the *Albright & Wilson* case (set out ante, para 13.01), at para 25. But the goods may still be regarded as in the course of transit: see s 45(1) SGA, set out post, para 24.18.

9   Eg, *Galbraith and Grant Ltd v Block* [1922] 2 KB 155; and see ante, para 22.06, note 5. As to the scope of s 32(1), see Goode, *Commercial Law* (2nd edn), pp 261–66. For the passing of property, see ante, para 20.17.

10 *Michael Gerson (Leasing) Ltd v Wilkinson* (set out ante, para 21.41); and see ante, para 21.40. See the definitions in Palmer, *Bailment*, 846; Bell, *op cit*, note 3, p 63; and ante, para 20.17. Distinguish mere receipt of a delivery order by the person having custody of the goods, eg, *Laurie & Morewood v Dudin* [1926] 1 KB 223, CA, from the situation where he 'attorns' to another, eg, *Henderson v Williams* (set out ante, para 21.11).

11 As to the implications of this for the unpaid seller's rights of lien and stoppage, see post, paras 24.11; 24.19. There can be no attornment in respect of an unidentified part of a larger bulk: Goode, *op cit*, note 9, pp 49, 278. But see note 6, above.

12 Eg, *Inglis v Robertson* (set out ante, para 21.47); *Wardar's Co Ltd v Norwood & Sons Ltd* (set out ante, para 20.17). See also Reynolds [1984] JBL 151.

(5) *Delivery documents.* In the ordinary course of business, a buyer is entitled to assume that contractual documents, eg, delivery notes, are correct and relevant to the goods to which they purport to relate.[13]

[23.04] The rules of delivery. Certain rules of delivery are set out in s 29 of the SGA; and the basic rule is to be found in s 29(1):

> Whether it is for the buyer to take possession of the goods or for the seller to send them to the buyer is a question depending in each case on the contract, express or implied, between the parties.

Thus the Act leaves it to the parties to decide the mode of delivery; and it has been regretted that there is no more definite *prima facie* rule.[1] However, this seems to reflect the common law that the seller's *prima facie* duty was merely to afford the buyer the opportunity of taking possession of the goods at the agreed place of delivery; and it is usually thought that these rules are also applicable to quasi-sales, hp and simple hiring.[2] There is discussed below the relationship of this rule to the buyer's right to examine the goods (post, para 23.10) and his duty to pay the price or rent (post, para 23.13). The SGA lays down a *prima facie* rule that the expenses of, and incidental to, putting the goods in a deliverable state (see ante, para 20.12) must be borne by the seller (s 29(6)) and then deals with the following aspects of delivery:

1   *The place of delivery.* Section 29(2) provides that *prima facie*:

> ... the place of delivery is the seller's place of business if he has one, and if not, his residence; except that, if the contract is for the sale of specific goods, which to the knowledge of the parties when the contract is made are in some other place, then that place is the place of delivery.

The underlying presumption is not that the seller will send the goods, but that the buyer will collect them; and this ties in with the buyer's duty to seek out his creditor, the seller (see post, para 23.13). However, this presumption may be displaced, whether in the export trade,[3] or in domestic transactions,[4] eg, home and internet sales, mail order[5] and Interflora. In retail supplies, home delivery may be offered as a collateral contract (see ante, para 11.06).

2   *The time of delivery.* The following rules as to the time of delivery are laid down (s 29):

> (3) Where under the contract of sale the seller is bound to send the goods to the buyer,[6] but no time for sending them is fixed, the seller is bound to send them within a reasonable time.[7]

---

13   The *Albright & Wilson* case (above), at para 13.

[23.04]

1   Chalmers, *Sale of Goods* (18th edn), p 179.

2   As to hp, see Guest, *Law of HP*, para 321; Goode, *HP Law and Practice* (2nd edn), p 220.

3   *Zenziper Grains and Feed Stuffs v Bulk Trading Corp Ltd* [2001] 1 All ER (Comm) 385, CA (free on truck). See also fob, cif and ex-ship contracts: ante, para 22.07.

4   *ICM Computer Solutions plc v Black Horse Finance Ltd* [2001] unreported, CA (see 55 CC6/12).

5   The Post Office is offering a new service, allowing customers to collect undeliverable goods from a local post office: [2001] 5 Credit Today 7.

6   Thus ousting s 29(2). Even then, *prima facie* delivery time is not usually of the essence: see post, para 23.18.

7   Eg, *Charles Rickards Ltd v Oppenheim* (set out post, para 26.25); and *Thomas Borthwick (Glasgow) Ltd v Bunge & Co Ltd* [1969] 1 Lloyd's Rep 17. What is a reasonable time is a question of fact: SGA, s 59. Cf SGSA, s 14: see ante, para 15.15.

(5) Demand or tender of delivery may be treated as ineffectual unless made at a reasonable hour, and what is a reasonable hour is a question of fact.[8]

The effect of s 37 may be that time runs from the buyer's request for delivery (see post, para 23.09). As to whether time of delivery is of the essence, see post, para 23.16 et seq. Where a consumer enters a distance contract (see ante, para 8.17), the Distance Selling Regulations assume that *prima facie* the parties have agreed that the supplier 'shall perform the contract within a maximum of 30 days beginning with the day after the day the consumer sent his order to the supplier' (reg 19(1)). Further, reg 19(2) provides that:

> Subject to paragraphs (7)[9] and (8),[10] where the supplier is unable to perform the contract because the goods or services ordered are not available, within the period of performance referred to in paragraph (1) or such other period as the parties agree ('the period of performance'), he shall –
>
> (a) inform the consumer; and
>
> (b) reimburse[11] any sum paid by or on behalf of the consumer[12] under or in relation to the contract to the person by whom it was made.[10]

Where a contract has not been performed within the 'period of performance' (see above), it 'shall be treated as if it had not been made, save for any rights or remedies which the consumer has under it as a result of the non-performance' (reg, 19(5)); any security shall be treated 'as never having had any effect' (reg 19(6)); and any credit agreement shall be cancelled (reg 20). As to the cancellation rules, see regs 15 and 16 (see ante, para 10.22A).

Duties of delivery

There are two facets of the duty of delivery: the supplier is under a duty to tender delivery; and the buyer or hirer is under a duty to accept delivery.

Tender of delivery

[23.05] Because delivery is the essence of bailment, the law puts great emphasis on the tender of delivery in hp and simple hiring transactions. The hiring does not commence until the owner tenders to the hirer goods which conform with the contract and the hirer accepts the same (see ante, para 15.23). If the hirer does not accept the goods, he cannot be sued for the instalments of rent, even if expressed to be payable in advance (see post, para 27.21). However, in the case of sale, the seller's duty is to tender delivery in accordance with the rules set out above (para 23.04); and the buyer is under a duty to accept them (see post, para 23.08). As these duties are reciprocal, if the seller tenders non-conforming goods, the buyer is under no duty to accept them (see post, para 23.09). Suppose the buyer indicates to the seller that he will not accept delivery: if he repudiates on an actual

---

8 Presumably, this will be related to the ordinary course of business: see ante, paras 21.34–35.

9 The supplier may supply substitute goods where all the following conditions are satisfied (reg 19(7)): (a) allowed by the contract; and (b) prior to the contract the consumer has been so informed under reg 7 (see ante, para 9.05A).

10 In the case of outdoor leisure events, the parties may agree that reg 19(2)(b) shall not apply: reg 19(8).

11 Reimbursement shall be as soon as possible and in any event within 30 days of expiry of the period of performance: reg 19(4).

12 This includes any sum paid by a third party creditor: reg 19(3).

tender, the question of whether it is a conforming tender so that the buyer is liable for non-acceptance, can be tested against the actual tender; but, if the buyer repudiates in anticipation of tender, the seller is clearly entitled to accept the anticipatory breach (see post, para 26.15) and need not make an actual tender of delivery.[1] On principle, it might appear that, if the seller is not ready and willing to deliver, the contract will be discharged by mutual abandonment (see post, para 26.18). The courts have therefore held that, if he wishes to sue the buyer for non-acceptance, the seller must remain ready and willing to perform his side of the bargain.[2] However, in *British and Benningtons Ltd v North West Cachar Tea Co Ltd*:[3]

> The buyer agreed to buy the crop of tea to be produced on a certain Indian estate, delivery to be made in bonded warehouse in London, but no date for delivery being specified. Subsequently, the buyer agreed to accept delivery at certain out-ports;[4] but after further delays the buyer repudiated the contract on the grounds that delivery had not been made within a reasonable time. In the seller's action for damages for non-acceptance, it was found that a reasonable time for delivery had not expired when the buyer repudiated.

The House of Lords held that, where there was such an anticipatory breach by the buyer, the seller need not tender actual delivery before commencing the action; nor need he **prove** that at the date of repudiation he was ready and willing to deliver in London; and they upheld the award of damages to the seller.[5] Lord Sumner accepted that a buyer could set up his seller's breach of contract in these circumstances,[6] but pointed out that in this case there was not yet a breach because the seller might still have tendered in London within the contract period.[7]

It would appear that the effect of the buyer's anticipatory repudiation upon the seller's duty of delivery depends on whether or not the seller elects[8] to accept that repudiation (see post, paras 23.06–07).

[23.06] Repudiation by the buyer. Where the buyer's anticipatory repudiation is accepted by the seller, the effect is to discharge both parties from any duty of further performance (see post, para 26.16), so that the seller is discharged from his duty of delivery. At the same time, a defaulting buyer remains liable for damages for non-acceptance.[1] Is it any

---

[23.05]

1 *Levy & Co v Goldberg* [1922] 1 KB 688, at 692.

2 *Per* Lord Abinger CB in *De Medina v Norman* (1842) 9 M & W 820 at 827. See also Dawson (1981) 96 LQR 239.

3 [1923] AC 48; [1922] All ER Rep 224, HL, discussed in *Benjamin's Sale of Goods* (5th edn), para 9-013.

4 The HL held that this waiver did not discharge the seller's duty to deliver in London: see post, para 26.25.

5 For the seller's action for non-acceptance, see generally post, para 27.24.

6 At 71–72. Three other Law Lords concurred with this judgment; and the relevant passage in Lord Sumner's judgment was cited with approval by Devlin J in *Universal Cargo Corporation v Citati* [1957] 2 QB 401, 445.

7 At 71. Does this rebut the argument that, as the seller was still in breach, the buyer was still entitled to rescind? See Stoljar (1957) 35 Can BR 485, 509; and post, para 26.26.

8 As to the effect of a repudiation, see generally post para 26.15.

[23.06]

1 *British and Benningtons Ltd v North West Cachar Tea Co Ltd* (set out ante, para 23.05); discussed by Treitel, *Law of Contract* (10th edn), pp 710–11.

answer for that buyer to show that, had the contract continued in existence up until the time for delivery, the seller would have been unable to deliver?[2] Benjamin[3] answers that it depends who has made the first, and therefore wrongful, repudiation; but, in applying that principle, two others must be borne in mind. First, a seller is not necessarily in breach of contract by making a defective tender, as the contract may allow him time to cure that defect by re-tendering.[4] Second, if at the time of his repudiation, the buyer (unknown to himself) has a good reason for repudiation and that repudiation is accepted (see post, para 26.16), his repudiation does not give rise to any liability in damages, because the fact that he gave no reason (or a bad one) for his repudiation is irrelevant (see post, para 26.26).

Wrongful repudiation accepted by seller. Suppose the buyer wrongfully repudiates and the seller accepts that repudiation (see post, para 26.15), the buyer cannot escape liability for that repudiation by showing that, had the contract continued in existence, the seller would have been unable to perform his promise. In *Gill & Duffus SA v Berger & Co Inc*:[5]

> There was a sale by sample of 500 tonnes of Argentine 'bolita' (white) beans cif Le Havre. Suspecting that some of the beans were coloured, the buyer rejected the documents on the grounds that they did not include a certificate of quality. The seller re-tendered the documents, together with such a certificate in respect of the 445 tonnes already unloaded. The buyer again rejected the documents.

The House of Lords accepted that in a cif contract the seller has two separate duties, first to submit conforming documents, second to deliver conforming goods (see post, para 29.30). However, the House unanimously agreed that, since conforming documents were tendered,[6] the buyer's rejection of them was a wrongful repudiation; and that the seller, having accepted that repudiation, was released from his obligation to deliver conforming goods.[7] It followed that the buyer could not plead as a defence to liability that part of the cargo consisted of coloured beans,[8] which issue went only to damages.[9]

[23.07] Wrongful repudiation not accepted by the seller. Where the buyer's wrongful anticipatory repudiation is not accepted by the seller, then on principle the contract is kept alive for the benefit of both parties (see post, para 26.12), so that a subsequent event may release both parties from liability.[1] It would follow that the seller would continue bound by his duty of delivery: whilst he need not tender actual delivery (see ante, para 23.05), he ought to continue ready and willing to deliver; and it should be a good defence for the buyer to show that the seller was unable to perform his obligations at the time

---

2   The doctrine of frustration would no longer be available: *Avery v Bowden* (1855) 5 E & B 714 (charterparty).

3   *Benjamin's Sale of Goods* (5th edn), para 9-017. Cf Dawson (1980) 96 LQR 239.

4   See *Borrowman Phillips & Co v Free & Hollis* (set out post, para 29.03).

5   [1984] AC 382; [1984] 1 All ER 438, HL.

6   HL held the certificate of quality was not part of the shipping documents required to be presented by the seller, so that the absence of a certificate in respect of 55 tons was irrelevant. See further below.

7   *Aliter*, if the buyer had accepted the documents: the *Kwei Tek Chao* case (set out post, para 29.30).

8   On this point, the HL reversed the CA, who had held that the buyer was entitled to rely on s 30 to repudiate (see ante, para 13.03).

9   HL held the buyer had not in fact proved that any cargo was defective and was therefore liable for non-acceptance of the whole 500 tons (see post, para 27.33). See generally Benjamin, *op cit*, note 3, para 9-019.

[23.07]

1   Eg, *Avery v Bowden* (1855) 5 E & B 714 (frustration, as to which, see generally ante, para 22.14).

appointed for performance.[2] However, these propositions would appear to run counter to *Braithwaite v Foreign Hardwood Co Ltd*:[3]

> There was a contract for the sale of rosewood to be paid for by cash against the bills of lading. When the seller tendered the bills of lading, the buyer refused to accept them for reasons subsequently found to be unjustifiable. Subsequently, the buyer discovered that some of the consignments covered by the bills presented did not answer the contract description; and he pleaded this fact by way of a defence to the seller's action for non-acceptance. This defence was rejected by the Court of Appeal on the grounds that by rejecting the bills of lading the buyer had impliedly waived the seller's breach, and could not thereafter complain of it.

In the Court of Appeal, Collins MR appeared to deal with the case on the footing that the contract had been kept alive (at 551). However, this has been re-interpreted by the House of Lords in *The Simona*, a charterparty case.[4] In delivering the judgment of the House of Lords, Lord Ackner indicated that unless *Braithwaite* could be treated as a case where repudiation was accepted (see ante, para 23.06), it was wrong (at 805, 751j).

Nevertheless, if the innocent seller elects to keep the contract alive after the buyer's wrongful repudiation, the seller may put himself in a difficult position.[5] Although not accepting the wrongful repudiation,[6] the innocent seller may, for instance, refrain from delivering; and he may consequently be met by the buyer's argument that the seller did not have the capacity to perform at the time of delivery. In *The Simona*, the House of Lords suggested the following answer: if the buyer has clearly represented to the seller that there is no point in the seller attempting to deliver the goods, in acting on that representation the seller raises an estoppel against the buyer.[7]

Acceptance of delivery

[23.08] Conforming goods. Only where the seller tenders goods in conformity with the contract is it the buyer's duty to accept them.[1] If the buyer then wrongfully refuses to accept delivery,[2] s 37(1) of the SGA provides as follows:

> Where the seller is ready and willing to deliver goods, and requests the buyer to take delivery, and the buyer does not within a reasonable time[3] after such request take delivery of the goods, he is liable to the seller for any loss occasioned by his neglect or refusal to take delivery, and also for a reasonable charge for the care and custody of the goods.

---

2   *Per* Lord Ackner, delivering the judgment in *The Simona* (below) with which his fellow judges agreed.
3   [1905] 2 KB 543, CA, discussed by *Benjamin's Sale of Goods* (5th edn), paras 9-012, 19-146 *et seq*.
4   *Fercometal SARL v Mediterranean Shipping Co SA, The Simona* [1989] AC 788, [1988] 2 All ER 742, HL, discussed by Benjamin, *ibid*, para 9-015.
5   Atiyah, *Sale of Goods* (10th edn), p 118.
6   But, as to the effect of the seller's resale under SGA, s 48(3), (4), see post, paras 27.08–10.
7   See Benjamin, *op cit*, note 3, para 9-018.
[23.08]
1   SGA, s 27. This is one of the reasons for getting the buyer to sign a delivery receipt acknowledging that he has received the goods in the contract state: see ante, para 23.02.
2   *Aliter* if the seller delays delivery for his own ends, or by exercising his unpaid seller's lien (see post, para 24.04): *Benjamin's Sale of Goods* (5th edn), para 9-009.
3   What is a reasonable time is a question of fact: SGA, s 59.

Whilst s 37 is not expressed to give way to a contrary intention, it is submitted that it will *prima facie* do so with the following result: if the contract stipulates a time for acceptance of delivery, the section is ousted and delivery must be made at that time; but, if the contract merely stipulates a time for tender of delivery, acceptance of delivery need only be made within a reasonable time thereafter; and, if there is no stipulation as to the time of delivery, s 37(1) requires the buyer to accept delivery within a reasonable time of the seller's request that he should do so. Section 37(2) expressly recognises that the buyer's delay in taking delivery may be so great as to evince an intention to repudiate the contract,[4] in which case it is treated as a non-acceptance (50(1): see post, para 27.27).

[23.09] Non-conforming goods. Where the goods tendered by the seller are not in conformity with the contract, the buyer is *prima facie* entitled to refuse to accept them,[1] in which case s 36 provides:

> Unless otherwise agreed, where goods are delivered to the buyer, and he refuses to accept them, having the right to do so, he is not bound to return them to the seller, but it is sufficient if he intimates to the seller that he refuses to accept them.

This section seems to assume that there is a contract of sale between the parties; but, if the delivery merely amounts to an offer to sell, the ordinary common law rules of acceptance apply.[2] Where there is a contract of sale, it is open to the buyer who rejects to return the goods to the seller; but s 36 reaffirms the common law rule that he need not do so, and that *prima facie* the buyer may reject the goods by 'any unequivocal act showing that he rejects them'.[3] Again following the common law, it would seem that the buyer who evinces an intention to reject becomes a mere involuntary bailee of the goods, and is only under a duty to exercise care of them as a gratuitous bailee:[4] the underlying risk is on the erstwhile seller,[5] in whom the property in the goods remains or revests;[6] and that seller acquires an immediate right to possession of the goods.[7] Whilst the buyer has no lien on the rejected goods for repayment of the price (see post, para 24.03), he may be able to recover the price in quasi-contract where the contract of sale is rescinded (see post, para 29.13); and he can maintain an action against the seller for non-delivery of the contract goods (see post, para 29.18).

---

4   For repudiation, see further post, para 26.15.

[23.09]

1   For the restrictions on the buyer's right to reject, see post, para 29.04.

2   Chalmers, *Sale of Goods* (18th edn), p 198: see further ante, para 10.02. As to unsolicited goods, see ante, para 8.18.

3   *Per* Brett J in *Grimoldby v Wells* (1875) LR 10 CP 391, at 395. For an express agreement to reject in a certain manner, see *Docker v Hyams* [1969] 3 All ER 808, CA.

4   *Benjamin's Sale of Goods* (5th edn), para 12-065; and generally ante, para 1.17.

5   It has been argued that the ordinary rules as to risk do not operate where the buyer validly rescinds for breach: Atiyah, *Sale of Goods* (10th edn), p 352; Goode, *Commercial Law* (2nd edn), p 255, note 30.

6   As to the retention in (or reversion to) the seller of the property in goods after the buyer's rescission for breach, see post, para 29.06; and as to the ordinary rule as to the passing of risk, see ante, para 22.01.

7   *Per* Bankes LJ in *E Hardy & Co (London) v Hillerns and Fowler* [1923] 2 KB 490, CA, at 496. See also *Commission Car Sales Ltd v Saul* [1957] NZLR 144.

[23.10] Examination.[1] Obviously, it is very important to the buyer to determine whether or not he must accept the goods tendered by the seller; and the SGA therefore gave him a right to examine the tendered goods before he accepted delivery of them (s 34).[2] This formulation was thought insufficiently generous to the buyer[3] and new s 34 provides:[4]

> Unless otherwise agreed, when the seller tenders delivery of goods to the buyer, he is bound, on request, to afford the buyer a reasonable opportunity of examining the goods for the purpose of ascertaining whether they are in conformity with the contract and, in the case of a contract for sale by sample, of comparing the bulk with the sample.

As will be seen later, the buyer loses his right to reject by accepting the goods (see post, para 29.05) and will normally be liable for the price when the property has passed (see post, para 27.17). However, subject to the terms of the contract, s 34 gives the buyer a right, **on request**, to a reasonable opportunity for examination (see post, para 23.11) **before** he accepts delivery or pays the price, so that he may ensure that the goods correspond with the contract, eg, in matters of description,[5] quantity[6] or quality[7] or with any sample.[8]

Delivery or acceptance notes. Particularly in those circumstances where the seller effects delivery at the buyer's premises,[9] it is common for the seller's delivery agent to demand that the buyer sign a delivery or acceptance note. Sometimes, such a note simply recites that the buyer acknowledges delivery and it is commonly so understood. However, the note may go further. It may state that the delivered goods were in the state required by the contract, though it seems doubtful whether such a clause will bar subsequent complaint by the buyer.[10] Alternatively, the note may be intended to operate as an acceptance of the goods by the buyer, so reducing him to the lesser claim for damages for any breach (s 35). The Law Commission recommended that this latter device was unfair to both consumer and non-consumer buyers.[11] This recommendation has been adopted by amendment to s 35 (see post, para 29.05). Further, where there is a consumer supply, such a deemed acceptance may be an unfair term.[12]

[23.10]

1   This right to examine before acceptance of delivery must not be confused with examination before contract: see ante, para 14.26.

2   Old s 34 embodied the common law: *Benjamin on Sale* (8th edn), pp 741, 753.

3   By the Law Commission: see *Sale and Supply of Goods* (1987, Law Com 160), para 5.20. For an explanation, see Bridge [1995] JBL 405–6.

4   As amended by the SGSA, s 2.

5   SGA, s 13: see ante, para 13.11.

6   SGA, s 30: see ante, paras 13.04–05.

7   SGA, ss 14, 15(2)(c): see ante, paras 14.07; 14.15; 15.11.

8   SGA, s 15(2)(a): see ante, para 15.06. The overlapping special opportunity to compare bulk with sample is defectively repealed: see ante, para 15.08.

9   Thus ousting the ordinary SGA presumption of delivery at the seller's premises (s 29(2)): see ante, para 23.04.

10   See *Lowe v Lombank Ltd* (set out ante, para 18.06).

11   *Op cit*, note 3, para 5.21.

12   OFT, *Bulletin No 14*, case 1; and see further ante, para 11.12 *et seq*.

[23.11] Reasonable examination. What constitutes a reasonable examination must depend on the nature of the goods[1] and any agreement between the parties.[2] The place of examination is *prima facie* the place of delivery;[3] but, if a reasonable examination is not possible at that place, the courts will try to read the contract so that the place where an effective examination is first possible is the place the parties have agreed upon for the examination.[4] This will commonly be the buyer's place of business,[5] or the place of delivery to a sub-buyer;[6] but it has been said that the latter will only be the place of acceptance where:[7]

> ... the original vendor must know, either because he is told or by necessary inference, that the goods are going further on, and the place at which he delivers must either be unsuitable in itself or the nature or packing of the goods must make inspection at that place unreasonable.

Such an approach has been adopted where the defect was a latent one not discoverable on delivery;[8] or where the delivery was to be made at a wharf where only a cursory inspection was possible;[9] or where the goods were specially packaged for carriage to a sub-buyer.[10] It has been held that the conduct of the seller must be taken into account in determining what is a reasonable time.[11] Presumably, the same is true for the nature of the goods, eg, the purchaser of a fitted carpet cannot effectively examine it until it has been fitted; the purchaser in January of a lawn mower cannot effectively test it until the Spring.

[23.12] Bailees. Whilst there is no authority on the point, it is thought that the position of a bailee under a hp or simple hiring agreement is similar to that of a buyer in respect of acceptance of delivery. Thus, it is the duty of the bailee to take delivery (see ante, para 15.24); and failure to do so will render him liable to damages,[1] and may even evince an intention to repudiate (see post, para 26.15). Furthermore, it would seem that, before accepting delivery and rendering himself liable to pay instalments of rent, the hirer has a right of examination similar to that of the buyer.[2]

[23.11]

1   See eg, *Esmail & Sons v Rosenthal & Sons Ltd* [1964] 2 Lloyd's Rep 447, CA; reversed on other grounds [1965] 2 All ER 860, HL.

2   *W Potts & Co Ltd v Brown, Macfarlane & Co Ltd* (1924) 30 Com Cas 64, HL.

3   *Perkins v Bell* [1893] 1 QB 193, CA (pre-SGA 1893); and *per* Pearce LJ in *Long v Lloyd* (set out post, para 26.13) at 407.

4   Eg, fob contracts: *Scaliaris v E Ofverberg* (1921) 37 TLR 307, CA; *Boks & Co v JH Rayner & Co* (1921) 37 TLR 800, CA; *Bragg v Villanova* (1923) 40 TLR 154, DC. See further *Benjamin's Sale of Goods* (5th edn), paras 20-093/5.

5   Eg, *B and P Wholesale Distributors v Marko* [1953] CLY 3266.

6   Eg, *Heilbutt v Hickson* (1872) LR 7 CP 438; *Molling & Co v Dean & Son Ltd* (1901) 18 TLR 217, DC.

7   *Per* Bailhache J in *Saunt v Belcher and Gibbons Ltd* (1920) 26 Com Cas 115, at 119.

8   *Heilbutt v Hickson* (above).

9   *B and P Wholesale Distributors v Marko* (above).

10   *Molling & Co v Dean & Son Ltd* (above).

11   *Lucy v Mouflet* (1860) 29 LJ Ex 110.

[23.12]

1   But not to any instalments of hire rent: see post, para 27.21.

2   *Farnworth Finance Facilities Ltd v Attryde* [1970] 2 All ER 774, CA (hp).

PAYMENT

[23.13] The duty to pay.[1] The SGA makes it clear that it is the duty of the buyer to pay the price (s 27); an hp or simple hiring agreement will usually impose a similar obligation on the hirer with respect to the instalments of hire rent (see ante, para 15.23); and a contract of loan will usually expressly provide for repayment, whether by lump-sum or instalments (see ante, para 7.03). This obligation to pay the price or other debt should be carefully distinguished from a claim for damages for breach of contract: in the former case the creditor need prove nothing more than the occurrence of the event or condition precedent to performance, eg, the passing of property in an action for the price (see post, para 27.16), whereas a claim for damages is subject to the ordinary rules, eg, as to remoteness, penalties and mitigation (see post, para 27.39).

At common law, payment is a consensual act requiring the consent of both creditor and debtor, whereas tender is a unilateral act by the debtor. The obligation of the buyer, hirer or debtor to pay or tender the debt[2] is balanced by the obligation (implied if not express) on the part of the seller, owner or creditor not to refuse the whole or part of the debt where this is tendered in conformity with the contract (see post, para 24.14). At common law, it is *prima facie* the duty of the debtor or his authorised agent[3] to tender the exact nominal amount of his debt to the creditor,[4] or to such agent as the creditor authorises to receive payment under the ordinary rules of agency, which are expressly saved by s 62(2) of the SGA,[5] eg, the Bank Giro system,[6] the dealer in a financed transaction (see ante, paras 2.21–22). Acceptance of that tender turns it into payment, whilst even an unaccepted valid tender produces certain legal effects: for instance, the seller is no longer 'unpaid' within s 38(1)(a) of the SGA (see post, para 24.03); and payment may include a valid tender (see above). Default in payment may give rise to express remedies[7] and those implied by law, eg, withholding performance (see s 28 of the SGA: set out post, para 23.16); damages (see post, para 27.28 *et seq*); termination (see post, para 26.08 *et seq*); remedies of an unpaid seller (see post, para 24.03 *et seq*). Normally, payments made are irrecoverable[8] and the creditor may be bound by a mistakenly low settlement figure (see post, para 26.04).

[23.13]

1   See generally Goode, *Payment Obligations in Commercial and Financial Transactions.*

2   As to what constitutes a valid tender, see post, para 23.14. Where the agreement is regulated, 'payment' is expressed to include tender: CCA, s 189(1).

3   Eg, *Bennett v Griffin Finance* [1967] 2 QB 46, CA. See generally *Chitty on Contract* (28th edn), para 22-041.

4   *Bradford Old Bank v Sutcliffe* [1918] 2 KB 833, CA. For the principle of nominalism, see Goode, *op cit*, note 1, 33. For exact performance, see post, para 26.04. For payment of a lesser sum in satisfaction, see post, para 26.18.

5   See further Chitty, *op cit*, note 3, paras 22-043; 22-096; Jones, *Credit Cards,* p 158; Arora, *Electronic Banking* (2nd edn), pp 10–12; Jacks, *Report on Banking Services* (1989, Cm 622), paras 7.22–81.

6   For discussion of the legal position of Bank Giro, see a DTI Paper (1990, Cm 1026), para 5.22. As to whether such a payment may be rejected, see [1992] JBL 335.

7   Eg, sometimes interest on overdue payments (see ante, para 7.03A); acceleration clauses (see post, paras 23.26, 26.19); crystallisation of a floating charge (see post, para 25.25); repossession (see post, para 24.23 *et seq*); termination (see post, para 26.08 *et seq*); liquidated damages (see post, para 27.29).

8   Exceptionally, payments may be recoverable, eg, where there is a condition subsequent as on sale or return (see ante, para 20.23 *et seq*); where there is a total failure of consideration (see post, para 29.12); under the equitable rule for relief against forfeiture (see post, para 27.20); where money is paid under a mistake (see Tettenborn, *Law of Restitution*, Chapter 3).

If the buyer, hirer or debtor owes more than one debt to the same person, he is *prima facie* entitled when making a payment to appropriate that payment to a particular debt; but, if the debtor remains silent, the creditor is entitled at common law to make such appropriation as he thinks fit;[9] but the creditor is deprived of this right where payments are due under two or more regulated agreements (s 81 of the CCA), though not where the debts are due under a single regulated agreement, eg, a single Visa card. Special rules obtain where the creditor or debtor is insolvent (see ante, para 19.12); or subject to a garnishee order (see post, para 27.04); or the payment is to be made by instalments (see post, paras 23.26–27) or by post (see post, para 23.14); or the debtor is unlawfully harassed (see post, para 24.24); or the right to receive payment has been assigned (see ante, para 7.16); or payment is of a lesser sum (see post, para 26.18); or unenforceable[10] or in respect of tracing (see post, para 27.13).

[23.14] Valid tender. What constitutes a valid tender will depend on the terms of the agreement creating the debt (see ante, para 23.13) and the ordinary law.[1] *Prima facie*, in a contract governed by English law the debtor must seek out the creditor[2] and proffer his debt in pounds sterling, which is the legal tender.[3] The position may vary where such payment is sent by post[4] or the initial debt is later discharged by subsequent agreement or set-off.[5] However, it may be that the supplier cannot be required to contract for cash;[6] and the agreement may instead provide another form of payment.

1   *In international sales governed by English law* (see ante, para 10.01), the parties may provide for a currency of payment other than sterling.[7] As to the means of payment, the creditor may agree to take a cheque or other bill of exchange (see ante, para 7.24), perhaps supported by a surety (see post, para 25.03 *et seq*). Alternatively, commonly agreed forms of payment are bankers' confirmed credit or telex.[8]

---

9   See Chitty, *op cit*, note 3, para 22-059 *et seq*.
10 As being a penalty (see post, paras 27.46; 27.38); or under the doctrines of frustration (see ante, para 22.14 *et seq*) or unconscionable bargain (see post, para 29.40).

[23.14]

1   See generally *Chitty on Contract* (28th edn), para 22-039.
2   See Chitty, *ibid*, para 22-054. This ties in with the duty of the seller to make delivery at his own premises (s 29(2)): see ante, para 23.04.
3   For discussion of legal tender, see *Halsbury's Laws* (4th edn rev), vol 9(1), para 975; and see further ante, paras 2.06; 7.24. If/when the UK joins the EMU, the Euro will presumably become the legal tender. For decimalisation, see ante, para 4.24.
4   The express or implied authority by a creditor for his debtor to post a cheque to him may transfer the risk of loss in course of post on the creditor: Chalmers, *Bills of Exchange* (13th edn), p 344. But this is not necessarily so: see (1994) 144 NLJ 419. Such possibility of loss may be obviated by using the 1992 Act cheque forms: see ante, para 7.28.
5   See *Sinochem International Oil (London) Co Ltd v Mobil Sales and Supply Corp* [2000] 1 All ER (Comm) 474, CA. As to variation, waiver or novation, see post, paras 26.18 *et seq*; and as to set-off, see ante, para 7.23; and *Hong Kong and Shanghai Banking Corp v Kloeckner & Co AG* [1990] 2 QB 514 (contracting out of set-off – which may in other cases be subject to UCTA: see ante, para 18.16).
6   White Paper on *Banking Services* (1990, Cm 1026), Annexe 8.22.
7   See for example the *Alan* case (set out post, para 26.21). For money of account and payment, see *Benjamin's Sale of Goods* (5th edn), paras 25-135/7; Goode, *Payment Obligations in Commercial and Finance Transactions*, p 5.
8   *The Chikuma* [1981] 1 All ER 652, HL (telex). For payment by bankers' confirmed credit, see Atiyah, *Sale of Goods* (10th edn), Chapter 23.

2 *In domestic transactions,* where the obligations will normally be in sterling, instead of legal tender (see above), the debt to the supplier may instead be settled by 'digital money' (see ante, para 2.24); or by bank giro (see ante, para 23.13); or by payment card or voucher;[9] or by credit note;[10] or by gift voucher or trading stamp or token, eg, electricity tokens (for gift vouchers, see ante, para 15.18; for trading stamps, see ante, para 15.19; and for debit cards see post, para 23.15. For early settlement, see post, para 26.19A); or by debit card (see post, para 23.15), perhaps effected by telephone or internet (see ante, para 8.17); or increasingly rarely by cheque.[11] Further, where there is an instalment credit transaction (see ante, para 1.03), the supplier may prefer to insist that payments are made by banker's standing order or by direct debit.[12] In such cases, the supplier may also require a deposit before delivery, perhaps partly as a test of creditworthiness: such a deposit may be paid by way of legal tender (see post, para 23.22), but frequently takes the form of a part exchange. In the last case, the parties will usually themselves agree a price to be put on the part exchanged goods (see ante, para 2.09); and the CCA expressly includes such part exchange allowance in the deposit (see ante, para 2.07).

[23.15] Debit cards.[1] These are plastic cards used to effect a transmission of funds from bank or other account of the debtor to the account of his creditor by way of EFT (see ante, para 2.17) and have been likened to an electronic cheque (see ante, para 2.25), although it would seem that the debit card arrangements make no provision for a debit to be stopped.[2] To operate one of these cards to transfer a sum of money from his account, the card holder inserts it into an electronic reader, which connects it by telephone to his account and then authorises the transaction either by signature on a flimsy or by PIN.[3] Such cards may involve two or three parties: a two party cash card is used by the holder to extract cash from his account via an ATM; whereas a three party card is used by the holder for making retail payments for goods and services at the point of sale, so they are known as EFTPOS cards.[4] Attempts to launch a nationally recognised EFTPOS card system have so far been unsuccessful.[5]

---

9 For payment cards and vouchers, see generally ante, paras 2.24 *et seq*; and for use of a credit card by telephone, see ante, para 8.17. Unlike payment by cheque, payment by credit or charge card *prima facie* amounts to absolute payment: *Re Charge Card Services Ltd* (set out ante, para 2.27).

10 As to which, see post, para 29.03A. Is it an assignable (see ante, para 7.21) promissory note (see ante, para 7.24)?

11 The number of (almost always 'account payee': see ante, para 7.28) cheques drawn is decreasing rapidly and now accounts for less than 8% of domestic purchases, commonly with a cheque guarantee card (see ante, para 2.26. For the rules regarding payment by cheque, see Macleod, *Consumer Sales Law,* Butterworths edn, 1989, para 23.14A.

12 Giving a DD has been held equivalent to a cash payment: *Weldon v GRE Life Assurance Ltd* [2000] 2 All ER 914 (not a goods case). See also *Esso Petroleum Ltd v Milton* [1997] 2 All ER 593, CA.

[23.15]

1 See generally *Chitty on Contract* (28th edn, paras 38.438/40).

2 Arora, *Electronic Banking* (2nd edn), p 74.

3 See ante, para 2.24. Is a flimsy a negotiable instrument (see ante, para 7.24)?

4 E(lectronic) F(und) T(ransfer) at P(oint) O(f) S(ale). For EFT generally, see ante, para 2.17.

5 See Arora, *op cit,* note 2, p 4.

Even at common law, the several different contracts necessary to effect debit card transactions[6] give rise to a number of problems. First, is payment by way of debit card conditional payment like a cheque (see ante, para 23.14); or is it absolute payment like a charge card (see ante, para 2.27)? It has been argued that it is absolute payment,[7] perhaps because it cannot be stopped (see above). Second, these systems are usually off-line, that is, recorded by the bank and processed subsequently, so that the debtor has a similar delay between use of his debit card and debiting of his account to that which he would have had if payment had been made by cheque.[8]

In neither case is credit an essential element of the transaction, though use of the card may draw down credit facilities already established on that bank or other account (see ante, para 7.03). As a significant deferment of payment is necessary for the credit essential for a transaction to fall within the CCA (see ante, para 5.21), it has therefore been argued that debit cards are not *per se* regulated,[9] though there has been disagreement as to whether or not debit cards can amount to credit tokens within s 14 (see ante, para 5.30). If, like charge cards (see ante, para 5.15), debit cards are also outside the ambit of the CCA, this will mean that the legal rules applicable to charge and debit cards differ substantially from those governing regulated credit cards, even though they may all be dealt with in an identical way by the Banking Code (see ante, para 3.13). It has been pointed out that this inconsistency of legal treatment is undesirable, as being unreasonable and confusing to customers;[10] and statutory reform is under consideration (see ante, para 7.03).

THE TIME OF DELIVERY AND PAYMENT

[23.16] Having analysed the duties of payment and delivery, the importance of the time element in their performance must now be examined.[1] First, reference must be made to the connection between payment and the right of the buyer or hirer to sue in conversion. It has been seen that a person can only maintain an action in conversion where he is entitled to the immediate possession of goods (see ante, para 19.06); and this in turn depends on whether the supplier is bound to deliver immediately. Second, it must be remembered that each party has two obligations: it is for the supplier to tender delivery of the goods and accept payment of the price or rent; and for the buyer or hirer to accept delivery of the goods and tender payment of the price or rent. The basic rule for sale is laid down in s 28 of the SGA as follows:

---

6   These follow a similar analysis to that in *Re Charge Card Services Ltd* (set out ante, para 2.27). If the debit card issuer is not debiting a (bank) account which it holds, there may be an extra contract between the card issuer and the card holder's bank.

7   Arora, *op cit*, note 2, p 71.

8   Arora, *op cit*, note 2, pp 63, 71.

9   Because it is purely a payment/debit mechanism: Goode, *Consumer Credit Law and Practice*, paras 3.43; 3.47; 24.84.

10 *The Jack's Report on Banking Services* (1989, Cmnd 622) paras 11.04–11, rejecting the call for a Payments Card Act; and the White Paper on *Banking Services* (1990, Cmnd 1026), Annex 8.3.

[23.16]

1   SGA, s 10(3), defines a 'month' as *prima facie* a calendar month.

Unless otherwise agreed, delivery of the goods and payment of the price are concurrent conditions, that is to say, the seller must be ready and willing to give possession of the goods to the buyer in exchange for the price and the buyer must be ready and willing to pay the price in exchange for the possession of the goods.

Two situations must be considered: (i) where the contract contemplates that the basic presumption of concurrent events applies (see below); and (ii) where it does not (see post, para 23.22). However, there should be noted the special rules for consumer distance contracts (see ante, para 23.04).

Where delivery and payment are concurrent terms

[23.17] Where the presumption in s 28 operates, delivery must be made in exchange for the price: that is, the SGA envisages that the seller will hold out the goods, the buyer will hold out the price, and price and goods will be exchanged simultaneously.[1] Thus, it is whilst the buyer is still holding out the price that the Act envisages that he will exercise his right under s 34 to inspect the goods (see ante, para 23.10). However, where the contract contemplates delivery of documents of title, these documents are equivalent to the goods (see ante, para 23.03), so that on delivery of the documents the seller is thereupon entitled to the price;[2] but the buyer retains the right to inspect and reject the goods.[3]

In order to appreciate the effect of delay in performance by either party, the status of the obligations of delivery and payment must first be examined. In *Bunge Corp v Tradax:*[4]

> There was a chain of contracts, including one for the sale of 5,000 tons of soya bean meal fob at an American Gulf Port nominated by the sellers. The contract required the buyers to provide a vessel at the nominated port. Clause 17 stipulated that the buyers should 'give at least 15 consecutive days' notice' of the probable readiness of the vessel so that the sellers could arrange for the goods to be available at a Gulf Port they would then nominate. The buyers were four days late in giving the notice required by clause 17, which the sellers claimed amounted to a repudiation. The buyers argued that clause 17 was an innominate term; and the sellers conceded that, if so, the breach was not sufficiently serious to entitle them to treat the contract as being repudiated.

The House of Lords unanimously found for the seller, holding that clause 17 was a condition[5] for the following reasons: stipulations as to time in mercantile contracts were generally to be treated as conditions, even minor breaches of which might amount to repudiations,[6] both to enable each party to organise his affairs and to meet the need for certainty, especially necessary in the case of strings of contracts.[7] Of course, such stipulations may be waived (see post, paras 26.23–25).

[23.17]

1   But see Oditah, *Legal Aspects of Accounts Receivable*, 1.
2   *Clements Horst v Biddell Brothers* [1912] AC 18, HL.
3   This dual right of rejection is explained ante, para 22.07.
4   [1981] 2 All ER 513, HL. See also *Gill & Duffus SA v Societe Pour L'Exploration des Sucres SA* [1986] 1 Lloyd's Rep 322, CA ('at latest').
5   For conditions and innominate terms, see ante, para 11.05.
6   *Contra* delay in acceptance of delivery (see post, para 23.19) or tender of payment (see post, para 23.20).
7   For criticism of this doctrine, see Goode (1983) 3 Legal Studies at 285–86.

[23.18] Tender of delivery. In the case of hp agreements, the hiring does not commence until delivery (see ante, para 15.23); but, subject to this, it is presumed that, insofar as the agreement does not cover delay in delivery, those rules of sale which relate to delivery apply by analogy. In fact, the SGA refrains from laying down any hard and fast rule as to whether the time of delivery is of the essence of the contract (s 10(2): set out post, para 23.20), but does require that the 'demand or tender of delivery' be made at a reasonable hour (s 29(5): set out ante, para 23.04) and makes the duty to tender delivery subject to the unpaid seller's lien (see post, para 24.10). According to McCardie J:[1]

> In ordinary commercial contracts for the sale of goods the rule clearly is that time is *prima facie* of the essence with respect to delivery.

This statement must obviously be read subject to the statutory rules just mentioned, and hides an ambiguity: the learned judge may have been saying that delay is always fatal; or only such delay as causes serious loss amounts to a breach entitling the other side to rescind.[2] In fact, the courts have decided that, if a commercial contract stipulates a time for delivery,[3] any breach by the seller entitles the buyer to rescind,[4] even if he has suffered no damage.[5] However, if the contract is not a commercial one, or does not stipulate a time for delivery,[6] the SGA merely requires that the seller must deliver within a reasonable time (s 29(2): set out ante, para 23.04), though the seller's delay may be so great as to show an intention to repudiate.[7] It may seem a pity that there does not appear to be a *prima facie* rule for retail sales. Should they be regarded as a sort of 'spot' contract (see post, para 23.19)?

[23.19] Acceptance of delivery. Bearing in mind the foregoing rules for tender of delivery (see ante, para 23.18), it might be thought that the law would impose reciprocal obligations with respect to acceptance of delivery. However, the law will only assume that acceptance of delivery is of the essence where the goods are perishable[1] or there is a 'spot' contract.[2] In all other cases, it is assumed that the time of acceptance of delivery is not of the essence;[3] that, if no time of acceptance is specified, the buyer is merely required to accept delivery within a reasonable time;[4] and that further delay merely gives the seller the right to damages,[5] unless it is so great as to show an intention to repudiate.[6] In a

---

[23.18]

1 *Hartley v Hymans* (set out post, para 26.24), at 484. See also *Bunge Corp v Tradax* (set out ante, para 23.17).

2 See Stoljar (1955) 71 LQR 527, at 532.

3 Or if a non-commercial contract stipulates a time for delivery and makes that time of the essence: *Charles Rickards Ltd v Oppenheim* (set out post, para 26.25).

4 *The Naxos* [1990] 3 All ER 641, HL.

5 *Bowes v Shand* (1877) 2 App Cas 455, HL.

6 Eg, *McDougall v Aeromarine of Emsworth Ltd* [1958] 3 All ER 431 (seller to use his 'best endeavours').

7 Cf *Pearl Mill Co v Ivy Tannery Co* [1919] 1 KB 78. For repudiation, see post, para 26.15.

[23.19]

1 *Sharp v Christmas* (1892) 8 TLR 687, CA; cf SGA, s 48(3): see post, para 27.08.

2 A 'spot' contract is one which envisages almost immediate delivery, eg, *Thames Sack & Bag Co Ltd v Knowles & Co Ltd* (1919) 88 LJKB 585.

3 *Woolfe v Horn* (1877) 2 QBD 355.

4 *Shearson Lehman Hutton v Maclaine Watson & Co* [1990] 2 Lloyd's Rep 570.

5 *Penarth Dock Engineering Co Ltd v Pounds* [1963] 1 Lloyd's Rep 359.

6 *Pearl Mill Co v Ivy Tannery Co* [1919] 1 KB 78. For repudiation, see post, para 26.15.

commercial contract, why should the time of tender of delivery normally amount to a condition, whilst the time of acceptance of delivery is only a warranty? It has been suggested that, apart from the cases of perishable goods and 'spot' contracts, the seller's prime interest is to obtain the price whereas that of the buyer is to obtain delivery, so that it is understandable that the tender of delivery is more important to the buyer than acceptance of delivery is to the seller.[7] Yet it ought to follow that the tender of the price by the buyer is also an essential term; but this is not so (see post, para 23.20).

[23.20] **Payment**. It is the duty of the buyer to tender the price and of the seller to accept the price at the time laid down in the contract,[1] or, if no time is stipulated, within a reasonable time.[2] Section 10 of the SGA provides as follows:

(1) Unless a different intention appears from the terms of the contract, stipulations as to time of payment are not of the essence of a contract of sale.

(2) Whether any other stipulation as to time is or is not of the essence of the contract depends on the terms of the contract.

However, s 10(1) appears to conflict with s 28 of the SGA, which states that payment and delivery shall be 'concurrent conditions'. Perhaps the explanation lies in the different usage of the word 'condition' (see ante, para 11.04): it may be that s 28 is referring to 'condition' exclusively in the sense of condition precedent, and not in the sense of a contractual promise,[3] whereas s 10(1) is dealing with the importance of the contractual promise. Certainly, the courts have acted on s 10(1), and held that its effect is to create a presumption that stipulations as to the time of payment are only warranties,[4] and it has been said that this reflects a more general common law rule.[5]

Of course, this presumption may be displaced, as when the contract provides for the payment of a deposit (see post, para 23.27), or the exercise of an option,[6] or where the buyer contracts to open a banker's confirmed credit,[7] or the goods are perishable (s 48(3) of the SGA: discussed post, para 27.08). It is fairly common to find time of payment expressly made of the essence in a standard form contract:[8] but in a consumer supply this may be an unfair term;[9] and in any standard form it may be unreasonable (s 3 of UCTA: see ante, para 18.24).

Even where time is not of the essence of the original contract, the delay in payment may be so great as to show an intention to repudiate (see post, para 26.15); or the seller

---

7 Stoljar (1955) 71 LQR 527, at 538. *Sed quaere?*

[23.20]

1 See Goode, *Payment Obligations in Commercial and Financial Transaction*, pp 64–69.

2 See *Brighty v Norman* (1862) 3 B & S 305 (stipulation for payment on request).

3 See Smith and Thomas, *Casebook on Contract* (11th edn), p 424.

4 *Payzu Ltd v Saunders* (set out post, para 27.44).

5 Goode, *op cit*, note 1, p 74.

6 *United Dominions Trust (Commercial) Ltd v Eagle Aircraft Services Ltd* [1968] 1 All ER 104, CA. See also credit cards (below).

7 *Trans Trust SPRL v Danubian Trading Ltd* (set out post, para 27.35).

8 See post, para 26.08. For acceleration clauses, see ante, para 7.03; and for standard form contracts, see generally ante, para 11.08.

9 OFT, *UCT Bulletin No 5*, p 121; and see generally ante, para 11.12.

may by giving notice make time of the essence.[10] In relation to credit cards, the debtor will usually have an option as to the amount payable; but if he breaks the terms of that option, the agreement will usually make time of the essence as to the whole debt, though it may not be able to require an increased **rate** of interest payable on default (default interest).[11]

[23.21] Delivery and payment. The relative importance of the stipulations as to the time of delivery and payment can now be examined. Leaving aside such delays as manifest an intention to repudiate, s 28 of the SGA appears to create a statutory stalemate; but what it really means is that each of the parties must be ready and willing[1] to perform his part of the bargain before the other party performs his obligations.[2] Moreover, the effect of s 10 would appear to be to allow the time of delivery to remain an essential undertaking, whilst making the time of payment a warranty: if the seller does not deliver on time, the buyer may treat the contract as repudiated; but if the buyer does not pay the price on time, the seller is only entitled to damages.[3] This state of affairs has been criticised as extending 'compulsory credit to the buyer'.[4] But it must be remembered that the unpaid seller is entitled to retain possession of the goods until payment under two provisions of the SGA: s 28 makes payment of the price a condition precedent to the duty of the seller to deliver the goods; and s 39 gives the seller a lien on the goods for the price (see post, para 24.04).

Where delivery and payment are not concurrent terms

[23.22] The parties to a contract for the supply of goods are quite at liberty to oust the presumption in s 28 (set out ante, para 23.16) and make performance on one side conditional on prior performance by the other, whether in whole or in part:

1   *Prior payment.* Where the contract provides for payment in advance of delivery, the seller is entitled to sue for the price without tendering delivery (s 49(2) of the SGA: set out post, para 27.18): he merely has to show an intention to continue with the contract (see ante, para 23.05). In relation to consumer transactions, this form of business is common for mail order,[1] double glazing, goods made-to-measure, eg, suits, and goods not held by a retailer in stock, eg, furniture. Any substantial delay between payment and delivery increases the risk that the consumer will lose his pre-payments,

---

10   Eg, under the SGA, s 48(3). See generally, Goode, *op cit*, note 1, pp 76–9.
11   Where the agreement is regulated, by reason of CCA, s 93: see Jones, *Credit Cards*, pp 163–65; and generally post, para 26.19.
[23.21]
1   And able? See ante, para 23.06.
2   As to concurrent conditions, see further post, para 26.01.
3   Because the only consequence is that he is deprived of the use of the money: Goode, *Commercial Law* (2nd edn), p 440.
4   Stoljar (1955) 71 LQR 527 at 540.
[23.22]
1   In a distance contract, the consumer should be aware of the pre-payment by reason of the notification provisions in the Distance Selling Regulations: see ante, para 9.05A.

eg, on the seller's insolvency.[2] Whilst some protection is offered by voluntary codes,[3] present legal safeguards are somewhat inadequate: some redress is obtainable if dishonesty can be proved (see ante, para 4.01), which may lead to a compensation order (see ante, para 3.20); or if a supplying company is liquidated;[4] or the consumer may avoid the problem by paying by credit card and using s 75 of the CCA (see post, para 16.11); or the supplier may help by putting such prior payments into a trust account,[5] or by insuring them.[6] Moreover, prior payment deprives the customer of the leverage of withholding payment where the goods supplied are defective, so it may amount to an unfair term;[7] but the OFT have negotiated a 'voluntary' scheme whereby on complaint the supplier will deposit 20% of the price with Qualitas.[8]

2   *Prior delivery.* Similarly, if the contract provides for delivery in advance of payment, eg, credit or conditional sale (see ante, paras 1.12–16), the buyer is entitled to sue for non-delivery without tendering the price (s 51(1), SGA: set out post, para 29.19). Alternatively, the buyer in this last situation may maintain an action in conversion against the seller, as he is *prima facie* entitled to immediate possession;[9] but he will lose this right if insolvent, because the unpaid seller's lien will arise by reason of the insolvency (s 41(1) of the SGA: set out post, para 24.10).

Finally, it must be borne in mind that delay in performance of the obligation to deliver or pay may show an intention to repudiate (see ante, para 23.19).

PERFORMANCE BY INSTALMENTS

[23.23] It is quite compatible with s 28 of the SGA that either or both of the obligations of delivery or payment may be discharged by instalments. Indeed, if the parties agree that both delivery and payment shall be by matching instalments, they are plainly adhering to the basic presumption of s 28, eg, a book club. On the other hand, it is open to the parties to provide that only one of the obligations shall be performed by instalments. However, in a consumer supply, this must not be done in a manner unfair to consumers.[1]

---

2   As to insolvency, see ante, para 19.12 *et seq.* And see generally OFT, *Don't Wave Your Money Goodbye* (1987); (1990) 7 Tr LR 229.

3   Eg, the Mail Order Protection and Double Glazing Schemes. See ante, para 3.13.

4   On the grounds of carrying on a business with intent to defraud creditors: see Insolvency Act 1986, ss 213, 215; and further ante, para 19.24.

5   See *Re Kayford* (set out ante, para 19.23). There are no OFT plans to make this compulsory: 91/2 Beeline, 14. For a failed scheme, see [2001] 7 Which? 4.

6   See post, para 25.07A. Cf product liability insurance (see ante, para 17.09). For creditors' rights, see ante, para 16.17.

7   OFT, *Bulletin No 13*, para 1.9; *No 14*, case 16; *No 15*, para 15 and case 1; *No 16*, case 9; and see generally ante, para 11.12 *et seq.*

8   An independent trust: see OFT, (2001) 29 Fair Trading 4. For Qualitas, see ante, para 3.13.

9   *Per* Bayley J in *Bloxam v Sanders* (1825) 4 B & C 941, at 948–49. It is sometimes said that this case conflicts with *Chinery v Viall* (set out post, para 29.24), though in both cases it was irrelevant whether the sale was on credit. See also *Healing (Sales) Ltd v Inglis Ltd* (1968) 42 ALJR 280; and generally ante, para 19.06.

[23.23]

1   See OFT, *Bulletin No 12*, case 13; *No 13*, case 1; *No 14*, case 3; and generally ante, para 11.12 *et seq.*

Delivery by instalments

[23.24] General. One consequence of the general duty to deliver the right quantity[1] is that after accepting a short delivery the buyer is *prima facie* not obliged to accept a subsequent tender of the balance.[2] Nor is he entitled to demand delivery by instalments.[3] Thus, to permit delivery by instalments, there must be some agreement between the parties to this effect. No doubt, the typical litigation situation where the parties agree to instalment deliveries involves a 'lengthy course of dealings and great quantities of goods';[4] but it should be remembered that the rules also cover cases such as a retail sale where the consumer takes some goods away with him and has the rest delivered.

Whether a contract provides for delivery by instalments is a question of construction;[5] and, where it does so, the contract may be susceptible of any one of the following interpretations:

(1) That the parties intend that there should be not one contract, but a series of contracts between them;[6] or

(2) That the parties intend that there should be a single contract, but that that contract should be divisible or severable in the sense that each instalment is to be paid for separately;[7] or

(3) That the parties intend that there should be a single contract, and that the price is to be paid as a single sum.[8]

Which interpretation is adopted may be important for several reasons:[9] first, in determining whether acceptance of part of the goods prevents the buyer subsequently rejecting the remainder (see post, paras 29.08–09); second, in deciding whether breach by the seller or buyer in respect of one of the instalments amounts to a repudiation of the whole contract;[10] third, in establishing the unpaid seller's real rights (see post, para 24.08); and fourth, to decide whether delivery is subject to the strict rules of s 30 (see post, para 23.25).

Where there is a series of contracts, then, however serious the breach of one of them, it cannot, without more, amount to a repudiation of the others. But in practice, the courts seem reluctant to treat an instalment contract as a series of contracts; and even a provision that each delivery shall be treated as a separate contract tends to be construed as

---

[23.24]

1 Under the SGA, s 30: see ante, paras 13.03–07. Cf the common law rule of exact performance: see post, para 26.02.
2 SGA, s 31(1); eg, *Behrend and Co v Produce Brokers Co* (set out ante, para 13.04).
3 Goode, *Commercial Law* (2nd edn), p 281.
4 Stoljar (1955) 71 LQR 527, at 543.
5 Eg, *Howell v Evans* (1926) 134 LT 570. See generally Goode, *op cit*, note 3, pp 282–87.
6 See *Benjamin's Sale of Goods* (5th edn), para 8-071. Cf SGA, s 57(1): see ante, para 10.10.
7 Eg, *Robert Munro & Co Ltd v Meyer* [1930] 2 KB 312; *Jackson v Rotax Motor and Cycle Co* (set out ante, para 14.05), CA.
8 Eg, *Longbottom & Co Ltd v Bass, Walker & Co* [1922] WN 245, CA; *J Rosenthal Ltd v Esmail* [1965] 2 All ER 860, HL.
9 See further Goode, *op cit*, note 3, pp 286–89.
10 See below and post, para 23.25. For repudiation generally, see post, para 26.15. As to the position of previous instalments, see Atiyah, *Sale of Goods* (10th edn), pp 506–07.

indicating that there is a single contract under which each instalment is to be paid for separately.[11] Assuming that there is a single contract, the next question is whether performance of that contract is divisible. Where performance is indivisible, a serious breach in respect of one instalment is treated as giving rise to a right to rescind in the same manner as partial breach of a non-instalment contract would do;[12] whereas a partial breach of a divisible contract will not necessarily have such an effect (see post, para 23.25).

[23.25] Divisible contracts. In this case, the 'question is whether the acts and conduct of the (guilty) party evince an intention no longer to be bound by the contract';[1] and in conducting this enquiry, the common law today generally assumes that the parties contemplated payment of damages rather than discharge, so that the guilty party can normally set up his willingness to perform the rest of the contract, subject to his compensating the innocent party for the breach.[2] Such divisible contracts are partly[3] covered by s 31(2) of the SGA, which provides:

> Where there is a contract for the sale of goods to be delivered by stated instalments, which are to be separately paid for, and the seller makes defective deliveries in respect of one or more instalments, or the buyer neglects or refuses to take delivery of or pay for one or more instalments, it is a question in each case depending on the terms of the contract and the circumstances of the case, whether the breach of contract is a repudiation of the whole contract or whether it is a severable breach giving rise to a claim for compensation but not to a right to treat the whole contract as repudiated.

In the case of short delivery in one instalment, this provision appears to overlap with, and to be preferred on grounds of flexibility to, s 30(1): the **short** delivery (s 30(1)) is treated as a defective delivery (s 31(2)).[4] However, even where it applies, s 31(2) poses rather than answers the question, and it is necessary to fall back on common law principles. In *Robert Munro & Co Ltd Meyer*,[5] Wright J found that the seller had no intention of breaking his contract, but nevertheless held that, as there was a persistent breach continuing for nearly half the contract total of goods, the buyer was entitled to rescind. He explained that (at 331):

> In such circumstances, the intention of the seller must be judged from his acts and from the deliveries which he in fact makes, and that being so, where the breach is substantial and so serious as the breach in this case and has continued so persistently, the buyer is entitled to say that he has the right to treat the whole contract as repudiated.

---

11   *Per* Lord Wright in *Ross T Smyth & Co Ltd v Bailey, Sons & Co* [1940] 3 All ER 60, at 73, HL.

12   *Longbottom & Co Ltd v Bass, Walker & Co* (above).

[23.25]

1   *Per* Lord Coleridge CJ in *Freeth v Burr* (1874) LR 9 CP 208, at 213. See also *per* Lord Blackburn in *Mersey Steel and Iron Co Ltd v Naylor Benzon & Co* (1884) 9 App Cas 434, HL at 443.

2   *Per* Lord Wright in *Ross T Smyth & Co Ltd v Bailey, Sons & Co* [1940] 3 All ER 60, at 71, HL. See, eg, *James Shaffer Ltd v Findlay* [1953] 1 WLR 106, CA; *Peter Dumenil & Co Ltd v Ruddin Ltd* [1953] 2 All ER 294, CA.

3   Whilst s 31(2) mentions the common cases, a number of others are listed in *Benjamin's Sale of Goods* (5th edn), para 8-073.

4   *Regent OHG Aisenstadt & Barig v Francesco of Jermyn St Ltd* [1981] 3 All ER 327, discussed by Atiyah, *Sale of Goods* (10th edn, pp 506–07. As to s 30(1), see ante, para 13.04.

5   [1930] 2 KB 312; [1930] All ER Rep 241 (5% adulteration with cocoa husks).

In *Maple Flock Co Ltd v Universal Furniture Products (Wembley) Ltd,*[6] the Court of Appeal said that (at 157):

> ... the main tests to be considered in applying the sub-section ... are, first, the ratio quantitatively which breach bears to the contract as a whole, and secondly the degree of probability or improbability that such a breach will be repeated.

In that case, the Court of Appeal found that the delivery complained of amounted to no more than one and a half tons out of a contract for the sale of 100 tons of rag flock and that the chances of the breach being repeated was for all practical purposes negligible; and the court therefore concluded that there was 'no sufficient justification to entitle the (buyer) to refuse further deliveries' (at 158). Should it make any difference that the breach is in respect of the first instalment? The cases are conflicting,[7] and commentators disagree; but the issue must be set against the modern background of reluctance on the part of the courts to find an intention to repudiate.[8]

Payment by instalments

[23.26] Whereas s 31(1) enacts that *prima facie* the buyer is not bound to accept delivery of the goods by instalments (see ante, para 23.24), the SGA contains no counterpart to s 31(1) in relation to the obligation to pay the price. However, it may be that it is to be implied from s 31(1) that payment is *prima facie* to be made in a lump sum.[1] Certainly, where the time for payment has arrived, there is no room for payment by instalments; but, where the contract provides for delivery by instalments, s 31(2) itself lays down no definite rule for the effect of non-payment of instalments (see ante, para 23.25). Of course, there is nothing to prevent the parties from stipulating in the contract for payment by instalments; and in this event, the contract will commonly specify the times of payment, make time of the essence[2] and provide that on any such default all the outstanding instalments shall be payable immediately.[3]

Sometimes, all the instalments of the price are payable before delivery of the goods,[4] eg, under certain types of retail 'Christmas Club', the goods being selected and set aside for delivery after completion of payment of the price by instalments; but the situation is rather more complicated where delivery is made in advance of payment of the whole or part of the price.[5] Naturally, the unpaid seller will lose his lien (see post, para 24.14); and, where the price is payable by instalments, the transaction might amount to a credit sale

---

6   [1934] 1 KB 148; [1933] All ER Rep 15, CA (judgment of Hewart LCJ, Lord Wright and Slesser LJ delivered by the LCJ).

7   Compare *Hoare v Rennie* (1859) 5 H & N 19 and *Honck v Muller* (1881) 7 QBD 92, with *Simpson v Crippin* (1872) LR 8 QB 14.

8   Compare *Benjamin on Sale* (8th edn), p 734 with Stoljar (1955) 71 LQR 527, at 543–44 and *Benjamin's Sale of Goods* (5th edn), para 8-077.

[23.26]

1   But if the contract provides for payment by instalments, would not s 28 (set out ante, para 23.16) imply that delivery should also be by matching instalments?

2   Thus reversing s 10(1): set out ante, para 23.20.

3   For acceleration clauses, see ante, para 7.03 and further post, para 26.19.

4   Eg, *Hyundai Heavy Industries Ltd v Papadopoulos* [1980] 2 All ER 29, HL (ship-building contract).

5   Pre-contract credit enquiries have already been considered: see ante, para 8.35 *et seq.*

regulated by the CCA (see ante, para 1.13). Moreover, if the seller attempts to protect himself by reserving the property in the goods until paid for, then the transaction may be a regulated 'conditional sale' within the CCA (see ante, para 1.14). Thus, if the transaction is a regulated one within the CCA, the real choice available to the supplier is whether or not to reserve the property in the goods: without a reservation of property, the transaction is a credit sale and offers him less protection, but is subject to only some of the CCA restrictions; whereas a transaction with a reservation of property – be it conditional sale or hp – offers some security (see post, para 24.27 *et seq*), but is subject to the full rigours of the CCA. Further problems connected with instalment payments are considered below.

[23.27] In considering the position of the instalments to be paid under a sale, hp or simple hiring, a distinction must be drawn between the initial payment and the subsequent instalments:

1 *The initial payment.* The supplier sometimes requires the first payment to be made before delivery, or even before contract. If the transaction proceeds, it will usually be possible to spell out a mutual intention that the initial payment is to constitute a part payment of the debt.[1] However, if the supply contract does not proceed, then, ignoring the supplier's insolvency (see ante, para 23.22), a distinction must be drawn in dealing with the initial payment:

(a) If the supply contract is never concluded, it may depend on whether the sum is simply an advance part payment, or a deposit.[2] If it is a part payment, the buyer or hirer can recover the sum on grounds of total failure of consideration.[3] If it is a deposit, or a deposit and part payment,[4] the position is as follows: generally, a reasonable deposit is irrecoverable by the defaulting buyer or hirer,[5] being in the nature of a preliminary contract guaranteeing completion, though there may be relief against forfeiture (see post, para 27.20) and, in a consumer supply, a retention of deposit clause may be unfair;[6] whereas, if the supply contract is a prospective regulated one (see ante, para 5.20), any preliminary contract is probably void under s 59 of the CCA, upon which the intended deposit becomes recoverable on grounds of total failure of consideration.

(b) Where the supply contract has been concluded, the position depends on whether or not it is regulated. Where the agreement is unregulated, then with the possible exception of sale or return transactions (see ante, para 20.23 *et seq*), the buyer or hirer cannot, except by subsequent agreement or lawful discharge (see Chapter 26), escape from his contract without breaking it, in which case the supplier may

---

[23.27]

1 See post, para 27.19. As to the ordinary rules regarding payment of a debt, see ante, paras 23.13–15.

2 For the distinction between part payments and deposit, see further post, para 27.19; and for prior payments, see ante, para 23.22.

3 For total failure of consideration, see post, para 29.12 *et seq*. As to the question from whom the sum is recoverable in a tripartite transaction, see ante, para 16.05.

4 Unless expressed to be a 'returnable deposit', which presumably is treated as a simple part payment.

5 *Contra* if the supplier is at fault, in which case the deposit ought to be recoverable by the buyer or hirer on grounds of total failure of consideration (as to which, see note 3, above). This may be spelt out in a standard form contract, eg, a new vehicle order form.

6 OFT, *Bulletin No 15*, cases 8 and 13. See generally ante, para 11.12 *et seq*.

elect either to affirm and sue for the agreed sum,[7] or treat the contract as discharged and claim damages.[8] In the latter event, the buyer or hirer may counterclaim to recover a part payment,[9] whereas the position of a deposit is different: a reasonable deposit already paid by the guilty buyer or hirer probably remains irrecoverable (see above), and the innocent supplier can recover by way of damages such a deposit payable but not yet paid.[10] Where the agreement is regulated, it may be cancellable in which case all sums paid are recoverable (s 70, of the CCA: see ante, para 10.33); or the protected goods rules may intervene (s 91 of the CCA: see post, para 24.38).

2   *The subsequent instalments.* In the case of an instalment sale, the buyer cannot normally[11] unilaterally terminate his obligations, remaining liable for the outstanding instalments, possibly at an accelerated rate; and, notwithstanding the *prima facie* rule (see ante, para 23.20), the sale contract will frequently make time of payment of the essence, so giving the supplier the right to treat the contract as discharged (see post, para 26.15). On the other hand, a hirer under a periodic hiring will have a unilateral right to terminate the agreement at the end of each period of the hiring: in this case, the hirer is *prima facie* not liable for hire rent in respect of any future period (see post, para 25.21); *contra* an agreement to hire for a fixed term (see ante, para 7.18). Moreover, attempts by suppliers to secure for themselves such payments under minimum payment clauses may amount to unfair terms (see ante, para 11.09); and are also bedeviled by the rule relating to penalties (see post, para 27.25) as regards unregulated agreements, or the CCA restrictions (s 100: see post para 27.49) as regards regulated agreements.

---

7   Unless the agreement contains an acceleration clause (see ante, para 23.26), he will have to await the dates of payment: see ante, para 23.20.

8   As to whether non-payment of one instalment shows an intention to repudiate, cf ante, para 23.25; and as to repudiation generally see post, para 26.15.

9   *Dies v British and International Mining and Finance Corp Ltd* [1939] 1 KB 724.

10 *The Blankenstein* [1985] 1 All ER 475, CA (criticised by Carter 104 LQR 207). As the deposit exceeded his actual loss, the supplier was entitled only to nominal damages for repudiation: see further post, para 27.20. See also *Pollway Ltd v Abdullah* [1974] 2 All ER 381, CA (auction buyer sued on stopped deposit cheque).

11 *Contra* where the sale is subject to a suitable condition subsequent: see ante, para 20.03.

CHAPTER 24

POSSESSION AND REPOSSESSION BY THE SUPPLIER

[24.01] It was seen in Chapter 23 that the basic assumption of a sale of goods is that the goods will be exchanged for the price (see ante, para 23.16), in which case the seller is secure in the knowledge that he will have either his goods or his price (see Chapter 2). On the other hand, the demands of the market place will frequently indicate that a supplier by way of sale or bailment should relinquish possession of the goods before payment. Leaving aside the general question of security (see Chapter 25), the purpose of this chapter is to compare the relative legal strength in the position of a supplier weighing the following alternative strategies:

(1) To retain possession until paid, relying on his possessory rights as an unpaid seller (see post, paras 24.02–20); or

(2) To relinquish possession by way of sale or bailment and instead rely on a right to recover possession in the event of default, what might be termed his 'ownership' rights (see post, paras 24.21–48).

Of course, the supplier can always ignore his security and simply sue for the price or rent (see post, paras 24.49; 27.15A *et seq*).

SECURITY THROUGH POSSESSION

[24.02] There is much truth in the old adage that possession is nine-tenths of the law: to retain possession of the goods to be supplied may well be the safest way in which the seller can ensure payment or, at least, minimise his loss. In part, this is because Part V of the SGA gives the unpaid seller in possession certain rights against those goods.

The unpaid seller's right

[24.03] The unpaid seller. Part V of the SGA is expressed to operate only in favour of an 'unpaid seller'. This expression is given a special meaning.

1　*A seller.* Section 61(1) defines a seller as 'a person who sells or agrees to sell goods';[1] but s 38(2) here extends the concept to include any person in the position of a seller, such as his agent[2] or assignee.[3] However, this does not include a buyer who justifiably rejects the goods after paying the price.[4] He should therefore reject (see

---

[24.03]

1　It has been proposed that these rules should not apply to conditional sellers whilst they retain possession: see post, para 25.34. Why should they not remain 'unpaid sellers' for any deposit?

2　See generally ante, para 10.06. Section 38(2) explicitly extends the category to an agent who has made himself personally liable on the contract as if he were the seller, eg, *Couturier v Hastie* (set out ante, para 22.10).

3　See ante, para 7.16 *et seq*. As to purely personal contracts and those expressed to be non-assignable, see ante, para 7.26.

4　*JL Lyons & Co Ltd v May and Baker Ltd* [1923] 1 KB 685.

post, para 29.03) only if satisfied of the seller's solvency, as rejection will revest the property in the seller, so allowing it to pass into an insolvent seller's estate (see ante, para 19.23) and reducing the buyer to a claim in quasi-contract for the return of the price.[5]

2   *An unpaid seller.* According to s 38(1):

> The seller of goods is deemed to be an 'unpaid seller' within the meaning of this Act –
>
> (a) When the whole of the price has not been paid or tendered;
>
> (b) When a bill of exchange or other negotiable instrument has been received as conditional payment, and the condition on which it was received has not been fulfilled by reason of the dishonour of the instrument or otherwise.

Notwithstanding that stipulations as to the time of payment are only warranties,[6] Part V of the SGA allows an unpaid seller who has not granted credit to retain possession of the goods until payment.[7] This fits in neatly with his duty under s 28 to deliver when the buyer is ready and willing to pay the price (see ante, para 23.21). Alternatively, where the seller has taken a cheque or negotiable instrument for the price,[8] his rights under Part V are suspended; but they revive if the cheque is not met, for s 38(1)(b) then deems him to be an 'unpaid seller' again.[9] Does this rule extend to 'account payee' cheques (see ante, para 7.28)? It is for consideration whether s 38(1)(b) can apply where the consumer buyer 'pays' by giving the seller a modern cheque: as we have already seen (ante, para 7.28), it seems unlikely that one of these instruments can amount to a 'bill of exchange or other negotiable instrument'.

[24.04] His rights against the goods. The rights of the unpaid seller against the goods are set out in s 39(1) as follows:

> Subject to this and any other Act,[1] notwithstanding that the property in the goods may have passed to the buyer, the unpaid seller of goods, as such, has by implication of law –
>
> (a) A lien on the goods or right to retain them for the price while he is in possession of them;
>
> (b) In the case of the insolvency of the buyer, a right of stopping the goods in transit after he has parted with the possession of them;
>
> (c) A right of resale as limited by this Act.

Thus, the rights of the unpaid seller are as follows:

1   *A right of lien.* At common law, a lien merely conferred a right to retain possession of goods until certain demands were met (see ante, para 1.23). The common law lien of

---

5   Atiyah, *Sale of Goods* (10th edn), pp 450–51; and see generally post, para 29.12.

6   See s 10(1), discussed ante, para 23.20.

7   As to payment or tender of the price, see ante, para 23.14. As to identifying the unpaid balance of the price in an instalment contract, see *Stocznia Gdanska SA v Latvian Shipping Co* (set out post, para 29.15), *per* Lord Goff at 893h–j.

8   Distinguish the situation where the cheque is merely taken by way of collateral security: see Butterworths edn,1989, para 23.14A.

9   As to cheque guarantee cards, see ante, para 2.26.

[24.04]

1   The provisions of the SGA directly relevant are ss 24, 25, 41–48. The most directly relevant other statute is the FA; and see further *Benjamin's Sale of Goods* (5th edn), para 15-039.

the unpaid seller of goods has now been embodied in the SGA (see post, para 24.08), which has been said to replace entirely the common law on the subject.[2] Generally speaking, once the unpaid seller relinquishes possession, his lien is lost (see post, paras 24.13–14); and it will not revive merely because he regains possession.[3] However, an exception to this rule is where the unpaid seller validly stops the goods in transit (see below).

2 *A right of stoppage*. Whilst that lien was lost where the goods passed into the possession of the buyer, the common law recognised an intermediate stage whilst the goods were in transit from seller to buyer. In this situation, the unpaid seller was given a limited right to stop the goods and recover possession from the carrier, whereupon the unpaid seller's lien arose once more.[4] This right of stoppage in transit has now been enacted in the SGA (see post, para 24.17), but is still limited in that it is only available where the buyer is insolvent.[5]

3 *A right of resale*. In some cases, the unpaid seller's rights of lien and stoppage will meet his primary object: they will exert enough pressure to ensure that he is paid the contract price for the goods sold. However, where the buyer is unable or unwilling to pay the price, the exercise of the rights of lien and stoppage is a mere preliminary to resale. The common law granted a limited right of resale to an unpaid seller in possession; and this right is now embodied in the SGA (see post, para 24.07).

It would seem that the exercise of the rights of lien or stoppage by the unpaid seller will not necessarily show an intention on his part to rescind the contract,[6] but it will defeat an action against him by the buyer for wrongful interference with goods.[7] On the other hand, where the unpaid seller wrongfully purports to exercise a lien or to stop the goods, he will be liable in tort, but damages will only be the value of the buyer's actual interest in the goods.[8] The effect of the exercise of the right of resale is considered later (see post, paras 27.08–11).

[24.05] Section 39(1) says that the three rights enumerated (see ante, para 24.04) are to arise 'by implication of law', thereby implying that they may be excluded or varied by the terms of the agreement.[1] Furthermore, care must be taken not to confuse two things: (1) the **powers** of the unpaid seller to pass a good title to a second buyer either by virtue of his property in the goods or one of the exceptions to the *nemo dat* rule (see ante, Chapter 21); and (2) the **rights** of the unpaid seller as against the first buyer, which are listed in s 39. In order to distinguish between the rights and powers of the unpaid seller, it is convenient to set out the four basic permutations of possession and property.

---

2 *Transport and General Credit Corp Ltd v Morgan* [1939] 1 Ch 531, at 546.
3 Even though he does so with the consent of the buyer: see *Pennington v Reliance Motor Works Ltd* [1923] 1 KB 127.
4 *Per* Buller J in *Lickbarrow v Mason* (1793) 6 East 21, at 27n.
5 According to s 61(4) of the SGA (as amended), 'A person is deemed to be insolvent within the meaning of the Act if he has either ceased to pay his debts in the ordinary course of business or he cannot pay his debts as they become due'; and see ante, para 19.21. See further post, para 24.10.
6 See s 48(1): set out post, para 27.09.
7 *Milgate v Kebble* (1841) 3 Man & G 100 (detinue has now been abolished: see ante, para 19.04).
8 *Chinery v Viall* (set out post, para 29.24).
[24.05]
1 See SGA, s 55(1): set out ante, para 18.09.

Case 1. The property has passed to the buyer, who has taken possession of the goods. In this situation, the unpaid seller can have no rights against the goods,[2] nor any power to sell them;[3] and he is reduced to a personal action against the buyer for the price (see post, para 27.16).

Case 2. The property has passed to the buyer, but the seller retains possession. The seller has power to pass title to a bfp under one of the exceptions to the *nemo dat* rule; but whether he has a right, as against the first buyer, to resell is another question.[4]

Case 3. The seller retains the property in the goods, but transfers possession to the buyer. In this case, the seller has the power to pass a good title to a third party by reason of his property in the goods; but it may be a breach of the original contract of sale to do so.

Case 4. The seller retains the property in and possession of the goods. He can, of course, pass a good title to a third party by reason of his property in the goods; and the resale could only be a breach of the first contract where it could be shown that the goods annexed to that contract had been resold (see ante, para 20.05).

This may be set out diagrammatically as follows:

	Seller	Buyer
Case 1		Po + Pr
Case 2	Po	Pr
Case 3	Pr	Po
Case 4	Po + Pr	

[24.06] Lien and stoppage. Strictly speaking, at common law a man could not have a lien over his own goods.[1] It would follow that the first two rights enumerated in s 39(1) are appropriate only to a seller who has retained possession of, but parted with property in, goods. Thus, where the property and possession have passed (*Case 1*), the unpaid seller can have no right of lien or stoppage under s 39(1); and the apparent object of s 39(1) is to confer on a seller who has parted with property but retained possession (*Case 2*) 'not merely the power to deal with the goods, but the right to do so as against the buyer'.[2] However, in the pre-1893 case of *Re Edwards ex p Chalmers*,[3] the Court of Appeal in Chancery held that an unpaid seller who had retained both property and possession (*Case 4*) should not have any less right to retain possession than one who had merely retained possession (*Case 2*). Perhaps the draftsman intended to reflect this in s 39(2), which provides as follows:

---

2   As to the *nemo dat* rule, see ante, para 19.11.
3   SGA, s 24: see ante, para 21.38.
4   As to resale, see post, para 24.07.
[24.06]
1   *Per* Lord Wright in *Nippon Yusen Kaisha v Ramjiban Serowgge* [1938] AC 429, PC, at 444; and Goode (1998) 114 LQR at 180.
2   Atiyah, *Sale of Goods* (10th edn), p 449.
3   (1873) LR 8 Ch App 289.

Where the property in goods has not passed to the buyer, the unpaid seller has, in addition to his other remedies, a right of withholding delivery similar to and co-extensive with his rights of lien and stoppage in transit where the property has passed to the buyer.

The question arises whether s 39(2) has the effect of restricting the unpaid seller who has retained property and possession to what Benjamin terms this 'quasi-lien'.[4] Presumably only applicable to specific or ascertained goods,[5] perhaps the better view is that s 39(2) merely ensures that a seller who has retained the property in the goods (*Cases 3* and *4*) will be no worse off than one who has not done so as regards the rights of lien and stoppage.[6]

[24.07] Resale. The third right enumerated in s 39(1) (set out ante, para 24.04) is a right of resale. Clearly, the unpaid seller has a power of resale where he has retained either or both of possession and property (see post, para 27.11); and the question is whether s 39(1) gives him a right to do so as against the original buyer. The obvious case where s 39(1) confers on the unpaid seller a right of resale is where he has retained possession but parted with the property in the goods (*Case 2*).[1] However, it is sometimes deduced from the existence of s 39(2) that s 39(1) is only applicable where the property has passed; and then inferred from the absence of any mention of a right of resale in s 39(2) (set out ante, para 24.06) that an unpaid seller who has retained both possession and property (*Case 4*) has no right of resale.[2] It would be possible to avoid this undesirable result by denying that the absence of a right of resale from s 39(2) has such a significance; but in *Ward v Bignall* (set out post, para 27.10) the Court of Appeal escaped from the dilemma by another route, deciding that the unpaid seller who retained property and possession had a right of resale under s 39(1).

Does the unpaid seller have any **right** of resale in *Cases 1* and *3*; that is, where possession of the goods has passed to the buyer? Section 39(1)(c) gives a 'right of resale as limited by this Act'; and these limitations are to be found in s 48(3) and (4).[3] In one case, Turner J said that the New Zealand equivalent of s 48 conferred a power only on 'those vendors who have never lost possession',[4] though the wording of s 48 does not appear to support this view. Where both property and possession have passed to the buyer (*Case 1*), clearly the unpaid seller has neither the **power** nor the **right** of resale. However, where the unpaid seller takes the precaution of reserving the property in the goods whilst parting with possession (*Case 3*), it is arguable that he has a statutory **right** of resale under s 39(2); he certainly has the **power** to do so by virtue of his retention of property.[5]

---

4 *Benjamin's Sale of Goods* (5th edn), para 15-029.
5 It has been argued that it is 'inconceivable' that s 39(2) should fetter the seller's discretion to deal with goods not yet earmarked to the contract: Atiyah, *op cit*, note 2, p 450.
6 Perhaps the words 'in addition to his other remedies' in s 39(2) will allow s 61(2) to save any other rights which the seller may have in respect of the goods.

[24.07]

1 Eg, *Gallagher v Shilcock* (set out post, para 27.10).
2 See Atiyah, *Sale of Goods* (10th edn), p 450, where the author suggests that the courts are likely to avoid such an incredible result.
3 Section 48(3) and (4) are discussed post, para 27.08.
4 *Commission Car Sales Ltd v Saul* [1957] NZLR 144, at 146.
5 For reservation of property, see post, para 25.29 *et seq*.

The unpaid seller's lien

Nature of the lien[1]

[24.08] Part delivery. The ordinary rule is that the seller's lien is for the whole of the price; but the question arises as to the effect of a part delivery. Leaving aside the situation where the non-payment manifests an intention to repudiate (see post, para 26.15), the seller's rights may depend on whether there is a single contract or a series of contracts (see ante, para 23.24). Where there is a series of contracts, the unpaid seller's statutory rights against the goods attach to each instalment only in respect of the price attributable to it;[2] but it may be otherwise where there is a single contract. Assuming that part delivery under a single contract does not constitute delivery of the whole,[3] and that the other requirements for the exercise of a lien are satisfied (see post, para 24.10), s 42 provides:[4]

> Where an unpaid seller has made part delivery of the goods, he may exercise his right of lien ... on the remainder, unless such part delivery has been made under such circumstances as to show an agreement to waive the lien.

Suppose there is a single contract for the sale of goods at a price of £100; the contract envisages payment on delivery; but the seller delivers half the goods, valued at £50, before receiving any payment. *Prima facie*, this part delivery indicates a waiver by the seller of his lien.[5] However, there are three possible interpretations of the seller's conduct: (1) the seller has waived his lien for the £100 and converted the transaction into a sale on credit; or (2) the seller has waived his lien over the goods delivered, but still retains a lien for £50 over the goods in his possession; or (3) the seller has waived his lien over the goods delivered, but retains a lien for £100 over the goods in his possession. Where the seller's conduct is not such as to indicate the first interpretation, the common law appears to have assumed that the lien over the remainder of the goods was for the £100, even where the contract was divisible;[6] and this presumed 'indivisibleness of the lien seems to have been recognised by the Act'.[7]

[24.09] Repairer's lien and storage charges. Whilst the SGA twice says that the lien granted thereby is for the price (ss 39(1)(a); 41(1)), it is submitted that this does not prevent the seller from exercising any other particular lien to which he may be entitled at common law.[1] Thus, a seller who agrees to repair goods for his buyer will have a lien in respect of the cost of those repairs:[2] where the sale and repair are two independent

---

[24.08]

1 For liens generally, see post, para 25.02.

2 *Steinberger v Atkinson* (1914) 31 TLR 110. Distinguish an all-monies clause: see ante, para 20.29.

3 As to which, see the cases cited in *Benjamin's Sale of Goods* (5th edn), para 15-041.

4 Cf the right of stoppage in transit, see s 45(7), set out post, para 24.19.

5 See s 43(1)(c), discussed post, para 24.15.

6 *Re Edwards ex p Chalmers* (1873) 8 Ch App 289. For the distinction between divisible and indivisible contracts, see ante, para 23.24.

7 *Benjamin on Sale* (8th edn), p 841. See also *Longbottom v Bass, Walker & Co* [1922] WN 245, CA. *Sed quaere?*

[24.09]

1 The rules of common law are expressly saved insofar as consistent with the SGA by s 62(2).

2 For the repairer's lien, see generally ante, para 1.23. Distinguish a lien from a pledge: see post, para 25.02.

transactions, he will have two separate liens, one for the price and the other for the cost of repairs; but, where there is a contract for the sale of repaired goods, it may be that the cost of repairs is subsumed under his seller's lien. On the other hand, there is no common law lien for storage charges,[3] and the unpaid seller may therefore wish to subsume these under his seller's lien. However, *Somes v British Empire Shipping Co*[4] is sometimes said to rule out indirectly any possibility of including storage charges in the lien,[5] though it does not preclude a claim for damages for such charges.[6] Moreover, storage charges may fall within the seller's lien if bargained for in the price.[7]

Conditions under which the lien is exercisable

[24.10] Section 41(1) provides as follows:

> Subject to the provisions of this Act,[1] the unpaid seller of goods who is in possession of them is entitled to retain possession of them until payment or tender of the price in the following cases, namely –
>
> (a) Where the goods have been sold without any stipulation as to credit.
>
> (b) Where the goods have been sold on credit, but the term of credit has expired.
>
> (c) Where the buyer becomes insolvent.

Not only does the lien granted by the SGA only exist for the price of goods sold (see ante, para 24.09), but s 41(1) insists that three conditions all be fulfilled before it is exercisable:

(1) The person seeking to exercise the lien must be an 'unpaid seller' within the meaning of s 38 (see ante, para 24.03).

(2) The price must be due, or the buyer insolvent. Leaving aside the case where the buyer becomes insolvent (see below), the position where the unpaid seller refuses to deliver the goods would appear to be as follows: in the absence of credit terms, the seller's lien and s 28 will prevent the buyer from having a right to immediate possession sufficient to succeed in an action in conversion against the seller (see ante, para 19.06); but, where the granting of credit terms shows an intention that delivery shall be made before payment (thereby ousting s 28),[2] the buyer may bring such an action.[3] However, even where the seller has agreed to deliver in advance of payment, the

---

3 See *Re Southern Livestock Producers Ltd* [1963] 3 All ER 801 (maintaining pigs).

4 (1860) 8 HL Cas 338, [1843–60] All ER Rep 844 (because he is detaining the goods for his own benefit).

5 See *Benjamin's Sale of Goods* (5th edn), para 15-041; Atiyah, *Sale of Goods* (10th edn), p 454.

6 The seller has an action for damages under s 37: set out ante, para 23.08.

7 *The Winson* [1981] AC 939, HL, *per* Lord Diplock (*obiter*) at 962–63; Benjamin, *op cit*, note 5; Atiyah, *op cit*, note 5.

[24.10]

1 Thus, this lien is subject to the express provisions of the contract (s 55(1): see ante, para 18.09), and the provisions for its termination (ss 43, 47: see post, paras 24.12–16).

2 Section 28 is set out ante, para 23.16. If the granting of credit shows no more than that delivery and payment are to be postponed, but are to remain concurrent terms, the buyer has no right to immediate possession before tendering the price.

3 See *per* Bayley J in *Bloxam v Sanders* (1825) 4 B & C 941, at 948–49.

unpaid seller's lien arises once more when[4] and if the term of credit expires[5] or the buyer becomes insolvent.[6] Insolvency does not necessarily amount of itself to a repudiation of the contract,[7] so that it is still open to the buyer, his representative, or a sub-buyer to tender the price and claim delivery;[8] but the effect of s 41(1)(c) is that the seller cannot, against his will, be reduced to claiming a dividend.[9] Nor can he be forced to supply goods: he is entitled to refuse to supply in the absence of payment at common law;[10] and such an application of ordinary commercial pressure is not an abuse of dominant position contrary to the Treaty of Rome.[11]

(3) The person claiming the lien must be in possession of the goods (see post, para 24.11).

[24.11] Possession. The seller's lien depends on one of the most difficult concepts in English law, namely, 'possession'. Not only does this term have different meanings in different branches of the law,[1] but the extent of the control necessary to exercise an innkeeper's lien differs from that required for a repairer's lien;[2] and neither may be applicable to the unpaid seller.[3] Whilst the SGA nowhere defines possession, that concept is important in three contexts within the Act: (1) the exceptions to the *nemo dat* rule (see Chapter 21, and especially paras 21.28; 21.40); (2) the seller's duty of delivery (see ante, paras 23.05–07); and (3) the unpaid seller's rights of lien (see below) and stoppage (see post, para 24.17). In the present context, difficult problems can arise where actual control and the legal (right to) possession are separated. Leaving aside the situation where actual control is being exercised by a third party,[4] possession may be divided between seller and buyer as follows:

(a) The seller is in actual control as agent for the buyer. Section 41(2) provides:

> The seller may exercise his right of lien notwithstanding that he is in possession of the goods as agent or bailee ... for the buyer.

On the other hand, these facts may be evidence that the seller has waived his lien.[5]

(b) The buyer is in actual control as agent of the seller. Whilst the common law rule may have been that the seller with 'legal possession' retained his lien, the SGA seems to

---

4   Presumably, the seller is liable in conversion for the period before payment fell due. For this action, see generally ante, paras 19.04–06.

5   But does not the granting of credit show an intention to contract out of the statutory lien?

6   And if the buyer is insolvent at the time of contracting? As to when a buyer is insolvent, see s 61(4), set out ante, para 24.04.

7   *Re Edwards ex p Chalmers* (1873) LR 8 Ch App 289.

8   As to repudiation, see generally post, para 26.15; and as to tender of price and delivery, see ante, Chapter 23.

9   As to the claim of the unsecured creditor for a dividend, see ante, para 19.22.

10   *Re Edwards* (above), *per* Mellish LJ at 291.

11   *Leyland Daf Ltd v Automotive Products plc* [1993] BCC 389, CA (Art 82 (ex-86)); and see generally ante, para 2.12.

[24.11]

1   See generally, Crossley Vaines, *Personal Property* (5th edn), Part 2; *Oxford Essays in Jurisprudence*, IV Possession (by Harris); Bell, *Personal Property*, Chapter 3.

2   See Atiyah, *Sale of Goods* (10th edn), p 453.

3   *Per* Lord MacNaghten in *Great Eastern Railway Co v Lord's Trustee* [1909] AC 109, HL, at 115.

4   The Act distinguishes different sorts of third party: (i) 'carrier or other bailee' (see post, para 24.13); (ii) other third party, eg a warehousekeeper (see post, para 24.18).

5   Waiver of lien is considered post, para 24.15.

suggest that, at least where actual control passes to the buyer, the lien is lost.[6] In other words, more regard may now be paid to actual control that to the legal right to control.[7]

Termination of the lien

[24.12] The seller may lose his right to exercise a lien for the price in any of the ways set out below:

1 *Where he ceases to be an 'unpaid seller'*. According to s 41(1), the seller's lien only lasts 'until payment or tender of the price';[1] but s 43(2) provides that the unpaid seller:

> ... does not lose his lien ... by reason only that he has obtained judgment ... for the price of the goods.[2]

One difficulty here is that s 41(1) appears to suggest that the seller's lien, and hence his right to retain possession, does not cease until the buyer at very least tenders the price, whereas s 28 expressly says that payment and delivery are concurrent conditions (see ante, para 23.16). Whilst the two provisions are usually reconciled by inferring that actual tender of the price is not necessary provided the buyer is ready and willing to pay the price,[3] it has been argued that it is difficult to avoid giving effect to the literal words of s 41(1).[4] It is submitted that a solution may be found as follows: that the buyer's duty to tender the price is similar to the seller's duty to tender delivery (as to which, see ante, paras 23.05–07); and that actual tender is not usually required because it is presumed that the buyer will perform his contract.[5]

2 *Delivery to a carrier* (see post, para 24.13).

3 *The buyer obtains possession* (see post, para 24.14).

4 *Waiver* (see post, para 24.15).

5 *Dispositions by the buyer* (see post, para 24.16).

[24.13] Delivery to a carrier. Section 43(1)(a) provides that the seller will lose his lien:

> When he delivers the goods to a carrier or other bailee ... for the purpose of transmission to the buyer without reserving the right of disposal of the goods.

The scheme of the Act is that the unpaid seller will have a right of lien whilst he retains possession of the goods, and a right of stoppage whilst they are in transit to the buyer.[1] Not surprisingly, the Act uses the same test both for the termination of the lien and the

---

6   See s 43(1)(b), considered post, para 24.14.

7   Schmitthoff, *Sale of Goods* (2nd edn), p 156. But see *Benjamin's Sale of Goods* (5th edn), para 15-038.

[24.12]

1   And see s 38(1)(a), considered ante, para 24.03.

2   *Quaere* whether in these circumstances the lien extends only to the price, or also to the costs on the judgment?

3   See Chalmers, *Sale of Goods* (18th edn), p 176; Schmitthoff, *Sale of Goods* (2nd edn), pp 121–22.

4   Atiyah, *Sale of Goods* (7th edn), p 344. But see note 5, below.

5   See also Atiyah, *Sale of Goods* (10th edn), 455, relying on Australian authority.

[24.13]

1   For the effect of successfully exercising a right of stoppage, see post, para 24.16.

commencement of the transit, namely, 'delivery to a carrier or other bailee for the purposes of transmission to the buyer'; and this expression will be examined in the latter context (see post, para 24.18). However, s 43(1)(a) allows one exception to the rule which it lays down: where the seller reserves 'a right of disposal'. In the context of sections dealing with the passing of property, this expression clearly denotes a reservation of property (see ante, para 20.28); but it has been argued that, to avoid any inconsistency with s 39(2), it must in s 43(1)(a) refer only to a reservation of possession.[2] Perhaps the better view is that in s 43 the phrase denotes a reservation of property and possession;[3] and that in s 43(1)(a) it is referring to the 'quasi-lien' under s 39(2) (see ante, paras 24.05–06).

[24.14] The buyer obtains possession. Section 43(1)(b) lays down that the lien is lost:

> When the buyer or his agent lawfully obtains possession of the goods.

The first issue here concerns the meaning of 'possession': there has already been explored the situation where 'legal possession' and control are divided between seller and buyer (see ante, para 24.11); but in other cases it probably extends to legal possession,[1] except where the goods are in the hands of an independent carrier.[2] The other problem in this subsection concerns the meaning of the word 'lawfully', as to which there are several theories. First, it may refer to the absence of criminal conduct on the part of the buyer.[3] However, there has been some reluctance to import the law of theft into this branch of the civil law. Second, Atiyah has suggested another possible meaning; namely, that 'lawfully' in this context means 'with the consent of the seller', so as to bring it into line with the provisions in respect of dispositions by buyers in possession found in s 25(1) and 9 of the SGA and FA respectively.[4] Perhaps the strongest argument in favour of this view is that the term 'lawfully' is used in ss 47 and 10 of the respective Acts. However, it has been pointed out that (1) this view rather strains the language of s 43(1)(b), and (2) there is no reason why s 43(1)(b) needs to be brought into line with this exception to the *nemo dat* rule.[5] Furthermore, it is quite conceivable that 'lawfully' has a different meaning in ss 47 and 10 from that which it bears in s 43(1)(b) (see ante, para 21.49); and it is submitted that it is logically possible that the seller's lien binds all except a bf transferee under one of the exceptions to the *nemo dat* rule. Third, Benjamin has suggested that 'lawfully' in s 43(1)(b) means that 'the possession must not be obtained tortiously as against the seller'.[6] Whilst this test may be circular if one thinks in terms of the tort of conversion, it does seem satisfactory in relation to the tort of trespass.[7] In the last analysis, then, it may be that

---

2   Schmitthoff, *Sale of Goods* (2nd edn), p 157.

3   See *Benjamin's Sale of Goods* (5th edn), para 15-046, citing *Saunders v Maclean* (1883) 11 QBD 327, CA at 341.

[24.14]

1   As where the goods are in the physical control of a third party, eg warehouseman, on behalf of the buyer or his agent.

2   In which case, the right of stoppage may arise: see post, para 24.18.

3   Eg, *Wallace v Woodgate* (1824) 1 C & P 575.

4   *Sale of Goods* (10th edn), p 456.

5   Smith (1963) JSPTL 225, at 226.

6   *Benjamin's Sale of Goods* (5th edn), para 55-055.

7   Is the point academic since both torts are now subsumed under the heading of wrongful interference with goods (see ante, para 19.04)?

'lawfully' in s 43(1)(b) denotes the absence of a trespassory taking by the buyer, irrespective of whether that taking amounts to theft.

[24.15] Waiver. Section 39(1) gives the unpaid seller a lien by implication of law (see ante, para 24.04); s 55(1) allows such rights to be waived expressly or by implication (see ante, para 18.09); and s 43(1)(c) expressly states that the lien may be lost by waiver. Thus, the unpaid seller may expressly waive his statutory lien, eg, a sale on credit; or waiver of it may be inferred. Examples of implied waiver are where the contract includes the reservation of an express lien;[1] or where the seller takes a cheque for the price (see ante, para 23.14); or where the seller wrongfully deals with the goods in a manner inconsistent with the rights of the buyer, eg, by consuming or reselling them;[2] or where the seller agrees to retain possession as agent of the buyer.[3] Can the unpaid seller who is still in possession go back on any waiver of his statutory lien? The Act envisages that, notwithstanding that the seller accepts payment by bill of exchange or sells on credit, he may exercise his lien where the bill is not met,[4] or the term of credit expired;[5] and it is possible to see these two instances in terms of an initial waiver and subsequent exercise of the unpaid seller's lien.[6]

Moreover, the common law will normally allow a party to go back upon a waiver of his rights if he gives adequate notice;[7] and it was decided before the 1893 Act that the unpaid seller might revive his waived lien where he was still in possession.[8] The better view would therefore appear to be that the statutory lien may be revived after waiver by giving adequate notice.[9]

[24.16] Dispositions by the buyer. Under the *nemo dat* principle (see ante, para 19.11), a sub-buyer will *prima facie* acquire title subject to the lien of the original unpaid seller.[1] However, the sub-buyer may claim title under one of the exceptions to the *nemo dat* rule (see ante, para 21.03); and sometimes the facts which bring a case within an exception may also operate to terminate the unpaid seller's lien under one of the rules discussed above. However, two such exceptions to the *nemo dat* rule which are especially likely to defeat both the unpaid seller's lien and his right of stoppage in transit (see post, paras 24.17–20) receive express treatment in s 47:

[24.15]

1   See Chalmers, *Sale of Goods* (18th edn), p 207.

2   Chalmers, *ibid*, p 208; Atiyah, *Sale of Goods* (10th edn), p 457.

3   See Atiyah, *ibid*; and ante, para 24.11.

4   Section 38(1)(b): set out ante, para 24.03.

5   Section 41(1)(b) and (c): set out ante, para 24.10. It seems to be sensible to read s 43(1)(c) subject to s 41(b) and (c): see Atiyah, *op cit*, note 2. But compare *Benjamin on Sale* (8th edn), p 853 and *Benjamin's Sale of Goods* (5th edn), para 15-056.

6   Alternatively, it may be agreed that the lien arises *de novo* upon the happening of these two events.

7   *Charles Rickards Ltd v Oppenheim* (set out post, para 26.25).

8   See *Townley v Crump* (1835) 4 Ed & El 58.

9   See Atiyah, *op cit*, note 2. For waiver generally, see post, para 26.23.

[24.16]

1   Section 47(1): see *Laurie and Morewood v Dudin* [1926] 1 KB 223, CA. Section 47(1) is expressed to give way to a contrary intent: s 55(1) – see ante, para 18.09.

(1) the original seller's rights are completely lost where he assents to the subsale;[2] and

(2) his rights are overridden *pro tanto* where he parts with a document of title relating to the goods.[3]

Such rules cause no difficulty where a document of title is transferred in respect of specific or ascertained goods. However, it has been pointed out[4] that in the case of a sale of a larger bulk where the goods remain unascertained at the time the document is transferred,[5] the rule here considered appears to conflict with s 16, which prohibits the passing of property until the goods are ascertained (see ante, para 20.05). Moreover, even assuming that the unpaid seller's rights against the goods are overridden by the bf transferee, does the unpaid seller have any right to the proceeds of the disposition?[6] At common law, the better opinion would appear to be that *prima facie* he did not;[7] and such a view would appear to be consistent with the terminology of the SGA,[8] so probably the position has not changed,[9] except with regard to co-owners (see ante, para 20.20A).

The unpaid seller's right of stoppage in transit

[24.17] In the 18th and 19th centuries, the right of stoppage in transit was an extremely valuable weapon in the armoury of the unpaid seller in both domestic and international sales; but in the 20th century the importance of this right declined.[1] In the field of international sales, the development of the system of payment by bankers' confirmed credits (see ante, para 23.14) and government export guarantees[2] may have rendered the doctrine more or less obsolete; and in domestic sales, the right of stoppage never applied to one of the largest carriers, the Post Office,[3] which developed its own alternative – the 'cash on delivery' service.[4] Modern treatment of the right of stoppage is in domestic sales restricted to private carriers, and may therefore be reduced to a minimum.

The basic principle is set out in s 44 of the SGA, which provides that:

---

2   Section 47(1): see ante, para 21.04.

3   Section 47(2). See also s 10 of the FA 1889: the effect of both provisions is examined in para 21.50.

4   Nicol (1979) 42 MLR 129. *Quaere*: whether this is simply an illustration of the fact that in case of conflict the rules as to transfer of title *pro tanto* override those as to the passing of property (see ante, para 19.09)?

5   See eg *Mount Ltd v Jay Ltd* (set out ante, para 21.04).

6   The specially created right to trace is considered post, paras 27.13–14.

7   *Per* Lord Selbourne in *Kemp v Falk* (1882) 7 App Cas 573, HL at 577.

8   See *Benjamin's Sale of Goods* (5th edn), para 15-100.

9   Benjamin, *ibid*; Atiyah, *Sale of Goods* (10th edn), p 463.

[24.17]

1   Perhaps partly because of better communications, speedier carriage, better credit control and a higher volume of trade compensating for occasional bad debts.

2   See *Benjamin's Sale of Goods* (5th edn), Chapter 24.

3   And now Parcelforce. The PO does not enter into any contract of carriage (*Whitfield v Le Despenser* (1778) 2 Comp 754); it is not generally liable for torts connected with the postal services (see now s 90 of the Postal Services Act 2000 and ante, para 3.07) and would not act on an order to stop (s 83 of the 2000 Act).

4   Post Office Inland Post Scheme 1989 (as amended), made under s 89 of the 2000 Act.

Subject to the provisions of this Act,[5] when the buyer of goods becomes insolvent,[6] the unpaid seller[7] who has parted with possession of the goods has the right of stopping them in transit, that is to say, he may resume possession of the goods as long as they are in course of transit, and may retain them until payment or tender of the price.[8]

The most difficult questions involved here are probably the meaning of 'possession' and the duration of the transit, matters upon which s 45 lays down a series of rules (see post, paras 24.18–19). The difficulty may be illustrated by the following facts: suppose the seller owns goods then in independent warehouse A; he agrees to sell them to the buyer, with delivery to independent warehouse C; and the transfer of the goods is to be undertaken by an independent carrier, during the course of which the goods will be temporarily lodged in independent warehouse B. The unpaid seller's real rights whilst the goods are being transferred depends on who has physical possession of them and may be illustrated diagrammatically as follows:

Right of lien	Right of stoppage	No real rights
Seller	Carrier	Buyer
Warehouse A	Warehouse B	Warehouse C

[24.18/19] Course of transit. According to s 45(1):

> Goods are deemed to be in course of transit from the time when they are delivered to a carrier by land or water, or other bailee ... for the purpose of transmission.

It is quite clear that, where goods are in the legal possession and actual control of the seller, he has the more efficacious right of lien (see ante, para 24.11); and that, where the legal possession and actual control of the goods have passed to the buyer, the seller has lost his rights of lien (see ante, para 24.14) and stoppage.[1] Thus, the right of stoppage can only exist in the intermediate situation, where the goods are in the hands of a third party, whom s 45 calls 'a carrier[2] or other bailee',[3] as agent for either seller or buyer. Difficulties immediately arise, however, if it is admitted that either the seller or the buyer may be in legal possession of goods under the actual control of an agent (see ante, para 23.03). Leaving aside the situation where either seller or buyer is in actual control as agent of the other (see ante, para 24.11), the ordinary rule is that the possession of the agent is regarded as being the possession of his principal in this context as elsewhere (see ante, para 24.14): where the seller's agent has actual control, the seller has the more efficacious right of lien; but, where the buyer's agent obtains control, the seller loses his real rights

---

5 This refers principally to ss 39, 45, 46, 55(1).

6 Notice the rather wider grounds which s 39(1) allows for the exercise of the unpaid seller's lien: see ante, paras 24.10–11. As to insolvency, see ante, para 24.04.

7 See ante, para 24.03.

8 See ante, para 24.12.

[24.18/19]

1 Section 45(3): set out post, para 24.19.

2 Presumably, the word 'carrier', is wide enough to cover a common carrier. What about an air freighter?

3 He has been variously described as a 'middleman' (*Schotsmans v Lancs & Yorks Ry Co* (1867) 2 Ch App 332 at 338) or an 'independent contractor': (Atiyah, *Sale of Goods* (10th edn), p 459).

entirely. However, if this rule were applied indiscriminately, there would be no room for a right of stoppage at all; and the law is therefore committed to distinguishing between the constructive possession of (1) 'a carrier or other bailee', and (2) any other agent in actual control of the goods, eg, a warehousekeeper. Even more difficult, it must distinguish between two different types of constructive possession of 'a carrier or other bailee'. For instance, the delivery by the seller of the goods to a carrier for transmission to the buyer operates under s 32(1) as a constructive transfer of possession to the buyer so as to discharge the seller's duty to deliver (see ante, paras 23.05–07); but that does not necessarily end the transit.[4] Support for this approach may be gained from s 45(5), which deals with one particular instance as follows:

> When the goods are delivered to a ship chartered by the buyer it is a question depending on the circumstances of the particular case, whether they are in the possession of the master as a carrier, or as agent to the buyer.

As might be expected, the matter which appears to have caused particular difficulty at common law was not so much when the transit commenced as when it ceased;[5] and s 45 concentrates on this latter point, dealing explicitly with a number of difficult cases.[6] Clearly, the transit can at most only last until the goods reach the place at which the contract contemplates that the transit will end;[7] and it will in any case be brought to an end where the 'carrier or other bailee' hands the goods to the buyer or his agent (s 45(1)).

[24.20] Exercise of right of stoppage. According to s 46(1):

> The unpaid seller may exercise his right of stoppage in transit either by taking actual possession of the goods or by giving notice[1] of his claim to the carrier or other bailee ... in whose possession the goods are.

In the latter event, s 46(4) provides as follows:

> When notice of stoppage in transit is given by the seller to the carrier or other bailee ... in possession of the goods, he must redeliver the goods to, or according to the directions of, the seller; and the expenses of the redelivery must be borne by the seller.

If the seller has no right of stoppage, the seller issuing the order and the 'carrier or other bailee' who complies are both liable to the buyer in conversion;[2] but, if the seller has the right to stop, but the 'carrier or other bailee' refuses to comply with such an order, he is liable to the seller in conversion, or possibly for breach of statutory duty:[3] if in doubt, the

---

4   This seems consistent with the views of Brett LJ in *Re Cock ex p Rosevear China Clay Co* (1879) 11 Ch D 560, CA, at 569. For another explanation, see Todd [1978] JBL at 40.

5   The moment of commencement of the transit would only be material where the buyer was not insolvent, in which case the unpaid seller would look to his ordinary remedies: see post, Chapter 27.

6   Section 45(2)–(7). See further my Butterworths edn, para 24.20.

7   *Jobson v Eppenheim* (1905) 21 TLR 468.

[24.20]

1   'The notice may be given either to the person in actual possession of the goods or his principal' (s 46(2)). In the latter event, see s 46(3) as to the time when the notice is effective.

2   Eg, *Taylor v Great Eastern Ry Co* (1901), as reported in 17 TLR 394. For conversion, see generally ante, para 19.04.

3   See SGA, s 60. As to the possible purpose of this section, see Chalmers, *Sale of Goods* (18th edn), p 261; and as to actions for breach of statutory duty, see generally ante, para 3.21.

safest course for the 'carrier or other bailee' is to interplead, or to make delivery dependent on an indemnity. Finally, whilst the Act does not define the relationship between the 'carrier or other bailee' and the seller, it has been decided that the stoppage of goods by the seller gives the 'carrier or other bailee' a prior lien over the goods for his charges;[4] and that, after stopping the goods, the seller is under a duty to give orders for their disposal.[5]

SECURITY WITHOUT POSSESSION

Agreements outside the CCA

[24.21] Title and repossession as security. The previous section considered the advantage in terms of security which may accrue to an unpaid supplier who retains possession, delivering the goods only on payment.[1] The present section seeks to contrast that with the position of a supplier who delivers goods without payment of the price. If he delivers under a credit sale, he will be an unsecured creditor[2] for the price.[3] However, there are a number of ways in which the unpaid supplier may seek to elevate himself to a status equal to a secured creditor: he may enter into a conditional sale,[4] a hp or a simple hiring agreement.[5] Under all three forms of contract, he will make early delivery of the goods, but reserve the property in them, which may give him priority in respect of his interest (see post, para 24.22) as against his transferee's insolvency,[6] or sub-transferee under the *nemo dat* rule (see ante, para 19.11). However, as bailee in possession, the transferee may be able to override the unpaid supplier's interest in favour of some creditors[7] or a bfp.[8] The best way for the unpaid supplier to avoid such overriding interests is to terminate the bailment (see post, para 26.08) and resume possession of the goods.[9] This he may seek to achieve by either (1) recaption (see post, para 24.23), possibly followed by court action for breach of contract (see post, para 27.33 *et seq*), or (2) action in tort.[10] Such actions will usually be in the defendant's county court (see ante, para 3.22).

---

4   See *United States Steel Products Co v Great Western Ry Co* [1916] 1 AC 189, HL.
5   *Booth Steamship Co Ltd v Cargo Fleetiron Co Ltd* [1916] 2 KB 570, CA. But see the comment by Atiyah, *Sale of Goods* (10th edn), p 464.

[24.21]
1   For cash and credit sales, see generally ante, paras 1.07–13.
2   For unsecured and secured creditors, see generally ante, para 19.22.
3   For actions for the price, see post, para 27.15A *et seq*. Additionally, the unpaid supplier may have taken out some bad debt insurance, though in domestic supplies this tends to be unusual. Distinguish insurance taken out by or on behalf of the debtor or hirer (see post, para 24.30).
4   See generally ante, para 1.14. Such a conditional sale may contain a *Romalpa* clause (see post, para 25.30).
5   As to simple hiring agreements, see ante, paras 1.17–19; and as to hp agreements, see ante, paras 1.20–25.
6   Generally, the trustee or liquidator takes only property owned by the insolvent: see ante, para 19.23.
7   See the special rules for distress (ante, para 19.18) and execution (ante, paras 19.19–20).
8   Amongst the exceptions to the *nemo dat* rule (see generally Chapter 21) especially relevant here are the power of a conditional buyer to pass title as one who has agreed to buy (see ante, para 21.43) or of a conditional buyer or hirer on hp to confer a Part III title (see ante, para 21.55).
9   As to when the right of repossession would arise at common law by reason of arrears of rent, see post, para 27.38.
10 See post, para 24.25. As to the assessment of the value of the goods in a tort action, see post, para 27.30.

[24.22] The supplier's common law interest in the goods. In the case of a cash or credit sale (see ante, paras 1.03–07), the supplier's entire proprietary interest in the goods passes to the buyer at latest on delivery (see Chapter 20); but, at the other end of the scale, where goods are supplied under a simple hiring agreement, the supplier retains the entire proprietary interest.[1] In between these two extremes lie conditional sales and hp, where it has already been pointed out that the value of the supplier's interest diminishes *pro tanto* with every payment made (see ante, para 1.14), though neither form of contract creates a mortgage.[2]

1 *Conditional sales*.[3] If the buyer defaults, the unpaid seller can repossess the goods,[4] exercise his real remedy of resale (see ante, para 24.04), so rescinding the contract,[5] and sue the defaulting buyer for damages to recover any loss (see post, para 27.34). In this case, the common law will not allow the seller also to sue for unpaid instalments due; but in respect of instalments already paid draws a distinction between a deposit, which is irrecoverable and a part payment which may, subject to the terms of the agreement, be recoverable (see post, para 27.19). However, conditional sale agreements almost always provide for the forfeiture of instalments already paid and it seems that equity offers little relief to the defaulting buyer (see post, para 27.20). Further, it follows from the fact that a conditional buyer has no equity of redemption (see *McEntire v Crossley Bros*: set out ante, para 1.14A) that, unless also suing for damages,[6] the conditional seller is under no duty of care to get the best price obtainable.[7]

2 *Hire purchase*.[8] If the hirer defaults, the unpaid supplier is entitled to repossess the goods, rescind the contract, sell at his own price and sue the defaulting hirer for damages to recoup any loss.[9] However, the position of the defaulting hirer is worse than that of the conditional buyer: as a matter of principle, whereas the **seller** is *prima facie* entitled to recover the goods or price (see above), the supplier of goods on hp is as **bailor** entitled to both goods and rent. Unfortunately, it seems an *a fortiori* case that the defaulting hirer has no equity of redemption[10] though equity may sometimes give relief against forfeiture (see post, para 27.22). It is this which provides the element of

---

[24.22]

1   Thus, the owner entitled to immediate possession may sue in conversion for the full value of the goods: *Manders v Williams* (1848) 4 Exch 338; and see further ante, para 19.06. As to simple hiring agreements, see generally ante, paras 1.17–19.

2   Compare the position of a mortgagee exercising a power of sale: see post, para 25.20. It is for consideration whether it would not be better if conditional sale and hp (and finance leases?) were turned into forms of chattel mortgage: see post, para 27.29.

3   As to conditional sales, see generally ante, paras 1.14–16; and as to hp, see generally ante, para 1.20. As to remedies of the supplier, see post, para 28.12 *et seq*.

4   As to reservation of a right of disposal, see ante, para 20.28. As to recaption, see post, para 24.23; and as to unlawful harassment, see post, para 24.24.

5   As to 'resale' amounting to a rescission of the first contract, see post, para 27.12.

6   In suing for damages, he is under a duty to mitigate by seeking the best price obtainable: see post, para 27.44.

7   *Contra Forward Trust Ltd v Best* (1983) unreported, discussed in 38 CC 3/26.

8   *Lombard North Central plc v Butterworth* (set out post, para 27.26).

9   *Alf Vaughan & Co Ltd v Royscot Trust plc* (set out post, para 27.22).

10   *Cramer v Giles* (1883) Cab & El 151, affd (1884) *The Times*, 9 May; but see Oditah (1992) 108 LQR 459 at 487, esp note 159. Nor has the court any discretion where the creditor seeks a writ of execution: *TC Trustees Ltd v JS Darwen Ltd* [1969] 2 QB 295, CA.

'double recovery' that helps to give rise to the snatchback (see post, para 26.08): the hirer is prevented by the legal fiction of hp (see ante, para 1.20) from pleading either that the owner/supplier has made a double recovery in the legal sense,[11] or that instalments paid are a part payment of the price.[12]

Repossession through self-help

[24.23] Recaption. A rightful recaption (repossession) of goods by the owner[1] will not deprive him of his other remedies under the agreement,[2] but a wrongful recaption will constitute both a tort and a repudiation of the agreement.[3] Leaving aside special statutory restrictions,[4] a recaption gives rise to the following legal problems. First, is the owner entitled to use force to repossess the goods? The position would appear to be that, on failure by the hirer to return the goods after a request, the owner may use reasonable force to recapt them,[5] but that unreasonable force may amount to an assault.[6] To avoid the uncertainty of what is reasonable force in a confrontation with a hirer, a recaption is sometimes achieved in the early hours. Second, is the owner entitled to enter the hirer's premises to recapt the goods? Because the common law is uncertain, the agreement will usually confer on the owner a licence to enter the hirer's land and seize the goods. Such a contractual licence is probably irrevocable:[7] unless unfair,[8] it will give the owner immunity from an action in trespass where only reasonable force is used,[9] though entry to recapt may amount to a criminal offence.[10] Third, recaption might amount to an offence under the Administration of Justice Act 1970 (see post, para 24.24). Fourth, effective recaption is, of course, part of the technique of the 'snatchback' (see post, para 26.08); but it cannot be used in respect of chattels after-acquired by a non-corporate hirer.[11] Fifth, even peaceable re-entry may infringe human rights (see ante, para 3.09). It is largely by reason of the foregoing legal difficulties that separate firms of repossession agents have flourished,[12] though their use might give rise to vicarious criminal liability (see post, para 28.09).

---

11 For double recovery, see post, para 27.39. *Contra* if the supplier sues in conversion: see post, para 27.31. For the uncertain value of the hirer's interest, see ante, para 1.25.

12 *Ellis v Rowbotham* [1900] 1 QB 740, CA; *Kelly v Lombard Banking Ltd* [1958] 3 All ER 713, CA.

[24.23]

1 The owner may have supplied the goods under a conditional sale, hp or simple hiring agreement, in each of which cases there will be a form of bailment so that the transferee may properly be described as hirer: see ante, para 24.21.

2 *Overstone Ltd v Shipway* [1962] 1 All ER 52, CA: see post, para 27.21.

3 *Abingdon Finance Ltd v Champion* [1961] CLY 3931. See generally ante, para 19.05 and post, para 26.15.

4 See Guest, *Law of HP*, p 531; and Goode, *HP Law and Practice* (2nd edn), pp 19–20.

5 *Blades v Higgs* (1861) 10 CBNS 713, *obiter* at 720.

6 *Dyer v Munday* [1895] 1 QB 742, CA.

7 *Hurst v Picture Theatres Ltd* [1915] 1 KB 1, CA; cf *Wood v Leadbitter* (1835) 13 M & W 838.

8 See OFT, *Bulletin No 15*, case 4; and ante, para 11.12 *et seq*.

9 *Hemmings v Stoke Poges Golf Club* [1920] 1 KB 720, CA.

10 Violent entry without consent or a court order may be an offence under s 6 of the Criminal Law Act 1977.

11 Because it would contravene the Bills of Sale Acts (see ante, para 9.05). *Contra*, where there is a corporate hirer: see post, para 25.28A. It follows that the ordinary consumer running-account credit gives no right of recaption: see ante, para 7.08.

12 It will be a matter of commercial judgment as to whether the financier will seek repossession (either on his own account or via a repossession agent), or whether repossession is left to the goods-supplier.

[24.24] Unlawful harassment of debtors. The Report of the Payne Committee recommended that the unlawful harassment of debtors be made a criminal offence;[1] and Parliament sought to give effect to this suggestion by the Administration of Justice Act 1970. Section 40(1) provides that:

A person commits an offence if, with the object of coercing another person to pay money claimed from the other as a debt due under a contract he:[2]

(a) harasses the other with demands for payment which, in respect of their frequency or the manner or occasion of making any such demand, or of any threat or publicity by which any demand is accompanied, are calculated to subject him or members of his family or household to alarm, distress or humiliation;

(b) falsely represents, in relation to the money claimed, that criminal proceedings lie for failure to pay it;

(c) falsely represents himself to be authorised in some official capacity to claim or enforce payment; or

(d) utters a document falsely represented by him to have some official character or purporting to have some official character which he knows it has not.[3]

The offence created by s 40[4] is intended to protect two classes of victims: (1) those who do not owe any money under a contract, either because they were never so indebted, or have repaid it, and (2) those who are so indebted.[5] On the other hand, the scope of the offence is limited by s 40(3), which excludes –

... anything done by a person which is reasonable (and otherwise permissible in law) for the purpose –

(a) of securing the discharge of an obligation due,[5a] or believed by him to be due to himself or to persons for whom he acts, or protecting himself or them from future loss; or

(b) of the enforcement of any liability by legal process.

Unlawful harassment. Section 40(1)(a) makes it an offence if –

(i) with the **object** of coercing payment,

(ii) a person **harasses** another with demands for payment (see below),

(iii) which are **calculated** to subject him or his family on household to alarm, distress or humiliation.[6]

[24.24]

1 The *Report of the Committee on the Enforcement of Judgment Debts* (1969), Cmnd 3909, para 1238 (see further post, para 27.01).

2 Section 40(2) extends the offence to any person who 'concerts with others in taking such action ... notwithstanding that his own course of conduct does not by itself amount to harassment'.

3 Eg, The OFT has revoked a CCA licence for regularly issuing statutory demands (see ante, para 19.21) without taking bankruptcy proceedings: 50 CC1/37.

4 For penalties, see s 40(4) (as amended)

5 Section 40 probably does not extend to suppliers of gas, water and electricity due under statute rather than contract: *Norweb plc v Dixon* [1995] 3 All ER 952, DC; and see generally ante, para 3.07.

5a This should not apply to statute-based debts (see post, para 26.17).

6 'Are calculated to' means 'likely to' not 'intended to': the *Norweb* case (above): see *per* Dyson J at 960–62.

Some idea of the type of conduct s 40(1)(a) was intended to prohibit may be gathered from the Report of the Payne Committee[7] which originated the idea; but it is to be regretted that the section is 'sadly lacking in precision'.[8] For instance, the Payne Report intended that the provision should cover 'visiting the home of the debtor ... under the guise of collecting chattels let under an hp agreement (para 1233(i)), though s 40 gives rise to several problems in this context. First, is the act of recaption done 'with the object of coercing another person to pay money claimed' contrary to s 40(1);[9] and is it a 'demand for payment' within s 40(1)(a)? Or is it only the threat[10] of recaption which is prohibited? The latter interpretation would produce the undesirable result of encouraging recaption without warning – because it would be safer to actually recapt than to threaten. Second, as s 40 is only expressed to be applicable where money is claimed 'as a debt due under a contract', can s 40 be avoided entirely by the expedient of obtaining a judgment for debt prior to recaption? Third, what is the criterion for the establishment by the recaptor of the defence that his action was 'reasonable' within the meaning of s 40(3)?[11]

Breach of s 40 by a person licensed under the CCA could jeopardise his CCA licence.[12]

Repossession through court action

[24.25] **Adverse possession**. As an alternative to recaption (see ante, para 24.23), the owner (see ante, para 24.23, note 1) might seek to obtain judgment for the return of the goods and have that judgment executed by court officers.[1] Leaving aside the summary process of replevin,[2] and a claim for restitution in criminal proceedings (see ante, para 3.20) or quasi-contract (see post, para 29.12), the only such cause of action which will normally be available to the owner is the statutory tort of wrongful interference with goods (see ante, para 19.04). To succeed in such an action, it is not sufficient for the owner to plead that another, eg, the hirer or buyer, has continued in possession of goods:[3] there must be shown a neglect or refusal to return the goods which is adverse to the owner's right to immediate possession. Normally, adverse possession is proved by showing that the owner demanded redelivery, but that the hirer or buyer unreasonably refused to

---

7   See generally paras 1230–44. For inertia selling, see ante, para 8.18. For 'look-alikes', see offences under the County Courts Act: ante, para 5.42.

8   Borrie and Pyke (1970), 114 NLJ 588, at 589. Eg, at what times of day or night may such demands be made? Can a trader publish a 'debtor's list' on his premises? In seeking an absconded debtor, can a creditor tell third parties why he wishes to find the debtor?

9   Presumably, it is an offence to imply falsely that there is a legal right of recaption, eg, where goods are protected (see post, para 24.34)?

10   See also Malicious Communications Act 1988.

11   See Borrie and Pyke (1970) 114 NLJ 588. For enquiries as to previous occupants, see (1992) 47 CC 3/12.

12   Eg, the *Allied Collection Agencies Affair*: see (1989) 44 CC 2/24.

[24.25]

1   For the commonly available forms of execution, see post, para 27.04.

2   See Guest, *Law of HP*, p 847; Winfield and Jolowicz, *Tort* (15th edn), p 616. Replevin is now a form of interlocutory relief as to which, see post para 24.26, note 1.

3   Though such continued possession may amount to a breach of the supply contract: *Heskell v Continental Express Ltd* [1950] 1 All ER 1033. Where non-return is due to destruction of the goods without fault on the part of the hirer or buyer, the supply contract will usually make him strictly liable, and the goods will probably be insured as well (see ante, para 11.09).

comply.[4] However, the battle of wits to which this may give rise is well illustrated by *Capital Finance Ltd v Bray*:[5]

> The owners of a car let on hp seized it. Because it was protected goods (see post, para 24.35) this was in contravention of the HPA. Within a few hours, the owners realised their mistake, took the car back, and left it outside the hirer's house. As the hirer failed to make any repayments, the owners some five months later sued to recover the car.

Despite evidence that the hirer had continued to use the car in the intervening five months, the Court of Appeal refused to imply that the agreement had been revived,[6] and held:

(a) the hirer was not liable in tort as there was no adverse possession, on the grounds that the hirer was under no legal obligation to return the car, as distinct from allowing them to collect it;[7] and

(b) the hirer was entitled under the HPA to recover all sums that he had paid under the agreement (for the CCA equivalent provision, see s 91: post, para 24.38).

[24.26] The forms of judgment. At common law, even a defendant to the now abolished action in detinue might have the option whether to return the goods or pay their value.[1] Statute has now vested this power in the court, once it has assessed the value of the litigated goods (see post, paras 27.30–32). Besides the power to order up delivery of any goods by way of interim relief,[2] s 3 of the Torts (Interference with Goods) Act 1977 provides for final judgment where goods are wrongfully detained in any one of the following alternative (s 3(3)(a)) forms:[3]

1 *For specific delivery of the goods and damages for any consequential loss* (s 3(2)(a)). This form gives the defendant no option to pay their value; and the plaintiff is allowed to recover the goods by execution.[4] This form of judgment is wholly discretionary (s 3(3)(b)), likely only to be granted where the goods are unique,[5] and even then the order may be conditional (s 3(6)).

2 *For goods or value.* This form of judgment orders, perhaps conditionally, delivery of the goods to the plaintiff **unless** there is payment of their value[6] made within a specified

---

4   The forms of judgment then available to an owner are considered post, para 24.26.
5   [1964] 1 All ER 603; [1964] 1 WLR 323, CA.
6   It would appear that a court would require cogent evidence before so concluding. Cf regulated agreements: see post, para 24.38.
7   Compare the position for regulated agreements: see post, para 24.42.
[24.26]
1   *Crossfield v Such* (1852) 8 Exch 159. For the abolition of detinue see ante, para 19.04.
2   Torts Act 1977, s 4. See *Howard E Perry & Co Ltd v BRB* [1980] 2 All ER 579.
3   Section 3(2). These forms appear to be modelled on the common law remedies for detinue: as to which, see *General and Finance Facilities Ltd v Cook Cars (Romford) Ltd* [1963] 2 All ER 214. According to s 3(8), these forms of judgment are without prejudice to the remedies afforded by s 133 of the CCA (see post, para 24.43).
4   But if the judgment is not satisfied, the court has power to revoke it (s 3(4)). As to execution, see post, para 27.04.
5   See *Cohen v Roche* [1927] 1 KB 169; and per Swinfen Eady MR in *Whiteley Ltd v Hilt* [1908] 2 KB 808, CA, at 319. See also *Howard E Perry & Co Ltd v BRB* (above). Cf claims for specific performance: see post, para 29.38.
6   As to the value of goods, and improvement allowances see post, para 27.30. Where the bailee has made improvements to the goods, that may be deducted from the assessed value: ss 3(6), (7).

time, plus damages for their detention.[7] Before the time limit expires, the defendant may prevent the initiation of process for recovery of their assessed value by returning the goods (s 3(5)); but thereafter he must pay their assessed value.[8]

3   *Payment of the value of the goods to the plaintiff,*[9] with damages for their detention.[10] A judgment in this form means that neither party can insist on the return of the goods;[11] but this does not prevent the owner from seizing the goods (see ante, para 24.23), which continue to belong to him until the judgment is satisfied.[12] If the plaintiff does recapt the goods, he is deemed to have waived his right under the judgment to their assessed value.

In a typical case, a county court judge is likely to consider his choice as lying between forms of judgment (2) and (3): for instance, if he believes the defendant is unmeritorious he may prefer judgment (2); whereas, if his sympathies be with the defendant he is more likely to choose judgment (3). In any event, any order for payment of money is likely to be by instalments (see post, para 27.03). Default may lead to a warrant for delivery (see post, para 27.04).

Regulated agreements[1]

[24.27] Even though the unpaid supplier may have reserved ownership of the goods supplied, statute has imposed a substantial number of restrictions on his power to recover possession of them.[2] However, eschewing the simple course of setting out the unpaid supplier's rights, the draftsmen instead produced a series of special statutory restrictions on the general rules previously considered (see ante, paras 24.21–26). The HPA 1938 forbad recaption after one-third of the hp price had been paid.[3] The HPA 1964 added the default notice procedure and death provisions, and made all three provisions applicable to conditional sales.[4] Following its normal practice (see ante, para 5.07), the CCA 1974 adopted all three of the above restrictions and simply applied them to a larger range of contracts:[5] indeed, some of the restrictions were made applicable to all regulated

---

7   Section 3(2)(b). As to whether the defendant must actually deliver the goods, see Winfield and Jolowicz, *Tort* (15th edn), 613, note 35.

8   *Metals and Ropes Ltd v Tattersall* [1966] 3 All ER 401, CA; *Astley Industrial Trust Ltd v Miller* [1968] 2 All ER 36. But the court has power to stay execution, even out of time.

9   If the plaintiff claims only this form, judgment must be in this form (s 3(3)(b)): Thornely [1990] CLJ at 367.

10 The court must put a separate figure on the value of the goods: *General and Finance Facilities Ltd v Cook Cars (Romford) Ltd* (above).

11 However, by returning the goods before trial, the defendant may reduce the damages by their value: *Hillesden Securities Ltd v Ryjak Ltd* [1983] 2 All ER 184.

12 *Brinsmead v Harrison* (1872) LR 7 CP 547. If judgment is satisfied, the plaintiff's title passes to the defendant: see post, para 26.17.

[24.27]

1   For regulated agreements, see ante, Chapter 5.

2   See ante, para 24.23, note 1.

3   As to the modern restrictions on the recaption of goods, see post, para 24.34.

4   As to the modern procedures in respect of default notices and death, see respectively post, paras 24.30; 24.44.

5   As recommended by the *Crowther Report* (see ante, para 5.03), para 6.7.17.

agreements, including credit sales, loans and consumer hirings. Additionally, the CCA sought to ensure that the supplier did not side-step the default notice procedure by acting under the terms of the agreement (see post, para 24.28); and it laid down in Part IX general powers of judicial control over the enforcement of regulated agreements,[6] including enforcement orders.[7] These orders are required for the enforcement of an improperly executed agreement (see ante, para 9.20), though the court can instead make a declaration (see ante, para 9.19).

Notice of enforcement by creditor or owner

[24.28] The contractual right of a creditor or owner under a regulated agreement to enforce that agreement may arise not only upon breach by the debtor or hirer, but also in accordance with a number of terms of the agreement (see post, para 26.08). As it may obviously be a matter of accident whether a debtor or hirer getting into financial difficulties ceases payments under his regulated or another agreement first, the CCA seeks to ensure that the debtor or hirer has seven days notice before activation of the acceleration clause (see ante, para 7.03) in both events. However, the Act makes separate provision for notice of enforcement according to whether it operates after default or in the absence of default for this reason: whereas the defaulting debtor or hirer is given the right to wipe the slate clean by remedying a default (see post, para 24.32), a non-default notice only suspends the rights of the creditor or owner.[1] On the other hand, where the regulated agreement involves a supply of goods, both notice requirements **suspend** the right of the creditor or owner to immediate possession of the goods, so temporarily preventing continued possession by the debtor or hirer from being adverse (see ante, para 24.25).

To the following extent, default and non-default notices share the same rules:

1   *Co-debtors.* Where there is more than one debtor, s 185 requires that the notice must be served[2] on each of them (see post, para 25.08).

2   *Form of notice.* Each of the provisions requires its notice to be in a prescribed form;[3] and regulations now provide in detail the form of such notices in a manner which allows default and non-default notices to be combined in one document.[4]

---

6   See post, para 24.39 *et seq.* As to the special rules for extortionate credit bargains, see post, para 29.40; and for the financial relief of defaulting hirer, see post, para 27.23.

7   Section 127: see ante, para 9.20. For enforcement orders in respect of negotiable instruments and security agreements, see post, paras 25.09–11; and upon death, see post, para 24.47.

[24.28]

1   Sections 76, 98: see post, para 24.29. Except that the debtor or hirer can always apply to the court for a time order (see post, para 24.40) or equitable relief against forfeiture: Goode, *Consumer Credit Law and Practice*, paras 45.17; 40.23.

2   'Serve' means 'deliver or send by post' (s 189(1)). Section 176 lays down how such a document may be served and may be of considerable assistance if the debtor/hirer has 'done a moonlight' or denies receipt: see *Lombard North Central v Power-Hines* [1994] CLY 501, Cty Ct; and Goode, *ibid*, para 45.33a.

3   Section 76(3), 88(1), 98(3). This refers to the forms prescribed by the Secretary of State (s 189(1)) by statutory instrument (s 182).

4   Consumer Credit (Enforcement, Default and Termination Notices) Regulations 1983, SI No 1561. Do the prescribed forms require too much information for optimum effect?

3   *Period of notice.* Each of the provisions requires that, prior to taking one of the steps listed in the relevant provision, the creditor or owner must give the debtor or hirer[5] not less than seven days notice of his intention to do so.[6]

4   *Exemptions.* Each of the provisions requiring such seven day notices lays down in identical form that (ss 76(4), 87(2), 98(4)):

> ... it does not prevent a creditor from treating the right to draw on any credit as restricted or deferred and taking such steps as may be necessary to make the restriction or deferment effective.

Thus, a bank may, without such a seven day notice, put a temporary embargo on a credit card facility or overdraft. Additionally, other types of agreement may be exempted by regulations.[7]

5   *Acting without notice.* If the creditor or owner takes one of the steps listed in the relevant provision without giving the requisite seven day notice, the effect is as follows: even if the creditor or owner is permitted to take such steps at common law, eg, because the debtor's landlord has levied distress (see post, para 26.08), he is not 'entitled' to do so in the absence of the requisite notice,[8] so that his taking that step without such notice may (notwithstanding s 170: see ante, para 10.19) be a breach of contract[9] or tortious.[10]

[24.29] Non-default notices. There are two notice provisions which may be applicable where the CCA requires the creditor or owner[1] to give notice (see ante, para 24.28) before exercising certain rights granted to him by the regulated agreement in the absence of default by the debtor or hirer (ss 76(6), 98(6)).

1   *Termination notices.* Where the right granted to the creditor or owner is to terminate the regulated agreement, the matter is governed by s 98; and, as a remedy, this is more properly considered later (post, para 26.10).

2   *Other notices.* Section 76(1) provides that:

> The creditor or owner is not entitled to enforce a term of a regulated agreement by[2]

---

5   As 'debtor' and 'hirer' are defined to include persons to whom their rights may have passed 'by operation of law' (s 189(1)), this obviates any problem relating to service of a notice where the debtor or hirer has died: notice may be served on his personal representative or at the last known address of the debtor or hirer. As to death, see further post, para 24.44 *et seq.*

6   Sections 76(1), 88(2), 98(1). In practice, a minimum of 12 days from posting is generally allowed: (1995) 50 CC 3/35.

7   Sections 76(5), 87(4), 98(5). See the regulations referred to above.

8   Sections 76(1), 87(1), 98(2). Eg, even if a creditor was entitled under the terms of an agreement to 'demand earlier payment of any sum', he would not be so entitled under a regulated agreement so long as he failed to serve a s 76 notice (see below).

9   Eg, breach of warranty of quiet possession (see ante, para 12.16).

10 For wrongful interference with goods, see ante, para 19.04.

[24.29]

1   Under any regulated agreement, whether by way of conditional or credit sale, hp, consumer hiring or loan.

2   Note that paras (a)–(c) correspond with s 87(1)(b)–(d) applicable where the debtor or hirer defaults: see post, para 24.30. Section 76 does not refer to the enforcing of any personal security: *contra* s 87(1)(e).

(a) demanding earlier payment of any sum,[3] or

(b) recovering possession of any goods or land,[4] or

(c) treating any right conferred on the debtor or hirer by agreement as terminated, restricted or deferred,[5]

except by or after giving the debtor or hirer not less than seven days' notice of his intention to do so.

As s 98(1) deals with termination of regulated agreements, it has been suggested that s 76(1)(c) only deals with some lesser termination, eg, of the hiring, so that a creditor or owner who wishes to terminate both the hiring and the agreement should give a combined ss 76 and 98 notice.[6]

It is further provided that the requirements as to non-default notices do not apply to either of the following types of case:

(i) Facilities where the credit is in the circumstances repayable on demand (ss 76(4), 98(4): set out ante, para 24.28);[7] or

(ii) Agreements where the whole of the specified credit period has expired.[8]

[24.30] Default notices. One of the most frequent causes of repossession at common law was default in payment of instalments: as neither the conditional buyer or hirer under a hp or simple hiring agreement had any equity of redemption (see ante, para 24.22), the supplier was not required to give him any latitude in this respect,[1] though in practice the courts were very willing to find that the supplier had waived the default by accepting late payment.[2] However, this dependence of the buyer or hirer on the whim of the supplier was thought to be wrong; and the CCA therefore requires the creditor or owner to give notice (see ante, para 24.28) before exercising certain rights granted to him by the regulated agreement after default[3] by the debtor or hirer. According to s 87(1):

Service of a notice on the debtor or hirer in accordance with s 88 (a 'default notice') is necessary before the creditor or owner can become entitled, by reason of any breach by the debtor or hirer of a regulated agreement –

(a) to terminate the agreement,[4] or

---

3   Eg, loans to buy goods which are then destroyed. For accelerated payments clauses, see generally ante, para 7.03. This will be subject to the time order procedure: see post, para 24.39.

4   For the repossession action in respect of goods, see post, paras 24.42–43; and in respect of land, see post, para 25.23.

5   Eg, terminate the hiring (see post, para 26.09). Cf s 87(1)(d).

6   Goode, *Consumer Credit Law and Practice*, para 45.16; and see post, para 26.09.

7   Eg, bank overdrafts or credit cards. Thus, without such seven day notice, these running accounts may be embargoed (see ante, para 24.28) or terminated. *Contra* credit granted for a specified period with an overriding right to call it in: Goode, *op cit*, note 6, para 28.66.

8   Sections 76(2), 98(2). Eg, a credit sale where all instalments are now overdue.

[24.30]

1   However, the debtor or hirer might have been persuaded to take out insurance against this event (see post, para 24.45): in this case, the insurance payment will prevent the default. *Contra* where the creditor or owner has insured himself against default. As to multiple agreements, see ante, para 5.27.

2   Eg, *Reynolds v General Finance Facilities Ltd* (1963) 107 Sol Jo 889, CA. See generally post, para 26.23. For refinancing, see ante, para 7.04A.

3   For non-default notices, see ante, para 24.29. As to the types of agreement requiring default notices, see ante, para 24.29, note 1.

4   For termination of the agreement, see further post, para 26.09.

(b) to demand earlier payment of any sum,[5] or

(c) to recover possession of any goods or land,[6] or

(d) to treat any right conferred on the debtor or hirer by the agreement as terminated, restricted or deferred,[7] or

(e) to enforce any security.[8]

Observe that s 87(1) is only applicable where the creditor or owner wishes to take any of the steps there listed, **and** where he becomes entitled to do 'by reason of any breach by the debtor or hirer':[9] if the listed right arises otherwise than by reason of breach, the case falls outside s 87(1),[10] though a non-default notice may be required before its exercise; and if, despite the breach, the creditor or owner does not wish to take any of the above-listed steps, no default notice is required.[11] The contents and effect of a default notice are considered below. Further, the supplier may register the default with a credit reference agency.[12]

[24.31] Contents. The required minimum contents[1] of a default notice (see ante, para 24.30) are spelt out by s 88(1).[2] As expanded by the Regulations, it requires that the default notice must be in the prescribed form (see ante, para 24.28) and contain the prescribed contents, including both the following:

1 *'The nature of the alleged breach'*. Whilst at common law it may not matter that one gives the wrong reason for doing that which one is entitled to do (see post, para 26.26), the CCA requires specification of the correct reason relied on by the creditor or owner for

---

5 For accelerated payments clauses, see ante, para 7.03. It has been said that the creditor or owner cannot rely on the default notice, but must instead make separate demand after its expiry: Goode, *Consumer Credit Law and Practice*, para 45.33. *Sed quaere?*

6 For repossession actions in respect of goods, see post, para 24.34; and for repossession actions in respect of land, see post, para 25.24.

7 Cf s 76(1)(c): see ante, para 24.29.

8 See post, para 25.14. According to s 87(3), 'The doing of an act by which a floating charge becomes fixed is not enforcement of a security'. This provision is only applicable in the exceptional case where an incorporated body is a joint debtor with an individual, and its effect there is explained by Goode, *op cit*, note 5, para 45.35. As to floating charges, see post, para 25.25.

9 Whether that right is expressly granted by the agreement, or given by the general law: Goode, *op cit*, note 5, para 45.32. However, if it is to the advantage of the debtor or hirer, his actions might be construed as an exercise of any statutory right of cancellation or termination (see respectively ante, para 10.29 and post, para 26.05) rather then a default (see post, para 27.26).

10 Eg, where the debtor wrongfully disposes of goods: Goode, *op cit*, note 5, 45.34; *sed quaere?*

11 Eg, recover arrears of rent or damages from the debtor, or rescind for misrepresentation (see Goode, *op cit*, note 5, 45.32).

12 As to credit reference agencies, see ante, para 8.36. Default information which may be filed is limited by DP Principles 1–5: see ante, para 3.28.

[24.31]

1 There is no reason why the notice may not also include other information, eg, a demand for the return of the goods (see ante, para 24.25). See further s 88(5): post, para 24.32.

2 The drafting seems to follow closely that of the Law of Property Act 1925, s 146: see Goode, *Consumer Credit Law and Practice*, para 45.36, who suggests that the authorities on s 146 may therefore be useful in interpreting s 88.

taking action,[3] and it may be that a waived breach will not suffice (see generally, post, para 26.23). The notice may specify more than one breach.[4]

2   *The action required of the debtor or hirer.* This will vary, according to whether or not the breach is remediable,[5] as follows:

(a) *Remediable breaches.* Section 88(1)(b) requires the default notice to specify:

> ... if the breach is capable of remedy, what action is required to remedy it and the date before which that action is to be taken.

The obvious example is non-payment of an instalment; but the notice is bad if it stipulates for a sum greater than was actually due.[6] The Act makes special provision for the relatively common occurrence that such a default may be expressed to activate an acceleration clause.[7]

(b) *Irremediable breaches.* Section 88(1)(c) requires the default notice to specify:

> ... if the breach is not capable of remedy, the sum (if any) required to be paid as compensation for the breach, and the date before which it is to be paid.

Thus, after an irremediable breach, the creditor or owner may demand some action by the debtor or hirer such as the return of the goods, in which event the debtor or hirer may apply for a time order (s 129: see post, para 24.40). Alternatively, the creditor or owner may demand compensation: so, if the debtor wrongfully passed a good Part III title to a bf private purchaser of a motor vehicle (see ante, para 21.55 *et seq*), or if the debtor wrote the hired vehicle off, the creditor or owner may demand its value in tort (see ante, para 24.26). Similarly, where a debtor fails to make the stipulated minimum payment due under a credit card, the creditor may demand payment of all arrears under an acceleration clause (see ante, para 7.03) and return of the card.[8]

[24.32/33] Effect. On receipt of a default notice in prescribed form (see ante, paras 24.30–31), the debtor or hirer may or may not comply with it.

1   *Compliance.* Within that statutory breathing space compulsorily granted to the debtor or hirer, s 89 lays down that:

> If before the date specified for that purpose in the default notice the debtor or hirer takes the action specified under section 88(1)(b) or (c) the breach shall be treated as not having occurred.

Unlike the case of non-default notices, where the effect of the notice is only suspensory (see ante, para 24.29), the defaulting debtor or hirer is thus given a right to

---

3   If any amount owing is overstated, does this not only make the default notice bad, but also amount to 'unlawful harassment' (as to which, see ante, para 24.24)?

4   *Ropaigealach v Allied Irish Bank plc* [1996] CLY 416, CA (16 Tr LR 32).

5   For discussion as to what amounts to a remediable breach, see Goode, *op cit*, note 2, para 45.37.

6   *Woodchester Lease Management Services Ltd v Swain & Co* [1999] 1 WLR 263, CA.

7   Only the first breach (which triggers the acceleration clause) is to be taken into account for the purposes of the default notice: s 88(3); and see further post, para 24.32. For acceleration clauses, see generally ante, para 7.03; and for early settlement, see post, para 26.19A.

8   The credit token agreement will normally provide that ownership of the card remains in the creditor, to whom it must be returned on demand: see ante, para 7.09.

make good the breach: *pro tanto* there is a compulsory[1] variation of the regulated agreement[2] on each default notice.[3]

2 *Non-compliance.* On the other hand, it may be that the debtor or hirer is not in a position to avail himself of this statutory right to make good the default, eg, where he suffers a distress or is otherwise impecunious. In this case, the effect of the default notice itself is only to suspend the listed rights of the creditor or owner for the period there mentioned, though the court will have jurisdiction to make a time order (see post, para 24.39). Moreover, s 88(5) makes it clear that a default notice may activate a provision in a regulated agreement that the agreement or hiring is terminable[4] for arrears by saying such as: 'If arrears of £x is not paid within ten days, the creditor will terminate the agreement, repossess the goods,[5] and levy a default charge'.[6] By s 134, the effect is to render the possession of the goods by the debtor or hirer adverse to the creditor or owner (see ante, para 24.25).

Additionally, the Act provides that, whilst the default notice may not require the making good of some promise only activated by breach, eg, an accelerated payments clause (see ante, paras 7.03; 24.31), if the specified breach, eg, arrears of instalments, is not remedied, such other clause, eg, the acceleration clause, may be relied upon free of the default notice procedure.[7]

Repossession

[24.34] The HPA 1938 introduced two statutory restrictions on the supplier's right to recover goods let on hp within the ambit of the Act. Today, they form just two items on a list of CCA restrictions (see ante, para 24.27).

1 *Licences to enter premises.* Whilst at common law instalment credit agreements might contain a contractual licence for the supplier to enter premises to recapt goods (see ante, para 24.23), such provisions in some hp agreements were avoided by the HPA 1938. However, that did not prevent the hirer from granting his supplier express permission to enter premises at the time of entry. Fundamentally, this would still appear to be the position, though the CCA protection has also been extended to include conditional sales and simple hirings.[1] Section 92(1) of the CCA provides:

[24.32/33]

1 Section 173(1): see generally ante, para 18.11.

2 Might acceptance of part of any arrears amount to a waiver of breach (see ante, para 24.30)? For compulsory variation of regulated agreements, see generally post, para 26.22. Cf mortgages of land: post, para 25.20.

3 The regular slow payer may be charged default interest if the agreement so provides: (1993) 48 CC 4/13. But the rate of interest must not be increased (see below).

4 For the situation where the agreement or hiring is terminable, see generally post, para 26.09.

5 For repossession actions in respect of protected goods, see post, para 24.42.

6 A default charge may amount to a penalty (see post, para 27.46) or an increased rate of interest (default interest): default interest is prohibited in the case of consumer credit agreements (see post, para 26.19), but not in the case of consumer hirings (see (1989) 43 CC 6/17).

7 Section 88(3). Thus, if the third of ten instalments is in default beyond the default notice period the acceleration clause operates, so that the creditor becomes entitled to claim immediately all the remaining seven instalments.

[24.34]

1 With a similar restriction being introduced in relation to recovery of land subject to a conditional sale (s 92(2): see post, para 25.24). For such conditional sales, see generally ante, para 1.16.

Except under an order of the court, the creditor or owner shall not be entitled to enter any premises to take possession of goods subject to a regulated hire-purchase agreement, regulated conditional sale agreement or regulated consumer hire agreement.

Presumably, 'premises' connotes land to which the public does not have access as of right and extends to car-ports and private driveways, whether or not 'premises' occupied by the debtor or hirer.[2] Within its ambit,[3] contravention of s 92(1) will give rise to an action for breach of statutory duty (s 92(3): see ante, para 3.21). Any common law right to recapt[4] protected goods is therefore only likely to remain of significance in relation to such goods in two circumstances: (1) where recaption is possible without entry on 'premises', eg, in respect of motor vehicles, especially where the vehicle cannot be shown to have been garaged at the time of repossession; or (2) where consent to entry on 'premises' is given at the time of entry under s 173(3).[5]

2   *Protected goods.* Where the hirer had paid more than one-third of the hp price, the HPA 1938 termed them 'protected goods': in respect of these, the exercise of any common law right of recaption was totally prohibited; and, if the owner alternatively sought to recover the goods through court action, the 1938 introduced a number of substantive and procedural protections. These provisions were subsequently extended to conditional sales and have now been reformulated in the CCA:[6] not only are such actions subject to prior observance of the notice procedure (see ante, paras 24.28–32), but an action to recover protected goods (see post, paras 24.35–38) must be brought in the debtor's local county court (s 141: see post, para 24.39), where there are alterations in the forms of judgment. The court may simply reschedule the payments under a time order (see post, para 24.40); and, even where that remedy is inappropriate, there are substantial restrictions (see post, paras 24.42–43) on the forms of judgment otherwise applicable (see ante, para 24.26).

3   *Unprotected goods.* Before the hirer had paid one-third of the hp price, under the 1938 Act the owner retained his power to recapt, though modified by the removal of any contractual licence to enter premises (see above). This last rule has now been extended to consumer hirings (see ante, para 1.19) and to any security (see post, para 25.13) or linked transaction (see ante, para 5.31).

Finally, it should be remembered that, if the goods are not commercially worth repossessing, the creditor can always instead sue for the price or rent (see post, para 27.15A *et seq*).

---

2   But does it include a private road, lock-up garage, a garage under a block of flats, a dormobile, a caravan, or any other structure not amounting to a dwelling house? This restriction may extend to premises occupied by third parties: see Goode, *Consumer Credit Law and Practice*, para 38.4.

3   What about exercise of a contractual right of entry to inspect goods? Or where goods are no longer subject to the agreement, eg, where the hiring has terminated?

4   For the right of recaption, see ante, para 24.23. Under s 80 of the CCA, the debtor must disclose the whereabouts of the goods: see ante, para 15.17. But what is to stop him then moving them?

5   See generally ante, para 18.11 and post, para 24.37. Whose consent is relevant if the debtor or hirer is not the occupier of the 'premises'? What if the debtor's trustee in bankruptcy consents? As to consent, see further post, para 24.37.

6   The substantive provisions do not apply to consumer hirings in respect of which the hirer's only substantive protection on repossession is financial (s 132): see post, para 27.23.

[24.35] Protected goods. According to s 90(1):

At any time when –

(a) the debtor is in breach of a regulated hire-purchase or a regulated conditional sale agreement relating to goods, and

(b) the debtor has paid to the creditor one-third or more of the total price of the goods, and

(c) the property in the goods remains in the creditor,

the creditor, is not entitled to recover possession of the goods from the debtor except on an order from the court.

Thus, goods only fall within s 90(1) where **all** three paragraphs are satisfied as follows:

Paragraph (a). The section does not extend to all regulated agreements,[1] but only a regulated hp or conditional sale (see ante, paras 1.24; 1.16). Further, s 90(5) makes it clear that the protection is lost where the debtor terminates (see post, para 24.37); but the sense of s 90(1) is that the creditor cannot escape its ambit by himself exercising any common law right of termination (see post, para 26.09). Finally, the creditor must be claiming repossession **after** a breach by the debtor,[2] though it does not require any connection between the debtor's breach and the creditor's claim.[3]

Paragraph (b). The concept of 'total price' is defined by s 189(1) as:

... the total sum payable[4] by the debtor under a hire-purchase agreement or a conditional sale agreement, including any sum payable on the exercise of an option to purchase,[5] but excluding any sum payable as a penalty[6] or as compensation or damages for a breach of the agreement.[7]

This paragraph requires that the 'total price of the goods' be compared with the sums paid[8] by the debtor:[9] the goods will fall within s 90 only if the latter is at least one-third of the former (see further, post, para 24.36). It may, however, be possible for a debtor in possession of unprotected goods even after termination of the agreement to claim protection from s 90 by making additional payments up to the one-third level,[10] eg, through the bank giro system (see ante, para 23.13).

[24.35]

1 So it does not extend to consumer hiring agreements. But see s 132: post, para 27.23.

2 The goods will not fall within s 90(1) where the debtor has not committed any breach and the creditor is terminating the agreement under a s 98 notice (as to which, see post, para 26.10). It has been remarked that this is a surprising reduction in the protection of the debtor: Goode, *Consumer Credit Law and Practice*, para 45.60.

3 What if there is no breach at the time a s 98 notice is served, but one occurs before expiry of the seven days – as is quite likely if the triggering event is, eg, insolvency? For death, see post, para 24.48.

4 This presumably includes part exchange allowances (as to which, see ante, para 2.09). What if there is a variable finance charge?

5 See ante, para 1.25.

6 See post, para 27.25.

7 This does not include extra interest and administration charges: *Julian Hodge Bank Ltd v Hall* [1998] CLY 2493, CA.

8 Does 'paid' include tendered? Section 189(1) provides that *prima facie* 'payment' includes tender; and as to tender, see generally ante, paras 23.14–15.

9 Or on his behalf, eg, by a surety. For the common law rules of payment, see ante, para 23.13.

10 See post, para 24.36, note 3. As to appropriation of payment where the debtor has more than one agreement, see *ibid*.

Paragraph (c). Whilst perhaps unlikely, it would seem that the property could pass in goods held under a regulated hp or conditional sale (see above) agreement before completion of the payments, upon which the goods would be taken outside s 90(1) and might seem unprotected in the hands of the hirer or buyer,[11] whilst safe in the hands of his purchaser.[12]

[24.36] The one-third rule.[1] Section 90(1)(b) brings a regulated hp or conditional sale agreement within the protection of s 90 only if the debtor has paid one-third of the 'total price' (see ante, para 24.35) 'of the goods'.[2] Suppose a total price of £900. In the ordinary case, the goods will fall within s 90 where the debtor has paid £900 x 1/3 = £300,[3] including any deposit.[4] However, the section also makes provision for the following special cases:

1   *Installation charges.*[5] According to s 90(2):

> Where under a hire-purchase or conditional sale agreement the creditor is required to carry out any installation and the agreement specifies, as part of the total price, the amount to be paid in respect of the installation (the 'installation charge') the reference in subsection (1)(b) to one-third of the total price shall be construed as a reference to the aggregate of the installation charge and one-third of the remainder of the total price.

Thus, suppose a total price of £900 plus a compulsory installation charge of £60, the goods will fall within s 90 where the debtor has paid £60 + (£900 x 1/3) = £360. On the other hand, if the installation charge was not compulsory under the regulated agreement,[6] the goods will fall within s 90 where only £300 has been paid.

2   *Successive agreements.* Between the two world wars, there became prevalent the device of linking one hp agreement to another in the following manner:[7] the hirer under an almost completed agreement was persuaded to abandon it and take the goods from the first agreement together with further goods under a second agreement; and in this manner the owner increased his security at no cost to himself.[8] The HPA 1964 sought to combat this device in controls subsequently re-enacted in the CCA: the result is

---

11   Is this a drafting slip? Would any contractual right of repossession then amount to a colourable licence to seize? See post, para 25.27.

12   The purchaser would have a title good enough to defeat a tort claim by the supplier: see ante, para 19.06.

[24.36]

1   As to multiple agreements, see ante, para 5.27.

2   Might the words 'of the goods' in s 90(1)(b) save from the section payments in respect of related services? The words do not appear in s 100 (see post, para 27.49), but are arguably assumed to cover services by s 90(2).

3   Even this simple rule may cause creditors practical difficulties, given that a payment may be made by or on behalf of the debtor at any of the creditor's branches, or even via the banking system: see ante, para 23.12. Might it be avoidable by not authorising receipt of payments; or does payment here include tender (see ante, para 23.13) ? See Goode, *Payment Obligations*, pp 21–23.

4   Distinguish the concept of credit, from which the deposit is excluded: see ante, para 5.22.

5   'Installation charges' are elaborately defined in s 189(1).

6   What if it was made compulsory under a prior collateral contract?

7   This became part of the technique of the 'snatchback': see post, para 26.08.

8   Eg, furniture trade. Unfortunately, the practice was to term these 'linked transactions'. However, the CCA reserves that expression for an entirely different device (see ante, para 5.31).

that, where the first agreement falls within s 90, both the old and new goods will fall within s 90, regardless of the amount paid under the second agreement.[9]

[24.37] Loss of protected goods status. Goods which fall within s 90 as above explained (ante, paras 24.35–36) are termed 'protected goods' (s 90(7)). However, there are a number of ways in which the status of protected goods may be lost by action on the part of the debtor, though he could still apply for a time order (s 129: see post, para 24.40):

1   *Consent to repossession.* At first sight, s 90(1) looks as though it prohibits any repossession by the creditor without court order (recaption), so ruling out voluntary surrender of the goods by the debtor. However, when read in conjunction with s 173(3) (see ante, para 18.11), it is clear that what the CCA does is only to avoid any device whereby the debtor consents **in advance** to repossession by the creditor.[1] However, *de facto* consent is frequently given by the debtor in the hope that resale by the creditor will discharge the balance due; and the question may be whether that consent is informed, and therefore *de iure*, consent.[2] Is s 173(3) wide enough to cover the case where goods are abandoned by the debtor?[3] Is it then needed?[4]

2   *Termination.* According to s 90(5), where a debtor[5] exercises his common law or statutory right of termination (see post, para 26.04), he loses the protection of s 90, though this would seem to follow only where that exercise were truly voluntary: this rule is an inducement to the court to find that the debtor's action amounts to a breach rather than the exercise of a right to terminate.[6]

3   *Transfer of possession.* Sometimes, a person taking goods on conditional sale or hp will transfer possession of those goods to a third party (as to the effect of such a transfer at common law, see ante, para 1.22). The effect of this on the protected goods status is as follows:[7] if the transfer of possession is by way of assignment, the goods remain protected because the expression 'debtor' includes his assignee;[8] if the debtor bails goods to another for a temporary purpose, eg, to a repairer, the goods remain protected because they can still be regarded as in the legal possession of the debtor;[9] but, where the goods are sold by the debtor, it would seem that they are no longer

---

9   Where the second agreement entirely discharges the first one, this effect is achieved by s 90(3); and, where the second agreement only modifies the first one, by s 90(4). For modifying agreements, see generally, post, para 26.22.

[24.37]

1   *Mercantile Credit Ltd v Cross* [1965] 2 QB 205, CA. As to consent by the debtor's agent, see ante, para 10.06.

2   No consent held: *FC Finance Ltd v Francis* (1970) 114 Sol Jo 568, CA (third party purported to consent on behalf of hirer); *Chartered Trust plc v Pitcher* [1988] RTR 72, CA (consent by hirer qualified and uninformed). Consent of one joint debtor is sufficient (s 185(1)(b)): set out post, para 25.08.

3   *Bentinck Ltd v Cromwell Engineering Co Ltd* [1971] 1 QB 324, CA (six months). See Goode, *Consumer Credit Law and Practice*, para 45.77; and Hudson (1984) 100 LQR, 110, especially 116–17, and 119 note 70.

4   Are abandoned goods repossessed from the debtor within the meaning of s 90(1)? See Goode, *op cit*, note 3, Div 11B, para 5.170.

5   Where the debtor is bankrupt, his position is taken by his trustee (see ante, para 5.24), who may disclaim the agreement as onerous property (see ante, para 19.22). Consider then the effect of s 92 (see ante, para 24.34).

6   See *Bridge v Campbell Discount Co Ltd* (set out post, para 27.25). For repudiation, see post, para 26.15.

7   Bear in mind the prohibition against such transfers frequently found in conditional sales and hp agreements: see ante, para 7.26.

8   Section 189(1). As to where the debtor dies, see post, para 24.48.

9   Goode, *op cit*, note 3, para 45.78. Cf *Re Atlantic Computer Systems plc* (set out ante, para 19.19).

protected, because s 90(1) only prohibits the creditor recovering possession from the 'debtor'.[10] Where the creditor takes the goods into protective custody under s 131 (see post, para 24.43), the goods seem to have lost their protected status.[11]

[24.38] The protection. The effect of s 90 (see ante, paras 24.34–37) is that 'the creditor[1] is not entitled to recover possession of [protected] goods from the debtor except by order of the court' (s 90(1)). The process for obtaining such a court order is examined below (see post, para 24.39 et seq). Contravention of s 90 attracts the severe[2] penalty of s 91:[3]

If goods are recovered by the creditor in contravention of section 90 –

(a) the regulated agreement, if not previously terminated, shall terminate, and

(b) the debtor shall be released from all liability under the agreement, and shall be entitled to recover from the creditor all sums paid by the debtor under the agreement.[4]

Not only is the effect of s 91(a) to terminate the regulated agreement forthwith,[5] but it also renders ineffective any security provided in relation to the agreement.[6] However, it gives rise to no further sanction.[7] The effect of a similar scheme in the HPA 1938 was considered by Goddard LJ in *Carr v James Broderick Ltd*:[8]

The owners of goods let under an hp agreement seized them in contravention of the Act after one-third of the hp price had been paid. Subsequently, the owners admitted their error, and offered to repay the sums already paid by the hirer. The hirer refused to accept the money, and sued to recover the goods.

His Lordship held that the agreement had been determined by the Act; and that the hirer was not entitled to claim the goods either in detinue or conversion (see now ante, para 19.04), but merely the sums paid under the agreement (detinue has now been abolished: see ante, para 19.04). Thus, once the owner recaps the goods, the hirer cannot recover their possession by court action.[9] Nor will the agreement be revived simply because the goods are returned to the hirer.[10]

---

10 Eg, a vehicle transfer agency (see ante, para 1.15). See *Kassam v Chartered Trust plc* [1998] RTR 220, CA. What if the goods are innocently given away by the debtor, perhaps to somebody within his immediate family?

11 *Lombank v Dowdall* (1973) 118 Sol Jo 96, CA (under narrower HPA 1965, s 34(3)). *Contra* where the owner does not obtain a court order before purporting to take the goods into protective custody: *UDT (Commercial) v Kesler* (1962) Sol Jo 15.

[24.38]

1 'Creditor' includes his assignee: s 189(1).

2 The penalty originated in the HPA 1938, when there did not exist the modern more flexible, licensing provisions (see ante, para 6.11 et seq).

3 If there is any doubt as to whether or not s 91 has operated, any 'interested party' may apply to the court for a declaration: s 142(2)(b).

4 Eg, *Humberclyde Finance Ltd v Thomson* (set out ante, para 5.22).

5 For the position where only part of the protected goods are repossessed, see Goode, *Consumer Credit Law and Practice*, para 45.93.

6 Sections 106, 113(3)(b). Eg, a guarantor who has paid some instalments may recover them.

7 Section 170(1): see ante, para 10.19. See further Goode, *op cit*, note 5, para 46.143.

8 [1942] 2 KB 275; [1942] 2 All ER 441.

9 What if the debtor seizes the goods? Is it conversion? Theft?

10 Because fresh documentation would be necessary to comply with the CCA: see Chapter 9. Cf unregulated agreements: see *Capital Finance Ltd v Bray* (set out ante, para 24.25).

Powers of the court

[24.39] Introduction. Thus far, this section has concentrated on the CCA rules designed to place fetters (see ante, paras 24.27–38) on the rights of the creditor or owner to exercise his ordinary proprietary rights (see ante, paras 24.21–26); to channel disputes into the relevant County Court (s 141(1): see ante, para 24.34); and to ensure that all parties are before the court.[1] Attention must now be turned to what happens when the dispute gets to court. Leaving aside the interim power of the court to make a protection order,[2] the CCA envisages that the normal situation will be this: the court will conclude that the sum claimed under the regulated agreement is due under the terms of the contract, but wish to allow the debtor or hirer time for payment; and the Act envisages that this is to be effected by means of time orders (see post, para 24.40 *et seq*). However, some special rules are provided for the case where the regulated agreement includes the supply of goods with a reservation of title (see post, para 24.42 *et seq*).

Where a case is instead brought in the High Court, it may be transferred to the relevant County Court;[3] or it may be struck out if the person bringing the proceedings ought to have known this.[4] However, there would appear to be a gap in the strategy of the CCA in its seeking to channel all disputes into the relevant County Court: it assumes that the creditor or owner will commence a court action under the agreement. However, it has been decided that the creditor or owner is entitled instead to make a 'statutory demand' leading to High Court insolvency proceedings (see ante, para 19.21); but it has been pointed out that the High Court may then exercise its discretion to set aside the demand.[5]

Further, the creditor or owner may always instead offer 'favourable' terms for a settlement: if before commencement of action, this may operate as discharge by subsequent agreement (see post, para 26.18); but, if offered after commencement of action, it may be embodied in a court consent order, in which case it will usually be binding on the parties as *res judicata*.[6]

[24.40] Time orders. Section 129(1) empowers the court 'if it appears just to do so' to make a time order[1] in any of the following circumstances:

    (a) on an application for an enforcement order;[2] or

    (b) on an application made by a debtor or hirer under this paragraph after service on him of –

[24.39]

1   This will include all co-principals and any sureties (s 141(5)): see further post, para 25.08.

2   Under s 131, the creditor may apply for a 'protection order' in respect of the goods if worried as to his interest in them, eg, if the debtor or hirer is driving uninsured, or trying to sell them. Repossession would then seem possible even of protected goods (see s 90(1): set out ante, para 24.35); but the efficacy of the proceedings may be reduced by court delays.

3   CCA, s 141(2); *Sovereign Leasing v Ali* [1992] CLY 3457, Cty Crt.

4   Section 40(1) County Court Act 1984 (as substituted); *Barclays Bank plc v Brooks* [1998] CLY 405.

5   Goode, *Consumer Credit Law and Practice*, para 46.23.

6   *Centrehigh Ltd v Amen* [2001] unreported, CA.

[24.40]

1   For the reasons why time orders are more potent than instalment orders under s 71(1) of the County Courts Act 1984, see Goode, *Consumer Credit Law and Practice*, para 46.174.

2   See ante, para 24.33.

(i)   a default notice,[3] or

(ii) a notice under section 76(1)[4] or 98(1);[5] or

(c) in an action brought by a creditor or owner to enforce a regulated agreement[6] or any security,[7] or recover possession of any goods[8] or land[9] to which a regulated agreement relates.

Powers of the court. Given that the court has jurisdiction by reason of s 129(1) to make a time order in respect of a regulated agreement, s 129(2) provides that:

A time order shall provide for one or both of the following, as the court considers just –

(a) the payment by the debtor or hirer or any surety of any sum owed under a regulated agreement or a security by such instalments, payable at such times, as the court, having regard to the means of the debtor or hirer and any surety, considers reasonable;[10]

(b) the remedying by the debtor or hirer of any breach of a regulated agreement (other than non-payment of money) within such period as the court may specify.

It will be observed that time orders under s 129(2) may be made in respect of either of the following types of default.[11]

1   *Monetary default*. This is the more common type of default. Where the debtor or hirer makes an instalment offer, the court may make a time order without hearing evidence of means (s 130(1)). In other cases, s 129(2)(a) implies that the court must hear evidence of means – what if the debtor simply fails to appear in court (see post, para 24.43)? For those cases where the debtor or hirer appears and does not make an offer, Leggatt LJ explained[12] that 'the power to make a time order under s 129 is essentially a social provision to assist debtors who find themselves unable to repay loans through no fault of their own. I see no reason to construe such a provision narrowly.' It is considered below (post, para 24.41).

2   *Non-monetary default*. The jurisdiction conferred in respect of this less common situation by s 129(2) is further regulated by s 130(5). The basic effect is to freeze the remedies of the creditor or owner for the period specified in the time order (as varied): if the debtor complies with the time order, then under s 130(4) he continues to enjoy his contractual right to retain possession[13] and expunge his default by compliance with the time order; but, if the debtor or hirer further defaults, the remedy

---

3   See ante, para 24.30.
4   See ante, para 24.29.
5   See post, para 26.10.
6   Eg, the terms of a loan: see ante, para 7.02 *et seq*.
7   For security agreements, see post, para 25.10.
8   See ante, para 24.34.
9   See post, para 25.24.
10 There is a special exemption for pledges (s 130(3): see generally post, para 25.18). For powers to reduce the sums payable, see ss 137–40: post, para 29.42.
11 The order can usually be made conditional or suspended (s 135: set out ante, para 9.20). But this power may not be exercised so as to extend the period of a consumer hiring (s 135(3)).
12 Delivering the judgment of the CA in *Southern District Finance plc v Barnes* (see post, para 24.41).
13 However, if the creditor has already recovered possession, the order does not entitle the debtor to resume possession, its sole effect being to freeze remedies which the creditor has not yet exercised: Goode, *op cit*, note 1, para 46.191.

of the creditor or owner is to apply for revocation of the time order,[14] upon which the restraints imposed by s 130(5) are removed and the position is as in the case of monetary default.

[24.41/42] Time order after monetary default. Where a time order is sought in respect of monetary default, the position is governed by s 129(2)(a) set out above, which refers to 'any sum owed' by the debtor or hirer. In the case of hp and conditional sale agreements, the Act expressly permits the court to deal with sums not yet due (s 130(2)); but in other cases, it was not clear whether the phrase referred just to arrears, or the entire sum which would become payable under the agreement. The matter was considered in *Southern & District Finance plc v Barnes*,[1] where the Court of Appeal dealt with three separate appeals concerning loans secured on land. Leggatt LJ laid down six principles:

(1) The court must first consider whether it is just to make an order, taking into account the position of both parties.[2]

(2) A time order should normally be for a stipulated period on account of temporary financial difficulty,[3] so that it is normally inappropriate if the debtor is unlikely to be able to resume paying at least the contractual instalments.[4]

(3) The 'sum owed' (see above) means every sum due and owing under the agreement (*Lewis*). But, where possession proceedings are brought, that will normally comprise the total indebtedness (as to possession actions, see post, para 25.24). The court must consider what instalments would be reasonable, having regard to the debtor's means (see ante, para 24.40).

(4) The court may include in a time order any amendment of the agreement which it considers just to both parties, and which is a consequence of a term of the order. The interest rate may be amended under s 136 (see ante, para 9.20); but, if the interest rate is not amended, it is relevant that the smaller instalments will result both in a liability to pay interest on accumulated arrears[5] and in an extended period of repayment.[6]

(5) If the order is made when the whole of the outstanding balance is due, there will inevitably be consequences for the term of the loan or rate of interest or both.[7]

---

14 Under s 130(6). For the position then in relation to default notices (see ante, para 24.30), see Goode, *op cit*, note 1.

[24.41/42]

1 [1995] GCCR 1935, CA. The Court also considered appeals in the following cases: *J & J Securities v Ewart*; *Equity Home Loans v Lewis* (leave to appeal to HL refused). See generally Lawson (1995) 14 Tr 527; Goode, *Consumer Credit Law and Practice*, para 46.173.

2 As the position of both parties is to be taken into account, this does not appear to offer an easy sanction against overselling credit: see *First National Bank plc v Syed* [1991] 2 All ER 250, CA.

3 As by reducing the amount payable under each monthly instalment for a finite time, eg, *Lewis*; *Ewart* (above).

4 Approved by Lord Bingham (at para 29) in the *First National Bank* case (set out ante, para 7.03A). It will then normally be more equitable to allow the regulated agreement to be enforced. But see the *Lewis* case (above).

5 To prevent any additional interest being payable: see *Barnes*; *Lewis*; *Ewart* (above); and the analysis by Hickman, etc in (1995) 145 NLJ 691.

6 To some extent the high rate of interest usually payable under regulated agreements already takes account of the risk that difficulties in repayment will occur.

7 Approved by Lord Bingham (at para 28) in the *First National Bank* case (above). See the eight principles deduced by Hickman, etc, *op cit*, note 5, 692.

(6) If justice requires the making of a time order, the court should suspend any possession order (see above) that it also makes (see below), so long as there is compliance with the terms of the time order.

This s 129 power is quite distinct from the power under s 138 to rewrite the agreement where the interest rate is extortionate (see post, para 29.40).

Effect of such a time order. With regard to a loan secured on land, the effect of a time order is considered later (see post, para 25.24). However, where a time order is granted in respect of a hp, conditional sale or consumer hiring agreement, the effect of the CCA is to turn the debtor or hirer into a sort of statutory bailee of those goods, though preserving any contractual power to acquire the creditor's title.[8] Moreover, the Act allows the court to make alterations in the terms of the regulated agreement or any security, either upon first making a time order under s 136 (see *Barnes*), or by means of subsequent variations (s 130(6)). Whilst rescheduling the instalments payable under an instalment credit agreement, a time order made solely[9] under this provision does not of itself restrict the creditor's remedies for default.[10] However, in relation to hp or conditional sales agreements, the court is empowered to make further orders under s 133 (see post, para 24.43).

[24.43] Special powers. It has already been seen that the CCA takes special steps so that a creditor may maintain an action for the recovery of goods. The CCA enables the creditor or owner to demonstrate adverse possession (s 134) and also provides for interim protection orders (s 131). However, besides the ordinary forms of judgment available at common law where the hirer or buyer defaults (see ante, para 24.26) and the powers granted to a creditor where a debtor exercises a statutory right of termination (s 100(5): see post, para 26.06), s 133(1) grants the court some overriding[1] powers in the following circumstances:

If, in relation to a regulated hire-purchase or conditional sale agreement, it appears to the court just to do so –

(a) on an application for an enforcement order or time order;[2] or

(b) in an action brought by the creditor to recover possession of goods to which the agreement relates ...[3]

These powers do not extend to consumer hire agreements;[4] but they are exercisable even where the creditor is seeking repossession after the debtor has terminated the agreement, though there is a special restriction on the power of the court to refuse specific delivery

---

8   Goode, *op cit*, note 1, para 46.178. This will be so even if the agreement has been terminated: s 130(4).
9   *Contra* if there is both a monetary and non-monetary default, in which case s 130(5) operates as for non-monetary default (see ante, para 24.40).
10 Eg, to recapt unprotected goods or bring an action to recover protected goods. See Goode, *op cit*, note 1, para 46.192.
[24.43]
1   Torts (Interference with Goods) Act 1977, s 3(8).
2   See ante, paras 9.20; 24.39; 24.40.
3   See ante, paras 24.34–38.
4   Transfer orders would not be appropriate to consumer hirings; and return orders are unnecessary as the owner can always seek a judgment under the Torts Act 1977, s 3: see ante, para 24.26.

(s 100(5): see further post, para 26.05). Section 133 envisages the two following types of order,[5] which can themselves be subsequently revoked:[6]

1   *Return orders.* This is an order for 'the return to the creditor of the goods to which the agreement relates' (s 133(1)). It may be made conditional or suspended,[7] but may not be suspended unless the court is satisfied that the goods are in the debtor's possession or control.[8] The form of return order most commonly used is where the order is suspended on condition that the debtor makes the rescheduled payments due under a time order (see ante, paras 24.40–41). Where the debtor fulfils the terms of a time order or return order, he will automatically acquire the creditor's title to the goods (s 133(5)); but, where the debtor further defaults, the form of the order may allow the creditor to execute judgment immediately, though this cannot deprive the debtor of the statutory option to pay the outstanding balance.[9]

2   *Transfer orders.* This is a Judgment of Solomon, ordering the transfer to the debtor of the creditor's title to certain of the goods to which the agreement relates ('the transfer goods') and the return to the creditor of the remainder of the goods,[10] again subject to the right of the debtor to pay off the outstanding balance. Transfer orders are sometimes used for the furniture trade.

After service of the above orders on the debtor, he sometimes wishes to negotiate so that he can keep the goods.[11]

Death

[24.44/46] On the death of the borrower, buyer or hirer, the general rule is that most causes of action subsisting against, or vested in, him survive against his estate or for its benefit.[1] However, the death of the borrower, buyer or hirer must usually at best result in a temporary cessation of payments; and over the years suppliers have therefore taken steps to safeguard their interests. Sometimes, they have taken the benevolent step of providing that the agreement shall then be treated as fully paid: this may be done either under the terms of the loan or supply contract,[2] or, more frequently, under a separate insurance.[3] Unfortunately, it has been rather more common for instalment credit contracts to provide

---

5   The orders can amend any agreement or security (s 136): set out ante, para 9.20.
6   Under s 133(6). This will be useful, eg, where the debtor has since the date of the order sold the goods.
7   Section 135(1): set out ante, para 9.20. There is a power of subsequent variation: s 135(4).
8   Section 135(2). What if the debtor does not appear, or no evidence of possession is led? See Goode, *Consumer Credit Law and Practice*, para 46.217. Compare the position under the Torts Act 1977, s 3(6): see ante, para 24.26.
9   'At any time before the goods enter the possession of the creditor': s 133(4).
10 Section 133(1). Section 133 contains special rules designed to compensate the creditor for having to accept the return of used goods: see further Goode, *op cit*, note 8, paras 46.218–19.
11 Lunn (1995) 49 CC 6/20.

[24.44/46]
1   Law Reform (Miscellaneous Provisions) Act 1934, s 1(1) (as amended).
2   This effectively insures the life of the borrower, buyer or hirer at the expense of the lender or supplier who in fact sometimes take out Credit Protection Insurance (CPI): see post, para 24.48.
3   Group insurance is normally offered as an optional extra with separate premiums payable by the borrower, buyer or hirer (Insurance Companies Amendment Act 1973, s 50). The modern group insurance frequently extends beyond death cover to embrace accident, illness and unemployment: see ante, para 7.03; and (1988) 43 CC2/4.

that the agreement shall terminate automatically upon the death of the borrower, buyer or hirer.[4] Such a provision tends to compound the distress caused by the bereavement.[5]

The only contribution made by the HPA 1938 to the above problem was to provide that 'hirer' should include the person to whom his rights or liabilities passed by operation of law; and this provision has been repeated in the CCA.[6] This has the effect of extending the statutory restrictions on recovery of possession in appropriate circumstances to the personal representative of the debtor or hirer;[7] but it did not prevent the operation of a clause providing in that event for the termination of the agreement, or the recovery of the goods. As a matter of grace, some suppliers were prepared to accept tender of the outstanding balance of the hp price from a personal representative or other interested party;[8] but it was felt that the hirer's interest should be given some measure of legal protection. However, statute has eschewed the simple, and benevolent, answer of a compulsory transfer of property and cessation of payments[9] in favour of another solution (see post, para 24.47), which itself causes difficulty over voluntary insurance premiums (see post, para 24.48).

[24.47] The CCA provisions. A distinction may conveniently be drawn between the effect of the death of the debtor or hirer on the payment obligations under a regulated agreement (see post, para 24.48) and the measures taken by the Act to combat clauses in the regulated agreement expressed to operate on death *simpliciter* (see ante, paras 24.44–46). In the latter connection, s 86 provides as follows:

(1) The creditor or owner under a regulated agreement is not entitled, by reason of the death of the debtor or hirer, to do an act specified in paragraphs (a) to (e) of section 87(1) if at the death the agreement is fully secured.

(2) If at the death of the debtor or hirer a regulated agreement is only partly secured or is unsecured, the creditor or owner is entitled, by reason of the death of the debtor or hirer, to do an act specified in paragraphs (a) to (e) of section 87 (1) on an order of the court only.

It will be noticed that, where s 86(1) applies because the agreement is 'fully secured', any such clause is void (s 173(1): set out ante, para 18.11); whereas, if the agreement is 'only partly secured or unsecured', the agreement may be enforced by court order (see ante, para 24.27). Unfortunately, this dichotomy between 'fully secured', eg, a pledge or mortgage of sufficient value to secure the debt, on the one hand and 'partly secured'[1] or 'unsecured'[2] on the other is not defined in the Act:[3] first, there is some doubt as to the

---

4 For such automatic termination of agreement, see generally post, para 26.08.
5 Commonly, the loan or supply agreement was in the name of the deceased breadwinner, so compounding the difficulties of the family caused by the cessation of income.
6 In the definitions of 'debtor' and 'hirer': see s 189(1). See ante, para 5.24.
7 Eg, as to notices, repossession and court orders: see ante, para 24.27 *et seq.*
8 Under s 97, a 'debtor' is entitled to notice of a settlement figure: see further post, para 26.19A.
9 It would have saved much subtle learning if this provision had also applied on the insolvency of the buyer or hirer. However, matters have been improved by the Insolvency Act 1986: see ante, para 19.12.

[24.47]
1 See Goode, *Consumer Credit Law and Practice*, Div 11B, para 5.166.
2 Presumably, this includes loans and credit sales. What about promissory notes?
3 See Guest and Lloyd, *Encyclopedia of Consumer Credit*, para 2-087.

meaning of the word 'secured';[4] and second, it is uncertain whether the fully/partially dichotomy refers to (i) whether the security extends to the full debt or (ii) the market value of the security, eg, suppose the market value of the goods in less than the balance outstanding.[1]

However, the distinction is clearly important as determining the rights of the creditor or owner which may arise simply by reason of the death of the debtor or hirer. If the agreements is 'fully secured', s 86(1) deprives the creditor or owner of those rights, eg, to accelerate payments; whereas, if the agreement is only partly secured or unsecured, s 86(2) allows the creditor or owner to apply for a court order to that effect, though s 128 adds the rider that:

> The court shall make an order under s 86(2) if, but only if, the creditor or owner proves that he has been unable to satisfy himself that the present and future obligations of the debtor or hirer under the agreement are likely to be discharged.

However, in any event the scope of s 86 is somewhat limited. It basically applies to rights exercisable 'by reason of the death of the debtor or hirer';[5] and then only where the creditor or owner is entitled under the terms of the agreement to do one or more of the acts specified in s 87(1).[6] It neither prevents a creditor from 'treating the right to draw on any credit as restricted or deferred',[7] nor affects the operation of any agreement providing for payment of instalments out of any life insurance,[8] nor prevent repossession by reason of default (see post, para 24.48).

[24.48] The effect of death on payment obligations. Section 86 is directed solely towards rights of the creditor or owner arising by reason of the fact of death of the debtor or hirer (see ante, para 24.47): it does not suspend any of the rights of the creditor or owner to payment of instalments.[1] Even supposing the debtor or hirer is up to date with his payments at death, there is a considerable likelihood that one or more instalments will fall into arrears before anyone can act on his behalf. The CCA therefore extends to the deceased's personal representatives all the protections conferred on the debtor or hirer as previously outlined in this chapter (see ante, para 24.27 et seq), whilst allowing service of any requisite notice as if the debtor had not died.[2] Where there are protected goods (see ante, para 24.35) at the date of death, the CCA expressly provides that they shall continue to be so until the grant of probate or administration (s 90(6): see ante, para 24.37), upon which the personal representative will fall to be treated as the 'debtor' or 'hirer'.[3]

---

4   Does it refer to the s 189(1) definition of 'security' (see post, para 25.11), which will exclude hp and conditional sale?

5   See s 86(6). Or, if there are joint debtors or hirers, the death of any of them: s 185(4).

6   See ante, para 24.30. Thus, s 86 will not prevent the creditor or owner exercising any other right, eg, to inspect the goods.

7   Section 86(4). Eg, to prevent further withdrawals under an overdraft agreement. Cf s 76(4): see ante, para 24.28.

8   Section 86(5). For insurance arrangements, see post, para 24.48.

[24.48]

1   But for the remarkable effect of s 86(6)(b), see Goode, *Consumer Credit Law and Practice*, para 45.96.

2   Section 176(6). In practice, the requisite notices are likely to be received by the deceased's spouse.

3   Because 'debtor' and 'hirer' are defined by s 189(1) to include their assignees by operation of law. See ante, para 5.24.

Whilst the foregoing CCA provisions are no doubt a substantial improvement on their HPA counterparts, they would still appear to be open to the following criticism: it might have been much simpler and fairer if the CCA had deemed the agreement automatically paid up on the debtor's death, so effectively giving compulsory life insurance cover (see ante, para 24.45). Instead, the present practice is to offer Credit Protection Insurance (CPI) as an optional extra.[4] Unfortunately, this gives rise to some difficulties with the CCA;[5] the Act does not expressly deal with negative option system used to maximise insurance sales;[6] and there may be problems on the cancellation of credit insurances which are linked transactions.[7]

Conclusions

[24.49] The common law denied that a buyer or hirer under a conditional sale or hp agreement was a mortgagor with an equity of redemption (see ante, para 24.22). It followed that, if the supplier managed to recover the goods either by recaption or court action (see ante, paras 24.22–26), he could keep for himself any surplus; and he was not answerable to the buyer or hirer where he realised less than the best price obtainable. Indeed, under the present system, there is little incentive for the supplier to dispose of the goods at any price in excess of his loss on the transaction; but *contra* where he needs to claim damages from the buyer or hirer in which case the duty to mitigate will go some way towards encouraging him to seek a good price (for the duty to mitigate, see post, para 27.44).

However, the CCA has created in respect of regulated conditional sale and hp agreements[1] an untidy approximation to a statutory equity of redemption.[2] This certainly accords with the policy of the *Crowther Report*,[3] and has substantially reduced the advantage of repossession. The logical result of this must be as follows:

(1) The total charge for credit will increase for all debtors and hirers – the good payers paying for the bad within each class of business, eg, customers may be stratified into 'status' and 'non-status' (see ante, para 7.04A).

(2) Wherever the domestic consumer is an adequate risk, the financier may prefer to divorce his loan from the supply of goods. Sometimes, he will enter into a Personal

---

4   This enables the financier to give competitive quotations (excluding CPI) and collect valuable commission on the additional insurance: see [1994] 3 Which? 30. For an optional payment waiver clause, see *Humberclyde Finance Ltd v Thompson* (set out ante, para 5.22).

5   The CPI premium may turn the regulated transaction into a multiple agreement (see ante, para 5.27).

6   This does not contravene the ordinary inertia selling rules (see ante, para 8.18). However, the OFT Director has threatened (eg (1993) 10 Tr LR 56) that, if inertia selling of CPI continues, he will use against it his CCA licensing powers (see ante, para 6.17) or Part III assurances (see ante, para 6.07); and he has suggested that such a prohibition should be included in trade codes of practice (ante, para 3.13).

7   See the regulations made under s 19(4) (see ante, para 5.31): Jones, *Credit Cards*, 71–72; (1993) 48 CC 1/13).

[24.49]

1   But not consumer hiring agreements, where the only relief for the hirer is provided under s 132: see post, para 27.23.

2   See Bridge [1992] JBL at 16–17; and ante, para 24.27–43.

3   Para 5.2.15. *Quaere* whether it would have been more satisfactory to convert all hp and conditional sales into chattel mortgages? See the *Crowther Report*, paras 5.2.5–7, 5.4.3, and ante, para 1.26.

Loan, which will deprive him of his security, but escape the 50% rule (s 100: see post, para 27.49). At other times, he may prefer running account credit, eg, a credit card (see also (4) below).

(3) Where security is indicated, a second mortgage of realty may be the preferred alternative,[4] with simple hiring agreements as a possible commercial alternative.[5]

(4) Particularly in relation to goods of a small unit value, it may be that the advantages of repossession have been so reduced that suppliers will instead prefer the unsecured credit sale or loan;[6] and creditors will favour the commercial advantages of running account credit, eg, a credit card, especially repeat business. The danger is that this has been achieved by accident rather than conscious policy, thereby reducing the chance of marginal customers obtaining such credit or increasing the cost of that credit.

(5) Inevitably, with every extra statutory restriction, there will be an increase in the number of domestic consumers who are such bad financial risks that they cannot obtain financial accommodation within the law at any price.[7] For them, the illegal lender and the 'baseball bat' method of collection.[8]

---

4   Where large sums are lent to householders to finance, eg, central heating, double glazing. See generally post, para 25.19. A similar result is achievable by making unsecured credit available to a householder, but on default placing a charging order on his house (see post, para 27.04).

5   Particularly favoured as regards goods with a high rate of obsolescence and servicing, eg, computers.

6   He may sue in debt (see post, para 27.15A *et seq*). It must be remembered that retention of title is often regarded as important for psychological as much as legal reasons.

7   As to extortionate credit bargaining, see post, para 29.40 *et seq*.

8   Cayne and Trebilcock (1973) 23 UTLJ 396, at 418–19; OFT, *Vulnerable Consumers and Financial Services* (1999), para 400. As to loan sharking, see ante, para 6.20.

CHAPTER 25

SECURITY FOR PERFORMANCE

SECURITY IN GENERAL

[25.01] This chapter will deal with the ways in which the supplier of goods can obtain security in respect of the performance by the other party of the latter's contractual obligations, which are principally to take delivery (see ante, para 23.08 *et seq*) and pay the price or rent (see post, para 27.16). Such security may be personal or real, and the various forms of security can often be used cumulatively.

1 *Personal security.* This offers the supplier a further action against a third party[1] and is fairly commonplace in instalment credit transactions, particularly when there is some doubt as to the efficacy of the legal obligation upon the buyer, hirer or borrower, eg, where he is a minor (see ante, para 10.18) or as to his financial status.[2] Personal security may take the form of requiring a third party to go surety for, or insure, the buyer, hirer or borrower (see post, paras 25.04; 25.14), or of a wage assignment;[3] and, particularly when the desire of a commercial buyer, hirer or borrower to make prompt payment (rather than his ability to pay) is questionable, the supplier may insist on his accepting bills of exchange or giving post-dated cheques for the instalments.[4]

2 *Real security.* This offers the creditor the right to look to particular property for the satisfaction of his debt in preference to the debtor's general creditors; and it is particularly useful in the debtor's insolvency (see ante, para 19.22). However, from the legal viewpoint a clear distinction must be drawn between two types of secured credit:[5]

 (a) *Supply credit.* Whilst undoubtedly creating a debt,[6] price deferment or rental due has always been regarded by English law as essentially different from loan credit (see below).[7] The major methods by which the purchase money 'lender' may seek to ensure payment of the deferred price or rent by *retaining* possession or property were considered in Chapter 24: they escaped the Bills of Sale Acts;[8] and, when property retention leads to resale, any surplus belongs to the supplier.[9]

[25.01]

1 Sometimes the supplier will separately buy the protection, as by taking out insurance against bad debts, eg, with trade indemnity (for domestic supplies) or the ECGD (for export sales).

2 Eg, where the buyer or hirer is a student, or is not a householder. As to married women, this may cause trouble with the Sex Discrimination Act 1975: see ante, para 4.23.

3 In the UK, wage assignments are more commonly used only after breach: see further post, para 27.05.

4 For bills of exchange, see ante, para 7.24; and for CCA regulation, see post, para 25.09. The advantage of taking a bill or cheque from the buyer or hirer lies in the simplified enforcement procedure available on default: see Butterworths edn, 1989, para 23.14A.

5 See Goode, *Commercial Law* (2nd edn), p 637.

6 For contracts of loan, see generally Chapter 7.

7 SGA s 62(4) (see ante, para 1.02) only applies to sham sales: see further post, paras 25.29; 25.33.

8 *McEntire v Crossley Bros* (set out ante, para 1.14A).

9 See *Armour v Thyssen* (set out ante, para 20.29).

(b) *Loan credit*. Where a debt does not arise out of a contract for the supply of goods, the lender may seek by *taking* possession or property to ensure payment (see post, para 25.02); and where the lender's acquisition of property rights leads to sale, any surplus value belongs to the debtor.

[25.02] Consensual real security for loans. These are rights over property granted by agreement[1] as a form of security for a loan:[2] they are not absolute rights, but conditional, collateral and outside the SGA (s 62(4): set out ante, para 1.08). The rights are **conditional** in the sense that they exist only to secure the payment of the debt, or the performance of some other obligation, and are discharged by that payment or performance. The rights are **collateral** in that they do not replace the primary obligation: if, for instance, the sale of an item pledged does not realise sufficient to pay off the secured debt, the debtor remains liable for the difference. Strictly, only three types of consensual real security are known to English law.[3]

1   *A pledge* is made by the deposit of personal property by way of security.[4] It is essential to the validity of a pledge that possession should have passed to the secured party (pledgee): it follows that it is not possible to pledge a pure intangible such as a chose in action (see ante, para 7.16). A pledge may be created where the goods are deposited before the sum to be loaned is agreed or advanced.[5] However, a mere agreement to pledge (hypothecation) creates only an equitable charge (see below): this does not operate as a pledge until delivery (see post, para 25.16); and it is inferior to a pledge in that it may be defeated under the *nemo dat* rule by a bfp.[6] Unlike a lien (see ante, paras 1.23; 24.08), a pledge is invariably created by agreement and gives the pledgee a special property in the goods pledged (see post, para 25.15). The normal remedy of a pledgee of goods is sale, not foreclosure.[7]

2   *A mortgage* involves a transfer by way of security of legal or equitable ownership in either realty or personalty by the owner/borrower (mortgagor) to another (the mortgagee) upon the express or implied condition that the asset be reconveyed when the sum secured had been paid (see post, para 25.20). Initially, the mortgagee's ownership is subject to the mortgagor's equity of redemption;[8] but after the mortgagor's default the mortgagee may extinguish (foreclose) that equity and become the absolute owner of the property (see post, para 25.20). Theoretically, it is this right of foreclosure which at common law distinguishes a mortgage from a pledge (see

---

[25.02]

1   Distinguish (a) purely **personal** rights, eg, set-off (see ante, para 7.23), retention of deposit (see post, para 27.20); (b) **reservation of title** and the rights it confers (see ante, para 25.01); (c) rights granted by operation of law, eg, liens (see below).

2   These rights against property have been described as rights of pursuit and preference: Goode, *Commercial Law* (2nd edn), p 673.

3   Goode, *ibid*, p 642.

4   See FA, s 1(5). Cf the Indian Contracts Act 1872, s 172 (now repealed). As to the consideration necessary for a pledge, see FA, s 5: ante, para 21.33.

5   *Blundell-Leigh v Attenborough* [1921] 3 KB 235, CA.

6   See *Harrold v Plenty* [1901] 2 Ch 314 (deposit of share certificate created only a charge). This equitable right will on principle give way to a bfp of the legal interest, notwithstanding the *nemo dat* rule (see ante, para 19.11).

7   See Oditah, *Receivables Financing*, p 83. As to trust receipts, see post, para 25.16.

8   See Jones, *Chattel Mortgages* (6th edn), paras 937–51. See further post, para 27.19.

post, para 25.26. But see s 120(1)(a) of the CCA: post, para 25.18). As the mortgagee was not required to take possession, the mortgage was an extremely flexible instrument: it could be applied to all classes of assets (land, goods and intangibles), and even to after-acquired property (*Holroyd v Marshall*: set out ante, para 9.05). However, in practice a mortgagor will normally remain in possession of the mortgaged property during the currency of the mortgage, which has led to the following conclusion:[9] 'in short, the essence of a pledge is the transfer of possession; of a mortgage, the transfer of property'.

3   *A charge* does not depend on either delivery of possession (a pledge) or the transfer of ownership (a mortgage), but upon an agreement between the creditor and debtor that the creditor may look to the proceeds of a disposal of an asset owned by the debtor which he charges to discharge his indebtedness.[10] Such an encumbrance on goods cannot exist at common law;[11] but it can be created in relation to both real and personal property by statute or equity (see post, para 25.20), which recognise that a charge may be one of two sorts:[12]

(a) *A fixed (or specific) charge.* Without more, this fastens on ascertained or ascertainable property, so that on default the chargee may recoup the debt thereby secured by selling the charged property (see ante, para 19.21).

(b) *A floating charge* hovers over the class of property it is intended to affect until some event occurs which causes it to fasten on all property then within that category (see post, para 25.25), so allowing the debtor-company prior to such an event to manage and dispose of the shifting assets in the ordinary course of its business without specific permission.

[25.03] Regulated agreements. The statutory restrictions on security rights (see ante, para 25.02) were scattered all over the statute book. However, in respect of regulated agreements (ante, para 5.13), the CCA for the first time attempted to collect those restrictions together in one place. Part VIII of the Act contains a coherent pattern of rules governing the taking and enforcement of security. It deals carefully with attempts to take both personal sureties (see post, paras 25.04–14) and pledges (see post, paras 25.15–18); but unfortunately, the pattern is a peculiarly lop-sided one. It will be recalled that the rules relating to rights against goods were to be left to the – as yet to be enacted – Lending and Security Act (see ante, para 5.03). Apart from some special provisions for second mortgages of land (see post, para 25.24), the chattel mortgage rules to be considered later (see post, para 25.19 *et seq*) therefore remain largely untouched by the CCA. Instead, the Act concentrates on ways in which the supplier may obtain personal rights against his transferee (see ante, paras 24.21–48) or a third party (see post, para 25.04–14). For this purpose, it defines 'security' very widely, terms the person who gives that security 'a surety' and a document embodying that security a 'security instrument' (see, post, paras 25.11; 25.12).

---

9   Goode, *HP Law and Practice* (2nd edn), p 536; and post, para 25.26.

10   This depends on the proper construction of the contract: *Smith v Bridgend CBC* [2002] 1 All ER 292, HL, *per* Lord Scott at para 53. See Megarry and Wade, *Law of Real Property* (6th edn), para 19-005.

11   Oditah, *op cit*, note 7, 95; and ante, para 2.13.

12   *Re Atlantic Computer Systems plc* (set out ante, para 19.19), *per* Nicholls LJ at AER 493–94; *Smith v Bridgend CBC* (above), *per* Lord Scott at paras 60, 63. For the borderline between fixed and floating charges, see Berg [2001] JBL 532; and post, para 25.25. For attempts to convert fixed into floating charges and vice versa, see ante, para 19.22.

PERSONAL SECURITY

Introduction

[25.04] It is fairly common in instalment credit transactions for the 'lender' to insist on the security of some personal rights of action against a third party in the event of default by the hirer or buyer.[1] Whilst it is true that since 1970 there has been an apparently viable system for the attachment of earnings (see post, para 27.05), that system is only available in respect of debts where there is a court order following a default in payment. Hence, there seems little possibility of obtaining such an order as security for payment when the credit transaction is set up; and, as the system only has significance as a remedy, it is considered later (post, para 27.05 *et seq*). This matter aside, the obvious form of personal security is a surety. Insofar as the government may contemplate acting as guarantor, say for the credit granted to public bodies or export credit guarantees, prior approval may be needed from the European Commission.[2]

[25.05] Types of surety. Sureties of instalment credit transactions will usually fall into one of the following categories: (a) a friend or relative of the hirer or buyer; or (b) a dealer or supplier signing a recourse provision (see ante, para 16.21); or (c) a director of the hiring or buying company;[1] or (d) one who makes a business of guaranteeing debts, eg, export credit guarantees (see ante, para 23.14). In any particular transaction, there may be sureties from any or all of these classes; and the owner, seller or lender may use any of the following techniques to achieve his object:

1   *Co-principals*. Particularly where the surety belongs to category (a), the 'lender' may make him a party to the supply contract,[2] a device commonly employed in instalment contracts where the first 'borrower' is a minor (see ante, para 10.18) and with credit cards.[3] It also makes it easier for the creditor to avoid having the transaction upset on grounds that he has constructive notice of any undue influence.[4] If the intention is that he should act as guarantor, the surety's liability is conditional on default by his

---

[25.04]

1   Eg, the provision of insurance (see ante, para 24.21). The alternative strategy is to sell the bad debt: see post, para 27.02.

2   Because of the competition implications (see generally ante, para 2.13).

[25.05]

1   Eg, *Silverburn Finance (UK) Ltd v Salt* [2001] 2 All ER (Comm) 438, CA.

2   Eg, *HFC Bank plc v Grossbard* [2001] 3 CL 313, Cty Ct. For joint obligations, see *Chitty on Contract* (28th edn), p 18.

3   For co-debtors on credit cards, see ante, para 7.10. Co-debtors under regulated cards share the CCA protections: see ante, paras 5.24, 7.12; and post, para 25.08.

4   *CIBC Mortgages plc v Pitt* [1993] 4 All ER 433, HL (see 110 LQR at 169). Their Lordships distinguished this situation from that of a guarantee (see post, para 25.06) on the grounds that in the latter case there is an increased risk of undue influence over a cohabitee because the transaction does not involve a joint advance and hence is not for the surety's financial benefit (at 441j).

co-principal;[5] but, if it is intended that he be a genuine principal, his liability may be joint only, or both joint and several,[6] eg, category (d) (see ante, para 19.25).

2   *Indorsees.* A form more frequently used with sureties from categories (b), (c) and (d) is to require them to 'back' (indorse) a bill of exchange drawn by the debtor.[7] Since the Cheques Act 1992, this form is most unlikely to arise in consumer transactions, category (a) (see post, para 25.09).

3   *Guarantors.* Into whatever category the surety may fall, a common technique is to require[8] the surety to guarantee[9] the principal contract.[10] On default by the principal 'debtor', the 'creditor' will then usually have the choice whether to sue the debtor or his guarantor (see post, para 25.06). Because guarantors of category (a) so frequently undertake guarantees for altruistic motives, the courts have adopted a protective attitude towards them, often insisting on precise compliance by the creditor with all relevant technical rules before he can succeed against the guarantor.[11] That aside, in recent years there has in domestic supply transactions been a significant increase in the activities of the above category (d) business, particularly in connection with the acceptance by retailers of cheques (see ante, para 23.14). First, for cheques below a stipulated minimum size, the clearing banks have introduced cheque guarantee cards (see ante, para 2.26). Second, above that figure a credit reference agency operates the following system: the retailer may obtain telephone approval, after which the agency guarantees the cheque.[12]

Sureties of unregulated agreements[1]

[25.06] Many of the difficulties in this subject may be traced back to the Statute of Frauds 1677; and to the distinction drawn in consequence of that provision between a surety who guarantees performance by the principal debtor, and one who takes the primary obligation upon himself by agreeing to indemnify the creditor. The distinction between contracts of guarantee and of indemnity is a question which is both important in law and uncertain in practice. For instance, the courts have had some difficulty in deciding to

---

5   Equity may regard him as a surety: *Overend, Gurney & Co v Oriental Financial Corp* (1874) LR 7 HL 348.

6   See further Goode, *HP Law and Practice* (2nd edn), p 471.

7   This would avoid the past consideration rule which might be troublesome with guarantors (see below): Bills of Exchange Act 1882, s 27(1)(b). See further Butterworths edn, 1989, para 25.05.

8   It will usually be safer for the lender to negotiate directly with the surety to avoid any taint of undue influence or fraud: see *Bank of Baroda v Shah* [1988] 3 All ER 24, CA.

9   Eg, cheque guarantee cards (see ante, para 2.26). Distinguish the completely different 'manufacturer's guarantee': see ante, see para 18.26.

10 Beware of the past consideration rule: see *Astley Industrial Trust Ltd v Grimston Ltd* (1965) 109 Sol Jo 149. It could be side stepped by getting the surety to: (i) back a bill of exchange (see above); or (ii) enter a deed (see ante, para 9.01).

11 Eg, *Levett v Barclays Bank plc* [1995] 2 All ER 615 (non-disclosure). The fact that this consideration does not apply to types (b) and (c) obviously causes difficulty with precedents.

12 The Transax system offered by Equifax: see (1995) 49 CC 6/27.

[25.06]

1   See generally Goode, *Commercial Law* (2nd edn), p 30; Goode, *Legal Problems of Credit and Security*, 3; Treitel, *Law of Contract* (10th edn), pp 165–70.

which class a surety belongs, where he is a friend of the borrower, hirer or buyer, or a dealer under a recourse provision.[2] We must now examine the position of the surety.

1   *Liability.* The surety will not be liable unless the other party's loss is caused by the act in respect of which he has agreed to act as surety[3] and unless any condition precedent to which his promise is subject has been fulfilled.[4] Further, the liability of a guarantor, but not of an indemnifier (nor signatory on a bill of exchange: see ante, para 25.05) is also subject to the following restrictions: a guarantee must be evidenced by a signed note or memorandum;[5] it is necessary for the secured party first to call on the borrower, hirer or buyer to make good his default (*Moschi v Lep Air Services Ltd* [1973] AC 331, HL); and at common law the guarantor's liability is co-extensive with that of the borrower, hirer or buyer.[6] However, the gap between guarantees and indemnities has been narrowed by statute, especially with regard to category (a) (see ante, para 25.04): guarantees of minor's contracts have become more onerous, in that they are enforceable even though the minor's contract is not enforceable against him (s 2 of the Minors' Contracts Act 1987: see ante, para 10.18), eg, cheque guarantee card issued to a minor; whilst indemnities have been rendered less onerous generally in that, as against a surety 'dealing as consumer', they are subjected to the test of reasonableness (s 4 of the UCTA: see ante, para 18.25) and equated with guarantees with regard to most regulated agreements (see post, para 25.07).

2   *Rights.* (See post, para 25.07.)

3   *Discharge.* The surety may be discharged from liability under his contract of guarantee in any of the ways in which a contract can normally be discharged (see post, Chapter 26), including all the following: by a plea of *non est factum* (see ante, para 10.16), by a variation (see post, para 26.21), by a misrepresentation (see post, paras 26.12–14), or by undue influence.[7] In addition, there are a number of situations where a surety may be discharged in pursuance of the rule that the creditor must not do anything to prejudice the rights of the surety (see above) without his consent: for example, where the supplier releases the borrower, hirer or buyer;[7a] or there is a novation or material alteration in the terms of the supply agreement;[8] or possibly a waiver of its terms.[9] Where the supply agreement is terminated, a surety who has agreed to indemnify the creditor, owner or seller may be liable for the full debt or 'price'; but a guarantor is

---

2   Cf *Western Credit Ltd v Alberry* [1964] 2 All ER 938, CA (guarantee); and *Goulston Discount Ltd v Clark* [1967] 2 QB 493, CA (indemnity).

3   *Bentworth Finance Ltd v Lubert* (set out ante, para 15.23); *United Dominions Trust Ltd v Beech* [1972] 1 Lloyd's Rep 546; *Perrylease Ltd v Imecar AG* [1987] 2 All ER 373.

4   *Midland Counties Motor Finance Ltd v Slade* [1951] 1 KB 346, CA; *James Graham & Co (Timber) Ltd v Southgate Sands* [1985] 2 All ER 344, CA; *Associated Japanese Bank (International) Ltd v Credit du Nord* [1988] 3 All ER 902. Eg, cheque guarantee card conditions (see ante, para 25.05).

5   1677 Act, s 4; *The Maria D* [1992] 1 AC 21, HL.

6   Eg, *Stadium Finance Ltd v Helm* (1965) 109 SJ 471, CA. And see Steyn (1974) 90 LQR 246.

7   *Barclays Bank plc v O'Brien* [1994] 1 AC 180, HL (Battersby (1995) 15 Legal Studies 35; Chandler 111 LQR 51); *Royal Bank of Scotland v Etridge (No 2)* [2001] 4 All ER 449, HL (62 QA 15).

7a   *Lloyd's TSB plc v Shorney* [2001] unreported, CA.

8   *Raiffeisen ZO AG v Crossseas Shipping Ltd* [2000] 1 All ER 76, CA. But see *Lombard Finance Ltd v Brookplain Trading Ltd* [1991] 2 All ER 762, CA (immaterial); *Samuels Finance Group v Beechmanor* [1995] CLY 402, CA (variation clause).

9   See *Midland Counties Motor Finance Ltd v Slade* (above). Distinguish a waiver by the surety of his right to discharge: see Goode, *Legal Problems of Credit and Security*, pp 66–68. The general effect of a waiver is considered post, para 26.23.

only liable to a maximum[10] of the accrued liabilities of the borrower, hirer or buyer.[11] Failure by the creditor to sell any security for its market value will be treated as if he had obtained that market value.[12]

[25.07] Rights of a surety. The surety who meets his liability under a contract of suretyship (see ante, para 25.05) has certain rights against the other parties.[1]

1   *As against the buyer, hirer or borrower,* the surety has a right of indemnity[2] in respect of sums paid out in discharge of his obligations under the contract of surety.[3] This right of indemnity may be granted to the surety expressly; or it may be implied, as where the surety undertook the obligation at the request of the borrower, hirer or buyer. *Contra* where the suretyship is a form of dealer recourse (see ante, para 16.22).

2   *As against the supplier,* the surety has the right to secure his discharge by paying the amount due (see ante, para 25.06); but he has no right to insist that the supplier first exercise any power of sale over mortgaged property.[4] However, the guarantor does have the right of exercising any set-off or counterclaim against a supplier that would have been available to a hirer or buyer.[5] When the surety pays the supplier, he is further entitled[6] to a right of subrogation;[7] that is, the supplier must assign (s 5, Mercantile Law Amendment Act 1856) to him all his rights against the hirer or buyer, including any securities,[8] insofar as those rights are not purely personal ones.[9]

3   *As against a co-surety,* the surety may have a right of contribution,[10] a rule which may operate between the different categories of surety above mentioned, even if unaware of each other's existence (see ante, para 25.04).

---

10 See *Hewison v Ricketts* (set out post, para 27.19).
11 *Western Credit Ltd v Alberry* (above: lawful termination by hirer); *Hyundai Heavy Industries Ltd v Papadopoulos* [1980] 2 All ER 29, HL (instalment of price due before cancellation). Difficulties have arisen over guarantees open-ended as to amount: Banking Ombudsman, AR 1990–91, Part 6.
12 *Skipton BS v Stott* [2000] 2 All ER 779, CA. Cf mitigation (see post, para 27.45).

[25.07]
1   For the situation where the surety assumed the obligation without antecedent request from a party to the transaction, see *Owen v Tate* [1976] QB 402, CA.
2   And see his rights in equity: *Ascherson v Tredegar Dry Dock and Wharf Co Ltd* [1909] 2 Ch 401.
3   This right was not affected by the fact that the liability was not enforceable against the debtor because of an infringement of the Moneylenders Acts (now repealed: see ante, para 6.09): *Re Chetwynd's Estate* [1938] Ch 13, CA. Would the same result follow under s 113 of the CCA (see post, para 25.14)? See *Chitty on Contract* (28th edn), vol 2, paras 44-100, note 72.
4   *China and South Sea Bank Ltd v Tan* [1990] AC 536, PC (a mortgagee of shares is under no duty to exercise his power of sale in a falling market: see generally, post, para 25.25).
5   *Sterling Industrial Facilities Ltd v Lydiate Textiles Ltd* (1962) 106 SJ 669, CA. Cf *American Express International Banking Corp v Hurley* [1985] 3 All ER 564. *Contra* a cross-claim: *Indrisie v General Credit* [1985] VR 251, SC of Vict.
6   Except in so far as he has expressly or impliedly waived such right: *Re Lord Churchill* (1888) 39 Ch D 174.
7   Much the same result may be achieved by taking a counter-indemnity: *Barclays Bank Ltd v TOSG Trust Fund Ltd* [1984] 1 All ER 628, CA.
8   *Prima facie,* any surplus realised from those securities must be paid over to the principal debtor: but see *L Lucas Ltd v Export Credit Guarantee Dept* [1974] 2 All ER 889, HL.
9   *Chatterton v Maclean* [1951] 1 All ER 761. Cf ante, para 7.26.
10 *Stimpson v Smith* (1999) 149 NLJ 414, CA. See generally Goode, *Commercial Law* (2nd edn), pp 840–41.

Sureties of regulated agreements

[25.08] Whilst the HPA 1938 offered little protection to sureties, their position was considerably improved by the HPA 1964, and further protected by the CCA. Of course, this protection is only available to persons who act as sureties of regulated agreements;[1] and in that context, it must be considered in relation to each of the following three surety techniques (already explained: see ante, para 25.04).

1 *Co-principals.* In all cases where there is more than one debtor or hirer (see ante, para 5.24), s 185(1) provides as follows:

> Where an actual or prospective regulated agreement has two or more debtors or hirers (not being a partnership or an unincorporated body of persons) –
>
> (a) anything required by or under this Act to be done in relation to the debtor or hirer shall be done in relation to each of them; and
>
> (b) anything done under this Act by or on behalf of one of them shall have effect as if done by or on behalf of all of them.

It should be noticed that this provision does not apply where the debtor or hirer is a partnership or other unincorporated association:[2] in these cases, whether the act of one binds another depends on the ordinary law.[3] These aside, s 185 does two things. First, where the Act requires the doing of something to the debtors or hirers, it must be done in relation to all of them,[4] except where they have dispensed with the periodic notices prescribed under s 78(4) for running account credit.[5] Second, when the Act allows something to be done by the debtors or hirers, any one of them may generally act on behalf of all of them,[6] but each debtor or hirer must usually sign the regulated agreement individually,[7] a rule extending to enforcement orders;[8] and the death of any of them triggers the death provisions (ss 86, 185(4): see ante, para 24.48). Finally, the sections makes special provision for the situation where one joint debtor or hirer is a body corporate,[9] with suitable amendment to the signature rule (s 185(6)).

2 *Indorsees* (see post, paras 25.09–10).

3 *Guarantors* (see post, paras 25.11–12).

[25.08]

1 Subject to the rules of court, all the parties to a regulated agreement must he before the court (s 141(5): see ante, para 24.39).

2 Even though the association would usually be an 'individual' within s 189(1): see ante, para 5.24.

3 For partnership, see Partnership Act 1890, s 6; for unincorporated associations, see the law of agency; and further Goode, *Consumer Credit Law and Practice*, paras 44.9–10.

4 See ante, para 5.24. For some difficult cases, see Goode, *ibid*, paras 44.4–5.

5 Section 185(2). So second joint credit card holders may dispense with a second copy of the monthly statement: see ante, para 7.12. For s 78(4), see ante, para 7.08.

6 Section 185(5): see ante, para 5.24. Eg, consent to repossession (see ante, para 24.37); statutory right of termination (see post, paras 26.06–07). For some difficult cases, see Goode, *op cit*, note 3, para 44.7.

7 Sections 61(1)(a), 185(3). Except in the case of a partnership or unincorporated association (s 61(4)): see ante, para 9.13.

8 Sections 127(3), 185(3): see ante, para 9.20.

9 Section 185(5): see ante, para 5.24.

[25.09/10] Indorsees. The use of bills of exchange to reinforce the consumer's payment obligations under instalment credit transactions has long been a cause of concern;[1] such bills were commonly negotiated even before the supply of the goods or services for which they were issued; and the consumer could then find himself committed to pay a holder in due course despite the supplier's breach, because such holder took free of any equities the consumer might have against his supplier.[2] The CCA sought to tackle this problem, not by attacking concept of a holder in due course, but by making it difficult for any bill or cheque issued in such circumstances ever to come into the hands of such a person (s 125(1)). Section 123 took the following two steps:[3]

(1) To prohibit the taking by way of payment of negotiable instruments in general (see ante, para 7.24). Section 123(1) provides:

> A creditor or owner shall not take a negotiable instrument,[4] other than a bank note[5] or cheque,[6] in discharge of any sum payable –[7]
>
> (a) by the debtor or hirer under a regulated agreement, or
>
> (b) by any person as surety in relation to the agreement.[8]

(2) A general prohibition on negotiating cheques otherwise than to a banker.[9]

The consequences of non-compliance is that the instrument and any security are normally enforceable on an order of the court only.[10]

Nowadays, it will be even less likely that the problems tackled by s 123 will arise. This is because, since the Cheques Act 1992, most banks no longer issue to their customers cheque forms which are negotiable, but instead non-negotiable ones under the 1992 Act (see ante, para 7.28).

[25.11] Guarantors. Whilst the HPA 1938 offered little protection to sureties of agreements within its ambit, their position was considerably improved by the HPA 1964, which assimilated the treatment of guarantees and indemnities as regards a limited range of safeguards. The CCA has gone much further, and now 'provides a reasonably comprehensive pattern of protection for guarantors and indemnifiers' of regulated

---

[25.09/10]

1 Eg, in relation to central heating and double glazing: Goode, *Consumer Credit Law and Practice*, para 37.161.

2 For holders in due course, see ante, para 7.24. *Contra* the position of an assignee: see ante, para 7.23.

3 Section 123 does not apply to (i) non-commercial agreements (s 123(5): as to these, see ante, para 5.18); (ii) international trade exempted by statutory order (s 123(6): cf UCTA, s 26 – see ante, para 18.15).

4 It therefore does not apply to cheques worded 'not negotiable' or postal orders, where it is not needed because there cannot be a holder in due course (see ante, para 7.24).

5 This will amount to legal tender: see ante, para 23.13.

6 Does this include post-dated cheques? See Goode, *op cit*, note 1, para 37.164.

7 Nor may this rule be circumvented by taking the negotiable instrument by way of security instead of payment: s 123(3), (4); Goode, *op cit*, note 1, para 37.166; and see generally Butterworths edn, 1989, para 23.14A.

8 See generally post, para 25.11.

9 Section 123(2). Usually a bank will only act as agent for collection and not itself become a holder of the cheque.

10 Section 124. Is the effect that it is 'not properly executed' (see ante, para 9.19)?

agreements,[1] subsuming both these common law categories under the expression 'surety', which is defined as follows by s 189(1):

> ... the person by whom any security is provided, or the person to whom his rights and duties in relation to the security have passed by assignment or operation of law.

However, the definition of 'security' is limited to that 'provided by the debtor or hirer or at his request',[2] which will effectively limit it to category (a) (see ante, para 25.05). Within that limitation, s 113(1) prevents the creditor or owner side-stepping the protection of the CCA by laying down that a security:

> ... shall not be enforced so as to benefit the creditor or owner, directly or indirectly, to an extent greater ... than would be the case if the security were not provided.

Without this provision, a creditor could simply sue an indemnifier to extract his full common law rights, leaving the indemnifier to recoup his loss from the debtor (see ante, para 25.07). However, the effect of s 113(1) is to deprive an indemnity of its principle advantage over a guarantee (see ante, para 25.06) and restrict the creditor to amounts recoverable by him from the debtor,[3] whether that security is provided in relation to any actual or prospective regulated agreement[4] or linked transaction.[5] Where a regulated agreement is enforceable only by court order, any security is not enforceable unless and until such enforcement order has been made.[6] However, there is an important saving from s 113(1) where the debtor or hirer is a minor, so that s 113(1) will not render the agreement unenforceable simply by reason of his minority.[7]

Besides making substantial provisions as to the formalities and enforcement of such 'securities' (see post, paras 25.12–14), the CCA also brings them within the following protections: the duty to provide information and copies during the continuance of the agreement;[8] service of default notice on the surety (s 87(1)(e): set out ante, para 24.30), together with copies of default or non-default[9] notices served on the debtor or hirer (s 111); time orders;[10] and extortionate credit bargains.[11]

[25.12] Formalities. In favour of a surety who has provided security in respect of a regulated agreement (see ante, para 25.11), the CCA provides protection in relation to the

---

[25.11]

1 Goode, *Consumer Credit Law and Practice*, para 37.64.
2 'Security' is widely defined by s 189(1) to mean 'a mortgage, charge, pledge, bond, debenture, indemnity, guarantee, bill, note or other right'. For criticism of this definition, see Goode, *ibid*.
3 Would the duty to mitigate (see post, para 27.44) enable a surety to make an offer for the repossessed goods (47 CC 6/25)?
4 Section 113(1)). For examples of the operation of s 113(1), see Goode, *op cit*, note 1, paras 37.196–99.
5 Section 113(8). See *Citibank International plc v Schleider* [1999] CLY 2505.
6 Section 113(2). As whether this might enfringe the Human Rights Act, see *Wilson v First County Trust Ltd* (set out ante, para 9.20), *per* Morritt VC at 151.
7 Section 113(7), as amended by the Minors' Contracts Act 1987, s 4. Without this saving, it would be impossible for the creditor or owner to take an effective security in respect of minors' regulated agreements (see ante, para 10.18), making it difficult for minors to obtain credit.
8 Sections 107, 108, 109, 110. For the counterpart duties towards a debtor or hirer, see ante, para 15.17.
9 Section 111. For non-default notices, see ante, para 24.29 and post, para 26.10.
10 Section 129(1)(c): see ante, para 24.40.
11 Section 139: see post, para 29.40.

formalities connected with the formation of the security agreement. Just as a regulated agreement must be in writing in the prescribed form (see ante, para 9.09), so must any security provided at the request of the debtor or hirer (see ante, para 25.11) by a third party:[1] the 'security instrument' must be expressed in writing (s 105(1)) in the prescribed form (s 105(2)) containing the prescribed information (ss 105(2), (3)). Further, ss 105(4) and (5) of the Act lay down that the security instrument is not properly executed unless it complies with the foregoing, embodies all the express terms of the security,[2] is signed 'by or on behalf of the surety'[3] 'in the prescribed manner', ie, in the Regulations, and that the debtor or hirer receive copies of both the security instrument and regulated agreement.[4] The sole (s 170(1): see ante, para 10.19) penalty for non-compliance with the above rules is that (s 105(7)):

> ... the security, so far as provided in relation to a regulated agreement, is enforceable against the surety on an order of the court only.

At any time before court action, a seven day notice must be served on the surety.[5] When the case comes before the court, the position depends on whether or not the defect is on 'technical grounds only', a test already discussed (see ante, para 9.19): if so, the position is governed by s 127 (see ante, para 24.27); whereas, if there is a substantive infringement, then s 105(8) provides that the case shall fall within s 106 (see post, para 25.13).

[25.13/14] Enforcement. The scheme of the Act is to bring within s 106 any security which it wishes to invalidate. Section 106 provides as follows:[1]

> Where, under any provision of this Act, this section is applied to any security provided in relation to a regulated agreement, then, subject to section 177[2] ...
>
> (a) the security, so far as it is so provided, shall be treated as never having effect;
>
> (b) any property lodged with the creditor or owner solely for the purposes of the security as so provided shall be returned by him forthwith;
>
> (c) the creditor or owner shall take any necessary action to remove or cancel an entry in any register, so far as the entry relates to the security as so provided; and
>
> (d) any amount received by the creditor or owner on realisation of the security shall, so far as it is referable to the agreement, be repaid to the surety.

[25.12]

1 These rules do not apply to a security provided by the debtor or hirer (s 105(6)), which are governed by s 60(1): s 105(9); and ante, para 9.10.

2 Under the Consumer Credit (Guarantees and Indemnities) Regulations 1983, SI 1556, the security instruments must contain, *inter alia*, a statement alerting the surety to the fact that he may have to pay instead of the debtor and drawing his attention to the availability of advice from *Trading Standards Depts and CABx*.

3 Section 105(4). Compare regulated agreements, which must be signed by the debtor or hirer personally (s 61(1)): see ante, para 9.13.

4 Section 105(4)(d), (5). Cf the rules for service of copies on the debtor or hirer: see ante, para 9.14 *et seq*.

5 As to default notices, see ss 87(1)(e), 111 (see ante, paras 24.30; 25.26). As to non-default notices, see Goode, *Consumer Credit Law and Practice*, 37.191.

[25.13/14]

1 Subject to the human rights point: see ante, para 25.11, note 6.

2 Savings for registered land charges: see post, para 25.24.

The section applies to securities in all the following cases (s 113(3)):

(1) Where the regulated agreement is cancelled under s 69,[3] or terminated by s 91 because of the repossession of protected goods (see ante, para 24.38).

(2) Except on technical grounds only, where an application to a County Court (see ante, para 24.39) to enforce a security is dismissed for breach of s 105 (s 105(8): see further ante, para 25.11), because the agreement was made by an unlicensed trader[4] or credit broker,[5] by reason of the fact that it was improperly executed,[6] or that it involved a negotiable instrument in breach of s 123,[7] or upon refusal of an enforcement order under s 142(2) (see ante, para 24.33. But see s 113(4)). As to where the security is a land mortgage, see s 126 (post, para 25.24); as to minors, see s 113(7) (ante, para 25.11).

(3) According to s 113(6), a surety may withdraw[8] at any time before the making of the regulated agreement for which he was to stand surety by giving notice to the creditor or owner,[9] in which case the security is brought within s 106.[10] What if the surety does not withdraw, but the regulated agreement is never made?[11]

POSSESSORY REAL SECURITY

Pawns and pledges

[25.15] Pledges at common law.[1] A pledge (or pawn) is a special form of bailment (see generally ante, para 1.17), whereunder the bailor/borrower (pledgor) transfers possession of the goods to another (the pledgee) by way of security for a loan (see ante, para 25.02). It being a species of bailment, the pledgor retains the general property in the goods (see ante, para 19.08), which he is entitled to sell to a third party subject to the pledge.[2] However, a pledge grants the pledgee/lender a special interest in the pledged goods, commonly referred to as a 'special property',[3] whose value equals the amount of the loan. During the continuance of the pledge, the pledgee may transfer that special property to

---

3   See further ante, para 10.32. But see s 113(5).
4   Under s 40(1): see further ante, para 6.20.
5   Under s 149(1): see further ante, para 6.28.
6   Under s 65(1): see further ante, para 9.19.
7   Under s 124: see ante, para 25.09.
8   Cf the protection of the debtor or hirer under s 59: see ante, para 5.20.
9   The debtor or hirer who has given real security can also use s 113(6) to recover that security: see Goode, *Consumer Credit Law and Practice*, para 37.198; and ante, para 10.26.
10   The complicated manner in which the draftsman has achieved this result is criticised by Goode, *ibid*, Div IIB, para 5.223.
11   Must the surety give notice under s 113(6) to escape, or is his obligation automatically terminated on common law principles (see ante, para 25.06)?

[25.15]

1   See generally Crossley Vaines, *Personal Property* (5th edn), p 23.
2   On tendering the amount of the pledge, the third party may sue for wrongful interference with the goods: *Franklin v Neate* (1844) 13 M & W 481; and generally ante, para 19.06.
3   Perhaps because of a tendency to extend the expression 'special property' to a lienee's interest (see ante, para 25.02), the expression has been criticised: see Chalmers, *Sale of Goods* (18th edn), p 269. Yet, if 'special property' is reserved for proprietary, rather than solely possessory interests (see ante, para 19.08), its use to describe the interest of a pledgee would seem appropriate.

another,[4] or sue for wrongful interference with the goods (see post, para 27.31); and on default by the pledgor/borrower, the pledgee has a power of sale to recoup his loan, holding any surplus for the pledgor.[5]

The essence of a pledge being a transfer of possession, only those species of personal property which admit of delivery may be pledged: so a chose in action, eg, a contract debt such as instalments due under a credit sale, may not be pledged,[6] though a negotiable instrument may because title passes by delivery (see ante, para 7.24). However, in relation to choses in possession (goods), the delivery may be actual or constructive.[7] On the other hand, except in the case of bills of lading (see post, para 25.16), a pledge of documents of title will not usually of itself amount to a pledge of the goods because it does not change the possession of the goods. It follows from this insistence on a transfer of possession that the owner of goods supplied on conditional sale, hp or simple hiring cannot create a pledge over those goods during the continuance of the agreement.[8] *Prima facie*, an attempted pledge by the conditional buyer or hirer will *ipso facto* determine the hiring,[9] though not an option to purchase (see ante, para 1.22). As between the pledgor (buyer/hirer) and the pledgee, such a pledge may break the implied condition that the pledgor is the owner of the pledged goods, or has the authority of the owner to pledge them.[10] As between the owner who supplied the goods and the pledgee (lender), under the *nemo dat* rule the pledgee cannot obtain a good title (see ante, para 21.02), except where one of the exceptions operates (see Chapter 21); and his receipt of the goods will be a conversion (see ante, para 19.05), as will his sale or refusal to deliver them to the owner.[11]

[25.16] Trust receipts.[1] Particularly in overseas trade, a buyer (importer) may need an advance from his own bank to pay for the goods, repaying this loan from his sub-sale of them. Usually, a bank will want to take a security interest in the goods so financed: although a mere agreement by the buyer to give the bank possession of goods on their later arrival can only amount to a letter of hypothecation,[2] his transfer of the bill of lading

---

4   *Donald v Suckling* (1866) LR 1 QB 585.
5   *Re Hardwick ex p Hubbard* (1886) LR 17 QBD 699, CA. In equity, interest is due on that surplus until paid, as in a mortgage (see post, para 25.20): *Matthew v TM Sutton Ltd* [1994] 4 All ER 793; and generally ante, para 7.03A.
6   *Harrold v Plenty* [1901] 2 Ch 314. For choses in action, see generally ante, para 7.16.
7   *Wrightson v McArthur and Hutchinson (1919) Ltd* [1921] 2 KB 807.
8   Goode, *HP Law and Practice* (2nd edn), p 537. Deposit of the instalment contracts will operate as a mortgage or charge: see Butterworths edn, 1989, para 16.27.
9   But see Goode, *ibid*, p 540, note 15.
10 *Sugar Manufacturing Co v Clark* (1879) 5 Ex D 37. See further Goode, *op cit*, note 8, p 538, note 16.
11 *Belsize Motor Supply Co v Cox* [1914] 1 KB 244.
[25.16]
1   See generally Goode, *Commercial Law* (2nd edn), pp 1026–29; Gutteridge and Megrah, *Law of Bankers' Commercial Credits* (5th edn), pp 173–75; *Benjamin's Sale of Goods* (5th edn), paras 18.182–86, 23.114; *Crowther Report*, para 4.1.7. As to the distinction from conditional sales, see Jones, *Chattel Mortgages* (6th edn), para 976.
2   See ante, para 25.02. Such a letter referring to a specific transaction is not a bill of sale within the 1878 and 1882 Acts (for the definition of a bill of sale, see ante, para 9.04): Bills of Sale Act 1891. *Contra* a general letter covering all transactions, which is outside the 1891 Act and does require registration under the chattel mortgage legislation: set post, para 25.28.

will create a pledge.[3] In order to re-imburse the bank (A), the buyer will need to obtain possession of the goods or bill of lading to complete the sub-sale. Whilst the mere release by A of the goods or bill to the buyer/pledgor (B) would destroy A's pledge, there emerged the letter of trust (trust receipt), whereby B undertakes to hold the property released and proceeds of sub-sale in trust for A. Thus, the trust receipt is a means of securing the continuance of the pledge rather than an independent security device,[4] and therefore does not require registration under the chattel mortgage legislation.[5]

It has been held that, as against a bfp (C), under the *nemo dat* rule A was entitled to the goods.[6] However, in English law a person in B's position may well be able to pass a good title to C under s 2(1) of the FA.[7]

Regulated agreements

[25.17] Pawnbroking. The specialised pawnbroker, for whom lending money on the security of pledges (see ante, para 25.15) was a principal form of business, has existed in this country for a long time, the first attempt at regulation being an Act of 1603.[1] In the 18th century, pawnbroking became a service principally utilised by the poor of the large cities, and a series of enactments aimed at the protection of that class was consolidated in the Pawnbrokers Acts 1872–1960.[2] The *Crowther Report* (see generally ante, para 5.03) recommended that the principles of those Acts should be retained and rationalised (para 6.2.60). However, the Report recognised that its general approach of restricting the taking of possession of the security[3] was inapplicable to pawnbroking, whose essence was a taking of possession (para 6.2.4). Accordingly, the Report recommended special provisions to regulate pawnbroking;[4] and these are now to be found in ss 114–22 of the CCA (see post, para 25.18), which replace the old Pawnbrokers Acts (above). More recently, there has been a renaissance in pawnbroking, which has even ventured into off-trade premises business on the weekly collected credit model.[5] Moreover, the repeal of the wide statutory definition of 'pawnbroking' in the 1872 Act has seen a resurgence of activities which appear to fall just outside the common law notion of pawning.[6] The result would appear to be that such activities fall outside the specialist CCA control of

---

3   Bills of lading are explained ante, para 20.09. This pledge of a bill of lading is by way of exception to the general rule: see ante, para 25.15.
4   *North Western Bank Ltd v Poynter* [1895] AC 56, HL(s).
5   *Re David Allester Ltd* [1922] 2 Ch 211. But see note 2, above.
6   *Mercantile Bank of India Ltd v Central Bank of India Ltd* (set out ante, para 19.11).
7   *Lloyd's Bank Ltd v Bank of America* [1938] 2 KB 147, CA (see ante, para 21.31).
[25.17]
1   See the *Crowther Report*, paras 2.1.15–18. For that Report, see generally ante, para 5.03.
2   For the principal requirements of those Acts, see the *Crowther Report*, para 4.1.31.
3   For these restrictions, see ante, para 24.27 *et seq*.
4   The *Crowther Report*, paras 6.2.37, 6.13.19.
5   See (1990) 11 CCA News 5/20; 11 CCA News 6/5.
6   Sales agency, exchange and repurchase: see Macleod [1995] JBL 155, esp 168–69.

pawnbroking and arguably outside the general CCA controls as well, depending on whether or not such activities amount to 'financial accommodation' (see ante, para 5.21).

[25.18] The CCA. The modern business of pawnbroking is now likely to be regulated by the CCA (see above). The pawnbroker will then require a category A licence (see ante, para 6.15); and his individual transactions will be governed by ss 114–22 of the CCA. According to s 114, these provisions apply to anyone 'who takes an article[1] in pawn[2] under a regulated agreement',[3] other than under a non-commercial agreement.[4] It may be an offence to take any article in pawn from a minor (s 114(2). Cf the sending of circulars to minors (s 50): see ante, para 8.33) or to canvas such loans.[5] Unless the agreement to pledge complies with all the ordinary formalities for a regulated agreement (ss 62–64: see Chapter 9), it is not properly executed, so that the creditor may be unable to enforce the security (s 113(2): see ante, para 25.14). Further, the creditor (pawnbroker) must also issue a pawn receipt in the prescribed form to the debtor/pledgor.[6] Under the Act, the debtor may redeem the pledge[7] by surrender of the pawn ticket[8] within the redemption period which expires upon the latest of the following events: expiry of six months or such greater period as the parties may agree (s 116(1), (2)); or realisation by the pawnbroker (s 116(3)). Unreasonable refusal by the pawnbroker to redeliver the pawned goods amounts to an offence;[9] but the failure by the debtor to redeem the goods will allow the creditor to forfeit the pledge for a small sum, or sell to repay himself any sum,[10] or sometimes to seek a time order (see ante, para 24.40). The burden of proving that he obtained the true market value lies on the pawnbroker;[11] and any surplus on sale by the creditor must be paid (plus interest) to the debtor (s 121(3)).

[25.18]

1 The sections do not extend to pledges of documents of title or bearer bonds (CCA, s 114(3)(a), as amended). As to these, see ante, para 25.15.

2 'Pawn' means any article subject to a pledge: s 189(1). For pledge, see ante, para 25.15.

3 Section 114(1). For regulated agreements, see ante, para 5.13. Can a pledge ever amount to a consumer hire agreement (as to which, see ante, para 1.19)?

4 Section 114(3)(b). For non-commercial agreements, see ante, para 5.18. Thus, strictly speaking, the provisions are not limited to pawnbrokers: Goode, *Consumer Credit Law and Practice*, para 37.126.

5 Section 49(1). But it is still possible to conduct such business on the basis of solicited weekly home visits: see ante, para 7.07.

6 Section 114(1). However, the sanction for breach of s 114(1) is more powerful in that it amounts to a criminal offence (s 115). Home pawnbroking may lead to cancellable agreements (ss 67–73: see ante, para 10.28 *et seq*): (1990) 11 CCA News 4/3.

7 For redemption charges, see s 116(4); and for the redemption procedure, see s 117.

8 For the situation where the debtor has lost the pawn ticket, see s 118.

9 Section 119. The onus lies on the pawnbroker to prove he had reasonable cause to refuse to allow redemption: s 171(6).

10 Sections 120(1)(a), 121. Forfeiture of small pledges looks very much like foreclosure of mortgages: as to which, see post, para 25.20.

11 Section 121(6). The OFT will usually require that the property is auctioned: see (1994–95) 9 Fair Trading 3. As to the pawnbroker's 'internal sales', see OFT, 1994 AR, 29.

PROPRIETARY REAL SECURITY

Introduction

[25.19] This section is concerned with the situation where a debtor obtains or retains **possession** of real or personal property,[1] whilst his creditor retains or is granted **proprietary** rights therein by way of security for the payment or repayment of a sum of money.[2] Such transactions have already been distinguished from both pledges and sales.[3]

Legislation. The statutory regimes which govern such transactions have to some extent been coloured by the typical circumstances in which they have been used. Mortgages or charges of land have tended to be associated with security for its purchase price, society's approval of the objective being mirrored by the evolution of a helpful legal framework.[4] On the other hand, mortgages or charges of chattels have frequently been given to secure cash loans; and the legislature has treated such loans with unsympathetic suspicion.[5] In more recent times, this dichotomy of usage has become less clear cut, a shift reflected in statutory treatment: mortgages of choses in action have become acceptable[6] and charges of a company's stock-in-trade positively supported;[7] whereas second mortgages of land, often to secure home improvements, have achieved sufficient notoriety to ensure their inclusion in the CCA (see post, para 25.24). The outcome of this varied legislative treatment is a present position as follows:

(1) Where realty is mortgaged or charged to anyone, the system set up by the Law of Property Acts (LPA) must be followed; and, if the borrower is a registered company, the transaction is **also** subject to the Companies Act.

(2) Where goods are mortgaged or charged by an individual, the matter is governed by the Bills of Sale Act 1882; but, if goods are mortgaged or charged by a company, the matter is **instead** dealt with by the Companies Act.

(3) Where choses in action (see ante, para 7.16) are mortgaged or charged, the transaction may be caught by the Companies Act, but not by the Bills of Sale Acts. **Additionally**, the transaction may in any event fall within some of the provisions of the LPA.

[25.19]

1 For real and personal property, see generally ante, para 19.02. Distinguish the different sense of 'real' as opposed to personal security: see ante, para 25.01.

2 In equity, security may be granted by the debtor not only over property he currently owns, but also over after-acquired property: see ante, para 9.05.

3 See respectively ante, paras 25.02; 25.01. How far, if at all, does the scheme that follows reflect the SGA rules?

4 See post, para 25.20 *et seq.*

5 See post, para 25.27 *et seq.*

6 See ante, paras 7.20–21. Eg, factoring (see ante, para 2.22).

7 See post, para 25.28 *et seq.*

Mortgages and charges of realty

[25.20] Introduction.[1] The mortgage was originally a common law invention; but equity later intervened to mitigate the common law's harshness. By the 17th century, the characteristics of a mortgage were clear. First, in the case of both real and personal property, a mortgage was effected by transfer of ownership: if the mortgagor (borrower) failed to redeem (repay) the mortgage, the property was forfeit to the mortgagee (lender), subject to the mortgagor's equity of redemption (see below). In the case of land, the usual form was a conveyance of land in fee simple with a covenant to reconvey if the money was paid by a fixed date;[2] but that rule was later changed by statute (see post, para 25.21). Equity allowed more informal modes of making mortgages.[3] Second, the rate of interest that could be charged was first governed by the usury laws, then by the Moneylenders Acts (now repealed: see ante, para 6.09). In modern times, regulated mortgages of any property are governed by the CCA (see post, para 25.24), whilst the modern statutory rules relating to mortgages of real property are referred to below (para 25.21). Third, equity discouraged the mortgagee from taking possession, so leading to the modern form whereby the mortgagor remained in possession (see ante, para 25.02). Fourth, the agreement commonly granted the mortgagee an express power to sell the security in default: in every modern mortgage by deed, such a power is now conferred by statute,[4] which also makes him a trustee of the proceeds of sale.[5] In any case, a mortgagee in exercising his power of sale is required to act in good faith and with reasonable care to obtain the best price reasonably obtainable.[6] Fifth, equity granted the mortgagor relief against forfeiture (see post, para 27.20) and a right to redeem (obtain reconveyance) even after the fixed date for repayment had long passed (the equity of redemption: see below), so compelling the mortgagee to treat the property as no more than security for the money actually owed. Any attempt in the mortgage to restrict this right to redeem is ignored by equity, a rule which is usually expressed as there may be no clog on the equity of redemption.[7]

Equity of redemption. This mortgagor's equity of redemption was regarded as an equitable interest in property, exercisable by repayment, eg, if property worth £50,000 is mortgaged to secure a loan of £40,000 the mortgagor's equity of redemption is worth £10,000 at the outset. However, if the money was not repaid, equity would foreclose (determine) the mortgagor's right of redemption, leaving the mortgagee with unfettered

---

[25.20]

1 See generally Megarry and Wade, *Law of Real Property* (6th edn), Chapter 19.

2 Equity regards the issue of a transfer of ownership by way of security instead of absolutely as a matter of substance rather than form: *Re Duke of Marlborough* [1894] 2 Ch 133 (transaction in form of conditional sale). Cf the right of a debtor or hirer under a regulated agreement: see ante, para 24.30.

3 Eg, by deposit of title deeds with the intention of creating a mortgage. Under s 2 of the LPA 1989, dispositions of an interest in land must be in signed writing (see ante, para 9.03).

4 LPA 1925, ss 101–07; Administration of Justice Act 1970, ss 36–39 (as amended). See generally Megarry and Wade, *op cit*, note 1, paras 19-056–66; Goode, *Commercial Law* (2nd edn), pp 749–50. But see the *Syed* case (post, para 25.24, at note 4).

5 LPA, s 105, including a statutory duty to pay interest on the surplus until paid over; and for interest payable in equity, see ante, para 7.03A.

6 See *Meftah v Lloyd's TSB plc* [2001] 2 All ER (Comm) 741. Cf the right of the hirer under the hiring or hp agreement: see ante, para 24.22.

7 Eg, *Cityland and Property (Holdings) Ltd v Dabrah* [1968] Ch 166; *Jones v Morgan* [2001] 8 CL 510, CA.

ownership,[8] but with an obligation to pay any surplus obtained on sale to the mortgagor. Thus, the market value of the equity is any excess obtained on such sale over the amount of the debt;[9] but any deficit is termed 'negative equity'.[10] A mortgage is enforceable not only as against the mortgagor, but also as against anyone to whom the mortgagor transfers his title, save only for a *bona fide* purchaser without notice. This infirmity of an equitable title may be compared with the common law exceptions to the *nemo dat* rule (see ante, para 19.03).

[25.21] Modern rules. The modern rules relating to mortgages and charges of realty generally are set out in Part III of the LPA 1925 (as amended). This allows only two formal types[1] of legal mortgage, of which the more common[2] is a charge[3] by deed expressed to be by way of legal mortgage.[4] However, where there is a land mortgage, by statute the borrower retains the estate.

Nowadays, most formal transfers of interests in land fall within the registration system,[5] which abandons the *nemo dat* principle (see ante, para 19.11) in favour of the indefeasibility of registered title.[6] The only other matters which require special mention for our purposes are the following: the rules as to the tying in of services[7] and priorities (see post, para 25.22); the position of fixtures (see post, para 25.23); the restrictions on the right of a mortgagee of a dwelling house to recover possession;[8] those special rules pertaining to mortgages and charges which fall within the CCA (see post, para 25.24); and the realisation of charges over company realty (see post, para 25.28). For the mortgagees remedies, see post, para 27.07.

[25.22] Priorities. Where there is more than one mortgage or charge on the same property, there is generally no question of each of the secured lenders sharing any loss should the proceeds of realisation of the security be insufficient to pay them all out.[1] Each secured

---

8   Because in the above example it would give the mortgagee a windfall of £10,000, the courts are reluctant in such cases to make foreclosure orders: Goode, *op cit*, note 4, p 751.

9   Compare the position of a hirer or conditional buyer: see post, para 24.22.

10 See *Palk v Mortgage Service Funding plc* [1993] 2 All ER 481, CA. If the sale or foreclosure leaves the mortgagor still indebted, this may be recorded in the credit register: see ante, para 8.35.

[25.21]

1   Compare informal mortgages: see ante, para 25.20.

2   The other form is a demise (lease) for a term of years absolute subject to a provision for cesser on redemption: LPA, ss 85(1), 86(1).

3   For charges, see generally ante, para 25.02.

4   LPA, ss 85(1), 86(1). This form involves no conveyance of any estate to the mortgagee, but grants him 'the same protection, powers and remedies' as if he had been granted a lease: s 87(1). This puts the chargee in much the same position as a mortgagee.

5   See the Land Registration Act 1925–66; the Land Registration and Land Charges Act 1971; and further Megarry and Wade, *Law of Real Property* (6th edn), Chapter 6.

6   See Megarry and Wade, *ibid*, para 6-004.

7   Sections 104–07 of the Courts and Legal Services Act 1990 prohibit the lender under a 'residential property loan' from requiring the borrower to also take from him 'controlled services', eg, conveyancing, surveying.

8   See Administration of Justice Act 1970, s 36 (as amended) and the cases decided thereunder. For the mortgagor's right to take possession generally, see Megarry and Wade, *op cit*, note 5, paras 19-045–55.

[25.22]

1   *Contra* the unsecured lender: see ante, para 19.22.

lender takes his claim in full in order of priority, and it is for a later secured lender to satisfy himself as to the value of the security before he takes his mortgage or charge.[2] The rules as to priority as between succeeding mortgages or charges depends on whether or not the borrower is a registered company.[3] Moreover, the 1925 legislation is displaced in respect of formally-created charges of equitable interests in land,[4] where, subject to the following rules, priorities are usually[5] determined by the *Dearle v Hall* (first to register) rule.[6]

Registered land. A charge of registered land should be registered under the Land Registration Act 1925 (LRA). Subject to any overriding interests (see below), a registered chargee *prima facie* has all the powers of a legal mortgagee (ss 27(1), 24(1), LRA), and priority is governed by the order of entry in the register (s 29, LRA). But failure to register incurs a loss of priority to later incumbrancers,[7] though it remains valid as between lender and borrower (see ante, para 25.20). By way of exception to the ordinary priority rule for registered charges (above), an overriding interest binds a transferee from the registered proprietor, whether he knows about it or not.[8] For our purposes, the principle importance of this rule concerns mortgages of land by a registered proprietor, eg, husband, where there may be an overriding interest arising from 'actual occupation', eg, a deserted wife, which takes precedence over the mortgagee.[9] Whilst it is normal practice for the lender to require any person 'in actual occupation' to agree to postpone their interest to the lender,[10] that is not always effective in subordinating that interest.[11]

[25.23] The borderline between realty and personalty: fixtures and fittings. English law draws a sharp distinction between land and chattels (see ante, para 19.03). Where chattels are brought onto land, it has to be determined whether to apply to those chattels the law relating to realty or personalty (see ante, para 9.03). Thus, materials used to build a house are thereby converted from personalty into realty.[1] On the other hand, 'fittings' are freestanding chattels which *prima facie* remain personalty, eg, curtains, unfitted carpets. In between those two categories are 'fixtures', which are chattels annexed (attached) to the

---

2 Goode, *Commercial Law* (2nd edn), pp 710–12.

3 If the borrower is a registered company, the mortgage or charge will also require registration under the Companies Act: see post, para 25.28A.

4 *Contra* goods: see post, para 25.25.

5 The rule in *Dearle v Hall* has not been applied to charging orders (see post, para 27.04): *United Bank of Kuwait plc v Sahib* [1995] 2 All ER 973, *ratio* 1 (affirmed on other grounds).

6 By the LPA 1925, s 137(1); and see Megarry and Wade, *Law of Real Property* (6th edn), para 19-208 *et seq.* For the *Dearle v Hall* rule, see ante, para 7.19.

7 LRA, ss 19(1), (2), 22(1).

8 Cheshire and Burn, *Modern Law of Real Property* (15th edn), p 797.

9 LRA, s 70(1)(g); and *Williams & Glyn's Bank v Boland* [1981] AC 487, HL. But see *Abbey National BS v Cann* [1991] 1 AC 56, HL.

10 Eg, *Equity & Law Home Loans Ltd v Prestidge* [1992] 1 All ER 909, CA. It is wise to ensure that she receives independent advice in doing this: as to undue influence, see ante, para 25.06; and as to unconscionable bargains, see post, para 29.40.

11 See Curwen [1995] JBL 373 at 391.

[25.23]

1 *Elitestone Ltd v Morris* [1997] 2 All ER 513, HL; Wilkinson (1997) 147 NLJ 1031. See also Megarry and Wade, *Law of Real Property* (6th edn), para 14-312. But such property might still be subject to Part I of the CPA: see ante, para 17.25.

land in such a way that they may be later detached (severed).[2] Thus, on sale of a house, *prima facie* fixtures pass with the land, whereas fittings remain with the vendor.

The general rule is that where a hired chattel is annexed to land so as to become a fixture, at common law it *prima facie* becomes the property of the owner of the land,[3] though the chattel owner retains an equitable interest in it as against the hirer[4] and, presumably, the hirer's execution creditor (see ante, para 19.15). Exceptions include the following:

1 *Landlord and tenant*. Generally speaking, a fixture becomes a landlord's and must be left for him; but, during the currency of a lease, it cannot be distrained.[5] Moreover, a fixture becomes the property of the landowner irrespective of the previous title to the chattel, in which case the *nemo dat* rule (see ante, para 19.11) is defeated and the erstwhile owner of the chattel has an action in conversion (see ante, para 19.05) against the person making the annexation, eg, tenant. Thus, a person who supplied goods to a tenant by way of hire, hp or conditional sale would lose his security unless that fixture was removable under the agreement.[6]

2 *Mortgagor and mortgagee*. Where land is mortgaged,[7] there will usually vest in the mortgagee all fixtures annexed to the land either at the date of the mortgage or thereafter (ss 62(1), 88(4), 89(4), 205(1)(ii) of the LPA), whereas fittings remain in the ownership of the mortgagor (*Botham v TSB* [1996] CLY 4999, CA). This can lead to conflicts of priority in fixtures as between the mortgagee of the land and a third person having an interest in the chattel, eg, as mortgagee[8] or supplier. In modern times, this has caused particular difficulty where the chattels which have been fixed to the land were supplied on simple hire (lease) or hp:[9] the mortgagee of the land may take priority over the lessor of the chattels;[10] but, if (as is usually the case) the chattel lease contains a licence to enter and seize the chattel on default, at common law (contra where that licence contravenes s 92 of the CCA: see ante, para 24.34) this would appear to create an equitable interest in the chattel good against all deriving title to the land from the goods-hirer except a bfp, which rule will include a mere

---

2 Eg, 'shop fittings'; fitted carpets. Whether a chattel becomes a fixture depends on the degree and purpose of annexation: see Megarry and Wade, *ibid*, paras 14-313–55; Gray, *Elements of Land Law* (3rd edn), p 44 *et seq*.

3 *Appleby v Myers* (1867) LR 2 CP 651; *Crossley v Lee* (1908) 1 KB 86; *Brookes Robinson Pty Ltd v Rothfield* [1951] VLR 405; *Aircool Installations v British Telecommunications* [1995] CLY 821, Cty Ct. There are similar rules with regard to the accession of goods (see ante, para 19.05) eg, a new gasket fitted to an engine. But what of a new car battery or radio telephone?

4 Guest, *Law of HP*, para 956.

5 See Crossley Vaines, *Personal Property* (5th edn), 4944; and generally ante, para 19.17.

6 See Gray, *op cit*, note 2, pp 54–55.

7 Unless separately assigned from the land, fixtures are not normally 'personal chattels' requiring registration under the Bills of Sale Acts: see ante, para 9.04. For criticism of the present rules, see the *Crowther Report*, para 5.7.78.

8 *Holland v Hodgson* (1872) 7 CP 328, Exch Ch; *Ellis v Glover & Hobson* [1908] 1 KB 388.

9 See Guest, *op cit*, note 4, Chapter 18; Goode, *HP Law and Practice* (2nd edn), Chapter 32. It has been suggested that similar rules obtain in respect of *Romalpa* clauses (see post, para 25.30): Parris, *Retention of Title on the Sale of Goods*, 54; McCormack [1990] Conv 275 at 280–87.

10 Compare *Lyon & Co v London City and Midland Bank* [1903] 2 KB 135 (lease); and *Vaudeville Electric Cinema Ltd v Muriset* [1923] 2 Ch 74. The goods supplier may save himself by taking a waiver from an existing mortgagee: see Soper and Munro, *The Leasing Handbook*, p 256 and Chapter 21.

mortgagee or chargee of the land.[11] The respective rights of chattel owner and land mortgagee may thus vary depending on whether the chattel is affixed to the land before or after the mortgage is created and whether that mortgage is legal or equitable.[12]

[25.24] The Consumer Credit Act. For the most part, first mortgages of domestic dwelling houses are outside ambit of the CCA (see ante, para 3.02), either because the amount borrowed is outside its financial ambit (see ante, para 5.22) or the agreement is exempt.[1] Such unregulated mortgages are subject to different rules, eg, as to powers to repossess in default (see ante, para 25.21). On the other hand, there were serious abuses in the second mortgage market, in particular in relation to straightforward secured lending,[2] home improvements,[3] and more recently remortgages (see ante, para 7.04A). Accordingly, the CCA regulates the second mortgage market, whilst taking regulated mortgages outside the ordinary (above) rules regarding repossession on default.[4]

Where a land mortgage[5] is undertaken to finance a regulated consumer credit agreement, it is subject to restrictions by the CCA in respect of all the following matters: advertising (see ante, para 7.04A); withdrawal from a prospective land mortgage (see ante, para 10.27); information during the currency of the agreement;[6] recovery of possession of land by the creditor under a conditional sale;[7] termination by the buyer (see post, para 26.06); and realisation of security.[8] Furthermore, the CCA ousts the ordinary rules governing the rights of a mortgagee to take possession of land and sell it (see ante, para 25.20), and provides that:[9]

> ... a land mortgage securing a regulated agreement is enforceable[10] (so far as provided in relation to the agreement) on an order of the court only.

In such event, the court has jurisdiction to make a time order (see ante, para 24.40), perhaps suspended (s 135), or the agreement may be varied (s 136). In *Barnes* (see ante,

---

11   *Re Morrison, Jones & Taylor Ltd* [1914] 1 Ch 50; and see Bennett and Davies (1994) 110 LQR 448 at 449–52. *Contra* a landlord.

12   See Giddins (1993) BJIBFL at 265; Bennet and Davies (1994) 110 LQR 448.

[25.24]

1   See ante, para 5.15. Except for the extortionate credit bargain provisions (see post, paras 29.40–41) and the advertising rules (see ante, para 8.29).

2   The *Crowther Report* pointed particularly to the activities of mortgage brokers (paras 6.4.22–25).

3   The *Crowther Report* was particularly worried about the use of promissory notes in relation to financing central heating installations (para 6.6.35): see ante, para 25.09.

4   Section 38A, Administration of Justice Act 1970 (inserted by CCA, Sched 4, para 30). This seems to have been overlooked in *First National Bank plc v Syed* [1991] 2 All ER 250, CA (see Hickman (1994) 110 LQR 221).

5   'Land mortgage' includes any security charged on land: s 189(1).

6   Sections 77, 78, 80: see ante, para 15.17.

7   This may only be achieved by court order (s 92(2)), contravention being a breach of statutory duty (s 92(3); and generally ante, para 3.21).

8   Section 113(6): see ante, para 25.14. Whilst s 112 contains a general power to make regulations concerning the 'sale or other realisation' of any security, it must be primarily significant in relation to mortgage securities because the realisation of pledges is dealt with elsewhere (s 121): see ante, para 25.18. No regulations have been made.

9   Section 126. But no sanction is provided for breach: see s 170 (ante, para 10.19), and Goode, *Consumer Credit Law and Practice*, para 38.7.

10   For difficulties as to whether enforcement includes repossession, see Guest and Lloyd, *Encyclopedia of Consumer Credit Law*, para 2-127.

para 24.41) the CA refused to allow separate actions for arrears (under s 129), holding that the s 129 proceedings covered the total indebtedness. Some of these controls may be transferred to the FSMA (see ante, para 3.02).

Mortgages and charges of personalty

[25.25] Introduction. Personal property may be mortgaged or charged; but remember that a mortgagee or chargee of goods may lose his interest in them if they are annexed to land (see ante, para 25.22).

1   *Mortgages of personalty*. This is a 'grant of an interest in an asset to secure payment of a debt or performance of some other obligation';[1] and it is subject to many of the same rules of common law and equity as a mortgage of realty.[2] However, whereas in a mortgage of land the borrower by statute retains the legal estate (see ante, para 25.21), a legal mortgage of personalty can be effected only by a transfer of title;[3] and this leaves the mortgagor only an equity of redemption, whilst the mortgagee has power of sale[4] and foreclosure (see ante, para 25.20). As between competing legal mortgages, the common law rule is that interests rank in order to creation.[5] On the other hand, unlike a modern equitable mortgage of realty (see ante, para 25.20), in an equitable mortgage of personalty the basic priority rule remains subject to the right of a bfp.[6] The written instrument recording the mortgage will be registrable: if the borrower is a natural person, such a mortgage may fall within the Bills of Sale Act 1882 (see post, para 25.26); and if he is a registered company, it may be governed by the Companies Acts (see post, para 25.28).

2   *Charges of personalty*. A charge of personalty conveys nothing and is necessarily equitable, giving the lender only a personal right of action against the borrower and an encumbrance over the goods (see ante, para 25.02), but no proprietary interest or right of foreclosure.[7] As usual with equitable rights (see ante, para 7.17), no special form of words is required for the creation of an equitable charge over goods.[8] The personalty so charged may be either choses in possession (goods)[9] or choses in action. It is broadly subject to the same statutory control and priority rules as mortgages of personalty (see above), except as regards personal borrowers (see post, para 25.26).

[25.25]

1   *Crowther Report*, para 1.2.15. See also *per* Lord Lindley MR in *Santley v Wilde* [1899] 2 Ch 474 at 474.

2   See Holdsworth, *History of English Law*, vii, 80–81, 455–58, iii, 352 *et seq*.

3   Cf mortgages of land before 1925; see ante, para 25.20. In the case of a legal mortgage of a chose in action, there must also be notice to the debtor: see ante, para 7.21.

4   *China and South Sea Bank Ltd v Tan* [1990] AC 536, PC.

5   Macleod [1995] JBL 155 at 156; Snell, *Principles of Equity* (29th edn), p 46. Because the first mortgage may be redeemed, this seems a better way to put it: see Thornely [1990] CLJ at 367. Cf the *nemo dat* rule: see ante, para 19.10.

6   The scope of the bfp rule in this context is limited by the statutory registration systems which may make it difficult for a purchaser to take without notice: see Goode, *Legal Problems of Credit and Security*, pp 20, 23–27.

7   Oditah, *Financing Receivables*, p 95.

8   Megarry and Wade, *Law of Real Property* (6th edn), para 19-040.

9   A charge on goods of which possession is retained by the chargor is sometimes called an hypothecation: see the *Crowther Report*, para 1.2.15; Goode, *op cit*, note 6, 19–20; and further ante, para 25.16.

Where the borrower is a registered company, the charge may be fixed; or it may float[10] over the assets for the time being falling within the generic description of the charge (see post, para 25.32) until crystallisation, upon which there occurs an equitable assignment to the chargee.[11] A floating charge is more vulnerable than a fixed charge on the insolvency of the chargor (see ante, para 19.21).

[25.26] Personal borrowers. Generally speaking, a mortgage or charge of personalty by a natural person (the mortgagor) is subject to rules which are the same as, or analogous to, those governing mortgages of realty (see ante, para 25.20). However, whereas the rights of a mortgagee of realty to enter into possession of, and sell, the mortgaged property are governed by the LPA (as varied), the position is not so simple with regard to personalty. Unlike choses in action (see ante, para 25.19), a licence to seize goods[1] by way of mortgage is governed by the Bills of Sale Act 1882,[2] which rules out the granting of charges by natural persons (see ante, para 9.05). With regard to written[3] chattel mortgages, even where the document complies with the formalities required by the 1882 Act, it severely limits the grounds upon which the goods may be seized (s 7). Further, as few written transactions do comply with the requirements of the Act, such chattel mortgages are normally absolutely void (s 9). This has caused difficulty in relation to instalment supplies and pledges.

1 *Instalment supplies.* Quite early, there were worries as to whether the traditional conditional sale might fall within the 1882 Act by reason of the fact that it invariably granted the supplier a licence to seize in default. However, we have seen that in *McEntire v Crossley Brothers* the House of Lords confirmed that an ordinary two party instalment supply transaction would escape the 1882 Act because the supplier had simply reserved a licence to seize (see ante, para 1.14A). More difficulty was caused by sale and rehiring transactions: after the passage of the 1882 Act, numerous attempts were made to disguise what were really chattel mortgages as sales and rehirings on hp. To prevent such evasions of the 1882 Act, the courts laid down the rule that a sale and rehiring would escape the Act if genuine,[4] but not if it was a mere cloak for a loan.[5] It was one thing to lay down such a rule, but quite another to apply it; and the courts have experienced difficulty with both financed instalment credit (see post, para 25.27) and *Romalpa* clauses (see post, para 25.29 *et seq*).

---

10 For floating charges, see Oditah, *op cit*, note 7, 110–12. For the borderline between fixed and floating charges, see Goode, *op cit*, note 6, 17–19; and ante, para 25.02. As to the ranking of floating charges, see Goode, *op cit*, note 6, 43 *et seq*; and for a summary of the advantages of fixed over floating charges, see Goode, *op cit*, note 6, 14.

11 See Oditah, *op cit*, note 7, 113, note 37; and ante, para 7.17. This prevents any subsequent arising of any set-off in respect of the debt: Grantham [1989] JBL 377 at 386.

[25.26]

1 'Goods' are defined as 'personal chattels': see ante, para 9.04.

2 If contained in a regulated agreement, the licence to seize is subject to the default notice procedure (as to which, see ante, para 24.30): Bills of Sale Act 1882, s 7A (added by the CCA, Sched 4, para 1). See the explanation in Goode, *Consumer Credit Law and Practice*, para 37.191.

3 A chattel mortgage can be made orally, in which case it is outside both the 1882 Act and the SGA (s 62(4)). Suppose the borrower/seller makes a subsequent sale, is the lender's title overridden by s 8 of the FA (see ante, para 21.38)?

4 Eg, *Yorkshire Railway Wagon G v Maclure* (1882) 21 Ch D 309, CA; *Staffs Motor Guarantee Ltd v British Wagon Ltd* (set out ante, para 21.28). See also sale and simple rehiring (ante, para 1.18).

5 Eg, *Re Watson ex p the Official Receiver* (1890) 25 QBD 27, CA.

2 *Pledges*. In theory, a pledge is distinguished from a mortgage because the former depends on a special property, whilst the latter rests on a right of foreclosure.[6] However, faced with a written note of the transaction, the courts have found it more helpful to see whether the secured party goes into possession at the outset:[7] a change of possession at, or before, the moment of loan has been held to create a pledge outside the 1882 Act;[8] but where that right was deferred, the transaction was held to be a mortgage within the Act.[9]

[25.27] Financed instalment supplies. Suppose an owner of goods (C) wishes to raise money from B on the security of goods whilst retaining possession of them. One way of achieving this would be by way of a chattel mortgage (see ante, para 25.25); but another would be for C to sell those goods to B and rehire them on hp from B. As Lord MacNaughten said in one 1888 case:[1]

> ... there is all the difference in the world between a mortgage and a sale with a right of repurchase. But if the transaction is completed by redemption or repurchase as the case may be there is no difference in actual result.

It has already been seen that whether a transaction amounts to a mortgage or a sale and rehiring is a matter of intention (see ante, para 25.26). Within a few years, this attitude was used in a line of cases where an impecunious tenant (C) sought to raise money to pay his rent by the following device: there was held to be a chattel mortgage where C colluded with his landlord (A) for the latter to levy distress for the rent on C's furniture, which was then sold to a third party (B), who let it to C under an hp agreement.[2] It will be observed that the foregoing was not a two party sale and rehiring, but a three party transaction, under which the property in the furniture was to go round in a circle: from C to A, to B, to C on hp; and it was soon settled that similar circular transactions might amount to chattel mortgages.[3] However, the issues involved have arisen in a much more straightforward manner in relation to directly finance transactions: if the customer (C) enters into a binding contract to purchase the goods from the dealer (A)[4] before the parties apply to the finance company (B), then the property in the goods may immediately pass from A to C; and there may subsequently be a colourable sale and

---

6 *Charlesworth v Mills* [1892] AC 231, HL. For a summary of the different transactions under which money may be advanced upon the security of personal property, see Crossley Vaines, *Personal Property* (5th edn), p 449.

7 Whilst the essence of a pledge is a taking of possession (see ante, para 25.02), it has been seen that a mortgagee may also go into possession (see ante, para 25.20).

8 *Re Hall ex p Close* (1884) 14 QBD 386; *Re Hardwick ex p Hubbard* (1886) 17 QBD 690, CA.

9 *Re Townsend ex p Parsons* (1886) 16 QBD 532. CA; *Dublin City Distillery Ltd v Doherty* [1914] AC 823, HL(I).

[25.27]

1 *Manchester, Sheffield and Lincolnshire Railway Co v North Central Wagon Co* (1888) 13 App Cas 554 at 567–68, HL.

2 *Beckett v Tower Assets Co* [1891] 1 QB 638, CA.

3 *Maas v Pepper* [1905] AC 102, HL, where the facts were unusual.

4 Because his primary interest is to effect a 'sale', A may at an early stage give C a 'sold note' (see ante, para 10.09). If that note was intended to evidence a contract of sale from A to C, with an option for C to take the goods on hp terms from B, then it might be contrary to *Scammell Ltd v Ouston* (set out ante, para 10.03) and also infringe s 59 of the CCA (set out ante, para 5.20).

rehiring between B and C in order to re-imburse B for the price which he has advanced on behalf of C to A.[5]

More recently, the courts seem to have been less acute to find that a financed instalment credit transaction was a disguised chattel mortgage. In *Stoneleigh Finance Ltd v Phillips*:[6]

> A Ltd, who dealt mainly in 'private' transactions, frequently did business with a finance company, B Ltd. B Ltd had made it quite clear to A Ltd that they would accept 'private', but not 'refinancing', transactions (see ante, para 7.04A). However, on one occasion, A Ltd agreed to obtain finance on the security of their vehicles for C Ltd by way of 'refinancing'; and, unaware of this, B Ltd accepted the proposal. Subsequently, C Ltd became insolvent, and the liquidator sold the goods. B Ltd sued the liquidator in detinue and conversion. McNair J held that no genuine sale was intended, and dismissed the actions on the following grounds: (1) the parties did not intend title to pass under this transaction, or were estopped from denying this; and (2) the documents involved were chattel mortgages and void for want of registration.

By a majority, the Court of Appeal reversed this decision on both points. Their Lordships held that B Ltd had obtained a good title to the vehicles for the following reasons:

(1) C Ltd and A Ltd intended a genuine sale, so that the title to the goods passed from C Ltd to A Ltd and thence to B Ltd;[7] but, even if this were not so, C Ltd was privy to the warranty of title given by A Ltd to B Ltd, and were therefore precluded from denying A Ltd's authority to sell.[8]

(2) The refinancing transaction did not operate as a chattel mortgage, because there was no obligation on C Ltd to pay or repay any money to A Ltd[9] and B Ltd had no intention of lending money on the security of the documents.[10]

Whilst it may be difficult to distinguish *Stoneleigh* from some of the earlier cases where the courts found a chattel mortgage, the distinction may be historical: perhaps pre-1960 suspicion of hp financing has been replaced by judicial familiarity with this modern form of financing.

[25.28] Company borrowers. Businesses frequently suffer from a shortage of working capital, and hence it is normal for them to raise as much money as they can on the security of their assets. Although the Bills of Sale Acts do not apply to incorporated companies,[1] Parliament has thought it important to keep a public record of these transactions so that persons lending money to registered companies have the means of ascertaining which of their assets are subject to mortgages or charges. The present rules

---

5   *Polsky v S & A Services Ltd* [1951] 1 All ER 1062, CA; *North Central Wagon Co Ltd v Brailsford* [1962] 1 All ER 502.

6   [1965] 1 QB 537, [1965] 1 All ER 513, CA.

7   At 569–71, 575–77; *contra* Sellers LJ at 562.

8   At 571, 577–78; and see Sellers LJ at 566; and ante, para 21.08. And see *Snook v London and West Riding Investments Ltd* [1967] 2 QB 786, CA (for another point, see post, para 27.06).

9   Davies LJ at 568. This echoes the reasoning of the HL in *Manchester Railway* case (see above, note 1).

10   *Per* Davies and Russell LJJ at 572–73, 579–80; *contra* Sellers LJ at 564–66. See also *per* Diplock LJ in *Snook's* case (above) at 802.

[25.28]

1   Section 17 of the 1882 Act; and see *Re Standard Manufacturing Co* [1891] 1 Ch 627, CA.

on the subject are to be found in Part XII of the Companies Act 1985, even though substantial amendments to it have been on the statute book since 1989.[2] Whilst full discussion of the 1985 scheme is beyond the scope of this work, its application must be noted in respect of certain registrable charges (see post, para 25.28A). Thus, although a document granting a mortgage or charge granted by an individual may fall within the Bills of Sale Act 1882 (see ante, para 25.27), a similar right created by a company may fall within the Companies Act.[3] Further, the extent of the avoidance of that mortgage or charge is different: where it is granted by an individual, the 1882 Act will make it void for non-perfection as against all persons, including the debtor (see ante, para 9.05); but not so under the Companies Act 1985. The Companies Act requires that a registrable charge be registered by the company granting it with the Registrar of Companies[4] within 21 days of its creation (s 400). Where insolvency occurs after the creation of the charge, failure to register makes the charge 'void' as against (s 395(1)) an administrator or liquidator[5] of the company, but not as against the company debtor,[6] or other third party.[7]

In practice, an unpaid seller of goods to a company who has arranged a proprietary interest by way of security is most unlikely to register the price as such a secured debt, in which case the security will be avoided by the above provision.[8] Thus, the real issue is likely to be whether that secured interest is registrable.

[25.28A] The ambit of registration. For our purposes, the vital matter is normally the ambit of the registration provisions (see ante, para 25.28). These do not encompass all charges within the common law notion (see ante, para 25.02); but s 396(1) lists the affected charges[1] as follows:

(a) a charge for the purpose of securing any issue of debentures,[2]

(b) a charge on uncalled share capital of the company,

(c) a charge created or evidenced by an instrument which, if executed by an individual, would require registration as a bill of sale,

---

2   By Part IV of the Companies Act 1989, which was intended to insert new sections into the 1985 Act. It has never been implemented: see post, para 25.33.

3   See post, para 25.28A.

4   Section 744. As to the register, see s 401; as to prescribed particulars, see s 415; as to the delivery of further particulars, see s 417; and as to the effect of errors and omissions in registered particulars, see s 404.

5   For administrators, see ante, para 19.19; and for liquidators, see ante, para 19.22.

6   But only if it survives an administration: *Smith v Bridgend CBC* [2002] 1 All ER 292, HL, *per* Lord Hoffman at paras 21, 31.

7   See *Stroud Architectural Systems Ltd v John Laing Construction Ltd* [1994] CLY 4028 (claimant not a creditor of person granting charge).

8   Eg, *Borden (UK) Ltd v Scottish Timber Products Ltd* (set out post, para 25.31); *Re Bond Worth Ltd* (set out post, para 25.32); *Orion Finance Ltd v Crown Financial Management Ltd (No 2)* [1996] CLY 953, CA.

[25.28A]

1   'Charge' includes mortgage: s 396(4); and used by itself the expression means a fixed (as opposed to a floating) charge. See further *per* Phillips J in *Tatung (UK) v Galex Telesure* (1989) 5 BCC 325 at 335. For the borderline, see Oditah, *Receivables Financing*, p 127; Harrison-Hall (2001) 151 NLJ 1062; and ante, para 25.02.

2   'Debenture' is a name applied to certain types of document evidencing indebtedness by a company, usually being secured by a fixed or floating charge, or both: Gower, *Company Law* (6th edn), pp 322–24.

(d) a charge on land (wherever situated) or any interest in it, but not including a charge for any rent or other periodical sum issuing out of the land,[3]

(e) a charge on book debts of the company,

(f) a floating charge on the company's undertaking or property,

(g) a charge on calls made but not paid,

(h) a charge on a ship or aircraft, or any share in a ship,[4]

(i) a charge on goodwill, on a patent or a licence under a patent, on a trademark or on a copyright or a licence under a copyright.

It will be noticed that s 396(1) says nothing about absolute transfers, eg, sales, or possessory security, whether granted by contract, eg, pledges (see ante, para 25.15 *et seq*) or by law:[5] instead it refers exclusively to charges granted; nor does it apply to simple title retention (see post, para 25.29). Of particular interest in our context are the types of charges listed in paragraphs (c), (e) and (f).

Paragraph (c). An absolute assignment of goods by a natural person falls within the Bills of Sale Act 1878 (see ante, para 9.05); whereas an absolute assignment by a registered company falls outside s 395.[6] However, a written mortgage or charge granted by an individual comes within the 1882 Act; and one granted by a company is registrable under s 395, eg, a *Romalpa* clause (see post, para 25.31). Because they fall outside the definition of a bill of sale (see ante, para 9.04), this category cannot include oral transfers of choses in action, though both may fall within other paragraphs.

Paragraph (e). This applies where book debts (see ante, para 7.18) are charged;[7] but where a negotiable instrument, eg, a post-dated cheque, is given to secure payment of any book debt, its deposit to secure an advance to the company is not for the purposes of s 395 to be treated as a charge on those book debts.[8] It has no counterpart in the Bills of Sale Acts, which do not apply to choses in action (see ante, para 9.04). Its primary significance for us is in relation to tracing the proceeds of sale under a *Romalpa* clause (see post, paras 25.29; 27.14).

Paragraph (f). This applies to floating charges:[9] but a floating charge created within 12 months of winding up may be invalid, except to the extent that it secures new cash paid to the company (s 245 of the Insolvency Act 1986), though this does not invalidate a repayment by realisation of that floating charge.[10] It has no counterpart in the Bills of Sale

---

3   For the methods of perfecting land charges required in addition by other legislation, see ante, para 25.22.

4   It must be registered in the shipping or aircraft registry as appropriate: see ante, para 9.02.

5   Eg, liens: see *Re Hamlet International plc* [1998] CLY 3338; and ante, para 1.23.

6   *Stoneleigh Finance Ltd v Phillips* (set out ante, para 25.27).

7   *Smith v Bridgend CBC* [2002] 1 All ER 292, HL, at para 41. Distinguish sums held in trust: see ante, para 19.22; ECGD policies (*Paul and Frank Ltd v Discount Bank (Overseas) Ltd* [1967] Ch 348); attempts to charge a book debt to the debtor (*Re Charge Card Services Ltd* (on another point set out ante, para 2.27)); and set-offs (see [1988] JBL at 136, 225–28, 198; and the *Smith* case).

8   Section 396(2)). *Contra* where given by way of conditional payment: *Dawson v Isle* [1906] Ch 633.

9   The *Smith* case (above). As to floating charges, see generally ante, para 25.02 and post, para 25.32. The charge may be over the whole or any part of the property: *Re Bond Worth Ltd* (set out post, para 25.32).

10 *Mace Buildings (Glasgow) v Lunn* [1987] Ch 191, CA.

Act 1882 (s 17: see ante, para 25.28); but it is highly relevant to *Romalpa* clauses (see post, para 25.32).

Title reservation

[25.29] Introduction. As has already been pointed out (see ante, para 25.01), with regard to proprietary rights to secure payment, English law has been accustomed to distinguish between those rights **granted** to a lender and those rights **reserved** by a supplier. Certainly, where common law rights in property were granted by an individual to a lender, the transaction was within the Bills of Sale Act 1882;[1] whereas common law rights reserved by a supplier were not, eg, a bf conditional sale, hp or simple hiring agreement (see ante, paras 1.14; 1.21; 25.27). However, the position was less clear where equitable rights were reserved: because equitable ownership in one person pre-supposes legal ownership in another, it might be presumed that the property in the goods has passed (as to proprietary interests, see generally ante, para 19.03); and so the transaction might be construed as a grant back of the equitable rights. The matter arose where suppliers of goods to businesses sought to obtain security for payment in respect of the goods supplied by taking or retaining an interest in those goods, products into which they were turned,[2] or proceeds of sub-sale.[3] In *Aluminium Industrie Vaasen BV v Romalpa Aluminium Ltd*:[4]

A manufacturer, B Ltd, bought from S some aluminium foil under a Dutch standard form contract which provided:[5] (1) the ownership of the foil was only to pass from S to B when all debts between them had been settled; (2) until then, B agreed that the ownership of all products made with any of the foil should be transferred to S; (3) until then, insofar as B sold such products, the proceeds to be held for S. B became insolvent at a time when there were still debts owing to S. In an action between S and B's receiver, the Court of Appeal held –

(a) By virtue of his property in the goods, S as (admitted) bailor was entitled to both the unworked and worked foil now in the possession of the receiver;[6] and

(b) Insofar as B had sold such goods, he was accountable to S for the proceeds of sale, by virtue of their fiduciary relationship as agents and bailees.

[25.29]

1 Goode, *Legal Problems of Credit and Security*, p 2; and generally ante, para 25.27.

2 For alteration, accession and intermixture, see generally Crossley Vaines, *Personal Property* (5th edn), p 19; *per* Staughton J in *Hendy Lennox Ltd v Graham Puttick Ltd* [1984] 2 All ER 152 at 159; Whittaker (1984) 100 LQR 25; and ante, para 19.05.

3 On resale, a good title may be obtained under the SGA, s 25(1): set out ante, para 21.43.

4 [1976] 2 All ER 552; [1976] 1 WLR 676, CA. See generally (1976) 39 MLR 587; Eastway (1978) 128 NLJ 439; Atiyah, *Sale of Goods* (10th edn), pp 473–74; Smith, *Property Problems in Sale*, p 126 *et seq*; Parris, *Retention of Title on the Sale of Goods*, Chapter 7; Goode, *Commercial Law* (2nd edn), pp 774–75.

5 The standard terms were in Dutch. It was held that those terms were incorporated in this transaction and that Dutch law applied; but, there being no evidence to the contrary, it was assumed that Dutch law was the same as English law: see ante, para 18.13.

6 For the bailment aspect of conditional sales, see ante, para 1.14; and for tracing the price, see post, paras 27.13–14. It has been argued that B could not have been a bailee: Atiyah, *op cit*, note 4, p 475; Williams (1991) 12 BCC at 57.

Of course, the right to trace the proceeds depends on the finding of a fiduciary relationship (see post, para 27.14); and the case has been criticised for assuming that there will be a fiduciary relationship where a bailment exists, which will not necessarily be the case.[7] Moreover, as Mocatta J expressly recognised at first instance,[8] the effect of the decision was to bypass the statutory system for the registration of charges on a company's property (see ante, para 25.28); but the registration provisions were not mentioned by the Court of Appeal because it was notionally applying Dutch law and their effect left to be worked out in subsequent cases (see post, paras 25.31–32). The decision has also been criticised for its artificiality: it resulted in S being entitled to all the value of the worked foil and proceeds, which will necessarily include the value added by B.[9]

The decision has the following practical result in the event of a company's (B's) insolvency: without such a clause, its bankers, who will normally have taken a first registered floating charge over its bank account and other property to secure its overdraft, therefore rank as a (prior) secured creditor; with such a clause, its bankers would be postponed to B's ordinary trade suppliers (S), even after delivery.[10] In practice, this proved far more useful to the suppliers of equipment than of raw materials or stock-in-trade.[11] Whilst the effect of *Romalpa* clauses, particularly as regards equitable proprietary interests, is outlined below, it should be borne in mind that the legislative changes made by the Companies Act 1989 could bring such clauses back within the registration system and restore the primacy of bankers over trade suppliers (see post, para 25.34). In a consumer supply contract, a *Romalpa* clause may be unfair.[12]

[25.30] *Romalpa* clauses at common law.[1] The almost immediate popularity of what came to be called '*Romalpa* clauses' (see ante, para 25.29), soon forced the courts to look with considerable care at the incorporation of such terms (see ante, para 18.04 *et seq*), their interpretation and the effect on them of the chattel mortgage legislation. In conducting this enquiry, it is convenient to distinguish the three major stages through which goods supplied by a manufacturer might pass, though it must be borne in mind that in this area so much turns on the precise wording of the *Romalpa* clause and of the facts in issue.[2]

1   *The goods supplied.* In the *Romalpa* case itself, the court accepted almost without argument that the reservation of title escaped the chattel mortgage legislation (see ante, paras 25.27–28). In *Clough Mills Ltd v Martin:*[3]

---

7   Bridge, *Sale of Goods*, pp 109–10.
8   [1976] 2 All ER at 557; [1976] 1 WLR at 682–83. A similar result may be obtainable by supplying on sale or return: see ante, para 20.23. See also Pollard [1988] JBL at 128–29.
9   Atiyah, *op cit*, note 4, p 473.
10 For enforcement, see *Lipe v Leyland Daf Ltd* [1993] CLY 2356, CA. Compare the rights of a supplier who has retained possession: see ante, para 24.02.
11 Bridge [1992] JBL at 20. For discussion of the feasibility of such registrations, see Hicks [1992] JBL at 413–14.
12 OFT, *Unfair Contract Terms Bulletin No 5*, 121; and see generally ante, para 11.13 *et seq*.
[25.30]
1   See generally Parris, *Retention of Title on the Sale of Goods*; Goode, *Proprietary Rights and Insolvency in Sale Transactions*, Chapter V; Spanier [1989] JBL 220; McCormack, *Reservation of Title* (2nd edn); Davies, *Retention of Title Clauses* (1991); *Benjamin's Sale of Goods* (5th edn), para 5.136 *et seq*; Bridge, *Sale of Goods*, pp 104–10.
2   Eg, *Chaigley Farms Ltd v Crawford Kaye & Grayshire Ltd* [1997] CLY 4478.
3   [1984] 3 All ER 982; [1985] 1 WLR 111, CA. See Farrer and Chai [1985] JBL at 163–64; Goodhart 49 MLR 96; Webb [2000] JBL at 529–30.

Yarn was supplied on credit to a buyer who intended to use it in the manufacture of fabrics. When the buyer became insolvent, the supplier claimed the unused yarn under a *Romalpa* clause (see ante, para 25.29), and the receiver resisted on the grounds that the supplier's interest was an unregistered charge. The Court of Appeal supported the supplier's action in conversion on the grounds that, since the yarn claimed remained identifiable, unused and unpaid for, the supplier had retained legal title to it.

The Court of Appeal explained how the chattel mortgage legislation was avoided as follows: the SGA allows for a reservation of property notwithstanding delivery (see ante, para 20.06), a right of recaption (see ante, para 24.23) and a right of disposal;[4] and the buyer was in no position to confer a valid charge on anyone.[5] Where a supplier/bailor validly retains legal title in the goods supplied, the goods are *prima facie* saved from the buyer's insolvency,[6] even where that retention is to support an 'all monies clause' (*Armour v Thyssen*: set out ante, para 20.29). On the other hand, notwithstanding the clause reserving the property in the goods, that property may pass to the buyer, as where the goods have become fixtures (see ante, para 25.23) or cease to be identifiable;[7] or the buyer may pass a good title to a bfp under an exception to the *nemo dat* rule (see ante, Chapter 21). If so, then assuming the buyer was registered company, a written sale agreement would require registration under the Companies Act (see ante, para 25.28): if the interest was restricted to the goods supplied, then it might amount to a bill of sale (see post, para 25.31); whereas, if the interest extended to other property, it might amount to a floating charge (see post, para 25.32).

2   *Products* (see post, para 25.30A).

3   *Proceeds* (see post, para 25.30A).

[25.30A] *Romalpa* **clauses: products and proceeds.** Whereas it was comparatively easy for the draftsman of a *Romalpa* clause to reserve title to the goods supplied (see ante, para 25.30), this was significantly more difficult with regard to products and proceeds.

Products. Where the goods supplied remain identifiable even after undergoing the buyer's manufacturing process,[1] the property in them may remain in the supplier, as where the goods supplied are merely worked, eg, the worked foil in the *Romalpa* case, or reversibly attached to other goods owned by the buyer. In *Hendy Lennox Ltd v Grahame Puttick Ltd*:[2]

---

4   See ante, para 20.28. As to whether such a clause may be effective as a reservation of a right of disposal (see ante, para 20.28) even though only included in a post contract delivery note, see Bradgate [1988] JBL 477.

5   Eg, the unworked foil in the *Romalpa* case; the *Clough Mills* case (yarn remained unused and identifiable); *Re Peachdart Ltd* (set out post, para 25.30A; unworked leather).

6   For the rule that goods not owned by an insolvent normally escape his insolvency, see ante, para 19.23.

7   For the reason explained ante, para 25.29. Eg, *Re Bond Worth Ltd* (set out post, para 25.32) at 256B, 945C; *Borden's* case (set out post, para 25.31). Would priorities be subject to the rule in *Dearle v Hall* (set out, para 7.19)? For an argument that there might be an equitable tenancy in common, see Ulph [1996] JBL at 501–02.

[25.30A]

1   *A fortiori* where the buyer is a wholesaler or importer who does not do anything to destroy the identity of the goods, eg, *Re Interview Ltd* (below).

2   [1984] 2 All ER 152; [1984] 1 WLR 485; and see Hicks [1993] JBL 485.

Manufacturing Co (B) wished to make some generating sets. To do so, B obtained a number of diesel engines on credit from a Ford main dealer (S) under a contract which contained a *Romalpa* clause. Whilst each engine formed the main element of a generating set, it remained readily identifiable by serial number and could be disconnected from the generating set comparatively easily. B went into receivership before paying S. Staughton J held that the parties had impliedly agreed that the proprietary rights of S in the engines were not affected when they were incorporated into generating sets; but they were lost by B's sub-sale (see below).

On the other hand, where the supplier's interest is expressed to extend to the products into which the goods are turned, this process may itself deprive the supplier of the property in the goods,[3] as where the goods supplied are used or altered in the manufacturing process.[4] Thus, in *Re Peachdart Ltd:*[5]

B Ltd was a manufacturer of handbags. B purchased some leather from S under a contract which contained a *Romalpa* clause. At the time when a receiver was appointed to B, its factory contained some of that leather unused; some had partly or completely been turned into handbags; and some handbags sold to sub-buyers. The Receiver conceded that the unworked leather belonged to S. Vinelott J held that once B had started work on a piece of leather to turn it into a handbag, the leather would cease to be the exclusive property of S and S thereafter had only an unregistered charge on it or its proceeds.

Thus, as the buyer was a registered company, the written sale agreement would require registration (see post, para 25.31): this is because the property in the newly created goods (handbags) arises in the buyer, who then grants rights in that property to the seller of the original goods (leather). This case may be distinguished from *Hendy Lennox* in that here the worked leather had been **irreversibly** altered; and the same principle has been applied to goods supplied and fitted by a repairer, which will usually become part of the repaired goods by accession.[6] Moreover, it would seem that the *Peachdart* rule has no application where the parties intend to be co-owners of goods.[7] As ever, everything turns on the precise drafting of the *Romalpa* clause and the circumstances of the case.

Proceeds. As a sub-sale by the buyer might in any event transfer either the property in the goods or products to a sub-buyer under the *nemo dat* rule,[8] or a good title to him under s 9 of the FA,[9] the *Romalpa* clause will normally attempt instead to confer on the original supplier rights in the proceeds of the sub-sale.[10] This will require proof of a

---

3   See *obiter* in the *Clough Mills* case (above), at 989–90, 983, 994.

4   Eg, *Borden (UK) Ltd v Scottish Timber Products Ltd* (set out post, para 25.31).

5   [1984] Ch 131; [1983] 3 All ER 204; discussed by Whittaker in (1984) 100 LQR at 38–41.

6   *Specialist Plant Services Ltd v Braithwaite Ltd* [1987] CLY 369, CA. This is normally termed 'accession' and will amount to an act of conversion (see ante, para 19.05).

7   Eg, *Re Stapylton Fletcher Ltd* (set out ante, para 20.05A); and as to co-owners, see ante, para 20.22A.

8   Eg, *Hendy* case (above).

9   Eg, *Four Point Garage Ltd v Carter* [1985] 3 All ER 12 (goods delivered direct to sub-buyer). Unless the sub-buyer has knowledge of the *Romalpa* clause: *Re Interview Ltd* [1974] IR 382; and see ante, para 21.49.

10 Eg, *Borden's* case (above); *Re Bond Worth Ltd* (above); *Re Peachdart Ltd* (above); *Hendy* case (above).

fiduciary relationship: the mere reservation of the property in the goods (see ante, para 25.30) will not create such a fiduciary relationship;[8] nor will a bailment necessarily do so.[8] However, a fiduciary relationship may be created expressly by the clause, as in the *Romalpa* case (set out ante, para 25.29); but it is unlikely that it will be implied.[11] Even where such a fiduciary relationship is created, it is unlikely to be over the entire proceeds of sale (an absolute interest), because it would be unlikely that the buyer would want to give his seller the right to the value which he has added to the product, eg, by manufacture; instead, it is more likely to be construed as granting the unpaid seller just a floating charge over the proceeds of sale to the extent of his price.[12] Such an interest by way of security will be registrable (see post, para 25.32). Take, for instance, the processed meat in *Mills and Lawrence v Harris (Wholesale Meat) Ltd* (set out ante, para 21.51): although the property in the meat had never passed from A to B, by the time it had been processed by C it had lost its identity and the property was thereupon vested in C (at 281F); and, by reason of s 9 of the FA, C had a good title to the meat as against A (at 281G). His Lordship held that the price of this processed meat must be treated as paid by C to B and then be subject at common law to A's reservation of title clause; but that this transaction was void for want of registration as amounting to a charge on the book debts of the buyer (see post, para 27.14).

[25.31] *Romalpa* clauses as bills of sale. The scope of the rule regulating chattel mortgages by individuals (see ante, para 25.27) is likewise applicable to registered companies by reason of s 396(1)(c) of the Companies Act (see ante, para 25.28A). The leading case on this provision is *Borden (UK) Ltd v Scottish Timber Products Ltd*:[1]

> There was a sale on credit of resin by S to a chipboard manufacturer. As S well knew, the manufacturer normally used the resin within two days as an ingredient in the product. The manufacturer became insolvent whilst S remained unpaid. S claimed that, under a reservation of title clause, any chipboard which had been manufactured using his resin was charged with the amount owing, so that S was entitled to trace the resin into the chipboard or any proceeds of its sale.

The trial judge held that the reservation of title clause created a charge over the chipboard which fell outside s 395, but he was reversed by the Court of Appeal on the following grounds:

(a) Once the manufacturer used the resin in making his product, it ceased to exist as resin: the effect of the clause was simply to reserve the property in the resin until it was used, when it passed automatically,[2] perhaps because the chipboard is created *de novo*.[3]

---

11 See *Benjamin's Sale of Goods* (5th edn), para 5.147.
12 See Benjamin, *ibid*, paras 5.148–50; 5.155.
[25.31]
1   [1981] Ch 25; [1979] 3 All ER 961, CA; discussed by Parris, *Retention of Title on the Sale of Goods*, pp 107–12, 123–27. See also *Specialist Plant Services Ltd v Braithwaite Ltd* [1987] BCLC 1, CA (repairer's security).
2   See also *Re Peachdart Ltd* (set out ante, para 25.30A). Perhaps there is just a strong presumption to this effect in respect of heterogeneous goods, but only a weak presumption as regards the mixture of homogeneous goods: Watts (1990) 106 LQR at 553. For conversion by co-owners, see ante, para 19.05.
3   Webb [2000] JBL at 537, citing *Holroyd v Marshall* (set out ante, para 9.05).

(b) As regards the proceeds, there was not the fiduciary relationship between S and the manufacturer necessary to create a right to trace them (see ante, para 25.30A).

(c) Even if S had acquired an interest in the chipboard, it would be void under what is now s 396(1)(c) as to the chipboard, and under s 396(1)(f) as to the proceeds.[4]

This decision may be compared with that in *Clough Mills v Martin* (set out ante, para 25.30), where the court accepted that the effect of its decision was to give the supplier security for the price of the yarn supplied. They explained that the registration provisions look, not to the purpose of a transaction,[5] but only at the way in which it is achieved: so, a genuine **retention** of title remained outside the provisions, because a buyer can only charge his own property (see ante, para 25.02) and he has not acquired the property in the goods;[6] and this retention principle has even been extended to an 'all monies clause'.[7] On the other hand, there may be a transfer of title to the buyer: this may occur where the buyer turns the goods supplied into something entirely new, eg, the *Borden* case (above), or by accession of the goods supplied;[8] or where a term to that effect is implied.[9] Where the property does so pass to the buyer, the effect of the *Romalpa* clause may be that the buyer is conferring of an interest on the supplier, which interest will be registrable.[10]

[25.32] *Romalpa* **clauses as floating charges.**[1] Floating charges were invented to enable a borrowing company to grant security over the shifting assets[2] of its business[3] by floating over them until the creditor needed to realise (crystallise) his security.[4] Crystallisation operates as an equitable assignment to the chargee (see ante, para 25.25). Whilst it is not possible for an individual to grant a floating charge,[5] an equitable floating charge over the assets of a registered company will on crystallisation take priority over unsecured ordinary creditors, though postponed to fixed charges[6] and preferential creditors (see ante, para 19.21). Floating charges granted by companies require registration by reason of

---

4   See ante, para 25.30. The *Romalpa* case was distinguished on the grounds that the predecessor of s 395 had not been argued before the CA (see ante, para 25.29).

5   *Contra* O'Donaghue J at first instance: [1984] 1 All ER 720, at 732.

6   This might include the situation where the goods supplied have been turned into a manufactured product without altering their identity or adding any other material, eg, the products made with the aluminium foil in the *Romalpa* case (set out ante, para 25.29). See further *Benjamin's Sale of Goods* (5th edn), para 5.145; Webb [2000] JBL at 532, 535–36.

7   *Armour v Thyssen* (set out ante, para 20.29).

8   See ante, para 25.30A. This may involve difficult questions of degree: Benjamin, *op cit*, note 6, para 5.144.

9   Eg, to give business efficacy where the buyer is a manufacturer: see Benjamin, *op cit*, note 6, para 5.139.

10 See *per* Robert Goff LJ (at 989d), Oliver LJ (at 992c), Donaldson MR (at 994a).

[25.32]

1   See ante, paras 25.02; 25.25; and generally Goode, *Commercial Law* (2nd edn), Chapter 25; Gower, *Company Law* (6th edn), p 362 *et seq*; Oditah, *Accounts Receivable*, p 110 *et seq*.

2   Eg, its trading stock of goods; receivables (trade debts); or classes of them.

3   The first step was to extend the fixed charge to after-acquired property (*Holroyd v Marshall* (see ante, para 9.05)); but it left the difficulty that the chargee's permission was still required to dispose of charged assets.

4   *Re Panama, New Zealand and Australian Royal Mail Co* (1870) 5 Ch App 318. For events of crystallisation, see Oditah, *op cit*, note 1, pp 113–14.

5   Bills of Sale Act 1882, s 17 (see ante, para 25.28); and the charge may be void under s 344 of the IA 1986 (see ante, para 19.24).

6   As to fixed charges over future book debts, see Pearce [1987] JBL 18. For a summary of the advantages of fixed charges, see ante, para 25.25.

s 396(1)(f) of the Companies Act 1985 (see ante, para 25.28A), which provision was considered in *Re Bond Worth Ltd*:[7]

> S sold synthetic fibre to a carpet manufacturer under a contract which provided that risk should pass on delivery, but 'equitable' and beneficial ownership' should remain in the seller until payment, or prior sale, in which latter case S's entitlement should attach to the proceeds of sale; or where the fibre was used to make carpet, S's beneficial interest should likewise attach to the proceeds of sale. When the manufacturer became insolvent, much of the fibre had been woven into carpets.

In a masterly judgment, Slade J held as follows:

(1) The property and risk in the fibre passed to the manufacturer on delivery,[8] subject to S's equitable interest, which amounted to a charge over the fibre, product or proceeds: the buyer had an equity of redemption.[9]

(2) This equitable charge was created by way of an implied grant back to S after the property in the goods had passed to the manufacturer under the sale;[10] and not by S reserving an interest out of the property passing.[11] Further, as the manufacturer had implied permission to use the fibre in his production, the charge must be a floating one rather than specific.

(3) S had therefore created a floating charge which was void for want of registration under s 396(1)(f), the *Romalpa* case (set out ante, para 25.29) being distinguishable on all the following grounds: it was decided *per incuriam*; it involved an express reservation of property; the goods and proceeds remained identifiable; it gave rise to a fiduciary relationship generating a duty to account (see post, para 27.14); and, in the last resort, the effect of a reservation of title clause was always a matter of construction (see ante, para 25.30).

The future

[25.33] Introduction. It has already been seen that the essence of a mortgage is the equity of redemption (see ante, para 25.20): this will distinguish mortgages of all types of property on the one hand, from conditional sales and hp on the other.[1] Whilst a first step would be to assimilate hp to conditional sales (see ante, para 1.26), a second would be to

---

7   [1980] Ch 228; [1979] 3 All ER 919; discussed by Guest (1979) 95 LQR 477 and Parris, *Retention of Title on the Sale of Goods*, pp 113–23.

8   Compare the position with regard to a purchase on mortgage of realty: see ante, para 25.22. Personalty has been distinguished on the grounds that, at the time of its creation, the charge is of future property and is therefore registrable: Hicks [1992] JBL 398, at 405–09.

9   Distinguishing *Re George Inglefield Ltd* [1933] Ch 1, CA. Compare *Re Goldcorp Exchange Ltd* (set out ante, para 20.22 (the PC on allocated claimants).

10 It has been argued that this charging back analysis has been overruled by a subsequent HL case on real property mortgages, which allows the seller to grant an equity of redemption: Gregory (1990) 106 LQR 550; Hicks [1992] JBL 398. But see Atiyah, *Sale of Goods* (10th edn), p 478, note 130.

11 *Contra* reserving legal title: *McEntire v Crossley Bros* (set out ante, para 1.14A); and *Clough Mills Ltd v Martin* (set out ante, para 25.30) See the criticism by Parris, *op cit*, note 7, pp 72–82, 121–22; Gregory (1990) 106 LQR 550; and Ulph [1996] JBL 482 at 499–501.

[25.33]

1   The conditional buyer has no equity of redemption: see ante, para 1.14. Nor does the hirer under a hp agreement: see ante, para 24.22.

establish a clear relationship between conditional sales and chattel mortgages.[2] With regard to individual debtors, there has already been demonstrated the difficulty of deciding whether a transaction falls within the Bills of Sale Acts (see ante, para 25.27 *et seq*); and in any event those Acts were designed to be difficult to operate (see ante, para 9.05). As to company debtors, most observers agree that the provisions in the Companies Act 1985 are also unsatisfactory (see ante, para 25.28–28A): this conclusion led to the promulgation of substantial amendments to that scheme by the Companies Act 1989 (ss 92–107), which would include the power to bring *Romalpa* clauses within the scheme;[3] but, apparently because of continuing disagreement as to the exact form these amendments should take, those provisions in the 1989 Act have never been implemented.

On a wider plain, it would seem that two alternative broad courses of reform are possible:

(1) Make all mortgages of personalty subject to the same rules as mortgages of realty (see ante, paras 25.21–23). One of the purposes of the LPA 1925 was to assimilate the law of real and personal property so far as possible; and such a proposal would have the advantage of building on a model presently working successfully here, whilst avoiding any difficulties at the interface of financing realty and personalty.[4]

(2) Introduce an entirely new system for mortgages of personalty. The model most often thought of in this context is Art 9 of the American Uniform Commercial Code.[5] First published as a official text in 1952, the Code has since been adopted in almost all the states of the Union, together with much of the rest of the common law world. Its purpose is 'to provide a simple and unified structure within which the immense variety of present-day secured financing transactions can go forward with less cost and with greater certainty'.[6] Article 9 abolishes, *inter alia*, all the conceptual differences between the chattel mortgage, conditional sales, hp agreements and other security devices and in their place substitutes the single concept of a 'security agreement'.[7] Over the years, it has proved very successful in regulating commercial transactions.[8]

[25.34] The *Crowther Report*.[1] Way back in 1971, that Report recommended the repeal of 'all existing legislation affecting the general law of lending and security in personal

---

2   The US Uniform Commercial Code treats all conditional sales as subject to the chattel mortgage legislation rather than the sales legislation (Arts 2-102, 9-102; see further below). And see the *Crowther Report*, para 5.3.1.

3   Even if the more generous definition of 'charge' does not include *Romalpa* clauses, there would be power to bring them within the CA s 395 scheme by means of regulations (s 396(4)).

4   Problems would be particularly likely to arise in the financing of building construction and fitting out over priority between mortgages: see ante, para 25.23.

5   See generally, Spivak, *Secured Transactions* (2nd edn): Coogan, Hogan and Vagts, *Secured Transactions under the UCC*; see also Goode and Ziegel, *HP and Conditional Sale*, pp 17–18; the *Crowther Report*, para 5.1.5.

6   Commentary to Art 9-101.

7   Article 9-102.

8   Article 9 has nothing to say about consumer protection *per se*, but it does have special perfection rules for consumers.

[25.34]

1   See generally ante, paras 5.03–04.

property' and its replacement by a Lending and Security Act,[2] which should be entirely separate from the then proposed statute (now enacted in the CCA 1974) to regulate consumer credit.[3] Faced with two alternative methods of achieving this (see ante, para 25.33), Crowther unhesitatingly recommended that the Act be drafted on the model of Art 9 of the Uniform Commercial Code.[4] As to what form the loan aspect of the transaction should take, Crowther recommended complete freedom of contract and the minimum of formality for non-consumer transactions (paras 5.2.15–16). As to the security aspect, Crowther envisaged the proposed Lending and Security Act applying to all security interests in pure personalty and fixtures, whether by way of hp or conditional sale,[5] finance leases, mortgages and charges of personalty, pledges and outright sales of accounts receivable (para 5.3.1). Its proposals extended to both the rights of the debtor and creditor *inter se* (5.6) and conflicts between the secured party and third parties, including a register of security interests (5.7). However, the government, whilst accepting that there were aspects of the then existing law in this field (not substantially changed since) which cause difficulty, said they did 'not have sufficient evidence either of a need for such a major recasting of existing law on new principles or of general support for the particular solution proposed by the Committee'.[6] Nevertheless, the demand for reform continued.[7] The trouble is, there are conflicting opinions as to how to reconcile the interests of trade suppliers and the buyer's other creditors, eg, bankers (see ante, para 25.29): supporters of trade creditors argue for the unfettered recognition of *Romalpa* clauses;[8] whereas supporters of the banks argue for the fairness of making such clauses subject to the registration provisions.[9] Bearing in mind the practical unlikelihood of registration of *Romalpa* clauses by unpaid suppliers (see ante, para 25.28), this debate is likely to settle the relative priority of suppliers and bankers.

---

2   Paragraph 5.3.4. The provisions which should be repealed are more particularly listed in para 5.3.7.

3   Paragraph 5.2.18. The latter provision was enacted as the CCA: see ante, para 5.05.

4   Paragraphs 1.3.9; 5.5.6. For technical aspects of the proposed system, see Appendix III of the Report.

5   This would include taking conditional sales outside Part V of the SGA (as to which see ante, para 24.03 *et seq*): *Crowther Report*, paras 5.2.3 and 19.

6   *Reform of the Law on Consumer Credit* (1973, Cmnd 5427) para 14. But see the remarks of Lords Edmund Davies and Fraser in *Moorgate Mercantile Co Ltd v Twitchings* (set out ante, para 21.17) at 660–61 and 665e.

7   See Goode [1984] JBL 79; (1984) 100 LQR 234; *Insolvency Law Review Committee* (1982, Cmnd 8558) paras 1623, 1639; Diamond, *A Review of Security Interests in Property* (DTI, 1989). A basis for a register of security interests might be provided by HPI: as to which, see ante, para 21.01.

8   Eg, the draft Council of Europe Convention: see Latham [1983] JBL 81.

9   Atiyah, *Sale of Goods* (10th edn), p 478. See also McCormack [2002] JBL 113.

PART 7

DISCHARGE, ENFORCEMENT AND REMEDIES

CHAPTER 26

DISCHARGE OF CONTRACTUAL OBLIGATIONS

This chapter is concerned with an examination of the ways in which contractual obligations may be discharged. Leaving aside such matters as discharge by frustration or illegality and rescission *ab initio* for mistake (as to frustration, see ante, para 22.14 *et seq*; as to illegality, see ante, paras 10.19, 22.14; and as to rescission *ab initio* for mistake, see ante, paras 17.11, 22.10), the subject may be divided on the basis of whether or not the discharge takes place in accordance with the terms of the contract.

DISCHARGE IN ACCORDANCE WITH THE CONTRACT

In considering the discharge of contractual obligations in accordance with the contract, a distinction may be drawn as to whether that discharge is brought about by (a) performance, or (b) the happening of some other event.

Discharge by performance[1]

[26.01] Performance by A of a contractual obligation owed to B may be important for two reasons: first, non-performance by A may prevent A enforcing B's promises to him; and second, performance will discharge A's obligations to B.

1   *Enforcement of B's obligations.* When sued by A, B may set up A's failure to perform as a defence; and the general rule is that A cannot succeed unless he can show that he has performed his side of the bargain to the letter (see post, para 26.02). This may be because performance by A is a condition precedent either to the existence of the contract or to performance by B (see ante, para 15.21): if precedent to contract, A is not bound to perform, though neither party is bound unless he does so; but, if precedent merely to performance, there is a binding contract. In the latter case, it may be that A cannot enforce B's performance until he has performed his own side of the bargain;[2] or that the promises on each side are concurrent, eg, s 28 of the SGA (set out ante, 23.16). However, it would seem that, notwithstanding the duty to mitigate (see post, para 27.45), A may be able to perform his promises against the wishes of B and then enforce B's obligations, eg, to pay the price[3] or rent,[4] but only if he has a legitimate interest in so doing.[5] For the relationship of the duty to mitigate and the right of rescission, see post, para 26.16.

[26.01]

1   See generally Treitel, *Law of Contract* (10th edn), Chapter 18.
2   Eg, *Trans Trust SPRL v Danubian Trading Co Ltd* (set out post, para 27.35). Cf *State Trading Corp of India v Golodetz* [1989] 2 Lloyd's Rep 277, CA.
3   *White and Carter (Councils) Ltd v McGregor* [1962] AC 431, HL(s) (action for price); discussed by Treitel, *op cit*, note 1, pp 945–49 (see especially note 29).
4   *The Odenfield* [1978] 2 Lloyd's Rep 357 (charterparty – action for agreed hire).
5   *The Alaskan Trader* [1984] 1 All ER 129 (charterparty). Does not this 'exception' deny the very basis of the decision in the *White and Carter* case (above)?

2   *Discharge of A's obligations.* Generally speaking,[6] A will only be discharged by exact performance of his obligations;[7] and, if A's obligation is the payment of money, it is normally insufficient to pay a lesser sum (see post, para 26.18). If the contract gives A discretion as to the mode of performance, eg, as to place of delivery, or time or amount of payment, he is entitled to perform in the manner least beneficial to B,[8] and, in giving up that discretion, A gives further consideration to support another promise.[9] The remedies available to B where A is in breach have already been discussed (see ante, para 11.04 *et seq*). What is A to do if B announces in advance that he **may** not be able to render due performance?[10]

[26.02] Exact performance. The common law normally takes an extremely strict view of contractual promises.[1] For instance, unless a supply contract is divisible (see ante, para 23.24), it usually[2] insists that performance be exact, even if allowing of alternative methods of performance (see ante, para 26.01). This principle may work particular hardship where A has partly performed his obligations under an 'entire contract'; that is, one where performance by A of all his obligations is a condition precedent to performance by B of **any** of his obligations. The effect may be unjustly to enrich B:[3] A cannot claim under the contract because he has not fully performed the condition,[4] nor may he claim in quasi-contract where B has no choice whether to accept/retain the benefit conferred.[5] Of course, sometimes contracts for the supply of goods will not give rise to such problems, as with deliveries of the wrong quantity or quality (see Chapter 13), where B may either reject the goods delivered or is liable because he voluntarily accepted them.[6] However, where such escape is not possible, the common law has sometimes sought to avoid injustice by accepting a lower standard than exact performance and allowing A to sue B for breach of contract notwithstanding his own non-performance:

---

6   Alternatively, he may be discharged by a condition subsequent: see ante, para 1.11.

7   As to exact performance, see post, para 26.02. In the case of a regulated agreement, the debtor or hirer may be entitled to a written confirmation ('termination statement') that he has discharged his indebtedness under the agreement: see post, para 26.04.

8   *The World Navigator* [1991] 2 Lloyd's Rep 23, CA.

9   May this be the explanation of *Williams v Roffey Bros & Nicholls (Contractors) Ltd* [1990] 1 All ER 512, CA (carpentry work on premises)?

10   B's statement being insufficiently unequivocal to amount to an anticipatory breach (see post, para 26.15): see Goode (1983) 3 Legal Studies 283 at 289–90.

[26.02]

1   Eg, *Arcos Ltd v Ronaasen & Son* (set out ante, para 13.12). Cf SGA, s 31(1): see ante, para 23.24.

2   Although it has been suggested that in the case of an hp contract the obligations of hiring and option may sometimes be treated separately: see Goode, *HP Law and Practice* (2nd edn), p 328.

3   But see the recommendations of the Law Commission, *Pecuniary Restitution on Breach of Contract* (1983, Law Com No 121, discussed by Burrows (1984) 47 MLR 76), which perhaps surprisingly excluded sales from its recommendations. What of other contracts for the supply of goods?

4   *Bolton v Mahadeva* [1972] 2 All ER 1322, CA (central heating installation).

5   *Foreman & Co Pty Ltd v SS Liddesdale* [1900] AC 190, PC (ship repair).

6   *Sumpter v Hedges* [1898] 1 QB 673, CA (building contract, materials left on site).

(1) Where B has wrongfully[7] prevented A from completing performance.[8]

(2) Where the contract provides for performance by B before performance by A, as where B sells on credit terms to A (see ante, para 23.22).

(3) Where there are in fact a number of separate contracts, or where a single contract (or obligation) is divisible (see ante, para 23.24). The effect of deciding that a particular obligation is divisible is that A may sue B for breach of contract notwithstanding his own non-performance of the divisible obligation, but is liable to a counterclaim for damages for non-performance.[9]

(4) Where B is only entitled to damages in respect of A's breach of contract (see ante, para 11.03). In these circumstances, A may sue B for his non-performance, subject to a counterclaim for damages. The only real question is how to fit the doctrine of substantial performance into this scheme[10] and whether it applies to sales (see ante, para 11.04).

(5) Where A has committed such a breach as would entitle B to rescind, but B elects to affirm and claim damages, as where a buyer voluntarily accepts goods of a different quality. For voluntary and statutory elections, see post, paras 26.17; 29.04.

Discharge by stipulated event

[26.03] The contract may provide for the discharge of one or both parties on the happening of some event other than performance.[1] Sometimes, that event is the unilateral choice of one of the parties, whether supplier or transferee of the goods[2] or services;[3] and in a consumer supply, it should be remembered that, if there is no balance between the rights and duties of the two parties, the contract may be unfair (see ante, para 11.14).[4] On other occasions, the event may be one outside the control of either party: an important example is to be found in the context of instalment credit contracts (see ante, para 1.03), where it is common to find stipulated events upon the happening of which one or both parties are to be discharged from some or all of their contractual obligations.[5] Termination by transferee and by other stipulated event are considered separately below (paras 26.04–10).

---

7 See Goode, *Payment Obligations in Commercial and Financial Transactions*, p 40. *Contra* if B is entitled to prevent A performing, as where A has already repudiated the contract: *British and Benningtons Ltd v Northwestern Cachar Tea Co Ltd* (set out ante, para 23.05).

8 Contrast the situation where A may complete performance against the wishes of B: see ante, para 26.01.

9 It may be more accurate to speak of divisible obligations rather than divisible contracts, for one contract may contain both divisible and entire obligations: Treitel, *Law of Contract* (10th edn), p 728.

10 As to which, see Treitel, *ibid*, p 729; Beck (1975) 38 MLR 413.

[26.03]

1 Eg, SGA, s 48(4) provides that a contract of sale is discharged where the seller exercises an express power of sale: see post, para 27.08.

2 Eg, where a contract for the supply of goods envisages that the transferee may not complete a contract of purchase but instead return the goods, as with sale or return (see ante, para 20.23) or hp (see ante, para 1.22).

3 Eg, a running-account credit contract will normally allow the consumer to close the account unilaterally at any time by paying off the outstanding amount.

4 OFT, *Bulletin No 12*, case 13, Grey Term 1(f): see ante, para 11.16.

5 See post, para 26.08. As to revival and reinstatement of instalment credit agreements, see Goode, *HP Law and Practice* (2nd edn), p 346; and *St Margaret's Trust Ltd v Byrne* [1976] CLY 1342, CA.

In instalment contracts, it should be noted that the common law produces a different measure of damages according to the circumstances of termination (see post, para 27.37).

Termination by the transferee (consumer)

[26.04] At common law, it was quite possible for a bailee under an instalment credit contract to be given the right to terminate or rescind the agreement at any time before all the instalments have been paid even where the supplier was not in breach of the agreement. However, it was only in hp and simple hiring that the common law required that the bailee had a right to terminate without cause,[1] so that it was hardly ever available in other such cases.[2] Even in the context of hp and simple hiring, the right to terminate was almost always subject to some restrictions: sometimes these were merely designed to ensure that the owner recovered the goods, eg, a requirement that the hirer give notice or return the goods to the supplier; but at other times the restrictions were intended to ensure that the owner did not make a loss on the transaction,[3] or to discourage the hirer from exercising his option to terminate,[4] or even primarily to increase the hirer's liability on a 'snatchback' (see post, para 26.08).

With regard to contractual limitations on the right of the bailee to terminate a conditional sale or hp agreement without cause, the HPA restrictions were substantially re-enacted in the CCA with an extension to simple hiring agreements. They are three fold:[5]

1 *Agency.* Section 102(1) facilitates the exercise by the debtor or hirer under a regulated agreement of any common law right of 'rescission' (see post, paras 26.11–16) by deeming certain persons to be the agent of the creditor or owner for the purposes of receiving notice of that 'rescission' (see ante, para 10.25). However, s 102(2) makes it clear that this is without prejudice to the exercise of any statutory right of cancellation (see ante, para 10.29) or termination (see below).

2 *Termination.* The Act includes statutory rights of termination by the debtor (see post, para 26.05) or hirer (see post, para 26.07), which are in addition to any right of termination which may exist on general principles, eg, under the terms of the agreement (see ante, para 26.03), or by reason of breach by the creditor or owner (see post, para 26.15).

3 *Termination statements.* Except in the case of non-commercial agreements (see ante, para 5.18), a debtor or hirer who has 'discharged his indebtedness' under a regulated agreement is entitled on written request[6] under s 103 on one occasion only to a statement from the creditor or owner ('trader') to that effect (s 103(1), (3), (4)). Where

---

[26.04]

1 This is the essence of any bailment (see ante, para 1.17); but its effect depends on whether or not the hiring is periodic (as to which, see ante, para 7.18).
2 For statutory intervention in respect of pyramid selling, see ante, para 1.09.
3 See the 'minimum payment clauses' discussed ante, para 11.09 and post, para 27.50.
4 The transaction being viewed essentially as a secured loan of the price rather than a sale.
5 These rights of the debtor or hirer may not be ousted by the terms of the agreement: CCA, s 173(1), as to which, see ante, para 18.11.
6 Section 103 actually says by serving 'a notice'; and s 189(1) defines 'notice' as a 'written notice'.

the trader disputes that the indebtedness has been discharged, he must say so (s 103(2)): otherwise he is bound by the customer's version or his written confirmation.[7]

[26.05] Termination of conditional sale or hp agreement. Sections 99–100 of the CCA grant the debtor under a regulated conditional sale or hp agreement[1] an indefeasible (s 173(1): set out ante, para 18.11) statutory right to terminate the agreement without cause. The key provision is s 99(1), which stipulates that:

> At any time before the final payment by the debtor under a regulated hire purchase or regulated conditional sale agreement falls due, the debtor shall be entitled to terminate the agreement[2] by giving notice to any person entitled or authorised to receive the sums payable under the agreement.

This statutory right to terminate by giving notice[3] lasts only whilst the agreement exists[4] and until the final payment 'falls due',[5] which moment may probably be advanced by the operation of any accelerated payments clause.[6] Moreover, its exercise is 'not to affect any liability under the agreement which has accrued before the termination (s 99(2)): so the creditor is entitled after such termination to recover arrears of instalments[7] and damages for previous breaches, eg, for failure to take reasonable care of the goods (see s 100(4) and post, para 27.24). The Act further provides that (s 100(5)):

> Where the debtor, on the termination of the agreement, wrongfully retains possession of goods to which the agreement relates, then, in any action brought by the creditor to recover possession of the goods from the debtor, the court, unless it is satisfied that having regard to the circumstances it would not be just to do so, shall order the goods to be delivered to the creditor without giving the debtor an option to pay the value of the goods.

This s 99 right may be compared with all the following: the common law right to terminate, which may be exercised in accordance with s 102 (see ante, para 26.04); the powers which a court will ordinarily have to order specific delivery in an action in tort (see ante, para 24.26), or where the debtor is in breach (see ante, para 24.43). As to the effect of ss 99–100, see post, para 26.06. Presumably, in respect of a non-cancellable agreement, a purported s 99 termination without cause which falls outside s 99, eg, an oral termination of hp, or a written termination of a cash or credit sale, is likely to amount to a common law repudiation (see post, para 26.15). *Aliter*, if there are other good reasons for discharge of which the transferee is unaware (see post, para 26.26). Nothing is said by the Act as to the place to which the debtor must return the goods.[8]

---

7   Section 172(2). Delay in giving a termination statement beyond one month is an offence (s 103(5)); as to offences, see further post, para 28.07 *et seq.*

[26.05]

1   For the definitions of regulated conditional sales and hp agreements, see respectively ante, paras 1.16, 1.24.

2   What of any linked transaction?

3   'Notice' means notice in writing: s 189(1). As to service of notice, see s 176. As to joint debtors, see s 185(1)(b): set out ante, para 25.08.

4   As to termination by the supplier, see post, para 26.08. What if the supplier has already served a statutory notice of termination (see post, para 26.10)?

5   As to the persons entitled to payment, see ante, para 23.13.

6   *Wadham Stringer Finance Ltd v Meaney* (set out post, para 26.19).

7   Eg, hire rent (as to which, see post, paras 27.21; 27.50). This includes any instalments due by reason of an acceleration clause operating before the debtor terminates: the *Wadham Stringer* case (above).

8   The debtor's premises, or those of a trade party? Any express term of the regulated agreement must be fair and reasonable (see ante, paras 11.15; 18.24A).

[26.06] So far as hp agreements are concerned, the effect of ss 99–100 (see ante, para 26.05) is simply to nullify any attempt to restrict the right of the hirer to terminate the agreement. However, in the case of a conditional sale, the provisions embody a right in the debtor to terminate without cause which would not necessarily exist at common law, thus taking yet another step towards the assimilation of conditional sales and hp. But this new right of the conditional buyer (debtor) to terminate without cause is a limited one: not only is there a special restriction in respect of conditional sales of land,[1] but s 99(4) provides that:

> In the case of a conditional sale agreement relating to goods, where the property in the goods, having become vested in the debtor, is transferred to a person who does not become the debtor under the agreement, the debtor shall not thereafter be entitled to terminate the agreement under sub-section (1).

Thus, a person (B) who as assignee stands in the shoes of the conditional buyer (A)[2] may enjoy the benefit of ss 99–100; but, if A sells to B the goods of which he is conditional buyer,[3] A can only later exercise those s 99 rights provided the property in the goods has not passed to B;[4] and B has no statutory right of termination in any event.[5] Where a conditional buyer who has not resold exercises the statutory right to terminate, the position is as follows: normally, under the terms of the agreement the property will remain in the conditional seller until payment of the last instalment; but, to meet the unusual case where the property has already passed to the conditional buyer,[6] s 99(5) provides that generally:

> ... the property in the goods shall thereupon vest in the person (the 'previous owner') in whom it was vested immediately before it became vested in the debtor.

[26.07] Termination of consumer hiring. Whilst the HPA gave no statutory right of termination to the bailee under a simple hiring agreement, the CCA sought to protect hirers under consumer hire agreements (see ante, para 1.19) from being locked into burdensome contracts for long periods.[1] Accordingly, s 101(1) provides that:

> The hirer under a regulated consumer hire agreement is entitled to terminate the agreement by giving notice to any person entitled or authorised to receive the sums payable under the agreement.

[26.06]

1 Section 99 does not apply after title to the land has passed to the debtor: s 99(3). For conditional sales of land, see further ante, para 25.23.

2 By reason of assignment or operation of law: see the definition of 'debtor' in s 189(1).

3 B cannot obtain a good title under s 25(2) of the SGA: see ante, para 21.45.

4 It has been said this will include the case where B obtains title under one of the exceptions to the *nemo dat* rule (as to which see ante, Chapter 21): Goode, *Consumer Credit Law and Practice*, para 36.204. *Sed quaere?*

5 Whether A has sold the goods to B, or simply assigned his interest in them to B, is a matter of interpretation. Should A be assumed to do that which is to his greater advantage (see post, para 27.47)?

6 Under the terms of the agreement or operation of law, eg, accession (see ante, para 19.05). Note the proviso to s 99(5), which makes special provision for the situation when the 'previous owner' has died or become bankrupt, etc, in the meantime.

[26.07]

1 Goode, *Consumer Credit Law and Practice*, para 36.221. But note that s 101 is in addition to any more advantageous contractual right of termination not caught by s 173.

It will be observed that this provision nominates the same persons as eligible to receive such notice as does s 99;[2] and s 101(1) is likewise expressed to operate without prejudice to 'any liability under the agreement which has accrued before the termination' (s 101(2)). On the other hand, s 101 does not derogate from any common law right of termination;[3] 'shall not expire earlier than 18 months after the making of the agreement';[4] and is subject to a minimum period of notice.[5] However, it does not matter whether the hiring is for a fixed period or periodic (see ante, para 7.18), so long as the hirer is an 'individual' (see ante, para 5.24).

The foregoing provisions could have been made applicable to small equipment leases (see ante, para 1.18A) made to sole traders and partnerships, in which event a minimum lease of only 18 months would have rendered this form of business uneconomic.[6] Not wishing to give a blanket exemption to equipment leases, Parliament therefore exempted three categories of lease which had been found not to generate abuse:[7]

Category (a), where the minimum rental exceeded £x per year.[8]

Category (b), where the goods are bailed to the hirer for the purposes of his business under a directly financed transaction.[9]

Category (c), where the hirer requires the goods for a sub-leasing business, eg, a car hire firm leasing its fleet.

As to the hirer's liability on termination, see post, para 27.49.

Termination by other stipulated event

[26.08] **Termination provisions**. In order to protect the interests of the supplier, an instalment credit contract with a reservation of property, ie, conditional sale, hp or simple hiring, would commonly stipulate a number of events that would either terminate the agreement or render it terminable.[1] Examples were death (see ante, para 24.44),

---

2 See ante, para 26.05. 'Notice' means notice in writing: s 189(1). As to service of such notice, see s 176.

3 Section 101(3). Eg, if the agreement provides for a minimum hiring period of only 12 months; or minimum notice of only one week.

4 Section 101(3). Note that the period runs from the making of the original agreement: not from the commencement of the hiring; nor from the making of any modifying agreement (s 101(9)).

5 Expiring not earlier than the above 18 months, there must be a period of notice which is the lesser of the following (s 101(3), (6)): the shortest payment interval or three months. See the example in Guest and Lloyd, *Encyclopedia of Consumer Credit*, para 2-102.

6 For an explanation, see Goode, *op cit*, note 1, para 36.223.

7 Section 101(7). Note the power of the Director to exempt certain other transactions: ss 101(8), 183.

8 Originally fixed at £300, the minimum annual rental has now been raised to £1,500: Consumer Credit (Further Increase in Monetary Limits) Order 1998, SI No 997. The figure includes any deposit. But does it extend to 'balloon payments'? As to service payments, see Goode, *op cit*, note 1, III para 102.

9 As to which, see ante, para 2.21. See the limitations suggested by Guest and Lloyd, *op cit*, note 5, para 2-102; and Soper and Munro, *The Leasing Handbook*, 279.

[26.08]

1 See post, para 26.09. The invocation of an acceleration clause does not terminate the agreement: *Wadham Stringer Finance Ltd v Meaney* (set out post, para 26.19). For termination of a loan facility, see ante, para 7.03.

insolvency,[2] appointment of a receiver or administrator,[3] or levying of distress (see ante para 19.17) against the buyer or hirer, eg, *Smart v Holt* (set out post, para 26.09), or any attempt on his part to assign his rights (see ante, para 1.22), or late payment of instalments.[4] Furthermore, to avoid any dispute as to whether the common law would allow the owner to terminate in the following situations, the agreement would usually expressly so provide in the case of: (a) any material inaccuracy in the proposal form (see ante, para 8.35); (b) any arrears in payment of any instalments; and (c) any other breach of the agreement.[5] The insertion of an enormous variety of such stipulated events is, of course, part of the technique of the 'snatchback' (see below).

Snatchbacks. This is a form of business which flourished before 1939 as follows: there was an hp agreement, but the hirer was probably not told the cash price, so that he could not work out the finance charge (see now ante, para 9.11); it was frequently for shoddy goods, from which the supplier would be protected by wide ranging exclusion clauses (see now ante para 18.19); it would be signed in blank, with terms more onerous than those agreed inserted thereafter (see now ante para 16.05); it would contain wide-ranging repossession clauses (as above), but, as the consumer had no copy, he would be unlikely to be aware of all the triggering events (for the modern copies rules, see ante, para 9.14 *et seq*). By ruthless use of these clauses, whose likelihood of operation was frequently enhanced by encouraging overindebtedness,[6] the supplier could almost ensure a right of repossession effected by recaption (see ante, para 24.23); if the hirer sought to exercise his option to terminate, he was often faced with intimidation and an exorbitant minimum payment clause (see now ante, para 26.04); if he delayed repossession until late in the day, the supplier could usually obtain most of the 'price' by way of rent and still recover the goods, because the hirer had no equity of redemption (see ante, para 24.22; but see now ante, para 24.34); and the supplier could then let the same goods again on similar terms, so recovering the 'price' of the goods several times over. Many of these ploys were outlawed by the HPA 1938 in provisions subsequently re-enacted in the CCA; and even where the agreement is unregulated, if the agreement is a consumer supply, it may nowadays infringe the Unfair Terms Regulations.[7]

[26.09] Their effect. In this paragraph there will be considered the effect at common law of the operation of termination provisions (see ante, para 26.08). In the leading case of *Smart Bros Ltd v Holt*:[1]

---

2   Eg, *Granor Finance v Liquidator of Eastore* 1974 SLT 296 (Sess), where the clause was held not to be operable on breach and therefore not a penalty (as to the latter, see post, para 27.25). As to whether such a condition is void as being a fraud on the bankruptcy law, see Oditah (1992) 108 LQR at 482–86. As to consumer supplies, see note 7, below.

3   *Alf Vaughan & Co Ltd v Royscot Trust plc* (set out post, para 27.22).

4   Eg, *The Laconia* [1977] AC 850, HL (charterparty); *Lombard North Central plc v Butterworth* (lease; set out post, para 27.26).

5   See post, para 26.09. However such a clause will not always be effective: compare *Schuler AG v Wickham Machine Tool Sales Ltd* [1974] AC 235, HL with *Lombard North Central plc v Butterworth* (above).

6   This effect was compounded by the 'linked-on' agreement: see ante, para 24.36, but now post, para 26.22. Distinguish CCA linked agreements (see ante, para 5.31) and running accounts (see ante, para 5.28).

7   Eg, insolvency: see OFT, *Bulletin*, cases 1 and 11: Grey Terms 1(f) and (g): see ante, paras 11.16–17.

[26.09]

1   [1929] 2 KB 303; [1929] All ER Rep 322, DC.

Clause 8 of the hp agreement provided that if the hirer was in breach the owner might alternatively –

(a) without notice terminate the hiring or

(b) by written notice terminate both the hiring and the agreement.

Acting under (b), the owner purported to terminate the agreement. Subsequently, the hirer's landlord levied distress on the hired goods. The owner successfully sued for illegal distress on the grounds that at the time levied the goods were no longer 'comprised in' the hp agreement for the purposes of s 4 of the Law of Distress Amendment Act 1908 (see ante, para 19.17).

It will be noted that clause 8 is drafted around two distinct dichotomies. First, there is the distinction between the following:[2] (i) automatic termination clauses, which take effect *ipso facto* on the occurrence of the stipulated event;[3] and (ii) clauses granting the owner a right to terminate, which will not cause termination unless and until the owner so elects. Moreover, a terminable agreement will commonly impose some condition precedent to termination, for example, that the owner gives notice to the bailee: if it does so, there will be no termination until notice is given;[4] but, if it does not so stipulate, the supplier is not obliged to give notice before terminating.[5] Second, whilst the phrase 'termination of the agreement' has so far been used, it is necessary to distinguish between termination of the bailment and termination of the agreement, as it is possible to terminate the bailment without terminating the agreement for all purposes.

1 *Termination of the bailment*. Prima facie, the bailment will be determined by any act of the bailee inconsistent with the terms of the agreement, eg, a sale or pledge of the goods; but in practice, it is normal for the agreement to make specific provision about this matter, eg, *Smart Bros Ltd v Holt* (above). The question of whether the bailment is terminated automatically or merely terminable used to be important for the purposes of the reputed ownership doctrine;[6] and it remains important for the following reasons: (1) whether the supplier is entitled to immediate possession of the goods;[7] (2) whether the bailee can create a lien over the goods, eg, a repairer's lien (see ante, para 1.23); and (3) to determine the bailor's right to hire rent.[8]

2 *Termination of the agreement*. This will also necessarily terminate the bailment (see above); but, unless the agreement manifests a contrary intention, it will not discharge either party from any obligations which have already accrued under the agreement

---

2 The matter is one of interpretation: for the difficulties this may cause, see *Jay's Furnishing Co v Brand & Co* [1915] 1 KB 458, CA; *Times Furnishing Co Ltd v Hutchings* [1938] 1 All ER 422; and Goode, *HP Law and Practice* (2nd edn), p 326.

3 Automatic termination is not possible with regulated agreements, because a termination notice is required: see post, para 26.10.

4 *Reliance Car Facilities Ltd v Roding Motors* [1952] 2 QB 844.

5 *Moorgate Mercantile Ltd v Finch and Read* [1962] 1 QB 70, CA; *Union Transport Finance Ltd v British Car Auctions Ltd* [1978] 2 All ER 385, CA.

6 This doctrine no longer obtains in insolvency (see ante, para 19.23) but still exists in the law of distress (see ante, para 19.17).

7 To enable him to sue in conversion (see ante, para 19.06). See the cases cited in notes 4 and 5 above.

8 Determination of the hiring extinguishes the owner's right to hire rent in respect of any period thereafter: see post, para 27.21. As to whether the owner may claim damages in respect of loss of future rentals, see post, para 27.38.

(see post, para 26.16). Once again, it may be important to know whether the specified event automatically terminates the agreement, or merely renders it terminable: (1) as regards the matters turning on termination of the bailment (see above); (2) whether the bailee has any proprietary interest which can be seized in execution or fall into his bankruptcy (see ante, paras 19.15; 19.23); and (3) whether the goods are still 'comprised in' any agreement for the purposes of the law of distress, eg, *Smart Bros Ltd v Holt* (above).

[26.10] Regulated agreements. Where there is an instalment credit contract with a reservation of property, the plight of the bailee at common law (see ante, paras 26.08–09) has to some extent been alleviated by statute. Perhaps the most significant innovations of the HPA, now elaborated by the CCA, are the interposition of default notices (see ante, para 24.30) and the restrictions on the repossession of protected goods (see ante, para 24.34 *et seq*). In the case of the death of the debtor or hirer, the Act has partly struck out a common stipulated event (see ante, para 24.47). In other cases, s 98 of the CCA has introduced a new restriction, applicable wherever the creditor or owner seeks to terminate a regulated agreement otherwise than by reason of the default of the debtor or hirer (s 98(6)). Section 98(1) provides:

> The creditor or owner is not entitled to terminate a regulated agreement except by or after giving the debtor or hirer not less than seven days' notice on the termination.

Like the notice required by s 76 before the creditor or owner can exercise one of the rights there listed (see ante, para 24.29), the seven day notice of termination required by s 98[1] is ineffective unless in the prescribed form (s 98(3)); there is the same saving with regard to credit repayable on demand (s 98(2)) and as to lines of credit;[2] and the Director has a similar power to exempt from the provisions (s 98(5)). Like a s 76 notice (see ante, para 24.29), a s 98 notice is **not** remediable by the debtor or hirer: whether the notice terminates the agreement or merely renders it terminable, the debtor or hirer can only avoid its consequences by applying to the court for a time order.[3] If the creditor or owner wishes in the absence of breach both to terminate the agreement and repossess the goods, then he must give both s 76 and s 98 notices, though they can be combined in one document.[4]

[26.10]

1 The s 98 notice need not necessarily terminate the agreement automatically on the expiry of the seven days: it is enough if it renders the agreement terminable: Goode, *Consumer Credit Law and Practice*, para 45.54.

2 Section 98(4). Eg, a store withdrawing budget account facilities as to future transactions.

3 As to time orders, see ante, para 24.40. If the debtor is in breach (although that breach is not relied upon by the creditor), the goods may in any event be protected goods: as to which, see ante, para 24.35 *et seq*.

4 Consumer Credit (Enforcement, Default and Termination Notices) Regulations 1983, SI No 1561, reg 2(8).

OTHER TYPES OF DISCHARGE

A party may be discharged from his contractual obligations otherwise than in accordance with the terms of the contract by (1) rescission of the contract, or (2) a subsequent act or event.

Discharge by rescission

[26.11] Introduction. Rescission is a self-help remedy, being regarded by the law as an act of a party to a contract (see post, paras 27.02; 29.02). A contract may be rescinded[1] on the grounds of (a) a misrepresentation or (b) a breach by the other party. However, it must be borne in mind that the 'rescissions' are of different sorts. Where a contract has been induced by misrepresentation (see ante, para 17.10), the defect is in the **formation** of the contract and the innocent party may be able to rescind the contract *ab initio* (see post, para 26.12); that is, it may be annulled in every respect so as to produce a state of affairs as though the contract had never been entered into.[2] Where a contract has been broken by one party, the defect lies in his **performance** and the other party may be entitled to treat the contract as discharged, in which case the contract is usually terminated as from that moment (see post, para 26.15); and, perhaps unfortunately, such discharge or termination of the contract for breach, is likewise frequently described as 'rescission', meaning rescission *de futuro*.[3]

Rescission ab initio *for misrepresentation*

[26.12] Wherever a party is induced to enter into a contract by a material misrepresentation, whether innocent or fraudulent, *prima facie* he has a right to rescind, though the contract will continue in force until he so elects. This election may be made in court, either by asking the court to declare the contract rescinded (see post, para 26.17), or by setting up rescission as a defence to a claim for specific performance (see post, para 29.38); or it may be made at some earlier date, as by avoidance of a voidable contract (see ante, para 21.21). Where the misrepresentation was fraudulent, the effect of rescission at common law was to avoid the contract *ab initio*;[1] and, whilst the common law would not allow rescission for innocent misrepresentation,[2] equity recognised a *prima facie* right to rescind *ab initio*.[3] However, it also accepted a number of ways in which that right may be lost (see post, paras 26.13–14).

[26.11]

1   Does 'rescission' refer to (a) the act of the party recognised by the court; or (b) the act of the court; or (c) either? Insofar as it means (a), the CCA contains some deemed agency provisions for the purposes of receiving notice of rescission: see ante, para 26.04.

2   *Per* Buckley LJ in *Buckland v Farmer & Moody* [1978] 3 All ER 929 at 938b (not a sale of goods case).

3   See generally Treitel, *Law of Contract* (10th edn), pp 342–43, 703–04.

[26.12]

1   *Per* Lord Atkinson in *Abram Steamship Co Ltd v Westville Steamship Co* [1923] AC 773, HL at 781. And see *Murray v Larsen* [1953] 2 Lloyd's Rep 453.

2   *Kennedy v Panama Royal Mail Co* (1867) LR 2 QB 580.

3   *Car & Universal Finance Co Ltd v Caldwell* (set out ante, para 21.21).

[26.13] Bars to rescission *ab initio*. Even assuming there is a *prima facie* right to rescind on grounds of innocent or fraudulent misrepresentation (see ante, para 26.12), there are a number of ways in which that right to rescind may be lost,[1] though the list has been reduced by statute (see post, para 26.14).

1   Restitutio in integrum *impossible*. The common law took the strict view that there could be no rescission for misrepresentation unless there could be a complete handing back and taking back of benefits transferred under the contract; and it is for this reason that rescission was barred at common law where the representor had transferred a benefit gained under the contract to a bfp (see below). Whilst equity recognised the overriding claims of the bfp, it took a rather more realistic view of the situation: in the case of fraud, the victim did not have to make restitution insofar as this was impossible by reason of the fraud; and, in the case of innocent misrepresentation, equity was prepared, within reason, to accept substantial restitution and a financial allowance for depreciation of the subject matter.[2]

2   *Affirmation*. If the representee, with knowledge of the misrepresentation,[3] elects to affirm the contract, the election is determined forever.[4] For instance, in *Long v Lloyd*[5] the court held that the buyer had elected to affirm in accepting the seller's offer to pay half the cost of making good the defect.

3   *Lapse of time*. How short such a period of time may be is demonstrated by *Long v Lloyd*:[5]

> The seller of a lorry innocently misrepresented to the buyer that it was in 'exceptional condition', and capable of 40 mph and 11 mpg. The buyer paid part of the price, took delivery, and used the lorry in the course of his business for three days. Having discovered several defects after the first day's outing, the buyer complained to the seller, who offered to pay half the cost of some of the repairs. The buyer accepted this; but, after two further days' use, he purported to reject on grounds of misrepresentation (see post, para 29.11). The Court of Appeal unanimously held that, from the nature of the representation, it must have been intended that the buyer be allowed a reasonable trial after delivery; but that one day's trial was reasonable, so that sending the lorry on a further journey amounted to a 'final acceptance';[6] and that in any event he had lost the right to rescind by accepting the offer to pay half the cost of repairs (see above).

It would seem that, where there is an innocent misrepresentation, time *prima facie* begins to run from the date the contract is executed;[7] but it has been suggested that in the case of

---

[26.13]

1   At one time, it was thought that the right to rescind for misrepresentation had not survived the SGA; but it is now clear that it has done so: see Howard (1963) 27 MLR 272, 282–85.

2   *Per* Bowen LJ in *Newbigging v Adam* (1886) 34 Ch D 582, CA at 594–95; and *per* Pearce LJ in *Long v Lloyd* (below) at 407.

3   Or perhaps, if he ought to have known: see Treitel, *Law of Contract* (10th edn), p 356.

4   *Per* Mellor J in *Clough v London and North Western Railway Co* (1871) LR 7 Exch 26, at 34.

5   [1958] 2 All ER 402; [1958] 1 WLR 753, CA.

6   This must be because of a lapse of a reasonable time, not because it constituted an affirmation, as there does not appear to be the intimation to the seller necessary for an affirmation. Cf *Butterworth v Kingsway Motors Ltd* (discussed post, para 29.13).

7   *Leaf v International Galleries* (set out post, para 29.11).

fraud time only runs from the date of discovery.[8] How much time must elapse is a question of fact, which will vary from case to case;[9] but in any event, it may be that it cannot exceed the time during which the innocent party might have rescinded *de futuro* for breach (see post, para 29.11).

4   *Rights acquired by a* bona fide *purchaser* (see ante, para 21.19).

[26.14] The Misrepresentation Act 1967. The Act made the following two types of change to the foregoing pattern.

1   *Bars to rescission.* At common law, there were two further possible bars to rescission; but these have been removed by s 1 of the 1967 Act, which provides as follows:

> Where a person has entered into a contract after a misrepresentation has been made to him, and –
>
> (a) the misrepresentation has become a term of the contract; or
>
> (b) the contract has been performed;
>
> or both, then, if otherwise he would be entitled to rescind the contract without alleging fraud, he shall be so entitled, subject to the provisions of this Act, notwithstanding the matters mentioned in paragraphs (a) and (b) of this section.

Paragraph (a) resolves a conflict as to the effect of the incorporation in a contract of an innocent misrepresentation made before contract. Two situations are possible. First, the misrepresentee acquires the right to rescind for breach of contract. Two questions arise: (i) does rescission for misrepresentation have the same effect as rescission for breach of contract (see post, para 26.16)? (ii) is the right to rescind for misrepresentation lost when the right to rescind for breach of contract is lost (see post, para 29.11)?[1] Second, the misrepresentee only acquires a right to damages for breach of contract. Section 1 appears to grant him also a *prima facie* right to rescind for misrepresentation.[2]

Paragraph (b) replaces the rule that rescission was barred by execution of a formal transfer.[3]

2   *Damages in lieu of rescission.* It was thought unsatisfactory that the representee should be able to rescind however minor the matter misrepresented.[4] Accordingly, s 2(2) of the Act now provides as follows:

> Where a person has entered into a contract after a misrepresentation has been made[5] to him otherwise than fraudulently,[6] and he would be entitled, by reason of the

---

8   Treitel, *op cit*, note 3, p 357.
9   Eg, *Oscar Chess Ltd v Williams* [1957] 1 All ER 325, CA (eight months too long); *Leaf's* case (above, five years).

[26.14]

1   As s 1(a) does not apply in the circumstances where there was no pre-contract misrepresentation, it may not be possible to grant rescission under s 1 in respect of a broken warranty which makes its first appearance in the contract.
2   Eg, the *Thomas Witter* case, at 167c.
3   The so called rule in *Seddon v NE Salt Co* [1905] 1 Ch 326 (see Howard (1963) 23 MLR 272).
4   Law Reform Committee, 10th Report, *Innocent Misrepresentation* (1962, Cmnd 1782) paras 11–12.
5   As to 'misrepresentation', and 'misrepresentation … made', see ante, para 17.10.
6   It is usually assumed that the 1967 Act has not touched the common law action for deceit: as to which, see ante, para 17.18.

misrepresentation, to rescind the contract,[7] then, if it is claimed, in any proceedings arising out of the contract, that the contract ought to be or has been rescinded, the court or arbitrator may declare the contract subsisting and award damages[8] in lieu of rescission, if of the opinion that it would be equitable to do so, having regard to the nature of the misrepresentation and the loss that would be caused by it if the contract were upheld, as well as to the loss that rescission would cause to the other party.

Unlike a claim under s 2(1) (see ante, para 17.10), the claim for damages under s 2(2) is a discretionary alternative to rescission for innocent misrepresentation.[9] Unfortunately, the wording of the provision does not make it clear whether the power to award damages under s 2(2) exists where a *prima facie* right to rescind arose, but was lost by one of the bars above considered (see para 26.13). In *Thomas Witter Ltd v TBP Industries Ltd:*[10]

> The parties decided to effect the sale of a carpet manufacturing business by selling the assets (goods), their price being fixed by reference to the profitability of the business. During the negotiations, the seller (S) altered the basis upon which the management accounts were drafted. Four years later, the buyer (B) claimed rescission of the elaborate written contract and damages for misrepresentation and breach of contract. In finding S liable for damages, Jacob J held as follows:
>
> (a) S's 'rough estimate' of one cost was not fraudulent (see ante, para 17.18), but negligent (see ante, para 17.20).
>
> (b) Rescission for misrepresentation was not available because *restitutio in integram* was no longer possible; but that would not preclude a claim for damages under s 2(2) (see below).
>
> (c) The profit forecasts were negligent misrepresentations within s 2(1) (see above), even though they were also (see below) breaches of contract.
>
> (d) The generalised exclusions clause would not be read as excluding liability for misrepresentation (see ante, para 18.06) and in any event contravened new s 3 as being unreasonable at the time the contract was made (at 170F). His Lordship refused to sever the clause to save part of it (see post, para 18.20).
>
> (e) S was also liable for breach of several express warranties (see ante, para 11.07).

Jacob J took the view that 'the power to award damages under s 2(2) does not depend upon an extant right to rescission – it only depends upon a right having existed in the past'.[11] As to the measure of damages, see post, para 27.24.

Rescission de futuro for breach of contract

[26.15] B may be entitled to rescind the contract on grounds of breach by A as follows: where A without lawful excuse, eg, frustration (see ante, para 22.14), or abandonment (see post, para 26.18), either performs his side of the bargain defectively or wrongfully

---

7 Does this mean right to rescind for (a) misrepresentation, or (b) misrepresentation or breach? Does it refer exclusively to the common law right to rescind; or to that right as enlarged by s 1 of the Misrepresentation Act 1967? See Atiyah and Treitel (1967) 30 MLR 369, 376–78.

8 It has been pointed out that rescission can be obtained without proof of damage, so that presumably the court could award nominal damages in lieu of rescission without proof of damage: *Street on Torts* (10th edn), p 126.

9 See further Treitel, *Law of Contract* (10th edn), pp 331–32. *Contra* Beale (1995) 111 LQR 385 at 386–88.

10 [1996] 2 All ER 573; (1995) 14 Tr LR 145 (Beale 111 LQR 385).

11 At 162c. *Contra Zanzibar v British Aerospace Ltd* [2000] 1 WLR 2333 (but see 117 LQR 524).

repudiates his obligations under the contract; but where the agreement is regulated and B is the creditor or owner, he will first have to serve a default notice (see ante, para 24.30). The effect of that 'rescission' will be considered later (see post, para 26.16).

1   *Defective performance.*[1] Whilst not every defective performance by A will justify B in refusing to continue with the contract,[2] it will do so in the following circumstances: where there is a breach of an essential stipulation (see ante, para 11.04), which will include a self-induced frustration (see ante, para 22.14); or a breach which deprives B of substantially the whole benefit of the contract (see ante, para 11.05); or where the contract expressly entitles B to refuse to continue if A commits any breach of contract (see ante, para 26.08); or where performance by A is a condition precedent to performance by B (see ante, para 26.01).

2   *Wrongful repudiation.* Any unequivocal refusal by A to perform a contractual obligation without good cause[3] may amount to a repudiation,[4] though it has been said that repudiation 'is a serious matter and not to be lightly inferred'.[5] The repudiation may be express, eg, anticipatory breach (see below); or it may be implied, either by statute (see s 11(3) of the SGA: ante, para 11.04), or at common law, as where A incapacitates himself from performing his contractual obligations,[6] or becomes insolvent,[7] or otherwise completely fails to perform his side of the bargain.[8] However, it has been held that an unjustified attempted rescission by A will not necessarily amount to an implied repudiation;[9] nor will an unjustified attempted price escalation necessarily do so.[10] Obviously, A may repudiate at the time when performance is due; but the common law has accepted that A may alternatively sometimes repudiate before that time, in which case there is what is termed an 'anticipatory breach'.[11]

[26.15]

1   This should be distinguished from repudiation: *per* Lord Denning MR in *Harbutt's Plasticine Ltd v Wayne Tank Ltd* [1970] 1 QB at 464, CA.

2   Eg, *State Trading Corp of India v Golodetz* [1989] 2 Lloyd's Rep 277, CA.

3   *Aliter,* where B is in breach of an essential stipulation, when A's repudiation will be rightful (cf s 11(3), SGA).

4   *Per* Lord Coleridge CJ in *Freeth v Burr* (1874) LR 9 CP at 213. For the difficulty this has caused with instalment contracts, see ante, paras 23.24–25; and for failure to pay a deposit on time, see post, para 27.19. Does the rule even extend to refusal to perform a warranty?

5   *Per* Lord Wright in *Ross T Smyth & Co Ltd v Bailey, Son & Co* [1940] 3 All ER 60 at 71, HL. See *The Sara D* [1989] CLY 415, CA; *Lombard North Central plc v Butterworth* (set out post, para 27.26); *Lloyds & Scottish Finance v Cyril Lord Carpet Sales* [1992] BCLC 609, HL; and post, para 27.47.

6   As by a supplier wrongfully reselling; but see the difficulties with *Smart v Holt* clauses (see ante, para 26.09). Compare the supplier's right to resell: see post, para 27.09.

7   *Edinburgh Grain Ltd v Marshall Food Group Ltd* 1999 SLT 15.

8   Eg, *Gill & Duffus SA v Berger & Co Inc* (set out ante, para 23.06); *Lawson v Supasink* [1984] Tr L 37, CA. Compare *Lombard North Central plc v Butterworth* (set out post, para 27.26).

9   *Woodar Investment Development Ltd v Wimpey Construction UK Ltd* [1980] 1 All ER 571, HL (not a sale case; supported by Treitel, *Law of Contract* (10th edn), p 749). Contrast *The Nanfri* [1979] AC 757, HL (charterparty; also supported by Treitel, p 750).

10   *Vaswani v Italian Motors* [1996] 1 WLR 270, PC (genuine mistake). For price escalation clauses, see ante, para 10.05.

11   Eg, *Tai Hing Cotton Mill Ltd v Kamsung Knitting Factory* (set out post, para 29.21). The terminology has been criticised by Lord Wrenbury in *Bradley v Newsom, Sons & Co* [1919] AC 16 at 53–54, HL. See generally Carter (1984) 47 MLR 422. As to an equivocal statement, see ante, para 26.01.

Whilst it is easy to draw the above distinctions in theory, it may be difficult to apply them in practice. This is particularly the case in instalment credit transactions, where an intimation by the borrower, buyer or hirer that he no longer intends to proceed with such a regulated transaction might amount to any of the following: (1) a notice of cancellation (see ante, para 10.29); or (2) a notice exercising a right to terminate (see ante, paras 26.05–07); or (3) a breach of contract or repudiation (see post, para 26.16).

[26.16] Effect of right to rescind *de futuro*. Assuming that B is entitled to rescind on the grounds of breach or repudiation by A, this does not automatically bring the contract to an end,[1] except possibly where further performance is impossible by reason of a frustrating breach.[2] It is thought that the general rule is that B merely has an option to treat the contract as discharged, the contract remaining binding on both parties unless and until B elects to rescind.[3] Nor is this option foreclosed by the duty to mitigate.[4] Thus, it would appear that at common law it is open to B to elect as to the following alternative rights:[5]

1   *To treat the contract as discharged*. It would now appear to be settled that the effect of discharge for breach is this: whether the discharge occurs automatically (upon a frustrating breach) or more commonly on unequivocal election by B,[6] the first effect is to discharge both parties from any duty of further performance of the ('primary') promises made under the contract, in a similar way to where the contract is frustrated (see ante, para 22.14 *et seq*). However, the two situations thereafter differ in that, whereas both parties to a frustrated contract walk free of any contractual[7] obligations, if a contract is discharged by A's breach, it was explained by Lord Diplock[8] that B is totally discharged from any future ('primary') obligations, because performance by A was a condition precedent to performance by B (see ante, para 26.01). However, with regard to all the other broken promises, the party in breach of that obligation remains liable to pay damages:[9] A remains liable for past and future breaches;[10] whereas B is only liable for past breaches, and can set these off when sued by A (s 53(1)(a) of the SGA: see generally post, para 29.26). It follows that B escapes from more of his obligations by rescinding *ab initio* for misrepresentation than *de futuro* for breach; and

---

[26.16]

1   *Heyman v Darwins Ltd* [1942] AC 356, HL; *Decro-Wall International SA v Practitioners in Marketing Ltd* [1971] 2 All ER 216, CA (franchise agreements).

2   *Harbutt's Plasticine Ltd v Wayne Tank Ltd* [1970] 1 QB 447, CA; and see further ante, para 22.13.

3   Per Diplock LJ in *Ward Ltd v Bignall* (set out post, para 27.10) at 548. See also *Garnac Grain Co v HMF Faure & Fairclough Ltd* [1968] AC 1130, HL.

4   *Tredegar Iron Co Ltd v Hawthorn Brothers & Co* (1902) 18 TLR 716, CA. But see Goode, *Commercial Law* (2nd edn), pp 130–32; and further post, para 27.44.

5   Per Diplock LJ in *Ward Ltd v Bignall* (above) at 550. Election to treat the contract as discharged does not amount to a variation: *Moschi v Air Services* [1973] AC 331, HL. See also CCA, s 89: ante, para 24.35.

6   *Vitol SA v Norelf Ltd, The Santa Clara* [1996] AC 800, HL.

7   See ante, para 23.06. Though not necessarily of quasi-contractual obligations: see ante, para 22.19.

8   In *Gill & Duffus SA v Berger & Co Inc* (set out ante, para 23.06) at 390, HL.

9   What Lord Diplock termed 'substituted or secondary obligations' in *Photo Production Ltd v Securicor Transport Ltd* [1980] AC 827 at 848, HL. See also post, para 27.29.

10 See *Hyundai Heavy Industries Co Ltd v Papadopoulos* [1980] 2 All ER 29, HL; and the *Stocznia* case (set out post, para 29.16). As to future rentals, see post, para 27.38 and as to part-payments, see post, para 27.19.

by using the Misrepresentation Act 1967, s 2, he may be able to recover damages from A (see ante, para 17.10. See further ante, para 26.14).

2   *Not to treat the contract as discharged.* If B elects to keep the contract alive, then it continues binding on both parties (see post, para 29.02), unless, perhaps there is a 'continuing breach' (see post, para 29.10): each must perform his side of the contract, but B may claim damages for that breach: *Wallis & Wells v Pratt & Haynes* (set out ante, para 11.04). In the case of an anticipatory breach, that election may operate to the advantage of either side in respect of subsequent impossibility[11] or the measure of damages.[12]

Discharge by subsequent act or event

[26.17] Leaving aside discharge by breach, there are certain other acts or events occurring subsequent to the formation of the contract and irrespective of the terms which may bring about its discharge.

1   *Subsequent agreement* (see post, para 26.18).

2   *Election of remedies.* Where a man is entitled to one of two inconsistent rights, any unequivocal act of election[1] to pursue one of them, made by him with knowledge of his rights, will shut him out from the other,[1a] as where an owner under an hp agreement accepts hire rent after breach (see post, para 27.22), or a seller exercises a licence to seize under a conditional sale.[2] However, normally it is not a question of choosing between two inconsistent rights, but merely of electing between two alternative remedies, in contract or tort, in which case the election is not *per se* irrevocable;[3] but a party will *prima facie* be bound by a final judgment of a court of competent jurisdiction,[4] eg, rescission *ab initio* (see ante, para 26.12).

3   *Judgment.* Prima facie, final judgment in any suit has the effect of merging the original cause of action in the judgment, and the plaintiff must rely as against the defendant on the rights created by the judgment, eg, a judgment debt (see post, para 27.04). Judgment alone will normally extinguish any alternative claims against the defendant,[5] but not those claims which are cumulative.[6] Nor will judgment alone discharge the claim upon which that judgment was obtained, though satisfaction of the judgment will do so: for instance, a judgment in conversion for damages

---

11   Eg, *Avery v Bowden* (1855) 5 E & B 714. See generally ante, para 22.14.

12   Eg, *Roper v Johnson* (1873) LR 8 CP 167. See generally post, para 29.21.

[26.17]

1   Whether he has made such an election is a matter of fact: *Bremer Handelsgesellschaft mbH v Deutsche Conti Handelsgesellschaft mbH (No 2)* [1983] 2 Lloyd's Rep 45, CA. For discussion of the use of the term 'waiver' in this context, see Spencer Bower, *Estoppel* (2nd edn), p 295.

1a *Aliter* where he has not so elected: the *Albright & Wilson* case (set out ante, para 13.01), at para 7.

2   *Hewison v Ricketts* (set out post, para 27.19). Or where he sues for the price (see post, para 27.16).

3   But see *Meng Leong Development Pte Ltd v Jip Hong Trading Co Pte Ltd* [1985] 1 All ER 120, PC (specific performance sought on sale of land). For waiver, see post, para 26.23.

4   *Forward Trust Ltd v Whymark* [1990] 2 QB 670, CA, *per* Lord Donaldson MR, AER at 921d; *DG of FT v First National Bank plc* (set out ante, para 7.03A).

5   What of claims against third parties? Compare the two authorities cited in note 4 above.

6   Eg, the right of an owner under an hp agreement to arrears of rentals and damages for breach (see post, para 27.21). See the *First National Bank* case (set out ante, para 7.03A), *per* Lord Bingham at paras 11, 12.

amounting to the assessed value of the goods claimed will vest the plaintiff's title in the defendant if satisfied,[7] but not if it remains unsatisfied.[8] Finally, it should be remembered that, where more than one person is liable in respect of the same damage, the position has been altered: whilst at common law even an unsatisfied judgment against one of them discharged the others,[9] by statute a contribution can now be claimed from 'any person liable in respect of the same damage'.[10]

4   *Repossession.* The recaption of 'protected goods' contrary to s 90 of the CCA terminates the agreement and releases the debtor from all liability thereunder (s 91: see ante, para 24.38).

5   *Early payment* (see post, para 26.19).

6   *Limitation of actions.* Under the Limitation Act 1980 (as amended) the ordinary rule is that no civil action may be brought on a simple contract or for a tort after the expiry of six years from the moment when the cause of action arose (ss 2, 3, 5, 9). However, there are many exceptions to this rule: for instance, there is a longer limitation period where a contract is made by deed (a specialty: s 8), or certain loans (s 6), or the plaintiff suffers from a disability (s 28), or there is acknowledgment or part payment of a debt (ss 29–31), or there is fraud, concealment or mistake (s 32), or in respect of product liability claims (see ante, para 17.23); and the limitation period is reduced to three years for personal injuries (s 11) and two years for some consumer remedies (see post, para 29.03A). Further consideration of this complicated subject is beyond the scope of this work.

[26.18] Subsequent agreement. On ordinary principles, any duty created by one contract may be discharged by another contract between the same parties; and there may therefore be a total or partial discharge of liability.[1]

1   *Total discharge.* Where the parties expressly agree that each shall be discharged from his contractual liability, this may be seen almost as a mutual repudiation (see ante, para 26.15); but a total discharge may also be brought about impliedly, as where the parties abandon the contract.[2] If the first contract is still executory on both sides at the time of the subsequent agreement, it generates its own consideration; but, if the first contract remains executory on one side only, it will usually[3] be necessary for that party to give some fresh consideration for his release, in which case it is termed an

---

7   *USA v Dollfus Mieg* [1952] AC 582, HL (see now the Torts Act 1977, s 5). There is a similar rule under the CCA, s 133(5) in respect of a satisfied time or return order (see ante, para 24.43).

8   *Ellis v John Stenning & Son* [1932] 2 Ch 81.

9   Eg, *Kendall v Hamilton* (1879) 4 App Cas 504, HL (partnership case).

10   Civil Liability (Contribution) Act 1978, s 1(1); and see s 1(5). See further generally ante, para 12.10.

[26.18]

1   The common law rule that release of one joint tortfeasor or contractor releases all the others appears to have been left open by the silence of the Civil Liability (Contribution) Act 1978: see s 1(4), the Current Law Annotation thereto and Dugdale (1979) 42 MLR at 189.

2   Eg, *Pearl Mill Ltd v Ivy Tanneries Ltd* [1919] 1 KB 78, DC; *GW Fisher Ltd v Eastwoods Ltd* [1936] 1 All ER 421. Alternatively, such a situation may be looked at as mutual breaches: see Treitel, *Law of Contract* (10th edn), p 763.

3   But see s 62 of the Bills of Exchange Act 1882, and the suggestion in Treitel, *ibid*, p 95.

'accord and satisfaction'.[4] Two forms of total discharge require special mention. First, the original contract may be replaced by an entirely new one: for instance, where the subject matter of the first contract is 'traded-in' in part exchange (see ante, para 2.09); or taken with further goods under the second agreement (see ante, para 26.08); or a fresh party is added to the agreement, an arrangement termed a 'novation' (see ante, para 7.27). Second, where a lesser sum is tendered in satisfaction of a greater, *prima facie* that lesser payment is no satisfaction of the greater, and the difference is still owed.[5] However, sufficient consideration to discharge the first agreement may be generated, as where the lesser payment is made early, or in kind,[6] or in a different currency,[7] or the claim was of an uncertain amount,[8] or bf disputed;[9] or it may be inequitable to claim the larger sum (see post, para 26.24).

2   *Partial discharge.* The terms of the original contract may be varied by contract or by mere waiver (see post, para 26.20). Whether there has been a contractual variation (see post, para 26.21) or total discharge and subsequent agreement is a question of intention.[10]

[26.19] Early payment. Particularly in the case of a contract which provides for payment by instalments, there may be situations where either creditor or debtor seeks early payment; and a distinction must be drawn according to which party activated the early payment.

1   *Activated by creditor.* Especially in instalment sales on credit (see ante, para 1.03), it is common to find an acceleration clause.[1] But distinguish a claim with regard to future hire rent: no hire rent is due after termination of the bailment (see post, para 27.21); and an acceleration clause in an hp agreement may turn that agreement into a conditional sale (see ante, para 1.22). In *Wadham Stringer Finance Ltd v Meaney*:[2]

> A conditional sale agreement within the HPA 1965 gave the seller an express right on the buyer's default to elect to accelerate payment of the price. The buyer having failed to pay any instalments, the seller successfully claimed the sum due under the accelerated payments clause, including charges.

Woolf J rejected all the following arguments by the buyer in trying to avoid that clause: (1) that it was void as being a restriction on his statutory right to terminate, because the sum payable under it was a 'final payment' for the purposes of what is

---

4   See generally, Treitel, *op cit*, note 2, pp 94–95; Goode, *HP Law and Practice* (2nd edn), pp 329–30.
5   *Foakes v Beer* (1884) 9 App Cas 605, HL; *D and C Builders Ltd v Rees* [1966] 2 QB 617, CA (payment by cheque); *Ferguson v Dawson* [1997] 1 All ER 315, CA (similar); *IRC v Fry* (2001) 151 NLJ 1820.
6   *Pinnel's case* (1602) 5 Co Rep 117a. For early payment, see generally post, para 26.19.
7   *Alan & Co Ltd v El Nasr Export & Import Co* (set out post, para 26.21).
8   What is termed an unliquidated sum: see *Wilkinson v Byers* (1834) 1 A & E 106. For liquidated damages clauses, see post, para 27.24.
9   *Re Warren* (1884) 53 LJ Ch 1016; *Auriema v Haigh and Ringrose* [1989] CLY 403.
10   See Guest, *Law of HP*, para 462.
[26.19]
1   See ante, paras 7.03, 23.26; and generally Goode [1982] JBL 148; Goode, *Payment Obligations in Commercial and Financial Transactions*, pp 51–53. As to damages for loss of future rentals, see post, para 27.38.
2   [1980] 3 All ER 789; [1981] 1 WLR 39; discussed by Davidson 1982 SLT 1.

now s 99(1) of the CCA – (see ante, para 26.05), or as seeking to impose an additional liability on him;[3] (2) that it was void as an attempt to impose on him liability after termination;[4] and (3) that it was void as being a penalty,[5] though nowadays such a clause might be attacked under other statutes as being unreasonable or unfair.[6] It is important to remember that reliance on an acceleration clause presupposes that the agreement is still in being, because the clause is treated (unrealistically?) as an alternative method of 'primary' performance (see ante, para 26.16): if the clause become operable on breach, reliance on it by the supplier may be an election to affirm the contract.[7] Normally, the agreement will provide for payment of interest on sums accrued (including charges) but unpaid (see ante, para 7.03A). However, sometimes an agreement will go further and provide for an increase in the rate of interest on default ('default interest'), supposedly to recompense the creditor for the extra administrative cost and increased risk.[8] In this respect, the CCA has in a number of respects altered the rules in favour of a debtor under a regulated consumer credit agreement: (a) it requires a prior seven day notice (ss 76(1)(a); 87(1)(b): see ante, para 24.28); (b) the agreement may be cancellable (s 67: see ante, para 10.29) or amount to an extortionate credit bargain (s 137: see post, para 29.40); (c) the buyer may seek a Time Order (s 129: see ante, para 24.40) or statutory rebate;[9] (d) a court may suspend the operation of an acceleration clause (s 135(1)(b): see post, para 9.20); and (e) directly protect him against such default interest in a consumer credit (but not consumer hire) agreement,[10] though interest can still continue at the previous rate, and once again, the home credit trade does things differently.[11]

2   *Activated by debtor* (see post, para 26.19A).

[26.19A] Early payment by the debtor. The debtor, buyer or hirer in a loan, instalment sale or hp agreement may seek to pay the whole outstanding sum ahead of time. At common law, he is *prima facie* entitled to make early settlement by tender to the lender,

---

3   The provision for the payment of interest was not an additional liability contrary to what is now s 100(1) of the CCA because it had accrued before termination under what is now s 99(2) of the CCA: see ante, para 26.05 and post, para 27.49. But see now post, para 26.19A.

4   Because the operation of the clause did not terminate the agreement (see ante, paras 26.08; 26.10), which remained in force until the parties had performed all their obligations under it. For the rights of the innocent party upon serious breach, see ante, para 26.16.

5   Because it contained provisions for rebate of charges on early settlement and was therefore a genuine pre-estimate of loss: see also *The Angelic Star* [1988] 1 Lloyd's Rep 122, CA; *Lordsvale Finance plc v Bank of Zambia* [1996] QB 752; and post, para 27.26.

6   Unreasonable under s 3 of UCTA (see ante, para 18.24) or unfair under the UTCC Regulations, Grey Term 1(e): see ante, para 11.16.

7   See *Hewison v Ricketts* (set out post, para 27.19); and generally ante, para 26.16. In this sense, invocation of an acceleration clause may be seen at common law as an alternative to recaption: as to which see ante, para 24.34.

8   Eg, *Mutual Loan Fund Association Ltd v Sanderson* [1937] 1 All ER 380.

9   CCA, s 95: see post, para 26.19A. Judgment should be entered for the unrebated sum: *Forward Trust Ltd v Whymark* [1990] 2 QB 670, CA (flat rate agreement).

10   Section 93, which effectively reduces the rate below the APR by excluding non-interest items from the tcc. However, this does not preclude the charging of any extra administration costs actually caused by the default (see (1999) 54 CC 1/33), so that they cannot amount to a penalty (see post, para 27.26).

11   They tend to await the end of the credit period (say 20 weeks) and then renew the facility for a further such period at the same APR, claiming that this does not breach CCA, s 93 (see above).

seller or owner of the capital sum plus interest due to date of payment;[1] and, where the lender/supplier mistakenly quotes too low a 'settlement figure' (see below) for this purpose, he may subsequently be estopped from claiming the difference.[2] Where there is a 'trade-in' (see ante, para 2.09), 'payment' may be effected by the dealer paying the 'settlement figure' on the old goods out of their trade-in price[3] to their supplier on behalf of the buyer or hirer.[4] Suppose the dealer does not make that payment. On general principle, the buyer or hirer is responsible for seeing his debt paid to the creditor (see ante, para 23.13) and it is not clear that the dealer is at common law the creditor's agent (see ante, para 16.06). But see below.

Rebates. In confirmation of the common law rule (see post, para 27.29), the agreement will sometimes provide for,[5] or the supplier allow,[6] a rebate for early settlement, though this may cause him financial embarrassment if he has funded his operation at rates of interest higher than those prevailing at the time of settlement.[7] Nevertheless, when the agreement is regulated, the CCA requires the creditor to take this merciful line: on written request,[8] the debtor has statutory rights to a written statement of the sum outstanding;[9] and, armed with that information, the debtor may elect to exercise by written notice a right to make early payment of that sum (s 172(1)) to the creditor,[10] upon which he is entitled to a minimum statutory rebate in respect of future instalments (s 95). This 'early settlement rebate' is at a minimum figure prescribed by the regulations, which is calculated by a complicated industry formula known as the 'Rule of 78'.[11] This formula is tolerable for agreements of between about two and five years' duration, but works unfairly for shorter or longer periods: *Falco Finance Ltd v Gough* (see ante, para 11.16). At

---

[26.19A]

1   *Lancashire Waggon Co v Nuttall* (1879) 42 LT 465, CA; and Goode, *HP Law and Practice* (2nd edn), p 268. Distinguish payment of a lesser sum on or after due date (see ante, para 26.01); or where the creditor is entitled to terminate the agreement: *Alf Vaughan & Co Ltd v Royscot Trust plc* (set out post, para 27.22).

2   *Lombard North Central plc v Stobart* (1990) 9 Tr LR 105, CA; CCA, s 172(1); and see generally post, para 26.24.

3   If the settlement figure exceeds the trade-in and is added to the new agreement, this may create difficulties: (i) there may then be a multiple agreement – a dcs supply and a dc loan (see ante, para 5.27); (ii) there may be difficulty over the 'total price' (see ante, para 24.35). See 46 CC 1/26; 46 CC 2/12.

4   See Goode, *Consumer Credit Law and Practice*, para 36.85.

5   If the interest is to be calculated daily, the debtor may be able to make an early 'capital repayment' and hence avoid any subsequent liability to interest on the sum repaid: [1990] Which? 492.

6   As to this displacing the prohibition on assignment, see ante, para 7.26. For payment at an earlier date of a lesser sum, see ante, para 26.18.

7   For the common law requirement of a rebate for accelerated payment made by way of the payment of damages, see post, para 27.29. Should such rebate affect any commission previously paid to the dealer for introducing the business?

8   *Home Insulation v Wadsley* [1988] CCLR 25, DC. The notice does not need to be signed by the debtor, nor of any minimum duration: Goode, *op cit*, note 4, para 36.13.

9   Section 97. For the prescribed form, see the Consumer Credit (Settlement Information) Regulations 1983, SI No 1564. For the effect of the Data Protection Act 1998 (see ante, para 8.36), see (1988) CC 5/10.

10 Section 94(1), together with any option to purchase (s 94(2)). Suppose the dealer never forwards payments to the creditor. Does s 56(1)(c) (see ante, para 16.08) place the debtor in a stronger position than at common law (see note 1, above)?

11 Consumer Credit (Rebate on Early Settlement) Regulations 1983, SI No 1562 (as amended); and further Guest and Lloyd, *Encyclopedia of Consumer Credit*, para 3-263 *et seq*. For reform proposals in respect of the rebate, see OFT, *Consumer Credit Deregulation* (1994) Ch 8; the DG (see (2000) 12 Credit Today 6 and 24; and generally ante, para 5.11.

the same time, such early payment will discharge any linked transaction (see ante, para 5.31) as regards future obligations (s 96(1). There is power to exempt by regulation: s 96(3)). It would seem that the right to a statutory rebate is drafted widely enough to be applicable also on refinancing (see ante, para 7.04A) or where it is the creditor who insists upon early payment by reason of the debtor's breach,[12] but not where there is no fixed date for repayment, eg, a loan repayable on demand.

Variation and waiver[1]

[26.20] The subject matter of this section is the variation and waiver of obligations, whether or not those obligations arise from a contract.[1a] Historically, this area is bedeviled by the Statute of Frauds 1677, though that body of law is no longer applicable to sales of goods,[2] and is only relevant here insofar as it relates to contracts of surety (see ante, para 25.06). Ignoring the now largely irrelevant usage under the Statute of Frauds, the terms 'variation' and 'waiver' will be used to mean the following:[3] 'variation' will be reserved for those situations where contractual rights are subsequently altered by another contract;[4] and any attempt to alter accrued rights otherwise than by contract will be called a 'waiver'.[5] Both variations and waivers bears some resemblance to the exclusion clauses and disclaimers considered in Chapter 18; but they must be distinguished from the subject matter of that chapter in that variation and waiver take effect, if at all, only **after** the accrual of contractual or tortious liability. In a consumer supply, a requirement that any variation must be in writing may be an unfair term.[6]

Variation of liability

[26.21] **Common law.** On ordinary principles, whilst an attempted unilateral variation of contract will usually only amount to a breach,[1] the parties may always make alterations to their contract by mutual agreement.[2] Thus, in *Alan & Co Ltd v El Nasr Export & Import Co*:[3]

---

12 Under an acceleration clause: see *Forward Trust Ltd v Whymark* [1990] 2 QB 670, CA. As to credit cards, see Jones, *Credit Cards*, 166–68.

[26.20]

1 See generally Stoljar (1957) 35 Can BR 484; Adams (1972) 36 Conv 245; Dugdale and Yates (1976) 39 MLR 680.

1a Distinguish the situation where the original contract itself allows alteration of its terms, eg, price adjustment formulae (see ante, para 10.05).

2 Section 4 of the SGA 1893 was repealed by the Law Reform (Enforcement of Contracts) Act 1954, s 1: see ante, para 9.02.

3 Unfortunately, the expression 'waiver' has not in practice been restricted as in the text, but has sometimes been used to mean rescission or variation: Treitel, *Law of Contract* (10th edn), p 97.

4 The distinction is whether or not the promise to give up contractual rights is itself supported by consideration: see ante, para 26.18.

5 In practice, it may be difficult to decide whether there has been a variation or a waiver: see Hoggett (1970) 33 MLR 518.

6 Grey Term 1(n): OFT, *Bulletin No 13*, case 16; *No 14*, case 16; and see generally ante, para 11.18.

[26.21]

1 See generally, ante, para 26.15. With regard to payment of a lesser sum than the debt due, this will usually be no satisfaction (see ante, para 26.01), except where there is a rebate (see ante, para 26.19A).

2 See *D and C Builders Ltd v Rees* [1966] 2 QB 617, CA (not a sale case).

3 [1972] 2 QB 189; [1972] 2 All ER 127, CA.

There were two contracts for the sale of coffee in Kenya, at a price of 'Shs 262/- ... per cwt', payment by confirmed irrevocable credit prior to shipment. In purported compliance with the contract, the buyers arranged a credit in sterling, which the sellers drew upon in relation to the September shipment. At the time of the contract, there was parity between sterling and Kenyan currency; but, before the sellers could draw on the credit in respect of the November shipment, sterling was devalued. The sellers claimed the amount of Kenyan shillings necessary to restore the amount paid in sterling to its pre-devaluation level.

The Court of Appeal held that the irrevocable credit should have been in Kenyan currency, because the money of account under the original contract was Kenyan currency; but that, in accepting a sterling irrevocable credit,[4] the sellers had either varied the original contract to substitute sterling for Kenyan currency[5] or waived the right to Kenyan currency (see generally post, para 26.23).

Prima facie, even a written contract may be varied by oral agreement;[6] but a guarantee required to be evidenced in writing may only be varied by written agreement,[7] though it may be discharged by oral agreement.[8] Leaving that complication aside, the only matter likely to cause general difficulty in this context is the requirement of consideration. If neither or both of the parties are in breach of contract, then the variation generates its own consideration;[9] but, if only one party is in breach of the original agreement, consideration by that party is not so generated automatically.[10] Quite apart from this, variation of regulated instalment credit transactions may give rise to particular difficulties in this context (see post, para 26.22).

[26.22] Regulated agreements. The CCA alters the general rules above considered with regard to both unilateral and consensual variations of regulated agreements.

1   *Unilateral variations*. The CCA allows one party to vary a regulated agreement without cause in several circumstances: cancellation (ss 67–73: see ante, para 10.32); early payment (ss 94–96: see ante, para 26.19A); remedying default (s 89: see ante, para 24.32. For the position where the default arises upon the death of the debtor or hirer, see ante, para 24.48); time orders (see ante, para 24.40) or other court orders utilising s 136 (see ante, para 9.20); and extortionate credit bargains (see post, para 29.40).

2   *Consensual variations*. Except in the case of non-commercial agreements (s 82(7). For non-commercial agreements, see ante, para 5.18), s 82 controls consensual variations of regulated agreements in a number of circumstances.

---

4   It was held that the giving of a credit was conditional payment, which became absolute when the credit was duly honoured: as to absolute and conditional payment, see Butterworths edn, 1989, para 23.14A. For money of account and irrevocable credits, see ante, para 23.14.

5   See also *Hartley v Hymans* (set out post, para 26.24). For a case where there was no variation because the parties were not *ad idem*, see *Woodhouse AC Israel Cocoa Ltd SA v Nigerian Produce Marketing Co Ltd* [1972] AC 741, HL.

6   A standard form instalment credit contract may purport to exclude oral variations and waivers: see post, para 26.23. As to the formation in respect of a variation of a sale of land, see ante, para 9.03.

7   *Goss v Nugent* (1833) 5 B & Ad 58.

8   *Morris v Baron* [1918] AC 1, HL. See further ante, para 25.06.

9   See ante, para 26.18. It may be important to determine whether, in the case of non-performance of the varied agreement, the consideration is the promise to vary, or performance of that promise.

10   For a case where consideration was found, see *Tommey v Finextra Ltd* (1962) 106 Sol Jo 1012.

(a) Section 82(1) envisages that the regulated agreement may confer on the creditor a power to vary the terms of the agreement. Such a power is common in relation to the rate of interest charged. In *Lombard Tricity Finance Ltd v Paton*:[1]

> P was minded to obtain an Amstrad computer from a retailer, Dixons, for a price of £244.98. Instead of a credit sale from Dixons, he entered a loan transaction under which Lombard provided him with running account credit within s 10 of the CCA (see ante, para 5.28). A box on the face of that credit agreement stated that interest payable on the credit balance was 'subject to variation by the creditor from time to time on notification as required by law'. After an interest rate increase P defaulted and Lombard sued for the outstanding loan.

P argued that the credit agreement was improperly executed because, contrary to Regulations made under s 60 (see ante, para 9.10), the agreement did not indicate 'the circumstances in which any variation ... may occur'. However, a unanimous Court of Appeal reasoned that, if it was lawful for a seller to vary unilaterally the price (see ante, para 10.05), it was in principle permissible for the creditor to vary unilaterally the rate of interest charged;[2] that there was nothing in the CCA regulations to make that unlawful; and that this power was stated with sufficient clarity in the box on the face of the agreement (see ante, para 9.11). As to the implementation of such rate changes,[3] s 82(1) insists that the variation does not take effect before notice is given to the debtor or hirer in the prescribed manner.[4] This rule does not apply to variations which are automatic in the sense of being outside the control of the parties.[5]

(b) Where, after the formation of a regulated agreement,[6] the parties subsequently agree[7] to 'vary or supplement' it,[8] the effect of the modifying agreement is to

---

[26.22]

1   [1989] 1 All ER 918; (1989) 8 Tr LR 129, CA (criticised 105 LQR 524). It does not apply where the variation is automatic in the sense of being outside the control of the parties: as to which, see ante, para 10.05.

2   If a lender treats old borrowers capriciously unfavourably, the OFT may take action under the CCA licensing provisions (see ante, para 6.23): *per* Staughton LJ in *Paton* (below) at 923d; and see [2001] 3 Credit Today 7. As to new borrowers, if the loan is a consumer supply, the variation may also be unfair: OFT, 2000-AR 35; and see ante, para 11.12 *et seq.*

3   If the power is utilised to make too radical a variation of the agreement, it might be struck down by s 3(2)(b) of UCTA (see ante, para 18.24). There being currently no statutory power to make minor alterations unilaterally, these are commonly effected by letters of waiver (see post, para 26.24): Rosenthal (1990) 45 CC 1/10.

4   Consumer Credit (Notice of Variation of Agreements) Regulations 1977, SI 328. See further Guest and Lloyd, *Encyclopedia of Consumer Credit*, paras 2-083, 3-224; Jones, *Credit Cards*, pp 171–73.

5   See ante, para 10.05. A newspaper advertisement announcing such variations would seem to be outside the advertising regulations (see ante, para 8.30), provided it referred only to existing (not potential) customers.

6   Could ss 82(2) and (3) be avoided by inserting a general power of unilateral variation by the creditor? But see note 3, above.

7   These provisions only apply where there is a contract of variation strictly so called. They have no application to waivers, eg, where the creditor unilaterally grants the debtor a 'payment holiday' (see post, para 26.24); nor to contracts which discharge earlier agreements, eg, novations (see ante, para 26.18). See Guest and Lloyd, *op cit*, note 4, para 2-083.

8   Eg, linked-on agreements (see ante, para 24.36); rescheduling of payments on default (see ante, para 24.32); replacement of defective goods (see post, para 29.03); debtor or hirer wishes to assign his interest to a third party (see ante, para 1.23); where an agreement is secured on land and the debtor moves house (see ante, para 25.24).

revoke the earlier agreement and replace it with a new agreement combining the effect of the two agreements.[9] If the earlier agreement is regulated, the effect of s 82(3) is that generally speaking the 'modifying agreement' is also regulated: so, once regulated always regulated,[10] though the variation may give rise to substantial extra CCA requirements, principally the Part V requirements (as to which, see generally Chapter 7). Instead of first taking out a fixed-sum agreement and later varying it, it may therefore be simpler and more attractive to the creditor instead to propose from the outset a running-account credit.[11]

(c) Where the parties agree to vary a non-regulated agreement, s 82(2) spells out how to decide whether the 'modifying agreement' has become regulated.[12]

The doctrine of waiver

[26.23] A party may waive the right to sue in either tort or contract.

1 *Waiver of tort.*[1] Where a party indicates before the commission of a tort against him that he will waive any right of action in respect thereof, this may amount to a consent to the commission of the tort against him, or a voluntary assumption of risk (see ante, para 18.03). A waiver after commission of the tort may operate to discharge the right of action by way of an election of remedies, or by reason of a judgment (see ante, para 26.17); but otherwise its effect is presumably similar to that in contract (see below).

2 *Waiver of contractual rights.* The common law has long accepted that contractual rights may be expressly or impliedly waived before or after breach. The effect of a waiver may be to discharge the whole contract: it may evince a mutual intention to abandon the contract;[2] alternatively, a party who wrongfully repudiates his own obligations, or disables himself from performing them, may thereby impliedly waive his own rights.[3] However, we are concerned here with those waivers which do not discharge the whole contract, but merely purport to relinquish certain rights under it. Whether a contractual right has been waived is primarily a question of intention,[4] with this limitation: if the contractual provision is for the benefit of one party alone, he may waive it unilaterally; but, if it is inserted for the benefit of both parties, it can only be

---

9   Section 82(2). Distinguish self-standing agreements: see Goode, *Consumer Credit Law and Practice*, para 35.62.

10 Eg, further loan advanced under a fixed-sum credit. But see the special rules for the modification of regulated running-account credit (s 82(4)) and cancellable agreements (s 82(5), (6)): ante, para 10.32. For protected goods, see ante, para 24.36.

11 He would, of course, thereby give up any recaption rights (see ante, para 24.23). For running-account credit, see ante, para 7.08.

12 See Goode, *op cit*, note 9, para 35.61 *et seq.* If so, matters become so complicated and expensive that such transactions are best avoided: Guest and Lloyd, *op cit*, note 4, para 2-083. For the difficulties raised by further advances, see Ferran, *Mortgage Securitisation*, pp 122–23.

[26.23]

1   The expression 'waiver of tort' may be misleading: see Burrows (1983) 99 LQR at 236–37.

2   Eg, *Fisher Ltd v Eastwoods Ltd* [1936] 1 All ER 421.

3   See the cases collected in *Benjamin on Sale* (8th edn, 1950), p 560, note (q).

4   See *per* Lord Denning LJ in *Charles Rickards Ltd v Oppenheim* (set out post, para 26.25). See also *Finance for Shipping v Appledore* [1982] Com LR 49, CA.

waived by mutual agreement.[5] Mere neglect or delay in enforcing an agreement does not *per se* amount to a waiver;[6] but, to avoid any doubt, standard form agreements (see ante, para 11.08) commonly provide that no relaxation or indulgence shall be construed as a waiver of rights. At any event, it is clear that a waiver has no effect unless unequivocal,[7] and perhaps then only where the representee acts on it to his detriment.[8] Examination of the basis of waiver in sale (see post, para 26.24) is followed by consideration of the general effect of such waiver (see post, para 26.25), and the relationship of waiver to rejection for the wrong reason (see post, para 26.26).

[26.24] The basis of waiver. The common law rules as to waiver of contractual rights (see ante, para 26.23) would appear to have been partially embodied in s 11(2) of the SGA, which provides as follows:

> Where a contract of sale is subject to a condition to be fulfilled by the seller, the buyer may waive the condition, or may elect to treat the breach of the condition as a breach of warranty and not as a ground for treating the contract as repudiated.

It should be noticed that the provision speaks of a 'waiver' of rights and an 'election' of remedies;[1] and the distinction between the two may become important when deciding whether a buyer may go back on his waiver or election. Where the buyer has several alternative remedies at his disposal, the **election** may be or become irrevocable (see ante, para 26.17); and in some circumstances the law may compel the buyer to accept damages rather than rescind for breach of condition (see post, para 29.05). On the other hand, the effect of a **waiver** of rights is illustrated by *Hartley v Hymans*:[2]

> A written contract for the sale of 11,000 lbs of cotton provided for delivery between September and 15 November 1918. By the latter date, the seller had only delivered 500 lbs; and the buyer subsequently repeatedly complained and requested early delivery. Instalments totalling 3704 lbs were delivered between 15 November 1918 and 27 February 1919. On 13 March 1919 the buyer without any previous notice, purported to cancel the order.

In the seller's action for non-acceptance (see post, para 27.24), McCardie J found that the time for tender of delivery was of the essence of the contract (see ante, para 23.18); but he held that the buyer was not entitled to insist on delivery in the period ending 15 November 1918 for the following reasons:

(1) he had waived his rights under what is now s 11(2); and

---

5   See *per* Tucker J in the *Fibrosa* case [1942] 1 KB 12, at 20–21 (reversed by the HL on other grounds: [1943] AC 32); and *per* Buckley J in *Manchester Diocesan Council v Commercial and General Investments Ltd* [1969] 3 All ER 1593 at 1598.

6   *Perry v Davis* (1858) 3 CB NS 769 (not a sale case).

7   *Mardorf Peach & Co Ltd v Attica Sea Carriers Corp* [1977] AC 850, HL (charterparty); *Woodhouse AC Israel Cocoa Ltd SA v Nigerian Produce Marketing Co Ltd* [1972] AC 741, HL (sale); *The Post Chaser* [1982] 1 All ER 19 (sale); *Bunge SA v Compagnie Europeane De Cereales* [1982] 1 Lloyd's Rep 306 (sale).

8   *The Post Chaser* (above). *Sed quaere?*

[26.24]

1   Are there (only?) two different sorts of waiver? See generally Treitel, *Law of Contract* (10th edn), pp 752–56.

2   [1920] 3 KB 475; [1920] All ER Rep 328.

(2) he was estopped from asserting that the contract ceased to be valid on that date;[3] and

(3) the parties had made a new agreement extending the period for delivery beyond 15 November 1918 (see ante, para 26.21).

Each of the first two reasons appears to refer to a different line of authority, and 'reveals the incredible confusion of thought the law has now reached'.[4] The binding effect of a waiver at common law had already been recognised in the converse case where the buyer was in breach, and the seller waived the breach;[5] but in a later case Denning LJ explained the rule in terms of estoppel.[6] However, a promise as to future conduct cannot amount to an estoppel at common law (see ante, para 21.12), and could only take effect under the alleged doctrine of equitable estoppel, a matter beyond the scope of this work.[7] The precise relationship of the doctrines of waiver and equitable estoppel are still being worked out.[8]

[26.25] The effect. Suppose A does waive a contractual duty owed to him by B, can either party later set up the subsequent non-performance of that waived term? It seems that the party for whose benefit the waiver was made (B) is estopped and cannot refuse to accept the varied performance.[1] Can A go back on his waiver? He cannot put the clock back; so that, if, for example, a delivery date is waived but the contract is not performed at all, damages are assessed on the footing that the breach took place at the end of the extended period.[2] On the other hand, the contractual promise still stands,[3] so A may go back on his waiver as regards future performance. Thus, in *Charles Rickards Ltd v Oppenheim*:[4]

> A ordered a Rolls Royce chassis from B and the latter agreed to build a body on it by 20 March. After B had failed to complete the work by that date A continued to press for delivery, but on 29 June gave notice that if the work was not completed within the next four weeks the contract was off.

The Court of Appeal unanimously held that time of delivery was of the essence of this contract (see ante, para 23.18); that this stipulation was impliedly waived by A's requests for delivery after 20 March;[5] but that A was entitled to make time of the essence again by reasonable notice. They decided that A's notice of 29 June had made time of the essence

---

3   See also *Lombard North Central plc v Stobart* (1990) 9 Tr LR 105, CA. Compare *Societe Italo-Belge etc v Palm and Vegetable Oils etc* [1981] Com LR 249.

4   Stoljar (1957) 35 Can BR 485, 503.

5   *Panoutsos v Raymond Hadley Corp* as reported in (1922) Com Cas 207, CA. Applied in *Plasticmoda Societe Per Azione v Davidsons Ltd* [1952] 1 Lloyd's Rep 527.

6   *Charles Rickards Ltd v Oppenheim* (set out post, para 26.25), at 623.

7   See Treitel, *op cit*, note 1, pp 99–113; Stoljar (1957) 35 Can BR 485, 520–28; Spencer Bower, *Estoppel* (2nd edn), Chapter XIV.

8   See Treitel, *op cit*, note 1, p 107.

[26.25]

1   *Hickman v Haynes* (1875) LR 10 CP 598; *Levy & Co v Goldberg* [1922] 1 KB 688.

2   *Ogle v Earl of Vane* (1868) LR 3 QB 272, Ex Ch: see further post, para 29.29. See also *The Eurometal* [1981] 3 All ER 533; and waiver of lien (ante, para 24.15).

3   *British and Benningtons Ltd v North Western Cachar Tea Co Ltd* (set out ante, para 23.05).

4   [1950] 1 KB 616; [1950] 1 All ER 420, CA. See also *Tool Metal Manufacturing Co Ltd v Tungsten Electric Co Ltd* [1955] 2 All ER 657, HL; *Etablissements Chainbaux SARL v Harbormaster Ltd* [1955] 1 Lloyd's Rep 303.

5   Compare *Nichimen Corp v Gatoil Overseas Inc* [1987] 2 Lloyd's Rep 46, CA.

again, so that B's failure to deliver within the four weeks amounted to a breach of condition, entitling A to rescind the contract.

[26.26] Rejection for the wrong reason. What if the seller intends to make a delivery which would be a breach of contract;[1] but, before he can tender the goods, the buyer, in ignorance of the seller's intention, intimates that he will not accept delivery and purports to repudiate for another reason insufficient in law. Can the buyer subsequently rely on the seller's intended breach as a waiver of performance so as to justify his refusal to accept delivery? In *Taylor v Oakes*,[2] Greer J at first instance noted *obiter* the general:[3]

> ... long established rule of law that a contracting party who, after he has become entitled to refuse performance of his contractual obligations, gives a wrong reason for his refusal, does not thereby deprive himself of the justification which in fact existed, whether he was aware of it or not.

His Lordship sought to reconcile this rule with *Braithwaite's* case (set out ante, para 23.07) by suggesting that his rule applies where there is a refusal to accept an actual tender of delivery, whereas in *Braithwaite's* case there was a mere offer to tender delivery (at 267). The point seems to be that the valid ground for repudiation must actually exist at the time of rejection: in *British and Benningtons Ltd v North West Cachar Tea Co Ltd* (set out ante, para 23.05), the buyer committed an anticipatory breach which was accepted by the seller before the time when the seller was required to deliver.[4] Assuming that a valid ground for repudiation does exist at the time the buyer gives the wrong reason, the above rule is only needed where the buyer elects to treat the contract as repudiated: if the buyer had affirmed after what he thought was a breach, the contract enures for the benefit of both parties, so that when the buyer discovers the seller's actual breach, he can anyway rely upon it to treat the contract as repudiated.[5]

Where the buyer does elect to treat the contract as repudiated, the above Greer principle that he can rely upon a then undiscovered valid ground to repudiate notwithstanding that he gave another invalid ground is subject to a number of exceptions.[6] One such exception appeared to arise in *Panchaud Freres SA v Etablissements General Grain Co*:[7]

> A cif sale of maize provided for shipment June/July 1965. The maize was shipped in August: the bill of lading was falsely dated July, though a certificate of quality tendered at the same time revealed the August shipment. Not noticing the date on the certificate, the buyer accepted the documents; but, when the goods arrived, the buyer rejected them on other insufficient grounds.

[26.26]

1 For the duty of delivery, see ante, para 23.05 *et seq*.

2 (1922) 27 Com Cas 261, CA. See also *per* Mocatta J in *The Mihalis Angelos* [1970] 1 All ER 673, at 676e; reversed on the other grounds [1970] 3 All ER 125, CA.

3 At 266. *Applied Glencore Grain Rotterdam BV v Lebanese Organisation for International Commerce* [1997] 4 All ER 514, CA.

4 See also *Gill & Duffus SA v Berger & Co Inc* (set out ante, para 23.06).

5 *The Simona* (see ante, para 23.07).

6 *Benjamin's Sale of Goods* (5th edn), para 19-139.

7 [1970] 1 Lloyd's Rep 53, CA.

Three years later, during litigation, the buyer discovered both that his original grounds for rejection was insufficient and that the bill of lading was wrongly dated. The Court of Appeal refused to allow the buyer to rely now on the misdating, when he could have cited it three years earlier, as not being 'fair conduct' (at 59). However, this exception has been criticised on grounds of vagueness and it has been argued that the case in fact decided only that the acceptance of the documents[8] precluded subsequent reliance on a valid reason apparent on the face of the documents.[6] If this last point is correct, the case is relevant only to cif sales and may be safely ignored in our context of domestic sales.

---

8   A cif buyer has two rights to reject: (i) to reject the documents; and (2) to reject the goods (see ante para 22.07; and post, para 29.30).

CHAPTER 27

REMEDIES OF THE SUPPLIER – 'CREDITOR OR OWNER'

INTRODUCTION

[27.01] Before considering the substantive rules relating to the remedies available to a supplier, brief mention must be made of the causes of indebtedness and procedures for enforcement of repayment, because the latter frequently have a considerable bearing on the efficacy of the remedies.

In our modern society, the use by consumers of debt, and especially of instalment debt (see ante, para 1.03), has become a widespread method of acquiring the lifestyle which our society assumes, this being particularly the case with young families (the 25–40 year olds with children). The demand is fostered by advertising (see ante, Chapter 8), eg, of interest free, low start and instant credit, whereas it is hoped that consumers will be helped to manage it by education (see ante, para 3.01), consumer codes of practice (see ante, para 3.13) and credit insurance (see ante, para 24.48). Even assuming an initial ability to pay,[1] a proportion of those consumers will not pay their debts lawfully due. Those who will not pay include not only 'professional debtors', but also those who misguidedly cease payment because they have a valid complaint, eg, about goods supplied (see Chapters 13–15), and those who cannot pay. The last group include the inadequate and a proportion of low income families with unexpectedly reduced income, eg, through illness or redundancy or divorce. Whilst there has been little increase in the level of consumer bad debts as a whole, among a significant minority there is a problem of overindebtedness. In 1999, it was estimated that there were about a quarter of a million consumers with actually unmanageable debt and two million consumers with potentially unmanageable debt.

Faced with a defaulting customer within the limitation period (see ante, para 26.17), the supplier in principle has two basic choices open to him, unless opting for arbitration (see ante, para 3.24): (1) **self-help** (see post, para 27.02), in the pursuit of which the creditor may be restrained by the offences with regard to forcible entry of premises and unlawful harassment of debtors;[2] or (2) **court action** (see post, para 27.03), which in the case of insolvency proceedings only is carefully controlled (see ante, para 19.18). Nevertheless, the present 'system' of enforcement by self-help and court action still gives significant advantages to the ordinary creditor who acts first as against other ordinary creditors, so unfortunately encouraging precipitate action rather than merciful forbearance.[3] For this 'Devil take the hindmost' philosophy, see ante, para 19.13. To some extent, it is possible for the OFT to control their treatment by use of the CCA licensing system (see ante, para 6.23); and the debtor is kept aware of his indebtedness by the compulsory statements of the level of indebtedness (see ante, para 15.16).

[27.01]

1   This is assessed in the application process: see ante, para 8.35 *et seq*. The Registry Trust (see post, para 27.03) has called for a policy of taking proceedings against 'won't pays': [2001] 1 Credit Today 7.

2   See ante, paras 24.23–24. But not by the Protection from Harassment Act 1997: *Tuppen v Microsoft Corp Ltd* [2000] CLY 46.

3   There may be this relationship: the greater the court delays, the more creditors may be tempted to early self-help to minimise the build-up of arrears.

As long ago as 1969 there were officially identified the following drawbacks to the enforcement system, still unremedied:[4] that in appropriate cases serial debtors should be restrained by court order from incurring further credit and creditors deterred from granting it by postponement to other creditors;[5] that the recovery of debts should be undertaken jointly by an enforcement office administering all methods of enforcement;[6] and that the present harsh system should be displaced by the same priority system as on insolvency.[7] In fact, there is a power for a debtor with multiple debts to seek a county court administration order (see post, para 27.04). Alternatively, a debtor could go further and petition for his own insolvency (see ante, para 19.21). Insofar as the serial debtor is inadequate, or simply overtaken by disaster, there are presently informal systems in the credit industry that may sometimes achieve some of these results.[8] In 1998, the Lord Chancellor began a Civil Enforcement Review;[9] and his Department has since produced some interim reports (see ante, paras 19.15; 19.17; and post, para 27.04). Furthermore, the DTI has looked at overindebtedness, which has two facets:[10] (1) preventing initial overindebtedness;[11] and (2) dealing with subsequent lapses into overindebtedness. The DTI Taskforce into overindebtedness has spawned a number of working groups, yet to formally report: the difficulty is to strike a balance between the majority of performing debtors advantaged by competition and the non-performing minority of debtors in need of protection.

[27.02] Self-help. As a first step, the creditor or owner is likely to seek to encourage payment by filing a default with a credit reference bureau, which may effectively debar the debtor or hirer from obtaining further access to such facilities (see ante, para 8.36) and rescind the contract for breach (see ante, para 26.11). Preferably before so doing (except in the case of fraud),[1] the creditor or owner should serve on the debtor or hirer a notice of intention to file, perhaps together with any Default Notice required (s 87, CCA: see ante, para 24.30) and do so in a manner which does not amount to unlawful harassment (see ante, para 24.24). The information filed must comply with the DPA[2] otherwise the IC may take enforcement action (see ante, para 3.27). Thereafter, the conduct of the creditor or owner against a solvent debtor may depend on whether the debt is secured (see below) or

---

4   The *Payne Report on The Enforcement of Judgment Debts* (1969, Cmnd 3903). See especially paras 38–44, 78.

5   Or might this result in lawful credit not being available to those who most need it?

6   Enforcement offices were introduced for a trial period in Northern Ireland, but never on the mainland. They proved slow and costly. See further *Enforcement of Debt*, paras 69–74, 195–219.

7   See paras 304, 1137; and *Enforcement of Debt*, paras 220–22.

8   Whilst it may be that creditor-repairers (see post, para 27.03) should be expressly outlawed, it may be that debt advisers and managers (see ante, paras 3,16; 5.42) should be more tightly controlled and perhaps financially supported. See also Reynolds (2001) 60 Quarterly Account 18.

9   For the terms of reference, see (1998) 53 CC 2/5–6. See further 50 Quarterly Account 1; [2001] 9 Credit Today 17.

10 OFT, *Report by the Task Force on Tackling Overindebtedness* (July, 2001).

11 There is a legislative trade-off to be made between the privacy of the creditworthy majority and rejection of applications by the uncreditworthy on the basis of data that could be held (see ante, para 3.26). Would it be feasible by statute to make unenforceable credit granted without adequate checks and specify allowable standard forms to outlaw the worst temptations of easy credit?

[27.02]

1   Notice after filing would, if inaccurate, render the creditor or owner liable to pay compensation to the consumer (the 'data subject': DPA, s 10: see ante, para 3.27.

2   It must be, eg, accurate, adequate, relevant and fair under the Data Protection Principles (see ante, para 3.28); it must comply with any relevant code of practice (see ante, para 3.13); and there must be no genuine dispute as to the existence of the debt. The DPC has produced *Guidance Notes on Defaults*.

unsecured; and, in the latter case, whether it is a 'priority' or ordinary debt.[3] This informal 'priority' category does not refer to priority on insolvency (see ante, para 19.22), but is normally accorded to the privatised utilities (see ante, para 3.07) in recognition of their public regulation and that they provide essential services:[4] where a consumer does not pay his gas or electricity bill (but not water), the undertakings have power to install a pre-payment meter or disconnect the service.[5]

Whether or not the creditor is secured, he may commonly resort to persuasion to get the debtor to pay up.[6] However, creditors have sometimes sought to distance themselves from the methods of collection employed by assigning[7] the (bad) debts to a debt collection agency (see ante, para 5.42), in which case it may be necessary to register the agency as a creditor to satisfy the DPA (see ante, para 3.27). Moreover, the OFT has the negative and positive licensing powers considered in Chapter 6, which should hopefully lead to the removal of the most undesirable creditors and debt collectors from the legitimate trade.[7a] It is questionable whether it is ever possible to eradicate from society illegal lending because of the apparently insatiable demand for credit. This imposes on legislators awkward policy problems as to how much legitimate lending to allow (see post, para 29.42).

Real security. The transaction may have been set up with some real security, which may take one of the traditional forms of pledge, mortgage or charge (see ante, Chapter 25); or security may be achieved by way of an instalment contract.[8] It remains to be noticed here the very small sums of money commonly realised on the sale of repossessed goods:[9] not only is the market price for second hand goods frequently low,[10] but in the case of instalment contracts there is not even any duty on the repossessing supplier to secure the best price obtainable because there is no equity of redemption (see ante, para 24.22), as compared with regulated pledges (s 121(6) of the CCA: see further ante, para 25.18), mortgages and charges (see ante, para 25.20).

[27.03] Court action. Leaving aside claims for restitution in criminal proceedings (see ante, para 3.20), normally, the appropriate first step will be civil proceedings by a supplier against a consumer in the consumer's local county court[1] for any of the following: (1)

---

3   The expression may come from the County Court Default Summons, which uses it to include also arrears on housing, community charge and maintenance.

4   A water board may not even know enough details of their customer to register default with a credit bureau (see ante, para 8.36).

5   Gas and electricity Boards may not use these powers to collect other debts: *South Wales Electricity plc v OFFER* [1999] CLY 2000. Water Boards lost their disconnection powers (see ante, para 3.07), which may lead to their being treated as non-priority debtors.

6   It is for consideration whether the law ought to put the creditor to his election – seize or sue. See Cranston, *Consumers and the Law* (3rd edn), p 282.

7   See ante, para 7.17. Without more, such an assignment will not be struck down as maintenance or champerty (see ante, para 7.26): *Camdex International Ltd v Bank of Zambia* [1998] QB 22, CA.

7a For the OFT Guidelines on debt management, see ante, para 5.42.

8   Ie, conditional sale, hp or simple hiring. For recaption of goods so supplied, see ante, paras 24.23–24.

9   Cranston, *op cit*, note 6, p 273; Goode, *HP Law and Practice* (2nd edn), pp 403–04. Cf the effect of court action: post, para 27.04.

10 Sales of repossessed goods tend to take place either at local auctions or through second hand dealers or specialist shops.

[27.03]

1   See ante, para 3.22. It should always be enforced as a judgment of the County, not High, Court: *per* Lord Donaldson in *Forward Trust Ltd v Whymark* [1989] 3 All ER 915, CA, at 921h. For a summary of County Court debt collecting procedure, see Sherriff (1992) 142 NLJ 1164.

repossession (see ante, para 24.25); (2) **debt**, as for the price of goods sold[2] or arrears of rentals (see post, para 27.21) or money lent (see ante, para 7.03); and (3) **damages** (see post, para 27.27). Frequently, such actions are undefended, in which case if the agreement is unregulated summary judgment may be obtained,[3] though it is sometimes more effective for the creditor to apply for adjournment and an order requiring the debtor's presence.[4] However, if the debtor puts in any sort of defence, eg, that it is an extortionate credit bargain (as to which, see post, para 29.40), or counterclaim for defective goods (see post, para 29.26), the creditor may have to choose between discontinuing the action because it is uneconomic, or continuing the proceedings to make an example of the debtor to encourage performance by other debtors.[5] If the creditor contemplates continuing proceedings, he will have to bear in mind the power of the county court to order payment by instalments as a way of redressing the inequality of bargaining power between creditors and debtors: such a general power has existed since 1846[6] and has been re-enforced as regards regulated debts by time orders (see ante, para 24.40).

Assuming the unsecured creditor does succeed in obtaining judgment he is then said to be a **judgment creditor**: that judgment will be registered[7] and the judgment creditor has available to him the range of remedies considered below (para 27.04). However, a very large proportion of debt cases continue to be settled at a late stage in proceedings,[8] suggesting that in many cases the threat of judicial proceedings[9] secures payment.[10] Whence can the judgment debtor obtain funds to pay off such judgments, other than from unlicensed moneylenders (see ante, para 6.09) or non-commercial sources?

Undefended claims. In over 90% of debt cases no defence is made so that proceedings are administrative rather than judicial, in that application may be made for summary judgment (see above). As part of this process, a public registry of unsatisfied county court judgments is kept;[11] but, despite assertions to the contrary, these records cannot

---

2   See post, para 27.16. Where there is an instalment contract, instalments in arrears at the time of proceedings will be recoverable anyway; and the future instalments may become due immediately by reason of an acceleration clause (see ante, para 26.19).

3   Under the CPR, Part 12 (which is not available as regards regulated agreements), if no defence whatsoever is put in; or if the sum exceeds the arbitration limit (see ante, para 3.23) and the reply put in is no real defence. See *Enforcement of Debt* (1987, LC's Dept) paras 13, 94–95.

4   Failure to appear would be a contempt of court, which may lead to arrest of the debtor and hence pressurise him to pay: see (1991) 12 CCA News 5/11.

5   See *Consumer Credit* (ed Goode) 302; and post, para 27.04. But some judgments are satisfied in whole or part: *Enforcement of Debt*, paras 96-100.

6   See County Courts Act 1984, s 71.

7   At the Registry Trust Ltd. This may itself be a sanction in that the judgment debtor may find himself barred from further credit (see ante, para 8.36); but it may be circumvented by a credit repair company (see note 12, below). Entitlement to statutory interest may also commence: see ante, para 7.03A.

8   See the *Crowther Report*, para 6.6.49; and post, para 27.04. Can attempts by the judgment creditor to pressure the debtor amount to unlawful harassment (see ante, para 24.24)?

9   Eg, as a prior step to initiating bankruptcy proceedings, a judgment creditor may issue a Statutory Demand for payment (see ante, para 19.13: and (1993) 47 CC 6/2).

10   See *Enforcement of Debt*, paras 228–33. However, from time to time financiers suggest that the security offered by conditional sale or hp has been so reduced (see Chapter 24) that they might just as well rely upon a credit sale with acceleration clause, summary judgment and execution. See eg, the *Crowther Report*, para 6.6.46.

11   County Courts Act 1984, ss 73, 73A (as inserted by the Administration of Justice Act 1985, s 54). The Registry is a company limited by guarantee, Registry Trust Ltd. Its record of judgments is computerised and routinely accessed by the major reference bureaux: see ante, para 8.36.

legitimately be 'repaired',[12] as by removing an adverse credit history so as to obtain a satisfactory credit score (see ante, para 8.39).

[27.04] **The judgment creditor's remedies.** Where an unsecured judgment debt remains unsatisfied,[1] it should be borne in mind that, if the debtor is without assets, use of the following remedies will not lead to recovery of any money but simply add to the costs.[2] Hence, enquiry agents are sometimes used at an early stage in the proceedings to establish whether the debtor is worth suing. The major remedies of a judgment creditor, including perhaps where an instalment order is in arrears,[2a] are as follows:[3]

1 *Execution* (see generally ante, para 19.15). In about half of the cases, the likely return may be so small that the court officer simply notifies the execution creditor that the process has been abortive. Even where the requisite minimum level of debt makes the remedy available, forced sales of goods by way of execution tend to produce a very small financial return, so that it may be more useful as a threat (see ante, para 27.02) or to trigger insolvency (ss 123(1)(b), 268(1)(b) of the IA. See below).

2 *Charging orders.* In respect of land or stock owned by the judgment debtor,[4] the judgment creditor may apply for a 'charging order' securing the payment of money due or to become due under the judgment (ss 1, 2 of the Charging Orders Act 1979). If granted, the effect is almost to turn the judgment creditor into a secured creditor,[5] though he will necessarily take subject to any prior charges, typically the judgment debtor's house mortgage. However, insofar as the judgment debtor has a significant equity of redemption in his home (see ante, para 25.20) it is unlikely that the judgment creditor will have to go so far as to apply to a court order for sale of the charged property, making this form of execution attractive.[6]

3 *Attachment of debts.*[7] The judgment debtor may himself be owed money, eg, in a bank or building society account. Once aware of this, the judgment creditor may be able to ensure that the third party debtor, eg, bank, pays the judgment debt direct to the judgment creditor in what are known as garnishee proceedings.[8] Leaving aside the

---

12 Eg, by applying to the county court to have judgments struck off the register using procedural excuses which lead to temporary removal. There have been warnings against these forms of activity by both the OFT (see (1992) 9 Tr LR 102) and the Lord Chancellor (see 9 Tr LR 229). See also (1994) 48 CC 5/33; 15 CCA News 2/3; (1996) 50 CC 6/32.

[27.04]

1 Distinguish a judgment for delivery of goods (see ante, para 24.26): if unsatisfied, this may lead to a warrant for delivery of goods.

2 The pattern of debt collecting is therefore likely to be affected by significant increases in court charges. See also the *Enforcement of Debt* (1986, LC's Dept) paras 101–02. For the use of scoring techniques (see ante, para 8.39). Before litigating, see (1991) 46 CC 4/11.

2a *Ropaigealach v Allied Irish Bank* [2001] unreported, CA.

3 For the new rules, see CPR, Parts 70–73. The Lord Chancellor is conducting a major review of the enforcement remedies.

4 Ownership of registered land can now be cheaply checked: see ante, para 25.22. In respect of land, even before a application for a Charging Order Nisi, it is possible to register a Caution at the Land Registry (1993) 48 CC 2/12. For a consumer's view of the process, see Sullivan (1999) 52 QA 4.

5 But see *Mercantile Credit Co v Ellis* [1987] CLY 2917, CA.

6 *Enforcement of Debt*, paras 43, 128. This explains why credit proposal forms ask for details as to whether an applicant owns his own home. See generally, ante, para 8.35.

7 See generally Crossley Vaines, *Personal Property* (5th edn), pp 486–89.

8 Supreme Court Act 1981, s 40; County Courts Act 1984, s 108. Subject to the difficulty of finding it, the most common source of garnished funds is the debtor's bank or building society account, eg, *Alcom Ltd v Republic of Colombia* [1984] 1 All ER 1, CA.

debtor's earnings (see below), this little used process is sometimes effective against consumers,[9] more often against traders.[10]

4   *Attachment of earnings and distress.* In England, unlike the US, attachment of earnings is not available when the contract is made (see ante, para 25.04), but only when the creditor has become a judgment creditor (see post, para 27.05). Whereas a house-owning debtor is subject to charging orders (see above), a tenant debtor is subject to distress (see ante, para 19.17).

5   *Bankruptcy.*[11] Where the bankrupt estate is comparatively small and the cost of full bankruptcy comparatively large, it is likely that recourse will be made to the summary administration procedure (s 275). Assuming that the bankruptcy court issues a certificate of administration under s 275, this will usually state that the Official Receiver shall be the trustee of the bankrupt's estate, so removing the control of proceedings from the creditors; and under s 275 the debtor will usually obtain an accelerated discharge.[12]

6   *Debt administration orders.*[13] First introduced in 1883, these are completely outside the bankruptcy system and are intended to enable a multiple consumer debtor to discharge his indebtedness by making regular payments into court for distribution *pro rata* to his creditors. Unfortunately, despite modification, the orders have not yet achieved their original purpose, the present rules being contained in s 112 of the County Courts Act 1984. It was intended that they be replaced by new provisions set out in s 13 of the Courts and Legal Services Act 1990; but it seems that s 13 is defective and cannot be implemented. Similar to Interim Orders in the High Court (see below) and often known as the 'poor man's bankruptcy', whilst a debt administration order remains in force, all the other creditors' remedies are usually unenforceable (s 114(1) of the 1984 Act). This procedure may be seen as a more formal (court sanctioned) alternative to a negotiated debt management plan (see ante, para 5.42). Perhaps negotiated by a money advice centre (see ante, para 3.08) or other debt counsellor or debt adjuster (see ante, para 5.43), it will be registered as a County Court judgment (see ante, para 27.03). The Lord Chancellor's Department are currently researching whether and how s 13 might be improved and implemented;[14] it is to be hoped that this project will be co-ordinated with the DTI's Enterprise Bill (see ante, para 19.18).

[27.05/06] Attachment of earnings.[1] As a *quid pro quo* for the abolition of imprisonment for judgment debt, in 1970 Parliament introduced attachment of earnings.[2] The new

---

9   *SCF Finance Co Ltd v Masri (No 3)* [1987] QB 1028, CA; *Fitzpatrick v DAF Sales* [1988] IR 464; and see generally *Enforcement of Debt*, paras 40, 125.

10   For use by a factor of receivables, see Oditah, *Receivables Financing*, pp 142–49.

11   See ante, para 19.18 *et seq.* It is not an abuse of process to file for insolvency against a solvent debtor wilfully failing to pay: *Cornhill Insurance v Improvement Services* [1986] 1 WLR 114. But the court has a discretion to reject the application where there is a substantial dispute as to liability.

12   See further, Fletcher, *Law of Insolvency* (2nd edn), pp 327–29.

13   See Fletcher, *ibid*, pp 60–61.

14   The present suggestion by the LCD is to effect the reform by 2003/04 by means of a Regulatory Reform Order (see ante, para 5.10), for implementation in 2006.

[27.05/06]

1   See generally Cranston, *Consumers and the Law* (3rd edn), pp 279–81; Crossley Vaines, *Personal Property* (5th edn), pp 489–91. Attachment is regarded as the most effective way to collect a debt: *Enforcement of Debt* (1987, LC's Dept) para 122.

2   Administration of Justice Act 1970, ss 11–12. See generally ante, para 27.01.

system was consolidated in the Attachment of Earnings Act 1971, whose orders may be made by the county court on application of either debtor[3] or creditor; but where application is made by the creditor, the court has slightly fewer powers. Under such an order, an amount will be deducted from the debtor's earnings which will not normally leave him with less than the basic level of Income Support;[4] and periodically paid into court, which may distribute the sums between multiple creditors.

Thus, where a judgment debtor continues in regular employment, this ought to be a procedure by which the creditor can depend on regular reduction of the debt in a simple and cheap manner. However, the scope for an attachment of earnings order is limited: it only applies to judgment debts; even when a debtor continues in employment, it is only knowing failure by his employer to comply with an order which amounts to an offence;[5] the unemployed draw their social security in full; the scheme has no application to the self-employed;[6] incomes paid by employers other than wages, salaries and pensions are immune from the process (s 24); if the debtor changes his job, the entire court process has to be started afresh;[7] and there is a minimum order.[8]

[27.07] Secured creditor's remedies. The powers of a pledgee to sell an unredeemed pledge depend on whether the pledge is regulated or not (see ante, paras 25.15; 25.18). The usual remedies of a mortgagee (foreclosure, sale, taking possession and appointment of a receiver) are beyond the scope of this work;[1] but there are additional restrictions in respect of a regulated mortgage (see ante, para 25.24). In respect of conditional sale and hp the ordinary remedies of repossession and resale have already been considered (see ante, paras 24.21–26), though there are substantial restrictions if the transaction is regulated (see ante, para 24.27 *et seq*).

The position of a secured creditor upon the insolvency of his debtor has already been mentioned (see ante, para 19.22).

THE SUPPLIER'S REMEDIES AGAINST THE GOODS

Remedies of an ordinary seller

This will cover cash and credit sales where the unpaid seller wishes to exercise his real rights of lien, stoppage and resale. It has already been pointed out that the SGA fails to draw a clear distinction between the power of sale and the right to resell (see ante, para 24.05); that is, between the effect of resale on (1) the original contract of sale and (2) the title to the goods resold.

---

3   In which case the debtor is perhaps more likely to co-operate in its operation.
4   But there is now a statutory power to transfer collection functions to designated officers: Courts and Legal Services Act 1990, Sched 17, para 5.
5   Section 23(2). But the employer is under no liability if he is unaware of the order; and there is no central register or provision for making employer's aware of orders, eg, to stamp them on the debtor's P45 (employment card).
6   The system requires the debtor to have an employer: s 6(2). Cf whether the debtor is on PAYE.
7   Section 9(4). Thus, an employer may avoid the obligations of the Act by sacking the debtor, whilst the debtor may make enforcement of such orders difficult, if not impossible, by frequently changing jobs.
8   Currently £50: (1991) 41 NLJ 887.
[27.07]
1   See generally Megarry and Wade, *Real Property* (6th edn), para 19-045 *et seq*.

[27.08] The original contract of sale. Even a 'resale' by the seller will not be a breach of the original contract of sale in any of the following circumstances.[1]

1 *The goods are not ascertained.* The very expression 'resale' pre-supposes that the goods 'resold' have become the subject matter of the prior contract of sale so that the original buyer has a contractual right to those goods, or to an as yet unascertained part of them (see ante, para 20.05).

2 *Discharge of the seller.* Even if the goods 'resold' were specific or ascertained in relation to the original contract of sale, the seller is entitled to resell if the original contract, or the obligation to deliver those particular goods, is discharged, as by rescission *ab initio* or *de futuro* (see ante, para 26.11). One instance of this receives special mention in s 48(4) of the SGA, which provides that:

> Where the seller expressly reserves the right of resale in case the buyer should make default, and on the buyer making default, resells the goods, the original contract of sale is thereby rescinded, but without prejudice to any claim the seller may have for damages.

Typical examples here are contractual provisions for resale on non-acceptance or non-payment;[2] but other types of default may also be stipulated.[3] However, in a consumer supply, such a clause may be unfair.[4]

3 *The statutory right of resale.* As the time for payment of the price is *prima facie* not of the essence (s 10(1): set out ante, para 23.20), the unpaid seller in possession may be in a quandary as to what to do with the goods;[5] so s 48(3) lays down that:

> Where the goods are of a perishable nature, or where the unpaid seller gives notice to the buyer of his intention to resell, and the buyer does not within a reasonable time pay or tender the price, the unpaid seller may resell the goods and recover from the original buyer damages for any loss occasioned by his breach of contract.

This makes time of the essence in two situations:

(a) The goods are of 'a perishable nature'.[6] Where the price for goods of this type is not forthcoming within a reasonable time,[7] s 48(3) allows the seller to resell.[8]

(b) The seller gives notice. Whatever the type of goods, s 48(3) allows the seller to resell if the price is not paid or tendered within a reasonable time of receipt of that notice.[9] As will be seen later (post, para 27.10), the wording of s 48(3) is unfortunate; but presumably, at very least, its effect must be to prevent the resale from being a breach of the original contract of sale, as it envisages that he may still sue the buyer for damages for non-acceptance (as to which, see post, para 27.34).

[27.08]

1 No comment on the passing of property is intended by the use of the term 'resale' in this context.
2 Cf the *Stocznia* case (set out post, para 29.16).
3 *Per* Diplock LJ in *Ward Ltd v Bignall* (set out post, para 27.10), at 550.
4 OFT, *Bulletin No 15*, case 13: Grey Term 1(d): see ante, para 11.16.
5 As to whether a seller out of possession can resell under s 48(3), see *Benjamin's Sale of Goods* (5th edn), para 15.123.
6 The expression 'perish' in the SGA was considered ante, para 22.13.
7 This is a question of fact: s 59. See *per* Finnemore J in *Gallagher v Shilcock* [1949] 2 KB 765, at 770.
8 The seller may also have a right to resell under the doctrine of agency of necessity (see ante, para 10.06) or a court order (see ante para 21.06).
9 See Benjamin, *op cit*, note 5, para 15.122.

[27.09] Exercise of real rights. It is necessary to consider the effect on the original contract of sale of the exercise by the unpaid seller of his real rights in respect of specific or ascertained goods.

1   *Lien or stoppage*. Section 48(1) of the SGA provides that:

> Subject to the provisions of this section, a contract of sale is not rescinded by the mere exercise by an unpaid seller of his rights of lien ... or stoppage in transit.

It has been suggested that the object of this sub-section was to protect the unpaid seller where time of delivery was of the essence;[1] but it actually only states the obvious fact that such an action by the seller does not, without more, demonstrate an unequivocal intention to repudiate the contract.[2]

2   *Resale*. *Prima facie*, a seller with a right to rescind for breach by his buyer has the following alternatives (see ante, para 26.16).

(a) He may elect to rescind the contract,[3] in which case the property in the goods will, if it has already passed, revest in him; and he may then resell the goods as his own,[4] and sue the first buyer for damages for non-acceptance (see post, para 27.24).

(b) He may affirm the contract, in which case the property will pass under the terms of the contract to the buyer, whom he may sue for the balance of the purchase price (see post, para 27.16), and damages for non-acceptance, meanwhile exercising his unpaid seller's lien until judgment is satisfied.[5] Does a resale by the seller show an intention to rescind or affirm (see post, para 27.10)?

[27.10] On whose behalf is a resale effected? It is clear that, once the goods have been delivered to the first buyer and the property has passed to him, the seizure and resale by the seller can have no effect on the first sale because it is executed, the resale being merely tortious;[1] and in *Gallagher v Shilcock* Finnemore J took the same view with regard to the resale by an unpaid seller who had remained in possession after the property had passed.[2] However, the Court of Appeal unanimously took the opposite view of the effect of such a resale on the original sale in *Ward Ltd v Bignall*:[3]

> The buyer (B) contracted to buy two motor vehicles for a total purchase price of £850, and paid a £25 deposit; but he later wrongfully refused to take delivery. After giving due notice, the seller (S) attempted to resell the vehicles: he only succeeded in reselling one, for which he obtained £350; and sued B for £497 10s,[4] being the net balance of the purchase price.[5] At

---

[27.09]

1   *Per* Diplock LJ in *Ward Ltd v Bignall* [1967] 1 QB 534 at 549, CA.

2   As to repudiation, see ante, para 26.15; as to the rights of lien and stoppage, see ante, para 24.04.

3   See ante, para 27.08. But note that his wrongful resale may amount to a repudiation.

4   There appears to be no legal obligation on the seller as to the manner in which he exercises any right of resale, nor as to the price he accepts. However, if he also seeks damages, he is under a duty to mitigate his loss: see post, para 27.44.

5   *Per* Diplock LJ in *Ward Ltd v Bignall* (above) at 547.

[27.10]

1   See *Stephen v Wilkinson* (1831) 2 B & Ad 320; *Page v Cowasjee Edulijee* (1866) LR 1 PC 127.

2   [1949] 2 KB 765; [1949] 1 All ER 921. Cf a mortgagee realising his security: see ante, para 25.20.

3   [1967] 1 QB 534; [1967] 1 All ER 449, CA.

4   This was assumed by the CA to be for damages for non-acceptance.

5   Ie, £825, less £325, plus the expenses of attempting resale (£22 10s).

first instance, S was awarded the sum claimed; but the Court of Appeal deducted from the award the market value of the unsold car which S still retained (£450), and reduced the award to £47 10s.

The difference between the attitude of the two courts lay in the inference to be drawn from the fact that s 48(4) expressly states that the contract is rescinded by the resale, whereas s 48(3) is silent on this point (see ante, para 27.08): in the earlier case, Finnemore J deduced that the resale under s 48(3) was therefore not intended to rescind the original contract of sale; but in the later case, the Court of Appeal took the view that rescission was expressly referred to in s 48(4) to remove doubt, and to bring it into line with s 48(3), where on ordinary principles resale would rescind the first contract (see post, para 27.12). At the same time, Diplock LJ in *Ward Ltd v Bignall* pointed out that, if the seller had affirmed and sued for the balance of the purchase price, the first instance award in the case before him would have been correct (at 547). The moral for an unpaid seller considering resale would appear to be as follows:[6] leaving aside the question of any deposit (see post, para 27.20), he should rescind and resell if he can thereby obtain a better price;[7] but he should affirm the contract if he cannot do better elsewhere.[8]

[27.11] The title to the goods. In discussing the effect of a resale by the seller on the title to the goods, it is convenient to distinguish according to whether or not the seller has ever delivered the goods to the first buyer.

1 *Before delivery.* Where the resale by the seller before delivery does not amount to a breach of the first contract of sale, the seller can pass the property in the goods to the second buyer, either because the property never passed to the first buyer, or because it revested in him on resale.[1] However, where the resale is a breach of the first contract of sale,[2] it does not revest the property in the seller; and therefore he can only pass a good title to the second buyer, either because he has retained the property in the goods, or under one of the following exceptions to the *nemo dat* rule:

(a) Sales by a seller in possession (see ante, para 21.38 *et seq*);

(b) Section 48(2) of the SGA, which provides that:[3]

> Where an unpaid seller who has exercised his right of lien ... or stoppage in transit resells the goods, the buyer acquires a good title thereto as against the original buyer.

---

6 See also *per* Turner J in *Commission Car Sales v Saul* [1957] NZLR 144, at 146 (resale by seller after delivery and subsequent repudiation by buyer); and *per* Robert Goff LJ in *Clough Mills Ltd v Martin* (set out ante, para 25.30) at 987–88.
7 Eg, *Gallagher v Shilcock* (above).
8 Eg, *Ward Ltd v Bignall* (above).
[27.11]
1 *Ward Ltd v Bignall* (set out ante, para 27.10).
2 In which case the buyer can sue the seller for non-delivery: see post, para 29.19 *et seq*.
3 Section 48(2) differs from the *nemo dat* provisions: (1) it does not require a delivery or transfer to the second buyer; nor (2) does it require the original buyer to be in default; nor (3) insist that the second buyer act bf and without notice of the first sale. As to the title passed to the second buyer, see Goode, *Commercial Law* (2nd edn), p 446, note 163.

It may be that s 48(2) is confined to the situation where the seller remains unpaid[4] and in possession.[5]

2   *After delivery.* Once the goods have been delivered to the first buyer, the seller can only pass a good title to the second buyer where he has either retained the property in the goods (s 19: discussed ante, paras 20.28–29), or it has revested in him:[6] a mere bargain and sale changes neither property nor possession,[7] nor does it rescind the first contract of sale. Nor should the seller have any greater power to pass title where he merely seizes the goods after delivery to the first buyer.[8] Thus, if the resale is a breach of the first contract of sale, the position is as follows: the seller does not ordinarily commit conversion by reselling without delivery,[9] though his seizure of the goods would be a trespass[10] and the resale an injurious falsehood (see ante, para 17.17); but, if the seller resells and delivers to the second buyer, the seller commits conversion (see ante, para 19.06), and the second buyer will do so unless he obtains good title under one of the exceptions to the *nemo dat* rule (see ante, Chapter 21).

Remedies where there is a reservation of property

[27.12] Where the goods are supplied on conditional sale, hp or simple hiring,[1] the conventional strategy for the unpaid supplier is as follows:[2] to terminate any bailment (see ante, para 26.09), repossess the goods (see ante, para 24.21 *et seq*) and resell or rehire them.[3] If a conditional seller legitimately resells whilst the contract subsists, he is entitled out of the proceeds only to the amount needed to discharge the outstanding balance;[4] but, where the conditional sale has been terminated, the conditional seller is entitled to retain the whole of any capital profit made on resale.[5] Presumably, the position is similar in relation to any hp or simple hiring, so making it important in all three cases to decide whether the instalment credit agreement has been terminated.[6]

---

4   If between exercise of the lien and resale the original buyer tenders the price, it has been argued that s 48(2) ceases to apply: *Benjamin's Sale of Goods* (5th edn), para 15-102.

5   It is argued that s 48(2) requires the seller to be in possession at the time of resale: Goode, *op cit*, note 3, p 447.

6   Eg, on repudiation by the buyer: *Commission Car Sales Ltd v Saul* [1957] NZLR 144. Cf *Jarvis v Williams* [1955] 1 All ER 108, CA (seller in whom property not revested could not sue in detinue).

7   *Lancashire Waggon Co v Fitzhugh* (1861) 6 H & N 502.

8   *Stephens v Wilkinson* (1831) 2 B & Ad 320.

9   *Lancashire Waggon Co v Fitzhugh* (above). But see ante, para 19.05.

10 See ante, para 19.04. If it is a conditional sale within the CCA there may also be a breach of s 90: see ante, para 24.35 *et seq.*

[27.12]

1   For the definitions of which, see ante, Chapter 1.

2   Where the buyer or hirer has disposed of the goods, there may be a right to trace: see post, para 27.13. For regulated agreements, see post, para 27.15.

3   If the repossession is in breach of the instalment contract, it will amount to a repudiation by the supplier (see ante, para 26.15), enabling the buyer or hirer to rescind and/or claim damages: see post, Chapter 29.

4   As to the small sums commonly realised, see ante, para 27.02.

5   *Clough Mills Ltd v Martin* (set out ante, para 25.30), *per* Robert Goff LJ (at 987j–88g), Oliver LJ (at 991–93g–h) and *per* Donaldson MR (at 994g–h). Compare resale by an ordinary unpaid seller: ante, para 27.10.

6   As to the distinction between terminating the bailment and terminating the agreement, see ante, para 26.09.

Bearing in mind the foregoing process, when the original supply contract is made, the supplier should aim to ensure for himself sufficient real security over the life of the instalment contract. To achieve this, he must estimate the likely resale value of the goods over the life of the instalment contract, and then arrange the repayments so that the estimated resale value always exceeds the outstanding instalments. Unlike a mortgagee (see ante, para 25.20), the supplier is under no duty to get the best price obtainable, because the buyer or hirer has no equity of redemption (see ante, para 24.22). In respect of creditors licensed under the CCA, the OFT has used its licensing powers (see ante, para 6.23) to discourage creditors from claiming damages from the debtors in such circumstances.[7] However, insofar as the supplier does not realise enough from the resale to make good his loss, he may be thinking in terms of an action in damages against the buyer or hirer.[8]

[27.13] Tracing generally.[1] Whilst the common law and equitable doctrines of tracing are familiar in the context of trust property, such rights may arise whenever there exists a fiduciary relationship between the parties in relation to any type of property. Moreover, such a fiduciary relationship may be created by contract,[2] as was demonstrated with the introduction of *Romalpa* clauses into this country in 1976 (see ante, para 25.29). This development dramatically drew the attention of lawyers to the potential of the doctrine of tracing in the commercial context,[3] where a clear distinction must be drawn according to whether or not the property in the goods had passed.

1 *Property in the supplier.* The simple case is where the supply contract reserves the property in the goods to the supplier, ie, a contract of conditional sale, hp or simple hiring (see generally ante, para 27.12); and nothing is done to disturb this arrangement. For instance, in the *Romalpa* case itself, the unpaid supplier was held entitled at common law as against the receiver to the unworked aluminium in the possession of the conditional buyer.[4]

2 *Property in the buyer or hirer.* On the other hand, the unpaid supplier may lose both the property in, and possession of, the goods supplied. For instance, in *Borden* (set out ante, para 25.31) the Court of Appeal held that, notwithstanding the express reservation of property, the property in the resin passed to the conditional buyer when the resin was irretrievably mixed with wood chips; and in *Re Bond Worth* (see ante, para 25.32) one of the reasons the property passed was because the fibre became unidentifiable, even the unused yarn not remaining marked out in any way as the

---

7 OFT, 1980-AR, 31.

8 In which case the duty to mitigate may require that the supplier resells for the best price obtainable: see post, para 27.45.

[27.13]

1 For the common law and equitable rules of tracing, see generally Pettit, *Equity* (8th edn), Chapter 24; Snell, *Equity* (29th edn), pp 297–305; Goff and Jones, *Restitution* (5th edn), p 76 *et seq*; Goode, *Commercial Law* (2nd edn), pp 58–59.

2 But there will be no constructive trust without the clearest evidence of the assumption of equitable as against merely contractual obligations: *Feuer Leather Corp v Johnstone & Sons* [1983] Com LR 12, CA; and generally post, para 27.14.

3 See Goode (1976) 92 LQR 401 and 528; Goodhart and Jones (1980) 43 MLR 489.

4 It is argued that the seller is not then an undisclosed principle (see ante, para 10.06) so as to render him liable to the sub-buyer for defects in the goods: McCormack (1990) 11 BLR 109.

supplier's goods.[5] Where the property has so passed, the unpaid supplier has lost his rights to the goods at common law and is reduced to a claim in equity.[6]

[27.14] Equitable tracing. Notwithstanding any reservation of property by the supply contract after the supplier has relinquished possession, he may also lose the property in the goods, either because of the way the goods have been dealt with by the buyer or hirer (see ante, para 27.13), or because they have been disposed of to a bfp under an exception to the *nemo dat* rule.[1] In such cases, the unpaid supplier has lost his right to the goods at common law, and is reduced to tracing his interest in equity insofar as the contract provides[2] and the law allows. Such interests may be avoided by the chattel mortgage legislation for non-registration (see ante, para 25.28 *et seq*).

1   *Tracing into products.* Where the unpaid supplier has lost his right to the goods supplied because they have been turned into other goods, the contract may purport to grant the supplier rights in such products. In the *Romalpa* case (set out ante, para 25.29), where there was both a reservation of property and an expressly created fiduciary relationship, the Court of Appeal held the unpaid supplier entitled to the worked aluminium into which the aluminium foil had been turned. On the other hand, in *Borden* (set out ante, para 25.31) the Court of Appeal held that the mere relationship of seller and buyer did not give rise to a fiduciary relationship between them, so that there was no right to trace; and it has subsequently been made clear that the question turns upon whether the parties expressly or impliedly intend to create such a fiduciary relationship.[3] Even if effective in equity, it has been suggested that such an interest is always registrable (see ante, para 25.31–32).

2   *Tracing the proceeds.* Where the unpaid supplier has lost his rights to the goods supplied, the contract may purport to grant him rights in the proceeds of later disposal of the goods.[4] Thus, in the *Romalpa* case the receiver was held bound to account for proceeds of sale of the products under the first-in-time rule (see ante, para 7.21), these being deposited along with other money in a mixed bank account which was in credit.[5] However, subsequent sellers have found it difficult to establish such a fiduciary relationship to the satisfaction of the courts (see ante, para 25.30A). Moreover, even assuming proof of the necessary fiduciary relationship, this interest may amount to a charge on the book debts of the buyer, in which case the equitable

---

5   See also *Re Peachdart Ltd* (set out ante, para 25.30A).

6   *Clough Mills Ltd v Martin* (set out ante, para 25.30), *per* Robert Goff LJ (at 989g–990e), Oliver LJ (at 993c–h) and Donaldson MR (at 994c–e). See further post, para 27.14.

[27.14]

1   Section 25 of the SGA (see ante, para 21.43), as limited by the *Mills & Lawrence* case (set out ante, para 21.51): see [1996] JBL at 496, note 78.

2   But not otherwise, the bailor-bailee relationship not necessarily being a fiduciary one: *Hendy Lennox (Industrial Engineer) Ltd v Grahame Puttick Ltd* (set out ante, para 25.30A); *Re Andrabell Ltd* [1984] 3 All ER 407; and [1985] JBL at 161–62.

3   *Per* Robert Goff LJ in *Clough Mills Ltd v Martin* (set out ante, para 25.30), at 987. This will not be lightly inferred: see ante, para 27.13. For argument that there should be no such requirement, see Millett (1991) 107 LQR 71.

4   Either by the express provisions of the contract of sale, eg, the *Romalpa* case (set out ante, para 25.29), or by operation of law, eg, *Re Hallett's Estate* (above): see Williams (1991) 12 Company Lawyer at 57.

5   Under the doctrine in *Re Hallett's Estate* (1880) 13 Ch D 696, CA. See also *Re Kayford Ltd* (set out ante, para 19.23). Distinguish overdrawn bank accounts.

right to trace into proceeds is subject to any statutory duty to register that interest;[6] and the question may be whether there has been created a true beneficial interest or only a charge.[7] It has been recommended that all such *Romalpa* clauses should require registration to be effective (see ante, para 25.34).

[27.15] The CCA. With regard to regulated conditional sale and hp agreements, the CCA makes the following alterations to the pattern observed above (para 27.12). Where the supplier wrongfully repossesses protected goods, the agreement automatically terminates, with the consequences spelt out in s 91 (see ante, para 24.38). Where the debtor exercises his statutory right to terminate under s 99 (see ante, para 26.05), his liability is limited by s 100 (see post, para 27.49). Upon the operation of either ss 91 or 99, the supplier has an unfettered right to dispose of the goods on his own account.

In the case of consumer hiring agreements, the rules relating to protected goods are inapplicable; but there is a parallel right under s 101 for the hirer to terminate the agreement (see ante, para 26.07), the hirer's liability being considered later (see post, para 27.49).

PERSONAL REMEDIES OF THE SUPPLIER

[27.15A] The supplier affirming the contract may also be able to maintain an action in debt against the buyer or hirer for the price or hire rent;[1] but, if he recovers the price or hire rent, this will be deducted from the damages awarded to avoid any double recovery (see post, para 27.39). Alternatively, the supplier may be suing for what his services are worth (*quantum meruit*) in the following circumstances:[2] (a) where there is a binding contract which does not stipulate the price or rent;[3] (b) where there is a binding contract which stipulates the price or rent, but that price or rent is not recoverable, either because of the contractual incapacity of the transferee,[4] or the buyer or hirer has wrongfully prevented the agreed price or rent becoming due (see ante, para 26.02); or (c) the contract was void *ab initio*, eg, for mistake (see ante, para 10.14 *et seq*), or the contract is frustrated.[5]

However, a clear distinction is drawn at common law between a claim in **debt**, as considered below, and a claim for **damages** (see post, para 27.24 *et seq*):

(1) An action in debt lies upon a primary obligation[6] to pay a definite sum of money fixed and made payable by the contract, eg, the price or hire rent, or a loan. That debt

---

6 Eg, *Re Interview Ltd* [1975] IR 382; *Borden's* case (set out ante, para 25.31); *Re Bond Worth Ltd* (set out ante, para 25.32); *Re Peachdart Ltd* (set out ante, para 25.30A); *Pfeiffer etc GmbH & Co v Arbuthnot Factors* [1987] BCLC 522.

7 See Goodhart and Jones (1980) 43 MLR at 513; Guest (1979) 95 LQR at 480.

[27.15A]

1 In electing to sue for the price or rent (as to election, see ante, para 26.17), the unpaid supplier has generally speaking elected not to exercise any right of rescission (see ante, para 26.16) and therefore cannot recover the goods: but see post, para 27.19.

2 *Benjamin on Sale* (5th edn), para 12-067.

3 Eg, SGA, s 8(2): see ante, para 2.06.

4 Eg, SGA, s 3: see ante, para 10.18.

5 For benefits conferred before frustration: see the FCA 1943, s 1(3); ante, para 22.19.

6 For primary and secondary obligations, see ante, para 26.16.

obligation may arise upon the happening of some condition precedent,[7] or as liquidated damages upon breach (see post, para 27.24). It is normally recoverable regardless of loss, except for the rule against penalties (see post, para 27.25); and it is *prima facie* assignable (see ante, para 1.23).

(2) A claim for **damages** for breach of contract is a secondary obligation arising from breach of a primary obligation. To recover more than nominal damages, proof of loss is required (see post, para 27.29); transfer of such a claim may offend the rules against maintenance and champerty (see ante, para 7.26); and the amount of damages recoverable is subject to a number of limitations (see post, para 27.39).

Being personal actions, both claims in debt and damages are subject to any restrictions applicable if the debtor/defendant is insolvent (see ante, para 19.18 *et seq*).

Action for price or rent

Action for the price of goods sold

[27.16] An action for the price (see ante, para 2.06) may be available to the seller under the rules considered below in the case of a cash sale, or as to an instalment sale (credit or conditional) in respect of the instalments of the price which are due.[1] There are special rules for deposits and part-payments (see post, para 27.20).

Prima facie, a breach by the buyer of his duty to pay the price (see ante, para 23.13) does not give rise to a right to rescind;[2] and, in considering the right of the unpaid seller to recover the price, two points must be borne in mind: first the additional leverage provided by the rights of stoppage and lien are lost on delivery (see ante, paras 24.18; 24.14); and secondly, for historical reasons a sharp distinction is drawn according to whether the property in the goods has passed to the buyer. Unfortunately, s 49 of the SGA has preserved the common law position that, generally speaking,[3] an action for the price is only maintainable where the property has passed (see post, paras 27.17–18); and that, if it has not passed, the seller is normally confined to an action for damages.[4] The significance of the distinction is as follows: not only may there be a substantial difference in monetary terms between the price and damages, but in an action for the price alone the seller is under no obligation to prove or mitigate his loss.[5] Further, he may apply for summary judgment for the price.

---

7   *Carlill v Carbolic Smoke Ball Co* [1893] 1 QB 256, CA (see ante, para 8.05).

[27.16]

1   Where the period of credit has expired, the whole of the price will be due under an instalment sale; and the same result may follow upon the operation of an acceleration clause. See ante, paras 7.03; 23.26.

2   Section 10(1): set out ante, para 23.20. For the situation where that *prima facie* rule is displaced, see post, para 27.19

3   It has been argued that this is only a *prima facie* rule, and that s 49 may be ousted by a contractual provision as to when the price shall be payable: *Benjamin's Sale of Goods* (5th edn), para 16-025. Cf ante, para 22.11.

4   This apparent principle has been described as simply faulty drafting: Goode, *Commercial Law* (2nd edn), p 424.

5   *Aliter*, if there is also a claim for damages for consequential loss. For the duty to mitigate, see post, para 27.44.

Rather than largely depending on the passing of property, Art 2 of the US Uniform Commercial Code uses the general yardstick of the transfer of possession.[6]

[27.17] After the property has passed. Section 49(1) of the SGA provides that:

> Where, under a contract of sale, the property in the goods has passed to the buyer, and the buyer wrongfully neglects or refuses to pay for the goods according to the terms of the contract, the seller may maintain an action against him for the price of the goods.

Under this general rule, an action for the price is only maintainable on certain conditions.[1]

1 *The property has passed to the buyer*. Unless the case falls within s 49(2) discussed below, no action for the price is possible before the passing of property, even where it is the buyer's fault that the property has not passed.[2] Thus, s 49(1) will typically be applicable where goods have been delivered under a cash sale.

2 *The buyer wrongfully neglects or refuses to pay the price*. The duty to pay the price has already been examined (see ante, para 23.13); and the most common cases where neglect or failure to pay the price is **not** wrongful are as follows: (1) where payment and delivery are concurrent terms and the seller has not yet tendered delivery;[3] and (2) where the goods have been delivered, but the sale is on credit terms which have not yet expired (see ante, para 27.16). However, the unpaid seller under a credit sale will be able to sue for the full price where either the whole of the credit term has expired,[4] or an acceleration clause has operated.[5]

[27.18] Before the property has passed. The exceptional case where an action is maintainable for the price before the passing of property is embodied in s 49(2), which provides that:

> Where under a contract for sale, the price is payable on a day certain irrespective of delivery, and the buyer wrongfully neglects or refuses to pay such price, the seller may maintain an action for the price, although the property in the goods has not passed, and the goods have not been appropriated to the contract.

Once again, the right of action is hedged around with restrictions: first, that the buyer wrongfully neglects or refuses to pay the price;[1] second, that the price is payable irrespective of delivery;[2] and third, that the price is payable on a day certain. With respect

---

6 Supported by Bridge [1991] LM & CLQ 52 at 68.

[27.17]

1 Nevertheless the unpaid seller who has parted with the property in the goods and is suing for the price may exceptionally be able to get an interlocutory injunction to restrain the buyer from disposing of the goods: *Flam Textiles (Canada) v McQueen of London Sportswear* [1976] CLY 2196, CA.

2 *Colley v Overseas Exporters* [1921] 3 KB 302.

3 Where s 28 operates: set out ante, paras 22.01; 23.16.

4 Cf SGA, s 41(1)(b): set out ante, para 24.10.

5 For acceleration clauses, see ante, para 7.03; and for instalment sales see post, para 27.19.

[27.18]

1 For the requirement, see generally ante, para 27.17. As to payment by instalments, see post, para 27.19.

2 *Stein, Forbes & Co v County Tailoring Co* (1916) 86 LJKB 448 DC; *Colley v Overseas Exporters* [1921] 3 KB 320.

to this last requirement, the question arises as to whether it should be interpreted literally, or whether that literal meaning can be extended by invoking the maxim *certum est quod certum reddi potest*. In *Workman Clark Ltd v Lloyd Brazileno*[3] the Court of Appeal were unanimously of the opinion that the wider meaning should be taken; but this view would appear to have been *obiter*, and it has been pointed out that, if it prevailed, the price would almost always be payable on 'a day certain'.[4] However, a strict construction was put upon this requirement in *Shell Mex Ltd v Elton Cop Dying Co Ltd*:[5]

> There was a contract for the sale of 1,000 tons of oil to be delivered 'as reasonably required' by the buyers in about 12 equal monthly quantities up to 22 June 1927, payment to be made within 14 days of the delivery of each consignment. The buyers failed to take delivery of the last 466 tons; and after 22 June 1927, the sellers sued for the price. The claim failed, Wright J holding that the price was not due because the property had not passed and the contract did not make provision for payment 'on a day certain'.

Whilst his Lordship was prepared to read into s 49(2) that 'the price is payable by instalments on days certain',[6] he was not willing to interpret it so that 'the price is payable by a day certain'. The better view would therefore appear to be that s 49(2) can only apply if the time for the payment of the price is 'fixed in advance by the contract in such a way that it can be determined independently of the action of either party or of any third person'.[7]

[27.19] Payment by instalments. Where the *prima facie* rule is displaced and non-payment of the price shows an intention on the part of the buyer to repudiate the contract, the seller must elect between two mutually exclusive alternatives:[1] he can affirm the contract, and sue for the outstanding part of the price under s 49;[2] or he can rescind, in which case he is entitled to seize the goods, but not to recover the price. Thus, ordinarily the seller cannot have his cake and eat it too: he cannot have both the goods and their price. For instance, in *Hewison v Ricketts*:[3]

> The buyer under a conditional sale defaulted, whereupon the seller seized the goods and sued the defendant under his guarantee. The Court held that the seller could alternatively seize the goods or sue for the instalments; that in electing to seize the seller had therefore lost his right to the instalments; and that as the principal debt was extinguished, so was the liability of the guarantor (see ante, para 25.06).

---

3   [1908] 1 KB 968, CA. See especially at 977, 978, 981.
4   *Benjamin's Sale of Goods* (5th edn), para 16-024.
5   (1928) 34 Com Cas 39.
6   So that conditional sales may fall within s 49(2), as in *McEntire v Crossley Bros* (set out ante, para 1.14A).
7   Benjamin, *op cit*, note 4; Goode, *Payment Obligations in Commercial and Financial Transactions*, p 70.
[27.19]
1   See ante, para 27.16. For recovery by an innocent depositor, see post, para 29.13.
2   See ante, paras 27.17–18, in which case he may have to give credit for any deposit paid: *Gallagher v Shilcock* (see ante, para 27.10); and ante, para 23.27. Frequently, he will be able to sue for the whole of the price immediately by reason of an acceleration clause (see ante, para 7.03).
3   (1894) 63 LJQB 711, DC.

However, there is one instance where the seller may seek both to have his goods and the price; and that is where he recovers the goods and retains instalments of the price already paid.[4] In 1842, the common law rejected an attempt by a defaulting buyer to recover a sum already paid on account of the price;[5] but subsequently Stable J drew a distinction between a deposit and a part-payment, allowing recovery of the latter.[6] This decision is not easy to reconcile with the 1842 case; but the distinction between a deposit and a part-payment would appear at common law to depend on the intention of the parties and to have been accepted by the courts.[7] Part-payments (or 'recoverable deposits') may be recoverable by the defaulting buyer if a contract goes off (see ante, para 23.27); but in principle a deposit may be retained by the innocent seller.[8] However, the courts have since decided that that principle should be limited to a 'reasonable sum'; and that this connoted a sum which would not be penal (see post, para 27.26A) under the rule against penalties.[9] The effect was to draw a sharp distinction between the following: a **reasonable** deposit, which the seller might at common law retain;[10] and an **unreasonable** (penal) deposit, which the rescinding seller must return. At common law, the courts have even gone so far as to award damages for breach of a promise to pay a deposit (see ante, para 23.27). On the other hand it seems clear that, if a seller retaining a deposit sues for damages, he must also bring into account that deposit.[11] It is another question as to whether equity or statute would intervene in relation to even a reasonable deposit (see post, para 27.20).

[27.20] Recovery of deposits.[1] At common law, after rescission an advance part-payment of the price was recoverable even by a party in default, but a reasonable (non-penal) deposit generally was not (see ante, para 27.19). However, since that distinction between deposits and part-payments has become settled, attempts have been made to show that even a deposit may be recoverable in equity by the party in breach. In *Stockloser v Johnson*:[2]

> The plaintiff agreed to buy plant and machinery under a conditional sale contract which provided that the price was payable by instalments, and that if there was default for more than 28 days in payment of any instalment the seller could rescind, forfeit the instalments already paid and repossess the goods.[3] After the buyer's default the seller exercised these rights, and the buyer sued for the return of the instalments paid. The Court of Appeal

---

4 As to what constitutes payment, see ante, para 23.13 *et seq.*

5 *Fitt v Cassanet* (1842) 4 Man & G 898; and see *Cramer v Giles* (1883) 1 Cab & E1 151; affd (1884) 9 May. See also ante, paras 20.28; 24.22; and post, para 29.15.

6 Treitel, *Law of Contract* (10th edn), p 937.

7 *Dies v British and International Mining and Finance Corp Ltd* [1939] 1 KB 724. Cf Salmond and Williams, *Contract* (2nd edn), p 569, note (b); and Guest, *Law of HP*, 596.

8 *Stockloser v Johnson* (set out post, para 27.20).

9 *Workers Trust and Merchant Bank Ltd v Dojap Investments Ltd* [1993] AC 573, PC (sale of land case, where there may be special rules: Beale 109 LQR 524). See further Treitel, *op cit*, note 6, p 938.

10 *Pye v British Automobile Commercial Syndicate Ltd* [1906] 1 KB 425.

11 *Benjamin's Sale of Goods* (5th edn), para 15.132. Presumably, this is on the basis of the rule against double recovery: see post, para 27.39.

[27.20]

1 See generally Goff and Jones, *Law of Restitution* (6th edn), pp 535–46; Treitel, *Law of Contract* (10th edn), pp 939–41; McGregor, *Law of Damages* (16th edn), paras 544–57.

2 [1954] 1 QB 476; [1954] 1 All ER 630, CA. See Polack [1965] CLJ 17; Crawford (1966) 44 Can BR 142.

3 This was not a licence to seize within the Bills of Sale Acts because it was not granted by the owner (seller): see ante, para 25.27.

unanimously held that the forfeiture did not constitute a penalty on the facts of the case (see ante, para 27.19), whilst of the opinion that in appropriate circumstances relief might be given.

Whilst the equitable power to grant relief against forfeiture is well established in relation to mortgages of land (see ante, para 25.20), the courts have been more circumspect about extending the protection to personal property, even where the defaulting buyer was willing to pay, albeit late.[4] In *Stockloser v Johnson*, Romer LJ was prepared to give the defaulting buyer an opportunity (which the buyer did not want) to pay off the arrears;[5] but he added *obiter* that (at 501):

... no relief of any other nature can properly be given, in the absence of some special circumstances such as fraud, sharp practice or other unconscionable conduct of the vendor to a purchaser after the vendor has rescinded the contract.

However, the majority took a rather wider view; and Denning LJ said *obiter* that (only?) two things were necessary before equitable relief would be granted:[6]

... first, the forfeiture clause must be of a penal nature, in the sense, that the sum forfeited must be out of all proportion to the damage,[7] and, secondly, it must be unconscionable for the seller to retain the money.

Whilst the majority view may be desirable, it would appear that the weight of authority was on the side of Romer LJ. Since then similar issues have arisen in relation to bailments;[8] and, in relation to sales the Privy Council have held that at common law in sales of land it is only **reasonable** deposits which are forfeitable (see above), which ruling gives rise to considerable uncertainties in relation to supplies of goods.[9]

Upon the above pattern, there has been some statutory interference in relation to the recovery of deposits, whether reasonable or unreasonable: several types of relief have been offered in respect of regulated agreements (see post, para 27.23); and, in relation to consumer supplies, the requirement of a deposit may amount to an unfair term.[10]

Action for arrears of rentals

[27.21] There must here be considered the situation where there is an hp or simple hiring agreement. If the hirer refuses to accept delivery, the hiring does not commence; so that the owner is not entitled to any hire rent,[1] but must sue for damages for non-acceptance (see post, para 27.27), and failure to pay any deposit (see ante, para 23.27). On the other

---

4   *Goker v NWS Bank plc* [1990] GCCR 1507, CA (hp; relief denied to a persistent defaulter).
5   See also *BICC plc v Burndy Corp* [1985] Ch 232, CA (not a sale case; noted 101 LQR 145).
6   At 490. See also Somervell LJ at 485, 486 488. See Goode, *HP Law and Practice* (2nd edn), p 381.
7   This first test appears the same as that for penalties: see post, para 27.26.
8   See also the cases dealing with forfeiture of instalments due under a hiring contract: post, para 27.21. Cf *Sport International Bussum BV v Inter-Footwear Ltd* [1984] 2 All ER 321, HL; *Jobson v Johnson* [1989] 1 All ER 621, CA.
9   Eg, does the same rule apply? See Beale (1993) 109 LQR 524 at 528–30.
10   *Benjamin's Sale of Goods* (5th edn), 16-038; and see unfair term, Grey Term 1(e), ante, para 11.16.
[27.21]
1   See ante, para 15.23. Any rental paid in advance would be recoverable from the owner on grounds of tfc (see ante, para 16.05); but a deposit would not (see ante, para 27.20).

hand, once the hirer has taken possession under the agreement,[2] the owner is entitled, without any duty to mitigate (see ante, para 27.16) to any hire rent which accrues due by reason of the period during which the hirer is in possession under the terms of the agreement,[3] but not for any rentals in respect of any period thereafter.[4] This action for arrears of rental is an entirely separate one from the claim for damages for breach of contract.[5]

Because the essence of a hiring is payment of rent at an agreed rate in return for possession, the House of Lords have confirmed that at common law there is no power to order relief against forfeiture where a vessel is withdrawn by the owner upon failure by the charterer to make due payment of hire,[6] at least where the payments 'represent the agreed rate of hire and not a penny more' (at 703). Moreover, it follows from the very nature of bailment that at the end of its term the owner will both recover the goods and be entitled to retain or recover the hire rent in respect of the period of the bailment. Whilst formally this involves no element of double recovery of goods and price (compare ante, para 27.19), in practice it may do so (see also post, para 27.37). Thus, in *Galbraith v Mitchenall Estates Ltd*:[7]

> The plaintiff entered into a five year simple hiring agreement in respect of a caravan, mistakenly thinking that it was a hp agreement, and paid a deposit of £550. The plaintiff failed to pay any instalments, whereupon the owner repossessed the caravan, and resold it for £775. The plaintiff's claim for the return of the deposit was dismissed.

Notwithstanding that he thought the agreement 'hideously harsh', Sachs J preferred the view of Romer LJ in relation to the recovery of deposits (see ante, para 27.20); but his Lordship did recommend statutory intervention to protect such hirers (at 659). It would seem that the answer should be otherwise if the consumer hired on a trial basis, the supplier promising that, if satisfied, the consumer could convert to a purchase, putting the rent paid towards the purchase price. Is this hp?

However, in a sale the Privy Council have sanctioned relief against forfeiture of an unreasonable deposit (see ante, para 27.19); and the question arises whether the equitable jurisdiction to relieve against forfeiture is applicable to leases. In *On Demand Information plc v Gerson*:[8]

---

2   If no agreement is ever concluded, there is no liability to pay hire rent: *Campbell Discount Co Ltd v Gall* [1961] 1 QB 431, CA (an hp case, overruled on other grounds: as to which, see ante, para 16.05).

3   Eg, *Yeoman Credit Ltd v Apps* (set out post, para 29.25); *Charterhouse Credit Ltd v Tolly* [1963] 2 QB 683, CA (hp cases).

4   *Belsize Motor Supply Co v Cox* [1914] 1 KB 244 (hp case, where the hiring was for a fixed period). Would the answer be the same if there had been an acceleration clause (see ante, para 26.19); or would such a clause be treated as a minimum payments provision (see post, para 27.49)? Cf *IAC (Leasing) Ltd v Humphrey* (1972) 46 ALJR 106 (HC).

5   *Overstone Ltd v Shipway* [1962] 1 All ER 52, CA.

6   *The Scaptrade* [1983] 2 AC 694, HL.

7   [1965] 2 QB 473, [1964] 2 All ER 653. But see *per* Pennycuick J in *Barton Thompson & Co Ltd v Stapling Machines Co* [1966] Ch 499 at 509; and also *San Pedro Compania Armadora SA v Henry Navigation Co Ltd* [1970] 1 Lloyd's Rep 32.

8   [1999] 2 All ER 811; [1999] 1 All ER (Comm) 512. See also *Alf Vaughan & Co Ltd v Royscot Trust Ltd* (set out post, para 27.22; the finance leases).

There was a three year finance lease (see ante, para 1.18A) of video equipment, which provided (cl 9) for termination of the agreement if the lessee went into receivership (see ante, para 26.08). However, after being appointed towards the end of the lease, the receiver was anxious to take advantage of another provision in the lease (cl 12) allowing the lessee to sell the equipment at the end of the lease as agent of the lessor, but largely for his own benefit. Under court order, the receiver sold the equipment. He then sought relief from cl 9, so that he could take advantage of cl 12.

The judge held that the doctrine of relief against penalties was applicable to finance leases; that in principle it would enable the court to relieve a lessee who had retained possession from forfeiture under clause 9; but that, because he had already sold the goods, no such relief was available to the lessee.[9]

The consumer under a distance or doorstep supply may be able to avoid the above problems by exercising any statutory right of cancellation (see ante, paras 10.21–22A). For the position in relation to hp agreements, see post, para 27.22; and in relation to consumer hirings, see post, para 27.23; and for the action for damages, see post, para 27.37.

[27.22] Hire-purchase. As a species of bailment, an hp agreement entitles the owner to both the rentals and the goods at the end of the term: it does not matter whether he repossesses and then claims the arrears of rentals;[1] or vice versa.[2] However, under an hp agreement there is additionally an option to purchase, which makes it a hybrid (see ante, para 1.25); and in fact the amount of the instalments will be calculated on the basis of an aliquot part of the price, eg, if there are to be 20 instalments, each instalment will be one-twentieth of the price plus charges. Accordingly, if there is applied to hp the rule for simple hiring, the owner in recovering both the goods and the hire rent will commonly obtain an element of double recovery (see ante, para 24.22), which element would be reduced to the extent that the goods were worth less than the owner's loss. Of course, in some circumstances this result may be avoided on ordinary principles: first, the owner may affirm the contract with knowledge of the breach,[3] in which case he loses the right to repossess (see ante, para 27.16); and secondly, the owner may rescind and recover a judgment in conversion, which is merely for the value of his interest in the goods.[4] However, where the owner rescinds and, either recapts the goods (see ante, para 24.23), or obtains a judgment for their full value in conversion, there *prima facie* exists the potential element of double recovery (see post, para 27.39) which gave rise to the 'snatchback' (see ante, para 26.08).

It has already been seen that the case law discourages any hope that the courts will grant the hirer under a hire-purchase agreement an equity of redemption (see ante, para

---

9   Perhaps administrative receivers (see ante, para 19.14) may avoid this case and plead the equitable relief by delaying sale: Walker (2001) 56 CC 2/21.

[27.22]

1   *Brooks v Beirnstein* [1909] 1 KB 98 DC; *Overstone Ltd v Shipway* [1962] 1 All ER 52, CA; *Financings Ltd v Baldock* [1963] 2 QB 104, CA; *UCB Leasing Ltd v Holtom* (set out post, para 29.10).

2   *South Bedfordshire Electrical Finance Ltd v Bryant* [1938] 3 All ER 580, CA.

3   Eg, *Keith Prowse & Co v National Telephone Co Ltd* [1894] 2 Ch 147; *Reynolds v General and Finance Facilities Ltd* (1963) 107 SJ 889, CA.

4   See post, para 27.30. If that judgment is satisfied, he will thereupon lose his title to the goods (see ante, para 26.17).

24.22). However, there is some indication that the courts may sometimes be prepared to grant the hirer relief against forfeiture. In *Transag Haulage Ltd v Leyland Daf Finance plc*:[5]

> T, a haulage company, went into administrative receivership (see ante, para 19.14). At that time T were possessed of three lorries under unregulated hp agreements which provided, *inter alia* that the owners might terminate the agreements and repossess the goods if a receiver was appointed to T. T's Receiver resisted the repossessions because he wanted to sell the business as a going concern.

An argument that the hirer was, after resale of the lorries by the owner, entitled to any surplus over the remaining rentals under an express or implied term of the hp agreements was rejected (367F–368C). However, the Receiver also argued that T was entitled to relief against repossession under the equitable doctrine of relief from penalties or forfeiture. Knox J accepted that, because the owners were not claiming a sum of money, the matter could not be decided by the common law rule against penalties (see post, para 27.25), but thought that T's loss of his option to purchase might amount to a forfeiture, even though it was contingent on completion of the payment of instalments (372G). His Lordship said that he had a discretionary jurisdiction[6] to grant exceptional relief against forfeiture: he listed the relevant factors to be taken into account (375C–376B); and said that relief would only be granted where, as here, the owner would otherwise obtain a substantial windfall over and above what he would have obtained if the agreement had run its course.[7] This equitable jurisdiction is confined to forfeiture of proprietary or possessory rights and does not extend to merely contractual rights,[8] eg, an acceleration clause (see ante, para 26.19) in an unsecured instalment loan; nor where the hirer has relinquished possession. In *Alf Vaughan & Co Ltd v Royscot Trust Ltd*:[9]

> RT owned a number of vehicles which had been supplied to AV on unregulated hp or finance leases. The Administrative Receiver (see ante, para 19.14) appointed to AV wish to sell the business as a going concern and, to this end, exercise AV's rights under the agreements to pay all outstanding sums: he would then be able to sell the hp vehicles as owner and the leased vehicles as RT's agent. However, when the Receiver sought a settlement figure (about £34,000: see ante, para 26.19A), RT responded that it was entitled to terminate the agreements upon appointment of a receiver (see ante, para 26.08) and sent repossession agents to the site (see ante, para 24.23). RT demanded £82,000 from the Receiver for not recapting the goods, which sum the Receiver paid under protest and then sold on the business with the vehicles.

As the Receiver had sold the vehicles, he could not ask for relief against forfeiture (see ante, para 27.22). Instead, he claimed that the £82,000 had been paid under duress of goods (economic duress). The judge pointed out that a plea of economic duress was only available where the commercial pressure used to bring about a contract was illegitimate;[10] and he rejected the Receiver's claim on the grounds that, in the absence of

---

5   (1994) 13 Tr LR 361; [1994] BCC 356.
6   He made it clear that such relief would not be granted 'if the conduct of the hirer had disentitled it to receive it' (at 375C), eg, *Goker v NWS* [1990] CLY 4032, CA (repeated default by hirer).
7   He made an order for payment by the Receiver of the balance of the hp price within a week. If the agreement had had longer to run, would have had a discount for accelerated payment have been appropriate?
8   *The Scaptrade* [1983] 2 AC 694, HL. What about a restitutionary claim (cf *Banque Financière de la Cité v Parc (Battersea) Ltd* [1998] 2 WLR 475, HL)?
9   [1999] 1 All ER (Comm) 856.
10 His Lordship (at 860; 863) adopted passages from Goff and Jones, *Restitution* (5th edn), p 316. For duress, see generally ante, para 10.18.

exceptional circumstances amounting to unconscionable behaviour, the threat of recaption by the owner was not illegitimate (at 863–64).

For the position where the agreement is regulated, see post, para 27.23. For statutory protection by cancellation rights where there is a distance or doorstep supply, see ante, paras 10.21–22A.

[27.23] Regulated agreements. There is no general power in the CCA enabling the court to grant relief against forfeiture as such; but certain of the provisions of the Act will, where applicable, prevent the creditor or owner from having his cake and eating it too.[1]

1 *Prohibition of preliminary agreements.* Section 59(1) will avoid any separate deposit agreement (see ante, para 5.20), eg, with a dealer who is to put forward a directly financed transaction.

2 *The right of cancellation.* Where a hirer under an hp or simple hiring agreement, or a buyer under a conditional or credit sale agreement exercises his statutory right of cancellation, the creditor may recover the goods, but the debtor or hirer is under no further liability and may recover any payments made (s 70: see ante, para 10.33).

3 *Protected goods.* Where the creditor wrongfully repossess protected goods, the hirer on hp or conditional buyer is released from all further liability and may recover all sums already paid (s 91: set out ante, para 24.38). Even if the creditor does not recapt, where the debtor follows the procedure laid down for time orders, s 130(5) freezes the creditor's contractual rights arising by reason of the debtor's default (see ante, para 24.41).

4 *Extortionate credit bargains.* In respect of 'credit agreements,[2] a court may be persuaded to exercise the re-opening powers conferred by ss 137–40 (see post, para 29.40).

5 *Financial relief for hirers.* To combat the injustice evinced in *Galbraith v Mitchenall Estates Ltd* (set out ante, para 27.21), s 132(1) provides as follows:

> Where the owner under a regulated consumer hire agreement[3] recovers possession of goods to which the agreement relates otherwise than by action, the hirer may apply to the court for an order that –
>
> (a) the whole or part of any sum paid by the hirer to the owner in respect of the goods shall be repaid,[4] and
>
> (b) the obligation to pay the whole or part of any sum owed by the hirer to the owner in respect of the goods shall cease,[5]
>
> and if it appears to the court just to do so, having regard to the extent of the enjoyment of the goods by the hirer, the court shall grant the application in full or in part.

[27.23]

1 Compare the position where the debtor or hirer makes a statutory election to terminate the agreement: see ante, paras 26.05–07.

2 This concept extends beyond regulated consumer credit agreements but does not include any simple hirings, whether regulated or not.

3 As to consumer hire agreements, see ante, para 1.19.

4 This could include substantial deposits, as in *Galbraith's* case. But see *Automotive Financial Services v Henderson* 1992 SLT (Sh Ct) 63.

5 'Sum owed' appears to restrict s 132(1)(b) to rent arrears, and does not extend to sums payable: Guest and Lloyd, *Encyclopedia of Consumer Credit Law*, para 2-133. Presumably this would extend the subsection to rent accelerated by an acceleration clause, but does not touch claims for damages under minimum payment clauses (as to which see post, para 27.46).

Whilst this provision applies where the owner recapts goods (see ante, para 24.23), if the owner instead brings a successful action for repossession (see ante, paras 24.25; 25.16), similar powers to order release of the hirer are conferred on the court under s 132(2) or the court could reschedule those payments by way of a time order (see ante, para 24.40). Compare the common law rule against penalties (see post, para 27.25).

Liquidated damages and penalties

[27.24] Liquidated damages. As the quantification of damages can be a very difficult matter (see post, para 27.27 *et seq*), the parties sometimes agree beforehand (usually in the contract) what sum shall be payable in the event of certain breaches or wrongs, eg, an administration fee, the price.[1] Provided such a clause is a genuine pre-estimate of damage, then, irrespective of the precise amount of loss actually suffered, it is termed a 'liquidated damages' clause: without proof of actual loss, a liquidated damages clause will be *prima facie* be given effect to by the courts,[2] unless it amounts to an unfair term.[3] However, if it works to the advantage of the innocent party, it may be struck down as being a penalty (see post, para 27.25); and, if it acts to protect the guilty party, it may amount to an exclusion clause (see Chapter 18).

As a claim for an agreed sum (a debt), a liquidated damages clause is usually assignable (see ante, para 27.15A). However, it will be free from the rules limiting the recovery of damages, such as those of causation, remoteness and mitigation.[4] Nor does it probably fall within the definition of an 'exclusion or restriction' of liability for the purposes of s 13 of UCTA.[5]

[27.25] The rule against penalties.[1] Whilst a contractual promise to pay an agreed sum on default may take effect as a liquidated damages clause (see ante, para 27.24), at common law it may be struck down by the rule against penalties, in which case the innocent party will only be able to recover damages which he proves represents his actual loss,[2] whether that be less[3] or more[4] than the sum stipulated in the penalty clause. However, it has been decided that this rule against penalties does not affect clauses providing for a deposit (see ante, para 27.20), or accelerating payment,[5] or requiring entire performance by one side

---

[27.24]
1   Eg, the *George Mitchell* case (set out ante, para 18.08); the *Watford Electronics* case (set out ante, para 18.24A).
2   *Robophone Facilities Ltd v Blank* [1966] 3 All ER 128, CA.
3   OFT, *Bulletin No 14*, case 6: no refund of fees paid within Grey Term 1(d): see ante, para 11.16.
4   See *Chitty On Contract* (28th edn), para 27-08.
5   Treitel, *Law of Contract* (10th edn), 227; and see generally, ante, para 18.16.
[27.25]
1   See generally Treitel, *Law of Contract* (10th edn), pp 929–37.
2   *Financings Ltd v Baldock* [1963] 2 QB 104, CA; *Bridge* (see below); *Jobson v Johnson* [1989] 1 All ER 621, CA (not a sale of goods case; [1990] LM & CLQ 158).
3   Eg, *Clydebank Engineering and Shipbuilding Co* case [1905] AC 6, HL.
4   See Treitel, *op cit*, note 1, p 933. Compare Hudson (1985) 101 LQR 480.
5   *Wallingford v Mutual Society* (1880) 5 App Cas 685, HL. But see *Wadham Stringer Finance Ltd v Meaney* (set out ante, para 26.19), at 796–97, discussed by Treitel, *op cit*, note 1, p 931.

before performance by the other (see ante, para 26.02), or liquidating damages,[6] or performance bonds,[7] or making time of the essence.[8]

One of the areas where the penalty principles have been particularly litigated is that of minimum payments clauses in instalment credit agreements.[9] Frequently, the largest element in this is the sum expressed to be 'compensation' for depreciation of the goods; and the real purpose of such a clause may be to allow the owner to recoup his 'loss of profit'. The leading case is *Bridge v Campbell Discount Co Ltd*:[10]

> There was a directly financed hp transaction in respect of a Bedford Dormobile van. The hp agreement provided (cl 9) that, if it be terminated by the hirer for any reason, then the hirer 'shall ... (b) pay to the owners ... by way of agreed compensation for depreciation of the vehicle such further sum as may be necessary to make the rentals paid and payable hereunder equal to two-thirds of the hp price'. Having paid the deposit and taken possession of the van, the hirer on 3 September 1959, wrote to the owner:
>
>> Owing to unforeseen personal circumstances I am very sorry but I will not be able to pay any more payments ... Will you please let me know where and when I will have to return the car. I am very sorry regarding this but I have no alternative.
>
> The owner did not reply; the hirer returned the vehicle to the dealer; and subsequently the owner commenced proceedings against the hirer under clause 9 for the balance of two-thirds of the hp price. The County Court Judge dismissed the claim as being for a penalty; but he was reversed by the Court of Appeal on the grounds that the rule against penalties could not apply where, as here, the hirer had lawfully terminated his agreement.[11] Reversing the Court of Appeal, the House of Lords held that the hirer had broken the agreement; that the owner was asserting rights under clause 9 consequent on that breach; that clause 9 was void as stipulating for a penal sum; and that the owner was therefore only entitled to damages for the loss suffered.

Two issues were involved, to both of which the House of Lords gave an affirmative answer: (1) whether the rule against penalties was applicable at all; and (2) if so, whether clause 9 stipulated for a penal sum (see post, paras 27.47–48).

Nowadays, the facts of *Bridge* would fall within s 100 of the CCA (see post, para 27.49).

[27.26] The scope of the penalty rule. On the traditional rule that the stipulated sum could only be a penalty if payable on breach,[1] it was at first held that a minimum payments clause could not be a penalty where the stipulated sum was payable not just on

---

6   *Dunlop Pneumatic Tyre* case [1915] AC 79, HL.

7   *ECGD v Universal Oil Co* [1983] 2 All ER 205, HL; *Cargill International SA v Bangladesh Sugar Industries Corp* [1996] 4 All ER 563.

8   *Lombard North Central plc v Butterworth* (set out post, para 27.26), especially *per* Mustill LJ at 273d–275d. See generally ante, para 26.08.

9   Explained ante, para 11.09: see the discussions in Goode, *HP Law and Practice* (2nd edn), pp 385–409; Guest, *Law of HP*, pp 625–50; Ziegel [1964] CLJ 108; Hughes [1962] JBL 252.

10   [1962] AC 600; [1962] 1 All ER 385, HL: see above and also *Chitty on Contract* (28th edn), para 27-103.

11   [1961] 1 QB 445; [1961] 2 All ER 97, CA.

[27.26]

1   *Associated Distributors Ltd v Hall* [1938] 2 KB 83, CA (determination by hirer); and as to determination by transferee, see generally ante, para 26.04; *Re Apex Supply Co Ltd* [1942] Ch 108 (automatic termination on liquidation of hirer: see ante, para 26.08).

breach but also on certain other events, such as lawful termination by the hirer.[2] However, this ruling offered such an obvious means by which a draftsman of a minimum payments clause could escape the rule against penalties that it was reversed: where the event which in fact brought the minimum payments clause into operation was a termination by the owner on grounds of breach by the hirer, the rule against penalties was held to be applicable.[3] Since then, the courts have sought to extend the rule against penalties in two ways. First, they have taken the view of the facts most advantageous to the hirer in deciding how the agreement has been terminated. Notwithstanding the ordinary rule of interpretation that a party should *prima facie* be assumed to have intended to do that which is lawful, in *Bridge's* case (set out ante, para 27.25) the House of Lords held that the hirer had broken rather than lawfully terminated his agreement.[4] Secondly, even though the common law rule is not applicable where the minimum payments clause is activated by an event other than breach by the hirer, it was suggested by Lord Denning in *Bridge* that a similar equitable principle might be invoked in these circumstances.[5] However, in *Lombard North Central plc v Butterworth*:[6]

> There was a lease for a period of five years of a computer which made payment of instalments of the essence. A number of instalments being overdue, the lessor terminated the lease and recovered possession. The Court of Appeal held: (a) in the absence of a repudiatory breach by the lessee, the minimum payments clause would be void as being a penalty; (b) repeated failure by the lessee to pay instalments punctually did not evince an intention by him to repudiate (see ante, para 26.15); but (c) as time was expressly made of the essence (see ante, para 26.08), default in punctual payment went to the root of the contract, enabling the lessor to terminate the contract and recover damages for loss of future instalments.

In holding that the clause making time of the essence was not of itself a penalty, the Court reluctantly accepted that by a mere drafting change the lessor had escaped the *Baldock* causation rule (see post, para 27.29) and could enforce the minimum payments clause, though their Lordships did not view the result with much satisfaction.

The common law rules may be displaced in the case of regulated agreements (see post, para 27.49) and may be subject to the Unfair Terms rules.[7]

[27.26A] A penal sum. Unlike the genuine pre-estimate of damage in a liquidated damages clause (see ante, para 27.24), a penalty clause will stipulate for a penal sum.[1] As Lord Dunedin explained,[2] it:

---

2   *Elsey Ltd v Hyde* (1926), unreported: see Guest, *Law of HP*, p 628.

3   *Cooden Engineering Ltd v Stanford* [1953] 1 QB 86, CA.

4   See also *United Dominions Trust (Commercial) Ltd v Ennis* [1968] 1 QB 54, CA (hirer's letter treated as invitation to owner to terminate; or, if it were a repudiation, the owner had affirmed by suing on the minimum payments clause); *Chartered Trust v Pitcher* [1988] RTR 72, CA.

5   At 631; and see Lord Devlin at 634. *Contra* Lords Simonds and Morton at 613, 614. See also *Penalty Clauses and Forfeiture of Moneys Paid* (1975, Law Com Working Paper No 26) para 26; Goode (1988) 104 LQR 25.

6   [1987] QB 527; [1987] 1 All ER 267, CA (discussed Treitel [1987] LMCLQ 143; Macassey 42 CC 1–2; Opeskin (1990) 106 LQR 293).

7   Treitel, *Law of Contract* (10th edn), pp 936–37; OFT, *Bulletin No 12*, case 6 (Grey Terms 1(b) and (e): see ante, para 11.16).

[27.26A]

1   See further Treitel, *Law of Contract* (10th edn), pp 930–32.

2   In *Dunlop Pneumatic Tyre Co Ltd v New Garage and Motor Co Ltd* [1915] AC 79 at 87, HL.

... will be held to be a penalty if the sum stipulated for is extravagant and unconscionable in amount compared with the greatest loss which could conceivably be proved to have followed from the breach.

However, a clause cannot be a penalty for some purposes but not for others, so that, if a clause is expressed to operate on more than one type of breach, it is to be tested against the smallest possible breach.[3] This is Lord Dunedin's 'weakest link' principle: in assessing whether a clause is penal, it will be judged on the highest amount payable for the most insignificant breach, regardless of the actual facts.[4]

On this weakest link principle, any attempt to exact a fixed percentage of the hp price would appear to be penal.[5] Nor will a sliding scale necessarily suffice: this may prove objectionable if the result is that the owner is always entitled to recover both the full hp price and the goods, or if the scale does not take into account either the acceleration in payments or the resale.[6] In the light of these considerations and of the difficulties thrown up by such cases as *Lombank Ltd v Excell*,[7] it may be that the inclusion of such a clause in any hp agreement is positively dangerous.[8] On the other hand, the law does allow clauses for payment of a variable sum whose variations adequately reflect the loss flowing from different breaches.[9] Thus, where simple hirings have not contained an element of double recovery, the courts have been rather more ready to uphold a minimum payment clause;[10] and the same may follow where the clause in effect gives the hirer an equity of redemption.[11]

Action for damages[1]

[27.27] The common types of action for damages available to a supplier[2] against the hirer or buyer are for breach of contract, tort or misrepresentation.[3]

1 *For breach of contract.* The SGA partially covers the possibilities: besides expressly recognising the right of action for damages where the price is not forthcoming (ss 48(3) and (4): set out ante, para 27.08), the Act in two places deals with the

---

3 *Ford Motor Co (England) v Armstrong* (1915) 31 TLR 267, CA.
4 See *Dunlop Pneumatic Tyre Co Ltd* case (above).
5 Eg, *Landom Trust Ltd v Hurrell* [1955] 1 All ER 839; see *McGregor on Damages* (16th edn), para 524.
6 Eg, *Cooden Engineering Ltd v Stanford* [1953] 1 QB 86, CA; *Anglo-Auto Finance Ltd v James* [1963] 3 All ER 566, CA; *Bridge's* case (set out ante, para 27.25).
7 [1964] 1 QB 415, CA. See Thornley [1964] CLJ 108; Downey (1964) 27 MLR 100; Guest, *Law of HP*, p 638.
8 Eg, *Ennis'* case [1968] 1 QB 54, CA: see ante, para 27.26.
9 Eg, the *Clydebank Engineering* case [1905] AC 6, HL.
10 *Robophone Facilities Ltd v Blank* [1966] 3 All ER 128, CA; discussed by Goode, *HP Law and Practice* (2nd edn), pp 397, 887–88. See also Goode, *Commercial Law* (2nd edn), pp 785–87; (1988) 104 LQR 25.
11 See Giddens (1993) BJIBFL at 265.

[27.27]
1 See generally *McGregor on Damages*, (16th edn).
2 For damages actions by lenders, see ante, para 7.03.
3 For declarations of non-liability, see post, para 29.01.

common situation where the buyer fails to take delivery,[4] on the basis of whether or not that delay is so great as to evince an intention to repudiate.[5] If not, s 37 (set out ante, para 23.08) expressly recognises the seller's right to damages for loss occasioned by the failure to take delivery and for storage charges. If so, s 50(1) provides that:

> Where the buyer wrongfully neglects or refuses to accept and pay for the goods, the seller may maintain an action against him for damages for non-acceptance.

It is usually assumed that these provisions apply by analogy where a hirer under an hp or simple hiring agreement fails to take delivery.[6] Under such a claim, the major head of *prima facie* loss is likely to be loss of profit (see post, paras 27.34–38). Claims for consequential loss are more likely to be made where it is the supplier who is in breach and will therefore be considered later (see Chapter 29).

2   *In tort.* The buyer or hirer might wrongfully deprive the supplier of the goods in several ways; and under the Torts Act 1977 these have all been subsumed under the new statutory tort of 'wrongful interference with goods' (see ante, para 19.04). If the wrong amounts to conversion, the supplier is entitled to the value of the goods (see post, para 27.30).

3   *For misrepresentation.* The common law offers a remedy for misrepresentation where it amounts to the torts of deceit or negligent misstatement (see ante, paras 17.18–19); and in the former case the measure of damages is the same as in conversion,[7] ie, the value of the goods (see above). Additionally, damages may now be awarded under s 2 of the Misrepresentation Act 1967 (see ante, para 17.10), in which case the measure of damages is tortious: for breach of s 2(1), damages may be measured as for the tort of deceit;[8] whereas, damages granted under s 2(2) are presumably based on some lesser tortious measure,[9] so giving more meaning to s 2(3).[10] As to misrepresentations by the supplier, see post, para 29.18.

In English law, a cause of action for breach of contract is complete on breach: it is said to be actionable *per se*, so that nominal damages are recoverable without proof of loss.[11] On the other hand, in some torts,[12] loss or damage is an ingredient of the cause of action, ie, there is no action without proof of loss.

---

4   *Prima facie*, it is the buyer's duty to collect the goods (s 29(2)): see ante, para 23.04.
5   This is the explanation of the apparent overlap between ss 37 and 50(1) preferred by Goode, *Commercial Law* (2nd edn), p 432.
6   See *Karsales Ltd v Wallis* [1956] 2 All ER 866, CA. See also Guest, *Law of HP*, p 321; Goode, *HP Law and Practice* (2nd edn), pp 354–55.
7   *Smith Kline & French Laboratories Ltd v Long* [1988] 3 All ER 887, CA.
8   Including damages for unforeseeable loss: *Royscot Trust Ltd v Rogerson* (set out post, para 27.28), *per* Balcombe and Ralph Gibson LJJ at AER 302e, 302c (criticised 107 LQR 547; [1992] JBL 311); and generally post, para 27.41.
9   Perhaps on the basis of indemnity only: see Treitel, *Contract* (10th edn), p 339; *Chitty on Contract* (28th edn), para 6-098. But why not as for negligent misstatement, ie, subject to a foreseeability test of remoteness (see post, para 27.41)? See *Cemp Properties (UK) v Deutsply Corp* [1991] 2 EGLR 197, CA (not a goods case; consequential loss recovered).
10   Ie, that more damages are recoverable under s 2(1) than under s 2(2). For the double recovery point, see post, para 27.39.
11   *Charter v Sullivan* (set out post, para 27.33). For the issues relevant to the recovery of substantial damages, see post, paras 27.28–29.
12   Eg, negligence (see ante, para 17.14 *et seq*); Misrepresentation Act 1967, s 2(1) (see ante, para 17.10). *Contra* wrongful interference with goods (see ante, para 19.04).

Quantification of damages

[27.28] Object of damages. It has been seen that a supplier will frequently have the choice of suing in either contract or tort in respect of damage caused by the wrong (see ante, para 27.27). Sometimes such claims will lie in the alternative; but, insofar as they are concurrent,[1] there may be no double recovery (see post, para 27.39). In any event, the object of compensatory damages in tort and contract are different.[1a]

1   *Damages in tort.* The object of damages in tort is *restitutio in integrum*; that is, so far as money can do it, to put the injured plaintiff back in the same position as if the wrong had not been sustained.[2] If the goods have been lost, this will *prima facie* be their value (see post, para 27.30), plus expenses, such as the cost of hiring a replacement;[3] but there may also be a claim for consequential loss, such as a loss of profit (see post, para 27.33). The same *prima facie* rule applies to claims for damages under the Misrepresentation Act 1967; and a similar result is obtained where there is a claim to recover money paid on grounds of total failure of consideration (see post, para 29.12). In *Royscot Trust Ltd v Rogerson*:[4]

> The dealer (D) was arranging a directly financed hp transaction in respect of a Honda Prelude car, through a finance company (RT) to a hirer (H). D arranged with H an hp price of £7,600, a deposit of £1,200 and finance of £6,400. As this would not meet RT's stipulation for a 20% deposit, D misrepresented to RT that the hp price was £8,000 and that H had paid a deposit of £1,600, leaving a balance of £6,400. After paying instalments amounting to some £2,275, H dishonestly passed a Part III title to a bf private purchaser (see ante, para 21.57). RT sued D for damages under s 2(1) of the 1967 Act for inducing RT to purchase the car by misrepresenting the financial arrangements.

The Court of Appeal held that the measure of damages for breach of s 2(1) was that in tort for fraudulent misrepresentation (see ante, para 27.27), which includes unforeseeable loss (see post, para 27.41); that H's sale was not a *novus actus*, such as would relieve D of all liability (see post, para 27.29), because it was foreseeable;[5] and that, as the essence of the transaction was for RT to finance H's instalments rather than purchase and resell to H,[6] RT was therefore entitled to recover £3,652 from D, being the difference between the amount it paid D (£6,400) and that received from H (£2,775).

[27.28]

1   Is the plaintiff entitled to elect whichever cause of action will give him the greater damages? See Street, *Law of Damages*, 252–53.

1a As to whether exemplary damages should sometimes be available as a deterrence for breach of a consumer contract, see Edelman (2001) 117 LQR 539.

2   *Swingcastle Ltd v Alastair Gibson* [1991] 2 AC 223, HL (loan). See Fuller and Perdue (1936) 46 Yale LJ 52, at 71; Burrows (1983) 99 LQR 217, at 253; Holyoak (1983) 99 LQR at 593. See generally Stoljar (1975) 91 LQR 68. As to exemplary damages, see Bell (1991) 20 Anglo-Am 371 at 372–76.

3   *Dimond v Lovell* (set out ante, para 5.13); but as to where impecuniosity precludes his so doing, see post, para 27.41. Support in hiring a replacement is unlikely to amount to champerty (see ante, para 7.26): *Giles v Thompson* [1993] 3 All ER 321, HL.

4   [1991] 2 QB 297; [1991] 3 All ER 294, CA (see Pugh (1993) 5 LN 20).

5   At AER 301d, 303a. Criticised by Hooley (1991) 107 LQR at 551. The fact that R's sale was foreseeable might lessen the force of the decision insofar as it suggests that unforeseeable loss was recoverable as in deceit: Cumberbatch [1992] JBL 311.

6   As to the measure of damages where a misrepresentation induced a purchase, see post, para 29.17.

2   *Damages in contract.* Whereas the object of damages in tort is to put the clock back, the object of damages in contract is to put it forward to the time when the contemplated contract would be fully performed; that is, so far as money can do it, to put the injured plaintiff in the same situation as if the contract had been performed. *Prima facie,* this will be the difference between the contract and market price (see post, para 27.34); but there may also be a claim for consequential loss, such as the business profit which could have been earned through the article bought (see post, para 27.33). This has been termed as giving the injured plaintiff 'the value of performance', or his 'expectancy interest'.[7] Of course, a business plaintiff, whilst expecting to make a profit from a venture, may not wish or be able to quantify that profit. In these circumstances, there is no objection to his simply claiming the wasted expenditure incurred in reliance on the contract;[8] that is, the expenses he would have set off against the gross profit of the venture to arrive at his net profit, what has been termed his 'reliance interest'.[9] However, except doubtfully in the case of pre-contract expenditure,[10] this should not enable the injured plaintiff to claim by way of his reliance interest expenses he would not have been able to recoup anyway, because it cannot then be said that the defendant caused the plaintiff's loss;[11] and this argument has been used to justify a refusal of expenses thrown away in the bad bargain cases.[12]

In pursuing the issue of damages, there will be examined first some special rules (see post, para 27.29), then some of the more important heads of damage (see post, para 27.30 *et seq*), and thereafter the restrictions on the amount recoverable (see post, para 27.39 *et seq*).

[27.29] Some special considerations. To recover more than nominal damages for breach of contract, the plaintiff must show that some loss has been sustained (*Thompson v Robinson* (set out post, para 27.33). Before proceeding to the rules by which the courts quantify damages (see post, para 27.30 *et seq*) within the limitation period (see ante, para 26.17), certain points of general application must be mentioned. First, bear in mind the distinctions between general and special damage (see ante, para 7.03A); and damages and debt (see ante, para 27.15A). Second, the impact of taxation or a foreign currency element

---

7   Waters (1958) 36 Can BR 360, 361. It is P's lost profit that is recoverable, not any extra profit accruing to D: *Surrey CC v Bredero Homes Ltd* [1993] 3 All ER 705, CA (not a goods case).

8   This will include the expenses of care and custody or resale (see ante, para 27.24) and recompense for damage to the goods caused by a bailee's wrongful acts (*Brady v St Margaret's Trust Ltd* [1963] 2 QB 494, CA).

9   Eg, *Mason v Burningham* (see ante, para 12.16); *Bacon v Cooper (Metals) Ltd* [1982] 1 All ER 397 (hp); interest (see ante, para 7.03A); and generally post, para 29.23. This has been seen as a completely separate principle: Treitel (1992) 108 LQR at 229.

10 See *Anglia Television Ltd v Reed* [1972] 1 QB 60, CA (not a sale case); but how can it be said that the defendant caused the plaintiff's pre-contract expenditure? See below; and Ogus (1972) 35 MLR 423; Treitel, *ibid*, p 226.

11 *C & P Haulage v Middleton* [1983] 3 All ER 94, CA (not a sale case). But the onus is on the defendant to show that the expenditure would not have been recouped: *CCC Films (London) Ltd v Impact Quadrant Films Ltd* [1984] 3 All ER 298 (licence and bailment).

12 *L Albert & Son v Armstrong Rubber Co* (1949) 178 F 2d 182 (US).

are beyond the scope of this work. Third, there is the question of putting a monetary value on the time element: there are statutory provisions for the award of interest on debt or damages (s 54 of the SGA; and ante, para 7.03A); and the common law *prima facie* insists on a rebate for accelerated payment.[1] Fourth, difficulty may sometimes be caused by questions of causation: the defendant is only liable for more than nominal damages where he caused a loss;[2] and, in an action in conversion, that is where he was 'the effective, natural and direct cause' of the loss.[3] Conversely, damages should only be diminished where he causes a benefit to accrue to the plaintiff.[4] Further, the test of whether the flow of damage has been interrupted by a *novus actus* is the same for contract and tort[5] and should be distinguished from the mitigation rule (see post, para 27.45). Fifth, where the defendant has the option of performing a contract in alternative ways, it is assumed that he would have performed in the manner most advantageous to himself,[6] but, where the defendant's act is merely one of two or more causes of the plaintiff's harm, the other cause is generally ignored,[7] unless it is subsequent to the defendant's act and involves questions of remoteness (see post, para 27.41), or there is the possibility of a contribution (see ante, para 12.10). Sixth, the impecuniosity of the contract breaker is irrelevant,[8] whilst that of the innocent party is considered in relation to remoteness (see post, paras 27.41–42). Seventh, in a commercial contract, no damages will be awarded for anguish, though the matter may be otherwise in a consumer contract to provide pleasure.[9] Eighth, the agreement may actually spell out some of the heads of damages arising from the breach, eg, reasonable expenses;[10] or it may go further and commute some or all of the damages into a liquidated damages clause, so turning them into a debt (see ante, para 27.24). Ninth, there may be an exclusion clause purporting to limit recoverable damage.[11] Tenth, especially in our field, there must always be borne in mind

---

[27.29]

1   *Interoffice Telephones Ltd v Freeman* [1958] 1 QB 190, CA; *Overstone Ltd v Shipway* [1962] 1 All ER 52, CA. For express provisions and a statutory requirement, see ante, para 26.19.

2   *Lambert v Lewis* (set out ante, para 17.06); *Dobell & Co Ltd v Barber and Garrett* (set out ante, para 18.35); *The Zinnia* [1984] 2 Lloyd's Rep 211 (repair contract); the bad bargain cases (see ante, para 27.28); misrepresentations (see ante, paras 17.10, 17.20); *Ackerman v Protim Services Ltd* [1988] 2 EGLR 259, CA (guarantee); *Royscot Trust Ltd v Rogerson* (set out ante, para 27.28); *Dimond v Lovell* (set out ante, para 5.13; [1999] JBL at 464–66); ante, para 17.24 and post, paras 29.35; 29.37. But see *Gran Gelato Ltd v Richcliff (Group) Ltd* [1992] 1 All ER 865 (criticised 109 LQR 539); *EE Caledonia Ltd v Orbit Value Co* [1993] 4 All ER 165.

3   *Kuwait Airways Corp v Iraqi Airways Co No 3* [2001] 1 All ER (Comm) 557, CA, *per* Brooke LJ at para 522.

4   Eg, sub-sales: *Slater v Hoyle* (set out post, para 29.33); *Hussey v Eels* [1990] 2 QB 227, CA (not a goods case). But see the difficult *British Westinghouse* case [1912] AC 673, HL; discussed by Treitel, *Law of Contract* (10th edn), pp 913–14.

5   *Beoco Ltd v Alfa Laval Co Ltd* [1995] QB 137, CA. Eg, *The Theresa Navigation SA* [2001] 2 All ER (Comm) 243.

6   Eg, *Re Thornett and Fehr and Yuills Ltd* [1921] 1 KB 219; *Paula Lee Ltd v Robert Zehil and Co Ltd* [1983] 2 All ER 390. See also Hudson (1975) 91 LQR 20.

7   *Financings Ltd v Baldock* [1963] 2 QB 104, CA (minimum payments clause in hp agreement: see ante, para 11.09). Compare *Lombard North Central plc v Butterworth* [1987] QB 527, CA (discussed Treitel [1987] LMCLQ 143).

8   *Raineri v Miles* [1981] AC 1050, HL (sale of land). But see McClaren (2001) 151 NLJ 1702 at 1706.

9   *Hayes v Dodd* [1990] 2 All ER 815, CA (lease of land; anguish); *Jarvis v Swan Tours* [1973] 1 QB 233, CA (package holiday); *Farley v Skinner* [2001] 4 All ER 801, HL (house purchase; noise).

10 Large suppliers to consumers tend to take this as authority to levy standard charges: see (1998) 50 Quarterly Account 8–9; (2000) 54 CC 6/32.

11 See eg, *British Sugar plc v NEI* [1997] CLY 1751, CA ('consequential loss'); and generally ante, Chapter 18.

the extent to which express terms may be struck down on the basis that they are unreasonable or unfair.[12]

[27.30] Value in tort. It has already been pointed out that a satisfied judgment in conversion is effectively a compulsory sale (see ante, para 26.17); and, if the defendant destroys the goods, an action in negligence will have a rather similar effect.[1] But it is a 'sale' with a difference: the defendant in that tort action is not required to pay the contract price (see ante, paras 27.16–19), but damages calculated by reference to the value of the goods.[2] *Prima facie*, the value is taken at the date of conversion, even where the value of the goods subsequently declines;[3] but, if the goods have increased in value by the date of trial, the plaintiff may be entitled to that increase.[4] However, where the increase is due to improvements made to the goods, the position is as follows: at common law an innocent improver was entitled to an allowance for his improvements;[5] and this rule has now been extended by s 6 of the Torts Act 1977 to protect a direct or indirect innocent purchaser (s 6(2)) or hirer (s 6(4)) from the improver, and also any intermediate purchaser sued in quasi-contract (s 6(3)). This will cover the situation where the end purchaser (himself made an allowance for prior improvements) sues his supplier in quasi-contract to recover his price as on total failure of consideration (see ante, para 12.06), and requires that a similar allowance be made to his supplier (for total failure of consideration generally, see post, para 29.12). Improvements aside, unless the defendant insists on returning the goods,[6] the plaintiff is entitled to the full value of the goods notwithstanding his own limited interest in them,[7] except where the defendant has a legal interest in them,[8] a rule which has caused difficulty with hp (see post, para 27.31).

For the purposes of the foregoing rules, the value of the goods in a tort action are assessed as follows: if the goods have a market value, that market value at the place of loss should *prima facie* be taken;[1] but, where the goods have no market value, the courts start with the assumption that the plaintiff should recover the replacement cost.[9] The effect of these rules in relation to second hand cars was considered in *Sargent Ltd v Motor Auctions Ltd*:[10]

A rogue stole from a motor dealer (P) a second hand Jaguar and sold it to an auctioneer (D1), who resold it to D2.[11] P had purchased the car only a few weeks before its theft for

---

12 As to unreasonable terms, see UCTA, s 3 (see ante, para 18.24); and as to unfair terms, see ante, para 11.12 *et seq*.

[27.30]

1 *Liesbosch Dredger v Edison Steamship (Owners)* [1933] AC 449, HL. Distinguish *Alcoa Minerals of Jamaica Inc v Broderick* [2000] 3 WLR 23, PC.

2 *Dominion Mosaics and Tile Co Ltd v Trafalgar Trucking Co Ltd* [1990] 2 All ER 246, CA.

3 *BBMB Finance (Hong Kong) Ltd v Eda Holdings Ltd* [1991] 2 All ER 129, PC (shares).

4 *IBL Ltd v Coussens* [1991] 2 All ER 133, CA – is a trade plaintiff entitled to the trade or retail value?

5 *Greenwood v Bennett* [1973] QB 195, CA, discussed in (1973) 36 MLR 89 and (1977) 93 LQR 273.

6 As the defendant may be entitled to do under s 3 of the Torts Act 1977: see ante, para 24.26. But see the *BBMB* case (above); and there may be a duty to account: see ante, para 1.17.

7 *The Winkfield* [1902] P 42, CA. For concurrent actions, see ante, para 27.27.

8 Eg, co-owners, as to which see ante, para 27.26; conditional buyers, as to which see post, para 27.31. Cf *Chinery v Viall* (set out post, para 29.24).

9 Eg, *J and E Hall Ltd v Barclay* [1937] 3 All ER 620, CA; *Harbutt's Plasticine Ltd v Wayne Tank Ltd* [1970] 1 QB 447, CA.

10 [1977] RTR 121, CA. Cf *Naughton v O'Callaghan* [1990] 3 All ER 191.

11 It was held that P was not precluded from denying the rogue's authority to sell: see ante, para 21.14.

£1,975, paying £25 more than the Glass's Guide price because the car had some extras. In his action for conversion, P proved that he had every expectation of being able to sell the car for £2,650.

Applying the same reasoning as is used in actions between seller and buyer for non-acceptance (see post, para 27.36), the Court of Appeal decided that a second hand car was a unique item, so that the market value of similar models (c £1,950) was not an appropriate measure, and P was entitled to what he could have got by selling it (£2,650).

[27.31/32] Valuing instalment contracts. This paragraph is concerned with the valuation of the supplier's interest in goods subject to a conditional sale, hp or simple hiring. In all three cases, the supplier retains the ownership of goods in the hands of another; but not until termination of the hiring (see ante, para 26.09) does the owner have sufficient interest in the goods to maintain an action in conversion (see ante, para 19.06). Where a simple bailment has been determined, the owner/supplier is entitled to recover in conversion[1] the full value of the goods as explained above (para 27.30). On the other hand, under a conditional sale the buyer has a contractual right to call for the property in the goods upon payment of the instalments; and on breach by the conditional buyer, if the supplier chooses to sue in conversion, he must make an allowance for that interest.[2]

Now, hp is a hybrid between bailment and sale (see ante, para 1.20). Whereas the right to sue in conversion arises upon termination of the bailment, there is still the question of the option to purchase (see ante, para 26.09). Where the agreement still subsists, the hirer or assignee sued in conversion is entitled to have deducted from the value of the goods the value of that option.[3] However, where the agreement has been terminated, the supplier should on principle be entitled to the full value of the goods; and he has been held so entitled as against a third party.[4] However, when the value exceeds the amount outstanding, as against the hirer or his assignee the courts have restricted the supplier to the outstanding balance of the hp price. Some cases are explicable on the basis that the agreement has not in fact been terminated for breach. For instance, in *Wickham Holdings Ltd v Brooke House Motors Ltd*:[5]

A Rover car was let to a hirer under a hp agreement which contained a prohibition against assignment. When the hirer tried to trade in the Rover to obtain another model from a dealer, the dealer sought a settlement figure from the owner. The dealer accepted the trade-in, but forgot to pay the settlement figure (£270) to the owner. On learning of the sale by way of trade-in of the Rover to the dealer, the owner terminated the hp agreement and sued the dealer for the return of the Rover or its value (£365).

[27.31/32]

1 *Manders v Williams* (1849) 4 Exch 339.

2 See ante, para 27.30. Cf *Johnson v Stear* (1863) 15 CB (NS) 330 (owner suing pledgor). Compare the supplier's right to sue in contract for the outstanding instalments: see ante, para 27.19.

3 *Whiteley Ltd v Hilt* [1918] 2 KB 808, CA; discussed in Goode, *HP Law and Practice* (2nd edn), pp 586–88.

4 *North Central Wagon Co Ltd v Graham* [1950] 2 KB 7, CA (auctioneer); *Union Transport Finance Ltd v British Car Auctions Ltd* [1978] 2 All ER 385, CA (auctioneer); *Chubb Cash Ltd v John Crilley & Son* [1983] 2 All ER 294, CA (against bailiff levying execution).

5 [1967] 1 All ER 117, [1967] 1 WLR 295, CA. Discussed by Goode, *op cit*, note 3, pp 584–86.

The Court of Appeal restricted the owner to the settlement figure:[6] in rather unsatisfactory judgments, the majority appeared to say that, in quoting a settlement figure, the owner had waived the prohibition on assignment.[7] However, others cases are not so easily reconcilable,[8] and it may be that this hp rule is just *sui generis*.[9]

[27.33] Loss of profit. Whilst loss of profit is commonly thought of as an expectancy interest recoverable in an action for breach of contract, such a claim may arise out of a tort action.

1 *Profit claims in tort*. Where a profit earning chattel is destroyed, a claim for consequential loss of profit is an alternative to claiming the cost of hiring a replacement.[1] The principles at issue here were discussed in *Strand Electric Ltd v Brisford Entertainments Ltd*:[2]

> D wrongfully detained some portable switchgear let to him by P. In an action for detinue,[3] P claimed for loss of profit. In allowing P to recover damages calculated at a rate for hiring from the detention to the date of judgment,[4] the Court of Appeal rejected as immaterial D's plea that he had not used the switchgear.

The Court of Appeal were careful to confine their remarks to (1) a profit earning chattel, which (2) the plaintiff owner normally hired out,[5] and which (3) the defendant detained for his own ends.[6] A claim for loss of profit has similarly been allowed in an action in deceit.[7]

2 *Profit claims in contract*. A claim for loss of profit for breach of s 50(1) of the SGA (set out ante, para 27.27) differs in two respects from that just considered: first, the plaintiff is not suing for a prospective profit that he might have made out of some third party, but the profit he would have made out of his contract with the defendant; and secondly, the plaintiff in contract must show that he has actually lost such a profit if he is to recover more than nominal damages.[8]

---

6 For trade-ins by way of part exchange, see ante, para 2.09. For settlement figures, see ante, para 26.19A.

7 For waiver, see ante, para 26.23. See Diamond (1967) 30 MLR 322; Guest, *Law of HP*, para 700; Goode, *op cit*, note 3, p 583 *et seq*; Oditah (1992) 108 LQR at 484–85.

8 *Belsize Motor Supply Co v Cox* [1914] 1 KB 244, discussed by Goode, *op cit*, note 3, pp 583–84; *Belvoir Finance Co Ltd v Stapleton* [1971] 1 QB 210, CA.

9 See *Street on Torts* (10th edn), p 48; and ante, para 1.25. Cf the recaption rule (see ante, para 24.23) and the loss of profit rule (see post, para 27.37).

[27.33]

1 See Street, *Law of Damages*, pp 206–10.

2 [1952] 2 QB 246; [1952] 1 All ER 796, CA. And see *Penarth Dock Ltd v Pounds* [1963] 1 Lloyd's Rep 359; *Astley Industrial Trust v Miller* [1968] 2 All ER 36; *Hillesden Securities Ltd v Ryjack Ltd* [1983] 2 All ER 184.

3 See now wrongful interference with goods: ante, para 27.25.

4 Denning LJ said *obiter* that, if the hirer had wrongfully disposed of the goods, the owner would have been entitled to loss of profit until the date of disposal, and the value in conversion at that moment (at 255). In the *Hillesden* case (above) the defendant returned the goods to the plaintiff after commencement of proceedings, and the plaintiff was held entitled to the loss of profit for the period it was out of possession.

5 Need this be to the knowledge of the defendant? See post, para 27.42. Cf the position of a third party: see post, para 27.41.

6 Compare *General and Finance Facilities Ltd v Cook Cars Ltd* [1963] 2 All ER 314, CA.

7 *East v Mauer* [1991] 2 All ER 733, CA (not a goods case; criticised 108 LQR 386; 55 MLR at 704–05; 20 Aust B LR 372); *Clef Aquitaine SARL v Laporte Materials Ltd* [2000] 3 All ER 493, CA (franchise case).

8 The same rule is applicable where there is an anticipatory breach: *The Mihalis Angelos* [1970] 3 All ER 125, CA.

The latter point may be neatly illustrated by reference to two cases, in both of which the defendant, a retail buyer of a new motor car at a price fixed by the manufacturer failed to take delivery of it; and the plaintiff, a retail seller, then disposed of the car and subsequently claimed for the loss of profit on the sale to the defendant. In *WL Thompson Ltd v Robinson (Gunmakers) Ltd*[9] it was found as a fact that the supply of that type of car exceeded demand in the area and Upjohn J held that the plaintiffs were entitled to recover the full sum, because they had lost a sale, and hence lost the profit they would otherwise have made.[10] On the other hand, in *Charter v Sullivan*[11] it was shown that there was a shortage of cars of that type and the plaintiff could dispose of all he could obtain; and the Court of Appeal therefore awarded the plaintiff only nominal damages for loss of profit, because he had not lost a (profitable) sale. Of course, in other circumstances the disappointed seller may be under a duty to mitigate his loss.[12] Assuming the plaintiff can show that he has lost a profit, how is that profit to be measured (see post, para 27.34)?

[27.34] Assessing loss of profit in contract. In the case of a sale (for bailments, see post, para 27.37), the unpaid seller will be able to sue in contract for either the price (see ante, paras 27.16–18) or damages for loss of profit. However, it must be remembered that claims for damages differ from claims for the price (see ante, para 27.15A) in that only the former are subject to the restrictions on damages (see post, para 27.39), eg, as to remoteness.

As regards damages claims, the 19th century common law took the view that the value of performance in a contract for the sale of goods was:[1]

> ... in general ... the difference between the contract price and the market price of such goods at the time when the contract is broken, because the purchaser, having the money in his hands, may go into the market and buy. So, if a contract to accept and pay for goods is broken, the same rule may properly be applied; for the seller may take his goods into the market and obtain the current price for them.

Thus, the approach was to be the same whether the seller or buyer was in breach; and this artificial market rule has been adopted by the SGA.[2] However, whilst it may be that in some cases this market rule will normally provide the disappointed seller with an adequate level of compensation (see the *Shearson Lehman* case (below)), in practice the rule may be overridden by the remoteness rule contained in s 50(2).[3] Further, the two sections only lay down a *prima facie* rule to apply where there is an 'available market',[4] and there has been some judicial disagreement as to whether this refers to a market place (a

---

9   [1955] Ch 177; [1955] 1 All ER 154 (see Bridge, *Sale of Goods*, pp 585–87).

10 This may be an over-simplification: see Goode, *Commercial Law* (2nd edn), pp 438–39.

11 [1957] 2 QB 117; [1957] 1 All ER 809, CA.

12 Bridge, *op cit*, note 9, pp 587–89.

[27.34]

1   *Per* Tindal CJ in *Barrow v Arnaud* (1846) 8 QB 604, at 609–10. See generally Bridge, *Sale of Goods*, pp 568–70.

2   In respectively SGA, s 50(3) for sellers and s 51(3) for buyers. See Waters (1958) 36 Can BR 360, 370; Bridge, *ibid*, pp 561–64.

3   *Bem Dis A Turk Ticaret S/A TR v International Agri Trade Co Ltd* [1999] 1 All ER (Comm) 619, CA. The same thing may happen with a buyer's claim for damages: see *Bence Graphics International Ltd v Fasson UK Ltd* (set out post, para 29.26).

4   See generally Waters (1958) 36 Can BR 360; Lawson (1969) 43 ALJ 52, 106; *McGregor on Damages* (16th edn), para 668.

geographical test),[5] or a level of supply and demand (an economic test);[6] but, if there is such a market, the rule also applies where it is deemed to be available. It may be thought that this principle was tested nearly to destruction in *Shearson Lehman Hutton Inc v Maclaine Watson & Co Ltd (No 2)*:[7]

> In 1985 B entered into forward contracts to purchase 7,755 tons of standard grade tin from S for a total price of £70M for delivery on 12 March 1986. Between the dates of contract and delivery the market collapsed. B refused to take delivery and was found liable for non-acceptance under SGA, s 50(1) (see ante, para 27.24).

In an action to assess the damages, Webster J argued as follows:

(1) Section 50(3) is the only statutory guide available to the courts for assessment of damages, which it does by laying down an arbitrary presumption:[8] strictly speaking, it is not an application of the mitigation rule (see post, para 27.44).

(2) The subsection requires an 'available market': if the seller actually offers the goods for sale, there is no available market unless there is at least one actual buyer on that day at a fair price; but, if there is no actual offer for sale, there is an available market where there are 'in the market sufficient traders potentially in touch with each other to evidence a market'.[9]

(3) In this case, it would not have been possible to find a single market buyer for the huge quantity sold. His Lordship accepted that the rule allowed him to contemplate a number of notional buyers; and, because it would be impossible to communicate with enough of them at once, he would assume that negotiations had been proceeding for several days before the breach.[10]

(4) He then turned to the appropriate price under s 50(3) (see post, para 27.35).

[27.35] Where there is an available market.[1] In such cases (see ante, para 27.34), the presumption is that the disappointed seller will go out into that market and resell the goods (s 50(3)); additionally, the supplier should be compensated for any expenses or other special damage under s 54, eg, return carriage, storage (see generally post, para 29.23). Section 50(3) of the SGA provides:

> Where there is an available market for the goods in question the measure of damages is *prima facie* to be ascertained by the difference between the contract price and the market or

---

5   See *per* James LJ in *Dunkirk Colliery Co v Lever* (1878) Ch D 20 at 25, CA. It has even been extended to a black market: *Mouatt v Betts Motors Ltd* [1959] AC 71, PC.

6   See *per* Jenkins LJ in *Charter v Sullivan* [1957] 2 QB 117 at 128, CA.

7   [1990] 3 All ER 723; [1990] 1 Lloyd's Rep 441 (see [1990] LMCLQ 305, esp 310–14).

8   At 726b. See also Goode, *Commercial Law* (2nd edn), pp 415, 416. In this sense the market rule may be seen as primarily lightening the burden of proof on the innocent party.

9   At 730j. This was to be tested on March 12–13 (at 726h).

10 At 732a. This shows how artificial the exercise was: S would not know for certain that the buyer would default until 12 March; and the court would then assume that he had been negotiating resales for several days beforehand.

[27.35]

1   Presumably, the terms of any sales franchise held by the innocent supplier ought to be relevant. But would this cause difficulties with the doctrine of remoteness (see post para 27.41)?

current price at the time or times when the goods ought to have been accepted or, if no time was fixed for acceptance, then at the time of the refusal to accept.

This provision contains two rules: (a) the damages are to be established by the artificial market rule (see ante, para 27.34); and (b) they are to be assessed at the time of breach (the 'breach date' rule), so that, if the seller chooses to speculate by staying out of the market, he does so at his own risk.[2] Further, it is only a *prima facie* measure: it may be increased by any consequential loss (cf post, para 29.33) or reduced by any counterclaim by the buyer.[3] The onus of proving the selling price (where this differs from the buying price) in that market at the time of acceptance[4] is on the seller.[5] The assessment of damages may now be explained by reference to the simplest case, where the buyer is in breach at the time fixed for delivery and the seller resells immediately.[6] In this case, the amount recoverable from the buyer is as follows:

(1) If the **market price** is below the **contract price**, the seller is *prima facie* entitled under s 50(3) to the difference between the two:[7] if he resells below the market price, he is not entitled to that extra loss because he has not mitigated his loss (see post, para 27.44); and if he resells above that market price, he will only recover his actual loss.[8] The position on a notional resale was considered in the *Shearson* case (set out ante, para 27.34), where Webster J held that:

(a) The appropriate price under s 50(3) is the fair market or current price at the moment of breach, not prices before or after that date.[9]

(b) The duty to mitigate would only have been relevant had there been an actual resale (at 731e).

(c) The court has a discretion (perhaps by reason of the words '*prima facie*' in s 50(3)) to select as the appropriate price one that is not the average market price.[10]

(2) If the **market price** is equal to or above the **contract price**, presumably the intention of s 50(3) is that the seller will only be entitled to nominal damages. However, the courts may be willing to oust s 50(3), as in *Trans Trust SPRL v Danubian Trading Ltd*:[11]

There was a chain of contracts for the sale of steel from the manufacturer to A, to the plaintiff, to the defendant, to B. It was known to the defendant that the manufacturer

---

2 The time element in fixing the price is examined later (see post, paras 29.20–21).

3 *Gill & Duffus SA v Berger & Co Inc* (set out ante, para 23.06).

4 'Acceptance' does not here refer to a s 34 acceptance (as to which see ante, para 23.10) but rather to receipt of delivery: see Goode, *Commercial Law* (2nd edn), p 433.

5 *Per* Diplock LJ in *RV Ward Ltd v Bignall* (set out ante, para 27.10) at 547, CA. The resale price, if any, may be evidence of this.

6 If he delays beyond this time, the seller carries the risk of any fluctuation in the market price: *Campbell Mostyn (Provisions) Ltd v Barnett Trading Co* [1954] 1 Lloyd's Rep 65, CA. For anticipatory breach, see Atiyah, *Sale of Goods* (10th edn), p 534 *et seq*.

7 *Gebruder Metelmann GmbH & Co v NBR London* [1984] 1 Lloyd's Rep 614, CA.

8 But compare the position of the innocent buyer: see post, para 29.20.

9 At 728a. But prices obtaining in the market before or after that date were admitted as indirect evidence of what that price was (at 732a–c).

10 At 731g. His Lordship took a price somewhat below the midpoint of that range (at 732d–e). For the factors he took into account, see [1990] LMCLQ at 312–13.

11 [1952] 2 QB 297; [1952] 1 All ER 970, CA.

would only release the steel against payment; but the defendant, in breach of his contract with the plaintiff, failed to procure the opening of a letter of credit.

The Court of Appeal unanimously (a) allowed the plaintiff substantial damages for loss of profit notwithstanding that the market price was higher than the contract price, because the plaintiff could not have taken advantage of that higher price; but (b) refused the plaintiff any damages to compensate him for any claim which might have been made on him by A on the grounds that it was too remote (see post, para 27.42). Similarly, the courts have shown very little enthusiasm for s 50(3) when dealing with fixed-price goods.[12]

[27.36/38] Where there is no available market. There may be no available market for a seller,[1] as where goods are specifically manufactured to order,[2] or supply exceeds demand;[3] and in such cases s 50(3) of the SGA is obviously inapplicable. *Prima facie*, such a seller will be entitled to be put in the same situation he would have been if the contract had been performed (see ante, para 27.28). Thus, he has been held entitled to the profit he would have made, even where he does manage to resell the goods;[2] and the rule has even been used to justify the award to the seller of substantial damages for breach of a promise to pay a deposit.[4] The same principles have been applied to a simple hiring agreement: the supplier's right to rentals having been terminated with the hiring (see ante, para 27.21), he has been awarded damages to compensate him for loss of future rentals.[5]

On the other hand, it is clear that the defaulting buyer or hirer is entitled to adduce evidence to show that the supplier would not have made the second profit as well:[6] and if he does so, the supplier will receive only nominal damages for loss of profit.[7] In *Lazenby Garages Ltd v Wright*:[8]

B agreed on 19 February to buy from S a second hand BMW 2002 for £1,670. The next day, B changed his mind and repudiated the contract. S resold the car in April for £1,770. Nevertheless, S claimed from B £345 loss of profit, this being the difference between the price B had agreed to pay and that for which S had purchased the car in mid-February (£1,325). B replied that S had lost nothing, having resold the car for £100 more than he promised to pay. The Court of Appeal unanimously found for B.

---

12 See *WL Thompson Ltd v Robinson Ltd and Charter v Sullivan* (ante, para 27.33).

[27.36/38]

1 As to available market, see ante, para 27.35; and as to the *prima facie* measure of damages where there is such a market, see ante, para 27.35.

2 Eg, *Re Vic Mills Ltd* [1913] 1 Ch 465, CA.

3 *Per* Upjohn J in *Thompson Ltd v Robinson Ltd* [1955] Ch 177 at 187.

4 See ante, para 23.27. For deposits, see ante, para 27.20. Why was this action not subject to the rule against penalties (as to which see ante, para 27.25)?

5 *Interoffice Telephones Ltd v Freeman Ltd* [1958] 1 QB 190, CA. Subsequently, this formula was reduced to take account of the accelerated payment: *Robophone Facilities Ltd v Blank* [1966] 3 All ER 128, CA (for another point, see ante, para 27.26A).

6 *Hill and Sons v Showell* (1918) 87 LJKB 1106, HL.

7 See *Charter v Sullivan* (set out ante, para 27.33).

8 [1976] 2 All ER 770; [1976] 1 WLR 459, CA (criticised by Bridge, *Sale of Goods*, pp 589–90).

Lord Denning MR pointed out that there could not automatically be applied to second hand cars the rule for new goods;[7] second hand goods may well (as here) be unique, so that there was no available market;[9] and damages would have to be assessed on the basis of the reasonable contemplation of the parties.[10] However, the Court of Appeal thought that it was not within B's reasonable contemplation that S would lose a sale by B's repudiation, so that B would only have to make good S's loss; and there was none.

Common law and statutory restrictions on damages

[27.39/40] Even where the damage caused to the supplier[1] has been quantified in accordance with the principles discussed above (see ante, paras 27.24–38), there remain a number of rules which will restrict the sum recoverable below the amount indicated by those principles.

1   *Public policy.* There may be sums irrecoverable on grounds of public policy, eg, fines (*Payne v Ministry of Food* [1953] CLY 3272, Cty Ct).

2   *The rule against double recovery.* As the primary function of the law of damages is to make good any loss (see ante, para 27.28), it follows that the plaintiff can only recover once in respect of any particular loss, even though that loss may be recoverable by more than one cause of action.[2] For instance, a seller may be entitled to recover the value of goods in conversion from more than one person, but he can only recover it once because satisfaction of a judgment in conversion extinguishes the plaintiff's interest in the goods (see ante, para 26.17); a conditional seller may be able at his option to sue the buyer for the price or recover the goods, but not both (see ante, para 27.19); and in an action for damages for non-acceptance, the seller will have to give an allowance for the price paid, eg, *Ward Ltd v Bignall* (set out ante, para 27.10); actions for loss of profit (see ante, paras 27.33–36).

Similarly, a disappointed buyer cannot recover his loss of profit twice over;[3] nor can he recover the price in contract and value in tort, eg, *Chinery v Viall* (set out post, para 29.24); and a misrepresentee will only be compensated once.[4]

3   *Contributory negligence.*[5] Whilst this was a complete defence at common law, the Law Reform (Contributory Negligence) Act 1945 provides for apportionment of damages

---

9   Cf the argument in tort as to the valuation of the goods: see ante, para 27.30.

10   SGA, s 50(2): see further post, para 27.42.

[27.39/40]

1   As to causation, see ante, para 27.29. In exceptional circumstances, the law may allow one who has not himself suffered loss to recover damages on behalf of another, eg, the owner: *The Winkfield* (tort; see ante, para 27.30). Compare the position in contract: see *The Albazero* [1977] AC 774, HL; and ante, para 22.08.

2   A further action may lead to the recovery of only nominal damages: *The Albazero* (above).

3   Eg, *Burdis v Livsey* [2001] 1 WLR 1751 (accident hire).

4   Even where more than one action may lie for damages under the Misrepresentation Act 1967: see s 2(3); and further ante, para 17.10.

5   See generally Glanville Williams, *Joint Torts and Contributory Negligence*, Part 2; Winfield and Jolowicz, *Tort* (15th edn), pp 233–35; Treitel, *Law of Contract* (10th edn), pp 915–19.

with regard to the 'fault' (s 4) of the plaintiff (P) and defendant (D), except where there is a overriding contractual or statutory provision.[6] D's liability creating 'fault' includes his negligence or breach of statutory duty (see respectively ante, paras 17.13 and 3.21), but does not extend to his wrongful interference with goods nor to fraud.[7] As regards simple breach of contract, only where D's liability for negligence is independently co-extensive and claimed in both contract and tort is the 1945 Act available to apportion damages in an action for breach of contract[8] or under s 2(1) of the 1967 Act.[9] Otherwise, the court must decide whether P or D caused the loss (see ante, para 27.29). As to the statutory contribution rules, see ante, para 12.10.

4 *Reasonableness.* In *Ruxley Electronics Ltd v Forsyth*[10] the House of Lords laid down the overriding principle that the damages must be reasonably proportionate to the loss suffered.[11]

5 *Remoteness of damage* (see post, paras 27.41–43).

6 *Mitigation of damage* (see post, paras 27.44–48).

7 *The CCA* (see post, para 27.49).

8 *Insolvency* (see ante, para 19.18 et seq).

[27.41/42] Remoteness of damage.[1] Whilst the criteria for quantifying damages have thus far been reasonably logical and scientific, the courts have always sought to retain an element of negative discretion, refusing compensation where damage was 'too remote', eg, *ex gratia* payments to customers.[2] In a sense, the courts have been very successful in retaining an unfettered discretion: there remains considerable doubts as to the tests of remoteness in tort and contract, and the extent to which they correspond (see post, para 27.43).

(1) *Remoteness in tort.* Intended consequences cannot be too remote:[3] for this purpose, recklessness amounting to deceit (see ante, para 17.18) is put on a par with intention,[4] and liability under s 2(1) of the Misrepresentation Act 1967 may be treated like deceit.[5] However, where the defendant did not intend the consequences of his act, it

---

6 As to contractual exclusion clauses, see ante, para 18.03. What about a non-contractual disclaimer? As to statutory provisions, see eg, CCA, s 100 (see post, para 27.49); UCTA, s 3 (see ante, para 18.24); CPA, s 6 (see ante, para 17.29).

7 See respectively Torts (Interference with Goods) Act 1977, s 11(1); and ante, para 17.18.

8 The *Albright & Wilson* case (set out ante, para 13.01), at para 13. See also the White Paper on *Banking Services* (1990, Cm 1026), Annexe 7. For a recommendation that the 1945 Act should be a defence to strict contractual duties, see *Contributory Negligence* (1990) Law Com WP No 114, para 5(2)(c) and (e).

9 *Gran Gelato Ltd v Richcliff (Group) Ltd* [1992] 1 All ER 865 (not a goods case: criticised because of the connection with fraud – 109 LQR 539).

10 [1996] AC 344, HL (not a goods case). See further, Treitel, *op cit*, note 5, p 883.

11 See *Southampton Container Terminals Ltd v Hansa Schiffarts GmbH* [2001] 6 CL 472, CA (negligent destruction of crane; reinstatement would be out of all proportion to loss).

[27.41/42]

1 See generally *Street on Torts* (10th edn), p 274 et seq; Treitel, *Law of Contract* (10th edn), pp 898–907.

2 *Anglian Water Services Ltd v Crawshaw Robbins & Co Ltd* (2001) BLR 173 (not a goods case).

3 *Scott v Shepherd* (1773) 2 WMB 1892; *Smith New Court Securities Ltd v Scrimgeour Vickers Ltd* [1997] AC 254, HL (not a goods case).

4 And see *per* Lord Denning MR in *Doyle v Olby Ltd* [1969] 2 All ER 119, CA at 122.

5 *Royscot Trust Ltd v Rogerson* (set out ante, para 27.28), at All ER 299 (see Wardsley 55 MLR at 701–04).

was decided that it was unreasonable to make him liable for more harm than he ought to have **foreseen** it would cause.[6]

(2) *Remoteness in contract.* The basic test of remoteness in contract laid down by *Alderson B* in *Hadley v Baxendale*[7] turned on what the guilty party could have **contemplated**; and as this depended on the state of his knowledge, it led to the formulation of two so called rules.

First rule. The guilty party is assumed to have the knowledge that every person possesses and to contemplate all the damage which would arise according to the ordinary course of things. In the case of sales, this rule has received statutory formulation in s 50(2) of the SGA, which provides:

> The measure of damages is the estimated loss directly and naturally resulting in the ordinary course of events, from the buyer's breach of contract.

Is the statutory rule for sale[8] synonymous with the common law rule applicable in quasi-sale, hp and simple hiring?[9]

Second rule. If the guilty party has knowledge of some special circumstance which would increase the loss naturally arising from the breach, he may[10] be liable for that other loss – what the SGA terms 'special damage' (s 54). Claims for special damage have rarely been successful, whether claimed by the sellers or buyers:[11] where successful, claims for special damage normally increase the recoverable loss.[12]

[27.43] Comparison of remoteness tests. In *The Heron II*,[1] four members of the House of Lords *obiter* strongly took the view that the **foreseeability** test of remoteness in tort was far removed from the **contemplation** test of remoteness in contract (see ante, para 27.41–42). This issue actually came before the court in *Vacwell Engineering Ltd v BDH Chemicals Ltd*,[2] where Rees J held that the damage was not too remote under either rule: as to the contractual claim,[3] he held (at 1696–97) that it was sufficient that some damage by explosion was reasonably contemplated within the rule in *The Heron II* and that the

---

6   *The Wagon Mound* [1961] AC 388, PC; *Saleslease Ltd v Davis* [1999] 1 WLR 1664, CA. It is no answer that the precise mechanics by which the harm is caused, and the extent of the harm, is not foreseeable: *Vacwell Engineering Ltd v BDH Chemicals Ltd* (set out ante, para 18.29).

7   (1854) 9 Ex 341 at 354. For a modern formulation, see *The Heron II* [1969] 1 AC 350, HL (carriage of goods; discussed post, para 27.43).

8   Eg, *Charter v Sullivan* (set out ante, para 27.33); *Lazenby Garages Ltd v Wright* (see ante, para 27.36); *Victoria Laundry Ltd v Newman Industries Ltd* (set out post, para 29.31).

9   Eg, *Liverpool and County Discount Ltd v AB Motors Ltd* [1963] 2 All ER 396, CA.

10 Liability depends on 'some knowledge and acceptance by one party of the purpose and intention of the other in entering the contract': *per* Lord Sumner in *Weld-Blundell v Stephens* [1920] AC 956 at 980, HL.

11 Eg, *Trans Trust SPRL v Danubian Trading Ltd* (seller: set out ante, para 27.35); *Victoria Laundry v Newman Industries Ltd* (buyer: see above).

12 But not necessarily: the *Bence Graphics* case (set out post, para 29.26).

[27.43]

1   [1969] AC 350; [1967] 3 All ER 686, HL.

2   Set out ante, para 18.29. This case was settled during appeal, [1970] 3 All ER 553. See Weaver (1970) 33 MLR 446.

3   Under (a) what is now SGA s 14(3) (see ante, para 14.07 *et seq*) and (b) the course of dealings (see ante, para 15.22).

position was similar with regard to the claim in tort.[4] The matter was again considered *obiter* by the Court of Appeal in *Parsons Ltd v Uttley Ltd*:[5]

> S supplied B with a hopper for storing pig food, but failed to provide for proper ventilation so that the food became mouldy and many of B's pigs died from a rare intestinal disease. In an action mounted solely for breach of s 14 of the SGA, the Court of Appeal unanimously held S liable.

However, their Lordships gave differing reasons. Lord Denning MR based his judgment on the view that the stricter test stated in *The Heron II* applied where a claim was only for purely financial loss; and that where, as here, the claim was for physical damage the test of remoteness was the same in contract and tort, the difference between reasonably **foreseeable** (the test in tort) and reasonably **contemplated** (the test in contract) being 'a semantic exercise' (AER at 532b). However, Orr and Scarman LJJ expressly disagreed with this reasoning, though it is far from clear what that majority thought.[6] They appear to have taken the view that there was no distinction between financial loss and physical damage for the purposes of remoteness; and that S was liable under the test laid down in *The Heron* because he should have contemplated a 'serious possibility' that the pigs might, as a result of the breach, suffer that type of illness, albeit in a less serious form.[7] Subsequent cases have shed little light on the matter.[8]

However, even if the test of remoteness is the same in contract and tort, it is by no means clear that the rules of remoteness will produce the same result in those situations where actions in contract and tort are available concurrently.[9] First, the object of damages is different in the two cases (see ante, para 27.28). Second, there is a difference in the time at which the remoteness test is directed: in contract, the material date is the time of contracting; and in tort, the time of the tort.[10] Third, there may be differences in attitude to concurrent causes.[11] Fourth, there may be differences in the degree of probability of consequences required.[12]

---

4   At 1698. As to the negligence claim, see ante, para 17.14.
5   [1978] QB 791; [1978] 1 All ER 525, CA. See (1978) 94 LQR 171; (1978) 41 MLR 483; Treitel, *Law of Contract* (10th edn), p 906. It was not very clear why this case was not also pleaded in tort: Winfield and Jolowicz, *Tort* (15th edn), p 214, note 22.
6   See ante, para 27.42; and Treitel, *ibid*, pp 900–01.
7   Before the CA, it was accepted that the loss had not been caused by B feeding the food to the pigs.
8   See Bell (1991) 20 Anglo Am LR 371–79. It has been held that the *Hadley v Baxendale* rules (see ante, para 27.42) are not applicable to tortious negligence: *Mortgage Corp plc v Halifax (SW) Ltd (No 2)* [1999] Lloyd's Rep PN 159.
9   See *per* Lord Reid in *The Heron* [1969] 1 AC 350, at 385–86, HL.
10 See Street, *Law of Damages*, p 249.
11 See *McGregor on Damages* (16th edn), paras 153–88; 237–45.
12 See McGregor, *ibid*, Chapter 18; Pickering (1968) 31 MLR 203, 208.

[27.44] Mitigation of damage.[1] Where an injured party makes a claim for damages, it is commonly said that he may be under a common law 'duty' to mitigate that damage,[2] whether the claim be in tort[3] or for breach of contract.[4] Thus, in *Payzu Ltd v Saunders*:[5]

> There was a contract for the sale of goods to be delivered by instalments, payment to be made within one month of each delivery. The buyer failed to make punctual payment for the first instalment. The seller claimed that this amounted to a repudiation, but offered to continue deliveries if the buyer would pay cash upon each delivery. Taking the view that this amounted to a repudiation by the seller, the buyer unsuccessfully sought to buy elsewhere on a rising market.

If there had been a repudiatory breach by the buyer, it seems that the doctrine of mitigation would not have interfered with the seller's right to treat the contract as discharged.[6] However, the Court of Appeal accepted that the buyer's delay in payment did not amount to a repudiation (see ante, para 23.20) and that the seller was therefore liable to pay damages for non-delivery (see post, para 29.18); but the court took the view that the buyer should have mitigated his loss by accepting the seller's offer to deliver for cash and that damages must be limited to the loss the buyer would have suffered if he had accepted that offer (one month's credit).

What the injured party must do to mitigate his loss is a matter of fact, which will vary from case to case: so the above case may be compared with the ordinary situation with regard to non-acceptance or non-delivery, where the innocent party is expected to go into any available market and sell or buy as the case may be (see ante, para 27.34; post, para 29.20). At very least, the duty to mitigate requires the injured party to consider whether he could take any reasonable steps to mitigate his loss; but the standard required of him is a fairly low one[7] and the burden of proof lies on the party in default.[8] Moreover, the injured party need not act so as to injure innocent persons and prejudice his commercial reputation,[9] nor risk his money too far,[10] nor accept a tender of goods of a lower quality

---

[27.44]

1 See generally Treitel, *Law of Contract* (10th edn), pp 910–15; *McGregor on Damages* (16th edn), Chapter 7. Does the duty to mitigate also apply to a claim for an agreed sum? See post, para 27.45.

2 It has been said to be incorrect to express this rule as that the law places him under a duty to mitigate: *The Solholt* (below).

3 *Moore v DER Ltd* [1971] 3 All ER 517, CA (negligence); *Standard Chartered Bank v Pakistan National Shipping Corp* [1999] 1 All ER (Comm) 417 (deceit).

4 The damages rule in s 50(3) of the SGA is not an example of this rule: *Shearson Lehman Hutton Inc v Maclaine Watson & Co Ltd (No 2)* (set out ante, para 27.34).

5 [1919] 2 KB 581; [1918–19] All ER Rep 219, CA (criticised by Bridge (1989) 105 LQR 398, esp at 412–16).

6 See ante, para 26.16. However, in *The Solholt* [1983] 1 Lloyd's Rep 605, the CA confirmed that, once the contract had been discharged, the mitigation rule required the buyer to accept late delivery (see below): but see the criticism by Bridge (1989) 105 LQR 398 at 417–23.

7 Examples of breach of duty to mitigate include: *Payzu Ltd v Saunders* (above); *Nedd v Cox* (1940) 67 Ll LR 5, CA; *The Soholt* (above; discussed 99 LQR 497); *Dimond v Lovell* (set out ante, para 5.13).

8 The burden lies on the party in default to prove that the injured party has not discharged his duty to mitigate: *Garnac Grain Co Inc v Faure & Fairclough Ltd* [1968] AC 110, HL; *Regent OHG Aisenstadt & Barig v Francesco of Jermyn St Ltd* [1981] 3 All ER 327.

9 *James Finlay & Co Ltd v NV Kwik Hoo Tong* [1929] 1 KB 400, CA; *Banco de Portugal v Waterlow & Sons Ltd* [1932] AC 452, HL.

10 *Lester Leather and Skin Co v Home Brokers Ltd* (1948) 64 TLR 569, CA. And see *Jewelowski v Propp* [1944] 1 KB 510.

than contracted for, even with an allowance for the inferiority.[11] What if the injured party is financially unable to take steps in mitigation?[12]

[27.45/48] Effect of mitigation rule. Where the injured party is required to take some steps to mitigate his loss (see ante, para 27.44), the position is as follows: any advantages which he obtains by taking those steps is taken into account in assessing damages;[1] whilst, if he fails to mitigate, any loss occasioned by that failure is irrecoverable.[2] On the other hand, the injured party can recover any extra expenses incurred in an unsuccessful attempt to mitigate if reasonable,[3] but not if unreasonable.[4] Three matters have caused particular difficulty: first, whether to take into account any reduction in the loss to the injured party brought about by his efforts to mitigate succeeding to a greater extent than required by the duty to mitigate;[5] second, the distinction between an act of mitigation and a *novus actus interveniens*;[6] and third, the relationship of the duty to mitigate to the doctrine of anticipatory breach. As to the last issue, if the innocent party accepts the anticipatory repudiation as bringing an end to the contract, then he will in claiming damages be under the ordinary duty to mitigate;[7] but, if he elects to keep the contract alive, it has been held that no question of mitigation arises.[8] This is consistent with the ordinary rule that the duty to mitigate does not interfere with any right of the innocent party after breach to elect whether to rescind or affirm (see ante, para 26.16); but in the case of an anticipatory breach it appears to enable the injured party to continue with the contract and so increase his loss.[9] Finally, an act of mitigation must be carefully distinguished from an accord and satisfaction (see ante, para 26.18).

It must be remembered that the common law mitigation rule may be displaced by a liquidated damages clause (see ante, para 27.24).

[27.49] The CCA and minimum payments clauses. The Act interferes with a number of clauses in instalment credit contracts which seek to entitle the supplier to a sum of money on the happening of some event. Reference has already been made to clauses which accelerate payment or provide for default interest (see ante, para 26.19) and the power to re-open extortionate credit bargains will be examined later (see post, para 29.40). In

---

11 *Heaven & Kesterton Ltd v En Francois* [1956] 2 Lloyd's Rep 316, at 321.
12 Cf *Clippens Oil Co Ltd v Edinburgh and District Water Trustees* [1907] AC 291, HL and *Liesbosch Dredger v Edison Steamship (Owners)* [1933] AC 449, HL; discussed in Street, *Law of Damages*, 41 and McGregor, *op cit*, note 1, para 216.

[27.45/48]

1 *Pagnan & Fratelli v Corbisa Industrial Agropacuaria Limitada* [1971] 1 All ER 165, CA.
2 *Payzu Ltd v Saunders* (set out ante, para 27.44); *Schering Agrochemicals Ltd v Resibel NVSA* [1993] unreported, CA (109 LQR 175); *Standard Chartered Bank v Pakistan National Shipping Corp* [2001] 1 All ER (Comm) 822, CA. But arguably not any loss due solely to inflation: Feldman and Libling (1979) 95 LQR 270.
3 *Lloyd's and Scottish Finance Ltd v Modern Cars Ltd* (set out ante, para 12.14); *Bacon v Cooper (Metals) Ltd* [1982] 1 All ER 397 (hp charges).
4 *The Borag* [1981] 1 All ER 856, CA (see ante, para 27.42).
5 See the *British Westinghouse* case [1912] AC 673, HL: ante, para 27.29.
6 *Mobil North Sea Ltd v PJ Pipe & Valve Co* [2001] 2 All ER (Comm) 289, CA; and see ante, para 27.29.
7 *Gebruder Metelmann GmbH & Co KG v NBR (London)* [1984] 1 Lloyd's Rep 614, CA.
8 See ante, para 26.16. But how can the extra loss then be said to be caused by the guilty party?
9 See further Treitel, *Law of Contract* (10th edn), pp 945–49.

relation to minimum payment clauses, the common law rules[1] have been supplemented by CCA provisions which have tended to concentrate on the event triggering the minimum payment clause, such as the death of the debtor or hirer,[2] his default[3] or exercise of his statutory right of termination (see ante, paras 26.05–07). In the last event, his liability is limited.

1   *Conditional sale and hp.* Where a debtor under a regulated conditional sale or hp agreement exercises his statutory right of termination, his further liability is limited by s 100. Whilst such termination does not affect any already accrued liability for price/rent[4] or damages and the debtor must return the goods to the creditor (s 100(5): set out ante, para 26.05), s 100 limits his further liability to whichever is the **least** of the following sums:

   (a) *A maximum of 50%.* The maximum amount recoverable under s 100(1) is such sum (if any) as will bring the sums paid and payable up to half the 'total price',[5] plus damages if the debtor has in breach of contract not taken reasonable care of the goods (s 100(4). For the position at common law, see ante, para 27.38).

   (b) *Actual loss.* Whilst the formula of 'loss sustained' in s 100(3) reproduces faithfully the HPA wording, it would unfortunately appear to be ambiguous.[6]

   (c) *The specified amount.* The foregoing rule does not apply where the agreement 'provides for a smaller payment, or does not provide for any payment' (s 100(1)). Whilst the Act does not expressly state what shall be payable in the latter event, presumably the amount recoverable is left to the common law and the penalties rule is inapplicable (see ante, para 27.26).

2   *Consumer hiring.* Where a hirer under a consumer hiring exercises his statutory right of termination (s 101(1): see ante, para 26.07), he remains liable to return the goods to the owner and for 'any liability under the agreement which has accrued before the termination';[7] but he is discharged from any liability for future rentals (s 101(2)). However, it has been argued that a minimum payments clause stipulating for further payments would be void;[8] and, in any event if the owner recapts or recovers possession by court order, the court has power under s 132 to grant a defaulting hirer financial relief in respect of both sums paid and payable (see ante, para 27.23).

[27.49]

1   See especially the rules as to causation (ante, para 27.29) and penalties (see ante, para 27.25).

2   Where the position depends on whether or not the agreement is fully secured: see ante, paras 24.47–48.

3   The matter is subject to the default notice procedure (see ante, para 24.30) and the debtor or hirer can ask for a time order (see ante, paras 24.40–41).

4   Section 99(2). Eg, arrears of rentals (as to which, see ante, para 27.21). It has been argued that an acceleration clause could lead to the entire balance being due under this rule: Goode, *Consumer Credit Law and Practice,* para 36.203.

5   As to 'total price' see ante, paras 5.23. Plus any compulsory installation charge: see s 100(2); and Goode, *ibid,* para 36.206.

6   *Booth & Phipps Garages Ltd v Milton* [2000] CLY 2601, Cty Ct. Compare Goode, *op cit,* note 4, para 36.207 and Guest, *Law of HP,* para 609.

7   Section 101(2). Eg, arrears of rentals. But see note 1, above.

8   Under s 173 (see ante, para 18.11): Guest and Lloyd, *Encyclopedia of Consumer Credit Law,* para 2-102; Goode, *op cit,* note 4, para 36.222. *Sed quaere?* What about acceleration clauses (see note 4, above)?

CHAPTER 28

ENFORCEMENT BY PUBLIC AUTHORITIES

INTRODUCTION

Enforcement authorities

[28.01] Historical development. At least from medieval times, it has been found necessary to regulate by criminal law the provision to consumers of bread, beer, fuel and credit.[1] It is therefore hardly surprising that during the 19th century we find major enactments, the direct predecessors of modern legislation, dealing with such matters as the following: weights and measures (see ante, para 4.24); food and drugs (see ante, para 4.26); merchandise marks (see ante, para 4.02); and moneylending (see ante, para 6.09).

The pattern which emerged over the centuries had a number of common characteristics. First, there was the imposition of statutory criminal offences of strict liability:[2] this process has continued apace during the last century (see ante, Chapters 4 and 5). Secondly, enforcement of these criminal offences has for the most part been left to local authorities,[3] who have usually been granted a number of ancillary powers (see post, para 28.05). Thirdly, the harshness of these locally enforced strict liability offences has been moderated by an elaborate series of increasingly common form defences (see post, para 28.13 *et seq*). It is for consideration whether this whole pattern is now sufficiently uniform to merit consolidation in a single enactment. Fourthly, the piecemeal nature of the foregoing developments inevitably led to a haphazard machinery of enforcement;[4] but, following some official recommendations,[5] this has in more recent times been substantially rationalised (see post, para 28.02). Fifthly, in place of criminal proceedings,[6] it may now be possible for the Authorities to obtain Stop Now Orders (see post, para 28.03).

[28.02] Modern enforcement. The modern pattern for the enforcement of statutory crimes of strict liability designed as measures of consumer protection has established two tiers.

(1) *Central supervision*. Central co-ordination of the administration of these provisions is undertaken by the Office of Fair Trading (OFT) under the political supervision of Whitehall (see ante, paras 3.02–03). Besides its licensing register (see ante, para 6.26), the OFT also keeps a register of convictions.[1]

[28.01]

1   See Harvey, *Consumer Protection and Fair Trading* (5th edn), pp 1–6.

2   As to strict liability, see post, para 28.08.

3   *R v Croydon Justices ex p Holmberg* (1993) 12 Tr LR 10, DC. See post, para 28.02. It does not follow that there should necessarily be a prosecution in respect of every breach: *Smedley Ltd v Breed* [1974] AC 839, HL, *per* Viscount Dilhorne.

4   For a modern exception designating no prosecuting authority, see the Mock Auctions Act 1961 (see ante, para 10.11).

5   1962, Cmnd 1781, paras 682–845, 719; the Review of the TDA (1976, Cmnd 6628), Ch X.

6   See Tench, *Towards a Middle System of Law* (1981).

[28.02]

1   For an account of this **private** register, see (1996) 15 Tr LR 257.

(2) *Local authority (LA) enforcement.* There is no single provision imposing on local authorities a general duty of enforcement, but there are two major strands of responsibility. In some areas of law the powers are divided between district authorities and the county councils, whilst in other areas they are all vested in district councils.

(a) *Food and drugs authorities.* The Food Safety Act 1990 designates certain bodies 'food authorities', which is in effect the LAs (s 5). These are under a duty to appoint a public analyst (s 27) and are made responsible for enforcing many of the provisions of the 1990 Act.[2] Similar arrangements are made in relation to medicines (s 108, Medicines Act 1968). The powers tend to be delegated to environmental health departments. Some idea of the types of consumer complaint fielded by LA Environmental Health Departments may be gathered from the Annual Reports of the OFT.

(b) *Weights and measures authorities.* The Weights and Measures Act 1985 designated certain bodies as 'local weights and measures authorities',[3] an expression it defined as local authorities (ss 52, 69). Additionally, local weights and measures authorities have been charged with the responsibility of enforcing certain other consumer protection statutes within their area,[4] such as s 26(1) of the TDA, s 27 of the CPA s 27, s 161(1) of the CCA and the UTCC Regulations (as 'qualifying bodies': see ante, para 11.19). Some of this work is contracted out, such as advising consumers as to the position under the TDA, CPA and CCA may be contracted out to CABx (see ante, para 3.08). However, the result was to so alter the burden of their work[5] that there was a tendency to rename them 'Consumer Protection' or 'Trading Standards' Departments, with their designated officers termed 'trading standards officers' (TSOs). Their professional association is the Institute of Trading Standards Administration (ITSA).

Whilst the foregoing designated local authorities have cast upon them a duty of enforcement, it is not an exclusive duty. Other LAs still have a **power** of prosecution where they consider this is in 'the interests of the inhabitants of their area' (s 222, Local Government Act 1972); and in some cases the OFT or other body is given a concurrent **power** of prosecution so that it may act where it is felt that an incident has national implications (eg, s 161(1)(a), CCA). Nor is there usually any legal impediment to a private prosecution.[6] However, it is to be expected that prosecution by anybody other than the

---

2   Section 6. For discussion of the work of these food authorities, which detects a greater emphasis on in-factory enforcement, see Bradgate and Howells [1991] JBL 320, esp at 321, 323 and 331.

3   See further Harvey and Parry, *Consumer Protection and Fair Trading* (6th edn), p 445.

4   Eg, Prices Act 1974, Sched, paras 6 and 8; FTA 1973, s 27(1) (in relation to statutory orders made under s 22 – see ante, para 4.22); Video Recordings Act 1984 (as amended by s 162 of the Criminal Justice Act 1988); Doorstep Selling Regulations, reg 4D – see ante, para 10.22); Estate Agents Act 1979, s 26 and Property Misdescriptions Act 1991, s 3 (see ante, para 4.03); Distance Selling Regulations, reg 26 (see ante, para 8.17).

5   Some idea of the modern balance of their work may be gained by looking in the Annual Reports of the OFT at the Appendix dealing with the classification of consumer complaints and details of convictions.

6   Eg, the Pharmaceutical Society who have statutory recognition, or some wholly private trade or other body. But sometimes the statute allows no room for private prosecution, eg, Weights and Measures Act 1985, s 83(1). Cf CPA, s 11(3)(c).

designated LAs will be unusual.[7] The duty of the prosecuting LA to report intended prosecutions to the OFT[8] should encourage uniformity in administration throughout the country, as should the statutory duty cast on the designated local authorities to report their activities to the OFT (see s 26(2), TDA; s 161(3), CCA). It should also ensure a more uniform observance of the law: the OFT might remove any CCA licence (see ante, para 6.23) or seek an order against the conviction under Part III of the FTA (see ante, para 6.08). A system has been set up to co-ordinate action between local authorities (LACOTS),[9] and there have been introduced uniform enforcement codes (see ante, para 5.10). There is concern that the current government initiative may replace the County Councils (currently the local authority normally designated under the above legislation) with new single tier authorities too small to provide a viable service,[10] but there are proposals for a high level Enforcement Forum.[11]

[28.03] **Stop Now Orders**. There will be many occasions where the ordinary remedies of rescission and damages for breach of contract are insufficient protection for a consumer, the obvious example being where the loss is too small to make individual court action a suitable remedy. In such cases, it has always been possible for the injured consumer to take out an injunction under the ordinary rules (see post, para 29.39). But again, the cost of individual court action make the remedy unattractive. Much more attractive to consumers is the continental system that such actions for injunctions may be brought by a public official on behalf of the consumer. Such a system had already been introduced into the UK in relation one piece of UK law, Part III of the Fair Trading Act 1973 (FTA) (see ante, para 6.08); and more recently this has been the case under some EU-inspired law, such as the Unfair Terms Regulations (see ante, para 11.20). However, under the Injunctions Directive,[1] consumer bodies have been given much wider powers to seek injunctions to stop traders infringing the interests of consumers under ten existing consumer protection Directives (see below). This Directive has been enacted in the UK by the Stop Now Orders (EC Directive) Regulations 2001 (SI No 1422), which collectively describes the ten other directives as 'Community infringements' (reg 2(1); Sched 1). The Regulations introduce a uniform injunction system for all the following pieces of law (reg 2(3)), a category perhaps extending beyond 'Community infringements': misleading advertising;[2] doorstep selling (see ante, para 10.21), eg, incorrectly dating order forms to reduce the cooling off period, or refusing to return the customer's furniture on cancellation; consumer credit (see ante, para 5.12), eg, infringements of credit licences (see

---

7   Remembering the cost of prosecution and the advantages to the consumer of a conviction being secured as a prelude to compensation: see ante, paras 3.20–21.

8   See post, para 28.06. Further, the convicting court is sometimes under a duty to notify conviction to the OFT: FTA, s 131; CCA, s 166.

9   Local Government Co-ordinating Body on Trading Standards. See generally Harvey and Parry, *op cit*, note 3, p 54, noting their explanation of the 'home authority' principle. The ambit of LACOTS is now being extended to food safety: see Roberts (1991) 8 Tr LR 212 at 214–15.

10 This view is taken by ITSA (see Borrie (1993) 14 CCA News 4/7; Street (1994) 15 CCA News 1/19).

11 DTI, *Modern Markets: Confident Consumers* (1999), para 7.24.

[28.03]

1   Directive 98/27/EC; set out in Goode, *Consumer Credit Law and Practice*, Part VI, para 1.401. See DTI, *Modern Markets: Confident Consumers* (1999), para 7.10.

2   See ante, para 8.12A. 'Except regulation specifically in relation to food, tobacco and tobacco products' (reg 2(3)(a)).

ante, para 6.23), inaccurate APRs (see ante, para 8.27), refusal to accept s 75 liability (see ante, para 16.11); television broadcasting (see ante, para 3.14); package holidays;[3] advertising of medicinal products (see ante, para 8.12); unfair terms in consumer contracts (see above); timeshare;[4] distance selling (see ante, para 8.17), eg, misdescribing goods, or making it difficult to cancel or obtain refunds; and (reg 2(3)(j)):

> ... regulations of the sale and supply to consumers[5] and the following services, and of guarantees in relation to such services –
>
> (i) services provided under a contract for the supply of goods to be manufactured or produced;[6] and
>
> (ii) installation of goods, where installation forms part of a contract for the sale or supply of goods, and where the goods are installed by the seller or supplier or under his responsibility.[7]

This should also encompass other UK consumer statutory protections, some home grown, both civil law, such as the statutory implied terms (see ante, para 11.11) and product liability (see ante, para 17.21 *et seq*); and also criminal law, such as the TDA (see ante, para 4.02 *et seq*) and safety offences (see ante, paras 4.33–37).

Instead of setting out an entirely new statutory framework, the Stop Now Order Regulations make use of the framework of Part III of the FTA (reg 3; Sched 2) in relation to 'Community infringements' (see ante, para 6.08). However, whereas the powers under Part III can only be exercised by the Director of the OFT, the Regulations extend those powers to any 'public UK qualified entity',[8] 'other UK qualified entities'[9] and 'Community qualified entities'.[10] The Director and 'public UK qualified' entities may also bring proceedings under these Regulations in other Member States or in the UK on behalf of any 'Community qualified entity' (reg 5), eg, as regards misleading websites (see ante, para 8.17). There is the usual duty on the Director to publicise the Regulations (reg 6: see ante, para 3.03) and on the other qualified entities taking action under these Regulations to notify the Director, who is given a co-ordinating function (reg 7). However, it is to be noted that the Regulations do not allow ad hoc consumer groups, eg, a class action (see ante, para 3.18) to obtain Stop Now Orders on behalf of individual consumers.

It may be that some regulators will see these new powers to seek a Stop Now Order an effective route for side-stepping the carefully constructed Parliamentary restrictions on

---

3   Directive 92/314. This is concerned with package holidays and is beyond the scope of this work.

4   Directive 94/47. This is concerned with timeshare and is beyond the scope of this work.

5   See ante, para 14.01.

6   See ante, para 15.15.

7   See ante, para 2.05.

8   'An independent public body specifically responsible for protecting the collective interests of consumers included in the Directives and listed in Schedule 3 to these Regulations' (reg 2(1)). These bodies include the following (Sched 3): the Information Commissioner (see ante, para 3.27); the Gas and Electricity Markets Authority and Director General of Water Services (see ante, para 3.07); and every Weights and Measures Authority (see ante, para 28.02).

9   By reg 2(1), this means 'an organisation designated by the Secretary of State in accordance with regulation 4'. These are applicant private organisations which meet the criteria set out in reg 4(2). Eg, the Consumers Association (see ante, para 3.08), which has applied for recognition.

10 By reg 2(1), these are entities from other EU Member States approved by the EU.

enforcement:[11] as a civil action, proceedings for such an Order will avoid the need to prove breach of consumer legislation to the criminal standard of proof, the carefully constructed tariff of penalties (see post, para 28.07) and the rules of interpretation of criminal statutes (see ante, para 1.05). Furthermore, it is intended that the scope of Stop Now Orders will be extended in due course by an Enterprise Bill, perhaps during the 2001–02 Parliamentary Session (see ante, para 5.11).

[28.04] Criminal offences. Presumably for policy reasons (see ante, para 28.01), many consumer protection statutes are not content to grant a civil right of action for breach[1] but also make it a criminal offence[2] of strict liability (see post, para 28.08). Penalties usually depend on the method of prosecution: so, for conviction on indictment under the TDA, the penalty is up to two years imprisonment and/or an unlimited fine; whereas, on summary prosecution under the TDA, the penalty is a fine up to 'the prescribed sum'.[3] Typically, prison tends to be reserved for situations where there is *mens rea* or repeated infringement.

However, these offences tend not to be absolute (see post, para 28.08), but to be subject to some wide ranging defences (see post, para 28.13 *et seq*) and, of course, the higher criminal burden of proof on the prosecution. Moreover, in practice the present system does not necessarily result in prosecution, except as a last resort;[4] but, on repeated conviction, the authorities sometimes seek an injunction, which may result in further criminal sanctions on default.

Injunctions.[5] The prosecuting authority may be faced with a defendant who finds it worthwhile to breach repeatedly a criminal provision involving a relatively mild sanction, eg, small financial penalty. In this case, the authority may consider seeking an injunction,[6] a course of action that has been much used by local authorities with regard to Sunday trading. In *Stoke on Trent City Council v B & Q (Retail) Ltd*[7] the House of Lords confirmed that this was a proper cause of action on the part of the local authority, that prior actual convictions were not required, but that the authority must show that the defendant was deliberately and flagrantly flouting the law.[8] Subsequently, the Sunday trading lobby sought to avoid this decision by two arguments. First, they unsuccessfully argued that the Sunday trading laws were invalidated by the Treaty of Rome (see ante, para 2.13). Secondly, they unsuccessfully argued that, in the (usual) application for an interim

---

11   McCalla (2001) 151 NLJ 751 at 752.

[28.04]

1   On principle, an action for breach of statutory duty may be available to a person injured thereby, but consumer protection statutes commonly expressly exclude this: see ante, para 3.21.

2   Eg, Prices Act 1974, Sched, para 5(1); TDA, s 18 (as amended by s 32(2) of the Magistrates Court Act 1980; DPA, s 19); FTA, ss 23, 122; CCA, s 167; CPA, ss 12(5), 20(4). See further post, para 28.07. Note the anomalous rule in TSA, s 9.

3   This is level 5 on the standard scale (Criminal Justice Act 1982, s 37). For a discussion of sentencing policy, see Bragg, *Trade Descriptions*, pp 218–20.

4   See Bragg, *ibid*, pp 201–02.

5   See generally Harper (1989) 139 NLJ 1016. For injunctions sought by a buyer or hirer, see post, para 29.39.

6   Eg, *Portsmouth City Council v Richards* (1989) 87 LGR 757, CA (against a sex shop). For a statutory power of the Director of Fair Trading to seek an injunction, see ante, para 8.12A.

7   [1984] AC 754; [1984] 2 All ER 332, HL.

8   Acting under s 222 of the Local Government Act 1972: see ante, para 28.03.

injunction, the local authorities was automatically required to give a cross-undertaking as to damages.[9]

Powers of enforcing authorities

Where consumer protection statutes (see ante, Chapters 4 and 5) are enforced by a designated local authority (see ante, para 28.03), there are a number of almost common form powers (see post, para 28.05) and duties (see post, para 28.06). In laying these down, the parliamentary draftsman has tended to reflect the general common law presumption in favour of the liberty of the subject, with any derogation being set out in detail.

[28.05] **Powers**. Over and above the powers of any prosecutor, the designated authorities tend to be granted by statute the following powers.[1]

1   *Test purchases*.[2] For the purposes of obtaining evidence of the commission of an offence, the authorised officer of a designated authority is empowered to purchase goods or obtain the provision of services at all reasonable hours (business hours?) and on production of his credentials. There is no requirement of reasonable cause, so that 'spot checks' may be made. In the case of the CCA, the Act also expressly deals with one particularly relevant exercise of the power, allowing the officer to enter as debtor or hirer into a regulated agreement (s 164(2)); and some other Acts allow the taking of samples.[3]

2   *Inspection and entry*.[4] For the purposes of ascertaining whether any offence has been committed under the relevant Act, the duly authorised officer is empowered (see above) to inspect any goods and enter any premises other than those used only as a dwelling house: if the premises are being used both as a dwelling and as business premises, the power exists; and failure to allow entry is an obstruction (see post, para 28.06. *Contra* a self-contained flat over a shop). Where entry is refused,[5] or it is desired to enter a dwelling house, a warrant must first be obtained.[6]

---

9   *Kirklees MBC v Wickes Building Supplies* [1993] AC 227, HL (undertaking not required: see 109 LQR 27).

[28.05]

1   Similar powers are granted under the Estate Agents Act 1979, s 11; Data Protection Act 1998, Sched 9; Property Misdescriptions Act 1991, Sched. For discussion of the codes of practice under the Food Safety Act 1990, s 40, see Roberts (1991) 8 Tr LR 212.

2   Prices Act 1974, Sched, para 7; TDA, s 27; FTA, s 28; CCA, s 164(1), (3); Weights and Measures Act 1985, s 42; CPA, s 28(1); Food Safety Act 1990, s 29(a). Can a trader refuse to sell? As to entrapment, see Roberts (1992) 9 Tr LR 158.

3   Eg, Prices Act 1974, Sched, para 9(2); Medicines Act 1968, s 112(2); Food Safety Act 1990, ss 29–31.

4   TDA, s 28(1)(a); Prices Act 1974, Sched, para 9(1); Medicines Act 1968, s 111(1); FTA, s 29(1)(a); CCA, s 162(1)(a); Video Recording Act 1984, s 17; Weights and Measures Act 1985, s 79(1); CPA ss 29(2), (3). See generally Feldman, *Law Relating to Entry Search and Seizure*.

5   Eg, *John v Matthews* [1970] 2 QB 443, DC; *Brunner v Williams* (1975) 73 LGR 266, DC.

6   TDA, s 28(3); Prices Act 1974, Sched, para 9(1); FTA, s 29(3); CCA, s 162(3); Weights and Measures Act 1985, s 79(2); CPA, s 29(2); Food Safety Act 1990, s 32. There are strict conditions on the issue of a warrant which *inter alia* do not allow its use for conducting spot checks unless perhaps entry has been refused. If in doubt as to whether a business is being carried on, it may be wiser to apply for a warrant.

3   *Production and copy of documents.*[7] Where he has a reasonable cause to suspect that an offence has been committed, the authorised officer may require the production of books and documents[8] by any person carrying on a trade or business[9] and take copies thereof, though there are special protections for documents in the hands of legal advisers, eg, s 28(7), TDA; s 162(7), CCA.

4   *Seizure and detention of material.* Where he has reasonable cause to **believe** that an offence has been committed under the relevant Act, the authorised officer may seize and detain **goods** to ascertain by test or otherwise whether an offence has been committed;[10] he may detain goods and documents which he has reasonable cause to **believe** may be required as evidence;[11] and he has power to break open containers to obtain that test or evidential material.[12] This last power does not extend to breaking open containers to inspect goods; and in any case, it is subject to the condition precedent that any person authorised to do so must first be invited to break open the container. Finally, there is provision for compensation in respect of goods seized (see post, para 28.06).

[28.06] Duties. In the exercise of the foregoing statutory powers by designated authorities for the purpose of enforcing these Acts (see ante, para 28.05), both sides are subject to a number of statutory duties.

1   *The general public.* There are a number of offences of obstructing the designated authorities in the exercise of their enforcement powers, such as wilfully obstructing, or failure without reasonable cause to supply information, or giving false information.[1] A convicted person may have to pay the expenses of enforcement (see s 35 of the CPA). What more than the general power of convicting courts as to costs, does this confer?

2   *The designated authorities.* An officer[2] seizing any goods or documents must give the person from whom they were seized notice of seizure (eg, s 28(2) of the TDA; s 29(2)

---

7   Prices Act 1974, Sched, para 9(1); TDA, s 28(1)(b); FTA, s 28(1)(b); CCA, s 162(1)(b); the Doorstep Selling Regulations 1987, reg 4E. Cf Medicines Act 1968, s 112(3)(b); CPA, s 29(4), (5). The power to take a copy does not authorise the taking away of the original: *Barge v British Gas Corp* (1983) 81 LGR 53, DC.

8   The CCA and CPA extend to computer held information. The drafting of CPA, s 29(4) is criticised in 50 MLR 626–28. See also the Bankers' Books Evidence Act 1879, s 7. There is sometimes protection against self-incrimination, eg, Doorstep Selling Regulations 1987, reg 4H; and *Walkers Snack Foods Ltd v Coventry CC* [1998] 3 All ER 163, DC (Food Safety Act 1990, s 33).

9   This need not be the suspected trade or business, eg, accountant. As to 'trade or business', see ante, para 4.03. But the officer must have grounds to suspect that an offence has been committed: *Dudley MBC v Debenhams plc* (1995) 14 Tr LR 182, DC.

10 Prices Act 1974, Sched, paras 9(2), 10; TDA, s 28(1)(c); FTA, s 29(1)(c); CCA s 162(1)(c); CPA, ss 29(6), 33. Cf Medicines Act 1968, s 112(4).

11 Prices Act 1974, Sched, para 9(2). Books are expressly mentioned only in some of the Acts: TDA, s 28(1)(d); FTA, s 29(1)(d); CCA, s 162(1)(d). Cf Medicines Act 1968, s 112(4); CPA, s 29(4). As to 'suspect' and 'believe', see Bragg, *Trade Descriptions*, p 207.

12 But some Acts expressly give permission only to open vending machines: TDA, s 28(1)(e); FTA, s 29(1)(e); CCA, s 162(1)(e); CPA, s 29(7).

[28.06]

1   TDA, s 29; FTA, s 30; CCA, s 165; Prices Act 1974, Sched, para 9(3); Medicines Act 1968, ss 114(2), (3); Weights and Measures Act 1985, s 81; CPA, s 32; Food Safety Act 1990, s 33; Doorstep Selling Regulations 1987, reg 4F. See Bragg, *Trade Descriptions*, pp 210–12.

2   Any person impersonating an officer commits an offence: TDA, s 28(6); FTA s 30(4); CCA, s 162(6); CPA, s 30(5).

of the FTA; s 162(2) of the CCA; s 30(1) of the CPA) and of the results of any test.[3] He must also give notice of intended prosecution to the OFT (eg, s 130 of the FTA (as amended); s 161(2) of the CCA; s 125(4) of the Medicines Act 1968), and sometimes also to the defendant.[4] On conviction, the authority is sometimes entitled to recover the special expenses arising from any seizure (eg, s 35 of the CPA). However, if the 'owner' of goods seized is not convicted, the goods must be returned and he must be compensated for any loss or damage to the goods during their detention,[5] a provision which may deter seizure in case of doubt.[6] Unauthorised disclosure of information acquired under these powers is an offence,[7] though authorisation now extends to civil proceedings[8] and is subject to any enforcement codes (see ante, para 5.10). Unfortunately, this (fairly standard) prohibition on disclosure may inhibit both naming-and-shaming and any feedback to consumer organisations trying to assess the efficacy of OFT activities.

OFFENCES[1]

[28.07] **Introduction.** The persons permitted to prosecute in respect of an offence against one of the consumer protection statutes have already been mentioned.[1a] There are also provisions to deal with activities which amount to an offence under more than one of the Acts, eg, s 22, TDA (as amended). Time limits for prosecution tend to some extent to depend on the manner of prosecution.

(a) *Summary prosecution.* The ordinary time limit for summary offences is six months.[2] However, where offences are triable either summarily or on indictment, the 1980 statute abolishes the special time limits, leaving all such prosecutions subject to the indictable time limits below.[3]

(b) *Indictments.*[4] Consumer protection statutes commonly require prosecution on indictment to be commenced before the expiry of the lesser of three years from the

---

3   TDA, s 30(1); FTA, s 31; CCA, s 164(4); CPA, s 30(6). As to the failure to give test results, see Bragg, *op cit*, note 1, pp 202–03.

4   Eg, where there is an offence under the Weights and Measures Act 1985 (s 83(3)) or also under the TDA (s 22(1), as amended).

5   TDA, s 33; FTA, s 32; CCA, s 163; Food Act 1984, ss 9(4), 28(5), CPA, ss 14(7), 34; Food Safety Act 1990, s 9(7). Cf *Hobbs v Winchester Corp* [1910] 2 KB 471, CA. The compensation powers do not extend to loss caused by breaking open containers. Do they extend to the seizure of documents? See generally Cardwell (1988) 6 Tr L 212.

6   See Cardwell (1987) 50 MLR 634–7; Bragg, *op cit*, note 1, pp 208–09.

7   TDA, ss 28(5), (5A, as amended); FTA, s 30(3); CCA, s 174 (as amended); Prices Act 1974, Sched, para 12; CPA, s 38; Estate Agents Act 1979, s 10(6); Medicines Act 1968, s 118; Doorstep Selling Regulations 1987, reg 4G.

8   Eg, under the SGA; but probably not until the writ has been issued. See Bragg, *op cit*, note 1, p 217.

[28.07]

1   See generally Cartwright, *Consumer Protection and the Criminal Law* (2000).

1a   See ante, para 28.02. For sentencing under the TDA, see Roberts (1991) 8 Tr LR 36, 9 Tr LR 205; *R v Hewitt* [1991] CLY 1122, CA; *R v Dobson Ltd* (1994) *The Times*, 8 March, CA.

2   Magistrates' Courts Act 1980, s 127(1). Nor can the time limit for summary trial exceed that for trial on indictment: s 127(4). For the purposes of the time limit, it has been held that the latest moment at which goods are 'supplied' is on delivery (cf ante, para 23.03): *Rees v Munday* [1974] 3 All ER 506, DC (TDA).

3   Section 127. See Bragg, *Trade Descriptions*, p 214.

4   Eg, *R v Nash* [1990] RTR 343, CA.

commission of the offence, or one year of its discovery by the prosecutor.[5] However, with regard to some consumer protection statutes the courts have side-stepped such limitations by holding that offences are continuing ones.[6]

At the trial of offences under consumer protection statutes, there are sometimes special rules as to the onus of proof[7] and evidence of sample analysis[8] or by certificate (s 31, TDA). A long chain of distribution (see ante, para 17.01) may cause problems,[9] as may an insistence that the interpretation of words used are matters of fact rather than law.[10] The tribunal may also take into account compliance by the prosecuting authority with any enforcement code (see ante, para 5.10).

There must now be considered the liability for these offences created by consumer protection statutes (see post, para 28.08 *et seq*) and the statutory defences available (see post, para 28.13 *et seq*).

Liability

[28.08] Strict liability. Whilst the presumption of the common law is that *mens rea* (a guilty mind) is normally required for the commission of a criminal offence, it is often said that consumer protection statutes tend to contain 'absolute prohibitions'.[1] However, this last expression is a misnomer in two senses: first, it is usually with regard only to a key element rather than all constituents of the offence that no *mens rea* is required;[2] and secondly, there is commonly a statutory defence where a person charged proves lack of negligence (see post, para 28.13 *et seq*). On these grounds, the expression 'strict liability' has been preferred.[3]

Whilst the imposition of strict liability has become common in this context,[4] this is only partly attributable to the statutory language, as it often arises from judicial interpretation, claiming to be based on the implied intention of Parliament.[5] For example, it has been said of the TDA that 'trading standards, not criminal behaviour, are its

---

5 TDA, s 19(1); FTA, s 129(1); FSA, ss 34–35. See *R v Beaconsfield Justices ex p Johnston & Sons* (1985) 4 Tr LR 212, DC (TDA).

6 See Clayson (1995) 14 Tr LR 6.

7 Eg, CCA, ss 171, 172, discussed by Goode, *Consumer Credit Law and Practice*, paras 52.1–2. See further Glanville Williams, *Criminal Law: The General Part* (2nd edn), para 292 *et seq*.

8 TDA, s 22(3). For sample analysis, see ante, para 28.05.

9 An earlier party in the chain of distribution, brought in because his act or default **caused** the offence by another (see post, para 28.12), is also entitled to the benefit of the time limit: *R v Bicester Justices ex p Unigate Ltd* [1975] 1 All ER 449, DC.

10 So preventing the appellate courts from curing inconsistencies between the sentences of magistrates courts: Bragg, *op cit*, note 3, 148.

[28.08]

1 Eg, *R v Bradish* [1990] 1 QB 981, CA. As to the rationale for imposing strict criminal liability under consumer protection statutes, see *Hobbs v Winchester Corp* [1910] 2 KB 471 at 483, *per* Kennedy LJ. Contrast the continuing judicial reluctance to do so as exemplified in *Tesco Supermarkets Ltd v Nattrass* [1972] AC 153 at 194, *per* Lord Diplock.

2 Thus, on a charge of selling unfit meat, innocence of unfitness is irrelevant, whilst knowledge of sale is probably still required: Smith and Hogan, *Criminal Law* (5th edn), p 87; and see generally (9th edn), pp 97–98.

3 Smith and Hogan, *Criminal Law* (9th edn), pp 102, 112.

4 Eg, *Sherras v De Rutzen* [1895] 1 QB 918 (liquor); *R v St Margaret's Trust Ltd* [1958] 2 All ER 289, CA (credit terms); *Sweet v Parsley* [1970] AC 132, HL (drugs).

5 Smith and Hogan, *op cit*, note 3, pp 101–02.

concern'.[6] However, it has been questioned whether this requires the imposition of strict criminal liability,[7] or even criminal liability at all (see ante, para 28.01). Yet Parliament has even gone beyond the imposition of strict liability on the principal actor,[8] be he an employee or agent:[9] that liability has been extended to third parties, such as the actor's employer or principal (see post, para 28.09), or corporations (see post, para 28.10) and other persons (see post, para 28.11), or sometimes 'bypassed' the actor to that third party (see post, para 28.12).

[28.09] Vicarious criminal liability.[1] Whilst in the law of tort a master may be vicariously liable for the acts of his servants or agents, this doctrine usually has no place in the criminal law (see post, para 28.10). However, if such an attitude were applied to consumer protection statutes, it would largely defeat their object, because the person whose conduct the statutes were designed to influence will frequently secure performance through another. After considerable hesitation, the courts therefore sought to uphold the purpose of such statutes by three means. First, principally in relation to liquor licensing, they held that, where the person upon whom the statute cast a duty delegated performance of that duty to another, the former was liable for the offence committed by the latter.[2] Secondly, where the central feature of the offence is some act such as selling, the courts have had little difficulty in convicting under the relevant statute the person who is the seller in law;[3] and the person who conducts the sale has also been held liable either as an abettor[4] or co-principal,[5] even though the seller in law escapes conviction by pleading a statutory defence (see post, para 28.13). However, in relation to sales of intoxicating liquor by an employee, there would appear to be a loophole.[6] Thirdly, there are special rules provided where a corporation is involved,[7] under which there may be convicted the corporation (see post, para 28.10), its officers (see post, para 28.11) or another (see post, para 28.12).

---

6   *Per* Lord Scarman in *Wings Ltd v Ellis* [1985] AC 272 at 293, HL. See generally Peiris (1983) 3 Legal Studies 117.

7   Smith and Hogan, *op cit*, note 3, pp 113–18. But see Stephenson, *Criminal Law and Consumer Protection*, 101–07.

8   There may be more than one such actor, as where there is a partnership eg, *Clode v Barnes* [1974] 1 All ER 1166, DC. A sleeping partner may have a defence under s 24 (see post, para 28.13): Bragg, *Trade Descriptions*, p 11, n 23.

9   Eg, auctioneer. As to clubs, see Bragg, *ibid*, pp 11–12.

[28.09]

1   See generally Smith and Hogan, *Criminal Law* (9th edn), p 171 *et seq*; Stephenson, *Criminal Law and Consumer Protection*, pp 109–11.

2   *Howker v Robinson* [1972] 2 All ER 786, DC; and see further Smith and Hogan, *ibid*, pp 149–52. Contrast *Jordan v White* (1945) 44 LGR 12 (club).

3   Eg, *Slatcher v George Mence Smith Ltd* [1951] 2 KB 631, DC (sells); *Evans v Clifton Inns* (1987) 85 LGR 119, DC (uses).

4   Even though he is in fact the only person present at the commission of the offence: *Ross v Moss* [1965] 2 QB 396, DC. Although the offence might be strict, the abettor requires *mens rea*: Smith and Hogan, *op cit*, note 1, p 182.

5   Eg, *Preston v Albury* [1963] 3 All ER 897, DC (sale by employee); *Clode v Barnes* [1974] 1 All ER 1166 (sale by partner); *Melias Ltd v Preston* [1957] 2 QB 380, DC (possession by employee).

6   Under the licensing Act 1964, s 169(1), an offence of selling to a minor may be committed by an employee of the licensee; but, in a chain of off-licences, the licensee (manager?) will not usually be the employer of branch staff, eg, *Russell v DPP* [1997] CLY 3415, DC.

7   Cf *Salomon v Salomon Ltd* (set out ante, para 19.25).

[28.10] Corporate criminal liability.[1] As consumer protection statutes commonly impose criminal liability on a 'person', which expression includes bodies corporate (s 5 and Sched 2, Interpretation Act 1978), there would *prima facie* appear to be no difficulty in charging a limited company with breach in the same manner as a natural person, notwithstanding that as an artificial person the company cannot perform the prohibited act or form the requisite intent.

1   *Vicarious liability.* In the same manner as a natural person (see ante, para 28.09), a corporation may be held vicariously liable for the torts of its servants or agents; but the common law has made no parallel extension of liability in the criminal law.[2] In relation to statutory offences, the courts have occasionally accepted that a statute intended to fix a corporation with vicarious criminal responsibility for the acts of its employees.[3] More commonly, a statute will expressly provide an innocent corporation with a good defence (see post, para 28.14), from which it has been deduced that Parliament did not intend to introduce vicarious criminal liability: the *Nattrass* case (see below).

2   *Corporate brains.* Where the actor is part of the brains of the corporation, his act is held to be that of the corporation. In *Tesco Supermarkets Ltd v Nattrass:*[4]

> In operating their chain of several hundred supermarkets, T Ltd set up a careful and elaborate system for the supervision of its employees in order to avoid the commission of offences under the TDA. Because a store manager failed to check the work of his staff in accordance with his duties under this system, a 'special offer' poster was displayed at a time when no goods were available at the special price, so that a s 11(2) offence was committed by T Ltd (now repealed: see ante, para 8.09).

The House of Lords held as follows:

(1) The store manager was insufficiently senior for his acts to be regarded as those of T Ltd (see below) so as to render liable its corporate officers,[5] though he himself might have been liable.[6]

(2) T Ltd was not vicariously liable for the acts of its store manager[7] as s 24(1) provided a good defence (see post, para 28.14).

[28.10]

1   See generally Smith and Hogan, *Criminal Law* (9th edn), p 179 *et seq*; Stephenson, *Criminal Law and Consumer Protection*, p 107 *et seq*.

2   As to the difficulty with corporate manslaughter, see Involuntary Manslaughter (1996) Law Com 237; Smith and Hogan, *ibid*, p 188; Slapper (1999) 149 NLJ 1031; Trotter (2000) 150 NLJ 454; Hickman (2001) 151 NLJ 912; Walker (2001) 151 NLJ 1494.

3   *Mousell Bros v LNWR Co* [1917] 2 KB 836, DC.

4   [1972] AC 153; [1971] 2 All ER 127, HL (discussed 34 MLR 676; and by Tench, *Towards A Middle System of Law*, pp 16–17).

5   See post, para 28.11.

6   See post, para 28.12. But compare *Bellerby v Carle* [1983] 2 AC 101, HL (discussed 99 LQR 360).

7   On the basis that the store manager was 'another person': see post, para 28.14. Does this allow the corporate employer a greater defence than a non-corporate employer? See Stephenson, *op cit*, note 1, pp 112–13.

As to point (1), their Lordships explained that the store manager is not the company's 'brains' and does not act as the company;[8] and Lord Reid indicated that a company would be criminally liable for the acts only of:[9]

... the board of directors, the managing director and perhaps other supervisor officers of [the] company [who] carry out the functions of management and speak and act as the company.

It is thus a question of law whether a company servant or agent in doing particular things is to be regarded as the 'brains' of the company (in the sense of a controlling officer), or merely as its 'hands'.[10] However, the decision has been criticised as requiring only a very low standard of supervision by the 'brains' of the company, seemingly concentrating on a paper system rather than looking at its implementation.[11] However, there are some more recent cases which suggest that, where a consumer protection defence requires knowledge, the knowledge of a more junior employee may be imputed to the employer/company.[12]

Finally, it should be borne in mind that, where the prohibited act is in fact done by a servant or agent of the corporation, there are two provisions under which the actor may be held liable, depending on whether he amounts to the 'brains' or mere 'hands' of the company.

[28.11] Corporate officers: the 'brains' of the company. Normally speaking, one employee could not possibly be criminally vicariously liable for the act of another employee. However, where a corporation is found criminally liable under one of the consumer protection statutes (see ante, para 28.10), that will generally be due to the action or inaction of an employee (see post, para 28.12). In such circumstances, it has been thought right that criminal responsibility should also be visited on those senior employees who constitute the 'brains' of the corporation in what amounts to a limited lifting of the corporate veil (see generally ante, para 19.25). Seemingly based on a similar provision in s 733(2), Companies Act 1985, such almost common form provisions[1] are to be found in s 20, TDA; s 132, FTA; s 40(2), CPA and the CCA, this last providing as follows (s 169):

---

8   *Per* Lords Reid (171), Dilhorne (187), Diplock (200).
9   At 171. Lords Dilhorne and Diplock drew an analogy from the statutory provisions rendering liable 'any director, manager, secretary or other similar officer': see post, para 28.11.
10 Smith and Hogan, *op cit*, note 1, p 182. For the unreality of this test, see Stephenson, *op cit*, note 1, p 109.
11 Bragg, *Trade Descriptions*, pp 186–88, pointing out that, because the HL gave no guidance as to the required degree of supervision, there have been inconsistent cases in inferior courts. See also Bergman (2000) 150 NLJ 316.
12 *Tesco Stores Ltd v Brent LBC* [1993] 2 All ER 718, DC (Video Recordings Act 1984, s 11: see further post, para 28.17); Cartwright (1996) 59 MLR 225, at 228–32; [1987] JBL 467–71; Wickens and Ong [1997] JBL 524.

[28.11]
1   See also Mock Auctions Act 1961, s 2; Gaming Act 1968, s 45; Prices Act 1974, Sched, para 13; Medicines Act 1968, s 124; Unsolicited Goods and Services Act 1971, s 5, British Telecommunications Act 1981, s 51; Food Act 1984, s 94 (as amended); Video Recordings Act 1984, s 15(1); Weights and Measures Act 1985, s 82; Health and Medicine Act 1988, s 23(5); DPA, s 20; Estate Agents Act 1979, s 28(2); Gas Act 1986, s 45; IA 1986, s 432; Doorstep Selling Regulations 1987, regs 4C(2) and (3); Electricity Act 1989, s 108; Property Misdescriptions Act 1991, s 4; FSA 1990, s 36; Water Industry Act 1991, s 210; Children and YP (Protection from Tobacco) Act 1991, s 4(6); Data Protection Act 1998, s 61; Competition Act 1998, s 72. Cf Companies Act 1985, s 733(2).

Where at any time a body corporate[2] commits an offence under this Act with the consent or connivance of, or because of neglect by, any individual,[3] the individual commits the like offence if at that time –

(a) he is a director,[4] manager, secretary or similar officer[5] of the body corporate, or

(b) he is purporting to act as such an officer,[6] or

(c) the body corporate is managed by its members of whom he is one.

It is to be noticed that the officer is not vicariously liable to quite the same extent as his corporation (see also s 40(3) of the CPA). In proceedings against an officer under this section, it would appear that the prosecution must prove the 'consent', etc of the officer, whereas in proceedings against the corporation, the latter must prove the facts necessary to make a good defence (see post, para 28.13). The reference to the officer's 'consent or connivance'[7] adds little to the ordinary rules of aiding and abetting (see generally ante, para 28.10); but the reference to his 'neglect' extends liability to his careless failure to prevent the offence.[8] However conviction of an officer under this provision also requires the commission of an offence by the corporation;[9] and it was made clear by the Divisional Court in *Tesco Supermarkets Ltd v Nattrass* that 'manager' in this context refers to one who manages the affairs of the company, not a mere store manager or other junior employee.[10]

Finally, it should be noted that in some cases statute expressly penalises any person who in the UK helps another person outside the UK to do an act which, if committed within the UK, would be an offence.[11]

[28.12] Act of another (bypass provisions), eg, the 'hands' of a company. Sometimes, the transgression under a consumer protection statute by A may be due to the conduct of B, eg, a retailer's offence may be due to the act of his employee, agent or supplier. In these circumstances, A may be entitled to an acquittal under one of the statutory general defences (see post, para 28.13) and the policy of the Act may be better implemented by convicting B. Sometimes, B may be liable to be convicted of the same offence as A on the basis that B acted as co-principal or abettor (see ante, para 28.09)). To cover those cases where B is not so liable, the TDA provides as follows (s 23):

---

2   Could this expression include a partnership? See *Douglas v Phoenix Motors* 1970 SLT 57, Sheriff Ct.
3   As to consent, connivance or neglect, see *R v Roussel Laboratories* (1989) 88 Crim App R 140, CA; *Southern BC v White* (1991) 11 Tr LR 65, DC.
4   Eg, *Elliott v DG* (set out ante, para 5.30). See generally the Companies Act 1985, s 741(1).
5   Cf *Registrar of Restrictive Trading Agreements v WH Smith & Sons Ltd* [1969] 3 All ER 1065, CA.
6   Cf 'shadow directors' (see Companies Act 1985, s 741(2)); *R v Boal* [1992] 1 QB 591, CA (Fire Precautions Act 1971).
7   Some statutes refer to 'consent and connivance', eg, TDA, s 20; Medicines Act 1968, s 124. Does this make any difference?
8   See *Lewis v Bland* [1985] RTR 171, DC (delegation); *Hirschler v Birch* [1987] RTR 13, DC (co-director). Does it require *mens rea*?
9   But see Bragg, *Trade Descriptions*, p 11.
10 [1971] 1 QB 133, at 142 (DC view unchallenged on this point. As to the facts, see ante, para 28.10). For the rationale, see Cartwright (1996) 59 MLR 225 at 235–36. A culpable junior employee can be prosecuted under another provision: see post, para 28.12.
11 TDA, s 21, eg, to help another outside the UK to give a false indication of Royal Approval (see ante, para 4.10).

Where the commission by any person of an offence under this Act is due to the act or default of some other person that other person shall be guilty of the offence, and a person may be charged with and convicted of the offence by virtue of this section whether or not proceedings are taken against the first mentioned person.

With the notable exception of the CCA, comparable bypass provisions are to be found in a number of consumer protection statutes.[1] Thus, in *Nattrass v Timpson Shoes*:[2]

A, owners of multiple shoe shops, issued to branch managers a warning against committing offences under the TDA and a procedure for repricing goods. In one of the shops where the manager (B) redressed the window, one pair of shoes in the display was by mistake left displaying the old price. A was charged with an offence under s 11(2), and B with an offence under s 23 on the grounds that it was due to his act or default. Held: A was rightly acquitted on the ground that the offence was due to B's default under s 24(1); but B's plea that it was due to the fault of his five assistants was rejected because he had not checked their work (see post, para 28.15).

However, the conviction of B is subject to the following limitations:

1   *Commission of an offence by A.* Whilst proceedings need not necessarily be taken against A,[3] the substantive position is as follows: it is sufficient if A commits only a *prima facie* offence, eg, through the actions of servant B, whilst able to plead one of the statutory defences;[4] but B cannot be convicted under this section where A has committed no offence whatsoever.[5]

2   *Act or default of B.*[6] This will commonly be carelessness by B in fulfilling his duties as, for example, junior employee or wholesaler.[7] However, for B to be so convicted, his act or default must cause the commission of the offence by A,[8] though perhaps B does not always need to be a trader[9] unless the statute so requires.[10] Nor does B himself need to commit a separate offence.

When charged, presumably B can raise the general defence (see post, para 28.13).

[28.12]

1   Eg, Prices Act 1974, Sched, para 5(3); TSA, s 8; Medicines Act 1968, s 121; FTA, s 24; Weights and Measures Act 1985, s 32; CPA, s 40(1); Doorstep Selling Regulations 1987, reg 4C(1); FSA 1990, s 20. See generally Roberts (1991) 8 Tr LR 145; and ante, para 8.09.

2   [1973] Crim LR 197, DC.

3   Thus, A or B or both may be prosecuted, perhaps depending on whom the prosecutor thinks is really responsible for the infringement: see *Meah v Roberts* [1978] 1 All ER 97, DC (both A and B convicted). A must disclose his reliance on B's fault before trial: see post, para 28.14.

4   *Tesco Supermarkets Ltd v Nattrass* (set out ante, para 28.10); *Nattrass v Timpson Shoes* (above). Contrast *K Lill Holdings (Trading as Stratford Motor Col) v White* [1979] RTR 120, DC (criticised Roberts, *op cit*, note 1, 149; Bragg, *Trade Descriptions*, pp 80–81, 197–98).

5   *Cottee v Douglas Seaton (Used Cars) Ltd* [1972] 3 All ER 750, DC; *Coupe v Guyett* [1973] 2 All ER 1058, DC (A was a sleeping partner).

6   As to whether B's act or default must be wrongful, see Stephenson, *Criminal Law and Consumer Protection*, pp 136–37. For the raising of this plea as a defence by A, see post, para 28.14. For B's use of the time limit, see ante, para 28.07.

7   Eg, *Hicks v Grewal* (1985) 4 Tr LR 92, DC (supplier). For the policy issues concerning the prosecution of employees, see Cartwright (1996) 59 MLR 225 at 237–38.

8   *Tarleton Engineering Co Ltd v Nattrass* [1973] 3 All ER 699, DC; the *Lill Holdings* case (above). B does not have to be the cause to be convicted: see 17 Tr LR 403.

9   *Olgeirsson v Kitching* [1986] 1 All ER 746, DC (see Roberts, *op cit*, note 1, p 145; Bragg, *op cit*, note 4, p 63; Cartwright, *op cit*, note 7, pp 238–39). It has been recommended that it should remain possible to convict under this provision fraudulent private individuals: *Review of the TDA* (1976, Cmnd 6628) paras 36–38.

10   *Warwickshire CC v Johnson* (set out ante, para 8.09).

Defences

Where under one of the consumer protection statutes there has *prima facie* been the commission of an offence (see ante, paras 28.07–12), there may be available a statutory defence as follows:[1] the general defence (see post, paras 28.13–15); or one of the special defences (see post, para 28.16 *et seq*).

The general defence

[28.13] The rule. Most of the offences created by consumer protection statutes being ones of strict liability (see ante, para 28.04), it is normal to ameliorate their effect by a provision which in effect entitles the defendant to be acquitted if he shows on the balance of probabilities that he took due care. The traditional, almost common form, general defence was laid down in s 24(1) of the TDA and repeated in the CCA in the following terms:[2]

> In any proceedings for an offence under this Act it is a defence for the person charged to prove –
>
> (a) that his act or omission was due to a mistake or to reliance on information supplied to him, or to an act or omission by another person, or to an accident or some other cause beyond his control, and
>
> (b) that he took all reasonable precautions and exercised all due diligence to avoid such an act or omission by himself or any person under his control.

To succeed in this defence, a defendant must on the balance of probabilities prove[3] both:

(1) that the commission of the *prima facie* offence was due to one of the statutory reasons specified in paragraph (a) (see post, para 28.14); **and**

(2) the two matters specified in paragraph (b) (see post, para 28.15).

If he satisfies all the above requirements, a defendant is entitled to an acquittal[4] for the following reasons: as Lord Reid observed, if a defendant has done all that can reasonably be expected of him, how can he do more?[5] He has 'done his best'.[6] Any disclaimer must be at the time of the *prima facie* offence.[7] It has been said[8] that this traditional general defence can also apply to offences under s 14 of the TDA (see ante, para 4.15 *et seq*).

[28.13]

1 The defendant must discharge the civil burden of proof: *R v Carr-Briant* [1943] KB 607, CCA (Prevention of Corruption Act 1906); *Whitehead v Collett* [1975] Crim LR 53, DC (TDA).

2 Section 168(1). See also FTA, s 25(1); Cf Medicines Act 1968, s 121(2); Weights and Measures Act 1985, s 34(1); CPA, s 39; DPA, s 47(3); FSA, s 20; Property Misdescriptions Act 1991, s 2; Children and YP (Protection from Tobacco) Act 1991, s 4(5).

3 *Coventry CC v Ackerman Group plc* [1996] CLY 1189, DC. See also *Waltham Forest LBC v TG Wheatley (No 2)* [1978] RTR 33, DC (Defendant offered no evidence on defence).

4 Eg, *Beckett v Kingston Bros (Butchers) Ltd* [1970] 1 QB 606, DC; *Naish v Gore* [1971] 3 All ER 737, DC; and see Fidler (1998) 148 NLJ 379.

5 *Tesco Supermarkets Ltd v Nattrass* (set out ante, para 28.10) at 174.

6 Compare (civil) product liability and development risks (see ante, para 17.30).

7 *Lewin v Fuell* (1991) 10 Tr LR 126, DC (see ante, para 4.09).

8 In *Wings Ltd v Ellis* (set out ante, para 4.17), *per* Lords Hailsham and Scarman.

However, it seems likely that it could only apply to those parts of the s 14 offence which do not require *mens rea*: if so, then the defence can apply to making a statement under s 14(1)(a), but not to doing so under s 14(1)(b).[9]

Experience with the above double-barrelled defence showed that defendants had little difficulty in overcoming paragraph (a), usually by claiming reliance or act of another, so that the real problem for defendants lay in paragraph (b).[10] Accordingly, more recent statutes have tended to dispense entirely with paragraph (a) (see post, para 28.17).

[28.14] Paragraph (a). In order for the defendant to plead successfully the general defence (see ante, para 28.13), he must prove *inter alia* that his act or omission was due to one of the matters specified in paragraph (a).

1 *Mistake.* This unusual[1] defence does not refer to ignorance of the statutory provision creating the offence, but to mistakes by the defendant personally (not by a third party) as to matters of fact known to him.[2] Thus, where a corporation is charged, the 'mistake' must be that of its 'brains' and not its 'hands' (see ante, para 28.10); and a mistake by its 'hands' is properly dealt with in (3) below.

2 *Reliance on information supplied.* It has been held that the odometer reading of a motor vehicle is 'information' for this purpose and statements printed on packaging or containers is also covered.[3] However, this defence will usually be dependent on the precautions taken by the defendant[3] and may even extend to the reliance on legal advice.[4] It is in any event subject to the requirement of prior notice.[5] It has been suggested that this defence should be narrowly construed by restricting it to information from an apparently authoritative source.[6]

---

9   Stephenson (1985) 135 NLJ 160, 162.

10 Lawson (1993) 137 SJ 144.

[28.14]

1 It seems to require proof of absence of *mens rea*, and anyway is usually inconsistent with due diligence (see post, para 28.15): Bragg, *Trade Descriptions*, pp 178–79.

2 If the mistake is by another employee, the proper defence would be 'act or default of another' (see below): *Birkenhead Co-op Ltd v Roberts* [1970] 3 All ER 391, DC. See also *Butler v Keenway Supermarkets* [1974] Crim LR 560, DC (TDA).

3 See the case discussed in Bragg, *op cit*, note 1, pp 180–85. As to disclaimer by odometer, see ante, para 4.09.

4 *Coventry CC v Lazerus* [1994] CLY 1165; see Lawson (1995) 139 SJ 826. Can a defendant rely under this defence on advice sought from a tso? What of LA non-compliance with an enforcement code (see ante, para 5.10)?

5 Prior notice to the prosecutor identifying the supplier of information is normally required so that he can pursue the person really responsible (see ante, para 28.12): TDA, s 24(2); FTA, s 25(2); CCA, s 168(2); Weights and Measures Act 1985, s 34(2); CPA, s 39(2); eg, *Wings Ltd v Ellis* (absence of notice precluded defence: see ante, para 4.17). But see *McGuire v Sittingbourne Co-op Society* [1976] Crim LR 268, DC (defence allowed although precise identification impossible; discussed Cmnd 6628, para 59). For argument that the defendant should himself be required to prosecute the third party, see Cmnd 6628, paras 64–66.

6 Stephenson, *Criminal Law and Consumer Protection*, 129. But see *Barker v Hargreaves* [1981] RTR 197 (reliance on MOT not allowed for this defence; but latency of defect allowed in another defence: see post, para 28.17). See now CPA, s 39(4).

3   *Act or default of another.* This will clearly cover both persons working within the same enterprise as the defendant, eg, employees,[7] and those outside, eg, suppliers;[8] and it may give rise to the opportunity to prosecute others (see ante, para 28.12). As regards employees, the effect of the decision in *Tesco Supermarkets Ltd v Nattrass* is to draw a distinction between those senior corporate officers who might be liable along with the corporation (see ante, para 28.11) and more junior employees. Where the senior officer is the 'brains' of the corporation, it may be vicariously liable for his conduct (see ante, para 28.10); whereas if he is only part of its 'hands', the corporation may escape criminal liability under the general defence, and the authorities may be reluctant to prosecute the 'hands' under the bypass provision (see ante, para 28.12) for mis-operating a system designed by the 'brains'.[9] This defence is subject to the requirement of prior notice.

4   *Accident, etc.* The defendant may escape if he can show that the prohibited act was the result of an 'accident or some other cause beyond his control'. Thus, the trader does not have to have a perfect system,[10] but it has been said that an employee cannot be beyond his control[11] and that some explanation must be given of an accident.[12]

[28.15] Paragraph (b). In order for the defendant to plead successfully the general defence (see ante, para 28.13), he must prove that before the event he took **both** the steps specified in paragraph (b) in order to 'avoid such an act or omission by himself or any person under his control'.

1   *All reasonable precautions.* In showing that he has taken all reasonable precautions, it may be a necessary, though not sufficient, precaution for a retailer to show that he obtained his stock from a reputable source;[1] that he relied on an assurance from his supplier, or a British Standard;[2] or that he had adequate expertise in the type of products sold;[3] or that, if he cannot verify the facts, that he made an adequate

---

7   *Tesco Supermarkets Ltd v Nattrass* (set out ante, para 28.10; store manager); *Nattrass v Timpson Shoes* (set out ante, para 28.12).

8   *Naish v Gore* [1971] 3 All ER 737, DC (TDA); *Sherratt v Gerald's the American Jewellers Ltd* (1970) 68 LGR 256, DC (TDA).

9   The effect may be that multiple traders are only effectively subject to *mens rea* liability, whereas single shops are strictly liable; and possible statutory amendments have therefore been considered: Cmnd 6628, paras 52–63; Cartwright (1991) 141 NLJ at 889–90. As to the possible significance of codes of practice (see ante, paras 3.11–14), see Bragg, *op cit*, note 1, p 189.

10 Eg, *Marshall v Herbert* [1963] Crim LR 506, DC (staff sickness); *Bibby-Cheshire v Golden Wonder Ltd* [1972] 3 All ER 738, DC (machine malfunction); *R v Swaysland* [1987] BTLC 299 (newspaper picture captions reversed).

11 *Hall v Farmer* [1970] 1 All ER 729, DC (Weights and Measures Act). What if the employee is on a frolic of his own? Cf *McGuire v Sittingbourne Co-op Society* (above); and Stephenson, *op cit*, note 6, pp 131–32.

12 *Urwin v Toole* (1976) 75 LGR 98, DC (weight labels missing from sacks).

[28.15]

1   *Sherratt v Gerald's, The American Jewellers Ltd* (1970) 68 LGR 256, DC; *Riley v Webb* [1987] CLY 3321, DC; *Hurley v Martinez & Co* [1990] TLR 189, DC. See also *Gale v Dixons Stores Group* [1995] CLY 751, DC (resold without testing goods returned as defective).

2   *Sherratt* (above) and *Taylor v Lawrence Fraser* [1978] Crim LR 43, DC (supplier assurances); *Ealing LBC v Taylor* (1995) 159 JP 460, DC (no enquiry from supplier); *Balding v Lew Ways Ltd* (1995) Tr LR 344, DC (British Standard: see ante, para 3.08).

3   *Aitchison v Reith and Anderson Ltd* [1974] SLT 282 (auctioneer with no previous experience of auctioning vehicles). Cf *Naish v Gore* [1971] 3 All ER 737, DC (car examined by independent expert).

disclaimer of them, or adequately consulted a tso.[4] Where the defendant is a large business, this will require him to lay down an adequate system for avoiding the commission of offences by persons under his control: in *Tesco Supermarkets Ltd v Nattrass* (set out ante, para 28.10), Lord Diplock pointed out that in a large organisation personal supervision of all employees by the 'brains' of the organisation was impractical, but an effective system operated by supervisory grades was required (at 197–98). Further, the business would require an adequate sampling system with regard to products manufactured beyond his control.[5]

2   *All due diligence.* Nor may the defendant rest on his laurels after showing that he took all reasonable precautions at the outset, but must continue to be vigilant.[6] As Lord Diplock explained in the *Nattrass* case (see above), at 199D:

> Due diligence is in law the converse of negligence ... To establish a defence ... a principal need only show that he personally acted without negligence ...

For instance, buying from a reputable source does not necessarily preclude his taking 'elementary precautions' for himself, such as asking his supplier meaningful questions,[7] or check-weighing goods supplied, or adequate random sampling.[8] Where the defendant is a large business, it is not sufficient just to lay down a proper system: the staff must be adequately trained in its operation,[9] the staff must apply it and the system itself must be able to cope with mistakes,[10] before such a defendant can rely on the 'act of another'.[11] Further, the phrase 'any other person under his control' (s 24(1)(b), TDA) has been omitted from some later statutes.[12]

Special defences

[28.16] Besides what is here termed the general defence to offences laid down in consumer protection statutes (see ante, paras 28.13–15), there are also to be found a number of special defences of more restricted application. These include the following:

---

4   *Zawadski v Sleigh* [1975] RTR 113, DC; *Simmons v Potter* [1975] RTR 347, DC (disclaimers: see ante, para 4.09); *a fortiori*, if he gives a warranty: *Norman (Alec) Garages v Phillips* [1985] RTR 164, DC; *Coventry CC v Lazerus* [1994] CLY 1165 (see Lawson (1995) 140 SJ 690).

5   *Rotherham MBC v Raysun (UK) Ltd* [1988] C & F LR 316, DC (importer of Hong Kong products). See also *Haringey LBC v Piro Shoes* [1976] Crim LR 462, DC; *Baxters (Butchers) v Manley* (1985) 4 Tr LR 219, DC; and Roberts (1994) 13 Tr LR 50.

6   *Denard v Smith & Dixons* (1991) 10 TLR 86, DC; *Turlington v United Co-operatives* [1993] Crim LR 376, DC. See also Cotter (1992) 142 NLJ 133 and 170; Lawson (1995) 14 Tr L 2.

7   *Richmond upon Thames LBC v Motors Sales (Hounslow) Ltd* [1971] RTR 116, DC; *Simmons v Potter* (above); *Riley v Webb* [1987] CLY 3321, DC; and see further Stephenson, *Criminal Law and Consumer Protection*, pp 133–34.

8   *Nattrass v Timpson Shoes Ltd* (set out ante, para 28.12); *Rotherham* (above; discussed by Weatherill [1990] JBL 36; *P & M Supplies v Devon CC* (1992) 11 Tr LR 52, DC. Cf *Hurley v Martinez & Co* (above).

9   *Tesco Supermarkets Ltd v Nattrass* (above); *Knowsley MBC v Cowan* (1992) 11 Tr LR 44, DC. It must be more than a mere paper scheme: Stephenson, *op cit*, note 7, p 133.

10 *Beckett v Kingston Bros (Butchers) Ltd* [1970] 1 QB 606, DC (chain store's remedial system omitted by one store manager); *Horner v Sherwoods of Darlington* [1990] 9 TLR 73, DC (staff did not apply system). But the business does not need to take all practical steps: *Berkshire CC v Olympic Holidays Ltd* (1994) 13 Tr LR 251, DC (computer malfunction).

11 It **may** be enough to rely on inspection by a tso: *Carrick DC v Taunton Vale Meat Traders Ltd* (1994) 13 Tr LR 258, DC.

12 As to the effect, see Bragg, *Trade Descriptions*, p 146.

1 *Reasonable diligence* (see post, para 28.17).

2 *Innocent publication.* For the owners of news media,[1] there is a special defence of innocent publication to some of the offences under the TDA and several other statutes.[2] The TDA provides that (s 25):

> In proceedings for an offence under this Act, committed by the publication of an advertisement[3] it shall be a defence for the person charged to prove that he is a person whose business it is to publish or arrange for the publication of advertisements and that he received the advertisement for publication in the ordinary course of business and did not know and had no reason to suspect that its publication would amount to an offence under this Act.

Like the reasonable diligence defence (above), this s 25 defence is one of excusable ignorance rather than mistake: he must not know that publication amounts to an offence (subjective) nor have any reason to suspect that it does (objective). There is no provision for corrective advertisements.[4]

3 *Exempted exports, etc.* To save UK exporters from competitive disadvantage, the TDA allows a lower standard to be applied to goods being exported (s 32 (as amended)). The Act also allows some exemption from certain registered trade marks and genuine market research (ss 34, 37), besides saving the wider defences available under some other Acts.[5]

4 *Wrong quantity.* Where the defendant is charged under the Weights and Measures Act 1985 in respect of goods marked with the wrong quantities (see ante, para 4.25), that Act provides special defences with regard to shrinkage after marking,[6] excess[7] or average quantity. As to the last, the 1985 Act lays down that, if other articles of the same type were available for testing, there shall be no conviction unless a reasonable number of those other articles were also tested.[8]

5 *Written warranty* (see post, para 28.18).

6 *Food Safety Act defences* (see post, para 28.19).

7 *Pricing regulations* (see ante, para 8.10)

8 *Innocent supplier pyramid selling* (s 121(2), FTA. See further ante, para 8.17).

[28.16]

1 Possibly s 25 does not extend to advertising agents because they do not receive advertisements.

2 See Medicines Act 1968, s 93(6); FTA, s 121(1); CCA, s 47(2); Food Act, s 6(3); CPA, s 24(3).

3 For the definition of 'advertisement', see ante, para 8.07.

4 As to whether there should be power to require corrective advertising, see the *Review of the TDA* (1976, Cmnd 6628), paras 194–97.

5 TDA, s 22 (as amended). Where the TDA overlaps with, eg, the Food Act or the Weights and Measures Act, these other Acts provide some more generous defences, and s 22 saves these, eg, the written warranty defence. As to prosecutions with regard to food, see Roberts (1993) 10 Tr LR 93.

6 Section 35. This defence is available not only to the manufacturing packer, but also to the retailer: *FW Woolworth & Co Ltd v Gray* [1970] 1 All ER 953, DC.

7 Section 36. This is to cover the situation where a machine is set to dispense a reasonable excess on average to try to avoid giving too little in any case.

8 Section 37. Eg, *Ellis v Price* (1968) 66 LGR 404, DC. However, where a member of the public tenders one article in complaint, the authorities are under no duty to seek out others so that this defence may be established: *Sears v Smiths Food Group Ltd* [1968] 2 QB 288, DC.

[28.17] Reasonable diligence. In relation to some of the less heinous offences, Parliament allows a rather more generous defence. For instance, where a defendant is charged with supplying goods to which another has applied a false trade description (see ante, para 4.05), s 24(3) of the TDA provides that:

> ... it shall be a defence for the person charged to prove[1] that he did not know, and could not with reasonable diligence have ascertained that the goods did not conform to the description or that the description had been applied to the goods.

Similar provisions are to be commonly found in more modern consumer protection statutes.[2] In essence, this defence only requires excusable ignorance, whilst the general defence looks for proof of mistaken belief:[3] as the former appears to set a lower standard, it will clearly be preferred by the defendant in those many cases where the two defences appear to overlap;[4] but it may be that the defence considered in this paragraph should be confined to defective goods, whereas the general defence extends also to verbal misdescriptions.[5]

The present defence seems to envisage two different situations; namely, that the defendant did not know (a subjective test)[6] **and** could not with reasonable diligence have ascertained (an objective test)[7] that **either:**

(i)   the goods did not conform to the description,[8] **or**

(ii) the description had been applied to the goods, eg, an importer has published a description.

Where the nub of the defence is the fault of an employee,[9] this may allow the possibility of prosecuting the latter (see ante, para 28.12) but gives rise to the same reluctance to prosecute as in relation to the general defence (see ante, para 28.14). In *Cottee v Douglas Seaton (Used Cars) Ltd:*[10]

[28.17]

1   On the balance of probabilities: *Wandsworth BC v Fontana* (1983) 146 JP 196, DC. As to food retailers, see post, para 28.19.

2   Eg, Weights and Measures Act 1985, s 34(1) (see *Bibby-Cheshire v Golden Wonder Ltd* [1972] 3 All ER 738, DC); CPA 1987, s 39(1); Doorstep Selling Regulations 1987, reg 4B(1); Food Safety Act 1990, s 21(1) (cf *Benfall Farm Produce v Surrey CC* [1983] 1 WLR 1213, DC).

3   See *Barker v Hargreaves* [1981] RTR 197, DC (MOT certificated but latent corrosion).

4   As to whether the two defences do require different standards, see Bragg, *Trade Descriptions*, pp 194–96. See also *Tesco Stores Ltd v Brent LBC* [1993] 2 All ER 718, DC (Video Recordings Act 1984, s 11).

5   Bragg, *ibid*, p 195, note 77.

6   *Furniss v Scott* [1973] RTR 314, DC (innocent; but culpability not considered).

7   This would appear to involve the same objective test as due diligence under the general defence (see ante, para 28.15): *Taylor v Lawrence Fraser (Bristol)* [1978] Crim LR 43, DC (consumer safety); *Simmons v Ravenhill* [1983] Crim LR 749, DC (TDA); *Denard v Abbas* [1987] Crim LR 424, DC (TDA); *Texas Homecare v Stockport MBC* [1988] CLY 851, DC.

8   *Naish v Gore* [1971] 3 All ER 737, DC.

9   In some statutes it is provided that, if the defendant relies on the act or default of another, he must give prior notice: ante, para 28.14; Food Safety Act 1990, s 21(5). Why is there not a similar requirement in relation to the TDA or CPA?

10 [1972] 3 All ER 750; [1972] 1 WLR 1408, DC.

Trader B acquired a car with a suspension arm so rusted as to make it unroadworthy. Rather than weld it properly, B merely used a plastic filling material, so totally concealing the defect without repairing it. B sold the car to trader A, who sold it to S.

At first sight, it looked as though the plastic filler caused the car to be supplied to S with a false trade description contrary to s 1(1)(b) (see ante, para 4.03). However the court held that A had committed no offence on the grounds that he had 'no knowledge' or means of knowledge of the defect' (per Widgery LCJ, at 757f. See also Milmo J at 759b). It followed that B could not be convicted under the bypass provision (see ante, para 28.12). The decision has been criticised as defeating the intention of Parliament:[11] it is argued that A should have been found to have breached s 1(1)(b), as knowledge should be irrelevant, but that A had a reasonable diligence defence; and that consequently it would have been possible to convict B under the bypass provision.[12]

[28.18] Written warranty. To prevent injustice to retailers, Parliament has sometimes thought it right to allow retailers charged with offences under consumer protection statutes to plead by way of defence that they reasonably relied on the written warranty of their supplier.[1] Provisions to this effect are to be found in the Medicines Act 1968 and the Weights and Measures Act 1985.[2] Reliance by the retailer on this defence is usually subject to prior notice to the prosecutor[3] and to proof by the retailer[4] of all the following conditions:

(1) the goods were lawfully supplied to him under their name or description and with a written warranty (see below) to that effect (respectively ss 122(1)(a); 33(1)(a), (b));

(2) he had no reason to believe at the time of commission of the alleged offence that this was not the case (respectively ss 122(1)(b); 33(1)(c), (d)); and

(3) the goods were in the same state as when purchased,[5] save for untampered natural deterioration.[6]

---

11 Bragg, *op cit*, note 4, pp 193–94, suggests the case was decided *per incuriam*. But the LCJ did point out that B could have been charged with supplying an unroadworthy car contrary to the RTA: see generally ante, para 4.37.

12 Instead of concentrating on the supply to S, the DC suggested B should have been charged under s 1(1) in relation to his supply to A.

[28.18]

1 This defence also used to be available under the now-repealed Food Act 1884. Instead, s 21 of the Food Safety Act 1990 replaces it with two defences: (a) reasonable diligence (see ante, para 28.17) and (b) innocent retailer (see post, para 28.19).

2 Respectively ss 122, 33. In the latter case, the defence relates only to offences connected with the quantity or pre-packing of goods. Is there any reason why this type of defence should not be extended to offences created under other consumer protection statutes? Cf the general defence of reliance on information supplied: see ante, para 28.14.

3 And to the alleged warrantor: respectively ss 122(3), 33(2). The alleged warrantor is entitled to appear in the proceedings: respectively ss 122(5), 33(4) because the giving of the warranty may amount to an offence by him: respectively ss 123(2), 33(6).

4 This defence is expressly extended to employees: respectively ss 122(5), 33(3).

5 Respectively ss 122(1)(c); 33(1)(e). In the latter case, he must take all reasonable steps to ensure that the quantity remains unchanged: s 33(1)(e). But see *Gateway Foodmarkets v Simmonds* [1988] CLY 1698, DC.

6 *Watford BC v Maypole Ltd* [1970] 1 QB 573, DC (pre-packed perishable food). *Contra* where goods have been processed: *Hall v Owen-Jones* [1967] 3 All ER 209, DC (pasteurised milk); *Tesco Stores Ltd v Roberts* [1974] 3 All ER 74, DC (liver bulk purchased, part thawed, cut up and repackaged). See generally Stephenson, *Criminal Law and Consumer Protection*, pp 123–26.

This defence requires a 'written warranty': whilst it must obviously be expressed,[7] this comprehends any contractual promise[8] and is specially extended to a name or description in an invoice.[9]

[28.19] Innocent food retailer. When the Food Safety Act 1990 was being enacted, food retailers were worried that it did not provide them with a defence of written warranty (see ante, para 28.18). Not content with a new reasonable diligence defence (s 21(1): see ante, para 28.17), they therefore insisted upon an additional (overlapping) defence with regard to the three types of offence most commonly charged under food legislation: *viz*, selling food not complying with the food safety requirements (s 8: see ante, para 4.27), selling food not of the nature, etc, demanded (s 14: see ante, para 4.28) and falsely describing food (s 15: see ante, para 8.11). Retailers argued that the above reasonable diligence defence would be unduly burdensome where they had neither prepared the food nor imported it (s 21(2)). Accordingly, whether the retailed food was own branded (s 21(4)(b)) or not (s 21(3)(b)), s 21(2) provided that the retailer shall be taken to have established the above reasonable diligence defence where he proves[1] both that:

(1) the commission of the offence was due to an act or default of another person who was not under his control, or to reliance on information supplied by such a person;[2] **and**

(2) he did not know and had no reason to suspect at the time of the commission of the alleged offence that his act or omission would amount to an offence under the relevant provision.[3]

---

7 *Jeynes v Hindle* [1921] 2 KB 581 (sufficient that buyer stipulates in contract for warranty). As to express promises, see generally ante, para 11.07.

8 *Laidlow v Wilson* [1894] 1 QB 74 (delivery note). But it may not extend to a mere representation (as to which, see generally ante, para 11.02).

9 Respectively ss 122(6); 33(8). See *Rochdale MBC v FMC (Meat) Ltd* [1980] 2 All ER 303, DC (brand name on invoice).

[28.19]

1 Section 21(3), (4). So the burden of proof is on the retailer as in the reasonable diligence defence.

2 Sections 21(3)(a), (4)(a).

3 Sections 21(3)(c), (4)(c).

CHAPTER 29

REMEDIES OF THE TRANSFEREE – 'DEBTOR OR HIRER'

[29.01] Introduction. It must be borne in mind that there are a number of difficulties which a hirer or buyer may face when seeking to pursue his remedies. First, the sheer complexity of the legal rules discussed in this work may make ascertainment of his substantive rights a daunting experience; and even finding competent, affordable and timely advice may be difficult (see Chapter 3). Second, a feasible way of avoiding the foregoing difficulties may be to identify a strict liability criminal offence in the supplier (see ante, Chapters 4 and 5), persuade a public authority to prosecute (see ante, para 28.03) and then use the conviction to obtain financial compensation (see ante, paras 3.20–21). Third, turning to civil proceedings, it may be possible to simplify and cheapen proceedings by going to arbitration (see ante, para 3.23), or by complaining to an ombudsman (see ante, para 3.25). Fourth, as regards the substantive civil law, there should be recalled the sharp distinction drawn in English law between remedies in contract and tort, which is often important in determining such issues as product liability (see Chapter 17), particularly if the transaction is financed (see Chapter 16); and there should also be remembered the differing limitation periods (see ante, para 26.17). Fifth, there is the difficulty in enforcing legal rights[1] or judgment debts,[2] though even more important to the hirer or buyer is likely to be the cost of litigation (see ante, para 3.22). However, consumers may avoid this by seeking enforcement on their behalf by Stop Now Orders (see ante, paras 6.08; 28.03).

Leaving aside termination of supply contracts (see ante, para 26.04), actions for breach of a collateral contract (see ante, para 17.09) or a declaration,[3] or statements of indebtedness or termination,[3a] loss caused by pricing and anti-competitive practices (see ante, paras 2.12–14) and defective regulated agreements,[4] the major substantive remedies which may be available to the transferee under a valid supply contract[4] are as follows: (1) rescission for breach of contract or misrepresentation;[5] (2) restitution in quasi-contract;[6]

[29.01]

1   As there is difficulty in identifying the seller by reason of eg, franchising (see ante, para 1.07), eponymous subsidiaries (see ante, para 16.06A), or one-off sales events (see [1995] 2 *Which?* 5).

2   See Borrie, *The Development of Consumer Law and Policy*, pp 39–44, referring in particular to the difficulties of consumers facing insolvent limited liability suppliers (see ante, para 19.25); and generally ante, para 27.04.

3   *Garnac Grain Co Inc v Faure and Fairclough Ltd* [1968] AC 1130, HL (that contract valid); *Camilla Cotton Co v Grandex SA* [1975] 1 Lloyd's Rep 470, CA (of non-liability); *Rogers v Parish* (set out ante, para 14.23; validly rescinded); *The Gladys* [1990] 1 All ER 397, HL (existence of contract); *Manatee Towing Co v Oceanbulk Maritime SA* [1999] 2 All ER (Comm) 306; *Messier-Dowty Ltd v Sabena SA* [2000] 1 All ER (Comm) 833, CA (non-liability); *Wilson v First County Trust Ltd* (set out ante, para 9.20; declaration under Human Rights Act). And see generally *Benjamin's Sale of Goods* (5th edn), para 17.095.

3a   Under a regulated agreement, the debtor or hirer has a right to (binding) statements of his indebtedness or termination: see ante, para 15.16; 26.04.

4   A regulated agreement may be unenforceable as not being properly executed; and both regulated and unregulated agreements may be cancellable or void for illegality: see Chapters 8–10.

5   See post, para 29.02 *et seq*. Possibly with recovery of any price already paid by way of tracing: see ante, para 20.22; and generally ante, paras 27.13–14.

6   See post, paras 29.12–16. While refund is delayed, sums retained may be financing the supplier's business or earning interest for him: see *DG v All-wear Trading Ltd*, reported by OFT in 1980-AR, 73 (Part III undertaking: see ante, para 6.08). Cf *The Manila* [1988] 3 All ER 843.

(3) damages for breach of contract, tort or misrepresentation (see post, para 29.17 *et seq*); (4) specific enforcement (see post, paras 29.38–39); (5) extortionate credit bargain (see post, para 29.40 *et seq*). Each of these remedies may be available alone; or more than one of them may be available alternatively or cumulatively,[7] depending on the duty broken and the nature of the breach.

Of great practical importance is the suspension of payments. Sometimes, there is a legal right of suspension because acting on the transferee's complaint is a condition precedent to the duty of payment, eg, under s 28 of the SGA (see ante, para 23.16). However, there are also suggestions that disaffected consumers of goods supplied on credit be given the explicit legal right to suspend payments,[8] a tactic frequently employed in any event.[9]

Inspired by an EU Directive, new Regulations should significantly improve the position of consumers as follows: (1) in relation to both breaches of statutory implied terms and manufacturers' guarantees (see ante, para 14.01; 17.09A); and (2) as regards the remedies available (see especially post, para 29.03A).

RESCISSION

Rescission for breach of contract

[29.02] It has already been pointed out that the innocent party to the contract will be entitled to rescind it *de futuro* where the other party repudiates, or sometimes where he defectively performs the supply contract (see ante, para 26.15); but that the innocent party may lose that right by waiver (see ante, paras 26.23–25) or by electing to affirm the contract (see ante, para 26.16). In a consumer supply, any term which gives the supplier the right to decide whether the goods supplied conform with the contract may be void as being an unfair term (Grey Term (m): see ante, para 11.18).

Of particular significance in the present context is the right of the hirer or buyer to reject the goods tendered and rescind on grounds of defective performance, and the fact that he may lose this right by accepting the goods with knowledge of the breach (see post, para 29.03 *et seq*). Such an acceptance of the goods may amount to an election to affirm, in which event the hirer or buyer can only sue for damages; or it may even be treated as an acceptance of an offer to enter a contract to vary the previous contract, in which case all remedies for breach of the previous contract might be extinguished (see ante, para 26.18). The present section is concerned with rescission for breach, in which respect it is convenient to consider separately the contracts of sale and bailment.

Rescission by the buyer

[29.03] Rejection. It will be recalled that it is the duty of the seller to tender goods in conformity with the contract (s 27, SGA: set out ante, para 23.01) and that the buyer has

---

7 Subject to the rule against double recovery: see ante, para 27.39.
8 NCC, *Buying Problems* (1984) 67; and see below.
9 There may already be a common law or statutory (CCA, s 75) right to set off payments due: see Chapter 16.

the right to inspect any goods tendered to ascertain whether they do so conform (s 34: set out ante, para 23.10). The buyer has a *prima facie* right to reject[1] the goods tendered on grounds of breach of contract in any of the following cases:[2] where there is an express or implied term of the contract to that effect;[3] where the seller has by defective tender or otherwise evinced an intention to repudiate the contract (see ante, para 26.15); or where the seller has committed a breach of condition or innominate term giving a right to treat the contract as repudiated (see ante, paras 11.04–05A). A *prima facie* right to reject may be lost by acceptance of the goods (see post, para 29.04), which leaves a claim for damages available.[4] An improper rejection amounts to a repudiation by the buyer,[5] whilst a lawful rejection will at least nullify delivery and, if already passed, revest in the seller the property[6] and risk.[7] The position after rejection is considered below.

From the above right to reject for breach, there must be distinguished three things: (1) the right to rescind *ab initio* on grounds of misrepresentation (see ante, paras 26.12–14); (2) a subsequent agreement between the parties to discharge the contract (see ante, para 26.18); and (3) any unilateral right on the part of the transferee to cancel the contract. This last right may occasionally exist by reason of the terms of the original supply contract, or more commonly by statute (see ante, para 10.28). For instance, sometimes the CCA gives him such a right without cause in respect of regulated conditional or credit sales (see ante, para 26.22).

After rejection. Where the defective tender does not amount to a frustrating breach (see ante, para 26.16), must the rejecting buyer (see above) also treat the contract as repudiated? Section 11(3) of the SGA runs together the notions of rejecting the goods and rescinding the contract, ie, treat the contract as repudiated by reason of the seller's breach (see ante, para 11.04); and it does so in a manner which seems to assume that the disappointed buyer will also want to rescind. No doubt, a buyer who can and does reject goods **may** also wish to rescind the contract (see post, para 29.04), in which case there will be no question of the seller making a second tender of conforming goods. However, in *Borrowman Phillips & Co v Free & Hollis*:[8]

[29.03]

1. Clauses limiting the right to reject are most often found in international commodity contracts: Yates and Hawkins, *Standard Business Contracts*, pp 229–30.

2. Rejection may take place before or after delivery. As to delivery, see ante, para 23.03. If there has been a delivery, it is the buyer's duty simply to hold rejected goods for collection: see ante, para 23.09. For the dual rights of rejection in cif contracts, see ante, para 22.07. As to rejection for the wrong reason see ante, para 26.26.

3. Eg, trade usage (see ante, para 15.11); sale or return (see ante, para 20.23), which may include 'money back' guarantees (see ante, para 20.24). Distinguish the common manufacturer's offer to replace goods with which the consumer is justifiably dissatisfied: see ante, para 17.09. Cf *Codes of Practice* (see ante, para 3.13).

4. See post, para 29.17. Or a right to reject may be lost by waiver of all remedies: see ante, para 26.25.

5. Even after *Woodar Investment Development Ltd v Wimpey Construction UK Ltd* [1980] 1 All ER 571, HL (not a sale case)? As to whether the improper rejection of one instalment constitutes a repudiation of an instalment contract, see ante, para 23.25.

6. Before rejecting a defective tender, the buyer who has paid the price should first ensure his seller is solvent: otherwise he will be reduced to claiming a dividend – see ante, para 19.22. As to the initial passing of property by appropriation, see ante, para 20.15.

7. But might the right to reject be lost by accidental damage or part consumption by way of trial? See *Sale and Supply of Goods* (1987, Law Com No 160), paras 5.39–40.

8. (1878) 4 QBD 500, CA. This rule certainly seems to be settled with regard to offers to tender the goods in cif sales (see ante, para 22.07): see *Benjamin's Sale of Goods* (5th edn), para 19-062; Bridge, *Sale of Goods*, p 199.

There was a contract for the cif sale of a quantity of maize under which the seller (S) was bound to tender shipping documents. In purported performance of this contract, S insisted on tendering a cargo for which he had no shipping documents. When the arbitrator found against him, S tendered another cargo for which he had shipping documents. The Court held that, since the buyer (B) had simply rejected the first tender, S was at liberty to make a conforming tender and that B was liable for non-acceptance of that second tender.

Whilst it will not always be possible to make a second tender within the contract period,[9] the case does appear to demonstrate that the contract may be kept alive for the benefit of both parties: so, the first defective tender will not necessarily preclude a second tender,[10] unless perhaps fatal to the buyer's confidence;[11] but that second tender may itself be so defective as to give the buyer a right to reject.[12] The foregoing issue of re-tendering is all bound up with the question whether the defect in the goods when first tendered may be cured (see post, para 29.03A).

[29.03A] The buyer's remedies: replacement and cure. This paragraph is concerned with the situation where a buyer has the right to rescind *de futuro* by reason of his seller's breach (see ante, para 29.03). Traditionally, English law has *prima facie* offered the disappointed buyer the following choices (s 11(3), SGA: see ante, para 11.04; 26.16):

1   *to treat the contract as discharged.* In this case, the buyer would 'return' the goods (s 36, SGA: see ante, para 23.09), recover the price (if paid) by way of restitution (see post, para 29.12), and claim damages for any consequential loss (see post, para 29.23); or

2   *not to treat the contract as discharged.* In this case, the buyer would accept the goods (see post, para 29.04) and just claim damages (see post, para 29.17 *et seq*).

Yet this dichotomy never did represent the whole picture of what actually happened to the disappointed buyer, particularly where goods were bought for consumption.[1] Commonly, two other courses of action were considered when the buyer returned the goods to his seller, normally before the above remedies were discussed:

1   **Credit note.** Retail suppliers frequently try to persuade complaining consumers to accept a credit note. This is where a buyer, usually a consumer, having properly refused to accept goods, does not exercise his right to treat the contract as discharged and immediately recover any price he has already paid (see post, para 29.15), but instead accepts the seller's 'credit note': the intention is that this credit note (acknowledgment of indebtedness) will later be exchanged for other goods which the buyer will subsequently (perhaps within a time limit) choose from the seller's stock. Any attempt by a retail supplier to provide in the supply contract that his consumer/buyer must in these circumstances accept a credit note would be void,

---

9   Or at all if the goods are specific goods rejected for breach of the undertaking as to description: Bridge, *ibid*; Goode, *Commercial Law*, pp 308–09.

10   Goode, *ibid*, pp 363–64; Atiyah, *Sale of Goods* (10th edn), pp 501, 508; Benjamin, *op cit*, note 8, para 14.014; and post, para 29.04. If the buyer is contemplating suing for damages, the duty to mitigate may require him to accept a second tender: see ante, para 27.44.

11   Benjamin, *op cit*, note 8, para 12-032.

12   Cf *The Wise* [1989] 2 Lloyd's Rep 451, CA.

[29.03A]

1   Compare the rights of replacement and cure found in the US Uniform Commercial Code, Arts 2.508 and 2.608. See *Benjamin's Sale of Goods* (5th edn), para 14-014. See also Bridge, *Sale of Goods*, p 201.

unfair[2] and amounts to a criminal offence.[3] Further, any subsequent attempt to persuade the consumer to accept a credit note is likely to fail as unfair.

2 **Replacement**. The seller might offer to replace free of charge the defective goods with an identical, or even just a comparable model. If the buyer agreed, the natural legal analysis of what transpired would appear to be this: the original contract of sale was mutually abandoned (see ante, para 26.18); and the parties made a second supply contract for the replacement goods, which would appear to be a barter or quasi-sale (see ante, paras 2.09–10).

3 **Cure/repair**. The seller might offer to cure the defect, whether by use of his own facilities, or by returning them to his supplier (the manufacturer, importer or wholesaler). If English law allowed the defaulting seller[4] a second tender (see ante, para 29.03), then the cure might be effected under the original contract of sale,[5] though the buyer's agreeing to repair would not itself amount to a deemed acceptance (s 35(6)(a), SGA: see post, para 29.06). If not, the cure was effected under a second contract, which perhaps amounted to a contract of repair which varied the original sale (see ante, para 26.21): the buyer would in effect bargain away his rights for breach of the original sale contract in return for the cure contract.

It should be noted that the above analysis gave neither seller nor buyer the **right** to replacement or cure; but, the buyer might **encourage** cure by a conditional rejection.[6] However, returning the goods may carry the danger of loss of evidence that the first tender was defective, so enabling the seller to argue that the rejection was improper and a repudiation (see ante, para 26.15). The rights of the disappointed 'consumer buyer' will be substantially increased by an EU Directive (see ante, para 14.01) 'for any lack of conformity which exists at the time the goods were delivered' (Art 3(1)). Unless the lack of conformity is minor (Art 3(6)), a 'consumer buyer' shall, in addition to his national remedies (Art 8):

> ... be entitled to have the goods brought into conformity free of charge[7] by repair or replacement, in accordance with paragraph 3, or to have an appropriate reduction made in the price or the contract rescinded with regard to those goods ...

Article 3 then establishes an order of preference for the minimum (Art 7) remedies of the consumer buyer within a two year limitation period (Art 5; and see generally ante, paras 14.05; 26.17) as follows (Art 3(2)):

First, by replacement or cure/repair. According to Art 3(3):

---

2 OFT, *Bulletin No 12*, case 19; *No 13*, case 13: Grey Term 1(b): see ante, para 11.16.

3 It is void under s 6 of UCTA (see ante, para 18.19) and an offence under the Restrictions on Statements Order (see ante, para 4.22).

4 Distinguish cure in the absence of breach by the supplier: see ante, para 17.09.

5 *BMBF (No 12) Ltd v Harland and Woolf Shipbuilding etc Ltd* [2001] 2 All ER (Comm) 385, CA. It has been suggested that, in the case of supplies of new motor vehicles the supplier may have a right to cure by reason of an implied term by trade usage: see ante, para 15.11.

6 Eg, 'if you do not repair the goods to my satisfaction, I will rescind the contract'. On the other hand, it has been held that rejection must be firm and not hedged around with qualifications: *Benjamin's Sale of Goods* (5th edn), para 14-013.

7 The term 'free of charge' 'refers to the necessary costs incurred to bring the goods into conformity, particularly the cost of postage, labour and materials': Art 3(4).

In the first place, the consumer may require the seller to repair[8] the goods or he may require the seller to replace them, in either case free of charge, unless this is impossible or disproportionate.

This provision introduces an objective definition of disproportionate;[9] and it restricts the time for repair or replacement to a reasonable time and without significant inconvenience.[10]

Second, to a price reduction or rescission. The consumer buyer is to have these rights where (i) he is not entitled to replacement or cure, or (ii) the seller has not completed the above remedy within a reasonable time, or (iii) without excessive inconvenience to the consumer (Art 3(5)). The following points should be noted: the burden of proof is reversed for the first six months after delivery;[11] but it may be that the consumer must exercise any such rights in good faith;[12] and the alternative is not restricted to damages for actual loss caused (see ante, para 27.29), but is for 'an appropriate reduction of the price'.

[29.04] Rescission *de futuro*. Even without any repudiation by the seller or especially enhanced rights in the buyer, under the scheme adopted by the SGA 1893 many of the seller's duties were conditions (see Chapters 11–16). In such cases, even minor infringements of those conditions would *prima facie* give the buyer the right to reject the goods (see ante, para 29.03), rescind the contract *de futuro*, even if the property had already passed to him,[1] and reclaim the price if already paid.[2] To counterbalance this very wide right of rescission, the draftsman of the SGA 1893 provided that the buyer could not exercise it unless he acted quickly (s 11(1)(c)). However, the last limitation has subsequently been whittled down by statute and new s 11(4) of the SGA lays down that (s 11(4) of the SGA 1979 was amended by s 3(2) of the SSGA 1994):

> Subject to section 35A below, where a contract of sale is not severable and the buyer has accepted the goods or part of them, the breach of a condition to be fulfilled by the seller can only be treated as a breach of warranty, and not as a ground for rejecting the goods and treating the contract as repudiated, unless there is an express or implied term of the contract to that effect.

---

8   'Repair: shall mean, in the event of lack of conformity, bringing consumer goods into conformity with the contract': Art 1(2)(f).

9   It is disproportionate if the cost is unreasonable as compared with the value of the goods in contract state, the significance of lack of conformity and whether an alternative remedy would cause significant inconvenience to the consumer: Art 3(3).

10 'Any repair or replacement shall be completed within a reasonable time and without significant inconvenience to the consumer, taking into account the nature of the goods and the purpose for which the consumer required the goods': Art 3(3).

11 Article 5(3). Clothing retailers fear that consumers will use this to wear new goods and then return them, claiming a fault: DTI, Impact Assessment (4.1.2001), Annex D, para 2; Annex E, para 3.

12 DTI, Impact Assessment (4.1.2001), Annex E, para 3. For good faith, see ante, para 11.15. Would this make any practical difference?

[29.04]

1   *McDougall v Aeromarine of Emsworth Ltd* [1958] 3 All ER 431. As to rescission, see ante, para 26.15; and as to revesting of property, see post, para 29.06.

2   As on total failure of consideration: see post, para 29.12. Alternatively, he may accept a credit note: as to which, see ante, paras 23.14; 29.03A. As to the failure of credit traders to make refunds, see ante, para 6.19; and as to refunds by credit or charge card, see ante, para 7.09.

New s 11(4) seems confined to those cases where (a) the contract is not severable[3] and (b) there is a breach of condition by the seller.[4] Even in those cases in which it is applicable, s 11(4) does not say that if a buyer can and does reject he must rescind the contract,[5] but merely imposes a *prima facie* restriction on his right to reject and rescind.[6] However, this does insert an important rigidity into the law, namely that the buyer's right to reject is lost by his acceptance of the goods.[7] True, the rule can be ousted expressly,[8] or impliedly, eg, by a contrary trade custom (see ante, para 15.11) and is varied in respect of severable contracts (see ante, para 23.24) and part acceptance.[9] Further, the scope of s 11(4) was subsequently reduced by the provision that s 11(4) shall not apply to a conditional sale agreement[10] where the buyer deals as consumer within Part I of UCTA (see ante, para 18.18): in such cases, the right to reject and rescind is the same as for hp.[11] The position of quasi-sales (see ante, para 2.10) in this respect remains unclear.[12]

[29.05] Acceptance. Under the scheme laid down in the SGA, after the buyer has acquired a right to reject the goods (see ante, para 29.03), he will *prima facie* have a right to rescind the contract *de futuro*. However, he will lose that right to rescind and be reduced to claiming damages where he has accepted the whole of the goods (see ante, para 29.04). Acceptance in this sense[1] is dealt with by new s 35 of the SGA, which deems the buyer to have accepted the goods in three situations,[2] though with special rules for cif contracts, sale or return transactions and breaches of the undertakings as to title or description (see respectively ante, paras 22.07; 20.24; 12.08; 13.04). Nowadays much hedged about with restrictions, the three situations of deemed acceptance by the buyer are these (new ss 35(1), (4)):

1   *He intimates his acceptance* (new s 35(1)(a)). As a buyer has a statutory right of inspection (s 34, SGA: see ante, para 23.10), even under the 1979 Act it followed that mere receipt of the goods by the buyer would not *per se* amount to an acceptance.[3]

---

3   For a curious drafting argument, see Atiyah, *Sale of Goods* (10th edn), p 524. Why is that argument necessary?

4   As to whether s 11(4) is applicable to the implied condition as to title, see ante, para 12.06A. As to s 35A, see post, para 29.09.

5   This would deprive him of any right to specific performance. But see *per* Devlin J in *Kwei Tek Chao v British Traders and Shippers Ltd* (set out post, para 29.30), at 480.

6   See *per* Salter J in *William Barker & Co Ltd v Agius Ltd* (1927) 33 Comm Cas 120, at 130.

7   As to which, see post, para 29.05. However, the earlier version of the rule (to be found in s 11(1)(c) of the SGA 1893) was significantly wider in effect: see ante, para 20.08.

8   Eg, *WE Marshall v Lewis and Peat Ltd* [1963] 1 Lloyd's Rep 562 (reducing buyer's rights); retailer's guarantee 'money back if not entirely satisfied'.

9   See post, para 29.08. Suppose the desired goods are supplied along with a 'free gift' (as to which see ante, para 2.08) and one of the items is defective. Is it possible to keep one and reject the other?

10   Conditional sales are defined by s 15(1) of SOGIT in a manner virtually identical to that in the CCA, except for the latter's reference to 'land': see ante, para 1.16. However, the present rule applies whether or not a conditional sale is regulated.

11   SOGIT, ss 14(1), (2), 15(3) as amended by the CCA, Sched 3. As to the effect, see post, para 29.10.

12   See Palmer (1983) 46 MLR at 622–23.

[29.05]

1   'Acceptance' seems to be used in different senses in ss 27, 35, 50(3): Goode, *Commercial Law* (2nd edn), p 367.

2   Does new s 35 apply where the seller is fraudulent?

3   *Libau Wood Co v H Smith & Sons Ltd* (1930) 37 Lloyd's Rep 296.

What was required before acceptance would bar the right to reject[4] was an intimation by the buyer to the seller that he had elected to accept the goods delivered as conforming with the contract.[5] Now, the buyer's signature on an acceptance note (see ante, para 23.10) might have done so and the Law Commission recommended that this was wrong for both consumer and non-consumer buyers.[6] In the event, Parliament only accepted part of the argument laying down in new s 35(2) as follows:

> Where goods are delivered to the buyer, and he has not previously examined them, he is not deemed to have accepted them under sub-section (1) above until he has had a reasonable opportunity of examining them for the purpose –
>
> (a) of ascertaining whether they are in conformity with the contract, and
>
> (b) in the case of a contract for sale by sample, of comparing the bulk with the sample.

Leaving aside sales by sample (see ante, para 15.08–09) and inconsistent acts (see post, para 29.06), it will be realised that new s 35(2) does not preclude an actual acceptance by the buyer before he has inspected the goods. Further, new s 35(3) just provides that, where the buyer 'deals as consumer',[7] he cannot lose his right to rely on the new s 35(2) above 'by agreement, waiver or otherwise'. Accordingly, in a consumer sale, the buyer's acceptance can no longer be inferred just because he allows the seller to effect a cure (new s 35(6)(a): set out post, para 29.06), or uses the goods for a reasonable time to try to overcome teething problems.[8] On the other hand, in a non-consumer sale actual acceptance before inspection remains possible, either by a term of the sale contract,[9] signature of an acceptance note, allowing a cure,[10] or otherwise.

2   *He does an inconsistent act.* (See post, para 29.06.)

3   *Lapse of a reasonable time.* (See post, para 29.07.)

[29.06] Inconsistent act. The position at common law would appear to have been that the buyer was deemed to have accepted the goods if he did any act which clearly showed an intention to affirm.[1] The SGA 1893 amended this in a rule now to be found reproduced verbatim in new s 35(1)(b), namely that the buyer is deemed to have accepted the goods:

> ... when the goods have been delivered to him and he does any act in relation to them which is inconsistent with the ownership of the seller.

---

4   It may be that much more is required before the buyer's acceptance will also act as a waiver of even his claim to damages (see ante, para 26.24): Atiyah, *Sale of Goods* (10th edn), p 514.

5   Eg, *Rosenthal & Sons Ltd v Esmail* [1965] 2 All ER 860, HL; *Long v Lloyd* (set out ante, para 26.13); the *Kwei Tek Chao* case (set out post, para 29.30); *Lee v York Coach and Marine* [1977] RTR 35, CA.

6   *Sale and Supply of Goods* (1987, Law Com No 160), paras 2.45; 5.20–24.

7   'Reference in this Act to dealing as consumer are to be construed in accordance with Part I of UCTA; and, for the purposes of this Act, it is for a seller claiming that a buyer does not deal as consumer to show that he does not': SGA, new s 61(5A) (inserted by SSGA 1994, Sched 2, para 5(9)(c)). For 'dealing as consumer' in UCTA, see ante, para 18.18.

8   See *Millicent v Hollick* [1956] CLY 7927, CA; and Whincup (1975) 38 MLR at 670–71. If the trial is prolonged beyond a reasonable time, that in itself is an act of acceptance: see post, para 29.07.

9   Such a clause may be subject to the UCTA reasonableness test (see ante, para 18.20) by reason of UCTA, ss 3, 6.

10 See *Jackson v Chrysler Acceptances Ltd* [1978] RTR 474, CA; *Leaves v Wadham Stringer (Clifton) Ltd* [1980] RTR 308. What if the same defect reappears? What if another defect appears after acceptance? What if the supply contract contains a post-delivery maintenance provision?

[29.06]

1   It has been argued that the common law rule is preserved by the SGA, s 62(2), so saving other grounds of acceptance: Goode, *Commercial Law* (2nd edn), p 380.

This statutory formula has given rise to a number of difficulties:

(a) What is the interest of the seller with which the buyer must act inconsistently? Clearly, this cannot mean simply the general property in the goods, because this will normally pass at latest at the moment of delivery,[2] so it may be that s 35 should be interpreted to read any act 'inconsistent with the **retention in or reversion of ownership to** the seller'.[3]

(b) What is the relationship of this rule with the buyer's right of examination (see ante, para 23.10)? Parliament first attempted to settle that the s 35 rule was subject to s 34 in 1967; but the matter has now been put somewhat more clearly in new s 35(2) (set out ante, para 29.05). The formula 'reasonable opportunity' ties in with the reasonable time rule (see post, para 29.07).

(c) What acts by the buyer will be inconsistent with the rights of the seller? In the commercial context, the commonest example of an inconsistent act is a sub-sale by the buyer.[4] Whilst a buyer should obviously lose the right to reject where his sub-buyer accepts and refuses to return the goods,[5] difficulty arose where the sub-buyer rejected the goods. The pre-1893 cases went no further than to say that a sub-sale by the buyer after he had an opportunity of inspecting the goods showed an intention to accept. Unfortunately, the Court of Appeal in *E Hardy & Co v Hillerns and Fowler*[6] took the view that any sub-sale must necessarily be inconsistent with the ownership of the seller; and the logical outcome of this was that a buyer who 'sub-sold' the goods before he purchased, or before the goods were delivered to him, or who ordered delivery direct to his sub-buyer, never had a right to inspect and reject.[7] After trying in 1967 to deal with the point indirectly simply by declaring s 34 to be paramount (see above), Parliament has now dealt with the issue directly in new s 35(6), which provides as follows:

> The buyer is not by virtue of this section deemed to have accepted the goods merely because –
>
> (a) he asks for, or agrees to, their repair by or under an arrangement with the seller, or
>
> (b) the goods are delivered to another under a sub-sale or other disposition.

So, the effect of a sub-sale would appear to depend on whether the buyer has a reasonable opportunity of inspection at the place of delivery (see ante, para 23.04): where he does not, then after rejection by the sub-buyer he may himself in turn reject,[8] eg, a finance company engaged in direct financing, whereas, if the buyer does have a reasonable chance of examination, he will lose his right to reject by dispatching the goods to his sub-buyer,[9] unless perhaps the defect is latent.[9a]

---

2   See the definition of the property in goods in SGA, s 61(1): ante, para 19.08; and the rules for the passing of property: ante, Chapter 20.

3   The *Kwei Tek Chao* case (set out post, para 29.30). See *Benjamin's Sale of Goods* (5th edn), para 12-046.

4   For analysis of the cases to find a rationale for the rule, see Benjamin, *ibid*, para 12-047 *et seq*.

5   Atiyah and Treitel (1967) 39 MLR 369, 386; and see post, para 29.13.

6   [1923] 2 KB 490; [1923] 3 All ER Rep 275, CA. It has been said that a transfer of cif documents is not such an act: *per* Devlin J in the *Kwei Tek Chao* case (set out post, para 29.30) at 488. Cf *Barrow Lane & Ballard Ltd v Phillip Phillips Ltd* (set out ante, para 22.12).

7   *E and S Ruben Ltd v Faire Brothers & Co Ltd* [1949] 1 KB 254. But see *Rowland v Divall* (set out ante, para 12.05).

8   Section 35(6)(b). Cf *Molling v Dean* (1901) 18 TLR 215, DC; see Atiyah, *Sale of Goods* (10th edn), p 517.

9   Section 35(2). Cf *Perkins v Bell* [1893] 1 QB 193, CA (common law: criticised by Atiyah, *ibid*, p 517).

9a   *Truk (UK) Ltd v Tokmakidis* (set out post, para 29.07), at 604j.

In relation to consumer sales, there was little direct authority as to what may be an act by the consumer buyer inconsistent with the rights of the (usually retail) seller.[10] However, it would now seem that the inconsistent act rule does not apply simply because the buyer makes a gift of his purchase (s 35(6)(b) 'other disposition') or has it repaired (see ante, para 29.06); and the (retail) seller can in turn reject the goods back to his supplier.[11] As to whether a third party could himself reject the goods back to the retailer, see ante, para 17.07.

[29.07] Lapse of time. The mere fact that the goods remain in the buyer's possession cannot without more amount to an acceptance, because s 36 of the SGA provides that he is under no duty to return the goods (see ante, para 23.09). However, assuming that the buyer has not rejected the goods, s 35 of the SGA 1893 deemed the buyer to have accepted the goods if he retained them beyond a reasonable time. The Law Commission carefully considered, but opposed, the suggestion that greater certainty should be introduced by spelling out a more precise time limit;[1] and, following their recommendation, the reasonable time rule remains,[2] what amounts to a reasonable time being a question of fact.[3] Thus, these proposals have been adopted in new s 35(4) in the following terms:[4]

> The buyer is also deemed to have accepted the goods when after the lapse of a reasonable time he retains the goods without intimating to the seller that he has rejected them.

Certainly, the seller may extend the period of a reasonable time, either by a contractual term[5] or by conduct, eg, by disregarding the time taken to negotiate a settlement,[6] or effect a cure.[7] However, the basic time limit may be quite short, presenting a particular dilemma to consumers, the classic case being the expensive consumer durable in which a number of small defects appear over a period of time (see ante, paras 14.23–24).

The running of time. On a related matter, however, Parliament did alter the law in 1994. In drafting the SGA 1893, Chalmers took the view that the reasonable time rule would not unduly circumscribe the buyer of defective goods because the loss of right to reject (s 35) would not take place until the buyer had under s 34 (set out ante, para 23.10) had a reasonable time to inspect the goods.[8] Unfortunately, in *Hardy v Hillerns and Fowler* (set

---

10 See *Sabir v Tiny Computers* [1999] CLY 840, Cty Ct (buyer installing upgraded software). See generally Atiyah, *op cit*, note 8, pp 520–21; Benjamin, *op cit*, note 3, para 12-051; *Sale and Supply of Goods* (1987, Law Com No 160), para 2.47.

11 Section 35(6)(b): Law Commission, *Sale and Supply of Goods* (above), para 5.38. Is this (possibly delayed) sub-buyer's rejection to be taken into account when deciding whether the retailer has rejected within a reasonable time (see post, para 29.07)?

[29.07]

1 *Sale and Supply of Goods* (1987, Law Com No 160), paras 5.14–19.

2 For consideration of this rule, see eg, the *Kwei Tek Chao* case (set out post, para 29.30; 20 week delay); *Lee v York Coach & Marine* [1977] RTR 35, CA (six months delay); Mullan (1988) 138 NLJ 280, 299; Thomas (1989) 139 NLJ 1188; and the cases cited by the Law Commission, *ibid*, para 2.48.

3 SGA 1979, s 59. This was to overcome previous uncertainty as to whether the matter was one of fact or law; and see the cases gathered by *Benjamin's Sale of Goods* (5th edn), para 12-054 *et seq*. Distinguish acceptance of offer, where lapse of time does not *prima facie* amount to acceptance: see ante, para 10.02.

4 New s 35(4) was imported into the SGA 1979 by s 2 of the SSGA 1994.

5 As by auctioneer's conditions of sale allowing a finite period of rescission in respect of 'deliberate forgery': Harvey and Meisel, *Auctions* (2nd edn), p 164. In a consumer supply, this may be an unfair term: OFT, Bulletin No 14, case 9: see generally ante, para 11.12 *et seq*.

6 *Manifatture Tossik Laniera Wooltex v JB Ashley Ltd* [1979] 2 Lloyd's Rep 28, CA, discussed 43 MLR 463.

7 New s 35(6)(a): set out ante, para 29.06. See the Law Com, *op cit*, note 1, para 5.31.

8 Cranston and Dehn [1990] JBL 346.

out post, para 29.08), the Court of Appeal held that s 35 was not so subject to s 34; and the effect of this on consumers was spelt out in *Bernstein v Pamson Motors Ltd*:[9]

> B bought a new Nissan car from S for just under £8,000. After three weeks, when the car had done 140 miles, it broke down. The cause was a piece of sealant which had entered the lubrication system during manufacture. During B's use, it cut off the oil supply and made the engine seize up. Whilst this rendered the car unmerchantable (see ante, para 14.22), it was held that B had by that use lost the right to rescind and was confined to a claim for damages (see post, paras 29.32; 29.35; 29.37).

Rougier J explained that the reasonable time in s 35 was related, not to B's opportunity to discover any particular defect, as would appear to be the rule in hp (see post, para 29.10); but it was 'solely to what is a reasonable practicable interval ... [between B] ... receiving the goods and his ability to send them back' (at 230g). However, the decision is reversed by the new s 35(5), which provides as follows:

> The questions that are material in determining for the purposes of sub-s (4) above whether a reasonable time has elapsed include whether they buyer has had a reasonable opportunity of examining the goods for the purpose mentioned in sub-s (2) above.

The two statutory purposes of examining the goods contained in new s 35(2) have already been set out (see ante, para 29.05); and in *Truk (UK) Ltd v Tokmakidis GmbH*[9a] it was suggested that a reasonable time may now be significantly longer:

> S agreed to supply and fit lifting gear to the chassis of B's recovery vehicle, S guaranteeing that the equipment would be installed in accordance with the recommendation of the chassis manufacturer and B promising to pay the price upon the earlier of resale or the expiry of six months. Almost on the expiry date, a potential buyer pointed out to B that the vehicle did not meet the manufacturer's recommendation.

The judge held that the supply of the lifting gear was a sale of goods, rather than a supply of services (see ante, para 2.05); that s 35(4) requires B to reject within a reasonable time (see above); that this involves a balancing of the opposing interests of B and S (at 603e–f) and cannot be less than the reasonable opportunity to examine (s 35(5)), though it may be more (s 35(6): see ante, para 29.06); that however many defects, there is only one reasonable time for the acceptance rule (at 603g–h); and that that time had not expired when B rejected the lifting gear (at 606f).

So, if it takes a consumer-buyer a number of days or weeks to test out the various cycles of his new washing-machine, he should still be able to reject if the last one he tests proves defective.[10] Further examples might be a lawnmower or skis bought at an end of season sale. On the other hand, new s 35(5) would not seem to preserve his right to reject where the delivered goods remain untested beyond a reasonable time,[11] eg, where a consumer cannot test the goods within the usual reasonable time, as where he is going on holiday or into hospital. To meet such problems, the EU Directive introduces a two year

---

9   [1987] 2 All ER 220; [1987] RTR 384 (discussed 104 LQR 16; [1988] JBL 56). An appeal on the basis that the right to reject had not been lost was settled when the manufacturer agreed to compensate B in full: (1987) 137 NLJ 962.

9a [2000] 2 All ER (Comm) 594.

10 See the Law Commision, *op cit*, note 1, para 5.16.

11 Cf *Leaf v International Galleries* (set out post, para 29.11). What if the retail-buyer keeps the goods for some time unopened, eg, where intended for a gift? In Parliament, it was suggested that this period of non-use would be ignored as irrelevant (Standing Committee C, March 1994, col 37). *Sed quaere?*

limit as from delivery (Art 5(1)), provided the buyer informs the seller of the lack of conformity within two months from the date on which he detected this lack of conformity.[12]

[29.08] Part acceptance. Whilst not absolutely clear, it would appear that the effect of s 11(4) of the SGA 1979 was to extend the acceptance rule (see ante, para 29.05) to partial acceptances.[1] Thus in *Hardy & Co v Hillerns & Fowler*:[2]

> There was a contract for sale of 2,365 tons of wheat cif Hull. When the wheat arrived at Hull, the buyer immediately resold part of the cargo, and dispatched it to sub-buyers. Subsequently, the buyer ascertained that none of the wheat complied with the contract description and sought to reject it all. Despite the fact that the buyer examined the wheat as soon as he reasonably could, the Court of Appeal unanimously held that:
>
> (1) by reselling part of the goods the buyer had accepted that part under s 35,[3] and
>
> (2) by accepting part the buyer had lost his right to reject any of the wheat, and must be content with damages.

However, the effect of this rule depends on the indivisibility of the contract (see ante, para 23.24):

(1) Where there is in fact not one, but a series of contracts between the parties, each of that series is to be considered as a separate contract for the purposes of the acceptance rule. It follows that acceptance of goods under one of those contracts[4] does not bar rejection of goods due under other contracts in the series, eg, suppose a consumer on the same occasion makes a number of unconnected purchases in different parts of a department store. The position is the same where there is a single severable contract.[5]

(2) Where there is a single entire contract, different considerations generally apply (see post, para 28.09), except in the following case.

A commercial unit. The Law Commission recommended that there should be introduced into English law the notion of a 'commercial unit' of goods, with the idea that it should not be possible for a buyer to accept some of the goods within such a unit whilst rejecting others,[6] eg, one shoe out of a pair. This recommendation was enacted by Parliament by means of new s 35(7):[7]

> Where the contract is for the sale of goods making one or more commercial units, a buyer accepting any goods included in a unit is deemed to have accepted all the goods making the unit; and in this sub-section 'commercial unit' means a unit division of which would materially impair the value of the goods or the character of the unit.

---

12 Article 5(2). As to the Directive and limitation periods, see generally ante, paras 14.01 and 26.17 respectively.

[29.08]

1 See Atiyah, *Sale of Goods* (10th edn), p 524. *De minimis* partial acceptances are presumably ignored, eg, the instruction book delivered in advance of a new car.

2 [1923] 2 KB 490; [1923] All ER Rep 275, CA.

3 SGA, s 11(4): set out ante, para 29.04. But see the alteration in the law made for part acceptances: see post, para 29.09.

4 The courts seem reluctant to treat transactions as a series of contracts in the ordinary commercial context; and generally ante, paras 23.24–25.

5 *Jackson v Rotax Motor and Cycle Co* (set out ante, para 14.05); and see new s 35A(2), post, para 29.09.

6 *Sale and Supply of Goods* (1987, Law Com 160), para 6.12, adopting a notion from the US Uniform Commercial Code, Arts 2-105(6); 2-601.

7 As inserted by s 2 of SSGA 1994.

According to the Law Commission, the effect of this should be as follows:[8]

(i) A buyer who accepted part only of a set, such as a single volume of an encyclopedia which is sold as a set, would normally be deemed to have accepted the whole set.

(ii) A buyer who accepted part only of a sack or other unit (whether measured by weight or in some other way) by which goods of the type in question are customarily sold in the trade would be deemed to have accepted the whole unit. The buyer would not be so restricted if it was merely the seller (and not the trade in general) who chose to sell the goods in that particular way.

(iii) A buyer who accepted one shoe of a pair would be deemed to have accepted the pair; but he would be entitled to accept one of a number of identical articles, even if more than one at a time was commonly bought, if each was in fact a self-contained unit.

[29.09] Partial rejection. Where, under a single entire contract (see ante, para 26.02), the buyer accepts one or more commercial units (see ante, para 29.08), the law has been changed. The Law Commission criticised the SGA 1979 because it did not normally[1] allow the buyer to reject any defective goods and keep the rest.[2] Instead, they recommended that there should be 'a general right of partial rejection in cases where some of the goods delivered to the buyer do not conform with the contract requirements' (para 6.9). This recommendation was adopted in the new s 35A of the SGA 1979 (as inserted by s 3(1) of the SGSA 1994). Subject to a contrary intention,[3] new s 35A(1) provides:

(1) If the buyer –

(a) has the right to reject the goods by reason of a breach on the part of the seller that affects some or all of them, but

(b) accepts some of the goods, including, where there are any goods unaffected by the breach, all such goods,

he does not by accepting them lose his right to reject the rest.

It will be observed that this new right of partial rejection only applies where the buyer has a right to reject all the goods under the ordinary rules,[4] so is subject to the inability to reject part of a single commercial unit (s 35(7): set out ante, para 29.08). Where applicable, new s 35A(1) gives the buyer the additional choice of accepting:

... some of the goods, including, where there are any goods unaffected by the breach, all such goods.

The new section makes it clear that the ordinary acceptance rule is subject to this new right of partial rejection;[5] that, in the case of an instalment contract, each instalment shall

---

8   *Op cit*, note 6, 6.13.

[29.09]

1   Such a right had only existed where the contract goods had been 'mixed with' goods of a different description under the now repealed s 30(4) SGA 1979: see ante, para 13.02.

2   *Sale and Supply of Goods* (1987, Law Com 160), para 6.6.

3   New s 35(4): so this rule may be ousted for both consumer and non-consumer sales.

4   New s 35A(1)(a). So this new right is not available to a non-consumer buyer after a slight breach of condition (new s 15A): see ante, para 29.03.

5   SSGA 1994, s 3(2). For the ordinary acceptance rule, see ante, para 29.04. What if the buyer accepts only part of the conforming goods?

be treated separately for the purposes of this new rule;[6] and that this new right of partial rejection is no longer confined to 'mixed goods', but applied wherever goods 'are not in conformity with the contract', which expression will extend to matters of both quality and quantity.[7] The expected effect of the 1994 changes were spelt out as follows:[8]

(a) If the buyer is a non-consumer and orders 100 objects, of which only one is defective (the breach being 'slight' or 'non-material'), he may not reject any but may claim damages.[9] If the buyer were a consumer, he could keep them all, reject them all, or keep the 99 and reject the defective one (and in all cases claim damages).

(b) If they buyer orders 100 objects of which 50 are defective, he may reject 100,[10] keep 100, or keep the 50 conforming objects and reject any or all of the 50 defective objects[11] (and in all cases claim damages).

(c) If the buyer order 100 objects and all are defective, he may reject all or any of claim damages.

(d) If the 100 objects in the previous examples comprised an instalment of a larger order, the result would be exactly the same as regards that instalment; the partial rejection rules do not affect any rights the buyer may have as regards other instalments.

Rescission by the hirer

[29.10] It is possible that a hirer under a simple hiring or hp agreement has a duty to accept delivery which is similar to that of a buyer (see ante, para 27.27), counterbalanced by similar *prima facie* rights to reject and rescind where the owner is in breach.[1] However, the following matters need to be taken into consideration:

1   *Slight breaches of condition.* Following the recommendation of the Law Commission[2] that the rule should be the same as for sale (see ante, para 29.03), a business hirer has no right of rejection for slight breaches under either an hp agreement[3] or simple hiring.[4]

2   *Continuous breaches.* In *Yeoman Credit Ltd v Apps* (set out post, para 29.25) the hirer under an hp agreement paid instalments and retained the defective car for a total of five months. Nevertheless, the Court of Appeal unanimously agreed that the hirer was entitled to reject for breach of condition at the end of that five months. Holroyd Pearce LJ explained:[5]

---

6   New s 35A(2). See generally ante, paras 23.24–25.
7   For defects of quality, see ss 13–15 (see ante, Chapters 13, 14, 15); and for defects of quantity, see s 30 (see ante, paras 13.03–06).
8   Law Commission, *op cit*, note 2, para 6.16.
9   Cf *Re Moore Ltd* [1921] 2 KB 519, CA.
10 Cf *Hardy v Hillerns & Fowler* (set out ante, para 29.08).
11 Cf *Barker v Agius* (1927) 33 Com Cas 120.
[29.10]
1   Eg, *Ditchburn Equipment Co Ltd v Crich* (1966) 110 Sol Jo 266, CA (simple hiring).
2   *Sale and Supply of Goods* (1984, Law Com 160), para 4.21.
3   New s 11A of SOGIT 1973, as inserted by SSGA 1994, Sched 2, para 4(6).
4   New s 10A of SGSA 1982, as inserted by SSGA 1994, Sched 2, para 6(9).
5   At 552. As a conditional buyer is in possession of the goods as bailee (see ante, para 1.14), why should he too not have the benefit of the doctrine of continuous breach?

Had this been a sale of goods on instalment payments, he could not, of course, have done so after payment of instalments and acceptance of goods. Had this been a simple hiring ... he would have been entitled to reject [the goods] and end the hiring, since the owner's breach was a continuing one. The owner's conduct would constitute a continuing repudiation. This hire purchase agreement was, at the material time, more analogous to a simple hiring than to a purchase.

The oddity of the doctrine of continuous breach becomes apparent when the measure of damages is considered (see post, paras 29.25; 29.34). The doctrine was subsequently rejected for simple hiring in *UCB Leasing Ltd v Holtom*:[6]

Under a directly financed transaction, UCB leased a new Alfa Romeo car to H for 37 months. The car was found to have electrical faults rendering it unfit for the purpose supplied. After four months, H stopped paying rentals. The car was returned to UCB after seven months, when it had done nearly 8,000 miles. Held that UCB rather than H had rescinded after seven months (see below); and, in diminution of UCB's claim for rentals (see post, para 29.26), H was awarded damages as assessed in *Tolly's* case (see post, para 29.34).

In refusing H's claim that he was entitled to rescind after seven months,[7] the Court of Appeal expressly dismissed the above reasoning of Holroyd Pearce LJ as *obiter*. Has the *Apps* rule of continuous breaches survived for periodic hirings? If not, to what extent does s 35 of the SGA apply by analogy to limit rescission of bailment?

3   *Acceptance.* In the case of most sales, but not some conditional sales, any right to rescind is lost by acceptance of the goods (s 11(4) of the SGA: set out ante, para 29.04). It has been said that this acceptance rule has no place in hp,[8] where the hirer instead 'loses his right to termination only when he becomes aware of the defect in the goods and then affirms the contract, or waives his right to terminate or is estopped from relying on his right to terminate'.[9]

4   *Lapse of time.* This has caused problems in relation to defective motor vehicles obtained by consumers on hp, there being no doubt that the right to reject lapses on expiry of a reasonable time.[10] Frequently, there is a long history of attempts by the hirer to get his supplier to repair the goods before he finally rejects them. Sometimes the courts have ignored these periods of time on the grounds of the doctrine of continuous breach (see above) or whilst repairs were attempted or negotiations conducted.[11] However, unlike in sale (see ante, para 29.07), the period itself seems to be measured by the opportunity to discover the defect.[12]

---

6   [1987] RTR 362, CA.

7   At 371, 375. The court adopted the argument by Goode, *HP Law and Practice* (2nd edn), pp 456–58.

8   Law Commission, *op cit*, note 2, para 5.43. The remark actually extends to 'other contracts for the supply of goods'. Presumably, this means simple hirings. What about quasi-sales (see ante, para 29.04)?

9   *Op cit*, note 2. As to whether SGA s 11(4) might apply by analogy, see Palmer (1983) 46 MLR at 626–27.

10 *Jackson v Chrysler Acceptances Ltd* [1978] RTR 474, CA.

11 *Farnworth Finance Facilities Ltd v Attryde* [1970] 2 All ER 774, CA (repairs); *Porter v General Guarantee Corp Ltd* [1982] RTR 384 (negotiations).

12 *Laurelgates v Lombard North Central* (1983) 133 NLJ 720; and see generally Mullan [1990] JBL 231. It has been recommended by the Law Commission that this position be allowed to continue: *op cit*, note 2, para 5.46.

Rescission for misrepresentation

[29.11] The principles upon which a supply contract may be rescinded on the grounds that it was induced by misrepresentation have already been outlined (see ante, paras 26.12–13). The effect of that misrepresentation subsequently becoming a term of the contract must now be considered. That incorporation will no longer *per se* bar the right to rescind for misrepresentation.[1] But will that right be lost where there is no right to rescind for breach of contract? The problem may arise (1) where there was never any right to rescind for the breach (see ante, para 26.14), or (2) the right to rescind for breach has been lost by acceptance (see ante, paras 29.05; 29.10). In *Leaf v International Galleries Ltd*:[2]

> There was a misrepresentation that the painting sold was by Constable, and this became a term of the contract. Five years later the buyer discovered the truth, and immediately sought to rescind for misrepresentation. The Court of Appeal held that, even if there had been a right to rescind, it was barred by lapse of time.

Denning LJ assumed in the buyer's favour that the statement was a condition, pointed out that the right to reject for breach of condition had been lost by lapse of time (see ante, para 29.07) and continued (at 90):

> An innocent misrepresentation is much less potent than a breach of condition; and a claim to rescission for innocent misrepresentation must at any rate be barred when the right to reject for breach of condition is barred.

His Lordship was careful to confine his remarks to innocent misrepresentations which became conditions of that contract;[3] but in *Long v Lloyd* (set out ante, para 26.13) they were applied by the Court of Appeal to acts by the buyer which would have amounted to acceptance after breach,[4] although no breach of condition was alleged.[5] Even granted this, certain problems arise. First, does the rule apply to fraudulent misrepresentations[6] or to innominate terms? Second, does it follow that at common law, if the misrepresentation become a warranty, the right to rescind for misrepresentation is lost?[7] Third, does the rule apply to quasi-sale, hp and simple hiring transactions?

RESTITUTION[a]

[29.12] Suppose one party (A) has performed his side of a 'contract' with B, so conferring a benefit B, but has not received the consideration for which he bargained. In the

---

[29.11]
1 Section 1(a) of the Misrepresentation Act 1967: set out ante, para 26.14.
2 [1950] 2 KB 86; [1950] 1 All ER 693, CA. See also *Miljus v Yamazaki Machinery UK Ltd* [1997] CLY 992, OR.
3 The other members of the CA do not appear to have gone any further than to say that it was too late to rescind for misrepresentation. See further Treitel, *Law of Contract* (10th edn), p 356.
4 As to what would have amounted to acceptance by the buyer after breach, see generally ante, para 29.05.
5 Grunfeld (1958) 21 MLR 550, 555.
6 Treitel, *op cit*, note 3, p 357.
7 If so, s 1 of the Misrepresentation Act 1967 appears to grant the representee a new right of rescission: see ante, para 26.14. But see Treitel, *op cit*, note 3, p 348.
[29.12]
a See generally Tettenborn, *Law of Restitution* (3rd edn).

following circumstances, A may be able to seek restitution from B by an action in debt,[1] depending on the nature of that benefit conferred:[2]

1 *Benefit in money*. In our context, this situation will typically arise where A is a buyer or hirer who has paid the price or rent. Where A has obtained no part of that for which he bargained, he may be able to recover any money paid on grounds of total failure of consideration.[3] In relation to such claims by a buyer[4] or hirer of goods, two questions arise: (1) as to the relationship of this remedy to rescission (see post, para 29.13); and (2) as to what amounts to a total failure of consideration (see post, para 29.15).

2 *Benefit in kind*. In a contract for the supply of goods, such a situation may arise where the supplier (A) has supplied goods for which he cannot recover the agreed price or rent (see ante, para 27.16 *et seq*), but is instead suing for what the service is worth (*quantum meruit*: see ante, para 27.15A).

[29.13/14] Relationship to rescission. Clearly, such a claim in debt by a buyer or hirer to recover sums paid will lie for total failure of consideration (see post, para 29.15) where the parties never reached agreement;[1] or where their agreement was rendered void *ab initio* on grounds of mistake or misrepresentation;[2] or sometimes where one party is a minor (see ante, para 10.19). But what if the contract was valid when made but was subsequently terminated before it was fully executed? In the *Fibrosa* case,[3] the House of Lords said that the test was not whether there had ever been a contract, but whether it had ever been performed: it followed that no such claim lay where a contract was illegal (see ante, para 10.20); but it was available in the event of frustration,[4] or abandonment,[5] or rescission for breach,[6] whether or not the goods have been delivered to him (see post, para 29.18). Indeed, in the *Kwei Tek Chao* case (set out post, para 29.30) Devlin J said that (at 475):

> If the goods have been properly rejected, and the price has already been paid in advance, the proper way of recovering the money back is by an action for money paid for a consideration which has wholly failed ... but that form of action is governed by exactly the same rules with regard to affirming or avoiding the transaction as in any other case.

It is, of course, logical that the innocent party must elect to rescind before he can recover the price paid on grounds of total failure of consideration; and that the quasi-contractual

---

1 For the distinction between actions in debt and for damages, see ante, para 27.15A.
2 This must be distinguished from the process of restitution on conviction: see ante, para 24.25.
3 See generally Treitel, *Law of Contract* (10th edn), p 977 *et seq*; *Chitty On Contract* (28th edn), para 30.048 *et seq*; Goff and Jones, *Law of Restitution* (5th edn), pp 523, 535.
4 The SGA preserves the common law in this respect: s 54.

[29.13/14]

1 Eg, *Branwhite v Worcester Finance Ltd* [1969] 1 AC 552, HL: see ante, para 16.05.
2 This would seem to follow from *Bell v Lever Brothers Ltd* [1932] AC 161, HL (not a goods case); and see Treitel, *Law of Contract* (10th edn), pp 985–88.
3 *Fibrosa Spolka Akcyjna v Fairbairn etc Ltd* [1943] AC 32; [1942] 2 All ER 122, HL.
4 The decision in the *Fibrosa* case (above); and see ante, para 22.17.
5 Similarly, where a wholly executory contract is rescinded by mutual agreement: see generally ante, para 26.18.
6 See ante, para 26.15. To secure his deposit against his seller's insolvency, a buyer should therefore insist on paying it into a joint trust account (see ante, para 19.23).

claim is not open to him if he affirms, or if he cannot rescind.[7] As such a view would entail making the availability of the quasi-contractual remedy dependent on the right to rescind,[8] it is difficulty to reconcile with the cases where the transferor has no title to the goods (see ante, para 12.06A): in *Rowland v Divall*[9] the plaintiff had resold the car to X, who had been in possession for two months;[10] and in *Butterworth v Kingsway Motors Ltd* (set out ante, para 12.06) Pearson J held that the intermediate buyers had lost the right to rescind, but that Butterworth was entitled to rescind notwithstanding his eleven months' use of the car.[11]

So far, we have been considering the right of the innocent buyer or hirer to recover the price paid on grounds of total failure of consideration. Suppose the buyer or hirer were the guilty party. Assuming that the supplier elects to rescind (see post, para 29.16), can the buyer or hirer recover any sums paid on grounds of total failure of consideration? In bailment, the hirer's possession may preclude any failure of consideration being total.[12] In sale, the early cases refused to countenance such a claim; but we have seen that Stable J subsequently drew a distinction between a deposit and a part payment, holding that the sum was recoverable in the latter case (see ante, paras 27.19–20).

[29.15] Total failure.[1] The courts have always stressed that money paid under a contract can only be recovered under this ground if the failure of consideration was total. The vital thing is not whether there was rendered to the payee any benefit, but whether there was rendered to him any part of that benefit which he was entitled to expect by way of performance of the contract.[2] Thus, a buyer to whom no title is passed suffers a total failure of consideration[3] as does a buyer of computer hardware to whom no software is delivered,[4] or a buyer who only uses goods long enough to discover that they are defective.[5] On the other hand, it has been held that a hirer under an hp agreement cannot so recover sums paid under the agreement where that agreement is subsequently determined but he has in the meantime enjoyed both possession of the goods under the

---

7 The *Kwei Tek Chao* case (set out post, para 29.30). This is accepted by most of the authorities as being the position: see Goff and Jones, *Law of Restitution* (5th edn), pp 47, 527.

8 The limitations on the right to rescind are considered ante, paras 26.13; 29.11.

9 Set out ante, para 12.05. But compare *Linz v Electric Wire Co Ltd* [1948] AC 371, PC.

10 It is arguable that the resale should not bar rescission because it was cancelled by mutual agreement: see also ante, para 29.06.

11 It is a little difficult to accept this in the light of other authorities, though the issue is essentially one of fact: see ante, para 29.07.

12 But the problem is not so avoided where the hirer wrongfully refuses ever to take possession but has already paid a first instalment of rent. *Aliter* a deposit (see ante, para 27.19).

[29.15]

1 See Treitel, *Law of Contract* (10th edn), p 976 *et seq*. The rule that failure of consideration must be total may be reconsidered: see *Chitty on Contract* (28th edn), para 30-057.

2 *Rover International Ltd v Cannon Film Sales Ltd [No 3]* [1989] 3 All ER 423, CA (not a sale case). See generally Samek (1959) 33 ALJ 392, 397; Chitty, *ibid*, para 30-053. In the case of frustration, this rule has been modified by the Law Reform (Frustrated Contracts) Act 1943: see ante, para 22.19. As to free gifts, see ante, para 2.08.

3 *Rowland v Divall* (set out ante, para 12.05).

4 *South West Water Services Ltd v International Computers Ltd* [2000] CLY 870.

5 *Baldry v Marshall Ltd* [1925] 1 QB 260, CA.

bailment[6] and a valid option to purchase.[7] On the other hand, he may do so where there has never been any agreement, notwithstanding his use of the goods for three months.[8]

However, the scope of the quasi-contractual remedy has been extended to several situations where the claimant has received part of the benefit for which he has bargained. First, where the contract is divisible (see ante, para 23.24), the courts have applied the doctrine to each part individually, so that there might be a total failure in respect of one or more parts notwithstanding that some other parts may have been performed.[9] Secondly, where under a single indivisible contract an obligation is entire (see ante, para 26.02), there is a total failure of consideration although that obligation has been partially performed because the other party has bargained exclusively for a complete performance.[10] Thirdly, the parties can always agree that the partial failure of the whole consideration is to be treated as a total failure of part of the consideration;[11] and, where the partial performance of the seller shows an intention to repudiate (see ante, para 23.25), the buyer will have an option to do so.[12] Fourthly, where a sum is paid in advance of delivery of the goods, it is recoverable if paid by way of part payment rather than a deposit (see ante, para 27.19). Fifthly, there is the matter of making restitution (see post, para 29.16).

[29.16] Making restitution. Even where the case cannot be brought within any of the above rules (see ante, para 29.15), the law does not say that the receipt of part of the benefit for which the buyer or hirer has bargained must be fatal to his quasi-contractual claim, eg, where defective goods are delivered.[1] As a first step, he must rescind the contract (see ante, para 29.14), which will usually involve rejecting the goods (see ante, para 29.03); but not, perhaps, where the goods are at the supplier's risk,[2] nor where the inability to return the goods is caused by the supplier's breach.[3] As it has been put, the claimant must make *restitutio* as a condition precedent to his claim.[4] On the other hand, making *restitutio* may not be sufficient, because the contract may require the supplier to do things other than transfer a returnable benefit, as where the contract involves the provision of services. In *Stocznia Gdanska SA v Latvian Shipping Co*:[5]

> There were six contracts, each to design, build and supply a ship. In each contract, 5% of the price was payable at the outset; 20% on notice that the keel was laid; 25% on notice of launch; and 50% on delivery. The property was not to pass until delivery; and each contract provided that, if the buyer (B) defaulted on any instalment, the shipbuilder (S) shall be entitled to rescind the contract. The first 5% was paid under each contract. B later

---

6   *Yeoman Credit Ltd v Apps* (set out post, para 29.25).
7   *Kelly v Lombard Banking Ltd* [1958] 3 All ER 713, CA.
8   *Branwhite v Worcester Finance Ltd* [1969] 1 AC 552, HL: see ante, para 16.05.
9   *Rugg v Minett* (set out ante, para 20.11). See also Chitty, *op cit*, note 1, para 29.040.
10   *Giles v Edwards* (1797) 7 Term Rep 181: explained by Goff and Jones, *Law of Restitution* (5th edn), p 523. *Contra* where the obligation broken is not an entire one.
11   See *Benjamin on Sale* (8th edn, 1950), p 419. See generally ante, para 26.18.
12   *Behrend & Co v Produce Brokers Ltd* (set out ante, para 13.04).

[29.16]
1   Eg, *Baldry v Marshall Ltd* [1925] 1 QB 260, CA.
2   See *Benjamin's Sale of Goods* (5th edn), para 12-057.
3   A possible explanation of *Rowland v Divall* (below; see ante, para 12.11).
4   *Towers v Barrett* (1786) 1 Term Rep 133.
5   [1998] 1 All ER 883, HL (for other litigation, see ante, para 7.26).

experienced cashflow problems. S gave notice that the first two keels had been laid, but the 20% payments were not made. S rescinded those contracts and sued for the two 20% payments as debts due before rescission. B claimed to recover all sums paid (the 5% deposits) and rebut S's claims for the two 20%s arguing that there had been a total failure of consideration.

The House of Lords held as follows:

(1) *In the law of contract.* The fact that the contract gave S an express right to rescind did not show that he had abandoned his common law right to instalments due before rescission (see ante, para 26.16). As to liquidated damages, see ante, para 27.24.

(2) *In the law of quasi-contract.* The contractual consideration required of S was to design, build and supply one ship under each contract. Whilst the contracts had been rescinded before the property in the ships had passed to B, nevertheless S had already designed and started to build the ships, so there had been no total failure of consideration (see ante, para 29.15). What mattered was not whether B had **received** any part of the contracted-for benefit, but whether S had **performed** any significant part of his duties.

However, this causes difficulty with regard to intermediate enjoyment of possession. It is easy to see that the enjoyment should be ignored where it was induced by the supplier's fraud, but the courts have also adopted this approach where the supplier is innocently in breach of the implied condition as to title.[6]

AN ACTION FOR DAMAGES

[29.17] A buyer or hirer may have at his disposal an action for damages against his supplier or some third party within the limitation period (see ante, para 26.17) as follows: (1) as against the supplier for breach of the supply contract (see post, para 29.18) or some collateral contract, or in tort, or under the Misrepresentation Act; and (2) as against a third party for breach of a collateral contract, or in tort.[1] Whilst the general principles for the measurement of damages have been previously outlined (see ante, para 27.28 *et seq*), two points may be made here concerning the measure of damages available to an innocent buyer induced to enter a contract by the misrepresentation of the seller: first, the *prima facie* measure of damages may be the difference between the contract price and value of the goods at the time any misrepresentation was discovered;[2] and second, the mitigation rule (see ante, paras 27.44–45) will not require the innocent buyer to bring into account any profit made on an uncontemplated sub-sale.[3]

[29.18] For breach of contract. In this section it is proposed to concentrate on the right of the buyer or hirer to damages for breach of the supply contract. The rules in this regard

---

6   *Rowland v Divall* (set out ante, para 12.05); *Butterworth v Kingsway Motors Ltd* (set out ante, para 12.06).
[29.17]
1   For collateral contracts, see ante, para 17.09; for tort actions, see post, para 29.24; and for the 1967 Act, see ante, para 17.10.
2   *Naughton v O'Callaghan* [1990] 3 All ER 191 (55 MLR at 699–701; Bridge, *Sale of Goods*, pp 593–94).
3   *Hussey v Eels* [1990] 2 QB 227, CA (not a goods case; [1990] CLJ 394).

will differ according to whether or not the breach amounts to a total failure to deliver the goods. *Prima facie*, the buyer or hirer will have a right of action for damages for non-delivery of the goods (see post, para 29.19 *et seq*) where no goods are delivered at all,[1] or where the goods tendered by the supplier are lawfully rejected and the contract rescinded on grounds that they do not conform with the contract in quantity or quality, or any other matter (see ante, para 29.03); and he will also be able to recover any part of the price paid on grounds of total failure of consideration.[2] However, whereas the supplier has an action in contract for price or rent (see ante, para 27.16 *et seq*), an action to recover the contract goods themselves is seldom available to the buyer or hirer;[3] and to this extent he may be deprived of his so called 'consumer surplus'.[4]

Damages for non-delivery

Sale

[29.19] The cause of action. The counterpart to the seller's action for damages for non-acceptance under s 50 of the SGA (see ante, paras 27.24–27) is the buyer's action for non-delivery under s 51. Section 51(1) provides:

> Where the seller wrongfully neglects or refuses to deliver the goods to the buyer, the buyer may maintain an action against the seller for damages for non-delivery.

This provision does not apply to a mere delay in tendering delivery, where damages will necessarily be assessed on different lines (see post, para 29.28); but it may be a nice question whether the delay is so great as to amount to a non-delivery.[1] Where there is a 'neglect or refusal to deliver' within the meaning of s 51(1), the SGA establishes a *prima facie* measure of damages in a manner similar to that used where the buyer is at fault in not taking delivery.[2] The law assumes that the buyer will mitigate his loss[3] if he can by going out into any available market and buying a substitute; so that, leaving aside the possibility of an express provision as to the amount payable by the defaulting seller,[4] the loss will *prima facie* be quantified by reference to whether there is at the place of delivery

---

[29.18]

1 For the duty to deliver, see ante, para 23.05 *et seq*.

2 *Comptoir D'Achat v Luis de Ridder* [1949] AC 293, HL: see generally ante, para 29.13.

3 Whether framed as an action for the specific performance of the contract or in tort: see post, paras 29.38; 29.24. But, if the supplier has wrongfully resold, could the buyer trace the proceeds of the second sale (see ante, para 27.14; cf *Lake v Bayliss* [1974] 2 All ER 1114)?

4 His subjective element of enjoyment: see Harris, Ogus and Phillips (1979) 95 LQR 581; Macdonald (1996) 15 Tr LR 239.

[29.19]

1 For this reason it is illogical to use the delivery date in the market rule: the buyer may not then know whether he is facing a late delivery or a non-delivery.

2 The first rule in *Hadley v Baxendale* is set out in s 51(2) and the second rule referred to in s 54. Cf ss 50(2): see ante, para 27.42. Cf post, para 29.26.

3 As to the mitigation rule, see ante, paras 27.44–45.

4 A liquidated damages clause (see ante, para 27.24), which may amount to an exclusion clause (see ante, Chapter 18) or offend the rule against penalties: see ante, para 27.25 *et seq*.

an available market (see ante, para 27.34) in which the buyer may purchase substitute goods.[5] There may additionally be consequential loss (see post, para 29.23).

[29.20] Where there is an available market. Section 51(3) of the SGA provides:

> Where there is an available market for the goods in question the measure of damages is *prima facie* to be ascertained by the difference between the contract price and the market or current price of the goods at the time or times when they ought to be delivered, or, if no time was fixed, then at the time of the refusal to deliver.

This 'duty' on the disappointed buyer to shop around is the converse of the position of an innocent seller faced with a buyer's breach (see s 50(3) of the SGA: ante, para 27.35); and it should be compared with the position as regards a late delivery (see post, para 29.28). The onus of proving the buying price in that market is on the buyer and the amount recoverable is as follows:

(1) If the market price is above the contract price, the buyer is *prima facie* entitled under s 51(3) to the difference between the two;[1] and any sub-sales by the buyer must be ignored, so that it is irrelevant that he has resold at an intermediate[2] or even a higher[3] price. If the buyer buys on the market at above the market price, he cannot recover that extra expenditure because he has not mitigated his loss;[4] but, if he buys at below the market price, he will only recover his actual loss.[5]

(2) If the market price is equal to or below the contract price, the intention of s 51(3) is presumably that the buyer will only receive nominal damages because he would suffer no loss by buying in the market. Unlike the predicament of the seller (see ante, para 27.35), this result will usually be fair and is therefore normally adopted by the courts.

Thus, the *prima facie* measure of damages for non-delivery is the amount by which the **market price** exceeds the **contract price** at the stipulated date[6] and place for delivery of the goods,[7] or of the documents of title in the case of a cif contract.[8] If the contract provides for delivery within a specified period, the last possible moment at which the seller is entitled to tender delivery is taken;[9] and, if delivery is to be by instalments (see

---

5   In practice, the courts have been fairly generous in deciding whether (a) the market is available and (b) what is a substitute: see generally Lawson (1969) 43 ALJ 52, 59–61. As to where there is no available market, see post, para 29.22.

[29.20]

1   *The Naxos* [1990] 3 All ER 641, HL.

2   *Williams Brothers v Agius Ltd* [1914] AC 510, HL.

3   *Williams v Reynolds* (1865) 6 B & S 495.

4   *Gainsford v Carroll* (1824) 2 B & C 624; and ante, para 27.44.

5   *Pagnan and Fratelli v Corbisa Industrial Agropacuaria Limitada* [1971] 1 All ER 165, CA (discussed by Atiyah, *Sale of Goods* (10th edn), p 492). *Contra* Goode, *Commercial Law* (2nd edn), pp 416–17.

6   *Toepfer v Cremer* [1975] 2 Lloyd's Rep 118, CA. This may be extended at the request of the seller (*Ogle v Earl of Vane* (1868) LR 3 QB 272, Ex Ch); or whilst there are negotiations for a settlement; or the seller reasonably considers his position (Atiyah, *ibid*, p 536).

7   *Melachrino v Nickoll and Knight* [1920] 1 KB 693; ABD (*Metal and Waste*) *Ltd v Anglo Chemical Co* [1955] 2 Lloyd's Rep 456. See further Goode, *op cit*, note 5, pp 393–96. If this is a foreign country, there will be a foreign currency element involved: see ante, para 27.29.

8   *Garnac Grain Co v HMF Faure and Fairclough Ltd* [1968] AC 1130, HL.

9   See *Leigh v Paterson* (1818) 8 Taunt 540.

ante, paras 23.24–25), the market price is fixed separately for each instalment at the time when it is due.[10] The provision that, if no time is fixed for delivery, the time of refusal to deliver is to be taken ought on principle to be relevant where delivery is to be made as required by the buyer;[11] but it is inapplicable where there is an anticipatory breach (see post, para 29.21). Finally, there is the question whether the buyer who has paid the price can be expected to go into the market and buy against the contract, which raises questions of remoteness and mitigation (see ante, paras 27.42; 27.44). If the buyer can be expected to buy a replacement, the above rules should apply; but otherwise, damages are presumably assessed on the basis that there is no market available to him.[12]

[29.21] Anticipatory breach. Where the supplier is in anticipatory breach (see ante, para 26.01), the foregoing *prima facie* rule for assessing damages for non-delivery is altered in the following respects: (1) the final limb of s 51(3) is ignored, the market price always being taken when the goods ought to be delivered;[1] and (2) the operation of s 51(3) is suspended until the buyer elects to accept the repudiation,[2] so possibly enabling the buyer to prolong the seller's duty to deliver more or less indefinitely.[3] The effect is illustrated by the *Tai Hing Cotton Mill* case:[4]

> There was a contract for the sale of 1500 bales of cotton, which was found to be for delivery as and when called for by B. S fell behind with deliveries and on 31 July 1973 repudiated the contract. B continued to press for delivery but eventually lost patience and issued a writ on 28 November 1973. The Privy Council held that B's election was not made until issue of the writ, until when B could have demanded delivery on reasonable notice; that reasonable notice was a month, so that delivery could have been demanded until 28 December 1973; and that the market price of the undelivered bales should be taken as at 28 December 1973.

When the buyer does elect to accept the repudiation, the position is as follows:[5] if the market is rising and the buyer elects to rescind, either immediately on repudiation or at a later time prior to the time of performance, he is then under a duty to mitigate his loss from the date of his election by purchasing substitute goods in the market at that date;[6] but, if the market is falling and buyer similarly elects to rescind either immediately or at an intermediate date, he is only entitled to the amount by which that price then exceeds the contract price as that is his actual loss.[7]

---

10 See *Brown v Muller* (1872) LR 7 Exch 319; *Roper v Johnson* (1873) LR 8 CP 167.
11 However, a tendency to ignore the last words of ss 50(3), 51(3) has been noted: Atiyah, *op cit*, note 5, pp 493–94.
12 But see *McGregor on Damages* (16th edn), para 831; Street, *Law of Damages*, pp 217–18.

[29.21]
1 *Millett v Van Heek & Co* [1921] 2 KB 369, CA; the *Tai Hing Cotton Mill* case (see below).
2 There is no duty to mitigate by buying in before the delivery date: *Brown v Muller* (1872) LR Exch 319, DC.
3 Atiyah, *Sale of Goods* (10th edn), p 535. The rules under the US Uniform Commercial Code, Art 2–712, have been preferred: Goode, *Commercial Law*, pp 417–18.
4 [1979] AC 91; [1978] 1 All ER 515, PC.
5 These qualifications apply conversely where the buyer is in anticipatory breach: see *McGregor on Damages* (16th edn), para 930.
6 *Melachrino v Nickoll and Knight* [1920] 1 KB 693, at 697. See also *Kaines (UK) v Osterreichische etc* [1993] 2 Lloyd's Rep 1, CA ([1994] JBL 152).
7 *Melachrino v Nickoll and Knight* (above). Cf *Rother v Taysen* (1896) 12 TLR 211, CA.

[29.22] Where there is no available market. There may be no available market, perhaps because the buyer has specifically sub-sold the same goods, or demand exceeds supply, or no reasonable substitute was available.[1] In such cases, s 51(3) is inapplicable,[2] and the court must make the best estimate it can with a view to putting the disappointed buyer in the situation in which he would have been if the contract had been performed (see ante, para 27.28). To some extent, this depends on the non-remote purpose for which the goods were required;[3] so a wholesale buyer has been given a normal trade mark-up.[4] In other cases, it may be appropriate to award the buyer the amount by which the value at the date of breach exceeds the contract price; and, if the buyer has effected a sub-sale, the sub-sale price is evidence of that value,[5] but not conclusive of that value.[6] Even the realisable scrap value has been given.[7]

[29.23] Consequential loss. This will be 'special damage' under s 54. Under his reliance interest (see ante, para 27.28), the disappointed buyer could recover his expenses, such as those for freight[1] and administration.[2] However, the more typical situation is one where the buyer is looking to recover his actual loss of the profit he expected to make on a sub-sale. The major difficulty here is whether the sub-sale is too remote (see generally ante, paras 27.41–43). The leading case is *Re Hall Ltd and WH Pim & Co*:[3]

> There was a contract for the sale of a cargo of wheat at 51s 9d per quarter, the contract clearly contemplating the possibility of a sub-sale by the buyer. Thereafter, the buyer sub-sold the cargo as such at 56s 9d per quarter. When the seller refused to deliver, the market price was 53s 9d per quarter. The seller argued that he should only be liable for the difference between the contract and market prices (2s per quarter); but the House of Lords held him liable for the difference between the contract and sub-sale prices (5s per quarter).

Clearly, the buyer in this case was awarded 5s per quarter only because of the non-remote sub-sale of that very cargo: if the sub-sale had been too remote, it would have been ignored; and, even if it were non-remote, the seller is normally entitled to expect the buyer to mitigate his loss by buying a substitute.[4] Thus, the decision turns on the finding that the sub-sale of that particular cargo as such was non-remote, and that there was no available market because the sub-sale contract would not have allowed the buyer to buy a substitute.[5] Everything therefore turns on what the seller could have contemplated under

---

[29.22]

1   As to available market, see generally ante, para 27.34.
2   As to s 51(3), see ante, para 29.20.
3   Goode, *Commercial Law* (2nd edn), p 397. For remoteness, see ante, para 27.42.
4   *Household Machines Ltd v Cosmos Exporters Ltd* [1947] KB 217.
5   *France v Gaudet* (1871) LR 6 QB 199, Ex Ch.
6   *The Arpad* [1934] P 189, CA; *Heskell v Continental Express Ltd* [1959] 1 All ER 1033.
7   *The Alecos* [1991] 1 Lloyd's Rep 120, CA (criticised 107 LQR 364).

[29.23]

1   *Braude (London) Ltd v Porter* [1959] 2 Lloyd's Rep 161.
2   *Robert Stewart & Sons Ltd v Carapanayoti Ltd* [1962] 1 All ER 418.
3   (1928) 139 LT 50; [1928] All ER Rep 763, HL. Cf *Hydraulic Engineering Co v McHaffie* (1878) 4 QBD 670, CA: see post, para 29.31.
4   Per Devlin J in the *Kwei Tek Chao* case (set out post, para 29.30), at 489–90.
5   It was a string contract: Goode, *Commercial Law* (2nd edn), p 414. If the sub-sale had been below the market price, would this have reduced the damages? See Atiyah, *Sale of Goods* (10th edn), pp 537–38.

the rules of remoteness: if a sub-sale was contemplatable in general terms, he is *prima facie* only liable for an ordinary loss of profit;[6] and the buyer can only recover the greater amount lost on a specially lucrative contract if the seller was aware of that sub-sale.[7] Where the sub-sale is non-remote, the seller should also be liable for any compensation which the buyer has to pay[8] his sub-buyer by way of damages and costs for breach of the sub-contract;[9] and, where there is a string (chain) of contracts contemplated, the buyer may recover in respect of compensation to the further buyers.[10] However, it seems unlikely that the buyer will ever receive any compensation for injury to his business connections.[11]

[29.24] An action in tort. Besides amounting to a breach of contract, non-delivery by the seller may also enable the buyer to maintain an action in tort for wrongful interference with goods (see ante, paras 19.04–06). Where the buyer is suing a third party in tort, the measure of his damages is *prima facie* the value of the goods (see ante, para 27.30); but, where he is suing the unpaid seller, the damages will be reduced by the unpaid price. Thus, in *Chinery v Viall*:[1]

> S sold some sheep on credit to B, but before delivery wrongfully resold and delivered them to X. B sued in contract and tort; and the court held –
>
> (1) in contract, B was entitled to damages for non-delivery calculated on the excess of the market value over the contract price (£5);
>
> (2) in tort, B was not entitled to the whole value of the sheep without deducting the unpaid price, but only the actual loss sustained (£5).

Since this case, it has become well established that a buyer suing for non-delivery cannot recover more in compensatory damages[2] by suing in tort than in contract.[3] Whilst it is clear that the buyer suing in tort is *prima facie* able to recover a non-remote loss of profit on a sub-sale,[4] it may be that the heads of damage in respect of which recovery may be made in a tort action are limited to the types of loss which would be non-remote in a contractual action,[5] so that to this extent it is irrelevant that the rules of remoteness may differ as between contract and tort.[6] Nor can the buyer suing in tort obtain an order for specific restitution (see ante, para 24.26) where he could not obtain a decree of specific performance of the contract (see post, para 29.38).

---

6   *Coastal International Trading v Maroil AC* [1988] 1 Lloyd's Rep 92.
7   Cf *Victoria Laundry Ltd v Newman Industries Ltd* (set out post, para 29.31).
8   Or an indemnity where he has not yet been sued by his sub-buyer: *Household Machines Ltd v Cosmos Exporters Ltd* [1947] KB 217.
9   *Grebert-Borgnis v Nugent* (1885) 15 QBD 85, CA.
10   Cf *Kasler and Cohen v Slavouski* [1928] 1 KB 78. On string contracts, see *Chitty on Contract* (28th edn), para 43-430.
11   *McGregor on Damages* (16th edn), para 851. Cf post, para 29.31.
[29.24]
1   (1869) 5 H & N 288.
2   What of exemplary damages, which are only available in tort?
3   See the authorities collected in *Benjamin's Sale of Goods* (5th edn), para 17-096, note 98.
4   See *France v Gaudet* (1871) LR 6 QB 199, Ex Ch.
5   *The Arpad* [1934] P 189, CA. See Goodhart (1937) 2 Univ of Tor LJ 1; *McGregor on Damages* (16th edn), paras 214; 1438.
6   See ante, para 27.43. Is the same true if contract damages would exceed tort damages?

Hire-purchase and hiring

[29.25] If the contract is one of simple hiring, the hirer will *prima facie* be entitled by way of damages to the amount by which the contract rate of hire is exceeded by the market rate at which the hirer could hire similar goods under similar terms. Logically, in the case of hp, the *prima facie* measure of damages should likewise be the amount by which the market hp price exceeds the contract hp price.[1] Whilst there has been no reported case where the measure of damages for physical non-delivery to a hirer under an hp agreement has been discussed,[2] the matter has been considered in relation to continuous breaches by the owner (see ante, para 29.10). Clearly, a hirer who lawfully rejects the goods tendered and rescinds the contract is entitled to sue on the basis of non-delivery.[3] But what of a hirer who has accepted delivery? In *Yeoman Credit Ltd v Apps*:[4]

> The consumer (C) entered into a directly financed hp transaction upon the dealer agreeing to do some repairs before delivery. After the car had been delivered, C ascertained that the repairs had not been done; and the car was found to have such an accumulation of latent defects as to render it unsafe and unroadworthy. C complained, but kept the car for five months and paid some instalments, hoping he could persuade the dealer to meet half the cost of the repairs. The plaintiff finance company (P) sued for arrears of instalments and C counterclaimed to recover the money he had paid on grounds of total failure of consideration.

The Court of Appeal implied into the hp agreement a common law condition as to fitness,[5] whose fundamental breach it said was outside the exclusion clause (see ante, para 18.07) and held:

(1) That since C had approbated the contract by paying some instalments, there was no total failure of consideration (see ante, para 29.15); and that P was therefore entitled to the hire rent up to the moment of C's rejection of the goods (see ante, para 27.21); but that

(2) C's rejection was lawful because there was a continuing breach of contract by P (but see ante, para 29.10) and that C was also entitled to recover by way of damages the estimated sum that would be necessary to put the car into repair.[6]

However, this measure of damages appears closer to the measure applicable to breach of warranty than non-delivery; and the decision has been criticised on the grounds that the hirer could have no possible interest in repairing the goods after rescinding the contract.[7] Of course, this very dilemma spotlights the oddity of the doctrine of continuous breach;

[29.25]

1 Goode, *HP Law and Practice* (2nd edn), pp 451–52. Even though the hirer could elect to terminate the agreement?

2 The issue arose in *Tommey v Finextra Ltd* (1962) 106 SJ 1012. See also *Kelly v Sovereign Leasing* [1995] CLY 720, Cty Ct.

3 But see *Farnworth Finance Facilities v Attryde* [1970] 2 All ER 774, CA.

4 [1962] 2 QB 508; [1961] 2 All ER 281, CA, discussed Goode, *HP Law and Practice* (2nd edn), pp 456–58.

5 For the statutory undertaking as to fitness, see ante, para 14.07.

6 Harman and Davies LJJ had some doubts about the matter (at 524, 526). Compare *Porter v General Guarantee Corp Ltd* [1982] RTR 384 (value of car and expenses).

7 Goode, *op cit*, note 1, pp 456, 458; Guest, *Law of HP*, p 283. *Contra* repair costs incurred whilst in possession: see post, para 29.34.

and the measure of damages where the hirer affirms is discussed below (see post, para 29.34).

Damages for other breaches of contract

[29.26] In respect of sales, the rules governing actions by the buyer for damages for breaches of contract other than non-delivery have partially been given statutory form in s 53 of the SGA; and, insofar as s 53 reflects the common law, it is also applicable in quasi-sale, hp and simple hiring.[1] Section 53(1) provides:

> Where there is a breach of warranty by the seller, or where the buyer elects (or is compelled) to treat any breach of a condition on the part of the seller as a breach of warranty,[2] the buyer is not by reason only[3] of such breach of warranty entitled to reject the goods; but he may –
>
> (a) set up against the seller the breach of warranty in diminution or extinction of the price, or
>
> (b) maintain an action against the seller for damages for breach of warranty.

Section 53(1) envisages that the buyer may *prima facie*[4] be able to do one of two things:

(a) Set up the seller's breach of contract by way of an answer to the seller's action for the price. Technically, this is not a defence (set-off), but a cross-action (counterclaim),[5] and therefore must arise in respect of the same contract.[6]

(b) Maintain an action against the seller for breach of contract or tort,[7] in which case the mere existence of a potential counterclaim by the unpaid seller for the price will not *per se* justify reducing the damages by the price.[8]

These two are alternative, in the sense that the buyer cannot recover compensation in respect of the seller's breach and then set up that breach when sued for the price; and a decision that there was no warranty or no breach operates as *res judicata* (see ante, para 26.17). However, in case the buyer's loss should exceed the price, s 53(4) says that:

> The fact that the buyer has set up the breach of warranty in diminution or extinction of the price does not prevent him from maintaining an action for the same breach of warranty if he has suffered further damage.

The SGA also deals with the question of remoteness of damage in contract in a manner similar to that used in the other sections: the first rule in *Hadley v Baxendale* is set out in

---

1 *UCB Leasing Ltd v Holtom* (set out ante, para 29.10).
2 This suggests that the draftsman thought that a condition became a warranty if the buyer only claimed damages; but this is not so: *Wallis, Son and Wells v Pratt and Haynes* (set out ante, para 11.04).
3 He may be able to reject for some other cause: see Chalmers, *Sale of Goods* (18th edn), p 242.
4 In a consumer supply, ouster of this rule may be an unfair term: OFT, *Bulletin No 14*, case 22: Grey Term 1(b): see ante, para 11.16.
5 *Bright v Rogers* [1917] 1 KB 917, DC. For set-offs, see ante, paras 7.23; 23.14.
6 See *Bow McLachlan & Co v Ship Camosun* [1909] AC 597, PC.
7 See *Benjamin's Sale of Goods* (5th edn) para 17-047.
8 *Gillard v Brittan* (1841) 8 M & W 575; *Healing (Sales) Pty Ltd v Inglis Electrix Pty Ltd* [1969] ALJR 533, HC. Compare non-delivery: ante, para 29.12.

s 53(2) and the second rule referred to in s 54.[9] In *Bence Graphics International Ltd v Fasson UK Ltd*:[10]

> There was a sale of vinyl film, promised to survive in good legible condition for the industry standard time of five years; but the film contained insufficient stabiliser against the effect of ultraviolet light. The buyer (B) used the film to manufacture container decals exhibiting identifying marks, some of which he supplied to his customers. Some of those customers having complained that the markings on decals became illegible in less than five years, B met one minor claim and returned to the seller (S) the small amount of film remaining unused. S admitted the latent breach; but there was a trial as to damages. Morland J applied the *prima facie* measure of damages set out in s 53(3) (see post, para 29.33), awarding B the diminution in value of the decals.

However, the majority of the Court of Appeal **reduced** B's damages to the small amount of unused vinyl returned, plus the actual loss B incurred to his customers.[11] They did this on the basis of the remoteness of damage rule in s 53(2), holding that, where S supplied goods containing a latent defect to B in circumstances where both parties contemplated that the goods would be sold on, the claims by the B's sub-buyers was to non-remote loss under s 53(2). In effect, the majority were saying that s 53(2) took precedence over s 53(3): in principle, this may be correct; but it has been strenuously argued that Morland J was correct, and that there was no remoteness issue on the facts of *Bence*.[12]

In applying these rules, it is convenient to distinguish between the claims of the buyer or hirer in respect of the following: (a) defective title (see post, para 29.27); (b) late delivery (see post, para 29.28 *et seq*); and (c) defective quality (see post, para 29.32 *et seq*).

[29.27] Actions in respect of a defective title. Where the supplier is in breach of the implied undertaking that he has the right to sell the goods under a sale, quasi-sale or hp agreement,[1] the buyer or hirer who is evicted from possession by a person with a superior title[2] has a right of election as to the remedy he pursues (see ante, paras 12.05–07): he may rescind the contract, recover the price on grounds of total failure of consideration and have his damages assessed on the basis of non-delivery (see below); or he may affirm the contract and recover by way of damages under his 'reliance' interest the purchase or hp price[3] and any expenses.[4] Even where the supplier is merely in breach of warranty as to quiet possession or as to freedom from encumbrances, if the buyer or hirer is rightfully evicted from possession by a third party, the buyer or hirer is similarly

---

9 Cf ss 50(2), 51(2): set out ante, paras 27.24; 29.19.
10 [1998] QB 87; [1997] 1 All ER 979, CA (criticised by Bridge [1998] JBL 259).
11 The majority cast serious doubts on the decision in *Slater v Hoyle & Smith Ltd* (set out post, para 29.33): Auld LJ thought the decision wrong (at All ER 994); and Otton LJ distinguished it (at All ER 988j), though Auld LJ thought the two cases indistinguishable (at All ER 992c). See Benjamin, *op cit*, note 7, para 17.055.
12 Treitel, *Law of Contract* (10th edn), pp 885–86. But see Benjamin, *op cit*, note 7, para 17-077.
[29.27]
1 See ante, para 12.02. There is a necessarily different undertaking in respect of simple hiring agreements: see ante, para 12.04A.
2 What if he is not evicted? See ante, para 12.11.
3 *Warman v Southern Counties Finance Corp Ltd* (set out ante, para 12.07).
4 *Warman's* case (above); and *per* Singleton LJ in *Mason v Burningham* [1949] 2 KB 545, CA, at 560. And see Treitel, *Law of Contract* (10th edn), p 984.

entitled to recover under his 'reliance' interest the purchase or hp price[5] and any expenditure thrown away.[6]

Where the buyer or hirer might have made a profit from the goods, he may alternatively claim under his 'expectancy' interest.[7] If he can and does rescind, then damages are measured on the basis of non-delivery (see ante, para 29.18). If not, it would appear that damages are assessed on the same basis as where the goods are defective in quality in respect of both the *prima facie* rule[8] and consequential loss (see post, para 29.35) flowing from the breach of an undertaking as to title.

Actions in respect of late delivery

[29.28] If the late delivery of goods supplied amounts to a repudiation (see ante, para 26.15), the buyer may elect to rescind, in which case damages will be assessed on the basis of non-delivery (see ante, para 29.18), though the duty to mitigate (see ante, paras 27.44–45) may reduce these damages if the buyer or hirer has acted unreasonably.[1] On the other hand, where the buyer cannot or does not rescind, the action for damages is something of a hybrid: the *prima facie* measure of damages has much in common with claims for breach of warranty because there has been a delivery,[2] whereas the measure of damages for consequential loss is akin to that for non-delivery.[3] Presumably, the rules are similar in the case of late delivery of goods supplied under a quasi-sale, hp agreement or simple hiring.

Prima facie measure on late delivery. Whilst there is no statutory formulation in the SGA which specifically refers to the measure of damages recoverable for late delivery of goods sold, it would appear that once again the *prima facie* measure of damages depends on whether there is an available market (see ante, para 27.34), though this time the assumption is that the buyer will sell the goods in such a market (see post, paras 29.29–30). Where an hp or simple hiring agreement contains the usual prohibition of sale by the hirer (see ante, para 7.26), presumably there is no available market in which the hirer can sell the goods during the continuance of the agreement. Claims for consequential loss will be considered later (see post, para 29.31).

Distinction from non-delivery. A significant difference between the two formulae for measuring damages in the event of a non-delivery or late delivery (see above) appears where the buyer or hirer made a bad bargain,[4] from which he can effectively escape by taking any opportunity to rescind. What is to happen where the buyer has lost the right to

---

5   *Lloyds and Scottish Finance Ltd v Modern Cars Ltd* (set out ante, para 12.14).

6   The *Lloyds & Scottish* case (above); *Mason v Burningham* (above).

7   The relationship of claims under the 'reliance' and 'expectancy' interest is explained ante, para 27.28.

8   The issue was avoided in the following case, where it was admitted that the goods were equal in value and price: *Healing (Sales) Pty Ltd v Inglis Electrix Pty Ltd* [1969] ALJR 533, HC. The *prima facie* rule for defective quality is considered post, para 29.33.

[29.28]

1   *The Solholt* [1983] 1 Lloyd's Rep 605 (failure to accept the late tender of the ship reducing the damages to nil). This may always be a factor where the buyer has not already gone into the market and obtained a replacement: Atiyah, *Sale of Goods* (10th edn), p 542.

2   *Per* Lord Dunedin in *Williams Brothers v ET Agius Ltd* [1914] AC 550, HL at 522.

3   See *McGregor on Damages* (16th edn), para 853.

4   Either because the market price falls, or he agreed to pay too much in the first place: see ante, para 27.28.

rescind through no fault of his own?[5] The dilemma has arisen in cif sales where the seller has shipped goods late but the buyer only discovered that the shipping documents were misdated after he had accepted them: in two cases, the courts have awarded the buyer the contract price less the fallen market price.[6] However, it is by no means obvious why the buyer in an ordinary sale should be afforded a method of escaping from his bad bargain;[7] and in a more recent cif case the buyer was confined to the ordinary measure of damages for late delivery, so denying him the fall in the market price.[8]

[29.29] Where there is an available market. Whilst the buyer or hirer will eventually obtain possession of the goods, so that his position is analogous to that where there is a breach of warranty of quality (see ante, para 29.28), what the buyer or hirer has lost depends on the purpose for which he is acquiring the goods[1] and the duty to mitigate.[2]

(1) Where a buyer or hirer is obtaining the goods for **use**, the appropriate measure of damages may be the loss of **use**, or cost of **hiring** a replacement, for the period of the delay.[3]

(2) Where a buyer is **buying** for resale, the normal *prima facie* measure is the amount by which the **market value** at the contractual time for delivery exceeds the **market value** at the actual time of delivery, the relevant price being the selling price.[4] It is the market value at the contractual time of delivery which is taken, not the contract price as in non-delivery (see ante, para 29.20), but the contract price is *prima facie* evidence of that value, just as any sub-sale price might be.[5] Similarly, a contemporaneous sub-sale price should be no more than evidence of the market value at the date of actual delivery, though this view might appear difficult to reconcile with *Wertheim v Chicoutimi Pulp Co*:[6]

> There was a sale of 3,000 tons of wood pulp at 25s per ton for delivery September/November. At the time fixed for delivery, the market price was 70s per ton; but when the pulp was eventually delivered and accepted the following June it was 42s 6d per ton. Whilst the buyers had *prima facie* lost 27s 6d per ton (70s – 42s 6d), they had in fact previously sub-sold[7] the pulp at 65s per ton. The Privy Council confirmed that the sellers could rely on the sub-sale to reduce damages to at 'highest' 5s per ton (70s – 65s).[8]

---

5   *A fortiori* where it is the act of the seller which has deprived him of the right to rescind.

6   *Finlay & Co Ltd v Kwik Hoo Tong* [1929] 1 KB 400, CA; applied in the *Kwei Tek Chao* case (set out post, para 29.30).

7   Atiyah, *Sale of Goods* (10th edn), 544. See also *McGregor on Damages* (16th edn), para 918.

8   *Procter & Gamble Philippine Manufacturing Corp v Kurt A Becher GmbH* [1988] 2 Lloyd's Rep 21, CA (see Cooper [1989] LM & CLQ 397).

[29.29]

1   Goode, *Commercial Law* (2nd edn), p 401. Cf post, para 29.34.

2   *The Solholt* [1983] 1 Lloyd's Rep 605, CA, as explained by Atiyah, *Sale of Goods* (10th edn), p 542.

3   The *Victoria Laundry* case (loss of profit: set out post, para 29.31); and see Goode, *op cit*, note 1, p 403.

4   *Per* Devlin J in the *Kwei Tek Chao* case (set out post, para 29.30), at 495. For the effect of a waiver of delivery date, see ante, para 26.25.

5   *McGregor on Damages* (16th edn), para 857.

6   [1911] AC 301; [1908–10] All ER Rep 707, PC.

7   The buyer actually used the goods to perform a contract made prior to the one presently litigated: see the explanation in Atiyah, *op cit*, note 2, p 543.

8   The figure of 5s per ton was the amount fixed by the Canadian court. It has been suggested that the reference to at 'highest' showed that the PC wished to award nominal damages as there had been no loss: Bridge, *Sale of Goods*, p 582.

This case has been the subject of much adverse criticism; and the facts are unclear.[9] If the sub-sale had been of the same goods as such, it is argued that there would have been no market available to the buyer, so that he would have made no loss;[10] but as the sub-sale had merely been of equivalent goods, it should have been irrelevant,[11] because the buyer need not have committed the goods to that contract but could have sold them on the market.[12]

[29.30] Where there is no available market. In this case, the measure of damages is *prima facie* the amount by which the contract price exceeds the **actual value** at the contractual time for delivery. In *Kwei Tek Chao v British Traders Ltd*:[1]

> There was a contract for the sale of 20 tons of Rongalite C cif Hong Kong at £590 per ton, shipment from Antwerp not later than 31 October 1951. The goods were actually shipped on 3 November 1951; but the bills of lading were forged by a third party to show 31 October 1951 as the date of shipment; and they were consequently accepted by the buyer, who paid the price. Owing to the later shipment, the buyer lost his contract for sub-sale in Hong Kong; but he accepted late delivery with knowledge of the breach. The buyer was unable to resell the goods, as a Chinese embargo had destroyed the market.

In a masterly judgment, Devlin J held as follows:

(1) *Prima facie*, the buyer in a cif sale (see ante, para 22.07) has two rights of rejection: (a) to reject the documents and (b) to reject the goods (at 480–81: see ante, para 22.07). He had accepted the goods with knowledge of the breach[2] and had therefore lost the right to reject them (see ante, para 29.06). Consequently, he was not entitled to recover the price on grounds of total failure of consideration;[3] but he was entitled to reject the documents.[4]

(2) There were two separate breaches of contract in respect of which the buyer might therefore claim damages, each with its own measure of damages.[5]

(3) *Prima facie*, the measure of damages for late delivery is the difference between the market values at the contractual and actual time of goods delivery (at 478: see ante,

---

9   See Bridge, *ibid*, pp 582–83.
10 *Contra* if the sub-sale had been non-remote: compare ante, para 29.23.
11 *Per* Scrutton LJ in *Slater v Hoyle* [1920] 2 KB 11, CA at 23–24. Accepted by *McGregor on Damages, op cit*, note 5; Treitel, *Law of Contract* (10th edn), p 885; Goode, *op cit*, note 1 (2nd edn), pp 402–03.
12 Compare *British Westinghouse Electric and Manufacturing Co Ltd v Underground Electric Railway Co Ltd* [1912] AC 673, HL: see ante, para 27.29. But see post, para 29.33.

[29.30]
1   [1954] 2 QB 459; [1954] 3 All ER 165.
2   By reason of delay (at 475): see further ante, para 29.07.
3   Because the forged documents were not nullities (at 477): see ante, para 29.13.
4   See Schmitthoff, *Export Trade* (10th edn), 2-026; Atiyah, *Sale of Goods* (10th edn), pp 544–45.
5   At 483: see post, para 29.33. Presumably this is subject to the rule against double recovery: see ante, para 27.39.

para 29.29) and document delivery.[6] In both cases, it is assumed that the buyer on discovering the breach will resell the goods on delivery to mitigate his loss, so that the relevant price is the selling price then (at 495, 497).

(4) Because of the Chinese embargo, there was no market in which the goods could be sold, so that the salvage value of the goods must be taken.

(5) His Lordship rejected the buyer's claim for loss of profit on the following grounds: whilst the sellers might contemplate sub-sales generally, they did not know that the goods had been sub-sold as such;[7] and it was therefore to be expected that the buyer would go out into the falling market and buy substitute goods, in which event he would suffer no such damage.[8]

[29.31] Consequential loss. Naturally, the buyer may recover any money expended in reliance on the seller's promise, such as extra freight charges,[1] or losses resulting from currency changes.[2] However, where he would have made a profit, the buyer may alternatively claim in respect of his expectancy interest;[3] and the major issue here is whether he may recover anything beyond the *prima facie* measure in respect of his intended use or sub-sale of the goods, subject always to the duty to mitigate (see ante, paras 27.44–45).

1 *Loss of use.* Obviously, the buyer may recover in respect of any expenses incurred as a result of the loss of use;[4] but he may also recover in respect of loss of profit he would have made from use of the goods. In *Victoria Laundry Ltd v Newman Industries Ltd*:[5]

> B decided to obtain a larger boiler to expand their laundry business in view of the prevailing shortage of laundry facilities. B contracted to buy one from S, who agreed to deliver and install it on B's premises. S knew that B needed the boiler in connection with their laundry business, though not the exact use to which it was to be put. When the boiler was delivered some five months late, B claimed damages for loss of profit as follows: (1) £16 per week for the new customers he would have taken on; and (2) £262 per week which he would have earned on a specially lucrative dyeing contract with the Ministry of Supply.

The Court of Appeal unanimously held that the seller could have foreseen that loss of business profits would be liable to result from the delay,[6] but did not know of the contract with the Ministry of Supply; and they therefore held that the buyer could recover (1) but not (2).

2 *Loss on a sub-sale.* Where the seller knew of the sub-sale of the goods *per se* and the sub-contract delivery date, he has been held liable for the loss of profit on the sub-

---

6 As the buyer had not rejected, the price at which he could have bought substitute goods in Hong Kong was irrelevant (at 479). Compare non-delivery: ante, para 29.20.
7 His Lordship was not even convinced that the goods had been resold *per se* (at 490): see post, para 29.31.
8 At 489–90. Cf ante, para 29.20.
[29.31]
1 *Borries v Hutchinson* (1865) 18 CBNS 445.
2 *Aruna Mills Ltd v Dhanrajmal Gobindram* [1968] 1 All ER 113.
3 The relationship of claims under the 'reliance' and 'expectancy' interest is explained ante, para 27.28.
4 *Henderson v Meyer* (1941) 46 Com Cas 209.
5 [1949] 2 KB 528; [1949] 1 All ER 997, CA.
6 For criticism of this test of remoteness, see ante, para 27.42.

sale.[7] However, such precise knowledge on the part of the seller is clearly unusual,[8] and anyway, such a claim will usually fail on the grounds that the buyer should have mitigated his loss by buying a substitute (see ante, para 29.23). Where the loss on the sub-sale is non-remote and there is no chance of mitigation, the buyer is entitled not only to his loss of profit, but also to a reasonable amount in respect of compensation that he has to pay to his sub-buyer.[9] He has, however, been refused damages arising because of loss of business connexion with his sub-buyer.[10]

Actions in respect of a defect in quality

[29.32] The present discussion is concerned with the situation where the goods delivered by the supplier do not comply with the contract description as to quality or undertakings as to quality (see Chapters 13 and 14), but the buyer or hirer elects, or is required (see ante, para 29.03), to accept the goods and claim damages.[1] This situation must be distinguished from the following cases: first, where the buyer or hirer accepts the goods delivered in full satisfaction of his rights under the contract, in which case those rights are thereby extinguished (see ante, para 26.18); and secondly, where the buyer or hirer properly rejects the goods, this is treated in law as a non-delivery (see ante, para 29.18). The *prima facie* measure for contractual defects of quality[2] is the shortfall between the **warranted** and **actual value** of the goods in the hands of the buyer or hirer. Additionally, claims for consequential loss are perhaps more common in this context than in respect of non-delivery (see post, para 29.35).

The *prima facie* measure must be contrasted with that available in non-delivery claims, the latter being the amount by which the **market price** exceeds the **contract price** (see ante, para 29.20), if any.[3] A significant difference between the two formulae for measuring damages in the event of a non-delivery or defective delivery (see above) appears where the buyer or hirer made a bad bargain (see ante, para 27.28), from which he can effectively escape by taking any opportunity to rescind (see ante, para 29.28). However, it is clear that where the buyer with knowledge of the breach accepts the goods, he will recover only the normal measure of damages for breach of warranty;[4] but it has been argued that this should not be the case where he accepts the goods without knowledge of the breach.[5]

---

7   *Hydraulic Engineering G v McHaffie* (1878) 4 QBD 670, CA.
8   Eg, the *Kwei Tek Chao* case (set out ante, para 29.30).
9   *Elbinger Aktiengesellschaft v Armstrong* (1874) LR 9 QB 473: cf non-delivery, ante, para 29.23.
10 *Simon v Pawson and Leafs Ltd* (1933) 148 LT 154, CA (criticised by Bridge 105 LQR at 411). Similarly defective quality: see post, para 29.36.

[29.32]

1   The ordinary common law rules of remoteness and measure of damage obtain: see generally ante, para 27.27 *et seq.*
2   SGA, s 53(3). As to the calculation of the *prima facie* measure of damages in the case of supply contracts, see post, paras 29.33–34. As to misrepresentations, see ante, para 29.17.
3   The *Bernstein* case (set out ante, para 29.07): nil difference.
4   *Vargas Pena Apezteguia y Cia Saic v Peter Cremer GmbH* [1987] 1 Lloyd's Rep 394.
5   Atiyah, *Sale of Goods* (10th edn), p 547.

[29.33] The *prima facie* measure in sale. Where in a contract of sale (or presumably quasi-sale?) the price has been paid, s 53(3) of the SGA provides as follows:

> In the case of a breach of warranty of quality such loss is *prima facie*[1] the difference between the value of the goods at the time of delivery to the buyer and the value they would have had if they had fulfilled the warranty.

1 *The warranted value*. As in actions for non-delivery or late delivery, the process of ascertaining the warranted value depends on whether or not there is an available market.[2] The contract price and any sub-sale price[3] are merely evidence of the value of the goods as warranted. In *Slater v Hoyle & Smith Ltd*:[4]

> B was a manufacturer of cloth and had already entered into a contract to sell bleached cloth to X. To fulfill this contract, B agreed to buy 3,000 pieces of unbleached cloth of a specified quality from S for 129s per piece. After S had delivered 1,629 pieces, B refused to accept any more because of its defective quality. Nevertheless, B used the defective unbleached cloth to fulfill his contract for bleached cloth with X, who complained but accepted the goods. S argued that B had therefore suffered no loss.

Nevertheless, the Court of Appeal awarded B the reduction in value of the goods on the basis of s 53(3), on the grounds that the chain of causation was breached by the facts that (i) B's contract with X was made before his contract with S and (ii) B altered the goods from unbleached to bleached cloth, so preventing reliance on the sub-sale to X (see ante, para 27.29). However, the authority of *Slater* would appear to be seriously undermined: in *Wertheim* the Privy Council did take account of sub-sales (see ante, para 29.29); and in *Bence* the Court of Appeal avoided *Slater* by giving primacy to the remoteness test in s 53(2) (see ante, para 29.26).

2 *The actual value*. There may be evidence of the actual value of the goods to a hypothetical buyer with knowledge of the breach,[5] eg, where there is a recognised price for 'seconds'; and the courts may recognise this in supporting the common commercial practice of taking defective goods at an allowance, perhaps fixed by an arbitrator.[6] Where the actual value cannot be ascertained, the courts may award damages based on the cost of repairs needed to bring the goods up to the contractual standard;[7] and, if that exceeds the warranted value, the actual value will be nil.[8] The buyer may sometimes be entitled to the cost of buying a substitute;[9] but, where this purchase exceeds the duty to mitigate (see ante, para 27.44), the question arises

---

[29.33]

1 But the rule may be ousted, as by a liquidated damages clause (see ante, para 27.24): the *Watford Electronics* case (set out ante, para 18.24A).

2 As to the *prima facie* measure for non-delivery, see ante, paras 29.20–22; and as to late delivery, see ante, paras 29.29–30.

3 *Loder v Kefak* (1857) 3 CBNS 128 (contract price); *Clare v Maynard* (1835) 6 Ad & El 519 (sub-sale price).

4 [1920] 2 KB 11, CA; discussed by Benjamin, *Sale of Goods* (5th edn), paras 17.054–55.

5 But the courts are wary of such evidence: Benjamin, *ibid*, para 17-050; and see *Jones v Just* (below).

6 *Biggin & Co Ltd v Permanite Ltd* [1951] 1 KB 422 (affd on different grounds).

7 *Minster Trust Ltd v Traps Tractors Ltd* [1954] 3 All ER 136; *Keeley v Guy McDonald* (1984) 134 NLJ 552. As to where the cost of repairs exceeds the value of the goods, see Bridge, *Sale of Goods*, p 593.

8 *Bridge v Wain* (1816) 1 Star 504. So the buyer will then be awarded as *prima facie* damages the market value of the goods in their warranted state. Cf motor insurance 'write offs'.

9 *British Westinghouse Electric and Manufacturing Co Ltd v Underground Electric Co Ltd* [1912] AC 673, HL. As to buying a substitute part, see *Bacon v Cooper (Metals) Ltd* [1982] 1 All ER 397.

whether his damages should be reduced to take account of any extra profit (see ante, para 27.29).

In providing that these two values are to be taken at the contractual time and place of delivery, s 53(3) of the SGA is clearly reflecting the common law.[10] However, this does not always make good sense and may be displaced, as where the defect is only discovered by a sub-buyer,[11] or the breached warranty refers to a future state.[12]

[29.34] The *prima facie* measure in hiring and hp. In the case of a simple hiring (leasing), the *prima facie* measure of damages should be like that for late delivery (see ante, para 29.29); that is, what the buyer or hirer has lost should depends on the purpose for which he is acquiring the goods and the duty to mitigate.

(1) Where a buyer or hirer is obtaining the goods for **use**, the appropriate measure of damages may be the loss of **use**, or cost of **hiring** a replacement, for the period of the delay.

(2) Where a buyer is **buying** for resale, the normal *prima facie* measure is the amount by which the **market value** at the contractual time for delivery exceeds the **market value** at the actual time of delivery, the relevant price being the selling price.[1]

However, in the case of hp allowance has to be made for the option to purchase; and, at first sight, it might appear that the *prima facie* measure should be the amount by which the hp price of the goods in their **warranted** condition exceeds the hp price obtainable in their **actual** condition.[2] Whilst this may be appropriate where the hirer is suing a third party under a collateral contract,[3] it ignores the possibility that the hiring may be determined, in which case the hirer would retain damages for a loss he has not suffered. All too commonly, this dilemma will arise because the hirer ceases payment of instalments on discovering the defects and the owner thereupon terminates the agreement.[4] Thus, in *Charterhouse Credit Ltd v Tolly*:[5]

> The hirer elected to affirm the agreement after discovering the owner's breach (in providing an unroadworthy vehicle). He paid £50 in repairs, but failed to pay any instalments. The owner therefore terminated the agreement, and claimed damages for breach; and the hirer counterclaimed for damages in respect of the defective state of the vehicle. The Court of Appeal unanimously held:

---

10 *Jones v Just* (1868) LR 3 QB 197 (after contract date market rose so that buyer able to resell damaged lamp at almost warranted value at delivery date). See Benjamin, *op cit*, note 4, para 17.051.

11 *Van den Hurk v Martens & Co Ltd* [1920] 1 KB 850 (chemicals packed in drums and contemplated will not be examined until reach sub-buyer).

12 *Ashworth v Wells* (1898) 14 TLR 227, CA (orchid sold warranted to flower purple: two years later first flowering white).

[29.34]

1 *McGregor on Damages* (16th edn), para 941. Cf the sale rule: see ante, 29.33.

2 Atiyah, *Sale of Goods* (6th edn), p 411 (chapter dropped from later editions).

3 *Brown v Sheen and Richmond Car Sales Ltd* [1950] 1 All ER 1102: ante, para 16.13; *Yeoman Credit Ltd v Odgers* [1962] 1 All ER 789, CA.

4 Arguably, the hirer's action arises from impecuniosity due to the need to meet repair bills and might be ignored.

5 [1963] 2 QB 683; [1963] 2 All ER 433, CA. See also *UCB Leasing Ltd v Holtom* (set out ante, para 29.10).

(1) As the owner had terminated, the hirer was only liable for arrears of instalments because he only caused the loss of those instalments (see ante, para 27.29);

(2) The appropriate measure of the hirer's damages was not the cost of repairs,[6] but the cost of hiring a similar car on a similar terms.[7]

Actually, Upjohn LJ suggested that, if the owner had not terminated, the hirer would only have been entitled to the amount required to put the vehicle in a proper state of repair, plus damages for loss of use.[8] However, in this circumstance repair will not always be a realistic option: so in *Doobey v Mohabeer*,[9] where the machine was useless in its defective condition, the Privy Council held that, after affirming the hp agreement, the hirer was entitled to recover by way of damages all the sums paid or payable under the agreement.[10] Yet where the contract remains afoot, the basic dilemma outlined remains.[11] A form of apportionment has been suggested.[12]

[29.35] Consequential loss. Naturally, the buyer or hirer may recover any money thrown away in reliance on the promise of the supplier.[1] However, when he would have made a profit, the buyer or hirer may, alternatively, claim the value of performance.[2] Here, he may have less opportunity to mitigate his loss as the breach may be less obvious than in the case of non-delivery or late delivery (see respectively ante, paras 29.23 and 29.31); and to this extent there may be greater scope for recovery in respect of consequential loss. Three difficulties have arisen: first, whether the supplier's breach has caused the loss;[3] secondly, following on from this, whether the buyer or hirer is under any duty to examine the goods with a view to discovering any patent or latent defects;[4] and thirdly, whether the buyer or hirer who takes steps to protect himself which go beyond the duty to mitigate is to have his damages diminished by way of any benefit accruing to him from such further steps, eg, the profit on a sub-sale (see ante, para 27.29).

There are several types of consequential loss commonly caused by the defective quality of the goods delivered.

---

6   Distinguish the situation where the hirer is not claiming recovery of repair costs incurred during the period of his possession, but future repair costs after he has relinquished possession: see ante, para 29.25.

7   The present agreement may be a good guide as to value: *per* Donovan LJ at 705–06.

8   At 711–12. His Lordship also suggested that each case should be judged on its own facts, and no general rule laid down (at 711). As to loss of use, see post, para 29.35.

9   [1967] 2 AC 278; [1967] 2 All ER 760, PC.

10 For criticism of the decision, see Goode, *HP Law and Practice* (2nd edn), p 463.

11 It was said that the hirer should not be in any worse position with regard to his claim for damages where he affirmed than where he rescinded: *per* Ormerod LJ in *Tolly's* case, at 715. See also *per* Lord Wilberforce in *Doobay v Mohabeer*, at 289.

12 Goode, *op cit*, note 10, pp 459–60.

[29.35]

1   Eg, *Bernstein v Pamson Motors Ltd* (set out ante, para 29.07; cost of car breakdown recovery and spoilt day); *Doobay v Mohabeer* [1967] 2 AC 278, PC (cost of installing engine); *Molling v Dean* (1902) 18 TLR 216 (cost of delivery).

2   The relationship of claims under the 'reliance' and 'expectancy' interest is explained ante, para 27.28.

3   *Beoco Ltd v Alfa Laval Co* [1995] QB 137, CA (buyer carelessly failed to check third party repair); and see generally ante, para 27.29.

4   *McGregor on Damages* (16th edn), para 885.

1   *Loss of use.* First, the defect may deprive the buyer or hirer of the enjoyment of using the goods for which he must be compensated.[5] Secondly, he may recover any non-remote loss of profit he would have made by utilising the goods to make some product for resale.[6] Thus, in *Cullinane v British 'Rema' Manufacturing Co Ltd*:[7]

> There was a sale of a machine warranted to pulverise clay at 6 tons an hour. The machine delivered only proved capable of handling 2 tons per hour. The court took it for granted that the buyer was entitled to compensation for loss of profit.

However, in calculating the damages recoverable, the Court of Appeal seems to have put themselves into a completely indefensible position:[8] first, there would not have been any profit in the period covered by the claim; and second, they erroneously thought that the buyer's claim (before amendment by the official referee) conflicted with the rule against double recovery (see ante, para 27.39).

2   *Loss on a sub-sale of goods* (see post, para 29.36).

3   *Loss caused by the defect* (see post, para 29.37).

[29.36] Loss on a sub-sale of the goods. Before the seller can be made liable for any loss suffered by the buyer in connection with any sub-sale, two things must be shown: first, that the sub-sales are not too remote;[1] and second, that the loss arising from the sub-sales was caused by the seller's breach of contract.[2] Whilst liability in respect of a non-remote sub-sale on identical terms is not in question,[3] the second requirement may give rise to difficulty where the terms of the sub-sale are not identical. Clearly, the buyer cannot recover in respect of liability to his sub-buyer arising out of substantially more onerous terms; but it would seem that he may do so where he would have been liable had the terms been identical,[4] or where the difference in terms was verbal rather than substantial.[5] Assuming that these criteria are satisfied, the buyer is entitled to recover from the seller by way of consequential loss, not just any loss of profit (cf the seller's claim for loss of profit: ante, para 27.33) and cost of recovering the goods,[6] but also in respect of

---

5   *Jackson v Chrysler Acceptances Ltd* [1978] RTR 474, CA (defective car spoilt French touring holiday); *Bernstein v Pamson Motors Ltd* (above); and see generally *Street on Torts* (10th edn), p 552.

6   *Holden Ltd v Bostock Ltd* (1902) 18 TLR 317, CA. See also *Ashworth v Wells* (1898) 78 LT 136, CA; *Central Meat Products Ltd v McDaniel Ltd* [1952] 1 Lloyd's Rep 562; *Hotel Services Ltd v Hilton International Ltd* [2000] 1 All ER (Comm) 750, CA.

7   [1954] 1 QB 292; [1953] 2 All ER 1257, CA. See also *Astley Industrial Trust Ltd v Grimley* [1963] 2 All ER 33, CA (liability of a dealer in a directly financed hp transaction).

8   See Macleod [1970] JBL 19; Fuller and Perdue (1936) 46 Yale LJ 52; Stoljar (1975) 91 LQR 68. See also *Benjamin's Sale of Goods* (5th edn), para 17-067; Goode, *Commercial Law* (2nd edn), pp 408–09; Bridge, *Sale of Goods*, pp 594–98.

[29.36]

1   *Clare v Maynard* (1835) 6 Ad & El 519; and see generally ante, para 27.41.

2   *Dobell & Co Ltd v Barber and Garrett* (set out ante, para 18.35); *Danecroft Jersey Mills Ltd v Criegee* [1987] CLY 3341, CA.

3   See *per* Scrutton LJ in *Dexters Ltd v Hill Crest Oil Co Ltd* [1926] 1 KB 348 at 359, CA.

4   *Per* Devlin J in *Biggin & Co Ltd v Permanite Ltd* [1951] 1 KB 422, at 434. Reversed on other grounds: [1951] 2 KB 314, CA.

5   *British Oil and Cake Co Ltd v Burstall* (1923) 39 TLR 406, *obiter.*

6   *Molling & Co v Dean & Son Ltd* (1902) 18 TLR 217, DC. But the cost of delivering the goods to the sub-buyer is only claimable as an alternative to recovery for loss of profit: see *McGregor on Damages* (16th edn), para 915.

any compensation reasonably paid to his sub-buyer[7] and cumulative costs.[8] Indeed, where his seller was impecunious, the court has even allowed the sub-buyer to enforce an assignment of the seller's rights against his supplier.[9] Only at the prospect of a claim in respect of loss of business connection do the courts appear to have called a halt.[10]

Whilst it is unlikely that the parties to a contract of hp will contemplate a sub-sale of the subject matter by the hirer,[11] similar principles have been applied against a dealer for breach of a collateral contract of warranty.[12]

[29.37] Loss caused by the defect. Normally, damage which the defect does to the goods themselves will be included in the *prima facie* measure of damages because it will reduce the value of the goods; but it is otherwise where the defective goods damage persons or other property. If such loss is caused to the buyer or hirer then, subject to the rules of causation[1] and remoteness (see ante, para 27.41 *et seq*), it is possible that an action will lie for the tort of negligence;[2] but it is more likely that he will wish to sue for breach of contract, because liability is strict. Where the goods have been put to their contemplated use and the defect amounts to a breach of the contract of sale, it has been held that the buyer may recover in respect of personal injury,[3] death of his wife[4] and injury to his other property;[5] and in a consumer case, he may also sometimes recover in respect of disappointment and distress.[6] The position is the same with regard to actions by a hirer under a simple hiring or hp agreement against the owner;[7] and it has been held that a dealer in a directly financed hp transaction is liable to the hirer both for breach of a collateral contract of warranty and the tort of negligence (*Andrews v Hopkinson*: set out ante, para 16.18).

Finally, it is necessary to consider the liability of the supplier for loss caused to any third party. Possibly that third party can sue the supplier directly under a collateral contract (see ante, para 17.09) or in the tort of negligence.[8] Alternatively, that third party

---

7   *Biggin Ltd v Permanite Ltd* (above); the *Bence* case (set out ante, para 29.26).

8   *Kasler and Cohen v Slovouski* [1928] 1 KB 78. See also *Parker v Oloxo* [1937] 3 All ER 524; *Butterworth v Kingsway Motors Ltd* (set out ante, para 12.06), as reported in [1954] 1 WLR 1297–1307; *Bowmaker (Commercial) Ltd v Day* [1965] 2 All ER 856.

9   *Total Liban SA v Vitol Energy SA* [2000] 1 All ER 267 (nor did the assignment amount to champerty: see ante, para 7.26).

10 Eg, *Bostock & Co Ltd v Nicholson & Sons Ltd* [1904] 1 KB 725. But see *GKN Centrax Gears Ltd v Matbro Ltd* [1976] 2 Lloyd's Rep 555, CA (recovered for loss of repeat orders to customers to whom defective goods supplied). As to late delivery: see ante, para 29.31.

11 Except where the hp agreement is used as a stocking device: see ante, para 16.20.

12 *Yeoman Credit Ltd v Odgers* [1962] 1 All ER 789, CA (cost of reasonably defending owner's action).

[29.37]

1   *Commercial Fibres (Ireland) Ltd v Zabaida* [1975] 1 Lloyd's Rep 27 (buyer received yarn in damaged cartons; but shipped it and so caused much more damage to yarn).

2   Eg, *Lambert v Lewis* (set out ante, para 17.06; fourth party proceedings).

3   Eg, *Geddling v Marsh* (set out ante, para 14.03); *Griffiths v Peter Conway Ltd* (set out ante, para 14.09); *Godley v Perry* [1960] 1 All ER 36; *Grant v Australian Knitting Mills Ltd* [1936] AC 85, PC.

4   Eg, *Jackson v Watson & Sons* [1919] 2 KB 193, CA.

5   Eg, *Bostock & Co Ltd v Nicholson & Sons Ltd* [1904] 1 KB 725; *Wilson v Rickett Cockerell & Co Ltd* (set out ante, para 14.03).

6   *Jackson v Chrysler Acceptances Ltd* [1978] RTR 474, CA; *Bernstein v Pamson Motors Ltd* (set out ante, para 29.07); see ante, para 27.29; and Atiyah, *Sale of Goods* (10th edn), pp 551–52.

7   *White v John Warwick & Co Ltd* [1953] 1 All ER 1021, CA (simple hire); *Jackson v Chrysler Acceptances Ltd* (above; hp).

8   Eg, *Lambert v Lewis* (above; plaintiff's claim).

may successfully sue the buyer or hirer in the tort of negligence; and, in either case, the buyer or hirer may be able to pass that loss back to his supplier. Leaving aside the possibility that the buyer or hirer and his supplier are joint tortfeasors (see ante, para 17.16), it may be that such a claim is a non-remote loss flowing from the breach of contract by the supplier; and in this event, the supplier[9] will be liable for the damages and costs paid by the buyer or hirer to a third party under a judgment[10] or a reasonable settlement,[11] or for any costs reasonably incurred in successfully defending such an action.[12]

SPECIFIC ENFORCEMENT[1]

[29.38] Specific enforcement. Whilst detailed discussion of the principles on which a decree of specific performance is granted or refused are beyond the scope of this work, it will be recalled that the remedy is discretionary; it is an **alternative** to damages and will only be granted where damages are not an adequate remedy;[2] and may not available in the case of fraud.[3] Moreover, in relation to contracts for the disposition of goods, the buyer or hirer will usually only be able to obtain specific performance of the contract where the subject matter is unique in some way.[4] Nor can he avoid this restriction by suing in tort (s 3 of the Torts (Interference with Goods) Act 1977: see ante, para 24.26).

In the case of sales, the remedy of specific performance was put in statutory form by s 52 of the SGA. This provides as follows (s 52(1)):[5]

> In any action for breach of contract to deliver specific or ascertained goods the court may, if it thinks fit, on the plaintiff's application,[6] by its judgment ... direct that the contract shall be performed specifically, without giving the defendant the option of retaining the goods on payment of damages.[7]

In the unlikely event of unique goods being supplied under a quasi-sale or hired, this provision would presumably apply by analogy. At any event, s 52 only applies where the

---

9   But as to causation, see *Lambert v Lewis* (above; third party proceedings); and ante, para 27.29.

10 *Vogan & Co v Oulton* (1899) 81 LT 435, CA (simple hire). Cf *Hadley v Droitwich Construction Ltd* [1967] 3 All ER 911, CA (simple hire).

11 *Kendall v Lillico* (set out ante, para 14.10).

12 *Britannia Hygienic Laundry Ltd v Thornycroft Ltd* (1925) 41 TLR 667. Reversed on facts: (1926) 42 TLR 198, CA.

[29.38]

1   See Treitel, *Law of Contract* (10th edn), pp 949–68; Bridge, *Sale of Goods*, pp 531–37.

2   *Société des Industries Métallurgiques SA v Bronx Engineering Co Ltd* [1975] 1 Lloyd's Rep 465, CA; and the criticism by Goode, *Commercial Law* (2nd edn), p 320. What if the parties bargain for specific performance (see Ogus (1985) 5 Legal Studies at 114)?

3   See *Geest plc v Fyffes plc* [1999] 1 All ER (Comm) 672, *obiter* (not a goods case).

4   Eg, *Behnke v Bede Shipbuilding Co Ltd* [1927] 1 KB 649; *Clarke v Reilly* [1962] ILTR 96 (part-exchange goods – see ante, para 2.09). Compare *The Stena Nautica (No 2)* [1982] 2 Lloyd's Rep 336, CA (damages only).

5   It may have been intended that s 52 should widen the scope of the remedy; but the post-Act cases do not appear to have so regarded it.

6   This means the buyer: *per* Wright J in *Shell Mex Ltd v Elton Cop Dying Co Ltd* (1928) 34 Com Cas 39, at 46.

7   The order may be conditional, eg, *BICC plc v Burndy Corp* [1985] Ch 232, CA. Compare the powers of the court in a tort action: see ante, para 24.26.

contract goods are identified and agreed upon either at the time of contracting (specific goods) or subsequently (ascertained goods);[8] and it does not apply to an unascertained part of a specific whole.[9] On the other had, it is unnecessary to prove that the property in the goods has passed in order to obtain specific performance; and, in this respect, the buyer is better off than the seller suing for the price (see ante, para 27.16). Where appropriate, the buyer may have the contract rectified[10] and then obtain specific performance of the contract as rectified.[11]

[29.39] Injunctions. Just as the buyer or hirer of unique goods may be able to obtain a decree of specific performance requiring his supplier to deliver the specific or ascertained goods to himself (see above), so he may be able to obtain an injunction preventing his supplier disposing of those goods to a third party,[1] perhaps on an interlocutory basis.[2] However, an injunction would appear to be available in somewhat wider circumstances, it being no defence to show that damages would be an adequate remedy,[3] nor that the good remain unascertained.[4] But it has been refused to prevent presentation of a post-dated cheque.[5] As to anti-suit injunctions, see ante, para 18.13.

Additionally, an injunction may be available to a stranger to a supply contract. First, where the formation or performance of a supply contract amounts to a criminal offence whose penalty is an insufficient deterrent, a public authority may seek an injunction against a contracting party (see ante, para 28.04). Second, where performance of a supply contract would amount to a tort, an injunction may be sought.[6] Third, an injunction may be obtained to enforce EU Competition law;[7] and the Competition Act 1998 has its own system of court orders for enforcement (see ante, para 2.14). Fourth, where a Local Authority takes action to enforce consumer protection statutes (see ante, para 28.04) by way of seeking an injunction, unlike a private plaintiff, it was usually under no obligation to give a cross-undertaking as to damages.[8] Fifth, whilst a consumer may always apply for an injunction under the above rules, qualified entities may in certain circumstances apply for injunctions on their behalf (see ante, para 28.03).

Moreover, as against a third party an injunction may be available to a contracting party to prevent the third party interfering with that contract.[9]

---

8   *Per* Atkin LJ in *Re Wait* [1927] 1 Ch 606, CA, at 630.
9   *Re Wait* (set out ante, para 20.22). But see post, para 29.39.
10   But see *Rose Ltd v Pim Ltd* [1953] 2 QB 450, CA.
11   *USA v Motor Trucks Ltd* [1924] AC 196, PC (realty).

[29.39]
1   *Contra* where statute prohibits further remedying eg, CCA, s 170.
2   To prevent his removing assets from the jurisdiction by what have become known as Mareva (or freezing) injunctions: see further Schmitthoff, *Export Trade* (10th edn), 22-030.
3   *Redler Grain Silos Ltd v BICC Ltd* [1982] 1 Lloyd's Rep 435, CA.
4   *Sky Petroleum Ltd v VIP Petroleum Ltd* [1974] 1 All ER 954 (P would be forced out of business if contract to deliver petrol not performed).
5   *Eldan Services Ltd v Clandag Motors Ltd* [1990] 3 All ER 459.
6   Eg, *Morris Motors Ltd v Lilley* [1959] 3 All ER 737, (passing-off); *BBC Enterprises Ltd v Hi-Tech Xtravision Ltd* [1991] 3 All ER 257, HL (breach of copyright).
7   *R v Secretary of State for Transport ex p Factortame No 2* [1991] 1 AC 658, HL (allowing injunction against Crown following ECJ's judgment); and see generally ante, para 2.13.
8   *Coventry CC v Finnie* [1996] CLY 841.
9   Eg, *Cutsforth v Mansfield Inns Ltd* [1986] 1 All ER 577 (for inducing breach of the supply contract – see ante, para 17.17); or amounting to an unlawful restraint of trade (see ante, para 2.13); *The Messiniaki Tolme* [1982] QB 1248, CA (against a banker under a documentary credit – see further [1983] 2 AC 787, HL); *The Iran Bohonar* [1983] 2 Lloyd's Rep 620, CA (against carrier).

EXTORTIONATE CREDIT BARGAINS

[29.40] Introduction. The old usury laws dealt with the problem of extortion by fixing a maximum rate of interest which a lender might charge – a rate ceiling (see ante, para 6.09). However, after the repeal of the usury laws and prior to the CCA,[1] the law had only very meagre weapons at its disposal with which to attack extortionate credit bargains.[2] First, leaving aside the common law doctrine of duress,[3] equity was sometimes prepared to intervene in unconscionable bargains. Besides the well established equity of redemption in respect of mortgaged land (see ante, para 25.22), equity might grant some relief in respect of forfeiture of goods (see ante, para 27.20; 27.22) or where a contract was procured by undue influence;[4] but it would seem that there is not yet any general principle that relief may be granted simply because of unconscionability and inequality of bargaining power.[5] Second, there was a limited statutory power under the Moneylenders Acts 1900 to 1927 to 'reopen' loans charging excessive interest, this being presumed if the rate of interest exceeded 48%.[6] In fact, this statutory jurisdiction led to the confusion of two separate policies:[7]

(a) the terms of the loan, including the interest rate, may be harsh and unconscionable in the light of the risks the lender was undertaking; and

(b) the re-introduction of a rate ceiling which would 'prohibit' lenders granting loans to bad credit risks even on terms reasonable in the light of that risk.[8]

The *Crowther Report* (see ante, para 5.03) considered whether a rate ceiling should be re-introduced on the grounds that such socially harmful lending should be prohibited (paras 6.6.3–6); but the Report rejected the idea (para 6.6.9), perhaps because of the tendency of such a rule to force that class of borrower onto the illegal, 'loanshark', market.[9] But, the Report did recommend continuation of the existing presumption that a rate in excess of

---

[29.40]

1 Doorstep transactions may now be cancelled without cause, whether made on a cash or credit basis: see respectively ante, paras 10.21; 10.28.

2 Under the FTA enacted the previous year, two avenues of attack are possible: (a) by way of delegated legislation under Part II of the Act (see ante, para 4.20); (b) for persistent breaches of the law under Part III of the Act (see ante, para 6.06).

3 Including economic duress: see ante, para 10.18.

4 Compare *Lloyds Bank Ltd v Bundy* [1975] QB 326, CA and *Goldsworthy v Brickell* [1987] Ch 378, CA with *Coldunell Ltd v Gallon* [1986] QB 1184, CA and *Woodstead Finance Ltd v Petrou* (1986) 136 NLJ 188, CA. See generally Treitel, *Law of Contract* (10th edn), p 378 *et seq*; *Chitty on Contract* (28th edn, vol I, para 7-041 *et seq*.

5 *Lloyd's Bank Ltd v Bundy* [1975] QB 326, CA, *per* Lord Denning MR (discussed in the authorities cited above; Treitel, *ibid*, pp 382–86; Chitty, *ibid*, para 7-088; Goode, *Consumer Credit Law and Practice*, para 47.91; OFT, *Trading Malpractices* (1990), Appendix 3).

6 1900 Act, s 1; 1927 Act, s 10 (now repealed). There was also a statutory tariff of charges laid down under the Pawnbrokers Acts (now repealed).

7 But the Moneylenders Acts did not themselves make this mistake: see the *Crowther Report*, para 6.6.3.

8 See Cayne and Trebilcock (1973) UTLJ 396, at 411–18; Johnson (1997) 51 CC 6/2, at 5–6.

9 For the CCA licensing penalties against loan sharking, see ante, para 6.20. The legal alternative would appear to be social lending, eg, government social loans: (see ante, para 27.01); credit unions (see ante, para 15.19).

48% was *prima facie* harsh and unconscionable (para 6.6.9). However, the CCA varied these proposals by abandoning the 48% rule, whilst confirming and extending the court jurisdiction to reopen (see post, para 29.40A) what it termed 'extortionate credit bargains' (see post, para 29.41).

[29.40A] The CCA jurisdiction. Abandoning the former 48% rule of thumb (see ante, para 29.40), the CCA introduced a new jurisdiction for the court to attack extortionate credit bargains (see post, para 29.41). This jurisdiction may be invoked by the debtor or any surety;[1] but the drawback of so doing is that the sub-prime market is quite small (see ante, para 7.04A): if the debtor does invoke the jurisdiction, he may find it difficult ever to get such credit again. Under it, the court[2] may reopen a 'credit agreement' (s 137(1)), which expression is defined by s 137(2)(a) as:[3]

> ... any agreement between an individual (the 'debtor') and any other person (the 'creditor') by which the creditor provides the debtor with credit of any amount.

It is immediately clear that this notion of a 'credit agreement' not only precludes entirely consumer hire agreements,[4] but is both narrower and wider than consumer credit agreements:[5] whilst both are only applicable to individual debtors, the notion of a 'credit agreement' is regardless of financial limit,[6] and whether the agreement is exempt (s 16(7): see ante, para 5.15), eg, a Building Society mortgage, or the creditor in business.[7]

In deciding whether to reopen a credit agreement[7a] within the limitation period (s 9 of the LA 1980: see ante, para 26.17), the court will have regard to the terms of that agreement, ignoring any concessions granted by the creditor.[7b] However, the court is empowered to look beyond the four corners of the agreement to what the Act conveniently terms a 'credit bargain' as defined in s 137(2)(b). Where there is no transaction other than the credit agreement, this excludes the tcc.[8] The rest of s 137(2)(b) would seem to be intended as an anti-avoidance device: if there is only a credit agreement, the court principally confines its attention to that; whereas, if there is a host of ancillary agreements within which the creditor may have hidden his excessive charges,[9]

[29.40A]

1   Section 139(1). As to whether a court can raise the issue, see *per* Dillon LJ in *First National Bank plc v Syed* [1991] 2 All ER 250, CA, at 252e.

2   Usually a county court: see s 139(5); and generally ante, para 3.22. Should the court be able to reopen of its own volition?

3   As to the meaning of 'credit', 'individual' and 'debtor', see ante, paras 5.21; 5.24. Cf 'personal credit agreement' in s 8(1).

4   See ante, para 1.19. For the power to 'grant financial relief to consumer hirers under s 132, see ante, para 27.23.

5   See ante, para 5.19. Insofar as the scope of s 138 extends to unregulated agreements, s 140 seeks to make the necessary adaption to the CCA definitions; but for criticism of s 140, see Goode, *Consumer Credit Law and Practice*, para 47.22.

6   As to the upper credit limit for consumer credit agreements, see ante, para 5.22, and as to a special lower limit, see ante, para 6.12.

7   The agreement may be non-commercial, so that even a loan between friends is caught.

7a *Broadwick Financial Services Ltd v Spencer* [2002] 1 All ER (Comm) 446, CA.

7b *Heffernan v Grangewood Securities Ltd* [2001] 61 QA 22.

8   Section 137(2)(b)(i); *Paragon Finance plc v Nash* (set out *sub nom Paragon Finance v Staunton*, ante, para 11.10.

9   Eg, maintenance or insurance contracts taken out by the debtor; or surety contracts by a third party.

the court may also look at those. Surveying that field, the court must decide whether the 'credit **bargain**' is extortionate (see post, para 29.41), in which case it has wide powers under s 139 to interfere with the 'credit **agreement**',[10] so as to reduce the obligations of the debtor or any surety.[11] Additionally, the OFT may exercise its licensing powers (see ante, para 6.11 *et seq*).

[29.41] Extortionate credit bargains. It is for the creditor to prove[1] that his is not an extortionate credit bargain.[2] Section 138(1) explains that:

A credit bargain is extortionate if it –[3]

(a) requires the debtor or a relative of his to make payments (whether unconditionally, or on certain contingencies) which are grossly exorbitant, or

(b) otherwise grossly contravenes ordinary principles of fair dealing.

Thus, a bargain is not 'extortionate' merely because it is harsh or even unconscionable;[4] nor even because it is unfair.[5] Before a transaction can be struck down, it must not only be exorbitant, but grossly so:[6] this applies not just to the primary obligations of the debtor, or his 'relative' (see ante, para 5.33), but also to any secondary ones operating on default[7] and linked transactions (s 138(5)). Such sums will mostly already be included in the total charge for credit (see ante, para 8.24). To help a court decide whether a credit bargain is grossly exorbitant, the Act lays down a number of guidelines (s 138), most of them based on decisions under the Moneylenders Acts.[8] A court is not obliged to take only these factors into account,[9] but they do provide a useful check list.[10]

---

10 But not so as to alter the effect of any judgment (s 138(4)); nor where the debtor is insolvent (see ante, para 19.16).

11 Compare time orders, which do not allow reduction of the sum owed, but only stretch the repayment period: see ante, para 24.40.

[29.41]

1 Section 171(7), eg, *Coldunell Ltd v Gallon* [1986] QB 1184, CA. But the debtor must first raise the issue (s 139(1)) so as to discharge an evidential burden: *Bank of Baroda v Shah* [1988] 3 All ER 24, CA. For the complicated process the debtor must follow, see Rosenberg (1999) 53 QA 4; 54 QA 11.

2 This is so, however low the interest rate, even if it is a low cost exempt agreement: see ante, para 5.15. Cf the definition of 'extortionate' in the Insolvency Act 1986: see ante, para 19.16.

3 It has been pointed out that the expression is 'extortionate' not 'unwise', connoting a 'substantial imbalance of bargaining power of which one party has taken advantage': *per* Donaldson MR in *Wills v Wood* (1984) 3 Tr LR 93 at 98, CA.

4 *Davies v Directloans Ltd* [1986] 2 All ER 783.

5 *Falco Finance Ltd v Gough* (set out ante, para 8.22). As to the test of unfairness in the UTCC Regulations, see OFT, *Bulletin No 14*, case 1; and ante, para 11.15.

6 So presumably it will not catch a standard commercial rate which is just not geared to the personal characteristics of a particular debtor: Goode, *Consumer Credit Law and Practice*, para 47.43.

7 That it does seems to suggest a far stricter test than that for a penalty. As to penalties, see ante, para 27.25. See generally Goode, *ibid*, para 47.29.

8 See Meston, *Moneylenders* (5th edn), Chapter 12. But see *per* Foster J in *Ketley Ltd v Scott* [1981] ICR 241, at 245. Nor does the section indicate on which side its listed factors weigh.

9 Eg, switch selling. The express reference to 'other relevant considerations' (s 138(2)(c)) was utilised in *Ketley Ltd v Scott* (above) so as not to reopen a transaction in view of the debtor's business experience, deceitful conduct and the rate of interest balanced against the risk.

10 So warning the creditor of the sorts of things on which he should lead evidence: *Woodstead Finance Ltd v Petrou* (1986) 136 NLJ 188, CA. Can there be taken into account (a) happenings **after** the agreement is concluded, (b) the defective state of any goods supplied under the regulated or any linked agreement? For a discussion of the statutory factors, see Bently and Howells [1989] Conv 164.

1 **Interest rates** prevailing at the time the bargain was made (s 138(2)(a)).[10a] As interest rates will differ for different classes of business and borrowers, much may depend on how a particular bargain in classified. The reference to rates prevailing at the time of contracting will exclude later falls in general interest rates.[10b]

2 The **debtor's** (a) 'age, experience, business capacity and state of health' and (b) the degree and nature of any financial pressure he was then under (s 138(3)).

3 The degree of risk accepted by the **creditor** having regard to (a) the value of any security and (b) his relationship to the debtor.[11]

4 Whether a colourable cash price was quoted, this being an anti-avoidance device (s 138(4)(c)), eg, by inflating the cash price and shrinking the credit charge.

[29.42] Reform. Interest rates charged by back street lenders have been recorded as high as 17.9 billion % (OFT, July 1987); yet in few reported cases have transactions been found to be extortionate. In 1989, it was suggested that ss 137–39 had failed for three reasons:[1] (i) the onus placed on the debtor to raise the issue; (ii) the statutory formulation employed; and (iii) judicial reticence to interfere with agreements voluntarily entered into by the parties. The statutory provisions were reviewed in 1991 by the OFT, who concluded that, whilst most credit caused no problems for most consumers most of the time, there was some socially harmful lending at the margins of the market.[2] The OFT recommended that ss 137–39 should be recast as 'unjust credit transactions' with the following major substantive changes:[3]

(1) The notion of 'grossly exorbitant' payments by the debtor (s 138(1)(a)) should be diluted to merely 'excessive'.[4]

(2) The notion of 'grossly contravenes the principles of fair dealing' (s 138(1)(b)) should be altered to the test of the fitness of a dealer to hold a CCA licence in s 25(2)(d).[5]

10a A high interest rate in the original contract will be saved from the UTCC Regulations as being a core term: see ante, para 11.14.

10b *Paragon Finance plc v Staunton* (set out ante, para 11.10). The fact that the implied term is that the creditor must act reasonably may make it more difficult to argue that it is unfair (see ante, para 11.15). See further, *Broadwick Financial Services Ltd v Spencer* [2002] 1 All ER 446, CA.

11 Section 138(4)(a), (b). See *Ketley Ltd v Scott* (above); *Davies v Direct Loans Ltd* (above). Does this encourage secured lending on the basis of the equity in the property rather than the debtor's ability to repay?

[29.42]

1 Bently and Howells [1989] Conv 164 and 234; and further Howells, *Aspects of Credit and Debt*, Chapter 6.

2 *Unjust Credit Transactions* (1991), para 1.5. The Report identified particularly non-status borrowers and roll-over loans.

3 *Ibid*, para 1.9. The Report also recommended that: (i) the court should have express powers to reopen a credit transaction of its own motion; (ii) the court should be required to notify the OFT where a credit transaction was unjust; and (iii) there should be tougher penalties for loan sharking (see ante, para 6.20). The government largely accepted the Report: see (1992) 9 Tr LR 105. The OFT continues to press for its implementation: 1998 AR, 12, 24.

4 In reply, the DTI preferred 'grossly excessive'. Compare the suggestion of 'good commercial practice' by Bently and Howells, *op cit*, note 1, at 239.

5 Set out ante, para 6.19. There may be a significant overlap here with the Unfair Contract Terms Regulations (see ante, para 11.08A).

(3) There should be added to s 138(2) an additional guideline of 'the lender's care and responsibility in making the loan, including steps taken to find out and check the borrower's creditworthiness and ability to meet the full terms of the agreement'.[6]

(4) The OFT and local authorities should be empowered to initiate proceedings for a declaration that a transaction was unjust.[7]

Yet, it has been argued that, whilst the present regime is quite adequate for most cases, what is needed is a specially protective regime of the most needy borrowers as against fringe lenders. The authors reject the imposition of interest rate ceilings (see ante, para 29.40) as ineffective,[8] and which would in effect brand all such commercial loans as loan sharking (see ante, para 6.20). Instead, they recommend the following:[9] a special licensing system under which high rates have to be justified; in these circumstances, additional factors for consideration as to whether a loan was colourable, such as the public interest; a presumption that high loan rates were colourable, as under the old Moneylenders Acts (see ante, para 29.40); and withdrawal of the issues from the courts to administrative tribunals.[10] Alternatively, the authors point out that loans to the needy could be removed entirely from the commercial sector: such loans could be obtained at less than commercial rates of interest from credit unions (see ante, para 15.17); or they might be brought within the government social fund.[11]

The government are currently considering the matter.[12]

---

6   In reply the DTI proposed alteration of the law by way of regulations under what is now the Deregulation Act 1994 (see ante, para 5.09).

7   In reply, the DTI suggested that such powers should be available to LAs only with permission of the OFT; and that, where such a declaration was sought, the burden of proving that the transaction was unjust should be on the OFT or LA.

8   Bently and Howells, *op cit*, note 1, at 236 and 240 respectively.

9   Bently and Howells, *op cit*, note 1, at 238 *et seq*.

10 This would usually mean the removal of such cases from the County Courts. But compare the original reason for the introduction of County Courts: see ante, para 3.22.

11 Social Security Act 1986, ss 32–35 (see ante, para 2.15).

12 DTI, *Modern Markets: Confident Consumers* (1999), para 5.21. For account of a 1999 Parliamentary Early Day Motion, see (1999) 51 QA 1.

INDEX